MW01258465

WORD
BIBLICAL
COMMENTARY

Thomas Nelson
Since 1798

NASHVILLE   DALLAS   MEXICO CITY   RIO DE JANEIRO

WORD
BIBLICAL
COMMENTARY

Volume 8

Judges

TRENT C. BUTLER

To the Spears bunch, who have supported me through a new stage of life
Bobby and Cordell
Ben and Mary
Martin and Allison
Adeline
and
Evelyn and Beatrice

וְאֹהֲבָיו כְּצֵאת הַשֶּׁמֶשׁ בִּגְבֻרָתוֹ
May those who love him be like the mighty sun as it rises. (Judg 5:31)

Published in Nashville, Tennessee, by Thomas Nelson. Thomas Nelson is a trademark of Thomas Nelson, Inc.

Thomas Nelson, Inc., titles may be purchased in bulk for educational, business, fund-raising, or sales promotional use. For information, please e-mail SpecialMarkets@ThomasNelson.com.

Scripture quotations in the body of the commentary marked NRSV are from the New Revised Standard Version of the Bible, copyright © 1989 by the Division of Christian Education of the National Council of the Churches of Christ in the USA and are used by permission. The author's own translation of the text appears in italic type under the heading *Translation*.

Library of Congress Cataloging-in-Publication Data
Main entry under title:

Word biblical commentary.

Includes bibliographies.
1. Bible—Commentaries—Collected works.
BS491.2.W67   220.7' 7   80–71768
ISBN 10: 084990207x (v. 8) AACR2
ISBN 13: 978-0-8499-0207-9

Printed in Mexico

5 6 7 8 9 EPAC 14 13 12 11 10

Contents

List of Tables

Editorial Preface

The launching of the Word Biblical Commentary brings to fulfillment an enterprise of several years' planning. The publishers and the members of the editorial board met in 1977 to explore the possibility of a new commentary on the books of the Bible that would incorporate several distinctive features. Prospective readers of these volumes are entitled to know what such features were intended to be; whether the aims of the commentary have been fully achieved time alone will tell.

First, we have tried to cast a wide net to include as contributors a number of scholars from around the world who not only share our aims, but are in the main engaged in the ministry of teaching in university, college, and seminary. They represent a rich diversity of denominational allegiance. The broad stance of our contributors can rightly be called evangelical, and this term is to be understood in its positive, historic sense of a commitment to Scripture as divine revelation and to the truth and power of the Christian gospel.

Then, the commentaries in our series are all commissioned and written for the purpose of inclusion in the Word Biblical Commentary. Unlike several of our distinguished counterparts in the field of commentary writing, there are no translated works, originally written in a non-English language. Also, our commentators were asked to prepare their own rendering of the original biblical text and to use the biblical languages as the basis of their own comments and exegesis. What may be claimed as distinctive with this series is that it is based on the biblical languages, yet it seeks to make the technical and scholarly approach to a theological understanding of Scripture understandable by—and useful to—the fledgling student, the working minister, and colleagues in the guild of professional scholars and teachers as well.

Finally, a word must be said about the format of the series. The layout, in clearly defined sections, has been consciously devised to assist readers at different levels. Those wishing to learn about the textual witnesses on which the translation is offered are invited to consult the section headed *Notes*. If the readers' concern is with the state of modern scholarship on any given portion of Scripture, they should turn to the sections on *Bibliography* and *Form/Structure/Setting*. For a clear exposition of the passage's meaning and its relevance to the ongoing biblical revelation, the *Comment* and concluding *Explanation* are designed expressly to meet that need. There is therefore something for everyone who may pick up and use these volumes.

If these aims come anywhere near realization, the intention of the editors will have been met, and the labor of our team of contributors rewarded.

General Editors: *Bruce M. Metzger†*
David A. Hubbard†
Glenn W. Barker†
Old Testament Editor: *John D. W. Watts*
Associate Editor: *James W. Watts*
New Testament Editor: *Ralph P. Martin*
Associate Editor: *Lynn Allan Losie*

Author's Preface

Should *fun* be the first word that comes to mind when describing the writing of a commentary? For this writer the word *fun* is quite apt. The book of Judges has a drearisome message of failure and disobedience, but it presents the theme through irony, satire, and humor. At times we have to laugh at others' mistakes and then at ourselves as we foolishly repeat the story we just honored with sarcastic laughter. Thus seeking to ferret out the instances of irony and humor and to solve the scholarly riddles the book so frequently presents have often engendered fun and laughter, both at the contents of the book and at my own feeble efforts to learn its lessons and avoid its mistakes.

The fun came at a most important moment in life as I adjusted to the loss of a wife, remarriage, adapting to a new family, being preserved from a deadly tornado with only the loss of a house, and then struggling through the process of moving into a temporary residence, finding builders, and constructing a new home. In all such endeavors I have made many mistakes and had to laugh at myself in doing so. Many times I sought refuge from life's demands behind a computer monitor as I tried to place new thoughts and helpful ideas on it.

Through it all, my sons, Curtis and Kevin; granddaughter Brynn; and new family, Mary Martin and Mary Webb, have given strong encouragement and love. Mary Martin's adult children and families have also supported me in ways beyond all expectations. Thus this book is dedicated to the Spears family, their faithfulness to the Judge of all the earth, their strong relationships to one another, and their example of love and acceptance for the new member of the family.

TRENT C. BUTLER

Gallatin, Tennessee
Spring 2008

Abbreviations

BIOSCS	*Bulletin of the International Organization for Septuagint and Cognate Studies*		T. Longman. Downers Grove, IL., 1998.
BK	*Bibel und Kirche*	DBSup	*Dictionnaire de la Bible: Supplément.* Ed. L. Pirot and A.
BLE	*Bulletin de littérature ecclésiastique*		Robert. Paris, 1928–.
BN	*Biblische Notizen*	DCH	*Dictionary of Classical Hebrew.* Ed.
BR	*Biblical Research*		D. J. A. Clines. Sheffield, 1993–
BRev	*Bible Review*	DDD	*Dictionary of Deities and Demons*
BS	The Biblical Seminar		*in the Bible.* Ed. K. van der
BSac	*Bibliotheca sacra*		Toorn, B. Becking, and P. W.
BSAC	*Bulletin de la Société d'archéologie copte*		van der Horst. Leiden, 1995.
		Did	*Didaskalia*
BSC	Bible Student's Commentary	DJD	Discoveries in the Judaean Desert
BT	*The Bible Translator*	DOTHB	*Dictionary of the Old Testament*
BTB	*Biblical Theology Bulletin*		*Historical Books.* Ed. B. T.
BV	*Biblical Viewpoint*		Arnold and H. G. M. William-
BWANT	Beiträge zur Wissenschaft vom		son. Downers Grove, IL, 2005.
	Alten (und Neuen) Testament	DTT	*Dansk teologisk tidsskrift*
BZ	*Biblische Zeitschrift*		
BZAW	Beihefte zur Zeitschrift für die	EAEHL	*Encyclopedia of Archaeological*
	alttestamentliche Wissenschaft		*Excavations in the Holy Land.*
			Ed. M. Avi-Yonah. 4 vols.
CaE	*Cahiers évangile*		Jerusalem, 1976–1978.
Car	*Carthagiensia*	EdF	Erträge der Forschung
CBC	Cambridge Bible Commentary	EHAT	Exegetisches Handbuch zum
CBQ	*Catholic Biblical Quarterly*		Alten Testament
CBQMS	CBQ Monograph Series	ErIsr	*Eretz-Israel*
CICR	*Communio: International Catholic*	ERT	*Evangelical Review of Theology*
	Review	EstBib	*Estudios bíblicos*
CJT	*Canadian Journal of Theology*	ETL	*Ephemerides theologicae lovanienses*
ConBOT	Coniectanea biblica: Old Testa-	ETR	*Etudes théologiques et religieuses*
	ment Series	EvQ	*Evangelical Quarterly*
COS	*The Context of Scripture.* Ed. W.	EvT	*Evangelische Theologie*
	W. Hallo. 3 vols. Leiden, 1997–	Exeg	*Exegetica* [Japanese]
	2000.	ExpTim	*Expository Times*
CTJ	*Calvin Theological Journal*		
CTM	*Concordia Theological Monthly*	FAT	Forschung zum Alten Testament
CTQ	*Concordia Theological Quarterly*	FB	Forschung zur Bibel
CurBS	*Currents in Research: Biblical Studies*	FCB	Feminist Companion to the Bible
CV	*Communio viatorum*	FoiVie	*Foi et vie*
		FOTL	Forms of the Old Testament
DB	*Dictionnaire de la Bible.* Ed. F.		Literature
	Vigouroux. 5 vols. 1895–1912.	FRLANT	Forschungen zur Religion und
DBAT	*Dielheimer Blätter zum Alten Testa-*		Literatur des Alten und
	ment und seiner Rezeption in der		Neuen Testaments
	Alten Kirche	FZPhTh	*Freiburger Zeitschrift für Philosophie*
DBI	*Dictionary of Biblical Imagery.*		*und Theologie*
	Ed. L. Ryken, J. C. Wilhoit, and	GBS	Guides to Biblical Scholarship

GKC	*Gesenius' Hebrew Grammar.* Ed. E. Kautzsch. Trans. A. E. Cowley. 2nd ed. Oxford, 1910.
GUOST	*Glasgow University Oriental Society Transactions*
HAL	Koehler, L., W. Baumgartner, and J. J. Stamm. *Hebräisches und aramäisches Lexikon zum Alten Testament.* 1967–1995.
HALOT	Koehler, L., W. Baumgartner, and J. J. Stamm. *The Hebrew and Aramaic Lexicon of the Old Testament.* Trans. and ed. under supervision of M. E. J. Richardson. 4 vols. Leiden, 1994–1999.
HAR	*Hebrew Annual Review*
HAT	Handbuch zum Alten Testament
HBA	Brisco, T. C. *Holman Bible Atlas.* Nashville, 1998.
HBS	Herders biblische Studien
HBT	*Horizons in Biblical Theology*
Hen	*Henoch*
HIBD	*Holman Illustrated Bible Dictionary.* Ed. T. Butler, C. Brand, C. Draper, and A. England. Nashville, 2003.
HKAT	Handkommentar zum Alten Testament
Hok	*Hokhma*
HolBD	*Holman Bible Dictionary.* Ed. T. C. Butler. Nashville, 1991.
Hor	*Horizons*
HOTC	Holman Old Testament Commentary
HS	*Hebrew Studies*
HSAT	*Die Heilige Schrift des Alten Testaments.* Ed. E. Kautzsch and A. Bertholet. 4th ed. Tübingen, 1922–1923.
HSM	Harvard Semitic Monographs
HTR	*Harvard Theological Review*
HTS	Harvard Theological Studies
HUCA	*Hebrew Union College Annual*
HvTSt	*Hervormde teologiese studies*
IB	*Interpreter's Bible.* Ed. G. A. But-

	trick et al. 12 vols. New York, 1951–1957.
IBC	Interpretation: A Bible Commentary for Teaching and Preaching
IBHS	*An Introduction to Biblical Hebrew Syntax.* B. K. Waltke and M. O'Connor. Winona Lake, IN, 1990.
ICC	International Critical Commentary
IDB	*The Interpreter's Dictionary of the Bible.* Ed. G. A. Buttrick. 4 vols. Nashville, 1962.
IDBSup	*Interpreter's Dictionary of the Bible: Supplementary Volume.* Ed. K. Crim. Nashville, 1976.
IDS	*In die Skriflig*
IEJ	*Israel Exploration Journal*
IES	Israel Exploration Society
IJT	*Indian Journal of Theology*
Int	*Interpretation*
IOS	*Israel Oriental Studies*
ISOCS	International Organization for Septuagint and Cognate Studies
ITC	International Theological Commentary
JAAR	*Journal of the American Academy of Religion*
JANESCU	*Journal of the Ancient Near Eastern Society of Columbia University*
JAOS	*Journal of the American Oriental Society*
JB	Jerusalem Bible
JBC	*Jerome Bible Commentary.* Ed. R. E. Brown et al. Englewood Cliffs, NJ, 1968.
JBL	*Journal of Biblical Literature*
JBQ	*Jewish Bible Quarterly*
JBR	*Journal of Bible and Religion*
JCS	*Journal of Cuneiform Studies*
JETS	*Journal of the Evangelical Theological Society*
JFSR	*Journal of Feminist Studies in Religion*
JJS	*Journal of Jewish Studies*
JLA	*Jewish Law Annual*

JNES	*Journal of Near Eastern Studies*	*LB*	*Linguistica Biblica*
JNSL	*Journal of Northwest Semitic Languages*	LD	Lectio divina
		Leš	*Lešonĕnu*
JPOS	*Journal of the Palestine Oriental Society*	*LTQ*	*Lexington Theological Quarterly*
JQR	*Jewish Quarterly Review*	*MdB*	*Le Monde de la Bible*
JRR	*A Journal for the Radical Reformation*	MdB	Le Monde de la Bible
JSem	*Journal for Semitics*	*MGWJ*	*Monatschrift für Geschichte und Wissenschaft des Judentums*
JSJ	*Journal for the Study of Judaism in the Persian, Hellenistic, and Roman Periods*	MPIL	Monographs of the Peshitta Institute, Leiden
JSJSup	Supplements to *JSJ*	NAC	New American Commentary
JSNTSup	Journal for the Study of the New Testament: Supplement Series	NCB	New Century Bible
JSOR	*Journal of the Society of Oriental Research*	*NEAEHL*	*The New Encyclopedia of Archaeological Excavations in the Holy Land.* Ed. E. Stern. 4 vols. Jerusalem, 1993.
JSOT	*Journal for the Study of the Old Testament*		
JSOTMS	Journal for the Study of the Old Testament Monograph Series	NEchtB	Neue Echter Bibel
		NedTT	*Nederlands theologisch tijdschrift*
JSOTSup	Journal for the Study of the Old Testament: Supplement Series	*NGTT*	*Nederduitse gereformeerde teologiese tydskrif*
JSP	*Journal for the Study of the Pseudepigrapha*	*NIB*	*The New Interpreter's Bible*
		NIBCOT	New International Biblical Commentary on the Old Testament
JSPSup	Journal for the Study of the Pseudepigrapha: Supplement Series	*NIDOTTE*	*New International Dictionary of Old Testament Theology and Exegesis.* Ed. W. A. VanGemeren. 5 vols. Grand Rapids, 1997.
JSS	*Journal of Semitic Studies*		
JTS	*Journal of Theological Studies*		
Jud	*Judaica*	NIVAC	The NIV Application Commentary
K&D	Keil, C. F., and F. Delitzsch. *Biblical Commentary on the Old Testament.* Trans. J. Martin et al. 25 vols. Edinburgh, 1857–1878. Repr., 10 vols. Peabody, MA, 1996.	*NJBC*	*The New Jerome Biblical Commentary.* Ed. R. E. Brown et al. Englewood Cliffs, NJ, 1990.
		NTT	*Norsk Teologisk Tidsskrift*
		OBO	Orbis biblicus et orientalis
KAI	*Kanaanäische und aramäische Inschiften.* H. Donner and W. Röllig. 2d ed. Wiesbaden, 1966–1969.	OBT	Overtures to Biblical Theology
		OLA	Orientalia lovaniensia analecta
		Or	*Orientalia*
		OrAnt	*Oriens antiquus*
KAT	Kommentar zum Alten Testament	*OTE*	*Old Testament Essays*
KD	*Kerygma und Dogma*	OTG	Old Testament Guides
KHC	Kurzer Hand-Commentar zum Alten Testament	OTL	Old Testament Library
		OTS	Old Testament Studies
		OtSt	Oudtestamentische Studiën
LASBF	*Liber annuus Studii biblici franciscani*		

PaVi	Parole di vita	RHR	Revue de l'histoire des religions
PEFQS	Palestine Exploration Fund Quarterly Statement	RIDA	Revue internationale des droits de l'antiquité
PEGLMBS	Proceedings of the Eastern Great Lakes and Midwest Biblical Society	RivB	Rivista biblica italiana
		RSO	Revista degli studi orientali
		RTL	Revue théologique de Louvain
PEQ	Palestine Exploration Quarterly	RTR	Reformed Theological Revue
Per	Perspectives		
PG	Patrologia graeca [= Patrologiae cursus completus: Series graeca]. Ed. J.-P. Migne. 162 vols. Paris, 1857–1886.	SA	Studia anselmiana
		Sacred Bridge	Rainey, A. F., R. S. Notley, et al. The Sacred Bridge: Carta's Atlas of the Biblical World. Jerusalem, 2006.
PIBA	Proceedings of the Irish Biblical Association	SANT	Studien zum Alten und Neuen Testaments
PL	Patrologia latina [= Patrologiae cursus completus: Series latina]. Ed. J.-P. Migne. 217 vols. Paris, 1844–1864.	SBFLA	Studii biblici Franciscani liber annus
		SBJT	Southern Baptist Journal of Theology
		SBL	Society of Biblical Literature
		SBLABS	Society of Biblical Literature Archaeology and Biblical Studies
POTT	People of Old Testament Times. Ed. D. J. Wiseman. Oxford, 1973.		
POTW	Peoples of the Old Testament World. Ed. A. J. Hoerth, G. L. Mattingly, and E. M. Yamauchi. Grand Rapids, 1994.	SBLDS	Society of Biblical Literature Dissertation Series
		SBLMS	Society of Biblical Literature Monograph Series
Preliminary and Interim Report	Preliminary and Interim Report on the Hebrew Old Testament Text Project. Vol. 2., Historical Books. Ed. UBS Committee. New York, 1979.	SBLSCS	Society of Biblical Literature Septuagint and Cognate Studies
		SBLSP	Society of Biblical Literature Seminar Papers
Proof	Prooftexts: A Journal of Jewish Literary History	SBLStBl	Society of Biblical Literature Studies in Biblical Literature
PRSt	Perspectives in Religious Studies	SBLSymS	Society of Biblical Literature Symposium Series
PSTJ	Perkins (School of Theology) Journal	SBS	Stuttgarter Bibelstudien
		SBT	Studies in Biblical Theology
QR	Quarterly Review	Scr	Scripture
		ScrHier	Scripta hierosolymitana
RANL	Rendiconti dell'Academia nazionale dei Lincei, Rome	SCS	Sino-Christian Studies
		SEÅ	Svensk exegetisk årsbok
RB	Revue biblique	Sem	Semitica
REJ	Revue des études juives	SemeiaSt	Semeia Studies
ResQ	Restoration Quarterly	SHANE	Studies in the History of the Ancient Near East
RevExp	Review and Expositor		
RevQ	Revue de Qumran	SJOT	Scandinavian Journal of the Old Testament
RGG	Religion in Geschichte und Gegenwart. Ed. K. Galling. 7 vols. 3rd ed. Tübingen, 1957–1965.	SMRS	Studi e materiali di storia delle religioni
RHPR	Revue d'histoire et de philosophie religieuses	SOTBT	Studies in Old Testament Biblical Theology

SOTSMS	Society for Old Testament Studies Monograph Series	*TRu*	*Theologische Rundschau*
SR	*Studies in Religion*	*TSK*	*Theologische Studien und Kritiken*
ST	*Studia theologica*	*TTJ*	*Trinity Theological Journal*
STDJ	Studies on the Texts of the Desert of Judah	*TWOT*	*Theological Wordbook of the Old Testament.* Ed. R. L. Harris and G. L. Archer, Jr. 2 vols. Chicago, 1980.
StPatr	*Studia patristica*		
SWBA	Social World of Biblical Antiquity	*TynBul*	*Tyndale Bulletin*
SwJT	*Southwestern Journal of Theology*	*TZ*	*Theologische Zeitschrift*
T&K	*Text & Kontexte*	*UF*	*Ugarit-Forschungen*
TA	*Tel Aviv*	*USQR*	*Union Seminary Quarterly Review*
TB	Theologische Bücherei: Neudrucke und Berichte aus dem 20. Jahrhundert	*VD*	*Verbum domini*
		VE	*Vox evangelica*
TBC	Torch Biblical Commentaries	*VT*	*Vetus Testamentum*
TBT	*The Bible Today*	VTSup	Supplements to Vetus Testamentum
TDOT	*Theological Dictionary of the Old Testament.* Ed. G. J. Botterweck and H. Ringgren. Trans. J. T. Willis, G. W. Bromiley, and D. E. Green. 15 vols. Grand Rapids, 1974–2006.		
		VyV	*Verdad y Vida*
		WBC	Word Biblical Commentary
		WHJP	World History of the Jewish People
THAT	*Theologisches Handwörterbuch zum Alten Testament.* Ed. E. Jenni and C. Westermann. 2 vols. Stuttgart, 1971–1976.	WMANT	Wissenschaftliche Monographien zum Alten und Neuen Testament
		WTJ	*Westminster Theological Journal*
Them	*Themelios*	WUANT	Wissenschaftliche Untersuchungen zum Alten und Neuen Testament
ThT	*Theologisch tijdschrift*		
ThWAT	*Theologisches Wörterbuch zum Alten Testament.* Ed. G. J. Botterweck and H. Ringgren. 15 vols. Stuttgart, 1970–1995.	*ZABR*	*Zeitschrift für altorientalische und biblische Rechtsgeschichte*
		ZAH	*Zeitschrift für Althebräistik*
TJ	*Trinity Journal*	*ZAW*	*Zeitschrift für altestamentliche Wissenschaft*
TLOT	*Theological Lexicon of the Old Testament.* Ed. E. Jenni and C. Westermann. Trans. M. E. Biddle. 3 vols. Peabody, MA, 1997.		
		ZDMG	*Zeitschrift der deutschen morgenländischen Gesellschaft*
		ZDPV	*Zeitschrift des deutschen Palästina-Vereins*
TLZ	*Theologische Literaturzeitung*	*ZS*	*Zeitschrift für Semitistik und verwandte Gebiete*
TOTC	Tyndale Old Testament Commentaries	*ZTK*	*Zeitschrift für Theologie und Kirche*
TRE	*Theologische Realenzyklopädie.* Ed. G. Krause and G. Müller. 36 vols. Berlin, 1977–2006.		

TEXTS, VERSIONS, AND ANCIENT WORKS

CEV	Contemporary English Version	MT	Masoretic Text (as published in *BHS*)
CJB	Complete Jewish Bible		
Ed(d)	Hebrew MSS according to Kennicott, de Rossi, and Ginsburg	NAB	New American Bible
		NASB	New American Standard Bible
		NASB95	New American Standard Bible, 1995 Update
ESV	English Standard Version		
GWT	God's Word Translation	NEB	New English Bible
HCSB	Holman Christian Standard Bible	NET	New English Translation
		NIV	New International Version
JB	Jerusalem Bible	NJB	New Jerusalem Bible
JPS	Jewish Publication Society translation	NKJV	New King James Version
		NLT	New Living Translation
K	Kethib, Hebrew written tradition	NRSV	New Revised Standard Version
KJV	King James Version	OG	Old Greek
LStB	*La Sainte Bible*	OL	Old Latin
LXX	Septuagint	Pesh.	Peshitta
LXX^A	LXX Codex, Alexandrinus	Q	Qere, Hebrew reading tradition
LXX^B	LXX Codex, Vaticanus	REB	Revised English Bible
LXX^C	LXX, Catenarum tradition	RSV	Revised Standard Version
LXX^L	LXX, Lucianic recension	Syr.	Syriac
LXX^{ll}	LXX, First sub-Lucian recension	TEV	Today's English Version (= Good News Bible)
LXX^{lll}	LXX, Second sub-Lucian recension		
		Tg(s).	Targum(s)
LXX^R	LXX, Codex Veronensis	TNIV	Today's New International Version
LXX^O	LXX, Origen recension	Vg.	Vulgate
Message	Contemporary rendering by E. H. Peterson		

BIBLICAL AND APOCRYPHAL BOOKS

OLD TESTAMENT

Gen	Genesis	Job	Job
Exod	Exodus	Ps(s)	Psalm(s)
Lev	Leviticus	Prov	Proverbs
Num	Numbers	Eccl	Ecclesiastes
Deut	Deuteronomy	Song	Canticles, Song of Solomon
Josh	Joshua	Isa	Isaiah
Judg	Judges	Jer	Jeremiah
Ruth	Ruth	Lam	Lamentations
1–2 Sam	1–2 Samuel	Ezek	Ezekiel
1–2 Kgs	1–2 Kings	Dan	Daniel
1–2 Chr	1–2 Chronicles	Hos	Hosea
Ezra	Ezra	Joel	Joel
Neh	Nehemiah	Amos	Amos
Esth	Esther	Obad	Obadiah

Jonah	Jonah	Zeph	Zephaniah
Mic	Micah	Hag	Haggai
Nah	Nahum	Zech	Zechariah
Hab	Habakkuk	Mal	Malachi

APOCRYPHA

Bar	Baruch	Ep Jer	Epistle of Jeremiah
Add Dan	Additions to Daniel	Jdt	Judith
PrAzar	Prayer of Azariah	1–2 Macc	1–2 Maccabees
Bel	Bel and the Dragon	3–4 Macc	3–4 Maccabees
SgThree	Song of the Three Young Men	Pr Man	Prayer of Manasseh
		Ps 151	Psalm 151
Sus	Susanna	Sir	Sirach/Ecclesiasticus
1–2 Esd	1–2 Esdras	Tob	Tobit
Add Esth	Additions to Esther	Wis	Wisdom of Solomon

NEW TESTAMENT

Matt	Matthew	1–2 Thess	1–2 Thessalonians
Mark	Mark	1–2 Tim	1–2 Timothy
Luke	Luke	Titus	Titus
John	John	Phlm	Philemon
Acts	Acts	Heb	Hebrews
Rom	Romans	Jas	James
1–2 Cor	1–2 Corinthians	1–2 Pet	1–2 Peter
Gal	Galatians	1–2–3 John	1–2–3 John
Eph	Ephesiams	Jude	Jude
Phil	Philippians	Rev	Revelation
Col	Colossians		

MISCELLANEOUS

B.C.E.	Before the Common Era	masc.	masculine
C.E.	Common Era	MSS	manuscript(s)
chap(s).	chapter(s)	n(n).	note(s)
diss.	dissertation	NS	new series
DSS	Dead Sea Scrolls	NT	New Testament
ed(s).	edition; edited by; editor(s)	OT	Old Testament
		p(p).	page(s)
esp.	especially	pl.	plural
fem.	feminine	sg.	singular
FS	Festschrift	trans.	translated by; translator
Heb.	Hebrew	v(v)	verse(s)
lit.	literally	§	section/paragraph

Main Bibliography

Commentary Bibliography

In the text of the commentary, references to commentaries on Judges are by author's name only or by author's name and year of publication if the author has produced more than one commentary.

Abadie, P. "Le livre des Juges." *CaE* 125 (2003). **Adams, H. C.** *The Judges of Israel.* London: Warne, 1866. *L'Ancien Testament: Traduction nouvelle d'après les meilleurs textes avec introduction et notes.* Vol. 2, *Les Prophètes.* Bible du Centenaire. Paris: Société Biblique de Paris, 1947. 41–84. **Amit, Y.** *Judges: Introduction and Commentary* (Heb.). Mikra Leyisra'el: A Bible Commentary for Israel. Tel Aviv: Am Oved, 1999. **Armerding, C. E.** "Judges." In *Laymen's Bible Commentary.* Ed. G. C. D. Howley. Grand Rapids: Zondervan, 1979. ———. "Judges." In *The New International Bible Commentary.* Ed. F. F. Bruce. Grand Rapids: Zondervan, 1986. **Arnold, D.** *Ces mystérieux héros de la foi: Une approche globale du livre des Juges.* Saint-Légier, Switzerland: Emmaüs, 1995. **Augustine.** *Quaestiones.* PL 34:791–824. **Auld, A. G.** *Joshua, Judges, Ruth.* The Daily Study Bible Series. Philadelphia: Westminster, 1984. **Auzou, G.** *La Force de l'esprit, étude du 'Livre des juges.'* Connaissance de la Bible 5. Paris: Éditions de l'Orante, 1966. **Bachmann, J.** *Das Buch der Richter: Mit besonderer Rücksicht auf die Geschichte seiner Auslegung und kirchlichen Verwendung.* Berlin: Wiegandt & Grieben, 1868. **Barber, C. J.** *Judges: A Narrative of God's Power: An Expositional Commentary.* Neptune, NJ: Loizeaux Brothers, 1990. **Barredo, M. A.** *La Iniciativa de Dios: Estudio Literario y Teológico de Jueces 9–21.* Publicaciones Instituto Teológico Franciscano Serie Mayor 40. Murcia: Espigas, 2004. **Bertheau, E.** *Das Buch der Richter und Rut.* EHAT 6. Leipzig: Weidmannische Buchhandlung, 1845. **Black, J. S.** *The Book of Judges.* The Smaller Cambridge Bible for Schools. Cambridge: Cambridge UP, 1892. **Block, D. I.** *Judges, Ruth.* NAC 6. Nashville: Broadman & Holman, 1999. **Bloomfield, P.** *Judges.* The Guide. Darlington, England: Evangelical Press, 2005. **Boling, R.** *Judges: A New Translation with Introduction and Commentary.* AB 6A. Garden City, NY: Doubleday, 1975. **Bonfrerius, J.** 1631. **Brensinger, T. L.** *Judges.* BCBC. Scottdale, PA: Herald, 1999. **Brettler, M. Z.** *The Book of Judges.* Old Testament Readings. New York: Routledge, 2002. **Brown, C. A.** "Judges." In *Joshua, Judges, Ruth.* NIBCOT 5. Peabody, MA: Hendrickson, 2000. **Budde, D. K.** *Das Buch der Richter.* KHC. Freiburg i. B.: Mohr (Siebeck), 1897. ———. *Die Bücher der Richter und Samuel, ihre Quellen und ihr Aufbau.* Gissen: Ricker, 1890. **Burney, C. F.** *The Book of Judges with Introduction and Notes.* 1903. Repr., New York: Ktav, 1970. **Bush, G.** *Notes Critical and Practical, on the Book of Judges.* 1844. Repr., Minneapolis: James and Klock, 1976. **Calmet, A.** *Commentarius literalis in librum Judicum, latinis literis traditus a J. D. Mansi.* Wirceburgi, 1790. **Campbell, A. F.** "The Book of Judges." In *Joshua to Chronicles: An Introduction.* Louisville: Westminster John Knox, 2004. **Campbell, D. K.** *Judges: Leaders in Crisis Times.* Wheaton, IL: Victor Books, 1989. **Cassel, B. P.** "The Book of Judges." In *Numbers-Ruth.* Vol. 1 of Lange's Commentary on the Holy Scripture. Trans. P. H. Steenstra. T&T Clark, 1871. Repr., Grand Rapids: Zondervan, 1960. Originally published in *Das Buch der Richter und Rut* (Bielefeld, 1865). **Celniker, M.** "The Commentary of Rabbi David Kimhi on the Book of Judges." PhD diss., University of Toronto, 1975 (Ottawa, National Library microfiche, 32757). **Clericus.** 1708. **Coffman, J. B.,** and **T. B. Coffman.** *Judges and Ruth.* Abilene, TX: Abilene Christian UP, 1992. **Cohen, A.** *Joshua and Judges: Hebrew Text and English Translation with an Introduction and Commentary.* London: Soncino, 1950. **Cook, F. C.,** ed. *The Bible Commentary: Exodus-Ruth.* Grand Rapids: Baker, 1953. **Cooke, G. A.** *The Book of Judges in the Revised Version with Introduction and Notes.* The Cambridge Bible. Cambridge: Cambridge UP, 1913.

Crossan, D. "Judges." In *The Jerome Bible Commentary*. Ed. R. E. Brown et al. London: Geoffrey Chapman, 1968. 149–62. **Cundall, A. E.** "Judges." In *Judges and Ruth: An Introduction and Commentary*. TOTC. Downers Grove, IL: InterVarsity Press, 1968. **Curtis, E. L.** *The Book of Judges*. New York: Macmillan, 1913. **Davis, J. J.** *Conquest and Crisis: Studies in Joshua, Judges, and Ruth*. Grand Rapids: Baker, 1969. **Davis, R. D.** *Such a Great Salvation*. Grand Rapids: Baker, 1990. **Dirksen, P. B.** *Richteren: Een praktische bijbelverklaring*. Tekst en Toelichting. Kampen: Kok, 1990. **Drusius.** Ca. 1610. **Dorsey, D. A.** *The Literary Structure of the Old Testament: A Commentary on Genesis-Malachi*. Grand Rapids: Baker Books, 1999. 105–20. **Ehrlich, A. B.** *Randglossen zur hebräischen Bibel: Textkritisches, sprachliches und sachliches*. Vol. 3, *Josua, Richter;* vols. 1 and 2, *Samuelis*. Leipzig: Hinrichs, 1910. **Elitzur, V.** *The Book of Judges* (Heb.). Da'at Miqra. Jerusalem: Mosad Harav Kook, 1976. **Enns, P. P.** *Judges: Bible Study Commentary*. Grand Rapids: Zondervan, 1982. **Ephrem Syrus.** *Opera*. 1.308–30. **Eves, A. E.** "Judges." In *The IVP Women's Bible Commentary*. Ed. C. C. Kroeger and M. J. Evans. Downers Grove, IL: InterVarsity Press, 2002. 128–46. **Exum, J. C.** "Judges." In *Harper's Bible Commentary*. Ed. J. L. Mays. San Francisco: Harper & Row, 1988. **Fausset, A. R.** *A Critical and Expository Commentary on the Book of Judges*. 1885. Repr., London: James & Klock, 1977. **Ferguson, B.** *Joshua, Judges, and Ruth*. Nashville: Graded Press, 1988. **Fewell, D. N.** "Judges." In *The Women's Bible Commentary: Expanded Edition*. Ed. C. A. Newsom and S. H. Ringe. Louisville: Westminster John Knox, 1998. 73–83. **Fraine, J. de.** *Rechters uit de grondtekst vertaald en uitgelegt*. Roermond; Maaseik: Romen Zonen, 1955. **Freedman, H.,** and **J. J. Slotki.** *Joshua and Judges*. Ed. A. Cohen. Soncino Books of the Bible. London: Soncino, 1950. **Garstang, J.** *Joshua, Judges*. Foundations of Bible History. London: Constable, 1931. **Gershon, Rabbi Levi ben.** In Buxtorf's Rabbinic Bible. Ca. 1350. **Görg, M.** *Richter.* NEchtB. Würzburg: Echter, 1993. **Goslinga, C. J.** *Het Boek der Richteren opnieuw uit den grondtekst verklaard*. 2nd ed. 2 vols. Kampen: Kok, 1951, 1952. ———. *Joshua, Judges, Ruth*. Trans. R. Togtman. BSC. Grand Rapids: Zondervan, 1986. **Gray, J.** *Joshua, Judges, and Ruth*. NCB. London: Nelson, 1967. ———. *Joshua, Judges, Ruth*. NCB. Grand Rapids: Eerdmans, 1986. **Gressmann, H.** *Die Anfänge Israels*. Vol. 2, *Mose bis Richter und Ruth*. Göttingen: Vandenhoeck & Ruprecht, 1922. **Grindel, J. A.** *Joshua, Judges*. Collegeville Bible Commentary, Old Testament 7. Collegeville, MN: Liturgical Press, 1985. **Gros Louis, K. R. R.** "The Book of Judges." In *Literary Interpretations of Biblical Narratives*. Ed. K. R. R. Gros Louis et al. Nashville: Abingdon, 1974. 1:141–62. **Gunn, D.** "Joshua and Judges." In *The Literary Guide to the Bible*. Ed. R. Alter and F. Kermode. Cambridge, MA: Belknap, 1987. ———. *Judges*. Blackwell Bible Commentaries. Oxford: Blackwell, 2005. **Gutbrod, K.** *Das Buch vom Lande Gottes: Josua und Richter*. 2nd ed. BAT. Stuttgart: Calwer, 1957. **Hamlin, E. J.** *At Risk in the Promised Land: A Commentary on the Book of Judges*. ITC. Grand Rapids: Eerdmans, 1990. **Harduf, D. M.** *Judges*. Willowdale, Ontario: Harduf, 1984. **Hertzberg, H. W.** *Die Bücher Joshua, Richter, Ruth*. ATD 9. Göttingen: Vandenhoeck & Ruprecht, 1965. **Holland, M.** *Das Buch der Richter und das Buch Ruth*. Wuppertaler Studienbibel. Zürich: Brockhaus, 1995. **Hoppe, L.** *Joshua, Judges*. Old Testament Message 5. Wilmington, DE: Glazier, 1982. **Inrig, G.** *Hearts of Iron, Feet of Clay*. Chicago: Moody Press, 1979. **Jackman, D.** *Judges*. Communicator's Commentary. Dallas: Word Books, 1991. **Jennings, F. C.** *Judges and Ruth: An Exposition*. New York: Gospel, 1905. **Jeter, J. R., Jr.** *Preaching Judges*. Preaching Classic Texts. Saint Louis: Chalice, 2003. **Jordan, J. B.** *Judges: God's War against Humanism*. Tyler, TX: Geneva Ministries, 1985. **Kaufmann, Y.** *The Book of Judges* (Heb.). Jerusalem: Kiryat Sepher, 1962. **Keil, C. F.** *Joshua, Judges, Ruth*. Trans. J. Martin. 1863. Repr., Grand Rapids: Eerdmans, 1950. **Kent, D. G.** *Joshua, Judges, Ruth*. Layman's Bible Book Commentary. Nashville: Broadman, 1980. **Kimchi, D.** *The Commentary of Rabbi David Kimchi on the Book of Judges*. Ed. M. Celniker. Ca. 1200. Repr., Toronto: Celniker Book Committee, 1983. **Kittel, R.** "Das Buch Richter." In *Mose bis Ezechiel*. Vol. 1 of *HSAT.* Ed. E. Kautzsch. 4th ed. Tübingen: Mohr (Siebeck), 1922. 367–407. **Lagrange, M. J.** *Le livre des Juges*. Paris: Lecoffre, 1903. **Lapide, C.** 1642. Translated as *The Great Commentary of Cornelius à Lapide*, by T. W. Moseman (London, 1876). **Lawrenz, J. C.** *Judges, Ruth*. People's Bible.

Milwaukee: Northwestern, 1997. **Lewis, A. H.** *Judges/Ruth*. Chicago: Moody Press, 1979. **Lias, J. J.** *The Book of Judges with Map, Notes and Introduction*. Cambridge Bible for Schools and Colleges. Cambridge: Cambridge UP, 1902. **Lindars, B.** *Judges 1–5: A New Translation and Commentary*. Ed. A. D. H. Mayes. Edinburgh: T&T Clark, 1995. **Lods, A.** *Bible du Centenaire*. Paris: Société Biblique de Paris, [1923]. **Malvenda, T.** *Commentaria in Sacram Scripturam, una cum nova de verbo ad verbum ex hebraeo translatione*. Lyons, 1650. **Martin, J. D.** *Judges*. CBC. Cambridge: Cambridge UP, 1975. **Matthews, V.** *Judges and Ruth*. NCB. Cambridge: Cambridge UP, 2004. **Mayes, A. D. H.** *Judges*. OTG. Sheffield: Sheffield Academic, 1985. **McCann, J. C.** *Judges*. IBC. Louisville: John Knox, 2002. **Montanus, A.** *De varia Republica siue commentaria in librum Judicum*. Antwerp: Plantin, Vidua & Joannes Moretus, 1592. **Moore, G. F.** *A Critical and Exegetical Commentary on Judges*. ICC. Edinburg: T&T Clark, 1895. **Münster, S.** 1534. **Myers, J. M.,** and **P. P. Elliott.** "The Book of Judges." In *IB*. Nashville: Abingdon, 1953. 2:675–852. **Nicholas a Lyra.** *Postillae perpetueae*. Ca. 1325. **Niditch, S.** *Judges*. OTL. Louisville: Westminster John Knox, 2008. **Nötscher, F.** *Josua; Das Buch der Richter*. EB. Würzburg: Echter, 1950. **Nowack, W.** *Richter, Ruth*. HKAT 1.4. Göttingen: Vandenhoeck & Ruprecht, 1900. **O'Connor, M. P.** "Judges." In *NJBC*. Ed. R. E. Brown, J. Fitzmyer, and R. Murphy. Englewood Cliffs, NJ: Prentice Hall, 1990. 132–44. **Oettli, S.** *Das Deuteronomium und die Bücher Josua und Richter*. Ed. H. Strack and O. Zöckler. Kurzgefasster Kommentar. Munich: Beck, 1893. **Olson, D. T.** "Judges." In *NIB*. Vol. 2. Nashville: Abingdon, 1998. 721–888. **Origen.** *Origenis in librum Judicum homiliae*. Ed. Rufinus. Ca. 230. Translated in *Die griechischen christlichen Schriftsteller der ersten Jahrhunderte*, 30.467 (Berlin: Academic, 1897–). **Penna, A.** *Giudici e Rut*. La Sacra Bibbia. Rome: Marietti, 1963. **Phillips, W. G.** *Judges, Ruth*. Ed. M. Anders. HOTC. Nashville: Broadman & Holman, 2004. **Procopius of Gaza.** PG 87:1041–80. Ca. 500. **Pressler, C.** *Joshua, Judges, and Ruth*. Westminster Bible Companion. Louisville: Westminster John Knox, 2002. **Rashi (Rabbi Shlomo Yitzchaki).** Ca. 1100. In Buxtorf's Rabbinic Bible: *Biblia sacra Hebraica et Chaldaica cum Masora*. 2 vols. Basel, 1618–19. **Reuss, E.** *Histoire des Israélites depuis la conquête de la Palestine jusqu'a l'Exil: Livres des Juges, de Samuel et des Rois*. Paris, 1877. German ed. 1892. **Rosenberg, A. J.,** ed. *Judges: A New English Translation: Translation of Text, Rashi, and Commentary*. Trans. A. Fishelis and S. Fishelis. New York: Judaica, 1983. **Rust, E. C.** *The Book of Judges*. Richmond, VA: John Knox, 1973. **Ryan, R.** *Judges*. Readings. Sheffield: Sheffield Phoenix, 2007. **Serarius, N.** *Judices et Ruth explanati*. Mainz, 1609; Paris, 1611. **Schmid, S.** 1684. **Schneider, T. J.** *Judges*. Ed. D. W. Cotter. Berit Olam: Studies in Hebrew Narrative & Poetry. Collegeville, MN: Liturgical, 2000. **Schulz, A.** *Das Buch der Richter und das Buch Ruth*. Bonn: Hanstein, 1926. **Slotki, J. J.** "Judges: Introduction and Commentary." In *Joshua and Judges: Hebrew Text and English Translation with Introductions and Commentary*. Ed. A. Cohen. London: Soncino, 1950. 152–318. **Soggin, J. A.** *Judges*. OTL. Trans. J. Bowden. Philadelphia: Westminster, 1981. **Stone, L. G.** "Judges." In *Asbury Bible Commentary*. Ed. E. E. Carpenter and W. McCown. Grand Rapids: Zondervan, 1992. 329–46. **Studer, G. L.** *Das Buch der Richter grammatisch und historisch erklärt*. 1st ed. Bern: Dalp, 1835. **Tamisier, R.** "Le livre des Juges traduit et commente." *LStB*. 3:135–299. **Thatcher, G. W.** *Judges and Ruth: Introduction; Revised Version with Notes, Giving an Analysis Showing from Which of the Original Documents Each Portion of the Text Is Taken*. Century Bible. New York: Frowde, 1904. **Tidiman, B.** *Le livre des Juges*. Edifac, 2004. **Tsang, J.** *Judges* (Chinese). Hong Kong: Tien Dao, 1998. **Ubach, B.** *Josuè-Jutges-Rut*. La Bíblia versió dels textos originals i comentari pels monjos de Montserrat. Vol. 4. Montserrat: Monestir de Montserrat, 1953. **Valema, J. H.** *Jozua, Richteren, Ruth*. Leeuwarden: Jongbloed, 1955. **Vincent, A.** *Le livre des Juges. Le livre de Ruth*. 2nd ed. Paris: Cerf, 1958. **Walton, J. H., V. H. Matthews,** and **M. W. Chavalas.** *The IVP Bible Background Commentary: Old Testament*. Downers Grover, IL: InterVarsity Press, 2000. 241–76. **Watson, R. A.** *Judges and Ruth*. New York: Oxford UP, 1904. **Webb, B. G.** *The Book of Judges: An Integrated Reading*. JSOTSup 46. Sheffield: JSOT Press, 1987. ———. "Judges." In *New Bible Commentary*. Ed. G. J. Wenham et al. 21st cent. ed. Downers Grove, IL: InterVarsity Press, 1994. 261–86. **Welton, D. M.** *The*

Book of Judges. Philadelphia: American Baptist Publication Society, 1931. **Wiersbe, W. W.** *Judges*. Wheaton, IL: Victor, 1994. **Wilcock, M.** *The Message of Judges*. Bible Speaks Today. Downers Grove, IL: InterVarsity Press, 1992. **Wolf, H.** "Judges." In *The Expositor's Bible Commentary*. Ed. F. E. Gaebelein. 12 vols. Grand Rapids: Zondervan, 1992. 3:375–506. **Wood, L.** *Distressing Days of the Judges*. Grand Rapids: Zondervan, 1975. **Wright, P.**, ed. *Joshua, Judges*. Shepherd's Notes. Nashville: Broadman & Holman, 1998. **Younger, K. L.**, Jr. *Judges, Ruth*. NIV Application Commentary. Grand Rapids: Zondervan, 2002. **Zapletal, V.** *Das Buch der Richter*. Münster: Aschendorff, 1923. **Ziegler, W. C. L.** "Bemerkungen über das Buch der Richter aus dem Geist des Heldenalters: Nebst Beurtheilung der griechischen Versionen und ihrer Abweichung von Originaltext." In *Theologische Abhandlungen*. Göttingen: Dietrich, 1791. 262–376.

General Bibliography

Cited in text by author's or editor's name and shortened title.

Ackerman, J. S. "Prophecy and Warfare in Early Israel." *BASOR* 220 (1975) 5–13. ———. *Warrior, Dancer, Seductress, Queen: Women in Judges and Biblical Israel*. ABRL. New York: Doubleday, 1998. ———. "What If Judges Had Been Written by a Philistine?" *BibInt* 8 (2000) 33–41. **Aharoni, Y.** "Nothing Early and Nothing Late: Rewriting Israel's Conquest." *BA* 39 (1976) 55–76. **Ahlström, G. W.** *The History of Ancient Palestine from the Paleolithic Period to Alexander's Conquest*. JSOTSup 146. Sheffield: Sheffield Academic, 1993. ———. *Who Were the Israelites?* Winona Lake, IN: Eisenbrauns, 1986. **Albertz, R.** *The History of Israelite Religion in the Old Testament Period*. Trans. J. Bowden. 2 vols. Louisville: Westminster John Knox, 1994. ———. "In Search of the Deuteronomists: A First Solution to a 'Historical Riddle.'" In *The Future of the Deuteronomistic History*. Ed. T. C. Römer. BETL 147. Leuven: Peeters, 2000. 1–17. ———. "Wer waren die Deuteronomisten? Das historische Rätsel einer literarischen Hypothese." *EvT* 57 (1997) 319–38. **Alonso-Schökel, L.** "Dos Obras Recientes Sobre el Libro de los Jueces." *Bib* 45 (1964) 543–60. ———. "Erzählkunst im Büche der Richter." *Bib* 42 (1961) 148–58. ———. "Narrative Art in Joshua-Judges-Samuel-Kings." In *Israel's Past in Recent Research: Essays on Ancient Israelite Historiography*. Ed. V. P. Long. Sources for Biblical and Theological Study 7. Winona Lake, IN: Eisenbrauns, 1999. 255–78. **Alt, A.** "The Formation of the Israelite State in Palestine." In *Essays*. 223–310. ———. "The Settlement of the Israelites in Palestine." In *Essays on Old Testament History and Religion*. Trans. R. A. Wilson. Garden City, NY: Doubleday, 1968. 173–221. **Alter, R.** *The Art of Biblical Narrative*. New York: Basic Books, 1981. ———. *The Art of Biblical Poetry*. New York: Basic Books, 1985. **Altman, A.** "The Development of the Office of 'Judge' in Pre-Monarchic Israel" (Heb.). In *Proceedings of the Seventh World Congress of Jewish Studies: Studies in the Bible and the Ancient Near East*. Jerusalem, 1981. 11–21. **Amit, Y.** *Book of Judges: The Art of Editing*. BibInt Series 38. Leiden: Brill, 1999. ———. "The Dual Causality Principle and Its Effect on Biblical Literature." *VT* 37 (1987) 385–400. ———. "The End of the Book of Judges" (Heb.). In *Proceedings of the Ninth World Congress of Jewish Studies*. Jerusalem: World Union of Jewish Studies, [1986]. 73–80. ———. *Hidden Polemics in Biblical Narrative*. Trans. J. Chipman. Leiden: Brill, 2000. ———. *Reading Biblical Narratives: Literary Criticism and the Hebrew Bible*. Trans. Y. Lotan. Minneapolis: Fortress, 2001. ———. "The Use of Analogy in the Study of the Book of Judges." In *Wunschet Jerusalem Frieden: Collected Communications to the XIIth Congress of the International Organization for the Study of the Old Testament*. Ed. M. Augustin and K.-D. Schunck. Frankfort: Lang, 1988. 387–94. **Anbar, M.** "La 'Reprise.'" *VT* 38 (1988) 385–97. **Andersen, F. I.** *The Sentence in Biblical Hebrew*. The Hague: Mouton, 1974. **Andersson, G.** *The Book and Its Narratives: A Critical Examination of Some Synchronic Studies of the Book of Judges*. Örebro Studies in Literary History and Criticism 1. Örebro, Sweden: Universitetsbiblioteket, 2001. **Armerding, C. E.** "A Charismatic Theology of Judges." In *Gott* *lieben, und seine Gebote halten.* FS K. Bockmühl, ed. H. Burckhardt and M. Bockmühl. Basel: Brunnen, 1991. ———. "The Heroic Ages of Greece and Israel: A Literary-Historical Comparison." PhD diss., Brandeis Univesity, 1968 (Ann Arbor, MI: University Microfilms, 1968). ———. "When the Spirit Came Mightily: The Spirituality of Israel's Charismatic Leaders." In *Alive to God: Studies in Spirituality Presented to James Houston.* Ed. J. I. Packer and L. Wilkinson. Downers Grove, IL: InterVarsity Press, 1992. **Assis, E.** *Self-Interest or Communal Interest: An Ideology of Leadership in the Gideon, Abimelech and Jephthah Narratives (Judges 6–12).* VTSup 106. Leiden: Brill, 2005. **Astour, M. C.** "The Amarna Age Forerunners of Biblical Anti-royalism." In *For Max Weinreich on His 70th Birthday: Studies in Jewish Languages, Literature and Society.* The Hague: Mouton, 1964. 89–111. **Auld, A. G.** "The Deuteronomists and the Former Prophets, or What Makes the Former Prophets Deuteronomistic?" In *Those Elusive Deuteronomists.* Ed. L. S. Shearing and S. L. McKenzie. JSOTSup 268. Sheffield: Sheffield Academic, 1999. 116–26. ———. "The Deuteronomists between History and Theology." In *Congress Volume Oslo 1998.* Ed. A. Lemaire and M. Saebø. VTSup 80. Leiden: Brill, 2000. 353–67. ———. "The Former Prophets (Joshua, Judges, 1–2 Samuel, 1–2 Kings)." In *The Hebrew Bible Today: An Introduction to Critical Issues.* Ed. S. L. McKenzie and M. P. Graham. Louisville: Westminster John Knox, 1998. 53–68. ———. *Joshua Retold.* Edinburgh: T&T Clark, 1998. ———. "Judges and History: A Reconsideration." *VT* 25 (1975) 261–85. ———. "Review of Boling's *Judges:* The Framework of Judges and the Deuteronomists." *JSOT* 1 (1976) 41–46. ———. "Tribal Terminology in Joshua and Judges." In *Convegno sul tema: Le origini di Israele.* Ed. J. A. Soggin et al. Rome: Accademia nazionale dei Lincei, 1987. 85–98. Reprinted in *Joshua Retold* (Edinburgh: T&T Clark, 1998) 69–76. **Aurelius, E.** *Zukunft jenseits des Gerichts: Eine redaktionsgeschichtliche Studie zum Enneateuch.* BZAW 319. Berlin: de Gruyter, 2003. **Auzou, G.** *La force de l'esprit: Etude du livre des Juges.* Connaissance de la Bible 5. Paris: L' Orante, 1965. **Bal, M.** "Dealing with Women: Daughters in the Book of Judges." In *The Book and the Text: The Bible and Literary Theory.* Ed. R. Schwartz. Oxford: Blackwell, 1990. 16–39. ———. *Death & Dissymmetry: The Politics of Coherence in the Book of Judges.* Chicago Studies in the History of Judaism. Chicago: University of Chicago Press, 1988. ———. *Lethal Love: Feminist Literary Readings of Biblical Love Stories.* Bloomington: Indiana UP, 1987. ———. "Murder and Difference: Uncanny Sites in an Uncanny World." *Literature and Theology* 5 (1991) 11–19. ———. *Murder and Difference: Gender, Genre, and Scholarship on Sisera's Death.* Trans. M. Gumpert. Bloomington: Indiana UP, 1988. ———. "The Rhetoric of Subjectivity." *Poetics Today* 5 (1984) 337–76. **Bal, M.,** ed. *Anti-Covenant: Counter Reading Women's Lives in the Hebrew Bible.* JSOTSup 81/Bible and Literature 22. Sheffield: Almond, 1989. **Barredo, M. A.** *La Iniciativa de Dios: Estudio Lierario y Teológico de Jueces 1–8.* Publicaciones Instituto Teológico Franciscano, Serie Mayor 31. Murcia: Espigas, 2000. **Bartelmus, R.** "Forschung am Richterbuch seit Martin Noth." *TRu* 56 (1991) 221–59. **Barthélemy, D.** *Critique textuelle de l'Ancien Testament.* Vol. 1, *Josué, Juges, Ruth, Samuel, Rois, Chroniques, Esdras, Néhémie, Esther.* OBO 50.1. Fribourg: Éditions Universitaires; Göttingen: Vandenhoeck & Ruprecht, 1982. **Bartusch, M. W.** *Understanding Dan: An Exegetical Study of a Biblical City, Tribe and Ancestor.* JSOTSup 379. Sheffield: Sheffield Academic, 2003. **Batten, L. W.** "The Age of the Judges." In *The Bible as Literature.* Ed. R. G. Moulton et al. New York: Crowell, 1986. **Batto, B. F.** "Images of God in Joshua and Judges." *TBT* 39 (2001) 217–23. **Bayley, R.** "Sources and Structures in the Book of Judges." PhD thesis, University of Exeter, 1986. ———. "Which Is the Best Commentary? 14. The Book of Judges." *ExpTim* 103 (1991–1992) 136–38. **Bechtel, L. M.** "Shame as a Sanction of Social Control in Biblical Israel: Judicial, Political, and Social Shaming." *JSOT* 49 (1991) 47–76. **Becker, U.** *Richterzeit und Königtum: Redaktionsgeschichtliche Studien zum Richterbuch.* BZAW 192. Berlin: de Gruyter, 1990. **Becking, B.,** and **M. Dijkstra,** eds. *On Reading Prophetic Texts: Gender-Specific and Related Studies in Memory of Fokkelien van Dijk-Hemmes.* BibInt 18. Leiden: Brill, 1996. **Bell, R. D.** "The Book of Ruth: The Conclusion to Judges." *BV* 35 (2001) 1–4. **Bendenbender, A.** "Theologie im Widerstand: Die Antiochoskrise und ihre Bewältigung im Spiegel der Bücher Exodus und Richter." *T&K* 76

(1997) 43–55. **Berlin, A.** *Poetics and Interpretation of Biblical Narrative.* Bible and Literature 9. Sheffield: Almond, 1983. **Beyerlin, W.** "Gattung und Herkunft des Rahmens im Richterbuch." In *Tradition und Situation: Studien zur alttestamentlichen Prophetie.* FS A. Weiser, ed. E. Wurthwein and O. Kaiser. Göttingen: Vandenhoeck & Ruprecht, 1963. **Bimson, J. J.** "Merneptah's Israel and Recent Theories of Israelite Origins." *JSOT* 49 (1991) 3–29. ————. *Redating the Exodus and Conquest.* JSOTSup 5. Sheffield: JSOT Press, 1978. **Blankenheim, L. M.** "Die Richtervorlesung Luthers." *ARG* 50 (1960) 1–18. **Bledstein, A. J.** "Is Judges a Woman's Satire on Men Who Play God?" In *A Feminist Companion to Judges.* Ed. A. Brenner. Sheffield: JSOT Press, 1993. 34–54. **Blenkinsopp, J.** "Ballad Style and Psalm Style in the Book of Judges." *Bib* 42 (1961) 61–76. ————. "Benjamin Traditions Read in the Persian Period." In *Judah and the Judeans in the Persian Period.* Ed. O. Lipchits and M. Oeming. Winona Lake, IN: Eisenbrauns, 2006. 629–46. **Bloch-Smith, E.** "Israelite Ethnicity in Iron I: Archaeology Preserves What Is Remembered and What Is Forgotten in Israel's History." *JBL* 122 (2003) 401–25. **Block, D. I.** "Empowered by the Spirit of God: The Work of the Holy Spirit in the Historiographic Writings of the Old Testament." *SBJT* 1 (1997) 42–61. ————. "The Period of the Judges: Religious Disintegration under Tribal Rule." In *Israel's Apostasy and Restoration.* FS R. K. Harrison, ed. A. Gileadi. Grand Rapids: Baker, 1988. 39–58. ————. "Unspeakable Crimes: The Abuse of Women in the Book of Judges." *SBJT* 2–3 (1998) 46–55. **Blok, H.** "'En het land had veertig jaar rust': De bewoners van Israël in het tijdperk van de Richteren." *ACEBT* 19 (2001) 37–53. **Blum, E.** "Der kompositionelle Knoten am Übergang von Josua zu Richter: Ein Entflechtungsvorschlag." In *Deuteronomy and Deuteronomic Literature.* Ed. M. Vervenne and J. Lust. BETL 133. Leuven: Peeters, 1997. 181–212. **Bodine, W. R.** *The Greek Text of Judges: Recensional Developments.* HSM 23. Chico, CA: Scholars Press, 1980. **Boling, R. G.** "In Those Days There Was No King in Israel." In *A Light unto My Path.* FS J. M. Myers. Philadelphia: Temple University Press, 1974. 33–48. ————. "Judges." *ABD,* 3:1107–17. **Bowman, R. G.** "Narrative Criticism of Judges: Human Purpose in Conflict with Divine Presence." In *Judges and Method.* Ed. G. A. Yee. Minneapolis: Fortress, 1995. 17–44. **Brenner, A.** *The Israelite Woman: Social Role and Literary Type in Biblical Narrative.* The Bible Seminar. Sheffield: JSOT Press, 1985. **Brenner, A.,** ed. *A Feminist Companion to Judges.* FCB 4. Sheffield: JSOT Press, 1993. ————, ed. *Judges.* FCB 4, 2nd series. Sheffield: Sheffield Academic, 1999. **Brett, M. G.** "Israel's Indigenous Origins: Cultural Hybridity and the Formation of Israelite Identity." *BibInt* 11 (2003) 400–412. **Brettler, M. Z.** "The Book of Judges: Literature as Politics." *JBL* 108 (1989) 395–418. ————. *The Creation of History in Ancient Israel.* New York: Routledge, 1995. **Bronner, L.** "Valorized or Vilified? The Women of Judges in Midrashic Sources." In *Feminist Companion to Judges* (1993). Ed. A. Brenner. 72–95. **Brueggemann, W.** "Social Criticism and Social Vision in the Deuteronomic Formula of Judges." In *Die Botschaft und die Boten.* FS H. W. Wolff, ed. J. Jeremias and L. Perlitt. Neukirchen-Vluyn: Neukirchener, 1981. 101–14. **Bruno, A.** *Die Bücher Josua, Richter, Ruth: Eine rhythmnische Untersuchung.* Stockholm: Almqvist & Wiksell, 1955. **Buber, M.** "Books of Judges and Book of Judges." In *Kingship of God.* 3rd ed. New York: Harper Torchbooks, 1967. 66–84. **Budde, K.** *Die Bücher Richter und Samuel, ihre Quellen und ihr Aufbau.* Giessen: Ricker, 1890. ————. "Richter und Josua." *ZAW* 7 (1887) 93–166. **Butler, T. C.** "Daily Meditations in the Book or in One's Own Eyes: Reverse Structures in Joshua and Judges." Paper presented at annual meeting, Evangelical Theological Society, 1996. ————. *Joshua.* WBC 7. Waco, TX: Word, 1983. ————. "The Royal Perspective of the Book of Judges." Paper presented at annual meeting, Society of Biblical Literature, 1989. **Callaway, J. A.** "The Settlement in Canaan: The Period of the Judges." In *Ancient Israel: A Short History from Abraham to the Roman Destruction of the Temple.* Ed. H. A. Shanks. Englewood Cliffs, NJ: Prentice-Hall, 1988. 53–84. **Campbell, A. F.** *Joshua to Chronicles: An Introduction.* Louisville: Westminster John Knox, 2004. 67–105. **Campbell, A. F.,** and **M. A. O'Brien.** *Unfolding the Deuteronomistic History: Origins, Upgrades, Present Text.* Minneapolis: Fortress, 2000. **Cangh, J.-M. van.** "Les livres de Josué confrontés à l'archéologie récente." *RTL* 28 (1997) 161–88.

Carr, D. M. *Writing on the Tablet of the Heart: Origins of Scripture and Literature.* Oxford: Oxford UP, 2005. **Castelbajac, I. de.** "Les juges d'Israël: Une invention du Deutéronomiste?" *RHR* 221 (2004) 83–97. **Castillo, R. D.** "Existío una época de los así llamados jueces." *Qol* 13 (1997) 3–8. **Cazeau, J.** *Le refus de la guere sainte: Josué, Juges et Ruth.* LD 174. Paris: Cerf, 1998. **Cazelles, H.** "Le livre des Juges." In *DBSup.* 1394–1414. **Chalcraft, D. F.** "Deviance and Legitimate Action in the Book of Judges." In *The Bible in Three Dimensions: Essays in Celebration of Forty Years of Biblical Studies in the University of Sheffield.* Ed. D. J. A. Clines et al. JSOTSup 87. Sheffield: Sheffield Academic, 1990. 177–201. **Chaney, M. L.** "Ancient Palestinian Peasant Movements and the Formation of Premonarchic Israel." In *Palestine in Transition: The Emergence of Ancient Israel.* Ed. D. N. Freedman and D. F. Graf. Sheffield: Almond, 1983. 39–90. **Chisholm, R. B.** "The Role of Women in the Rhetorical Strategy of the Book of Judges." In *Integrity of Heart, Skillfulness of Hands.* Ed. C. H. Dyer and R. B. Zuck. Grand Rapids: Baker, 1994. 34–49. ———. "What's Wrong with This Picture? Stylistic Variation as a Rhetorical Technique in Judges." Paper presented at the Evangelical Theological Society, Washington, DC, 2006. **Coote, R. B.,** and **K. W. Whitelam.** *The Emergence of Early Israel in Historical Perspective.* SWBA 5. Sheffield: Almond, 1987. ———. "The Emergence of Israel: Social Transformation and State Formation following the Decline in Late Bronze Age Trade." *Semeia* 37 (1986) 107–47. **Cortese, E.** *Deuteronomistic Work.* Trans. S. Musholt. Studium Biblicum Franciscanun Analecta 47. Jerusalem: Franciscan Printing Press, 1999. **Craigie, P. C.** *The Problem of War in the Old Testament.* Grand Rapids: Eerdmans, 1978. **Creason, J. F., Jr.** "A Biblical Theology of Judges." PhD thesis, Bob Jones University, 1985. **Cross, F. M.** *From Epic to Canon: History and Literature in Ancient Israel.* Baltimore: Johns Hopkins UP, 1998. ———. "The Themes of the Book of Kings and the Structure of the Deuteronomistic History." In *Canaanite Myth and Hebrew Epic: Essays in the History of the Religion of Israel.* Cambridge, MA: Harvard UP, 1973. 274–89. **Crüsemann, F.** *Der Widerstand gegen das Königtum: Die antiköniglichen Texte des Alten Testaments und der Kampf um den frühen israelitischen Staat.* WMANT 49. Neukirchen-Vluyn: Neukirchener Verlag, 1978. **Culley, R. C.** *Studies in the Structure of Hebrew Narrative.* Philadelphia: Fortress, 1976. ———. *Themes and Variations: A Study of Action in Biblical Narrative.* Atlanta: Scholars Press, 1992. **Cundall, A. E.** "Antecedents of the Monarchy in Ancient Israel." *VE* 3 (1964) 42–50. ———. "Judges—An Apology for the Monarchy?" *ExpTim* 81 (1970) 178–81. **Davidson, E. T. A.** "Can Sources of Judges Be Found in Ugaritic Myths?" *PEGLMBS* 25 (2005) 434–57. ———. "Comedy of Horrors." *PEGLMBS* 24 (2004) 39–44. **Davies, P. R.** *In Search of 'Ancient Israel.'* JSOTSup 148. Sheffield: JSOT, 1992. ———. "Whose History? Whose Israel? Whose Bible? Biblical Histories, Ancient and Modern." In *Can a 'History of Israel' Be Written?* Ed. L. L. Grabbe. JSOTSup 245. Sheffield: Sheffield Academic, 1997. 104–22. **Davis, D. R.** "A Proposed Life Setting for the Book of Judges." PhD diss., Southern Baptist Theological Seminary, 1978 (Ann Arbor, MI: University Microfilms, 1978). **Day, P.,** ed. *Gender and Difference in Ancient Israel.* Minneapolis: Fortress, 1989. **Dearman, J. A.** "Baal in Israel: The Contribution of Some Place Names and Personal Names to an Understanding of Early Israelite Religion." In *History and Interpretation.* FS J. H. Hayes, ed. M. P. Graham, W. P. Brown, and J. K. Kuan. JSOT Sup 173. Sheffield: Sheffield Academic, 1993. 173–91. **Desnoyers, L.** *Histoire du peuple hébreu des Juges à la captivité I.* Paris: Picard, 1922. **Dever, W. G.** "Ceramics, Ethnicity, and the Question of Israel's Origens." *BA* 58 (1995) 200–213. ———. *What Did the Biblical Writers Know and When Did They Know It? What Archaeology Can Tell Us about the Reality of Ancient Israel.* Grand Rapids: Eerdmans, 2001. **Dexinger, F.** "Ein Pladoyer für die Linkshander im Richterbuch." *ZAW* 89 (1977) 268–69. **Dietrich, W.** "Histoire et Loi: Historiographie deutéronomiste et Loi deutéronomique à l'example du passage de l'époque des Juges à l'époque royale." In *Israël construit.* Ed. A. de Pury et al. 297–323. Translated as "History and Law: Deuteronomistic Historiography and Deuteronomic Law Exemplified in the Passage from the Period of the Judges to the Monarchical Period," in *Israel Constructs Its History: Deuteronomist Historiography in Recent Research,* ed. A. de Pury, T. Römer, and J.-D. Macchi, JSOTSup

306 (Sheffield: Sheffield Academic, 2000) 315–42. ———. *Prophetie und Geschichte: Eine redaktionsgeschichtliche Untersuchung zum deuteronomistischen Geschichtswerk.* FRLANT 108. Göttingen: Vandenhoeck & Ruprecht, 1977. **Di Lella, A. A.** "The Book of Tobit and the Book of Judges." *Hen* 22 (2000) 197–206. **Dinur, B. Z.** *Studies in the Book of Judges* (Heb.). Publications of the Israel Bible Society 10. Jerusalem: Israel Bible Society, 1966. **Disse, A.** *Informationsstruktur im biblischen Hebräisch: Sprachwissenschaftliche Grundlagen und exegetische Konsequenzen einer Korpusuntersuchung zu den Büchern Deuteronomium, Richter und 2 Könige.* Arbeiten zu Text und Sprache im Alten Testament 56.1, 2. St. Ottilien: EOS, 2000. **Dornseiff, F.** "Das Buch der Richter: I. Die Literarische Absicht." *AfO* 14 (1944) 319–28. **Dragga, S.** "In the Shadow of the Judges: The Failure of Saul." *JSOT* 38 (1987) 39–46. **Driver, G. R.** "Problems in Judges Newly Discussed." *ALUOS* 4 (1964) 6–25. **Dumbrell, W. J.** " 'In those days there was no king in Israel; every man did that which was right in his own eyes': The Purpose of the Book of Judges Reconsidered." *JSOT* 25 (1983) 23–33. **Dus, J.** "Moses or Joshua? On the Problem of the Founder of the Israelite Religion." *Radical Religion* 2 (1975) 26–41. ———. "Die 'Sufeten' Israels." *ArOr* 31 (1963) 444–69. **Easterly, E.** "A Case of Mistaken Identity: The Judges in Judges Don't Judge." *BR* 13 (1997) 41–43. **Edzard, D.** "Das Wechselverhältnis von Richter und Gesellschaft: Mesopotamien und Peripherie bis Ur III." *Maarav* 12 (2005) 19–26. **Eissfeldt, O.** *Die Quellen des Richterbuches: In synoptischer Anordnung ins Deutsche übersetzt, samt einer in Einleitung und Noten gegebenen Begründung.* Leipzig: Hinrichs, 1925. **Elazar, D. J.** "The Book of Judges: The Israelite Tribal Federation and Its Discontents." Jerusalem Center for Public Affairs <http://www.jcpa.org/dje/articles/judges.htm>. **Emmerson, G. I.** "Women in Ancient Israel." In *The World of Ancient Israel.* Ed. R. E. Clements. Cambridge: Cambridge UP, 1989. 371–94. **Exum, J. C.** "The Centre Cannot Hold: Thematic and Textual Instabilities in the Book of Judges." *CBQ* 52 (1990) 410–31. ———. "The Ethics of Biblical Violence against Women." In *The Bible in Ethics.* Ed. J. W. Rogerson et al. JSOTSup 207. Sheffield: Sheffield Academic, 1995. 248–71. ———. *Fragmented Women: Feminist, (Sub)versions of Biblical Narratives.* JSOTSup 163. Sheffield: JSOT Press, 1993. ———. "Murder They Wrote: Ideology and the Manipulation of Female Presence in Biblical Narrative." In *The Pleasure of Her Text: Feminist Readings of Biblical and Historical Texts.* Ed. A. Back. Philadelphia: Trinity Press International, 1990. 45–67. ———. *Plotted, Shot, and Painted.* JSOTSup 215. Sheffield: Sheffield Academic, 1996. ———. *Tragedy and Biblical Narrative: Arrows of the Almighty.* Cambridge: Cambridge UP, 1992. ———. *Was Sagt das Richterbuch den Frauen?* SBS 169. Stuttgart: Katholisches Bibelwerk, 1997. **Exum, J. C.,** ed. *Signs and Wonders: Biblical Texts in Literary Focus.* Atlanta: Society of Biblical Literature, 1988. **Faiman, D.** "Chronology in the Book of Judges." *JBQ* 21 (1993) 31–40. **Fensham, F. C.** "Literary Observations on Historical Narratives in Sections of Judges." In *Storie e tradizioni di Israele.* FS J. A. Soggin, ed. D. Garrone and F. Israel. Brescia: Paideia, 1991. 77–88. **Fewell, D. N.** "Feminist Reading of the Hebrew Bible: Affirmation, Resistance, and Transformation." *JSOT* 39 (1987) 77–87. **Finkelstein, I.** *The Archaeology of the Israelite Settlement.* Jerusalem: Israel Archaeology Society, 1988. ———. "Pots and People Revisited: Ethnic Boundaries in the Iron Age I." In *The Archaeology of Israel: Constructing the Past, Interpreting the Present.* Ed. N. A. Silberman and D. Small. JSOTSup 237. Sheffield: Sheffield Academic, 1997. 216–38. ———. "The Rise of Early Israel: Archaeology and Long-Term History." In *The Origin of Early Israel—Current Debate.* Ed. S. Ahituv and E. D. Oren. Beer-sheva: Ben-Gurion University of the Negev Press, 1998. 7–39. ———. "Searching for Israelite Origins." *BAR* 14 (1988) 34–45, 58. **Fishbane, M.** *Biblical Interpretation in Ancient Israel.* Oxford: Clarendon, 1986. **Flanagan, J. W.** "Chiefs in Israel." *JSOT* 20 (1981) 47–73. **Fontaine, C. R.** *Traditional Sayings in the Old Testament: A Contextual Study.* Bible and Literature 5. Sheffield: Almond, 1982. **Frankenberg, W.** *Die Composition des Deuteronomischen Richterbuches (Richter II, 6–XVI) nebst einer Kritik von Richter XVII–XXI.* Marburg: Elwert, 1895. **Freedman, D. N.,** and **D. F. Graf,** eds. *Palestine in Transition: The Emergence of Ancient Israel.* Sheffield: Almond, 1983. **Frick, F. S.** "Ecology, Agriculture and Patterns of Settlement." In *The World of Ancient Israel.* Ed. R. E. Clements. Cambridge:

Cambridge UP, 1989. 67–94. **Fritz, V.** "Conquest or Settlement? The Early Iron Age in Palestine." *BA* 50 (1987) 84–100. ———. "Kanaaniter in frühen Israel." In *Vielseitigkeit des Alten Testaments.* FS G. Sauer, ed. J. A. Loader and H. V. Kieweler. Wiener Alttestamentliche Studien 1. Frankfurt a. M.: Lang, 1999. 207–13. **Fuchs, E.** "The Literary Characterization of Mothers and Sexual Politics in the Hebrew Bible." *Semeia* 46 (1989) 151–66. **Gaß, E.** *Die Ortsnamen des Richterbuchs in historischer und redaktioneller Perspektive.* Abhandlungen des Deutschen Palästina-Vereins 35. Wiesbaden: Harrassowitz, 2005. **Gerbrandt, G. E.** *Kingship according to the Deuteronomistic History.* SBLDS 87. Atlanta: Scholars Press, 1986. **Geus, C. H. J. de.** *The Tribes of Israel: An Investigation into Some of the Presuppositions of Martin Noth's Amphictyony Hypothesis.* Amsterdam: Van Gorcum, 1976. **Gillmayr-Bucher, S.** "Die Richter." In *Die Bibel in der deutschsprachigen Literatur des 20. Jahrhunderts.* Vol. 2, *Personen und Figuren.* Ed. H. M. Schmidinger. Mainz: Matthias-Grünewald, 1999. 137–50. **Glassner, J. J.** "Women, Hospitality, and the Honor of the Family." In *Women's Earliest Records.* Ed. B. S. Lesko. Atlanta: Scholars Press, 1988. 71–90. **Globe, A.** "'Enemies Round About': Disintegrative Structure in the Book of Judges." In *Mappings of the Biblical Terrain: The Bible as Text.* Ed. V. L. Tollers and F. Kermode. Lewisburg, PA: Bucknell UP, 1990. 233–51. **Good, R. M.** "The Just War in Ancient Israel." *JBL* 104 (1985) 385–400. **Gooding, D. W.** "The Composition of the Book of Judges." *ErIsr* 16 (1982) 70–79. **Gottwald, N. K.** "The Hypothesis of the Revolutionary Origins of Ancient Israel: A Response to Hauer and Thompson." *JSOT* 7 (1978) 37–52. ———. "The Israelite Settlement as a Social Revolutionary Movement." In *Biblical Archaeology Today.* Jerusalem: IES, 1985. 34–46. ———. *The Tribes of Yahweh: A Sociology of the Religion of Liberated Israel, 1250–1050 B.C.E.* Maryknoll: Orbis, 1979. **Greenspahn, F. E.** "Recent Scholarship on the History of Premonarchic Israel." *Journal of Reformed Judaism* 30 (1983) 81–93. ———. "The Theology of the Framework of Judges." *VT* 36 (1986) 385–96. **Grether, O.** "Die Bezeichnung 'Richter' für die charismatischen Helden der vorstaatlichen Zeit." *ZAW* 57 (1939) 110–21. **Gross, R. M.,** ed. *Beyond Androcentrism: New Essays on Women and Religion.* Missoula, MT: Scholars Press, 1977. **Groves, A.** "Saul Bashing: An Appropriate Agenda for the Book of Judges." Paper presented to Evangelical Theological Society, Jackson, MS, 1996. **Guest, P. E.** "Can Judges Survive without Sources? Challenging the Consensus." *JSOT* 78 (1998) 43–61. ———. "Dangerous Liaisons in the Book of Judges." *SJOT* 11 (1997) 241–69. **Guillaume, P.** "From a Post-monarchical to the Pre-monarchical Period of the Judges." *BN* 113 (2002) 12–17. ———. *Waiting for Josiah: The Judges.* JSOTSup 385. Sheffield: Sheffield Academic, 2004. **Gunn, D. M.** "The 'Battle Report': Oral or Scribal Convention?" *JBL* 93 (1974) 513–18. ———. "Narrative Patterns and Oral Tradition in Judges and Samuel." *VT* 24 (1974) 286–317. **Gunn, D. M.,** and **D. N. Fewell.** *Narrative in the Hebrew Bible.* Oxford: Oxford UP, 1993. **Hackett, J. A.** "'There Was No King in Israel': The Era of the Judges." In *The Oxford History of the Biblical World.* Ed. M. D. Coogan. New York: Oxford UP, 1998. 132–64. ———. "Violence and Women's Lives in the Book of Judges." *Int* 58 (2004) 356–64. ———. "Women's Studies and the Hebrew Bible." In *The Future of Biblical Studies: The Hebrew Scriptures.* Ed. R. Friedman et al. Atlanta: Scholars Press, 1987. 141–64. **Halpern, B.** *The Emergence of Israel in Canaan.* SBLMS 29. Chico, CA: Scholars Press, 1983. ———. *The First Historians: The Hebrew Bible and History.* San Francisco: Harper & Row, 1988. **Hamilton, V. P.** *Handbook on the Historical Books.* Grand Rapids: Baker Academic, 2001. **Hanson, P. D.** "War, Peace & Justice in Early Israel." *BR* 3 (1987) 32–45. **Harlé, P.** *La Bible d'Alexandrie.* Vol. 7, *Les Juges.* Paris: Cerf, 1999. **Hasitschka, M.** "Die Führer Israels: Mose, Josua und die Richter." In *Alttestamentliche Gestalten im Neuen Testament: Beiträge zur biblischen Theologie.* Darmstadt: Wissenschaftliche Buchgesellschaft, 1999. 117–40. **Hauser, A. J.** "Israel's Conquest of Palestine: A Peasant's Rebellion?" *JSOT* 7 (1978) 2–19, 35–36. ———. "The Revolutionary Origins of Ancient Israel: A Response to Gottwald." *JSOT* 7 (1978) 46–49. ———. "Unity and Diversity in Early Israel before Samuel." *JETS* 22 (1979) 289–303. **Helyer, L. R.** "Hero and Heroine Narratives in the Old Testament." *SBJT* 2 (1998) 34–45. **Hens-Piazza, G.** "Violence in Joshua and Judges." *TBT* 39 (2001) 196–203. **Herr-**

mann, S. "Basic Factors of Israelite Settlement in Canaan." In *Biblical Archaeology Today* (1985) 47–53. ———. "Das Werden Israels." *TLZ* 87 (1962) 561–74. **Hess, R. E.** "Early Israel in Canaan: A Survey of Recent Evidence and Interpretation." *PEQ* 125 (1993) 125–42. ———. "Israelite Identity and Personal Names from the Book of Judges." *HS* 44 (2003) 25–39. ———. "The Name Game." *BAR* 30 (2004) 38–41. **Hess, R. E., G. A. Klingheil,** and **P. J. Ray, Jr.,** eds. *Critical Issues in the Early History of Israel.* Winona Lake, IN: Eisenbrauns, 2008. **Hobbs, T. R.** "Aspects of Warfare in the First Testament World." *BTB* 25 (1995) 79–90. ———. "Hospitality in the First Testament and the Teleological Fallacy.'" *JSOT* 95 (2001) 3–30. **Hodgetts-Guest, P. E.** "In Search of Judges." PhD thesis, University of Birminghan, 1996. **Hollyday, J.** "Voices out of the Silence: Recovering the Biblical Witness of Women." *Sojourners* 15 (1986) 20–23. **Holzinger, H.** "Richter 2 ^{6}–16 ^{31} untersucht." Unpublished manuscript. **Howard, D. M., Jr.** "The Case of Kingship in Deuteronomy and the Former Prophets." *WTJ* 52 (1990) 101–15. ———. "The Case for Kingship in the Old Testament Narrative Books and the Psalms." *TJ* 9 NS (1988) 19–35. ———. *An Introduction to the Old Testament Historical Books.* Chicago: Moody, 1993. 99–123. **Hurvitz, A.** "The Historical Quest for 'Ancient Israel' and the Linguistic Evidence of the Hebrew Bible: Some Methodological Observations." *VT* 47 (1997) 301–15. **Isaksson, B.** "Infinitiven som adverbiellt komplement i domarboken: En komparativ studie." *SEÅ* 70 (2005) 107–18. ———. "Semitic Circumstantial Qualifiers in the Book of Judges: A Pilot Study on the Infinitive." *Orientalia Suecana* 56 (2007) 163–72. **Ishida, T.** "The Leaders of the Tribal League 'Israel' in the Premonarchic Period." *RB* 80 (1973) 514–30. ———. "SOFET: The Leaders of the Tribal League 'Israel' in the Monarchical Period." In *History and Historical Writing in Ancient Israel.* Ed. T. Ishida. Studies in the History and Culture of the Ancient Near East 16. Leiden: Brill, 1999. 36–56. **Ish Shalom, M.** *Meʾir ʿAyin—Comments on the Book of Judges* (Heb.). Wien, 1891. **Isserlin, B. S. J.** *The Israelites.* New York: Thames & Hudson, 1998. **Jenni, E.** "Vom Zeugnis des Richterbuches." *TZ* 12 (1956) 257–74. ———. "Zwei Jahrzehnte Forschung an den Bücher Joshua bis Könige." *TRu* 27 NS (1961–1962) 1–32, 97–146. **Jobling, D.** "Deuteronomic Political Theory in Judges and 1 Samuel 1–12." In *The Sense of Biblical Narrative.* Vol. 2. Sheffield: JSOT Press, 1986. 44–87. **Josipovici, G.** "The Rhythm Falters: The Book of Judges." In *The Book of God: A Response to the Bible.* New Haven: Yale UP, 1988. 108–31. **Jost, R.** *Frauenmacht und Männerliebe: Egalitäre Utopien aus der Frühzeit Israels.* Stuttgart: Kohlhammer, 2006. ———. *Gender, Sexualität und Macht in der Anthropologie des Richterbuches.* BWANT 164, NS 4. Stuttgart: Kohlhammer, 2006. **Kaiser, O.** "Pentateuch und Deuteronomistisches Geschichtswerk." In *Studien zur Literaturgeschichte des Alten Testaments.* FB 90. Würzburg: Echter, 2000. **Kallai, Z.** "The Conquest of Northern Israel in Joshua and in Judges" (Heb.). In *Proceedings of the Fifth World Congress of Jewish Studies.* Vol. 1. Jerusalem, 1969. 129–34. ———. "Joshua and Judges in Biblical Historiography." In *Biblical Historiography and Historical Geography: Collection of Studies.* Ed. K. Zecharia. BEATAJ 44. Frankfurt: Lang, 1998. 243–60. ———. "The Twelve-Tribe Systems of Israel." *VT* 47 (1997) 53–90. **Kang, S.-M.** *Divine War in the Old Testament and in the Ancient Near East.* Berlin: de Gruyter, 1989. **Kaswalder, P. A.** "I Giudici di Israele." *LASBF* 41 (1991) 9–40. **Kaufmann, Y.** *The Biblical Account of the Conquest of Canaan.* 2nd ed., with preface by M. Greenberg. Jerusalem: Magnes, 1985. ———. "Traditions concerning Early Israelite History in Canaan." In *Studies in the Bible.* Ed. C. Rabin. ScrHier 8. Jerusalem: Magnes, 1961. 303–34. **Keefe, A. A.** "Rapes of Women/Wars of Men." *Semeia* 61 (1993) 79–97. **Keel, O.,** and **C. Uehlinger.** *Gods, Goddesses and Images of God in Ancient Israel.* Trans. T. Trapp. Minneapolis: Fortress, 1998. **Kellermann, D.** "Das Buch der Richter." In *Höre, Israel! Jahwe ist einzig: Bausteine für eine Theologie des Alten Testaments.* Ed. E. Sitarz. Stuttgart: Katholisches Bibelwerk, 1987. 80–87. **Kitchen, K. A.** "Humble Beginnings—around and in Canaan." In *On the Reliability of the Old Testament.* Grand Rapids: Eerdmans, 2003. 159–239. **Kittel, R.** "Die pentateuchischen Urkunden in den Büchern Richter und Samuel." *TSK* 1 (1892) 44–71. **Klaus, N.** *Pivot Patterns in the Former Prophets.* JSOTSup 247. Sheffield: Sheffield Academic, 1999. **Klein, L. R.**

"The Book of Judges: Paradigm and Deviation in Images of Women." In *Feminist Companion to Judges* (1993). Ed. A. Brenner. 55–71. ———. "A Spectrum of Female Characters in the Book of Judges." Paper presented to Society of Biblical Literature, 1989. ———. "A Spectrum of Female Characters in the Book of Judges." In *Feminist Companion to Judges* (1993). Ed. A. Brenner. 24–33. ———. "Structure, Irony and Meaning in the Book of Judges." In *Proceedings of the Tenth Congress of Jewish Studies; Division A: The Bible and Its World.* Ed. D. Assaf. Jerusalem: World Union of Jewish Studies, 1990. 83–90. ———. *The Triumph of Irony in the Book of Judges.* JSOTSup 68. Sheffield: Almond, 1987. **Knoppers, G.,** and **J. G. McConville,** eds. *Reconsidering Israel and Judah: Recent Studies on the Deuteronomistic History.* Sources for Biblical and Theological Study. Winona Lake, IN: Eisenbrauns, 2000. **Kochavi, M.** "The Israelite Settlement in Canaan in the Light of Archaeological Surveys." In *Biblical Archaeology Today: Proceedings of the International Congress on Biblical Archaeology, Jerusalem, April 1984.* Jerusalem: Israel Exploration Society, 1985. 54–60. **Koizumi, T.** "Toward the Establishment of a Scientific History of Israel—from the Nomadic Period to the Organization of the Four Leading Tribes." *AJBI* 12 (1986) 29–76. **Kort, W. A.** *Story, Text, and Scripture: Literary Interests in Biblical Narrative.* University Park: Pennsylvania State UP, 1988. 29–35. **Kratz, R. G.** *The Composition of the Narrative Books of the Old Testament.* Trans. J. Bowden. New York: T&T Clark, 2005. Originally published as *Die Komposition der erzählender Bücher des Alten Testaments* (Göttingen: Vandenhoeck & Ruprecht, 2000). **Kreuzer, S.** "Max Weber, George Mendenhall und das sogenannte Revolutionsmodell für die 'Landnahme' Israels." In *Altes Testament—Forschung und Wirkung.* Ed. P. Mommer et al. Frankfurt a. M.: Lang, 1994. 283–305. ———. "Eine Schrift, zwei Fassungen: Das Beispiel des Richterbuches." *BK* 56 (2001) 88–91. **Kruger, H. A. J.** "Sun and Moon Grinding to a Halt: Exegetical Remarks on Joshua 10:9–14 and Related Texts in Judges." *HTS* 55 (1999) 1077–97. **Lamadrid, A. G.** "Historia Deuteronomista." In *Historia, Narrativa, Apocalíptica.* Introducción al Estudio de la Biblia 3b. Estella: EVD, 2000. 17–216. **Lambert, F.** "Tribal Influences in Old Testament Traditions." *SEÅ* 59 (1994) 33–58. **Landy, F.** "Between Centre and Periphery Her Story." Paper presented to Society of Biblical Literature, 1989. **Lang, B.** "The Social Organization of Peasant Poverty in Biblical Israel." *JSOT* 24 (1982) 47–63. **Lanoir, C.** *Femmes fatales, filles rebelles: Figures féminines dans le livre des Juges.* Actes et recherches. Geneva: Labor et Fides, 2005. ———. "Le livre des Juges, l'histoire et les femmes." *FoiVie* 96 (1997) 55–71. **Lapp, P. W.** "The Conquest of Palestine in the Light of Archaeology." *CTM* 38 (1967) 283–300. **Latvus, K.** *God, Anger and Ideology: The Anger of God in Joshua and Judges in Relation to Deuteronomy and the Priestly Writings.* JSOTSup 279. Sheffield: Sheffield Academic, 1998. **Leder, A. C.** "Reading the Former Prophets by the Rivers of Babylon." *CTJ* 37 (2002) 9–27. **Lemche, N. P.** *Ancient Israel: A New History of Israelite Society.* Sheffield: JSOT Press, 1988. ———. *The Canaanites and Their Land: The Tradition of the Canaanites.* JSOTSup 110. Sheffield: JSOT Press, 1991. ———. *Early Israel: Anthropological and Historical Studies on the Israelite Society before the Monarchy.* VTSup 37. Leiden: Brill, 1985. ———. "Early Israel Revisited." *CurBS* 4 (1996) 9–34. ———. "The Greek 'Amphictyony'—Could It Be a Prototype for the Israelite Society in the Period of the Judges?" *JSOT* 4 (1977) 48–59. ———. "Is It Still Possible to Write a History of Ancient Israel?" *SJOT* 8 (1994) 165–90. ———. "'Israel in the Period of the Judges'—The Tribal League in Recent Research." *ST* 38 (1984) 1–28. ———. *The Israelites in History and Tradition.* Library of Ancient Israel. Ed. D. A. Knight. Louisville: Westminster John Knox Press, 1998. ———. "The Judges—Once More." *BN* 20 (1983) 47–55. ———. "On the Problems of Reconstructing Pre-Hellenistic Israelite (Palestinian) History." *JHS* 3 (2000). ———. *Prelude to Israel's Past: Background and Beginnings of Israelite History and Ideology.* Peabody, MA: Hendrickson, 1998. **Leuchter, M.** "Jeroboam the Ephratite." *JBL* 125 (2006) 51–72. **Lilley, J. P. U.** "A Literary Appreciation of the Book of Judges." *TynBul* 18 (1967) 94–102. **Lindars, B.** "A Commentary on the Greek Judges?" In *VI Congress of the International Organization for Septuagint and Cognate Studies, Jerusalem 1986.* Ed. C. E. Cox. SCS 23. Atlanta: Scholars Press, 1987. 167–200. ———. *Interpreting Judges Today.* London:

University of London Press, 1983. ———. "The Israelite Tribes in Judges." In *Studies in the Historical Books of the Old Testament.* VTSup 30 (1979) 95–112. **Linden, N.** *The Story Goes . . . 3: The Stories of Judges and Kings.* Trans. John Bowden. London: SCM Press, 2000. **Lohfink, N.** "Gab es eine deuteronomistische Bewegung?" In *Jeremia und die Deuteronomistische Bewegung.* Ed. W. Gross. BBB 98. Weinheim: Beltz Athenäum, 1995. 313–82. ———. "Der Zorn Gottes und das Exil: Beobachtungen am deuteronomistischen Geschichtswerk." In *Liebe und Gebot: Studien zum Deuteronomium.* FS L. Perlitt, ed. R. G. Kratz and H. Spieckermann. FRLANT 190. Göttingen: Vandenhoeck & Ruprecht, 2000. **Long, V. P.** *The Art of Biblical History.* Foundations of Contemporary Interpretation 5. Grand Rapids: Zondervan, 1994. **Longman, T. III.** *Literary Approaches to Biblical Interpretation.* Grand Rapids: Zondervan, 1987. **Machinist, P.** "Outsiders or Insiders: The Biblical View of Emergent Israel and Its Contexts." In *The Other in Jewish Thought and History: Constructions of Jewish Thought and Identity.* Ed. L. J. Silberstein and R. L. Cohn. New York: New York UP, 1994. 35–60. **Mafico, T. L.** "Judge, Judging." *ABD,* 3:1104–05. ———. "Were the 'Judges' of Israel like African Spirit Mediums?" In *Text and Experience: Toward a Cultural Exegesis of the Bible.* Ed. D. Smith-Christopher. BS 35. Sheffield: JSOT Press, 1995. 330–43. **Malamat, A.** "Charismatic Leadership in the Book of Judges." In *Magnalia Dei: The Mighty Acts of God.* FS G. E. Wright, ed. F. M. Cross et al. Garden City, NY: Doubleday, 1976. 152–68. ———. "How Inferior Israelite Forces Conquered Fortified Canaanite Cities." *BAR* 8 (1982) 24–35. ———. "Israelite Conduct of War in the Conquest of Canaan according to the Biblical Tradition." In *Symposia Celebrating the 75th Anniversary of the Founding of the ASOR.* Ed. F. M. Cross. Cambridge, MA: ASOR, 1979. 35–55. ———. "The Period of the Judges." In *A History of the Jewish People.* Ed. H. H. Ben-Sasson. Cambridge, MA: Harvard UP, 1976. 67–87. ———. "The Proto-History of Israel: A Study in Method." In *Essays in Honor of David Noel Freedman in Celebration of His Sixtieth Birthday.* Ed. C. Meyers and M. O'Connor. Winona Lake, IN: Eisenbrauns, 1983. **Manley, G. T.** "The Deuteronomic Redactor in the Book of Judges." *EvQ* 31 (1959) 32–37. **Marais, J.** *Representation in Old Testament Narrative Texts.* BibInt 36. Leiden: Brill, 1998. **Marcos, N. F.** "The Hebrew and Greek Text of Judges." In *The Earliest Text of the Hebrew Bible: The Relationship between the Masoretic Text and the Hebrew Base of the Septuagint Reconsidered.* Ed. A. Schenker. SBLSCS 52. Atlanta: SBL Press, 2003. 1–16. **Margalith, O.** "On the Origin and Antiquity of the Name 'Israel.'" *ZAW* 102 (1993) 225–37. **Martin, J. D.** "Israel as a Tribal Society." In *The World of Ancient Israel.* Ed. R. E. Clements. Cambridge: Cambridge UP, 1989. 95–118. ———. "The Office of Judge in Pre-Monarchic Israel." *GUOST* 26 (1979) 64–79. **Matthews, V. H.** "Female Voices: Upholding the Honor of the Household." *BTB* 24 (1994) 8–15. ———. "Settlement and Judges Bibliography." <http://courses.missouristate.edu/VictorMatthews/bib/JUDGES.html>. **Matthieu, Y.** "Les livres historiques du premier testament: La synchronie ouvre-t-elle de nouvelles pistes de recherche?" In *Traduire la Bible Hébraïque: De la Septante à la Nouvelle Bible Segond.* Ed. R. David and M. Jimbachian. Sciences Bibliques 15. Montreal: Médiaspaul, 2005. 375–411. **Mayer, D.** "Passages dans le livre des Juges." *Sémiotique et Bible* 92 (1998) 35–44. **Mayes, A. D. H.** "Deuteronomistic Ideology and the Theology of the Old Testament." *JSOT* 82 (1999) 57–82. ———. *Israel in the Period of the Judges.* SBT 2.29. Naperville, IL: Allenson, 1974. ———. "Israel in the Pre-Monarchy Period." *VT* 23 (1973) 151–70. ———. "The Period of the Judges and the Rise of the Monarchy." In *Israelite and Judean History.* Ed. J. H. Hayes and J. M. Miller. OTL. Philadelphia: Fortress, 1977. 285–331. ———. *The Story of Israel between Settlement and Exile: A Redactional Study of the Deuteronomistic History.* London: SCM Press, 1983. **Mazar, A.** "Bronze Bull Found in Israelite 'High Place' from the Time of the Judges." *BAR* 9 (1983) 34–40. ———. "The Bull Site—An Iron Age I Open Cult Place." *BASOR* 247 (1982) 27–42. ———. "The Israelite Settlement in Canaan in the Light of Archaeological Excavations." *BAT* (1985) 61–71. **Mazar, B.,** ed. *Judges.* WHJP 3. Tel Aviv: Masada; New Brunswick, NJ: Rutgers UP, 1971. **McCarthy, W. B.** "Lang Lang May the Ladies Stand: A Ballad Motif in the Book of Judges." *Acta Ethnographica Hungarica* 47 (2002) 7–18. **McConville, J. G.** *Grace in the End: A Study in Deuteronomic Theology.* SOTBT. Grand

Rapids: Zondervan, 1993. **McKenzie, D. A.** "The Judge of Israel." *VT* 25 (1975) 118–21. **McKenzie, J. L.** *The World of the Judges.* Englewood Cliffs, NJ: Prentice-Hall, 1966. **McKenzie, S. L.** "Deuteronomistic History." *ABD,* 2:160–68. **McKenzie, S. L.,** and **M. P. Graham,** eds. *The History of Israel's Traditions: The Heritage of Martin Noth.* JSOTSup 182. Sheffield: JSOT Press, 1994. **McNutt, P.** *Reconstructing the Society of Ancient Israel.* Louisville: Westminster John Knox, 1999. **Mendenhall, G. E.** "The Hebrew Conquest of Palestine." *BA* 25 (1962) 66–87. **Metzger, M.** "Probleme der Frühgeschichte Israels." *VF* 22 (1977) 30–43. **Meyers, C.** *Discovering Eve: Ancient Israelite Women in Context.* New York: Oxford UP, 1988. ———. "Of Seasons and Soldiers: A Topological Appraisal of the Premonarchic Tribes of Galilee." *BASOR* 252 (1983) 47–59. ———. "Procreation, Production and Protection: Male and Female Balance in Early Israel." *JAAR* 51 (1983) 569–93. ———. "The Roots of Restriction: Women in Early Israel." *BA* 41 (1978) 91–103. ———. "To Her Mother's House: Considering a Counterpart to the Israelite *bêt 'ab.*" In *The Bible and the Politics of Exegesis.* FS N. K. Gottwald, ed. D. Jobling et al. Cleveland: Pilgrim, 1991. 39–51. ———. "Women and the Domestic Economy of Early Israel." In *Women's Earliest Records.* Ed. B. S. Lesko. Atlanta: Scholars Press, 1988. 265–78. **Midden, P. van.** "Lees maar: er staat niet wat er staat: Verborgen theologie in Richteren." *ACEBT* 19 (2001) 55–63. **Milgrom, J.** "Priestly Terminology and the Political and Social Structure of Pre-Monarchic Israel." *JQR* 79 (1978) 65–91. ———. "Religious Conversion and the Revolt Model for the Formation of Israel." *JBL* 101 (1982) 169–76. **Millard, A. R.** "Story, History, and Theology." In *Faith, Tradition, and History: Old Testament Historiography in Its Near Eastern Context.* Ed. A. R. Millard, J. K. Hoffmeier, and A. D. Baker. Winona Lake, IN: Eisenbrauns, 1994. 37–64. **Miller, J. M.** "Archaeology and the Israelite Conquest of Canaan: Some Methodological Observations." *PEQ* 109 (1977) 87–93. ———. "The Israelite Occupation of Canaan." In *Israelite and Judaean History.* Ed. J. H. Hayes and J. M. Miller. Philadelphia: Westminster, 1977. 213–79. **Miller, P.** "Moral Formation and the Book of Judges." *EvQ* 75 (2003) 99–115. **Miller, P. D.** *The Religion of Ancient Israel.* Library of Ancient Israel. London: SPCK; Louisville: Westminster John Knox, 2000. **Miller, R. D. II.** *Chieftains of the Highland Clans: A History of Israel in the Twelfth and Eleventh Centuries B.C.* The Bible in Its World. Grand Rapids: Eerdmans, 2005. ———. "Identifying Earliest Israel." *BASOR* 333 (2004) 55–68. **Mills, M. E.** *Historical Israel: Biblical Israel. Studying Joshua to 2 Kings.* Cassell Biblical Studies Series. London: Cassell, 1999. **Moyer, J. C.** "Weapons and Warfare in the Book of Judges." In *Discovering the Bible: Archaeologists Look at Scripture.* Ed. T. Dowley. Grand Rapids: Eerdmans, 1986. 42–50. **Mullen, E. T., Jr.** *Narrative History and Ethnic Boundaries: The Deuteronomistic Historian and the Creation of Israelite National Identity.* SemeiaSt. Atlanta: Scholars Press, 1993. **Müller, R.** *Königtum und Gottesherrschaft: Untersuchungen zur alttestamentlichen Monarchiekritik.* FAT 2.3. Tübingen: Mohr (Siebeck), 2004. **Nel, P. J.** "Character in the Book of Judges." *OTE* 8 (1995) 191–204. ———. "From Violence to Anarchy: Plot and Characters in Judges." In *'Lasset uns Brücken Bauen': Collected Communications to the XVth Congress of the Organization for the Study of the Old Testament, Cambridge, 1995.* BEATAJ 42. Frankfurt: Lang, 1998. 125–33. **Nelson, R. D.** *The Double Redaction of the Deuteronomistic History.* JSOTSup 18. Sheffield: JSOT Press, 1981. **Nelson, W. S.** "The Book of Judges: Its Structure and Paradigmatic Figures." Part 2. *JRR* 2 (1992) 49–60. **Neu, R.** *Von der Anarchie zum Staat: Entwicklungsgeschichte Israels vom Nomadentum zur Monarchie im Spiegel der Ethnosoziologie.* Neukirchen-Vluyn: Neukirchener Verlag, 1992. **Niditch, S.** *Ancient Israelite Religion.* New York: Oxford UP, 1997. ———. *Oral Word and Written Word: Orality and Literacy in Ancient Israel.* Louisville: Westminster John Knox, 1997. ———. *Underdogs and Tricksters: A Prelude to Biblical Folklore.* San Francisco: Harper & Row, 1987. ———. *War in the Hebrew Bible: A Study in the Ethics of Violence.* New York: Oxford UP, 1993. **Niditch, S.,** ed. *Text and Tradition: The Hebrew Bible and Folklore.* SemeiaSt. Atlanta: Scholars Press, 1990. **Niehr, H.** *Herrschen und Richtern: Die Wurzel špṭ im Alten Orient und im Alten Testamentum.* Wurzburg: Echter, 1986. **Nielsen, F. A. J.** *The Tragedy in History: Herodotus and the Deuteronomistic History.* JSOTSup 251. Copenhagen International Seminar 4. Sheffield: Sheffield

Academic, 1997. **Niemann, H. M.** *Herrschaft, Königtum und Staat.* FAT 6. Tübingen: Mohr, 1993. **Nöldeke, T.** "Die Chronologie der Richterzeit." In *Untersuchungen zur Kritik des Alten Testaments.* Hildesheim, 1869. 173–98. **Noth, M.** "Das Amt des 'Richters Israels.'" In *Festschrift Alfred Bertholet.* Ed. W. Baumgartner et al. Tübingen, 1950. 404–17. ——. "The Homes of the Tribes of Israel." In *Old Testament Issues.* Ed. S. Sandmel. London: SCM Press, 1969. 121–56. ——. Review of *Traditionsgeschichtliche Untersuchungen zum Richterbuch,* by W. Richter. *VT* 15 (1965) 126–28. ——. *Das System der zwölf Stamme Israels.* BWANT 4.1. Stuttgart: Kohlhammer, 1930. ——. *Überlieferungsgeschichtliche Studien.* 2nd ed. Tübingen: Niemeyer, 1957. Translated by D. Orton as *The Deuteronomistic History,* JSOTSup 15 (Sheffield: JSOT Press, 1981) 43–52. **Oberhuber, K.** "Zur Syntax des Richterbuches: Der einfache Nominalsatz und die sog. Nominale Apposition." *VT* 3 (1953) 2. **O'Brien, M. A.** *The Deuteronomistic History Hypothesis: A Reassessment.* OBO 92. Göttingen: Vandenhoeck & Ruprecht, 1989. ——. "Judges and the Deuteronomistic History." In *The History of Israel's Traditions: The Heritage of Martin Noth.* JSOTSup 12. Sheffield: JSOT Press, 1994. 235–59. **O'Connell, R. H.** *The Rhetoric of the Book of Judges.* VTSup 63. Leiden: Brill, 1996. **O'Connor, M. P.** "The Women in the Book of Judges." *HAR* 10 (1986) 277–93. **Orlinksy, H. M.** "The Tribal System of Israel and Related Groups in the Period of the Judges." *OrAnt* 1 (1962) 11–20. **Otwell, J.** *And Sarah Laughed: The Status of Women in the Old Testament.* Philadelphia: Westminster, 1977. **Page, H. R.** "Boundaries: A Case Study Using the Bible Book of Judges." *Research in the Social Scientific Study of Religion* 10 (1999) 37–55. **Parrott, B. W.** "Ontology of Humor: A Basis for Biblical Exegesis." *PSTJ* 32 (1978) 14–34. **Patton, C. L.** "From Heroic Individuals to Nameless Victims: Women in the Social World of the Judges." In *Biblical and Humane.* FS J. F. Priest, ed. L. B. Elder, D. L. Barr, and E. S. Malbon. Atlanta: Scholars Press, 1996. 33–46. **Penchansky, D.** "Up for Grabs: A Tentative Proposal for Doing Ideological Criticism." *Semeia* 59 (1992) 35–42. **Pennant, D. F.** "The Significance of Rootplay: Leading Words and Thematic Links in the Book of Judges." PhD diss., University of Bristol, 1988. **Person, R. F., Jr.** *The Deuteronomic School: History, Social Setting, and Literature.* SBLStBl 2. Atlanta: Society of Biblical Literature, 2002. **Polliack, M.** Review of *The Book of Judges: The Art of Editing,* by Y. Amit. *VT* 45 (1995) 392–98. **Polzin, R.** *Moses and the Deuteronomist: A Literary Study of the Deuteronomistic History.* Part 1, *Deuteronomy, Joshua, Judges.* New York: Seabury, 1980. **Preuss, H. D.** "Zum deuteronomistischen Geschichtswerk." *TRu* 58 (1993) 229–64, 341–95. **Provan, I. W.** "Ideologies, Literary and Critical: Reflections on Recent Writing on the History of Israel." *JBL* 114 (1995) 585–606. **Provan, I. W., V. P. Long,** and **T. Longman III.** *A Biblical History of Israel.* Louisville: Westminster John Knox, 2003. 138–92. **Pury, A. de, T. C. Römer,** and **J. D. Macchi,** eds. *Israel Constructs Its History, Deuteronomistic Historiography and Recent Research.* JSOTSup 306. Sheffield: Sheffield Academic, 2000. Originally published as *Israël construit son histoire: L'historiographie deutéronomiste á la lumière des recherches récentes,* MdB 34 (Geneva: Labor et Fides, 1996). **Radday, Y. T.** "Chiasm in Joshua, Judges, and Others." *LB* 27–28 (1973) 6–13. **Radday, Y. T.,** and **H. Shore.** "An Inquiry into Homogeneity of the Book of Judges by Means of Discriminant Analysis." *LB* 41–42 (1977) 21–34. **Radday, Y. T., G. Leb, D. Wickmann,** and **S. Talmon.** "The Book of Judges Examined by Statistical Linguistics." *Bib* 58 (1977) 469–99. **Radjawane, A. N.** "Das deuteronomistische Geschichtswerk: Ein Forschungsbericht." *TRu* 38 NS (1973) 177–216. **Radner, K.** "The Reciprocal Relationship between Judge and Society in the Neo-Assyrian Period." *Maarav* 12 (2005) 41–68. **Rainey, A. F.** "Who Is a Canaanite? A Review of the Textual Evidence." *BASOR* 304 (1996) 1–16. **Rainey, A. F., R. S. Notley,** et al. *The Sacred Bridge: Carta's Atlas of the Biblical World.* Jerusalem: Carta, 2006. **Raschke, C.** "Thunder at the Torrent: A Postmodern Theological Reading of the Book of Judges." *Mars Hill Review* 12 (1998) 31–39. **Rasmussen, C. G.** "Conquest, Infiltration, Revolt, or Resettlement? What Really Happened during the Exodus-Judges Period?" In *Giving the Sense: Understanding and Using Old Testament Historical Texts.* Ed. D. M. Howard, Jr., and M. A. Grisanti. Grand Rapids: Kregel, 2003. 138–59. **Reviv, H.** "Leadership during the Period of the Judges" (Heb.). *Be'er Sheva* 1 (1973) 204–21. **Richter,**

W. *Die Bearbeitungen des "Retterbuches" in der deuteronomischen Epoche.* BBB 21. Bonn: Hanstein, 1964. ————. *Traditionsgeschichtliche Untersuchungen zum Richterbuch.* BBB 18. Bonn: Hanstein, 1963. ————. "Zu den Richtern Israels." *ZAW* 77 (1965) 40–71. **Rogers, M. G.** "Judges, Book of." *IDBSup.* 509–14. **Rogerson, J. W.** "Was Early Israel a Segmentary Society?" *JSOT* 36 (1986) 17–26. **Römer, T. C.** "The Form-Critical Problem of the So-Called Deuteronomistic History." In *The Changing Face of Form Criticism for the Twenty-first Century.* Ed. M. A. Sweeney and E. Ben Zvi. Grand Rapids: Eerdmans, 2003. 240–52. ————. *The Future of the Deuteronomistic History.* BETL 147. Leuven: Leuven UP; Peeters, 2000. ————. *The So-Called Deuteronomistic History: A Sociological, Historical, and Literary Introduction.* London: T&T Clark, 2005. ————. "Transformations in Deuteronomistic and Biblical Historiography: On 'Book Finding' and Other Literary Strategies." *ZAW* 109 (1997) 1–11. **Rösel, H. N.** "The Books of the Former Prophets—Their Formation and Their Function." *Beit-Miqra* 154–55 (1998) 244–55. ————. "Die 'Richter Israels': Rückblick und neuer Ansatz." *BZ* 25 (1981) 180–203. ————. "Studien zur Topographie der Kriege in den Büchern Josua und Richter 1." *ZDPV* 91 (1975) 159–91. ————. "Studien zur Topographie der Kriege in den Büchern Josua und Richter 2." *ZDPV* 92 (1976) 10–46. ————. "Die Überlieferungen vom Joshua ins Richterbuch." *VT* 30 (1980). 342. ————. *Von Josua bis Jojachin: Untersuchungen zu den deuteronomistischen Geschichtsbüchern des Alten Testaments.* VTSup 75. Leiden: Brill, 1999. **Rosenmüller, E. F. C.** *Scholia in Vetus Testamentum—Judices et Ruth.* 1835. **Rozenberg, M.** "The Sofetim in the Bible" (Heb.). *ErIsr* 12 (1975) 77–86. **Saldarini, A. J.** *Targum Jonathan of the Former Prophets: Introduction, Translation and Notes.* ArBib 10. Wilmington, DE: Glazier, 1987. **Sasaki, T.** *The Concept of War in the Book of Judges: A Strategical Evaluation of the Wars of Gideon, Deborah, Samson, and Abimelech.* Tokyo: Gakujutsu Tosho Shuppaan-Sha, 2001. ————. "Structure and Redaction of the Book of Judges" (Japanese). *Exeg* 10 (1999) 77–88. **Sasson, J.** "On Choosing Models for Recreating Israelite Premonarchic History." *JSOT* 21 (1981) 13–24. **Satterthwaite, P. E.** "Judges." *DOTHB,* 580–92. **Satterthwaite, P. E.,** and **J. G. McConville.** *Exploring the Old Testament 4: The Histories.* Downers Grove, IL: InterVarsity Press, 2006. **Schäfer-Lichtenberger, C.** "Bedeutung und Funktion von *ḥērem* in biblisch-hebräischen Texten." *BZ* 38 (1994) 270–75. **Scham, S.** "The Days of the Judges: When Men and Women Were Animals and Trees Were Kings." *JSOT* 25 (2002) 37–64. **Schearing, L. S.,** and **S. L. McKenzie,** eds. *Those Elusive Deuteronomists: The Phenomenon of Pan-Deuteronomism.* JSOTSup 268. Sheffield: Sheffield Academic, 1999. **Schenker, A.,** ed. *The Earliest Text of the Hebrew Bible: The Relationship between the Masoretic Text and the Hebrew Base of the Septuaginta Reconsidered.* SBLSCS 52. Atlanta: Scholars Press, 2003. **Schibler, D.** "L'enjeu du livre de Josué et du livre des Juges." *Hok* 61 (1996) 1–14. **Schlauri, I.** "Wolfgang Richter's Beitrag zur Redaktionsgeschichte des Richterbuches." *Bib* 54 (1973) 367–403. **Schmid, K.** *Erzväter und Exodus: Untersuchungen zur doppelten Begründung der Ursprünge Israels innerhalb der Geschichtsbücher des Alten Testaments.* WMANT 81. Neukirchen-Vluyn: Neukirchener Verlag, 1999. **Schmitt, H.-C.** "Das spätdeuteronomistische Geschichtswerk Genesis 1–2 Regum xxv und seine theologische Intention." In *Congress Volume Cambridge 1995.* Ed. J. A. Emerton. Leiden: Brill, 1997. 261–79. **Schoors, A.** "The Israelite Conquest: Textual Evidence in the Archaeological Argument." In *The Land of Israel: Cross-Roads of Civilizations.* Ed. E. Lipiński. OLA 19. Leuven: Peeters, 1985. 77–92. **Schunck, K.-D.** "Falsche Richter im Richterbuch." In *Prophetie und geschichtliches Wirklichkeit im alten Israel.* FS S. Herrmann, ed. R. Liwak and S. Wagner. Stuttgart: Kohlhammer, 1991. 364–70. ————. "Die Richter Israels und ihr Amt." In *Volume du Congrès. Genève, 1965.* VTSup 15. Leiden: Brill, 1966. 252–62. **Schüpphaus, J.** "Richter-Prophetengeschichten als Glieder der Geschichtsdarstellung der Richter—und Königszeit." Thesis, University of Bonn, 1967. **Seppo, S.** *Between Literalness and Freedom: Translation Technique in the Septuagint of Joshua and Judges regarding the Clause Connections Introduced by ו and כ.* Publications of the Finnish Exegetical Society 75. Göttingen: Vandenhoeck & Ruprecht, 1999. **Simpson, C. A.** *The Composition of the Book of Judges.* Oxford: Blackwell, 1957. **Skjeggestad, M.** "Ethnic Groups in Early Iron Age Palestine: Some Remarks on the Use of the Term

'Israelite' in Recent Research." *SJOT* 6 (1992) 159–86. **Small, D. B.** "Group Identification and Ethnicity in the Construction of the Early State of Israel: From the Outside Looking In." In *The Archaeology of Israel: Constructing the Past, Interpreting the Present.* Ed. N. A. Silberman and D. Small. JSOTSup 237. Sheffield: Sheffield Academic, 1997. 271–89. **Smelik, W. F.** *The Targum of Judges.* OtSt 36. Leiden: Brill, 1995. **Smend, R.** "Das Gesetz und die Völker: Ein Beitrag zur deuteronomistischen Redaktionsgeschichte." In *Probleme biblischer Theologie.* FS G. von Rad, ed. H. W. Wolff. Munich: Kaiser, 1971. 494–509. Also published in *Die Mitte des Alten Testaments: Exegetische Studien* (Tübingen: Mohr [Siebeck], 2002) 148–61. ———. *Yahweh War and Tribal Confederation.* Nashville: Abingdon, 1970. **Soggin, J. A.** "Ancient Israel: An Attempt at a Social and Economic Analysis of the Available Data." In *Text and Context: Old Testament and Semitic Studies for F. C. Fensham.* Ed. W. Claassen. JSOTSup 48. Sheffield: JSOT Press, 1988. 201–8. ———. *Das Königtum in Israel: Ursprünge, Spannungen, Entwicklung.* BZAW 104. Berlin: Töpelmann, 1967. ———. *When the Judges Ruled.* London: Lutterworth, 1965. **Sparks, K. L.** *Ethnicity and Identity in Ancient Israel: Prolegomena to the Study of Ethnic Sentiments and Their Expression in the Hebrew Bible.* Winona Lake, IN: Eisenbrauns, 1998. **Spronk, K.** "Het boek Richteren: Een *overzicht* van het recente onderzoek." *ACEBT* 19 (2001) 1–36. **Stager, L. E.** "The Archaeology of the Family in Ancient Israel." *BASOR* 200 (1985) 1–35. **Steinmann, A. E.** "The Mysterious Numbers of the Book of Judges." *JETS* 48 (2005) 491–500. **Sternberg, M.** *The Poetics of Biblical Narrative: Ideological Literature and the Drama of Reading.* Bloomington: Indiana UP, 1985. **Stone, L. G.** "From Tribal Confederation to Monarchic State: The Editorial Perspective of the Book of Judges." PhD diss., Yale University, 1988. ———. "Judges, Book of." *DOTHB*, 592–606. **Summer, W. A.** "Israel's Encounters with Edom, Moab, Ammon, Sihon and Og according to the Deuteronomist." *VT* 18 (1968) 216–28. **Sweeney, M. A.** "Davidic Polemics in the Book of Judges." *VT* 47 (1997) 517–29. **Tanner, P.** "The Gideon Narrative as the Focal Point of Judges." *BS* 149 (1992) 146–61. **Täubler, E.** *Biblische Studien: Die Epoche der Richter.* Ed. H.-J. Zobel. Tübingen: Mohr (Siebeck), 1958. **Ter Linden, N.** *The Story Goes . . . : The Stories of Judges and Kings.* London: SCM Press, 2000. **Thomson, H. C.** "Shophet and Mishpat in the Book of Judges." *GUOST* 19 (1961–1962) 74–85. **Thompson, J. L.** *Writing the Wrongs: Women of the Old Testament among Biblical Commentators from Philo through the Reformation.* Oxford: Oxford UP, 2001. **Thompson, T. L.** *The Early History of the Israelite People: From the Written and Archaeological Sources.* SHANE 4. Leiden: Brill, 1992. ———. "Historiography of Ancient Palestine and Early Jewish Historiography: W. G. Dever and the Not So New Biblical Archaeology." In *The Origins of the Ancient Israelite States.* Ed. V. Fritz and P. R. Davies. JSOTSup 228. Sheffield: Sheffield Academic, 1996. 26–43. ———. *The Mythic Past: Biblical Archaeology and the Myth of Israel.* New York: Basic Books, 1999. **Tollington, J. E.** "The Book of Judges: The Result of Post-Exilic Exegesis?" In *Intertextuality in Ugarit and Israel: Papers Read at the Tenth Joint Meeting of the Society for the Study of the Old Testament and het Oudtestamentisch Werkgezelschap in Nederland en België Held at Oxford, 1997.* Ed. J. C. de Moor. OtSt 40. Leiden: Brill, 1998. 186–96. **Townsend, T. P.** "The Kingdom of God as a Reality: Israel in the Time of the Judges." *IJT* 32 (1983) 19–36. **Trible, P.** *God and the Rhetoric of Sexuality.* Philadelphia: Fortress, 1978. ———. *Texts of Terror: Literary-Feminist Readings of Biblical Narratives.* OBT 13. Philadelphia: Fortress, 1984. **Ulrich, D. R.** "Does the Bible Sufficiently Describe the Conquest?" *TJ* 20 NS (1999) 53–68. **United Bible Societies Committee,** eds. *Preliminary and Interim Report on the Hebrew Old Testament Text Project/Compte rendu préliminaire et provisoire sur le travail d'analyse textuelle de l'Ancient Testament hébréu.* Vol. 2, *Historical Books.* New York: United Bible Societies, 1979. **Van Der Toorn, K.** "From Patriachs to Prophets: A Reappraisal of Charismatic Leadership in Ancient Israel." *JNSL* 13 (1987) 191–218. **Van Midden, P. J.** "A Hidden Message? Judges as Foreword to the Books of Kings." In *Unless Some One Guide Me.* FS K. A. Deurloo, ed. J. W. Dyk et al. Maastricht: Shaker, 2001. 77–85. **Van Selms, A.** "The Title 'Judge.'" *Die Ou Testamentiese Werkgemeenskqap in Suid-Afrika* 2 (1959) 41–50. **Van Seters, J.** *In Search of History: Historiography in the Ancient World and the Origins of Biblical History.* New

Haven, CT: Yale UP, 1983. **Veijola, T.** "Deuteronomismusforschung zwischen Tradition und Innovation (II)." *TRu* 67 (2002) 391–424. ———. *Das Königtum in der Beurteilung der deuteronomistischen Historiographie: Eine redaktionsgeschichtliche Untersuchung.* AASF 198. Helsinki: Suomalainen Tiedeakatemia, 1977. **Vollborn, W.** "Die Chronologie des Richterbuches." In *Festschrift Friedrich Baumgärtel.* Ed. J. Hermann and L. Rost. Erlangen: Universitätsbund, 1959. 193–97. **Warner, S.** "The Period of the Judges within the Structure of Early Israel." *HUCA* 47 (1976) 57–79. **Washburn, D. L.** "The Chronology of Judges: Another Look." *BibSac* 147 (1990) 414–25. **Weinfeld, M.** *Deuteronomy and the Deuteronomic School.* Oxford: Oxford UP, 1972. ———. "Judge and Officer in the Ancient Near East." *IOS* 7 (1977) 65–88. ———. "The Pattern of the Israelite Settlement in Canaan." In *Congress Volume: Jerusalem 1986.* Ed. J. A. Emerton. VTSup 40. Leiden: Brill, 1986. 270–83. ———. "The Period of the Conquest and of the Judges as Seen by the Earlier and the Later Sources." *VT* 17 (1967) 93–113. ———. *The Promise of the Land: The Inheritance of the Land of Canaan by the Israelites.* Taubman Lectures in Jewish Studies 3. Berkeley: University of California Press, 1993. ———. "The Tribal League at Sinai." In *Ancient Israelite Religion.* FS F. M. Cross, ed. P. D. Miller, Jr., et al. Philadelphia: Fortress, 1987. 303–14. **Weippert, H.** "Das deuteronomistische Geschichtswerk." *TRu* 50 (1985) 213–49. ———. "Das geographische System der Stämme Israels." *VT* 23 (1973) 76–89. **Weippert, M.** "The Israelite 'Conquest' and the Evidence from Transjordan." In *Symposia Celebrating the Seventy-Fifth Anniversary of the Founding of the American Schools of Oriental Research (1900–1975).* Ed. F. M. Cross. Zion Research Foundation Occasional Publications. Cambridge, MA: ASOR, 1979. 15–34. ———. *The Settlement of the Israelite Tribes in Palestine.* Trans. J. D. Martin. SBT 2nd series 21. London: SCM Press, 1971. **Weisman, Z.** "Charismatic Leaders in the Era of the Judges." *ZAW* 89 (1977) 399–411. ———. "Did a National Leadership Exist in the Era of the Judges?" (Heb.). In *Studies in the History of the Jewish People and the Land of Israel.* Ed. B. Oded et al. Vol. 5. Haifa: University of Haifa, 1980. 19–31. **Wellhausen, J.** *Die Composition des Hexateuchs und der historischen Bücher des Alten Testaments.* 4th ed. Berlin: Reimer, 1899. Reprinted, Berlin: de Gruyter, 1963. ———. *Prologomena zur Geschichte Israels.* 4th ed. Berlin: Reimer, 1895. **Wenham, G. J.** "The Rhetorical Function of Judges." In *Story as Torah: Reading Old Testament Narrative Ethically.* Grand Rapids: Baker Academic, 2000. 45–71. **Westbrook, R.** "Judges in Cuneiform Sources." *Maarav* 12 (2005) 27–39. ———. *Property and the Family in Biblical Law.* JSOTSup 113. Sheffield: Sheffield Academic, 1991. **Westermann, C.** *Die Geschichtsbücher des Alten Testaments: Gab es ein deuteronomistisches Geschichtswerk?* TB 87. Gütersloh: Kaiser; Gütersloher Verlagshaus, 1994. **Whitelam, K. W.** "The Identity of Early Israel." In *Social-Scientific Old Testament Criticism.* Ed. D. J. Chalcraft. BS 47. Sheffield: Sheffield Academic, 1997. 172–203. ———. "The Identity of Early Israel: The Realignment and Transformation of Late Bronze-Iron Age Palestine." In *The Historical Books.* Ed. J. C. Exum. Sheffield: Sheffield Academic, 1997. 14–45. Originally published in *JSOT* 63 (1994) 57–87. ———. *The Invention of Ancient Israel: The Silencing of Palestinian History.* London: Routledge & Kegan Paul, 1996. ———. "Israel's Traditions of Origin: Reclaiming the Land." *JSOT* 44 (1989) 19–42. ———. "Recreating the History of Israel." *JSOT* 35 (1986) 45–70. **Wiener, H. M.** *The Composition of Judges II 11–I Kings II 46.* Leipzig, 1929. **Wieringen, W. C. G. van.** "De wederwaardigheden van de dochters in het boek Richteren als teken van verval." *ACEBT* 19 (2001) 125–38. **Wiese, K.** "Zur Literarkritik des Buches der Richter." In *Studien zu Ezechiel und dem Buch der Richter.* Ed. S. Prank and K. Wiese. BWANT 40. Stuttgart: Kohlhammer, 1926. 1–61. **Wifall, W. R.** "Israel's Origins: Beyond Noth and Gottwald." *BTB* 12 (1982) 8–10. ———. "The Tribes of Yahweh: A Synchronic Study with a Diachronic Title." *ZAW* 95 (1983) 197–209. **Williams, J. G.** "The Beautiful and the Barren: Conventions in Biblical Type-Scenes." *JSOT* 17 (1980) 107–19. ———. "The Structure of Judges 2:6–16:31." *JSOT* 49 (1991) 77–85. ———. *Women Recounted: Narrative Thinking and the God of Israel.* Sheffield: Almond, 1982. **Williams, R. J.** *Hebrew Syntax: An Outline.* 3rd ed. Toronto: University of Toronto Press, 2007. **Wilson, R. R.** "Israel's Judicial System in the Preexilic Period."

JQR 74 (1983) 229–48. **Winther-Nielsen, N.** "Fact, Fiction, and Language Use: Can Modern Pragmatics Improve on Halpern's Case for History in Judges?" In *Windows into Old Testament History: Evidence, Argument, and the Crisis of "Biblical Israel."* Ed. W. P. Long, D. W. Baker, and G. F. Wenham. Grand Rapids: Eerdmans, 2002. 44–81. **Wiseman, L. H.** *Men of Faith: Or, Sketches from the Book of Judges.* London: Hodder & Stoughton, 1870. **Wong, G. T. K.** *Compositional Strategy of the Book of Judges: An Inductive, Rhetorical Study.* VTSup 111. Leiden: Brill, 2006. ———. "Is There a Direct Pro-Judah Polemic in Judges?" *SJOT* 19 (2005) 84–110. **Wood, B. G.** "From Ramesses to Shiloh: Archaeological Discoveries Bearing on the Exodus-Judges Period." In *Giving the Sense: Understanding and Using Old Testament Historical Texts.* Ed. D. M. Howard, Jr., and M. A. Grisanti. Grand Rapids: Kregel, 2003. 256–82. ———. "Let the Evidence Speak." *BAR* 33 (2007) 26, 78. **Wood, L. J.** *Distressing Days of the Judges.* Grand Rapids: Zondervan, 1975. **Wood, R. A.** "The Major Judges and the Judgment of the Deuteronomist." Paper presented to the Society of Biblical Literature, 1989. **Wright, D. P., D. N. Freedman,** and **A. Hurvitz,** eds. *Pomegranates and Golden Bells: Studies in Biblical, Jewish, and Near Eastern Ritual, Law and Literature.* FS J. Milgrom. Winona Lake, IN: Eisenbrauns, 1995. **Würthwein, E.** *Studien zum Deuteronomistischen Geschichtswerk.* BZAW 227. Berlin: de Gruyter, 1994. **Yadin, Y.** "Is the Biblical Account of the Israelite Conquest of Canaan Historically Reliable?" *BAR* 8 (1982) 16–23. **Yee, G. A.,** ed. *Judges and Method: New Approaches in Biblical Studies.* Minneapolis: Augsburg Fortress, 1995. **Younger, K. L., Jr.** "Early Israel in Recent Biblical Scholarship." In *The Face of Old Testament Studies: A Survey of Contemporary Approaches.* Ed. D. W. Baker and B. T. Arnold. Grand Rapids: Baker, 1999. 176–206. **Zakovitch, Y.** "The Associative Arrangement of the Book of Judges and Its Use for the Recognition of Stages in the Formation of the Book" (Heb.). In *Isaac Leo Seeligmann Volume—Essays on the Bible and the Ancient World I.* Ed. Y. Zakovitch and A. Rofé. Jerusalem, 1983. 161–83. **Zertal, A.** "Israel Enters Canaan: Following the Pottery Trail." *BAR* 17 (1991) 28–49, 75. **Zevit, Z.** *The Religions of Ancient Israel.* New York: Continuum, 2001. ———. "Three Debates about Bible and Archaeology." *Bib* 83 (2002) 1–27.

Introduction

Introduction to the Riddle of Judges

The book of Judges, filled with fables and riddles, proves to be a riddle for modern scholars and commentators. On a surface reading, the Judges narratives preserve Israel's history between the conquest of Joshua and the kingships of Saul and David. First, the individual tribes attempt to establish control of the territories Joshua distributed to them as a tribal and clan inheritance (Josh 13–21), but with more failures than successes. The narrator then establishes a pattern for Israel's history—a pattern of obedience to Yahweh followed by worshiping other gods, then suffering divine punishment at the hands of other nations, crying to God for deliverance, and seeing God raise up a leader who delivers Israel from the enemy and judges over Israel for a certain time period but does not leave a lasting positive influence. The reader expects, then, to observe this cyclical framework. But, as will be seen, the framework quickly breaks apart, applying only in pieces to each judge. The first judges—Othniel, Ehud, and Shamgar—follow the pattern of obeying God and delivering God's people. The story for each of these includes a brief note regarding the unexpected nature of his leadership. Othniel let his wife secure a reasonable wedding dowry for them. Ehud was left-handed and worked alone in his most significant action. Shamgar bore a foreign name and may well have been a foreigner.

Then the pattern begins to break down as Barak refuses to accept God's invitation through the female prophetess and judge Deborah to lead God's people and so forfeits the honor of victory to a nomadic Kenite woman. Gideon continues testing God and finally goes across the Jordan on a rampage of personal revenge. The people want to honor him as king, but he piously refuses, saying only that Yahweh will be king. Still, he establishes a royal lifestyle; sets up an ephod that the people begin to worship; names his son Abimelech, "my father is king"; and dies, leaving the people to return to worship the Canaanite gods.

Abimelech then breaks out of the pattern completely, killing his brothers, fighting against the city where Joshua reestablished the covenant between God and people, and suffering death at the hands of a woman and a millstone.

A series of "minor judges" appears but without accompanying narratives. Albrecht Alt apparently coined the term "minor judges" in comparing them to twelfth-century Icelandic leaders. Thus Alt wrote: "If the whole series is taken together, it gives a picture of an uninterrupted succession of members of noble families from different tribes, exercising some form of legal jurisdiction over all Israel" ('The Origins of Israelite Law," in *Essays on Old Testament History and Religion,* trans. R. A. Wilson [Oxford: Blackwell, 1966] 102; compare E. T. Mullen, Jr., "The 'Minor Judges': Some Literary and Historical Considerations," *JBL* 44 [1982] 185). In discussing the monarchy, Alt notes that these minor judges "had held the only office common to the whole of Israel in the period before the national state was founded" ("The Monarchy in the Kingdoms of Israel and Judah," in *Essays on Old Testament History and Religion,* 247; originally published as "Das Königtum in den

Reichen Israel und Juda," *VT* 1 [1951] 2–22). Mullen concludes that the distinction between "major" and "minor" judges reflects "only a difference in literary purpose and not a difference in office. The accounts of the 'minor judges' are used to 'frame' and hence draw attention to the critical story of Jephthah (10:5–12:7), which serves as a theological focus in the accounts of the judges" (*JBL* 44 [1982] 201). In this view the judges have nothing to do with courts and judicial authority, and so all the figures in the book of Judges hold the same office. Block (338) refers to them as governors who function as local rulers or, more loosely stated, as kings. But this is just the role of the deliverers when they are not fighting Israel's battles. Younger (22) speaks of cyclical and noncyclical judges without drawing a strong functional line between them.

These minor judges serve as an important transition point for the writer of Judges. They apparently display lifestyles repugnant to Israel and represent the weak side of leadership. Finally, sinful, unfaithful Israel cries desperately for God's deliverance from the Philistines and Ammonites. Jephthah comes to deliver from the Ammonites but does so only through a foolish vow resulting in the sacrifice of his daughter. His frustration with the tribe of Ephraim and its military result in bloody battle and 42,000 dead Ephraimite soldiers. Another series of minor judges leads to Samson, who is anointed to begin to deliver Israel from the Philistines but instead chases women and defeats Philistines in individual combat, increasing his ego and infuriating the tribe of Judah. His greatest victory comes during a Philistine victory celebration and worship as he pulls the building down on the worshipers and on himself.

The last chapters of Judges surprise the reader by introducing the need for a king and showing how atrocious the religious and social systems have become in Israel. False worship, thievery of gods and religious paraphernalia, the establishment of a tribal worship center with pagan symbols and false priests, the rape of a secondary wife, civil war, the virtual destruction of an entire tribe, the annihilation of an Israelite city to capture virgin daughters, and the kidnapping of daughters of Shilo during a worship festival all point to the religious, political, and social nadir of Israel.

Let the riddles begin.

The first riddle is the nature of the authority and function of the people designated as judges (שׁפטים), deliverers (מושׁיעים), and those who judge Israel (את ישׁפט ישׂראל). Terms related to שׁפט appear to refer to a judicial or mediatorial position keyed to establishing justice in Israel. But only Deborah is given any such position, and that is before she acts in battle. Niditch (1) refers to them as "swashbuckling, charismatic military leaders." She compares them to both epic heroes and social bandits. Yet only a select few receive the Spirit to give them true charisma. The majority of the minor judges do not participate in battles. Apparently, Deborah does not either. Gideon for the early part of his career can hardly be termed "swashbuckling." Abimelech occupies a large portion of the narrative but stands quite apart from the other judges in character and religious devotion. Deborah lends a prophetic quality to the judges' characteristics, a quality not exhibited by any others. The book of Judges may be built on stories of epic heroes, but such heroic qualities are quickly abandoned by most of the political/military leaders in Judges. Social bandits rob the rich to help the poor, but most of the judges seem to enrich their own pockets and egos much more than they help anyone else.

Perhaps to solve this riddle, we must separate the activities as military deliverers from those as political/judicial leaders, activities that at least some of these deliverers engage in following their military successes. In that case, Samuel would assume the judicial portion of the judge's role and combine it with priesthood, while Saul would perform the military deliverer role and then assume political leadership. David would eventually combine all the roles, acting in judicial, military, and even priestly functions.

Why write such a book featuring Israel's failed leaders and aberrant religious, social, and political worlds? Could it have been written to justify a religious reform like Josiah's—or Hezekiah's? Or perhaps it was inspired by the opposition to the great rebellion in Israel's history, that of Jeroboam I, who divided the Israelite monarchy in two and used the false gods and sanctuaries featured in Judges. Perhaps an original collection of hero stories from the north has been subtly transformed by southern writers into a polemic against the entire northern religious, social, and political system.

The riddle of the overall history of Judges rests on a series of other riddles. Its textual history is so complex that Septuagint scholars print two Greek versions of the text rather than one. The history behind the stories of the Judges receives little credence from critical historians. Gösta Ahlström sees the theological pattern set out in Judg 2 as sufficient evidence to claim,

> It is self-evident that such a literary pattern does not have as its highest priority the description of actual events. Thus, it cannot be used for writing history. . . . The 'history' we find in the Book of Judges, therefore, is as an ideological reconstruction and as such is a product of the later pure-Yahwistic circle. Thus the goal of the book is not to present history but to advocate a religious ideal. (*History of Ancient Palestine*, 375–76)

Lemche even says that "as far as ancient Israel is concerned, there can be no doubt that it is an artificial creation of the scholarly world of the modern age" (*Israelites in History*, 163). Since Martin Noth, scholars have attributed the book to the "Deuteronomistic Historian" of a late preexilic or exilic age and dismiss the historical questions. But now the existence and meaning of "Deuteronomistic Historian" is coming more and more into question. The theology of the book is often dismissed as advocating violence, war, and rape. Barnabas Linders asks: "Should it perhaps be banned from liturgical use on the grounds that it does nothing to promote faith and Christian living?" (*Interpreting Judges Today*, 1). Thus in seeking to show ministers how to preach Judges, Jeter resorts to five "oblique approaches" (5) to the text and concludes, "Sometimes I preach under their guidance. Sometimes I have to preach against them" (14).

Riddles continue to puzzle scholars as they look at the structure of the book and its narrative and theological purpose. Most commentators agree on a division into three main parts: an introduction in 1:1–3:6, the basic narrative body in 3:7–16:31, and an appendix or epilogue in 17:1–21:25. (See D. Dorsey, 105, esp. n. 1.) Chap. 2 apparently gives an outline for the book, but this soon breaks down; all the elements do not appear in all the individual narratives, and the minor-judges lists do not contain these narrative elements at all. A repeated chorus in Judg 17:6, 18:1, 19:1, and 21:25—"in those days Israel had no king"—appears to give the purpose for the book, but recent readings question whether this statement is supportive of kingship or opposed to kingship.

Thus riddles in every area of scholarship face a commentator who begins the study and exposition of the book. Commentary readers are invited to join in the detective work as we seek to solve these riddles and many more rampant in the pages of this book. Is it really beset with an unsettled text, narrated without historical base, plagued with untenable theology, prepared only to be preached against, and so subtly designed that its structure and purpose must remain mysteries? I hope to be able to show in the following explanation of the text that efforts to understand Judges are not quite as impossible as they might appear.

Introduction to the Text of Judges

Select Bibliography

Abegg, M., Jr., P. Flint, and **E. Ulrich.** *The Dead Sea Scrolls Bible: The Oldest Known Bible Translated for the First Time into English.* San Francisco: Harper San Francisco, 1999. 208–12. **Andersen, F. I.** *The Sentence in Biblical Hebrew.* The Hague: Mouton, 1974. **Barthélemy, D.** *Critique textuelle de l'Ancien Testament.* Vol. 1, *Josué, Juges, Ruth, Samuel, Rois, Chroniques, Esdras, Néhémie, Esther.* OBO 50.1. Fribourg: Éditions Universitaires; Göttingen: Vandenhoeck & Ruprecht, 1982. **Barthélemy, D.,** and **J. T. Milik.** "1QJudg." In *Qumran Cave I.* DJD 1. Oxford: Clarendon, 1955. 62–64. ———. *Les Devanciers d'Aquila.* VTSup 10. Leiden: Brill, 1963. **Billen, A. V.** "The Hexaplaric Old Latin Version of Judges." *JTS* 43 (1942) 12–19. ———. "The Old Latin Version of Judges." *JTS* 43 (1942) 140–49. **Bodine, W. R.** *Greek Text of Judges.* ———. "*Kaige* and Other Recensional Developments in the Greek Text of Judges." *BIOSCS* 13 (1980) 45–57. **Boling, R. G.** "Some Conflate Readings in Joshua-Judges." *VT* 16 (1966) 293. **Bruno, A.** *Bücher Josua, Richter, Ruth.* **Chepey, S. D.** "Samson the 'Holy One': A Suggestion regarding the Reviser's Use of *hagioi* in Judg 13,7; 16,17 LXX Vaticanus." *Bib* 83 (2002) 97–99. **Cooper, C. M.** "Studies in the Greek Text of the Book of Judges: I. The Synonyms of the Alexandrian and Vatican Codices." Diss., Dropsie College, 1941. ———. "Theodotion's Influence on the Alexandrian Text of Judges." *JBL* 67 (1948) 63–68. **Dirksen, P. B.** *Judges.* The Old Testament in Syriac 2. Leiden: Brill, 1978. ———. *The Transmission of the Text in the Peshitta Manuscripts of the Book of Judges.* MPIL 1. Leiden: Brill, 1972. **Doorninck, A. van.** *Bijdrage tot de Tekstkritiek van Richteren I–XVI.* Leiden, 1879. **Fernández Marcos, N.** "The Genuine Text of Judges." In *Sofer Mahir.* FS A. Schenker, ed. Y. Goldman, A. van der Kooij, and R. D. Weis. VTSup 110. Leiden: Brill, 2006. ———. "The Hebrew and Greek Texts of Judges." In *The Earliest Text of the Hebrew Bible: The Relationship between the Masoretic Text and the Hebrew Base of the Septuagint Reconsidered.* Ed. A. Schenker. SBLSCS 52. Atlanta: Society of Biblical Literature, 2003. 1–16. ———. *The Septuagint in Context: An Introduction to the Greek Versions of the Bible.* Trans. W. G. E. Watson. Leiden: Brill, 2000. **Harl, M., G. Dorival,** and **O. Munnich.** *Le Bible grecque des Septante.* Paris: Cerf, 1988. 90–103. **Harlé, P.** *La Bible d'Alexandrie.* Vol. 7, *Les Juges.* Paris: Cerf, 1999. ———. "Flavius Josèphe et la Septante des Juges." In *Kata tous o' = Selon les septante.* FS M. Harl, ed. G. Dorival and O. Munnich. Paris: Cerf, 1995. 129–32. **Hess, R. S.** "The Dead Sea Scrolls and Higher Criticism of the Hebrew Bible: The Case of 4QJudgᵃ." In *The Scrolls and the Scriptures: Qumran Fifty Years After.* Ed. S. E. Porter and C. A. Evans. JSPSup 26. Sheffield: Sheffield Academic, 1997. 122–28. **Jellicoe, S.** *The Septuagint and Modern Study.* Oxford: Clarendon, 1968. **Le Bonnardière, A. M.** *Biblia Augustiniana.* Vol. 2, *Les Livres Historiques.* Paris: Études Augustiniennes, 1960. **Lindars, B.** "Commentary on the Greek Judges?" ———. "Some LXX Readings in Judges." *JTS* 22 (1971) 1–14. **Marcos, N. F.** "The Genuine Text of Judges." In *Sôpher Mahîr.* FS A. Schenker, ed. Y. A. P. Goldman, A. van der Kooij, and R. D. Weis. VTSup 110. Leiden: Brill, 2006. 33–45. ———. "The Hebrew and Greek Text of Judges." In *The Earliest Text of the Hebrew Bible: The Relationship between the Masoretic Text and the Hebrew Base of the Septuagint Reconsidered.* Ed. A. Schenker. SBLSCS 52. Atlanta: SBL, 2003. 1–16. ———. "L'histoire textuelle: Les livres historiques (Juges)." In *L'enfance de la Bible* *hébraïque: L'histoire du texte de l'Ancien Testament à la lumière des recherches récentes.* Ed. A. Schenker and P. Hugo. MdB 52. Geneva: Labor et Fides, 2005. 148–69. **Moore, G. F.** *The Book of Judges: Critical Edition of the Hebrew Text.* Leipzig: Hinrichs, 1900. **Pretzl, O.** "Septuagintaprobleme im Buch der Richter: Die griechischen Handschriftengruppen im Buch der Richter untersucht nach ihrem Verhältnis zu einander." *Bib* 7 (1926) 233–69, 353–83. **Robert, U.** *Heptateuchi partis posterioris versio latina antiquissima e codice Lugdunensi: Version latine du Deutéronome de Josué et des Juges antérieure à Saint Jerôme, publié d'après le manuscript de Lyon.* Lyon: Rey, 1900. **Rofé, A.** "The End of the Book of Joshua according to the Septuagint." *Shnaton* 2 (1977) 217–27. **Rösel, H. N.** "Die Überleitungen vom Josua ins Richterbuch." *VT* 30 (1980) 342–50. **Rudolph, W.** "Textkritische Anmerkungen zum Richterbuch." In *Festschrift Otto Eissfeldt.* Ed. J. Fück. Halle: Niemeyer, 1947. 199–212. **Schreiner, J.** *Septuaginta-Massora des Buches der Richter: Eine textkritische Studie.* AnBib 7. Rome: Pontifical Biblical Institute, 1957. ———. "Textformen und Urtext des Deboraliedes in der Septuaginta." *Bib* 42 (1961) 173–200. ———. "Zum B-Text des griechischen Canticum Deborae." *Bib* 42 (1961) 333–58. **Schulte, A.** *De restitutione alque indole genuinae versionis graecae in libro Judicum.* Leipzig, 1889. **Smelik, W. F.** *Targum of Judges.* **Soisalon-Soinomem, I.** *Die Textformen der Septuaginta-Übersetzung des Richterbuches.* AASF, series B, 72.1. Helsinki: Druckerei-A.G. der Finnischen Literaturgesellschaft, 1951. **Sperber, A.** *The Bible in Aramaic.* Vol. 2, *The Former Prophets according to Targum Jonathan.* Leiden: Brill, 1959. **Tov, E.** "The Nature of the Large-Scale Differences between the LXX and MT S T V, Compared with Similar Evidence in Other Sources." In *The Earliest Text of the Hebrew Bible: The Relationship between the Masoretic Text and the Hebrew Base of the Septuaginta Reconsidered.* Ed. A. Schenker. SBLSCS 52. Atlanta: Scholars Press, 2003. 121–44. ———. *Textual Criticism of the Hebrew Bible.* Minneapolis: Fortress, 1992. ———. "The Textual History of the Song of Deborah in the A Text of the LXX." *VT* 28 (1979) 224–32. **Trebolle Barrera, J.** "4QJudg^a 4QJudg^b." In *Qumran Cave 4.* Vol. 9, *Deuteronomy, Joshua, Judges, Kings.* Ed. E. Ulrich et al. DJD 14. Oxford: Clarendon, 1995. 161–69. ———. "La aportación de 4QJueces^a al estudio de la historia textual y literaria del libro de los Jueces." *Miscelánea de Estudios Árabes y Hebraicos* 40 (1991) 5–20. ———. "Édition préliminaire de *4QJudg^b*: Contribution des manuscrits Qumrâniens des Juges à l'étude textuelle et littéraire du livre." *RevQ* 15 (1991) 79–100. ———. "Light from 4QJudg^a and 4QKgs on the Text of Judges and Kings." In *The Dead Sea Scrolls.* Ed. D. Dimant and U. Rappaport. STDJ 10. Leiden: Brill, 1992. 315–24. ———. "Textual Affiliation of the Old Latin Marginal Readings in the Books of Judges and Kings." In *Biblische Theologie und gesellschaftlicher Wandel.* Ed. G. Braulik. Freiburg: Herder, 1993. 315–29. ———. "Textual Variants in *4QJudg^a* and the Textual and Editorial History of the Book of Judges." *RevQ* 14 (1989) 229–45. **Troyer, K. de.** "Reconstructing the OG of Joshua." In *Septuagint Research: Issues and Challenges in the Study of the Greek Jewish Scriptures.* Ed. W. Kraus and R. G. Wooden. SBLSCS 53. Atlanta: Society of Biblical Literature, 2006. 105–18. **Ulrich, E.** *The Dead Sea Scrolls and the Origins of the Bible.* Leiden: Brill, 1999. **Ulrich, E., et al.,** eds. *Qumran Cave 4.* Vol. 9, *Deuteronomy, Joshua, Judges, Kings.* DJD 14. Oxford: Clarendon, 1995. 161–69. **United Bible Societies Committee,** eds. *Preliminary and Interim Report on the Hebrew Old Testament Text Project/Compte rendu préliminaire et provisoire sur le travail d'analyse textuelle de l'Ancient Testament hébréu.* Vol. 2, *Historical Books.* New York: United Bible Societies, 1979.

The following commentary includes extensive notes comparing LXX readings with MT as well as notes coming from Meyer's suggestions in *BHS*. I wish to thank Chris Conver and the staff of Westminster John Knox for providing a prepublication copy of Niditch's new commentary on Judges, from which I take most of the information relating to OL readings. I have not had an opportunity to judge the value of all these readings or to incorporate her tantalizing oral literature approach into my textual explanations.

Block seems to have removed the text riddle of Judges as he writes, "Compared to the rest of the historiographic writings of the Old Testament, the Hebrew text of Judges preserved in the Leningrad Codex of 1008 C.E. (upon which *BHS* is based) and the Aleppo Codex from the early tenth century C.E. is relatively pure" (Block, 72). Soggin supports his witness: "The Masoretic text of Judges is particularly pure" (12).

The Dead Sea Scrolls from Qumran offer little new, though much has been made of one small piece of evidence. 4Qjudg[a] from after 50 B.C.E. contains Judges 6:2–6, 11–13, omitting vv 7–10. In the publication of the Judges scrolls, Trebolle Barrera concludes, "This fragment represents a form of the text independent from any other known text-type, although it shares readings with the proto-Lucianic text. It is the only extant witness which does not include the literary insertion found in vv 7–10 of MT, LXX. . . . 4Qjudg[a] can confidently be seen as an earlier literary form of the book than our traditional texts" ("4QJudg[a] 4QJudg[b]," 162). See *Notes* on Judg 6 in this commentary. Trebolle Barrera concludes that both of the Greek texts of Judges and the OL source text can be traced back to an Egyptian Hebrew text, while the MT stems from a Palestinian Hebrew text (*RevQ* 15 [1991] 99–100).

1QJudg appears to contain 8:1 and 9:1–6, 28–31, 40–43, 48–49, with a few insignificant variant readings. See *Notes* on Judg 9 in this commentary. 4QJudg[b] consists of three fragments of 19:5–7 and 21:12–25. It differs from MT only in the spelling of Benjamin, although Trebolle Barrera wants to leave open the possibility that Judg 21:18b is missing in the Qumran text, but then gives evidence to dispute his own suggestion.

Even after a thorough examination of recent evidence from the Dead Sea Scrolls and the earliest Greek evidence, Fernández Marcos can conclude that "the Hebrew text known by the Greek translator of Judges was one only slightly different from the Masoretic text" ("Hebrew and Greek Texts," 15).

Abegg, Flint, and Ulrich in *The Dead Sea Scrolls Bible* note the sparse evidence and then quickly claim, "4Qjudg[a] reveals that this earlier text is shorter than all other extant Hebrew manuscripts. . . . 4Qjudg[a] retains the original, unembellished narrative" (208–9). This is all based on one text lacking Judg 6:7–10, evidence that led Trebolle Barrera ("4QJudg[a] 4QJudg[b]," 163) to claim that two editions of the book of Judges circulated, one lacking the latest Deuteronomistic additions. Tov ("Nature of the Large-Scale Differences," 138) appears to support this to a point even as he dates 4QJudg[a] to 50–25 B.C.E. He concludes, "If this minus did not stem from a textual accident, such as the omission of a complete paragraph ending with open sections, it could reflect an earlier edition of the book, in which part of the deuteronomistic framework, contained in these verses, was lacking" (135–36). He recognizes, however, the paucity of evidence with which he works since "only four or five biblical texts from Qumran, and none at all from the other sites in the Judaean Desert, provide *early* material relevant to the editorial development of the Hebrew Bible" (137, emphasis original).

One long-known piece of evidence has to be considered. Editions of the Septuagint deviate from their normal practice and print both the Alexandrinus (LXX[A]) and the Vaticanus (LXX[B]) texts because of "a series of quite remarkable variants between the text of LXX[B] and that of LXX[A], which are without parallel in the Old Testament. So great are the discrepancies, that we might speak of two different translations" (Soggin, 12). Soggin (13) finally notes the majority preference for "successive revisions of the same text." Tov explains:

> To date no conclusive evidence has been produced for any of the suggested theories. One may nevertheless speak of a common opinion, namely that the A text is closer to the original translation than the B text, and that the B text probably incorporates an early revision of the original translation. . . . The A text . . . should not be considered as reflecting the Old Greek translation itself because it contains various doublets as well as interpolations from the B text and from the Hexapla. (*VT* 28 [1979] 224)

Alexandrinus is generally considered to be the more reliable and older of the two texts. The question still at issue is whether Vaticanus represents a separate, freer translation of the same basic Hebrew tradition, a translation of a different Hebrew tradition, or a conscious effort to create a freer edition of Alexandrinus.

Recently, Chepey reported on the "general relationship between the two MS families of Judg."

> They represent either preserved revisions of one another or separate revisions of a common Greek text now lost, rather than separate competing translations. In terms of their respective dates the recent works of Bodine have substantiated the theory of Barthélemy that LXX[B] Judg represents, in general, part of the early καίγε recension dating back to the turn of the era. LXX[A] . . . represents a much later version similar in character to Origen's Hexaplaric recension of the third century AD. An early date respecting the reading in LXX[B] is suggested by its probable use in the Synoptic Gospels. (*Bib* 83 [2002] 97–98)

Boling (297–301) provides evidence in Judges of the infamous *Kaige* (καίγε) recension, finding seventy-one instances in LXX[A] and ninety-two in LXX[B], leading him to conclude: "It is clear that neither A nor B preserves a consistent Kaige text, although that recension has clearly influenced both and is especially prominent in B. The pattern shifts significantly midway through the book" (301).

Niditch (21–25) approaches the text from the nearly unique perspective of oral tradition studies, paying particular attention to the Old Latin version. Regarding the MT, she concludes:

> A work such as Judges no doubt existed in multiple versions, even once its various stories were combined along the lines with which we are now familiar. Oral versions of larger or smaller portions of Judges would have existed side by side with accounts that were written down. . . . Variations in manuscript traditions, which are essentially set in this sense, reflect an oral-world mentality in which different versions exist side by side in the tradition. . . . The attitude is typical of a traditional world in which variant texts are deemed valid and authentic. (22)

Seeing that there were "always multiple versions of the tradition before the Common Era" (23), Niditch chooses not to reconstruct a whole text or to seek an original or urtext. She recognizes the consequence of such a decision for "some of the differences between readings make for genuine differences in the plot or in characterization." The many examples and methods of filling out a text "point to the border where translation decisions, textual variants, targum, midrash, inner-biblical variants, and intertextuality meet on oral-world terms." Such an approach to texts alive in a world strongly devoted to oral transmission and memorization of texts points us close to reality in dealing with the varied textual traditions. Compare the work of David Carr, *Writing on the Tablet of the Heart.*

Thus riddles remain in the Judges text tradition. I will deal with as much of the evidence as possible in the commentary without attempting to create new riddles and new theories. I summarize my findings below.

Introduction to the Narrative Composition of Judges

THE LARGER CONTEXT: THE DEUTERONOMISTIC HISTORY

Select Bibliography

Albertz, R. "In Search of the Deuteronomists: A First Solution to a 'Historical Riddle.'" ———. "Wer waren die Deuteronomisten? Das historische Rätsel einer literarischen Hypothese." *EvT* 57 (1997) 319–38. **Ash, P.** "Jeroboam I and the Deuteronomistic Historian's Ideology of the Founder." *CBQ* 60 (1988) 16–24. **Auld, A. G.** "Deuteronomists between History and Theology." ———. "What Makes Judges Deuteronomistic?" In *Joshua Retold.* 120–26. **Aurelius, E.** *Zukunft jenseits des Gerichts: Eine redactionsgeschichtliche Studie zum Enneateuch.* **Bach, R.** "Deuteronomistisches Geschichtswerk." *RGG,* 2:100–101. **Bartelmus, R.** "The Deuteronomists and the Former Prophets, or What Makes the Former Prophets Deuteronomistic?" In *Those Elusive Deuteronomists.* Ed. L. S. Schearing and S. L. McKenzie. 116–26. ———. "Forschung am Richterbuch seit Martin Noth." *TRu* 56 (1991) 221–59. **Beck, M.,** and **U. Schorn,** eds. *Auf em Weg zur Endgestalt von Genesis bis II Regum.* FS H.-C. Schmitt. BZAW 370. New York: de Gruyter, 2006. **Becker, U.** "Endredaktionelle Kontextvernetzungen des Josua-Buches." In *Die deuteronomistischen Geschichtswerke.* Ed. M. Witte et al. 139–59. **Beyerlin, W.** "Gattung und Herkunft des Rahmens im Richterbuch." **Brueggemann, W.** "The Kerygma of the Deuteronomic Historian." *Int* 22 (1968) 387–402. ———. "Social Criticism and Social Vision in the Deuteronomic Formula of Judges." **Campbell, A. F.,** and **M. A. O'Brien.** *Unfolding the Deuteronomistic History.* **Carr, D. M.** "Empirisches Perspektiven auf das Deuteronomistiche Geschichtswerk." In *Die deuteronomistischen Geschichtswerke.* Ed. M. Witte et al. 1–17. ———. *Writing on the Tablet of the Heart.* **Carrière, J.-M.** "L'historiographie deutéronomiste: une manière d'écrire l'historie." In *Comment la Bible saisit-elle l'histoire? XXI' Congrès catholique française pour l'étude de la Bible. Illy-les-Moulineaus, 2005.* Paris: Cerf, 2007. 115–54. **Castelbajac, I. de.** "Les juges d'Israël: Une invention du Deutéronomiste?" *RHR* 221 (2004) 83–97. **Coggins, R.** "What Does 'Deuteronomistic' Mean?" In *Those Elusive Deuteronomists.* Ed. L. S. Schearing and S. L. McKenzie. 22–35. Reprinted from *Words Remembered, Texts Renewed,* FS J. F. A. Sawyer, JSOTSup 195 (Sheffield: Sheffield Academic, 1995) 135–48. **Cortese, E.** *Deuteronomic Work.* **Cross, F. M.** "The Structure of the Deuteronomistic History." *Perspectives in Jewish Learning* 3 (1968) 9–24. ———. "Themes of the Book of Kings and the Structure of the Deuteronomistic History." **Davies, G. I.** "The Origin of the History of Israel: Herodotus' Histories as Blueprint for the First Books of the Bible." *JTS* 55 (2004) 805–6. **Davies, P. R.** *In Search of 'Ancient Israel.'* ———. "Whose History?" **Dietrich, W.** *Prophetie und Geschichte.* **Dutcher-Walls, P.** "The Social Location of the Deuteronomists: A Sociological Study of Factional Politics in Late Pre-exilic Judah." *JSOT* 52 (1991) 77–94. **Eissfeldt, O.** *Geschichtsschreibung im Alten Testament: Ein kritischer Bericht über die neueste Literatur dazu.* Berlin: Evangelische Verlagsanstalt, 1948. **Fretheim, T. E.** *Deuteronomic History.* Interpreting Biblical Texts. Nashville: Abingdon, 1983. **Galil, G.** "The Chronological Framework of the Deuteronomistic History." *Bib* 85 (2004) 413–21. **Geoghegan, J. C.** "'Until This Day' and the Preexilic Redaction of the Deuteronomistic History." *JBL* 122 (2003) 201–27. **Gerbrandt, G. E.** *Kingship.* **Greenspahn, F. E.** "The Theology of the Framework of Judges." *VT* 36 (1986) 385–96. **Hjelm, I.** *Jerusalem's Rise to Sovereignty: Zion and Gerizim in Competition.* JSOTSup 404. London: T&T Clark, 2004. **Hoffman, H. D.** *Reform und Reformen: Untersuchungen zu einem Grundthema der deuteronomistischen*

Geschichtsschreibung. ATANT 66. Zürich: Theologischer Verlag, 1980. **Hoffman, Y.** "The Deuteronomist and the Exile." In *Pomegranates and Golden Bells: Studies in Biblical, Jewish and Near Eastern Ritual, Law, and Literature.* FS J. Milgrom, ed. D. P. Wright, D. N. Freedman, and A. Hurvitz. Winona Lake, IN: Eisenbrauns, 1995. **Hurwitz, A.** "The Historical Quest of 'Ancient Israel' and the Linguistic Evidence of the Hebrew Bible: Some Methodological Observations." *VT* 47 (1997) 301–15. **Jenni, E.** "Zwei Jahrzehnte Forschung an den Bücher Joshua bis Könige." *TRu* 27 NS (1961–1962) 1–32, 97–146. **Jobling, D.** "Deuteronomic Political Theory." **Kaiser, O.** "Pentateuch und Deuteronomistisches Geschichtswerk." **Knoppers, G.,** and **J. G. McConville,** eds. *Reconsidering Israel and Judah.* **Kraus, H.-J.** "Gesetz und Geschichte: Zum Geschichtsbild des Deuteronomisten." *EvT* 11 (1951–52) 415–27. **Lamadrid, A. G.** "Historia Deuteronomista." **Lohfink, N. F.** "Bilanz nach der Katastrophe: Das deuteronomistische Geschichtswerk." In *Wort und Botschaft: Eine theologische und kritische Einführung in die Probleme des alten Testaments.* Ed. J. Schreiner. Würzburg, Echter, 1967. 196–208. ———. "Was There a Deuteronomistic Movement?" In *Those Elusive Deuteronomists.* Ed. L. S. Schearing and S. L. McKenzie. 36–66. **Mayes, A. D. H.** "Deuteronomistic Ideology and the Theology of the Old Testament." *JSOT* 82 (1999) 57–82. **McCarthy, D. J.** "The Wrath of Yahweh and the Structural Unity of the Deuteronomistic History." In *Essays in Old Testament Ethics.* FS J. P. Hyatt, ed. J. L. Crenshaw and J. T. Willis. New York: Ktav, 1974. 97–110. **McConville, J. G.** *Grace in the End.* **McKenzie, S. L.,** and **M. P. Graham,** eds. *History of Israel's Traditions.* **Miller, R. D. II.** "Deuteronomistic Theology in the Book of Judges?" *OTE* 15 (2002) 411–16. **Moran, W. J.** "A Study of the Deuteronomic History." *Bib* 46 (1965) 223–28. **Mullen, E. T., Jr.** *Narrative History and Ethnic Boundaries.* **Nelson, R. D.** *Double Redaction of the Deuteronomistic History.* **Nielsen, F. A. J.** *Tragedy in History.* **Noll, K. L.** "Deuteronomistic History or Deuteronomic Debated? (A Thought Experiment)." *JSOT* 31 (2007) 311–45. **Noth, M.** *Deuteronomistic History.* **O'Brien, M. A.** *Deuteronomistic History Hypothesis.* ———. "Judges and the Deuteronomistic History." **Otto, E.** "Das Deuteronomistische Geschichtswerk im Enneateuch: Zu einem Buch von Erik Aurelius." *ZABR* 11 (2005) 323–45. **Peckham, B.** *The Composition of the Deuteronomistic History.* HSM 35. Atlanta: Scholars Press, 1985. **Person, R. F., Jr.** *Deuteronomic School.* **Plöger, O.** "Reden und Gebete im deuteronomistischen und chronistischen Geschichtswerk." In *Festschrift für Günther Dehn.* Ed. W. Schneemelcher. Neukirchen: Neukirchener Verlag, 1957. 35–49. **Polzin, R.** *Moses and the Deuteronomist.* **Preuss, H. D.** "Zum deuteronomistischen Geschichtswerk." *TRu* 58 (1993) 229–64, 341–95. **Provan, I. W.** *Hezekiah and the Book of Kings: A Contribution to the Debate about the Composition of the Deuteronomistic History.* BZAW 172. Berlin: de Gruyter, 1988. **Pury, A. de, T. C. Römer,** and **J. D. Macchi,** eds. *Israel Constructs Its History.* **Rad, G. von.** "The Beginnings of Historical Writing in Ancient Israel." In *The Problem of the Hexateuch and Other Essays.* 1944. Repr., London: SCM Press, 1966. 166–204. **Radjawane, A. N.** "Das deuteronomistische Geschichtswerk: Ein Forschungsbericht." *TRu* 38 NS (1973) 177–216. **Richter, S. L.** *The History and the Name Theology.* BZAW 318. Berlin: de Gruyter, 2002. **Richter, W.** *Bearbeitungen des "Retterbuches."* **Rofé, A.** "Ephraimite versus Deuteronomistic History." In *Storia e tradizioni di Israele.* FS J. A. Soggin, ed. D. Garrone and F. Israel. Brescia: Paideia, 1991. 221–35. **Römer, T. C.** "Entstehungsphasen des 'deuteronomistischen Geschichtswerkes.'" In *Die deuteronomistischen Geschichtswerke.* Ed. M. Witte et al. 45–70. ———. "Form-Critical Problem of the So-Called Deuteronomistic History." ———. *So-Called Deuteronomistic History.* **Römer, T. C.,** ed. *Future of the Deuteronomistic History.* **Rose, M.** *Deuteronomist und Jahwist: Untersuchungen zu den Berührungspunkten beider Literaturwerke.* ATANT 67. Zürich: Theologischer Verlag, 1981. **Rösel, H. N.** *Von Josua bis Jojachin.* **Schearing, L. S.,** and **S. L. McKenzie,** eds. *Those Elusive Deuteronomists.* **Simpson, C. A.** *Composition of the Book of Judges.* **Smend, R.** "Das Gesetz und die Völker." **Soggin, J. A.** "Deuteronomistische Geschichtsauslegung während des babylonischen Exils." In *Oikonomia: Heilsgeschichte als Thema der Theologie.* FS O. Cullmann. Hamburg-Bergstedt: Reich, 1967. 11–17. **Stipp, H. J.** "Ahab's Busse und die Komposition des deuteronomistischen Geschichtswerks." *Bib* 76 (1995)

471–97. **Thiel, W.** *Unabgeschlossene Rückschau: Aspekte alttestamentlicher Wissenschaft im 20. Jahrhundert* [with appendix]: *Grundlinien der Erforschung des 'Deuteronomistischen Geschichtswerkes.'* Biblisch-Theologische Studien 80. Neukirchen-Vluyn: Neukirchener Verlag, 2007. **Van Seters, J.** "The Deuteronomist from Joshua to Samuel." In *Reconsidering Israel and Judah.* Ed. G. Knoppers and J. G. McConville. 204–39. ———. "The Deuteronomist—Historian or Redactor? From Simon to the Present." In *Essays on Ancient Israel in Its Near Eastern Context.* FS N. Na'aman, ed. Y. Amit et al. Winona Lake, IN: Eisenbrauns, 2006. 359–75. ———. *In Search of History.* **Veijola, T.** "Deuteronomismusforschung zwischen Tradition und Innovation (II)." *TRu* 67 (2002) 391–424. ———. *Die ewige Dynastie: David und die Enstehung seiner Dynastie nach der deuteronomistischen Darstellung.* AASF B 193. Helsinki: Suomalainen Tiedeakatemia, 1975. ———. *Das Königtum in der Beurteilung der deuteronomistischen Historiographie.* **Weinfeld, M.** *Deuteronomy and the Deuteronomic School.* **Weippert, H.** "Das deuteronomistiche Geschichtswerk: Sein Ziel und Ende in der neueren Forschung." *TRu* 50 (1985) 213–49. ———. "The Emergence of the Deuteronomic Movement: The Historical Antecedents." In *Das Deuteronomium Entstehung, Gestalt und Botschaft.* Ed. N. Lohfink. Leuven, 1985. 76–83. ———. "Geschichten und Geschichte: Verheissung und Erfüllung im deuteronomistischen Geschichtswerk." In *Congress Volume.* Ed. J. A. Emerton. VTSup 43. Leiden: Brill, 1991. 116–31. Translated as "'Histories' and 'History': Promise and Fulfillment in the Deuteronomistic Historical Work by P. T. Daniels," in *Reconsidering Israel and Judah,* ed. G. Knoppers and J. G. McConville, 47–61. **Weiser, A.** *The Old Testament: Its Formation and Development.* Trans. D. M. Barton from 4th ed., 1957. New York: Association Press, 1961. **Westermann, C.** *Die Geschichtsbücher des Alten Testaments.* **Witte, M., K. Schmid, D. Prechel,** and **J. C. Gertz,** eds. *Die deuteronomistischen Geschichtswerke: Redaktions- und religionsgeschichtliche Perspektiven zur 'Deuteronomismus'-Diskussion in Tora und Vorderen Propheten.* BZAW 365. Berlin: de Gruyter, 2006. **Wolff, H. W.** "Das Kerygma des deuteronomistischen Geschichtswerks." *ZAW* 73 (1961) 171–86. Trans. F. C. Prussner as "The Kerygma of the Deuteronomistic Historical Work," in *The Vitality of the Old Testament Traditions,* ed. W. Brueggemann and H. W. Wolff (Atlanta: John Knox, 1975) 83–100, 141–43. Reprinted in *Reconsidering Israel and Judah,* ed. G. Knoppers and J. G. McConville, 62–78. **Würthwein, E.** *Studien zum deuteronomistichen Geschichtswerk.*

Since the publication of Martin Noth's pioneering work, *Überlieferungsgeschichtliche Studien,* the great majority of scholars have begun discussion of the composition of Judges by speaking of the Deuteronomistic Historian's final editorial shaping and interpretation of Judges along with Joshua, Samuel, and Kings. Noth presupposed that an undisputed result of scholarly investigation was the establishment of a Deuteronomistic author in Joshua, Judges, Samuel, and Kings. Noth also assumed that Deuteronomistic language and style are easy to recognize. A major indication of Deuteronomistic style appears in the tendency to open and close major narrative sections with speeches by leading characters, such as those that appear in Josh 1 and 23, 1 Sam 12, and 1 Kgs 8. At times the Deuteronomistic author simply provides a narrative summary, as in Judg 2 and 2 Kgs 17. Noth argued against seeing two Deuteronomistic authors, preferring to speak of later additions in Deuteronomistic style. Thus, for Noth, the Deuteronomistic book of Judges begins at 2:6, not at 1:1, since the opening chapter has no Deuteronomistic language. This Deuteronomistic author used traditional materials of quite different styles, origins, types, and purposes to fill out his narrative. Unlike the case of the conquest traditions and the Saul and David traditions, Noth found no trace of a pre-Deuteronomistic connection between the individual stories of the Judges or of the Kings narratives. Thus the Deuteronomist is the first author to collect and arrange Israel's traditions into a meaningful whole, a job accomplished shortly after 562 B.C.E.

Noth saw the Deuteronomist's period of the Judges reaching from Judg 2:6 to 1 Sam 12, proof for him that the Deuteronomist worked on materials not yet divided into separate books. To describe this epoch, the Deuteronomist had two sources available. The first was a collection of hero stories that had not been literarily combined, so that the author had to erase the original introductions to the stories and insert transitional texts to bind the stories together. In so doing he maintained the length of foreign rule from the original stories. The Deuteronomist's second source was a list of what we call the minor judges with a few details about each one. The appearance of Jephthah in both lists gave ample reason to unite the two sources into one narrative, and the title of *judge* in the list of minor judges gave the Deuteronomist cause to so entitle the charismatic heroes of the hero stories also. Finally, the Deuteronomist took over the all-Israel context of the minor judges and applied it to the charismatic heroes, some of whose stories already contained the name *Israel*. Noth even conceded that the early collection of hero stories was compiled under the assumption that they applied to Israel's battles against foreign neighbors. The Deuteronomist placed the heroes in an order to show how the nation fell away from Yahweh, with each generation behaving worse than the previous one.

In dealing with the individual stories, Noth saw the Othniel notice as a puzzle formulated strictly in Deuteronomistic language. The Deuteronomist has framed the Ehud narrative with Judg 3:12–15a and 30b. The Shamgar notice is also the work of the Deuteronomist, though it may have some foundation in the tradition. The Deborah and Barak story is framed by Judg 4:1a, 2, 3a and 5:31b and augmented by 4:4b. The secondary combination of Sisera and Jabin appeared in the old sources, as did the destruction of Hazor that clashed with the previous story in Josh 11. The Deuteronomist added Judg 6:1 to the old introduction of the Gideon narrative in 6:2–6a. Then he introduced the prophetic narrative in 6:6b–10, utilizing the Deuteronomistic style of introducing an important moment with a Deuteronomistic speech. The Deuteronomistic conclusion to the Gideon narrative (8:27b–28, 30–35) is extended to introduce the Abimelech story. The Deuteronomist added another long introduction (10:6–16) to the Jephthah narrative, which contains in 11:12–28 a later addition to the Deuteronomistic History. Also Judg 17–21 never had any connection to the Deuteronomistic History. Noth found judgment difficult concerning the Samson narrative's place in the Deuteronomistic History but finally decided that its lack of Deuteronomistic language, the absence of Samson from 1 Sam 12:11, and the opposition of the Philistines in Samuel's time lead to the conclusion that the Samson narrative is also a late addition to the history. (Radjawane, *TRu* 38 NS [1973] 184–86, shows how Noth divides materials into received traditions without editing, materials with Deuteronomistic editing, passages the Deuteronomist created, and materials later inserted into the history.)

Looking at the lack of prophetic eschatological hope and the lack of priestly cultic interests, Noth placed the origin of the history in unofficial circles as the work of a creative individual seeking to understand the recent catastrophe. Such an individual would have had access to traditions more readily in Palestine than in Babylon and so must have lived among the remnant in Judah, probably near Bethel and Mizpah, whose traditions he knew.

Noth's views of the Deuteronomistic History gradually became an accepted consensus among Hebrew Bible scholars with a few dissenters. (See Radjawane, *TRu* 38 NS [1973] 186–87.) Weiser argued that Joshua was an independent work connected to the Hexateuch until Ezra's time and that Judges was an independent Deuteronomic book growing out of oral tradition but not necessarily part of a larger Deuteronomistic History. Still, Weiser saw a decisive role for the Deuteronomist only in the editing of Kings, the Deuteronomic editorial style being quite distinctive in each of the constituent books. Thus Weiser argued for a "more sharply differentiated and varied history of the transmission and its connexion with cultic traditions" (*Old Testament*, 182). Various studies have disputed the origin of the history in Palestine, its date, its attribution to one author, and its pessimistic message. I will not be able to follow all those threads in this brief review.

Weinfeld gave great help to the study by listing basic Deuteronomic phraseology and the passages where each phrase occurs (*Deuteronomy and the Deuteronomic School*, 320–65). In Judges such language appears in 2:7, 10, 11, 12, 13, 14, 17, 19, 20, 21, 22, 23; 3:1, 4, 7, 12; 4:1; 6:1, 10; 10:6, 10; 11:23–24 (?); 17:6 (?); and 21:25 (?). Weinfeld also pointed to a few Judges passages that appear to be pre-Deuteronomic but use some Deuteronomic phrase: 1:32, 2:2, 5:31a, 6:8, 11:23–24 (?), 17:6 (?), 18:9, and 20:13. Taken by itself, this linguistic evidence would point only to 2:7–23; 3:1, 4, 7, 12; 4:1; 6:1, 10; 10:6, 10; 11:23–24; 17:6; and 21:25 as possible Deuteronomistic passages. This would mean the Deuteronomist introduced the book in chap. 2, the testing motif in 3:1, the Othniel narrative in 3:7, the Ehud narrative in 3:12, Deborah and Barak in 4:1, Gideon in 6:1, the prophet's conclusion in 6:10, and Jephthah in 10:6, 10. It would be possible that Deutronomic language was responsible for Jephthah's summary of salvation history in 11:23–24 and for the final theological teasers in 17:6 and 21:25. This would certainly validate Noth's excision of large parts of the book as post-Deuteronomistic. But it also raises the question of whether the scarcity of true Deuteronomistic language can validate the materials as Deuteronomistic.

From a different standpoint, R. D. Miller (*OTE* 15 [2002] 411–16) examined the theology in Judges. He concluded that Deuteronomistic theology is not present. Moreover, he claimed that Judges sets up a challenge to Deuteronomistic theology.

This question becomes even more vital as scholars begin to dissect the history into multiple Deuteronomists following Weiser's suggestions. Frank Cross ("Themes of the Book of Kings") set the stage for a large part of American scholarship as he followed the suggestion of von Rad ("Beginnings of Historical Writing") that Judges and Kings could not come from the same editorial hand and that the history sounded a note of grace. Cross followed the note of grace through 2 Sam 7 and Kings, showing that the history joined the threat of the Deuteronomic covenant theology with the promise of the Judean royal ideology to write a great sermon to rally the people of Josiah's day to faithfulness and hope. Cross then showed that Noth's final assessment of the history as pessimistic was true only after an exilic Deuteronomist had added the explanation of Judah's final demise seen in Manasseh's sins. Cross attributed about twenty passages to this second Deuteronomist. Nelson (*Double Redaction of the Deuteronomistic History*) and Campbell and O'Brien (*Unfolding the Deuteronomistic History*) have extended this theory through a broader textual base.

Smend ("Das Gesetz und die Völker") introduced a German perspective by attributing Deut 1:5; Josh 1:7–9; 13:2–6; 23:1–16; and Judg 1:1–2:5; 2:17, 20–21, 23 to an exilic editor he labels DtrN, or nomistic, because of the emphasis on the law. He speaks in one place of the possibility of four Deuteronomistic redaction layers but then backs off by saying that fortunately that is probably not the case. He comes later to warn that the editorial work of the Deuteronomistic School did not come to an end with DtrN. His students Dietrich *(Prophetie und Geschichte)* and Veijola *(Die ewige Dynastie* and *Das Königtum in der Beurteilung)* carried this further and introduced a Priestly editor DtrP. Becker *(Richterzeit und Königtum)* has followed this pattern through the book of Judges, finding a basic DtrH work expanded by DtrN and given a framework by a priestly redactor related to the Pentateuch redactor. DtrH opposes monarchy. DtrN underlines the people's guilt. The Priestly editor sees the period of the judges as a total failure with the monarchy the only hope for success.

In reviewing Becker, Brettler decided:

> These conclusions, and the textual analysis on which they are based, are quite plausible, but should not be seen as definitive. In contrast to the classical source criticism of the Pentateuch, where clear linguistic and stylistic features may be found which distinguish between sources, no such features are apparent within Judges. The use by the first Deuteronomic author of earlier pre/non-deuteronomic materials, as well as the likelihood that a "real" author may use a range of formulaic expressions, further complicates the possibility of neatly dissecting layers of Judges. Furthermore, no one has yet developed clear linguistic criteria which might uncover the chronological layers of Judges. *(JBL* 111 [1992] 517–19)

Finally, Van Seters and others reversed the normal theory of the origins of the biblical text and claimed that the Pentateuch simply formed the introduction to the Deuteronomistic History, which was written prior to the publication of any Pentateuchal source. In Judges in particular, the Priestly writer introduced 1:1–2:5 and 2:22–3:4 into the Deuteronomistic History, much or all of the material representing ad hoc creations. P may also have introduced the so-called minor judges of chaps. 10 and 12. The rest of Judg 2–16 is a literary creation of the Deuteronomist based on some old, previously unconnected folk legends and tied together by an artificial chronology. The Deuteronomist also created the role of judge/deliverer/savior on the basis of Phoenician practices. Judges thus came into existence only as a part of the larger history, having little relevance as a stand-alone work. Van Seters concluded, "The history of the books of Kings is the intellectual prerequisite for the history of the judges" ("Deuteronomist from Joshua to Samuel," 229).

This and other extensions of Deuteronomistic editing into various prophetic and other books led to a call for a stop to pan-Deuteronomism. Already in 1986 Greenspahn showed that the framework is not really consistent and that its major sections are not Deuteronomistic (*VT* 36 [1986] 386). He asserted that "virtually all elements characteristic of Deuteronomic thought are lacking from the Judges' framework. The only possible exception is idolatry. . . . It becomes readily apparent that only chapters ii and x contain a significant array of other characteristically Deuteronomic terms" (390–91). P. R. Davies sees talk of a Deuteronomistic History as meaningless and a tradition that should be abandoned (*In Search of 'Ancient*

Israel, '131). Coggins finds himself confronted with Deuteronomistic influence at its height from the eighth to the third centuries but notes significantly that "yet of so wide-ranging and influential a movement there is no external evidence of any kind; the whole history of tradition has to be worked out by inference. Deuteronomistic influence may be traced, but there is still no agreement as to who the Deuteronomists were" ("What Does 'Deuteronomistic' Mean?" 26). Coggins differentiates three implications of the related terms *Deuteronomic* and *Deuteronomistic:* the production of the book of Deuteronomy, the collection of existing literary pieces into a final (or perhaps penultimate) form, and an ideological movement that played a major role in shaping Jewish self-understanding. He suggests that continual usage of the same terminology for three separate realities is too confusing to be profitable ("What Does 'Deuteronomistic' Mean?" 34–35).

Auld uses his text-critical practices to decide that "the first two-and-a-half chapters of Judges are not part of, but depend on, material widely reckoned late Dtr." Thus his preference "increasingly is to read the influence backwards from Kings, not forwards from Deuteronomy" ("Deuteronomists between History and Theology," 123). For Auld the Former Prophets become "pre- or proto-Deuteronomic" (122). This pushes Deuteronomy much later than normally thought.

Carr *(Writing on the Tablet of the Heart)* argues for memory as the standard for education, textual study, and copying in ancient Israel. He contends that the typical text is reproduced from memory, not from a written scroll, thus attesting to many of the differences found in parallel texts. (See also D. M. Carr, "Empirisches Perspektiven, " 1–17.) Hjelm *(Jerusalem's Rise to Sovereignty,* 303) goes so far as to advocate a context of the third- through second-century Hasmonean struggles for control of Judea. On the other end of the spectrum, Winther-Nielsen finds pragmatics shows that "Judges is a record of language use and situations in a real past world rather than in a totally fictionalized world" ("Fact, Fiction, and Language Use," 77).

Römer ("Entstehungsphasen des 'deuteronomistischen Geschichtswerkes,'" 62–63) points to a current trend in recent research to set the original insertion of Judges between Joshua and Samuel in the postexilic period, Judges not appearing to know of 1 Sam 1:1. For Römer, Judges has less Deuteronomistic editing than any of the other books and certainly had a prehistory independent of Deuteronomism. He sees three Deuteronomic stages based on a study of Deut 12, but joins Cross in placing the initial Deuteronomistic writing under Josiah. Judges, however, was not included in this editing even though an original northern book of saviors probably existed. The exilic Deuteronomists used the book of saviors, to which they added Othniel to create a "period of the Judges" without historical basis. (See T. Römer, *The So-called Deuteronomistic History,* 136–39.) He sees a postexilic editing that inserted Judg 2:1–20 and Josh 23 among other texts and that started with Exodus, probably Exod 3.

U. Becker ("Endredaktionelle Kontextvernetzungen des Josua-Buches," 139–59) decides that Joshua was originally part of the Hexateuch material, but a collection without Genesis and Deuteronomy. Joshua became part of an Enneateuch.

Having reviewed the perspectives of these earlier commentaries, it is interesting to note how the many recent Judges commentaries handle the Deuteronomistic History question. In *The New Interpreter's Bible,* neither Peter Miscall in his "Introduction to Narrative Literature" (2:539–52) nor Dennis Olson in his introduction to Judges (2:723–29) mentions the Deuteronomist, though Olson speaks of a later editor and gives a footnote reference to the work of Lawson Stone. Block sees Judges as "an independent literary composition, written in light of the authentically Mosaic theology of Deuteronomy and in light of the written accounts of the conquest found in the Book of Joshua. . . . A single mind has deliberately selected, arranged, linked, and shaped the sources available to him" (49). Block explains the so-called Deuteronomistic elements as deriving not from "a single hand but from the common Mosaic theological and literary tradition in which the Yahwistic authors of all of these books were schooled" (50). Brensinger simply assumes a Deuteronomistic History without discussion. Schneider sidesteps the issue as not relevant to the nature of the commentary series in which she writes and as not conducive to the literary unity that she emphasizes (xii–xiii). Brettler notes interestingly, "Judges is not a typical Dtr book (but what is?). . . . It is not infused with Dtr terminology and ideology" (114). Brown (129) and Pressler (1–2) follow Cross in postulating a Josianic DtrH with an exilic redaction. McCann speaks of a possible early shaping of the material "as political propaganda for the claims of David over Saul" but sees the book as part of the Deuteronomistic History having gone through several "editions" (8). Phillips (5) uses internal chronology to support the Talmud's contention that Samuel or someone in Samuel's time period authored Judges. Matthews (5) points to a late sixth-century Deuteronomistic editor using oral materials.

Niditch (9–13) finds not three "editors" but, in her oral-tradition emphasis, "three voices." The "epic bardic" voice "may be as old as the stories themselves." Its interests include "distribution of booty, the workings of temporary charismatic leadership and a decentralized polity, and aspects of religious life that sometimes differ, for example, from portrayals in the book of Deuteronomy" (9). Judg 5 is used as the best example of this voice.

What scholars usually refer to as the Deuteronomic or Deuteronomistic editor, Niditch refers to as the "voice of the theologian" but refuses to "attempt to distinguish between various contributors within this layer or to deal with the knotty larger issue of Deuteronomism" (10). This theologian's voice has a strong covenant emphasis and is responsible for framing the hero stories of Judg 3–16. The tradition behind this voice appears among northern Levites who may have influenced Josiah's reform. Judg 2, 3:7–15, 4:1–3, 6:1–10, 10:6–16, and 13:1 represent this voice. It preserves practices Deuteronomy opposes and has an irrepressible appreciation for the old stories. She tentatively dates this voice in the seventh to sixth centuries B.C.E. (11).

The final voice, most clearly heard in Judg 1 and 17–21, is that of the "humanist." It is "noncritical about the ancient protagonists" (Niditch, 11). The chief themes of the humanist are the vagaries of power and the transience of military and political control. It appears to echo voices from the Persian or early Hellenistic period. For this voice "the monarchy is inevitable if not always glorious" (13). All these voices use epic style and agree on essential features of Yahwism (13). One wonders why anyone should go to such effort to speak of different voices when they maintain so much agreement. They may preserve different kinds of stories rather than come from different times.

We are left with confusing evidence. One can identify Judges as Deuteronomistic only by deciding certain theological motifs are Deuteronomistic or by curtailing the book to a section without the present introduction and conclusion. On the other hand, the present book clearly presupposes the stories of Joshua preceding it and at least some part of the story of monarchy following it. Thus we must look closely at the structure of the present book.

THE IMMEDIATE CONTEXT: THE STRUCTURE OF THE BOOK OF JUDGES

Select Bibliography

Alonzo Schökel, L. "Erzählkunst im Buche der Richter." *Bib* 42 (1961) 148–58. **Amit, Y.** *Book of Judges.* **Campbell, A. F.**, and **M. A. O'Brien.** *Unfolding the Deuteronomistic History.* **Cross, F. M., Jr.** "The Structure of the Deuteronomistic History." *Perspectives in Jewish Learning* 3 (1968) 9–24. **Exum, J. C.** "The Centre Cannot Hold: Thematic and Textual Instabilities in the Book of Judges." *CBQ* 52 (1990) 410–31. **Gooding, D. W.** "The Composition of the Book of Judges." *ErIsr* 16 (1982) 70–79. **Gros Louis, K. R. R.** "Book of Judges." **Lilley, J. P. U.** "A Literary Appreciation of the Book of Judges." *TynBul* 18 (1976) 291–304. **Mullen, E. T., Jr.** *Narrative History and Ethnic Boundaries.* **O'Connell, R. H.** *Rhetoric of the Book of Judges.* **Polzin, R.** *Moses and the Deuteronomist.* **Stone, L. G.** "From Tribal Confederation to Monarchic State: The Editorial Perspective of the Book of Judges." PhD thesis, Yale University, 1988. **Sweeney, M. A.** "Davidic Polemic in the Book of Judges." *VT* 47 (1997) 517–29. **Wong, G. T. K.** *Compositional Strategy of the Book of Judges: An Inductive, Rhetorical Study.* VTSup 111. Leiden: Brill, 2006.

Much recent skepticism about the role of the Deuteronomistic History in Judges comes from studies that show a unified literary structure not only for individual units or parts of the present book of Judges but also for the entire twenty-one-chapter book. Gros Louis ("Book of Judges") described recurring motifs that unify these narratives. Particularly important is his attempt to take the two extended narrative episodes in chap. 1 and relate motifs in them to motifs in later narratives. Lilley (*TynBul* 18 [1976] 291–304) rebelled against critical scholarship's fragmentation of the book and argued for a literary unity by one author, though he still did not deny some later editing. Lilley also introduced the idea of a progressive deterioration in the depiction of the Judges rather than repeated examples of the "Deuteronomistic formula" of 2:11–19. Polzin *(Moses and the Deuteronomist)* used Russian formalism to show the distinct perspectives within the narration of Judges. He joined Gros Louis in pointing to the Samson narratives as the climactic presentation of most, if not all, the motifs of the Judges narratives. Polzin also saw chaps. 1 and 19–21 as consciously framing the larger narratives.

Gooding (*ErIsr* 16 [1982] 70–79) proposed the thesis that one unifying mind formed the present book of Judges. He began his study with a basic structural analysis with which virtually all scholars agree:

1:1–3:6	A two-part (1:1–2:5; 2:6–3:6) introduction
3:7–16:31	A body of narratives
17:1–21:25	A two-part (chaps 17–18; 19–21) epilogue

He placed these in a chiastic scheme with pairs:

Introduction 1 with epilogue 2	Disintegration of the tribes
Introduction 2 with epilogue 1	Idolatry rampant
Othniel with Samson	The problem of foreign women
Ehud (and Shamgar) with Jephthah, Ibzan, Elon, Abdon	Foreign kings at the fords of the Jordan
Deborah, Barak, and Jael with Abimelech, Tola, Jair	Heroic women end the war

This leaves Gideon alone at the center of the chiasm illustrating in his own narrative the decline of the judges.

These studies led to Webb's major exploration of literary unity in Judges. He emphasizes the narrative form of the entire book and the indirect manner of stating the text's point of view or religious instruction. The narrative creates a plot as it presents history rather than chronicling a series of events. Webb finds that such a narrative plot is best revealed by means of rhetorical criticism rather than through structuralist methods. Interestingly, Webb does not claim to show either unity of authorship or authorial intention. He simply seeks to "demonstrate that the work in its final form is a more meaningful narrative work than has been generally recognized" ([1987] 39). To achieve this aim, Webb looks at organization, characterization, and points of view. His investigation discovers connecting motifs between successive narrative units and overarching issues that find their climax in the Samson narratives. The four major issues for Webb are

1. Israel's special status as a nation separated to Yahweh
2. Israel's going after other gods in willful violation of this special status
3. The implied contest between Yahweh and these other gods
4. The freedom of Yahweh's activity over against Israel's presumption that it knows him and can use him, as required to secure its own future

Examining the two epilogue narratives in Judg 17–21, Webb finds that they simply complement the themes of the narratives in the main body of the book. Here, however, Judah plays a significantly different role from that in the opening prologue. Judg 1 paints a favorable view of Judah in the leadership position in contrast to the other tribes. This favorable picture of Judah makes itself known in redactional levels rather than in the traditional narrative material. This appears again in 20:18, showing that it joins 1:1–2 as part of the "literary shaping of the finished form of the work" ([1987] 201). This progressively more negative portrayal of Judah brings into question, for Webb, any support the book might give to a Judean monarchy. Indeed, "there is no correlation between the portrayal of Judah and the alleged pro-monarchical and anti-monarchical tendencies of the book" (202).

Monarchy is an important motif for Webb:

The refrain of 17.6, 18.1, 19.1, and 21.25 intimates that kingship will be the subject matter of a sequel to the present work and that the positive contribution of kingship will be to bring a measure of order and stability to Israel's internal affairs. But the clear message of the two narratives brought together in these chapters is that no institution can make Israel proof against divine chastisement and, paradoxically, that it is that very chastisement which preserves Israel, not its institutions. ([1987] 202–3)

O'Connell *(Rhetoric of the Book of Judges)* presents the most comprehensive literary analysis of Judges. He sees the book as an apologetic for the Judean Davidic monarchy and thus a polemic against the Benjaminite Saulide monarchy. Sweeney (*VT* 47 [1997] 517–29) extends this viewpoint, speaking of a limited polemic against Benjamin but a pervasive polemic against Ephraim and Bethel for Canaanizing Israel and thus being the causes for the dissolution of the Deuteronomic Historian's ideal for Israel. Judah and its Davidic king thus become the Deuteronomist's hope for achieving the ideal for God's people.

On this foundation Block writes a massive commentary arguing for Judges as an

> independent literary composition, written in light of the authentically Mosaic theology of Deuteronomy and in light of the written accounts of the conquest as found in the Book of Joshua. . . . A single mind has deliberately selected, arranged, linked, and shaped the sources available to him to achieve a specific ideological agenda, which has yielded a coherent literary work. Few biblical compositions present a plot as tightly knit as that found in the Book of Judges. (49)

Block's analysis of the composition differs from that of his predecessors. He follows closely the Hebrew syntactical clues to divide the introduction into three parts (1:1–36; 2:1–23; 3:1–6) that present a "military and theological context to the 'Book of Deliverers' that follows" (77). Block then divides the body of the book into seven cycles with three parentheses, though the Shamgar parenthesis has to be counted with the other cycles to achieve the number seven (143–45). Each cycle concerns an enemy and a deliverer while the parentheses relate to the governorships of the minor judges:

Cycle One: Aram-Naharaim and Othniel (3:7–11)
Cycle Two: Moab and Ehud (3:12–30)
    Parenthesis One: Shamgar's governorship (3:31)
Cycle Three: Canaan and Barak (4:1–5:31)
Cycle Four: Midian and Gideon, including "the Canaanite Kingship of Gideon's Son Abimelech" (6:1–9:57)
    Parenthesis Two: Governorships of Tola and Jair (10:1–5)
Cycle Five: Ammon and Jephthah (10:6–12:7)
    Parenthesis Three: Governorships of Ibzan, Elon, and Abdon (12:8–15)
Cycle Six: Philistine and Samson Cycle (13:1–16:31)

Block sees the order here determined not by chronology but rather by rhetoric and logic to present the Canaanization of Israel. The presentation reflects "the downward spiraling of the Israelite condition during this period" (145). This is reflected in the breakdown of the structures in Judg 2:11–23 that appear in almost complete form in the introductions to the early narratives but then disappear (146–47). Including the minor judges, or parentheses, one finds "that the entire picture of twelve rulers and their respective tribes corresponds to the cycle of the solar year, beginning with Othniel (Judah) in early winter and ending with Samson in late autumn" (145; compare J. G. Williams, "The Structure of Judges

2:6–16:31," *JSOT* 49 [1991] 77–85). Finally, turning to the third major section of the book (chaps. 17–21), Block sees a change from emphasis on God's working with foreign peoples to how ordinary Israelites, especially the heartland tribes of Dan and Benjamin, fared. A nameless Levite with connections to Bethlehem-Judah and to Mount Ephraim and a priest play an important part in each of the two narratives (Judg 17–18; 19–21). Both narratives conclude at Shiloh and feature military units of six hundred men. And the refrain "in those days Israel had no king" (17:6; 18:1; 19:1; 21:25) unites the two originally independent narratives. This shows that "the Israelites do not need either a governor (Samson) or a king to lead them into sin. They will do it on their own" (476). Thus chaps. 17–18 show religious and cultic Canaanization of Israel while chaps. 19–21 point to Israel's moral and ethical Canaanization.

David Dorsey has presented the most complex analysis of the structure of Judges and, indeed, of the entire Hebrew Bible. Dorsey believes ancient texts were intended to be read aloud, thus requiring that the structure be identified through "verbal structure indicators" (16). Modern readers must learn to listen for such indicators, aware that "Hebrew structuring patterns and techniques were different from ours" (16). Dorsey outlines a three-step listening process (16–18):

1. Identify the composition's constituent parts
2. Analyze the arrangement of these parts
3. Consider the relationship of the composition's structure to its meaning and message

Working from Gooding's article, Dorsey (105–20) discovers two themes in Judges: (a) Israel's spiritual and political decline and (b) Yahweh's gracious and repeated deliverance of Israel. These themes present an intricate literary structure prominently featuring chiasms. The prologue has the traditional two parts (1:1–2:5 and 2:6–3:6). The main body uses only seven parts to narrate the adventures of thirteen judges. Each of these seven units follows a pattern of eleven elements with "minor variations." The eleven elements are divided among three major components—beginning, story proper, and conclusion.

Dorsey asserts the seven major stories "are designed in seven-part symmetries" except for the three-part introductory story of Othniel (*Literary Structure of the Old Testament*, 108). The fourth or central episode represents each story's turning point. The narratives of Othniel, Ehud, and Deborah center on Yahweh's intervention, while the other four narratives emphasize Israel's deterioration. Similarly, the seven major narratives as a whole form a chiastic pattern that pairs Othniel and Samson, Ehud and Jephthah, Deborah/Barak and Abimelech. This isolates the Gideon narrative as the turning point of the main body of the book.

A different but still chiastic structure appears in the epilogue, which in turn forms a chiasm with the two-part introduction. The two stories here are prime examples of Israel's moral and political decline. Thus the author of Judges has shown that the days of the Judges were in no way "the good old days." Rather, they were shameful days (*Literary Structure of the Old Testament*, 120).

Younger, in his commentary, reads Judges against Deuteronomistic law. He sees the double introduction forming an inclusio with the double conclusion. The introduction deals with foreign wars and idols while the conclusion deals with domestic wars and idols. In Younger's reading the introduction is structured to create literary expectations for the main cycle section. These expectations include (1) the increasing inability to drive out the Canaanites mirrored in the moral degeneration of the judges and (2) the south to north sequence of Judah to Dan. The paradigms of Judg 2:6–3:6 lay the groundwork for the irony that permeates the book. Younger places special emphasis on the repeated refrain of 17:6, 18:1, 19:1, and 21:25—"in those days Israel had no king"—as a double entendre pointing to the lack of an earthly king and of a spiritual or divine king.

Younger finds in the main body a macrostructure that should control the reading of each episode. The framework statements do not force the individual narratives into a fixed grid. Rather each narrative focuses on one element of the grid, "giving depth and texture to the plots and also heightening the reader's interest with numerous surprising turns" (35). This allows the author to picture the "progressive deterioration in Israel's condition: in relation to Yahweh, in relation to its enemies, and in relation to its own internal stability" (35). In this view the Samson cycle becomes both the literary climax and the moral nadir of the main body or cycles section (36). Even the length of a cycle reflects the morality of the judge involved: the longer the cycle, the less moral the judge (37). Another clue to deterioration comes from the depiction of women: "the book evinces a clear degeneration from the outspoken (in a positive sense) Acsah (1:12–15), to Deborah and Jael (chs. 4–5), to the '[certain] woman' (9:53), to Jephthah's daughter (11:34–40), to Delilah (16:4–22), and finally to the dependent and silent women of chapters 19–21" (37).

Younger identifies Othniel, not Gideon, as the exemplary judge, but does find the Gideon cycle "pivotal in every sense" as the "beginning of the Out-group judges" with their disturbing moral character traits and their searches for revenge (38). Younger also sees strong thematic links between the two middle cycles (Deborah/Barak and Gideon/Abimelech) and significant links between each of the other two pairings among the six cyclical judges (Othniel/Ehud; Jephthah/Samson). Even in the parenthetical minor judges Younger finds moral declivity (42): "Thus in every way, the cycles section of the book reflects a progressive degeneration. By the end of the story of Samson, the reader is left questioning the value of judgeship altogether. This is precisely what the narrator has planned so that his double conclusion to the book will be exactly the proper ending in which the issue of kingship is raised" (43).

Olson emphasizes the dialogical character of the book, saying it "holds together seemingly opposed or disjunctive viewpoints on the same subject," including kingship, religion and politics, well-being of women and the health of society, relationships with other nations, human character, divine and human agency, hope and chaos, and divine justice and mercy (726–27). Building on Webb and Stone, he sees 1:1–2:5 built around three uses of עלה, "to go up," in 1:1–2, 22 and 2:1. The content is built around materials taken from Joshua and reshaped for the editor's purpose of supporting Judah and David. The second introduction (2:6–3:6) contrasts Joshua's generation with following ones, preparing for the moral and spiritual declines to follow in the major narratives. In the central body of the book Olson, following Stone and Webb, finds "a downward progression in three stages" (762). Fairly faithful and victorious judges appear in 3:6–5:32. A transition to the downward slide appears in 6:1–10:5, while the judges of the third group, in 10:6–16:31, "descend further into military failure, religious unfaithfulness, and personal tragedy" (762). The dramatic conclusion (17:1–21:25) then portrays Israel "in religious and social chaos" (863). Here the era of the judges has ended.

Schneider contends that "the book of Judges is organized to show a degenerative progression; each cycle shows a generation beginning yet lower on the scale of legitimate behavior regarding the Israelites' relationship to their deity than the previous generation had" (xii). This degeneration involves several important themes for Schneider: differing forms of leadership, role of women, north/south polemic, David and Saul, and the nation's relationship to Yahweh. Judges, then, must be seen as "a well-integrated theological narrative which builds its story and supports its thesis until its conclusion" (xiii). The basic question for Judges is simply, "Who is going to lead Israel?" (xiv). The basic issue is Israel's relationship to deity (xv). Schneider's study thus looks for recurring words and phrases, use of irony, and repeated themes.

Hamilton views the book as living between "no Joshua" and "no king," with hope that removing the no-king vacuum will answer the no-Joshua problem, the book not being brought to closure (*Handbook*, 97–98). He, too, emphasizes the literary integration of the book, the process of degeneration introduced in chap. 1, and the south to north movement (103). Hamilton concludes his exposition by noting a gruesome fact: "Every Israelite in Judges who dies violently at the hand of another dies at the hand of a fellow Israelite! No Israelite is said to be put to death by any Midianite or Moabite or Philistine. It is a book about kindred killing kindred. That is a gruesome part of the savagery of the era" (169).

McCann begins with the startling claim "that the book of Judges may be the most timely and relevant of all the books in the Old Testament" since it deals with "tension and strife between rival groups (in the Middle East or elsewhere), disputes over land and territory, uncertainty over the roles of men and women, power-hungry political leaders, child abuse, spouse abuse, senseless and excessive violence, male political leaders who chase women, excessive individualism, moral confusion, and social chaos" (1–2). He sees basic material coming from the years 1200 to 1020 B.C.E. but "reworked, supplemented, and arranged, probably multiple times" (8). The earliest of the shaping supported David over Saul. There followed several editions of the Deuteronomistic History reaching to the restoration from exile (8). McCann then seeks to offer a theological interpretation of the book from its place in the canon.

Matthews also begins with a description of the progressive growth of the book from early, often fragmentary oral traditions to final editing, noting the ironic and violent, even scandalous, nature of much of the material. He concludes, "The editors constructed the narrative in such a way that it becomes an intentional caricature of events and thus an argument for law and order. The Judges material therefore is supposed to be rough, uncouth, and in places very exciting and comical" (4). He sees two possible purposes: legitimation of Josiah or demonstration of Yahweh's kingship. These purposes are accomplished by shaping stories to demonstrate progressive chaos with decline in moral standards and authoritative leadership (8).

A. F. Campbell sees Judges structured to present a "witness to the failure of leadership after Joshua" ("Book of Judges," 68). The book is one of "dysfunction," showing the failure of conquest of deliverer-judges and serving as "a horrible hinge between the Israel of Moses and Joshua and the Israel of prophets and kings"

(70). He thus sees the book as having three parts: (1) "occupation of the land: a different picture" (1:1–2:5); (2) "transition of generations" (2:6–10); and (3) "life in the land: new generations and degeneration" (2:11–21:25), including "God's action repeated regularly" (2:11–9:57) and "repeated sporadically" (10:1–16:31), and "God's absence" (17:1–21:25) (71). Working with O'Brien, Campbell admits the uncertainty of source distinctions and of structural divisions in Judges (*Unfolding the Deuteronomistic History,* 165–66) and then divides the text into at least six sources.

The discussion of structure could be expanded to include a number of other theories. These examples should be sufficient to point to some conclusions. More and more, scholars see the book as a literary unit describing the deterioration of Israel socially, politically, morally, and religiously. The author is credited with complex structures, elegant use of literary figures, complicated characterization and plotting, and exquisite use of irony. Granting such unity and literary dexterity, many scholars continue to trace literary additions and growth within the book. Such theories resurrect the imbecilic editors described by previous generations of scholars and redeem them into literary giants repeatedly able to take previous material and reshape it into new theological patterns for new social and religious conditions.

My view of the shape of Judges begins with taking seriously its opening and closing verses. The opening refers to the death of Joshua, and the closing refers to the lack of a king. The first thus obviously refers back to the book of Joshua, a reference made even more clearly in Judg 2:6–12. One can naturally assume that the final verse points forward to the story of at least one king, a king who would lead the people, not one who would simply do right in his own eyes and lead the people to do the same. At least three candidates appear to fit this description—David, Hezekiah, and Josiah. A closer look at the structure of the book may help to narrow the list. The book of Judges clearly and consciously reverses all that Joshua accomplished. In a real sense, the death of Joshua represents the death of Israel. Thus a comparison of the structure of the two books is in order.

Joshua has a three-part structure (Butler, *Joshua*): possessing the promise (chaps. 1–12), lots for the land (chaps. 13–19), and life in the land (chaps. 20–24). Judges also has a three-part structure: the situation after Joshua (1:1–2:23); Israel's sagging fortunes under the judges (3:1–16:31); and epilogue: who is king when all is right in my eyes? (17:1–21:25). The overall plot of the two books represents a total reversal. Joshua starts with no Moses, no land, and a people threatening to divide between east and west. The first part ends with a unified people having conquered the land and proved the merits of its leader. Judges starts with Joshua dead, a leading tribe with few allied tribes to follow, no person like Moses as leader, a broken covenant, a pattern of apostasy, and a divine promise not to keep the promises.

The second part of Joshua fairly divides the land among the tribes under divine leadership, including even those families left bereft of male leadership. The second part of Judges pictures one futile leader after another winning battles for God but not bringing the people back to covenant obedience, tribal unity, or possession of the land. Shechem, the key cultic site for Joshua, becomes the home of a murderous, self-proclaimed king and of military atrocities. Ammonites and Philistines continue to threaten Israel, and leadership has dwindled to a one-man show. Tribes begin fighting tribes rather than helping one another. The brightest spots come from the first three judges and some faithful women.

The final part of Joshua shows a plan for religious leadership, a plan to curb jealous vengeance, an agreement between eastern and western tribes, and a renewal of the covenant with God so that the people of Israel can go to their inheritances in a time of rest, peace, unity, and covenant obedience. The final part of Judges shows the need to start all over again under a new system. Families, cult sites, normal rules of hospitality and intertribal cooperation, and national unity have disappeared. The covenant established at the end of Joshua and broken at the beginning of Judges now disappears. Everyone does what seems right in their own eyes. The tribal cooperation of Josh 1 reverts to civil war, two tribes of Israel having been slaughtered. A divinely appointed leader no longer emerges. Female heroes vanish from the scene, replaced by female victims raped or kidnapped. Religious ritual brings defeat rather than victory. Holy war aims at another Israelite tribe to secure wives for a decimated tribe rather than at the enemies as in Joshua's days. Judges has thus systematically destroyed all that Joshua created. (See table I.1 in the appendix for a thorough comparison of Joshua and Judges.)

The thesis can be argued, I believe persuasively, that the content, themes, and structure of the Judges narrative together reflect a conscious effort to reverse the content, themes, and structure of the Joshua narrative. In canonical form, the book of Judges obviously presupposes the book of Joshua. The content of the first two chapters with their repeated references back to Joshua and his death make this abundantly clear as does Olson's listing of materials in chap. 1 that depend upon or refer back to Joshua.

The similarity of structural themes is at least intriguing, if not absolutely convincing, as one considers the relationship of Judges to its canonical predecessor. The structure shows Judges negating each accomplishment and theological claim of the book of Joshua. Joshua's first two parts are each introduced by a divine command that Joshua immediately obeys (Josh 1:2–5 and 13:7). Joshua uses clear theological statements to conclude sections of the work in Josh 5:1, 11:23, 19:51, 21:43-45, and 24:28. The structure in Joshua leads to geographical progression with the conquest of central, southern, and northern parts of the land followed by allotment of the land, including both eastern and western tribes, with particular emphasis on the unity with and loyalty of the eastern tribes (Josh 1:12–18; 13:8–32; 22:1–34). Joshua also shows cultic progression. Major sanctuaries at Gilgal, Shechem, and Shiloh are claimed for God with major cultic actions, climaxing in settlement of a cultic argument in Josh 22 and covenant renewal at Josh 8:30–35 and 24:1–28. Finally, Joshua shows thematic unity in its presentation of God's faithful gift of the land, God's expectation of obedience to the law, God's demands to be the only Lord, and God's elevation of Joshua to Moses' position as servant of Yahweh (Josh 1:16–18; 3:7, 14; 5:15; 6:27; 10:14; 24:29).

When we turn to Judges, we expect this same type of clear literary and thematic structure. Judges refuses to live up to Joshua's literary standards or Joshua's thematic consistency. Instead, Judges takes everything that unifies Joshua into a book describing the leader who succeeds Moses and reverses it, creating a book whose lack of unity and lack of consistency portray its message by its broken structure. Judges is simply a literary collection of historical vignettes loosely tied together by a chronological framework (1:1; 3:8, 11, 14, 30; 5:31; 8:28; 9:22; 10:2, 3, 8; 12:7, 9, 11; 13:1; 15:20; 16:31). Judges begins with a clear theological framework in 2:11–23 and utilizes elements of it in the following narratives, but they quickly disintegrate so that, according to Block, "the breakdown of the structures of the accounts is a rhetorical device, paralleling the general moral and spiritual disintegration of the nation" (147). The stories never again refer to God's covenant. They never refer to God's testing. Indeed, the stories begin with some part of the intricate judgment pattern of 2:11–23, but the schema never becomes a repetitive pattern, as table I.2 shows. (See table I.2 in the appendix.)

The "ideal" example of Othniel in 3:7–11 incorporates many of these elements as the table shows but also adds some of its own that are variously, but not consistently, repeated in the following narratives. For a comprehensive list of the new elements from the "ideal narrative," see table I.3 in the appendix.

The new elements from the "ideal narrative" appear more frequently than do those from the theological introduction, but still none of the elements appears in all the individual narratives. Portions of the schema reappear in all but the most compact narratives, but nowhere does the full-blown schema appear in pure literary form. The schema gives us a mirror through which to read the narratives rather than giving the author a plan by which to write the narratives.

The individual narratives themselves have long been admired for their literary skill and mastery. That is not denied. What is denied here is that any literary plan really unites the separate vignettes into a discernible whole with a literary, dramatic, narrative plan. The author produces a whole that communicates more through the feelings and impressions it produces than through any unified writing plan. The theological introduction seems intended to signal that Israel could not follow the planned pattern, while the ideal narrative is the starting point from which Israel quickly goes downhill. Here the irony of the book of Judges introduces itself. A people without a second Joshua cannot even follow God's pattern for a generation. As Exum summarizes the structural situation,

> Although we are led to expect a consistent and regular pattern, what happens is that the framework itself breaks down. Rather than attributing the lack of consistency in the framework pattern to careless redaction, I take it as a sign of further dissolution. The political and moral instability depicted in Judges is reflected in the textual instability. The framework deconstructs itself, so to speak, and the cycle of apostasy and deliverance becomes increasingly murky. (*CBQ* 52 [1990] 412)

Rather than looking for a clear literary structure, perhaps we should look for a thematic one as in Joshua, where battle stories and allotment narratives both follow clear geographical progressions. (The following is taken from T. C. Butler, "Daily Meditations in the Book.") The opening battle summaries in chap. 1 appear to parallel the Joshua allotment narratives, supplying information about the land that remains in Joshua. Instead, we find here that what has been apportioned is not taken. More land remains to be possessed after Judg 1 than was the case in Josh 13. Whereas chap. 1 at least appears to transform Joshua's east-west orientation into a north-south one, the individual narratives in the remainder of Judges follow no particular geographical pattern. Some battles have no geographical locale (3:7–11, 31). Ehud appears to have to retake Jericho, "the City of Palms" (3:13), and the fords of the Jordan (3:28). Deborah and Barak fight the fortified cities in the north. Gideon confines himself to the central country between Tabor and Shechem, where Abimelech remains. Jephthah battles in his Gilead homeland east of the Jordan. Samson confines his exploits to the Philistine territory, including Philistine-controlled parts of Judah and Dan. Thus the geographical "pattern" skips from central Palestine to the far north, then back to the north central area, then across the Jordan to the east, and finally to the far western stretches of Palestine. The strongholds of Judah disappear from the narrative.

Judges makes no pretense of organized warfare to capture the land. Rather Judges shows a desperate defensive strategy to repel victorious intruders. Similarly, the enemies of Israel expand rather than contract when compared with Joshua. Instead of a comprehensive battle plan against native inhabitants as in Joshua, in the book of Judges Israel fights Mesopotamia (3:8), Moab (3:12), Philistia (3:31; chaps. 13–16; compare Josh 13:2–3), the king of Canaan in Hazor (4:2; compare Josh 11), Midianites (chaps. 6–8), and Ammonites (chaps. 10–12). This means the victories of Moses in East Jordan must be repeated as must victory over the northern tribes centered in Hazor.

Sadly, the enemy list is still incomplete. Abimelech turns the sanctuary where Joshua renewed God's covenant with Israel (Josh 8:30–35; 24:1–28) into a war zone, killing off the inhabitants of Shechem and finally falling prey himself to an unexpected murderer. Ephraim constantly picks fights with judges from other tribes (8:1; 12:1), resulting finally in a civil war in which Gilead destroys 42,000 Ephraimites (12:6). This theme of violence reappears in chaps. 17–21 when a lurid story of false worship, rape, and the splitting of a woman's body into twelve pieces erupts into a confrontation between all Israel and Benjamin, whereby the tribe of Benjamin is almost eliminated from existence.

The latter story stands in sharp contrast to Joshua's picture of a unified Israel from east and west fighting together (chap. 1) and solving their differences (chap. 22). In Joshua, Israel expands to take in Rahab and her family (chap. 2) and the people of Gideon (chap. 9). Conversely in Judges, the people of Israel contract. Opening chapters refer to all the sons of Israel. The following narratives subtly define who Israel is in each instance. Othniel leads "the sons of Israel" (Judg 3:9). Ehud from Benjamin works solo to kill the king of Moab but then calls the "sons of Israel" from the hill country of Ephraim (3:27). Shamgar apparently works alone (3:31). Deborah, Barak, and their surprise compatriot Jael originally work with Zebulun and Naphtali (4:10). The poem of Judg 5 increases this to Ephraim, Benjamin, Machir, Zebulun, Issachar, and Naphtali (5:14–15a, 18) while noting with concern the absence of Reuben, Gilead, Dan, and Asher (5:15b–17) but passing without mention Judah and Simeon. Gideon works with Manasseh, Asher, Zebulun, and Naphtali (6:35; 7:23), with Ephraim issuing complaints for being called on only at a late date (7:24; 8:1). Abimelech works with "hired worthless and reckless fellows" (9:4). Jephthah from Gilead is first expelled from his home and then bribed back to lead Gilead against Ammon (11:1–10). His core army consists of "worthless fellows" (11:3). Finally, Samson never bothers to gather an army from anywhere. He simply thrives on individual exploits of strength. Thus all Israel devolves from the twelve tribes Joshua worked with continuously to individual heroes often working alone, or with a limited number of tribes, and finally to worthless fellows. In a real sense Samson epitomizes these worthless fellows.

The book of Judges has opportunity to picture geographical consistency, unity of enemies, and growth of Israel into a unified people. Instead, it depicts a happenstance geographical situation depending on enemy initiative, not Israelite initiative. It pictures enemies already conquered by Joshua and Moses or enemies who should have nothing to do with maintaining a hold on the promised land. It transforms Israel from a united group of tribes overcoming potential east/west conflict into a group of small tribal alliances plagued by jealousy, internal strife, and finally, near-fatal civil war. No story elements or contents thus provide thematic unity. Hauser finds the following pattern for Israel during the period of the judges:

> There were various independent, autonomous groups that had different degrees of commitment to Yahweh, such commitment often being blended with one or more other religions, which had various interpretations of the religion of Yahweh and which had different understandings of the laws associated with the worship of Yahweh. . . . In such a context of local autonomy and divergent understandings of what constituted Yahwism, highly varied practices and rituals (some of which would later be considered heterodox and scandalous by a more standardized Yahwism) were likely to proliferate due to the vacuum left by the lack of any central authority. (*JETS* 22 [1979] 293)

Surely at least the cultic unity of Joshua has carried over. Here the surprise grows. Gilgal is the angel's departure point on the way to Bochim and Israel's cultic weeping over God's disastrous announcement of judgment (Judg 2:1) and is mentioned in passing in the Ehud narratives (3:19). Never is it the center of worship or cultic acts. Shechem is Abimelech's birthplace and the center of worship for Baal Berith (9:4) or El Berith (9:46). It is the center of disastrous fighting between Abimelech and the people of Shechem, resulting in the city's destruction (9:45). Shiloh serves only as a contrast to the sanctuary at Dan with its graven image and a priest stolen from Micah (18:31) and as the site of the unusual feast where daughters are kidnapped to serve as Benjaminite wives (21:12–21). Israel has to have specific directions just to find Shiloh.

For Judges, then, the standard cult places of Joshua disintegrate into passing reference or destroyed city without any use for authentic worship and renewal. Judges knows that Shiloh is the house of God (Judg 18:31) but substitutes its own, quite unexpected, set of cult sites and cult acts. Gideon sets up a cult at Ophrah, eventually instituting worship of an ephod he has had made (6:24; 8:27). Jephthah speaks words before the Lord at Mizpah, probably in Gilead (11:11; compare 10:17; 11:29, 34; Gen 31:49). Israel gathers at what is apparently a different Mizpah to determine how to deal with the unruly tribe of Benjamin (20:1, 3; 21:1, 5, 8). For Judges, Bethel becomes the central cult place, even though it was a defeated city in Joshua (7:2–8:17; 12:16) and in Judges (1:25). Deborah judges Israel between Ramah and Bethel (4:5). Israel convenes at Bethel to determine who should lead the battle against Benjamin (20:18, 26; 21:2–4), the ark of the covenant being there (20:27).

Cultic activities abound, but not of the kind usual for normative Yahwism. Israel uses cultic means to find leadership (Judg 1:1), offers sacrifice with weeping (2:4–5), builds altars on the site of a destroyed Baal cult (6:24–27), worships on the battle field (6:15), worships an ephod (8:27), prostitutes itself with Baal Berith (8:33–34) and the gods of the nations (10:6; compare 10:10, 15), institutes a new festival for Jephthah's sacrificed daughter (11:31–40), offers family sacrifices (13:19), and prays during a Philistine festival (16:28–29). False worship, idols, greedy individualism, and disloyal priests mark the cultic activities of Judg 17–21.

Thus cult sites and cultic activity give no unity to the book of Judges. Rather, they show a nation in cultic disarray, not knowing where to worship, whom to worship, or how to worship. Israel's religion gradually disintegrates from lamentation over broken covenant to robbery, murder, tribal intrigue, false gods and images, and stolen priesthood. The religion of Israel in the book of Judges mirrors the literary form of the book—chaos.

The tour de force that marks the literary unity so strongly argued by Webb (1987) and Gooding (*ErIsr* 16 [1982] 70–79) lies in the masterfully ironic use of language and contrasting use of themes that will appear repeatedly throughout the commentary. The lack of structural and thematic controls is a macro sign of the irony that appears in all levels of structure and theme in the book. This deep level of irony is seen in the two features that hold the book of Judges together, namely description of failure and lack of leadership. The description of failure begins in Judg 1 as the tribes other than Judah and Joseph fail to control their land. Chap. 2 gives the overarching theme: covenant is broken, so God must punish. Even then covenant fades from the picture, appearing only in the name of enemy gods (8:33; 9:4, 46) and in a brief mention of the ark of the covenant (20:27). The cultic cries of the people avail nothing. So Israel must face punishment (2:3; compare Josh 23:13). For Judges, even Joshua failed, because he did not institute a successful training program, making God an alien among his people (2:10). Israel fails God by worshiping the Baals, bringing divine anger (2:12) that leads God to hand them over to plunderers (2:14). The threats of Deut 28 and Josh 23 become reality. Still, God has a solution, deliverers he will send, but people fail to listen to deliverers (2:17). The only hope is divine pity, but this leads only to further corruption. Even divine pity cannot make them abandon their corrupt practices. So when the people Israel return to their stubborn ways, God declares the covenant to be broken and refuses to continue driving out the people Joshua left (2:21). Chap. 3 then sets up the problem in terms of the commandments of Moses, so central to the book of Joshua (1:8; compare Judg 2:17). Judges then ironically ignores this term for the remainder of the book. The theological introduction having outlined Israel's points of failure, each of the individual narratives then describes failure in its own way (see table I.4 in the appendix).

The irony of Judges is that God's people lose their religion, their moral ideals, their political unity, and their political power. Progressively, Israel fails until no tribes are acting together except to annihilate another tribe, worship is directed to the gods of all Israel's enemies, Israel's armies comprise only worthless fellows, vows to God become insignificant and violent, personal lifestyle bears no resemblance to divine commands, and one tribe of Israel virtually vanishes from sight. Only Othniel and Ehud stand above the rest without personal fault. Failure grows until the leaderless anarchy of Judg 17–21 emerges. As Joshua was a story of progressive victory and obedience of a covenant people, so Judges is an ironic story of progressive decadence and destruction.

The second uniting theme of the book is lack of leadership. This appears immediately in Judg 1:1, where the leaderless people have to ask God for strategy. The tribes then go individually to battle, no leader being able to unite them. Such failure in leadership is uncannily traced back to Joshua, the inerrant leader of Israel in the book of Joshua, who suddenly is blamed for what he did not do. It seems that Joshua's failure to train future leaders has led to Israel not knowing

Yahweh, not obeying Yahweh, and thus not driving out the people who remain. In Judges, this portrayal of Joshua's leadership sets the pattern for leadership. No judge trains someone to follow. The death of a judge immediately thrusts Israel into spiritual chaos. No judge teaches the traditions and laws of Israel, so they do not follow Yahweh beyond the judge's life. Sadder still, several of the judges create false worship.

The failure of leadership appears in the ironic structure of the book. The story moves from (1) complete victory over an enemy with Othniel, Ehud, and Shamgar to (2) complete victory for some of the tribes under the feminine leadership of Deborah and Jael made necessary by Barak's fear to (3) the timid leadership of Gideon leading to victory over an an enemy but also to dispute among tribes and spiritual harlotry to (4) the presumptuous reign of Abimelech, instigating civil war and bringing down God's punishment. This is followed by (5) minor judges who gradually assume a royal lifestyle without leaving behind narrative exploits to show any accomplishments, leading to divine refusal to act except out of pity; (6) a judge—Jephthah—of illegitimate birth who assumes royal roles, displays sound theology based solely on historical memory, has piety without reason, and is willing to fight and destroy part of Israel rather than mediate and unite the people; and (7) a judge—Ibzan—who builds a royal lifestyle by outside relationships and leading other judges to adopt the same lifestyle. Finally, (8) the Philistines rule Israel while the designated leader—Samson—seeks to do what is right in his eyes until his own foolish self-confidence leads to his calling on the Lord to let him avenge himself against his enemies in an act of violence and suicide.

Judges thus poses the question, what kind of leadership can Israel establish that will lead to orderly succession and consistent religious and moral obedience? The answer is kingship. But even this answer is ironic, for Yahweh is Israel's king (8:23); yet, the very judge who utters such clearly correct theology is the one whose son is named Abimelech (my father is king) and whose lifestyle is evidently bordering on the royal.

The body of the narrative of Judges thus builds up the narrative tension by developing a growing mood of failure on the human side despite the repeated faithful intervention from the divine side. The people of Israel lose control of the land while they grow morally corrupt, spiritually naïve, religiously pagan, and nationally separated and decimated. Without the servant leadership of Joshua, the Israelite tribes and individuals seek personal prosperity no matter what the cost to others. At the end of the story Israel has Gideon's pagan shrine, Jephthah's pagan festival, and Philistine rulers.

How can these massive problems be resolved? Judges has no narrative resolution. It represents tragedy, not comedy. Its irony leads to dark humor, not vaudeville laughter. Judges explains only how the Israelites hit bottom, not how they rose again to the top. The resolution waits for David's story. The only answer found in the book of Judges appears to be in the person of a king, but Judges never shows how a king could actually help. Indeed, Judges has shown how aspiring kings destroyed Israel's religion, Israel's unity, Israel's cult center, and Israel's tribes. The structure of Judges is thus consistent. In describing its solution for Israel's problems, Judges paints only the dark side. No rays of hope for kingship shine through, even for kingship under the Spirit of Yahweh. Such kingship can bring tribal decimation, false religion, and the horrors of anarchy. Thus just as Judges consciously began the story in midstream with the death of Joshua, so it ends the story unfinished, pointing forward to a type of king it knows not. In so doing, it has disassembled the structure of Joshua, destroyed the unity Joshua created, ransacked the cultic loyalty Joshua renewed, and ignored the Mosaic law Joshua so carefully followed and taught. Everything Joshua created politically, literarily, theologically, religiously, and geographically, Judges has done away with. Samuel must start over from scratch. As he does, he faces a choice. Will he lift his eyes to the opening of the book of Joshua and meditate on the law of Moses? Or will he turn back to the end of the book of Judges and continue to lift his eyes only to selfish desires? The choice will determine Israel's future. But then that's for another commentary.

Introduction to the Historical Context: The Setting and Nature of the Judges Narratives

INTRODUCTION TO THE CHRONOLOGY OF JUDGES

Select Bibliography

Galil, G. "The Chronological Framework of the Deuteronomistic History." *Bib* 85 (2004) 413–21. **Guillaume, P.** *Waiting for Josiah.* 159–62. **Hayes, J. H.,** and **J. M. Miller,** eds. *Israelite and Judean History.* OTL. London: SCM Press, 1977. **Howard, D. M., Jr.** *An Introduction to the Old Testament Historical Books.* Chicago: Moody Press, 1993. **Kaiser, W. C., Jr.** *A History of Israel.* Nashville: Broadman & Holman, 1998. **Leuchter, M.** "'Now There Was a [Certain] Man': Compositional Chronology in Judges–1 Samuel." *CBQ* 69 (2007) 429–39. **Merrill, E.** "Paul's Use of 'about 450 Years' in Acts 13:20." *BSac* 138 (1981) 246–57. **Nöldeke, T.** "Die Chronologie der Richterzeit." In *Untersuchungen zur Kritik des Alten Testaments.* Hildesheim, 1869. 173–98. **Noth, M.** *Überlieferungsgeschichtliche Studien: Die sammelnden und bearbeiten Geschichtswerke im Alten Testament.* 2nd ed. Tübingen: Niemeyer, 1957. **Peet, J. H.** "The Chronology of the Judges—Some Thoughts." *Journal of Christian Reconstruction* 9 (1982–1983) 161–81. **Provan, I., V. P. Long,** and **T. Longman.** *Biblical History of Israel.* **Ray, P. J., Jr.** "Another Look at the Period of the Judges." In *Beyond the Jordan.* Ed. G. A. Carnagey, Sr. Eugene, OR: Wipf & Stock, 2005. 93–104. **Sauer, G.** "Die chronologischen Angaben in den Büchern Deuteronomium bis 2. Könige." *TZ* 24 (1968) 1–14. **Steinman, A. E.** "The Mysterious Numbers of the Book of Judges." *JETS* 48 (2005) 491–500. **Vaux, R. de.** *The Early History of Israel.* 2 vols. Trans. D. Smith. London: Darton, Longman & Todd, 1978. Originally published as *Histoire ancienne d'Israel* (Paris: Gabalda & Cie, 1971). **Vollborn, W.** "Die chronologie des Richterbuches." In *Festschrift F. Baumgärtel.* Ed. J. Hermann and L. Rost. Erlanger Forschungen A10. Erlangen: Universitätsbund, 1959. 192–96. **Warner, S. M.** "The Dating of the Period of the Judges." *VT* 28 (1978) 455–63. **Washburn, D. L.** "The Chronology of Judges: Another Look." *BibSac* 147 (1990) 414–24. **Wellhausen, J.** *Prolegomena zur Geschichte Israels.* 229–47.

The historical problems that confront a commentator on the book of Judges form a long list of complex, interlaced issues. Chronology constitutes the most obvious problem. Wellhausen *(Prolegomena zur Geschichte Israels)* summarized the critical solution more than a century ago: the 480 years of 1 Kgs 6:1, reaching from the exodus to the building of the temple in Solomon's fourth year, is simply a mathematical formulation multiplying the ideal twelve generations by 40 years for each generation, similar to the twelve high priests in 1 Chr 5:29–34. It is not simple, however, to reconcile this number with the number of years cited elsewhere in Scripture, including in Judges. The years from the exodus through Solomon's reign are enumerated in table I.5 in the appendix.

Historians and commentators take many paths to solve this chronological riddle. They generally use one or more basic assumptions to attack the problem—rounded numbers based on a multiple-of-twenty system, symbolic numbers like twelve for the tribes of Israel, counting a generation as forty years, overlapping of periods within the list, limited areas of authority for some rulers, literary additions, and lack of intention by the biblical writer to actually describe chronological continuity. See table I.6 in the appendix for a small sampling of the use of these assumptions.

Each author included in the survey in table I.6 points to Old Testament introductions and other materials that could expand the chart almost endlessly. To illustrate the problem, I will examine one of the standard critical assessments, that of Richter, and then the latest and most precise system, that of Steinmann. Such precision is possible only with the assumption of an early exodus. A thirteenth- or twelfth-century exodus leaves no room for all the succeeding numbers.

Richter's calculations, shown in table I.7 in the appendix, do not include Abimelech, Shamgar, Judg 10:8; 13:1, and 1 Sam 7:2. Aware of its weaknesses, both Boling and Soggin tentatively adopt it. Galil on the other hand decides:

> In my opinion, the notices of the minor judges were not included in the deuteronomistic edition of the Book of Judges, and therefore cannot form part of the Dtr's chronology or of the schematic framework spanning 480 years from the Exodus to the fourth year of Solomon. The notices of the minor judges are clearly secondary in the Book of Judges. They are devoid of any theological aspect: in these passages we find no sin, no repentance, and no forgiveness. Salvation is mentioned, but no salvation stories are related, and even the typical round figures are not mentioned. Moreover, the interpolation of these passages in chapters 10 and 12 evidently contradicts the Dtr's attitude towards the period of the judges, since, in his opinion, the Israelites were on a road downward. (*Bib* 85 [2004] 416)

Galil seeks then to use Deuteronomy through Samuel without the minor judges to show how the Deuteronomist created a chronological framework reaching 480 years from the exodus to the opening of the temple (1 Kgs 6:1).

Steinmann has created an interpretation of the numbers that allows him to conclude, "A careful examination of the book and its structure and a knowledge of ancient Judean practices regarding the recording of chronological data make it possible to construct a chronology of this period of Israel's history that is consonant with the rest of the Old Testament" (*JETS* 48 [2005] 500). He begins by seeing that reports on reigns of Judah's kings include the final year of a king's reign both in the passing king's total and in that of the new king, so one year is counted twice. He allows ten to twenty years for Joshua and the elders who succeeded him. Othniel's cycle requires forty-eight years. Shamgar was active during the eighty years of Ehud's peace, since Ehud's death is recorded after mention of Shamgar. Ehud thus requires ninety-eight years; Deborah, sixty; Gideon, forty-seven; Abimelech, three; Tola, twenty-three; and Jair, twenty-two. "That year" of Judg 10:7 looks back to 10:5 and indicates that the Ammonite and Philistine oppressions were simultaneous, the eighteen-year Ammonite story east of Jordan preceding the forty-year Philistine narrative west of Jordan. This included, then, the time of Jephthah, Ibzan, Elon, Abdon, and Samson, the last three, at least, overlapping.

Steinmann sees the beginning of Saul's reign as the end of Philistine oppression and uses Josephus to credit Saul with eighteen years before and twenty-two years after Samuel's death. He thus creates a dated chronology for the entire period, shown in table I.8 in the appendix.

Steinmann's system leaves several questions. For instance, can one accept ending the Philistine oppression with the beginning of Saul's reign, when Saul and David appear to be the people most involved in combating the Philistines? This also places Eli in the middle of the minor judges and prior to Samson. Steinmann's carefully worked out system may demonstrate the impossibility of combining three basic assumptions about Judges. First, the literary pattern of Judges combines a south to north orientation with a linear chronological system. Second, the judges appear to be local military (and judicial?) leaders who represent all Israel at a time when the tribes actually showed little consciousness of the larger body. The third major assumption comes from 1 Kgs 6:1. The entire effort to make such a precise chronology rests on the total provided here and the assumption that the writer of 1 Kgs 6:1 had all the numbers and information now present in the books preceding 1 Kings in our Bibles and thus had some such theory as the ones scholars now create to arrive at his total. That this can be proved is far from obvious. Thus Younger is most likely correct in his assessment that "the amount or degree of overlap is difficult to discern, and so the precise chronology of the period of the judges is unknown" (25).

Still, a thought continues to bounce through my head and demand to be put on paper. The appearance of Phinehas the priest (20:28) and of Jonathan, the immediate descendant of Moses (18:30), in the later chapters of Judges shows that chaps. 17–21, when not excised as later insertions outside the chronological scheme, are far out of chronological order. Throughout the commentary, I will identify other evidence that Judges does not intend to present a straight chronological story. Rather, Judges presents a theological history with a geographic and moral framework rather than a strict chronological framework. Can it be that Judges gives the raw data for a relative chronology rather than for an absolute one? Such a relative chronology might look something like that illustrated in table I.9 in the appendix. Obviously, the relative placement shown in table I.9 is quite tentative. It represents one starting point for creating a relative chronology among events when an absolute chronology seems impossible to create.

INTRODUCTION TO THE HISTORY BEHIND JUDGES

Bibliography

Ahlström, G. W. *History of Ancient Palestine.* **Assis, E.** *Self-Interest or Communal Interest.* **Barr, J.** *History and Ideology in the Old Testament.* Oxford: Oxford UP, 2000. **Coote, R. B.,** and **K. W. Whitelam.** *Emergence of Early Israel.* **Davies, P. R.** *In Search of 'Ancient Israel.'* **Dever, W. G.** *Who Were the Early Israelites and Where Did They Come From?* Grand Rapids: Eerdmans, 2003. **Faust, A.** "Abandonment, Urbanization, Resettlement and the Formation of the Israelite State." *Near Eastern Archaeology* 66 (2003) 147–61. ———. *Israel's Ethnogenesis: Settlement, Interaction, Expansion and Resistance.* London: Equinox, 2007. **Finkelstein, I.,** and **A. Mazar.** *The Quest for the Historical Israel: Debating Archaeology and the History of Early Israel.* Ed. B. B. Schmidt. SBLABS 17. Atlanta: Society of Biblical Literature, 2007. **Frendo, A. J.** "Back to Basics: A Holistic Approach to the Problem of the Emergence of Ancient Israel." In *In Search of Pre-exilic Israel.* Ed. J. Day. JSOTSup 406. New York: T&T Clark, 2004. 41–64. **Gottwald, N. K.** *Tribes of Yahweh.* **Grabbe, L. L.** *Ancient Israel: What Do We Know and How Do We Know It?* New York: T&T Clark, 2007. **Halpern, B.** *First Historians.* **Hawkins, R. K.** "The Date of the Exodus-Conquest Is Still an Open Question: A Response to Rodger Young and Bryant Wood." *JETS* 51 (2008) 245–66. ———. "Propositions for Evangelical Acceptance of a Late-Date Exodus-Conquest: Biblical Data and the Royal Scarabs from Mt. Ebal." *JETS* 50 (2007) 31–46. **Hermann, S.** *Geschichte Israels.* Munich: Kaiser, 1973. **Hess, R. S.** *Israelite Religions: An Archaeological and Biblical Survey.* Grand Rapids: Baker Academic, 2007. **Kamlah, J.** "Das Ostjordanland im Zeitalter der Entstehung Israels." *TQ* 186 (2006) 118–33. **Kitchen, K. A.** *The Reliability of the Old Testament.* Grand Rapids: Eerdmans, 2004. **Kofoeda, J. B.** *Text & History: Historiography and the Study of the Biblical Text.* Winona Lake, IN: Eisenbrauns, 2005. **Lemche, N. P.** *Israelites in History.* **Liverani, M.** *Israel's History and the History of Israel.* London: Equinox, 2005. **Machinist, P.** "Outsiders or Insiders." 35–60. **Miller, J. M.,** and **J. H. Hayes.** *A History of Ancient Israel and Judah.* 2nd ed. Louisville: Westminster John Knox, 2006. **Noth, M.** *The History of Israel.* Trans. P. R. Ackroyd. New York: Harper & Row, 1960. **Provan, I., V. P. Long,** and **T. Longman.** *Biblical History of Israel.* **Römer, T. C.** *Future of the Deuteronomistic History.* **Sasson, J. M.** "On Choosing Models for Recreating Israelite Pre-Monarchical History." *JSOT* 21 (1981) 3–24. **Soggin, J. A.** *A History of Ancient Israel.* Trans. J. Bowden. Philadelphia: Westminster, 1984. **Stager, L. E.** "Forging an Identity: The Emergence of Ancient Israel." In *The Oxford History of the Biblical World.* Ed. M. D. Coogan. New York: Oxford UP, 1998. 123–75. **Van Seters, J.** *In Search of History.* **Vaux, R. de.** *The Early History of Israel.* 2 vols. Trans. D. Smith. London: Darton, Longman & Todd, 1978. Originally published as *Histoire ancienne d'Israel* (Paris: Gabalda & Cie, 1971). **Whitelam, K.** "The Death of Biblical History." In *In Search of Philip R. Davies: Whose Festschrift Is It Anyway?* Ed. D. Burns and J. W. Rogerson. LHBOTS. London: Continuum, 2008. See <http://tandtclark.typepad.com/Davies_FS_Files/Davies_FS_Whitelam.pdf>. ———. "The Identity of Early Israel: The Realignment and Transformation of Late Bronze-Iron Age Palestine." In *The Historical Books.* Ed. J. C. Exum. Sheffield: Sheffield Academic, 1997. 14–45. **Winther-Nielsen, N.** "Fact, Fiction, and Language Use." 44–81. **Young, R. C.,** and **B. G. Wood.** "A Critical Analysis of the Evidence from Ralph Hawkins for a Late-Date Exodus-Conquest." *JETS* 51 (2008) 225–43.

Another part of the riddle one faces in studying Judges involves the value the book has as a historical source. Again, historians and commentators provide a wide variety of answers. Historical decisions are most often based on one or more of the following thirteen pieces of evidence:

1. The contrast between the information in Judg 1 and the conquest stories of Josh 1–12
2. The obvious theological ideology that guides the book and is sharply stated in chap. 2
3. The chronological problems sketched above
4. The appearance that geography takes precedence over chronology in the original arrangement of the narratives
5. The sense that materials in chaps. 17–21 represent historical events much earlier than those of the Samson stories and other materials preceding them in the present order of the book of Judges
6. The division of the book into sources, leading to the understanding that a late preexilic or exilic editor compiled the present book

7. The compressing of the narratives of the minor judges into one section in which they follow one another rather than being interspersed among the major judges
8. The all-Israel framework of the narratives contrasted to the narratives themselves, which appear to represent only local or, at most, regional skirmishes
9. The happenstance that exactly twelve judges appear in the narratives, each apparently intended in one way or another to represent a different tribe
10. The relationship of narratives that appear to parallel similar narratives in Joshua and Judges, such as the battle with Jabin in Josh 11 and in Judg 4 or the different tribes fighting for Jerusalem (Josh 10:1–27; 15:8, 63; 18:16, 28; Judg 1:8, 21; 19:10–11; 2 Sam 5:5–10; 1 Kgs 2:11)
11. The use of Shamgar without any story information and of Othniel among the Judges as a perfect type figure
12. The literary skill of the narratives and the apparent dependence on oral tradition
13. The relationship between archaeological remains and biblical narrative as the major sources for historical research

These and other issues have brought forth strongly conflicting opinions based on strongly differing assumptions about how to interpret the evidence.

Keil represents the traditional view that this was written in the time of Samuel based on oral and written records. He argues, "The historical fidelity, exactness, and vividness of description apparent in every part of the book are only to be explained in a work which embraces a period of 350 years, on the supposition that the author made use of trustworthy records, or the testimony of persons who were living when the events occurred" (248).

At the turn of the twentieth century Moore argued that the earliest collection of stories dated to the first half of the ninth century and that the stories "reproduce the state of society and religion in the early days of the settlement in Palestine with a convincing reality which is of nature, not of art, and exhibit a knowledge of the conditions of the time which can hardly have been possessed by an author of the 8th century, after the changes which two centuries of the kingdom and of rapidly advancing civilization had wrought" (xxvii).

Allowing for an original limitation of geographical area and tribal participation, de Vaux can still claim that Judges "preserved genuine traditions concerning this period during which the people of Israel was formed" (*Early History of Israel*, 693). In his sociological presentation Gottwald could still say the narratives "vividly presented the bald, unvarnished weaknesses, divisions, and apostasies of the time. The stories buttressed in detail D's conviction that Israel backslid after the death of Joshua" (*Tribes of Yahweh*, 149). For him Judges represents "refracted history—indeed, a collage of many histories" (187).

Coming from different presuppositions, Ahlström represents the postmodern Scandanavian approach as he decides that the theological introduction is a sign that the description of actual events was not the author's primary purpose since such a literary pattern cannot be used for writing history and is part of the Near Eastern tradition of describing the past in terms of chaos and order (*History of Ancient Palestine*, 375). Judges presents, then, an ideological reconstruction advocating a religious ideal, not history (376). Whitelam continued this approach emphasizing sociology and archaeology, an approach that seeks to do Palestinian history without reference to biblical narrative or to ethnic Israelites. He writes, "It is no longer possible to distinguish an 'Israelite' material culture from an indigenous material culture in terms of the archaeological data. The implication of this is that the term 'Israelite' becomes unusable in the context of the discussion once it is accepted that the biblical traditions do not bear upon the problem" ("Identity of Early Israel," 24). Economic disruption is the major explanatory tool for describing Late Bronze Age Palestine so that the historian need make no recourse to class struggle or external invasion or infiltration ("Identity of Early Israel," 39–40).

Lemche carries Whitelam's sociological approach further, concluding that ancient Israel "is an artificial creation of the scholarly world of the modern age. . . . It simply developed out of the usual bad habit of paraphrasing the biblical text" (*Israelites in History*, 163). So he finds, "At the end we have a situation where Israel is not Israel, Jerusalem is not Jerusalem, and David not David. No matter how we twist the factual remains from ancient Palestine, we cannot have a biblical Israel that is at the same time the Israel of the Iron Age" (166). Winther-Nielsen builds on the work of Halpern and argues against Lemche that his argument "rests on the curious notion that unless proved to be true by sources from the ancient Near East the data in the Hebrew Bible are false" ("Fact, Fiction, and Language Use," 50). Winther-Nielsen looks at the role of the reader in Judges, noting that the reader must decide "whether or not he believes that the biblical narrative is a true and accurate description of events with a valuable message for the present" (66). For him, Judges represents "recorded oral tales," and research shows that in the Middle East such tales are told in memorized form checked by "village memory." The language of Judges resembles everyday conversation without the "prototypical form of fiction" (75–76). He concludes:

> The only positive line of evidence may then turn out to be that Hebrew narrative reports on a great number of very different historical contexts from everyday life and not just some narrow poetic world. This is no final, absolute proof of the author's historical intentions, but it does provide some actual evidence of what he accomplished: portraying significant aspects of an intellectual-religious past along with a strong persuasive address to future generations. . . . In the final analysis, however, all current and past history writing will call on our hermeneutical trust, and the days of confessionalist, positivist, or minimalist absolute "proof" are gone forever. ("Fact, Fiction, and Language Use," 76)

Working from a more literary viewpoint, Brettler concedes the historical search in Judges, seeing that "Judges should not be studied to reconstruct ancient Israelite history of the pre-monarchic period. Nor should we examine it as a historical work by asking how it recreates the past that it is purporting to narrate, since (1) we have no independent method to create that past; and more significantly, (2) its main objective was not recreating the past" (8). In a slightly less critical vein, McCann sees stories of heroes whose exploits were remembered, embellished, and passed on through oral sources and credits a ring of historical authenticity to the minor judges. The Song of Deborah and some of the stories even go back to premonarchical Israel. Still, in the final analysis for McCann, Judges does not present "even a roughly chronological account of actual events, and so it is highly misleading to speak of 'the period of the judges.'" This period was created hundreds of years later by the Deuteronomistic Historian (6).

Sketching the development of the Deuteronomistic History, Römer speaks of the invention of the period of the judges, saying "this period is nothing other than a literary invention of the Deuteronomistic school" from a book of saviors preserved in the north (*So-called Deuteronomistic History*, 136).

Block emphasizes the prophetic and inspired side of the literature, admires the rhetorical unity of Judges, admits its homiletical agenda, and sets it out as an extended sermon or series of sermons based on the "real historical experiences of the Israelites in the premonarchic period" (52). Still, Block insists such categorization and description do not remove Judges from the "category of authentic historiography" (53). Niditch, on the other hand, concludes, "matching biblical events in the Hebrew Bible with Israelite history is always an uncertain task" (35). Still, she "takes seriously the idea that Judges includes material that would have been meaningful in some form to Israelite audiences before there were kings in Israel (pre-tenth century B.C.E.), during the northern and southern monarchies (tenth-sixth centuries B.C.E.), after the collapse of the southern kingdom (586 B.C.E.). Judges is multilayered" (8).

Richard Hess stops in his study of *Israelite Religions* (210–25) to trace at least five theories of the conquest and settlement of Israel, finally settling for a complex judgment in which all theories have some validity. He does seem to think that the major Israelite sanctuary shifted in order from Ebal to Shiloh to Bethel to Gilgal (at Khirbet ed-Dawwara and separate from the Gilgal of the early chapters of Joshua). For Hess, the divinely appointed judge is unique to Israel. But Israel's seemingly ideal system does not work because "Judges exhibits a pattern of appointments to this office that become increasingly deviant from the divine will and gradually spirals out of control in terms of their own lives and effectiveness" (226).

Provan, Long, and Longman give a different perspective to reading historical narratives. They see all history as interpretive testimony, defining knowledge of the past as faith in the testimony to the past (*Biblical History of Israel*, 37). They define historical knowledge as a choice of belief: "We 'know' what we claim to know about the history of Israel . . . by listening to testimony, to interpretation, and by making choices about whom to believe" (53). They prefer to give biblical texts the benefit of the doubt and use a falsification principle rather than a verification principle (55). They argue that "there is no reason to think, then, that biblical historians of the monarchic period could not have had access to written as well as oral sources of information about that period as well as the earlier period" (59). Seeing all Near Eastern accounts as ideological, they find that the biblical texts do not appear to reflect the "vivid imaginations of late postexilic authors" (60). It comes down to the awareness that "history is the telling and retelling of unverifiable stories. . . . Knowing any history aside from the history in which we are personally involved requires trust in unverified and unverifiable testimony" (74). "*Testimony* about the past can comfortably combine compositional technique, didactic intent, *and* historical information" (161, emphasis original). This does not mean that Judges is told in strict chronological sequence. Still, after judging all the biblical, archaeological, and extrabiblical texts, they conclude: "We see little reason that an attempt to write a history of Israel's emergence in Canaan should take a path radically different from the one that the biblical texts already suggest. . . . We have found nothing in the evidence considered that would invalidate the basic biblical contours" (192).

In somewhat the same vein Matthews asserts that Judges is "supposed to be rough, uncouth, and in places very exciting and comical." Still he says "the episodes in Judges provide a somewhat more realistic (than Joshua) portrayal of life in the Central Hill Country and in the Transjordanian area of Gilead before the monarchy" (4).

The last two mentioned positions form the basis for the present commentary. The thirteen issues dealt with above will be addressed piecemeal as they arise in the commentary itself. Here a basic position can be set out. The book of Judges is a literary masterpiece that is intentionally written against the grain—with violence, irony, uncouth acts, and comic relief. Its structure is geographical, literary, and theological rather than primarily historical or chronological. The framework gives an interpretation to the stories that helps explain the entire history of Israel and that sets it in polar opposition to the framework and structure of Joshua. The stories themselves make known the reality of life before David. They contain elements that make heroes of the leading figures rather than making them ironic causes of Israel's decline as the final collection does. These heroic elements lead to the inclusion of these figures in the roll call of faith in the Letter to the Hebrews (Heb 11). Combined, the framework collection and the original oral hero stories set up a tension for the historian who follows Provan, Long, and Longman and chooses to believe "the basic biblical contours."

The period of the judges is a historical construct by the editor who collected and combined the hero stories, but it is at the same time a necessary construct. Both Israel's cultic worship and its annalistic tradition set up Israel as a landless people from outside Palestine, a people with patriarchal roots and Egyptian slave experience. These same traditions celebrate Israel as the people of David and Solomon in Jerusalem. One can argue the historical details of who and how many were in Egypt; and where Yahwistic worship originated; and how non-Israelites like Rahab, the Gibeonites, the people renewing the covenant at Shechem, and the Kenizzite Caleb (Josh 14:6) came to be included among the Israelites.

Many historical issues lie open. Indeed, if one follows the minimalist approach of the Scandinavian school and others, the basic history of Palestine from Amarna to Omri lies open waiting for verifiable evidence outside the biblical text. Surely common sense dictates that neither Merneptah nor Omri—nor the Deuteronomist—invented the people Israel. Still, the biblical narrative, buttressed by materials like the Amarna letters, indicates a time when Israel did not live in or control Palestine followed by a time when Israel began to show strength and control large portions of the country.

The concept of outsiders coming in and David ruling from Jerusalem requires some type of interim period. Why not accept the biblical contours of this interim period as that of local heroes performing in ironic ways to become both revered in tribal memory and pictured as the ultimate cause of Israel's moral and political downfall? Does not the very human picture of the heroes provide some degree of authentication? Mythic, fictional pictures would idealize the founding fathers much more than did Israel. Thus, the Judges narratives may not provide the chronology or clues to political organization that a historian would like to have, but they do show the nature of life and the lack of organization experienced by a people whose descendants became Israel, sons of David, and sons of Omri. They show how an Israel without a Moses or Joshua managed to maintain a toehold on various tribal possessions despite strong outside opposition. They remember very human, even violent and immoral, sides of their characters. In so doing they testify to an Israel unlike Israel in any other period of history.

INTRODUCTION TO DATING THE BOOK OF JUDGES

Select Bibliography

O'Connell, R. H. *Rhetoric of the Book of Judges.* **Provan, I., V. P. Long,** and **T. Longman.** *Biblical History of Israel.*

Obviously, the author of Judges remains unknown despite clever guesses past and present. Without knowing the author, a commentator must search in the text for clues that point to a range of dates within which the text may have been created. Writing within a history of scholarship that has repeatedly pointed to a series of authors and editors for the text makes the task of assigning a date to that text even more complex. Table I.10 in the appendix demonstrates the wide range of available options.

Dating issues are almost too numerous to list. They include:

1. Unity of the book as creation of one author or of several editors
2. Nature of original materials as ancient traditions/collections of traditions or as fiction created by much later "historians"
3. Evidence of Deuteronomic and/or Priestly language and themes
4. Interpretation of "until this day" passages (Judg 1:21, 26; 6:24; 10:4; 15:19; 18:12; 19:30)
5. Correlating theological/historical themes with historical events
6. Relationship of Judges with preceding and succeeding books in the canon
7. Date of latest literary activity in canonical books
8. Validity and extent of Pentateuchal "sources"
9. Nature of preservation and passing on of oral and written traditions

Each of these issues would require a monograph to discuss, and then a large percentage of the conclusions would result as much from assumptions as from evidence. At various times I have represented differing positions on this issue of sources and dating. As seen in the above discussions of the structure and of the Deuteronomistic History, the evidence now points to a unified structure and purpose for the entire book with few if any Deuteronomistic touches. As will be seen below in the discussion of theological themes, leadership—in particular, kingship—has to be regarded as a major reason for collecting these materials into the present format. The Philistines have to be seen as the ongoing oppressor. Ephraim and Benjamin are the trouble-making tribes. And Judah bears the responsibility for leadership.

The interesting feature in the narratives is the place of the northern sanctuary Bethel. God is with the Joseph tribes as they take Bethel (Judg 1:22). Deborah judges Israel in the proximity of Bethel (4:5). Bethel is the home of the ark of the covenant and is served by Aaron's grandson as priest (20:27–28). Yet Bethel is the place where Israel makes the decisions that cost thousands of their own soldiers and that lead to the decimation of the tribe of Benjamin. Israel itself cannot understand this "decision of God" (21:3). Does the narrative support Bethel as a legitimate center of Israelite worship? Or does the text parody Bethel as an illegitimate center where divine decisions prove to be deadly? Or is Bethel simply part of the tradition on which the final collector of traditions and author of Judges makes no judgment?

The answer to the Bethel issue is crucial for dating Judges. If Bethel is a central concern of the author, several options arise:

1. A very early author supports Bethel as the central sanctuary prior to the emergence of Jerusalem.
2. An early author parodies Bethel in support of a southern alternative but without mentioning the alternative.
3. An author living during the early part of the divided monarchy supports the validity of Bethel over against the claims of Jerusalem.
4. An author living during the early part of the divided monarchy parodies Bethel in support of Jerusalem.
5. An author shortly after 722 B.C.E. and the fall of the northern kingdom explains the fall as an internal affair of a false worship center and civil war.
6. An author supports either Hezekiah's or Josiah's attempt to reclaim a defeated Bethel for an expanding southern kingdom.
7. A southern author under Manasseh draws on a northern collection from Bethel and creates a book supporting Assyrian appeasement.
8. An exilic or postexilic author draws on a northern collection from Bethel and creates a book explaining the destruction of the south as rooted in a tradition of evil leadership reaching back to the northern tribes.
9. An exilic or postexilic author draws on a northern collection from Bethel and creates a book supporting Bethel as a center for exilic/postexilic Israel.

This does not limit the possible theories based on seeing Bethel as a central concern of the author. It does show that the Bethel evidence can be read from many perspectives and can lead to a wide variety of conclusions. Below, I will argue that the Bethel materials must be combined with those of Benjamin, Ephraim, and Dan to show the author's judgment on these four entities. If one eliminates the Deuteronomistic History hypothesis as a dating clue, then one faces the question of where and when treatment of kingship theology and allegiance to one God became a major issue for the people of Yahweh. At the same time, one must solve the problem of why Benjamin, Ephraim, and Dan receive such bad press in Judges. Here one must acknowledge that after the kingdom divided, kingship was not the problem. The type of kingship was a problem, but not kingship itself. The closest Israel came to questioning kingship occurred at the time of the division of the monarchy or in the time of Manasseh, when the king apparently became a puppet of the Assyrian empire rather than an independent ruler of the nation Israel. At the same time, allegiance to Assyrian gods competed with, if it did not replace, worship of Yahweh.

This apparently leaves four moments in Israel's history as viable candidates for the time of composition of the unified structure we call the book of Judges. This could be an exilic/postexilic document looking to a new brand of kingship in the future. It could be a book opposing the non-Israelite kingship of Manasseh. It could be a book involved in the dispute between Rehoboam and Jeroboam as the kingdom split. Or it could be a book looking forward to kingship for the first time in Israel and involved in the Saul/Ishbosheth rivalry with David. The present commentary sees the last of these as a strong possibility, knowing that this goes against the grain of most modern scholarship (but see Dorsey; O'Connell, *Rhetoric of the Book of Judges;* and implications that can be drawn from Brettler and Sweeney) and that it implies an acceptance of the basic historical contents of Judges and Samuel at a time when much scholarship sees the beginning of Israel under Omri.

I prefer to follow the approach of Provan, Long, and Longman in acknowledging the chronological problems of the book, accepting that the structure is not a chronological one, and still concluding that Joshua and Judges "seem quite complementary and, broadly speaking, sequential" (*Biblical History of Israel,* 167). Block is correct in saying, "The exilic and/or postexilic contexts are unlikely candidates. Not only had the consequences of persistent apostasy fallen upon Israel/Judah by then; the nation was already being weaned from its pagan past" (66). Block thus opts for a date in the realm of Manasseh (see Guillaume, *Waiting for Josiah*), but this does not account clearly for what Block refers to as the "pronounced anti-Ephraimite stance evident throughout the book." Rather, the strong stand against Ephraim must come at a decisive moment in Israel's history when Israel had to decide between Judah leading first or an Ephraimite following the path of Joshua and leading Israel. Such a time came under Rehoboam, when the kingdom split and Jeroboam the Ephraimite (1 Kgs 11:26) led the northern tribes away from the south. At that time the judgment on Bethel and Dan becomes clearest, and at that time, the third player in the background would be Benjamin, a swing tribe between south and north and the carrier of the Saul tradition of kingship. The fate of Jabesh-gilead in Judg 21 would also hint at disgust with that city because it buried Saul (2 Sam 2:4). Benjaminites and Saul's followers both remained identified as suspicious under David's rule (2 Sam 19:16–30, 41–43; 20:1–22; 21:1–14). Thus, the working hypothesis of this commentary is that Judges represents an artful narration of the period of the Judges for an audience experiencing the opening years of the divided monarchy and having to decide which king to follow and which sanctuary to recognize as the true center of worship. The writer of Judges obviously places Judah first and condemns Bethel and Dan—and the entire northern kingdom with them—because of their idolatrous worship.

Introduction to the Purpose of Judges

Bibliography

Brettler, M. "The Book of Judges: Literature as Politics." *JBL* 108 (1989) 395–418. **Cundall, A. E.** "Judges—An Apology for the Monarchy." *ExpTim* 81 (1970) 178–81. **Dumbrell, W. J.** "'In those days there was no king in Israel; every man did that which was right in his own eyes': The Purpose of the Book of Judges Reconsidered." *JSOT* 25 (1983) 23–33. **Greenspahn, F. E.** "The Theology of the Framework of Judges." *VT* 36 (1986) 385–96. **Hess, R. S.** "The Name Game: Dating the Book of Judges." *BAR* 30 (2004) 38–41. **Lilley, J. P. U.** "A Literary Appreciation of the Book of Judges." *TynBul* 18 (1967) 94–102. **Mueller, E. A.** *The Micah*

Story: A Morality Tale in the Book of Judges. SBLStBl 34. Berlin: Lang, 2001. **Satterthwaite, P. E.** "Judges." *DOTHP,* 580–92. **Sweeney, M.** "Davidic Polemics in the Book of Judges." *VT* 47 (1997) 517–29. **Yee, G. A.** "Ideological Criticism: Judges 17–21 and the Dismembered Body." In *Judges and Method.* Ed. G. A. Yee. 146–70.

One's perception of the purpose of the book of Judges is tied to one's understanding of the editorial history of the book, its sources, its date, its literary structure, its rhetoric, and its opening and conclusion. Various theories on each of these topics have given rise to various theories concerning the purpose of the book.

Keil emphasizes the prophetic viewpoint applying the standard of the law to the spirit of the age so as to pronounce "a stern and severe sentence upon all deviations from the path of rectitude set before it in the law" (243). Moore is a bit more concrete in seeing the purpose as religious, not historical: "to impress upon his readers the lesson that unfaithfulness to Yahweh is always punished; that whenever Israel falls away from him, he withdraws his protection and leaves it defenceless before its foes" (xvi)—or stated in a different manner: Yahweh is Israel's God, and the religion of Israel is to keep itself to him alone. Burney (cxx–cxxi) makes the same points with less clarity. More recently, Younger (23) succinctly states: "The book's selective presentation of the period is clearly designed to instruct the reader on the consequences of disobedience to God and his law." In so doing, Younger approves Block's statement: "The theme of the book is the *Canaanization of Israelite society during the period of the settlement*" (58, emphasis original), a theme brought out in Sweeney's outline if not his article (*VT* 47 [1997] 517–29). Recently Mueller (*Micah Story*) has spoken of a morality tale calling Israel to forsake covenant unfaithfulness, repent, and hope in God. In similar fashion Ryan in his afterword (169–212) has taken an optimistic view of Judges and seen the book as intended to make exilic listeners feel ashamed for their failures to keep the covenant, to impress them with the ability and honor of the judges, and to remind them of their monotheistic religion. Thus Ryan understands "the 'book' of Judges in its final form to be an exilic voice of hope addressed to marginalized readers/listeners who—even though they have brought oppression upon themselves—ache for a better world and cry out for their home (Ps. 137)" (188).

For Gray ([1986] 243; compare Greenspahn, *VT* 36 [1986] 395–96; Pressler, 4–5) the Deuteronomistic message is the paradox of justice and grace so that even the principle of sin and retribution does not impair God's constructive purpose for Israel. Boling (38) sees the final segment (Judg 17–21) as presenting an Israel finally reunited after the separation of chap. 1 and thus sees a positive answer to how Israel can sing the Lord's song in a foreign land (see Ps 137). The book calls on exilic Israel for faith. In like mind, Hoppe (21) sees Judges as explaining why the promised land was lost and encouraging God's chosen people to obedience.

Cundall (*ExpTim* 81 [1970] 178–81; compare Lilley, *TynBul* 18 [1967] 101) sees the book as pointing to the need for a king. Wolf sees that the purpose of Judges is to show "that Israel's spiritual condition determined its political and material situation. . . . Israel failed to realize her divinely intended goal without a king" (3:378–79). Olson (726–27) also points to the kingship theme but sees the point as showing that "kingship in Israel, like the judges, will in time be replaced by another form of human leadership, which will be necessary but also provisional and imperfect." Olson also points to the dialectical interplay among many themes, especially divine justice and mercy. Matthews (5–6) underlines the leadership theme as first a legitimization of Josiah and also possibly a demonstration that Yahweh is Israel's true king. A. F. Campbell sees Judges painting "an increasingly miserable picture of a dysfunctional Israel, portrayed as a very creaky hinge between the heroic past of Moses and Joshua and the possible future under prophets and kings" (103).

Stone (594) traces three stages of the Deuteronomistic History with Judges providing a different purpose in each. For Stone, Judges shows the social crisis leading to the need for a new structure, a monarchy best illustrated by Hezekiah. Attached to the Deuteronomic law under Josiah, Judges underlines divine retribution and the need for a moral reforming king like Josiah as the true successor to Joshua. The exilic edition then projects the need for a king into the future as a hope for exiled people.

Several more recent writers have placed the purpose in the midst of the political battle between Saul and David. O'Connell sees the book defending the Davidic monarchy against supporters of Saul. Brettler (113–16; *JBL* 108 [1989] 395–418) and Sweeney (*VT* 47 [1997] 517–29) underline the Saul/David polemic but see it coming long after the demise of Saul and the fall of the northern kingdom, a strange time to denigrate the tribe of Benjamin. (Compare Hamilton, *Handbook*, 169.) Sweeney, at the same time, emphasizes the Canaanization of Israel, another theme with great importance for the time of David but with increasingly less importance for the period of the monarchy. Dorsey phrases this in an interesting way: "The book may have been written to counter the popular view current in the author's day (perhaps the early united monarchy) that the period of the judges was 'the good old days' when Israel's heroes of old led the nation to glorious victories, when 'there was no [oppressive] king' over the land and when each person could do as he or she saw fit" (120). McCann (8–11) accepts the political propaganda motif for the "earliest shaping" of the material. He sees, however, the exilic Deuteronomist offering an explanation for the exile and hope beyond the exile. He warns that people and institutions will perish if they do not worship God exclusively and do not follow his will.

Kratz outlines a complex literary growth beginning as a secondary Deuteronomistic piece intended to serve as "a bridge over which the sin responsible for the judgements of 720 and 587 BC can be loaded on the people of Israel, the people of Yhwh, and not just on the kings of Israel and in part of Judah" (*Composition*, 207). Satterthwaite sees the basic theme as "Israel's increasing unfaithfulness and distance from God". He "wanted people to see how the *power of God* operated through ordinary men and women whom He chose to speak and act on His behalf," the key being the Holy Spirit ("Judges," 589, emphasis original). Similarly, Schneider reduces the theme simply to "the relationship of Israel to its deity" (xv).

For Polzin, Judges represents the Deuteronomist's "sustained reflection on the limitations of any ideology to test reality or to understand the historical vicissitudes man encounters in his lifetime" (*Moses and the Deuteronomist*, 210–11). Thus, Judges pictures "the mystery of God's dealings with man and the comedy of man's efforts to overpower and master the events that make up his existence." Similarly, Webb ([1987] 208–9) sees the fundamental issue to be the nonfulfillment of God's promise to the patriarchs, answered by pointing to Israel's apostasy and God's freedom, thus building dramatic tension between Israel's weakness and Yahweh's choice.

Yee ("Ideological Criticism," 167) concentrates on Judg 19–21 as a part of the original Josianic Deuteronomistic History. She discovers a propaganda war against the Levites (who are trying to get Levitical income from the state treasury), along with a plea for central government over against the tribal form that collapsed in the time of the Judges.

How can so many excellent scholars read the same literature and come up with quite distinct understandings of its basic purpose? One reason for this is the differing answers to the various issues and riddles I have posed to this point. Another explanation is the perspective one brings to the text. Finally, the nature of the material itself influences its interpretation. Judges is a complex work of literature that cannot be easily reduced to a thesis sentence or to one single purpose statement.

Most obviously, the book deals with leadership, indeed a crisis in leadership. This crisis occurs because Joshua and his generation did not properly train the next generation (Judg 2:10). This leads to an attempt to find tribal leadership rather than individual leadership (1:1), but this style of leadership proves ineffective in trying to settle the land's cities left unsettled by Joshua, as the various failures in chap. 1 demonstrate. Consequently, the people rely on individual tribal heroes, who are effective to varying degrees in their lifetimes but consistently fail to provide continuity and faithfulness to Yahweh (chaps. 3–12). This reliance on individuals produces a self-centered hero who virtually ignores the need for tribal or national leadership until he commits suicide (chaps. 13–16). His death leads to political and religious anarchy (chaps. 17–21). Thus Israel needs a king. But two problems stand in the way. First, experience with Gideon and Abimelech have shown the dangers of kingship. Second, Israel's theology claims that only Yahweh is king (8:23), though Israel patently does not live out this theology at the national, tribal, or individual level as the various stories illustrate. Thus Judges points the leadership question forward toward monarchy, not backward to the theocracy of Joshua's day. But will the king be a servant of Yahweh as were Moses and Joshua (Deut 34:5; Josh 1:1, 13, 15; 8:31, 33; 11:12; 12:6; 13:8; 14:7; 18:7; 22:2, 4–5; 24:29; Judg 2:8)? Or will the king emulate self-serving Gideon and Abimelech? Is any king better than the anarchy of chaps. 17–21? Judges raises the leadership issue in its most complex and puzzling form without providing the answer.

Second, Judges deals openly with obedience, for Israel does evil in God's eyes (Num 32:13; Deut 4:25; 9:18; 17:2; 31:29; Judg 2:11; 3:7, 12; 4:1; 6:1; 10:6; 13:1). The book defines this evil twice at 2:11 and 3:7. Doing evil means forsaking Yahweh as God and serving the Canaanite gods called the Baals and Asherahs. The list of gods served is expanded in 10:6 to include gods of all the oppressive foreign nations—Syria, Sidon, Moab, Ammon, and Philistia. This implies that the deeper into the Judges experience Israel went, the more members they added to their illicit pantheon. The basis of all Israel's political and social troubles is explained as departing from the first of the Ten Commandments. Yet Judges does not refer to law or statutes or judgments. Twice it mentions commandments (מצות)—2:17 and 3:4. The people of Israel did not follow the example of Joshua's generation (Judg 2:17; compare Josh 24:16–18). They did not pass God's test (Judg 3:4). In fact, the ensuing stories of the individual judges never refer to the law or commandments or statutes or judgments of God. Israel never renews the covenant. The people never hold themselves accountable to God's commands. More and more the people of Israel do what is right in their own eyes (Judg 17:6; 21:25). Even Israel's cries to God in the most tragic times are cries for deliverance, not cries of repentance. God's commandments represent God's standard by which one must measure Israel's conduct. Only God bothers to measure. Israel ignores the standard and thus falls into evil in the broadest of senses. The people worship evil gods. They do evil in forsaking their savior God. They practice evil in their daily life and in their international affairs. Judges wants to deal with obedience but has to tell, instead, a constant narrative of disobedience.

Third, Judges deals with the political scene. This is done a bit more through literary artistry than through explicit statement. The writer of Judges takes materials that are basically confined to the northern tribes and skillfuly adds to the collection his own interpretation. Judah is placed at the head of the list as the only truly successful tribe in inhabiting its territory (Judg 1:1–20). Israel's evil leads to the Ammonites daring to move across the Jordan and involve Judah in their oppressive attacks (10:9). Philistine oppression also spreads to Judah (15:9–11), but Judah is not involved in the battle. Several of Samson's exploits lie in territory on the Judean border with the Philistines. The Judeans decide to hand the judge Samson over to the Philistines. Additionally, the Levite of chap. 17 is from Bethlehem in Judah but cannot find work there. This Judahite Levite is seen as a promise of peace and prosperity (17:13). The Danite troubles begin at Kiriath-jearim in Judah (18:12). Again the narrative of chap. 19 begins in Judah (19:1), where its featured citizen is no moral example, but then turns to Gibeah in Benjamin, where the real trouble ensues. The central character is from Ephraim (19:1, 18). Finally, Judah appears as God's choice to lead the battle against the Benjaminites, but there is no report that Judah actually took the lead. Judges does not picture Judah as a perfect example of faithfulness, but Judah is the least of the evils among the tribes and the one twice designated as God's chosen leader.

This portrayal of Judah stands in contrast to the image of Benjamin, Ephraim, and Dan. Benjamin took the blame for Israel not occupying Jerusalem (Judg 1:21; contrast 1:7–8). Benjamin sent the lone messenger Ehud to dispatch the king of Moab (3:12–30). Benjamin did play a leading role for Deborah (5:14) and faced opposition from the Ammonites (10:9). Benjamin stands at the center only in the closing episode. An elderly man from the hill country of Ephraim shows great hospitality (19:20–21), but the Benjaminite residents in Gibeah are characterized as "sons of Belial" (19:22; 20:13) and live up to their reputation (19:25). They have committed sacrilege or shameful folly in Israel (20:10). They fought their brothers rather than handing over the guilty party (20:13). Despite initial successes, Benjamin eventually becomes a tribe cut off or hewn down from Israel (21:6). Nonparticipating Jabesh-gilead then becomes the source of wives for the Benjaminites (21:14). Finally, more wives come from Shiloh in Ephraim (21:20–23).

Interesting at this point is the place of Bethel, the sanctuary border town that became a worship center for the northern kingdom. Jeroboam I made Bethel into the worship center, along with Dan, for the northern kingdom. Abijah, king of Judah, then captured it (2 Chr 13:19); Baasha, king of Israel, retook the city. When Israel fell to the Assyrians, Bethel reverted to Judah (Ezra 2:28; Neh 7:32). Thus Bethel, a frontier town between two provinces, shifted back and forth in political ownership. (See H. Brodsky, *ABD*, 1:710–12.) In Judges the Joseph tribes (Ephraim and Manasseh) capture and destroy Bethel (1:22–26), the city allotted to Benjamin

(Josh 18:22). Thus Bethel was located in the hill country of Ephraim when Deborah judged there (Judg 4:5). The tribes of Israel first meet at Mizpah in Benjamin (20:1) to determine guilt and plan strategy against the inhospitable Benjaminites (20:1) but then shift to Bethel to gain God's direction in their battle plans. There in the northern sanctuary southern Judah is named leader of the tribes (20:18). After each defeat, Israel returns to Bethel (20:23, 26), a sanctuary legitimized by the ark of the covenant and the Aaronic priest Phinehas. The final consultation at Bethel results in victory, decimating a tribe of Israel. This leads to a return to Bethel in weeping and a plan that destroys yet another part of Israel—Jabesh-gilead. The Ephraimite city of Bethel, having been slyly captured from Benjamin, thus plays an ambiguous role in Judges. There the people of Israel get word from God pointing to Judah as leader and find a battle strategy that leads to losses before victory, and to victory at the expense of two major groups of Israelites.

The civil conflict that results in the loss of important segments of Israelites leads to the rest of the Ephraimite story. Ephraim is apparently meant in Judg 1:22–23 in the capture of Bethel, but mysteriously not named. The tribe is named in its inability to capture Gezer (1:29). The replay of Joshua's burial (2:9) locates it in the hill country of Ephraim, identifying Ephraim as the tribe of Joshua and thus possibly the place to look for a successor to Joshua (2:9). The model judge, Othniel, appears first (3:9), but the first narrative about a judge features Ehud of Benjamin, who gathers his troops from the hill country of Ephraim (3:27). In that hill country Deborah judges Israel (4:5), and Ephraim loyally joins Deborah's forces for battle (5:14). Gideon, the next judge, is from Ophrah in Manasseh but calls forth the men of Ephraim (7:24), who fulfill their assignment. The men of Ephraim, however, are not satisfied, thinking they have been summoned too late in the battle (8:1). This time Gideon is able to pacify them. Tola has Issachar roots but lives in the hill country of Ephraim (10:1). Ephraim joins Judah and Benjamin in facing Ammonite forces from east of the Jordan (10:9). Jephthah of Gilead calls Ephraim to fight the Ammonites. Again the Ephraimites complain that they were called too late (12:1) and threaten Jephthah. Jephthah retorts that they had not answered his first and dire call to arms. Jephthah and the men of Gilead then defeat the Ephraimites and show that the Ephraimites even speak a distinct dialect, separating them from their comrades. Abdon also appears to be from Ephraim, and his lifestyle resembles that of royalty (12:13–15).

In chaps. 17–18 Micah, the central character, lives in the hill country of Ephraim. He is a thief who builds an idol, a shrine, an ephod, and a teraphim and then makes his own son the priest. Such action introduces the overt statement that Israel needs a king because everyone does what is right in his or her own eyes (17:6). When opportunity arises, Micah deposes his son and hires a traveling Levite from Judah. Micah can rest assured of prosperity because he has a Levite priest (17:13). Prosperity does not last long, for the men of Dan steal the shrine, the idol, the ephod, and teraphim, and the priest.

Chaps. 19–21 also begin with a Levite in the hill country of Ephraim. Eventually, coming to Gibeah he meets an old man from the hill country of Ephraim. The old man shows him hospitality but cannot protect him from the lusts and rage of the Benjaminite citizens of Gibeah. Ephraim is thus the center of or at least strongly involved in many of the Judges narratives—the original occupation narratives, Joshua's burial, Ehud, Deborah, Gideon, Tola, the Ammonite invasion, Jephthah,

Abdon, Micah and his illicit cult, the Danite migration, and the Benjaminite wars. Ephraim is set up to be a leader in Israel following the example of Ehud and Deborah. But Ephraim does not play the central role in any of these narratives. (See the relative chronology shown in table I.9 in the appendix.) Instead, it becomes a prideful, interfering, self-centered tribe with a distinctive dialect and false worship. This leads to the people of Ephraim being soundly defeated by fellow Israelites under Jephthah and to having the false shrine of one of their members stolen by another tribe.

Dan receives similar treatment in Judges. Not only could they not conquer the towns in their inheritance, but the Amorite armies pressed them back to the hill country, not allowing them to enter the valley (Judg 1:34). They apparently become laborers for the Amorite seafarers (5:17). The only judge from Dan is the notorious woman-chaser Samson, who did nothing at all to further the Israelite cause except for killing Philistines by killing himself (chaps. 13–16). Finally, the Danites have to move north. In so doing they steal their shrine, idol, and priest from an Ephraimite (chap. 18). Then they burn down a defenseless, unprepared people to establish their own city. Dan then joins in the war against the Benjaminites (20:1).

Three tribes thus receive the brunt of the author's judgment in Judges. Benjamin could not take Jerusalem, could not hold on to Bethel in the face of Ephraim's strength, acted with lust and violence against Micah's concubine, refused attempts at reconciliation, and suffered the consequences. Ephraim proved strong militarily but weak spiritually in its pride and demands to be first. Ephraim's sanctuary in Bethel had all the proper accoutrements as the central sanctuary, but the decisions made there led to defeat and then to the decimation of a whole tribe of Israel and the people of Jabesh-gilead. The major positive decision at Bethel was for Judah to take the lead. Dan became a servant tribe to Canaanite or Amorite seamen, eventually losing its foothold in the foothills and having to move to the far north. In so doing, it took over by force a private sanctuary with its idol, teraphim, and priest.

Why these three tribes? Ephraim and Bethel became the center of northern Israelite worship and political power. Dan and Bethel became the center of northern Israel's cult. And Benjamin was the home of Saul, the first king of Israel. The authors who collected the materials of Judges into a final "book" apparently wanted Judah to go first ahead of the shameful trio of Benjamin, Ephraim, and Dan.

The book of Judges deals with leadership, obedience, and politics. At least one other subject must join the list—God. Here a commentator must step carefully through the bits and pieces of evidence to come to a complex presentation. Too easily one speaks of God's sovereignty and grace. Too quickly one sees God's sovereign hand behind all events. Too seldom does the reader look with eyes from the perspective of the narrative participants. Judges nowhere connects God with loving kindness (חֶסֶד) or mercy (רַחֲמִים) or other words of love and grace. One time in the framework God has compassion (נחם; Judg 2:18). The end of the story of Judges is one of disaster—waiting to see if an age of grace and compassion might come under the proper king. The narrator sets up a framework that puts God in control (2:1–3:4), but Israel lives by a different standard. God seldom appears in the narratives themselves. Israel chooses other gods and alien ways of worship. Israel turns to God only under direst distress.

An enemy king (Judg 1:7) attributes just retribution to God (אלהים). God is "the God of their fathers" (2:12; compare 2:17), but this generation forgets God (3:7) and does not remember God (8:34). Only in 10:10 do they confess they have forsaken God, a fact God acknowledges, refusing to deliver Israel again (10:13). Finally, Israel turns from foreign gods to serve Yahweh (10:16).

Ehud does have a message from God addressed to Eglon, not Israel (3:20). Deborah receives a message from Yahweh, the God of Israel (compare 5:3, 5), for Barak (4:6), who sidesteps it; and God gives the victory (4:23). An unnamed prophet has a message for Israel from Yahweh, the God of Israel (6:8), who must reintroduce himself to the people Israel (6:10). The angel of God meets Gideon and shows him how to build an altar for Yahweh, your God (6:20, 26), so Gideon bargains with God (6:36, 39–40). A Midianite can recognize God's purpose through a dream (7:14). Gideon defends himself against the Ephraimites by saying God has delivered the leaders of Midian into their hands, not his (8:3). Jotham prays that God may listen to the people of Shechem (9:7). But God sends an evil spirit between Shechem and Abimelech (9:23), letting Abimelech be killed to return Abimelech's evil against his brothers upon him as well as Shechem's evil upon them (9:56–57). Jephthah knows God's past work for Israel (11:23) but equates God's gift with that of Chemosh (11:24). Samson's parents consecrate him to God (13:5; compare 16:17), obeying a "man of God" (13:6) or "angel of God" (13:9). God hears the prayer of Samson's father (13:9), but the father fears he will die because he has seen God (13:22). God performs a miracle for Samson (15:19). Finally, Samson prays to die to gain revenge against the Philistines (16:28). Micah with all his pagan paraphernalia and the gods he has made (18:24) can still inquire of God and receive an answer (18:5–6). The Danites declare God has given the northern territory into their hands (18:10) shortly before stealing Micah's house of God with its idol and other sanctuary items. The house of God at Shiloh simply gives a time reference rather than functioning as an intimate part of Israel's life (18:31).

Still, the people of Israel in preparing to destroy Benjamin are "the assembly of the people of God" (20:2) who ask God for direction (20:18; 21:2). The ark of God is in Bethel but plays no role in the story (20:27). Ultimately, Israel laments before Yahweh, the God of Israel (21:3). In fact, אלהים (god or gods) frequently represents the pagan gods (Judg 2:3, 12, 17, 19; 3:6; 5:8; 6:31; 8:33; 9:9, 13, 27; 10:6, 13, 14 ,16; 11:24; 16:23, 24; 17:5; 18:24) rather than Israel's true God. The same term, אלהים (Elohim), occasionally shows a direct action of God for Israel or a positive action of God towards Israel, and in several of those cases one wonders if the narrator truly refers to Yahweh or is ambiguously leaving open the possibility of reference to foreign gods.

The personal name *Yahweh* (יהוה) occurs 175 times in Judges in 137 verses. Israel asks Yahweh for direction (1:1) and receives it (1:2). Yahweh hands the Canaanites to Judah (1:4), being with Judah (1:19) and also with Joseph (1:22; compare 6:12–13, 21–22). Yahweh's angel warns Israel (2:1, 4; compare 5:23; 6:11–12; 13:3, 13, 15, 16, 17, 18, 20, 21), leading Israel to sacrifice to Yahweh (2:5; compare 20:26). This had been their standard procedure under Joshua's leadership (2:7; compare 2:17). Joshua was the last servant of the Lord (2:8) in the biblical histories, David receiving the title only in the titles to Pss 18 and 36. The Judges period is marked as a generation who does not know Yahweh or the works Yahweh had done for

Israel (2:10). They do evil in Yahweh's sight (2:11; 3:7, 12; 4:1; 6:1; 10:6; 13:1), forget God (3:7; compare 8:34), and abandon Yahweh (2:12, 13), thus enraging Yahweh (2:12, 14, 20; 3:8; 10:7), who brings evil on them, fulfilling his warnings (2:15) by selling Israel or handing them over to the enemy (4:2, 9; 6:1; 13:1).

God allows nations to test Israel (2:22–3:4) and to see if they will keep the commandments. In desperation Israel cries out to Yahweh (3:9, 15; 4:3; 6:6–7; 10:10). On one occasion the people of Israel even confess sin and worship Yahweh (10:10, 15–16) as they plead for deliverance. Yahweh does raise up judges to deliver them (2:16, 18; 3:9) and puts the Spirit of Yahweh on them (3:10; 6:34; 11:29; 13:25; 14:6, 19; 15:14) because of Yahweh's response to their groans (2:18). Yahweh hands enemy nations over to the judges (3:10, 28; 4:14; 11:21, 32; 12:3; compare 4:15; 11:36). Yahweh commands Barak through Deborah (4:6) and goes before Barak (4:14). Deborah and Barak praise Yahweh, the God of Israel (5:2–3, 9) describing divine battle actions (5:4–5, 11, 23) for the people of Yahweh (5:11, 13). They pray a curse down on Yahweh's enemies and blessing on those who "love him" (5:31). Yahweh finally sends a prophet to remind the people of all that Yahweh has done for them and of their disobedience (6:8–10; compare 10:11–14). Gideon shows his skepticism about Yahweh's presence, being able to confess only Yahweh's abandonment (6:13). Still, Yahweh commissions Gideon (6:14–15) and reassures him (6:23). Gideon responds by building an altar to Yahweh and following Yahweh's instructions to destroy his father's Baal altar (6:24–27). Yahweh keeps Gideon from having reason to brag (7:2–6) and promises to deliver him (7:7). Yahweh shows Gideon the Midianite's dream and resulting fear (7:9–15), Gideon coming to believe Yahweh has given Midian into their hands (7:15) so that the battle cry becomes the sword of Yahweh and of Gideon (7:18, 20). Yahweh then provides victory (7:22; compare 8:7). Gideon gains proper theology about Yahweh as king but does not live it out (8:23–27).

Jephthah speaks of Yahweh's deliverance in a conditional manner (11:9). The Gileadite elders use an oath formula (11:10) and then ritually install Jephthah in Yahweh's presence (11:11). Jephthah knows Yahweh's history with his people (11:23) but then apparently puts Yahweh on a par with Chemosh (11:24) before declaring Yahweh to be judge between nations (11:17) and making a foolish vow to Yahweh (11:30–31, 35–36; compare 21:5,7). Samson's father prays to Yahweh, asking for the angel to return (13:8). Obeying the angel, Manoah offers sacrifice to Yahweh. Still his wife has to assure Manoah that Yahweh does not intend to kill him. Yahweh blesses the young Samson (13:24), but his mother and father cannot discern Yahweh's will (14:4). Having seen Yahweh's victory, Samson prays in exasperation for water (15:18) and finally for death (16:28). Yahweh wearily leaves Samson (16:20). Micah's mother sees him as blessed by Yahweh because he returns to her what he stole (17:2). Micah then dedicates the money to Yahweh and uses it to make a carved image (17:3). Hiring a Levite as his priest for his personal house of God, he thinks he has life made and Yahweh's blessings assured (17:13). The young priest outside any Levitical city or official worship place and officiating with Micah's idol still promises Yahweh's blessings (18:6). Forsaken by all people, the man of chap. 19 plans to go to the house of Yahweh (19:18). Seeking how to deal with inhospitable Benjamin, Israel has a series of assemblies before Yahweh (20:1, 23, 26, 27). Yahweh appoints Judah to lead the way (20:18) and orders the people to fight (20:28). So Yahweh defeats Benjamin (20:35). Then Israel speaks to Yahweh lamenting Benjamin's absence (21:3). They have to find a city that does not prove true to the group and does not assemble with the rest of the tribes (21:8). They credit Yahweh with causing a gap in the tribes (21:15). And so they use a festival of Yahweh to steal wives for Benjamin (21:19).

All this points to the glaring absence in Judges of any theological statements about God or Yahweh, the God of Israel. A large percentage of the statements including God refer to the angel of Yahweh or to false gods. Many more refer to people with false practices still trying to serve Yahweh. Only frameworks point to the one major statement Judges wants to make about God. Yahweh deserves worship for all that Yahweh has done for Israel. No other god should share any part of that worship. The framework shows that part of that worship is obeying commandments, but this is seldom repeated in the book. The framework has one statement about divine pity or compassion or relenting before Israel's groaning but makes no other statements about God's reasons for consistently sending deliverers to Israel. To understand the nature of this God one must read the larger story of God and Israel, a story told in Torah and especially in Joshua and Samuel.

If Judges does not attempt to say much about God, it does point strongly to the nature of Israel, the people of God. The author has made clear his concept that Israel is one people under one God created for the one purpose of worship. He does this by collecting local tribal anecdotes and hero stories and combining them into an all-Israel context. The age of these stories belongs to the period of the judges, as Hess (*BAR* 30 [2004] 38–41) has recently shown. See table I.11 in the appendix.

The Israel of the traditional narratives does not appear as a united group of twelve tribes. Rather, each judge works in a specific territory and calls to battle those tribes or clans in the immediate vicinity. The Song of Deborah (chap. 5) is conscious that tribes and clans do not always answer the call. Gideon and Jephthah show that Ephraim complains bitterly when not called to lead the battle. The abbreviated narratives of the so-called minor judges do not reveal the identities of the tribes that are involved or their enemies. Samson and Jephthah lead the way to the final chapters of the book by fighting representatives of other tribes in Israel. Most often the north-central tribes appear in the narratives, though occasionally a narrative will spill across the Jordan to include eastern tribes.

None of the narratives involves all the tribes, but Ephraim appears in more narratives than any other tribe. Yet the book is clearly written to describe the nature of all Israel and to teach lessons to all Israel. The editor has let each of the parts represent the whole. All Israel should see its own actions in those of any one or more parts of Israel. All Israel must share responsibility and accountability for the actions of the parts. No one individual part of Israel can claim leadership for itself, nor can any one part separate itself from the rest. Israel is the one people of God under the leadership of the God-chosen person and responsible to God for the faithlessness of any of its constituent members. This becomes especially important for the biblical story in the days of Rehoboam and Jeroboam. God has shown that he can choose and use leaders from any of the segments of Israel. God has also shown that when the people seek a leader for all the people, Judah goes first. Under Jeroboam and Rehoboam, both leaders share blame. Rehoboam disregarded good advice and refused to be a servant of God or a servant of the people. Rehoboam chose rather to be a tyrant, like the kings who oppressed Israel in the days of the judges. Jeroboam and the northern tribes refused to commit themselves to the whole of Israel or to let Judah go first. They returned to the days of the judges when a northern coalition led in most of the battles and did not include the southern tribes. The writer of Judges shows that lack of commitment to the people Israel and to the God of Israel can lead only to anarchy and self-destruction.

Outline of the Book of Judges

I. The situation after Joshua (1:1–2:23)
   A. The territorial situation (1:1–36)
      1. Judah's conquests (1:1–20)
         a. Divine consultation and human collaboration (1:1–3)
         b. Conquest of Bezek and divine retribution (1:4–7)
         c. Conquest of Jerusalem (1:8)
         d. Conquest of southland (1:9–17)
             (1) Introductory summary (1:9)
            (2) Conquest of Hebron (1:10)
            (3) Caleb's challenge and gift (1:11–15)
               (a) Judah attacks Debir (1:11)
               (b) Othniel accepts Caleb's challenge (1:12–13)
               (c) Caleb accepts his daughter's challenge (1:14–15)
            (4) Kenites join the southern people (1:16)
            (5) Conquest of Hormah (1:17)
         e. Conquest of Philistines (1:18)
         f. Conquest summary with divine-presence formula (1:19)
         g. Gift to Caleb for obedience (1:20)
      2. Failures of the tribes of Joseph and Benjamin (1:21–29)
         a. Benjaminites' failure in Jerusalem so Jebusites live with Benjaminites (1:21)
         b. Joseph with divine-presence formula and spy strategy destroys Bethel but lets informant escape (1:22–26)
         c. Manasseh does not possess Beth-shan, Taanach, Dor, Ibleam, Megiddo against determined Canaanite opposition, and only later Israel puts them to corvée (1:27–28)
         d. Ephraim does not possess the Canaanites in Gezer, so Canaanites live in their midst in Gezer (1:29)
      3. The northern tribes' failures (1:30–35)
         a. Zebulun does not possess Kitron or Nahlol, so Canaanites live in their midst and become corvée (1:30)
         b. Asher does not possess Acco, Sidon, Ahlab, Achzib, Helbah, Aphek, or Rehob, so Asherites live in midst of Canaanites, the residents of the land because they could not dispossess them (1:31–32)
         c. Naphtali does not possess Beth-shemesh or Beth-anath and lives in the midst of the Canaanites; the residents of the land and the residents of the two cities become corvée (1:33)

1. Uniquely evil Benjamin violates law of hospitality by violating concubine (19:1–30)
   a. Irate concubine leads to lingering Levite (19:1–9)
      (1) Editorial refrain: no king in Israel (19:1a)
      (2) Ephraimite Levite takes Judean as concubine (19:1b)
      (3) Irate concubine returns to father for four months (19:2)
      (4) Levite received joyously by concubine's father (19:3)
      (5) Father's hospitality forces Levite to stay four days (19:4–7)
      (6) Levite refuses to stay on fifth day (19:8–9)
   b. Traveling Levite finds no hospitality in Benjamin (19:10–15)
      (1) Levite refuses to stay in foreign Jerusalem (19:10–12)
      (2) Levite finds no hospitality in Benjaminite Gibeah (19:13–15)
   c. Ephraimite resident in Gibeah offers hospitality (19:16–21)
   d. Perverse Benjaminites serially rape concubine (19:22–26)
      (1) Benjaminites demand access to visiting Levite (19:22)
      (2) Host refuses demand but offers virgin daughter and concubine (19:23–24)
      (3) Benjamin refuses offer (19:25a)
      (4) Levite forces concubine to go to them (19:25b)
      (5) Benjaminites rape concubine until dawn (19:25c)
      (6) Woman falls down at host's door (19:26)
   e. Perverse Levite cuts concubine in twelve pieces for tribes (19:27–30)
      (1) Insensitive Levite ignores concubine's needs and rides on (19:27–28)
      (2) Butcherous Levite dissects concubine into twelve pieces (19:29a)
      (3) Vengeful Levite gives each tribe a piece as a summons to Israel to battle (19:29b–30)
2. All Israel gains revenge on inhospitable Benjamin (20:1–48)
   a. Israel decides to fight Benjamin (20:1–11)
      (1) Israelites assemble at Mizpah to hear testimony (20:1–3)
      (2) Levite testifies and asks for counsel (20:4–7)
      (3) Israel decides to repay Benjamin for the stupid sin (20:8–11)
   b. Benjamin refuses to hand over guilty Gibeanites, so sides assemble for war (20:12–17)
   c. Assembly at Bethel finds Judah to lead (20:18)
   d. First battle lost, but new battle finds divine affirmation (20:19–23)
   e. Second battle lost, but new battle finds divine promise (20:24–28)
   f. Third battle uses ambush (20:29–35)
   g. Benjamin's retreat (20:36–41)
   h. Israel's mop-up action completes holy war requirements (20:42–48)
3. Israelites work around vow and provide wives for surviving Benjaminites (21:1–25)
   a. Israel recalls vow not to give wives to Benjaminites (21:1)
   b. Israel laments and offers sacrifices (21:2–4)
   c. Israel seeks way around oath so Benjaminites will have wives (21:5–8a)

d. Israel slaughters nonparticipating Gileadites to secure wives (21:8b–11)
e. Israel finds four hundred virgins of Jabesh-gilead and gives them to Benjamin (21:12–14)
f. Israel seeks wives for rest of Benjamin (21:15–18)
g. Israel authorizes Benjamin to kidnap wives from Shiloh festival (21:19–22)
h. Benjamin gets wives at Shiloh, and Israel returns to homes (21:23–24)
i. Editorial refrain: no king, right in his own eyes (21:25)

I. The Situation after Joshua (1:1–2:23)

A. The Territorial Situation (1:1–36)

Bibliography

Abramsky, S. "On the Kenite-Midianite Background of Moses' Leadership" (Heb.). *ErIsr* 12 (1975) 35–39. **Aharoni, Y.** "New Aspects of the Israelite Occupation of the North." In *Near Eastern Archaeology in the Twentieth Century*. FS N. Glueck, ed. J. A. Sanders. Garden City, NY: Doubleday, 1970. 254–67. ————. "The Stratification of Israelite Megiddo." *JNES* 31 (1972) 302–11. **Auerbach, E.** "Untersuchungen zum Richterbuch 1." *ZAW* 48 (1930) 286–95. **Auld, A. G.** "Judges 1 and History: A Reconsideration." *VT* 25 (1975) 261–85. **Barredo, M. A.** "Convergencias redaccionales sobre la conquista de la tierra prometida en Jue 1,1–2,5." *Car* 14 (1998) 1–42. **Belz, W.** *Die Caleb-Traditionen im Alten Testament*. BWANT 5.18. Stuttgart: Kohlhammer, 1974. **Bieberstein, K.** *Josua—Jordan—Jericho: Archäologie, Geschichte und Theologie der Landnahmeerzählungen Josua 1–6*. OBO 143. Göttingen: Vandenhoeck & Ruprecht, 1995. **Blum, E.** "Der kompositionelle Knoten am Übergang von Josua zu Richter: Ein Entflechtungsvorschlag." In *Deuteronomy and Deuteronomic Literature*. FS C. H. W. Brekelmans, ed. M. Vervenne and J. Lust. BETL 133. Leuven: Peeters, 1997. 181–212. **Brettler, M. Z.** "Jud 1,1–2:10: From Appendix to Prologue." *ZAW* 101 (1989) 433–35. **Cortese, E.** "Gios. 21 e Giud. 1 (TM o LXX?) e l''abbottonaura' del 'Tetrateuco' con l''Opera deuteronomistica.'" *RivB* 33 (1985) 375–94. **Dahood, M.** "Scriptio Defectiva in Judges 1:19." *Bib* 60 (1979) 570. **DeVries, L. F.** *Cities of the Biblical World*. Peabody, MA: Hendrickson, 1997. **Doherty, E.** "The Literary Problem of Judges I,1–III,6." *CBQ* 18 (1956) 1–7. **Drews, R.** "The 'Chariots of Iron' of Joshua and Judges." *JSOT* 45 (1989) 15–23. **Elitzur, Y.** "Two Adjacent and Contradictory Verses (Judges 1:18–19)" (Heb.). In *Sefer Deem*. Publications of the Israel Bible Society 5. Jerusalem, 1958. 192–97. **Eslinger, L. M.** "A New Generation in Israel." In *Into the Hands of the Living God*. SBLStBl 24. Sheffield: Almond, 1989. 55–80. **Fensham, F. C.** "Did a Treaty between the Israelites and the Kenites Exist?" *BASOR* 175 (1964) 51–54. **Fewell, D. N.** "Deconstructive Criticism: Achsah and the (E)razed City of Writing." In *Judges and Method*. Ed. G. A. Yee. 119–45. **Fleishman, J.** "A Daughter's Demand and a Father's Compliance: The Legal Background to Achsah's Claim and Caleb's Agreement (Joshua 15,16–19; Judges 1:12–15)." *ZAW* 118 (2006) 354–73. **Fritz, V.** "Das 'negative Besitzzeichnis' im Judicum 1." In *Gott und Mensch im Dialog*. FS O. Kaiser, ed. M. Witte. 2 vols. BZAW 345. Berlin: de Gruyter, 2005. 375–89. **Gal, Z.** "The Settlement of Issachar, Some New Observations." *TA* 9 (1982) 79–86. **Garsiel, M.,** and **I. Finkelstein.** "The Westward Expansion of the House of Joseph in the Light of the 'Izbet Sartah Excavations." *TA* 5 (1978) 192–98. **Geus, C. H. J. de.** "Richteren 1.1–2.5." *Vox Theologica* 36 (1966) 32–53. **Gibson, A.** "ṢNḤ in Judges 1:14: NEB and AV Translations." *VT* 26 (1975) 275–83. **Gitin, S.** "The Rise and Fall of Ekron of the Philistines: Recent Excavations at an Urban Border Site." *BA* 50 (1987) 197–222. **Goff, B.** "The Lost Jahwistic Account of the Conquest of Canaan." *JBL* 53 (1934) 241–49. **Gomes, J. F.** *The Sanctuary of Bethel and the Configuration of Israelite Identity*. BZAW 368. Berlin: de Gruyter, 2006. **Grintz, J. M.** "Judges Ch. I." In *Studies in the Bible*. FS M. H. Segal, ed. J. M. Grintz and J. Liver. Jerusalem: Kiryat Sepher, 1964. 42–71. **Guillaume, P.** "An Anti-Judean Manifesto in Judges 1?" *BN* 95 (1998) 12–17. ————. "Dating the *Negative Besitzverzeichnis* (Judges 1,27–34): The Case of Sidon." *Hen* 23 (2001) 131–37. **Gunn, D.**

M., and **D. N. Fewell.** *Narrative in the Hebrew Bible.* 158–63. **Gurewicz, S. B.** "The Bearing of Judges i–ii 5 on the Authorship of the Book of Judges." *ABR* 7 (1959) 37–40. **Haag, H.** "Von Jahweh geführt: Auslegung von Ri. 1,21–2,5." *BibLeb* 4 (1963) 174–84. **Hamlin, E. J.** "Adoni-Bezek—What's in a Name (Judges 1:4–7)?" *PEGLMBS* 4 (1984) 146–52. ———. "The Significance of Bethel in Judges 1:22–26." *PEGLMBS* 5 (1985) 67–72. **Hawkins, R. K.** "The Survey of Manasseh and the Origins of the Central Hill-Country Settlers." In *Critical Issues in the Early History of Israel.* Ed. R. S. Hess, G. A. Klingsheil, and P. J. Ray. 165–79. **Hertzberg, H. S.** "Adonibeseq." *JPOS* 6 (1926) 213–21. Reprinted in *Beiträge zur Traditionsgeschichte und Theologie des Alten Testaments* (Göttingen: Vandenhoeck & Ruprecht, 1962) 28–35. **Hess, R. S.** "Judges 1–5 and Its Translation." In *Translating the Bible: Problems and Prospects.* Ed. S. E. Porter and R. S. Hess. JSNTSup 173. Sheffield: Sheffield Academic, 1999. 142–60. **Hubbard, R. P., et al.** "The Topography of Ancient Jerusalem." *PEQ* (1966) 137. **Jost, R.** "Achsas Quellen: Feministisch-sozialgeschichtliche Überlegungen zu Jos 15,15–20/Ri 1,12–15." In *'Ihr Völker alle, klatscht in die Hände!'* FS E. S. Gerstenberger, ed. R. Kessler et al. Münster: LIT, 1997. 110–25. **Kalimi, I.** "Three Assumptions about the Kenites." *ZAW* 100 (1988) 386–420. **Kaswalder, P. A.** "Le tribù in Gdc 1,1–2,5 e in Gdc 4–5." *LASBF* 43 (1993) 80–113. **Keel, O.** *Die Geschichte Jerusalems und die Entstehung des Monotheismus.* 2 vols. Göttingen: Vandenhoeck & Ruprecht, 2007. **Kenyon, K.** *Digging Up Jerusalem.* New York: Praeger, 1974. ———. *Jerusalem: Excavating 3000 Years of History.* New York: McGraw Hill, 1967. **Klein, L.** "Achsah: What Price This Prize?" In *Judges* (1999). Ed. A. Brenner. 18–26. **Knauf, E. A.** "Jerusalem in the Late Bronze and Early Iron Ages: A Proposal." *TA* 27 (2000) 75–90. ———. "Bethel: The Israelite Impact on Judean Language and Literature." In *Judah and the Judeans in the Persian Period.* Ed. A. Lipschits and M. Oeming. Winona Lake, IN: Eisenbrauns, 2006. 291–349. **Kochavi, M.** "Malḥata, Tel." *EAEHL,* 3:771–75. **Köhlmoos, M.** *Bet-El-Erinnerungen an eine Stadt: Perspektiven der alttestamentlichen Bet-el-Überlieferungen.* FAT 49. Tübingen: Mohr Siebeck, 2006. **Könen, K.** *Bethel: Geschichte, Kult, und Theologie.* OBO 192. Freiburg: Universitätsverlag; Göttingen: Vandenhoeck & Ruprecht, 2003. **Landy, F.** "Judges 1: The City of Writing, the Sacred, and the Fragmentation of the Body." In *Voyages in Uncharted Waters.* FS D. Jobling, ed. W. J. Bergen and A. Siedlecki. Hebrew Bible Monographs 13. Sheffield: Sheffield Phoenix, 2006. **Lindars, B.** "Some Septuagint Readings in Judges." *JTS* 22 (1971) 1–14. **Livingston, D.** "The Location of Biblical Bethel and Ai Reconsidered." *WTJ* 33 (1970) 20–44. ———. "Traditional Site of Bethel Questioned." *WTJ* 34 (1971) 39–50. **Long, B. O.** *1 Kings.* FOTL 9. Grand Rapids: Eerdmans, 1984. ———. *2 Kings.* FOTL 10. Grand Rapids: Eerdmans, 1991. **Lurie, B. Z.** "Bezek and Adoni-Bezek." *Beit-Miqra* 29 (1982–1983) 103–6. ———. "Early and Late in Judges 1." In *Proceedings of the 9th World Congress of Jewish Studies: Period of the Bible.* Ed. R. Giveon et al. Jerusalem: World Union of Jewish Studies, 1986. 65–72. **Mazar, A.** "Jerusalem in the 10th Century B.C.E.: The Glass Half Full." In *Essays on Ancient Israel in Its Near Eastern Context.* FS N. Na'aman, ed. Y. Amit et al. Winona Lake, IN: Eisenbrauns, 2006. 255–72. **Mazar, B.** "The Sanctuary of Arad and the Family of Hobab the Kenite." *JNES* 24 (1965) 297–303. **Meyers, C.** "Of Seasons and Soldiers: A Topological Appraisal of the Premonarchic Tribes of Galilee." *BASOR* 252 (1983) 47–59. **Miller, J. M.** "Jebus and Jerusalem: A Case of Mistaken Identity." *ZDPV* 90 (1974) 115–27. **Minkoff, H.** "Coarse Language in the Bible: It's Culture Shocking." *BRev* (1989) 22–27, 44. **Mittman, S.** "Ri. 1,16f und das Siedlungsgebiet der Kenitischen Sippe Hobab." *ZDPV* 93 (1977) 213–35. **Mojola, A. O.** "The 'Tribes' of Israel? A Bible Translator's Dilemma." *JSOT* 91 (1998) 15–29. **Mosca, P. G.** "Who Seduced Whom? A Note on Joshua 15:18//Judges 1:14." *CBQ* 46 (1984) 18–22. **Mullen, E. T., Jr.** "Judges 1:1–36: The Deuteronomistic Reintroduction of the Book of Judges." *HTR* 77 (1984) 33–54. **Na'aman, N.** "Bethel and Beth-aven: An Investigation into the Location of the Early Israelite Cult Places" (Heb.). *Zion* 50 (1985) 15–25. ———. *Borders and Districts in Biblical Historiography.* Jerusalem Biblical Studies 4. Jerusalem: Simor, 1986. ———. "Canaanite Jerusalem and Its Central Hill Country Neighbours in the Second Millennium B.C.E." *UF* 24 (1992) 275–91. ———. "Canaanites and Perizzites." *BN* 335 (1988)

42–47. ———. "The Inheritance of the Sons of Simeon." *ZDPV* 96 (1980) 136–52. ———. "When and How Did Jerusalem Become a Great City? The Rise of Jerusalem as Judah's Premier City in the Eighth-Seventh Centuries B.C.E." *BASOR* 347 (2007) 21–56. **Neef, H.-D.** *Studien zur Geschichte des Stammes Ephraim von der Landnahme bis zur frühen Königszeit.* BZAW 238. Berlin: de Gruyter, 1996. **Nelson, R. D.** *Double Redaction.* 43–53. **Nicholson, E. W.** "The Problem of *ṣnh.*" *ZAW* 89 (1977) 259–65. **Niditch, S.** "Reading Stories in Judges 1." In *The Labour of Reading: Desire, Alienation, and Biblical Interpretation.* FS R. C. Culley, ed. F. C. Black, R. Boer, and E. Runions. SBLSymS 36. Atlanta: SBL, 1999. 193–208. **North, R.** "Israel's Tribes and Today's Frontier." *CBQ* 16 (1954) 146–53. **Noth, M.** "Jerusalem and the Israelite Tradition." In *The Laws in the Pentateuch and Other Studies.* Philadelphia: Fortress, 1966. 132–44. **O'Doherty, E.** "Literary Problem of Judges 1:1–3:6." *CBQ* 18 (1956) 1–7. **Penna, A.** "L'introduzione al libro dei Giudici (1,1–3,6)." In *Miscelánea Bíblica: Andrés Fernández.* Ed. J. Sagües et al. Madrid, 1961. 521–29. **Poplutz, U.** "Tel Miqne/Ekron: Geschichte und Kultur einer philistäischen Stadt." *BN* 87 (1997) 69–99. **Rainey, A. F.** "Looking for Bethel: An Exercise in Historical Geography." In *Confronting the Past.* FS W. G. Dever, ed. S. Gitin, J. E. Wright, and J. P. Dessel. Winona Lake, IN: Eisenbrauns, 2006. 269–74. **Rake, M.** *'Juda wird aufsteigen!' Untersuchungen zum ersten Kapitel des Richterbuches.* BZAW 367. Berlin: de Gruyter, 2006. **Rose, M.** "Siebzig Könige aus Ephraim." *VT* 26 (1976) 447–52. **Rösel, H. N.** "Judges 1 and the Settlement of the Leah Tribes" (Heb.). In *Proceedings of the Eighth World Congress of Jewish Studies.* Jerusalem: World Union of Jewish Studies, 1982. 2:17–20. ———. "Das 'Negative Besitzverzeichnis'—Traditiongeschichtliche und historische Überlegungen." In *Wünschet Jerusalem Frieden: Collected Communications to the XIIth Congress of the International Organization for the Study of the Old Testament, Jerusalem 1986.* Ed. M. Augustin. Frankfurt: Lang, 1988. 121–34. ———. "Die Überleitungen von Josua zum Richterbuch." *VT* 30 (1980) 342–50. **Rosenberg, R.** "The God Ṣedeq." *HUCA* 36 (1965) 161–77. **Rowley, H. H.** "Zadoq and Nehushtan." *JBL* 58 (1939) 113–41. **Schmitt, G.** *Du sollst keinen Frieden schliessen mit dem Bewohnern des Landes.* BWANT 5.11 (1970) 39–41. **Schunk, K. D.** "Juda und Jerusalem in vor- und frühisraelitischer Zeit." In *Schalom: Studien zu Glaube und Geschichte Israels.* FS A. Jepsen. Stuttgart: Calwer, 1971. 50–57. **Sima, A.** "Nochmals zur Deutung des hebräischen Namens Otni'el." *BN* 106 (2001) 47–51. **Spreafico, A.** "Giud 2,3 'Isdym.'" *Bib* 65 (1984) 390–92. **Stevenson, J. S.** "Judah's Successes and Failures in Holy War: An Exegesis of Judges 1:1–20." *ResQ* 44 (2002) 43–54. **Storch, W.** "Zur Perikope von der Syrophoniziern MK 7:28 und Ri. 1:7." *BZ* 14 (1970) 256–57. **Streck, M. P.**, and **S. Weninger.** "Zur Deutung des hebräisches Namens Otniel." *BN* 96 (1999) 21–29. **Szpek, H. M.** "Achsah's Story: A Metaphor for Societal Transition." *AUSS* 40 (2002) 245–56. **Talmon, S.** "Judges Chapter 1" (Heb.). In *Studies in the Book of Judges.* Publications of the Israel Bible Society 10. Jerusalem, 1966. 14–29. **Ussishkin, D.** "Was the Earliest Philistine City of Ekron Fortified?" *BAR* 32 (2006) 68–71, 76. **Van Seters, J.** "The Deuteronomist from Joshua to Samuel." In *Reconsidering Israel and Judah.* Ed. G. Knoppers and J. G. McConville. 204–39. **Vaux, R. de.** "The Settlement of the Israelites in Southern Palestine and the Origins of the Tribe of Judah." In *Translating and Understanding the Old Testament.* Ed. H. T. Frank and W. L. Reed. Nashville: Abingdon, 1970. 108–34. **Weinfeld, M.** "Judges 1.1–2.5: The Conquest under the Leadership of the House of Judah." In *Understanding Poets and Prophets.* FS G. W. Anderson, ed. A. G. Auld. JSOTSup 152. Sheffield: JSOT Press, 1993. 388–400. **Welten, P.** "Bezeq." *ZDPV* 81 (1965) 138–65. **Westbrook, R.** *Property and the Family in Biblical Law.* **Wright, G. E.** "The Literary and Historical Problem of Joshua 10 and Judges 1." *JNES* 5 (1946) 105–14. **Younger, K. L., Jr.** *Ancient Conquest Accounts: A Study in Ancient Near Eastern and Biblical History Writing.* JSOTSup 98. Sheffield: Sheffield Academic, 1990. ———. "The Configuring of Judicial Preliminaries: Judges 1:1–2:5 and Its Dependence on Joshua." *JSOT* 68 (1995) 75–92. ———. "Judges 1 in Its Near Eastern Literary Context." In *Faith, Tradition, History: Essays on Old Testament Historiography in Its Near Eastern Context.* Ed. A. R. Millard, J. K. Hoffmeier, and A. D. Baker. Winona Lake, IN: Eisenbrauns, 1994. 207–27.

Translation

¹*After Joshua*[a] *died, the sons of Israel inquired of* [b] *Yahweh, "Who will go up for us against the Canaanites*[c] *at the start of the fighting against them?"* ²*Yahweh said, "Judah will go up. See, I have given the land into his hand."* ³*Judah said to Simeon, his brother, "Go up with me into my allotted territory so we may fight against the Canaanites.*[a] *Then I will surely go with you in your allotted territory." And Simeon went with him.*

⁴*Judah went up, and Yahweh gave the Canaanites and the Perizzites into their hand. They struck*[a] *ten thousand*[b] *men dead in Bezek.* ⁵*In Bezek they found Adoni-bezek*[a] *and fought against him. They struck*[b] *the Canaanites and the Perizzites dead.* ⁶*Adoni-bezek fled, and they pursued*[a] *after him and caught him. They chopped off his thumbs and his big toes.* ⁷*Adoni-bezek said, "Seventy kings with their thumbs and big toes chopped off are eating scraps under my table. Just as I have done, so God has repaid me." They brought him to Jerusalem, and he died there.*

⁸*The sons of Judah fought against Jerusalem and captured it. They struck it dead with the edge of the sword and sent the city up in flames.* ⁹*Later the sons of Judah went down to fight against the Canaanites who lived in the hill country, in the Negev, and in the Shephelah.* ¹⁰*Judah*[a] *went against the Canaanites who resided in Hebron.*[b] *(Now the previous name of Hebron was Kiriath-arba.*[c]*) They*[d] *struck Sheshai, Ahiman, and Talmai*[e] *dead.*

¹¹*From there they went*[a] *against the residents of Debir. (Now the previous name of Debir was Kiriath-sepher.*[b]*)* ¹²*Caleb said, "Whoever will strike Kiriath-sepher dead and capture it, to him I will give Achsah,*[a] *my daughter, as his wife.* ¹³*Othniel, son of Kenaz and youngest*[a] *brother of Caleb, captured it, and he*[b] *gave him Achsah, his daughter, as his wife.*

¹⁴*When she arrived,*[a] *she persuaded him*[b] *to ask her father for the*[c] *field. She dismounted*[d] *from her donkey, and Caleb said to her, "What do you want?"* ¹⁵*She*[a] *said to him, "Give me a blessing. Since you have given me land in the Negev, now give me flowing springs*[b] *of water." Caleb gave her the upper and the lower springs.*[c]

¹⁶*At that time the sons of the Kenite,*[a] *Moses' father-in-law,*[b] *had gone up from the city of palms with the sons of Judah to the Judean*[c] *wilderness that is into the Negev of Arad.* [d] *They*[e] *went and resided with the people.*[f]

¹⁷*Judah went with Simeon, his brother, and struck*[a] *the Canaanites who resided in Zephath dead. They devoted it to the ban and named the city Hormah.*[b] ¹⁸*Judah captured*[a] *Gaza and its surrounding territory, Ashkelon and its surrounding territory, and Ekron and its surrounding territory.*[b] ¹⁹*Yahweh was with Judah,*[a] *and he took over possession of the hill country, except for taking over possession*[b] *of the residents of the valley because they owned chariots utilizing iron.*[c]

²⁰*They*[a] *gave Hebron to Caleb just as Moses promised. From there he*[b] *took over possession from the three sons of Anak.* ²¹*But the sons of Benjamin*[a] *could not take over possession*[b] *from the Jebusites, the residents*[c] *of Jerusalem, and the Jebusites reside with the sons of Benjamin in Jerusalem*[d] *to the present day.*

²²*The house*[a] *of Joseph also went up against Bethel, and Yahweh*[b] *was with them.* ²³*The house of Joseph spied out*[a] *Bethel. (Now the previous name of the city was Luz.)* ²⁴*The spies saw a man going out of the city*[a] *and said to him, "Show us the entrance to the city, and we will deal with you in covenant faithfulness.* ²⁵*He showed them the entrance to the city, and they struck the city dead with the edge of the sword. But the man and all his family they set free.* ²⁶*The man went to*[a] *the land of the Hittites and built*[b] *a city. He called*[c] *its name Luz. That is its name to the present day.*

[97] *But Manasseh did not take over possession*[a] *of Beth-shan*[b] *with its dependent villages,*[c] *Taanach with its dependent villages, nor of the residents*[d] *of Dor and its dependent villages, the residents of Ibleam*[e] *and its dependent villages, nor the residents of Megiddo*[f] *and its dependent villages. The Canaanites had determinedly prepared themselves to reside in this land.* [28] *When Israel became strong, they put the Canaanites to corvée labor,*[a] *but they never took over possession from them.* [29] *At that time Ephraim did not take over possession from the Canaanites who resided in Gezer. The Canaanites resided among them in Gezer.*[a] [30] *Zebulun did not take over possession from the residents of Kitron*[a] *or from the residents of Nahalol.*[b] *The Canaanites resided among them and became subject*[c] *to corvée labor.* [31] *Asher did not take over possession from the residents of Acco*[a] *or the residents of Sidon or of Ahlab,*[b] *Achzib, Helbah,*[c] *Aphik,*[d] *or of Rehob.* [32] *The Asherites resided among the Canaanites who resided in the land, but they did not take over*[a] *possession from them.* [33] *Naphtali did not take over possession from the residents of Beth-shemesh or the residents of Beth-anath. They*[a] *resided among the Canaanites who resided in the land. The residents of Beth-shemesh and of Beth-anath became corvée labor for them.* [34] *The Amorites pushed the sons of Dan into the hill country. Indeed, they did not allow*[a] *them to go down into the valley.* [35] *The Amorites were determined to reside in Har-heres, in Aijalon, and in Shaalbim.*[a] *Then the hand of the house of Joseph grew heavy,*[b] *and they became corvée labor.* [36] *At that time the Amorites' territory went from the Ascent of Akrabbim, that is, from Sela and on up.*[a]

Notes

1.a. *BHS* proposal to emend to Moses because of Judg 2:6 has no textual evidence and is based strictly on literary and redactional theories. The Syr. adds from Josh 24:29, "the son of Nun the servant of the Lord."

1.b. LXX[A] reads ἐν κυρίῳ, while LXX[B] reads διὰ τοῦ κυρίου, obvious translation alternates.

1.c. LXX[A] reads sg. with MT, while LXX[B] reads pl., a proper rendering of the Heb. collective noun; also in v 3.

3.a. LXX[A] reads πολεμήσωμεν ἐν τῷ Χαναναίῳ, "so that we may wage war with the Canaanite," while LXX[B] reads παραταξώμεθα πρὸς τοὺς Χαναναίους, "so that we may set up in battle line over against the Canaanites," both acceptable translation variants used consistently throughout Judges (see Lindars, 79–80).

4.a. LXX[A] reads ἔδωκεν κύριος τὸν Χαναναῖον καὶ τὸν Φερεζαῖον ἐν χειρὶ αὐτοῦ καὶ ἐπάταξεν αὐτοὺς ἐν Βεζεκ, "gave the Canaanite and the Perizzite in his hand, and he struck them dead in Bezek," while LXX[B] reads παρέδωκεν κύριος τὸν Χαναναῖον καὶ τὸν Φερεζαῖον εἰς τὰς χεῖρας αὐτῶν καὶ ἔκοψαν αὐτοὺς ἐν Βεζεκ, "the Lord gave over the Canaanite and the Perizzite into their hands and cut them off in Bezek."

4.b. Some scholars think אלף refers to a military company of soldiers or a clan as a social unit above the family. See *HALOT*, 1:59–60; Hess, "Judges 1–5," 144.

5.a. Or "the lord of Bezek."

5.b. LXX[A] reads καὶ εὗρον τὸν Αδωνιβεζεκ ἐν Βεζεκ καὶ ἐπολέμησαν ἐν αὐτῷ καὶ ἐπάταξαν, "they found Adoni-bezek in Bezek and warred with him and struck dead," while LXX[B] reads καὶ κατέλαβον τὸν Αδωνιβεζεκ ἐν τῇ Βεζεκ καὶ παρετάξαντο πρὸς αὐτὸν καὶ ἔκοψαν, "they overtook Adoni-bezek in the Bezek and set up in battle line over against him and cut off."

6.a. LXX[A] reads κατεδίωξαν, "they pursued," while LXX[B] reads κατέδραμον, "they ran."

10.a. The *BHS* proposal to read Caleb with Josh 15:13 seeks to harmonize narratives and misses the tribal motif central to chap. 1.

10.b. LXX adds καὶ ἐξῆλθεν Χεβρων ἐξ ἐναντίας, "and Hebron went out against (him)." This could be seen as a narrative clarification by LXX, but since LXX does not make such clarifications elsewhere in the chapter, this is more probably a part of the original text omitted by haplography, though Lindars (81–82) sees it as a corrupt doublet of the following clause.

10.c. LXX^A and LXX^B use variant spellings, each representing a combination of Kiriath-arba and Kiriath-sepher of v 11 into one name, a somewhat complex case of dittography.

10.d. LXX^A reads sg., maintaining grammatical consistency, but should not be adopted as *BHS* proposes.

10.e. LXX reads "and Talmai, offspring of Anak," a gloss copied from Num 13:22 and Josh 15:14; for a complex theory of the development of this text tradition, see Lindars (25). Niditch (33) sees such variants in the tradition as a testimony "to the oral-world quality of these written texts in which multiplicity is not harmonized away and in which variants coexist within the tradition."

11.a. LXX^B (compare OL) reads ἀνέβησαν, "they went up." This combined with ויעל of Josh 15:15 does not justify the *BHS* proposal of וירל.

11.b. LXX and Arabic translate city name to "city of letters (or) of writings"; also in the following verse.

12.a. LXX transposes the name to Ασχαν throughout.

13.a. Josh 15:17 does not have הקטן ממנו, "younger than he," leading Lindars (28) to see its awkward syntax as evidence that it is not original here but dependent on 3:9. Such minor syntactical awkwardness does not justify such a complex reading of the textual history. LXX^B makes Othniel the nephew of Caleb, but OL and LXX^A make them brothers. This may again reflect oral variants in the tradition.

13.b. LXX^B reads "Caleb," clarifying a possible misunderstanding of pronominal antecedents.

14.a. LXX^A reads εἰσπορεύεσθαι, while LXX^B reads εἰσόδῳ, simply translation variants. Schneider's reading of the Heb. as a "directional *h*," resulting in translating "he came (sexually) to her," is strained and unnecessary.

14.b. LXX^A reads καὶ ἐπέσεισεν αὐτὴν αἰτῆσαι, "and he persuaded her to ask"; LXX^B clarifies further, making the subject *Othniel* explicit. In Josh 15:18 LXX supports MT; see Butler, *Joshua*, 180, on 15:18. On the possibility that the LXX reading is original in Judges with MT reintroducing the reading from Joshua, see Barthélemy, *Critique textuelle*, 1:35–36. Still, the Judges LXX appears to be a simplification of the narrative and not an original reading. See Hess, "Judges 1–5," 144.

14.c. Unlike LXX and OL here or MT or LXX of Josh 15:18, MT adds a definite article, making this a request for a specific piece of land. This may be a part of the ironic touch of the Judges editor.

14.d. LXX^A reads καὶ ἐγόγγυζεν τοῦ ὑποζυγίου καὶ ἔκραξεν ἀπὸ τοῦ ὑποζυγίου εἰς γῆν νότου, "she grumbled on the donkey and cried out from the donkey, 'You have handed me over to the south (or the Negev).'" LXX^B does not have the first reference to donkey. This apparently represents a complex textual history of dittography within the verse and with the next verse along with oral variants. Niditch (33) sees "sound-alike" variations on the root ṣnḥ with LXX and OL translating Heb. ṣrḥ or ṣwḥ.

15.a. LXX reads "Ascha," making clear the distinction between her and Othniel after making Othniel the subject in v 14a.

15.b. LXX reads λύτρωσιν ὕδατος, "the ransom of water," apparently based on hearing Heb. גאל rather than MT גלת. Niditch (33) suggests that this could be scribal error or wordplay. OL has "blessing of water."

15.c. LXX (compare OL) reads, ἔδωκεν αὐτῇ Χαλεβ κατὰ καρδίαν αὐτῆς λύτρωσιν μετεώρων καὶ λύτρωσιν ταπεινῶν, "according to his heart, Caleb gave her the ransom of the upper ones and the ransom of the lower ones." *BHS* suggests, probably correctly, that this may represent haplography of the Heb. כלבה. The Heb. adjectives are sg. in the Judges text but pl. in the parallel in Josh 15:19, where LXX uses adverbs. The Heb. term appears only in these two passages and may be seen as a collective noun for water sources or as a proper place name as in the NRSV Upper Gulloth and Lower Gulloth or CEV's Higher Pond and Lower Pond. OL reads "a redemption of the upper ponds and a redemption of the lower ponds."

16.a. The Heb. requires an article before קיני, as seen in 4:11, but note Barthélemy *(Critique textuelle)*, who sees the lack of the article transforming this into a quasi proper name.

16.b. LXX^A reads οἱ υἱοὶ Ιωβαβ τοῦ Κιναιου πενθεροῦ Μωυσῆ, "the sons of Hobab the Kenite, Moses' father-in-law," while LXX^B reads οἱ υἱοὶ Ιοθορ τοῦ Κιναιου τοῦ γαμβροῦ Μωυσέως, "the sons of Jethro the Kenite, the father-in-law of Moses." Each tradition inserts information from other passages—Jethro from Exod 18:9; for Hobab, compare Num 10:29 and Judg 4:11. In LXX πενθεροῦ usually refers to the wife's father-in-law, while γαμβρός to the husband's father-in-law (Kutsch, *TDOT*, 5:276). Lindars, followed by NRSV and NJB, inserts Hobab as haplography, but this is an unnecessary simplification, supplying information the audience was expected to know. *Preliminary and Interim Report* (2:70) allows two translations: the descendants of the Kenite <who was> Moses' father-in-law or the Kenites <who descended> from Moses' father-in-law. Rainey (*Sacred Bridge*, 134) creates a new text of vv 16–19 from the Septuagint: "the sons of Hobab the Kenite, Moses' father-in-law, went up from the city of Palms to the sons of Judah to the wilderness of Judah which is in the descent of Arad, and they went and lived with the Amalekites."

16.c. lxxᴬ reads πρὸς τοὺς υἱοὺς Ιουδα εἰς τὴν ἔρημον τὴν οὖσαν ἐν τῳ νότῳ ἐπὶ καταβάσεως Αραδ καὶ ἐπορεύθη καὶ κατῴκησεν μετὰ τοῦ λαοῦ, "to the sons of Judah to the wilderness which was in the south on the descent of Arad, and he went and lived with the people"; lxxᴮ reads μετὰ τῶν υἱῶν Ιουδα εἰς τὴν ἔρημον τὴν οὖσαν ἐν τῳ νότῳ Ιουδα ἥ ἐστιν ἐπὶ καταβάσεως Αραδ καὶ κατῴκησαν μετὰ τοῦ λαοῦ, "with the sons of Judah into the wilderness which was in the south of Judah that is on the descent of Arad, and he lived with the people." lxxᴬ thus has the Kenites come to Judah rather than with Judah and does not witness Judah in the description of the wilderness. The phrase מִדְבַּר יְהוּדָה, "Judean wilderness," without an introductory preposition is awkward in Heb., leading *BHS* to suggest deleting מִדְבַּר יְהוּדָה. Heb. apparently points to the Negev of Arad as a more definite part of the wilderness or desert of Judah.

16.d. Both Gk. witnesses point to the descent of Arad rather than the Negev or south of Arad (see Num 21:1; 33:40), leading to many scholarly hypotheses; see Lindars, 37–39. Apparently lxx did not understand ancient geography, for "descent of Arad" is not used elsewhere in мт or in lxx. However, νότῳ Ιουδα may represent a standard geographical term, the Negev of Judah (1 Sam 27:10; 2 Sam 24:7). Gk. may thus represent a reading of the text from a different geographical viewpoint.

16.e. Lit. "he went and lived with," another of the grammatical difficulties in this text, which switches from pl. to collective sg. with some regularity. lxxᴮ does not witness "and he went," thus ignoring a Heb. idiom (compare Gen 21:16; 38:11; Judg 8:29; 9:21; 1 Kgs 17:5).

16.f. Some witnesses to lxxᴮ and a few minor Heb. мss read Amalekites in apposition to "with the people." This leads many commentators, looking to 1 Sam 15:6, to substitute Amalekites for "with the people" (see BHS, cev, reb, nab, nrsv; *Preliminary and Interim Report*, 2:71; Barthélemy, *Critique textuelle*, 1:73–74; *Sacred Bridge*, 134). Lindars (39–40) gives reasons for rejecting the emendation, particularly the fact that the various proposals do not correspond to any surviving text.

17.a. lxxᴬ reads ἐπάταξαν, "they struck," while lxxᴮ reads ἔκοψεν, "he cut down." Two Heb. мss also read the sg., leading to the proposal to read the sg. here, but this goes against the sense of the text, which includes Simeon with Judah in the pl. subject.

17.b. lxxᴬ reads ἀνεθεμάτισαν αὐτὴν καὶ ἐξωλέθρευσαν αὐτὴν καὶ ἐκάλεσαν τὸ ὄνομα τῆς πόλεως Ἐξολέθρευσις, "they cursed (or devoted) it and completely destroyed it and called the name of the city Destroyed," while lxxᴮ reads ἐξωλέθρευσαν αὐτοὺς καὶ ἐκάλεσαν τὸ ὄνομα πόλεως Ἀνάθεμα, "they completely destroyed them, and he called the name of the city Accursed." OL has "completely destroyed and devoted it to the ban and called the name of the city Destroyed." Niditch (33) sees here more indication of oral tradition introducing alternate ways of expressing the same idea. Again the sg./pl. inconsistency of the text appears, giving rise to suggestions to read the pl. וַיִּקְרְאוּ, but this misses the emphasis on the action by Judah or can be explained, with Lindars (84), as an "inherent indefinite subject" often used with this verb. ἀνεθεμάτισαν αὐτὴν represents a double reading of the same Heb. verb and may incorporate a double tradition in the lxx renderings based on Num 21:3 (see Lindars, 85).

18.a. lxx (compare OL and мт of Josh 13:3; Judg 3:3) reads καὶ οὐκ ἐκληρονόμησεν, "and Judah did not inherit," leading *BHS* to read וְלֹא הוֹרִישׁ, parallel to v 18b. Lindars (42–44) sees Gk. as obviously original with мт rejected on literary and historical grounds, seeing vv 18 and 19 as contradictory in мт. Barthélemy (*Critique textuelle*, 1:74) rightly retains мт as obviously the most difficult reading.

18.b. Gk. and OL add Ashdod to the list of Philistine cities, an inclusion that Boling sees as original, lost by haplography. Lindars (85) more correctly attributes it to a glossator.

19.a. Tg. avoids literalism of God going with Judah by saying his arm accompanied them.

19.b. lxx reads ὅτι οὐκ ἐδύνατο κληρονομῆσαι τοὺς κατοικοῦντας τὴν κοιλάδα ὅτι Ρηχαβ διεστείλατο αὐτήν, "because he was not able to dispossess (lxxᴮ ἠδυνάσθησαν ἐξολεθρεῦσαι, 'they were not able to completely destroy') the residents of the valley because Rechab (Heb. *rekeb*) separated (or ordered) it (lxxᴮ 'them')." The addition of "were not able" clarifies a Heb. text that appears to require כְּלוֹ, "to be able" (found in a Heb. мs; compare GKC, §114l; Josh 17:12). But мт text can be interpreted as negating a gerundive use of the construct infinitive (R. J. Williams, *Hebrew Syntax*, § 397; compare Amos 6:10). Niditch (34) points to "this formulaic indicator of military inferiority" in Josh 17:16, 18 applied to Joseph. She sees this as a scribal error becoming "a new bit of narrative content. The resulting multiplicity is within the purview of an oral-world mentality."

19.c. lxx has garbled the last line, transliterating the Heb. רֶכֶב as "chariot" and apparently reading בַּרְזֶל, "iron," as הַבְדִּיל, "to separate." See Lindars, 85. Rainey (*Sacred Bridge*, 134) sees a contradiction between vv 18 and 19 and thus uses lxx to gain a new reading of these two verses: "Judah did not take

Gaza with its territory and Ashkelon with its territory and Ekron with its territory. Now YHWH was with Judah, and they took possession of the hill country, but they could not dispossess the inhabitants of the valley because they had iron chariots. Then they gave Hebron to Caleb, as Moses had promised, and he drove out from there the three sons of Anak." This simplifies the Heb. text, removing the more difficult reading, and making unnecessary harmonizations.

20.a. LXX^A reads "he"; the indefinite pl. subject here would seem to refer either to Judah and Simeon or to "the sons of Israel" of v 1. The Gk. sg. would make explicit the implicit action of God behind all this. Both Lindars (46) and Auld (*VT* 25 [1975] 273) interpret the impersonal plural as reference to God.

20.b. The *BHS* suggestion that perhaps several words have dropped out is based on Josh 11:21 or 15:13–14 but calls for unneeded harmonization. LXX^A reads ἐκληρονόμησεν ἐκεῖθεν τὰς τρεῖς πόλεις καὶ ἐξῆρεν ἐκεῖθεν τοὺς υἱοὺς Ενακ, "and he inherited from there the three cities, and he carried away from there the three sons of Anak," while LXX^B reads ἐκληρονόμησεν ἐκεῖθεν τὰς τρεῖς πόλεις τῶν υἱοῶν Ενακ, "he inherited from there the three cities of the sons of Anak," leading commentators such as Boling to accept LXX^A and see haplography causing the omission in MT. Lindars (46–47) shows the growth of the Gk. text. MT certainly represents the more difficult reading.

21.a. *BHS* proposes to read "sons of Judah" with Josh 15:63, based on a theory of literary copying and harmonizing that cannot be established for Judg 1. See Auld, *VT* 25 (1975) 274–75. Lindars (47) is more to the point in understanding the issue to be Jerusalem's inclusion in Benjaminite territory in contrast to Jerusalem's conquest by the tribe of Judah.

21.b. LXX^A reads ἐξῆραν, "did not carry away."

21.c. Several MSS read ישׁבי, which may be original but is the easier reading, whereas MT takes the היבוסי as collective. The disjunctive fronting of the direct object shows the contrast to the previous statements about Judah and Caleb.

21.d. LXX^A does not have "in Jerusalem."

22.a. LXX joins several Heb. MSS in reading בני, "sons of," for בית, "house of," harmonizing the usage to the rest of the chapter. MT represents the more difficult reading.

22.b. LXX^A and OL read, "Judah was with them," adopted by Boling as original, with MT repeating v 19 here, but that goes against the structure of the text that clearly separates the work of the northern tribes from that of the southern ones. Niditch sees this as a "common formulaic expression of God's approval and blessing," disrupted here, resulting in the enhancement of the human leader.

23.a. LXX^A reads "the house of Israel set up camp," while LXX^B reads "they set up camp and spied out Bethel," using the normal structure of battle narratives. OL has "and the sons of Israel began to fight." See Niditch (34), who sees the "interesting minor variations, typical of the sort of multiplicity available to the traditional storyteller."

24.a. LXX and OL read "and they took him and said to him," smoothing out the narrative. See Lindars, 54.

26.a. Some MSS "improve" the grammar by adding a preposition here; LXX follows its grammatical structure with εἰς here, but the more difficult MT may be retained.

26.b. LXX reads " built there (ἐκεῖ) a city," again smoothing the narrative flow. Lindars (86) sees a misplaced dittography from אֹתָה.

26.c. Some MSS add the sign of the direct object here.

27.a. LXX^B reads ἐξῆρεν, "did not carry away."

27.b. LXX (compare OL) reads Βαιθσαν ἥ ἐστιν Σκυθῶν πόλις, "Beth-shan, city of the Scythians." As Niditch (35) notes, "throughout 1:27–36 the traditions exhibit variations in the names assigned to places and in the number of towns named." Compare also Josh 17–19. Niditch correctly supposes that "such variations, no doubt, reflect differing views of geography and ethnography within these ancient traditions."

27.c. Lit. "and her daughters" consistently in this chapter; LXX adds "nor the open country," though the two versions use different Gk. words.

27.d. K here represents accidental loss of ', which must be read with Q, Heb. MSS, and versions.

27.e. For Ibleam, LXX^A reads καὶ τοὺς κατοικοῦντας Βαλααμ καὶ τὰς θυγατέρας αὐτῆς, "and the residents of Balaam and its daughters," while LXX^B reads τὸν κατοικοῦντα Βαλακ οὐδὲ τὰ περίοικα αὐτῆς οὐδὲ τὰς θυγατέρας αὐτῆς, "neither the residents of Balak nor its open country nor its daughters." Both are readings of Ibleam using an abbreviated version of the story of Balaam and Balak from Num 22.

27.f. LXX^A adds οὐδὲ τοὺς κατοικοῦντας Ιεβλααμ οὐδὲ τὰς θυγατέρας αὐτῆς, "nor the residents of Ibleam and its daughters," while LXX^B reads οὐδὲ τοὺς κατοικοῦντας Ιεβλααμ οὐδὲ τὰ περίοικα αὐτῆς οὐδὲ τὰς θυγατέρας αὐτῆς, "nor the residents of Ibleam nor its open country nor its daughters." Auld (*VT* 25 [1975] 279) may well be correct in seeing this as a "late 'correction' by an editor who had not realised that Balaam (A)/Balak (B) in fourth place render יבלעם in fourth place in the мт."

28.a. LXX reads φόρον, "tribute," its consistent rendering of Heb. מס, "corvée labor," each version using a different verb before the noun.

29.a. LXX adds ἐγένετο εἰς φόρον, "he came into tribute," apparently a dittography from the next verse if not an intentional paralleling to that verse.

30.a. OL reads Hebron for Kitron.

30.b. LXX^B reads Δομανα; see Lindars' explanation (86).

30.c. BHS suggests changing Heb. pl. to sg., but the text takes the grammatically sg. subject as a collective pl.

31.a. LXX adds καὶ ἐγένετο αὐτῷ εἰς φόρον καὶ τοὺς κατοικοῦντας Δωρ, "and he came under tribute to him, and the residents of Dor." Again the LXX appears to fill out texts from other contexts (vv 30 and 27, respectively).

31.b. LXX reads κατοικουντας Ααλαφ, "and the residents of Aalaph"; BHS suggests reading מַחֲלֵב on the basis of transposing two letters in Josh 19:29 and is supported by Lindars (65). Barthélemy (*Critique textuelle*, 1:58) finally concludes that in this confused situation it is better not to interfere with the мт. A firm decision here is impossible due to the frequent misunderstanding or reinterpretation of place names in the ongoing textual tradition.

31.c. LXX^A reads "and Akzib and Helba and Aphek and Roob," while LXX^B reads "and Askazi and Helbah and Nai and Ereo." BHS suggests deleting Helbah as dittography from Ahlab and is supported by Lindars (65).

31.d. אֲפִיק is spelled אֶפֶק in Josh 19:30.

32.a. LXX provides basis for inserting יְכֹל, "to be able," here, contrary to the structure of Judg 1. See Lindars, 66; Boling, 66.

33.a. Lit. "he lived"; LXX^A reads "Israel," while LXX^B reads "Naphtali."

34.a. BHS uses LXX, Syr., and Tg. along with LXX of Josh 19:47 to change נַחֲתוּם to נתנום.

35.a. LXX^A reads ἤρξατο ὁ Αμορραῖος κατοικεῖν ἐν τῷ ὄρει τοῦ Μυρσινῶνος οὗ αἱ ἄρκοι καὶ αἱ ἀλώπεκες, "The Amorites began to live in the mountain of the myrtle grove where there are bears and foxes," while LXX^B reads ἤρξατο ὁ Αμορραῖος κατοικεῖν ἐν τῷ ὄρει τῷ ὀστρακώδει ἐν ᾧ αἱ ἄρκοι καὶ ἐν ᾧ αἱ ἀλώπεκες ἐν τῷ Μυρσινῶνι καὶ ἐν Θαλαβιν, "The Amorites began to live in the mountain full of potsherds in which were the bears and in which were the foxes in the myrtle grove and in Thalabin." This represents a misunderstanding of the Heb. place names with attempts to translate some of them. See Lindars, 87. Niditch (35) sees an imaginative elaboration here.

35.b. LXX adds "on the Amorites" for clarity. BHS notes differing places in the text of this verse where a prepositional phrase is added to clarify the recipients of the powerful hand of Joseph.

36.a. LXX^A reads "and the coast of the Amorites the Edomite over the Akrabin on Petra (or the rock) and upward," while LXX^B reads "and the coast of the Amorites was from the ascent of Akrabin from Petra and upward." "The Edomite" may well have fallen out by haplography. BHS and Barthélemy (*Critique textuelle*, 1:75) adopt this as the correct reading, but Lindars is more on target, seeing it as a corrupt dittography in the Heb. text tradition. *Sela* and *Petra* both mean "rock" and refer to a mountain stronghold in Edom.

Form/Structure/Setting

The extent of the introductory section of Judges. Judg 1–2 opens the book to summarize briefly the history of Israel between the death of Joshua and the onset of kingship. Israel is presented as a loose federation of tribes. The body of the narrative will then give more details, backing up this summary report.

Current German scholarship has moved from documentary/source theories to highly involved redaction studies dividing the biblical structures into an almost infinite series of the work of editors, redactors, glossators, and later inserters. The supreme examples of this come from Kratz (*Composition*) and Rake. The latter reduces the primary narrative of chap. 1 to vv 1, 2a, 4a, 5, 6, 8b, 10a, 11, 19a, 21, 22, 23a, 24, 25, 26, 27, 29, 34a, 35, placing it in the Persian period ('*Juda wird aufsteigen!*'

156–57). The basic narrative of 2:1–5 from another hand involves only part of v 1 and 2a, the rest added by two subsequent editors. Space does not allow arguments against the several varieties of such work in each chapter. Rather, I simply do not see the presuppositions behind such work as valid. The process ignores the literary unity of biblical reports as displayed by modern literary critics and generally results in isolated sectors that do not represent complete narrative units or genres and that come from supposed dates far too long after the events reported to be anything but figments of an anonymous Hebrew scholar's imagination.

Other scholarly discussion centers on isolating the narrative breaks in this opening section. Does the first main narrative extend through 2:5, or does it end with the chapter break in 1:36? Does the parallel introduction beginning at 2:1 (or 2:6) extend through 3:6 or conclude at the end of chap. 2? The Hebrew syntax appears to help us answer these questions. As so often, conversation dominates much of the narrative, yet the major syntactical thread remains easy to follow. See table 1.1 in the appendix for an examination of the syntactical breaks in Judg 1.

Chap. 1 forms a complete narrative unit without 2:1–5. The major actor is Israel (1:1, 28). In 1:1 Judah leads Israel. In 1:28–33 syntax may tie Israel together with northern tribes. Mention of Joseph in 1:22 and 1:35 sandwiches all the northern action within the "house of Joseph" designation. Yahweh appears only in 1:1, 2, 4, 19, commissioning and bringing victory to Judah, and in 1:22, being present with Joseph, who then sends out spies to see how to win the battle with Bethel. Ironically, the military summary yields only three anecdotes: (1) The lord of Bezek confesses God's justice. (2) Caleb gains a wife for his daughter, who subtly takes center stage and gains from him an addition to her dowry. (3) Spies of the house of Joseph deal in covenant faithfulness with the informant from Bethel by letting him retreat to a foreign country and build a city rather than letting him become a part of their people as Joshua had with Rahab. The greatest irony comes at the end as the Amorites take center stage and the narrator lists their territory rather than that of Judah or Joseph, foreshadowing the stories to come when enemies continue to make inroads on Israelite territory. With this, the military story is complete.

Scholarly debate rages over the relationship of Judg 2:1–5 to what precedes and follows it. Noth saw this as a secondary Deuteronomistic addition (*Überlieferungsgeschichtliche Studien*, 9). Smend ("Gesetz und die Völker," 506–7, followed by Becker, *Richterzeit und Königtum*, 6) attributed its insertion along with chap. 1 to his Dtr^N, who did no editing on it. For Boling (30), Judg 2:1–5 serves as the introduction to the seventh-century Deuteronomistic framework, as opposed to those who identify chap. 1 as the introduction to the sixth-century edition. Auld ("Review of Boling's Judges: The Framework of Judges and the Deuteronomists," *JSOT* 1 [1976] 45) sees the entire outer framework of 1:1–2:5 and chaps. 17–21 as belonging to a post-Deuteronomistic Judean editor.

Webb ([1987] 102–3), followed by Younger (62, 73; "Judges 1," 215; and Dorsey, 105–6), argues that 2:1–5 is tied to chap. 1 by the appearance of the Hebrew verb עלה, "to go up"; by the parallel structure with 1:1–2; and by the reviewing of the going up in 1:3, 22. This structural assessment ignores the "going up" of the sons of the Kenite (v 16). Dorsey (105–6, n. 2) admits 2:1–5 could be seen as an independent unit or as part of the following. Webb (104) notes that the divine speech here "anticipates the divine speech in 2:20–22" and that the lapse into apostasy

(2:11–19) "is foreshadowed" in 2:3d. Webb thus unintentionally offers as much if not more evidence to tie 2:1–5 to the following verses than he does to tie the passage to the preceding chapter. Blum ("Kompositionelle Knoten," 192–93; compare Kratz, *Composition,* 208, 321) argues that 2:1–5 cannot be the conclusion to chap. 1, which separates Judges from the Hexateuch and belongs to a post-Deuteronomistic and postexilic editor. Van Seters (*In Search of History,* 341–42) joins 2:1–5 with chap. 1 but makes the verses part of the Priestly work.

Lindars sees Judg 1:1–2:5 as a "prelude" smoothing the transition from Joshua's conquest and land allocation to Judges' war stories. This prelude has three purposes: (1) 1:3–21 presents the story of Judah's conquests since Judah is the "first tribe to claim its territory in accordance with the list in Joshua 15"; (2) 1:22–36 prepares for the subsequent wars in Judges by showing the limits of Joshua's conquest; and (3) 2:1–5 prepares the reader for what happened after Joshua's time. This prelude is a literary "pastiche" (Lindars, 4–5) presupposing the lists of tribal territories in Josh 13–19. Vv 1–3 are modeled on the conquest of land by an imperial conqueror such as Cyrus, who then distributes the land to his lieutenants. Vv 4–7 reflect an underlying Judah tradition, while v 8 is an editorial insertion of another tradition taking Judah's campaign further south. V 9 then serves as a heading for the tradition of vv 10–16 (Lindars, 15–16). For Lindars, many archaic-appearing anecdotes actually are inserted by a "second hand of DtrN" that is "concerned to preserve these scraps of information by inserting them into appropriate parts of the tribal lists" (so Josh 15:13–19, 63; 16:10; 17:11–13; 19:47 and parallels in Judges). DtrN is responsible for links between the prelude and Judg 20. But this literary "pastiche" "has been carefully composed to achieve the two main purposes of bringing Judah into the history and preparing the reader for the situation presupposed in the following stories" (5–6). This Judahite bias comes from its setting in the exilic or early postexilic period. This prelude is intended "to give a fuller account of the circumstances of the period between the tribal assembly under Joshua and the end of the generation which outlived him" (6).

Guillaume (*Waiting for Josiah,* 113) separates the developmental history of Joshua and Judges, refusing to accept Noth's Deuteronomistic History. Thus Judg 2:1–5, along with the oldest parts of Joshua and Kings, belongs to the Josianic period and interprets the list of unconquered cities in chap. 1 in a negative light. This represents the third of Guillaume's (255) seven-stage history of the book reaching from 720 to 150 B.C.E.

Amit admits that 2:1–5 differs from chap. 1 in both content and form, but still connects the two, seeing the two connected by cause and effect so that 2:1–5 becomes a "summary of the results of non-possession and its conclusions" (*Book of Judges,* 152–53). Campbell connects 2:1–5 with chap. 1 but as "a somewhat disassociated explanation" (*Joshua to Chronicles,* 73). Somehow he sees two statements of Joshua's death bracketing 2:1–5, but the second statement occurs only in 2:8. Thus Campbell and O'Brien see 2:1–5 as a late independent insertion "to account for the situation portrayed in the traditions of 1:1–3:6" (*Unfolding the Deuteronomistic History,* 171).

Schneider (26–27) sees 2:1–5 as beginning a new unit, providing the background material for chap. 1, which set the stage for the major issues of the book, and introducing the characters and the new situation. McCann (27) thinks 1:1–2:5 presents a military introduction from Israel's perspective, while 2:6–3:6 introduces

God's perspective on religious failure. The problem here is that 2:1–5 deals with blatantly religious issues, particularly the covenant and altars and pagan gods. On the basis of Mullen (*HTR* 77 [1984] 33–54) and Stone ("From Tribal Confederation to Monarchic State," 190–259), Olson (732) portrays 1:1–2:5 as a new introduction drawing material from Joshua. Block (76) summarizes reasons for tying 2:1–5 to chap. 1 but then shows conclusively why 2:1–5 belongs with chap. 2: it uses theological language; the verses of Judg 2:1–23 are joined by a sequence of *wāw*-consecutive clauses; Judg 2:6–10 gives an exposition of 1:1a; and the speech in 2:20–22 is linked theologically and linguistically with 2:1–3.

Thus the first basic unit encompasses only chap. 1. Chap. 1 is closely tied, however, to the so-called second introduction of chap. 2 or 2:1–3:6.

This leads to the question of where this second introduction ends. Answering that question lets us determine how the two introductions are parallel and how they function individually and together. A complex syntax and narrative structure ties chap. 2 together. The narrative features first the messenger of Yahweh (vv 1–3), then the sons of Israel (vv 4–9), and then a new generation of sons of Israel (vv 10–23). Joshua, Yahweh, ancestors, and judges all appear in the narrative, but the focus remains on Israel.

Chap. 2 thus presents a contrast. First Yahweh appears as a messenger and promises to keep the covenant with Israel as he did with the first faithful generation. Then Israel is portrayed as an unfaithful nation who passed over or transgressed the covenant. The nations are set up as God's ploy to provide Israel an opportunity to keep or transgress covenant. Only chap. 2 in Judges mentions God's covenant. Chap. 2 plays on the work of Joshua, even ending the chapter with Joshua as an inclusio to 1:1. The divine speech in 2:20b–22 parallels similar vocabulary in the divine messenger's speech in 2:1–3.

Syntax separates 3:1 from chap. 2, using a disjunctive clause to introduce the exposition to a new narrative and a traditional opening formula to begin the new unit. Chap. 3 ignores Joshua. The transition in 3:7 is parallel to 2:11, requiring in both cases an expository introduction to set the stage. Finally, chap. 2 focuses on nations surrounding Israel, the residents of the land, plunderers, enemies, or nations Joshua left. Chap. 3 centers on specific nations and geographical regions: Canaan, Philistines, Sidonians, Hivites, Mount Lebanon, Mount Baal Hermon, Lebo-hamath, Hittites, Amorites, Perizzites, Hivites, Jebusites. Judg 3:1–6 functions in chap. 3 as 2:1–10 does in chap. 2, setting the stage for the action to follow, action that involves the geographical and national names. The structure of Judges then deals with 1:1–2:23 as a military and then religious introduction with 3:1–16:31 as the body of the narrative. (See the conclusive discussion by Block, 76–77, who argues for following the current chapter division and then in his commentary works with 1:1–3:6.)

I conclude then that the first segment of Judges comprises only the first two chapters. Chap. 3 begins the body of the narrative proper. Chap. 1 gives the military situation of Israel immediately after Joshua's death as a prologue to the military expeditions of the judges to follow. Chap. 2 gives the religious situation of Israel during the time of the judges and prepares for the divine punishment to come when the summary description becomes reality.

Supposed patterns in Judg 1. Judg 1 provides a most unusual narrative introduction to the entire book of Judges. Van Seters ("Deuteronomist from Joshua to Samuel,"

220) decides that "the fundamental problem of the Hexateuch is, perhaps, how to view Judg 1:1–2:5 and its relationship to what comes before and after it." Describing a "rather advanced historiography" here, Van Seters notes the ongoing difficulty of source attribution in light of the unity of the material, the impossibility of removing redactional frame material, and the lack of any clear historical genres. Van Seters (222) thus attributes both Josh 13–19 and Judg 1:1–2:5 to the same Priestly writer who intentionally repeated his account to emphasize that the land promise was not entirely kept. Comments about Jerusalem, Gezer, and forced labor come from the later Deuteronomistic Historian based on 1 Kgs 9:20–21.

Younger shows that genre analysis is not impossible, comparing Judg 1 with Assyrian summary inscriptions in contrast to Assyrian annalistic texts. Summary inscriptions are arranged geographically, not chronologically, and are shorter than the royal annals. Inscribed on a commemorative stele or a slab, these summaries contained four parts: "(a) a prologue, consisting of invocation to the gods and the king's titulature; (b) a geographically arranged summary of events; (c) the main section explaining the circumstances leading to the composition of the inscription, introduced by the formula *ina umeshuma* = 'at that time'; (d) an epilogue with maledictions" ("Judges 1," 211). Younger, however, does not, and probably cannot, show how Judg 1 relates to this form, as Niditch (36) also notes, pointing to the first-person form of the Assyrian materials. Rather, Younger is interested in parallel content items. He points to the tendency to summarize time in nonspecific and nonconcrete terms. Similarly Younger sees that Judg 1 "neutralizes and reshapes our very sense of time and distance," bringing together "under one umbrella events that are remote chronologically" and clothing "simultaneity in the guise of sequence" (219). He also describes how Assyrian materials show that certain battles are conquest battles whereas others simply soften the enemy up for later conquest. Judg 1 is thus presented as a second series of battles intended to subjugate or destroy an enemy Joshua previously softened up. Lindars sees this from another direction. He reads the material from a postexilic viewpoint and sees that "Joshua has acted like an imperial conqueror, Cyrus perhaps, who breaks the resistance of a whole nation and then divides the land among his lieutenants as their areas of rule" (10).

Niditch finds the closest parallel to Judg 1 in the journey reports of Num 21, which she describes as "a series of brief annals that reflect richer and fuller traditions about military encounters and their participants." But Num 21 as a whole is a journey report or itinerary, not a battle report. The battles described feature enemies attacking Israel, not Israel attacking enemies. The battle reports here are not tied to the form D. M. Gunn ("The 'Battle Report': Oral or Scribal Convention?" *JBL* 93 [1974] 513–18) finds in the books of Samuel. Rather, they do reflect the abbreviated skeletal form of a much richer tradition. (See B. O. Long, *I Kings*, 244: "A schematic recounting of a military encounter typically organized around the following elements: [1] the confrontation of forces, [2] the battle, [3] the consequences of battle, whether defeat or victory, usually with summarizing and characterizing statements.") Thus Niditch herself begins the paragraph describing Judg 1 as a "combination of brief battle reports in the third person, punctuated by vignettes related to the battles and their participants."

In his commentary, Younger, following Webb's study, has attempted to show patterns in this narrative. The first depends on repetition of the Hebrew verb

עלה, "to go up" (Judg 1:1–4, 16, 22; 2:1). Younger sees a chiastic pattern of asking Yahweh who will go up (v 1), Judah going up (v 2b), Joseph going up (v 22), and the messenger going up (2:1). It is a stretch to parallel Israel asking who will go up with the messenger going up. The pattern skips lightly over Simeon going up (v 3) and the sons of Kenite going up (v 16). It also ignores the causative form in 2:1 with Yahweh as subject. The pattern looks nice and offers a basis for teaching and preaching, but does not rest on firm enough evidence in the text.

Younger also notes the geographic pattern flowing from south to north. This has stronger foundations in the text, but it requires one to place Dan in the north with chap. 18, not in the west as in chap. 1 and in the Samson narratives. It also ignores in part the shifts to the east with Jephthah and to the west with Samson. Thus the pattern fits to an extent from the viewpoint of the monarchical author, not from the viewpoint of the historical context. See, in the Introduction, "The Immediate Context: The Structure of the Book of Judges."

Younger's third pattern he calls "moral movement" as he traces a moral decline in chap. 1. We shall certainly discover such a moral decline in the body of the book, but one has to stretch and ignore a bit to find the pattern here. What part do the Kenites living among the Judahites play in this pattern? Or Adoni-bezek in Jerusalem? Or Caleb's daughter in the Negev? How does the informant in Bethel relate to Canaanites living in the land in Manasseh? Is there a moral distinction in Israel becoming strong (v 28) and causing forced labor and the house of Joseph having a heavy hand and placing the Amorites into forced labor (v 36)? How does Zebulun (v 30) rate a place higher in the moral standard than does Naphtali (33) when both brought the enemy to forced labor, something not attributed to Ephraim at the head of the line nor to Asher just ahead of Naphtali? How is their ability as a tribe to cause corvée not somehow more enhanced than that of Manasseh and the house of Joseph who had to become strong before accomplishing this?

The pattern is solely based on who resided among whom. It works nicely at first glance; see table 1.2 in the appendix for an analysis of the tribal conquests and failures in Judg 1.

The pattern appears to be much more in the eye of the modern beholder than in the heart of the author/editor. This is especially the case when one looks at all the instances of ישׁב, "to reside, live," in this chapter. See table 1.3 in the appendix.

The use of ישׁב does not so much create a pattern of moral decline as it paints an absorbing portrait of continued Canaanite (Amorite) residence in the land. Repeatedly, the Canaanites are referred to as the residents of the land. Israel under Joshua may have conquered the land, but already in the first chapter of Judges that conquest is reversed. The conquered can only partially be dispossessed and only later be put under corvée control. Even Judah, the major victor here, fights battles where dispossession or victory is glaringly missing in the battle report. The report does not use moral terms to condemn Israel or any part of it. That will come in the next chapter. The report simply leaves the impression of extensive Canaanite presence, control, and power in the land Joshua left behind. What Josh 13:1 hinted at in saying "very much of the land still remains to be possessed" (NRSV), Judg 1 now makes explicit. God gave the whole land to Israel in battle (Josh 11:23) as an inheritance. When the aged Joshua died, the generation left behind did not finish the task of possession. Joshua softened the land up for inhabitance. Israel never followed up and subjugated much of the land until many generations after

Joshua. Judg 1 does not attribute blame. It simply reports the military status of the generation following Joshua.

The structure of Judg 1. Here the reading of the whole provides an introductory slant on the narrative different from simply listing its parts and their narrative genres. The parts can easily be distinguished by the abrupt change of subjects. Two major sections contain first a series of battle reports (vv 1–26) and then an annotated listing of tribal failures (vv 27–35). The two sections are not as clear-cut in content as the opening lines of each section might lead one to expect, and the content repeatedly invites comparison to other biblical literature dealing with similar content. Such intratextual analysis gives a different flavor to the overall purpose and setting of the reports. A flat first reading of Judg 1:1–26 appears to show that both Judah, the leading southern tribe, and the Joseph tribe(s), the leading northern tribe residing in central Palestine, accomplished their tasks, while all the rest of the tribes belong to the list of failures (vv 27–35). A closer analysis provides a structure more distinct than that provided by genre analysis.

The outline provided in my Introduction would seem to indicate that chap. 1 comprises three well-rounded narrative units: Judah's conquests (vv 1–20), the Rachel tribes' failures (vv 21–29), and the northern tribes' failures (vv 30–35), followed by a one-verse epilogue.

Strangely, this is precisely what does not appear. The depiction of Judah's conquest consists of a series of brief reports, not a connected narrative. The expected narrative summary conclusion appears in v 19 but leads immediately to negative results and an unexpected addendum. This alerts us that the book's opening narrative structure is fractured and that the observant reader should look for narrative dissonance more than for narrative symmetry in the book of Judges. Genres, narrative structure, and content combine to leave a negative impression.

As Lindars expresses it, Judg 1:1–21 "brings together some old traditions which the editor regarded as related to the conquests of Judah, but it is evident that there was no connected narrative source at his disposal. The available items are odd scraps of information" (9).

A quick look at the other two major sections echoes this conclusion. Content joins vv 21–29, since it deals with the closely related tribes of Benjamin and Joseph, the two sons of Rachel (Gen 30:24; 35:18), but no introduction or conclusion joins the narrative. Instead, a distinctive battle report is sandwiched among lists of negative results, and the house of Joseph suddenly splits into Ephraim and Manasseh. Vv 30–36 appear to continue the list of negative results, broadening it to include more than the house of Joseph, but the concluding epilogue (v 36) deals with the spread of Amorites rather than the results of Israelites. Thus we see a shot-gun narrative approach with little discernible order except for the south to north orientation. A look at the individual formal elements will enhance this impression.

The narrative elements of Judg 1. This narrative brokenness gains a clue in 1:1. This does not pretend to be a narrative beginning. It is a narrative continuation that mirrors the opening of Joshua, Joshua's name simply replacing Moses' name. Such mirroring causes one to compare further and see that the first purpose of Judg 1 is not to serve as an introduction to what follows. Rather it serves as a contrast to what precedes. This means that we must first read Judg 1 in its relationships to the book of Joshua before we too quickly rush ahead to see how it compares to the following narratives of Judges. The reader first notices apparently duplicate content in several places but with some strongly apparent discrepancies. The textual notes above seem to indicate that Judges knew at least some form of the material in Joshua and added notes for clarity while telling the story for its own purposes. It may well be that Joshua represents a northern version of the materials while Judges represents a southern rendition. This would fit with the oral tradition perspective Niditch represents in her commentary. See table 1.4 in the appendix for a comparison of Judges with Joshua.

Josh 1 reflects a divine military commission to Israel's new chosen leader calling for dedication to divine law and for immediate action. It shows immediate commitment on the part of the Israelite tribes to the new leaders. Judg 1 features human initiative rather than divine initiative. The human question appears to call for the name of an individual to lead the armies. Instead, Yahweh provides a tribe to lead as an example for the other tribes. This formal breakdown of an opening commissioning report gives the first hint that Judges is about separate tribal actions rather than about a united Israelite front. Israel has no individual leader; therefore, Israel has little national loyalty and little national military action.

Chap. 1 sets the stage for the book of Judges as a book of military confrontations between individual tribes or tribal coalitions and local enemies. Judah leads the first confrontation, to which it invites the tribe of Simeon (vv 3, 17—the only appearances of this tribe in the book). The "battle reports" that follow fit the terse description of Simon de Vries: "A schematic recounting of a battle encounter typically containing (1) the confrontation, (2) the battle, and (3) the consequences" (*1 and 2 Chronicles*, FOTL 11 [Grand Rapids: Eerdmans, 1989] 428). B. O. Long notes that "summarizing and characterizing statements" usually appear and that "often, the report will include a scene of consultation with priests for divine guidance" (*I Kings*, 293).

Judg 1:1–7, the first battle report, opens with the consultation but without mention of priests (v 2). The divine answer in v 2 is expressed by means of the typical "conveyance formula" (Long, *I Kings,* 320). A second "consultation" follows, but this is among humans rather than with God, the tribe of Judah inviting the tribe of Simeon to join in the battle (v 3). The battle description simply repeats the conveyance formula (v 4a) before the consequences are summarized (v 4b). V 5a expands the battle report slightly and is followed by another statement of consequences (v 5b). The battle is then described from yet another perspective, that of the capture of the enemy leader and his admission of the justice of the consequences (vv 6–7a). A final statement of consequences (v 7b) concludes this somewhat convoluted and ironic battle report.

A series of brief battle reports follows (vv 8–10) without repetition of the consultation. Then the narrative of Caleb, Othniel, and Achsah reappears (vv 10–15) almost verbatim from Josh 15:15–19, explaining the battle of Debir. In Joshua the Caleb narrative functions as part of the allotment-of-the-land theme of Josh 13–22 and of the Joshua-obeyed-God theme. Caleb is the leading actor in conquering Hebron and dispossessing Sheshai, Ahiman, and Talmai, identified specifically as descendants of Anak. Judges places the Caleb narrative squarely in the middle of an individual tribal battle report and in parallel to a similar report concerning the activities of the sons of the Kenite, Moses' father-in-law (v 16). Judges, in accord with its tribal theme, gives the tribe of Judah credit for taking Hebron. (See Younger,

"Judges 1," 226.) It then inserts, somewhat awkwardly, part of the Caleb narrative from Joshua. In Judg 1:11 MT reads וַיֵּלֶךְ מִשָּׁם אֶל־יוֹשְׁבֵי דְּבִיר, "and he went from there to the inhabitants of Debir,"with Judah the natural subject of the sentence. The parallel Josh 15:15 reads וַיַּעַל מִשָּׁם אֶל־יֹשְׁבֵי דְּבִר, "and he went up from there to the inhabitants of Debir," with Caleb the natural subject. Judges introduces Caleb a bit jarringly only in v 12. In so doing Judges transforms the story's genre from the battle report of its Joshua setting. Joshua easily accommodates the story to its allotment-of-the-land theme, showing that Caleb got the promised allotment and distributed it to his family. Judges stretches the story a bit to fit it into its battle-report context, for the story of the daughter's request has little place in a battle report. Rather, Judges makes two points. Judges introduces the battle hero—Othniel, the first and model judge (see Judg 3:9–11). Then it shows the controlling power of Achsah, Caleb's daughter and Othniel's wife, introducing the theme of the power and ability of women that will consistently reappear.

V 16 apparently introduces a travel report featuring the Kenites, who have Mosaic connections. This stands totally outside the battle-report context to incorporate Moses' people along with Caleb's into the tribe of Judah.

V 17 presents another brief battle report, this time explicitly involving the tribe of Simeon. V 18 is yet another battle report expanded to include three cities of the Philistines but contracted to eliminate any narrative information. V 19 provides a formulaic surprise. The assistance formula stating divine presence (see G. W. Coats, *Genesis*, FOTL 1 [Grand Rapids: Eerdmans, 1983] 320; Long, *I Kings*, 319) appears to introduce a summary formula of success (compare Gen 39:2, 21; Josh 6:27), but shifts suddenly to describe failure.

V 20 provides an unexpected addendum or correction to the previous Caleb narrative, adding the Mosaic component and providing an interesting, if inconclusive, conclusion to the narrative of the tribe of Judah.

V 21 employs the etiological formula עַד הַיּוֹם הַזֶּה, "until this day," creating an etiological motif rather than an etiological narrative (see Butler, *Joshua*, 28–30; B. O. Long, *2 Kings*, FOTL 10 [Grand Rapids: Eerdmans, 1991] 299). This is attached to the negative-results list, which itself employs a strange form. V 21 begins with the disjunctive וְאֶת־הַיְבוּסִי יֹשֵׁב יְרוּשָׁלַם, "the Jebusites, the inhabitants of Jerusalem," rather than with בְּנֵי בִנְיָמִן, "the sons of Benjamin," fronting and calling attention first to Jerusalem and its Jebusites, not to Benjamin. Again, content belies form. V 8 underlines this with its reference to Jerusalem in a victorious battle report. See also the *Comment* on vv 5–7. All this calls attention to Jerusalem, not to a tribe of Israel.

Vv 22–26 appear to constitute another battle report but again with a twist. What does גַּם־הֵם, "even they," indicate? Is this simply a literary way to include the house of Joseph in the list, or does it mean "even they," with a bit of irony—adding them to the list despite the readers' expectations? (Compare 1 Sam 14:15, 21–22; Jer 12:6.) The battle report breaks off, and the divine-assistance formula appears. This gives way to an introduction to an Israelite spy narrative. (See Butler, *Joshua*, 29–30; S. Wagner, "Die Kundschaftergeschichten im Alten Testament," *ZAW* 76 [1964] 255–69.) The spy narrative develops intrigue as a native accomplice turns informant. The Israelite spies promise to deal with the informant with חֶסֶד, "covenant faithfulness, loyalty, grace," the only time in the book such behavior is even suggested, behavior central to the Israelite covenant (compare 8:35). The addition to the battle report shows that the Israelites treat this native inhabitant with covenant faithfulness, allowing him to go free. In so doing they ignore the holy war commandments of their God. A final etiological motif rounds off the narrative.

Negative-results lists complete the remainder of the chapter (vv 27–35), but each has its own nuance. The first list points to the dogged determination of the Canaanites to live in the land despite Israelite efforts. Does this represent a progression from v 21, where the Jebusites live with the Benjaminites in Jerusalem? Vv 29–30 repeat the situation of v 21, Canaanites living among the Israelites. Vv 32–33 change that, for Asherites and Naphtalites live among Canaanites. V 34 advances a step further. Amorites defeat Danites and push them off their allotted territory. Here the determination of the Amorites rounds off the narrative form, repeating the situation and language of v 27. But eventually, both groups of determined people face corvée labor under Israelite rule. The conclusion (v 36) has nothing to say about Israel. The Amorite boundaries are traced, in contrast to the extensive tracing of Israelite boundaries in Josh 13–21.

The broken narrative structure, repetitive content, and emphasis on Canaanites, Jebusites, and Amorites reveals a literary artistry that suits form to content and uses formal breakdown to alert the reader to national breakdown.

Comment

1–3   The opening of Judges imitates that of Joshua (1:1) and will be repeated in 2 Sam 1:1 to provide periodization for the narratives. The editor sees Israel's history in four stages: the Mosaic period, the Joshua period, the period without a king, and the royal period introduced by David. Only the period of the book of Judges does not mention a new leader. This hints at the problems to come. Israel faces a new national era without a national leader. This opening verse also anticipates the ending of Judges, where in a last desperate effort to maintain national unity the tribes inquire of Yahweh whether they should fight Benjamin (20:23, 27–28). Battle situations often formed the backdrop for Israel's leaders to inquire of the Lord (1 Sam 23:2, 4; 30:8; 2 Sam 2:1; 5:19, 23), so that Fuhs sees this as the original setting for the language (*ThWAT,* 7:921). Apparently priests normally made such inquiry (1 Sam 22:10), following a practice of religions around the world (compare Fuhs, *ThWAT,* 7:920). Answers came in different manners (1 Sam 28:6). The expression can substitute אלהים (Elohim) for the divine name יהוה (Yahweh) (Judg 18:5; 20:18; 1 Sam 14:37; 22:13, 15; 1 Chr 14:10). Interestingly, the expression שאל ב יהוה, "inquire of Yahweh," occurs only in the judges, Saul, and David narratives, apparently pointing to an old priestly practice at sanctuaries that finally gave way to seeking God's word from the prophet (Fuhs, *ThWAT,* 7:922; compare *HALOT,* 4:1372). The call for Judah to go up first takes up the theme of Judah's leadership from Gen 49:8–10 and Num 10:14 (see Olson, 736).

Judges uses בני ישראל, "sons of Israel," "Israelites," sixty-one times in fifty-six different verses to refer to the nation; an interesting lacuna occurs between chaps. 12 and 19, where the term appears only in 13:1 before resuming its regular appearance in 19:13. Joshua and Judges have 118 occurrences. This usage alone indicates the importance of all Israel to the book of Judges. The work of individual tribes may be described, but the underlying understanding is that the work of a tribe or tribes is simply part of the work of all Israel.

The Israelites ask God who will lead the way in fighting the Canaanites. This unites Israel's opponents under one title rather than enumerating them in the long list of peoples familiar in the book of Joshua (3:10; 9:1; 11:3; 12:8; 24:11) but comparable to the descriptions in the distribution-of-the-land narrative (Josh 13–22). Despite the efforts of many modern scholars such as N. P. Lemche (*The Canaanites and Their Land: The Tradition of the Canaanites,* JSOTSup 110 [Sheffield: JSOT Press, 1991]) to "vaporize the Canaanites and to erase the land of Canaan from the map" (A. F. Rainey, *BASOR* 304 [1996] 1), Canaan was a significant geographical and ethnic term for Israel and her contemporary nations reaching back to 3000 B.C.E. or even before. Rainey includes a map (compare the physical description by K. N. Schoville, "Canaanites and Amorites," in *Peoples of the Old Testament World,* ed. A. J. Hoerth et al. [Grand Rapids: Baker, 1994] 161; compare map 27, in T. Brisco, *Holman Bible Atlas* [Nashville: Broadman & Holman, 1998] 58) showing the land of Canaan stretching from Mount Hor on the northern Mediterranean coast through Lebo to Ziphron and Hazar-enan in the northeast. The eastern boundary runs due south from Hazar-enan and turns westward to a point just south of the Sea of Galilee, where it runs southward along the Jordan River just east of Beth-shan. The southern boundary is not shown but now appears in *Sacred Bridge,* 34. It runs from Zoar at the end of the Dead Sea between Kadesh and Hazar-addar to the Brook of Egypt that empties into the Mediterranean (compare Gen 10:15–19; Josh 13:3).

Scholars continue to dispute the origin and meaning of the term *Canaan.* A. H. W. Curtis ("Canaanite Gods and Religion," *DOTHB,* 132) gives the simplest definition: "the Canaanites are the pre-Israelite inhabitants." Schoville ("Canaanites and Amorites," 159) opts for "Sundowners, Westerners," following M. C. Astour ("The Origin of the Terms 'Canaan,' 'Phoenician,' and 'Purple,'" *JNES* 24 [1965] 346–50). H.-J. Zobel (כנען, *TDOT,* 7:215) sees a relationship to the West Semitic term for "merchant," though the land name may have come from being associated with merchants or merchants may have derived their occupational title because Canaan was their home. This follows B. Mazar (Maisler) ("Canaan and the Canaanites," *BASOR* 102 [1946] 7–12) and R. de Vaux ("Le pays de Canaan," *JAOS* 88 [1968] 23–30). The Canaanites, according to Lindars (12), cannot be connected with purple-dye merchants as long thought (see B. Landsberger, "Über Farben im Sumerisch-akkadischen," *JCS* 21 [1967] 167–68) but may be "lowlanders" and lowly servants (Gen 9:25–27). (See Millard, *POTT,* 34.) Canaanites are inhabitants of the region, not an ethnic group. D. T. Tsummura ("Canaan, Canaanites," *DOTHB,* 123) believes the etymology and meaning of *Canaanite* to be obscure without much basis for "merchant," "blue-dyed cloth," or "bend/bow" and thus "low." The Bible traces Canaanites back to a grandson of Noah placed under a curse because his father disgraced Noah (Gen 9:18–27; compare 10:15). Canaan was the land promised to Abraham (Gen 12:1–7).

In light of Joshua's death, one would expect the answer to the question of who will lead Israel to be an individual. The narrator's unexpected answer names a tribe, not an individual. The tribe is Judah, the same tribe chosen to lead the fight against Benjamin in Judg 20:18. Elsewhere a fighting force from Judah appears only in Judg 15:9–11, where Judah complains to Samson about his making the Philistines angry. The Ammonites attack Judah in Judg 10:9. Thus Judah sandwiches the delivery stories of the book without playing a significant role in them. Judah is the southernmost tribe, descended from the fourth son of Leah (Gen 29:31–35).

נָתַתִּי אֶת־הָאָרֶץ בְּיָדוֹ, "I gave the land into his hand," represents the "conveyance formula" (B. O. Long, *2 Kings*, 320). It "occurs in military and legal settings and signifies the delivery or abandonment of a person(s) or matter into the power of another (M. A. Grisanti, נתן, *NIDOTTE*, 3:210). (Compare Deut 19:12; 2 Sam 10:10; 1 Chr 19:11; Jer 26:13; 38:16). It is particularly significant with God as the subject (Deut 7:24; 21:10; Josh 2:24; 21:44; Judg 3:8; 11:21; 18:10). The formula can also have other gods as subject (Judg 16:23–24). Israel's faith centered on God's acts for his chosen people. Other nations also attributed historical direction to their gods as B. Albrektson (*History and the Gods* [Lund: Gleerup, 1967]) has shown. Still, Israel stands alone in its choosing of historical narrative as the form for the central section of its religious literature and historical recitation as the content for a significant part of the non-narrative literature. Israel tells its history not as human achievement but as divine gift.

Another surprise appears. Judah does not immediately assume leadership of the twelve tribes and go to battle with the Canaanites. Instead, Judah calls on Simeon for help, while apparently ignoring the other tribes. Simeon is pictured as a southern tribe bound within Judah (Josh 19:1–9) and is grouped with Benjamin and Judah in the allocation of priestly cities (Josh 21:4, 9–19). Simeon is grouped with the larger southern constellation of "blessing" tribes in Deut 27:12. The smallest of the tribes in Num 26, Simeon has only 22,200; Ephraim, the next smallest, has 32,500; while Judah, the largest, has 76,500. Simeon has decreased from 59,300 (Num 2:12–13). In 1 Kgs 11:26–40, Judah and Benjamin form the southern kingdom, so Simeon must be connected to the north (compare 2 Chr 15:8–9; 34:6). Simeon and Levi seem to have northern connections in Gen 34:25–31 and 49:5–7, both referring to their battling Shechem. Ezekiel's ideal Israel has Simeon bordering Benjamin and Issachar. Thus, through history, Simeon was apparently aligned with different tribes for different purposes.

4–7 Judah goes to battle with no mention of Simeon. No battle is reported. Rather the conveyance formula (compare Deut 3:3; Josh 2:24; 21:44; Judg 3:10, 28; 4:14; 7:15; 8:7) stresses divine, not human, action (see B. O. Long, *2 Kings*, 320).

The Perizzites appear in twenty-one of the twenty-seven lists of pre-Israelite inhabitants of Canaan. Their pairing with the Canaanites here and in Gen 13:7 and 34:30 in two-name lists may suggest these two groups include larger groups of peoples (S. A. Reed, "Perizzites," *ABD*, 5:231; compare T. Ishida, "The Structure and Historical Implications of the Lists of Pre-Israelite Nations," *Bib* 60 [1979] 461–90). God promised Abraham their land (Gen 15:20). Perizzites are not mentioned outside the Bible (Lindars, 16) unless the term appears in a mention of Perizzi (or the Perizzite) as a representative of Tushratta of Mitanni in the Amarna Letters (Lindars, 16). This would connect the Perizzites to the Hurrians. Lindars prefers to connect them with the Hebrew term referring to those who live in unwalled settlements (Deut 3:5; 1 Sam 6:18; Esth 9:19; compare Judg 5:7, 11; Ezek 38:11; Zech 2:8). Josh 11:3 and 17:15 locate them in the hill country. The Perizzites would then be the rural population of the hill country as opposed to "successful invaders of an earlier time who lived in the cities" (Lindars, 17). They stood among the peoples God commanded Israel to "utterly annihilate" (Deut 20:17, NET).

Josh 11:8–9 reports victory over them as part of a Hazor coalition (compare 12:8; 24:11). Still, Perizzites remained, and Israel settled down among them (Judg 3:5). Solomon eventually subjected them to forced labor (1 Kgs 9:20–21).

Bezek is modern Khirbet Ibzik or nearby Khirbet Salhab, whose archaeological remains fit the biblical narratives better (A. Zertal, "Bezek," *ABD*, 1:17–18). These sites are twelve miles (19.3 km) northeast of Shechem, thirteen miles (20.9 km) southwest of Jabesh-gilead, and nine miles (14.5 km) north of Tirzah. There Saul mustered and counted his troops on the way to deliver Jabesh-gilead (1 Sam 11:9) and traveled on the road that led from Shechem through the eastern valleys of Manasseh to the Jordan.

If this is the correct location for Bezek, it brings mystery into the narrative. Why were Judah and Simeon so far north? Block (89), Lindars (17), and Boling (55) seek another location near Jerusalem, perhaps Khirbet Bizqa near Gezer. Gaß (*Ortsnamen*, 10–11) says ceramic evidence points only to the seventh century B.C.E. The name may have moved there from Khirbet Salhab. Gaß entertains the possibility that the biblical author has projected later conditions and names back into the earlier period. Lindars (9) says the battle at Bezek was inserted here because it points forward to the capture of Jerusalem. Does this narrative join with Judah's attack on Jerusalem (v 8) to illustrate Judah's true leadership of all Israel as v 1 indicated?

Adoni-bezek means either "My Lord, Bezek" or "the lord of Bezek." For Lindars (15), *Adoni-bezek* is the corruption of a theophoric name (one which describes a god), the divine name (possibly Adoni-zedek of Josh 10) being replaced by the geographical name central to this tradition. It may be a title rather than a name, indicating the ruler of Bezek. For the narrative, Adoni-bezek is strong enough that he can claim to have conquered seventy kings and that his defeat is a defeat of both Canaanites and Perizzites. This is the first king mentioned in the book of Judges, a book about the disintegration of leadership. His confession of failure shows that improper, Canaanite kingship is not the type Israel wants. Niditch says the narrative is not about Israelite or Judean triumphalism but a "warning colored with pathos about the vagaries of power" (40). That is certainly one implication from the story, but the material still features Judah and its victorious leadership.

Rainey sees Bezek as too small for such a conflict and suspects "a veiled allusion to some phase in the conquest of the Jerusalem area" (*Sacred Bridge*, 134). For Lindars, Adoni-bezek is king of Jerusalem (v 8), not of Bezek, which is only a battleground in the story (compare Rainey). In some way the defeat of Adoni-bezek gave Judah an entrée to Jerusalem that even Joshua had not obtained (Josh 15:63; compare 12:10), though Lindars sees Adoni-bezek's own soldiers taking him back to Jerusalem. Certainly the Hebrew narrator saw his own Israelite people in action here, entering Jerusalem for the first time, apparently delivering one of Jerusalem's allies back to them to foreshadow things to come for Jerusalem. As Joshua defeated a Jerusalem-led coalition (Josh 10:3–23), so now Judah enters Jerusalem with the beshamed Canaanite partner.

Cutting off "thumbs and big toes" brings "savage and vindictive humiliation" and reflects a widespread ancient custom witnessed in sources from Mari to Persia and Arabia to Greece to Hannibal (Lindars, 18). Here Younger finds parallels to reports in the Assyrian Annals ("Judges 1," 226; compare E. Bleibtreu, "Grisly Assyrian Record of Torture and Death," *BAR* 17 [1991] 52–61). Seventy is "the indefinite large number of saga" (Gray) seen in many passages (Exod 24:2; Num 11:16ff.; Judg 8:30; 9:2, 5, 56; 12:14; 2 Kgs 10:1ff.). The mutilated kings are presumably chieftains of clans which posed a threat to Adoni-bezek's expansion of his local hegemony.

God (אלהים, "Elohim") in the present context certainly refers to Yahweh, the God of Israel, but on Adoni-bezek's lips could have referred to his own pagan god. The story thus illustrates the power and justice of Israel's God in dealing with Canaanite enemies. He is doing no more to them than they have done to their own enemies. But their kind of kingship leads eventually to receiving the same punishment they have dished out. It is not Israel's kind of kingship.

8   The following verses combine battle reports, an anecdote from Joshua, and a negative note on Benjamin to show Judah's superiority to Benjamin and its qualifications to lead Israel. Again Judah does Joshua one better, burning Jerusalem. This does not need to be seen as some kind of literary doublet to Josh 10 or as a literary invention. Nothing indicates Judah exercised political control or even dispossessed the inhabitants of Jerusalem. As Matthews sees it, "Judah's action in the Judges account might be better understood as a raid" (40). For Judges, this stands in stark contrast to Benjamin's abject failure here (v 21) when Jerusalem belonged in Benjamin's territory (Josh 18:28).

9–10   Judah then retraces Joshua's route into the hill country, the Negev, and the Shephelah (Josh 10:40). Judah has thus led Israel just as Joshua did and even better, successfully entering and raiding Jerusalem.

The story centers not on capturing cities but on defeating Canaanites. The major example is the city of Hebron or, as earlier named, Kiriath-arba, literally, "the city of the four," but taken as a proper name for the father of Anak (Josh 14:15; 15:13; 21:11). Niditch (40) sees the possibility of reference to four locations: Aner, Eshcol, Mamre, and Hebron (compare J. M. Hamilton, *ABD*, 4:84).

Joshua obediently destroyed the city (10:37; 11:21). Hebron's history reaches back prior to 3000 B.C.E. and includes strong patriarchal ties (Gen 13:18; 23:1–20; 25:9–10; 35:27–29; 37:14; compare chap. 18). A Levitical city (Josh 21:11–13), it became David's first royal residence (2 Sam 2:3–11).

Num 13:22 says Hebron was founded seven years before Tanis. A stele of Seti I (about 1330 B.C.E.) was found at Tanis but may have been carried there from Qantir. Rainey (*Sacred Bridge*, 132) says Tanis is first mentioned in the twenty-third year of Rameses XI of Dynasty XX (c. 1076 B.C.E.). Rainey concludes that "in the eyes of the narrator (or annotator) the presence of the sons of Israel in the Kadesh area was during the last days of the XXth Dynasty" (119). F. F. Bruce (*Baker Encyclopedia of Bible Places*, ed. J. J. Bimson [Grand Rapids: Baker, 1995] 152; compare Lindars, 23) sees the Numbers mention as reference to a rebuilding of Hebron in the eleventh century. Hebron was earlier called Kiriath-arba (Gen 23:2) and Mamre (23:19).

Judah only kills the three heroes: Sheshai, Ahiman, and Talmai—the three leaders of the Anakim, a people noted for their gigantic size who cast fear into the Israelites (Deut 1:28; 9:2)—whom Moses had found there (Num 13:22) and Caleb dispossessed (Josh 15:14). Younger has shown that the attempt to see contradictions here goes against normal historical writing since "credit in battle can be and often is given to individuals, regiments, and/or generals" ("Judges 1," 226). He might have added "or to nations." Judah acts as and for the entire nation in subduing the leaders of Jerusalem and Hebron, the two cities most important to David in acquiring his kingship (Weinfeld, "Judges 1.1–2.5," 392; Matthews, 40).

11–15 A major task for understanding the nature of Judges involves relating these Calebite traditions (vv 11–15, 20) with those in Josh 15:13–19. The two traditions agree in connecting Caleb with the tribe of Judah and with the Kenizzites. The two passages agree word for word except for the opening verb, Judges identifying Othniel as the youngest brother of Caleb, and Judges inserting the name Caleb in v 15. The last two are obviously clarifications made in the Judges text, which is thus copying the Joshua original. If that is the case, then one wonders why the historian would insert the text here, knowing its original context in Joshua. The answer is complex but has mostly to do with the literary intention of Judges. Judges is not trying to place material in chronological order; this is obvious from the geographical rather than chronological order of the rest of the chapter and especially of chaps. 17–21 with mention of immediate descendants of Moses and Aaron. See Introduction, "Introduction to Chronology of Judges."

Obviously the editor of Judges expects the reader to know the story of Caleb and Achsah from knowing the book of Joshua. He could easily rephrase the narrative as he has done with the Hebron materials from Josh 14. Instead, he quotes Joshua word for word, even retaining in Judg 1:11 the מִשָּׁם ("from there") from Joshua (15:15), which, in the Judges narrative, ties the Debir narrative in close consecution to the exploits of the tribe of Judah.

Niditch sees the story following "the traditional pattern that links the fighting of enemies with the exchange of women" (40). In Judges she argues that the story becomes a comment on the "serendipitous nature of power and on the capacity of unexpected ones to take control" (41). The editor must want the audience to read this as a "remember when" narrative even though no syntactical markers indicate this. Amit must be right in saying that Judg 1 "proves to the reader how important it was for the editor of the exposition to stress the [sic] Judah's part in the act of conquest" (*Book of Judges*, 129–30). The tradition already showed a major act by a family connected to the tribe of Judah, and the editor picked this up to remind the audience of that heroic part. As Schneider puts it, the "text focuses on the new situation in Judges where the focus and answer to the call for leadership is Judah" (9).

Debir was originally Kiriath-sepher or "city of the book" or "city of scribes." It served as a Levitical city (Josh 21:15). Gaß (*Ortsnamen*, 25–30) offers four possible sites: edh-Dahariye, Tell Beit Mirsim, Tell Tarrame, and Khirbet er-Rabud, pointing to the last as the seemingly assured site. Niditch (40) still sees the site as undetermined.

The story itself is full of irony and humor (see T. Butler, *Joshua*, 185–86; see the variety of possible interpretations of the narrative and its parts in Fewell, "Deconstructive Criticism"). For Judges it not only emphasizes the role of Judah, but it also highlights the strength of the female character and prepares the way for Othniel to be Israel's first judge (3:9). Schneider goes so far as to call Achsah "a model to which other women's situations in Judges are evaluated" (17). Caleb's oath before battle may also prepare the way for Jephthah's oath in 11:30–31 and the Israelites' oath in chap. 20.

16 The narrator connects Judah to the Moses tradition by incorporating the Kenites as part of Judah. In so doing he prepares for the appearance of the

Kenites in chap. 4–5 with Deborah and Barak, and possibly for the father-in-law narrative of chap. 19. The Kenites not only go with Judah; they also settle down with Judah. Niditch thinks that "as in any folk tadition, details vary and sometimes contradict one another" (41).

The early translations added a name for Moses' father-in-law, but the writer of Judges presupposes the readers know the name. Exod 3:1, 4:18, and 18:1–27 identify him as Jethro, the priest of Midian who lived in the desert near the holy mountain, called Horeb. Exod 2:18 and Num 10:29 identify him as Reuel, again a Midianite. Judg 4:11 names him Hobab, who appears to be the brother-in-law in Num 10:29. Apparently Kenites originally allied themselves with the Midianites but then later with the tribe of Judah. They moved from the southern wilderness to Jericho—the City of Palms six miles (9.6 km) north of the Dead Sea—to the Judean Negev of Arad. In the Deborah narrative, a family of Kenites had moved much farther north. Apparently the Kenite clans were loosely tied together and could make individual political and religious treaties with other clans and nations, and apparently Moses' father-in-law was known by various names in different Hebrew circles.

17 Judah completes a task with a long history in Israel's traditions. Hormah first represented Canaanite victory over Israel (Num 14:40–45; Deut 1:41–46) and then fulfillment of a vow after defeat by the king of Arad (Num 21:1–3). Joshua listed it among his victories (Josh 12:14) and allotted the city to Simeon (Josh 19:4) within the allotment of Judah (Josh 15:30). The city became an important ally for David (1 Sam 30:30). Judges thus credits Judah with final victory over the city, preparing it for the connection with David, the king. Hormah's location is debated. Rainey (*Sacred Bridge*, 122) places it at Tell el-Khuweilfeh after listing four other possibilities. Negev (*AEHL*, 177) opts for Tell el-Meshash, eight miles (12.9 km) southeast of Beersheba. Gaß (*Ortsnamen*, 47) uses biblical information to isolate a position for Hormah on the border of Judah and Simeon near Ziklag in the Negev and near the wilderness. Having looked at other possible locations, Gaß (*Ortsnamen*, 57) agrees with Rainey.

Since the city is in Simeon's territory, Simeon joins Judah for this battle. Judah's cooperation with Simeon has nothing to do with disobedience to God's call to lead, as many recent commentators assume (see Klein, *Triumph of Irony*, 23; Younger, 65; Hess, "Judges 1–5," 143–44; Matthews, 38). It simply shows Judah's leadership ability over the smaller tribe living within its boundaries. Simeon represents a model for what happens to tribes who follow Judah. Mullen (*HTR* 77 [1984] 33–54) points out that, unlike the northern tribes, Judah was God's elected leader, followed God's orders in devoting a city to the ban (v 17), and carried out Moses' promise (v 20). Judah also prepared the way for David by making the first inroads on Jerusalem, killing the fearful and fabled leaders of Hebron, incorporating the Mosaic family into its midst, incorporating Hormah into Judean territory, capturing the Philistines and thus preparing the way for David's final capture of them, and doing everything possible with God's presence. The editor also reminds his audience that the faithful spy Caleb, who had assured the conquest of Debir and thus brought Israel's first judge to the forefront, also belonged to Judean tradition.

18–20 Gaza, Ashkelon, and Ekron were three of the five major Philistine cities (the other two being Ashdod and Gath). Philistines sailed from the Aegean area (Amos 9:7 and Jer 47:4 trace them to Caphtor or Crete), destroying cities along the Mediterranean coast and finally settling on the southeastern coast of Canaan. Between 1200 and 1150 b.c.e. they destroyed Canaanite cities and Egyptian strongholds, replacing them with even larger Philistine settlements. Egypt under Rameses III planted military outposts in the proximity of the Philistine settlements. The Philistines incorporated Canaanite population into their urban centers and gradually modified their Aegean material cultural elements under the influence of Canaanite patterns. Two things they did not modify were a preference for pork and a refusal to be circumcised. Their preference of goddesses also gradually incorporated Canaanite gods such as Baal and Dagon into their pantheon. The Philistines perpetually opposed Israel's military, political, and religious plans. Though these five cities had similar ethnic connections, the amount of political unity or cooperation can be debated since most sources, biblical and extrabiblical, show independent city-states with their own rulers (Hebrew סֶרֶן used only for Philistine rulers; Josh 13:3; Judg 3:3; 16:5, 8, 18, 23, 27, 30; 1 Sam 5:8, 11; 6:4, 12, 16, 18; 7:7; 29:2, 6–7; 1 Kgs 7:30; 1 Chr 12:19 [Heb. 12:20]).

Joshua left the Philistine cities as territory that remained to be conquered (Josh 13:3). Between 1150 and 1050 b.c.e. the Philistines used Egyptian weakness to expand their territory, reaching north to Tel Aviv, east into the Shephelah, and southeast into the Wadi Gaza and the Beer-sheba basin. During this period they built Tell Qasile and forced the people of Dan to give up their attempts to settle on the coast and to migrate to the north as seen in Judg 17–18. The Philistines even expanded into the hill country (1 Sam 10:5; 13:3, 11; 2 Sam 23:13–14), where they met Saul and then David. David first made an alliance with the ruler of Gath and by 975 b.c.e. established control over the Philistines.

The editor of Judges emphasizes that Judah, the tribe of David, led the way in establishing a beachhead against Israel's strongest opponents, the Philistines. Even the early translators questioned this, as seen in the lxx's use of ἐκληρονόμησεν, which normally renders a form of Hebrew נחל, "inherit,"or ירש, "possess, dispossess," in Judges but nowhere renders לכד, "captured," which is always rendered by a form of καταλαμβάνω or συλλαμβάνω. lxx thus used the information of Josh 13 that the Philistine cities were not seized or disinherited from Philistines to Israelites and interpreted Judg 1:18 in the same light, inserting the negative (see Rainey, *Sacred Bridge,* 134, for a defense of lxx as original). We have no way of knowing the tradition or narrative behind the Judges report. It is not beyond the realm of reason that Judah was able to make successful raids on these cities as well as on Jerusalem. It is interesting that the earliest stage of Philistine settlement with Mycenaean IIIC1b pottery is in the southern cities up to Ekron (Rainey, *Sacred Bridge,* 134), precisely the area mentioned in Judg 1:18, so that this could represent an early clash between newly appearing Philistines and Israelites. (See Block, 99.) As Olson concludes, this text "corresponds to the note in Josh 15:45–47 that these cities were part of the inheritance of the tribe of Judah" (739). This is also the area of the Samson narratives, as Hamlin (35) and Schneider (18) point out. (For further information on Philistines, see L. E. Stager, *The Oxford History of the Biblical World,* ed. M. D. Coogan [New York: Oxford UP, 1998] 152–75; R. Drews, "Canaanites and Philistines," *JSOT* 81 [1998] 39-61; C. S. Ehrlich, "Philistines," *DOTHB,* 782–92, and bibliography listed there.)

Judah's unique success as compared with the other tribes has one explanation: Yahweh was present "with Judah," allowing Judah to take possession of the hill country from its original inhabitants. This points back to Josh 6:27 to show that Judah maintained the true tradition connected with Joshua and points ahead to Judg 1:22. (For the tradition history and use of the formula, see H. D. Preuss, *TDOT,* 1:449–63.) The second half of v 19 has occupied and troubled scholars for several reasons. First, it indicates that the Iron Age (ca. 1200–586 B.C.E.) has begun in Palestine. (See Block, 99–100; P. M. McNutt, *The Forging of Israel: Iron Technology, Symbolism, and Tradition in Ancient Society,* JSOTSup 108 [Sheffield: Almond, 1990].)

Second, it distinguishes Israelite culture from that of its neighbors. (See Hackett, "There Was No King in Israel," 193–207, for discussion of the cultural change and contrasts.) Third, it shows military advances in technology as iron is used to strengthen the axle and wheel base of the wooden chariots. Note that R. Drews (*JSOT* 45 [1989] 15–23) points to a much later date, either to Assyrian chariots with bronze wheels or to Persian chariots with iron scythes (compare Niditch, 42). Fourth, it raises theological issues. How did God's promises of victory over the nations (Deut 7:1, for example, and more particularly Josh 1:3–5) suddenly find limits? Why was an "obedient" Judah unable to carry out victory thoroughly if God was with that tribe? Superior weaponry should not be an explanation. Scholars make this more difficult by emending the text to say Judah "could not" (Hebrew לא יכל). The translation above understands the Hebrew to mean "except for," indicating some volition on Judah's part. They apparently chose not to face the settlers in the valley, being content to remain in the hill country. Thus, typical of Israelite history writing, no one gets a clean slate. Even the heroes are painted with their faults clearly showing, David being example number one. Certainly Josh 11 and Judg 4–5 show God's ability to defeat enemy chariots, while Josh 17:16 shows no fear of iron chariots.

The Judahites face a fabulous opportunity to complete Joshua's task and conquer the land that remained in Josh 13. Instead, they quit before the task is done. Either they become satisfied with controlling the southern region or they lose their courage and faith and refuse to go further afield to complete God's command to conquer the land. They apparently let human evidence prevent them from experiencing more divine miracles. Thus, Israel must wait until the Judahite king David before they can accomplish the task.

V 20 at first glance seems superfluous in view of vv 10–15. Instead, it plays a vital role. This is the only place in Judges that credits Israel or a part thereof of obeying or fulfilling Mosaic commands. The story of Judah is rounded off by showing that the Judahites follow Joshua's example in fulfilling God's promises through Moses (see Josh 21:45; compare Judg 3:4).

21   As indicated by the Hebrew disjunctive clause opening v 21, Judah's example stands in contrast to Benjamin, the tribe of Saul. Judah and Caleb displace the gigantic inhabitants of Hebron, David's first capital; but Benjamin has to remain content to live with the Jebusites in Jerusalem until David appears to take over the chosen capital city of Israel. Perhaps Judg 1:8 indicates that Benjamin could live with the Jebusites only because of Judah's first success in Jerusalem.

22–26   Judah (with Simeon) stands in contrast to the other ten tribes, gathered together as the inclusio created by vv 22 and 35 shows under the name of the "house of Joseph." Here is clear indication that the writer of Judges faces a situation in which the two kingdoms strongly oppose one another, each seeking legitimization of its position before God and in the world of politics. The launching point is Bethel, the major cultic center of the northern kingdom (1 Kgs 12:29, 32–33) with strong patriarchal roots (Gen 12:8; 13:3; 28:19; 31:13; 35:1, 3, 6–8, 15–16) but only a subsidiary role in the conquest stories in Joshua (Josh 7:2; 8:9, 12, 17; 12:9, 16). See Introduction, "Introduction to the Chronology of Judges." Joshua used it to describe the boundary of the sons of Joseph (16:1–2) but allotted it to Benjamin (18:13, 22). Judg 1:22–23 represents another indication of the ironic literary attack on Saul's tribe of Benjamin, who could take neither of the important cities in their territory—Jerusalem and Bethel. Niditch continues to fight against any type of tribal polemic, seeing simply a lesson acknowledging "the way in which power and control fluctuate" (43).

Israel asked who should go first and got the answer, "Judah will go up" (Hebrew עָלָה, vv 1–2), and Judah invited Simeon to go up (v 3) before Judah went up (v 4). Later the Kenites went up with Judah (v 16). Here Joseph goes up without divine oracle but with divine presence. Yet divine presence is not sufficient for the tribe of Joseph. They must try human ruse to win the battle. They imitate the method Joshua used in attacking Jericho by seeking help from a native resident (see Butler, *Joshua*, 34). They promise to "deal with you in covenant faithfulness" (חֶסֶד). Whereas in the Jericho story this resulted in incorporating Rahab into the covenant community, in Joseph's case this results in the man from Bethel being set free to go and begin a new Luz in the land of the Hittites, an enemy Israel was supposed to destroy (Deut 7:1), not strengthen. Here *Hittites* refers to the remnant of the Anatolian kingdom who settled in Syria and gave their name, in at least some circles, to that area.

The cities Joshua allotted the northern tribes composing "the house of Joseph" now comprise cities where Canaanites continue to live because the various tribes did not drive them out. The historical implications here raise many questions in relationship to the book of Joshua. K. L. Younger, Jr., uses Near Eastern parallels to claim that the Joshua narratives are built on the use of hyperbole and thus give "no reason to maintain that the account in Josh 9–12 portrays a *complete* conquest" (*Ancient Conquest Accounts: A Study in Ancient Near Eastern and Biblical History Writing*, JSOTSup 98 [Sheffield: JSOT Press, 1990] 243, emphasis original). Thus, parallel to Assyrian and Egyptian sources, conquest can mean to temporarily gain possession, not to subjugate and colonize the entire territory. Provan, Long, and Longman clarify further in relationship to Joshua's northern exploits (Josh 11):

> All the royal cities are captured, along with their kings, and they are "utterly destroyed." While this language might give English readers the impression that the cities themselves were destroyed, and not just their populations, the text is at pains to clarify that Hazor alone was burned (vv 11–14). Thus far, then, only three cities are explicitly said to have been burned in the taking of the land: Jericho (6:24), Ai (8:28), and Hazor. (*Biblical History*, 154)

They thus see that the reports may seem exaggerated but in one sense may be "quite accurate, claiming only that Joshua gained the upper hand throughout the land as a whole" after long warfare (11:18). Josh 18 showed that the tribes had to occupy their territory after Joshua's military successes.

The book of Judges thus briefly notes the failures of the northern tribes in occupying land they should have held long ago, before Joshua's death, repeating much of the information from the source in Joshua to underline the northern failures. Manasseh had territories east and west of the Jordan. Judges points only to the western sites. In the plains and lowlands within the boundary lines of Asher and Issachar (Josh 17:11), the listed towns "represent a geographical and population belt reaching from the seacoast to the Jordan Valley" (Rainey, *Sacred Bridge*, 135). Apparently the Canaanite battle strategy against Israel centered on maintaining control of this central territory, especially the Jezreel Valley. Israel won some battles, but until David's time, they lost the long-term war. Even the united monarchy did not exterminate the people and rid the country of their influence as Mosaic law demanded. Instead Israel treated the Canaanites as foreign invaders (Deut 20:1–18) and made them laborers on David's and especially Solomon's massive building projects (2 Sam 20:24; 1 Kgs 9:15–24). Solomon's treatment of Israelites as foreigners, forcing them to corvée eventually led to northern revolt against Rehoboam (compare 1 Kgs 5:13 [Heb. 5:27]; 12:18). Judges thus sets up the background for the north/south dispute that eventually leads to disaster and division.

27–29 Beth-shean was an important city for Egyptian control of Israel and then for Canaanite and Philistine forces. It appears somewhat frequently in Egyptian texts. It represented the place where the Philistines shamefully treated Saul's corpse (1 Sam 31:8–10). Located at Tell el-Ḥuṣn on the intersection of the Jordan and Jezreel valleys, it was a major trade center and also housed important Canaanite temples. Beth-shean came under Israelite control only under David. Thus, as Rainey concludes, "This passage in the first chapter corresponds to the final verse of the book in proclaiming that only under the monarchy was the country organized at last into a cohesive entity, geographically, administratively and socially" (*Sacred Bridge*, 135). Israel needed a united monarchy to be able to control its alloted, God-given territory and to subdue the enemies. (See LaMoine F. DeVries, "Bethshan City at the Crossroads," in *Cities of the Biblical World*, 156–62.)

Taanach lies about five miles (8 km) south of Megiddo overlooking the Jezreel Valley and will play a role along with Megiddo in Deborah's battles (Judg 5:19). Joshua defeated its king (12:21) and set it aside for the Levites (21:25). Egyptian sources often refer to it, especially in connection with Megiddo. It is located at Tell Ti'innik or Ta'annek.

Dor lies on the Mediterranean at Khirbet el-Burj, fourteen miles (22.5 km) south of modern Haifa and about nine miles (14.5 km) north of Caesarea. Its king allied with Hazor (Josh 11:1–2) and met defeat (Josh 12:23). The Egyptian source describing the travels of Wen-Amon about 1100 B.C.E. names its king as Beder, king of the Sikil, one of the Sea Peoples. Excavations show habitation from about 2000 B.C.E. onward. (See E. Stern, *NEAEHL* 1:357–68; Gaß, *Ortsnamen*, 100–106.)

Ibleam stood at Khirbet Bel'ameh near modern Jenin in the Jezreel Valley on the easternmost pass through the hill country of Ephraim. Bronze Age Egyptian sources describe it as a royal city. (See Lindars, 58; M. Hunt, *ABD*, 3:355; Gaß, *Ortsnamen*, 106–8.)

Megiddo, dating back to Chalcolithic times, lay on the great International Coastal Highway at Tell el-Mutesellim, where it veered off the coast into the mountains. Megiddo controlled the Jezreel Valley and finds frequent mention in Egyptian sources. Joshua defeated its king (Josh 12:21), but Manasseh did not control it (Josh 17:11). Megiddo frequently served as a major battlefield (for example, 2 Kgs 9:27; 23:29–30). It was important for Solomon's government (1 Kgs 4:12) and defense system (1 Kgs 9:15). See DeVries, *Cities of the Biblical World*, 215–23; Gaß, *Ortsnamen*, 93–100.

Ephraim, the other Joseph tribe, coexisted with Canaanites in Gezer. Gezer's history reaches back to 3500 B.C.E. Its location on Tell Gezer near the International Coastal Highway and on the road connecting Jerusalem and the port of Joppa gave it political and commercial importance. Egyptian Bronze Age sources frequently mention it. The Amarna letters apparently paint it as a rebel city making alliances against Egypt. Joshua killed its king (Josh 10:33; 12:12) as he fulfilled his treaty obligations with Lachish. Joshua allotted the city to Ephraim (Josh 16:3) and made it a Levitical city (Josh 21:21). David defeated the Philistines, making Gezer the new boundary line between the two enemies (2 Sam 5:22–25), but Israel only controlled the city when the Egyptian pharaoh made it a wedding gift for his daughter's politically arranged marriage with Solomon (1 Kgs 9:15–17). Thus the central northern tribe that will play a fascinating role in the book of Judges owed possession of one of its most important defense cities to Solomon. But Ephraim could not control its important border city without Davidic help. Unless one follows the easier reading of LXX, Judges does not even view Gezer as subject to corvée. Ephraim simply has a foreign enclave living in its midst. See DeVries, *Cities of the Biblical World*, 176–81; Gaß, *Ortsnamen*, 108–17.

30 Joshua had conquered the central portion, then the south, and finally the north. Judges loses territory directly from south to central to north. Thus the northern failures climax the list. Zebulun's fortune stood connected to the Mediterranean Sea (Gen 49:13; Deut 33:19). This tribe played a central role under Barak and Deborah (Judg 4:10; 5:14, 18) and, according to the Chronicler, its people were also important members of David's army (1 Chr 12:33). Even later some parts of Zebulun supported King Hezekiah (2 Chr 20:10–11, 18). Joshua allotted Kitron to Zebulun (Josh 19:15, Kitron and Kattah apparently being variant spellings of the same site). Its precise location is not known. Gaß (*Ortsnamen*, 117–19) looks at Tell el-Far, Tell Kerdane, and Khirbet Quttene and decides on Tell el-Far.

Rainey (*Sacred Bridge*, 135; compare Gaß, *Ortsnamen*, 119–21) follows rabbinic tradition as he identifies Nahalol with Mahalul, modern Maʿlul. Rainey points to Tell el-Beida in the north central section of the Plain of Jezreel or Esdraelon as the ancient tell. John Peterson (*ABD*, 4:994–95) follows Albright in locating it at Tell en-Nahl, six miles (9.7 km) east of the Mediterranean east of Haifa, but this lies outside the boundaries of Zebulun. Joshua allotted it to Zebulun (Josh 19:15) and made it a Levitical city (Josh 21:35). Judges again points to the rule of David and Solomon before this important northern tribe controlled its territory and inhabitants.

31–32 Asher's blessing promised royal delights (Gen 49:20; compare Deut 33:24–25), and the tribe received fertile land from Joshua near the Mediterranean coast, ideally reaching northward to Tyre and Sidon (Josh 19:24–31). Egyptian documents from Seti I (1294–1279 B.C.E.) and Rameses II (1279–1212 B.C.E.) apparently mention Asher (Rainey, *Sacred Bridge*, 135). But Asher weakly remained at home while Deborah fought (Judg 5:17). Only under David and Solomon could Israel control even parts of this territory, and Solomon had to cede much of it to King Hiram of Tyre to get provisions to build the temple, but the cities did not please Hiram (1 Kgs 9:10–14). Thus Judges cleverly prepares for another of Israel's trouble spots. An important highway crosspoint, Acco appears only here in the Old Testament, unless one emends Josh 19:30 to create a reference to Acco. It is identified with el-Fukhkhar in modern Acre (Gaß, *Ortsnamen*, 121–25). It appears frequently in Bronze Age Egyptian documents and in Ugaritic texts.

Sidon's gods proved a particular temptation for Israel (Judg 10:6; compare 1 Kgs 11:5; 2 Kgs 23:13). The city located at modern Saïda was too far from Dan's new territory to help the people resist Dan's onslaught (Judg 18:28), but it was included in David's census (2 Sam 24:6). The city's mercantile importance appears in strong prophetic oracles against it (Isa 23:2, 4–12; Jer 25:22; 27:3; 47:4; Ezek 27:8; 28:21–22). It joined Tyre, twenty-five miles (40.2 km) to the south, as the two strongest Phoenician cities. They controlled the Mediterranean sea lanes. The Amarna letters picture Sidon's leadership in opposing Egypt. See Gaß, *Ortsnamen*, 125–28.

Most scholars locate Ahlab at modern Khirbet el-Machalib, about four miles (6.4 km) northeast of Tyre, on the basis of Sennacherib's mention of Mahhalliba in this area and on the reading Mahalab from the LXX of Josh 19:29. Gaß (*Ortsnamen*, 128–29) wants a more southern location and points to Ras el-Abyad but without much supporting evidence.

Achzib was a Mediterranean port nine miles (14.5 km) north of Acco on the International Coastal Highway. It is located at ez-Zib. (See Gaß, *Ortsnamen*, 131–32.) Settlement goes back to about 1750 B.C.E. with at least two destructions in the Late Bronze Age. Pottery from the Sea Peoples appears at the end of the Bronze Age. Sennacherib destroyed it.

Helbah appears to be a spelling variant for Ahlab or Mahalab (Josh 19:29). See Melvin Hunt, *ABD*, 3:117; Gaß, *Ortsnamen*, 135–37.

Aphik or Aphek is one of several Apheks in Scripture. This one is apparently located at Tell Kabri, about three miles (4.8 km) east of Nahariya. See Rafael Frankel, *ABD*, 1:275–77; Gaß, *Ortsnamen*, 138–46.

Rehob is often seen as a Levitical city on the northern border of Israel. See John L. Peterson and Rami Aray, *ABD*, 5:660–61. Gaß (*Ortsnamen*, 151–54) identifies at least three towns by this name and sets the Judges one south of Aphek at Tell Bir el-Garabi, which controlled entrance to the sea.

Asher failed in its occupation mission, having to live among the Canaanites, the original occupants of the land. The people of the tribe of Asher may well have worked as agriculturalists for the Canaanites and Phoenicians, who were occupied with maritime activities. See Rainey, *Sacred Bridge*, 135.

33   Naphtali receives promises of blessings (Gen 49:21; Deut 33:23) and the sixth land lot distributed by Joshua (Josh 19:32–39). Barak belonged to the tribe of Naphtali, and his tribe loyally led the way into battle (Judg 4:6, 10; 5:18). Naphtali also fought for Gideon (6:35; 7:23). Yet this important military tribe receives notice here only for what they could not accomplish. They, like Asher, lived among the Canaanite natives; but at least they finally, perhaps in the time of David, subjected the troublesome cities to corvée. Much of Naphtali's territory was mountainous, so Naphtali settled in the highlands of Mount Meron.

The lower Canaanite worship centers of Beth-shemesh and Beth-anath, literally "House of the Sun" and "House of Anath," resisted Israelite occupancy. Both towns were fortified and had dependent villages (Josh 19:38). Neither town has been definitely located, though Beth-shemesh may have been Khirbet Tell er-Ruweisi in northern Galilee with Beth-anath at Safed el-Battikh. See Rainey, *Sacred Bridge*, 135; Gaß, *Ortsnamen*, 158–66. Gaß differentiates three distinct towns called Beth-shemesh, one in Judah, one in Naphtali, and one in Issachar, but places the town in Naphtali at Khirbet Tell er-Ruweisi.

Gaß (*Ortsnamen*, 166–69) lists seven possible locations for Beth-anath before pointing to el-Biʾne, almost nine miles (14 km) from Khirbet Tell er-Ruweisi. This closeness is a major reason for Gaß's decision. Meir Lubetski (*ABD*, 1:680–81) sees Hîneh and Safed el-Battikh as the two possibilities and opts a bit unsurely for the latter.

34 The tribe of Dan had the least good fortune of all. Dan appears anachronistically in Gen 14:14 in connection with Abraham. A play on its name gave Dan the "blessing" of achieving justice but also the reputation of being a dangerous snake attacking the heels of military horses, perhaps a reference to its final ability to find a home in the north (Gen 49:16–17). Moses' blessing similarly describes Dan's strength with the image of a lion (Deut 33:22). The wilderness sanctuary arrangement credits Dan with the second highest increment of troops, Judah having the most (Num 2). Josh 19:40–48 (compare 21:23–24) lists the southern coastal cities in Dan's inheritance but then explains Dan's failure to settle on the coast as the territory "going out from them," possibly meaning that it "slipped through their fingers" (D. M. Howard, Jr., *Joshua*, NAC 5 [Nashville: Broadman & Holman, 1998] 377, n. 232). Thus they moved north to their permanent home. Judges is most explicit, saying the Amorites pushed the Danites into the hill country away from the coastal plain. Guillaume notes that "Dan is set in a geographical and cultural zone distinct from Israel. From every point of view, Dan is closer to Damascus than to Samaria" (*Waiting for Josiah*, 131).

The determined Amorites refuse to give up Har-heres, Aijalon, and Shaalbim. Har-heres represents the mountain (Hebrew הר) on the eastern side of the Aijalon Valley. Aijalon, a Levitical city (Josh 21:24), lay on the western end of the Valley of Aijalon guarding the trade road from the coast to Jerusalem. Gaß (*Ortsnamen*, 174) places it at Yalo. Thus it became a battle scene (Josh 10:12; 1 Sam 14:31; 1 Chr 8:13; 2 Chr 28:18). Rehoboam fortified it against Israel (2 Chr 11:10). Shaalbim appears to lie at Silbit, three miles (4.8 km) northwest of Aijalon on the western edge of the Aijalon Valley, though Gaß (*Ortsnamen*, 176–78) raises many questions about the identification, accepting it simply because he has no better alternative.

35 The enemies suddenly become Amorites (Gen 10:16; 14:7; 15:16, 21; 48:22; Exod 3:8, 17; 13:5; 23:23; 33:2; 34:11; Num 13:29; 21:13, 21, 25–26, 31–32, 34; 22:2; 32:33, 39; Deut 1:4, 7, 19–20, 27, 44; 3:2, 8–9; 4:46–47; 7:1; 20:17; 31:4; Josh 2:10; 3:10; 5:1; 7:7; 9:1, 10; 10:5–6, 12; 11:3; 12:2, 8; 13:4, 10, 21; 24:8, 11–12, 15, 18; Judg 1:34–36; 3:5; 6:10; 10:8, 11; 11:19, 21–23; 1 Sam 7:14; 2 Sam 21:2; 1 Kgs 4:19; 9:20; 21:26; 2 Kgs 21:11; 1 Chr 1:14; 2 Chr 8:7; Ezra 9:1; Pss 135:11; 136:19; Isa 17:9; Jdt 5:15). Mesopotamian sources from before 2000 B.C.E. refer to Amurru or nomadic people invading from the west. Eventually, the term referred to Syria and then to all of Syria/Palestine. Texts found in Syria show that Amorites lived in cities such as Mari before 2000 B.C.E. and during the Late Bronze Age ruled a kingdom in the mountainous parts of Syria. When these peoples entered Palestine and the kingdoms east of the Jordan is not certain.

The Bible speaks of victories over the Amorites east of the Jordan (Num

21:21–35) and west of the Jordan (Josh 10; 11:3; compare Amos 2:9), the latter including Amorite kings of Jerusalem, Jarmuth, Eglon, Hebron, and Lachish. These inhabitants of Palestine's hill country (Num 13:29) became powerful and important enough to give their name to the general population of Palestine (Gen 15:16; Josh 24:15; Judg 6:10). Eventually Solomon forced them into corvée labor (1 Kgs 9:20–21). See K. N. Schoville, "Canaanites and Amorites," in *Peoples of the Old Testament World*, ed. A. J. Hoerth, G. L. Mattingly, and E. M. Yamauchi (Grand Rapids: Baker, 1994) 157–82; E. C. Hostetter, *Nations Mightier and More Numerous: The Biblical View of Palestine's Pre-Israelite Peoples*, BIBAL Dissertations Series 3 (N. Richland Hills, TX: BIBAL Press,1995) 51–57.

Unexpectedly, we return to the "house of Joseph" in a literary inclusio with v 22. Joseph, not Judah or Dan, subjects these cities to corvée. Despite Niditch's (44) insistence that the end of the chapter does not picture "consummate defeat," the contrast with Judah's lengthy opening narrative must indicate a strong distinction between Judah's results and those of the northern tribes. Why does the list of northern failures find such a conclusion? The structure at least raises some issues. The house of Joseph first went up against Bethel (v 22). Now they exercise a heavy hand on Dan's territory. Only these two reports deviate from the northern failure list's annalistic style. From a Judean viewpoint, Bethel and Dan represent the evil of the northern kingdom, for they house the shrines Jeroboam built for calf images in opposition to southern worship in Jerusalem. Jeroboam was from Ephraim (1 Kgs 11:26) and was the chief administrator in Solomon's corvée labor ventures "of the house of Joseph" (1 Kgs 11:28). Thus Judges places the house of Joseph, and by implication Jeroboam, at the center of corvée. By wrapping mentions of the house of Joseph around all the northern tribe listings, the house of Joseph is extended to include the entire northern territory from Bethel to Dan. The corvée labor tactics of the house of Joseph stand in strong contrast to Judah's reverence for justice and obedience to God.

36 Ironically, the section ends by describing the Amorite borders, not the Israelite ones. The "Ascent of Akrabbim" represents the southern edge of Judah's territory and thus of the promised land (Num 34:4; Josh 15:3). The exact location is not known, though Gaß (*Ortsnamen*, 179) wants to place it at Naqb Safa, a pass leading from the Arabah into the Negev. Nor can Sela be located, though Gaß (*Ortsnamen*, 183–84) would like to put it as es Silʾ. As Webb explains,

> By the time this note is introduced the focus of the narrative has shifted from conquest to co-existence. When the whole process of conquest and settlement has run its course, Israel dwells within "the border of the Amorites." The Amorites/Canaanites are still "the inhabitants of the land" among whom Israel dwells (see especially 32a, 33b). This note provides a final sardonic comment on the chapter as a whole, and on VV. 22–35 in particular. ([1987] 101)

Or as Matthews notes, "The sober reality of Israel's inability to conquer and occupy territories beyond the central highlands explains much of the nation's subsequent history and fits the archaeological record. . . . The failures of the settlement period contributed to the eventual failures of the monarchy" (46–47).

Explanation

Chap. 1 apparently introduces Judges as a chronological narrative following directly upon the book of Joshua. The astute reader quickly realizes that Judg 1 repeats and reinterprets material from Joshua much more than taking it forward to a new era. Judg 1 splits the record into two major parts, one covering Judah and Benjamin, the other encompassing the northern tribes as the house of Joseph. Judah, with its compatriot Simeon, follows the divine oracle in taking leadership; provides an example of tribes working together; delivers tough retributive justice to the king of Bezek; captures and thus lays claim to Jerusalem, the most important city of all; establishes control of Hebron, David's original capital; rids the country of the legendary giants; fulfills the promise to Caleb, the original hero among those who spied out the land; gives prominence to the wisdom and wit of Achsah, the first of many women featured in the book; introduces Othniel, the first judge; incorporates Moses' clan into Judah; obeys God's commands by devoting Hormah to the ban; establishes a foothold and precedent of victory among the Philistine cities who would be David's chief enemies; and fulfills Moses' promises by giving Hebron to Caleb. Only a lack of technology prevents their completely fulfilling their mission. Judah could claim Jerusalem, because Benjamin, the rightful owner of the city could not take possession of it.

The story of the northern tribes, the house of Joseph, takes an entirely different path. Yahweh was with the house of Joseph as well as the house of Judah. Joseph did not execute or drive out enemy citizens. Rather Joseph made treaties with them in "covenant faithfulness" and allowed them to reestablish themselves in Hittite or Syrian territory, from which would come opposition for David and Solomon. The first priority for the house of Joseph was gaining Bethel, the site of Jeroboam's heretical sanctuary.

Partners in the house of Joseph did not succeed against the enemies as had Judah. They could not take possession of major cities. Instead, the determined Canaanites and Amorites deterred them. Rather than instituting the ban, they institute corvée, which will become the point of contention between Rehoboam and Jeroboam. They left Canaanites and Amorites as residents of the land rather than imitating Judah in incorporating families with historic connections to Israel like the Kenizzites of Caleb and the Kenites of Moses. Gradually, the northern tribes moved from conquering the Canaanites and Amorites to corvéeing them and coexisting with them in a land with Amorite borders.

Judg 1 thus sets the stage for (1) the "period of the judges" (3:1–16:31) with its continued attempts to control the land and its continued temptations to be like the nations they lived with; (2) the total breakdown of the Israelite coalition, revealing its need for a king (Judg 17–21); (3) the disputes between Judah and Benjamin in the persons of David and Saul; (4) the establishment of the Davidic monarchy first at Hebron and then in Jerusalem through victory over the Philistines; (5) the division of the monarchy because of the cruel corvée policies implemented by Solomon but carried out in the house of David by Jeroboam; and (6) the unending dispute over the proper worship places between Jerusalem in the south and Bethel and Dan in the north.

Theologically, the opening chapter of Judges quietly hints at the basic question of Old Testament and even biblical theology: who are the people of God? Judg 1 uses political/military narrative to approach the question. The following chapter will approach it from a religious perspective. The question has many elements to it. Are they an elect people under God's presence no matter how they act? Or do they have responsibilities under God that they must fulfill to show they truly are people of God? Does the designation people of God come from our fathers or from our faithfulness? The book of Judges sets the stage for Israel to wrestle with this question through days of turmoil, days of rebellion, and days of power.

New Testament followers of the new David continue to wrestle with these issues. Are people of God a covenant people who hand their identity down to the next generation through ritual and education? Must people of God personally incorporate certain doctrines into their belief system? Do people of God find guaranteed protection in the trials and temptations of life? Or does God call believers in the Christ to follow him in the journey crossward, denying self and serving others?

B. The Religious Situation (2:1–23)

Bibliography

Amit, Y. "Bochem, Bethel and the Hidden Polemic (Judg 2,1–5)." In *Studies in Historical Geography and Biblical Historiography.* FS Z. Kallai, ed. G. Galil and M. Weinfeld. VTSup 81. Leiden: Brill, 2000. 121–31. **Ausloos, H.** "The 'Angel of YHWH' in Exod. xxiii 20–33 and Judg. ii 1–5: A Clue to the 'Deuteronom(ist)ic' Puzzle?" *VT* 58 (2008) 1–12. **Barredo, M. A.** "Aspectos literarios y lectura teológica de Jue 2,6–3,6." *Anton* 73 (1998) 291–340. **Bartelmus, R.** "Menschlicher Misserfolg und Jahwes Initiative: Beobachtungen zum Geschichtsbild des deuteronomistischen Rahmens im Richterbuch und zum geschichtstheologischen Entwurf in Ez 20." *BN* 70 (1993) 28–47. **Blum, E.** "Der kompositionelle Knoten am Übergang von Josua zu Richter: Ein Entflechtungsvorschlag." In *Deuteronomy and Deuteronomic Literature.* FS C. H. W. Brekelmans, ed. M. Vervenne and J. Lust. BETL 133. Leuven: Peeters, 1997. **Dus, J.** "Herabfahrung Jahwehs auf die Lade und Entziehung der Reuerwolke: Zu zwei Dogmen der mittleren Richterzeit." *VT* 19 (1969) 290–311. **Foster, J. F.** "A Prototypical Definition of בְּרִית, 'Covenant,' in Biblical Hebrew." *OTE* 19 (2006) 35–46. **Frolov, S.** "Joshua's Double Demise (Josh. xxiv 28–31; Judg. ii 6–9): Making Sense of a Repetition." *VT* 58 (2008) 315–23. **Greenspahn, F. E.** "The Theology of the Framework of Judges." *VT* 36 (1986) 385–96. **Haag, H.** "Zwischen Jahwe und Baal." *BibLeb* 4 (1963) 240–52. **Hamlin, E. J.** "Structure and Meaning of the Theological Essay in Judg 2:6–3:6." *PEGLMBS* 6 (1987) 114–19. **Jericke, D.** "'Josuas Tod und Josuas Grab: Eine redaktionsgeschichtliche Studie.'" *ZAW* 108 (1996) 347–61. ———. *Die Landnahme im Negev: Protoisraelitische Gruppen im Süden Palästinas. Eine archäologische und exegetische Studie.* ADPV 20. Wiesbaden: Harrassowitz, 1997. **Kooij, A. van der.** "'And I Also Said': A New Interpretation of Judges ii 3." *VT* 45 (1995) 294–306. **Linington, S.** "The Term בְּרִית in the Old Testament: Part III, An Enquiry into the Meaning and Use of the Word in Joshua and Judges." *OTE* 18 (2005) 664–80. **Marx, A.** "Forme et Fonction des Juges 2:1–5." *RHPR* 59 (1979) 341–50. **McKenzie, D. A.** "The Judge of Israel." *VT* 17 (1967) 118. **Miller, P. D.** *The Religion of Ancient Israel.* Ed. D. A. Knight. Library of Ancient Israel. Louisville: Westminster John Knox, 2000. **Neef, H. D.** "'Ich selber bin in ihm' (Ex 23,21): Exegetische Beobachtungen zur Rede vom 'Engel des Herrn" in Ex 23,20–22; 32,34; 33:2; Jdc 2,1–5; 5,23." *BZ* 39 (1995) 54–75. **Noort, E.**

"Josua 24,28–31, Richter 2,6–9 und das Josuagrab: Gedanken zu einem Strassenchild." In *Biblische Welten*. FS M. Metzger, ed. W. Zwickel. OBO 123. Göttingen: Vandenhoeck & Ruprecht, 1993. 109–33. **Penchansky, D.** "Up for Grabs: A Tentative Proposal for Doing Ideological Criticism." *Sem* 59 (1992) 35–42. **Rofé, A.** "The Composition of the Introduction of the Book of Judges (Judges II,6–III, 6)" (Heb.). *Tarbiz* 35 (1966) 201–13. **Rösel, H.** "Die Überleitungen vom Josua ins Richterbuch." *VT* 30 (1980) 342–50. **Spronk, K.** "A Story to Weep About: Some Remarks on Judges 2:1–5 and Its Context." In *Unless Some One Guide Me*. Maastrict: Shaker, 2001. 87–94. **Stemmer, N.** "Introduction to Judges 2:1–3:4." *JQR* 57 (1967) 239–41. **Trebolle Barrera, J.** "Historia del texto de los libros históricos e historia de la redacción deuteronomística (Jueces 2,10–3:6)." In *Salvación en la Palabra: Targum-Derash-Berith*. FS A. D. Macho. Madrid: Cristiandad, 1986. 245–58. **Vaccari, A.** "Parole rovesciate e critiche errate nella Bibbia ebraica." In *Studi orientalistici*. FS G. Levi Della Vida. Rome, 1956. 2:553–66. **Wessels, J. P. H.** "Persuasion in Judges 2:20–3:6: A Celebration of Differences." In *The Rhetorical Analysis of Scripture*. Ed. S. Porter et al. Sheffield: Sheffield Academic, 1997. 120–36. ———. "'Postmodern' Rhetoric and the Former Prophetic Literature." In *Rhetoric, Scripture & Theology: Esssays from the 1994 Pretoria Conference*. Ed. S. E. Porter and T. H. Olbricht. JSNTSup 133. Sheffield: Sheffield Academic, 1996. 182–94. **Williams, J. G.** "The Structure of Judges 2:6–16:31." *JSOT* 49 (1991) 77–86.

Translation

[1] *The angel of Yahweh went up from Gilgal to Bochim.[a] He said, "I brought[b] you up from Egypt and brought you to the land that I swore to your fathers.[c] I said, 'I will never break my covenant with you,* [2] *but you must not enter into a covenant with the residents of this land:[a] their altars you must tear down.' But you did not obey my voice. How could you do this?* [3] *I also said, 'I will not drive them out before you.[a] They will be with you at your sides,[b] while their gods will become a trap for you.'"* [4] *As the angel of Yahweh spoke these words to all the sons[a] of Israel, the people raised their voices and wept.* [5] *They[a] named that place Bochim and sacrificed to Yahweh there.*

[6] *Joshua sent the people away, and the sons of Israel went[a] each to his inheritance to take possession of the land.* [7] *The people served Yahweh all the days of Joshua and all the days of the elders whose days stretched out after Joshua, those[a] who had seen all Yahweh's great actions which he did for Israel.* [8] *Joshua, the son of Nun and the servant of Yahweh died when he was 110 years old.* [9] *They buried him in the territory of his inheritance, that is, in Timnath-heres[a] in the hill country of Ephraim north of Mount Gaash.* [10] *That entire generation was also gathered to their fathers, and another generation rose up after them who did not know either Yahweh[a] or the actions that he had done for Israel.*

[11] *The sons of Israel did evil in Yahweh's eyes: they served the Baals.* [12] *They abandoned Yahweh, the God of their fathers who brought them out from the land of Egypt. They followed after other gods, the gods of the peoples who surrounded them. They worshiped them and infuriated Yahweh.* [13] *They abandoned Yahweh and served Baal and the Ashtaroth.[a]* [14] *Yahweh burned with anger against Israel, and he gave them into the hand of plunderers. They plundered them and sold them into the hand of their enemies all around. They were no longer able to stand before their enemies.* [15] *Any time they went out,[a] the hand of Yahweh was against them to bring evil just as Yahweh promised and just as Yahweh swore to them. They were in extreme trouble.[b]* [16] *[a]Yahweh raised up judges,[b] and they[c] delivered them from the hand of their plunderers.* [17] *But they did not obey, even their judges,[a] because they became harlots with other gods. They worshiped them,[b] turning quickly from the way their fathers followed, who obeyed the commandments of Yahweh. They did not act that*

way. [18] *But when Yahweh raised up judges for them, Yahweh was with the judge so that he delivered them from the hand of their enemies all the days of the judge. This was because Yahweh showed compassion on account of their groaning before those who tormented and oppressed them.* [19] *At the death of the judge, they again*[a] *behaved more corruptly than their fathers. They followed other gods, serving them and worshiping them. They did not abandon their deeds*[b] *or their obstinate way.*

[20] *Yahweh's anger burned against Israel. He said, "Because this nation has disobeyed the covenant that I commanded their fathers and did not obey my voice,* [21] *I also will not again drive out anyone before them from the nations which Joshua left when he died.*[a] [22] *This will be to use them to test Israel to see whether they will keep the way*[a] *of Yahweh to walk in them as their fathers kept it."*

[23] *Yahweh had caused these nations to remain without driving them out rapidly. He did not give them into the hand of Joshua.*[a]

Notes

1.a. LXX (compare OL) adds "and to Bethel and to the house of Israel," representing later scribal glosses seeking to clarify the location of Bochim or the place of weeping. See Barthélemy, *Critique textuelle*, 1:75–76.

1.b. LXX^A (compare OL) reads "and the Lord said to them, 'The Lord brought you,'" while LXX^B reads "and he said to them, 'thus says the Lord, "I brought you."'" *BHS* suggests that some words have fallen out, indicating that the Gk. offers evidence for proper replacements. But the Gk. represents later glosses seeking to clarify that God, not the angel, brought Israel up from Egypt. The parallel use of the prefix form and the consecutive prefix form perplexes linguists. Lindars (77) says it "defies solution." GKC, §107b, says the "imperfect serves in the sphere of past time to express actions, etc, which *continued* throughout a longer or shorter period . . . very frequently alternative with a perfect . . . or when the narration is continued by means of an imperfect consecutive." Waltke and O'Connor (*IBHS*, 498) suggest that "in some prose texts it seems that some prefix forms without *wāw* must be taken as *preterites.*"

1.c. LXX^A reads "your fathers to give you." This represents an updating or contextualizing of the text to show that the promise to the fathers was intended to be fulfilled in the present generation.

2.a. LXX (compare OL) reads ἐγκαθημένοις εἰς τὴν γῆν ταύτην οὐδὲ τοῖς θεοῖς αὐτῶν οὐ μὴ προσκυνήσητε ἀλλὰ τὰ γλυπτὰ αὐτῶν συντρίψετε καὶ τὰ θυσιαστήρια αὐτῶν κατασκάψετε καὶ οὐκ εἰσηκούσατε τῆς φωνῆς μου ὅτε ταῦτα ἐποιήσατε, "those lying in wait in this land, neither are you to fall down in worship to their gods, but their carved images you must break to pieces and their altars you must destroy . . . because you have done these things," picking up the thought of Exod 34:13–14 and introducing it here. Niditch (47) speaks of "oral-style recurring idioms of the Israelite tradition" and refers to the final clause as "language of judgment."

3.a. Several Heb. MSS read מלפניכם rather than the virtually synonymous מפניכם.

3.b. LXX^A (compare OL) reads οὐ προσθήσω τοῦ μετοικίσαι τὸν λαόν ὃν εἶπα τοῦ ἐξολεθρεῦσαι αὐτοὺς ἐκ προσώπου ὑμῶν καὶ ἔσονται ὑμῖν εἰς συνοχάς, "I will not continue to drive out the people whose destruction from your presence I promised, and they will be to you for affliction." Niditch (48) refers to this as expansion with "language of the ban." LXX^B reads ὁ μὴ ἐξαρῶ αὐτοὺς ἐκ προσώπου ὑμῶν καὶ ἔσονται ὑμῖν εἰς συνοχάς, "I will not carry them away from your presence, and they will be an affliction to you." Most translators (see Lindars, NASB, NIV, GWT, HCSB, NLT, ESV) see a case of haplography here, with the original reading in Judg 2 being לצנים בצדיכם, "as thorns in your sides," of Num 33:55. Judg 2 MT has only לכם לצדים, "with you at (your) sides." Others follow Gk. in emending the *dālet* to a *rêš* to read לצרים, translated either "oppressors" (NAB, JPS, NJB) or "distress," with the Gk. and other versions or see a secondary meaning of צר, "snares," in parallel with מוקש (*Preliminary and Interim Report*, REB, NET). MT remains the most difficult text and may well represent the original, but the idiom from Numbers seems to represent a standard reading that would be expected here.

4.a. LXX^A does not have "sons of," which may reflect the addition of a common phrase in MT, but the frequency of the term in Judges points to the longer text being original here.

5.a. LXX^A reads "because of this, they," providing a literary touch to the text or, as Niditch (48) understands it, using an "etiological rubric."

6.a. LXX^A reads ἀπῆλθαν οἱ υἱοὶ Ισραηλ ἕκαστος εἰς τὸν οἶκον αὐτοῦ καὶ εἰς τὴν κληρονομίαν αὐτοῦ, "and the sons of Israel each went away to his house and to his inheritance," while LXX^B reads ἦλθεν ἀνὴρ εἰς τὴν κληρονομίαν αὐτοῦ, "and each man came into his inheritance." The former is an expansive, clarifying translation, while the latter is a terse rendition. Neither points to a reason to modify MT. OL has God send the people away. Niditch (48) sees this as "continuing the frame of a divinely sent message with which the scene begins."

7.a. Several MSS add an unneeded *wāw* before the relative.

9.a. Josh 19:50 and 24:30 read Timnath-serah, "left-over portion," for Timnath-heres, "portion of the sun," thus erasing memory of sun worship there. See Lindars, 96.

10.a. OL has Joshua for Yahweh, either reducing the theological indictment or continuing the theme of human leadership.

13.a. The Heb. vocalization substitutes the vowels of בֹּשֶׁת, "shame," for Astarte, the normal name of the Canaanite goddess.

15.a. LXX^A (compare OL) reads ἐν πᾶσιν οἷς ἐπόρνευον, "in everything by which they committed sexual immorality." This may be a copyist's hearing error using Heb. זוּ (compare v 17) instead of MT יִצְאַ or a Gk. copyist's error replacing ἐξεπορεύοντο with ἐπόρνευον.

15.b. LXX reads ἐξέθλιψεν αὐτοὺς σφόδρα, "he (Yahweh) oppressed them greatly."

16.a. For symmetry, *BHS* and commentators insert "and they cried to Yahweh," without textual support. See Judg 2:3, 9, 15; 6:6; 10:10. This is unnecessary without further evidence.

16.b. In Judges the term שֹׁפְטִים, "judges," refers more to military deliverers and political leaders than to people with judicial function.

16.c. LXX has sg. verb, with LXX^B and OL inserting κύριος, "Lord," as explicit subject. This represents a theological interpretation of the text, but the more difficult MT must be retained.

17.a. Omitting "judges," OL reads "they did not listen to his judgment," perhaps a scribal error reading מִשְׁפָּט instead of שֹׁפֵט.

17.b. LXX^A (compare OL) adds the traditional note "and they made the Lord angry."

19.a. For this rendering, see Lindars, 107.

19.b. LXX^A adds "and they did not depart from." Lindars (107–8) and Boling insert שָׂרוּ, "turn," here.

21.a. LXX^A reads "nations which Joshua left behind and he left (or dismissed)"; LXX^B reads "nations which Joshua, son of Nun, left behind in the land; and he left." OL does not have "and he died." Nothing indicates, however, strong reason to change MT.

22.a. Tg. reads pl., "ways," to agree with the following pl. pronoun, "to follow it" (lit. "them"). A few Heb. MSS, the Masoretic marginal Sebir ("supposed" or "expected") notation, LXX, Syr., and Vg. read בָּהּ, the sg. "in it." The text may be explained as the writer indicating a double meaning for "way(s) of Yahweh," introducing both a devotion to the path God sets out for Israel to follow and to the commandments that indicate that path. One *yôd* may have fallen out in copying דַּרְכֵי יהוה, "ways of Yahweh." A copyist may have written the wrong pronoun through familiarity with the expression "ways of Yahweh." Boling sees an example of what he calls a double-duty consonant.

23.a. Niditch (48) cites OL reading, "And the Lord handed these nations into the hand of Joshua/Iesu so that he would not quickly destroy them from their face. And the Lord put them into the hand of Joshua/Iesu." This is a theological rendering seeking to maintain the understanding that God fulfilled all his promises and Joshua defeated all the enemies.

Form/Structure/Setting

See table 2.1 in the appendix to compare one possible example of narrative analysis with form-critical analysis for chap. 2. The narrative elements follow the typical pattern of Hebrew narrative while the genre elements show the genre of each section with its component parts. Note how the narrator can use different genre elements and markers within or even across various narrative elements.

As described in *Form/Structure/Setting* for chap. 1, chap. 2 forms a complete unit within itself, describing the religious situation of Israel just as chap. 1 described the military/political situation. The oft-noted use of עלה, "to go up," ties the chapter back to the previous narrative without being the driving structural

force that separates 2:1–5 from the remainder of chap. 2. Continuity of subject is
more important in determining the structure than is the repetition of one lexical
marker. The opening oracle serves to open this section as did the oracle of 1:2
and also forms an inclusio with 2:20–21, marking the end of the section except
for the narrator's conclusion in vv 22–23. The chapter thus includes an angelic
theophany (vv 1–5); an interpretive flashback rearranging Josh 24:28–31 based on a
burial account (vv 6–10); a narrative preview describing the cycle of disobedience,
punishment, and deliverance that will provide an interpretation for each of the
following stories (vv 11–19); a divine judgment speech reinforcing the theophany
of vv 1–5 (vv 20–22); and the narrative summation (v 23). Niditch (48) sees four
segments here, all framed in terms of covenant, giving a theological explanation
for Israel's lack of success.

In 2:6–10 Judges again takes up material virtually word for word from Joshua.
But Judges uses the same material for a radically different purpose. Judges obviously steps outside its own chronological framework, having reported Joshua's
death in 1:1. This repetition of the death of Israel's perfect leader serves a literary purpose. It identifies Joshua as a leader from Ephraim, a people subsequent
events will show have indeed forgotten their founding fathers' tradition. It also
allows the writer of Judges to set the stage for the body of his work about Israel's
less than perfect leaders (chaps. 3–16) in two stages, one military/political and
the other religious. It thus lets the writer quietly move from describing Judah to
describing the "sons of Israel," which for his day under Jeroboam pointed directly
to the northern kingdom. The story of the judges becomes the story of a divided
people. It becomes a southerner's report of the northern heresy. It pictures a divine oracle opening the way for southern successes, and a divine oracle pointing
toward judgment of the rebellious north.

In Joshua, the material represents a burial report honoring Joshua, showing
obedience through the burial of Joseph's bones, and reporting the burial of Eleazar,
the priest, in land he had been able to pass on to his son for an inheritance. (See
the discussion in Butler, *Joshua,* 280–84.) Judges has an entirely different form
and function. Judges presents a different order:

Judg 2:6	=	Josh 24:28
Judg 2:7	=	Josh 24:31
Judg 2:8	=	Josh 24:29
Judg 2:9	=	Josh 24:30
Judg 2:10	=	No parallel

The shifting forward of Josh 24:31 and the addition of the concluding Judg
2:10 reveal the form and purpose Judges has adopted. So does the subtle change
of the verb ידע, "know," in Josh 24:31 to ראה, "to see," in Judg 2:7 as well as the
insertion of "and to take possession of the land" in Judg 2:6. The intention in
Judges is not to honor Joshua but to dishonor disobedient Israel and show that
this people did not keep the tradition Joshua initiated. The dying generation did
not just know of the "great" acts of Yahweh. They had seen them. Each Israelite
had to explicitly go (Judg 2:6 adds וילכו, "they went") to the land assigned for an
inheritance, but the purpose there was more than gaining title to the land. They
had to take possession of the land. Judges thus proceeds beyond Joshua's story of

total fulfillment (Josh 21:43) to a story of Israel's total disobedience and failure. This occurred in one generation. The covenant of Josh 24 has disappeared into forgetfulness and the weeping ritual of Judg 2:5. The idyllic rest of Josh 21:44 has disappeared into divine threat of Judg 2:3. And the remnant of the nations of Josh 13 serves to test the disobedient people of Judg 2:20–23.

Judg 2:11–23 represents an introductory summary report that sets the religious tone for all that follows in the book of Judges. The disjunctive clause and separate genre of 3:1 sets it clearly off as an introduction to a new section.

Comment

1 Unexpectedly, we encounter the "angel of Yahweh" (מַלְאַךְ יְהוָה). Nothing has prepared us for the messenger's entrance. This mysterious figure appears fifty-eight times in the OT. The messenger of God (מַלְאַךְ הָאֱלֹהִים) appears nine times (Gen 31:11; Exod 14:19; Judg 6:20; 13:6, 9; 2 Sam 14:17, 20; 19:28; 2 Chr 36:16). Before Judges, the last meeting with the Lord's messenger appeared much earlier, in Num 22:35 with Balaam. Josh 5:14 had a similar abrupt appearance from the commander of Yahweh's army (שַׂר־צְבָא־יְהוָה). Here we see the ability of Hebrew narrative to switch focus without warning and to interrupt any chronological sequence we may be expecting.

The Hebrew term for angel is simply מַלְאָךְ, the common word for messenger. Those who encountered the messenger often considered the person to be a human being and then discovered that a divine reality faced them. The messenger found Hagar in the wilderness and promised the birth of Ishmael (Gen 16). Gen 19:1 seems to indicate that God has a plurality of messengers. The messenger prevented Abraham from slaughtering his son Isaac (Gen 22). The messenger appeared to Moses in the wilderness of Midian to call him to deliver his people (Exod 3:2). The messenger opposed Balaam and his talking donkey (Num 22) then directed Balaam in his negotiations with Balak of Moab. Next the angel will tell Deborah and Barak to curse Meroz, whoever or whatever Meroz is (Judg 5:23), then, mysteriously, to visit Gideon (Judg 6) and Samson's parents (Judg 13), at which points I will discuss this divine messenger further. Here it suffices to see that the messenger that summoned Moses to deliver Israel now summons the people of Israel to a rite of weeping because they will not be delivered.

The angel appears from Gilgal, Israel's first camping place after they crossed the Jordan. Here, apparently, was their first major place of worship (Josh 4:19; 5:9). Joshua was at Gilgal while they began apportioning the land by lot (Josh 14:6). Gilgal was located near the border of Judah (Josh 15:7) and easily accessible to Benjamin, Ephraim, and Manasseh. Gilgal was one of Samuel's three stopping points on his circuit judging Israel (1 Sam 7:16). Later Amos (4:4; 5:5) and Hosea (4:15) pointed to heretical worship at Gilgal. Bochim's identification with Bethel goes back to Bethel's patriarchal connections (Gen 12:8; 13:3; 28:19; 31:13; 35:1, 3, 6, 8, 15–16) and the "Oak of Weeping" (Gen 35:8; compare Judg 4:5). Yahweh was the God of Bethel (Gen 31:13), and the city was no longer Luz (Gen 28:19) even though the Joseph tribes had allowed Luz to reappear on the map (Judg 1:26). Bethel played a minor role in Joshua's campaigns (Josh 7:2; 8:9, 12, 17; 12:9, 16; 16:1–2; 18:13, 22). Later, along with Gilgal, it would be central to Samuel's attempts to judge Israel and renew the people's relationship with Yahweh (1 Sam

7:16; compare 10:3) and would serve as a military center for Saul (1 Sam 13:2–4). And of course it became Jeroboam's central sanctuary. The angel moved from holy Gilgal to unknown Bochim, the "place of weeping or weepers," apparently symbolizing the situation of Israel as a people in the era of the Judges: a people weeping instead of worshiping, a people who deserted the chosen sanctuary of Joshua for a sanctuary promising only sadness. Of course, all Israel would return to Bethel in time of civil war to try again to find an oracle from Yahweh (Judg 20:18), only to weep again (Judg 20:26; 21:2).

The angel's message calls on Israel to remember history (Exod 6:8; Num 14:3, 8; Judg 2:1; Ezek 20:15). As J. Goldingay affirms, "the basis of the covenant has now changed. Whereas it was previously based on what God intended to do, it is now based on what God has actually done" (*Old Testament Theology,* vol. 1, *Israel's Gospel* [Downers Grove, IL: InterVarsity Press, 2003] 370). The angel reaffirms God's faithfulness to do what he promised (Gen 12:1–7; 13:15; 15:7, 18; 24:7; 26:3–4; 28:13; 35:12; 48:4; 50:24; Exod 3:8; 6:8; 12:25; 23:29–31; 32:13; 33:1; 34:12, 15; Num 14:23; Deut 6:10, 23; 10:11; Josh 1:6; Judg 2:1). Everything God did, even setting forth the legal codes of Leviticus, anticipated Israel's life in the land sworn to the patriarchs (for example, Lev 18:25–28; 19:23, 29; 20:22; 23:10, 39; 25:2, 18–23; 26:4, 6; compare Num 15:18; 26:53; 34:2–13; 35:33–34).

Even before the people entered the promised land, God planned how he would exile a disobedient people then renew the promise of land to his people (Lev 26:20–43). And the land was just what Israel needed, the best possible of lands for a farming people (Num 13:27; 14:7). Still, lack of faith kept Israel from conquering the land for forty years (Num 14:3, 23, 30, 34). And lack of obedience denied Aaron and Moses entrance into the land (Num 20:12, 24). Even then Yahweh had a plan to fulfill his promise to the fathers (Num 14:31; 27:12). When some tribes found land to their liking outside the boundaries of the promised land, that is, east of the Jordan River, still God incorporated that into his plans to give the land promised to the patriarchs (Num 32:4–55).

Why was God so careful to ensure that he gave the land to the descendants of Abraham? Because God had to be true to his own character! He could not break his covenant (Lev 26:44). This was true even though God knew Israel would not be true and would break the covenant (Gen 17:14; 26:15; Deut 31:16, 20).

2 Having pledged his faithfulness to his people, God then warns them of the covenant obligations they are expected to fulfill (Exod 24; Josh 24; see Butler, *Joshua,* on Josh 24). They can be covenant partners with only one party, God himself. As W. Brueggemann phrases it, "Yahweh designates Israel as Yahweh's covenant partner, so that Israel is, from the outset, obligated to respond to and meet Yahweh's expectations. As covenant partner of Yahweh, Israel is a people defined by obedience. . . . Israel was to respond in love to the self-giving love of Yahweh. As in any serious relationship of love, the appropriate response to love is to resonate with the will, purpose, desire, hope, and intention of the one who loves" (*Theology of the Old Testament* [Minneapolis: Fortress, 1997] 417, 420).

P. D. Miller observes of God's covenant, "There does not seem to have been any period in Israel's religious history where the specific recognition of the relationship of deity and tribe or people was not expressed in such a pact, though it took different forms prior to the monarchy and during it and may have been formulated differently in the North and in the South" (*Religion of Ancient Israel,*

5). This covenant theology may well have its roots deep in the northern kingdom and thus serve as a most appropriate theme to use in condemning the sins of the sons of Israel, the house of Joseph, or Ephraim. (See B. W. Anderson, *Contours of Old Testament Theology* [Minneapolis: Fortress, 1999] 138; for study of the covenant see S. L. McKenzie, *Covenant,* Understanding Biblical Themes [Saint Louis: Chalice, 2000].)

Thus Israel could not enter into treaties or covenants with other people who served other gods (compare Exod 23:32; 34:12, 15; Deut 7:2). Such a covenant with the land's native inhabitants would be attested to and preserved in the worship places of each of the covenant partners. Therefore, God makes one further stipulation. Israel must pull down all the altars dedicated to pagan, Canaanite gods in the land of promise (Exod 34:13; Deut 7:5; 12:3).

Before we are introduced to a single judge, we find the status of the people: they are disobedient, literally, "You did not listen to my voice." Thus Israel is called to the witness stand to witness against themselves. They must answer the messenger's question: "What is this that you have done?" That question stands over the entire book of Judges. Each generation needs to answer the question, but each generation stands self-incriminated before the question.

3 Israel's guilt leads God's messenger to change his tune. He reverts to his threats to withdraw his promise (see Exod 23:28–31; 33:2; 34:11–16; Deut 33:27; Josh 24:12, 18–20) to drive the inhabitants out of the land. Rather, these people remain a great threat. They stay right at Israel's "sides" (or if the common text-critical change is made, they are thorns in Israel's side) with their gods standing in the immediate vicinity to trap Israel. As Israel had been a "trap" to Egypt (Exod 10:7), so now the Canaanites and their gods will trap Israel as God had previously warned (Exod 23:33; 34:12; Num 33:55; Deut 7:16; Josh 23:13). A disobedient Israel has brought its own worst punishment on itself by leaving the source of temptation close at hand. Here we see the religious application of the military affairs described in Judg 1:22–36. The northern tribes cannot drive out the Amorites and Canaanites, the inhabitants of the land, because God chooses to carry out his threat rather than his promise and "not drive" the enemies out of the promised land.

4 The people of Israel respond appropriately at the moment with great lamentation. But is the lamentation caused by sorrow for sin and commitment to God, or is it simply a reaction to the announcement of punishment and of God's backing away from fulfilling promises for a disobedient people? Did they expect to hold God to his promises when they had not kept theirs? Or did God maintain the freedom to act in judgment and punishment in response to the people's actions? Their weeping only foreshadows further weeping to come (11:37–38; 14:16–17; 20:23, 26; 21:2). This theme thus ties the introduction of Judges into the Samson cycle and to the concluding epilogue.

5 Their weeping explains the name of the place—Bochim, "weeping" or "weepers." Often a biblical story concludes with an etiological statement giving the name of a person or a place, as is seen in the first chapters of Joshua. This has no bearing on the historicity of the materials. An etiological explanation has as much claim to historical accuracy as does an explanation of the inventive power of much later generations of narrators.

Israel appears to be on the right course of action as the people offer sacrifices to God. They ignore the gods of the land; they avoid the traps and snares around them. They appear to offer true, covenant worship to their covenant God. That is the starting point for the book of Judges: a repentant people have failed politically and religiously. Standing convicted before God's messenger of judgment, they react appropriately in sorrow and sacrifice. Have they renewed the covenant the previous generation made in Josh 24? Apparently so, but how long will this last?

6 The scene changes abruptly once more. We return to the days of Joshua, just as earlier we had turned back to the days of Caleb's conquests. We are constantly reminded that chronological order is not the writer's intention in the book of Judges. Rather, we have had the stage set in Judg 1:1–2:5, showing us the people's inability to complete the mission God set before them through Joshua and showing us God's refusal to carry out the mission of fulfilling any more of his promises for such a disobedient people. Thus from two perspectives we discover one central truth: life is going to be more difficult in the promised land than we expected and than we experienced in most of the book of Joshua.

We have suddenly returned to the exact phrasing of Josh 24:28 with important additions. Now the directive is given explicitly to the "sons of Israel," and they are to "go" each to his inheritance "to take possession of the land." This is a distinct refinement of Josh 21:43, where "Yahweh gave to Israel all the land which he had promised to give to their fathers, and they possessed it [וַיִּרָשׁוּהָ] and lived [וַיֵּשְׁבוּ] in it." Here we see clearly how Judges seeks to consciously provide the dark side of Joshua's bright side. The book of Joshua emphasizes the greatness of its obedient leader and the fullness of the divine faithfulness. (See T. C. Butler, *Understanding the Basic Themes of Joshua* [Dallas: Word, 1991]; idem, "The Theology of Joshua," *RevExp* 95 [1998] 203–25.) The book of Judges shows what happens to a people without leadership, a people after Joshua dies. They lose all God's gifts because they choose to coexist with the enemy and the enemy's gods rather than obey the God of promises and covenant. The faithful God must deal with an unfaithful people. Joshua can talk of having rest on all sides. Judges can only talk of a people living amid the enemies.

7–10 Judges moves Joshua's climactic verse for this section to the top of the order. Why? Because this sets the stage for his story, a story in direct opposition to the situation in Joshua's day. Joshua's generation, as long as it lasted, could bear eyewitness to God's great acts. But the generation with the revered servant of the Lord leading them died out. For Judges the importance lies in the situation v 10 describes. The previous generation was inevitably replaced by a new generation, an ignorant generation. They did "not know" Israel's God or the "actions" that God had done for Israel. In one generation true religion, the religion of Josh 24, vanished from the promised land. The weeping and sacrifice of v 5 did not suffice. True religion knows the tradition and the God of the tradition. A generation that does not teach its children, as Josh 4:6, 21 advised, would lose its children to false religion.

11 Without knowing God or the tradition of the fathers, the new generation follows the only example they have before them, the example of the Canaanite Baal worshipers. The plural הַבְּעָלִים represents the various manifestations of the high god Baal in the various Canaanite worship sites. As the northern tribes had failed to evict and eliminate the Canaanites in the various parts of the country, so the "sons of Israel" now serve Baal in every part of the country. *Baal* means "lord," "master," or "husband" and was the name often given to the high god of a state.

By 1550 B.C.E. *Baal* came to be used as the title or name of the Canaanite weather and war god also know as Hadad. Ugaritic materials show Baal as the major god, the son of the ancient high god El, with Anat and Astarte as his consorts. Baal often fought with Yam, the god of the sea; Mot, the god of death and the underworld; and Ashtar, the morning and evening star. Baal is a fertility god in the sense that he controlled the weather and, more specifically, the rain for crops. Ugarit may have celebrated his death and resurrection as part of the annual agricultural cycle. The texts do not reveal sacred prostitution, but the Canaanite enemies accuse them of such lewd worship behavior. Thus J. M. Hadley can conclude:

> In none of these passages do we have anything that corresponds to the modern concept of "Canaanite religion"—a figment of scholars' imaginations. Hosea and Ezekiel use sexual imagery as a metaphor of Israel's behavior (similarly in Jer 3). Scholars have derived a "sex cult" from this, but there is no evidence for lascivious orgies or sacred marriages. . . . The concept of prostitution belongs not to cultic practices but to the vocabulary of the writers. (*NIDOTTE*, 4:426)

On the other side J. Day (*ABD*, 1:548) argues from the plethora of Old Testament evidence that sacred prostitution must have been connected to Baal worship.

Baal appears only sporadically in the Old Testament. The singular referring to a specific god appears in Deut 4:3; Judg 6; 1 Kgs 16:29–19:18; 22:51–53; 2 Kgs 1; 3:2; 10:1–18, 27; 11:18; 17:16; 21:3; 23:4–5; 2 Chr 23:17; Jer 2:8; 7:9; 11:13, 17; 12:16; 19:5; 23:13, 27; 32:29, 35; Hos 2:8 (2:10); 13:1; Zeph 1:4; compare Rom 11:4. Baal (of) Peor appears in Num 25:3, 5; Deut 4:3; Ps 106:28; Hos 9:10. The plural appears in Judg 2:11; 3:7; 8:33; 10:6, 10; 1 Sam 7:4; 12:10; 1 Kgs 18:18; 2 Chr 17:3; 24:7; 28:2; 33:3; 34:4; Jer 2:23; 9:13; Hos 2:13, 17 (15, 19); 11:2. Looking at inscriptional and onomastic evidence, P. D. Miller (*Religion of Ancient Israel*, 58) warns against exaggerating the degree of Baalistic syncretism in Israel. See W. Herrmann, "Baal," *DDD*, 249–63. J. Day is correct in concluding that

> the Baal cult . . . provided the greatest and most enduring threat to the development of exclusive Yahweh worship within ancient Israel. The fact that the Israelites were settled among the Canaanites, for whom the worship of Baal was so important, and that Palestine is a land utterly dependent for its fertility upon the rain, which was held to be Baal's special realm of influence, accounts for the tempting nature of this cult as well as the strength of the OT polemic against it. (*ABD*, 1:545)

They did what was right in their eyes (compare 14:3, 7; 17:6; 21:25). That proved to be "evil in Yahweh's eyes," a favorite biblical phrase used to describe Israel's disobedience, particularly its false religious practices borrowed from the nations as instigated by Israel's kings (Gen 38:7; Num 32:13; Deut 4:25; 9:18; 17:2; 31:29; Judg 2:11; 3:7, 12; 4:1; 6:1; 10:6; 13:1; 1 Sam 15:19; 1 Kgs 11:6; 14:22; 15:26, 34; 16:19, 25, 30; 21:20, 25; 22:53; 2 Kgs 3:2; 8:18, 27; 13:2, 11; 14:24; 15:9, 18, 24, 28; 17:2, 17; 21:2, 6, 16, 20; 23:32, 37; 24:9, 19; 1 Chr 2:3; 2 Chr 21:6; 22:4; 29:6; 33:2, 6, 22; 36:5, 9, 12; Jer 52:2).

12 By serving Baal they "abandoned Yahweh" (compare Judg 10:6; 1 Sam 12:10; 1 Kgs 9:9; 2 Kgs 21:22). In renewing the covenant the people swore not to forsake (עזב) Yahweh and serve other gods. Now the situation is reversed. They cannot worship the God they do not know, so they forsake him for other gods. Joshua had given them the consequences of such an act, but they forgot all that

Joshua did (Josh 24:20). Yahweh was now the "God of their fathers," not the God of the present generation. This generation worships the "gods of the peoples who surrounded them," in direct opposition to the teaching in Deut 6:14 (compare Deut 13:6–8). Joshua claimed that Yahweh gave them rest all around and gave their enemies into their hands (21:44), but now Israel gives its worship (literally, "bows face to the ground," יִשְׁתַּחֲווּ) to the gods of these defeated enemies.

The Israelites thus quickly turn victory into defeat and obedience into heretical worship. This "infuriated" Yahweh. כעס, *hip̄ʿil*, "irritated," means "to grieve, to provoke to anger, to make indignant, to infuriate." Most often creating and worshiping idols and other false religious practices lie behind God's fury. This fury is usually directed at Israel's unfaithful leaders who encourage the people in false religious rituals and worship (Deut 4:25; 9:18; 31:29; 32:16, 21; Judg 2:12; 1 Kgs 14:9, 15; 15:30; 16:2, 7, 13, 26, 33; 21:22; 22:54; 2 Kgs 17:11, 17; 21:6, 15; 22:17; 23:19, 26; 2 Chr 28:25; 33:6; 34:25; Neh 3:37; Pss 78:58; 106:29; Isa 65:3; Jer 7:18–19; 8:19; 11:17; 25:6–7; 32:29–30, 32; 44:3, 8; Ezek 8:17; 16:26; Hos 12:15).

13 V 13 reduces the previous two verses to their essence: a people bound to Yahweh in a covenant acknowledging his grace and lordship follows the false gods of Canaan. Ashtaroth represents the plural of Astarte, apparently given the vowels of the Hebrew word בֹּשֶׁת, *bošet*, "shame," and originally spelled Ashtoreth. The Mesopotamian counterpart is Ishtar. The Egyptians also worshiped the Canaanite Astarte from 1500 B.C.E. onward. In Ugaritic materials Astarte, one of Baal's consorts, plays a subordinate role to Asherah and Anath. The war goddess, she was also the god of fertility and sexuality and closely associated to the Phoenician city of Sidon, especially in Solomon's day (1 Kgs 11:5, 33; 2 Kgs 23:13). Astarte may be the "queen of heaven" in Jer 7:18 and 44:17, 18. Only under Samuel's leadership did Israel forsake the worship of the Ashtaroth (Judg 10:6; 1 Sam 7:4; compare 1 Sam 12:10). See J. M. Hadley, *NIDOTTE*, 3:562–63; N. Wyatt, *DDD*, 203–13; J. Day, *ABD*, 1:491–94.

14 The infuriated Yahweh "burned with anger" (חרה אף; Exod 4:14; 22:24 [Heb. 23]; 32:10–11; Num 11:1, 10; 12:9; 22:22; 25:3; 32:10, 13; Deut 6:15; 7:4; 11:17; 29:26; 31:17; Josh 7:1; 23:16; Judg 2:14, 20; 3:8; 6:39; 10:7; 2 Sam 6:7; 2 Kgs 13:3; 23:26; 1 Chr 13:10; 2 Chr 25:15; Job 42:7; Ps 106:40; Isa 5:25; Hos 8:5; Zech 10:3). This metaphoric expression refers literally to the burning of God's nostrils. G. A. Herion notes that with חרה and חֲרוֹן "the source of provocation often is 'transgression of the covenant' (Josh 7:1; 23:16; Judg 2:20) or 'pursuit of other gods' (Deut 6:14–15; 11:16–17; 31:16–17)" (*ABD*, 6:990). From this Herion finds "a specialized use designating the legitimate rage of a suzerain against a disobedient vassal." He further differentiates human passion and loss of self-control from divine pathos, "an act formed with care and intention, the result of determination and decision. It is not a 'fever of the mind' that disregards standards of justice and culminates in irrational and irresponsible action; it is intricately linked to 'ethos' and approximates what we mean by 'righteous indignation'" (*ABD*, 6:991). This, however, sounds too much like a modern theologian with theodicy in mind rather than the biblical writer who used an idiom from the common language and applied it anthropomorphically to God. Herion is certainly correct when he concludes that divine wrath "is a reaction to human history, an attitude called forth by human (mis)conduct." As J. F. D. Creach says, "the most consistent use of חָרָה, when it connotes the anger of God, is in the narrative report of Israel's unfaithful response

to Yahweh's steadfast love. Rarely does divine rage seem arbitrary (2 Sam 24:1)"
(*NIDOTTE*, 2:267). I must note and disagree with K. Latvus (*God, Anger, and Ideology*, 36–41), who uses Smend's progression of Deuteronomists to isolate divine
anger as a theme only of the exilic Deuteronomists (DtrN). Certainly the theme
of divine anger to explain defeat is much more widespread in the ancient Near
East and in Israel than to refer only to the nation's ultimate destruction.

Divine anger leads to divine action. God hands Israel over to "plunderers,"
that is, arrogant raiders who defeat nations and steal their treasures (Ps 44:10; Isa
10:13; Hos 13:15). Saul, in the line of the judges, would temporarily deliver Israel
from such plunderers (1 Sam 14:48), but the Philistines continued plundering
Israel's towns (1 Sam 23:1). Plunderers eventually brought Israel's downfall (2 Kgs
17:20). But Yahweh always controlled the plunderers, selling Israel to them (Isa
42:22–25) and punishing them for unjustly mistreating God's people Israel (Jer
50:11). The stories of Judges are stories of deliverance from such plunderers, a
deliverance that continues through Israel's history (Isa 17:14).

15 Enemies take charge of the promised land, and Israel's Divine Warrior joins
the enemy forces. Yahweh brings evil on the people who did evil (v 11). Israel should
not have been surprised. God had promised this, sworn an oath to do it. The biblical
text does not point back exactly to a previous text, so scholars debate the reference.
Lindars (104) points to Deut 6:14–15; Block and Brown prefer Deut 31:16–21; Burney
and Wolf look to the curses of Deut 28:25; Gray finds the source in Deut 27:15–26;
Younger adds Deut 28:25–37 alongside 31:16–21 to the list; Olson posits Deut 7:4 as
an example. Moore is more accurate in sensing "the reference is not to any single
passage expressly containing this threat, but to the whole tenor of such chapters as
Dt. 28 and Lev. 26" (71). Or even more abstractly, the reference is to the very nature
of the covenant relationship. Olson is on target: "According to the covenant, God has
the legal right to impose the death penalty on Israel as a people; such is the severity
of the transgression of bowing down to other deities" (756). Certainly they were "in
extreme trouble" (צרר, "tied up, restricted, confined, constricted").

16 As we come to expect in Judges, the unexpected occurs. "Yahweh raised
up judges." Here we obviously turn to a cycle involving the following generations,
whereas the preceding verses appear to refer to the generation after Joshua. The
Hebrew participle שׁפֵט used in a nominal function carries a wide range of meanings. It can refer to one carrying out legal functions as a judge (Exod 2:14; Deut
1:16; 17:9, 12; Isa 3:2; Mic 7:3). The same meaning appears in the plural (Num
25:5; Deut 16:18; 19:17–18; Josh 8:33; 23:2; 24:1; 1 Sam 8:1; 2 Chr 1:2; 19:5–6; Ezra
10:14; Job 9:24; Pss 109:31; 141:6; Prov 8:16; Isa 1:26; Zeph 3:3), though some
plural uses may be interpreted as "rulers," as is the case in 2 Chr 26:21, Pss 2:10,
148:11, Isa 40:23, Dan 9:12, Hos 13:10, Amos 2:3, and Mic 4:14. The ambiguity
in meaning appears clearly in Gen 18:25, Isa 33:22, and Jer 11:20 when applied
to God's function over all the earth. This ambiguity hangs over several passages,
especially those in Judges and ones referring back to the book of Judges (2 Sam
7:11; 2 Kgs 23:22; compare Isa 1:26). Surprisingly, the nominal participle appears
very seldom in the book of Judges itself—2:16–19, 4:4, and 11:27.

Outside the present passage, the term for "judge" is used in reference to
Deborah functioning in a legal setting (4:4) and God operating in a legal setting
(11:27). As Bal notes, "The only character-judge who does something beyond
killing enemies is Deborah" (*Murder and Difference*, 52). The verb appears more

frequently (3:10; 10:2–3; 12:7–14; 15:20; 16:31), in the phrase וַיִּשְׁפֹּט אֶת־יִשְׂרָאֵל, "he judged Israel," and is not applied to the central judges—Ehud, Deborah, Barak, Gideon, and Abimelech. What function, then, does the author of chap. 2 expect these leaders to perform? Is the writer pointing ahead only to those explicitly said to have judged Israel? Or are all the book's leading characters enveloped in this term? These questions may be variously answered.

Brown's understanding is typical:

> The book of Judges is not about judges, at least not in the way we commonly understand the English term. . . . The Hebrew word *špt* has a broader semantic range than does the English term "judge." The Hebrew can also mean "leader" or "deliverer." . . . The type of leadership that judges provided was unique in the ancient Near East. They were charismatic figures, divinely raised up in times of crisis from outside the traditional power circles to meet a specific threat, namely, enemy oppression. . . . It was a nondynastic leadership. (123)

Gray points to Ras Shamra or Ugaritic texts from the fourteenth century to indicate that "'ruler' is the basic meaning of the Canaanite cognate of the Hebrew *shopet,* who was thus one who upheld *mishpat,* or ordered rule" ([1986] 202). Hoppe sees the Deuteronomist using the term in a way distinct from the rest of the book by picturing the judge here as a "prophet who calls Israel to obedience" and "fulfilling the vacuum of leadership caused by the death of Joshua" (115).

Block (22–25) has summarized the discussion well and shown the expansive leadership roles the judges filled. Akkadian, Ugaritic, and Phoenician cognates point to the meaning of "rule or govern," "exercise leadership." Block uses the present passage to infer that the author applied the term "judge" to all the leaders in the book, extending through 1 Sam 7. These leaders then "functioned more as deliverers than as legal functionaries." They gained power and authority from Yahweh for a soteriological, not a legal purpose, delivering Israel from external enemies rather than settling internal disputes. Israel's judges were "tribal rulers, leaders, governors."

Younger (21) follows Block, seeing the judges both as "deliverers" or "saviors" and as "instigators" or "stimuli" "for godly living. In essence, their purpose was not judicial, but soteriological." In external affairs their role was "restoring *shalom,* harmonious relations," as shown by T. L. J. Mafico, "Judge, Judging" (*ABD,* 3:1104–5). McCann, leaning on J. Berquist's translation (*Reclaiming Her Story: The Witness of Women in the Old Testament* [Saint Louis: Chalice, 1992] 91) as "bringer of justice," expands the judge's role a bit to "persons entrusted with the enactment of God's will for the world." For McCann this "encompassed deliverance from external oppression (2:16, 18), leadership exercised to ensure the exclusive worship and service of God (2:19), and hence the creation of internal conditions that support life as God wills it to be" (4).

Scholars may be too determined to define something the biblical text leaves tantalizingly ambiguous. Lindars points out that "the function of judging (or ruling) is not characteristic of the stories," judges being chosen to "import the idea of rule into the scenario of the period" (105). Certainly none of the judges, with the possible exception of Deborah, performs prophetic functions leading the nation to do the will of God. It appears that the editor of Judges has played his introduction of leadership over against that of Joshua. Josh 1:1–9 provided Joshua an explicit job description in both a military and a religious sense. Judges receive no such instruction from God. The narrative simply tells the historical reality. God acts unilaterally to raise up a judge with no mention of qualifications or expectations. These judges deliver or save Israel from plunderers. Such action does not bring the judges the response from the people and from God that Joshua received. God exalted Joshua, and the people feared him with reverent awe just as they had feared Moses (Josh 4:14). Eventually, Joshua received Moses' title as the "servant of Yahweh" (Josh 24:29). The judges cannot even get the people to listen to them. Instead the people "became harlots" with foreign gods. This means at least that they were unfaithful to God (Judg 8:27, 33). It most likely means they joined in the fertility practices of their neighbors (Exod 34:15–16; compare Deut 31:16; Lev 17:7; 20:5–6; Pss 73:27; 106:39; Ezek 6:9) involving cultic prostitution, though this is the subject of heated debate. Ackerman can declare, "The notion that sacred prostitution ever existed in Israel or anywhere in the ancient Near East, for example, has been widely discredited" (*Warrior, Dancer,* 156). (See the arguments against cultic prostitution by E. A. Goodfriend, *ABD,* 5:507–9; K. van der Toorn, *ABD,* 5:510–13.)

The Hebrew זָנָה refers to adultery, illicit sex, and prostitution (G. H. Hall, *NIDOTTE,* 1:1123). So Schneider astutely notes that "this terminology is powerful in a text where some of the major characters have close relations with prostitutes (Judg 11:1; 16:1 and 19:2 where the final conflict is initiated by a woman carrying out this action)." The lure of Canaanite religion is obvious. Canaanite gods have a history of providing for the people living in Canaan. Israel's God has only shown power in war and desert. Do not the Israelites, as much as the Canaanites, need a god who provides food, fertility, and fun in the new land? Israel has married Yahweh in their covenant relationship, but Block points out that the "lusty young fertility gods" of Canaan "offered exciting and often erotic cult rituals" (129).

17 Scholars quickly dismiss v 17 as a later addition that credits the judges with religious leadership. Block notes the difficulty of the verse because it "interrupts the flow of thought and casts the rulers in the roles of spiritual reformers, preachers of the way in which their fathers walked in the commandments of Yahweh" (128). Block prefers to see the editor interrupting his own train of thought and looking "back at the period of the governors/judges through the filter of the last governor, Samuel, who clearly functioned in this capacity." Webb ([1987] 243, n. 6) sees the proclamation of 2:17 involved in Othniel's work of judging. V 17 stands in direct contrast to the work of Joshua in Josh 1:7–8 and chaps. 23–24. Joshua studied the commandments given to Moses and led the people to follow. This is the standard for all leaders in Israel. Leaders after Moses instill the commandments and bring the people to renew the covenant with Yahweh. This generation after Joshua's death have forgotten both the acts and the words of God. Their leaders refuse to follow the pattern Joshua set. The editor of Judges thus assumes this role for the judges but knows from each of the stories that no one accepted and assumed the role. Instead they "quickly" turned the other direction to the gods with experience in the land. The angelic warning of v 3 had quickly become reality without the ensuing weeping of v 4.

18 Boling (76) dismisses vv 18–19 as adding little. However, the verses are important for the editor, for they stand in stark contrast to vv 14–15. God has unexpectedly raised up judges. No longer does God stand against Israel. Rather God stands with Israel, or more particularly with the judge. God's presence, not the judge's leadership or military skills, brings victory. Yahweh remains faithful to the judge even when Israel does not, as seen in v 17.

Yahweh does not reward the judge or the people for their attitude and actions. They do not deserve victory. Yahweh brings victory out of divine "compassion," not out of human morality or repentance. This compassion contrasts with the anger of v 14 and is connected to Israel's "groaning," an infrequent root (נאק) in the Hebrew Bible (Exod 2:24; 6:5; Job 24:12; Ezek 30:24) but one connected with the exodus event. Thus Israel has forgotten the deeds of Yahweh for the fathers but acts like the fathers in groaning about their condition. The groaning has nothing to do with their sins or with a sense of repentance. Their groaning comes strictly from their condition "before those who tormented and oppressed them." Such groaning mirrors Israel's weeping in v 4 without mention of the sacrifice of v 5. Yahweh's compasssion (נחם) is related to the verb for comfort in times of bereavement (Gen 24:67; 37:35; 2 Sam 12:24; 13:39). The psalmists thank God and declare that God is a God of comfort (Pss 69:20 [Heb. 21]; 71:21; 86:17). God's compassion here leads to the irony of Israel's compassion in 21:6, 15. The term also means to relent or change courses of action and describes a basic part of God's nature (Joel 2:13; Jonah 4:2) by which he turns away from anger at people to bring a comfortable condition to them (Gen 6:6–7; Exod 32:14; Jonah 3:9–10).

The holy God reacts in anger against sin but always holds a warm spot in his heart for a hurting, suffering people. Still, in certain situations part of the character of this God who is so distinct and different from humans consists in his refusal to lie or deceive (Hebrew שקר), interpreted as his refusal to relent or change his mind (1 Sam 15:29). This shows the freedom of God to stand above all human definitions and to respond to the human condition in personal care, not in a legal courtroom decision.

19 The editor summarizes the cyclic sin of Israel. As Joshua died (v 8), so do the judges. As the generation after Joshua forsook Yahweh, so do the generations following the judges. This assumes that the judges succeeded to some extent in bringing Israel back to Yahweh for a time, an assumption standing in some tension with v 17. Together vv 18 and 19 picture a people constantly shifting allegiance, always on the lookout for a way and reason to abandon Yahweh quickly in favor of the gods with history in the land rather than in Egypt and the wilderness. The editor prepares us for the worst behavior that we will encounter in the following narratives. Whereas the people of Israel learned from the sin at Ai (Josh 7–8), the people of Israel never learn the lesson of God's compassionate presence with their judges. They can never surrender their fascination with the allure of Canaanite religion.

20–21 Ultimately, the people's fascination with foreign gods attracts Yahweh's anger. The situation with the generation after Joshua in v 14 becomes God's permanent attitude toward the stubborn people. Joshua had led the people to covenant renewal (Josh 24–24) even when nations remained in the land unconquered (Josh 13:1–6). Israel chooses covenants with Canaan's gods (v 2), so the threat of v 3 becomes reality. The divine plan for the generation after Joshua had apparently been for them to follow God and conquer those remaining nations in the same way Joshua defeated the cities of Canaan. That required an obedient generation like that under Joshua. When generation after generation shows that obedience no longer characterizes Israel, God exercises divine freedom, changes the plan, and decides not to drive out the nations. Divine anger replaces divine compassion as the central emotion towards Israel.

Amit gives up on Judg 2:20–3:4 and relegates the section to "editing that sought answers to the question as to why Joshua did not drive out all the Canaanites and why the other nations remained in the country" (*Book of Judges*, 156–57). I see no reason for such skepticism about the narrator's ability to use all the materials to create one total picture of God allowing nations to remain for a complex set of reasons, all tied eventually to Israel's obedience or disobedience of God's commandments, especially his commandments with regard to staging warfare.

22 So God decides to use the nations to test Israel's obedience. Would the people ever return to the ways of the fathers, the ways of Joshua's generation? (Notice that Moses' generation could not be described as an obedient one.)

23 The final verse reiterates the situation that made it possible for nations to remain and tempt Israel as reported in v 21 and also prepares the way for the next section, which will also deal with the problem of testing Israel with remaining nations. We are ready to read the stories of the judges, knowing the overarching plot from the beginning. Judges is a book of narratives detailing God's judgment of a disobedient people lured by foreign gods and sacrificing to them rather than to Yahweh.

Explanation

Chap. 1 showed the political and military disobedience of Israel and the leadership role of Judah after Joshua died. Chap. 2 pictures the religious rebellion of the covenant people. They do not learn the lessons that Joshua's life and actions should have taught them. They do not remember God's works or words. They weep and sacrifice for a moment but renege on covenant promises for centuries. God's presence with the judges and compassion for the oppressed, groaning people do not sway Israel to return to the God of their fathers and the commandments that the Joshua generation obeyed. Instead, they let fascination with the gods of the country's history—the gods of fertility and crops, the gods of sexuality and weather—lure them into worship that infuriates the God of their history. How could a people so quickly transform themselves from covenant servants of Yahweh to fascinated worshipers of Baal and his cohorts? The following stories will illustrate how that happens and will justify Yahweh's destructive actions against a disobedient people of the covenant.

II. Israel's Sagging Fortunes under the Judges (3:1–16:31)

A. Bright Beginning in the South (3:1–31)

Bibliography

Alonso-Schökel, L. "Erzählkunst im Buche der Richter." *Bib* 42 (1961) 143–72. **Alter, R.** *Art of Biblical Narrative*. 37–41. **Amit, Y.** "The Story of Ehud (Judges 3:12–30): The Form and the Message." In *Signs and Wonders: Biblical Texts in Literary Focus*. Ed. J. C. Exum. Decatur, GA: Scholars Press, 1989. 97–123. **Andersson, G.** *The Book and Its Narratives: A Critical Examination of Some Synchronic Studies of the Book of Judges*. Örebro Studies in Literary History and Criticism 1. Örebro: Universitetsbiblioteket, 2001. **Auerbach, E.** "Untersuchungen zum Richterbuch II: Ehud." *ZAW* 51 (1933) 47–51. **Barré, M. L.** "The Meaning of *pršdn* in Judges iii.22." *VT* 41 (1991) 1–11. **Barredo, M. A.** "Los relatos sobre los primeros jueces (Jue 3,7–14): Enfoques literarios y teológicos." *Anton* 73 (1998) 407–57. **Berman, J.** "The 'Sword of Mouths' (Jud. iii 16; Ps. cxlix 6; Prov. v 4): A Metaphor and Its Ancient Near Eastern Context." *VT* 52 (2002) 291–303. **Braslavy, J.** "On the War of Ehud: 'To Seir' and 'The Crossings of the Jordan'" (Heb.). *Beit-Miqra* 13 (1968) 37–42. **Brettler, M. Z.** "Never the Twain Shall Meet? The Ehud Story as History and Literature." *HUCA* 62 (1992) 285–304. ———. "The Ehud Story as Satire." In *The Creation of History in Ancient Israel*. New York: Routledge, 1995. 79–90. **Cahill, J., K. Reinhard, D. Tarler,** and **P. Warnock.** "It Had to Happen Sometime—Scientists Examine Remains of Ancient Bathrooms." *BAR* 17 (1991) 64–69. **Chisholm, R. B., Jr.** "What's Wrong with This Picture: Stylistic Variation as a Rhetorical Technique in Judges." Paper presented to Evangelical Theological Society, 2006, Washington, DC. **Christianson, E. S.** "A Fistful of Shekels: Scrutinizing Ehud's Entertaining Violence (Judges 3:12–30)." *BibInt* 11 (2003) 53–78. **Craigie, P. C.** "A Reconsideration of Shamgar Ben Anath (Jdg 3:31 and 5:6)." *JBL* 91 (1972) 239–40. **Culley, R. C.** *Themes and Variations: A Study of Action in Biblical Narrative*. Atlanta: Scholars Press, 1992. 99–100. **Danelius, E.** "Shamgar ben Anath." *JNES* 22 (1963) 191–93. **Deist, F.** "'Murder in the Toilet' (Judges 3.12–30): Translation and Transformation." *Scr* 58 (1996) 263–72. **Deurloo, K. A.** "Net als het lemmer: Ehud." In *Om voor te lezen—Miqra*. FS F. J. Hoogewoud, ed. H. Blok, K. A. Deurloo, et al. ACEBTSup 4. Maastricht: Shaker, 2005. 57–62. **Dexinger, F.** "Ein Pladoyer für die Linkshander im Richterbuch." *ZAW* 89 (1977) 268–69. **Donner, H.** *Geschichte des Volkes Israel und seiner Nachbarn in Grundzügen*. Vol. 1. Göttingen: Vandenhoeck & Ruprecht, 1984. **Eisenberg, D. N.,** and **B. Halpern.** "Readers Reply: Did Ehud Escape through the Toilet?" *BAR* 15 (1989) 12–13. **Elitzur, Y.** "The Story of Ehud Son of Gera" (Heb.). In *Studies in the Book of Judges*. Publications of the Israel Bible Society 10. Jerusalem, 1966. 403–13, 430–34. **Feldman, L. H.** "Josephus's Portrait of Ehud." In *Pursuing the Text*. Ed. J. C. Reeves and J. Kampen. JSOTSup 184. Sheffield: Sheffield Academic, 1994. 177–201. **Fensham, F. C.** "Shamgar ben Anath." *JNES* 20 (1989) 197–98. **Garsiel, M.** "The Story of Ehud Son of Gera in the Book of Judges" (Heb.). *Beit-Miqra* 16 (1973) 285–92. ———. "The Story of Ehud Son of Gera (Judges 3:12–30)" (Heb.). In *Reflections on Scripture—Selections from Studies of the Yishai Ron Memorial Bible Circle*. Vol. 2. Tel Aviv, 1977. 57–77. **Glaser, O.** "Zur Erzählung von Ehud und Eglon." *ZDPV* 55 (1932) 81–82. **Good, E. M.** *Irony in the Old Testament*. Philadelphia: Fortress, 1965. **Greenspahn, F. E.** "The Theology of the Framework of Judges." *VT* 36 (1986) 385–96. **Grottanelli, C.** "Un passo del Libro dei Giudici alla luce della comparazione storico-religiosa: Il Giudice Ehud e il valore della mano sinistra." In

Atti del Primo Convegno Italiano sul Vicino Oriente Antico. Rome, 1978. 35–45. **Hadley, J. M.** *The Cult of Asherah in Ancient Israel and Judah.* Cambridge: Cambridge UP, 2000. **Halpern, B.** "The Assassination of Eglon: The First Locked-Room Murder Mystery." *BR* 4 (1988) 32–41, 44. ———. *First Historians.* 39–75. **Handy, L. K.** "Uneasy Laughter: Ehud and Eglon and Ethnic Humor." *SJOT* 6 (1992) 233–46. **Hänsler, H.** "Der historische Hintergrund von Richter 3:8–10." *Bib* 11 (1930) 391–418; 12 (1931) 3–36, 271–96, 395–410. **Hartmann, T. A. G.** "נמד in Richter 3,16 oder die Pygmäen im Dschungel der Längenmaße." *ZAH* 13 (2000) 188–93. **Hostetter, E. C.** *Nations Mightier and More Numerous: The Biblical View of Palestine's Pre-Israelite Peoples.* BIBAL Dissertation Series 3. N. Richland Hills, TX: BIBAL Press, 1995. **Hübner, U.** "Mord auf dem Abort? Überlegungen zu Humor, Gewaltdarstellung und Realienkunde in Ri 3,12–30." *BN* 40 (1987) 130–40. **Ishida, T.** "The Structure and Historical Implications of the Lists of Pre-Israelite Nations." *Bib* 60 (1979) 461–90. **Jagersma, H.** "Geen andere goden: Richteren 3:1–6." *ACEBT* 19 (2001) 65–69. **Jobling, D.** "Right-Brained Story of Left-Handed Man: An Antiphon to Yairah Amit." In *Signs and Wonders.* Ed. J. C. Exum. 125–31. ———. "Structuralist Criticism: The Text's World of Meaning." In *Judges and Method* (1995) 91–118. **Jugel, E.,** and **H.-D. Neef.** "Ehud als Linkshänder: Exegetische und medizinische Anmerkungen zu Ri 3,15." *BN* 97 (1999) 45–54. **Jull, T. A.** "מקרה in Judges 3: A Scatological Reading." *JSOT* 81 (1998) 63–75. **Kallai, Z.** "'Dan Why Abides He by Ships'—and the Rules of Historiographical Writing." *JNSL* 23 (1997) 35–45. ———. "The Twelve-Tribe Systems of Israel." *VT* 47 (1997) 53–90. **Knauf, E. A.** "The Cultural Impact of Secondary State Formation: The Cases of the Edomites and Moabites." In *Early Edom and Moab.* Ed. P. Bienkowsky. Sheffield Archaeological Monograph 7. Sheffield: Collis, 1992. 47–54. ———. "Eglon and Ophrah: Two Toponymic Notes on the Book of Judges." *JSOT* 51 (1991) 25–44. **Kraeling, E. G. H.** "Difficulties in the Story of Ehud." *JBL* 54 (1935) 205–10. **Kutsko, J.** "Eglon." *ADB*, 2:319–20. **Maisler, B.** "Shamgar ben 'Anat." *PEQ* 66 (1934) 192–94. **Malamat, A.** "Cushan Rishathaim and the Decline of the Near East around 1200 b.c." *JNES* 13 (1954) 231–42. **Margalith, O.** "The Meaning and Significance of Ashera." *VT* 40 (1990) 264–97. **Mazar (Maisler), B.** "Shamgar ben 'Anat." *PEFQS* 66 (1934) 192–94. **Millard, A. R.** "Back to the Iron Bed: Og's or Procrustes'?" In *Congress Volume: Paris 1992.* Ed. J. A. Emerton. VTSup 61. Leiden: Brill, 1995. 193–203. **Miller, G. P.** "Verbal Feud in the Hebrew Bible: Judges 3:12–30 and 19–21." *JNES* 55 (1996) 105–17. **Mobley, G.** "Ehud and the Monoliths." In *The Empty Men.* ABRL. New York: Doubleday, 2005. 75–112. **Na'aman, N.** "Israel, Edom, and Egypt in the Tenth Century bce." *TA* 19 (1992) 71–79. **Oded, B.** "Cushan-Rishathaim (Judges 3:8–11): An Implicit Polemic" (Heb.). In *Texts, Temples, and Tragedies.* FS M. Haran, ed. M. V. Fox et al. Winona Lake, IN: Eisenbrauns, 1996. 89–94. **Ogden, G. S.** "The Special Features of a Story: A Study of Judges 3:12–20." *BT* 42 (1991) 408–14. **Quinn, A.** "Rhetoric and the Integrity of the Scripture." *CICR* 13 (1986) 326–41. **Re'em, H.** "The Story of Ehud Son of Gera Taken at Face Value" (Heb.). *Beit-Miqra* 17 (1972) 109–12. **Rösel, H. N.** "Ehud und die Ehuderzählung." In *Meilenstein.* FS H. Donner, ed. M. Weippert und S. Timm. Ägypten und Altes Testament 30. Wiesbaden: Harrassowitz, 1995. 225–33. ———. "Zur Ehud-Erzählung." *ZAW* 98 (1977) 270–72. **Scherer, A.** "Simson und Schamgar: Zur Frage nach der ursprünglich Position der Schamgarnotiz im Richterbuch." *ZAW* 114 (2002) 106–9. ———. *Überlieferungen von Religion und Krieg: Exegetische und religionsgeschichtliche Untersuchungen zu Richter 3–8 und verwandten Texten.* WMANT 105. Neukirchen-Vluyn: Neukirchener, 2005. **Shupak, N.** "New Light on Shamgar ben 'Anath." *Bib* 70 (1989) 517–25. **Sima, A.** "Nochmals zur Deutung des hebräischen Namens Otniel." *BN* 106 (2001) 47–51. **Soggin, J. A.** "Ehud ed i guadi di Moab, Giud. 3,28b." *BeO* 15 (1973) 252. English translation in *Old Testament and Oriental Studies*, BibOr 29 (Rome: Biblical Institute Press, 1975) 237. ———. "Ehud und Eglon: Bemerkungen zu Richter iii 11b–31." *VT* 39 (1989) 95–100. **Snyman, S. D.** "Samgar ben Anat oder die Rigtyers." *HvTSt* 60 (2004) 831–41. ———. "Shamgar ben Anath: A Farming Warrior or a Farmer at War." *VT* 55 (2005) 125–29. **Sternberg, M.** *Poetics.* 331–37. **Streck, M. P.,** and

S. Weninger. "Zur Deutung des hebräischen Namens ʿOṯnīʾēl." *BN* 96 (1999) 21–29. Sweeney, M. A. "Davidic Polemic in the Book of Judges." *VT* 47 (1997) 517–29. Täubler, E. "Cushan Rishathaim." *HUCA* 20 (1947) 126–42. Van Selms, A. "Judge Shamgar." *VT* 14 (1964) 294–309. Williams, J. G. "The Structure of Judges 2.6–16.31." *JSOT* 49 (1991) 77–85. Wong, G. T. K. "Ehud and Joab Separated at Birth?" *VT* 56 (2006) 399–402. Yadin, Y. "The Story of Ehud Son of Gera" (Heb.). In *Studies in the Book of Judges*. Publications of the Israel Bible Society 10. Jerusalem, 1966. 413–15, 429–30.

Translation

[1] *These are the nations that Yahweh[a] allowed to remain to use them to test all the Israelites who had not experienced any of the wars in Canaan.* [2] *The only reason[a] he did this was in order for the generations of the sons of Israel to know, that is, to teach them warfare. This was only for those who had no previous experience.[b]* [3] *Included were the five governors of the Philistines, all the Canaanites, the Sidonians, and the Hivites[a] who lived in Mount[b] Lebanon from Mount Baal[c] Hermon to the entrance of Hamath.[d]* [4] *They were to test Israel with them to determine if they would obey Yahweh's commandments which he had commanded their fathers by the hand of Moses.* [5] *But the sons of Israel lived among the Canaanites, the Hittites, the Amorites, the Perizzites, the Hivites, and the Jebusites.* [6] *They took their daughters as their wives and gave their own daughters to their sons. They served their gods.*

[7] *The sons of Israel did evil in Yahweh's eyes. They forgot Yahweh, their God, and served the Baals and the Asheroth.[a]* [8] *Yahweh's anger burned against Israel, and he sold them into the hand of Cushan Rishathaim, king of Aram Naharaim. The sons of Israel served Cushan Rishathaim[a] eight years.* [9] *The sons of Israel cried out to Yahweh, and he raised up a deliverer for the sons of[a] Israel, who delivered them, namely, Othniel, Kenaz's son and Caleb's youngest brother.[b]* [10] *The Spirit of Yahweh was upon him, and he judged Israel. He went out to battle,[a] and Yahweh gave Cushan Rishathaim, the king of Aram,[b] into his hand. His hand proved to be too strong for Cushan Rishathaim.* [11] *The land was quiet for forty[a] years, and then Othniel, Kenaz's son, died.*

[12] *The sons of Israel continued to do evil in Yahweh's eyes, and Yahweh strengthened Eglon, king of Moab, to oppose Israel because they did evil in Yahweh's eyes.* [13] *He massed the sons[a] of Ammon and Amalek and went and defeated Israel. They[b] took possession of the City of Palms.* [14] *The sons of Israel served Eglon, king of Moab, eighteen years.*

[15] *The sons of Israel cried out to Yahweh, and Yahweh raised up a deliverer for them—the Benjaminite Ehud, the son of Gera. He was left-handed.[a] The sons of Israel sent him with tribute to Eglon, king of Moab.* [16] *Ehud made for himself a double-edged[a] sword about a foot[b] long. He strapped it under his clothing[c] on his right thigh.* [17] *He carried the tribute to Eglon, king of Moab. (Now Eglon was a man who was quite well-fed.[a])* [18] *As he[a] finished giving the tribute, he sent the people[b] bearing the tribute away,* [19] *but he[a] turned around at the images near Gilgal.*

He said, "I have something secret for you, O king."

He[b] said, "Hush!"[c] All those standing around him went out from his presence. [20] *Now Ehud came to him; but he was alone, sitting in his cool, elevated throne room.[a]*

Ehud said, "I have something secret from God for you," and he[b] rose from his throne. [21] *Ehud[a] reached with his left hand, took the sword from his right thigh, and plunged it into Eglon's[b] belly.* [22] *Even the handle went[a] in after the blade, and the fat covered behind the blade so that he did not draw the sword out of his belly. Then he had a bowel move-*

ment.[b] [23]*Ehud went out through the private room,*[a] *closed the doors of the elevated throne room*[b] *behind him, and locked them.*[c]

[24]*After he went out, then Eglon's*[a] *servants entered. They looked around. The doors of the elevated throne room were locked. They said, "He must be using the bathroom*[b] *in a throne room chamber."*[c] [25]*They trembled with fear*[a] *to their own shame: "Look. He is not opening the doors of the elevated throne room." They took the key and opened the doors.*[b] *Look! Their lord was fallen to the ground, dead.*

[26]*But Ehud had escaped during their delay.*[a] *He had passed over the Images*[b] *and escaped to Seirah.* [27]*When he arrived,*[a] *he blew the ram's horn*[b] *in the hill country of Ephraim. The sons of Israel went down with him from the hill country,*[c] *but he was in the lead.*[d] [28]*He said to them, "Follow after me*[a] *for Yahweh*[b] *has given your*[c] *enemies—Moab—into your*[c] *hands." They went down after him and captured the fords of the Jordan at the entrance to Moab. They allowed no one to cross.* [29]*They struck the Moabites dead at that time,*[a] *about ten thousand men. Every one of them was fat and fit for battle.*[b] *Not a single man escaped.* [30]*Moab was subdued in that day under the hand of Israel. The land was quiet eighty years.*[a]

[31]*Afterwards, Shamgar, the son of Anath, came and struck the Philistines dead—six hundred men—with an ox goad.*[a] *He was the one who saved Israel.*

Notes

1.a. LXX[A], along with Syrohexapla, Old Latin, Armenian, and Theodotian, reads "Joshua let remain." Compare OL reading of Judg 2:23. Lindars (113–14) sees that this is not original and points to Moore's understanding of this as an assimilation to 2:21. Lindars prefers a theological explanation, the avoidance of "ascribing temptation to God." Both factors may have played into the textual tradition's change here.

2.a. MT reads, literally, "only for the sake of knowing of generations." LXX (compare OL) does not have דעת, "knowing of." Lindars points to the awkward construction and sees a Heb. dittograph here with the following דרות. The construction is awkward, but the combination of דעת, "knowing," and ללמד, "to teach," accents Israel's inexperience and ignorance.

2.b. MT reads, literally, "only who before them did not know them." BHS sees this as an enclitic *mêm* on ידע. Apparently, the antecedent is the pl. "wars" in v 1 even though the pronoun is masc., whereas the noun מלחמה is normally fem. Lindars (114) sees this as an easier reading than a final enclitic *mêm*.

3.a. BHS suggests, with older commentators, to read "Hittites" for Hivites, but this is unnecessary.

3.b. LXX does not have "Mount" before "Lebanon." This is the only occurrence of "Mount of Lebanon" in the MT and appears to represent a part of Lebanon where the Hivites live.

3.c. LXX[B] does not have "Baal," which appears with "Hermon" only here in MT. The reference may be to a peak above Hermon or may be a derogatory reference to a "home" or worship center of Baal.

3.d. Or "Lebo-Hamath" or "Lebo in the land of Hamath."

7.a. LXX translates *Asheroth* as "sacred groves"; two Heb. MSS, Syr., and Vg. read העשתרות, "Ashtaroth," substituting Astarte for Ashera.

8.a. LXX[A] simplifies to "and they served him eight years."

9.a. LXX does not have "sons of," representing either a simplification avoiding unnecessary repetition by LXX or the addition of familiar terms by the MT tradition.

9.b. LXX[A] reads "his youngest brother, and he listened to him," filling in the obvious. See *Note* 1:13.a.

10.a. LXX[B] reads "he went out to war with Cushan Rishathaim," introducing the enemy earlier in text for clarity.

10.b. LXX[B] reads "king of Aram Naharaim," repeating the full reading of the name from v 8. For detailed textual evidence, see Lindars, 159.

11.a. LXX[A] reads "fifty," a reading Lindars (160) classifies as an "error" that is "difficult to account for."

13.a. LXX reads "all the sons of," emphasizing the all-out effort needed to fight Israel.

13.b. LXX, OL, Syrohexapla, and Tg. read sg., giving the victory to Eglon in continuity with the preceding syntax. Lindars (138) accepts this reading, though MT represents the more difficult reading in underlining the diverse population that took over the City of Palms.

15.a. *HALOT* and *DCH* suggest "ambidextrous" here following the LXX (compare OL) ἀμφοτερο-δέχιον, while Syr. has "crippled" and Tg. "withered."

16.a. Lit. "two mouths"; see Berman, *VT* 52 (2002) 291–303. Many Heb. MSS read שְׁתֵי, the fem. form, for MT masc. שְׁנֵי, fitting it to the usually fem. pl. ending of פִּיּוֹת.

16.b. The unique Heb. term גֹּמֶד apparently means about twelve inches (30.5 cm), though this is quite uncertain. See Younger, 115, n. 11, and Hartman, *ZAH* 13 (2000) 188–93.

16.c. LXX translates מַד, "clothing," as μανδύας, "woolen cloak."

17.a. Lit. "an exceedingly fat man," a term not necessarily holding negative connotations; consequently, LXX translates as ἀστεῖος, "handsome, charming, refined."

18.a. LXX makes "Ehud" the explicit subject.

18.b. LXX omits "people" as unnecessary repetition.

19.a. LXXᴬ makes "Eglon" the subject, apparently to avoid connecting Ehud with contact of any kind with pagan images. This necessitates making "Ehud" the specific subject of "he said" later in the verse.

19.b. LXXᴬ makes "Eglon" the specific subject whereas Heb. emphatically inserts וְהוּא, pointing directly to Ehud. Gk. apparently avoided placing Ehud, the hero, near the Images.

19.c. LXXᴬ reads καὶ εἶπεν Εγλωμ πᾶσιν ἐκ μέσου καὶ ἐξῆλθον ἀπ' αὐτοῦ πάντες οἱ παραστήκοντες αὐτῷ, "Eglon said to all from the midst, and they went out from him all those who were standing around him"; LXXᴮ, with codex Ephraemi Syri rescriptus and Aquila, reads, καὶ εἶπεν Εγλωμ πρὸς αὐτόν σιώπα καὶ ἐξαπέστειλεν ἀφ' ἑαυτοῦ πάντας τοὺς ἐφεστῶτας ἐπ' αὐτόν, "Eglon said to him, 'Silence.' And he sent out from himself all those waiting on him." From earliest translation to present commentators, the meaning of Heb. הָס has provided food for argument and research. Other occurrences (Neh 8:11; Amos 6:10; Hab 2:20; Zeph 1:7; Zech 2:17) point to a meaning, "be still; hush." Boling (86), following a private suggestion from Freedman, argues for a meaning of "depart" but has not found a strong following. This leads to reading a *hip̄'il* form of יצא, "he caused them to leave," as suggested by LXX. For a detailed analysis see Lindars, 144, 161; compare Barthélemy, *Critique textuelle*, 1:76–77. Both authors argue cogently for retention of MT.

20.a. LXX (compare OL) reads ἐν τῷ ὑπερῴῳ τῷ θερινῷ, "in his upstairs summer room." See *Comment* on v 20.

20.b. LXX (compare OL) reads σέ βασιλεῦ καὶ ἐχανέστη ἀπὸ τοῦ θρόνου Εγλωμ ἐγγὺς αὐτοῦ, "you, O king, and Eglon rose up from his throne near him." This interjects the formal royal title (accepted as original by commentators such as Soggin and Boling) and the royal personal name, relieving the subject ambiguity of the Heb. "Near him" would apparently modify throne, but this would require "him" to refer to Ehud or be an obvious tautology. Lindars (145) is correct to see here and in the opening of the next verse "a scribal addition to heighten the narrative." Niditch (54) says "near him" blocks "the scene beautifully."

21.a. LXX (compare OL) opens the sentence, καὶ ἐγένετο ἅμα τῷ (LXXᴬ reads τοῦ) ἀναστῆναι αὐτόν, "and it came to pass at the same time he rose." See *Note* 20.b.

21.b. Heb. reads "his"; LXX made "Eglon's" explicit.

22.a. LXX (compare OL) ἐπεισήνεγκεν, "he drove in," apparently read the causitive *hip̄'il* וַיָּבֵא for MT *qal* וַיָּבֹא, again narrative enhancement in the tradition, but Barré (*VT* 41 [1991] 8–9) seeks to demonstrate narrative composition demanding the *hip̄'il* with Ehud as subject.

22.b. LXXᴬ does not represent the final sentence, whose meaning is unclear in Heb. Lindars (148) notes that LXX often "omits untranslatable words in Judges." See Barré, *VT* 41 (1991) 1–11; Mobley, "Ehud and the Monoliths," 81–85. KJV follows Vg. and Tg. in reading "dirt" for "feces." It is variously translated as "the filth came out" (JPS); "the dirt came out" (NRSV); "protruding behind" (REB); "stuck out in back" (GWT); "stuck out behind his legs" (TEV); "came out his back" (NIV); "Eglon's insides came out" (HCSB); "the king's bowels emptied" (NLT); "dung came out" (ESV); "refuse came out" (NASB); "entrails came out " (NKJV). LXXᴮ reads, ἐχῆλθεν Αωδ τὴν προστάδα, "and Ehud went out to the porch." Niditch (54) uses "exit way," seeing an architectural term following L. E. Stager ("Key Passages," *ErIsr* 27 [2003] 244–45). Lindars (146) follows H. Ewald (*Geschichte des Volkes Israel,* 8 vols. [Göttingen: Dietrichschen Buchhandlung, 1864–66]; translated as *The History of Israel,* ed. R. Martineau [London: Longmans, Green, and Company, 1869–86]) and Boling in seeing this as a doublet restating the opening of the next verse originating as a gloss on the misunderstood הַמִּסְדְּרוֹנָה in v 23. Thus NAB, NET, NJB do not translate. The text may represent a type of coarse humor that later versions did not understand or tried to hide. See Barré, 9; Mobley, 84; and the *Comment* on v 22.

23.a. Niditch (54) finds alternate versions of the escape in the last part of v 22 and the opening words of v 23. Meaning of Heb. הַמִּסְדְּרוֹנָה is uncertain; compare *HALOT. DCH* suggests "porch, lavatory or armoury, perh. air-shaft" with bibliography (5:861). Niditch (54) looks to root נדר, "to order," and translates "colonnaded portico." LXX^A reads προστάδα, "porch," while LXX^B has διατεταγμένους, "the appointed place." See *Comment* on v 23.

23.b. Or simply, "upper room."

23.c. MT has no pronoun, "them" being added in translation to conform to English syntax. The Heb. "perfect consecutive" is surprising here. *BHS* suggests the imperfect verb וַיִּנְעַל, to create the expected consecution of Heb. verb tenses. Gray and Boling—following a private note by D. N. Freedman—repoint to an infinitive absolute. Perhaps a result or purpose clause is intended by the unusual syntax: "so that" or "with the result that" it locked.

24.a. Lit. "his." OL adds "as Ehud was going out."

24.b. Lit. "he is covering his feet," a euphemism (see Deut 28:57; Isa 7:20; Ezek 16:25). LXX^A reads μήποτε πρὸς δίφρου κάθηται ἐν τῇ ἀποξωρήσει τοῦ κοιτῶνος, "perhaps he sits on the seat in the latrine of the bedroom," while LXX^B reads, μήποτε ἀποκενοῖ τοὺς πόδας αὐτοῦ ἐν τῷ ταμειείῳ τῷ θερινῷ, "perhaps he is emptying his foot in the summer chamber." OL asks if he does not sit on a stool. Niditch sees either נסך, "to pour," or סכך, "to cover," as possible Heb. roots for this difficult term. Niditch finally translates as "indisposed."

24.c. חדר appears here unexpectedly in place of the previously used הָעֲלִיָּה, apparently as a literary variant implying darkness (see *HALOT;* compare Judg 16:9, 12).

25.a. *BHS* sees וַיְּחִילוּ as doubtful, suggesting either וְיִחֲלוּ (*pi'el*) or וַיּוֹחִילוּ (*hip'il*) from יחל, "they waited," the reading in most modern translations. Lindars (150) and Block (168, n. 82) support this on the basis that עַד־בּוֹשׁ means "for an embarrassingly long time," finding Ugaritic evidence reinforced by the Tg. for a root *bš* meaning "remained, delayed," used here and in Exod 32:1 and Judg 5:28. We may doubt that a Heb. ear would recognize such an esoteric meaning here any more than modern readers of Heb. do without searching for something that fits the way we read the context. But OL reads "confounded." Certainly, shame and embarrassment would be heard by the text's original audience.

25.b. "The doors" added for clarity; Heb. reads simply "they opened."

26.a. LXX reads, ἐθορυβοῦντο καὶ οὐκ ἦν ὁ προσνοῶν αὐτῷ, "they were agitated (or tumultuous) and no one was observing him," but this most likely represents narrative embellishment in the transmission. Niditch (55) translates OL as "while they ran amok."

26.b. הַפְּסִילִים, "the Images," as a geographical designation is not clear. See *Comment* on v 26.

27.a. LXX^B reads, καὶ ἐγένετο ἡνίκα ἦλθεν Αωδ εἰς γῆν Ισραηλ, "when Ehud entered into the land of Israel," another narrative enhancement for clarity. OL has "and it was that a voice came, and the crowd sounded the shofar."

27.b. Heb. שׁוֹפָר, "shofar," originally a ram's horn used for signaling in war and in worship.

27.c. LXX^A does not have "from the hill country," representing either a mistake in copying or a deletion to avoid unnecessary repetition.

27.d. Lit. "and he was before them."

28.a. LXX uses the present or aorist pl. imperative form of καταβαίνω, "Come down," so *BHS* suggests changing MT רִדְפוּ to רְדוּ. Lindars (154) explains this argument by saying that the MT reading always means "pursue an enemy" (Judg 1:6; 4:16; 7:23; 8:5, 12). Perhaps the reading means, "pursue the enemy with me." But limiting the idiom to one precise meaning is probably making overly exacting demands for consistency on the language.

28.b. LXX reads, "the Lord God," a narrative enhancement using a common divine title.

28.c. LXX^B reads "your" for "our," giving a psychological edge to Ehud's speech. Lindars (154) calls this an itacism.

29.a. Heb. Genizah MSS read masc. הַהוּא for MT fem. הַהִיא here and in v 30. The antecedents עֵת and יוֹם, respectively, both appear sometimes as one gender and sometimes as the other, especially in later texts.

29.b. That is, "healthy and strong." LXX^A reads, πάντας τοὺς μαξητὰς τοὺς ἐν αὐτοῖς καὶ πάντα ἄνδρα δυνάμεως, "all of them fighters, those among them, and each a man of strength," while LXX^B reads, πᾶν λιπαρὸν καὶ πάντα ἄνδρα δυνάμεως, "all of them oily (luxurious, bright) and each a man of strength." The diverse readings show an early interpretation of the text as pointing to selected military heroes from among the army.

30.a. LXX (compare OL) reads "eighty years, and Ehud judged them until he died," another literary smoothing of the text, moving this information from 4:1.

31.a. LXX^A reads μόσχων τῶν βοῶν, "calf of an ox," while LXX^B reads ἀροτρόποδι τῶν βοῶν, "plow-share of an ox." The tradition had difficulty defining the unique Heb. term בְּמַלְמַד, normally taken as "with the goad." Lindars (162–63) argues from Gk. evidence that the original Heb. reading was מַלְמַד, "apart from" or "not including," the cattle. This smooths the reading and may account for the Gk. evidence, but it minimizes the narrative flavor that marks the book of Judges. Niditch (55) notes that OL reads, "'six hundred men besides the old men,' perhaps reflecting Hebrew *millĕbad hazzāqēn*. . . . One sees here a typical text-critical pattern whereby sound-alike or look-alike words are copied mistakenly from one version and then made sense of. MT and OL are at the beginning and end of the process, whereas A is somewhere in the middle."

Form/Structure/Setting

See table 3.1 in the appendix to compare one possible example of narrative analysis with form-critical analysis for chap. 3. The narrative elements follow the typical pattern of Hebrew narrative while the genre elements show the genre of each section with its component parts. Note how the narrator can use different genre elements and markers within or even across various narrative elements.

The opening disjunctive clause with the beginning of a list formula, וְאֵלֶּה ה, "these the," separates chap. 3 as a distinctive unit, though many commentators try to connect it to the preceding unit because of the catchword נסה, "to test." See Sweeney (*VT* 46 [1997] 6) and Schneider (36) for arguments supporting the independence of chap. 3. Chap. 3 sets up the testing conditions and then provides three examples of how the tests were met by Othniel, Ehud, and Shamgar. The opening exposition (vv 1–6) reflects complex Hebraic structure. The opening words prepare the reader for a list to follow (compare Gen 36:31; Exod 21:1; 28:4; Judg 3:1; 1 Kgs 4:2; 1 Chr 1:43; 6:18; 12:1; 2 Chr 24:26; Ezra 2:59; Neh 7:61; 12:1; Jer 30:4), but we have to wait until v 3 for the actual list. First we have the qualifications for those making the list (vv 1b–2) given with a pair of exclusive clauses introduced by רק, "only." Finally, v 4 gives the purpose of the test, and vv 5–6 give the result of the test, including a different list of nations.

Vv 7–11 present the first Judges "narrative," but close scrutiny shows it is a narrative pattern based on the framework of chap. 2 with names filled in at vital spots. As Olson suggests,

Many of the Judges stories probably originated as entertaining heroic tales about the military victories or exploits of a local tribal ancestor. These independent tales were retold and gradually came to be collected and edited into a coherent series of deliverers or judges. The resulting series of judge stories may have been formed on the model of a common genre of ancient Near Eastern literature called the royal annals or chronicles, in which a succession of rulers and their stories were brought together into a coherent whole. (763)

(Compare Lindars, 99, 125.) Brettler (27) concludes that the narrative "lacks verisimilitude on too many levels to function as that type of history. Instead, it was meant as a type of allegory for the ability of a good, righteous Judean judge to defeat the wicked enemy 'from the North.'"

Othniel and Shamgar present the problem cases for this description. Not one clause in these narratives is devoid of stereotypical language. (See the schema elements in table I.4 in the appendix.) Not one word about heroic action occurs. Nothing deviates from the norm to make them entertaining. Othniel and Shamgar leave as little trace of themselves as possible in the stories. These two narratives, then, do not represent a narrative so much as a pattern-fulfillment description. And this is the way all the tales should be. The judges narratives should tell tales of God's deliverance of Israel from intruding foreigners or from the people who remain in the land. God should take and remain in center stage with little said about the human "hero." But each of the stories, instead, gets more and more detailed about the deliverer's problems and includes less and less of God's actions. Near Eastern chronicles generally function as political documents praising the king. Israel's judges documents do just the opposite. They highlight the weaknesses of the judges and the strength of deity alone. As Olson phrases it, "the later judge stories gradually lessen the attention on God and increase the amount of biographical detail dedicated to the individual judges" (764). Olson sees this trend beginning with Gideon, ignoring the central story of Deborah and Barak, the central theme of which is the glory departing from the expected judge and being given to a most unlikely woman. Even the victory song in chap. 5 concentrates as much on the failure of tribes to participate as it does on praising God.

Vv 12–25 present an ironical test of wits between a left-handed Israelite and an obese enemy king. Guillaume carries the story into the realm of mythology and the storm god on the lofty mountain: "Mythology is turned into a daring farce, the storm-god into a urinating calf, his lofty abode into a lowly chamber in Jericho" (*Waiting for Josiah*, 27–28). He denies any Moabite existence before Mesha and so dates the narrative between Mesha (840) and Josiah (640). Here, as in most of his reading of Judges, Guillaume has more ahistorical imagination than he does faith in the basic testimony of the narrator. The story is almost a farce, but that does not deny its historical base.

Amit sees

> a series of tactics which bring out the role of human planning and execution and, on the face of it, leave little room for divine involvement and providence. . . . The author is interested in conveying the lesson that the effectiveness of Ehud's planned or improvised tactics could only have been assured by his having been set up as a deliverer by God. . . . This rhetorical technique, in which chance events and planned tactics appear alongside one another, convinces the reader that Ehud's ability to act as a tactician depends upon God's wish to deliver his people. (*Book of Judges*, 172–73)

Brettler (33–34) classifies it as "a humorous satire mocking the Israelites' enemy" but then cautions that humor has different forms in different societies. Still he defends this story as both humorous and satirical, lifting the spirits of the Israelites and encouraging hostility against the enemy Moabites with sexual and scatological humor. I join Mobley ("Ehud and the Monoliths," 85) in not being convinced that sexual humor is intended here. Brettler uses the humorous, satirical genre elements to cast doubt on the story's historicity. However, truth may often be funnier than fiction. Reality offers as much room for laughter as does farce. I contend with Provan, Long, and Longman that it is not necessary to suppose that "proof is necessary as the foundation of faith in testimony." The much more interesting question is

> what constitutes "reasonable belief"; and the contention that, in order reasonably to exercise faith in testimony, we ourselves must actually be acquainted individually with a testimonial chain stretching back to past events and situations, is patently absurd. All

that needs to be shown . . . is that we may reasonably believe that conditions existed in the ancient Near East, particularly Palestine, such that we cannot assume disjunction between the early testimony about Israel's past and the later forms of tradition in which this testimony has come down to us. We are not required to produce all the intervening texts. (*Biblical History of Israel*, 60–61)

It appears more difficult to believe that long-removed historians created materials to construct a previously unknown identity for Israel than it is to believe that the people of Israel at an early stage of their existence gained an appreciation for the character of their God as one who chose history as the main artery by which to reveal the divine nature to the chosen people. Israel thus collected orally and possibly in writing the narratives that tied them to Yahweh and gave them identity as a specially responsible people under Yahweh. It is much easier to believe that they preserved stories that cast their people in such bad light than it is to believe that generations much later created such self-denigrating materials.

V 12 represents a use of the chap. 2 framework with the addition of "Yahweh strengthened" (וַיְחַזֵּק יְהוָה), a phrase used nowhere else in Judges, though the verb in its *pi'el* form appears in 9:24 with the lords or Baals of Shechem strengthening Abimelech in his murderous activities and again in Samson's prayer for renewed strength from Yahweh to pull down the Philistine temple on himself and the enemy party goers (16:28). The same verb brings back remembrance of the exodus deliverance when God hardened Pharaoh's heart (Exod 4:21; 9:12; 10:20, 27; 11:10; 14:4, 8) and the Egyptians' hearts (14:17; compare Josh 11:20) so that they disobeyed Yahweh, a precisely opposite meaning to that in Judg 3. Rather, the meaning here is closer to Deut 1:38 and 3:28, where God encourages or strengthens Joshua (compare 1 Sam 23:16; 2 Sam 11:25). That is, God's giving strength or hardness to an enemy becomes the divine method for enemy victory rather than for enemy defeat as in the traditional exodus narrative. This term replaces the more familiar "God gave into the hand of" or "sold into the hand of."

The appearance of this "addition" to the framework elements forces us to rethink the complex relationship between the pattern of chap. 2 and the "frameworks" of the individual narratives. The pattern is not simply a collection of all the materials already present in the narrative frameworks. Neither is the pattern an editorial creation that is then used to frame each of the narratives. The pattern of chap. 2 serves its own theological purpose in introducing the book and is then used selectively and creatively to introduce in various creative ways the framework of the narratives. Again v 13 opens with an element unique to the frameworks of Judges—the enemy king massed or gathered (וַיֶּאֱסֹף) allied armies—and then introduces נכה, "smite, defeat, kill," a term strongly at home in the exodus tradition (Exod 2:11–13; 3:20; 7:17, 20, 25; 8:12–13; 9:15, 25; 12:12–13, 29; 17:5–6; 21:12, 15, 18–20, 26) and in Deuteronomy (Deut 1:4; 2:33; 3:3; 4:46; 7:2; 13:16; 19:4, 6, 11; 20:13; 21:1; 25:2–3, 11; 27:24–25; 28:22, 27–28, 35; 29:6). Joshua also features נכה in its military narratives (Josh 7:3, 5; 8:21–22, 24; 9:18; 10:4, 10, 20, 26, 28, 30, 32–33, 35, 37, 39–41; 11:8, 10–12, 14, 17; 12:1, 6–7; 13:12, 21; 15:16; 19:47; 20:3, 5, 9). Similarly, the Judges battle narratives feature the term, though the frameworks do not (Judg 1:4–5, 8, 10, 12, 17, 25; 3:13, 29, 31; 6:16; 7:13; 8:11; 9:43–44; 11:21, 33; 12:4; 14:19; 15:8, 15–16; 18:27; 20:31, 37, 39, 45, 48; 21:10). This narrative framework in 3:12–25 does not simply take its elements from the pattern of chap. 2 or the framework vocabulary of the other narratives. Rather, it uses vocabulary at home in military contexts to fill out the narrative framework here. The framework vocabulary of vv 12–15a sets the stage for the narrative. Even this framework has elements unique to this narrative interspersed within it: massing of the coalition partners, mention of the City of Palms, and the left-handedness of the new deliverer. The narrative proper begins with v 15b as Israel sends tribute to Eglon, setting up the narrative tension regarding how Israel can escape the tribute obligation.

The answer comes not with a battle narrative between opposing armies but with an ironic battle-of-wits story. Battle preparations begin not with a massing of armies as the narrative framework described but with a lone hero strapping his weapon to the wrong (right) thigh because of his being left-handed. The foe is introduced not with terms of royal respect but with a description of the king's "fatness," a term most often used as a compliment, not a disparagement (Ps 73:4; Dan 1:15). This is one of many examples of double entendre in the narrative. V 18 retards the narrative action, apparently ending a report with no narrative tension or resolution, but it also sets the stage by reducing Israelite forces to one person. V 19b thrusts him quickly before the king again, this time as a messenger from God—not from the people—bearing a secret דָּבָר, "word, thing, message, matter." The king calls for silence, a sign his people take as one of dismissal. This reduces the ironic story to a one-on-one confrontation. Eglon's fatness, which could be interpreted as well-fed and healthy, becomes the clue to Ehud's deadly success. Ehud has outwitted Eglon and his staff. The denouement then represents the ineptness of the staff as they tarry to find a dead king. Thus the narrator's summary exclamation, "Look! Their lord falling to the ground, dead!"

Vv 26–30 continue the Ehud story but in a new form. Now we have a typical battle report (see B. O. Long, *I Kings*, FOTL 9 [Grand Rapids: Eerdmans, 1984] 244), with the battle itself introduced by the conveyance formula of 28a, which in the context again places Ehud in a dual role as military deliverer and as prophetic spokesman (Long, *I Kings*, 264). This narrative is tied back to the battle of wits through description of the defeated army as שָׁמֵן, "well-nourished, fat"—a synonym for בָּרִיא, v 17. V 30 presents a typical framework closing, but the death-of-the-judge element is delayed until 4:1.

V 31 represents the shortest report of a judge in the book. Critics like Brettler (25) see it as an exegetical patchwork from Judg 5:6 and 10:11. Still, Brettler must fumble around to find how the narrative element of the ox goad entered, possibly as an etiological element. This battle report has no opening or closing framework elements, nor does it report the judge's death. Indeed, it uses the formula connected to the introduction of the minor judges (see Younger, 43). Thus the report on Shamgar is tied syntactically to the Ehud story, Ehud's death being reported only in 4:1, and is tied formally to the minor judges reports. It does foreshadow the mention of Shamgar in 5:6.

Comment

1–2 Judges picks up where Josh 13 left off. God has left nations in the land that Israel has not conquered. The difference lies in the nature of the new generation. They have land left to conquer, but they "did not know either Yahweh or the actions that he had done for Israel" (2:10). They are a generation living under God's anger (2:12, 14, 20). They are a generation who has forfeited God's promise to conquer the nations (2:21). Thus they are a nation under test (2:22). The test has two prongs. One seeks to see if Israel will obey Yahweh (2:22; 3:4). The other tests them in warfare so they will know how to conduct holy war (3:1–2). Niditch takes the theological holy war element out and decides, "warring is a learned skill, a matter of training" (55).

The book of Joshua introduces its hero by issuing a divine command that he be careful to obey the law of Moses (Josh 1:7–8). Judges begins not with a command that expects obedience but with a test that expects disobedience. Joshua begins with a nation expecting to drive out the peoples of the land. Judges begins with the people settled down among those same peoples, its tribes unable to drive them out of the land. Rather than enemies in holy war, we now find one big happy clan, all giving and receiving one another's children in marriage to cement the clan ties.

3 Having extended the explanations for having a list of nations that remain, the editor supplies the list of nations. They form a semicircle around Israel to the west and north. Here we see the complexity of the narrative in Judges and its total lack of a consistent chronological element in its narrative structure. The first chapter presented basically a summary of tribal activities ranging in time from Caleb's capture of Debir and Hebron to Judah's capture of Jerusalem and from the capture of Bethel to Dan's loss of its seaside territory and its trek to the north. The latter will be replayed in the Samson narratives in juxtaposition to the following chaos description leading to the Danites' northern trek.

Chap. 3 can thus ignore the description in chap. 1 of Judah's capture of Philistine cities and turn to an era, whatever that time may have been, when all five Philistine cities headed up the "land that remained" (compare Josh 13:2). The Philistines' unique form of government is represented by the term סְרָנִים, "governors" or "rulers" (Josh 13:3; Judg 16:5, 8, 18, 23, 27, 30; 1 Sam 5:8, 11; 6:4, 12, 16; 7:7; 29:2, 6, 7; 1 Chr 12:20; Sir 46:18). Apparently each of the five major Philistine cities had a city-state ruler called a סֶרֶן *seren,* or city-state king. The term may have originated among the Neo-Hittites with the city-state organization owing much to Greek and/or Anatolian sources. The *seren* served as military commander, also, with his subjects being a combination of Philistine immigrants and conquered Canaanites and Israelites. The Philistines' technological superiority is witnessed by their monopoly of iron forging (1 Sam 13:19–22). Their military superiority is shown in archaeological testimony to their presence in many cities in interior Palestine. Their ethnic distinctiveness is shown by their dress in Egyptian wall carvings and by their contributions to the Palestinian pottery collections (stirrup jars, kraters, pyxis, strainer spout jugs, kernos rings, bottles) and decoration (bichrome in black and red over a coating of white slip, with spirals, geometric bands, or figures with stylized swan or fish motifs). The pottery and other cultural remains also display a gradual acculturation, adapting native wares brought from the Aegean to Canaanite customs learned in Palestine.

See J. P. J. Olivier, *NIDOTTE,* 3:631; T. Dothan, *The Philistines and Their Material Culture* (Jerusalem: Israel Exploration Society, 1982) 94–218; A. E. Killebrew, *Biblical Peoples and Ethnicity: An Archaeological Study of Egyptians, Canaanites, Philistines, and Early Israel 1300–1100 B.C.E.,* SBLABS 9 (Atlanta: Society of Biblical Literature, 2005) 197–245; D. M. Howard, Jr., *POTW,* 231–250.

The list appears to move up the Mediterranean coast to the north, Canaanites representing the land between the Philistine cities and Sidon. This would represent a pristine and very narrow identification of Canaan, but would fit with what is presented in v 5. For Canaanites, see *Comment* on 1:1.

Sidonians are the occupants of Sidon and the territory it controlled, apparently in this list including Tyre. For Sidon, see *Comment* on 1:31.

Hivites (Gen 10:17; 34:2; 36:2; Exod 3:8, 17; 13:5; 23:23, 28; 33:2; 34:11; Deut 7:1; 20:17; Josh 3:10; 9:1, 7; 11:3, 19; 12:8; 24:11; Judg 3:3,5; 2 Sam 24:7; 1 Kgs 9:20; 1 Chr 1:15; 2 Chr 8:7) are a non-Semitic people listed in the reappearing notations on inhabitants of the promised land, peoples Israel is called to exterminate (Exod 3:8; 23:23; Deut 20:17; Josh 9:1; 24:11). They are closely tied to Gibeon (Josh 9) and to Mount Hermon (Josh 11:3). Eventually, Solomon conscripted them to build the temple (1 Kgs 9:20–21). For the little that is known about the Hivites see Hostetter, *Nations Mightier and More Numerous*, 72–76. The text here explicitly places the Hivites in northern Palestine. The Lebanon Mountains represent the range running parallel to the Mediterranean coast and rising to ten thousand feet (3048 m) elevation. Baal Hermon is apparently an Israelite designation for Mount Hermon, identifying it as a place of Baal worship. It marked the limits of Joshua's northern conquests (Josh 11:16–17). Lebo Hamath is often called the "entrance to Hamath," but more likely refers to the border city of Lebweh on one of the sources of the Orontes River north of Baalbek on the border of the Syrian city-state of Hamath. (See *Sacred Bridge*, 35.)

These identifications make this list hover beyond the major territory that the state of Israel actually occupied, pointing to territories only David and Solomon controlled to any extent. Chronologically, the list takes us back to Josh 13 in setting up boundaries that extend beyond Israel's reach under Joshua. The list ignores Judah's conquests of Philistine cities in Judg 1 as well as Israel's failures in chap. 1. Again we face the task set out for the generation after Joshua, a generation unlike that described in Judg 1, for the generation of Judg 3:1–5 has not faced battle. The nations God allowed to coexist because of Joshua's old age (Josh 13:1) are now facing a generation too young to have participated with Joshua's conquering army. Will this generation carry on the tradition of Joshua and testify that "Yahweh gave to Israel all the land which he had sworn to give to their fathers, and they possessed it and lived in it" (Josh 21:43)? Or will they succumb to the lures of Canaanite history and religion and settle down among the Canaanites without learning holy war?

4 Commentators too easily contrast this verse to the previous verses that relate the testing to war. The war test is defined in terms of obedience to "Yahweh's commandments which he had commanded their fathers by the hand of Moses." In Josh 1:7–8 God instructed Joshua to obey carefully all the commandments if he wished success. In Judg 2:17 the commandments to the fathers centered on false worship. Here the commandments join the laws on holy war to the commandments forbidding false worship, just as the Deuteronomic law had (Deut 7:1–5; 20:16–18). The rest of the book of Judges stands under this call to obedience in warfare and worship even though "commandments" and "Moses" disappear from the book at this point.

5 Summarily, the editor reports the results of the tests, results that reign through the rest of the book. Israel lived with the enemy instead of obeying the law and destroying the enemy. As Amit sees it, "In the days of the elders the Israelites still subjugated the Canaanites, while during the period of the judges, there was tendency toward assimilation" (*Book of Judges*, 157). Judges illustrates how God's people neglected God's law and accommodated themselves to life among the foreign nations. The chronological perspective here lengthens past the first generation after Joshua to describe the ongoing experience of Israel. They do not obey the holy war laws. They do not exterminate the enemies. Thus they have to live among the peoples in the traditional lists of the inhabitants of Canaan.

Note that this list includes those nations Israel had to fight for the heartland of Canaan, not nations on the periphery. *Canaanites* here takes the meaning it had in chap. 1, not that of v 3. *Hittites* in ancient literature most frequently refers to an Anatolian kingdom reaching back to 1750 B.C.E. and lasting to at least 1180 in the city of Hattusha, modern Bogazkoy. Hittites continued to control Carchemish and Tarhuntashsha. The Hittites thus gave their name to Syria, for Assyrian records referred to the territory as Hatti. Apparently, Hittite immigrants also reached Palestine and settled down, becoming part of the society there. See H. A. Hoffner, Jr., *POTW*, 127–55; A. Kempinski, "Hittites in the Bible: What Does Archaeology Say?" *BAR* 5 (1979) 20–45; Hostetter, *Nations Mightier and More Numerous*, 66–72.

For the Amorites see *Comment* on Judg 1:34. The Perizzites (Gen 13:7; 15:20; 34:30; Exod 3:8, 17; 23:23; 33:2; 34:11; Deut 7:1; 20:17; Josh 3:10; 9:1; 11:3; 12:8; 17:15; 24:11; Judg 1:4–5; 3:5; 1 Kgs 9:20; 2 Chr 8:7; Ezra 9:1; Jdt 5:16; 1 Esd 8:69; 2 Esd 1:21) lived in the forests of Samaria in the land of the Joseph tribes (Josh 17:15). See Hostetter, *Nations Mightier and More Numerous*, 80–83; S. A. Reed, *ABD*, 5:231.

The Jebusites controlled Jerusalem (Gen 10:16; 15:21; Exod 3:8, 17; 13:5; 23:23; 33:2; 34:11; Num 13:29; Deut 7:1; 20:17; Josh 3:10; 9:1; 11:3; 12:8; 15:8, 63; 18:16; 24:11; Judg 1:21; 3:5; 19:11; 2 Sam 5:6, 8; 1 Kgs 9:20; 1 Chr 1:14; 11:4, 6; 2 Chr 8:7; Ezra 9:1; Zech 9:7; Jdt 5:16; 1 Esd 8:69). See S. A. Reed, *ABD*, 3:652–53; Hostetter, *Nations Mightier and More Numerous*, 76–80.

6 Israel's second failure comes at the second point of the law: intermarriage resulting in false worship. Joshua had sternly warned them at this point (Josh 23:12–13), but Israel after Joshua refused to listen. This was more than the political marriages of Solomon. This represented a new identity for Israel, an identity that ignored God's law, repudiated a sense of separateness and uniqueness, and was willing to be like the nations. Israel refused marriage only with their own depleted tribe (21:1).

7–8 Thus we come to the first story of a judge. It is a strange story, for it is simply a framework taken from Judg 2:11–23 with names added to give it a peculiar identity.

Judg 3:7	=	Judg 2:11–13
Judg 3:8	=	Judg 2:14
Judg 3:9	=	Judg 2:16
Judg 3:10	=	Judg 2:18
Judg 3:11	=	Judg 2:18–19

Amit finds that "the Othniel passage contains the largest concentration of formulaic phrases in the book" (*Book of Judges*, 163). As patterned as the story is, one
new element appears immediately: Israel "forgot" (שׁכח) God. God had warned
Israel not to forget the covenant (Deut 4:23), but the people have obviously done
so (Judg 2:2). Most of all they should not forget Yahweh, who brought them from
Egypt (Deut 6:12). Forgetting shows in failing to keep God's commands (8:11;
see Judg 3:5–6). Forgetting God is the product of proud hearts (Deut 8:14). The
result of forgetting God is clear: you perish (Deut 8:19). The beginning statement
concerning Israel after Joshua is "they forgot Yahweh" (Judg 3:7). The summary
of the entire period before monarchy is "they forgot the LORD their God" (1 Sam
12:9, NRSV). Between the two summary statements stands all the evidence without
any explicit judgment that Israel has forgotten God. Still, the Deuteronomic threat
hangs over the people's heads.

Forgetting God leads to remembering other gods, the Baals discussed earlier and
the Asheroth. *Asheroth* is the plural form of *Asherah*, a Canaanite goddess distinct
from Astarte of 2:13. This is a fertility goddess represented by a wooden pole. As
the people of Israel learned war, they should follow God's covenant instructions
and tear down all emblems and totems representing Asherah and the other gods
and goddesses (Exod 34:13; Deut 7:5; 12:3). The danger stood that Asherah worship would invade the cult of Yahweh. Indeed, it must have done so, or the laws
against such action would have no basis in fact (Deut 16:21; compare 2 Kgs 23:6,
15). Gideon had to cut down his father's Baal altar and Asherah pole (Judg 6:25).
Archaeologists at Taanach have provided a clear representation of Asherah (R.
Hendel, "Aniconism and Anthropomorphism in Ancient Israel," in *The Image and
the Book: Iconic Cults, Aniconism, and the Veneration of the Holy Book in Israel and the
Ancient Near East,* ed. K. van der Toorn [Kampen: Kok, 1999] 205–28). In fact,
archaeological discoveries have led Matthews to this startling conclusion:

> Because Asherah can be equated with the Ugaritic goddess Athirat, the consort of Baal,
> it is quite likely that the Israelites, who borrowed many of El's attributes and ascribed
> them to Yahweh, also saw Asherah as Yahweh's consort. The argument for this position
> has been strengthened, or at least ignited, by the discovery of the drawing and inscrip-
> tions at Kuntillet 'Ajrud, which contains the phrase *lyhwh . . . wl'šrth* (by Yahweh and
> by his *'ăšērâ*). . . . It is perhaps enough to say that the Israelites, in their daily fight to
> survive in a marginal environment, found that calling on both Yahweh and a Canaanite
> goddess or her cult object was not incongruous. (80)

See among the vast recent literature J. Day, *Yahweh and the Gods and Goddesses of
Canaan,* JSOTSup 265 (Sheffield: Sheffield Academic, 2000) 43–45; John Emerton, "'Yahweh and His Asherah': The Goddess or Her Symbol?" *VT* 49 (1999)
316–17; N. Wyatt, "Asherah," *DDD,* 183–95; *COS,* 2:47, 52; R. S. Hess, "Yahweh
and His Asherah? Religous Pluralism in the Old Testament World," in *One God,
One Lord: Christianity in a World of Religious Pluralism,* ed. A. D. Clarke and B. W.
Winter (Grand Rapids: Eerdmans, 1993) 13–42; Z. Zevit, *Religions of Ancient Israel,*
370–405; S. Olyan, *Asherah and the Cult of Yahweh in Israel,* SBLMS 34 (Atlanta:
Scholars Press, 1988); O. Keel and C. Uehlinger, *Gods, Goddesses, and Images of
God in Ancient Israel* (Minneapolis: Fortress, 1998); O. Keel, *Goddesses and Trees,
New Moon and Yahweh: Ancient Near Eastern Art and the Hebrew Bible,* JSOTSup 261

(Sheffield: Sheffield Academic, 1998); C. Uehlinger, "Anthropomorphic Cult Statuary in Iron Age Palestine and the Search for Yahweh's Cult Images," in *The Image and the Book: Iconic Cults, Aniconism, and the Rise of Book Religion in Israel and the Ancient Near East*, ed. K. van der Toorn (Louvain: Peeters, 1997) 97–155; C. Frevel, *Aschera und der Ausschliesslichkeitsanspruch YWHWs: Beitrag zu literarischen, religionsgeschichtlichen und ikongraphischen Aspekten der Ascheradiscussion*, 2 vols., BBB 94 (Weinheim: Eelz Athenäum, 1995).

Patrick Miller (*The Religion of Ancient Israel* [Louisville: Westminster John Knox, 2000] 30–40) has provided a nuanced view of Asherah outlining several possibilities. He does not take our text into view, thinking it has a textual error and originally referred to Astarte, not Asherah. He proposes that "the extreme integration of divine characteristics, roles, and powers in Yahweh carried with it an absorption of the feminine dimension in deity represented in ancient Near Eastern religions by the worship of a goddess" and sees this occurring at an early date in the religion. Still he must admit that the data suggest "the possibility that the feminine dimension did not disappear altogether" (30). He finds that "there was no worship of a separate goddess Asherah in Israel and that the asherah [i.e., the wooden pole symbol] in some fashion could be acceptable to a radical Yahwist like Jehu" (35). He admits that this cult symbol could easily be identified in some quarters with the goddess. The asherah especially attracted women who used normal household activities such as weaving and cooking to serve this "hypostatized or mediating dimension of Yahweh," who may have been conceived of as a goddess (40).

Miller's description here is too sophisticated to reflect reality. The biblical and extrabiblical evidence points to a worship of a goddess alongside Yahweh, one apparently connected to fertility and represented by a pole symbolizing trees and growing things. In some quarters only the symbol may have been used, even in worship of Yahweh. In other quarters, worship incorporated the goddess herself into the cult either as a separate deity or as a partner or consort of Yahweh. Astarte may have stayed outside the Yahweh cult as a strong separate goddess, while Asherah, through her pole and local household practices, gained a foothold in the Yahweh cult itself in some of its manifestations. Forgetting the nature, promises, and demands of Yahweh, Israel worshiped Baal and Asherah, even in worship places dedicated originally to Yahweh.

The story of victory is told with no action verbs, no characterization, no narrative tension that has to be resolved, no climax. It simply serves as the perfect illustration of the frame set out in chap. 2. Everything else will go downhill from here.

Even the villain of the story, Cushan Rishathaim, has a somewhat contrived name, meaning Cushan the Doubly Wicked. He is from the distant land of Aram-Naharaim (Gen 24:10; Ps 60 title), that is, Syria of the Two Rivers. Rainey (*Sacred Bridge,* 136) sees the name here as enigmatic, seeking a southern location for the action rather than the northeast as represented by Aram.

Aram-Naharaim is located between the Tigris and the Euphrates rivers, extending even westward of the Euphrates to include the cities of Harran, Nahor, Pethor, and Tunip. Egyptian sources between 1500 and 1000 B.C.E. and the Amarna letters mention it as simply Naharaim, "Between the Rivers" (see W. T. Pitard, *ABD,* 1:341). The LXX translates "Mesopotamia" and adds Deut 23:4 and 1 Chr 19:6 to the list of texts. Taken at face value, this text stretches the borders of 3:3 eastward to incorporate the territories David conquered in that direction. The additions of "Rishathaim" and "Naharaim" convey upon the enemy a dimension of fearfulness, strangeness, and distance. The description of the wicked king coming from a far-off land fulfills the exhortatory threats of Deut 28:49–50.

The battle is portrayed as between a God-appointed deliverer who judges Israel and a dark, doubly wicked villain who is king of a far-distant land. This is one of many clues that the book is about leadership, and more precisely about kingship. Othniel, like Joshua, does things God's way. Doubly Wicked goes his own way and thus goes the way of all the earth.

The chronological note of the eight-year reign gives some verisimilitude to the story, departing from the twenty, forty, eighty scheme of much of the book (see Introduction, "Introduction to Chronology of Judges"). This concern for chronology marks the book through 16:31, showing that this is the major narrative composition, with chaps. 17–21 representing the epilogue to the narrative. As Webb phrases the situation, "Those who chose to serve (עבד) foreign gods (7d) are made to serve (עבד) a foreign tyrant (8e)" ([1987] 128).

9 The phrase "sons of Israel" (בְּנֵי־יִשְׂרָאֵל) appears fifty-six times in Judges as the major designation of the nation of Israel, tying the people to the patriarchal fathers. The editor adds a new element to the framework. In 2:18 God had compassion (יִנָּחֵם) because of Israel's groaning (מִנַּאֲקָתָם). Here Israel's cry (זעק) results in God raising up a "deliverer" (מוֹשִׁיעַ), not a judge. Here again we see the complex relationship between the opening outline in chap. 2 and the actual frameworks around the narratives. The individual stories prior to their collection must, of necessity, have had narrative introductions. It is doubtful that each of those introductions followed the same patterned framework as we have in the present book of Judges. This may well point to a smaller collection of deliverer narratives given standardized introductions prior to the final editor's "publication" of the entire book. Or it may show how the final editor ironically interpreted the stories, describing the individual "heroes" as deliverers in the stories because that is all that they did when they should have assumed a much broader role of judge, bringing unity to the people, establishing justice among the tribes, and leading the nation to obey God's commandments as the fathers had done. They should have used the example of Joshua as the model of a leader after Moses. Instead, they tended much more to resemble the Canaanite plunderers God used to punish them.

"Cried out" (זעק) occurs thirteen times in Judges (3:9, 15; 4:10, 13; 6:6–7, 34–35; 10:10, 14; 12:2; 18:22–23), but only a few (3:9, 15; 6:6–7) function as framework pieces, with 10:10, 14 playing a specific theological role (see *Comment* on 10:10 and 10:14). Though the term can serve as a cry of prayer (2 Chr 20:9; 32:20; Joel 1:14) or even repentance (Judg 10:10), it generally echoes a call of distress, particularly in a losing battle (Isa 14:31; 15:4–5, 8; Jer 47:2; 48:20; cf. Jer 48:31, 34) and in "large-scale calamity" (Jer 25:34; Ezek 9:8; 11:13), as A. H. Konkel points out in *NIDOTTE*, 1:1131–32. Israel cried because of foreign oppression, not because of internal revival. The story here reports that God responds simply because Israel cries. The overarching interpretation of chap. 2 categorizes this response under God's compassion. See R. Boyce, *The Cry to God in the Old Testament* (Atlanta: Scholars Press, 1988).

The "deliverer" or savior (מוֹשִׁיעַ) brings help to people in the midst of their trouble rather than in rescuing them from it. The verb is almost exclusively a theological term with Yahweh as its subject and his people as its object (R. L. Hubbard, Jr.,

NIDOTTE, 2:556). The Hebrew deliverer is thus doing God's work. The opening framework saw this as the function of all the judges (2:16, 18), but only Othniel and Ehud receive this specific title. Samson's birth announcement uses the verb to describe his function, one he fulfilled only in his death. This distinguishes the two main "heroes" of this chapter as distinct from their successors. They stand out as examples of what the framework editor expected of judges but only rarely saw. Gideon is commissioned to deliver Israel but claims he can't (6:14–15) and sets God to the test (6:36–37) to see if he can. Thus the God who tests Israel suddenly must take a test to determine his choice of agents of deliverance.

The editor hides the deliverer's identity as long as possible. He brings Othniel center stage for an encore performance after he has answered Caleb's challenge and conquered Debir (Kiriath-sepher) in 1:11–13. His role in his wife's wiles to gain new territorial gifts from Caleb is obscure as is the effect they might have on his qualifications to serve as the first deliverer. At least he has proper family qualifications. As Caleb's son-in-law, he cannot be said to have married a foreign wife without loyalty to Yahweh.

Othniel is too frequently seen as an afterthought in the book of Judges because of its framework's lack of detail. More recently Stone ("From Tribal Confederation to Monarchic State," 260–89) has shown how Othniel sets the standards by which all other judges must measure themselves. Othniel places the tribe of Judah at the head of the list of deliverers just as it stood at the head of the list of tribes who would go up to conquer for Yahweh (1:1–2). Othniel lets God remain in center stage. Othniel delivers Israel after only eight years of oppression. Othniel does nothing to intrude his own personality, his fears, his doubts, or his greed into the narrative. Amit comments, "The impression created is that only a judge from Judah would set out to do battle in a remote region, and that he does not confine himself to worrying about the needs of his own tribe, but displays concern for 'national' needs. In this respect, Othniel is a kind of precursor of David, who shall in the future rule over areas close to Aram Naharaim" (*Book of Judges,* 165). The book of Judges should reflect a boring string of framework narratives like this. Instead it has to add the many stories of disobedience and ego.

10 "The Spirit of Yahweh" empowered Othniel. Again the narrative adds a note absent from the opening framework in chap. 2. The Spirit will also empower Gideon and Jephthah, but will play its most prominent role with Samson (Judg 3:10; 6:34; 11:29; 13:25; 14:6, 19; 15:14). The Saul and David narratives also feature this empowering Spirit, called at times the evil spirit of Yahweh (1 Sam 10:6; 16:13–14; 19:9; 2 Sam 23:2). Spirit language here functions to underline God's sovereign power and plan as operative so that readers cannot attribute results to human operatives.

The *NIDOTTE* writers remind us,

> Frequently the Spirit of God represents the agent/agency by which God exercises his sovereign control over individuals. Occasionally the effects are calamitous, as in those instances when the LORD's Spirit is described as destructive or disruptive (not evil in a moral sense; Judg 9:23; 1 Sam 16:14–16, 23; 18:10; 19:9). But usually God's Spirit operates on behalf of his people by energizing them (Ezek 2:2), transporting them (1 Kgs 18:12; 2 Kgs 2:16; Ezek 3:12, 14; 8:3; 11:24; 37:1, though sometimes in visionary form), endowing ("filling") them with his Spirit, and giving them special gifts and power for

sacred service (Exod 35:31; Mic 3:8). Often the Spirit of God comes/falls on those divinely chosen and commissioned for the work of God. This was particularly true of those who prophesied under the inspiration of the LORD (the seventy elders, Num 11:17, 25; Saul, 1 Sam 10:6, 10), as opposed to false prophets, who were inspired from within (Ezek 13:3), though occasionally the Scriptures speak of the LORD deceitfully inspiring false prophets (1 Kgs 22:21–23; cf. Ezek 14:9). (M. V. Van Pelt, W. C. Kaiser, Jr., D. I. Block, *NIDOTTE*, 3:1075–76)

The other recipients of the Spirit do not produce perfect results. Gideon stops to test God (6:34–40). Jephthah makes a foolish vow leading to his daughter's death, and Samson's acts are self-serving. Schneider can thus say, "Othniel is the example of how 'the spirit of the Israelite deity' should affect one, confirming his role as the model Judge" (43).

Basing her conclusion on the actions of Jephthah and Samson, Schneider may go too far in claiming that "'the spirit of the Israelite deity' gives characters physical strength to carry out the physical and military actions necessary, but possibly blinds them from making intelligent choices."

By the Spirit's enabling, Othniel "judged Israel." The chap. 2 framework has prepared us for this (2:16–19), but chap. 2 used only the participle as a title for the official. Outside chap. 2, the editor reverts to verbal references to judging, not utilizing the title. Thus Deborah (4:4), the minor judges (10:2–3; 12:7–9, 11, 13–14), Samson (15:20; 16:31), and Yahweh (11:27) judge Israel. The number of years assigned the minor judges and Samson set this off as an ongoing function, not a one-time activity. Nowhere is the function described. The chap. 2 framework hinted at the office as seeking to maintain obedience to divine law, while Deborah appears to be settling disputes among fellow citizens. See further discussion in chap. 10. Whatever the function, chap. 2 reminds us what the stories constantly teach us, namely, the ineptness of the judges in establishing long-term influence. People might follow them in brief military encounters but will not obey them in either the things of the court or the things of the tabernacle. Such ineptness finally leads to everyone doing right in their own eyes, forcing Israel to seek a king (21:25).

Cushan Rishathaim, the king of Aram or of Aram Naharaim, that is, Syria between the rivers, poses impossible demands for the commentator. Younger (106–7) lists six different solutions to the problem of this foreign king's identity:

1. Irsu from Egypt, a Syrian usurper
2. Otherwise unknown Cushan from Edom, making a minor correction in Hebrew text from Aram to Edom; compare Hab 3:7, which parallels Cushan and Midian
3. Tushratta, king of Mitanni
4. Artatama II, king of Mitanni
5. Sharri Kushkh, Hittite ruler of Carchemish
6. Ruler of displaced Hurrians seeking a new home

Younger concludes, quite correctly, that "all of these proposals, however, are speculative. At the end of the day, we simply must admit that we do not know the identity of this individual." Egyptian sources point to Naharin as part of the Hurrian kingdom of Mitanni under Thutmose III about 1450 (see Younger, 107).

What we do know is that the king is a foreigner whose name would not be Hebraic, yet the text yields a strong Hebrew wordplay, translated by Younger as "dark doubly wicked" with the telling comment that the name "is clearly a pejorative (parents do not typically name their children such)" (104). Thus we do not know the king's real name. We know only how Israel saw his character and how the editor's fourfold mention of his name emphasizes the double trouble Israel faced.

God thus gives Israel to Double Trouble as his prize and then, through Othniel, overpowers him because "Yahweh gave Cushan . . . into [Othniel's] hand." Previously, God had given the land into Judah's hand (1:2). Often God gives Israel into the hand of plunderers and enemies as promised in the chap. 2 framework (2:14; compare 6:1; 13:1) but does not give the remaining lands into Joshua's hand (2:18). He promises to give Sisera into Barak's hand (4:7, 14). But being given the enemy must not call forth bragging from Israel (7:2, 9, 14–15). Jephthah asks God to give the enemy into his hand and gets his wish at the price of his daughter's life (11:30, 32). Again God gives the enemy into Jephthah's hands, only to cause an intertribal dispute (12:3). Once Judah gives Judge Samson into the hands of the Philistine enemies (15:12–13), Samson can confess that God has given into his hand the victory and yet lament his lack of water (15:18). Even enemy soldiers can celebrate that their gods had handed the enemy over to them (16:23–24). The spies from Dan proclaim that God has given the northern territory into their hands before they settle there and establish their unholy cult. Just as in 1:1 so in 20:28 Israel receives an oracle from God, but this time it tells them God has handed the enemy—Benjamin, one of their own tribes—into their hands.

The formula of giving into the hand may be a recurring one that seems to be closely related to the opening framework, but closer examination shows that its recurrence comes at different places within the narrative, not just in the framework, and that it carries vastly different meanings in the different occurrences. It is anything but sterile, repetitive language. It is a formula that the editor uses creatively and unexpectedly in various places in the narrative.

11 The quiet activity of Othniel, whose time in office elicits only a one-sentence battle report, leads to a quiet time for the people of God. Still Othniel, the almost inert judge, proves to be a model judge. The judge as leader is not called to devote his life to battle and violence. Josh 11:23 and 14:15 paint the securing of rest or quiet (שׁקט) as the goal of all Israel's Canaanite wars. The judge is to be used of God to lead God's people in war, but the judge's ultimate goal is to lead them to and in peace. Othniel, Ehud, Deborah and Barak, and Gideon succeed in gaining such quiet (Judg 3:11, 30; 5:31; 8:28). The tribe of Dan also manages to disrupt the quiet life of the inhabitants of Luz (Judg 18:7, 27). Thus Hamilton can conclude, "Othniel, who lives in Israel after the death of Joshua and the elders who outlived Joshua, models true judgeship for all who follow him in that position. There never is another Joshua, a survivor of a faithless generation, and there never is another Othniel, a survivor of a faithful generation" (*Handbook*, 112).

12 The Ehud story opens with only one brief framework verse, underlining Israel's evil and God's empowering of Eglon of Moab. Even the verb (חזק in the *pi'el*) used in the framework is foreign to all other framework formulations. The whole emphasis is on Israel's evil, repeated twice in the short verse and introduced by "continued to do evil." This framework verse is, however, an essential part of the exposition in vv 12–15 and points to the narrator's skill in using only those parts of the framework necessary for the present narrative and using them in unique ways to set up the tension within the narrative. The story that follows presents a series of almost unconnected tableaux with important parts of the action not mentioned. (See Amit, *Book of Judges,* 174–75, 180.)

Moab is Israel's perpetual enemy (Exod 15:15; Num 21:29; 22–24; Deut 23:4; 1 Sam 14:47; compare 1 Sam 12:9) and the original example of a foreign power tempting Israel to serve fertility gods (Num 25:1; compare Judg 10:6; 1 Kgs 11:7, 33; 2 Kgs 23:13). Still God did not allow Israel to conquer Moab (Deut 2:9; compare Judg 11:15, 17–18). At some point David established peaceful relationships with the king of Moab (1 Sam 22:4), but he soon made the Moabites his tributaries and subjects (2 Sam 8:2; 8:12; 23:20). Later, Moab gained the upper hand (2 Kgs 1:1; 3:4–5; compare the Moabite stone) for only a short period (2 Kgs 3:7–26). Constant provocation occurred between the enemy nations (2 Kgs 13:20). Finally, God used Moab in the destruction of Jerusalem (2 Kgs 24:2). The prophets repeatedly promised victory over Moab (Isa 11:14; 25:10) and issued oracles against Moab (Isa 15–16; Jer 48; Ezek 25:8–11; Amos 2:1–3).

13 Israel faces not just one enemy but a coalition that Eglon forms using military force. Ammon was Moab's northern neighbor, while the Amalekites were a nomadic or seminomadic group of Esau's descendants based in Edom but wandering in various places. See Gen 14:7; 36:12, 16; Exod 17:8–11, 13–14, 16; Num 13:29; 24:20; 14:25, 43, 45; Deut 25:17, 19; Judg 5:14; 6:3, 33; 7:12; 10:12; 12:15; 1 Sam 14:48; 15:2–3, 5–8, 15, 18, 20, 32; 27:8; 28:18; 30:1, 13, 18; 2 Sam 1:1; 8:12–13; 1 Chr 1:36; 4:43; 18:11; Ps 83:8. The editor blatantly makes one of many puns or ironic comparisons here. Eglon is closely associated phonetically to עֶגְלָה, "calf or heifer," and to עֵגֶל, "young bull" or "ox." This phonetic pun might be stretched to include עָגֹל, "round" or "rotund."

The City of Palms was apparently near Jericho (Deut 34:3; Judg 1:16; 3:13; 2 Chr 28:15), though S. Mittmann ("Ri. 1,16f und das Siedlungsgebiet der kenitischen Sippe Hobab," *ZDPV* 93 [1977] 213–35) would place it at Tamar southwest of the Dead Sea. Eglon dispossesses it (יָרַשׁ) from Israel, turning the tables on the people God had called to dispossess the inhabitants of Canaanite territory (Josh 1:11, 15; 3:10; 8:7; 12:1; 13:1, 6, 12–13; 14:12; 15:14, 63; 16:10; 17:12–13, 18; 18:3; 19:47; 21:43; 23:5, 9, 13; 24:4, 8; compare Judg 1:19–21, 27–33; 2:6, 21, 23; 11:21–24; 14:15; 18:7, 9). If, indeed, this is Jericho, then Eglon has begun to dismantle the very cities Joshua dispossessed and to accomplish what the powerful prophet Balaam could not (Num 22–24). But is this done through the power of political coalition or from the strength God gives Eglon? How do the two explanations of history relate to one another? This question appears throughout Judges and will be seen in Israel naming Ehud its leader, in bringing tribute to Eglon, and in God raising him up as a deliverer. See Amit (*Book of Judges,* 176–80) for more on the problem of dual causality.

14 The period of service is interesting, totaling eighteen years, an unusual, not rounded number. See Introduction, "Introduction to the Chronology of Judges."

15 Suddenly we return to framework language. We meet our champion, Ehud, "a left-handed Benjaminite." This sets him up as the representative of the smallest tribe and of the tribe from which Saul will come. Jericho stood in Benjamin's tribal allotment (Josh 18:21). Ehud is not described as a שׁוֹפֵט, "judge," but as a מוֹשִׁיעַ, "deliverer." His name may mean "Where is the glory or majesty?" At the moment it lies in the hands of Eglon. The narrative tension is formed here as Israel sends their deliverer, "Where is majesty?" to pay tribute to his majesty Eglon. How can tribute be a form of deliverance?

Ehud is a Benjaminite, literally, "a son of the right hand." Yet Ehud is left-handed, literally "impeded on the right side," but possibly meaning ambidextrous (LXX; HALOT; DCH; Block 161). Impeded cannot mean injured or deformed in any way, for as Younger notes (114), "Ehud's plot only works if he appears normal to the Moabite guards." Nor does ambidextrous add anything to this narrative. Seven hundred Benjaminites have this condition or gift in Judg 20:16. Ehud will eventually work individually, but he does so in the framework of being a messenger the sons of Israel have sent to Eglon with "tribute" (מִנְחָה), a common word for a present or a gift that becomes a technical term in at least two spheres—politics (Judg 3:15, 7–18; 2 Sam 8:2//1 Chr 18:2; 2 Sam 8:6//1 Chr 18:6; 2 Kgs 17:3–4; 2 Chr 17:11; 26:8; Hos 10:6) and worship, where it represents a food offering (Exod 29:41; 30:9; 40:29; Lev 2:1–23:37; Num 4:16–29:39; Ezek 42:13–46:20), certainly apropos for King Eglon and his appetites.

The text emphasizes that this enemy Eglon is the king of Moab. The book of Judges is determined to ensure that readers notice the way kings live and function.

16 Ehud has made a special dagger for himself, sharp on two sides (literally, "to it two mouths"). The Hebrew measuring term גמד, translated as "foot," appears only here, and so its precise meaning or measurement is uncertain. Ehud carefully hides the weapon on his right side, where he could easily reach it with his left hand but guards would most likely not detect it. Niditch (57–58) draws out the explicitly sexual imagery here saying that as in chap. 4 "an act of deception begins to weave an erotic theme that links the sexual with the aggressive and agonistic." She concludes that "the defeated soldier is the one who is knocked down, raped, and made the conquered woman" (58).

17 The narrator's attention focuses on Eglon and his body build. Again, irony controls the narrative. The description "exceedingly fat" (בְּרִיא מְאֹד) does not necessarily imply criticism. Rather, wicked people whose bodies are בְּרִיא gain worldly admiration (Ps 73:4). Daniel and his friends proved their good health with their בְּרִיא (Dan 1:15). This adjective can also indicate rich, enticing food (Hab 1:16; Zech 11:16). Most often it signifies good-quality animals, ready for sacrifice (Gen 41:4, 20; 1 Kgs 4:23; Ezek 34:3, 20). Eglon is thus pictured as very pleasingly plump on the one hand and as a perfect creature for sacrifice on the other. His physique also sets him up for Ehud's plan.

18 The temporal clause, "as he finished giving the tribute," deliberately slows down the Hebrew narrative, preparing the audience for the central, unexpected moment. Ehud has completed his earthly assignment, but he is just beginning his heavenly mission. He sends his own servants away since they have finished their task as tribute bearers and will only be in the way for the next step in the plan.

19 The Hebrew disjunctive clause sets this statement in direct contrast to the preceding one and adds new pace to the narrative. The tribute bearers turn back. Ehud does not. The geographical situation lacks clarity here. Ehud finds himself at Gilgal, the center of action for Joshua (Josh 4:19–20; 5:9–10; 9:6; 10:6–7, 9, 15, 43; 14:6; 15:7). Having suddenly appeared at 2:1 and here, Gilgal disappears from Judges. Has Israel abandoned its central military post, the people having dispersed to their "inheritances"? Has the center of worship moved to Bethel (see Introduction) or to Shiloh (Judg 18:31; 21:12, 19, 21)? Under Joshua, Israel repeatedly came back to its worship and military center. Under the judges the central shrine is ignored.

Israel's central shrine under Joshua now has "images," apparently symbols of pagan gods (Deut 7:5, 25; 12:3; Judg 3:19, 26; 2 Kgs 17:41; 2 Chr 33:19, 22; 34:3–4, 7; Ps 78:58; Isa 10:10; 21:9; 30:22; 42:8; Jer 8:19; 50:38; 51:47, 52; Hos 11:2; Mic 1:7; 5:12). One might read the Hebrew to see Gilgal as the site of the confrontation that follows. One might decide Eglon was camped nearby at Jericho, "the City of Palms" (v 13). Most probably, the narrator hastens the pace so much that he assumes the reader will understand that Ehud turned away from his people at Gilgal and returned to where the king was, in the capital city. This lets Ehud pull off his deception by suddenly returning after having left because he had received "something secret for you."

The Moabites would see the place of idols as an appropriate and likely place to receive such a divine secret. Eglon pays attention to the secret. Here the Hebrew reads דְּבַר־סֵתֶר. *Dābār* can mean "word," "thing," or "matter." Often it appears as "word of God" or "prophetic oracle." Eglon has to get to the root of the matter and determine what the secret is. He knows such secrets can only be shared on a one-on-one basis. Thus he calls for quiet from his servants and sends them out of his royal presence.

20 Ehud approaches as the king sits "in his cool, elevated throne room." The narrator underlines unnecessarily that Eglon is alone. Ehud has succeeded in creating the situation he desires. Ehud adds an eerie, awesome note to the conversation, saying his *dābār* comes "from God" (אלהים), a much more comprehensive and less definite term than the personal name יהוה, "Yahweh," to be used later. At the mention of deity, the king rises from his throne, perhaps in reverence, perhaps in consternation. In so doing he leaves himself open to Ehud's plot.

21–22 Now we find the reason for the careful manipulation of the dagger to his right leg and for getting the servants on both sides out of the picture. We also find the reason for mentioning the royal obesity. The dagger fits the belly perfectly. The "fat" (הַחֵלֶב) represents another vocabulary item closely connected to the sacrificial language (Gen 4:4; Exod 23:18; Lev 4:26; 6:5; 8:25; 9:19–20, 24; 10:15; 16:25; Deut 32:38; 1 Kgs 8:64; 2 Chr 7:7; 29:35; 35:14; Isa 43:24). The narrator quickly closes the scene with a bit of dark humor, if our understanding of the enigmatic Hebrew term is correct. The only explanation for the guards' refusal to act quickly has to come from bathroom humor of some type here. For Near Eastern examples of such injury in battle, see Younger, 118, n. 26; compare Halpern, *First Historians,* 40.

23–24 Ehud leaves the king alone on his "throne" and disappears alone down the escape hatch, locking the doors behind him. Chisholm ("What's Wrong with This Picture?") argues that an audience hall separated the king's chamber from an outer room where the king's servants were waiting. Thus Ehud could have locked the doors of the king's chamber without being seen. (For a reconstruction and explanation of such a lock, see P. J. King and L. E. Stager, *Life in Biblical Israel* [Louisville: Westminster John Knox, 2001] 31–33.) He would have left the audience hall, walked past the guards in the outer area, and left the same way he came in. As Ehud passes by the servants in the outer room, they reason correctly that his business with the king is finished, so they enter the audience hall between the outer room and the king's chamber. Finally, unsummoned for so long, the servants reenter without royal permission. They find something unexpected—locked doors—and come to a simple explanation: the king is relieving himself. Here the · Hebrew uses a euphemistic idiom: he was covering his feet. Mobley nicely phrases the literary result: "Even Eglon's offal, and its odor, aids Ehud's escape" ("Ehud and the Monoliths," 84).

25 The servants expect something. Fear and shame grip them. Have they neglected their duties? Have they failed their king? Finally, when the king fails to act, they do, unlocking the doors. What a sight! Their lord and majesty, before whom they have so often fallen to the ground in obedient submission and devotion, has "fallen to the ground, dead!" Killed in the toilet. Such is the end of a fat king so unwary that a left-handed man paid him the final tribute. God's secret was a deadly one leading to the sacrifice of Eglon, the royal fatted calf.

26 The narrator uses a disjunctive sentence to change course and switch scenes, back to the escaping Ehud, retracing his steps past Gilgal's Images. This time he "passed over the Images," certainly receiving no secret message from them. He arrives at Seirah, a town mentioned in Ugaritic materials that geographers have yet to locate. Rainey (*Sacred Bridge*, 137) sees this not as a town but as a geographical feature, "the woody hills." The context with its mustering of troops, however, seems to favor a town. The return to the Images (see v 19) brackets the basic Ehud narrative action. "The twin references to the *pĕsîlîm* articulate the decisive and dramatic core of the adventure. Everything that precedes 3:19–26 is preliminary; everything which follows is anticlimactic (Mobley, "Ehud and the Monoliths," 90).

27 The Hebrew verb חקע plays an important role here. It describes the sounding of the "ram's horn" or *shofar* as featured in Josh 6. The same verb appeared in Judg 3:21 describing the thrusting of the dagger into Eglon's belly. It will appear again as Jael hammers the tent peg into Sisera's temple. Gideon sounds the shofar to muster the troops (6:34) and scares the Midianites into fleeing by having the people sound their shofars (7:18–22). Finally, Delilah will thrust a peg into Samson's hair in a fruitless effort to discover the secret of his strength (16:14). Thrusting and blowing thus mark the narratives with action, summon the troops to battle, and celebrate the heroism of one woman and the dastardly deception of another.

The shofar was not a musical instrument. It was used in solemn occasions to celebrate God's approach in theophany (Exod 19:16, 19; 20:18; Zech 9:14; compare 2 Sam 6:15; Pss 47:6; 98:6; Joel 2:1; Zeph 1:16), to call people to holy days on the religious calendar (Lev 25:9; Ps 81:3 [Heb. 4]), to instigate national fasts (Joel 2:15), and to announce a new king (1 Kgs 1:34, 39, 41; 2 Kgs 9:13). A major function involved battle signals and warnings (Josh 6:4–20; Judg 6:34; 7:8–22; 1 Sam 13:3; 2 Sam 2:28; 18:16; 20:1, 22; Isa 18:3; Jer 42:14; 51:27; Ezek 33:3–6; Hos 5:8; 8:1; Amos 2:2; 3:6).

"The hill country of Ephraim," Rainey says, "is a generic geographical term for the entire block of hills that included the territory of Benjamin, Ephraim, and Manasseh. However, it seems likely that the participants in this action would have been from Ehud's own tribe" of Benjamin (*Sacred Bridge*, 137). The "sons of Israel" answer the summons. This phrase appears to give a national flavor to a very local narrative. Could it be that "sons of Israel" originally represented only the armies of the central tribes, especially Benjamin and the sons of Joseph? The narrator carefully points to Ehud's position in front of the troops. This is the place for an Israelite leader in the shadow of Moses and Joshua.

28 Ehud rallies the troops to follow in the assurance that Yahweh has given Moab into their hands. No longer does Yahweh have to deliver a king to Israel to defeat as he delivered the kings in the long list in Josh 12. Ehud has dispatched the king one on one. Now the battle strategy is simple: cut off the river crossing so the enemy cannot cross into your territory. Ehud's mention here of Yahweh raises issues about the nature of the narrative, of Ehud, and of Yahweh. In v 15 the framework says Israel cried to Yahweh and Yahweh raised up Ehud. From then until now in v 28, Yahweh disappears from the narrative.

Does the narrator use this narrative tactic to let the audience assume Yahweh has planned and directed all the intervening action? Or does the narrator want us to assume Ehud has craftily taken things into his own hands and left God out? Does Yahweh approve or disapprove of Ehud's tactics? The scholarly argument swings on and on. Block (171) calls the narrator's silence "deafening" so that Yahweh has to use a "crude" tool to do his will because that is all that is available. He compares Ehud to a Canaanite acting for his own glory. Younger has (124–25) no doubt that the account emphasizes God's ability to use "flawed individuals" to accomplish his purposes. For Younger, Ehud is no Othniel but is instead "treacherous and brutal," and "God does not endorse or condone his methods." Still, Younger praises Ehud's willingness to risk everything for God (126). Klein (*Triumph of Irony*, 39) sees Yahweh as opposed to the deception of Ehud. Such judgment puts our "refined, sophisticated" moral conscience to work against an ancient civilization's conduct of war and self-defense. One must doubt that any early reader of the narrative would have heard any condemnation of Ehud's action. Both he and Shamgar use untraditional ways to deliver God's people from their plunderers. Such unexpected military strategy gives the stories their unique flavor and appeal.

29 Enemy soldiers, like their king, are "fat" (שָׁמֵן, not בָּרִיא), again a positive attribute, not a negative one as seen by the parallel "fit for battle" (אִישׁ חַיִל). Outside warfare contexts (Judg 3:29; 20:44, 46; 1 Sam 31:12; 2 Sam 11:16; 24:9; 1 Chr 10:12; 11:22; 26:8; Neh 11:6; Ps 76:6; Jer 48:14; Nah 2:4), the term applies to people capable of accomplishments in various fields of endeavor (Gen 47:6; Exod 18:21, 25; 1 Kgs 1:42; compare Isa 5:22). A battle fought under God's leadership ends the way it is supposed to: no enemy escapes. Under Othniel and Ehud, Israel's soldiers have passed the test and know how to conduct warfare. The language here reverses the theme and action of v 13. There Eglon's coalition had to cross the Jordan to defeat (Heb. נכה). Here the murdered king's armies attempt to cross the Jordan, and Israel strikes them dead (Heb. נכה).

30 Thus Israel has its longest rest—eighty years. Polzin decides that "the eighty years of peace mentioned in 3:30 are not to be construed as dependent upon any supposed repentance of Israel, but solely upon the length of Ehud's life" (*Moses and the Deuteronomist*, 161). The editor of Judges uses the rest theme to show God's blessing on the work of the deliverers. Such came not as something earned by obedience or repentance. Neither is mentioned here. Israel again has attained Joshua's goal—quiet rest from war (Josh 11:23; 14:15; compare Judg 3:11; 5:31; 8:28). For the prophets this became a future hope (Isa 14:7; 30:15; 32:17; Jer 46:27).

31 Judges devotes one verse to Shamgar, preparing for his appearance in the Song of Deborah in Judg 5. None of the full framework elements appear. In fact, the Ehud narrative does not close until the next verse (4:1). Shamgar is thus enveloped in the Ehud narrative to bring a closure to the testing narratives among the nations introduced by 3:1. Othniel saved Israel from the distant enemy on its far eastern border. Ehud saved his people from the neighboring Moab, separated by the Jordan River. Shamgar delivered Israel from the Philistines, the first of the nations that remained (3:3).

Shamgar's credentials are suspect. His parent Anath carries the name of one of the three great Canaanite goddesses. See W. A. Maier III, *ABD*, 1:225–27. P. C. Craigie ("A Reconsideration of Shamgar ben Anath [Judg 3:31 and 5:6]," *JBL* 91 [1972] 239–40) argues that the name ben Anath is a military title based on the "warlike character of the goddess" and used by people like the Haneans in the Mari texts. (Compare F. C. Fensham, "Shamgar ben Anath," *JNES* 20 [1961] 197–98.) Soggin (57) would see the name as Canaanite.

Ben Anath may also be seen as a place name (Josh 19:38; Judg 1:33). N. Shupak ("New Light on Shamgar ben 'Anath," *Bib* 70 [1989] 517–25) connects the name with an Egyptian military contingent of *'prw* containing some Hurrian names and appearing in Egyptian sources at the beginning of the Iron Age. Matthews (62–63) takes this further to say,

> ben Anath was a common name used by the 'Apiru/Habiru mercenaries employed by the Egyptians during the twelfth-tenth centuries BCE. They took on the name of the Canaanite goddess of war to mark both their ferocity in battle and their membership in a military cadre. Shamgar's mention in the Jael story could therefore reflect the activities of Pharaoh Rameses III (1198–1190 BCE) against the Philistines in northern Canaan.

Shamgar is assigned no tribal designation among the Israelites. His name appears to be Hurrian (B. Maisler, "Shamgar ben 'Anat," *PEQ* 66 [1934] 192–94; P. C. Craigie, "A Reconsideration of Shamgar ben Anath [Judg 3:331 and 5:6]," *JBL* 91 [1972] 239–40). Thus Younger can decide that "the only scholarly agreement is that Shamgar son of Anath was not an Israelite" (129–30). Even this agreement may be questioned. Would original readers truly draw this conclusion from such oblique evidence? Did the editor expect the audience to know more about Shamgar than the narrative here or the poem in 5:6 tells?

Shamgar operates with an ox goad as an individual hero much like Samson in his later escapades among the Philistines. Still, Shamgar with his presence in this section of Judges and his indirect praise in the Song of Deborah stands with Othniel and Ehud as examples of how to pass the test God set down for the people of Israel as they faced the nations. Younger (130) draws a parallel with Othniel and sets Shamgar up as "a type of ideal noncyclical (i.e. minor) judge." Othniel was a Kennazite who was incorporated into Judah. Ehud was left-handed, and Shamgar had no explicit tribal connections. Yet each delivered Israel. The judges to come—Barak, Gideon, Abimelech, Jephthah, Samson—will not fare so well under testing. Each will show a flaw in carrying out God's commission.

Explanation

The period of the judges began with an inexperienced nation tested in its ability, and willingness to carry out war as God's commandments stipulated. They got off to a good start under three judges—Othniel, Ehud, and Shamgar. These judges represented those who still knew Joshua and God's works under him (Othniel), those who represented the nation after Joshua's generation, and those who served under the minor judges (Shamgar). Each saved Israel from powerful enemies, carrying out God's commission in different fashions but still following God's commands in defeating the enemy to the east, south, and west. In so doing they showed that God's way with judges remained superior to the enemy ways with coalitions of kings or with the unique governors of the Philistines. As with Joshua, so with these first three judges, God could take an individual and lead a nation to victory in ways consonant with God's commandments. As with Joshua, so with these judges, God could bring quiet rest from war. Despite the evidence of the following narratives, God's plan for the judges could work. The problem was not a bad plan from God. The problem was a bad people.

The three nations represented here provoke questions. Moab represents the arch enemy from Transjordan, while Aram-Naharaim represents the Syrian threat under David and his successors. D. C. Browning notes, "The rise of Aram-Damascus' power was facilitated by the division of Israel following the death of Solomon" (*HIBD*, 1548). The Philistines remained the strongest threat among the peoples living in Cisjordan after the division of the monarchy. The narrator probably collected his materials and edited them in this period shortly after the kingdoms divided and placed the three major powers of his day as the victims of the three judges who passed God's test.

The three stories show how God successfully brings victory through quite different procedures and methods. God uses a left-handed warrior with a dagger strapped to his right leg, a man full of tactics and tricks. God uses a son-in-law of a famous generation past who simply lets God give the enemy into his hand. Finally, God uses an individual warrior with a strange weapon—an ox goad—to defeat an enemy army. God may be teaching his people warfare, but the lesson is not one of tactics and tools. The lesson is one of depending on God and following God's laws for warfare. Throughout the Ehud narrative as well as with Othniel and Shamgar, we learn "that the success of human tactics depends upon the divine will" (Amit, *Book of Judges*, 181). Or as Olson (772) aptly affirms: "The story is first and foremost about the 'left-handed' ways of God both to judge and to deliver Israel."

B. Foreboding Failures in the North (4:1–16:31)

1. Barak: Surrendering Glory to a Woman (4:1–5:31)

a. The Prose Version (4:1–24)

Bibliography

Ackerman, J. S. "Prophecy and Warfare in Early Israel: A Study of the Deborah-Barak Story." *BASOR* 220 (1975) 5–13. ———. "Why Is Miriam Also among the Prophets? (And

Is Zipporah among the Priests?)." *JBL* 121 (2002) 47–80. **Adler, R.** "A Mother in Israel, Aspects of the Mother Role in Jewish Myth." In *Beyond Androcentrism: New Essays on Women and Religion.* Ed. R. M. Gross. Missoula, MT: Scholars Press, 1977. 237–55. **Aharoni, A.** "The Battle on the Waters of Merom and the Battle with Sisera" (Heb.). In *The Military History of the Land of Israel in Biblical Times.* Ed. J. Liver. Tel Aviv, 1964. 91–109. ———. "Jael the Wife of Heber the Kenite and Shamgar the Son of Anath" (Heb.). In *All the Land of Naphtali—The Twenty-Fourth Archaeological Convention, October 1966.* Ed. H. Z. Hirschberg and J. Aviram. Jerusalem, 1968. 55–61. ———. *The Land of the Bible: A Historical Geography.* Trans. A. F. Rainey. London: Burns & Oates, 1967. **Albright, W. F.** "Jethro, Hobab, and Reuel in Early Hebrew Tradition." *CBQ* 25 (1952) 1–11. **Alejandrino, M.** *Deborah and Barak: A Literary-Historical Analysis of Judges 4 and 5.* Rome: Université Grégorienne, 1998. **Alonzo-Schökel, L.** "Erzählkunst im Buche der Richter." *Bib* 42 (1961) 143–72. **Amit, Y.** "Judges 4: Its Content and Form." *JSOT* 39 (1987) 89–111. **Asen, B. A.** "Deborah, Barak and Bees: *Apis mellifera.* Apiculture and Judges 4 and 5." *ZAW* 109 (1997) 514–33. **Assis, E.** "The Choice to Serve God and Assist His People: Rahab and Yael." *Bib* 85 (2004) 82–90. ———. "'The Hand of a Woman': Deborah and Yael (Judges 4)." *The Journal of Hebrew Scriptures* 5 (2005) 1–12. ———. "Man, Woman and God in Judg 4." *SJOT* 20 (2006) 110–24. **Ausloos, H.** "Exod 23:20–33 and the 'War of YHWH.'" *Bib* 80 (1999) 555–63. **Bakon, S.** "Deborah: Judge, Prophetess, Poet." *JBQ* 34 (2006) 110–18. **Bal, M.** *Murder and Difference: Gender, Genre, and Scholarship on Sisera's Death.* Trans. M. Grumpert. Bloomington: Indiana UP, 1988. **Barbaosa, R. F., Z. R. Morais, and S. S. Silva.** "Debora e Jael: Mulheres que fazem historia." *EstBib* 29 (1991) 59–65. **Becking, B.,** and **M. Dijkstra,** eds. *On Reading Prophetic Texts: Gender-Specific and Related Studies.* FS F. van Dijk-Hemmes. BibInt 18. Leiden: Brill, 1996. **Bedenbender, A.** "Biene, Fackel, Blitz: Zur Metaphorik der Namen in der Deborageschichte (Ri 4–5)." *T&K* 76 (1997) 43–55. **Blessing, C.** "Judge, Prophet, Mother: Learning from Deborah." *Daughters of Sarah* 21 (1995) 34–37. **Block, D. I.** "Deborah among the Judges: The Perspective of the Hebrew Historian." In *Faith, Tradition, and History: Old Testament Historiography in Its Near Eastern Context.* Ed. A. R. Millard, J. K. Hoffmeier, and D. W. Baker. Winona Lake, IN: Eisenbrauns, 1995. 229–53. ———. "'Israel-Sons of Israel': A Study in Hebrew Eponymic Usage." *SR* 13 (1984) 301–26. ———. "Why Deborah's Different." *BRev* 17 (2001) 34–40, 49–52. **Bos, J. W. H.** "Out of the Shadows: Genesis 38; Judges 4:17–22; Ruth 3." *Semeia* 42 (1988) 37–67. **Brenner, A.** "A Triangle and a Rhombus in Narrative Structure: A Proposed Integrative Reading of Judges iv and v." *VT* 40 (1990) 129–38. ———. "Who's Afraid of Feminist Criticism? Who's Afraid of Biblical Humour? The Case of the Obtuse Foreign Ruler in the Hebrew Bible." *JSOT* 63 (1994) 38–55. **Burnette-Bletsch, R.** "At the Hands of a Woman: Rewriting Jael in Pseudo-Philo." *JSP* 17 (1998) 53–64. **Butler, T. C.** "Praising God by Praising Women: Interaction of Praise and Poetry in Judges 4–5." Paper read at Society of Biblical Literature, Toronto, 2002. ———. "Reading the Whole: More than the Sum of the Prose and Poetic Parts, An Analysis of the Literary Purpose of Judges 4 and 5." Paper read at Evangelical Theological Society, Toronto, 2002. **Calder, N.** "The *sa'y* and the *jabīn:* Some Notes on Qur'ān 37.102–3." *JSS* 31 (1986) 17–26. **Christianson, E. S.** "The Big Sleep: Strategic Ambiguity in Judges 4–5 and in Classic 'Film Noir.'" *SBL Forum* <http://www.sbl-site.org/Article.aspx?ArticleId=393>. **Couturier, G.** "Debora: Une autorite politico-religieuse aux origins d'Israel." *SR* 18 (1989) 213–28. **Culley, R. C.** *Themes and Variations.* 100–104. **Davies, G. I.** "Megiddo in the Period of the Judges." In *Crises and Perspectives: Studies in Ancient Near Eastern Polytheism, Biblical Theology, Palestinian Archaeology and Intertestamental Literature.* OtSt 24. Leiden: Brill, 1986. 34–53. **Deibner, B.-J.** "Wann sang Deborah ihr Lied? Überlegungen zu zwei der ältesten Texte des TNK (Ri 4 und 5)." *ACEBT* 14 (1995) 106–30. **Dijk-Hemmes, F. van.** "Blessed among Women: A Mother in Israel and a Virgin in the Church." In *The Double Voice of Her Desire.* Ed. J. Bekkenkamp and F. Dröes. Trans. D. E. Orton. Leiden: Deo, 2004. 89–109. ———. *Sporen van vouwenstudies in de Hebreeuwse bijbel.* Utrechtse Theologische Reeks 16. Utrecht: Universiteit Utrecht, 1992. **Drews,**

R. "The 'Chariots of Iron' of Joshua and Judges." *JSOT* 45 (1989) 15–23. **Duran, N.** "Having Men for Dinner: Deadly Banquets and Biblical Women." *BTB* 35 (2005) 117–24. **Eshel, H.** "A Second Fragment of Judges." *JJS* 54 (2003) 139–41. **Exum, J. C.** "'Mother in Israel': A Familiar Figure Reconsidered." In *Feminist Interpretation of the Bible.* Ed. L. M. Russell. Philadelphia: Westminster, 1985. 73–85. **Fager, J.** "Chaos and the Deborah Tradition." *QR* 13 (1993) 17–30. **Fensham, F. C.** "Did a Treaty between the Israelites and the Kenites Exist?" *BASOR* 175 (1964) 51–54. **Fewell, D. N.,** and **D. M. Gunn.** "Controlling Perspectives: Women, Men and the Authority of Violence in Judges 4 and 5." *JAAR* 58 (1990) 389–411. **Finkelstein, I.,** and **D. Ussishkin.** "Back to Megiddo." *BAR* 20 (1994) 30–43. **Fokkelman, J. P.** "The Song of Deborah and Barak: Its Prosodic Levels and Structure." In *Pomegranates and Golden Bells: Studies in Biblical, Jewish, and Near Eastern Ritual, Law, and Literature.* FS J. Milgrom, ed. D. P. Wright, D. N. Freedman, and A. Hurvitz. Winona Lake, IN: Eisenbrauns, 1995. 595–628. **Fritz, V.** "The Complex of Traditions in Judges 4 and 5 and the Religion of Pre-state Israel." In *I Will Speak the Riddles of Ancient Times: Archaeological and Historical Studies.* FS A. Mazar, ed. A. M. Maeir and P. de Miroschedji. Winona Lake, IN: Eisenbrauns, 2006. ———. "Das Ende der spätbronzezeitlichen Stadt Hazor Stratum XIII und die biblische Überlieferung in Josua 11 und Richter 4." *UF* 5 (1973) 84–139. **Garnot, M.** "The (Deborah) Prophecy in the Book of Judges" (Heb.). *Beit-Miqra* 25 (1979) 256–68. **Gilead, C.** "The Simple Meaning of the Story of Deborah and Barak's War against Sisera (Judges 4–5)" (Heb.). *Beit-Miqra* 34 (1988–89) 292–301. **Goldingay, J.** "Motherhood, Machismo, and the Purpose of Yahweh in Judges 4–5." *Anvil* 12 (1995) 21–33. **Gottlieb, F.** "Three Mothers." *Jud* 30 (1981) 194–203. **Grossfeld, B.** "A Critical Note on Judg 4,21." *ZAW* 85 (1973) 348–51. **Grottanelli, C.** "The Story of Deborah and Barak: A Comparative Approach." *SMRS* 11 NS (1987) 149–64. **Hackett, J. A.** "In the Days of Jael: Reclaiming the History of Women in Ancient Israel." In *Immaculate and Powerful: The Female in Sacred Image and Social Reality.* Ed. C. W. Atkinson, C. H. Buchanan, and M. R. Miles. Boston: Beacon, 1985. 15–38. **Halpern, B.** *Emergence of Israel.* 116–23, 146–49. ———. "Sisera and Old Lace: The Case of Deborah and Yael." In *First Historians.* 76–103. **Hanselman, S. W.** "Narrative Theory, Ideology, and Transformation in Judges 4." In *Anti-Covenant.* Ed. M. Bal. 95–112. **Hauser, A. J.** "Two Songs of Victory: Exodus 15 and Judges 5." In *Directions in Biblical Hebrew Poetry.* Ed. E. R. Follis. JSOTSup 40. Sheffield: JSOT Press, 1987. 265–84. **Hess, R. H.** "Israelite Identity and Personal Names from the Book of Judges." *HS* 44 (2003) 25–39. ———. "The Name Game: Dating the Book of Judges." *BAR* 30 (2004) 38–41. **Houston, W. J.** "Misunderstanding or Midrash? The Prose Application of Poetic Material in the Hebrew Bible." *ZAW* 109 (1997) 342–55, 534–48. **Jacobson, H.** "Bedan and Barak Reconsidered." *VT* 44 (1994) 108–9. **Jason, H.** "Judges 4–5: An Epic Work? (Preliminary Remarks)" (Heb.). *Shnaton* 5–6 (1982) 79–87. **Kallai, Z.** "Judah and Israel: A Study in Israelite Historiography." *IEJ* 28 (1978) 251–61. **Kaswalder, P.** "Le Tribù in Gdc 1,1–2,5 e in Gdc 4–5." *SBFLA* 43 (1993) 89–113. **Kawashima, R. S.** *Biblical Narrative and the Death of the Rhapsode.* Indiana Studies in Biblical Literature. Bloomington: Indiana UP, 2004. **Kegler, J.** "Debora—Erwägungen zur politischen Funktion einer Frau in einer patriarchalischen Gesellschaft." In *Traditionen der Befreiung.* Vol. 2, *Frauen in der Bibel.* Ed. W. Schottroff and W. Stegemann. Munich: Kaiser, 1980. 37–59. **Kooij, A. van der.** "On Male and Female Views in Judges 4 and 5." In *On Reading Prophetic Texts.* Ed. B. Becking and M. Dijkstra. 135–52. **Kutscher, Y.** "a) 'He makes his dwelling between his shoulders' [Deut 33:12]; b) 'So he turned aside to her into the tent and she covered him with a rug' [Jdg 4:18]" (Heb.). *Leš* 7 (1936) 266–68. **Layton, S. C.** "Yaʿel in Judges 4: An Onomastic Rejoinder." *ZAW* 109 (1997) 93–94. **Levine, M. H.** "A Biblical Protest against the Violation of Woman." *Dor le Dor* 8 (1979) 194–96. **Lewy, I.** "The Feminine Element in Biblical Judaism." *Judaism* 2 (1953) 339–44. **Lipiński, E.** "Juges 5,4–5 et Psaume 68,8–11." *Bib* 48 (1967) 185–206. **Manor, D. W.** "The Topography and Geography of the Jezreel Valley as They Contribute to the Battles of Deborah and Gideon." *Near East Archaeological Society Bulletin* 28 (1987) 25–33. **Margalith, B.** "Observations on the Jael-Sisera

Story (Judges 4–5)." In *Pomegranates and Golden Bells*. Ed. D. P. Wright et al. 629–41. **Matthews, V. H.** "Hospitality and Hostility in Judges 4." *BTB* 21 (1991) 13–21. **Matthews, V. H., and D. C. Benjamin.** "Jael: Host or Judge?" *TBT* 30 (1992) 291–96. **Mayes, A. D. H.** "The Historical Context of the Battle against Sisera." *VT* 19 (1969) 353–60. ———. "Israel in the Pre-monarchic Period." *VT* 23 (1973) 151–70. **Mazar, B.** "The Sanctuary of Arad and the Family of Hobab the Kenite." In *Biblical Israel: State and People*. Ed. S. Ahituv. Jerusalem: Magnes, 1992. 67–77. **Miller, P. D.** "Animal Names as Designation in Ugaritic and Hebrew." *UF* 2 (1970) 177–86. **Moor, J. C. de.** "Deborah." *Daughters of Sarah* 21 (1995) 34–37. **Moore, G. F.** "Shamgar and Sisera." *JAOS* 19 (1898) 160–95. **Murray, D. F.** "Narrative Structure and Technique in the Deborah-Barak Story, Judges iv 4–22." In *Studies in the Historical Books of the Old Testament*. Ed. J. A. Emerton. VTSup 30. Leiden: Brill, 1979. 155–89. **Na'aman, N.** "Literary and Topographical Notes on the Battle of Kishon (Judges IV–V)." *VT* 40 (1990) 423–36. **Neef, H. D.** "Deboraerzählung und Deboralied: Beobachtungen zum Verhältnis von Jdc. iv und v." *VT* 44 (1994) 47–59. ———. *Deboralied: Studien zu Jdc 4,1–5.31*. Biblisch-Theologische Studien 49. Neukirchen-Vluyn: Neukirchener Verlag, 2002. ———. "Der Sieg Debora und Baraks über Sisera: Exegetische Beobachtungen zum Aufbau und Werden von Jdc 4,1–24." *ZAW* 101 (1989) 28–49. **Nicholson, E. W.** "The Problem of צעה." *ZAW* 89 (1977) 259–66. **Niditch, S.** "Eroticism and Death in the Tale of Jael." In *Gender and Difference in Ancient Israel*. Ed. P. Day. Minneapolis: Fortress, 1989. 43–57. **Ogden, G. S.** "Poetry, Prose, and Their Relationship: Some Reflections Based on Judges 4 and 5." In *Discourse Perspectives on Hebrew Poetry in the Scriptures*. Ed. E. R. Wendland. UBS Monograph Series 7. New York: United Bible Societies, 1994. 111–30. **Patella, M.** "Women of Mystery." *TBT* 44 (2006) 94–97. **Rasmussen, R. C.** "Deborah the Woman Warrior." In *Anti-Covenant*. Ed. M. Bal. 79–93. **Reis, P. T.** "Uncovering Jael and Sisera: A New Reading." *SJOT* 19 (2005) 24–47. **Sakenfeld, K. D.** "Deborah, Jael, and Sisera's Mother: Reading the Scriptures in Cross-Cultural Context." In *Women, Gender, and Christian Community*. Ed. J. Douglass. Louisville: Westminster, 1997. 13–22. **Sauge, K.** "Jael-tradisjonene I Dommerne 4 og 5." *NTT* 88 (1987) 109–13. **Scippa, V.** "Due donne forti dell'A.T." *PaVi* 40 (1995) 12–16. ———. "Giaele, una donna forte dell'Antico Testamento: Analisi strutturale di Gdc 5,23–27 e 4,17–23." *RivB* 39 (1991) 385–422. **Shaw, J.** "Constructions of Women in Readings of the Story of Deborah." In *Anti-Covenant*. Ed. M. Bal. 113–32. **Soden, J. M.** *Prose and Poetry Compared: Judges 4 and 5 in Their Ancient Near Eastern Context*. Ann Arbor, MI: University Microfilms, 1990. **Soggin, J. A.** "'Heber der Qenit': Das Ende eines biblischen Personennamens?" *VT* 31 (1981) 89–92. **Spronk, K.** "Deborah, a Prophetess: The Meaning and Background of Judges 4:4–5." In *The Elusive Prophet: The Prophet as a Historical Person, Literary Character and Anonymous Artist*. Ed. J. C. de Moor. OtSt 45. Leiden: Brill, 2001. 232–43. **Stadelmann, A.** "Le origini del profetismo nella prospettiva teologica del 'Deuteronomista.'" In *Mysterium Christi: Symbolgegenward und theologische Bedeutung*. FS B. Studer, ed. M. Löhrer and E. Salmann. SA 116. Rome: Pontificio Ateneo S. Anselmo, 1995. 15–38. **Stek, J.** "The Bee and the Mountain Goat: A Literary Reading of Judges 4." In *A Tribute to Gleason Archer*. Ed. W. C. Kaiser, Jr., and R. Youngblood. Chicago: Moody Press, 1986. 53–86. **Sternberg, M.** *Poetics of Biblical Narrative*. 270–83. **Strom, D.** "Where Are the Deborahs and Baraks." *ERT* 10 (1986) 19–26. **Tsang, S.** "Violence and Gender: The Ugaritic 'Violent Female' Tradition and the Story of Deborah in Judges 4." *SCS* 4 (2007) 95–108. **Urbrock, W. J.** "Sisera's Mother in Judges 5 and Haim Gouri's אIMMO." *HAR* 11 (1987) 423–34. **Watts, J. W.** "Song and the Ancient Reader." *PRSt* 22 (1995) 135–47. ———. "'This Song': Conspicuous Poetry in Hebrew Prose." In *Verse in Ancient Near Eastern Prose*. Ed. J. C. de Moor and W. G. E. Watson. AOAT 42. Neukirchen-Vluyn: Neukirchener Verlag, 1993. 345–58. **Weimar, P.** "Die Jahwekriegserzählungen in Exodus 14, Josua 10, Richter 4, und 1 Samuel 7." *Bib* 57 (1976) 38–73. **White, S. A.** "In the Steps of Jael and Deborah: Judith as Heroine." SBLSP 28 (1989) 570–78. Reprinted in *'No One Spoke Ill of Her': Essays on Judith*, ed. J. C. VanderKam (Atlanta: Scholars Press, 1992) 5–16. **Wilkinson, E.** "The Hapax Legomenon of Judges 4:18." *VT* 33 (1983)

512–13. **Wilson, B. E.** "Pugnacious Precursors and the Bearer of Peace: Jael, Judith, and Mary in Luke 1:42." *CBQ* 68 (2006) 436–56. **Wind, R.** "Widerstand ist möglich—Funf Frauengeschichten aus der Bibel." In *Wer ist unser Gott: Beiträge zu einer Befreiungstheologie im Kontext der ersten Welt.* Ed. L. Schott-roff and W. Schottroff. Munich: Kaiser, 1986. 173–84. **Wit, H. de.** "Leyendo con Yael: Un ejercicio en hermenéutica intercultural." In *Los caminos inexhauribles de la Palabra (Las relecturas creativas en la Biblia y de la Biblia).* FS J. Severino Croatto, ed. G. Hansen. Buenos Aires: Lumen-ISEDET, 2000. 11–66. Published in German in *ACEBT* 19 (2001) 71–96. **Wolde, E. van.** "Deborah and Ya'el in Judges 4." In *On Reading Prophetic Texts.* Ed. B. Becking and M. Dijkstra. 283–95. ———. "Ya'el in Judges 4." *ZAW* 107 (1995) 240–46. **Yee, G.** "By the Hand of a Woman: The Metaphor of the Woman Warrior in Judges 4." *Semeia* 61 (1993) 99–132. **Younger, K. L., Jr.** "Heads! Tails! Or the Whole Coin?! Contextual Method and Intertextual Analysis: Judges 4 and 5." In *The Canon in Comparative Perspective.* Ed. K. L. Younger, Jr., W. W. Hallo, and B. F. Batto. Scripture in Context 4. Lewiston, NY: Mellen, 1991. 109–45. **Zakovitch, Y.** "Siseras Tod." *ZAW* 93 (1981) 364–75.

Translation

[1] *The sons of Israel again did evil in the eyes of Yahweh, but Ehud was dead.*[a] [2] *Yahweh sold them into the hand of Jabin, the king of Canaan. He ruled in Hazor, and the commander of his army was Sisera. He lived in Harosheth Haggoyim.*[a] [3] *The sons of Israel cried out to Yahweh because he owned nine hundred iron chariots. But he vehemently tormented the sons of*[a] *Israel for twenty years.*

[4] *Now the woman Deborah was a prophetess and the wife of Lappidoth.*[a] *She*[b] *judged Israel at that time.* [5] *She was sitting under the palm tree of Deborah*[a] *between Ramah and Bethel in the hill country of Ephraim. The sons of Israel went up to her to get justice.*

[6] *She*[a] *sent and summoned Barak, the son of Abinoam, from Kedesh in Naphtali. She said to him, "Did not Yahweh, the God of Israel, command you, 'Go,*[b] *deploy the army*[c] *in Mount Tabor. Take with you ten thousand men from the sons of Naphtali and Zebulon.* [7] *I will deploy*[a] *Sisera, Jabin's army commander, for you in the Kishon River valley along with*[b] *his chariots and his enormous army. I will give him into your hand.'"*[c] [8] *Barak answered her, "If you will go with me, then I will go; but if you do not go with me, then I will not go."*[a] [9] *She*[a] *said, "I will surely go with you, but*[b] *you will not receive your glory on the way you are following. For into a woman's hand Yahweh will sell Sisera." Deborah rose and went with Barak to*[c] *Kedesh.*

[10] *Barak called out*[a] *Zebulun and Naphtali to*[b] *Kedesh. He went up on foot with ten thousand*[c] *men, and Deborah went up with him.* [11] *But Heber*[a] *the Kenite had separated himself from the Kenites, who were from the sons of Hobab, Moses' father-in-law.*[b] *He pitched his tent*[c] *by the oak tree*[d] *in Zaanannim*[e] *near Kedesh.*[f] [12] *The report came to Sisera that Barak, the son of Abinoam, had gone up to Mount*[a] *Tabor.* [13] *Sisera called out all his chariots—nine hundred iron chariots*[a]*—and all the people who were with him from Harosheth Haggoyim to*[b] *the river Kishon.*

[14] *Deborah said to Barak, "Get up, for this is the day that Yahweh has given Sisera into your hand.*[a] *Has not*[b] *Yahweh gone out before you? Barak went down from Mount Tabor while ten thousand men followed him.* [15] *Yahweh threw Sisera and all his chariots and all his army into panic at the edge of the sword*[a] *in the face of Barak. Sisera stepped down from his chariot and fled on foot.* [16] *Meanwhile, Barak pursued*[a] *the chariots and the army as far as Harosheth Haggoyim.*[b] *All Sisera's army fell to the edge of the sword. Not even one remained alive.*

[17] *But Sisera fled[a] on foot to the tent of Jael, the wife of Heber the Kenite,[b] since peace prevailed between Jabin, the king of Hazor, and the house of Heber the Kenite.* [18] *Jael came out to meet Sisera and said to him, "Turn aside, my lord, turn aside to me. Don't be afraid." He turned aside to her to her tent, and she placed a covering[a] over him.* [19] *He[a] said to her, "Please give me a little water to drink, for I am thirsty."[b] She opened the skin milk bottle[c] and gave him a drink and then covered him.[d]* [20] *He[a] said to her, "Stand[b] at the opening of the tent. If a man comes and asks you if a man is here, you must say, 'No.'"[c]* [21] *Jael, Heber's wife, took a tent peg and picked up a hammer in her hand. She approached him secretly,[a] hammered the peg into his temple,[b] and it went clear down into the ground. But he had slept soundly,[c] being exhausted.[d] And he died.[e]* [22] *Just then Barak was pursuing Sisera. Jael came out to meet him. She said to him, "Come. I will show you the man you are seeking." He came to her. Right there was Sisera, fallen dead, and the peg was in his temple.*

[23] *On that day God[a] subdued Jabin, the king of Canaan, before the sons of Israel.* [24] *The hand of the sons of Israel continued growing strong and was harsh on Jabin, king of Canaan, until they had cut off Jabin, the king of Canaan.[a]*

Notes

1.a. Or "Ehud died"; not in LXX[A] since LXX reports Ehud's death in 3:30.

2.a. Or "Harosheth of the nations" as LXX translates it.

3.a. LXX and a few Heb. MSS do not have "sons of," perhaps the addition of a familiar phrase into MT.

4.a. Niditch (62) sees LXX[B] as indicating Lappidoth as a place of origin rather than the name of a husband. Niditch opts for a nominal translation: "woman of fire."

4.b. Many Heb. MSS add the conjunction here, but this is not necessary in Heb. apposition.

5.a. OL does not have "of Deborah."

6.a. LXX reads "Deborah," a common case of making explicit what the base text keeps implicit.

6.b. LXX (compare OL) reads σοι, "to you" (Heb. לְךָ), for Heb. לֵךְ, "go," an easy misinterpretation of an early text, but see Lindars (205) for the complicated evidence of OG, OL, Pesh., Tg.

6.c. Heb. וּמָשַׁכְתָּ "pull along, march forth, deploy the army." OL reads, "sit" or "take your position."

7.a. LXX[A] reads ἀπάξω, "I will lead away, march away," for וּמָשַׁכְתִּי, for which LXX used ἀπέρχομαι in v 6; LXX[B] reads ἐπάξω, "I will bring on, lead an army against." For the full complexity of the text tradition, see Lindars, 187, 205. LXX apparently makes "Deborah" the subject here. (See Boling, 95.)

7.b. Many MSS do not appear to point אֵת, the sign of the direct object, which may be read as אֵת, the preposition "with," which is similarly pointed.

7.c. A number of MSS read the pl. בְּיָדִי, an unimportant scribal change.

8.a. LXX[A] (compare OL) continues: ὅτι οὐκ οἶδα τὴν ἡμέραν ἐν ᾗ εὐοδοῖ κύριος τὸν ἄγγελον μετ' ἐμοῦ, "because I do not know the day in which the Lord will give success to the messenger with me."

9.a. LXX[A] reads "Deborah said to him," making the implicit explicit.

9.b. LXX reads πλὴν γίνωσκε ὅτι οὐκ ἔσται τὸ προτέρημά σου, "but know that success (or victory) will not be yours," a reading making a difficult text easier but accepted by Boling (96). Lindars (189) is correct in calling this a "stylistic insertion."

9.c. LXX[B] reads ἐκ Καδης, "from Kadesh" or "out of Kadesh," a different reading of the context.

10.a. LXX[A] reads, παρήγγειλεν, "commanded," while LXX[B] reads ἐβόησεν, "cried out" or "called out."

10.b. LXX[B] reads ἐκ Καδης, "from Kadesh" or "out of Kadesh." See *Note* 9.c.

10.c. A few MSS and Sebir ("supposed" or "expected") read the absolute form אֲלָפִים.

11.a. OL reads "friends of Cina were kings from the sons of Joab," translating *Heber* as a common collective noun. See Niditch, 63.

11.b. BHS suggests reading here and in Num 10:29 חֹתֵן, "son-in-law," rather than חֹתֵן, "father-in-law"; REB, NLT, NIV translate "brother-in-law." This is all based on the sometimes unclear relationships between Jethro, Hobab, and Reuel. See *Comment*.

11.c. A few MSS use the fuller form of the suffix אׇהֳלָה; see GKC, §§7c, 91e.

11.d. Tg., followed by KJV, reads ישר, "plain." For the complex Gk. evidence, see Lindars, 206–7.
11.e. Q has בצעננים, as in Josh 19:33, while K has a dual form. See Lindars, 192.
11.f. LXX^A (compare OL) reads καὶ οἱ πλησίον τοῦ Κιναίου ἐχωρίσθησαν ἀπὸ τῶν υἱῶν Ιωβαβ γαμβροῦ Μωυσῆ καὶ ἔπηξεν τὴν σκηνὴν αὐτοῦ πρὸς δρῦν ἀναπαυομένων ἥ ἐστιν ἐχόμενα Κεδες, "and the neighbors of the Kenites separated from the sons of Iobab, the father-in-law (or son-in-law) of Moses, and put up their tent toward the oak tree of the resting ones which is outside of Kedesh," while LXX^B reads καὶ Χαβερ ὁ Κιναῖος ἐχωρίσθη ἀπὸ Καινα ἀπὸ τῶν υἱῶν Ιωβαβ γαμβροῦ Μωυσῆ καὶ ἔπηξεν τὴν σκηνὴν αὐτοῦ ἕως δρυὸς πλεονεκτούντων ἥ ἐστιν ἐχόμενα Κεδες, "And Heber the Kenite separated from Caina (or an alternate spelling of Kenite) from the sons of Iobab, the father-in-law (son-in-law) of Moses, and they put up their tent unto the oak tree of the greedy ones which is outside of Kedesh." Lindars (206) sees this as a reading in light of the interpretation of 1 Sam 15:6, concluding that "a plausible interpretation of the situation has led to an erroneous translation."
12.a. A few MSS add the preposition to read "in Mount Tabor." LXX^A reads ἐπ' while LXX^B has εἰς.
13.a. LXX^A reads "iron chariots which were with him."
13.b. A few MSS read עד for MT את.
14.a. A few MSS and the Syr. and Vg. read the pl., "your hands"; compare Note 7.c.
14.b. LXX^A reads οὐκ ἰδοὺ κύριος ἐλεύσεται, inserting ἰδοὺ, "look! see!" after the negative, while LXX^B reads ὅτι κύριος ἐξελεύσεται, "because the Lord will go out."
15.a. BHS, followed by Lindars, Boling, and others, suggests deleting "at the edge of the sword," as an insertion based on v 16. For a complex theory on the development of the text in this verse, see Lindars, 195.
16.a. LXX reads a participle here, evening the text to repeat the participle of v 22.
16.b. LXX^A reads ἕως δρυμοῦ τῶν ἐθνῶν, "unto the thicket of the nations."
17.a. LXX^A reads ἀνεχώρησεν, "departed," for ἔφυγεν, "fled," in LXX^B.
17.b. LXX^B reads γυναικὸς Χαβερ ἑταίρου τοῦ Κιναίου, "wife of Heber, the companion (masc.) of the Kenite." Lindars (207) identifies this addition of ἑταίρου as a Gk. gloss giving the meaning of Heber's name.
18.a. LXX^A (compare OL) reads συνεκάλυψεν αὐτὸν ἐν τῇ δέρρει αὐτῆς, "she covered him with her leather skin"; LXX^B reads περιέβαλεν αὐτὸν ἐπιβολαίῳ, "she clothed him with a garment"; BHS suggests במכסה, "overlay, cover." See Lindars (198) for explanation. Two Heb. MSS have בסמיכה for Leningrad's בשמיכה, a frequent Heb. interchange of the two sibilants. See Niditch, 63.
19.a. LXX reads "Sisera," making the subject explicit.
19.b. Many MSS read the more usual form without the 'ālep.
19.c. The Heb. tradition used vowel letters in different ways to spell this word.
19.d. OL, Syrohexapla, LXX^A read καὶ συνεκάλυψεν τὸ πρόσωπον αὐτοῦ, "and she covered up his face," while LXX^B reads καὶ περιέβαλεν αὐτόν, "and she clothed him," representing different understandings of the text.
20.a. LXX^B reads "Sisera."
20.b. Syr. and Tg. evidence point to the imperative form עמדי; the MT has masc. imperative עמד. Grammatical purists change the MT. GKC, §110k, shows exceptional examples of third-person masc. sg. imperative in place of third-person fem. sg. imperative but concludes we should probably read the fem. here.
20.c. LXX^A repeats "she covered him with her leather skin."
21.a. Many MSS reflect the more common spelling without the 'ālep.
21.b. LXX^A reads ἐν τῇ γνάθῳ αὐτοῦ, "into his jaw"; also in v 22. Lindars (208) sees this as possibly original.
21.c. Several MSS read the perfect נרדם for MT participle נרדם.
21.d. BHS suggests reading the adjective ועיף for MT imperative consecutive from עיף.
21.e. LXX^A (compare OL) reads ἀπεσκάρισεν ἀνὰ μέσον τῶν γονάτων αὐτῆς καὶ ἐξέψυξεν καὶ ἀπέθανεν, "he struggled between her knees and became unconscious and died," while LXX^B reads ἐξεστὼς ἐσκοτώθη καὶ ἀπέθανεν, "he becoming confused (or having lost consciousness he) was darkened and died"; compare Lindars' discussion (200–204). Niditch concludes: "Thus the alternate traditions describe Sisera's passage from the living, whereas MT relates that Sisera's weary sleep allowed Jael to strike, paradoxically creating sympathy for the deceived enemy" (63).
23.a. LXX^A reads "the Lord God"; Syr. reads יהוה, "Yahweh."
24.a. LXX^A reads "they cut him off," avoiding the Heb. repetition of "Jabin, the king of Canaan."

Form/Structure/Setting

See table 4.1 in the appendix to compare one possible example of narrative analysis with form-critical analysis for chap. 4. The narrative elements follow the typical pattern of Hebrew narrative while the genre elements show the genre of each section with its component parts. Note how the narrator can use different genre elements and markers within or even across various narrative elements.

Chaps. 4 and 5 provide a prose and a poetic version of the same incident from Israel's ancient history. Such a dual highlighting marks a transition in the narrative much as that at 1:21 from the obedient example of what should be to the disobedient example of the majority of the tribes and judges. The title "Judges" may bring stirring portraits of valor and heroism to our minds, but a close study shows that the judges described in the remainder of the book are anything but stirring, patriotic heroes. Rather, they represent almost caricatures of what a hero and leader should be, and they lead Israel from a unified nation cementing its covenant relationship with God, as in Josh 24, to a nation becoming an independent group of jealous tribes who compete with one another, steal priests from one another, and eventually decimate one whole tribe of their people and then have to resort to a desperate measure to repopulate the tribe. It gets to the point where no one wants to be the judge, where no one is the judge, and where every individual does right in his own eyes because there is no ruler in Israel. And that is how the book ends. Chap. 4 marks the beginning of that end.

Judg 4 apparently comprises two components: a framework in 4:1–3, 23–24, replete with the language of the editor introduced in chap. 2, and the narrative itself in 4:4–22, which follows the normal patterns of Hebrew stories. Judg 4:1–3 makes us expect a completely formulaic account of an Israelite judge or savior. Making small modifications to the work of Block (146–47), table 4.2 (in appendix) illustrates the use of structural formulas in Judg 4.

Our expectations of a formulaic framework in Judg 4 are not realized. Most formulaic elements are missing: divine anger, weakness, divine opposition, provision of leadership, human deliverance, divine presence, divine compassion, and the death report, while the land-rest or tranquility formula is attached to chap. 5. The death formula appears, but it appears at the introduction, not the conclusion, and applies to Ehud, not to the characters in Judg 4–5 nor to Shamgar, the immediately preceding judge. Expositional elements intrude into the framework in vv 2b and 3b, while the cry of distress leads to a description of the enemy's power, not to a statement of God's raising up a judge. The subjection formula appears here for the first time. God is the explicit active subject in contrast to the passive voices in 8:28 and 11:23. The object of subjection is the enemy king, not the enemy nation, and the statement of subjection immediately modifies the subjection by describing the long process of subjugation.

Again selection of, addition to, and modification of framework elements reveal the editor's freedom and creativity in presenting the various judges. None of the stories of the judges are tied into an editorial straitjacket clearly repeating all that went before and all that will come afterward. The introductions to the stories are needed for an exposition to create narrative tension in each story. The sum of the framework parts of all the narratives provides the framework elements for the editor to use in composing the full framework of chap. 2. Even there freedom reigns so that all the elements of the frames of each story do not appear in the overarching framework of chap. 2.

Such evidence of editorial freedom leads to the conclusion that too much has been made of the difference between framework and narrative. Neither framework nor narrative is complete without the other element. Rather, the editor has artistically shown the larger story in the introductions and conclusions to each narrative, using the more strictly narrative elements to entertain and instruct the readers with more complex elements that show how Israel's leadership or lack of it led to the situation described in the introductions. This led Polzin to remark, "The distanced and estranged viewpoint of the body of the stories about the judges, as opposed to the evaluative utterances that form their framework, puts the reader into the very experiencing of chaos and ambiguity that is portrayed as the inner experience of Israel during this period. This is why the Deborah story is filled with equivocation and opposition" (*Moses and the Deuteronomist*, 166).

To understand the structure of the Hebrew narratives in Judges, the commentator must examine both the use of the individual formulae within the narrative and the overall narrative structure. I will begin with the latter and then turn to the former.

One approaches narrative by examining the various components that create and resolve narrative tension. Here I follow Amit in her work (*Reading Biblical Narratives*, 47) where she talks of plots and their structures, including exposition, complication, change, unraveling, and ending. I would separate the unraveling of the narrative into two parts, the unraveling and the resolution or climax. Thus in *Book of Judges* (201–2; compare *JSOT* 39 [1987] 90), Amit takes a different approach, analyzing Judg 4 as having exposition (vv 1–5), first unit (vv 6–9), second unit (vv 10–13), third unit (vv 14–16), fourth unit (vv 17–22), and a conclusion (vv 23–24). This analysis ignores the true plot structure unearthed by Amit's structural analysis noted above and forces far too much material into the overloaded first unit. Amit's analysis of the complex of units leads to this conclusion: "Perhaps the editor, who shaped the openings and endings, also designed the body of the narratives? Perhaps the original version was edited in such a manner that it lost its pristine form and we are unable to extricate it from the present text. In light of the degree of harmony between the openings and conclusions, these possibilities are quite likely" (*Book of Judges*, 221). Still, despite the obvious unity of the narrative, Amit uses the old theory of Deuteronomistic editing of the frames to throw into question any early dating or historical verity for the unit. Amit's own observations on the text seem to have negated any need of a late editor and opened the way for pushing the material back to the original collection of Israelite traditions.

Thus I will examine the story under the following structure, using Amit's categories but dividing the story a bit differently:

Narrative Element	Function	Passage	Signal of change
Exposition	Introducing the main characters	vv 1–5	Disjunctive sentence opening
Complication	Conditional acceptance of the call to arms	vv 6–8	Change of characters
Change	Search for a woman's glory	vv 9–11	Conditional sentence

Unraveling	Man's victory without glory	vv 12–15	Change of place
Climax	Woman gaining glory in unmanning generals	vv 16–21	Two disjunctive sentences
Ending or denouement	Glory revealed	v 22	וְהִנֵּה, "just then"

The exposition establishes the setting in which the narrative proper will take place. The setting rises from Israel's unspecified disobedience and the absence of a leader in light of the death of the heroic Ehud.

The exposition also introduces the major players in the drama. God sells the disobedient people to Jabin, king of Canaan. Jabin is the major antagonist as seen by his double mention here and his reappearance in the conclusion (vv 23–24). His realm is so large and strong that he does not go to battle. He puts Sisera in control of the troops so that Sisera is the central enemy figure in the narrative action if not in the larger story. Then Israel cries out to Yahweh because of Jabin's technological superiority. The reader expects Yahweh to raise up a hero to judge Israel and defeat the enemy. Instead, the exposition turns to the central Israelite character, Deborah, the female prophetess and wife of Lappidoth, who judges Israel. This emphasis on the character's gender and multiple offices turns the reader's world upside down. The hope for Israel lies not in a man Yahweh calls specifically for the situation but in a female judge and prophet. This turn of events might not seem so radical to today's audience, but it would have seemed unthinkable to the Israelites of the time. What has happened to leadership in Israel?

The exposition often supplies the time and place of the narrative action. The time here is an era of disobedience after Ehud's death with the oppressive forces of Canaan holding the upper hand. But the scene of action lies wide open somewhere between Deborah's hill country of Ephraim and Jabin's Hazor.

The complication appears to restore the reader's normal expectations, as the prophet calls forth a male leader to defeat the enemy and restore order. This recalls the prophetic oracle and answer in 1:1–2. Restoration soon turns to chaos. The chosen leader refuses to go. Perhaps he needs the promise of divine presence as had been given to Moses and Joshua (see Josh 1:5, 9). No! For Barak, the presence of Deborah suffices. The prophetess's presence is strong enough evidence of divine presence for Barak. Thus the fate of Israel apparently returns to Deborah's hands, complicating the plot.

The change represents the turning point of the plot. The change occurs mysteriously here as Deborah's threat turns attention away from Barak to an as-yet-unknown woman. The unexpected information in v 11 gives us clues about that woman without the reader realizing the significance of those clues. Now Israel's fate rests in the arms of an unknown woman. Who will she be? How will she change Israel's fortunes? What is the unexplained connection to Moses? And what does this say about leadership in Israel when the chosen male leader will not receive the glory?

The unraveling comes as Barak wins a battle, but the key parts of the section feature Sisera, not Barak, as Barak takes orders from the female prophet. Now the reader searches to find the chief character and the movement in the plot structure. Is the narrator turning the reader's attention to Sisera, Deborah, or Barak, or whom?

The climax comes with Barak pursuing and destroying Sisera's entire army, apparently in obedience to holy war regulations. But the narrator shifts attention from Barak to Sisera, placing long geographical distance between them. The whole army does not somehow include the general. As Sisera flees, the narrator introduces yet another character, the wife of the man with the unexplained Moses connection. She is supposedly on Jabin's side so that Jabin can flee there comfortably. Once there, Sisera gives the commands that lead to his own death.

The denouement brings Barak back into the picture to witness that Sisera is dead and to realize that the turning-point prophecy is fulfilled. A woman has gained Barak's glory, but not the woman Barak and the readers thought would do so. So the ending framework can return again to the long-absent Jabin and announce his slow destruction.

What type or genre does this complex narrative belong to? It is a battle narrative, but that is only one of its components, not the central thrust. It is a story of prophecy and fulfillment, and yet that is only one element of the narrative. The genre may be expressed in more human terms as the story of a riddle and its solution (Amit, *Book of Judges,* 207), but Deborah casts her speech in the form of prophecy, not riddle. It is a story of reversal in which the final hero emerges only after the reader has formed entirely different expectations. It is a story of seduction and murder, but that lets the ending determine the nature of the entire narrative.

Ultimately, the story must be fit into the widest of categories, that of divine punishment and deliverance. Niditch describes this version as "the traditional motif of the 'iron fist in the velvet glove'" (64). In this sense Amit is correct in pointing to God as the main hero of the story (*Book of Judges,* 214–18). But the criteria Amit sets up for such a decision do not work on a story with as many twists and complications as this one. Certainly, the internal framework of the story points to Jael as the unsuspecting hero of a battle narrative driven by prophecy. This battle narrative becomes the major component of the larger narrative in which the editor wishes to show God's preeminence over all enemies in his punishing and delivering Israel and Israel's lack of leadership. Chap. 4 then is a well-crafted Hebrew parody of a normal prophetic battle story. It highlights the most unexpected of heroines, while at the same time painting a narrative portrait of Israel's general in the weakest possible tones. It centers not on a battle between armies but on a confrontation between a man and a woman in her sleeping quarters as the woman breaks a peace treaty to destroy one general's life and another's honor.

Having looked at the narrative structure of Judg 4, we turn to its peculiar use of narrative formulae. The editorial framework of Judg 4 shows the editor's perspective on the prose narrative. The entire narrative is subsumed under the negative-evaluation formula, but with a significant omission. The pagan gods are not mentioned. May this be an indication that Israel's evil has expanded beyond false worship to include false leadership as will be illustrated in each of the ensuing deliverer narratives?

This would mean that an explicit contrast is drawn to the theme of Joshua as perfect leader after Moses, a theme illustrated throughout the book of Joshua and introduced explicitly again in Judg 2:6–10. This is reinforced by the unexpected contrast clause, "but Ehud had died." Some might see Ehud as the next Joshua, but at his death many nations still remained in the land. He had only defeated a nearby neighbor. Block (148) notes the contrasting use of this formula in 2:19 and in the narrative frameworks. In the introduction of chap. 2 the formula "highlights the tenuous nature of Israel's fidelity to Yahweh during a ruler's tenure." In the individual narrative frameworks the formula represents the "tenuous nature of Israel's tranquility."

One must note the Hebrew sentence order here. First, Israel does evil. Then Ehud's death is contrasted. Schneider rightly sees that the "response to the Israelites' misbehavior was Ehud's death. Only after that proclamation were they punished" (63). Polzin understands the period after Joshua's death to be one where "because of Israel's constant apostasy, they clearly deserved each setback they experienced but not the years of peace their judges' lives and God's compassion brought them. . . . Nothing in Israel's history is more remarkable than that they continued to exist in spite of their sustained apostasy in the days between Joshua's death and the establishment of kingship" (*Moses and the Deuteronomist*, 161).

The editorial introduction to Judg 4 highlights a new situation in Israel's history in the promised land. They have become a people without leadership and so cannot totally subdue the enemy and bring extended rest to the land. No leader will equal Ehud's accomplishment.

Having set this tone, the editor sets the stage for his understanding of the following narrative with the divine-sale formula. In so doing he chooses not to place the following narrative under the explicit focus of divine anger. God's favor for Jabin, not his anger at Israel, is underlined by the divine-sale formula. The basic narrative tension for the editor is the rule of Jabin in Hazor: a Canaanite king remains in the land promised Israel and taken by Joshua. Jabin is the first introduced and the last disposed of (vv 23–24). This is one of the complications of this convoluted plot structure. The chief antagonist is Jabin, but the only antagonist called to action is his general Sisera. How can the crowning triumph of Josh 11 suddenly disappear into the hands of a dynastic follower who rules over Israel?

Next the editor uses the cry-of-distress formula to set up the tension between Sisera—not Jabin—and Israel. The cry of distress does not introduce God's provision of leadership, a human-deliverance formula, a divine-presence formula, a divine-deliverance formula, or a divine-compassion formula. Rather it simply shows the enemy's strength, a strength maintained for twenty years against Israel.

Schneider (63) cleverly notes that "Israel did not consider their own actions or an absence of leadership as the cause of their distress, but technology, a new event in the book. The Israelites' lack of faith in their deity is highlighted by the previous savior's victory with a low technology weapon" (applying both to Ehud's knife and Shamgar's ox goad).

Now we expect the editor to use the formula that Yahweh raised up a judge. That is exactly what we do not get. We simply get the introduction to the main character, who will stand opposed to Jabin with words, not actions. Thus neither the chief antagonist nor the chief human character appears on the battle scene. Both are instigators and enablers for the narrative action that will feature their subordinates. The hero of action will be a latecomer on the scene. The narrator thus reduces the following narrative to a battle against an overwhelming oppressor, a battle with a surprise ending.

Another significant formula appears in 4:7 (compare v 14) as Deborah delivers the divine oracle to Barak. The committal formula appears only in a negative sense in the opening framework of 2:13, 23, having appeared in the positive sense in the framework of chap. 1 (v 2). Otherwise this common formula appears in Judges frameworks only in 6:1 and 13:1.

Vv 8–9 introduce a parody of the divine-presence formula as Barak demands Deborah's presence, but the formula then disappears from Judges.

By using formulaic language in the framework and even within the narratives, the editor provides a rhythm to the book, yet one with many variations. Framework formulas may reflect positively or negatively on Israel, and they may combine with other framework elements to provide varied pace and surprise elements in the narrative flow.

The overarching narrative structure of chap. 4 and its artistic use or lack of use of a variety of framework formulas calls the reader to an attentive reading of a simple narrative that suddenly reveals a complex structure and style.

Comment

1   Much has been made of the editor's skipping over Shamgar, mentioned in Judg 3:31, to refer again to Ehud here. Block surmises that the Shamgar narrative was a late addition "artificially determined by a desire to bring the total number of rulers in the book to twelve or to bring the number of 'deliverers' to seven," the name coming from Judg 5:6 (172). Similarly, Soggin writes, "Shamgar is mentioned here only for the purpose of dating the text: our ignorance about his chronology prevents us from making valid use of this information" (85). Schneider rightly sees Ehud as the one "who must be considered the primary protagonist in the text. . . . The reference to Shamgar is to a key episode, but one in which Shamgar should not be considered a major player, and the place from which the story continues is Ehud's reign" (59).

I would argue that the poet of Judg 5:6 knew a Shamgar tradition in the same way a Jael tradition was known. In addition to needing to set the historical context for the poem, the narrator needed a minor judge to show that all classes of people could fit in the calling of a successful judge. Thus Younger includes Shamgar among the "noncyclical/minor" judges on literary grounds and concludes: "Shamgar seems to be the most successful in fulfilling the role" (130).

Shamgar also extends Israel's victories to the western coast, thus introducing Israel's battle with the Philistines, which will be central to the final chapters with Samson and to the first chapters of Samuel with Samuel and Saul. Quite importantly Shamgar prepares the way for seeing fringe members of Israel, or even non-members of Israel, used as deliverers since Shamgar's name is not an Israelite name. Here Schneider correctly sees that this represents "another indictment of the men of Israel who were no longer saving their people but instead relied on foreigners (or at least fringe members) and women to carry out the task for them" (58).

The editor had to include anything he knew about Shamgar for the reader to be able to comprehend the allusion in Judg 5:6. But the editor did not set up Shamgar as a major leader who brought peace to the land. Rather Shamgar is included inside the Ehud narrative as representative of the best of the minor judges. Ehud had been the obedient, successful leader who brought rest to the land for eighty years (3:30). The editor's return to Ehud in Judg 4:1 sets up the contrast of what Ehud created for Israel and how the situation crumbled under the following leaders. The defeat of King Jabin of Hazor introduces a period of struggle before Israel is able to subdue the enemy (4:23–24) in contrast to Ehud's ability to subdue Moab "that day" and bring rest (3:30). Deborah and Barak's work will bring rest for only forty years (5:31b), as will that of Gideon (8:28).

Scholars have spilled much ink seeking to identify Shamgar. Schneider (55–56) sees him as "part of the pre-Israelite population of Canaan." She lists various suggestions concerning Shamgar:

- Native of pre-Israelite population of Beth-anath in Galilee
- Devotee of the goddess Anath
- Member of a military unity dedicated and named for Anath
- Son of a man named Anath

Schneider stretches the evidence a good bit to see in the mention of the goddess Anat here "a foreshadowing which prepares the reader for other women who engaged in warfare and politics and were not controlled by clear male authority" (56).

Soggin describes Shamgar as a "Canaanite lordling who fought against the Philistines: in this sense he could have 'saved' Israel even if Judg 5:6 then presents him as one of the oppressors. . . . So here we would have a Canaanite allied with Israel against the Philistines, while in Judg 5 a Philistine is at the head of the anti-Israelite coalition" (59). Lindars also positions Shamgar as an oppressor, not a deliverer-judge, whose origin comes from "a mythical person of long ago, a son or devotee of the warrior-goddess, whose name is sufficient to suggest oppression by an enemy. . . . Shamgar is not an oppressive ruler, but a legendary bandit who took advantage of the weakness of the Canaanite city-states to harass the Israelite settlers" (236).

It is difficult to justify such an imaginative reading of the evidence. That Shamgar was one of Israel's oppressors must be strongly questioned. In the following Song of Deborah, Shamgar is presented as parallel to Jael, the heroine, not in contrast to her. See *Comment* on 5:6. Younger sagely writes: "The identity of Shamgar is obscure. The only scholarly agreement is that Shamgar son of Anath was not an Israelite" (129). He then gives extensive evidence supporting the theory that Shamgar was part of an Egyptian army unit composed of *apiru*, restless nomadic fugitives or outlaws and devoted to the goddess Anat. Block (174) reaches a similar conclusion, noting that *ben 'anat* is more likely to have been read as a devotee of Anat than as a resident of the city Ben-anath. The military unit explanation stretches the evidence quite a bit but may have some foothold in reality.

Webb goes too far in another direction, arguing that Shamgar's name suggests that the catalyst of the battle was an "influx of Sea Peoples" ([1987] 134). Fensham tries to show that *ben 'anat* "may refer to a nomadic group known from the Mari tablets and other sources as the Hanaeans. The expression in Judges may be translated by 'the son of a Hanaean'" ("Shamgar ben Anath," *JNES* 20 [1961] 197–98). Such a theory may be judged improbable at best.

At most we can say that Shamgar apparently demonstrates that Israelite leadership reached such a weak position that a foreigner tied in some way to a foreign deity could be called on to deliver Israel from strong opponents.

2   This Jabin is not just king of Hazor; he is "king of Canaan." Niditch opines,

"Canaan was never a single political entity, but was composed of various city-states. Jabin's title, 'king of Canaan,' however, provides legendary stature to the defeated enemy in this epic tale" (64).

Here the editor identifies Canaan as a separate nation, rather than a geographical entity comprising several city-states. Canaan is thus parallel to Aram or Syria (3:10) defeated by Othniel, to Moab (3:30) subdued by Ehud, and to the Philistines (3:31) from whom Shamgar saved Israel. This identity of Canaan as the enemy is reinforced twice more in the editor's framework (4:23, 24). The editor found a basis for this understanding in the poetic composition he used, for the poem identifies the enemy as the "kings of Canaan" (5:19).

The editor thus places this battle as even more important than the previous confrontation with a King Jabin of Hazor in Josh 11. That battle led to the conquest of the northern part of Canaan. This battle results in the subjugation of Canaan, a subjugation made possible in part by the unbelievable ineptitude of the enemy king and general. Schneider is at least on the right path in saying:

> In Joshua's time kings fought battles. In the period of the Judges, the king, if he existed at all, was overshadowed by both his general and even the general's mother. The kings did not take counsel with other kings as in the time of Joshua, but the queen's mother took counsel with her counselors (5:29). . . . This may be an indictment or a mockery of the role of the king who is completely absent in this episode. (60)

Jabin ruled from Hazor, apparently part of a dynasty of kings there, as seen in Josh 11 (Younger, 138). Hazor plays no role in the narrative except as the place from which Jabin quietly awaits reports from the battlefield. Its mention, however, brings to the reader a set of memories about the importance of the city and its size in dominating at least the northern portion of Israel. Jabin is the antagonist for the larger arena of the book of Judges, but his general Sisera becomes the actual antagonist within the following narrative. Soggin (63) characterizes Sisera's name as Luvian, connected with the "sea peoples" and thus with the Philistines. Block (189) situates Sisera as a Hurrian or Hittite through the linguistic evidence of his non-Hebrew name. Younger (139) speaks of the name's Anatolian origin. Both Block and Younger see Sisera as an enemy general that Jabin of Hazor was able to attract as a mercenary to lead his forces. This may be true, but it would have to be a fact the author assumed his audience knew, for the author does not make this point.

Sisera lives in Harosheth Haggoyim, a town that plays a major role in the following narrative. It represents the western limits of the battle scene. Lindars reviews the scholarly suggestions for the meaning and location of the term while concluding that "the underlying tradition knew of no particular city associated with Sisera and so used the phrase as a vague designation of the location" (177–78). Lindars then suggests that the historian behind the book subsequently changed the designation into a city. Such a negative conclusion reflects an unduly skeptical use of biblical critical tools.

Our ignorance of the location and significance of the place is not surprising and is no basis for deleting the geographical location from history. Rainey ("Toponymic Problems," *TA* 10 [1983] 46–48), followed by Younger (138, n. 4), decides the name means "cultivated field of the Gentiles" and represents an area between

Taanach and Megiddo. Younger suggests that the text may thus be "an intima-
tion of the involvement of the nations." Along similar lines Soggin (63) thinks it
could have been a colony of the sea peoples located near Jezreel. Amit (*Book of
Judges,* 205, n. 45) identifies al-Hartiyeh near Sha'ar Ha'amakim in the Zebulun
Valley as the "accepted identification." Y. Aharoni (*Land of the Bible,* 203) says the
term refers to wooded groves of trees in Galilee. Boling points to Muhrashti in
the Tel-Amarna letters in the Sharon plain. Gaß (*Ortsnamen,* 236–40) lists three
suggestions scholars have made—al-Hartiyeh, Tell Amr, and Tell Harbagh—but
eliminates all three on the basis of archaeological remains, topographical presuppositions, or linguistic criteria. Thus he agrees it is a region, not a town, indeed the
fertile farmland in the Plain of Megiddo parallel to and synonomous with "waters
of Megiddo" in 5:19. Ultimately, I must agree with Younger that "the precise location of the town is unknown."

3 Israel cries under oppression. The oppression is represented by the military
and technological advantages Jabin (not Sisera) enjoys. For the editor, then, the
episode covered by Judg 4–5 appears to have one central focus: how can Israel
overcome the overwhelming force and technical superiority of its enemy? In accomplishing the task, Deborah and Barak stand in contrast to Judah in Judg 1:19.
The narrator reduces the following narrative to a battle against an overwhelming
oppressor with "nine hundred iron chariots," a battle that will determine who will
control Canaan. Israel must face this battle without knowing that God has raised
up a judge. This hints at a theme of weakened leadership in Israel. It also prepares
the way for divine intervention and feminine heroics.

4 Yahweh, God of Israel, remains the main force behind what is happening,
but he does not receive any credit for his feelings toward Israel or for his positive
actions on behalf of Israel. That will come only as the narrative is completed in
4:23–24. Instead of explicitly raising up a judge, God works behind the scenes. The
editor used a disjunctive clause with a bit of biographical information to set off
Sisera as the central character. He uses the same technique to introduce Deborah
without mention of God. Nouns describe her as "woman," "prophetess," and "wife
of Lappidoth." Only then does a participle describe her activity as judging Israel.
(Compare Murray, "Narrative Structure and Technique," 156; Brown, 171.) The
writer does everything the Hebrew language allows to emphasize that this is a
female, not a male. Brenner argues that in chap. 4 "not much distinction is made
between the sex of the participants, apart from Deborah's self-deprecating remark
in v. 9. . . . Still the emphasis is on Jael fulfilling God's words, rather than on Barak's
humiliation" (*VT* 40 [1990] 131). Yee gives a much more satisfying reading of the
text with the blunt statement: "For the author, the one who confronts Barak with
the oracle of God is first and foremost a woman" (*Semeia* 61 [1993] 115).

The editor appears to endorse Deborah as the savior who will supply the
answer to the people's cry. But she is a woman and already judging Israel. So
Amit describes the narrative situation: "The reader assumes that the mention
of Deborah after the crying-out stage means she was chosen to be the savior . . .
although at this stage there is no explicit support for such an assumption" (*JSOT*
39 [1987] 91). Amit (92) gives three reasons to doubt the assumption: avoidance
of the provision-of-leadership formula, the double stress on Deborah's sex, and
the stress on her role as judge settling disputes rather than as military deliverer.

Thus the editor leaves the question in the mind of the audience: did God raise up Deborah as the savior or not?

Ackerman does not want to grant historical existence to Deborah but says that what makes such a portrayal of Deborah possible "is that premonarchic Israel was a rural, nonhierarchical decentralized and domestically based society in which positions of power could be held by women" (*JBL* 121 [2002] 54). Yee, too, sees the sociological circumstances making this possible: "the lines between domestic and public domains were blurred" (*Semeia* 61 [1993] 111). Women's residential connections with the clan units created a condition in which "men in pre-monarchic Israel would have been more willing to accept and trust their leadership in warfare than a group of strangers" (112). Still, Yee is able to see that this is not the norm, so that Deborah's "leadership in war was one response to emergency situations of conflict which were prevalent in Israel during the time of the Judges. . . . The sudden confusion of gender roles in such anomalous situations during war was only temporary; it was assumed that when the emergency had passed women would return to their ordinary occupations." Such sociological conclusions are too limiting for any society, for it is precisely the unique quality of the woman Deborah, not the unique sociological situation, that makes her capable of fulfilling such multiple, masculine-dominated roles.

Commentators easily make too much of Deborah. Block calls her "without doubt the most honorable human figure in the Book of Judges" (246). He describes her as "the only unequivocally positive major personality and as the only one involved in the service of God prior to her engagement in deliverance activities" (184–95) in relation to all the other deliverers in the book of Judges. Similarly, Yee may make Deborah too strong a leader: "The biblical text represents Deborah as the leader to whose counsel Barak and his soldiers defer before and during the battle. Her leadership is decisive for the battle's conclusion, whose success by the hand of a woman she had prophesied. Deborah performs in this authoritative capacity normally and in all its complexity" (*Semeia* 61 [1993] 110). Yee even comprehends the actions of Jael as "a crucial part of Deborah's whole guerrilla war plan" (114). Deborah and Jael thus become metaphors for military leadership and covert involvement in military activity, respectively. Brensinger echoes this assessment: "Even a cursory glance at 4:1–5:31 leads the reader to suspect that Deborah, rather than being inferior to the male protagonists in the book of Judges, actually possesses greater influence and authority. She serves as both prophet and judge, and she exercises leadership during the episode that affects the single largest number of tribes" (61).

Bal (116) claims that the writer emphasizes Deborah as woman in 4:4 so that in 4:9 she may prophesy in her capacity as woman. For Bal "the class of woman is at stake, not Deborah the individual." I would counter that the extensive modifiers defining Deborah show that the story celebrates the feat(s) of a particular woman, not just the class of woman. In fact, it shows how exceptional Deborah, the woman, is rather than how typical. Still, her exceptional qualifications do not make her the heroine of the narrative; she is only the transitional character needed to prepare for Jael's emergence and Barak's decline.

Closer reading of the narrative shows that Deborah does not appear in all the episodes of the narrative. When she does appear, she points away from herself to a mysterious woman glory-getter or to a hesitant God-called leader. The narrative presents her not as a strongly defined character but almost as a stereotypical prophetic spokesperson. The major difference for the writer between Deborah and other somewhat stock characters is her gender and her accumulation of offices, not her actions. Thus Olson concludes his exposition with the understanding that "neither Deborah, Barak, nor Jael emerges as the singular hero or judge in this story" (782). Amit works with the thesis that "the available data do not enable one to decide who saved Israel—was it Deborah, Barak, or Jael? So one is impelled to examine the extent of the partial participation of the human heroes, coming ultimately to the conclusion that God is the redeemer, who pulls the strings and activates the historical heroes of the human reality" (*JSOT* 39 [1987] 89).

But one must also see that the prose narrative focuses on the lack of a human hero as a problem for Israel. They have no Moses, nor even a Joshua. Leadership roles must be separated and shared because the all-purpose leader has disappeared from history. Amit's thesis about the nature of the story leads her astray as she structures and reads the narrative. The narrative's question is not, who is the Savior? The question is, can Israel survive without a savior? Deborah, then, stands out as a female prophet and judge. Her female gender is played over against the expected male leadership of Barak and supplies the uncertainty and mystery behind her threat to Barak that a woman, and not he, will receive honor or glory.

The editor's description of Deborah runs from woman to prophet. Younger correctly sees that "it is her role as prophetess that is catalytic in this narrative" (140). Ackerman (*BASOR* 220 [1975] 12) needlessly pushes the title of prophet aside as anachronistic. She sees Deborah as an intermediary between people and God, which is the basic role of a prophet. Schneider sees that "Deborah's primary affiliation is not to a family or a spouse, as would be expected for a married woman, but to her profession, prophecy" (65). Block probably goes too far in saying the prophetic designation "deliberately places Deborah in the succession of Moses (Deut 18:15–22)" (192). Brown follows a similar trail saying, "Deborah is a multi-gifted woman whose roles parallel those of Moses" (170). (Compare Reid, *NIDOTTE* 4:512–13.) Lindars is on target in emphasizing Deborah's role as a "war prophet" (183). I cannot follow his downplaying of the prophetic prediction role, since she does predict Yahweh's deployment of Sisera's troops, his giving of Sisera into Barak's hands, and the giving of Barak's glory to a woman.

Schneider goes too far, then, in trying to say that Deborah was not married and that "wife of Lappidoth" should be read as "a fiery one" (87). Fewell and Gunn also dismiss family relationships, saying *'eshet lappidot* "promises family relationship but never produces it in any tangible way" (*JAAR* 58 [1990] 391). Block is surely correct in speaking of "how equally misguided are more recent attempts to rob Deborah of a husband by interpreting *'eshet lappidot* as an adjective, that is, 'fiery woman'" (192). Lindars (182) makes the same point. See F. Gottlieb, *Jud* 30 (1981) 195; R. Rasmussen, "Deborah the Woman Warrior," 79–94, esp. 93, n. 3; Bal, *Murder and Difference*, 57–58.

Such traditional, yet ironic, use of titles is what one would expect in a narrative filled with satire and irony. Deborah is first and foremost a woman. Next she is a prophetess, the role she will play in the following narrative. Then she is wife, the role that identifies her fulfilling the woman's normal place in Israelite society. The family designations rouse expectations and set the reader up for the surprise that comes through the climax of the narrative.

Finally, Deborah functions as a judge in central Israel. Lindars (182) would delete all mention of Deborah judging or ruling as a late editorial addition by the "historian." This again is taking critical methodology too far without sufficient evidence. For Bal "verse 4 allows of no misunderstanding: Deborah was an autonomous judge, in office." This means, in turn, that "Barak is neither hero, nor deliverer, nor judge" (*Murder and Difference*, 57–58). Soggin (72) is too critical in trying to make Deborah a creation of Deuteronomistic redactors with Barak being the story's original protagonist. Many scholars do not display such reticence in speaking of the historical Deborah, and rightfully so. It proves much more difficult to identify a time in Israel's life when a creative literary genius would create such a person and find believability from an Israelite audience than it is to believe that a unique individual would give rise to such a narrative, a narrative preserved in not one but two distinct literary formats.

Bal brings up the significant fact that "the only character-judge who does something besides killing enemies is Deborah" (*Murder and Difference*, 52). Similarly, Schneider decides that all the other judges "attained their position only after leading a military event. . . . Deborah held an office prior to her involvement in military affairs. This may be another ironic situation since the only person qualified for the office prior to military battle was a woman" (68). As Brown notes, "From the beginning, the focus is upon her—her identity and her special role in the life of Israel" (171). Here the term שפט in its feminine form has no relationship to military deliverance as Block has shown with his twelve questions (193–94). This special role seems to be so strongly emphasized to show not only her qualifications but also the absence of any man to fill the role, another way of showing the weakness of leadership in Israel. The text does not criticize Deborah implicitly or explicitly as it does the succeeding deliverers. Rather, the text implicitly criticizes the nation of Israel for having to rely on women to deliver them from danger and to fulfill the major roles in their society.

5 A second disjunctive clause describes Deborah's situation prior to the narrative plot. This is the only place in Judges where judging is given any definition, and that definition is not what one would expect from either 2:16, 18 or 10:2–3 and 12:7–13. Ackerman sees that both judge and prophet are roles in which she "serves as an intermediary between the human world and the divine, bringing the word of God to the people of Israel" (*Warrior, Dancer,* 29). Block (192–97) argues that Deborah's main role was as a prophet and that the writers did not intend to include her among either the judges or the deliverers. Certainly, the text in vv 4 and 5 means to underline strongly her role as judge, but as case-hearing judge, not as deliverance-bringing judge. Block concludes: "By stationing herself near Bethel, Deborah represents an alternative to the priesthood which had lost its effectiveness as mediator of divine revelation, and her pronouncements function as a substitute for Urim and Thummin" (196). (Block argues this point more fully in "Deborah among the Judges," 229–53, and summarizes and updates in *BRev* 17 [2001] 34–40, 49–52.) Here Block reads into the text more than the text will carry. Evidently, Israel's priesthood was not exceptionally strong at this time, but one can in no way say that Deborah entered that definitely all-male dominion or in any way served as a substitute for it.

Soggin is closer to the biblical text when he concludes that "there does not seem to be any reason why it should not be taken as the administration of justice in general and all the problems connected with it" (64). Brensinger shows how the task of judging turned to that of battle prophet: "It is probably in her position as judge that the latest commotion under Sisera first comes to Deborah's attention, for her home is located some fifty miles from the battle scene (4:6–7). It is certainly in her position as prophetess, however, that she sends for Barak; her message to him takes the form of a prophetic oracle" (64).

Bal makes the interesting suggestion that the difference in the major and minor judges is simply one of the "state of the land over which they preside" rather than in "the functions of the official" (*Murder and Difference*, 53–55). Both dispel chaos, whether that is caused by internal sin or external oppression. The minor judges had no need for exploits of deliverance. For Bal, then, the book of Judges centers on chaos and the act of remedying it. With this understanding, a new definition of *judge* emerges: "to pronounce the right word in a given situation," that is, "to establish order in the chaos by means of the right word" (56–57).

Deborah then is first and foremost a woman. As such she holds offices most commonly held by men—judge and prophet—while also conforming to expectations as a wife. The emphasis on her gender points to the lack of men to fill such roles and to Deborah's extraordinary talents. She points away from herself, and the climax confirms that she is not the central character or hero of the story. That role belongs to the surprise character who makes a late entrance into the narrative.

The phrase "palm tree of Deborah" raises more questions than it provides answers. It has an uncertain connection to the Oak of Weeping (Gen 35:8) under which Rebekah's nurse, also named Deborah, was buried. Nor is it necessary to conclude with Lindars (183) that Deborah's location under a tree near Bethel is derived from Gen 35:8. In fact Soggin states unequivocally "there does not seem to have been any connection between the two trees, which differ in both species and in function" (64). The site placed Deborah near but not at the cultic sites of northern Israel and still accessible to the southern tribes, if they indeed maintained identity with the northern tribes at this time. Younger notes that Barak's home was near the enemy stronghold of Hazor, while Deborah's was definitely not. "This heightens the irony that the one far away is the one who takes the initiative to deliver those whose 'general' lives near the palace of the oppressor king and the home of the oppressing general, Sisera" (139, n. 10).

6 The complication "reveals how and why the opening conditions have changed" (Amit, *Reading Biblical Narratives*, 47). Here the context changes radically. The plot or narrative action begins in Hebrew consecutive style as Deborah summons Barak to action. From statements about a judge under a tree near Bethel, we turn suddenly to a call to arms. Unexpectedly, the peaceful judge turns into a war prophet. We appear to be entering a typical battle narrative. Murray reveals a new twist at this point: "From this point the story-line develops basically around the actions of the men," suggesting "that it is the men who play the decisive roles in this story" ("Narrative Structure and Technique," 168). That is true until Jael emerges and again shifts the spotlight to a woman.

This leaves us with the amazing fact that the previous exposition has introduced only one character and has ignored the scenes of action that will appear in the following narrative. The exposition is thus more important for what it omits than for what it includes. It omits God raising a leader to deliver an oppressed people. It omits any reference to the normally expected male general/judge/deliverer. It omits any action by the character introduced seemingly as the leading character.

It focuses only on a female judge, prophetess, wife far removed from the enemy leaders.

The plot complication moves Deborah from static sitting in the hill country of Ephraim to military action in Mount Tabor. Here we find what Olson calls "one of the unique wrinkles in Judges 4–5." "It is not altogether clear who the actual judge is in this account. . . . This ambivalence about the real judge or hero of this story will play an important role in the narrative's plot as well as in the theological interpretation of the account" (774).

Younger (140) thinks Barak is the "designated deliverer . . . who ought to have served as the main character of the account." Ackerman goes further as she tries to demonstrate that in Judg 4 "Deborah's role in leading this war is minimized . . . in favor of that of Barak." This is because "for Deborah to be a believable character within such a context, her status as war leader in Judges 5 must be downplayed and in essence eliminated" (*Warrior, Dancer,* 70–71).

Quite to the contrary! It is precisely the reversal of role expectations that gives interest and entertainment value to the narrative and allows an audience to follow its depiction of Deborah as the supposed heroine. Barak is introduced almost as Deborah's foil. Deborah is not so much a participant or even a leader in battle as she is the instigator of action. Deborah accompanies Barak to the battlefield, but only Barak leads the charge against the enemies.

The complication or change in the plot comes when Barak refuses to go unless Deborah accompanies him, only to find that this will place all glory for victory into an unnamed woman's hands. Block asserts that "the request to be accompanied by the prophet is a plea for the presence of God" (199–200). Block thus understands Deborah as the alter ego of God so that her promise of presence represents the promise of divine presence in the call narrative and her warning of loss of glory is simply the sign given in such a narrative. Similarly, Soggin defends Barak as a man of "reticence pure and simple. . . . Barak, who is a leader and a man of the world, and therefore accustomed to weigh up the odds, cannot share the charismatic enthusiasm of Deborah: he cannot endanger himself and others without the necessary guarantees. . . . It is clear that in the end it is Barak who goes out at the head of the troops, and not Deborah" (72–73).

Nothing else in the narrative shows Barak as one piously seeking and obeying God, and the ending points to his weakness, not to the confirmation of a divine sign. Both Barak and Sisera are generals leading troops to war, and both are objects of intense satire and ridicule in the narrative. Nothing points to any heroic quality in either. As Amit asserts, "his dependence on Deborah and refusal to accept an exclusive and independent appointment cancel out that possibility" (i.e., the possibility of being Israel's savior) (*JSOT* 39 [1987] 93).

Mention of "Kedesh in Naphtali" has led scholars on a long search for its location. See J. L. Peterson, "Kedesh," *ABD,* 4:11, for locations at Tel Abu Kudeis in the Jezreel Valley between Taanach and Megiddo, at Khirbet Qedish a mile west of the southern end of the Sea of Galilee, and at Tell Qades in the hill country northwest of Lake Huleh. Margalith ("Observations," 630–31) works from אלון בצענים, "the tree in Zaanannim" (v 11), and, using Josh 19:33, locates it "on or near the southwestern shore of the Sea of Galilee in the vicinity of modern Khirbet Kdish." He identifies its meaning as the "Oak-Home of the Wanderers." Soggin (66) points to a location a short distance southeast of Megiddo; Lindars (185) looks to Khirbet Qedish as the "historian's understanding" because Tell Qades is "much too far away from the scene of action," but then argues that the historian was wrong, with Tel Abu Kudeis as the original location. In so arguing Lindars (190) has to excise vv 10–12 as later additions of the historian.

Ackerman says the "prose redactor of Judges 4" defies "topographic logic" and makes this "illogical choice" because Kedesh "is the only logical choice if Jael's tent is to be interpreted as a sanctified haven" (*Warrior, Dancer,* 97–98). Aharoni points to Tell Qades in upper Galilee as the "generally accepted" location identified with the Levitical city of Joshua (Josh 19:37; 20:7; 21:32), but then describes this as "absurd" and argues for a place near Mount Tabor in the vicinity of the Jabneel Valley (*Land of the Bible,* 204). Aharoni finds the location on the slopes leading down to the Sea of Galilee at Khirbet Qedesh. He is followed by Bimson (*Baker Encyclopedia of Bible Places,* 187), Gaß (*Ortsnamen,* 249), and Rainey (*Sacred Bridge,* 138). Block (198) prefers the northern site as near Jabin's power base in Hazor.

Deborah faces Barak with a rhetorical question: "Did not Yahweh, the God of Israel, command you . . . ?" This device will appear again in v 14. GKC includes this usage under what it calls "the conviction that the contents of the statement are well known to the hearer, and are unconditionally admitted by him" (§150e). This text most probably belongs, however, to GKC's next category: "a surprising communication is introduced in this way in order to show it to be absolutely true" (§150e). Here, then, as most modern translations show, the rhetorical question serves as what W. Schneider calls a *bekräftigenden Behauptung,* that is, an "empowering assertion" (*Grammatik des biblischen Hebräisch* [Munich: Claudius, 1974] 226). The prophet's words empower Barak to carry out the military command, a command whose validity he does not call into question.

Yahweh is identified as אֱלֹהֵי־יִשְׂרָאֵל, "the God of Israel." Canonically, this divine title goes back to Jacob's building of an altar to God at Shechem (Gen 33:20). It is closely tied to the plague narratives (Exod 5:1), the covenant ceremony in Exod 24:10 (compare 34:23), and the covenant breaking of Exod 32:27. Ringgren (*TDOT,* 1:278) connects the title to Israel's holy war traditions (Josh 7:13; 10:40, 42; 14:14; Judg 4:6; 5:3, 5; 6:8; 11:21, 23) and the ark of the covenant (1 Sam 5:7–11; 6:3, 5). The antiquity of the expression is shown by its occurrence in the Song of Deborah (5:3, 5) and most probably by its occurrence in Josh 24:2, 23. It must be more than accidental that "God of Israel" appears so frequently in connection with Shechem. It appears to represent an ancient patriarchal title for God used in Israel's covenant and war tradition, particularly in Shechem.

God's command has specific geographical directions leading Barak to Mount Tabor. Lindars (186–87) unnecessarily removes Mount Tabor as a later addition by the historian who did not understand the geography of the battle; this is too easy an escape route from the admittedly difficult geographical problems of the text. The mountain stood at the juncture of the tribal territories of Zebulun, Issachar, and Naphtali and may have served as a worship place for the three tribes (Deut 33:18–19; Hos 5:1; compare Brisco, *HBA,* 85). Its almost flat plateaued top rising above the major crossroads in the Jezreel Valley makes its appearance stick in the memory of any tourist who visits the site. (See R. Frankel, *ABD,* 6:304–5.)

The original command includes troops from only two tribes—Zebulun and Barak's tribe of Naphtali. The significance of this will become even greater in the study of the central section of the Song of Deborah. Here we begin to see the fragmentation of

Israel as only a few tribes fight the battle. Heretofore, the "sons of Israel" have joined the fray. Now only two tribes appear. Barak's response joins with the paucity of tribal participation to show we have stepped down from the model heroism of Othniel, Ehud, and Shamgar. Younger writes, "Deborah's charge to Barak in 4:6–7 indicates that he is destined for a role comparable to that played by Othniel in 3:7–11. His response, however, to Deborah's command from Yahweh with its great assurance of victory is hardly the stuff of an Othniel, or even an Ehud" (141).

7 A twist occurs as Barak is called to deploy his forces, while Yahweh will deploy the army of Sisera, Jabin's army commander. The introduction of Jabin here is more than a late editorial addition from the narrative framework. It maintains the entire narrative's focus on Jabin as the overarching enemy.

So far we have the introduction to a prophetic battle story (B. O. Long, *1 Kings*, FOTL 9 [Grand Rapids: Eerdmans, 1984] 257), but one that introduces its generals in strange, ironic ways. Deborah summons Barak to battle without previous introduction, and Sisera is simply placed as a pawn to be deployed by God's hand. Polzin expresses the remarkable insight that "we thus see how the phraseological composition of a story so surrounded by the certainty of Israel's victory and Sisera's defeat can still strongly suggest the inability of man, even God's elect, fully to understand either God's words or his own, or to predict his own destiny" (*Moses and the Deuteronomist,* 164).

Bal, following others, seeks to limit the concept and identity of Yahweh in these compositions, particularly chap. 4. She writes: "the narrative of chapter 4, with the exception of 4:14, represents a rather abstract warrior god, a moral support rather than an active character, and entirely bound, for Barak, to the person of Deborah. . . . In the song, the god is omnipresent" (*Murder and Difference,* 45). Bal takes this to the extreme when she cleverly writes: "Deborah's vision is indeed a highly specific blending of Yahwist and Canaanite elements, in which above all the profound unity between Yahweh, nature, and the Hebrew people predominates. . . . The Canaanite civilization . . . is more advanced and by this fact has lost its unity with nature. In a sense Deborah shows herself more Baalist than the Baalists" (46–47). Such a comment belies the limits the audience places on the narrator, for both audience and narrator know much more about Yahweh than is revealed in any part or the whole of a single narrative. Deborah will not accede to Baal any powers or realms, claiming all areas, even nature and its powers, for Yahweh.

The Kishon River, about ten miles (16.1 km) west of Tabor, is the Wadi al-Muqatta, a deceptively small wadi that flows northwesterly from hills south and east of Taanach through the Jezreel Valley into the Mediterranean Sea north of Mount Carmel. Normally a small rivulet if not dry, the wadi explodes with the spring rains. God, who commands both generals, knows the wadi's conditions better than does either general. Thus God uses the committal formula to promise Barak victory.

8 Webb asserts, "The bargain struck in vv. 8–9 . . . is the axis along which tension is developed and resolved here." Thus "mystification is of the very essence of the story's narrative art" ([1987] 137). This occurs with an interesting twist in v 8 when Barak responds in a fashion resembling the objections in the biblical-call narratives or vocation account. (See M. A. Sweeney, *Isaiah 1–39,* FOTL 16 [Grand Rapids: Eerdmans, 1996] 542–43.) Just as Moses said he could not speak, Gideon said he was too insignificant, and Jeremiah said he was too young, so Barak says he had to have the prophet as proof of God's presence. Niditch argues,

Barak's declaration that he will go to battle only if accompanied by Deborah (4:8) is not to be interpreted as cowardice; rather, within the context of the worldview of the literature, he is wise to know that victory comes with the presence of God's favorite. Thus Elisha declares concerning the prophet Elijah, who has ascended to his Master in a chariot of fire, "My father, my father, the chariots of Israel and its horsemen" (2 Kgs 2:12); Elijah is worth battalions. Barak's words to Deborah in v. 8 enhance her prestige as woman warrior, and her oracle emphasizes a favorite theme of Judges and the larger Hebrew Bible concerning the victory of the unlikely hero. Sisera will be undone by a woman. (65)

This interpretation of the narrative ignores Deborah's summons and Barak's loss of honor, the center of the narrative presentation. Deborah serves as an intermediary when we would expect a direct confrontation with God himself. Barak's objection is not voiced as a call for God to supply a need. Rather, Barak calls for Deborah, the woman prophetess, to do so. In a normal call or commissioning narrative, the expected answer would come from God or his messenger promising divine presence. Instead, Deborah promises her presence.

9 Narrative change is the crisis that the story must resolve. It appears that the crisis in this story is the presence or absence of Deborah. V 9 seems to solve that crisis by describing Deborah's participation with Barak. This promise, however, contains a twist that creates the narrative tension or change: Deborah's presence robs Barak of honor or glory. Instead, a woman will get glory. Here the translation "glory" does not represent the Hebrew word כָּבוֹד so often used of God's glory. The Hebrew here, תִּפְאֶרֶת, refers primarily to ornamental beauty and then to honor. "The semantic link seems to be that the beauty is expressive of the dignity of the bearer and elicits ascriptions of glory" (J. Collins, *NIDOTTE*, 3:573). But such ascription may come from the bearer in terms of boasting rights, a meaning Collins applies to Barak (574). One probably needs to acknowledge both meanings here. Barak would lose the praise and honor that go to the victorious general and the resulting boasting rights.

Bal (*Murder and Difference*, 63) raises shame and honor to a repeating theme in Judges. She continues this thematic exposition (116–24) in a complex and not totally satisfying manner, her thesis being that "what is at stake here is the honor-shame opposition, linked to that between the sexes." She concludes that precisely because they are not subject to the difficult test of military honor the "two women, characters portrayed in a man's discourse, are capable of assuming their function in this discourse so distinctly biased by the masculine code. . . . Honor, equivalent to existence itself, is from the masculine perspective threatened by women." Barak and Sisera become "interchangeable. Each the enemy of the other, they are inseparable, indistinguishable before the shame represented by the woman as executioner."

Olson tries to relieve Barak of shame, saying, "That Barak received help from God (4:6–7, 15) and from Deborah (4:8–9, 14) as well as from Jael is not a matter of great shame" (*NIB*, 2:775). This misses the entire narrative structure of the prose, which turns on the prophetic warning that Barak will lose his honor and glory to a woman. Yee defines the "Shame Syndrome" in terms of "a warrior queen" who "functions primarily to shame the weaker males who surround her." She notes, "This shaming by a woman is only effective if war is defined solely as a male activity. . . . Instead of celebrating women's military leadership, the story places women as adversaries of men" (*Semeia* 61 [1993] 115). Thus Yee agrees with Bal that women "become the means by which men are 'unmanned' or shamed" (Yee, 115, referring to M. Bal, *Murder and Difference,* 115–24).

Here Younger is on target in writing, "The Barak narrative is much less interested in who fought in the battle than it is in Barak's hesitation and its results" (158). Olson would argue that "the narrator does not provide an explicit evaluation of Barak's statement, and so we are left to wonder about Barak's inner motivation" (780). Making such an explicit statement would rob the story of its narrative tension, its irony, and its climax. The final scene, in which Barak enters the tent of Jael to meet his dead opponent, shows clearly enough that Barak is not painted as a strong character and that his motivation is not to be interpreted positively. Olson is more on target in describing the ambiguity of Deborah's statement as part of a larger narrative strategy of ambiguity.

The threat to give glory to the woman is done with the divine-sale formula. Instead of Israel being sold into the enemy's hands, the enemy is being sold into the hands of Israel's leader, though here the leader's identity remains shrouded in mystery. So Barak finally obeys Deborah by going to Kedesh, and Deborah keeps her promise. Kedesh is apparently the home of Barak (v 6). By keeping her promise, Deborah appears to be the woman lurking in the background ready to grab Barak's glory. Block points to this as the place where the narrative, in contrast to the poetic composition, "explicitly raises gender as an issue" (183). But one must respond that this is precisely the point of tension around which the entire narrative turns. Deborah's complex feminine introduction raised gender as the issue. The narrative is told to reveal how a woman, rather than a general, obtains glory. Lindars concludes that "in the prose the point is the prowess of a woman, which upsets the expected conventions of the heroic tale, and creates the interest of the story for the audience" (168). Block himself (183) concludes that the narrator deliberately highlights the initiative and power of female participants while humiliating the male characters. Here one must raise the question of which of these topics is the most important: the success of women or the humiliation of men?

10 Next the narrator employs a twist on the cry-of-distress formula. The children of Israel do not cry. Barak does. The cry is not to God but to two lone tribes in Israel. Note the similar use of זעק in Judges 12:2 and 18:23. Soggin (65) sees it as a technical military term for "mobilize," "call to arms." The cry is for a specific kind of help at a specific place, so translators often use the phrase "mustered to Kedesh" or "called out to Kedesh." Then comes the punch line to this prophetic battle story: ten thousand men went at his feet, "and Deborah went up with him." Ten thousand men do not suffice, though that has been the enemy strength in 1:4 and 3:29. Barak depends not on the ten thousand men but on the one woman, knowing all the while that glory goes to the woman not to himself. The audience can anticipate the resolution of the narrative already. It appears to be the simple transfer of glory to Deborah from Barak. The narrator artfully emphasizes this by making *Deborah* the last word in this section of the narrative. Soggin claims that "the figure 10,000 is evidently an exaggeration. . . . It seems obvious that the epic narrative tends rather to exaggerate figures" (65). These appear to be more traditional battle descriptions than exaggerations.

11 We are prepared for a full battle report, but that is not where the author goes next. Rather, he unexpectedly introduces another character with a disjunctive clause. Again this character receives brief biographical attention. Heber, the Kenite, related to Moses' in-laws, separates from them to move to Kedesh, right where God has deployed Sisera. Olson makes the provocative suggestion that despite familial relations with Israel, Heber separates from the other Kenites "in order to ply his trade with the 900 iron chariots of the Canaanites" (781). Margalith suggests that Heber was "a local nomadic chieftain employed by the king of Hazor to protect his trade route along the lucrative Way of Hauran along the Wadi Fejjas from bandits" ("Observations," 633). He tries somewhat unsuccessfully to make the narrative of Judg 4 a mirror image of the Ugaritic poem of Aqht. Schneider (77) tries to rob Heber of a wife—or Jael of a husband—but this is certainly bending the text a bit too far to fit the desires of feminist exegesis and literary study.

Attempts by A. Malamat ("Mari and the Bible: Some Patterns of Tribal Organizations and Institutions," *JAOS* 82 [1962] 146) and J. A. Soggin (*VT* 31 [1981] 89–92) to remove the individual Heber from the narrative in favor of an association or a clan have been adequately refuted by Lindars (191) and H.-D. Neef (*ZAW* 101 [1989] 43, n. 88). Still, Ackerman (*Warrior, Dancer,* 108) thinks Judg 5 refers to the "Kenite community," but Judg 4 reinterprets this as an individual, Jael's husband.

Such efforts to eradicate Heber steal the irony and narrative tension from the story. Amit rightly sees Heber's sudden appearance as "a further complication, for no key is available for understanding the relevance of that information to the narrative" (*JSOT* 39 [1987] 94). Much of the story's narrative tension and resolution hangs on the struggle Jael faces in choosing which allegiance to honor at the present moment. Chisholm ("What's Wrong with This Picture?") notes that at the literary level Jael supplants Heber, just as, in fulfillment of Deborah's prediction (4:9), she supplants Barak as the hero of the story. The narrator's variation on normal Hebrew story-telling style mirrors one of the themes of the story: "This is a story that downplays the role of a hesitant male leader . . . and highlights the role of a cunning and daring woman."

Younger (142, 143, n. 26) argues that a formal treaty is not meant here, but the text implies at least a formal oral agreement, which would be tantamount to a treaty. Ackerman goes so far as to contend that the peace treaty "is no more than a clumsy fiction, intruding into the Judges 4 story imperfectly and only temporarily" (*Warrior, Dancer,* 92). In truth the treaty is the entry point for the narrative tension that brings Sisera and Jael together. The treaty makes plausible Sisera's visit to Jael's tent. So Soggin writes, "It is a positive relationship of friendship or quite simply an alliance. . . . This is the only explanation of why the general took refuge in the woman's tent" (66–67). Schneider shows us that "the information is conveyed here so that when suspense surrounding Sisera's death builds later in the story, all the characters are in place, allowing the story to continue without interruption" (71). Later, she sees the great importance in giving the reader information the characters do not have and says, "This one line insertion ties the Kenites to the Israelites and places them precisely where a major battle is about to occur" (73).

Neither the narrative nor the poem answers one question about Jael: why? Why would she decide to kill the Canaanite general with whom her husband had a mutual nonaggression, support, or peace treaty? The answer to this question does not play a role for either writer, but it generates great heat among scholars.

In their brief review Fewell and Gunn decide the reason lies not in commitment to Yahweh (Amit), nor in her family relationships as a true Israelite (Garstang), nor as a woman loyal to the Israelite covenant (Boling). For Fewell and Gunn, Jael had no greater tie to Israel than did her husband. "Jael's motivation may be understood in much more pragmatic terms," for they see Jael caught in the middle with her husband on the losing side of the battle and the Israelite army approaching to capture and rape the women on the losing side. Thus "gender and politics put Jael in jeopardy. . . . Her desire for survival drives her to wield the authority of violence" (*JAAR* 58 [1990] 395–96). This goes to the extreme when they say, "Conveniently the song loses sight of the fact that Jael is not Israelite, that she is not fighting the oppression of Jabin king of Hazor, that she probably couldn't care less about YHWH and his people, that she must act for herself" (404). This is one reading among many possible ones, and in light of the last mention of the poet's convenient forgetting, one that they themselves must see as going against the obvious surface meaning of the total text. The narrative introduces Heber to show the family commitments to the Canaanite forces in order to picture Jael heroically breaking the commitments to save Israel. Margalith sees Jael in opposition with her husband, who is appears to be "betraying his own kin and coreligionists. . . . By acting as she did, Jael sought to restore the family honor sullied by her husband's defection" ("Observations," 640).

Kedesh represents the northern geographical limits for the story. Murray ("Narrative Structure and Technique," 180–82) shows the narrative skill in introducing Heber at this point: occupying a gap in narrative time, postponing the expected appearance of the enemy Sisera, intensifying the suspense by apparently introducing a fresh narrative, arousing curiosity as to Heber's significance, and preparing for the entrance of Jael. Amit thinks there is "no key available for understanding the relevance of the information to the narrative" (*JSOT* 39 [1987] 94). Brown rightly comments: "Far from being superfluous, the information is important in setting up the events that will follow; the fact that the author draws attention to it out of place, as it were, serves to highlight its importance even more" (173). The author has prepared the reader for the unexpected story ending via this foreshadowing without the reader comprehending the sense or purpose at this point.

The mention of Kenite flashes us back to 1:16 and brings expectations of peace between Kenite and Israelite or at least with the tribe of Judah. Connections with Moses increase this expectation, as do mentions of Kedesh, apparently the home of Barak. But the word נפרד, "separated," may alert us to observe more carefully. Zaanannim is a town on the southern border of Naphtali (Josh 19:33). It may be Khan et-Tujjar, a caravan station between Beth-shean and Damascus, four miles (6.4 km) southeast of Adam. This caravan station was part of the Via Maris and was located near Tell Abu Qedeis, which is to be identified with the Kedesh in Judg 4:11. See S. A. White, *ABD*, 6:1029.

12–13 Quickly, the narrator flashes back to Sisera and the reports coming to him about Barak. No spy narrative appears in this battle report, but spies were obviously at work. Now Sisera musters or cries for help to get his army ready for battle. He appears to be in charge, but the narrator has already informed us that Yahweh is the one (v 7) deploying Sisera's troops. The troops apparently moved from the home base (v 2) to the battlefield near the Kishon.

14 We move quickly from Heber to Sisera to Deborah in a few short verses.

This is the staccato nature of Hebrew narrative. Deborah assumes the role of commander in chief, or even of the voice of deity, in ordering Barak to march. Again the conveyance formula is used to bring assurance of victory and to give credit to the one responsible for victory. Now Deborah is no longer the one who has marched out with Barak. Rather, Yahweh has marched out ahead of Deborah's general. So Barak leads his ten thousand men down the mountain, apparently without his one woman. Younger (164) correctly observes, "There is nothing in the text that indicates any warrior status or abilities on the part of Deborah." This contrasts with the interpretation by Yee (*Semeia* 61 [1993] 99–132) noted above. Soggin (75) hints at an original stage of the battle led by Deborah and a central Palestinian group, later joined by Barak in a second-stage reinforcement. Such a reconstruction is pulled out of thin critical air, not from the narrative.

Sisera hears the reports and immediately orders his troops to deploy. On Israel's side Deborah again initiates the action, calling Barak to get up and spring into action for this is God's day of deliverance. As in v 6, she uses a rhetorical question to underline the truth of what she claims: Yahweh has marched out in front of Barak and his troops. Thus Yahweh is present with Barak and his army, though Barak asked only for Deborah's presence. Barak's full contingent of men follows him down Mount Tabor to battle.

15   The battle report is brief, formed in terms of holy war. Israel does not fight. Yahweh does. Yahweh throws Sisera and his army into panic (see המם; Exod 14:24; 23:27; Josh 10:10; Judg 4:15; 1 Sam 7:10; 2 Sam 22:15; 2 Chr 15:6; Pss 18:15; 144:6; Isa 28:28). Brensinger vividly catches the spirit of the story: "What is surely envisioned here is a sudden and unexpected downpour following the close of the latter rains. Miraculously, the same God who turned water into dry land (Exod 14:21–22; Josh 3:14–17) now turns dry land into a sea of mud!" (65). One must admit that this description may lie behind the narrative composition, but it becomes explicit only in the poem.

Block sets v 15 up as "the key to the entire chapter" (204). This is true if one is determined that this is an ordinary battle report with God as the hero. But here we have a parody of a battle report. The parody depicts only the height of the battle action to show again Barak's lack of involvement and to prepare for further evidence of his weakness. Amit observes, "The Lord is the savior and Barak's part parallels that of the Israelites in wars in which the outcome is determined by direct divine action and not by human military might. . . . The narrative of the battle is still not concluded, and the prophecy Deborah enunciated at the onset has yet to come true" (*JSOT* 39 [1987] 95).

But the way is left open for the rest of the story, for "Sisera stepped down from his chariot and fled on foot." Margalith ("Observations," 632) shows the route Sisera took as he fled (see *Comment* on v 17).

Amit encounters trouble here with her thesis that the plot centers on who is savior and has its basic resolution in vv 14–16. She must first write that "this scene therefore contains a solution to the question of the savior: The Lord is the savior, and Barak's part parallels that of the Israelites" (*JSOT* 39 [1987] 95). But then she must continue: "But even as one finds the solution the reader realizes that the narrative of the battle is still not concluded and the prophecy of Deborah enunciated at the outset has not yet come true." So she calls vv 17–22 "The Solution Scene"

(96). But this scene does not solve the question she puts at the center of the narrative. It solves the question of who gets glory, not of who is the savior.

16 In the unraveling the "consequences of the change are revealed" (Amit, *Reading Biblical Narratives,* 47). The narrator dwells on the resolution of the plot, describing the battle and then entering a surprise element to show that glory did go to the woman. The biblical narrator resolves his narrative tension in a slow, drawn-out fashion, gradually building tension by ignoring the point of crisis. He appears to be telling a simple battle narrative but repeatedly uses narrative twists to do so. Though Lindars makes unnecessary excisions attributed to a later editor, he correctly observes that "the narrative can be seen to concentrate on one issue, the defeat of Sisera by a woman" (179–80). Block sees that "the description of the conflict [which he sees in vv 11–22] is unusually long and takes some unexpected turns" (201). Here Murray is certainly to be followed: "The battle and rout is but a necessary stage in the working out of the plot: in fact, a plot-complicating, rather than plot-unraveling, stage, since it is the very fact of Sisera's escape from Barak's hands at the battle, that leads on to the third and fourth episodes" ("Narrative Structure and Technique," 165). The battle is over for all practical purposes, but the story is just about to begin.

A disjunctive clause opens this section of the story, a section dominated by dialogue. Such dialogue normally marks the climax of a narrative, so that is what we expect here. Webb ([1987] 136) sees the murder rather than the battle as the "high point of dramatic interest" both here and in the Ehud narrative. Soggin dismisses this episode as not historical because of its individualistic and anecdotal character, but does see v 17–22 as the "earliest part of the narrative" that "doubtless constitutes the climax of the story" (77). Barak chases an illusive enemy westward all the way to Harosheth Haggoyim, Sisera's home and base of operations (4:2). Meanwhile, Sisera's entire army is killed. Not even one remains alive. Thus Barak and his army appear to have fulfilled the call of holy war against the inhabitants of Canaan. The battle appears to be down to Sisera and Barak, a one-on-one confrontation. Barak is hunting. Where is Sisera? He has fled eastward and is hiding. Margalith posits Heber's location on the southwestern shore of the Sea of Galilee and then traces Sisera's escape route: "From the vicinity of the Jezreel Valley and its northern extension near Mt. Tabor, he flees eastward toward the Sea of Galilee, a distance of about 15 km as the crow flies and the shortest as well as the easiest route to Hazor" ("Observations," 632).

17 Where is Sisera hiding? He is in the tent of that mysterious man with Mosaic connections mentioned in passing in v 11. But Heber is not at home. Only his wife, Jael, is keeping the home fires burning. Block wants to take the hero's role from Jael, saying, "Her actions and character are patently ambiguous. . . . The narration offers no hint of any spiritual motivation on her part or any concern for Israel" (209). But the author does not seek to provide a characterization of Jael and explain her motives. Jael is more of a type character who performs her function as an instrument fulfilling the deity's plan and moves on. As Amit sees it,

The background information (v. 17b) prevents the reader from suspecting that Jael is planning the murder of Sisera, or that she is the woman referred to in Deborah's prophecy. Moreover, that information endows the meeting between Jael and Sisera with the serene atmosphere of hospitality. Her exemplary hospitality . . . (vv. 18, 19) is necessarily interpreted as a manifestation of compassion for the tired hero fleeing on foot. The description of the murder in v. 21 is sudden and surprising and cannot be connected with or explained by any motives suggested in the text. (*JSOT* 39 [1987] 97)

Later Amit will conclude that "a retrospective look at vv. 18–22—after the emergence of the feeling that events take place according to a plan predetermined by God—shows careful planning on Jael's part" (98).

Thus I agree with Younger: "Finally, Jael emerges as the real heroine of the narrative. But this is ironic, too. She is hardly an orthodox hero. Rather, she shares the unorthodox qualities of Ehud and Shamgar . . . a lone assassin who accomplishes her ends by deception . . . alone in a private chamber . . . she improvised a weapon from a domestic implement" (146).

Webb concludes:

> It is Jael who finally emerges as the real hero of the narrative. But she is not an orthodox hero on the Othniel model, as Barak was destined to be; she partakes rather of the unorthodox qualities of Ehud and of Shamgar. . . . Her action is morally ambiguous, but her courage and the sheer virtuosity of her performance are sufficient to silence criticism on that score (5.24). The crowning aspect of her unorthodoxy as a hero is her sex. ([1987] 137)

Notice the complex argument of Bal (*Murder and Difference*, 34–35) against either the literary critical elimination of Jael from the original narrative or the focus on condemning Jael for treachery, lying, assassination, or another list of "sins." Why would Sisera flee there? Because his boss Jabin, introduced briefly again here, had formed a peaceful alliance with Heber. This destroys all our expectations! How can a people who had allied themselves with Judah and had Mosaic connections make peace with the Canaanites? This represents only one step in the book's descriptions of Israel acting more like Canaanites than do the Canaanites. Apparently, however, wife Jael was not part of that alliance or withdrew from it in commitment to a higher allegiance. Fokkelman speaks of Jael as "the woman [who] belongs to the enemy side" and says "it takes courage to change sides on her own, as she finally does. Her radical decision to break with her husband and the alliance by killing Sisera is the big surprise of both ch. 4 and ch. 5" ("The Song of Deborah and Barak," 605).

18 V 18 introduces the allure of romance as Jael goes out to meet Sisera and invites, "Turn aside to me, my Lord. Don't be afraid." So he turns to her, that is, to her tent. Schneider (78) shows that women had their own tents separate from the husband's. Niditch notes that "the supposed sympathizer does not assist Sisera or hide him from his enemies, but uses her allure and his trust to destroy him. . . . The interaction between Sisera and Jael is characterized by the mix of sex and slaughter discussed in connection with the assassination of Ehud. Here, however, the ravisher is herself a woman!" (66). Lindars says, "Jael's deed can be seen as a parody of a sexual encounter in which Jael plays the part of the man, so that the roles are reversed" (275).

Brensinger notes, "Jael initially and inappropriately offers Sisera hospitality; her husband, the male head, could alone make such an offer" (66). Schneider emphasizes that "all her actions led him into a sense of comfort, an ironic sense" (79). And what does she do? She covers him with a rug, or perhaps better with one of the sleeping mats used to sleep on the floor of the tent. The atmosphere is set for romance. Here we have escaped the limits of holy war battle report. We have even stepped beyond the bounds of normal battle story. The battlefield has disappeared. One army is dead, the other off with its general on a wild goose chase. The story is down to the intrigue of either romance or murder.

Brown says, "Sisera thought he had to fear a male, but it was a woman who did him in when he least expected it" (174). From the other perspective Olson notes that Jael's "motives remain a mystery" (782). Ackerman (*Warrior, Dancer,* 92–109) argues that Judg 5 allows Jael to murder Sisera because as a religious functionary she has the divine will revealed to her. Ackerman strains at every straw of evidence possible to prove that Jael is seen in both Judg 4 and in Judg 5 as a cult functionary. The evidence is a relationship to Moses and Jethro, who both exercised cultic functions and supposedly established a family of priests, making Heber a priest. Also, Zipporah is seen as a cultic professional because of her actions in Exod 4:24–26. This, too, becomes a family tradition inherited by Jael. Finally, the association of Kedesh with the law of sanctuary or refuge and with cult points to their participation in this cult. Such a conclusion is built on too large a stack of hypotheses to be believable. The point is Jael's expected allegiance to Jabin and thus to Sisera because of her marriage, not because of her profession.

Lindars (197) sees the sexual interpretation of this scene by R. Alter (*The Art of Biblical Poetry* [New York: Basic, 1987]) and Y. Zakovitch ("Sisseras Tod," *ZAW* 83 [1981] 364–74) as "not to be dismissed out of hand." Lindars' further statement may take this line of thought a bit far: "It may well be a conscious irony that Sisera's position is comparable to that of a proverbial young man who falls into the clutches of a harlot." Alter (*Art of Biblical Narrative,* 49) says the story gives "an ironic glance at the time-honored martial custom of rape."

From a feminine point of view, Schneider sees that "clearly the sexuality of the majority of the women in Judges is significant to plots concerning them and would not be out of place in this context" (93). Ackerman totally ruins her case in trying to argue that Jael's role is also radically reinterpreted in Judg 4 because "the redactor seems unable to present Jael as a woman who can murder a foe in cold blood." She transforms the murder scene in 4:21 so that "the initial and primary focus of Judg 4:21 becomes Jael's role as a seductress" (*Warrior, Dancer,* 72). This stands in strong contradiction to the chapter's depiction of Sisera's murder. It is interesting that Deborah appears as the focal character but without sexual allusions.

I must in the end agree with Lindars that "the sexual details are mere suggestions, weaving a secondary theme into the narrative" (275). Fewell and Gunn put it another way: "while Jael is neither, literally, mother nor lover to Sisera, this scene is filled with maternal and sexual imagery" (*JAAR* 58 [1990] 393). They may well overfill the scene with some of their searches for such imagery, especially those based on new definitions of Hebrew vocabulary. Using her ritualistic perspective, Bal probably goes too far in thinking that "Sisera gets more than he asks for. . . . Jael forces on Sisera the superposition of one ritual upon another. The request for love receives as its response the gift of love, but a different kind of love. The elementary love requested is maternal love. The love given is sexual" (*Murder and Difference,* 122). One can see sexual intimations here without having to find actual sexual acts described or even hinted at. Indeed, Olson sees Sisera being "turned into a little child, tucked into bed for the night and hiding from any monsters who might threaten him . . . his masculinity has been reduced to that of an infant" (781).

19 First, though, the most primary of needs has to be met—thirst must be quenched. Bal informs us that since curdled goat's milk was always available in a nomad's tent, "to substitute milk for the water requested thus represents in itself nothing extraordinary" (*Murder and Difference*, 62). Again she writes, "The man who was once so powerful in the superiority of his chariots must now ask for water, the minimal element of survival, from a woman. He gets more than he asks for: he is nourished" (121). Block rightly decides that "the significance of Jael's substitution of milk for water is not clear" (207). Brenner sees water as a male image and milk as a female one so that milk "represents a transference from the male into its corresponding female symbolism. . . . Both stand for false nurture and death" (*VT* 40 [1990] 132). Brensinger may be right in surmising Jael's action is "an indication of generosity that probably gives him a sense of false security" (66). Ackerman sees that Jael "makes a special occasion of the war leader's visit, providing him with the only hints of support and compassion that he has seen in his long day of battle" (*Warrior, Dancer,* 90). Younger properly interprets the scene: "Jael demonstrates ancient Near Eastern hospitality in giving him milk and covering him. These actions disarm Sisera even more" (144). Bal contends that "what Jael offers him are the basic attributes of maternity: protection, rest, and milk" (*Murder and Difference,* 121). But Schneider (79) follows Boling (98) in seeing the milk as having a "soporific effect on him and so the milk was served to drug him." Bal (*Murder and Difference,* 62–63) wants to talk in terms of ritual enactment in the presentation of this scene and see this on multiple levels, so that the offer of water is not only a sign of hospitality but also part of the ritual of wife selection.

Repeating the description of v 18, this verse ends with the imagination-stirring statement: she covered him. Lindars is right in rejecting any interpretation that the poet suggests true sexual intimacy occurring between Jael and Sisera, for this "confuses the distinction between the actual narrative and the ironical overtones" (277).

20 Lying in Jael's bed, so to speak, Sisera takes command of the situation like a true general, ordering her to stand guard in the doorway of the tent and lie to whoever appears on the scene. Schneider describes the scene well: "Since he was an army leader he was presumably used to issuing commands, particularly in the masculine imperative. Its use here magnifies how comfortable and unsuspecting he was" (80). Similarly, Bal says, "it is possible to see in the masculine form a final attempt on Sisera's part to regain his former role as commander: he is accustomed to giving orders to men" (*Murder and Difference,* 121).

Sisera does not realize it, but his words are full of irony. Jael is told to answer, "no one" or "no man." When a man does come to Jael's door, the answer will be true: no one is there, only a corpse. Bal goes even further: "Sisera ceased being a man from the moment he entered the tent, bereft of his chariots and his army, shirking the battle of men against men, giving himself up 'into the hand of a woman.' . . . At the end of the narrative, there are no men left" (*Murder and Difference,* 92).

21 Jael does not obey orders well. She calmly picks up a tent peg and places the hammer in her hand and approaches Sisera secretly. She drives the tent peg into his temple and on into the ground. He is pegged down for good. Lindars says "these tools belong to Jael's way of life, and so explain why she used them for this purpose" (276). Similarly, Bal emphasizes that "the task of pitching the tent was the woman's responsibility" (*Murder and Difference*, 59) so we should not be surprised that Jael has "the instruments of murder at her disposal" (60). Meanwhile all this time Sisera has slept soundly, being exhausted. One Hebrew word gives the climax of the story: וַיָּמֹת, "and he died." What a climax: the great general dies in a woman's bed as she disobeys orders and pegs him down to death. As Fewell and Gunn describe it, "The mighty man has become a vulnerable child; the virile man lies impotent" (*JAAR* 58 [1990] 393). Or as Niditch points out, "Expectations about her own soft side as a woman make her deadly. The Israelite writer identifies with the power of the feminine. She who is expected to be weak turns the male warrior into the woman raped, a theme drawn much more overtly in the version in 5:27" (67).

22 The denouement, introduced by וְהִנֵּה, "just then," quickly wraps up the loose ends. The story's ending or denouement comes not where the story began but in the tent of Jael. Barak suddenly appears on the scene still pursuing Sisera. Block realizes that Barak is "doing everything in his power to negate the divine word." He "succumbs to the call of ambition" (208). As she had done to Sisera, so Jael comes out to meet Barak. She has an unexpected message for him. Murray notes that "Barak is twice summoned with the same imperative by a woman, but with what different prospects!" ("Narrative Structure and Technique," 173). Continuing to disobey Sisera's orders, Jael invites Barak into her tent to see "the man you are seeking." Look here: Sisera fallen dead, the peg in his temple. Amit suggests that "Jael's statement to Barak shows that she recognized her guest and all her actions were planned in advance" (*JSOT* 39 [1987] 98).

Webb says the denouement (which he sees as beginning with the Sisera and Jael incident) "is reached with the ironic juxtaposition of victor and vanquished in the tent of Jael, the woman who has in effect conquered them both: Sisera, by depriving him of his life, and Barak, by depriving him of the honour that should have been his as the chosen deliverer" ([1987] 135).

Yee provides an excellent summary of the author's portrait of potential leader Barak: "Through his emphasis on Deborah's gender at her introduction, through her reminder to Barak of God's command, through Barak's reluctance to enter the battle without Deborah, and through her foretelling of Barak's loss of honor, not only in his inability to kill Sisera but also in witnessing a woman accomplish what he has failed to do, the author cumulatively throws into relief Barak's shaming by the female" (*Semeia* 61 [1993] 116).

Story complete, all characters accounted for, the prose narrative has ended. And the glory has gone not to Barak, not to Deborah, but to Jael, the woman with the tent peg. And yet, as Grottanelli underlines, "Jael's deed is not only the behavior of a heroic female deceiver, but also the (doubly) guilty action of a breaker of covenant relationship" (*SMRS* 11 NS [1987] 160). Must Israel rely on covenant breakers, guilty of treason in their own family, to provide leadership?

Soggin tries to set up a historical situation that could explain how Israel could glorify "an action which, while it turned out well for Israel, could in no way be reconciled with existing practice among all civilized peoples from time immemorial" (78). So he posits a double relationship of the Kenites, one based on kinship with Israel and one based on an alliance with the Canaanites, that came to a head and forced a decision when Canaanites joined forces with Philistines against Israel. He also explains Jael's individual actions as what is necessary for a weak, defenseless woman: "the woman, incapable because of her own weakness of preventing the fugitive general from entering her tent, pretended to accede to his request, only at a later stage to act in accordance with what she considered to be her real duty." Still Soggin thinks "the scene remains sinister." It "cannot but raise negative reactions in us." The episode "seems to add to Yahweh's victory in a superfluous, not to say damning way." So he explains its incorporation into the Deuteronomistic history despite its "not very clear function." This "small local feud" featuring "a wretched assassination against all accepted rules . . . was probably rooted too deeply in the tradition for the Deuteronomists to be able to suppress it."

Aside from missing the important theme of the weakness of Israel expressed in the weakness of leadership, Soggin assumes that local tradition determined the choice of material for the final editor of Judges. One might argue on the opposite side that the editor picked up whatever traditions still remained current at his date of writing if one sees this truly as a seventh-century compilation. I would rather think that the editor in the late tenth century chose from the current traditions those materials that helped him explain the nature and purpose of Israel. He could assume his audience knew the traditions, as seen in the poet's casual references to Jael and Shamgar. He spotlighted how far a person loyal to Israel's traditions would go in defeating Yahweh's enemies even if it meant violating rules of ethics and hospitality.

23–24 In the closing verses of the chapter, the narrator lays out the historical significance of this story of reversal of gender roles, loss of honor, and betrayal of treaties. Even here, he attaches a bit of a surprise ending. The credit goes to God, not to any human. "God subdued Jabin." Even when God subdues the enemy, however, in the "period of the judges" the enemy does not stay subdued. Rather, the fight against Jabin continued for a long time before the sons of Israel totally subdued him. With only women for leaders and without a God-raised leader, the Israelites could turn only to the wiles of women and the decisions of Yahweh to know when to be gracious to the Canaanites as they fought those who remained in the land.

Explanation

Here then is an ironic prophetic battle story with four main characters: Deborah, Sisera, Barak, and Jael. Two subordinate characters play supporting roles—Jabin and Heber. Amit (*JSOT* 39 [1987] 89–111) would argue that Yahweh is the only main character, all others being equal to one another and subordinate to God. She might be right if she were correct in assuming that the basic question of the story is, who is savior? But the story hinges not on the question of who is savior but on the issue of leadership, as in the entire book, and how the leader can forfeit justified glory. God as savior is assumed. Barak as unwilling general is central to the narrative. Jael as surprise character is the ultimate hero even though she appears only in the final scene.

The story itself plays out on three levels: (1) Behind the scenes stands Jabin, king of the Canaanites, and the Israelites.

(2) The opening scene features Deborah the prophetess sending for and com-

missioning Barak the general. Also featured is Yahweh, the God of Israel, promising to deploy Sisera, Jabin's general, and sell him into Barak's hands. The scene concludes with the tension-forming statement that the narrative must resolve: "You will not receive your glory. . . . For into a woman's hand Yahweh will sell Sisera" (v 9). Now the framework language of "selling into the hand of" is reduced from the level of nations to that of individuals. It is no longer Jabin and Canaan against the children of Israel. Now it is Sisera versus an unnamed woman, apparently Deborah. But Deborah quietly vanishes from the scene, and Barak reappears only in the denouement after the climax of the narrative has been reached.

(3) The climactic scene is reduced to Sisera and the wife of Heber. What at first glance appears to open the door to romance quickly transforms itself into a murder account. Placed in the setting of the introduction, the murder account becomes the climax to a prophetic-battle account. But the climax creates not a normal battle story but a parody on a battle story. For the tension that must be resolved is not who will win the battle but who will get credit for the victory. And the resolution is not that the children of Israel win the battle and get credit. It is not that the God-called general is the hero and gets credit for the victory. It is not even that God's faithful prophetess accompanies the general into battle and gets credit for victory. The parody of the prophetic-battle story reduces the battle to a one-on-one confrontation between a man and a woman with the man sleeping in the woman's sleeping quarters. Here Jael, the woman with Mosaic connections, wins the battle, kills the enemy general, and gains credit for victory.

Brensinger concludes: "The story itself gives only limited attention to the important battle, placing stress instead on the individual conquest of the opposing general at the hands of an unlikely foe. Throughout, the all-consuming issue focuses not so much on who wins the battle, but on who among the earthly participants receives the credit (4:9). As such, the climax of the story comes not in verse 15, but in verse 21" (62).

Here, then, is an entertaining way of highlighting the problem of leadership in Israel. Murray phrases the theme as "the subjection, at once self-imposed but divinely-ordered, of presumed authority-bearing men to presumed subservient women" ("Narrative Structure and Technique," 177). As Schneider summarizes chap. 4, "The story focuses on Israel's plight and her need to rely on foreigners and women as a result of the decline in Israel's leadership. The decline is not because of Deborah's actions, which are praised in Judges, but because she had to carry them out at all, since the men would not. Following this episode the dichotomy between military and political leadership changed in Israel" (82).

Or as Grottanelli phrases it, "The whole textual evidence, both in the prose narrative and in the Song, may be seen as a play on the rather ridiculous helplessness of *both* male protagonists, Baraq and Sisera . . . and on the power of the female figures, who are the only really active figures in the whole narrative" (*SMRS* 11 NS [1987] 159).

In this story, then, we see a hesitant man; a woman who functions to bring justice among God's people and to announce God's word to his people without the text reporting that she was officially raised to do; and a woman who breaks a peace treaty her husband had made—and by doing so conquers the enemy of God's people. Obviously, the latter gains the glory, while Deborah faithfully fulfills her functions for God.

b. The Poetic Version (5:1–31)

Bibliography

Ackerman, J. S. "Why Is Miriam Also among the Prophets? (And Is Zipporah among the Priests?)." *JBL* 121 (2002) 47–80. **Ackroyd, P. R.** "The Composition of the Song of Deborah." *VT* 2 (1952) 160–62. ———. "Note to **parzon* = 'iron' in the Song of Deborah." *JSS* 24 (1979) 19–20. **Adler, R.** "A Mother in Israel: Aspects of the Mother Role in Jewish Myth." In *Beyond Androcentrism: New Essays on Women and Religion*. Ed. R. M. Gross. Missoula, MT: Scholars Press, 1977. 237–55. **Ahlstrom, G. W.** "Judges 5:20f and History." *JNES* 36 (1977) 287–88. **Albright, W. F.** "Some Additional Notes on the Song of Deborah." *JPOS* 2 (1922) 284–85. ———. "The Song of Deborah in the Light of Archaeology." *BASOR* 62 (1936) 26–31. **Alter, R.** *Art of Biblical Poetry*. 43–50. **Amit, Y.** "Judges 4: Its Content and Form." *JSOT* 39 (1987) 89–111. **Auffret, P.** "En ce jour-là Debora et Baraq chantèrent: Étude structurelle de Jg 5,2–31." *SJOT* 16 (2002) 113–50. **Ballentine, S.** *Prayer in the Hebrew Bible*. Overtures to Biblical Theology. Minneapolis: Fortress, 1993. 220–24. **Barredo, M. A.** "El cántico de Débora (Jue 5,1–31): Perfiles literarios y teológicos." *VyV* 56 (1998) 327–70. **Basser, H. W.** "History of Interpretation to Judges 5:4–5 with Special Attention to Rabbi Yosef Kara." *REJ* 164 (2005) 9–32. **Bechmann, U.** *Das Deboralied zwischen Geschichte und Fiktion: Eine exegetische Untersuchung zu Richter 5*. St. Ottilien: EOS, 1989. **Becker-Spörl, S.** "Krieg, Gewalt und die Rede von Gott im Deboralied (Ri 5)." *BK* 51 (1996) 101–6. ———. *Und sang Debora an jenem Tag: Untersuchungen zu Sprache und Intention des Deboraliedes (Ri 5)*. Europäische Hochschulschriften 620. Theology Series 23. Frankfurt am Main: Lang, 1998. **Beyerle, S.** "Der Name Issachar." *BN* 62 (1992) 51–60. **Blenkinsopp, J.** "Ballad Style and Psalm Style in the Song of Deborah: A Discussion." *Bib* 42 (1961) 61–76. **Brachman, A. J.** "Judges 5:2." *JQR* 39 (1949) 412–14. **Brekelmans, C. H. W.** "Some Translation Problems in Judges V 29." *OTS* 15 (1970) 170–73. **Caquot, A.** "Les tribus d'Israël dans la Cantique de Débora (Juges 5, 13–17)." *Sem* 36 (1986) 47–70. **Cathcart, K.** "The 'Demons' in Judges 5.8a." *BZ* 21 NS (1977) 111–12. **Cazelles, H.** "Débora (Jud. V 14), Amaleq et Makir." *VT* 24 (1974) 235–38. **Chaney, M. L.** "ḤDL-II and the 'Song of Deborah': Textual, Philological, and Sociological Studies in Judges 5, with Special Reference to the Verbal Occurrences of ḤDL in Biblical Hebrew." PhD diss., Harvard University, 1976. **Coogan, M. D.** "A Structural and Literary Analysis of the Song of Deborah." *CBQ* 40 (1978) 143–66. **Craigie, P. C.** "Deborah and Anat: A Study of Poetic Imagery (Judges 5)." *ZAW* 90 (1978) 374–81. ———. "A Note on Judges V 2." *VT* 18 (1968) 397–99. ———. "Parallel Word Pairs in the Song of Deborah." *JETS* 20 (1977) 15–22. ———. "A Reconsideration of Shamgar Ben Anath (Judg 3.31 and 5.6)." *JBL* 92 (1972) 239–40. ———. "Some Further Notes on the Song of Deborah." *VT* 22 (1972) 349–53. ———. "The Song of Deborah and the Epic of Tukulti-Ninurti." *JBL* 88 (1969) 253–65. ———. "Three Ugaritic Notes on the Song of Deborah." *JSOT* 2 (1977) 33–49. **Cross, F. M.** "The Ideologies of Kingship in the Era of the Empire: Conditional Covenant and Eternal Decree." In *Canaanite Myth and Hebrew Epic*. Cambridge: Harvard UP, 1973. 220–73. **Crown, A. D.** "Judges v. 15b–16." *VT* 17 (1967) 240–42. **Dehan, N.** "Concerning מחצצים and בפרע פרעות in the Song of Deborah (Judg 5:2,11)" (Heb.). *Beit-Miqra* 45 (2000) 171–76. **Dempster, S.** "Mythology and History in the Song of Deborah." *WTJ* 41 (1978) 33–53. **Diebner, B. J.,** and **H. Schult.** "Wann sang Debora ihr Lied?" *ACEBT* 14 (1995) 106–30. **Dijk-Hemmes, F. van.** "Blessed among Women: A Mother in Israel and a Virgin in the Church." In *The Double Voice of Her Desire*. Ed. J. Bekkenkamp and F. Dröes. Trans. D. E. Orton. Leiden: DEO, 2004. 89–109. ———. "Mother and a Metaphor in the Song of Deborah." In

Feminist Companion to Judges (1993). Ed. A. Brenner. 110–14. **Eissfeldt, O.** "Der Gott des Tabor und seine Verbreitung." In *Kleine Schriften*. Ed. R. Sellheim and F. Maass. Vol. 2. Tübingen: Mohr, 1963. 29–54. **Elliger, K.** "Debora, 'Mutter in Israel.'" In *Zwischen Ohnmacht und Befreiung: Biblische Frauengestalten*. Ed. K. Walter. Freiburg: Herder, 1988. 53–61. **Engberg, R. M.** "Historical Analysis of Archaeological Evidence: Megiddo and the Song of Deborah." *BASOR* 78 (1940) 4–9. **Eynde, S. van den.** "Are Jael (Judg 5:24) and Mary (Luke 1:42) Blessed *Above* or *Among* Women?" In *XII Congress of the International Organization for Septuagint and Cognate Studies, Leiden, 2004*. SBLSCS 54. Atlanta: SBL, 2006. 81–94. **Fewell, D. N.,** and **D. M. Gunn.** "Controlling Perspectives: Women, Men and the Authority of Violence in Judges 4 and 5." *JAAR* 58 (1990) 389–411. **Fokkelman, J. P.** "The Song of Deborah and Barak: Its Prosodic Levels and Structure." In *Pomegranates and Golden Bells*. Ed. D. P. Wright et al. 595–628. **Freedman, D. N.** "Early Israelite History in the Light of Early Israelite Poetry." In *Unity and Diversity*. Ed. H. Goedicke and J. J. M. Roberts. Baltimore: Johns Hopkins UP, 1975. 3–34. ———. *Pottery, Poetry, and Prophecy*. Winona Lake, IN: Eisenbrauns, 1980. 147–60. **Fritz, V.** "Das Ende der Spätbronzezeitlichen Stadt Hazor Stratum XIII und die Biblische Überlieferung in Josua 11 und Richter 4." *UF* 5 (1973) 123–39. **Gal, Z.** "The Settlement of Issachar: Some New Observations." *Tel Aviv* 9 (1982) 79–86. **Garbini, G.** "Il cantico di Debora." *La parola del passato* 178 (1978) 5–31. ———. "*Parzon* 'Iron' in the Song of Deborah." *JSS* 23 (1978) 23–24. **Gerleman, G.** "The Song of Deborah in the Light of Stylistics." *VT* 1 (1951) 168–70. **Gillingham, S. E.** *The Poems and Psalms of the Hebrew Bible*. Oxford: Oxford UP, 1994. **Globe, A.** "Judges v. 27." *VT* 25 (1975) 362–67. ———. "The Literary Structure and Unity of the Song of Deborah." *JBL* 93 (1974) 493–512. ———. "The Muster of the Tribes in Judges 5.11e–18." *ZAW* 87 (1975) 169–84. ———. "The Text and Literary Structure of Judges 5,4–5." *Bib* 55 (1974) 168–78. **Goodwin, C.** "The Meaning of Judges v. 8b–13." *JBL* 63 (1944) 257–62. **Graetz, H.** "Das Deborah-Lied." *MGWJ* 31 (1882) 193–207. **Grant, E.** "Deborah's Oracle." *AJSL* 36 (1919–20) 295–301. **Gray, J.** "A Cantata of the Autumn Festival: Psalm LXVIII," *JSS* 22 (1977) 2–26. ———. "Israel in the Song of Deborah." In *Ascribe to the Lord*. FS P. C. Craigie, ed. L. Eslinger and G. Taylor. JSOTSup 67. Sheffield: JSOT Press, 1988. 421–55. **Grether, O.** *Das Deboralied: Ein metrische Rekonstruktion*. Gütersloh: Bertelsmann, 1941. **Grottanelli, C.** "L'Inno a Hermes e il Cantico di Deborah: Due facce di un tema mitico." *RSO* 56 (1982) 27–37. ———. "The Story of Deborah and Barak: A Comparative Approach." *SMRS* 11 NS (1987) 149–64. **Guillaume, P.** "Deborah and the Seven Tribes." *BN* 101 (2000) 18–21. **Gunneweg, A. H. J.** "Über den Sitz im Leben der sogenannten Stammesprüche (Gen 49 Dtn 33 Jdc 5)." *ZAW* 76 (1964) 244–55. **Halpern, B.** "The Resourceful Israelite Historian: The Song of Deborah and Israelite Historiography." *HAR* 76 (1983) 379–401. **Harrington, D. J.** "The Prophecy of Deborah: Interpretative Homiletics in Targum Jonathan of Judges 5." *CBQ* 48 (1986) 432–42. **Hauser, A. J.** "Parataxis in Hebrew Poetry." *JBL* 99 (1980) 23–41. ———. "Two Songs of Victory: A Comparison of Exodus 15 and Judges 5." In *Directions in Biblical Hebrew Poetry*. Ed. E. R. Follis. JSOTSup 40. Sheffield: JSOT Press, 1987. 265–84. **Hendel, R. S.** "Where Is Mount Sinai?" *BRev* 16 (2000) 8. **Hillers, D. R.** "A Note on Judges 5,8a." *CBQ* 27 (1965) 124–26. **Janzen, J. G.** "The root *pr* in Judges v 2 and Deuteronomy xxxii 42." *VT* 39 (1989) 393–406. **Kallai, Z.** "The Twelve Tribe Systems of Israel." *VT* 47 (1997) 53–90. **Keller, S.** *Parallelism in Hebrew Poetry*. HSM 20. Missoula, MT: Scholars Press, 1979. 156–63. **Knauf, E. A.** "Zum Text von Ri 5,14." *Bib* 64 (1983) 428–29. **Lapp, P.** "Taanach, by the Waters of Megiddo." *BA* 30 (1967) 9–20. **Levin, C.** "Das Alter des Deboralieds." In *Fortschreibungen: Gesammelte Studien zum Alten Testament*. BZAW 316. Berlin: de Gruyter, 2003. 124–41. **Levin, M. Z.** "A Protest against Rape in the Story of Deborah" (Heb.). *Beit-Miqra* 25 (1979) 83–84. **Lewis, T. J.** "The Songs of Hannah and Deborah: *ḥdl-II* ('growing plump')." *JBL* 104 (1985) 107. **Lindars, B.** "Deborah's Song: Women in the Old Testament." *BJRL* 65

(1982–83) 158–75. ———. "The Israelite Tribes in Judges." In *Studies in the Historical Books of the Old Testament.* VTSup 30 (1979) 95–112. **Lipiński, E.** "Juges 5, 4–5 et Psaume 68, 8–11." *Bib* 48 (1967) 185–206. **Longman, T.** "Psalm 98: A Divine Warrior Victory Song." *JETS* 27 (1984) 267–74. **Margulis, B.** "An Exegesis of Judges v 8." *VT* 15 (1965) 66. **Mathys, H.-P.** *Dichter und Beter: Theologen aus spätalttestamentlichen Zeit.* OBO 132. Freiburg: Universitätsverlag, 1994. **Mayes, A. D. H.** "The Historical Context of the Battle against Sisera." *VT* 19 (1969) 353. **Miller, G. P.** "A Riposte Form in the Song of Deborah." In *Gender and Law in the Hebrew Bible and the Ancient Near East.* Ed. V. H. Matthews, B. M. Levinson, and T. Frymer-Kensky. JSOTSup 262. Sheffield: Sheffield Academic, 1998. 113–27. **Miller, P. D., Jr.** *The Divine Warrior in Early Israel.* HSM 5. Cambridge: Harvard UP, 1973. 87–102. **Moor, J. C. de.** "Poetic Fragments in Deuteronomy and the Deuteronomistic History." In *Studies in Deuteronomy.* FS C. J. Labuschagne, ed. G. G. Martínez et al. VTSup 53. Leiden: Brill, 1994. 183–96. ———. "The Twelve Tribes in the Song of Deborah." *VT* 43 (1993) 483–93. **Moor, J. C. de,** and **W. G. E. Watson,** eds. *Verse in Ancient Near Eastern Prose.* AOAT 42. Neukirchen-Vluyn: Neukirchener Verlag, 1993. **Müller, H.-P.** "Der Aufbau des Deboraliedes." *VT* 16 (1966) 446–59. ———. "Die hebräische Wurzel *śyḥ.*" *VT* 19 (1969) 361–71. **Murray, D. F.** "Narrative Structure and Technique in the Deborah-Barak Story, Judges iv 4–22." In *Studies in the Historical Books of the Old Testament.* Ed. J. A. Emerton. VTSup 30. Leiden: Brill, 1979. 155–89. **Na'aman, N.** "Literary and Topographical Notes on the Battle of Kishon (Judges IV–V)." *VT* 40 (1990) 423–36. **Neef, H.-D.** "Meroz: Jdc 5,23a." *ZAW* 107 (1995) 118–22. ———. "Der Stil des Deboraliedes (Ri 5)." *ZAH* 8 (1995) 275–93. **Niebuhr, C.** *Versuch einer Reconstellation des Debora-liedes.* Chicago: University of Chicago Press, 1893. **Niemann, H. M.** "Taanach und Megiddo: Überlegungen zur strukturell-historischen Situation zwischen Saul und Salomo." *VT* 52 (2002) 93–102. **O'Connor, M.** *Hebrew Verse Structure.* Winona Lake, IN: Eisenbrauns, 1980. 487–93. **Ottoson, M.** *Gilead: Tradition and History.* ConBOT 3. Lund: Gleerup, 1969. **Patterson, R.** "The Song of Deborah." In *Tradition and Testament.* FS C. L. Feinberg, ed. J. S. Feinberg and P. D. Feinberg. Chicago: Moody, 1981. 123–60. **Pfeiffer, H.** *Jahwes Kommen von Süden: Jdc 5; Hab 3; Dtn 33 und Ps 68 in ihrem literatur- und theologiegeschichtlichen Umfeld.* FRLANT 211. Göttingen: Vandenhoeck & Ruprecht, 2005. **Piatti, T.** "Una nuova interpretazione metrica, textuale, exegetica del canto di Debora." *Bib* 27 (1946) 65–106, 161–209. **Poethig, E. B.** "The Victory Song Tradition of the Women of Israel." PhD diss., Union Theological Seminary, New York, 1985. **Rabin, C.** "Judges 5:2 and the Ideology of Deborah's War." *JJS* 6 (1955) 125–34. **Rainey, A. F.** "The Military Camp Ground at Taanach by the Waters of Megiddo" (Heb.). *ErIsr* 15 (1981) 61–66. **Rietzschel, G.** "Zu Jdc 5,8." *ZAW* 81 (1969) 236–37. ———. "Zu Jdc 5, 14b–15a." *ZAW* 83 (1971) 211–25. **Robertson, D. A.** *Linguistic Evidence in Dating Early Hebrew Poetry.* SBLDS 3. Missoula, MT: Society of Biblical Literature, 1972. **Rose, M.** "'Siebzig Könige aus Ephraim' (Jdc V 14)." *VT* 26 (1976) 447–52. **Sáenz-Badillos, A.** "Tradición griega y texto hebreo del Canto de Débora (Jue 5)." *Sefarad* 33 (1973) 251–52. **Sawyer, J. F. A.** "'From heaven fought the stars' (Judges v 20)." *VT* 31 (1981) 87. **Scherer, A.** "Der Rhythmus der Schlacht: Die poetische Sprachgestalt von Jdc 5,19–22." *ZAW* 117 (2005) 529–42. **Schloen, J. D.** "Caravans, Kenites, and *Casus Belli:* Enmity and Alliance in the Song of Deborah." *CBQ* (1993) 18–38. **Schreiner, J.** "Textformen und Urtext des Deboraliedes in der Septuaginta." *Bib* 42 (1961) 173–200. ———. "Zum B-Text des griechischen Canticum Deborae." *Bib* 42 (1961) 333–58. **Schulte, H.** "Richter 5: Das Debora-Lied: Versuch einer Deutung." In *Die Hebräische Bibel und ihre zweifache Nachgeschichte.* FS R. Rendtorff, ed. E. Blum et al. Neukirchen-Vluyn: Neukirchener Verlag, 1990. 177–91. **Seale, M. S.** "Deborah's Ode and the Ancient Arabian Qasida." *JBL* 81 (1962) 343–47. **Seeman, D.** "The Watcher at the Window: Cultural Poetics of a Biblical Motif." *Proof* 24 (2004) 1–50. **Segond, A.** *Le Cantique de Débora.* Geneva: Kündig, 1900. **Sellin, E.** "Das Deboralied." In *Festschrift O. Procksch zum 60. Geburtstag.* Ed. A. Alt. Leipzig: Hinrichs, 1934. 149–66. **Shaw, J.** "Constructions of Women in Readings of the Song of Deborah." In *Anti-Covenant*. Ed. M. Bal. 113–32. **Sharon, D. M.** "Choreography of an Intertextual Allusion to Rape in Judges 5:24–27." In *Bringing the Hidden to Light: The Process of Interpretation*. FS S. A. Geller, ed. K. F. Kravitz and D. M. Sharon. Winona Lake, IN: Eisenbrauns, 2007. 249–70. **Smend, R.** *Yahweh War & Tribal Confederation: Reflections on Israel's Earliest History*. Trans. M. G. Rogers. Nashville: Abingdon, 1970. 13–25. **Soggin, J. A.** "Amalek und Ephraim, Richter 5,14." *ZDPV* 98 (1982) 58–62. ———. "Bemerkungen zum Deboralied, Richter Kap. 5: Versuch einer neuen Übersetzung und eines Vorstosses in die älteste Geschichte Israels." *TLZ* 106 (1981) 625–39. ———. "Il canto de Debora, Giudici, cap. V." *RANL* 8.32 (1977) 97–112. ———. "'Heber der Qenit': Das Ende eines biblischen Personnamens?" *VT* 31 (1981) 89–92. **Speier, S.** "On *tsdqt prznw,* Judg 5:11." *JBL* 82 (1963) 216. **Stager, L. E.** "Archaeology, Ecology, and Social History: Background Themes to the Song of Deborah." In *Congress Volume: Jerusalem, 1986*. Ed. J. A. Emerton. VTSup 40. Leiden: Brill, 1988. 221–34. ———. "The Song of Deborah: Why Some Tribes Answered the Call and Others Did Not." *BAR* 15 (1989) 50–64. **Stuart, D. K.** *Studies in Early Hebrew Meter*. HSM 13. Missoula, MT: Scholars Press, 1976. 121–36. **Taylor, J. G.** "The Song of Deborah and Two Canaanite Goddesses." *JSOT* 23 (1982) 99–108. **Tournay, R. J.** "Le Cantique de Débora et ses relectures." In *Texts, Temples, and Tragedies*. FS M. Haran, ed. M. V. Fox et al. Winona Lake, IN: Eisenbrauns, 1996. 195–207. **Tov, E.** "The Textual History of the Song of Deborah in the Text of the LXX." *VT* 28 (1978) 224–32. **Tsevat, M.** "Some Biblical Notes." *HUCA* 24 (1953) 107–14. **Vaccari, P. A.** *Studii critici sopra le antiche versioni latine del Vecchio Testamento*. Vol. 1, *Il cantico di Debora*. Rome: Pontifical Biblical Institute, 1914. **Vincent, M. A.** "The Song of Deborah: A Structural and Literary Consideration." *JSOT* 91 (2000) 61–82. **Walsh, J. P.** *The Mighty from Their Thrones*. OBT. Philadelphia: Fortress, 1987. 70–75. **Waltisberg, M.** "Zum Alter der Sprache des Deboraliedes Ri 5." *ZAH* 12 (1999) 218–32. **Watts, J. W.** "Biblical Psalms outside the Psalter." In *The Book of Psalms: Composition and Reception*. Ed. P. W. Flint and P. D. Miller, Jr. VTSup 99. Leiden: Brill, 2004. 288–309. ———. *Psalm and Story: Inset Hymns in Hebrew Narrative*. JSOTSup 139. Sheffield: Sheffield Academic, 1992. 82–98. **Weinfeld, M.** "'They Fought from Heaven'—Divine Intervention in War in Ancient Israel and in the Ancient Near East" (Heb.). *ErIsr* 14 (1979) 23–30. **Weippert, H.** "Das geographische System der Stämme Israels." *VT* 23 (1973) 76–89. **Weippert, M.** *The Settlement of the Israelite Tribes in Palestine*. London: SCM Press, 1971. **Weiser, A.** "Das Deboralied—Eine gattungs- und traditionsgeschichtliche Studie." *ZAW* 71 (1959) 67–97. **Weisman, Z.** "שרותיה (Judg v 29)." *VT* 26 (1976) 116–20. **Weitzman, S.** *Song and Story in Biblical Narrative: The History of a Literary Convention in Ancient Israel*. Bloomington: Indiana UP, 1997. **Wong, G. T. K.** "Song of Deborah as Polemic." *Bib* 88 (2007) 1–22. **Yadin, Y.** "And Dan, Why Did He Remain with the Ships?" *AJBA* 1 (1968) 8–23. **Yee, G.** "By the Hand of a Woman: The Metaphor of the Woman Warrior in Judges 4." *Semeia* 61 (1993) 99–132. **Younger, K. L., Jr.** "Heads! Tails! Or the Whole Coin?! Contextual Method and Intertextual Analysis: Judges 4 and 5." In *The Canon in Comparative Perspective*. Ed. K. L. Younger, Jr., W. W. Hallo, and B. F. Batto. Scripture in Context 4. Lewiston, NY: Mellen, 1991. 109–45. **Zobel, H.-J.** *Stammesspruch und Geschichte: Die Angaben der Stammessprüche von Gen 49, Dtn 33, und Jdc 5 über die politischen und kultischen Zustände im damaligen 'Israel.'* BZAW 95. Berlin: Töpelmann, 1965.

Translation

[1][a]*That day Deborah and Barak, son of Abinoam, sang:*[b]

> [2]*When the tresses flow freely*[a] *in Israel,*
> *when the people offer themselves freely*[b]*—bless Yahweh!*

³*Listen, O kings! Pay attention, O dignitaries!*
   I for Yahweh,^a *I will sing;*
   I will make music^b *for Yahweh, the God of Israel.*^c

⁴*Yahweh, when you marched out from Seir,*
   when you tramped forth from Edom's territory,
the land shook;
   even the heavens dripped;^a
   yes, the clouds dripped down water.
⁵*The mountains streamed*^a *in Yahweh's*^b *presence;*
   this one of Sinai,^c
   in Yahweh's presence, the God of Israel.

⁶*In the days of Shamgar, son of Anath,*
   in the days of Jael^a *the pathways disappeared;*^b
   those walking^c *the roadways were walking winding ways.*^d
^{7a}*The peasant population*^b *disappeared in Israel;*
   they disappeared until I, Deborah, took a stand.
   I took a stand, a mother in Israel.^c
⁸*They*^a *chose new gods;*
   then war was in the gates.
But shield and spear were not visible
   among forty thousand in Israel.^b
⁹*My heart goes out*^a *to Israel's commanders*
   who offer themselves freely among the people^b—
   blessed be Yahweh.

^{10 a}*Riders of tawny*^b *donkeys,*
   those sitting on blankets,^c
   and pedestrians^d *along the way, ponder this with praise.*^e
¹¹*Amid the sounds of those distributing water*^a *among the watering holes*^b
   there they recite the righteous^c *acts of Yahweh,*
   the righteous acts of the peasant population in Israel.^d
Then the people of Yahweh went down^e *to the gates.*^f

¹²*Get up! Get up, Deborah!*^a
   Get up! Get up! Speak out in song!^b
Stand up, Barak!
   Take captive your captives, son of Abinoam!^c
¹³*Then survivors came down*^a *to face the noble ones;*
   the people of Yahweh came down to me^b *against the warriors.*^c

¹⁴*From*^a *Ephraim they came,*^b *their roots in Amalek,*
   after you, Benjamin, with your armies.^c
From Machir came down leaders,^d
   and from Zebulun those bearing the commander's scepter^e
¹⁵*The officers among Issachar*^a *are with Deborah;*
   indeed, Issachar^b *is right there with Barak*^c

    dashing through the valley stride for stride.[d]
  Among Reuben's clans came great resolution of heart.[e]
[16] *Why did you remain between the campfires*[a]
  listening to the piping for the flocks?
For Reuben's clans came great heart-searching.[b]
[17] *Gilead was settled down across the Jordan.*
  And Dan, why[a] *do you live an alien's life by the ships?*
Asher lived by the sea coast,
  and on its harbors they settled down.[b]
[18] [a] *Zebulun is a people surrendering their own lives*[b] *to death,*
  while Naphtali is on the heights of the battlefield.[c]

[19] *Kings came; they fought;*
  yes, then the Canaanite kings fought
at Taanach by the waters of Megiddo,
  but they took no silver as spoils[a] *of battle.*
[20] *The stars*[a] *fought from heaven;*[b]
  from their orbits they fought[c] *with Sisera.*
[21] *The Kishon River swept them away*[a]—
  the ancient[b] *river,*[c] *the river Kishon.*
  March, my soul; stay strong.[d]
[22] [a] *The horses'*[b] *hoofs beat the ground,*
  galloping, galloping mighty stallions.[c]

[23] [a] *"Curse Meroz,"* *said the angel*[b] *of Yahweh.*
  Place a powerful curse on its[c] *residents,*
for they did not come to help Yahweh,
  to help Yahweh[d] *against the warriors.*
[24] *Blessed above all women is Jael,*
  wife of Heber the Kenite.[a]
  She is blessed above all women in tents.
[25] *"Water," he asked; milk, she gave.*[a]
  In a bowl for nobles
  she offered cream.
[26] *Her hand*[a] *reached out*[b] *for the tent peg,*
  her right hand for the workman's hammer.[c]
She struck Sisera,
  caving his head,
  shattering,[d] *piercing his temple.*
[27] *Between her feet his knees gave way; he fell.*[a]
  He lay between her feet.
His knees gave way; he fell.[b]
  Where his knees gave way, there he fell—destroyed.

[28] *Through the window she looked;*
  she cried[a]—*the mother of Sisera*—*through the lattice,*
"Why does his chariot linger in coming?
  Why the delay in the rumbling of his chariots?"

²⁹ *The wisest*ᵃ *of her staff answer her;*
*even she turns her words to herself.*ᵇ
³⁰ *"Aren't they finding, dividing the spoil?*
A young girl, or two for the chief hero,
*colored cloth as spoil for Sisera,*ᵃ
yes, spoil of colored embroidery—ᵇ
*two pieces of colored embroidery*ᶜ
*from the necks of the spoil. "*ᵈ

³¹ *So may all your enemies face destruction, O Yahweh,*
*but may those who love him*ᵃ *be like the mighty sun as it rises.*

The land had rest for forty years.

Notes

1.a. Tov (*VT* 28 [1978] 225) notes, "Within the complicated text history of the Greek texts of Judges, the text of the Song of Deborah suffered more than any other chapter probably because of its wide diffusion and possible liturgical use."

1.b. LXXᴮ reads ἦσαν, "they were," instead of MT, LXXᴬ's תָּשַׁר, ᾖσεν, "they sang."

2.a. The meaning of בִּפְרֹעַ פְּרָעוֹת is much discussed; *HALOT* suggests "to let the hair on the head hang loosely" either in locks or hanging free and unplaited, but also points to a possible meaning of "for the leaders, the leaders in Israel" and to Craigie's suggestion, "to devote oneself wholly to" (*VT* 18 [1968] 397–99). LXXᴬ reads ἐν τῷ ἄρξασθαι ἀρχηγούς, "while the rulers ruled," while LXXᴮ reads ἀπεκαλύφθη ἀποκάλυμμα, "the revelation was revealed." See Lindars (225–27) and Niditch (70) for a list of theories with supporting evidence for a variety of translations.

2.b. LXXᴬ reads ἐν προαιρέσει λαοῦ, "in the people's choice," while LXXᴮ reads ἐν τῷ ἑκουσιασθῆναι λαόν, "when the people volunteered themselves freely." Niditch takes a different tack: "Vat and OL read *akousiasthēnai* rather than the equivalent to *ndb, hekousiasthēnai*, resulting in 'when the people had sinned through ignorance' (Vat) and 'in the stubbornness of the people' (OL). A misreading of an earlier translation of Hebrew *ndb* thus leads to an interesting image that plays on the recurring theme of Israel's backsliding" (71).

3.a. A few Heb. MSS do not have "I for Yahweh."

3.b. LXXᴬ reads δυνατοί ἐγὼ τῷ κυρίῳ ᾄσομαι ψαλῶ τῷ θεῷ Ισραηλ, "strong rulers; I will sing to the Lord; I will make music to the God of Israel," while LXXᴮ reads ἐγώ εἰμι τῷ κυρίῳ ἐγώ εἰμι ᾄσομαι ψαλῶ τῷ κυρίῳ τῷ θεῷ Ισραηλ, "I myself am in the Lord; it is I who will sing; I will make music to the Lord, to the God of Israel." Thus LXXᴬ joins a few Heb. MSS in not witnessing the second אָנֹכִי, "I," which is redundant in Heb.

3.c. *BHS*, apparently on metrical grounds, suggests that the last line of the verse is a later addition to the text.

4.a. LXXᴬ reads ἐξεστάθη, "confused, wavered, amazed," for MT נָזֹלוּ; LXXᴮ ἔσταξεν, "dripped." LXXᴮ adds δρόσους, "dew." *BHS* uses Gk. evidence to suggest reading נָמֹסּוּ, "they melted away," or נָמֹשׁוּ, "they were moved or shaken." Niditch (71) notes, "OL reads that heaven 'was in an uproar' or 'disturbed,' an appropriate variant in the scene of cosmogonic activity."

5.a. MT נָזֹלוּ from נזל, "to flow, stream," is often emended (see *BHS*) to זָלֲלוּ *nip̱ʿal* from זלל, "to quake," the interpretation of LXX (compare OL, Syr., Tg.) with ἐσαλεύθησαν.

5.b. LXXᴮ adds Ελωι, "my God," in Aramaic.

5.c. *BHS* says "this one of Sinai" is a later addition to the text, for which the OL may give support.

6.a. Auld (157) wants to read "the days of the yoke" for "the days of Jael," but without sufficient support.

6.b. LXXᴬ (compare OL) reads ἐξέλιπον βασιλεῖς καὶ ἐπορεύθησαν τρίβους ἐπορεύθησαν ὁδοὺς διεστραμμένας, "kings disappeared and they went on paths, they went on winding ways." Block translates "the roads stopped (being used); travelers took to the side trails" (225, n. 335).

6.c. Several Heb. MSS do not have the initial connective *wāw*.

6.d. *BHS* suggests that אָרְחָה might be deleted.

7.a. *BHS* suggests transposing v 7 after v 8.

7.b. The meaning of Heb. פְּרָזוֹן is disputed; *HALOT* offers three meanings: "peasantry, people from the open country" (see LXX^A); "leaders or warriors"; and "iron." LXX^B (compare OL) reads δυνατοί, "strong ones" or "leaders." A few Heb. MSS read פְּרָזוֹת, "open country without walls." Niditch (72) opts here and in v 11 for "ways of life in the unwalled towns" "derived from the term *pĕrāzâ*, meaning 'open region, hamlet' (BDB 826), found in Ezek 38:11; Zech 2:8, lengthened with the ancient adjectival ending."

7.c. LXX^A reads ἐξέλιπεν φραζων ἐν τῷ Ισραηλ ἐξέλιπεν ἕως οὐ ἐξανέστη Δεββωρα ὅτι ἀνέστη μήτηρ ἐν τῷ Ισραηλ, "Peasantry were lacking in Israel; they were lacking until Deborah arose because a mother arose in Israel," while LXX^B (compare OL) reads ἐξέλιπον δυνατοὶ ἐν Ισραηλ ἐξέλιπον ἕως οὐ ἀναστῇ Δεββωρα ἕως οὐ ἀναστῇ μήτηρ ἐν Ισραηλ, "Strong ones were lacking in Israel; they were lacking until Deborah rose up, until a mother in Israel rose up." Lindars (238) demands a first-person pronoun preceding "Deborah" to retain the first-person verbs and so points to the LXX third-person rendering as evidence to change the text and prefers to change it to second person. This may be requiring too much linguistic rigidity of an ancient poetic text. Bal gets even more subtle, seeing the ambiguity as intentional in that "it allows the poetess to suspend the distincton between the voice that sings and those for whom, with whom, it sings, in order to inculcate even more effectively in her audience the value of the community" (*Murder and Difference*, 113–14).

8.a. Lit. "he chose" or "he is choosing" with reference to Israel.

8.b. LXX^A (compare OL) reads ᾑρέτισαν θεοὺς καινοὺς ὡς ἄρτον κρίθινον σκέπην ἐὰν ἴδω σιρομαστῶν ἐν τεσσαράκοντα χιλιάσιν, "they selected new gods as bread made of barley. Protection if I should see a spear among forty thousand." LXX^B reads ἐξελέξαντο θεοὺς καινούς τότε ἐπολέμησαν πόλεις ἀρχόντων θυρεὸς ἐὰν ὀφθῇ καὶ λόγχη ἐν τεσσαράκοντα χιλιάσιν ἐν Ισραηλ, "They chose new gods for themselves. Then the cities of rulers waged war. If a shield or a spear is seen among forty thousand in Israel!" See Lindars (240) for various attempts to emend the text. *HALOT* concludes, "unexplained and still without any clear emendation." REB reads: "They chose new gods, they consorted with demons." The Message (compare NET) interprets, "God chose new leaders, who then fought at the gates." *BHS* emends to read מָאֹז לֹא לָהֶם שְׁעָרִים, "which were unknown to them from that time on." Niditch sees an oath formula here: "the line literally reads, 'Shield, if it was seen.' The implication is, 'I swear, there wasn't one,' or 'May I be cursed if there was one'" (72).

9.a. Lit. (compare OL) "my heart is to those who decree for Israel." *BHS* sees this as a late addition copied from v 2. Niditch writes, "Vat [i.e., LXX^B] and OL translate with the 'law' nuance of the root *ḥqq*, but within the context reference to the head warriors is preferable, a translation that is also possible within the root (i.e., those who make the rules in war)." The Gk. term διατεταγμένα refers to putting something in order, giving commands or orders, and may have a military context.

9.b. LXX^A (compare OL) reads Ισραηλ οἱ δυνάσται τοῦ λαοῦ εὐλογεῖτε τὸν κύριον, "Israel. O rulers of the people, bless the Lord."

10.a. *BHS* suggests transposing v 12 here.

10.b. A. Brenner (*Colour Terms in the Old Testament*, JSOTSup 12 [Sheffield: JSOT Press, 1982] 116–20) places צָחֹר among the secondary colors, describing it as "light-colored" or "bright." *HALOT* says the exact shade is uncertain and points to suggestions of white, yellowish-red, reddish-grey.

10.c. The translations here vary. NKJV (compare Boling, 102) reads "who sit in judges' attire." Niditch (72) points to Ps 83:9 (Heb. 10) to translate "those who dwell in Midian." Most translations use some form of "saddle blankets" or "carpets"; Moore (148) honestly notes that the meaning of the noun is unknown. Niditch (72) points to OL's "Those who go up on chariots, sitting amid the clattering sounds" with no mention of donkeys.

10.d. A few Heb. MSS do not have the connective *wāw;* see *Note* 6.c.

10.e. שִׂיחַ describes some type of personal speaking or expression. Müller (*VT* 19 [1969] 361–71) points to the following possible meanings (see *HALOT*): "1. loud, enthusiastic, emotionally laden speech—praising, lamenting, taunting, mocking, instructing, teaching; 2. to meditate with thanks and praise." *NIDOTTE* notes, "Fluctuating between the act of speaking and thinking, שִׂיחַ takes on more specific connotations in contextual usage. In the present context the emphasis is either on praise, parallel to the previous verse or on personal meditation and pondering." LXX^A reads ἐπιβεβηκότες ἐπὶ ὑποζυγίων καθήμενοι ἐπὶ λαμπηνῶν, "those mounted on mules, sitting in shaded chariots," while LXX^B reads ἐπιβεβηκότες ἐπὶ ὄνου θηλείας μεσημβρίας καθήμενοι ἐπὶ κριτηρίου καὶ πορευόμενοι ἐπὶ ὁδοὺς συνέδρων ἐφ' ὁδῷ, "those mounted on female donkeys at noon (or to the south) sitting on the judgment seat and traveling on the way of council members on the way."

11.a. מְחַצְצִים is a *pi'el* participle from חצץ and occurs only here. The basic meaning is "division," with an apparent reference to those who distribute water among families at the community watering holes or wells. JPS, KJV, NKJV translate "archers," deriving the term from חץ, "arrow." NLT, NRSV, NAB, NIV follow cognate languages that point to a basic meaning of "strike" in reference to playing a musical instrument. (See Robert H. O'Connell, *NIDOTTE*, 4:2; LXX; OL.) NASB and NET see a reference to dividing the flocks of sheep. For the sources of the various conjectures, see Lindars (246). *BHS* looks to the Gk. and suggests that the text is corrupt and should perhaps be read as קוֹל מְחַצְצְרִים, "the sound of blowing (trumpets)." Niditch (72) acknowledges the difficulty of the word as she translates "sound of tambourines" but provides a list of possibilities.

11.b. OL has "in the midst of feasters."

11.c. צְדָקָה refers to "loyalty to the community" (see *HALOT*). The pl. in reference to God often refers to his saving acts that express his loyalty to his covenant oaths with his people; compare 1 Sam 12:7; Ps 103:6; Isa 45:24; Mic 6:5.

11.d. *BHS* suggests that a stich has probably dropped out at this point. For translation options, see *Note* 7.b. above.

11.e. Niditch (73) points "went down" (from ירד) as being from רדד (beat down, subdue) and carries this over to v 13. Stager ("Archaeology, Ecology, and Social History," 226) comes closer to reality in seeing the common word for "go down" as a technical military term indicating an army marching down to battle.

11.f. Lindars (245) wants to delete v 11b as "too fragmentary for metrical analysis and . . . as a misplaced variant of v. 13." LXX^A reads φθέγξασθε φωνὴν ἀνακρουομένων ἀνὰ μέσον εὐφραινομένων ἐκεῖ δώσουσιν δικαιοσύνην κυρίῳ δίκαιοι ἐνίσχυσαν ἐν τῷ Ισραηλ τότε κατέβη εἰς τὰς πόλεις αὐτοῦ ὁ λαὸς κυρίου, "Utter a sound of musical instruments [possibly meaning "those pushing back water"] among those rejoicing there; Let them give forth the righteous acts of the Lord; the righteous ones prevailed in Israel; Then the people of the Lord went down into his city." LXX^B reads διηγεῖσθε ἀπὸ φωνῆς ἀνακρουομένων ἀνὰ μέσον ὑδρευομένων ἐκεῖ δώσουσιν δικαιοσύνας κυρίῳ δικαιοσύνας αὔξησον ἐν Ισραηλ τότε κατέβη εἰς τὰς πόλεις λαὸς κυρίου, "Tell from the sound of the musical instruments among those carrying water there. Let them give forth the righteous acts of the Lord; make righteous acts grow in Israel. Then the people of the Lord went down into the city." *BHS* sees the last line as an addition.

12.a. *BHS* suggests transposing v 12 before v 10. LXX^A reads ἐξεγείρον μυριάδας μετὰ λαοῦ, "wake up ten thousands with the people." *BHS* back translates this to הָעִירִי רְבבוֹת עַם.

12.b. LXX^A ᾠδῆς ἐνισχύων ἐξανίστασο Βαρακ καὶ ἐνίσχυσον Δεββωρα τὸν Βαρακ, "prevailing ones (or strong ones); rise up, Barak! Strengthen Barak, Deborah."

12.c. *BHS* reads שְׁבְיָך, the participial form rather than the noun, on the basis of Isa 14:2 Syr. and Arabic. Niditch (73) translates the OL variant as "Rise up, Deborah, and arouse a thousand, thousands with the people. Rise up, speak with a song in power. Rise up, Barak, and Deborah, strengthen Barak. Take your human booty, son of Abinoam."

13.a. Lindars (250) proclaims the "verse is clearly corrupt." OL opens the verse with "then his strength is magnified." In the MT, ירד appears twice in this verse and has roused commentators to strong debate. Burney notes the early Jewish interpreters seeking to create a *pi'el* form of רדה, "to rule, have dominion over." The form might be seen as a *qal* imperative of ירד, "to go down," as listed in *DCH*. Burney adopts some readings of LXX^B and emendations of the verbs to translate: "Then down to the gates gat the nobles; Yahweh's folk gat them down mid the heroes." This requires extensive amendment and destroys the poetic repetition of the verbs. Most translators agree with Lindars' conclusion that "the existing text can be accepted, if *yrd* is read as perfect as in Targ Pesh LXX, *lāmed* is given possessive force, and '*am* is taken with 13b." The *Translation* follows Lindars except in his interpretation of the preposition ל. For MT אָז יְרַד שָׂרִיד לְאַדִּירִים עָם יְהוָה יְרַד־לִי בַּגִּבּוֹרִים, *BHS* proposes יְרַד יִשְׂרָאֵל בָּאַדִּירִים יְרַד עַם יְהוָה יְרַד־לוֹ בַּגִּבּוֹרִים, "Israel with the nobles went down, the people of Yahweh went down to him with the warriors."

13.b. LXX^B reads κατέβη αὐτῷ, "came down to him."

13.c. Following LXX^B; accents of MT lead to reading "Then the survivors ruled over the nobles, the people; / The Lord ruled over me with the mighty warriors." LXX^A reads πότε ἐμεγαλύνθη ἡ ἰσχὺς αὐτοῦ κύριε ταπείνωσόν μοι τοὺς ἰσχυροτέρους μου, "then his strength (or strong one) was increased (or boasted of). / O Lord, humble for me my strong ones."

14.a. lxx did not recognize מִנִּי as a dialectical or chronological variant to the common preposition and so translated it as if it contained the first personal pronoun, "from me."

14.b. "They came" added for English clarity; lxx cared for the lack of a verb by reading שָׁרְשָׁם as a verb, "to root out." *BHS* says the verse is corrupt and that the versions have a verb. OL has "valley" for Amalek. *BHS* proposes reading אָשְׁרוּ, "they strode" or "they led." See Fokkelman ("Song of Deborah and Barak," 613, with n. 50) for reasons to retain mt's *lectio difficilior* and not read שָׂרִים בְּעַמֵק, "princes in the valley."

14.c. lxx (compare OL) did not understand מְחֹקְקִים in its meaning of "commander" or "ruler" (see *HALOT*) and so apparently derived it from חקק, "to search out."

14.d. *BHS* wants to read the third-person pronoun rather than the second, again with no textual evidence. Niditch (73) follows Coogan (*CBQ* 40 [1978] 164) in comparing this phrase to Hos 5:8 and classifying it as a war cry.

14.e. lxx^A reads λαὸς Εφραιμ ἐτιμωρήσατο αὐτοὺς ἐν κοιλάδι ἀδελφοῦ σου Βενιαμιν ἐν λαοῖς σου ἐξ ἐμοῦ Μαχιρ κατέβησαν ἐξερευνῶντες καὶ ἐκ Ζαβουλων κύριος ἐπολέμει μοι ἐν δυνατοῖς ἐκεῖθεν ἐν σκήπτρῳ ἐνισχύοντος ἡγήσεως, "The people of Ephraim took vengeance on them. In the valley of your brother, O Benjamin, among your people. From me Machir went down searching out. And from Zebulun the Lord waged war for me among the strong ones. From there with a scepter they were issuing strong commands." OL has "from Zebulun the Lord fights for me with the powerful." Soggin (88) says that without some conjecture "the text is incomprehensible." He and *BHS* use the lxx^A reading to change בְּעַמֵלֵק to בְּעַמֵק. Tov (*VT* 28 [1978] 225) considers this a "remote 'doublet,'" that is, "a double translation, one of whose elements is transmitted in a completely different place." Compare the discussion of Lindars, 252–53. Craigie (*VT* 22 [1972] 351–52) uses Egyptian vocabulary to translate שָׁרְשָׁם as "high-ranking officers." Gray ([1986] 285) translates, "From Ephraim they set out thither into the valley," reading מִנִּי אֶפְרַיִם שֻׁרוּ שָׁם בְּעַמֵק. *BHS* wants to read סֵפֶר and interpret it in light of Akkadian *siparru*, "bronze." *BHS* then would transpose v 18 to the end of v 14. All such changes result from our inability to interpret a terse poetic statement that makes linguistic sense, the problem being more a historical one. See *Comment*.

15.a. Based on lxx, Syr., Tg., Vg., and v 18, *BHS* reads for mt וְשָׂרַי, "my princes," שָׂרֵי, the construct form meaning, "princes of."

15.b. *BHS* wants to insert a כ to create a double comparison statement, "and as Issachar so Barak."

15.c. Lit. "and Issachar just so Barak in the valley being sent at his feet." lxx^A reads ἐν Ισσαχαρ μετὰ Δεββωρας ἐξαπέστειλεν πεζοὺς αὐτοῦ εἰς τὴν κοιλάδα ἵνα τί σὺ κατοικεῖς ἐν μέσῳ χειλέων ἐξέτεινεν ἐν τοῖς ποσὶν αὐτοῦ, "In Issachar with Deborah she (or he) sent his infantry into the valley so that you may somehow live in the midst of the shore. He extended his infantry." lxx^B reads ἀρχηγοὶ ἐν Ισσαχαρ μετὰ Δεββωρας καὶ Βαρακ οὕτως Βαρακ ἐν κοιλάσιν ἀπέστειλεν ἐν ποσὶν αὐτοὺς εἰς τὰς μερίδας Ρουβην, "with Deborah and Barak. Thus Barak into the valley he sent on foot into the shares of Reuben." *BHS* notes that the OG did not have "indeed, Issachar is right there with Barak." OL renders, "in Shechem from the tribe of Issachar with Deborah, he/she sent his/her foot soldiers in the valleys."

15.d. *BHS* suggests moving the *soph passuq*, that is, the Hebrew verse divider, up to the next to last line just following בְּרַגְלָיו, "at his feet."

15.e. Lit. "great statutes of heart"; often emended (see *BHS* on basis of a few Heb. mss and Syr.) from חִקְקֵי-לֵב to חִקְרֵי-לֵב, "searchings of the heart," following v 16 below and lxx, where lxx^A reads ἀκριβασμοὶ καρδίας, "careful investigations of the heart," while lxx^B reads ἐξικνούμενοι καρδίαν, "reachings (or searchings) of the heart." One should notice that both lxx versions use different renderings in the phrase in v 16 from that used in v 15. Niditch translates:

> And the princes of Issachar are with Deborah.
> And Issachar, support of Barak,
> > in the valley was sent on foot.
> In the divisions of Reuben,
> > great are the stout of heart.

16.a. Meaning of הַמִּשְׁפְּתַיִם is widely debated. *DCH* (5:564–65) lists five possible meanings: "1. fireplaces or ash heaps; 2. saddlebags; 3. divided sheepfolds; 4. double wall; 5. grazing places." The main argument is from the context. lxx^A simply transliterated the Heb. word. lxx^B reads διγομίας, "double burden or load," basically a guess from the Heb. dual form.

16.b. See *Note* 5:15.b. In v 16 both lxx versions offer significantly different readings. lxx^A reads ἵνα τί μοι κάθησαι ἀνὰ μέσον τῶν μοσφαθαιμ τοῦ εἰσακούειν συρισμοὺς ἐξεγειρόντων τοῦ διελθεῖν εἰς τὰ τοῦ Ρουβην μεγάλοι ἐξιχνιασμοὶ καρδίας, "why do you sit with me in the middle of the *mosphathaim* [Heb. transliteration] to listen to the hissings (or bleatings) of the vigilantes (or of those awakened) of the one who passes through into the things of Reuben. There were great searchings of heart." LXX[B] reads εἰς τί ἐκάθισαν ἀνὰ μέσον τῆς διγομίας τοῦ ἀκοῦσαι συρισμοῦ ἀγγέλων εἰς διαιρέσεις Ρουβην μεγάλοι ἐξετασμοὶ καρδίας, "why did they sit between the double load to hear of the bleatings (hissings) of the messengers ['angels' or 'herds' through an inner Gk. error ἀγγέλων for αγέλων]. In the divisions of Reuben there were great examinations of heart." *BHS* sees the last line as a duplication from v 15. Niditch (74) follows Cross ("Ideologies of Kingship," 235, n. 74) and Halpern (*HAR* 76 [1983] 383) in applying Ugaritic grammar to the Heb. text, transforming "why" into "indeed" or "verily," and moving the nonparticipant tribes into the participant category. Thus Niditch develops here a "catalogue of fighters."

17.a. *BHS* deletes "why" on the basis of two Heb. MSS, Tg., and Vg.

17.b. *BHS* would transpose v 23 here, following v 17.

18.a. *BHS* would transpose v 18 to follow v 14.

18.b. Lit. "Zebulun (is) a people who taunts (or reviles) his own soul."

18.c. *BHS* wants to read שָׂדֵהוּ, "their fields."

19.a. LXX[A] reads πλεονεχίαν ἀργυρίου, "the greediness (or gain or share) of money," while LXX[B] reads δῶρον ἀργυρίου, "the gift of money." OL reads "they dwelled at the waters," removing mention of Megiddo.

20.a. *BHS* transposes the disjunctive accent 'atnāḥ to הכוכבים, "the stars," a move followed by virtually all translations, including the one above.

20.b. A few Heb. MSS place the definite article on "heavens."

20.c. LXX[A] reads ἐκ τοῦ οὐρανοῦ ἐπολέμησαν ἀστέρες ἐκ τῆς τάχεως αὐτῶν ἐπολέμησαν μετὰ Σισαρα, "from the heavens the stars fought; from their battle line they fought with Sisera," while LXX[B] reads ἐξ οὐρανοῦ παρετάχαντο οἱ ἀστέρες ἐκ τρίβων αὐτῶν παρετάχαντο μετὰ Σισαρα, "from heaven the stars lined up for battle; from their paths they lined up in battle with Sisera." OL reads "from their order." *BHS* wants to transpose v 22 here, following v 20.

21.a. LXX[A] reads ἐξέβαλεν αὐτούς, "cast them out."

21.b. LXX[A] reads καδημιμ, a transliteration of Hebrew קדומים, "ancient." OL reads, "The rivers of Kishon threw them out / My foot trampled them / My soul is powerful." *BHS* sees a corrupt text here and says perhaps we should read קדמם, "going into action against them." REB reads, "The torrent of Kishon swept him away, / the torrent barred his flight." NET translates: "The Kishon River carried them off; / the river confronted them—the Kishon River." The Message renders, "The torrent Kishon swept them away, / the torrent attacked them, the torrent Kishon."

21.c. *BHS* deletes the second of three appearances of "river" (נחל) in this verse as redundant and unmetrical.

21.d. LXX reads καταπατήσει αὐτὸν (LXX[A] αὐτούς) ψυχή μου δυνατή, "My mighty soul will trample him (them) down." NET note on 5:21 attributes its translation to Lindars: "This line is traditionally taken as the poet-warrior's self-exhortation, 'March on, my soul, in strength!' The present translation (a) takes the verb (a second feminine singular form) as addressed to Deborah (cf. v. 12), (b) understands נפש *(nefesh)* in its well-attested sense of 'throat; neck' (cf. Jonah 2:6), (c) takes the final *yod* (y) on נפשי *(nafshiy)* as an archaic construct indicator (rather than a suffix), and (d) interprets עז *(oz,* 'strength') as an attributive genitive (literally, 'necks of strength,' i.e., 'strong necks')." NET translates: "Step on the necks of the strong!" *BHS* sees the final line as a later addition to be deleted.

22.a. *BHS* transposes v 22 after v 20.

22.b. LXX[A] (compare OL) reads τότε ἀπεκόπησαν πτέρναι ἵππου αμαδαρωθ [transliteration of Heb. מדהרות] δυνατῶν αὐτοῦ, "then they cut off his horse's hooves, the galloping of his mighty ones," while LXX[B] reads τότε ἐνεποδίσθησαν πτέρναι ἵππου σπουδῇ ἔσπευσαν ἰσχυροὶ αὐτοῦ, "then the horse's hooves were hindered; hurriedly his strong ones hurried on." *BHS* wants to read the MT sg. as a pl., "horses" (סוסים), on the basis of their reading of the original OG and Vg., seeing a case of haplography. As the parallel pl. in the final line, MT apparently intends "horse" to be seen as a collective."

22.c. OL reads, according to Niditch (75), "My foot will assuage them regarding the injustice of his folly."

23.a. *BHS* transposes v 23 to follow v 17.

23.b. *BHS* sees מלאך, "angel," as a later addition.

23.c. LXX[B] reads πᾶς ὁ κατοικῶν αὐτήν, "all its residents."

23.d. LXX[A] reads κυρίου βοηθὸς ἡμῶν κύριος ἐν μαχηταῖς δυνατός, "of the Lord; our help is the Lord; the Mighty One is against the fighters." LXX[B] does not have the second "of the Lord." OL reads,

"Let them see pain; let them see curses. The angel of the Lord cursed those who dwell in it, because they were not found to help, the Lord our helper, the Lord among the powerful fighters." *BHS* follows many Heb. MSS and Syr. in deleting the second "to help Yahweh."

24.a. *BHS* says "the wife of Heber the Kenite" is an addition from 4:17.

25.a. LXX^A inserts pronouns after the verbs: "asked her"; "gave him." OL reads, "He asked for water from her. She gave milk to him in a basin of water. She offered butter to the prince."

26.a. LXX inserts "left" hand.

26.b. Lindars (278) says the "pointing of the MT as a plural form is clearly wrong." He reduces the possibilities to "regular singular with *nun energicum* form of the suffix תִּשְׁלַחְנָה . . . and a postulated energic form of the singular תִּשְׁלְחֶנָּה."

26.c. LXX^A reads εἰς ἀποτομὰς κατακόπων καὶ ἀπέτεμεν Σισαρα ἀπέτριψεν τὴν κεφαλὴν αὐτοῦ καὶ συνέθλασεν καὶ διήλασεν τὴν γνάθον αὐτοῦ, "to the workmen's (or wearied ones') cutting tools and cut off Sisera. She skinned his head and shattered and pierced his jaw." LXX^B reads καὶ ἐσφυροκόπησεν Σισαρα διήλωσεν κεφαλὴν αὐτοῦ καὶ ἐπάταξεν διήλωσεν κρόταφον αὐτοῦ, "and she hammered Sisera. She drove a nail in his head and she struck. She drove a nail into his temple."

26.d. *BHS* says a verb has probably dropped out. Lindars (278) sees מָחֲקָה as an Aramaic gloss on מָחֲקָה.

27.a. *BHS* finds the first line—"between her feet his knees gave way; he fell"—to be deleted as dittography since several Heb. MSS do not witness it. OL reads, "he slept under her feet. Trembling, the miserable one fell."

27.b. LXX^A does not translate "his knees gave way; he fell."

28.a. LXX did not understand וַתְּיַבֵּב, "she cried." LXX^A reads ἡ μήτηρ Σισαρα διὰ τῆς δικτυωτῆς ἐπιβλέπουσα ἐπὶ τοὺς μεταστρέφοντας μετὰ Σισαρα, "the mother of Sisera peered carefully through the lattice work for those returning with Sisera," while LXX^B reads μήτηρ Σισαρα ἐκτὸς τοῦ τοξικοῦ διότι ἠσχύνθη ἅρμα αὐτοῦ διότι ἐχρόνισαν πόδες ἀρμάτων αὐτοῦ, "the mother of Sisera out of the loophole. Why was his chariot ashamed? [reading the more frequent meaning of בֹּשׁ] Why did the feet of his chariot delay?" *BHS* looks to Gk. evidence and Tg. to read וַתֵּבֶא from נבט, "she looked."

29.a. *BHS* follows a few Heb. MSS, supported by Syr. and Vg., in reading the sg. construct חַכְמַת rather than the MT pl. חַכְמוֹת.

29.b. LXX^A reads καὶ αὐτὴ ἀπεκρίνατο ἐν ῥήμασιν αὐτῆς, "and she answered with her words," while LXX^B reads καὶ αὐτὴ ἀπέστρεψεν λόγους αὐτῆς ἑαυτῇ, "and she returned her words to herself." OL interprets, "the wisdom of her virtue will respond to him."

30.a. *BHS* transposes the disjunctive *'atnāḥ* accent to Sisera.

30.b. *BHS* deletes "yes, spoil of colored embroidery" as dittography.

30.c. *BHS* deletes "colored embroidery."

30.d. Lit. "for the necks of the spoil," but in context שָׁלָל must mean either "the one who takes spoil," or שָׁלָל should be repointed to שֹׁלֵל, "the spoiler," or the LXX tradition is correct in distributing the spoil to Sisera so that the preposition here reflects former ownership rather than future ownership. The last option is reflected in the translation above. LXX^A reads οὐχὶ εὑρήσουσιν αὐτὸν διαμερίζοντα σκῦλα φιλαίζων φίλις εἰς κεφαλὴν δυνατοῦ σκῦλα βαμμάτων Σισαρα σκῦλα βαμμάτων ποικιλίας βαφὴ ποικίλων περὶ τράχηλον αὐτοῦ σκῦλον, "Will not they find him dividing the spoil? He will show friendship to his friends, to each powerful head. The spoil of dyed garments for Sisera. The spoil of dyed garments with embroidery dyed in many colors—the spoil is for his neck." LXX^B reads οἰκτίρμων οἰκτιρήσει εἰς κεφαλὴν ἀνδρός σκῦλα βαμμάτων τῷ Σισαρα σκῦλα βαμμάτων ποικιλίας βάμματα ποικιλτῶν αὐτά τῷ τραχήλῳ αὐτοῦ σκῦλα, "He will surely show compassion to the head of a man. The spoil of dyed garments is to Sisera, the spoil of dyed garments with embroidery. Dyed garments from the embroiderer are these, the spoil for his neck." *BHS* suggests reading שֵׁגָל, "queen," or a preferred solution is to delete שָׁלָל and read it before לְצַוְּארוֹ, "spoil of his neck."

31.a. *BHS* wants to read a second-person rather than a third-person pronominal suffix.

Form/Structure/Setting

See table 5.1 in the appendix to compare one possible example of narrative analysis with form-critical analysis for chap. 5. The narrative elements follow the typical pattern of Hebrew narrative while the genre elements show the genre of each section with its component parts. Note how the narrator can use different genre elements and markers within or even across various narrative elements.

Form. Writing in 1963, Rudolph Smend could casually begin his monograph, "It is a commonplace of Old Testament scholarship that we have before us in the Song of Deborah (Judges 5) the most authentic, if not the only truly authentic, source concerning the time of the Judges." Scholarship over the last forty years has certainly shifted the category to something quite different from commonplace. (See Pfeiffer, *Jahwes Kommen,* 19–116, for a review of the history of research.) One must agree with Younger: "This song poses one of the most difficult passages in the Old Testament. Its date, authorship, text, unity, vocabulary, and structure have been debated by scholars for centuries" and "would easily produce a book in and of itself" (147). Most recently, Niditch has returned to the former position: "The 'Song of Deborah' may be one of the most ancient works of the Hebrew Bible. . . . It may well be that the artistic rendering is rooted in actual wars and battles" (76–77).

One may discuss innumerable problems scholars find with the song. The first is its genre. It is usually allocated to Israel's "victory songs" along with Exod 15. Ackerman points to the literature showing that "women . . . seem to have held the exclusive responsibility for singing victory songs after an Israelite triumph in holy war" (*JBL* 121 [2002] 48). Matthews (78) sees common elements with victory hymns in the repetition of the divine name, the stress on Yahweh's role in victory, use of a water motif, mocking of the enemy's failures, and use of the fall motif for the enemies, leaving room for irony and satire. The basic reference in a victory hymn would be to military victories. See Lindars, 247; Boling, 111. Webb ([1987] 141) sees Yahweh's victories as the "chief burden of the song," but I would argue that Yahweh and his victories must share the thematic spotlight with the celebration of volunteer participation with the people of Yahweh and with the solemn listing and even cursing of those who refused to participate.

Grottanelli decides that "at least these three aspects of the Deborah-Baraq story, i.e., the 'lightning' motif, the heroic duplicity of Jael and the breaking of the peace relationship between Jabin and the Qenite splinter group by that heroine, may be explained only by considering the narrative comparatively and typologically as a specific example of the 'battle' type of myth" (*SMRS* 11 NS [1987] 153). Dempster compares the Song of Deborah to the Baal and Anat texts of Ugarit and finds that "mythical motifs, characteristic of Baal and Anat, are applied to Yahweh and Deborah-Jael" (*WTJ* 41 [1978] 44). Ultimately, Dempster admits, "Although there is the prominence of Canaanite mythological elements in this song, these must be seen as denuded motifs having been extracted from a mythological fertility cycle and transferred into a radical Israelite eschatology. The Song of Deborah itself provides the perfect paradigm for demonstrating this Israelite historical framework, thereby evincing that there is no myth present" (52). Again he notes, "Deborah and Jael . . . take on the warlike characteristics of Anat in this text, but it is at once easily noticed that they are far from being goddesses, consorts of Yahweh; they are creatures of history" (53).

Webb recognizes that much of the problem connected to interpreting the hymn and its structure and genre rests in the "mixed genre (part ballad, part hymn)" ([1987] 139). Blenkinsopp (*Bib* 42 [1961] 61–76) and Lindars (*BJRL* 65 [1982–83] 158–75) point to a secular setting for the material as a war ballad later augmented with hymnic materials. This separates Israel's warfare from her worship, a separation that is far too modern in cast. Weiser (*ZAW* 71 [1959] 67–97) creates an elaborate cultic ritual for the song that is much too complex to result from the simple song. Olson settles simply for a poem that "combines elements of a hymn of praise and a ballad that recounts a story in poetic form" (787). This defines the elements of the poem but does not assign a genre and purpose to the whole artistic piece.

The form of the poem, then, is as complex as its contents. Epic narrative, battle calls, cultic blessings and curses, tribal evaluations, and poetic satire blend together into one complex work that defies categorization into one simple form. If author intentionality carries the greatest weight in assigning form or genre to a piece of literature, then hymnic praise becomes the dominant form here. If quantity of formal elements prevails, then epic narrative ballad comes to the fore. If function in literature has the last say, then a call to tribal unity may be the appropriate category.

Structure. The poem is variously divided into stanzas. Soggin is one of many commentators who would divide the song into sources as well as stanzas. Yet his own discussion shows the difficulty in such source division:

> Thus a different atmosphere seems to prevail in each of the two sections which make up the song: furthermore, the one which is rich in cultic elements seems to have been composed in the train of the second [for Soggin, vv 6–8, 13–30], as it were "lay," song, which is considerably older; however, the operation has been performed with skill, so that the two sections reflect a style and a complex of imagery which is not very different. (96)

Soggin is following the pioneer source-critical work of Wolfgang Richter (*Traditionsgeschichtliche Untersuchungen zum Richterbuch* [1963], 91). The latest to follow this trail are Schulte ("Richter 5: Das Debora-Lied" [1990], 177–91), with a complex story of growth beginning only with 19–22, 24–30 and the story of Sisera, and Pfeiffer (*Jahwes Kommen* [2005]), who sees the oldest part in 5:12*–13a, 18, 19–21a, 22, 24*–27, 28–30 coming from the ninth or eighth century with at least five further layers of redaction.

Coogan gives sufficient evidence to substantiate his claim that "the stanzas in the Song are not independent units but are linked by an extraordinary degree of repetition" (*CBQ* 40 [1978] 154–56). This evidence also shows the literary unity of the poem and so speaks against the many efforts to lop off verses as later additions, even Coogan's desire to ignore v 31 as a cultic addition. Coogan (143–66) gives the most extensive discussion of the structure of the poem and is followed by Webb ([1987] 139–41) in seeing the pattern as vv 2–8, 9–13, 14–18, 19–23, 24–30, thus seeing vv 9 and 23 as each closing a strophe rather than opening a new one. These are transitional verses that close out the preceding theme and lead into the new one.

Lindars (209–10) analyzes the final poem (though he deletes much of it—vv 2–5, 9–11, 31a—as not belonging to the oldest original poem [p. 218]) as vv 2–5, 6–8, 9–11, 12, 13–15a, 15b–17, 18, 19–22, 23, 24–27, 28–30, 31. Jan P. Fokkelman ("Song of Deborah and Barak," 595–628) gives the most detailed analysis of poetic structure, finding 864 syllables, 352 words, 108 cola, 50 verses, 20 strophes, 7 stanzas (2–5, 6–8, 9–13, 14–18, 19–23, 24–27, 28–31ab), and 3 sections or parts (vv 2–8, 9–23, 24–31ab). Younger (147–48) builds on Coogan and Fokkelman to arrive at a structure with five acts made up of seven stanzas comprising twenty strophes. He describes the basic structure as vv 2–8, 9–13, 14–18, 19–22, 23 as transition, 24–31c, narrowing the focus from the nation to ten tribes to two female individuals.

I will look at each stanza in turn and describe its contribution to the narrative description and to the emotional atmosphere the poem creates. The form and function of the parts of the poem gain new meaning and function when placed beside chap. 4 and introduced by 5:1 in the larger narrative. An original historical hymn featuring a call to unity through the use of blessings and curses has been transformed into a victory hymn sung by the victorious leaders.

1. Opening call to individual praise (vv 2–3). The poem opens with a call to praise that moves in two directions: (a) a call to the congregation to praise God for committed leaders and (b) a call to foreign, that is, enemy, kings to hear the individual poet raise praise to God. This gives the entire poem an emotional note of praise and subsumes its entire content under the genre of praise despite the many twists and turns the following content may take. Bal (*Murder and Difference*, 81–82) notes somewhat unexpectedly that the lyric parts of the song "do not affect the factual content of the statements; hence, there is no reason whatsoever to depreciate the historical truth of the narrative parts."

The poem's use of the Hebrew ברכו, "bless," sets the tone for the blessing and curses that follow and almost transforms the poem into a ritual blessing and curse within a national call for unity. Within the victory-song context, these blessings and curses play the subsidiary role of distinguishing participants from nonparticipants, those who share in victory celebration and those who do not.

Ackerman (*Warrior, Dancer*, 34) makes the intriguing, if unlikely, suggestion that v 3 is not a call to listen to a postwar victory song but instead is a "reveille" that summons Yahweh, the divine warrior, to go forth to battle against Sisera. Vv 4–5 would then be Yahweh's response to the call to arms, but this traditional theophany language looks backwards in time before marching forward. Younger sees that "the purpose of the Song of Deborah is to acknowledge and praise Yahweh and those who participated" (158). Block agrees that "the poem draws the reader into the ancient celebrants' praise to God for his gracious intervention in the affairs of the people when they had nowhere else to turn." The poem "was able to express feelings of joy and delight in God (and ridicule the enemy) with an intensity denied him in the conventions of narrative discourse" (184).

2. Report of a theophany (vv 4–5). The reason for praise is theophany, God coming to his people in what Matthews (77) sees as possibly the oldest example of this genre in the Bible. E. S. Gerstenberger observes that the report of a theophany gives "the account of Yahweh's coming, accompanied by an upheaval of nature, in order to rule and judge peoples. . . . Its original setting was perhaps the preparation for holy war, but in psalmic texts it was incorporated into worship services of praise and petition" (*Psalms, Part 2, and Lamentations*, FOTL 15 [Grand Rapids: Eerdmans, 2001] 533). These can be detected in Pss 18, 60, 68, 77, 97, and 114 and Hab 3. McCann points to the nature and theological meaning of theophany. Describing God's appearing, McCann says,

is to portray God's sovereignty on a cosmic scale. . . . The language in verses 4–5 is similar to that in other theophanies (such as Pss. 18:7–15; 29:3–9; 50:1–6; 68:7–8; 97:1–5; 99:1). . . . In short the theophany in Judges 5:4–5 reinforces the conclusion that God is behind all the action described in chapters 4–5, and that it all has ultimately to do with the establishment of life as God intends it. (59–60)

Or as Matthews (77) states it, "The purpose of this divine appearance is to intervene in history to liberate or provide military victory to Israel."

Theophany here presents the emotional setting of past divine experience as a backdrop for present praise of current divine experience and clearly identifies the God to whom praise is being offered. Fokkelman decides that "because it is not connected by the poet to the actual battle that occurs much later in the song, I venture to call this strophe the zero stage. It represents the spiritual origins of the people as the covenantal partner of God" ("Song of Deborah and Barak," 598). This disconnect with the latter parts of the Psalms is hard to justify. The theophany does not stand isolated in the structure of the song. Rather it prepares for all that follows. Hauser shows that

> the power of God through the forces of nature is thus heavily stressed at the beginning of the song, and the reader is led to conclude that in the face of this power the Canaanite kings, their armies, and their chariots (vv. 19–22) are puny and easily swept away. Since vv. 4–5 set the tone with Yahweh in power as the God of creation who controls the forces of nature, there is no need to mention him specifically in vv. 19–22 as a warrior; his might has already determined the outcome of the battle. ("Two Songs of Victory," 269)

Every other unit in the psalm, the Song of Deborah, derives emotional and theological meaning from this theophany report.

3. Historical setting (vv 6–9). The poem turns quickly from past experience and praise to the present situation. Interestingly, the name chosen to place the present events in their context is Shamgar, the one judge who sits so loosely in the formulaic framework of Judges (3:31). Fokkelman sets up Shamgar as representative of the situation in v 8cd, creating "an underlying opposition between the instruments of war and the tools of the peasant" ("Song of Deborah and Barak," 605). This represents a much more modern perspective than that of the poet. Younger decides that in the present context "the mention of Shamgar, son of Anath (see 3:31) is a reminder (resumptive repetition) that a non-Israelite—who used a peasant tool rather than a conventional weapon—delivered Israel" (150). In the original poem this is not resumptive but a reminder of shared knowledge. It becomes resumptive only in the literary context.

Olson observes that "the three judge stories—Ehud, Shamgar, and Deborah-Barak-Jael—are tied together as examples of temporary victories that God leads on behalf of an oppressed Israel through the agency of unexpected human agents" (782). Olson sees only the faithful and effective side of these leaders without noting their signs of weakness. He does admit that "chapters 4–5 contain some seeds of Israel's future deterioration, but these chapters largely celebrate a positive victory over Israel's Canaanite enemies" (74).

Parallel to Shamgar stands Jael, the heroine of chap. 4. Thus Shamgar and Jael are set up as contemporaries, not far removed in time from Deborah and Barak. Fokkelman explains that by mentioning Jael so early in the poem, the poet "sets up an opposition between the old Jael (neatly obeying husband and alliance; in short, totally adapted) and the new Jael, who, for her own reasons, develops into a highly original individual who implements a unique, totally personal, if not lonesome and courageous break. . . . The old Jael . . . represents a class of prominent people who are not genuine Canaanites themselves but are allied with them" ("Song of Deborah and Barak," 605).

Again, this explanation, as with the descriptions of Shamgar, represents modern sophistication. Readers are expected to know the stories of Shamgar and Jael before they read the poem. The poet calls upon knowledge the audience shares to set the stage for the poetic narrative and place it in a "recent" historical situation. By so doing the poet exalts the achievements of these two "foreigners" and prepares Israel to hear again in a poetic genre a description of the sad state of leadership in Israel.

The emphasis in this section is not on the people named but on the situation described: a time of devastation, population loss, fear, and idolatry. Fokkelman refers to a "bleak picture of an economy that has ground to a halt" ("Song of Deborah and Barak," 604). Israel had no defenses. Still Israel has some positive elements: Deborah—a mother in Israel—and commanders ready to serve their country. These two positives outweigh all the negatives, so the call to praise is repeated from v 2. This section sets up the narrative tension, so to speak. Can a devastated, defenseless country truly face its enemies simply by praising Yahweh, the God of theophany?

4. Call to ponder peasant praise (vv 10–11). The imperatives of the poem continue. Block (228) sees descriptions of rich Canaanite merchants continuing to ply their trade and ironically called upon to join in Israel's praise. Brensinger rightly decides that "all members of the community from the highest ranking officials . . . to the common laborers are summoned to the task of reciting and thereby affirming Israel's sacred traditions in which God delivers his people" (71). Israel's rich who can ride and the poor who must walk are all enjoined to ponder Israel's daily life. Such pondering is marked with joy and praise. What could possibly elicit such emotion-filled reaction?

Boling thinks these verses "celebrate how the force was mustered" in an assembly of tribal representatives. Singers like Deborah and Barak gather at the populace's daily gathering place praising God by recalling all "the righteous acts of Yahweh," righteous acts accomplished through the peasant population in Israel. Holy memory should incite the people of Yahweh to hope and action in a desperate situation.

5. Call to battle (vv 12–13). The function of these verses within the larger whole causes difficulties for the interpreter. This section shows the dual perspective of the song. Within the song itself, this is a call to battle. The present literary context presents it as celebration of a battle won. Such a celebration has elements of celebration (vv 1–5), of setting the scene (vv 6–11), of preparation (vv 12–13), of evaluation (vv 14–18), and of reenactment (vv 18–22), which are followed by the concluding curse (v 23) and blessing (vv 24–27) leading to the satiric denouement (vv 28–31).

Moore and his predecessors saw the problem here of Deborah calling on herself to sing a song of victory. Burney represents one side of the argument: the song comes after the battle and calls upon Deborah to "recount the main facts in poetic strain, and upon Barak to fight his battles o'er again" (122). Pressler sees this as a flashback "that recalls the mustering of Israel's troops . . . calling them to battle" (163). Hoppe (135) focuses too tightly on a victory-song milieu as he says Deborah was called on to rouse the troops with songs of past victories. Cundall misses the description of both leaders in saying, "Before the tribes could be aroused to action, she herself, at the word of the Lord (4:6), must be awakened from an apathetic acceptance of the situation. Similarly, Barak, who fought so valiantly and gave such outstanding leadership, had to be shaken out of his weak acquiescence in the Canaanite bondage" (97; compare Wolf, 3:412).

Schneider (90) sees the deity summoning Deborah and Barak. Moore (149) set the right direction as he perceived that Deborah is called on to strike up the song of battle and Barak is called on to attack the enemy. (Compare Hertzberg, 179, who speaks of Barak being called on to turn the tables: "den Spiess umdrehen"; and Olson, 788.) Similarly, Webb eventually decides that vv 9–13 are "perhaps best summed up as a call to participate in the battle" ([1987] 140). According to Lindars, "12a is the poet's appeal to Deborah to perform her task of prophecy in preparation for war and 12b his exhortation to Barak to act in the light of it" (249).

Ackerman pictures Deborah's role correctly as the one who "receives the command to sing out, which is the command to stand forth and sound the cry of reveille that will summon the Israelite troops into battle," but her subordination of Barak as "merely a recipient of this call" goes too far (*Warrior, Dancer*, 31). Block rightly sees that "Deborah imaginatively portrays God summoning to action the principal Israelite protagonists in the battle." She is called to "prophetic action," while his call is "more martial in tone" (230).

So the call went out—first to the leaders, then to the survivors among the decreasing population. Get up! Answer God's call to battle. Schneider (90) pushes the evidence too far in saying that the reader is supposed to read the call for Barak to take prisoners (v 12) in light of the prose narrative information that Sisera escaped him and thus to see that "the poetic reference functions as an indictment on Baraq." She even admits this was not the poem's original intent. Ackerman (*Warrior, Dancer*, 44) rightly sees the call to awake as a call to battle, based on other psalmic use of עורי, "awake."

The moment of decision has come. The commanders volunteered freely. Will God's chosen leaders and his peasant army do the same? Block aptly describes the situation: "The motley remnant of Israelite survivors of the oppression dares to attack the vastly superior might of the Canaanites for Deborah, that is for Yahweh, since as his prophet she represents him before the troops" (231).

6. Response to the call (vv 14–18). The heart of the poem deals with how Israel's tribes respond to the call to battle. Webb describes this stanza as building up "expectancy that there is to be a truly great battle such as the theophany of vv. 4–5 foreshadowed" ([1987] 142). Younger rightly calls vv 14–18 "a focal point of the song" (151). Coogan goes so far as to say, "All commentators agree that the center of the poem is the descriptive catalogue of the tribes" (*CBQ* 40 [1978] 152). For Coogan, what we are dealing with here is "a literary form which was modified according to the situation and inspiration of the poet," a conclusion supported by comparison with Canaanite and Homeric poetry, though no evidence is cited for this comparison.

The poem emphasizes the distinctions between obedient and disobedient tribes. Schneider makes the interesting observation that "this is the first time that someone in the book condemns Israelite tribes for not appearing" (91). Again Barak is mentioned with Deborah as leading the charge in contrast to v 7 but in parallel to v 12.

In an independent setting prior to being joined to the narrative, the poem functions not so much as a condemnation of specific tribes as it does as a reminder of the unity of Israel. Brensinger is on track in saying "the criticism leveled against the non-participants appears varied and in some cases restrained" (71). A call to Israel is a call to all its tribes, not just to the ones for whom the battle may be geographically important or chronologically convenient. I agree with Bal: "The purpose of the song is to reunite the tribes in order to celebrate the event together; the solidarity of the most remote members, represented by Jael—a woman on the fringe of the people—was decisive but only barely established" (*Murder and Difference*, 114).

The audience who participates in worship by singing this hymnic composition should turn for a moment to contemplate a lesson from history, namely, the lesson that participation with God brings blessing, while refusal to participate brings his curse.

7. Holy war (vv 19–22). Reciting the poetic story of God's victory is a part of emotional praise, of describing to God precisely, or as precisely as poetic language gets, what has happened in Israel's experience that brings forth praise to their God. Lindars reminds us that "its historical foundation should not be dismissed on the grounds that it is a topos of folklore, for the description keeps entirely within the bounds of normal experience, and without such a coincidence the Israelites would have been decimated and there would have been no story to tell" (266).

The war itself is quickly described, though the participants are not those we expect. Schneider emphasizes correctly that "the poetic version is not so much focused on the Deborah versus Baraq elements of the story as it is on the victory over the Canaanites" (92). Kings of Canaan fight "natural" resources—rivers and stars. No Israelite is mentioned. Sisera appears quite late. Lindars notes that the late mention of Sisera (v 20) is another indication "that the audience are expected to be familiar with the story. The mention of the name confirms their understanding of it" (267). The poetic battle then is not ordinary war. It is holy war in which Israel's unnamed God uses natural forces to destroy a coalition of kings commanded by Sisera. Here when war occurs in the poem, neither deity nor human volunteers take center stage, yet the poet strongly implies for the observant reader that Israel's God has defeated Canaan's kings on the field and with the resources that the fertility and war gods Baal and Anat should control.

Despite the brevity of the battle account, Lindars argues that this is the "climax of the poem" (217–19; similarly, Brensinger 69). I would argue, however, that the liturgical parts, not the narrative parts, offer the heart of the poem, and it is precisely the heart of these parts (vv 2–5, 9–11, 23–27, 31a) that Lindars would omit as not original. Such sharp use of critical methodology for one who wants to study the song as a piece of poetry seems inexcusable. Precisely these "omitted" parts give the song its vibrancy, its emotion, and its purpose.

8. Curse and blessing (vv 23–27). From holy war comes one lesson: curse on those who do not help Yahweh but blessing on those who do (compare Deut 27–28). So the description of war is both a way to praise and a way to teach with the element of praise dominating the content though the form juxtaposes blessing and curse. The intriguing factor here is that the elements of Israel raised up as examples of blessing and curse are fringe elements, elements with no other ties to Israel in its literature outside these chapters and this event. And this is the climax of the poetic narrative, much as the same episode climaxes the prose narrative. (See Soggin, 95, relying on H.-P. Müller, *VT* 16 [1966] 446–59. Soggin notes the typical way in which "the stress in stories falls on people and events which are really marginal.") Four verses (24–27) relate why Jael receives blessing. This stanza

calls Israel to celebrate and praise God for using the people he chooses to use to bless Israel and destroy their enemies.

9. A mother's mourning (vv 28–30). Sisera lies dead. The poem should be finished except for a formulaic ending of a hymn with its repeated call to praise. That is not what is found here. Rather, we have almost a denouement to a typical narrative. An entirely new character now dominates the stage—Sisera's mother. A new emotion controls the narrative—mourning and grief. Bal points to the irony of false wisdom here compared to Deborah's true wisdom and to the irony of "the shadow of a prophetic gift" misused contrasted to Deborah, the true prophet. She concludes: "The contrast between the two 'mothers' has nothing to do with the sugar-sweet idea of maternity so predominant in our culture" (*Murder and Difference,* 62–64).

Webb concludes: "The scene evokes strong and conflicting emotions. The bereaved mother-figure, the psychological realism, and the heavy irony in combination are powerful generators of pathos" ([1987] 143). A staff member gives almost comic relief as she lists the normal activities for a victorious army. Fokkelman describes the emotional aura of the scene: "moments before the ladies realize that their words of mutual reassurance are no more than self-delusion in the face of utmost terror" ("Song of Deborah and Barak," 623). Lindars speaks of "the wicked delight in the innocent hopes of Sisera's mother" (213). Fokkelman notes that "the item that opens the list [of hoped-for spoil] highlights a greed and nationalist mentality that totally overrides the gender aspect. . . . Women are reduced here to items of booty. However, the persons speaking like this are themselves women. What they are not aware of for one more hour is that they are describing their own imminent destiny" ("Song of Deborah and Barak," 623–24).

This is the reaction Israel was expected to display after the battle. An Israel without arms should be an Israel in fear, anxiety, and mourning. Instead, Israel was doing what the Canaanite staff lady hoped her heroes were doing. Israel was counting out the spoil. Bal (*Murder and Difference,* 65) notes that the emphasis on "embroidered cloth" sets up an ironic foreshadowing of the colorless sackcloth soon to clothe the mourning mother. In a fascinating reversal, Israel uses Canaanite fear, Canaanite mourning, and Canaanite false hopes to praise God. From a different perspective Brensinger sees that "as Deborah, the mother in Israel, arises in victory, so the mother of Sisera sinks deeper into despair" (73). Contemplation and repetition of the enemy's sadness bring new joy and praise to Israel's lips.

10. Concluding petition (v 31). The concluding petition demonstrates clearly the contrast of moods reflected by Israel and the enemies. Israel calls down a perpetual curse on Yahweh's enemies and an eternal blessing on those who love Yahweh. Here we see the blessing-and-curse element of the poem raised to be the climactic element of the entire composition. The people of Israel sing to bless or praise their God, to remember the greatness of their God, to revel in the defeat and hurt of their enemies. Most of all, Israel sings to guide history into the future. Soggin says the song's "aim is to arouse among the audience a sense of identification with the tribes which responded positively to the call and condemnation for those who stayed at home" (96). He points to Richter, who categorizes the song as a "*Werbelied,* that is, a song aimed at arousing dedication in the community in which it is sung" (*Traditionsgeschichtliche,* 104). May the righteous acts of Yahweh continue to be experienced by God's people and celebrated where God's peasants and local

dignitaries gather. May the single event now celebrated become the model for all Israel's experiences with God. But a solemn note reigns even amidst celebrations of victory, blessings on heroes, and celebration of brave volunteer leaders. Curse remains a possibility, even curse on Israel or some of its parts. Failure to participate remains a possibility. Israel can celebrate and push the present forward into the future only as Israel learns the lessons of the past and is truly a united Israel participating fully as it comes to help Yahweh in his holy wars.

Setting. Having examined the structure and contents of the poem, what have we learned about its genre, its function, and its message? In looking at these, we must take Coogan's warning seriously. This is not a naïve, primitive, or emotion-driven composition. Rather, "the author of the Song was disciplined and sophisticated" (*CBQ* 40 [1978] 145). The following commentary and explanation seek to survey important views and then offer a quite different viewpoint. I see no overwhelming reason to doubt the essential viewpoint of Israel's historians nor any reason to credit exilic or later writers with such creativity that they can devise a historical identity for Israel in such powerful prose and poetry that a nation without power will buy into the newly created identity without historical basis.

Block concludes that "the traditional view that Deborah was responsible for its composition rests on fairly solid ground" (214). But Amit would join a minimalist approach and say, without giving evidence, that

> thus the time of the formation was relatively late. If we accept the argument of current research that the redaction of the book of Judges represents the writing of the Deuteronomistic or pre-Deuteronomistic school, that means that this later period—the end of the eighth century BCE or beginning of the seventh—was when the story was completed, and it is doubtful whether it is possible to separate its early sources from its later reworking or whether we have the tools that would enable us to reconstruct the story in the version it had before its late formation. (*JSOT* 39 [1987] 104)

This very negative approach gives, from my perspective, far too much creativity and freedom to the Deuteronomistic writers without showing one piece of evidence that any part of the narrative aside from the narrative framework has any reason to be called Deuteronomistic. And as I pointed out in my Introduction, Deuteronomistic claims to Judges rest on very weak assumptions and theories.

Lindars (215–17) outlines the history of genre research on Judg 5 as victory song, thanksgiving hymn, and festal liturgy, then concludes that what is needed is study of the song as poetry. He apparently agrees with R. Alter, who concludes that the song is not an epic or narrative poem, but a "vivid and allusive presentation of a familiar tale, aimed at entertaining the hearers" (quoted in *Art of Biblical Poetry*, 216).

A longstanding designation of the poetic composition in Judg 5 has been victory hymn, a designation Alan J. Hauser ("Two Songs of Victory," 280) has recently given more definition. In doing so, however, he ignores Coogan's warning cited above. Even though Hauser has followed faithfully the lead of the framework editor, he has still not shown how either Exod 15 or Judg 5 could have functioned in a victory celebration. Block says, "The composite nature of the poem complicates its generic classification," its form and contents representing a mixed genre, but "in the present context . . . the song as a unit functions as a victory hymn of praise to Yahweh analogous to Egyptian victory odes" (212–13). Brettler points to 1 Sam 18:6–7 as the primary exemplar of the victory-song genre and argues that "the fact that Judges 5 is so very different from this certain 'victory song' should make us extremely cautious about claiming that it is a victory song" (67).

Fokkelman argues that lack of God as subject rules out "thanksgiving" as a possible genre for the song and contends that "because there is no plot, it could not be called an epic" ("Song of Deborah and Barak," 597–600). Still, Amit contends that "the poem is a song of thanks to the praise of God for the salvation he brought his people" (*JSOT* 39 [1987] 103).

Soggin calls the song "a heroic poem surrounded with liturgical elements (vv. 2–5, 9–11, 31a)" (96). Harris Lenowitz suggests that Ps 137 and the Song of Deborah may be classified as mock songs of joy, "celebrating immediate or long-withheld victory" ("The Mock-*simcha* of Psalm 137," *Directions in Biblical Hebrew Poetry,* ed. E. R. Follis, JSOTSup 40 [Sheffield: JSOT Press, 1987] 154). Auld decides, "This song is religious but not cultic. It celebrates the work of God, but it does not belong in the sanctuary." He continues: "But this song of triumph originated in what we often call the 'market place'" (157).

Soggin would modify this conclusion to say "in the pre-Dtr period, the heroic song in the strict sense was integrated into the cult," emphasizing that "this, however, is an insertion and not its original setting" (97). Such a generalized cultic usage should probably not be made more specific and related to a "fall covenant festival," as do Weiser (*ZAW* 71 [1959] 67–97) and Gray ([1986] 191–204, 261–62). It is tempting but much too theoretical to agree when Gray writes of

> the cultic occasion of rededication . . . the renewal of the sacral solidarity of the people of Yahweh (v. 13), doubtless at Mt. Tabor. There the territories of Zebulun, Issachar, and Naphtali met and there was their boundary-sanctuary of Yahweh, where the three groups might express their solidarity as the people of Yahweh and at which groups of worshippers of Yahweh from beyond the Jordan, in western Galilee and in the center of the country might realize their solidarity as the people of Yahweh. ([1986] 204)

Bal (*Murder and Difference,* 23) uses evidence amassed by Millard C. Lind (*Yahweh Is a Warrior: The Theology of Warfare in Ancient Israel* [Scottdale, PA: Herald, 1980] 66) to conclude that a mixed genre of hymn and epic is characteristic of the ode, the "conception of unified literary genres" being "anachronistic." Later Bal addresses the genre question further:

> The song of Deborah has distinct characteristics of the ode and to a lesser degree, of the satire. The ode to Yahweh is mimicked first by the ode to the tribes bound by allegiance and, then, by the ode to Jael, "blessed among women." The satire attacks the tribes not engaged in the holy war, and further on, the Canaanite women. If these genres apply here, then the song is hybrid. (*Murder and Difference,* 125)

Brettler (67) goes in a unique direction. He argues, against John Gray (*JSS* 22 [1977] 2–26; "Israel in the Song of Deborah," 421–55) and Artur Weiser (*ZAW* 71 [1959] 67–97), that the song does not represent an Israelite liturgy, especially a liturgy for a supposed fall festival. Brettler concludes, "Even though Judges 5 shares certain elements with various liturgies, it is difficult to characterize it in its entirety as a liturgy. The role of YHWH is not significant enough." From a different perspective Brettler (68) argues against Geoffrey P. Miller ("Riposte Form in the Song of Deborah"), who sees the song as a riposte, that is, a verbal feud seeking to restore Israel's honor "by projecting the enemy's cultural stereotypes of Israel back on Israel's enemies." Brettler correctly notes that the theory is impossible to prove, since we really do not know what the "average Canaanite" felt about the "average Israelite" at the time of this poem's composition.

Brettler suggests "in a very tentative fashion" that "Judges 5 functioned as a poem recited before war, and one of its main functions was to muster the troops to battle" (69). The liturgical elements that scholars have often wanted to delete as later accretions show that the song was meant to be used in religious contexts. The shame for the enemies is highlighted as a theme "in order to recreate similar shame for the current enemies." Thus "Judges is structured to convince groups of people to volunteer."

Brettler has accounted for several elements in the poetic composition that bring difficulty to Hauser's victory-song theory. A call to muster troops is much less spontaneous than the victory song. Such a call might well be issued in the cultic setting that the song appears to reflect. Most importantly, the strong blessing-and-curse or shame-and-praise motif is much more likely to be at home in the troop-muster setting than in that of a spontaneous victory celebration. I would conclude, then, that Brettler may well have pointed to a strong possibility for one place where the song was at home, but hopefully genre studies have come far enough to realize that such materials seldom remain fastened to one facet of a people's life. Such a popular poetic piece would surely find its way into national and more regionalized cultic celebrations as the tribes and clans celebrated their identity as Israel, people of Yahweh.

Guillaume says the "earliest form of Deborah's song can be set in a group living in the periphery of the Jezreel valley in the post-Amarna period . . . and evoke a particularly memorable victory of the inhabitants of the hill country (between the Jezreel plain and the Ephraimite mountains, around modern Jenin) over the dwellers of the plain. . . . The song belonged to the Zebulunite folklore and entered Israelite traditions at the same time than [sic] Zebulun joined Israel" (*Waiting for Josiah*, 37–38). Such a view eliminates too much of the song with its references to several tribes participating.

Several key elements point us toward identifying the genre of Judg 5. First are the opening and closing elements of blessing in 5:2 and 31 complemented by blessings in vv 9 and 24 and curses in vv 23 and 31, and the implied curses on the nonparticipating tribes. These represent cultic acts and give a cultic flavor to the entire poem.

Second is the address to Yahweh in vv 2, 3, 4, 9, and 31, which frames and subsumes the rest of the material as the work of Yahweh even when the divine name does not appear for long stretches of poetry. This is supported by the introductory report of a theophany. The righteous acts of Yahweh serve as the only connecting link holding the poetry together.

Third is the emphasis on the tribes of Israel and their participation or nonparticipation. This holds up a conception of an entity known as Israel and formed by the "merger" in some way of various tribes. It also shows the weakness of these links.

Fourth is the repeated change of subjects and locations. Does this point to liturgical reenactment or to poetic license?

Fifth is the last major unit's reversion to narrative with Sisera and his family as the central subject. This lends a strong element of satire and irony to the poem.

Sixth is the martial tone of so much of the poem with its vocabulary of willing participation and perverse absence.

Such diverse elements challenge an interpreter to find a common form and function for the whole. The element chosen as central to the poem becomes the defining factor for genre definition even when this means glossing over other elements. I choose to take the final blessing-and-curse element as the defining element of the poem and interpret the rest of the poem in light of that theme. This approach is easily dismissed when one, with Brettler (73), removes v 2 as an incipit or, with Lindars (286) following Richter, excises the final verse as a "liturgical addition."

In light of the assumption of a blessing-and-curse theme, one can interpret each section of the song as follows:

- The opening call to individual praise (vv 2–3) directs blessing two ways—to willing volunteers and to Yahweh—while implicitly directing a curse to enemy kings, who are called on to join in praise to Yahweh even though Yahweh is not their god.
- The report of a theophany (vv 4–5) again directs blessing to the God of the theophany and uses his coming to promise blessing for Israel.
- The historical setting (vv 6–9) shows the reasons for war in Israel—God's curse on Israel for choosing new gods—yet implies blessing on willing commanders.
- The call to ponder peasant praise (vv 10–11) anticipates blessing on an Israel who remembers and recites the righteous acts of God and goes to the city gates either to prepare for war or to secure justice.
- The call to battle (vv 12–13) expects a positive answer and thus a blessing on a people willing to fight against a strong enemy because Yahweh's praise is on their lips.
- The response to the call (vv 14–18) separates Israel into those deserving blessing and those deserving curses.
- The holy war (vv 19–22) description indirectly describes the curse on the enemy who took no spoil and galloped off.
- Curse and blessing (vv 23–27) explicitly pronounces curse on Meroz, and thus by allusion on all those who do not come to help Yahweh, and blessing on Jael, the unexpected heroine, who kills the accursed Sisera.
- A mother's mourning (vv 28–30) plaintively shows the curse on the family and leaders of the nation that opposes Yahweh.
- The concluding petition (v 31) generalizes the curse and blessing on God's enemies and on those who love God.

The setting for such a blessing-and-curse ritual is certainly a cultic affair, one that at least in theory includes all Israel's tribes, however many may have actively participated and identified themselves with Israel at the particular time. This would probably represent an early time in the period of the judges before the Philistine threat began to call the tribes together in unified defense and while instability within the individual tribes allowed leading clans such as Machir and Gilead to represent the entire tribe. We cannot discern details of such a ritual nor expect that each episode in the poem became a cultic scene. Such a ritual could eventually be used for many purposes in different cultic settings. Prior to battle, the song could muster the troops, encourage them, and promise assurance of victory by the God of the theophany. In times without imminent warfare, such a ritual could call the tribes of Israel to unity and perhaps covenant renewal. In times of victory after battle, such poetry could ridicule a defeated enemy, praise God for victory, and applaud the participating warriors. Taken outside the cult into daily life, the song could encourage peasants in their daily struggles, call forth memories and songs of God's righteous acts in the past, and enhance patriotism and loyalty among the tribes.

Thus the song of chap. 5 stands in stark formal contrast to the battle report of chap. 4. Yet the battle report of chap. 4 seems dependent on the earlier poetic version. The theory that chap. 4 is dependent on chap. 5 at least, as Watts notes, "does indeed explain many details of the prose account" (*Psalm and Story*, 93). Still Watts is right as he continues: "It does not, however, explain the underlying themes of Judges 4, which we have found to be focussed on Barak's humiliation when Jael destroyed his enemy." The narrative thus "borrows selectively" to make its own point, "but the amount of borrowing makes the hypothesis of direct dependence more likely" (94).

Younger describes the situation: "In the case of the battle against Sisera, the prose account provides a logical account with a carefully constructed point. The song, however, provides an emotional and more figurative account with special themes and purposes. The two are complementary in relationship" (157–58). Bal looks at the two accounts from the perspective of religious feeling as a motivational power. She determines that in chap. 4 Deborah uses such motivation to "push Barak to overcome his terror before the superior strength of the enemy," while "the song is penetrated with religious feeling. . . . Deborah makes it the *raison d'etre* of the entire community in 5" (*Murder and Difference*, 38). Amit appears far too simplistic when she reduces the two stories to two sides of the same coin, saying the poem's "purpose is identical with that of the story. Both express the divine salvation, but the technique differs for each genre. . . . Deborah and Barak, the speakers of the poem, repeat the message of the story explicitly and openly" (*JSOT* 39 [1987] 103). Quite to the contrary, the battle report shows how an untrusting general yields his victory glory to an unexpected, foreign woman. Chap. 5 looks at God's blessing on his volunteers and his curses on his enemies outside and inside Israel.

Block sees the editors presenting "the reader with two lenses with which to view a single event. . . . The versions do not contain any significant differences that cannot be attributed to differences in genre and function. Both versions of the story go back to a common source, the historical victory of the Israelites under the prophetic inspiration of Deborah and the military leadership of Barak over the Canaanites" (183–84). Lindars, however, wants to modify this: "There is no reason to doubt that the tradition preserves the memory of an episode of decisive importance in the early history of Israel," but he adds "even if the accounts of it are largely legendary" (164). Soggin excludes "the possibility that the Canaanites could have formed some such coalition only against Israel." Rather, mention of the two tribes of Naphtali and Zebulun "admits the local and therefore limited character of the battle; if we accept the substantial historicity of the note and therefore of the figures, it would be likely that the object of the concentration was a more powerful enemy, for example Egypt. . . . And once the army was available, why not also use it in a local policing operation?" (71). Coogan (*CBQ* 40 [1978] 143–44) decides from the outset that C. M. Bowra (*Heroic Poetry* [London: Macmillan, 1961] 535) is correct in judging that "poetry, especially heroic poetry, is a poor substitute for history." Thus Coogan finds "no indication of date" and sees it as "likely that Sisera's mother was unknown to our poet; Jael's action may originally have had nothing to do with Israel. The historical significance of the battle at Wadi Qishon may have been negligible." All this because "poets are not historians." For Coogan, the use of formulaic material—adapted not created—"makes historical conclusions even more tenuous."

Watts (*Psalm and Story*, 82–98) cannot find the confusion and contradictions that other writers find in the two versions. Nor can he find in the text a dichotomy between divine providence and human interactions (87). Elsewhere Watts ("Biblical Psalms outside the Psalter") provides a survey of recent work on the editorial insertion of psalms into historical narrative frames. Judg 5 does not fit his plan, being "the only clear example of an inset hymn in earlier biblical literature." It "seems to have been placed after the battle narrative in Judges 4 prior to or during the composition of the book of Judges" (290) and "simply concludes and amplifies the battle account in the previous chapter" (293), being the only inset hymn whose role "seems to be limited to its immediate context" (302). Watts does point to the Egyptian Piye Stela from the eighth century with its two victory hymns as representing the same "literary convention" as the placement of Judg 5 after Judg 4. (The stele is translated in M. Lichtheim, *Ancient Egyptian Literature: A Book of Readings* [Berkeley: University of California Press, 1980] 3:66–84, and in M. Lichtheim, "The Victory Stela of King Piye [Piankhy]," *COS*, 2:42–51.) Watts points to Weitzman's analysis (*Song and Story in Biblical Narrative*, 19) showing that the songs in the Egyptian example "model the desired reader response."

Comment

1 Commentary on Judg 5 may be the most difficult task that an interpreter of the Old Testament attempts. Soggin (92–93) shows why:

a. lxx^A in vv 7, 16, 21, and 22 has had to transliterate Hebrew words, having no translation value for them, while lxx^B simply offers "the fantastic interpretation of a translator" (see Garbini, *La parola del passato* 178 [1978] 8).

b. At least twenty-two verses have at least one word for which the translation is only a conjecture.

c. Vv 2, 10, 11, 13, 14, 21, 22, and 26 "are not completely comprehensible."

d. The prose version may have been written because the poem was barely comprehensible even in antiquity.

e. Comparison with Ugaritic poetry is an inadequate basis for dating the materials.

Schneider adds, "Many of the words which appear in it [i.e., Judg 5] are otherwise unknown or difficult to translate because the forms are so archaic. It is

poetry, rather than prose, and it is difficult to translate poetic license" (85). She
continues, "The poem plays with words and their sounds and is elegantly written,
though its meaning is obscure" (87). Still the commentator on Judges must make
a stab at translation and give the best explanation of the text possible, all the while
knowing the fallibility of such an effort.

The editor's framework has Deborah and Barak sing together in that day,
though the feminine singular verb form gives precedence to Deborah but gives
no indication of a parody on General Barak. This framework consciously joins
the two chapters, placing the action of chap. 5 in temporal sequence after the
action of chap. 4. Younger correctly notes that 5:1 "provides the narrative setting
for the song and does not speak directly to the issues of authorship" (147). Watts
observes that v 1 is "not intended to be an exhaustive description of the singers,
but simply serves to designate Deborah and Barak as the song leaders" (*Psalm
and Story,* 95).

2   The song's opening words bring its first problems. Beginning with the early
Greek tradition, the meanings of the words have escaped translators. Most modern
translations waver between references to locks of hair (NJB, JPS, NRSV) and to rulers
or leaders (REB, NIV, HCSB, NET, NLT, NASB, ESV, NAB, NKJV). Soggin (81) suggests,
"because the people have regained liberty," while Boling, similarly, translates, "when
they cast off restraint in Israel." If the reference to free-flowing hair is correct, the
tribute is to warriors who have vowed not to cut their hair for battle (compare
Deut 32:42) or who have simply let their hair grow during a military campaign in
their intense devotion to Israel's military cause. Such vows were part of the Nazirite
vow (Num 6:5; Judg 13:5). Israel's armies volunteer to do God's work against the
enemies and thus bring cause for praising and blessing God.

בָּרֲכוּ יְהוָה appears here and in Ps 103:20–22. The phrase refers to people "speaking well of [Yahweh], attributing 'blessing' (good qualities) to him, and so he is
'blessed' *(baruk)—i.e.,* praised and praiseworthy" (M. L. Brown, *NIDOTTE,* 1:764).
Block (221) characterizes this call to praise as "a rare and welcome expression of
devotion to Yahweh" in the book of Judges. Hauser points to the cluster of references to the divine name in vv 2–5 and concludes that "the clustering of so many
references at the beginning rivets the audience's attention on Israel's victorious
God." This clustering is unusual because of "the frequency and intensity with which
God is mentioned" ("Two Songs of Victory," 266).

Fewell and Gunn think this

> ring composition of verses 2 and 9 . . . brackets out YHWH and re-establishes the human
> focus of the celebration. . . . Despite these gestures of acknowledgement towards YHWH
> there emerges an underlying assumption of human indispensability. . . . The song implies
> that YHWH's deliverance was contingent upon human assistance. Consequently, the
> song gives more attention to celebrating YHWH's helpers and ridiculing those who left
> YHWH in the lurch, than it gives to YHWH himself. (*JAAR* 58 [1990] 401)

One must modify this observation to say that the song focuses attention on
blessing in two directions—to the deity and to human volunteers—just as it focuses
blessing and cursing in two directions—those loving Yahweh and his enemies. In
either case one must take into account both recipients. The entire biblical narrative
is a relationship narrative with human and divine partners each playing a role. We

must also note that the song's actual battle description leaves everything to forces the deity controls, offering no part for human participation or glory until the story of Jael. It is most difficult to see in this battle description that "with a deft stroke the singers remove YHWH from the most crucial moment of the campaign, the battle itself (vv. 20–21). That is won not by the divine warrior but by the stars in their courses, the stars in league with the torrent Kishon." Thus Fewell and Gunn (*JAAR* 58 [1990] 402) agree with Bal (*Murder and Difference*, 46) that we have here a pantheistic element in the poem.

Surely no one in the original audience of the poem nor anyone reading the final text would have understood these references to stars and Kishon as pantheistic. They would naturally have understood these phenomena as natural features controlled and directed by deity, indeed by the God of Israel, who thus disproved the claims of the gods of the Canaanites.

3 As is typical for this poem, the scene and participants shift quickly and unexpectedly. The addressees become "kings" and "dignitaries," apparently those of foreign nations, since Israel had no kings. The singer shifts to first-person singular address, affirming her intention to sing for Yahweh. Thus she chooses a musical method of doing what she called on the people to do in the previous verse. Watts (*Psalm and Story*, 94) shows that the "internal evidence" indicates that the "Song of Deborah" seems to be multi-voiced. Some parts belong in the mouths of Deborah and Barak. Other parts do not. For discussion of the first person in the song, see Fokkelman, "Song of Deborah and Barak," 596.

For "God of Israel," see *Comment* on 4:6. זמר in *pi'el* means

> playing a musical instrument in the context of worship, usually a stringed instrument (Pss 33:2; 98:5; 147:7), but also a percussion instrument (149:3). More often it has the developed sense of singing to a musical accompaniment (cf. 71:22–23). . . . Both the vb. and the nom. זִמְרָה are used to introduce communal hymns in extended calls to praise (Pss 33:2; 66:2, 4; 68:4 [5]; 81:2 [3]; 95:2; 105:2; 135:3; 147:1; compare Exod 15:2) or a renewed call to praise in a double or multiple hymn (47:6–7 [7–8]; 68:33; 98:4–5; 147:7; 149:3). (L. Allen, *NIDOTTE*, 1:1116)

Thus combined with שִׁיר, "sing," זמר gives the poem a hymnic overtone.

4–5 The theophany report is addressed to Yahweh and describes a past action, either from a traditional report of God's coming to Israel's aid from the mountains of Edom (see Deut 33:2) or in a freshly tailored variation making a play on the sounds of Canaanite chariots compared to Yahweh's footsteps and the provision of rain to rout those chariots in battle. *Seir* is another name for Edom (Gen 32:3), probably derived from a mountain in the region. It stood on the way from Mount Sinai or Horeb to Kadesh-barnea (Deut 1:2; compare 2:1), but God forbade Israel to provoke the Edomites there (Deut 2:5). The theophany report uses the responses of natural elements to display God's sovereign power. The mountains would stream with melted snow and make the valleys below unfit for strategic use of chariots.

Yahweh is referred to as "this one of Sinai," a phrase that has caused commentators to ponder long. Moore (141–42) dismissed it as a misplaced gloss on the *montains*. Burney (113) and Hertzberg (178) agreed. Albright (*BASOR* 62 [1936] 26–31) and Cross ("Yahweh and the God of the Patriarchs," *HTR* 55 [1962] 239,

225–59) provided linguistic evidence that זֶה, "this one," represents an archaic pronoun *du*, creating a divine epithet, "this one of Sinai," that also appears in Ps 68:8 (compare C. Brockelmann, *Hebräisches Syntax* [Neukirchen-Vluyn: Neukirchener Verlag, 1956] 68; J. M. Allegro, "Uses of the Semitic Demonstrative Element *z* in Hebrew," *VT* 5 [1955] 309–12; H. Birkeland, "Hebrew *zoe* and Arabic *du*," *ST* 2 [1948] 201–2). Albright and Cross are followed by Boling (108), Gray ([1986] 278), Wolf (3:409), and Soggin (85). Lindars (233) points out that H. Grimme ("Abriss der biblischen-hebräischen Metrik," *ZDMG* 50 [1896] 529–84) had already proposed this translation. Based on the paucity of Hebrew evidence, Lindars concludes that "the name, if accepted, must be regarded as a chance survival of an obsolete title, perhaps that of a god worshiped by proto-Israelite groups (mentioned with the Shasu in Egyptian texts) before the arrival of the Moses group in Palestine." Lindars (234) appears more attracted to Fishbane's conclusion that זֶה represents a gloss on the entire verse and "means [the theophany of] Sinai" (*Biblical Interpretation in Ancient Israel* [Oxford: Oxford UP, 1985] 54–55, 75, n. 30; compare C. Levin, "Der Dekalog am Sinai," *VT* 35 [1985] 189–90). The ancient nature of the poetry and the unusual form points to Lindars' "obsolete title" as being the most likely explanation here. As such it would be set in parallel with the old title "the God of Israel." The poem celebrates Yahweh from the south, marked by Mount Sinai as his home, rather than Baal of the northern Mount Zaphon, and shows Yahweh, not the fertility gods of Canaan, as the source of rain and water. This is what Block calls "a deliberate polemic against the perspectives cherished by the kings whom the poet has summoned to listen" (223).

6   In establishing the historical setting, the poem distances itself chronologically from the event. It looks back to the days of Shamgar and Jael, a time when the peasant population, quite probably limited to the hill country, suddenly found the "pathways" to the valleys closed, blocking their trade. They had to resort to the unused back roads that wound through the hill country between the various small settlements. Block assumes "Israelite caravaneers have ceased to travel on their normal trade routes for fear of attack and/or extortionary tolls demanded at crossroads by the Canaanite oppressors" (225). Lindars says, "The verse describes the effect of the conditions of the time on Israelite society. If the highways were impassable to caravans and individual travelers, it surely implies lack of adequate control to prevent constant risk from brigands" (236). Brown bluntly calls it "a picture of chaos. No security, no freedom, no order—in a word, no *shalom*" (179). The use of heroes with foreign names may point to Israel's lack of homegrown leadership.

7   Economic woes and enemy oppression threatened the growth of the population. In poetic hyperbole, Deborah sings, "The peasant population disappeared in Israel." Block notes the debate over the meaning of the Hebrew *pĕrāzôn* (פְּרָזוֹן) but is correct in understanding it as a "collective designation for residents of rural unwalled settlements" (225). This may well refer more to the people's activities outside their home villages than to actual decimation of the people. Again Block notes, "Afraid of attack from the enemy in the open field, these folks stayed at home—farmers refused to go out to the fields, and trade among the tribes of Israel came to a standstill" (225). Niditch decides that "such a picture tallies with historians' views of the political and economic uncertainties of the Late Bronze Age" (78).

What could change such a disastrous, hopeless situation? Deborah points to her own activity. She stood on her feet, meaning that when all looked hopeless and no masculine leaders stepped forward, this woman—known as prophetess, wife, and judge—took a stand, opposing Israel's weakness and the Canaanites' strength. She stood up as "a mother in Israel." Block sees this highly disputed phrase as simply "highlighting Deborah's surprise that a woman should have played the decisive role in turning the tables" and as evoking "affectionate maternal images, as if Deborah is the agent through whom Yahweh expresses his protective care over a people in a stressful and bewildering period" (226). Lindars thinks "a prophet discloses divine knowledge and as such has the teaching responsibility of a father, and the same would be true of a prophetess (cf. Prov. 1:8). . . . The phrase is a way of pointing to Deborah as a figure of national salvation, whose initiative restored the fortunes of the people" (238–39). (See J. C. Exum, "'Mother in Israel': A Familiar Figure Reconsidered," in *Feminist Interpretation of the Bible*, ed. L. Russell [Philadelphia: Westminster, 1985] 73–85.) Schneider, ever ready to highlight feminine greatness, goes a bit overboard in claiming, "Deborah is described as the person who saved Israel both militarily and spiritually" (89). Dempster thinks "'mother' need not be taken as a passive and submissive role here—an interpretation that hardly makes sense—but should mean a 'fierce protector and guardian of her people'" (*WTJ* 41 [1978] 48). Dempster surely goes too far in crediting the rain to Deborah and giving her authority to call the stars into battle. One may surely question whether Deborah had military functions outside of her prophetic role in summoning the general to action or had spiritual functions outside her role as judge giving God's response to the people's queries.

I can come much closer to following Schneider when she claims that "the reference to Deborah as 'a' mother in Israel may serve the literary function of paralleling Deborah with Sisera's mother." Still, one would expect that this is a more technical term with deeper meaning than simply a literary parallel, and one cannot use the absence of mention of children to claim there is no evidence for her as a biological mother. Webb ([1987] 141–42) sees an equivalence between the power of Yahweh in the theophany and its historical revelation in Deborah's arising as a mother in Israel but notes that this remains "a muted note in the song." Ackerman (*Warrior, Dancer,* 37–44) builds on this parallel and on the work of Claudia V. Camp ("The Wise Women of 2 Samuel: A Role Model for Women in Early Israel?" *CBQ* 43 [1981] 14–29) to see "mother in Israel" as being "a good and effective counselor" who uses her "skills in counseling to protect the heritage of Yahweh," occasionally using military force and so being "willing to step forth as a commander who leads those under her protection in military encounters" while having a "commitment to Israel's covenantal unity and wholeness." All this is derived from the application of the term "mother in Israel" to a city, not a person, in 2 Sam 20:19.

Ackerman readily applies the richness of meaning found here to Deborah while admitting "Deborah's attributes of 'good and effective counsel' are less obviously indicated in the text." So she concludes that Deborah and Yahweh are "thus the worthiest of partners. . . . Yahweh represents the cosmic, the divine, and the male in the role of war leader who extends protection to the community of Israel. Deborah represents the earthly, the human, and the female as she steps forth as military commander to ensure the security of Yahweh's people" (43–44).

Such conclusions come from building hypothesis upon hypothesis. Fewell and

Gunn see Deborah, in the end, repeating the traditional beliefs of the patriarchal system and thus "trapped in the very value system which we imagine her to be subverting" (*JAAR* 58 [1990] 397). Olson, following James W. Watts (*Psalm and Story*, 90), may be on the right trail in suggesting that the title "may represent the place and office of a wise woman prophet who delivers divine oracles to resolve disputes" (787). Or as Boling phrases it, the honorific title is "bestowed by the poet for the entertainment of folk who customarily associated oracular technique with the priestly title of 'father'" (118). Whatever the specific meaning, Deborah uses the title to underline her authority and leadership in an Israel sadly lacking in authoritative leaders.

8 Block (226) notes the notorious difficulty in translating v 8 and suggests that rather than Israel choosing new gods, the verse actually refers to God choosing new leaders for Israel. In a similar fashion, Soggin sees the statement "they chose new gods" as "nonsensical in the present context" (87). Lindars (239–41) agrees. Younger calls Block's solution "somewhat forced" (150, n. 48). Olson prefers to interpret the phrase as "Deborah's choosing new recruits for Israel's army" (787). The Hebrew יבחר אלהים חדשׁים has a singular verb that may be taken as having a collective subject, no marker of the direct object or accusative, and a plural adjective for "new." The subject may be "God" with the adjective as the object, or "Israel" may be the unstated collective subject with the adjective modifying the plural "gods." One's interpretation of the context is the only criteria for decision. The problem with Block's interpretation is the identification of the leaders, since Deborah has already been introduced earlier. Is this Barak and Jael? Barak and other unnamed tribal or military leaders? Rather, the emphasis appears to be on the problems and disobedience of Israel in these bewildering days. Fewell and Gunn (*JAAR* 58 [1990] 400) see the new gods chosen for Israel or rather imposed on Israel by foreign rulers, more specifically, by the Canaanites. Again, as with so many of their interpretations, in isolation one might consider the possibility of this, but when it is joined by a slew of such "possible but not the most immediately apparent" interpretations, one begins to question all of them. Boling (109) looks to gods as treaty witnesses and sees a collapse of trade route agreements but then speaks of "an Israel that was prosperous and complacent and turning to other gods" (118–19).

I would see rather a desperate Israel, defeated by the Canaanite forces and turning to Canaanite gods instead of remembering and adhering to the Sinai, theophanic traditions of Israel's warrior God. They may well have relied on new treaties they agreed to as witnessed by Canaanite gods and goddesses as well as by Yahweh. Even so "war was in the gates." The Canaanite leaders did not honor such treaties and came demanding more from Israel. Israel stood without weapons as they watched the enemy advance. Na'aman notes the importance of the Hebrew אז, "then," as a structural marker here and in vv 11, 13, 19, and 22, "deliberately selected to open the five major stages of the struggle between Israel and the Canaanites" (*VT* 40 [1990] 424).

9 Deborah expresses the emotions of a mother in Israel. She has empathy and sympathy for overmatched Israelite commanders. They volunteered freely just as the people or army of v 2 had done. Thus the poet repeats the call to bless Yahweh. This sandwiches the first major section of the poem between the two cultic calls. Yet the tone has shifted dramatically from rejoicing over a volunteer army's courage to fearful sympathy for volunteer commanders facing overwhelming odds. Fokkelman sees in vv 9–10 a beginning of the differentiation between "leaders and troops." He sees, in order, a "small and exclusive group of commanders," "a group of rich possessors, probably tradesmen," a group that makes "a less exclusive impression," and a final group that "does not want to exclude anybody at all" ("Song of Deborah and Barak," 608). But the repetition sealing vv 2–9 off as a separate unit seems to prohibit our joining vv 9 and 10 so closely.

10 As the peasants are called to praise, the enemy stands at the gate of an Israel depleted of forces and weapons. Thus we can take a look inside life in Israel. The phrase "riders of tawny donkeys" refers to the upper-class merchants who appear to have life easy amidst Israel's struggle. "Those sitting on blankets" may refer to a separate group who sit on carpets or blankets in the commerce in the city gate or to the same people who ride on donkeys. "Pedestrians" may represent the ordinary people visiting the market stalls on the pathway or may represent the poor class in contrast to the upper-class donkey riders. All elements of Israel's society are invited to ponder the theophanic One of Sinai and move to praise of that God even in the face of the enemy. One can, with Block, see this as a call to enemy merchants, parallel to v 3, but the close ties to the next verse appear to restrict these references to Israel.

11 We move from the pathways connecting the villages to the center of village communication, "the watering holes." Block (228) confesses that "every phrase in v 11 is difficult," but Block's solution (229) that "the Canaanite travelers stop and listen and join in the celebration of Yahweh's victory" appears far from reality. Scholars give educated guesses about the people described here—musicians, shepherds, archers, or "recruiters," the latter being suggested by Younger (151). It may simply be those who help one another draw and distribute water from the village well. The central theme is the recitation of God's "righteous acts." This is unexpected in the context of Judges, where the people generally show more loyalty to Baal or Astarte than to Yahweh and where a generation has forgotten the acts of God (2:10). In the context of Judges, does this then mean that a new generation had turned to Yahweh and could recite only the acts in the period of the Judges? Or does this change the interpretation of 2:10 into a bit of hyperbole so that a faithful remnant retained the memory of the stories of patriarchs, exodus, and conquest? Whatever the precise understanding, telling God's past encouraged and motivated God's people in the present. The righteous acts of God are victorious acts bringing righteous vindication for God's people. Thus they can be described by their source—Yahweh—and by their benefactors—Israel. Block separates the parallelism, seeing vv 14–18 as giving the acts of the villagers while vv 19–23 give Yahweh's acts. This makes v 11 look forward rather than providing the more likely glance back into history.

They "went down to the gates," apparently volunteering and assembling for battle, war being in the gates (v 8). Block (230) notes that this is the only place in Judges where Israel is called the "people of Yahweh."

12 In the call to battle, the speaker abruptly changes. Lindars sees v 12a as "the poet's appeal to Deborah to perform her task of prophecy in preparation for war" and 12b as "his exhortation to Barak to act in the light of it" (249). This could be right, but שׁיר would be used in a unique way here in referring to prophecy rather than music, and the genre of the poetic composition makes a call to sing natural. Here Deborah is more likely given the role of the women singing victory songs as in Exod 15 than that of a prophet. The prophetic role more likely appears in v 7 and possibly in v 15 as well as the certain depiction of her prophetic role in the narrative of chap. 4. Auld minimizes the prophetic aspect of the entire tradition when he claims, "Just like Miriam before here [sic] (Exod. 15:20), she [Deborah] is a prophetess because she leads the singing" (153).

The people of Yahweh apparently take the stage. They see that the time for action has arrived and challenge their leaders to action. Deborah's call is to call the people to battle. Barak's is to lead the troops into battle to take the enemies captive. "Enemies" is plural, pointing forward to what will actually occur, the major enemy not being captured. (See Schneider, 90.) T. H. Gaster refers to 1 Sam 18:7–8 and Ps 68:12 to conclude, "The reference is not to the present song but to that customarily chanted by the womenfolk when the warriors return with the loot" (*Myth, Legend, and Custom in the Old Testament* [New York: Harper, 1969] 419). Boling (111) and Schneider (89–90), among others, follow him. This separates the parallellism between Deborah's call and Barak's chronologically, something the poet gives no hint of. It also places the emphasis on Deborah as a woman among women rather than as a prophetic leader of Israel's commander.

13 Israel has become a remnant, "survivors" of the Canaanite oppression as described in v 7. Responding to Deborah's prophetic call, the remnant rises up, mustering at the gates for battle.

Na'aman (see *Comment* on v 8) translates v 13 as "Then down to Sarid he marched towards the mighty ones; the people of Israel marched down for him *(lw)* with warriors." Thus the verse mentions Sarid, "a well-known Israelite town on the southern border of Zebulun (Josh. xix 10,12)" (*VT* 40 [1990] 425).

This ingenious solution is unnecessary in light of the Hebrew parallelism showing the surviving members of the "people of Yahweh" facing the noble warriors of the Canaanites, using two terms for Israel's sadsack army and two for Canaan's mighty warriors (compare Block, 231). Fokkelman ("Song of Deborah and Barak," 609, n. 36) correctly argues that "nobles" and "warriors," or as he translates, "the mighty" and the "warriors," are Israel's foes, not friends. Block sees here "an apparent allusion to the oppression under which they had languished. . . . The motley remnant of Israelite survivors of the oppression dares to attack the vastly superior might of the Canaanites for Deborah, that is, for Yahweh" (231). Interestingly, the Israelite armies come to Deborah, not to the commander, in answer to her mustering song. Prophetic action, not military protocol, springs Israel to noble action against the Canaanite nobles. Olson correctly summarizes the section: "The war against Canaan begins with an already weak Israel at half strength but, more important, with God fighting on Israel's side" (788).

14 Here begins a roll call of Israelite tribes, some answering the call to battle and others not. Fokkelman asserts that technically this is not a roll call but a temporal sequence of actions in which "every colon is judgmental" ("Song of Deborah and Barak," 614). Younger believes that

> the Barak narrative is much less interested in who fought in the battle than it is in Barak's hesitation and its results. . . . But the purpose of the Song is to acknowledge and praise Yahweh and those who participated. The Song, therefore, presents three groups: those who did not respond (5:15b–17), those who responded (5:14–15a), and those who distinguished themselves in battle (5:18). Moreover, Judges 4 clearly describes an

initial victory of a longer campaign. . . . The song appears to include the entire campaign, recounting all that in the end participated. To this effect, the Song seems to have telescoped the entire campaign, just like the Tukulti-Ninurta Epic and the Ramesses Bulletin. ("Heads! Tails!" 130)

This early Israelite poem thus becomes the center of attention for identifying the nature of early Israel. The answer one finds here sheds light for interpreting the rest of the battles in Judges. In what way can Israel be identified as twelve tribes when this early poem does not name twelve? Why do some of the tribal names here reflect clans within a tribe rather than the more usual name for the tribe? Is Israel simply a northern coalition with the southern tribes going their own way until later in history? What unites the tribes outside of self-defense and self-interest?

Barnabas Lindars offers too minimal a view of the tribes and of Israel when he sees them as being without "any internal cohesion," being rather "groups of clans banded together for military purposes," the "evolution of the tribes" being "haphazard." A tribe is simply "a regional unit of clans, providing a wider circle for intermarriage." The simple tribal organization is limited to "judicial officers recognized by the whole tribe" due to "family matters." In time of war they "look to an outstanding warrior." As a sense of "national self-consciousness" grows, a "genealogical system" is formed "embracing all the tribes in one family." Then "geographical names become the personal names of eponymous ancestors" ("Israelite Tribes in Judges," 95–112).

Lindars does admit that the Song of Deborah shows "a real ethnic basis in the consciousness of belonging to Israel," even though not all clans were related, and an acknowledgement of "Yahweh as their only, or at least their principal, God," but this "covenant with Yahweh" entailed "no defined obligations to one another" and no "pan-Israelite cultic gatherings at a central sanctuary." "Landless Levites" ultimately brought the religion of Yahweh with its exodus traditions to the originally El-worshiping Israel ("Israelite Tribes in Judges," 110–11).

J. A. Dearman proposes that early Israel is connected to the decline of Egyptian power in Palestine along with a decline in urban settlements in the transition from Late Bronze Age to the Iron Age. Israel was "prominent among the builders of new dwellings in the depopulated hill country. . . . Israel would be not an ethnic term or primarily a territorial reference but the name of a tribal ancestry which was used to designate a decentralized tribal association" (*Religion & Culture in Ancient Israel* [Peabody, MA: Hendrickson, 1992] 34). Religious ideology and economic self-interest both played important roles in defining earliest Israel, which may or may not have comprised twelve tribes. For several generations "Israel's ancestors had moved about from Egypt to Syria, as had a number of similar groups. Some elements in these mobile population groups were native to Palestine and some not" (34). Trying to tie Israel to Canaan for its origins with no outside influence "is probably an overreaction to earlier theories that identified tribal Israel too closely with a romanticized notion of nomadic outsiders" (49). Culturally Canaanite, they identified themselves over against the city-state system of Palestine. They had enough cohesion to oppose Late Bronze Age Canaanite social policies and to form a "loose coalition of tribes and clans related to one another through lines of kinship and obligations of mutual support" (35). Individual tribes and clans moved in and out of the coalition. The God of the larger coalition became

Yahweh, who delivered one group of slaves from Egypt and brought them to Canaan. Yahweh is identified with or supplants the high god El, assuming many of El's characteristics. The people of Israel were not polytheistic nor monotheistic. They practiced monolatry, devoted to Yahweh but recognizing the existence of other gods. Israel's opposition to the city-state culture included opposition to temples and divine images. Still Yahwism must be considered a Canaanite religion. Dearman concludes, "From its beginnings, therefore, one can see the identity of Israel being formulated in cultural and theological terms" (35).

R. W. Younker ("The Iron Age in the Southern Levant," in *Near Eastern Archaeology: A Reader*, ed. S. Richard [Winona Lake, IN: Eisenbrauns, 2003] 367–82) sets three groups in southern Palestine by 1180 B.C.E.: Philistines, Egyptian-dominated Canaanites, and Israelites and other "highlanders." The result was destruction and then rebuilding of many if not most of the major towns in Palestine. Younker is willing to give some credence to each of the settlement models—conquest, peaceful infiltration, peasants' revolt, and ruralization—in explaining the emergence of Israel in various parts of Palestine. He separates origins into two categories—ethnic and socio-political.

R. B. Coote ("Tribalism: Social Organization in the Biblical Israels," in *Ancient Israel: The Old Testament in Its Social Context*, ed. P. F. Esler [Minneapolis: Fortress, 2006] 35–59) sees Israel emerging as a "tribal coalition" in the Late Bronze Age between the great powers of Egypt and Hatti. He reads the Merneptah Stele as evidence that "Israel was the main, if not sole, rural power in this region" (35). He sees a "run of unstable tribal monarchies" in the central highland, Israel's having a wider extent than any "urban-based local sovereignty in Palestine for the entire New Kingdom and Early Iron periods" (36).

Coote wants to remain "intentionally vague about Israelite social organization," sensing that it was "not always of one kind or ever one of a kind" ("Tribalism," 37). Indeed what we know of tribal organization comes from the later royal courts, the twelvefold Israelite system having arisen under David and showing great fluidity in its twenty different biblical orders. This results from clans moving geographically and changing tribal affiliations.

The designations of kinship levels within a tribe also appear fluid. *Šēbeṭ* (שׁבט) can refer to a tribe or a subgroup within a tribe. Clan terms *mišpāḥâ* (מִשׁפּחה) and *'elep* (אלף) can also refer to a whole tribe. Tribal territories are not intrinsic to tribal identity and often represent land also claimed by other groups. Such territory can be competed for or negotiated for. Tribal organization is shaped from the political top for military political reasons and not from local needs. It took shape "especially in relation to regional powers or states" ("Tribalism," 43). Ethnicity does not relate to tribalism, so we have "reason to doubt that in the biblical period 'Israel' was ever used as an ethnic entity" (45). Coote agrees with others that ceramic differences demonstrate the ethnic distinctions as opposed to ethnic homogeneity among tribes such as Asher and Benjamin. Genealogical descent is based on politics rather than on actual physical descent. Tribalism with its origins in royal courts "has no necessary connection with pastoralism or pastoral nomadism" (47).

P. McNutt (*Reconstructing the Society of Ancient Israel*, ed. D. A. Knight, Library of Ancient Israel [Louisville: Westminster John Knox, 1999] 64–103) surveys studies on Israelite tribal organization and repeatedly shows the dearth of information and consensus. So nowhere in the biblical traditions "do we find an explanation of how the notion of tribe was conceptualized, what the composition of tribes was, how the tribes related to one another on the economic and political levels, or the structure of society in general" (75). The various terms related to the social organization of Israel have yielded "no clear consensus on exactly what these terms mean or what level in the organization they refer to" (76). Genealogies function "not to produce and transmit accurate lists of biological relationships through time, but to define social, political, and economic relations, which are always open to revision" (76–77). The highland population of Iron Age I "probably consisted of nomads, seminomads, semisedentary peoples, and sedentary farmers and village residents" (78). The society had "no permanent 'governmental' authority" (79). The tribe "existed more as a means of providing a range of potential identities than as a base for sustained collective action" (81). Tribalism is not "a single phenomenon" but is "a complex system that brings people together for many different purposes in the context of many different competing or alternative principles of alignment" (82). The "concept of blood relatedness rather than actual blood relations . . . motivates common activities" (84). When not pulled together by crisis situations, the tribe maintains some sense of unity and loose bonding "through economic and religious ties" (84).

N. P. Lemche (*The Israelites in History and Tradition*, ed. D. A. Knight, Library of Ancient Israel [Louisville: Westminster John Knox, 1998]) sees Israelite history writing as something quite different from a report of what really happened. It is a dramatic creation of later writers "who had their idée of what constituted the people of God" (130). Lemche thus calls for a return to Noth's amphictyonic understanding but one created by Israelite writers of the late Persian or Hellenistic times. Ancient Israel, then, "is an artificial creation of the scholarly world of the modern age. . . . It simply developed out of the usual bad habit of paraphrasing the biblical text" (163).

J. A. Hackett ("'There Was No King in Israel': The Era of the Judges," in *The Oxford History of the Biblical World*, ed. M. D. Coogan [New York: Oxford UP, 1998] 193–201) infers from the Merneptah Stele that "Israel was a group of Canaanite people, self-identified as 'Israel' but not occupying any territory called 'Israel,' and therefore not a stable political entity" (196). It was a "segmentary tribal society lacking a central administration and a standing army" and was based on kinship relations. For leadership the tribal group had to rely on charismatic leaders. Throughout the period of the judges the tribal "system" was undergoing change—territorial, tribal name, allegiances, commitments. For Hackett, "this settlement-era tribal league, if it can be so called, apparently functioned under an arrangement for mutual defense, but did not have power to punish any members who failed to honor the arrangement" (199). Signs of centralization and amassing of wealth also appear, and the population doubles in two hundred years.

I would argue that the Song of Deborah at least shows a sense of unity among a large group of northern tribes and a sense of responsibility to answer the call to arms against an enemy. I would surmise from the song that it presupposed a gathering of the larger tribal group at which all tribes were expected to be present. The song would have been sung at such a "national" gathering. Worship of Yahweh was a central function of such a gathering as was affirmation of identity as a responsible people of Yahweh. The remainder of the book of Judges will show how lax leadership allowed the sense of unity and common purpose to dissolve amidst tribal isolation, jealousy, and warfare.

Remaining open is the question of how many tribes felt such loyalty, participated in such gatherings for worship, and answered the muster to battle. The book of Judges, with its opening chapter and its placing of Othniel as the first judge, obviously includes the southern tribes and sees twelve tribes composing "all Israel." Still, even chap. 1 omits mention of Issachar and the Transjordan tribes. Two verses from 1 Samuel either clarify or further confuse the picture: 1 Sam 11:8 and 15:4. They imply that Saul mustered armies from two distinct territories—Israel and Judah. M. W. Chavalas ("History of Israel 2: Premonarchic Israel," *DOTHB*, 441) correctly states: "This either implies an authentic historical situation or an anachronism on the part of the writer living in the period of the divided monarchy." Apparently, the writer of Judges, whom I would place in the period of Jeroboam I, had traditions like Judg 1:21–36 and the Song of Deborah that showed an early division between north and south but did his best in ordering his book to mask such a division. Compare the extent of the Israel that Ishbosheth ruled (2 Sam 2:9).

The total absence of Judah and Simeon from the song adds strength, albeit silent strength, to the supposition that a cleft between north and south reigned long before Saul and David. Judah and Simeon apparently come under no condemnation because they had, at the time of the song, no obligation to the larger group. Block instead reads this either as showing that the song "antedates the ascendancy of Judah under David's reign or that it reflects a subtle anti-Judahite posture" (234). Most commentators would accept the pre-Davidic date for the song, but that does little to explain the absence of Judah. The polemics of the song are anything but subtle. Younger is closer to reality as he sees that "although they are theoretically united by their worship of Yahweh and the covenant with him, the Israelites manifest a serious deficiency of political and military solidarity. The nonparticipant tribes refused to sacrifice their individual interest and well-being for the sake of the nation and are severely rebuked" (152). In his note Younger, a bit secretively, alludes to a possible military confederation as the "basis on which tribes can be chastened for noninvolvement," perhaps implying but not stating the lack of membership by the southern pair of tribes. Gray is more forceful in surmising that "it is questionable if Judah, unmentioned in the passage, was yet a member of the confederacy" ([1986] 284).

Ephraim was Joseph's second son (Gen 41:52) and became the eponymous ancestor of one of Israel's tribes when the Levites became a priestly tribe no longer listed as part of the twelve (Josh 14:4). He received his grandfather's blessing above his brother Manasseh (Gen 48:5, 19–20; compare Num 1:10; Deut 33:13–17) and the promise of extra land from Joshua (Josh 17:17–18). The name may have its origins in geography—the hill country of Ephraim (Josh 17:15; 19:50; 24:30), Deborah's home territory (Judg 4:5). In Judges, the people of Ephraim cannot drive the Canaanites from Gezer (1:29); they do answer Deborah's call to battle (5:14), as well as Gideon's (7:24). They argue with Gideon for calling them late in the battle (8:1–2; compare 12:1). The Ammonites attack them (10:9). The armies of Gilead decisively defeat Ephraim and show that dialect distinctions prevailed within all Israel (12:4–6). Abdon the judge (12:15) and Micah (17:1) were from Ephraim. Ephraim was part of Ishbosheth's kingdom (2 Sam 2:9). Eventually, Ephraim became a name for the entire northern kingdom (Isa 7:5, 8; 9:9; Jer 31:9; Hos 5:3).

The description of the people of Ephraim as having "their roots in Amalek" is unexpected and strange. Amalek refers to country near Kadesh-barnea in the south (Gen 14:7) in the Negev (Num 13:29; 1 Sam 27:8). Israel avoided the Amalekites' territory (Num 14:25). The Amalekites were apparently a nomadic tribe who occasionally attacked sedentary peoples or allied themselves with other groups for battle. Genealogies related Amalek to Esau (Gen 36:12, 16). The Amalekites fought Moses at Rephidim in the Sinai wilderness (Exod 17:8–13), causing God to put them under a curse (Exod 17:14–16; compare Num 24:20; Deut 25:17–19; 1 Sam 15:2). Still, God used them to punish Israel (Num 14:43–45). Judg 1:16 points to some interface with the Amalekites and portions of Judah (compare 1 Sam 15:6), but 3:13 shows them joining Eglon in attacking Israel (compare 6:3, 33; 7:12; 10:12). If the text of 12:15 is correct, then the Amalekites possessed part of Ephraim's territory (but see Soggin, 224). That being the case, the present verse builds off such Amalekite "occupation" to commend Ephraim for participation even when their own homeland, their "roots" stood under foreign dominion. Later Saul (1 Sam 14:48–15:32; compare 1 Sam 28:16–19) defeated the Amalekites, as did David (1 Sam 27:8; 30:1–18). (See G. L. Mattingly, "Amalek," *ABD*, 1:169–71.) A quaint reminiscence appears in 1 Chr 4:43 from "the days of Hezekiah" in which Simeonites defeat the remnant of the Amalekites.

Benjamin was Jacob's youngest and favorite (Gen 42:4) son, whose mother, Rachel, died giving him birth (Gen 35:18). Despite the portrayal of the Benjaminites as weak in Judg 1:21, Jacob described Benjamin as a "ravenous wolf" (Gen 49:27, NRSV; compare 1 Chr 12:2). Moses sang of Benjamin as "the beloved of the LORD" (Deut 33:12, NRSV). In assigning towns to the priests, Joshua grouped Benjamin with Simeon and Judah (Josh 21:4), while in Judg 10:9 Ammonites attack Judah, Benjamin, and Ephraim. The last chapters of Judges (19–21) describe the destruction of the tribe of Benjamin in civil war. Of great significance is Saul's descent from Benjamin (1 Sam 9:1, 16, 21; 10:21). His son Ishbosheth's short-lived kingdom included Benjamin, Ephraim, and Transjordan. Finally, Abner handed Benjamin over to David (2 Sam 3:19; compare 19:16–30). At the split of the kingdom, Benjamin fought with the southern Rehoboam (1 Kgs 12:21; compare 2 Chr 15:8; 25:5; 34:2; Ezra 4:1; Neh 11:4; Jer 17:26). Benjamin thus led his armies (or peoples) to support Deborah.

The name "Machir" puzzles the knowledgeable reader of the Bible, for Machir is not one of the twelve tribes. Rather, Machir was Jacob's grandson, the son of Manasseh (Gen 50:23; Num 26:29). Yet the people of Machir acted independently to gain land (Num 32:39) and apparently represented the eastern, Transjordan portion of Manasseh (Num 32:40; Deut 3:15; Josh 13:31; 17:1). Here mention of the name may call attention to the fact that western Manasseh did not answer the call to arms. The people of Machir sent not just soldiers, but commanders who bore the staff of authority.

Similar leaders came from Zebulun. Zebulun was Leah's sixth son (Gen 30:20). Jacob's blessing places Zebulun on the sea by the ships (Gen 49:13). Judg 1:30 shows the Zebulunites' inability to control their assigned territory. With Naphtali, Zebulun was a central tribe supporting Barak (Judg 4:6, 10; 5:18; compare Isa 9:1; Matt 4:13–15). Zebulun also supported Gideon (6:35) and David (1 Chr 12:33, 40 [Heb. 34, 41]). Zebulun is uniquely connected with Reuben and Gad in 1 Chr 6:63 (Heb. 6:48). Seen as a far-distant tribe, they were divided in their support of Hezekiah (2 Chr 30:10–11, 18).

15–16 Issachar, Leah's fifth son (Gen 30:18), also sent leaders into battle for

Deborah and also proved loyal to Barak. Jacob describes him as "a strong donkey, lying down between the sheepfolds" who "became a slave at forced labor" (Gen 49:14–15, NRSV), apparently describing a lazy tribe more ready to be slaves to Canaanites in the fruitful valley than to labor in the less fertile hills. Moses' blessing (Deut 33:18) places them in tents. Manasseh controlled some towns in Issachar's territory (Josh 17:11). Whatever the social status of the tribe in Deborah's day, they showed willingness and determination to join the battle. Representatives of the tribe participated in rebellions in the northern kingdom (1 Kgs 4:17; 15:27). Issachar represented the furthest extent of those supporting David (1 Chr 12:40 [Heb. 41]) and of those Hezekiah invited to his passover (2 Chr 30:18). Issachar displays courage in joining Barak in the valley, where Canaanite chariots appear to have an overwhelming advantage.

Reuben heads the other tribal listing, that of those not showing loyalty to the confederation. Reuben has "great resolution of heart." See *Notes* above, noticing the similarity yet distinction in the final parts of vv 15 and 16 and how Niditch can argue for ten tribes in a fighting confederation without condemnation of any of them (compare Niditch, 79–80). The Reubenites considered their options and decided to stay home tending their flocks. Economics and daily duties took precedence over the call to battle. These shepherd folks sat around the campfires listening to the pipes played to signal the flock and possibly to entertain the shepherds. Even second thoughts coming to their hearts (Boling, 112) do not change their resolution to stay put.

Reuben was Jacob and Leah's firstborn (Gen 29:32). His gift of mandrakes to his mother led to Rachel's jealousy of Leah and of the birth of Leah's fifth son, Issachar (Gen 30:14–18). Reuben also violated his father's concubine (Gen 35:22), resulting in the loss of his prerogatives as the firstborn (Gen 49:3–4; 1 Chr 5:1). As older brother, he protected his younger brother (Gen 37:21–22, 29; 42:22, 37). Along with Gad, the tribe of Reuben persuaded Moses to let them occupy the pasture lands east of the Jordan if they would send their armies with the Israelites in their occupation of land west of the Jordan (Num 32; compare Deut 3:12, 16; 29:8; Josh 1:12–13; 4:12; 12:6; 13:8, 15–23; 18:7). Moses' song prayed for the survival of sparsely populated Reuben (Deut 33:6). The altar of the eastern tribes led to threats from the western tribes (Josh 22). In the days of Saul the Reubenites faced Ammonite oppression (1 Sam 10:27). Saul delivered them from the Ammonites, leading to recognition of Saul's kingship (1 Sam 11). The tribe had a strong military reputation (1 Chr 5:18). The wavering Reubenites were apparently a small population and did not think they had resources to sacrifice for people so far removed from them.

17 Gilead is another unusual name among the tribes. Gilead appears to be a geographical designation (Gen 31:21; 37:25; Deut 2:36) described as well-suited for livestock (Num 32:1, 29) and given to Machir (Num 32:40; Deut 3:15; Josh 13:31; compare 1 Chr 27:21). It was included in the description of the land from Dan to Beersheba (Judg 20:1) and could be called the "land of Gad and Gilead" (1 Sam 13:7). Hosea referred to a city called Gilead (Hos 6:8; compare 12:11).

Gilead was the grandson of Manasseh and son of Machir (Num 26:29, a list that appears to demonstrate the use of the genealogical form to represent political conditions; Josh 17:1). Gileadites acted as a separate political entity in protecting their land (Num 36). Jephthah, a Gileadite, sired by Gilead (Judg 11:1; 1 Chr

2:21, 23; 7:14), agreed to lead the "people of Gilead" (Judg 10:18). The Gileadites had commanders (10:18) and elders (11:5–11). Jephthah mustered Gilead's
army—"the men of Gilead" (12:4), seen by Ephraim as "fugitives from Ephraim"
(12:4), as if the residents of Gilead had crossed over the Jordan west to east. Yet
the Ephraimites had developed a dialect distinct from that of Gilead (12:5–6).
Ishbosheth was king over Gilead in a list combining tribal and geographic names
(2 Sam 2:9). Gileadites participated in a rebellion in the northern kingdom (2 Kgs
15:25). Pss 60:7 and 108:8 (Heb. 60:9; 108:9) preserve a traditional poetic line
claiming tribal and national territories for Yahweh and placing Gilead parallel
with Manasseh, Ephraim, and Judah. The embryonic tribal system shown by the
poem may here incorporate a geographical term for an area distinct from that
controlled by Machir and parallel to that designated for Gad but not at the time
populated by any Israelite tribe. Otherwise, Gilead is a poetic name for Gad or a
tribe controlling part of the Transjordan in a revolving door of tribal names early
in Israel's fight for the land. Gilead only becomes involved in Israelite life when
the Ammonites bring the fighting into their territory (Judg 10–12).

As a tribe, Dan endured a checkered history. The name appears anachronistically as a geographical designation in Gen 14:14. Genealogically, Dan is the son
of Rachel's maid Bilhah (Gen 30:6; 35:25). Jacob's blessing makes a play on the
name of Dan, "to judge," but also describes Dan as a sly snake catching travelers
unawares and biting them (Gen 49:16–17). Moses' song places Dan in the north
by Bashan and refers to him as an attacking lion cub (Deut 33:22). Dan became
identified with Israel's northern border (Deut 34:1; Judg 20:1; 1 Sam 3:20; 2 Sam
3:10; 17:11; 24:2, 15; 1 Kgs 4:25; 1 Chr 21:2; 2 Chr 30:5). Dan lost its original land
allotment and moved north (Josh 19:47), but its Levitical cities were in the original
southwestern allotment (21:23). Judg 1:34 apparently records an intermediate
stage when Dan could not occupy the territory's coastal valleys, and the Amorites
pushed them back into the Shephelah. This is evidently the Dan in which Samson
operates (Judg 13–16). In Judg 18 Dan finally moves to the far north. Dan's noto-
riety came for the shrine Jeroboam established there for the northern kingdom
(1 Kgs 12:29–30; 2 Kgs 10:29; Amos 8:14). Deborah's song places Dan in its earliest
coastal location and views the people of Dan as landless resident aliens working
for the local shipping industry (compare Judg 18:1; see L. E. Stager, "Archaeology, Ecology, and Social History"; idem, *BAR* 15 [1989] 55). A. F. Rainey's attempt
("Who Is a Canaanite?" *BASOR* 304 [1996] 11, reprinted in *Sacred Bridge*, 138–39)
to locate Dan in the far north at the foot of Mount Hermon and explain the sea
connections as trading connections with Tyre and Sidon with some of the people
having "signed on for a tour of sea duty" is not comprehensive enough to explain
why the whole tribe can be castigated for not participating and does not really
place Dan living as an alien with ships.

Asher's territory lay to the far north above the Kishon River, not all that far
removed from Barak's battlefield. But Asher, too, had settled down to participate
in a maritime economy and had neither time nor inclination to go to war. Gray
may be right in surmising that "the absence of Asher in the foothills east of Acco
may indicate that Harosheth, Sisera's fortress, was still an effective barrier" ([1986]
284), but economic reasons probably played a stronger role. Asher was the son of
Zilpah, Leah's maid (Gen 30:13; 35:26). Jacob's blessing cryptically predicts that
Asher "shall provide royal delicacies" (Gen 49:20, NRSV). Does this mean Asher

had to serve in the kitchens for foreign kings? Or that Asher was wealthy enough to eat like a king? Moses' blessing appears quite positive for Asher (Deut 33:24–25). Manasseh held cities within Asher's territory (Josh 17:11). Asher could not occupy several of the Canaanite cities and lived among the Canaanites (Judg 1:31–32). Asher did answer Gideon's call (6:35; 7:23). Asher had representation, if limited, at Hezekiah's passover (2 Chr 30:11).

18 Zebulun's central role is emphasized, while adding Naphtali, Barak's tribe (Judg 4:6), to the list of brave participants. These two played the crucial roles in the opening stages of the call to battle (Judg 4:6, 10). Naphtali was the son of Bilhah, Rachel's maid (Gen 30:8; 35:25), described poetically as "a doe let loose that bears lovely fawns" (Gen 49:21, NRSV). Moses describes Naphtali as "sated with favor, full of the blessing of the LORD," who is to "possess the west and the south" (Deut 33:23, NRSV). Only after much struggle could Naphtali take control of the Canaanites in their cities (Judg 1:33). The people of Naphtali also fought for Gideon (6:35; 7:23). They provided provisions for David (1 Chr 12:40). Josiah carried out his cultic reform as far away as Naphtali (2 Chr 34:6).

This tribal roll call is unique. It includes the geographical designation of Gilead; the eastern clan designation for Machir as part of Manasseh, but no mention of the other part of Manasseh; the central role of Zebulun and Naphtali—otherwise somewhat minor tribes; the participation of Ephraim, Benjamin, and Issachar with their somewhat central location; and the designation of Dan, Asher, Reuben, and Gilead as nonparticipants. The most likely explanation remains that of Stager:

> The Song of Deborah depicts a ten-tribe confederation—the "kindred (or people) of Yahweh"—out of which only six tribes actively participated in the battle against the Canaanites. Those tribes who failed to respond to the call suffered the scorn of those who rallied to the battle, but they could not be coerced to join the fight. There were times when "ethnic" bonding did not prevail over more compelling realities, such as those non-tribal economic and political alignments that . . . caused Dan, Asher, Reuben, and Gilead/Gad to sit out the battle. . . . The tribes who answered the call . . . had far fewer economic entanglements with non-Israelites than those tribes whose livelihoods depended to a large extent on maritime trade or on specialized pastoralism. (*BAR* 15 [1989] 62)

The latter would be tied to the sedentary population required to trade for essential food and household items who thus would lack motivation to go to battle. One might note a lack of loyalty to commitments moving the other direction in the case of Heber and Jael.

These tribal assessments lie at the center of the poem, but they are not central to the message and meaning of the poem. They represent only one part of the blessing-and-curse motif that drives the poem forward to its unexpected end, which provides the central meaning.

19 The poem celebrates Yahweh, as do all Israelite hymns, but its specific uniqueness lies in its celebration of Israel's volunteer warriors and its curse on those who refuse to participate and on enemy forces who do. Vv 19–22 tell the tale of holy war.

Enemy kings come to Taanach expecting victory but end up with no "spoils of battle." Lindars (267) thinks, based on archaeological results, that neither Taanach nor Megiddo was a major city at the time of the battle. Their mention reflected rather the situation at the time of writing of the poem, or at least of this element of the poem. Younger follows A. R. Rainey (*ErIsrl* 15 [1981] 61–66), who sees Taanach as a traditional place for mustering armies for battle and surmises that military exploits were registered and prizes awarded there. From this Younger concludes that the narrative preserves "the location of the battle," while the song preserves "the location where the Canaanite kings would have divided the booty, but didn't" ("Heads! Tails!" 134).

Taanach is located at Tell Ta'annek, whose mound is 131 feet (40 m) above the Jezreel Valley and five miles (8 km) southeast of Megiddo on the road to Ibleam. Thutmose III in 1468 B.C.E. and Shishak I in 918 B.C.E. claim to have captured it. Captured by Joshua (Josh 12:21), it became part of Manasseh in territory originally belonging to Issachar and Asher (Josh 17:11). Only after a slow process could Manasseh occupy it (Jdg 1:27). Under Solomon, it became the administrative center of the fifth district (1 Kg 4:12). From 1450 to 1200 B.C.E. the site had "no significant occupation" (A. E. Glock, "Taanach," *NEAEHL*, 4:1432). Occupation in the 1100s was destroyed about 1125. Limited occupation occurred in the 1000s with heavier occupation in the next century, that being destroyed in 918. K. A. Kitchen (*On the Reliability of the Old Testament* [Grand Rapids: Eerdmans, 2003] 185) identifies the 1100s occupation with Deborah, but note the reservations of I. Finkelstein (*The Archaeology of the Israelite Settlement* [Jerusalem: Israel Exploration Society, 1988] 88–89, 92), who sees "no Israelite Settlement in the Jezreel Valley before the beginning of the 10th century BCE."

Megiddo at Tell el-Muteselim rises 130 to 200 feet (40–60 m) above the valley and controls access to the Via Maris running through the valley. Thus major battles often occurred there. Thutmose III claims to have defeated a coalition of rebellious Canaanite kings at Megiddo about 1468. Amenhotep II marched to Megiddo about 1430. At least six of the Amarna letters come from Megiddo, indicating it was one of the most powerful of the Canaanite city-states. Rameses II (1304–1237) mentions the city and its road system. Conquered by Joshua (Josh 12:21) and allocated to Manasseh (Josh 17:11–13), Megiddo resisted for a long period (Judg 1:27–28). Solomon fortified the city (1 Kgs 9:15; compare 1 Kgs 4:12). Shishak conquered it about 925. It became a provincial capital when Tiglath Pileser III of Assyria captured Israel in 721. Josiah died there, fighting the Egyptians (2 Kgs 23:29). Kitchen (*On the Reliability of the Old Testament*, 207) dates Deborah about 1165 to 1150 B.C.E., the same time he dates (148) Megiddo stratum VIIA or VIB. Finkelstein (*Archaeology of the Israelite Settlement*, 93) points to Stratum VIA as a Canaanite-Philistine city, attributing its conquest to David and thus leaving no room for pre-Davidic Israelites at Megiddo.

The poet uses Taanach and Megiddo as place markers, situating the fight, giving no indication of the size of either town at the moment of this battle. Archaeological reports here are insignificant as long as some form of occupation, even occupation difficult for archaeologists to discover, existed. The size of that occupation has more significance for Judg 1 and Josh 17. The significant point here is not geography but participants in battle. Canaanite kings, masters of the valley through use of their chariots, came forth in their favorite arena to meet the upstart highlanders coming down to face them. But the poet skips over any mention of the Israelite army. Lindars (265) describes the battle report as brief and ironical, the mention of war spoils pointing to the expectations of Sisera's mother in the final stanza. The battle is not the central theme of the poetic narrative. The battle is the preliminary action pointing ahead to the featured attraction.

20 Expecting to face an amateurish militia, the Canaanite army instead discovers an unexpected enemy—the entire natural universe, stars, and rivers. Block remarks that the poet "alludes to his [i.e., God's] involvement only obliquely" (182). Lindars sees the real motive in the poem as "the battle itself in which Yahweh fights on behalf of his people" (168). It is this victory that gives rise to a victory song praising Yahweh. A victory song would be expected to concentrate on the battle, as is seen much more vividly in Exod 15:1–18. That Judg 5 treats the battle in such brief, terse terms, leaving divine participation to the reader's or listener's discernment, provides further evidence for arguing against the victory song as the primary genre of this composition.

Canaanite kings might defeat Israel's army without weapons, but they cannot stand before God's weapons. Canaanite kings might pay allegiance to the fertility power of Baal in the north to send the rains, but Yahweh comes from the south accompanied by clouds streaming rain.

Lindars (268–69) discusses various theories about the stars, favoring the traditional image, boosted by Ugaritic evidence, that the stars poured the rain down. He rejects any suggestion that they represent Deborah's army with Deborah taking the position traditionally occupied by the goddess Anat in mythological texts. Lindars also denies any connection to the eclipse of the sun in 1131 B.C.E. Block sees the use of the forces of nature as a sign that Yahweh "usurps the signs of theophanic advent which Canaanites had associated with Baal" (237).

Younger explains that in the ancient Near East "an army was often composed of troops from numerous small vassal states with their kinglets or chiefs leading them" (133). Block calls the reference to Canaanite kings a "poetic hyperbolic flourish," explaining that "to Deborah the Israelite triumph over Sisera represented a victory over all the Canaanite kingdoms of the land" (236). One must note at this point that the prosaic framework (4:1, 23–24) sets the poem in a context of war with all of Canaan by referring to Jabin as the king of Canaan. In some way for Israel from its earliest celebration of this tradition, the battle God won for Deborah and Barak represented not just a local skirmish or a northern triumph, but a decisive victory over the land and nation(s) of Canaan. Soggin (95) points to the strange absence of the figure of God in these verses, but God is absent only to those who cannot read the poetic allusions to elements controlled only by the deity. Olson expands the discussion to talk of "widely divergent views of human and divine agency" that scholars hold in comparing the prose narrative and the poetic composition. He concludes that such divergence is due to "a complex intertwining and subtle dialectic between the divine plan and human freedom that cannot be easily distinguished or separated in either the prose or the poetic account" (775). Surely the simple explanation of Younger is to be followed here: "according to their emphases, these are simply complementary ways of describing the great victory that took place" ("Heads! Tails!" 134).

21 Mention of the Kishon River or wadi occurs only in reference to this section (see Ps 83:9 [Heb. 10]) and in Elijah's adventure on Mount Carmel (1 Kgs 18:40). The Kishon drained the western Jezreel Valley, supplying water for its great agricultural productivity, but heavy rains could turn it into a marshland, inhibiting all movement. The Kishon apparently served as the boundary line between Asher and Manasseh and between Zebulun and Manasseh. It may also have formed part of the border of Issachar and Manasseh. (See R. Frankel, "Kishon," *ABD*, 4:89.)

Hauser insists that such use of water goes beyond literal description to poetic metaphor yet does not enter the mythic world of a cosmic struggle with primordial chaos. The theophany shows that God comes to battle as "the powerful God of the storm." Hauser points to the "watering places"; the association of Gilead with the Jordan River, Dan with his ships, and Asher with the sea coast; and the Kishon torrent as artistic uses of water to contrast peaceful water and water as battle-determining torrent. Reference to the reluctant tribes is "teasing the reader, suggesting that, despite vv. 4–5, water may not be under Yahweh's control, may not be available to help with the Israelite victory." Then "the image of the torrent Kishon in v. 21 will automatically bring to the mind of the audience the theophany of Yahweh" ("Two Songs of Victory," 270–72). Niditch views the Kishon as including "notions of world creation, fertility, and destructive power" (80).

As the river rolls over the enemy, Deborah encourages herself to remain strong and continue marching until the battle is concluded. This intrusive jussive form somehow demonstrates the courage and determination of the Israelite army, but its exact meaning is widely debated. (For various views, see Lindars, who concludes: "the colon jars so badly with the form and character of the stanza that it cannot be regarded as original, however it is explained" [270–71].) As it stands, one must conclude with Schneider (91) that "the text stresses the role of Deborah." That this stress places her "over Barak" in this instance may be strongly contested. A self-address summoning courage to continue the fight does not necessarily place the addressee above anyone else. Block is on the right trail, saying the "self-exhortation to 'advance with strength' is triumphalist, conjuring up images of a conqueror treading the neck of the vanquished" (237).

22 Using "wonderful onomatopoeia" (Younger, 153), the poet draws the reader or listener into the battle, sensing the sound of galloping horses' hoofs. But the audience stands in wonder: whose horses going where? The expected answer would be Canaanite horses advancing. The most obvious and popular interpretation is that enemy troops famous for their chariots and cavalry are fleeing the battle scene, at least momentarily, before meeting their death; perhaps riderless horses are meant, signifying the enemy's total defeat. Block sees the reference to the horses as a description of stallions rearing wildly and flailing frantically in the frenzy of the torrent, thus a picture of "the incapacitation of the horses" (238). Younger writes of "the chaos of the horses galloping wildly over the field, missing their riders or free of their chariots" (153). The previous verse has shown the impossibility of Canaanite horses attacking Israel on the Kishon battlefield. Either we must allow the poet some poetic license and inconsistency here, or the horses are galloping away from the battlefield, beyond the marshes of the Kishon, in defeat. Perhaps the poet leaves the reader to wonder for a moment.

23–24 Lindars is correct in seeing that beginning here in v 23 "the triumphant success of the battle is impressed on the reader in three vivid scenes, which need not be considered as successive events, but are rather comments from three different angles" (272). The poetic theme of blessing and cursing reaches its climax here.

We know nothing of Meroz. Lindars uses "a little imagination" to see Meroz as a clan that "was in a position to cut off the flight of the main body of the enemy and refused to do so" (272). Such a clan, in his view, "need not have had obligations to either side, but being so close to the action was appealed to for help to cut off the Canaanites in their flight" (273). He sees this as another possible instance of the poet using existing verses and stanzas in composing the form that we have.

But Meroz is central to the repeated theme of blessing on freewill volunteering, battle participation, and personal initiative to defeat the enemy contrasted to cursing on those who do not participate and thus show love for Yahweh. Such a curse in this context reflects a group expected to show loyalty to Yahweh and to one's own people, not a group without obligations whose refusal brought forth frustration that expressed itself in a curse. Younger sees a structural parallel with the cursing of two cities in the Gideon narrative (Judg 8:7, 9): "If one considers this parallel of the Gideon narrative to the Song of Deborah, Meroz may be such an Israelite city that failed to aid the pursuing forces of Barak when they needed it rather than when the initial call to war went out" (153). "Meroz represents those Israelites who have taken their stand on the side of the Canaanites; [Jael in the next stanza] represents those non-Israelites who have taken their stand on the side of Israel" (154). Block, likewise, concludes on the somewhat tenuous basis of other contexts in which the *mal'ak yhwh* (יהוה מלאך) or "messenger of Yahweh" appears that "Meroz represents those Israelites who have taken their stand on the side of the Canaanites" (239). Compare H.-D. Neef, *ZAW* 107 (1995) 118–22.

Auld (159) goes the other way to see Meroz and Jael as not being Israelite, the argument concerning Meroz being that it is not listed among the tribes. This argument is dubious, for nowhere could Meroz merit tribal consideration. The point is that not just tribes, but also every component of Israel, even the most insignificant, has responsibility to the whole and is expected to display unity with the whole on every occasion. Perhaps Meroz stands here a bit obliquely for the entire nonparticipating Israelite contingent. At least, Israel is to understand that every component of Israel from tribe to the basic family unit has obligations to fight for the defense of every other component of Israel. Those who refuse stand under the curse of Yahweh.

Webb argues that "the battle itself is the climax of the song; the two strophes in the final stanza show how completely his enemies were undone" ([1987] 144). I would argue that the poet is much more interested in praising and blessing than in describing battle outcomes. The point is the praise of unexpected heroes. As Younger notes, "one of the Song's purposes is to exalt and praise Jael . . . and taunt Sisera" ("Heads! Tails!" 131).

We know Jael as the heroine of this story, but her identity comes only through her husband. She married Heber, the elusive Kenite, with only fringe ties to Israel. Israel is now identified through the actions and attitudes of their fringe members, not their core constituency. Schneider is surely right as she claims, "Jael's blessed status is important because it indicates that the actions Jael is about to take (and has already performed in Judges 4) are condoned" (92). Fokkelman says, "Her [Jael's] act is praiseworthy and unique because she is not an Israelite; her act, however, makes her an Israelite, poetically speaking" ("Song of Deborah and Barak," 620, n. 64).

Soggin notes that "a semi-nomadic group like the Kenites must have been particularly dependent on relationships of this kind, if it wanted to be able to obtain pasturage and water along its route" (77). He sees no evidence that the Kenites were robbers or brigands living off the spoils of other people's battles. As with Deborah in chap. 4, so here heroine Jael's gender is specifically emphasized. She is among the "women in tents." Younger asserts, based on Near Eastern parallels, that "since Jael is being portrayed as the most blessed of women, she is described with the stereotyped head-smashing motif. . . . The point is not the *modus operandi* but the implication. Hence, the means of death is not as important as the meaning of the death. Jael's praise takes precedence over the description of the event" ("Heads! Tails!" 131–32).

Lindars (274) argues that the warriors are really *heroes* of Israel and translates "alongside the heroes." This is possible, but the poem has emphasized the weakness of Israel and the strength of the enemy so that the נבורים most likely are the mighty enemy warriors, a translation Lindars admits as a possibility. When enemy warriors face off against Israel, every unit in Israel has the opportunity to join Yahweh in battle and in victory. Those who answer the call, no matter how tenuous their ties to Israel, find blessing.

25–27   Lindars sees these verses as part of a pre-formed unit the poet used, "an item for which the audience have been waiting," and "welded . . . into his composition with great skill" (274). The very nature of oral poetic composition may plead for this interpretation, but nothing can prove or disprove it. Niditch introduces the murder story nicely:

> The language is of eroticism and death and describes motherly or loverlike nurturing that masks murderous intentions. He asks for water, but she gives him milk, rich curds fit for a prince. Even as she offers the food to him, the poet's language swoops into another motion, as Jael reaches for the hammer and stake with which to impale the man. The overt violence of v. 26 is followed by the double entendres of v. 27 in which images of defeated warrior play upon those of would-be lover. (81)

Niditch then explicates each of the sexual nuances of the language, concluding, "The defeated enemy becomes the woman who is raped, the victor her rapist. Here, ironically, it is a woman who is in the position of rapist, the enemy male general her victim" (81).

Fewell and Gunn assert that "the song celebrates Sisera's world gone awry. His desire for control, for spoil, for glory, the song parodies in images of aborted sexual desire" (*JAAR* 58 [1990] 404). They read the prose narrative, on the other hand, as treating violence differently:

> The narrator's version revels in the reversal of expectations, the upturning of stereotypes. . . . The reader (if not Sisera) is forced to reconsider stereotypical expectations of women's behavior and power. . . . The point is that both Sisera and patriarchal reader fail to consider the woman's wider social/political interest. They do not want to imagine that, under duress, she might herself invade the male monopoly of power, claim the authority of violence. (405–6)

This is a fine statement if the narrative truly centers on feminine interests, but if the center of interest is not on self-interest but on how women illustrate the weakness of Israelite leadership and show they can fill the gap when needed, then the statement needs much revision. The distinction in presentation of the Jael-Sisera confrontation between the narrative and poetic accounts does not mean contradictory understandings of the event. As Lindars remarks, "Jael's action is really the same [in ch. 5] as in 4.19–21, and the differences noted by the majority of commentators are due to failure to observe the economy of the narrative" (274).

Yee observes that "the fact that she [i.e., Jael] uses trickery is no different from the guerrilla tactics that the Israelite forces already employ. Moral condemnations singling out her clandestine actions are therefore unwarranted" (*Semeia* 61 [1993] 113). Yee explains, "Jael's alleged violations of hospitality must be situated in the context of guerrilla war tactics" (113, n. 10). Yee accepts the arguments of Matthews ("Hospitality and Hostility in Judges 4," *BTB* 21 [1991] 13–21) that Sisera deserves more condemnation for violating hospitality codes than does Jael: "Jael would then be acting in defense of her household's honor" (Yee, *Semeia* 61 [1993] 113, n. 10). Webb notes that "unlike the corresponding scene in chapter 4 this one is not concerned with how the honour was taken away from Barak and given to a woman, but solely with the fate that Sisera suffered" ([1987] 143). Such a statement demands modification, for Jael is the commanding subject throughout. The poetic narrative shows why she is blessed, not why Sisera suffers. The loss and gain of honor motif from chap. 4 disappears, but the motif of the leadership and victory by a woman remains central. Chap. 4 subtly borrows the "woman wins" motif and transforms it into a more blatant ironic chastisement of Barak and the lack of male leadership in Israel.

Hauser observes that "the drawn-out description of his fall to the ground provides the cathartic moment of release for the audience, who can vent in their savoring of the downfall of the Canaanite leader the intense hatred of the Canaanites that had built up for so many years" ("Two Songs of Victory," 276). Again, I must add, not just before Israel, but before the peripheral Israelite, the woman Jael.

28–30 Chap. 4 turns the focus from Jael to Barak and his foolish and unsuccessful attempts to destroy his one last enemy, thus openly comparing Barak's weakness to Jael's strength. The poetic chap. 5 climaxes in a totally unexpected manner, with an ironic eavesdropping on the women left behind in Sisera's stronghold, including Sisera's mourning mother. Lindars justifiably sees this last stanza as "not merely a tail-piece, but a satisfying conclusion, which rounds off the poem as a whole" (280). Similarly, Bal notes, "the poetess knew exactly how to exploit the specific lyric form to enhance—impressively, it cannot be denied—the agony of the enemy and his definitive annihilation" (*Murder and Difference*, 84).

Younger concludes: "This stanza frees the reader from any positive sympathetic feelings toward Sisera and negative feelings toward Jael. The horrors that Sisera (directly) and his mother (indirectly) have mercilessly dispensed on others come back on them" (162). Fewell and Gunn note that "by forcing the Canaanite women to approve unconsciously their own imminent rape, the singer victors can end their recital in mocking triumph." They see that

> in reality, however, it is the authority of violence that is justified. And in the face of that authority, the woman, Deborah, has offered no real alternative. A woman in a man's world, her voice hardening, merging with a man's voice, defines that world by oppositions and so finds her place in it. . . . The singers, like their imagined Canaanite women, dispose of others without conscience because there is no middle ground. Once the trapped, the non-aligned, go unrecognized, it is a world set for oppression, domination by the mighty. And the mighty, this time, is, of course, Israel. (*JAAR* 58 [1990] 408)

Here is the interpreter's dilemma in Judges. When we go to Judges seeking a new moral outlook, a breakthrough in the realm of social ethics and realigning societal factions, we face great disappointment. The best we can say is that the book of Judges paints the crimes so black that one should see the need for a new ordering of society, though one will not find that new order here.

Bal (*Murder and Difference*, 84) notes the irony of women waiting hidden behind latticed windows rather than running out to meet the returning victors with a song of victory. Instead of singing, the women worry. This contrasts with Deborah singing a victory song, not only for other soldiers but also for her own part in prodding Israel and its general to victory. Schneider observes that the use of the term שׂר in this context, used here for women for the first and only time in the Hebrew Bible, "places these people in some official capacity *vis à vis* Sisera's mother, who would then in turn be seen to function in an official political position as the queen mother" (95). Fokkelman points out that "the single voice of the mother now merges with the voices of her wisest court-ladies" (Song of Deborah and Barak" 623). Coogan aptly describes the scene as "a combination of pathos and satire" (*CBQ* 40 [1978] 154). Schneider underlines the irony of the situation: "without knowing it she acted appropriately for the situation since she had just lost her son" (94). Further irony appears in the ensuing conversation as "suddenly the mother is not just a mother but someone with advisors and concerned with the booty she hoped her son was collecting. . . . She was visualizing her son having a good time raping captive women and bringing in booty while the reader knows that a woman, possibly a potential rape victim, just killed him" (Schneider, 96).

So the poetic narrative comes to an abrupt end. Meroz, Jael, Sisera, and his mother disappear into narrative oblivion. Yet they have made their point. No one can expect victory in opposition to Yahweh. No one can refuse to fulfill vows of loyalty to Yahweh and to Israel and escape Yahweh's angry curse. The normal rules of battle do not apply when Yahweh marches forth from his southern fortress to battle. And blessing from Yahweh falls on anyone who displays love for Yahweh by performing even the most insignificant role in fighting with Yahweh's forces.

31a Appropriately enough, the song ends with a liturgical curse on Yahweh's enemies and a blessing on those who love Yahweh. Polzin says this concluding petition of 5:31a "strongly suggests that even Israel may be a part of the company of the Lord's enemies" (*Moses and the Deuteronomist*, 167). Such a call to love Yahweh has roots in the formulation of the Decalogue (Exod 20:6; Deut 5:10; compare Josh 22:5; 23:11). Love of God is shown by obedience (Deut 7:9; 11:1; 30:20; 1 Kgs 3:3; Isa 56:6) and faithfulness (Ps 31:23 [Heb. 24]). Els (*NIDOTTE*, 1:283) traces all such language to Deuteronomistic theology, seeing the Decalogue and Judg 5:31 as late Deuteronomistic editiorial additions. This assumes a pristine, short version of the Decalogue and Deborah's song not being rounded off by the blessing and curse that aptly summarize and represent the major content and form of the song. Els can be followed when he ties human love for God to covenant obligations while maintaining a human, emotive "personal feeling of love of the Israelite for Yahweh, in some instances as a grateful response to his deeds of redemption and care." Brown defines "love the Lord" as "to be faithful to covenant commitment(s) to the Lord" (181). Lindars (287) also sees covenant language here as shown by W. L. Moran ("The Ancient Near Eastern Background of the Love of God in Deuteronomy," *CBQ* 25 [1963] 77–87).

Such human love for God results from a divine operation on the human heart (Deut 30:6). Els concludes:

Human love for God is therefore far from being expressed merely in sheer *legalism or external observance* of the cult; on the contrary, it engages the *whole person*, with all his/her powers; it must come from one's whole heart (Deut 4:29; 6:5; 10:12; 11:13; 13:3 [4]; 30:6) and must lead to a cleaving to God (דָּבַק) that is living and dynamic (Deut 10:20; 11:22; 13:3 [4]; 30:20; Josh 22:5; 23:8; 2 Kgs 18:6). (*NIDOTTE*, 1:286, emphasis original)

31b The editor inserts the framework element of forty years of rest. Conspicuous by its absence is any mention of either Barak or Deborah judging the land or dying and being buried. Was she perhaps buried under the "palm tree of Deborah" (4:5)? Did the editor seek to avoid encouraging people to make her burial place a pilgrimage shrine of some type? Many arguments can be made here by supposition and silence. Still, the absence of these important elements does force the commentator to ask questions if not give answers.

Explanation

The two accounts of the story of Barak, Deborah, and Jael show quite distinct purposes and emotional settings. Judg 4 proves to be a historical parody on holy war showing how God brings victory through a woman with only marginal Israelite identity and despite the uselessness of his chosen general. Judg 5 proves to be a unique poetic composition blending praise of God and of marginalized people who become his servants with cursing and implicit condemnation of people who do not answer his call to action. It blends cultic elements with instructional elements. It blends satirical narrative elements with epic narrative elements. It joins divine theophany language to a review of a roll call that some tribes answered and others ignored. In so doing, it may well have originated in an early Israelite community to inspire loyalty to Yahweh, to give identity to Israel as the people of Yahweh, and perhaps to muster volunteers for the army of Yahweh. The poem calls Israel to celebrate God's righteous acts, to petition God to push those past victories into the ongoing future, and to teach its people of the ever-present danger of curse on an Israel that is not unified. Fokkelman summarizes the poem:

> The importance of passing judgment is indeed so central that the act of passing judgment permeates the whole poem. It is a ferment that has penetrated every stanza. And it has given the poet a set of oppositions that are fertile material for shaping and charging his structures dynamically. ("Song of Deborah and Barak," 615)

The two chapters accomplish their quite distinct purposes by relating a basic set of facts common to both. Webb emphasizes the differences between the two versions of the story ([1987] 141). Olson (774) finds both similarities and key differences. Both versions have the same list of main characters, recount the battle and victory over Sisera, feature the leadership roles of Deborah and Barak, and tell the story of Jael's hospitality and murder. Younger figures that "about one third of each account corresponds with the other although even in this the material is not necessarily identical." He sees this as comparable to other Near Eastern parallel accounts, concluding that the "unmatched material reveals the different emphases of the respective accounts" ("Heads! Tails!" 129). Deborah and Barak are the titular heroes leading into battle, but Jael is the most blessed of the heroes, for she actually kills the enemy leader, Sisera. Naphtali and Zebulun are central tribes in the battle. Canaanites are the enemies. The river Kishon is the central point of battle. Heber the Kenite is Jael's husband. Jael fools Sisera by not obeying his orders. A tent peg and hammer are the murder weapons. A peg through the temple is the cause of death. Lindars concludes, "It can, then, reasonably be claimed that the common tradition told of Jael as using her skill in pitching tents to murder a mighty warrior in a way that no ordinary woman could do" (200–201). Niditch is certainly on target: "It is a particular self-image of the underdog that Israelite authors savor in various guises" (82).

With this list of similar elements, one must conclude that a common store of narrative elements lay behind each of the descriptions of the battle. Whoever has joined the two together has done so in the recognition that the individual compositions, so distinct in style and genre, still refer to the same event. Younger ("Heads! Tails!" 109–46) compares cuneiform and Egyptian reports preserved in both annalistic and poetic forms and discovers that

> ancient scribes could write different accounts about the same referents. But differences in purpose could determine differences in detail. If the scribe's purpose was to praise the king and/or the gods, poetry naturally offered a medium to heighten the emotions of the praise through rhetorical embellishments. Hence, divine activity and praise of the deities is encountered more often in the poetic versions. . . . But in most instances the poetic (or more rhetorical) text also added significant historical details so that the complementary nature of the accounts is manifest. (127)

Excursus: Unique Attributes of the Two Deborah Stories

Each account of the Deborah story has unique features not appearing in the other account. Here I will identify those unique features and highlight how they help the total account in which they appear achieve its unique purpose. I will also pose the question of why a feature might have been intentionally left out of the other account, knowing the hypothetical nature of such a question.

Unique features in the prose narrative of Judg 4. In chap. 4 there are twelve unique features, which I will examine in turn.

1. Jabin, king of Hazor. Jabin is introduced as the central figure of the prose framework, but he is also integral to the arc of narrative tension in the prose narrative, for it is he who has peace with Heber the Kenite. This peace agreement lures Jabin's general, Sisera (4:7), into Jael's tent, allowing her to gain the glory promised a woman in the crisis or change point of the narrative.

Both the narrative framework (1:2, 23–24) and the poetic composition (5:19) picture the Canaanites as the enemies. On the other hand, the prose narrative does not mention Canaanites, while the poetry does not refer to Jabin. The prose narrative centers attention on Jabin of Hazor rather than Jabin, king of the Canaanites, as the political leader (vv 7, 17). (See Amit, *JSOT* 39 [1987] 106, n. 12, for discussion of the title "king of Canaan.") This is interesting from two perspectives as compared to the book of Joshua. First, the Joshua conquest narrative features many kings in Canaan, each king of a town or city-state (Josh 2:2; 6:2; 8:1; 9:10; 10:1, 3, 5, 23, 28, 33, 41–42; 11:1, 2, 5, 10, 12, 18; 12:1–24; 13:10, 30; compare 5:1; 9:1). The book of Judges, including the poetic composition of chap. 5, also knows of different kings in Canaan (5:3, 19; 8:5; 9:6). Israel's lament was that it had no king as the Canaanites did.

The second perspective comes from Josh 11, the story of a Jabin, king of Hazor. Later tradition also connected Hazor to the oppression of Israel (1 Sam 12:9; Ps 83:9 [Heb. 10]). Brensinger aptly states: "The king appears as nothing more than an afterthought in the story itself. . . . Jabin is absolutely motionless and mute" (62). See Lindars (165–66) for discussion of the relationship of the two traditions. Lindars understands all references to Jabin as imported by a historian from the tradition behind Josh 11 "to enlarge the significance of the event." Olson thinks the mention of kings of Canaan in 5:19 may have occasioned the link to Josh 11, but states that "in any case, King Jabin remains a shadowy figure in the background to Judges 4; general Sisera is the one Canaanite who grabs the spotlight and generates any narrative interest in the story" (779). Volkmar Fritz (*UF* 5 [1973] 123–39) attempts to show that a Deuteronomistic redactor has introduced Jabin secondarily into both narratives, and Soggin (70) agrees. Auld offers his own feeling that "one decisive historic battle for the north has been reported to us in two quite separate traditions: one associated with Joshua, and the other with Deborah and Barak. . . . Israel's action against the chariotry of the north was only secondarily associated with Joshua" (152).

Auld makes the interesting observation that if Judg 4–5 was written without knowledge of Josh 11, then Jabin is an external enemy, but if it was written in light of Josh 11, then Jabin becomes an internal enemy. I would claim that at least the editor of the framework saw this as a climactic battle against the Canaanites as Israel's only internal enemy. Younger sees the two different titles for Jabin in the two narratives as evidence that "the writer of Judges 4 seems to have deliberately made sure that we not confuse this man with the one in Joshua 11, even though they have the same name" ("Heads! Tails!" 133).

One thing is sure here, the reader of Judg 4 is expected to know the story of Josh 11 and feel the horrendous threat Jabin of Hazor posed. Otherwise, questions abound. Is Judges in some way a type of literary doublet of Josh 11? Is Jabin a dynastic name passed down through several generations of kings at Hazor? Block (188, with nn. 154–56) shows various perspectives on this issue. Does the repeated name give historical validity to the story or show the historical fiction involved? And how can a city so totally razed by Joshua suddenly appear again as a major city terrorizing Israel for twenty years? Block (189) reaches a bit to explain this as a short-lived revival of the dynasty on Hazor's ruins, yet a more satisfactory explanation has yet to be developed. So Brensinger simply notes: "The strategic location of the city along the major trade route between Egypt and Mesopotamia makes it easy to imagine that it could have been resettled within a hundred-year span" (62). Scholarship, however, must be built on more evidence than simple imagination. I must admit that I cannot decide this historical issue, but I can see that the two forms of this narrative take two different approaches in identifying Israel's enemy. The framework and the poem point to Canaanites. The prose narrative points only to Jabin, king of Hazor, and his general from Harosheth Haggoyim.

But why would the poetic version not at least mention Jabin if he is a solid part of the tradition? Most likely because the poem takes two somewhat contrasting strategies. First, it focuses on a large plural enemy, the kings (v 3), that is, the kings of Canaan (v 19). It is an attempt to picture not the defeat of just one enemy but the defeat of all the peoples of the land of Canaan. All royal names are omitted in order to eliminate any attempt to minimize or reduce the significance of this victory. Just as Joshua took the entire land and all the kings (Josh 11:16), so the book of Judges begins with Israel defeating kings east of the Jordan, the Philistines to the west, and all the kings of Canaan. Israel's moral disaster that brought on its political disaster started from a strong base: complete renewed control of what Joshua conquered. Thus the Song of Deborah shifts the focus from one king to one general, who appears to represent all the kings of Canaan. The one king of Canaan disappears in silence, whereas the death of the general and the mourning for him become the climactic focus of the poem.

2. The identity of Deborah. The prose narrative and the narrative framework take pains to introduce the main characters, using disjunctive clauses as markers of such introduction. This becomes highly significant in its handling of Sisera, Deborah, and Barak. The framework highlights Sisera but ignores Deborah. The prose narrative opens with an extensive introduction of Deborah, but Barak enters the narrative only as the object of Deborah's summons, while Sisera is only a tool God uses for his purposes.

The extensive introduction of Deborah underlines her importance to Israel's history, but it also plays an important part in the narrative strategy of the story. Such a build-up makes the reader join Barak in assuming later that Deborah must be the one to whom glory will be given, Barak having willingly surrendered the opportunity for personal glory.

The poem treats Deborah in a different way. It presents her as a national hero. The narrator assumes the readers know the story of Deborah and Barak and need no introduction to her. Without the narrative motif of "who gets the glory?" the poet has no reason to highlight Deborah in order to present a false clue in the trail to the woman of glory. Rather, Deborah is somewhat reduced in the poem. Without the loss-of-glory motif, Barak can gain parallel status to Deborah. Barak retains such parallel status to Deborah in v 12, where his role is one of battle and Deborah's role is one of song, and in v 15, where Issachar rallies behind first one, then the other in parallel lines. The single appearance of Deborah alone in v 7 represents a separate poetic strategy that does not diminish the role of Barak.

Thus the strongly marked identifying characteristics of Deborah contrast her importance over against Barak's in the prose account as well as prepare for the "who gets the glory?" motif where Jael becomes the star. This motif disappears in the poetic version, where Barak shares center stage with Deborah until both disappear in favor of Jael. In the narrative framework Barak joins Deborah in singing, though admittedly he is placed in the second position in the introduction and given a patronym to identify him when none is needed for Deborah, even though the prose narrative does provide the name of her husband as a mark of identity.

3. The call and identity of Barak. The summons to action that brings Barak into the prose narrative is essential to the identity-of-Deborah motif. Barak is introduced when a female prophet relays God's summons to him. Schneider points out that, in contrast to the spirit coming on Ehud and Othniel, "in this case there is no evidence that the deity was working through Deborah, but the text is explicit that she viewed herself as acting on behalf of the deity. The narrator implies that Deborah was the deity's representative through her victory and the actualization of her predictions" (69–70).

Deborah is wife, prophet, and judge to whom all Israel comes and to whom word of God comes. Barak is son of Abinoam from Kedesh to whom Deborah alone comes. The call of Barak subtly sets the reader up for the next element of the narrative, one that retards the action of the story but opens the door for the narrator's surprise ending. Again, no such narrative motif calls for the poet to introduce Barak. Both poet and framework narrator assume the reader knows the partnership between Deborah and Barak.

4. Barak's hesitation to go without Deborah. Judg 4:8 freezes the reader and the narrative action. The general summoned to action lays conditions on his participation in the war. The woman who summoned him must accompany him. The prose narrator is not interested in providing a character study of Barak. He simply pictures Barak as unwilling to go for whatever reason or character weakness. Barak's unwillingness allows the narrator to set up his narrative tension by adding the next element to the story. The poet, in a mood to praise and not to set up narrative tension, has no need to feature Barak's call and his surprising response to it. The poetic theme of volunteer leaders in Israel does not permit Barak to become a half-hearted participant in the struggle. Lindars notes that "his apparent cowardice is a special feature of this prose version of the

tradition," its lack in the poem indicating that Jael's achievement does not necessarily "derogate from Barak's honour." He does claim that "Deborah punishes Barak for his lack of faith" (188–89).

Fewell and Gunn see Barak's response not as cowardly but as questioning Deborah's authority. They identify Shamgar, not Deborah, as the recognized military leader of the time, the one with authority to call forth the army: "Barak is being asked to risk his life as well as the lives of ten thousand men on the strength of this woman's unconfirmable word. Barak's conditional proposal, then, is a test: If Deborah is willing to stake her own life on this word, then he will believe and obey" (*JAAR* 58 [1990] 398–99). This is quite a stretch of the role of Shamgar. It ignores the fact that Deborah sees Barak, not Shamgar, as the natural military leader of Israel and negates the obvious prophetic authority Deborah asserts, an authority the people respond to in a positive manner.

5. The prophecy of delivery into a woman's hand. Deborah assumes her prophetic role and announces "but you will not receive your glory on the way you are following" (Judg 4:9). Schneider raises the interesting possibility that the text implies that "men, or maybe especially Israelite men, fought for glory or renown, not, as Deborah stated, because the deity commanded it" (70). Barak makes no protest. Deborah the prophet paints the other side of the picture: "For into a woman's hand Yahweh will sell Sisera" (Judg 4:9). Barak meekly complies, going with Deborah to his home in Kedesh. Meanwhile, the reader smugly continues, waiting to see how God gives glory to Deborah and not to Barak. Again, the poet has no mysterious glory-getting woman, and so the poet need not introduce this segment that retards the narrative action.

Fewell and Gunn argue that the song is told from the victors' perspective and has no concern for gender: "The song conveniently forgets Barak's earlier reluctance to act upon Deborah's word. The song forgets Deborah's mocking prediction that a woman will steal Barak's glory. Instead, the participants are portrayed as uniting in immediate, voluntary response to the cause. No concern for glory, no questioning of authority—just a courageous rallying to fight oppression" (*JAAR* 58 [1990] 399–400). This reading of the poem derives from Fewell and Gunn's attempt to read the two chapters as a whole and to see chap. 5 as a recapitulation from a different perspective. If one reads chaps. 4 and 5 as a true whole, then one does not emphasize what is missing in one chapter or the other but reads the missing ingredients from one chapter into the other, that is, interprets one reading of the event in light of the other reading of the event.

6. The call to Zebulun and Naphtali and the battle report. Here we meet perhaps the most controversial part of the narrative, involving a complex of problems. Is the book of Judges a collection of stories originally involving only a local leader with local tribes? In a narrative focusing on a mysterious movement of glory from a general to a woman with marginal Israelite connections, the story reduces the participants to a bare minimum to focus on leaders, not battles, on narrative surprise, not victory celebration. Battle narrative occupies as little space as possible. (See the discussion of Schneider, 74, concluding, "the battles are not the focus of the narrative.")

The battle report is used for four purposes much more germane to the narrative strategy. First, the battle report reiterates the motif of Deborah's presence. Armies are present; however, the climactic statement is not about armies but about Deborah. After the interruption to introduce the other two purposes of the battle report, Deborah again steps front and center, giving battle orders to Barak. Ackerman thinks Judg 4 "relegates Deborah to an advisory role in the war against Sisera" but "Judges 5 is unambiguous and emphatic in its depiction of Deborah as Israel's chief military commander" with Barak in Judg 5 "only as Deborah's second-in-command" (*Warrior, Dancer,* 31). This far overstates the evidence of Judg 5. The battle report gives credit to Yahweh, not to humans, for victory. Yahweh is on the battle scene before Barak has had a chance to answer the call to battle: "Yahweh threw Sisera and all his chariots and all his army into panic at the edge of the sword in the face of Barak" (Judg 4:15). Yahweh is the cause of victory.

Second, a disjunctive clause is used to focus attention on the unknown Heber the Kenite. The reader can only ask, where did he come from? And then file the information in the back of the mind to see where he is going to pop up again. But the narrative structure places more importance on Heber than on Barak and the armies.

Third, the battle report shows the superiority of and focus on Sisera, giving more information about him and his army than about Barak and his. Fourth, the battle report prepares for the central action, Sisera's escape and Jael's invitation to murder.

The poetic account, focusing on the voluntary response of Israel's leaders, shows the weakness of the Israelite army, having no shield or spear (Judg 5:8). The song summons both Barak and Deborah, apparently switching speakers from Deborah and Barak to the people marching down to the gate. Fokkelman shows the strength of the verb עוּר, "awake," as "a decisive move that starts or marks an intervention or a similar manifestation of power" ("Song of Deborah and Barak," 611). Each of the battle heroes has a particular calling: Deborah to sing and Barak to fight. Fokkelman is insightful in noting that "the poet skips . . . the hottest phase of all, the actual fighting, and chooses words that simply report the favorable outcome on the battlefield," thus preparing for the similar "ellipsis" (vv 19–22). "As a consequence all honor goes to the deity and the cosmic forces" (611).

The battle itself pits Israel's "survivors" against the Canaanite nobles, the people of Yahweh against the warriors (v 13). For the poet, the fight is all Israel against all Canaan. The narrative tension, if it can be called that, is created by concern for who will participate for Israel and who will not. This is not a question of Barak's participation. It is a question of all Israel's participation. Each tribe is measured by its willingness to get involved with Yahweh's war, to become part of Yahweh's unarmed people. Of significance is the climax of the roll call, in which Zebulun and Naphtali are featured, just as in the prose account (v 18). As with the prose, the poetic battle report has more to say about the Canaanite kings than about Israel's army. The enemy forces find they are not so much facing Israel as they are facing the heavens and the forces of nature (5:20–21). A sound bite ends the battle report, as we hear horses' hoofs pounding. But whose horses going in which direction? The poet cares not, as long as he etches a vivid picture of chaos and retreat in the reader's mind and emotions. He is pointing forward to his real center of interest, the Jael story. The intricacies of interplay between Deborah and Barak fall far beyond his purpose. He wants to celebrate what Yahweh has done through Deborah and Barak by bringing all God's hosts into play.

7. The introduction of Heber the Kenite. As at least inferred above, introducing Heber is of great importance to the prose narrator, for this is his surprise weapon. The narrative introduces Heber in disjunctive style to prepare for the significance a few verses later. Heber retards the action, removes the focus from Barak, provides identity for Jael as a marginal member of Israel at best, and explains how Jael can be geographically located for her special role.

The poet? He will mention Heber in passing (5:24) when the time comes to introduce Jael, but Heber plays no real role in the poet's work. Again, Jael does not have to be gradually prepared for and introduced as a surprise character. The poet presumes the audience knows the story of Jael and will join in celebration of Yahweh's righteous acts, one of which is illustrated by the work of Jael. The point made by the poet is simply that one marginal member of Israel—Meroz—refused to help Israel and was cursed, while the other marginal member—Jael—answered the call and was blessed.

The poet contrasts Jael with Meroz, seemingly assuming that each has a responsibility to help Israel without clarifying what makes them responsible. It is not some personal issue, but a corporate issue. Any tie to the people of God makes you responsible to act in the interest of the people of God, no matter your own personal circumstances. The same goes for the tribes who used personal circumstances as an excuse not to join the battle. They, too, stand condemned.

8. The report to and troop deployment by Sisera. As noted above, the battle report has more to say about Sisera than about Barak. The narrator underlines Sisera's intelligence reports and his weaponry, military assets that make his army far superior to Barak's. This sets the stage to display Yahweh's superior might over "all his chariots and all his army" (Judg 4:15).

The poet is more interested in displaying Yahweh's might than Sisera's, as seen in the opening theophany. The poem centers on who Yahweh is and what Yahweh does. The contrast is drawn between Yahweh's might and Israel's weakness rather than between Sisera's strength and Yahweh's overwhelming superpower strength. Israel had no weapons and was a divided people with several tribes not answering the call to arms. All the poet says about the enemy is that "kings came; they fought; yes, then the Canaanite kings fought at Taanach by the waters of Megiddo" (Judg 5:19). This sets up the poet's punchline—they carried off no silver, no spoils of war. Subtly the poet has introduced Canaanite kings in order to prepare for the last scene of his composition.

9. Emphasis on Mount Tabor and geography. Geography plays a role in both accounts, particularly in the prose narrative as seen in the mention of Hazor, Harosheth Haggoyim, the palm tree of Deborah between Ramah and Bethel in the hill country of Ephraim, Kedesh in Naphtali, Kishon River, the oak tree in Zaanannim near Kedesh, and Mount Tabor. All these create interesting literary contrasts for the narrator. Hazor is the imposing, historically famous center of activity for Canaanites in the north even though it suffered mightily under Joshua (Josh 11). But it remains aloof from action here.

Harosheth Haggoyim is Sisera's home and the staging place for his troops. As such, it is the place Barak expects to find a defeated, retreating Sisera and assumedly the place where his family waits anxiously for Sisera's return. The palm tree of Deborah is Israel's current center of activity, quite a contrast from the reputation of Hazor and isolated even further to the south of the action than Hazor is to the north. The tree is located in the central part of Israel, the hill country of Ephraim.

Kedesh in Naphtali is Barak's home, as insignificant a place as Harosheth Haggoyim, the Canaanite general's home base. Apparently, Barak copies the Canaanites in calling soldiers to his home town (Judg 4:10), but they soon move on to Mount Tabor, unless Kedesh is viewed as being on Mount Tabor. Tabor is where God tells Barak to deploy his troops. Deborah, God's prophet, will not let Barak remain on Mount Tabor. She calls him off the mount down to the field of battle to attack rather than to wait in more secure defensive positions.

The Kishon River is the battle site. A human observer would say Sisera chose the site and deployed his troops there (Judg 4:13), but the narrator has another perspective: God has deployed Sisera's troops for him (Judg 4:7). The river plays no further role in the narrative. It simply indicates a battle site and lets the narrator show that God chose the battle site. The Kishon River is crucial for the poet. It is apparently the same as the "waters of Megiddo at Taanach," where the Canaanite kings fight the battle (Judg 5:19, 21). The poet lifts up the "ancient river" as God's major weapon.

Poet and narrator agree on the battle site. The narrator mentions it as a normal part of a battle report and as a way of showing Yahweh's superiority and ability to control Sisera, even to deploy Sisera's troops. The poet uses the Kishon not only as the Canaanites' battle site but also as Yahweh's weapon against the technical superiority of the enemy.

10. Yahweh throwing Canaanite troops into panic. Panic (המם) is a holy war theme (Exod 14:24; 23:27; Deut 2:15; Josh 10:10; 1 Sam 7:10; 2 Sam 22:15; 2 Chr 15:6; Pss 18:15; 144:6) the narrator uses (4:15) to depict Yahweh as the victorious general. The poet, on the other hand, accomplishes the same purpose with a different literary strategy. The poet simply describes God's weapons—heavenly bodies and River Kishon—and their

effect on the enemy (Judg 5:20–21).

11. Sisera's flight and Barak's chase. Battle reports often reduce the battle to a one-on-one confrontation between the leaders of the respective forces. The prose narrator here apparently does the same, showing the Canaanite army defeated, its general fleeing on foot, and the Israelite general swift in chase. One problem. Sisera flees eastward to Barak's home in Kedesh of Naphtali, but Barak chases westward to Sisera's home in Harosheth Haggoyim. Sisera thus appears safe as he comes to the tent of Heber, who has a mutual nonaggression treaty with his boss, Jabin of Hazor, while Barak goes the only place he might be in danger, the staging ground and home base of Sisera and his troops. The one-on-one chase scene evaporates quickly, for the two combatants are on opposite sides of the country. The chase motif thus functions for the narrator in a far different manner from that which the reader might expect. The scene separates the generals rather than bringing them together in a final, decisive confrontation.

The poet sets up the Jael scene in an entirely different manner. The only fighting is by the kings of Canaan and God's heavenly and earthly weapons. The poet only introduces Sisera into his composition as the one the heavenly bodies attack (Judg 5:20). For the poet, Sisera, by name, never takes action. He is the object of attack, first from the stars and then from Jael. God and his servant Jael stay in the spotlight, pushing Sisera to a bit role in the shadows of the poetry.

12. The scene with Barak and Jael. The narrator reserves the denouement for one last opportunity to display Barak's humiliation. The general who would charge into battle only if a woman was at his side, the general who continued on knowing God had taken away any hope of glory, the general who went off on a wild goose chase going the wrong direction to find the general God had defeated—this general now stoops to enter a woman's tent and find his prey at his feet, dead, the victim of a woman's guile. The scene makes obvious how the narrative tension has been resolved. The honor shifts from Barak to Jael, not to Deborah. General Barak has done nothing right. Marginalized Israelite Jael has killed public enemy number one.

The poet has no theme of humbling Barak and giving the glory to a woman, so the poet has no use for the scene with Barak and Jael. Rather, the poet shifts attention in his denouement to another woman, the victim's mother.

Unique features in the poetic composition of Judg 5. Because of its completely different style and genre, the poetic composition of chap. 5 includes many elements not found in the prose narrative of chap. 4.

1. Blessing on people who volunteer. The poem's opening verse challenges the translator while setting the emotional mood and literary theme for the entire poem. The central word is הִתְנַדֵּב, "to volunteer freely" (Judg 5:2). N. K. Gottwald rightly interprets this disputed word as signifying "the spontaneity and enthusiasm of the citizens in arms in their spirited response to the call to battle" (*Tribes of Israel*, 539). The entire poem celebrates an Israel dedicated unselfishly to Yahweh. The reason to bless or praise God is because his people are giving themselves to him. This leitmotif proves interesting to the careful reader or listener, for much of the poem shows people who did not volunteer so freely.

Volunteering and participation in battle are not the major themes for the prose narrative. Instead, the question is, who gets the glory for participation? Barak hesitates, but participates. The poem highlights participation. The prose narrative highlights hesitation and its cost.

2. Call to song. The soloist invites the audience to praise Yahweh, but then switches quickly to an audience of kings and dignitaries, inviting them to enjoy the poet's solo performance. The call to song thus has multiple purposes for the poet. It identifies the piece of literature as musical poetry, as praise to Yahweh. It raises Deborah up as the central figure to be reckoned with and listened to. It centers attention on the acts of

the enemies, the kings, not on the acts of Israel.

The defeated kings of Canaan (Judg 5:19) are summoned (5:3) to listen to a musical tribute to those who led out in defeating these same kings. The narrative account, of course, centers on the battle, not on post-battle activities (except for the Jael/Barak scene) and has no time or place for music. The call to song belongs to poetic genres, not to narrative ones.

3. Theophany. Similarly, a description of a theophany belongs to the poetic genres, not to a battle report. The theophany paints the theological and dramatic backdrop against which all else is to be heard. The poetic focus is on God coming to his people, a people who are freely volunteering themselves to fight God's war. The theophany ties Israel's previous experiences in holy war, particularly experiences in the exodus, to Israel's present situation. The God of the exodus is still the God who comes to help his dedicated people. Thus the theophany also establishes reason to praise Yahweh from the beginning, even before the battle results are reported. Secondarily, it contrasts Yahweh's coming from the southern mountain to that of Baal's residence on the northern mountain.

4. The disappearance of the peasant population and the weakness of Israel. Here may be the most surprising element of the poem. In stark contrast to the volunteers among the people and to the aura of strength and power left by the description and experience of theophany stands the weakness of God's people, a people no longer able to travel the major highways, a peasant population disappearing from the earth, and a people without spear or shield. The poet uses every means available to show the greatness of God's victory and the amazing quality of people willing to volunteer out of such weakness. On the other side, the prose narrator paints a picture of the enemy's strength, their great hoard of chariots and soldiers. Israel had thousands available to fight, but that was nothing compared to Sisera's technological advantage.

5. Call to ponder in the gates. Deborah addresses the rich riding on donkeys and the poor walking along the path. She calls on both groups to "ponder this" (Judg 5:10). The object of such pondering follows, namely, the people of Yahweh sitting around the community gathering places—the water holes and wells—and singing songs to Yahweh, remembering his righteous acts of salvation. This is another slant on the volunteering-and-praising motif of Judg 5:2 and 9. The people are doing just what Deborah is summoning them to do. They are dedicating themselves to the God of the past theophanies, the God of past deliverance. They have not forgotten. They have not lost hope. Again, the narrative genre of chap. 4 gives no room to call people to ponder or to look in on people celebrating God's victories. The battle report adheres to those elements that strictly report battle action.

6. Call of Deborah and Barak to attention. Apparently, the peasants around the watering hole or the travelers on the way respond to Deborah's song by commanding her and Barak, the general, to get to work and bring victory yet again for God's people. They mete out two distinct roles, however: singing for Deborah; battle and the taking of prisoners for Barak. So despite the strong focus on the contribution of women in this account, the roles assigned are the traditional ones for battle. The prose narrative also calls people to action, but in a different way. Deborah the prophet summons Barak to battle once (Judg 4:6) and again (Judg 4:14), and Barak summons the two tribes to battle (Judg 4:12). For the prose narrator, summoning the troops is another element in deprecating the role of Barak, while for the poet the summons is an introduction to the larger summons of all the tribes.

7. Tribal roll call. The tribal roll call is the central element carrying out the volunteering motif of Judg 5:2, 9, and 13. As such, it introduces somewhat obliquely the blessing-and-curse motif that will follow in Judg 5:23 and 24. Interesting is the repeated reference to Zebulun (Judg 5:14, 18) and the climactic position given Zebulun and Naphtali, the very tribes central to the prose narrative (Judg 4:6). These two stand out

as prime examples of volunteering to fight with Yahweh no matter the cost.

The prose narrative has no such roll call. It has neither the volunteering motif nor the blessing-and-cursing motif that requires such a list of the poet. On the other hand, the prose narrator well might have listed all the tribes in the summons to battle in Judg 4:6 since such a summons to participate is integral to a battle report. The difficult question to answer is, why the difference in the list of participating tribes? It is somewhat simple to see why the poet included the large number of tribes; only a more extensive list would illustrate the volunteering motif effectively. One would expect the prose list to include at least Ephraim, the tribe where Deborah resided, and Issachar, in or near whose territory the major confrontations occurred. The prose narrative raises the motif of the might of the Canaanites against the limited resources of Israel. Ten thousand men are pitted against nine hundred chariots and no telling how many men (Judg 4:6, 7, 10, 12, 14). Limiting the number of tribes is another way of showing what few resources the Lord had to work with as he and a hesitant general faced the mighty Canaanites. This motif of scarcity of forces and resources may account for the prose narrative noting only two tribes.

8. Emphasis on Taanach. Taanach was a city inside the territory of Issachar but allotted to Manasseh by Joshua (Josh 17:11). It became a Levitical city (Josh 21:25). But the Canaanites did not allow Manasseh to gain control of the city (Judg 1:27–28), though Joshua had captured its king (Josh 12:21). The Kishon River originated southeast of Taanach and flowed to the northwest and into the Mediterranean Sea. Taanach was thus the logical city to mention in locating a battle near Kishon. Megiddo lay five miles (8 km) northwest of Taanach, so the river could also be referred to as the "waters of Megiddo" (Judg 5:19). Such lengthy geographical names fill out the poetic meter and emphasize the strength of two Canaanite towns still not under Israelite control. Fighting by the waters of the Kishon means invading Canaanite territory. For the poet, the important issue is to place the battle at the Kishon since the river will become one of the Lord's major weapons against Sisera (5:21).

The prose narrative, on the other hand, emphasizes God's creation of panic among Sisera and his troops, so that they die by the sword of Barak and Israel (Judg 4:15). The Kishon is not so much a weapon God uses as it is the battle place God determines (4:7) when Sisera thinks he has devised the perfect confrontation point (4:13). And the Kishon is not the final point of battle, for Barak chases the enemy chariots all the way to Sisera's base in Harosheth Haggoyim (4:16), showing that the battle probably entailed more action than either account reports.

9. Participation of heavenly bodies in battle. The poet pictures the battle purely on the heavenly plane. God uses his own unique weapons to attack Sisera. Human armies are not mentioned as necessary for the victory. For the prose account, God is at work sending panic among the enemy so Barak and his troops can easily finish them off and prepare for the chase scene to follow. Thus, different perspectives and points of emphasis in describing the battle determine the weapons and the warriors credited with victory.

10. Curse on Meroz. Central to the poet's concern is the curse on the town that did not assist the Lord in his battle. The poet has chosen to separate the statement of this curse from the tribal roll call and make it a distinct element. Those who do not voluntarily answer the call to battle stand under divine curse. Obviously, we have little hope of determining who Meroz was or why Meroz chose not to participate. This makes little difference. What is important for the poet is the curse God brings on those who refuse to serve voluntarily. The lack of the volunteer motif and the limitation of participants to Zebulun and Naphtali eliminate this cursing motif from the prose narrator's consideration. The parody of a battle report might use satire in its reporting of events, but its concentration on scenes featuring two or three people eliminates any thought of picturing a tribal assembly in any form.

11. Blessing on Jael. Here is the narrative climax for the poet. This is the most unlikely

of volunteers. Jael is a woman. Jael lives in a tent, not in a city or a village. Jael is married into, if not from, the Kenite clan, which has strong historical ties, but only marginal tribal ties, with Israel. Yet this nomadic, marginalized woman is the central hero, the one person or group worthy of blessing. Of all the battle scenes involving people, the poet selects only one to tell. All the rest God did at the Kishon River. Israel's powerful enemy met ignominious defeat, nailed by a tent peg to the floor, "destroyed." The prose narrator has just as much interest in Jael as does the poet. Here is where their interests merge, in proclaiming the greatness of Jael and her feat. But for the prose narrative, the issue is not a curse on nonparticipants and a blessing on unlikely volunteers. For the prose narrative, the issue is honor for the least likely woman and dishonor for the man summoned to be general of God's troops.

12. Sisera's waiting mother. The poet adds a moving denouement to the narrative. This almost becomes an Israelite taunt song of the cruelest type, peeping in on an anxious mother about to receive news of her valiant son's death. But the woman's closest advisors turn the theme from war, battle, and death to greedy grabbing of the spoils of war. And with such talk the scene ends.

That which Israel is practicing at the very moment, the Canaanite women are chattering about. Here is the ultimate contrast in the poem between the lone female hero in Israel and the cluster of defeated Canaanite women showing their true colors just before tragedy invades their conscious lives. Brown describes it aptly: "What began with a 'mother in Israel' (v. 7) ends with a mother in Canaan—one victorious and one vanquished, one singing a victory song and one a mourner's dirge. The reversal is complete" (181).

This brief Canaanite conversation spans the bridge between curse on Meroz and blessing on Jael on one side and imprecation on enemies and blessing on the faithful on the other side. In so doing it gives one more side of the picture portraying why Canaanites should be cursed and volunteer Israelites blessed. Again, without a blessing-and-curse motif and in a narrative genre where blessings and curses do not fit snugly, the prose narrator does not need this scene. His final touch is not a curse on Canaanite women to parallel the deadly curse on Sisera. The prose narrator's final touch is simply the picture of Jael, standing over her dead enemy in all her glory, while Barak ends his futile chase having to admit that the woman deserves the glory.

13. Final imprecation on Yahweh's enemies and blessing on his followers. The poet brings resolution to his blessing on volunteers and cursing on enemies, including those who do not volunteer, by praying to God that this will be the pattern in Israel: God's enemies will face destruction while those who love him, showing their love through volunteering, will be as strong and bright as the rising sun. This imprecation and the oblique blessing tantalize the reader into seeing that enemies cannot be confined to the military opponents but may include the militarily inactive who refuse to volunteer. Likewise, the recipients of blessing cannot be expanded to include all Israel, but must be confined to those who "love you" (Judg 5:31), that is, the volunteers faithful to God's covenant. The prose narrator easily skips over such a conclusion since it does not fit the battle-report genre, nor does he consciously extend his glory theme to anyone beyond Jael.

The perspective gained by joining the accounts. We thus have examined two accounts, each with its own perspective and its own choice of materials. The compiler or editor who joined the two accounts is apparently to be identified with the editor who compiled the entire book of Judges or at least the editor who compiled the stories of the individual deliverers if one sees a book of Deliverers being brought together into a source that the final editor used. This editor's hand is not apparent at all within either the prose narrative (4:4–22) or the poetic composition (5:2–31a). The editor's contribution is simply fitting these two approaches to the same historical tradition into one literary work. As Olson observes, in so doing the editor points "ultimately to the overarching and integrating agency of God" (782) even when God can be seen only as a background character in the explicit narratives themselves.

But why include both versions? Block concludes simply that the poem lends credibility and authority to the author's perception of the monarchic era by giving "early objective evidence." For Block the poem gives credit both to "courageous and gifted individuals and primarily to Yahweh" (6). Certainly the author is seeking more than self-justification and praise to Yahweh.

Brettler (77–79) reviews more recent literature and chooses to follow N. Na'aman ("The 'Conquest of Canaan' in the Book of Joshua and in History," in *From Nomadism to Monarchy: Archaeological and Historical Aspects of Early Israel*, ed. I. Finkelstein and N. Na'aman [Jerusalem: Israel Exploration Society, 1994] 229): the Deuteronomistic Historian quoted several accounts "to present before his audience his divergent 'sources' on whose authenticity he did not wish to decide or was unable to do so" (78). If this were the case, we would expect to see a great many more double accounts in the history books. One must certainly see purpose, not cowardice, behind the use and placement of sources.

Schneider (53) points us in the right direction by explaining that "Judges 4 preceding Judges 5 means that information included in Judges 4 colors how the reader views the following poem." One must also reverse the argument and note that reading Judg 5 forces the reader to rethink the meaning of Judg 4. Schneider summarizes the differences in emphasis:

> Topics such as how Deborah knew it was time to attack, how the Israelites won, and what happened to all those chariots are not explained by the prose but are described in the poetic account. The prose account stresses issues that are important to the book of Judges such as: leadership, responsibilities of a leader, the role of women, and the role of the deity in Israel's battles. The poetic account fills in many of the details of the episode. . . . The poem was certainly modified by its placement following the prose. The prose account introduces most of the major players and events which are retold in the poem. The characters portrayed in the poem are viewed through the lens of the information already recounted in the prose section. This means that aspects of the poem, which may have had certain meanings if the poem stood alone, are now modified by the information already provided the reader in the prose account. . . . The prose does not address issues better or already more elegantly described by the poem, demanding the inclusion of the poem, and therefore, both chapters, into the text. (82)

Watts concludes that "the use of the Song of Deborah in the context of the Deborah narrative enriches the latter with more explicit praise, celebration, and ridicule than Hebrew prose narrative style usually contains" (*Psalm and Story*, 96). Again Watts believes the limitations which Hebrew and Egyptian realistic narrative imposed were crossed through poetry in which "the writer was able to express feelings of praise, condemnation, and delight which were denied to the (realistic) narrator by the conventions of narrative discourse" (97).

The editor subsumes the two works under the editorial framework of Judges described in Judg 2:10–23. Carefully, however, the editor utilizes only part of the framework as he introduces and as he marks the brief conclusion of each of the two independent compositions. Though Shamgar is explicitly mentioned in the poetic narrative, the editor ties the Deborah-and-Barak narrative to Ehud, who preceded Shamgar in the account, since Ehud is the example of a judge who achieved total victory at once and established peace for eighty years. Shamgar was included among the deliverers to allow the reader of the poem to put that composition into the historical context the poem hinted at (5:6). Note Schneider's conclusion: "This case presents the transition from a non-judge (Ehud), to a foreign savior (Shamgar), to a female judge. The model judge embodied in Othniel has diminished considerably" (58).

I would read the evidence a bit differently. Even if Ehud does not explicitly receive the title "judge," the editor of the framework sees that he established rest in the land for a longer period than anyone else and so certainly intends with the long Ehud narrative to describe one of Israel's deliverers. Shamgar may have Anat connections from his parents, community, or occupation, but surely the editor would have given stronger clues than just the unclear reference to "ben Anath" if Shamgar were intended to be seen as a non-Israelite. Similarly, the conclusion that we have a woman judge is not at all certain as we have seen above. Rather the mention of "ben Anath" simply shows that a pagan goddess has in some way invaded Israelite life while the confusion of leadership in the Deborah/Barak/Jael triangle underlines the fact that the definition of a judge has begun to blur.

The negative-evaluation formula is reduced (Judg 4:1) so that no mention is made of serving foreign gods. The entire account, both prose and poetic, is then told without reference to such gods except in the enigmatic 5:8a. The divine-anger formula disappears, to appear again only under Jephthah (10:7). The central feature of the editorial framework to chaps. 4 and 5 is the divine-sale formula. The editor's emphasis here appears to be on the strength of the enemy, who had not only a king in Hazor but also a general far distant in Harosheth Haggoyim. Here the enemy is so strong that one faces only the general, and not the king, in battle, and the general is superbly equipped with nine hundred iron chariots. This general, or perhaps King Jabin, "vehemently tormented" (Judg 4:3) or "cruelly oppressed" (NIV) Israel for twenty years. *Oppression* is a term tied to the exodus narrative (Exod 3:9; 22:20; 23:9; Judg 6:9; 1 Sam 10:18; compare Judg 10:11–12). The editor of the book of Judges introduces oppression in his opening framework (2:18), but applies it specifically to an enemy of Israel during the period of the Judges only at 4:3. The editor then does not apply the weakness formula, the divine-opposition formula, the divine-presence formula, the divine-deliverance formula, or the divine-compassion formula. This makes the editorial framework stand out in its emphasis on the strength and cruelty of the opposition, rather than on the emotions, actions, or purposes of God. The framework introduction concludes with the cry-of-distress formula. Brensinger observes that "in previous episodes, such an Israelite gesture brought an immediate and favorable response. Here, for the first time, ambiguity is introduced, an ambiguity that will in subsequent accounts give way to even greater reluctance on the Lord's part" (63). Most significant here is the absence of the provision-of-leadership formula. The narrator does not name a judge that God raised up. The editor lets the story itself introduce the judge.

The editor then selects the prose narrative to illustrate not only the subjugation of the enemy but also the power of Yahweh to control and defeat the enemy. More importantly, the prose narrative demonstrates the weakness of Israel reduced to the leadership of a woman as both judge and prophet because the chosen general refuses to respond to the prophetic call to battle. Olson contends that "the story of Deborah, Barak, and Jael remains for the most part a positive portrait of a time in Israel when judges ruled effectively and faithfully as the Canaanites are defeated" (777). Earlier Olson had argued that the story hinged on the mystery of who was the real hero and who was the judge in this story. There he is headed more in the right direction, for Judg 4–5 paints a picture of Israel seeking leadership and having to depend on people who are only marginally related to them for ultimate victory. Jael stands out as the blessed one, not Deborah or Barak. Deborah does her job effectively but is not credited even by the framework editor with having given Israel rest. Barak leads in battle but then runs off in the wrong direction, leaving Sisera's capture and murder, as well as his own glory, to a woman. Here we find many more signs of weak leadership than we do of effective and faithful leadership.

This weakness also shows itself in the narrative's final scene. Here Bal's summary can be followed: "The shame of Sisera is paralleled with the shame of Barak and . . . the coming and going in the tent of Jael is organized around deceived hospitality" (*Murder and Difference*, 72). The editor has utilized the themes of shame and deceived hospitality to show again Israel's weakness and shame when a woman from a marginalized segment of Israel gains the glory due Israel's fearful general.

After the prose narrative, the editor interjects the subjugation formula but in an interesting manner. Subjugation was incomplete. Israel's hand had to grow stronger before it was able completely to cut off Jabin. The editor, then, has taken the prose narrative and used it as an example and expansion of his framework, but by eliminating most of the framework elements he has concentrated his attention and that of his readers on the strength of the Canaanite forces and the weak leadership of Israel in order to highlight the power of God in subjugating the enemy. At the same time the editor shows the continuing strength of the Canaanites that required yet more work on the Israelites' part, somewhat in parallel to the nations who remain in the Joshua conquest narrative after Joshua has conquered the long list of kings in Canaan (Josh 11–13). In his framework, the editor makes no mention of God using a judge or raising up a judge for Israel. This leaves some ambiguity about whether Deborah or Barak is to be seen as the God-called deliverer. The version of the prose narrative he chooses to preserve describes Deborah doing the work of a judge under a tree as Israel comes to her. The narrative, however, does not describe her in any way in the military deliverer role played by those who are called שֹׁפְטִים and lead in military victory. Here Bal's concept of the judge as the one with the right word at the right time may have relevance.

The editor maintains this ambiguity in penning only one line to open the Song of Deborah, for despite the song's strongly first-person-singular content, the editor attributes it to both Deborah and Barak. In so doing, he transforms the song into a part of his narrative. The song becomes an event occurring after the battle and recounting the battle from one central perspective, that of the volunteering of God's people. The poetic composition thus subordinates "the narrative of the past to the celebration of the present" (Bal, *Murder and Difference*, 81–82). As we have seen, the song gives much greater place to Barak as a hero than does the prose narrative. Thus, with his narrative introduction in 5:1 the editor supplements the emotional atmosphere created by the song in which both Deborah and Barak gain praise as those who lead God's volunteers. Having presented the song, the editor then completes his framework of the work of Deborah and Barak with one simple statement: "The land had rest for forty years."

Here again we find an amazing indifference to any judge involved. There is no death report for the judge. This stands in stark contrast to the editor's treatment of the other judges. Othniel died (3:11). Ehud died (4:1). Gideon died (8:32, 33). Abimelech died (9:54–55). Tola died (10:2). Jair died (10:5). Jephthah's daughter died (11:39). Jephthah died (12:7). Ibzan died (12:10). Elon died (12:11). Abdon died (12:15). Samson died (16:30–31). Every judge died except for the judge featured in chaps. 4 and 5. What explains this pregnant omission of the central fact that ties all the other Judges narratives together? Perhaps here the editor backs off from officially designating Deborah, the woman, as a judge even though she was obviously a stronger leader than was Barak. With the strong emphasis in both prose and poetry on the role of Jael as ultimate human deliverer here, could it be that the editor intentionally makes this narrative the featured piece in his narrative of the judges? Can it be that the volunteerism of the poetry and the individual heroism of the rank outsider in the prose narrative serve as the true ideal for the editor? Is this story a true counterpart to Joshua, the perfect leader after Moses though he was not a priest, not a prophet, not a king, not a judge? However one explains the framework's pregnant omissions, it must be noted that the final narrative picture is one of a volunteering Israel letting God fight its battles and giving praise to those on Israel's margins. It is a picture of Israel not accused of idolatry but coming to its prophet to learn God's will. It is Israel with a pair of leaders cooperating to let God bring blessing to his people.

It is also an Israel of weakness waiting to complete the job of victory over the Canaanites, having subdued Aram, Moab, and the Philistines. It is a picture that parallels Israel's situation when Joshua died except that now Israel has leaders who know and can sing about Yahweh and his righteous acts. The editor has created an ambiguous portrait of Israel and its leaders. It is an Israel whose leadership features role reversals, an Israel whose subjugating power is not as strong as before, an Israel whose rest is not as long as the previous rest, an Israel relying on marginal members of its community for heroic acts, an Israel whose own components are not always reliable and faithful. From this ambiguous picture of Israel, the editor is ready to retell the stories of Israel's other deliverers, men who are even less reliable and have even fewer moral inhibitions than are depicted in Ehud, Othniel, Deborah, Barak, and Jael and who are devoid of Deborah's prophetic voice.

Excursus: The Nature of Old Testament Historical Narrative

Three parts of Israel's history-writing tradition coalesce in the story of Deborah, Barak, and Jael: a prose narrative, a poetic paean, and an editorial combination. All three share central common elements. One produces a prose parody of a prophetic battle report. A second creates a marvelous poetic composition used probably to muster the troops for battle and more certainly for creating a common identity among the Israelites as the people of Yahweh. The poetic composition praises God for his righteous victory, calls blessing on Israel's volunteers, and brings curse on those who oppose God either by fighting him or by not volunteering to help him. The third part of Israel's history writing quickly and expertly wraps the other two together into a historical narrative of event and reaction to event. The editor interprets the new narrative with brief interpretive frames emphasizing Israel's ultimate victory over the king of Canaan, giving the Israelites control of Canaan in parallel to their control of Aram, Moab, and the Philistines.

If this analysis is correct, then certain historical questions arise. First, how did such independent narratives emerge? Scholars have long noted the unique language, poetic structure, and syntax of the poetic composition. These unique markings are most often used to position the Song of Deborah as one of Israel's oldest poetic pieces, quite possibly composed immediately following the events it describes.

The prose narrative without the editorial framework is a complete narrative in itself but offers little evidence for dating the original, most likely oral, form of the narrative. One interesting element is the connection of Deborah with the tribe and territory of Ephraim. This is made even more interesting when it is noted that the tribe of Ephraim is the first tribe in the song's listing of tribes who followed Deborah and Barak into battle (5:14). It is also Joshua's tribe (2:9) and apparently the only tribe (or at least the center of the mustering of the tribes) Ehud utilized (3:27). Elsewhere in the book of Judges, Ephraim is painted in quite different shades. This tribe failed to drive out the Canaanites in Gezer (1:29). They complained when Gideon called them out in the last stages of battle (7:24–8:3). They raised similar complaints against Jephthah (12:1), resulting in a war with Gilead in which 42,000 men of Ephraim died. Micah, the man with the idol and image and his own private priest, was from Ephraim (17:1). The Levite with the concubine was also from Ephraim (19:1).

Chap. 4, with its favorable view of Ephraim, may depict a period of history when Ephraim was strong and its sanctuary at Bethel was the central worship place for Israel. This would portray the same sociological setting as is found in the poetic composition, so the two traditions may both go back close to the historical event itself.

Second, how were such narratives preserved? At least two possibilities arise. The song may well have lived among the troops of Israel's army as a rousing military song, encouraging the troops to prepare for and answer the call to battle. At some point it probably became part of Israel's cultic poetry. The prose narrative, on the other hand, has such an explicit prophetic and feminine cast that one must ask if a prophetic guild, especially one with women in its membership, did not preserve and perpetuate this battle narrative, using it to remind the people of Israel of God's ability to fulfill his promises and defeat their enemies despite Israel's weaknesses.

A third issue that drives much modern study of these chapters is an ideological one. To what extent does this text encourage legitimate exegesis to create a theological, ideological, or sociological program from its contents? One can look at attempts to justify feminist concerns from the text. J. Cheryl Exum ("Feminist Criticism: Whose Interests Are Being Served?" in *Judges and Method: New Approaches in Biblical Studies*, ed. G. A. Yee [Minneapolis: Fortress, 1995] 64–93) demonstrates the questions feminist scholars have been asking in their historical and literary studies: "Can a woman's perspective be discovered in, or read into, this androcentric literature?" What is a text's "underlying assumptions about gender roles" (67)? Thus "feminist literary criticism attempts to subvert the hierarchy that has dominated not only readers but also culture itself" (69). Such reading "encourages multiple, even contradictory, readings of the same text" (69). Thus the basic questions raised include:

> Is there a woman or a woman's point of view in the text? . . . How are women portrayed in the text? . . . Are we given access to their point of view? Who has the power in this text? How is power distributed? How do women get what they want? . . . What do women want? How does the text represent uniquely female experiences such as childbearing, or traditionally female experiences, such as child rearing? How have women's lives and voices been suppressed by this text? Are women made to speak and act against their own interests? What hidden gender assumptions lie behind this text? ("Feminist Criticism," 69)

Thus Exum sees in Judges 4–5 "the way male ideology co-opts a woman's voice."

> Both Sisera and Barak fall short of what is expected of a hero-warrior. . . . Men fight for glory, for acclaim, and to have their valor praised in victory song. . . . But (so this song implies) because Barak behaved in a womanly way, showing uncertainty (cowardice?), he will suffer an insult to his male pride: a woman will snatch his glory from him. ("Feminist Criticism," 71)

The men in the story "are in the symbolic position of little boys," and the women "are their mothers." Deborah is a life-giving mother, while Jael is a "death-dealing" mother. The text in the end actually demonstrates that "it is not possible to experience only one side of the mother and not the other. Jael is both nurturing and deadly. Deborah not only gives life to Israel but also sends her 'sons' off to war, where many of them will die." Jael's story is a "mixture of erotic imagery and maternal imagery," but Deborah is the good mother who "is not a sexual mother" ("Feminist Criticism," 72–73).

The third mother, Sisera's real mother, "serves as the mouthpiece for the male ideology of war, in which pillage and rape go together." The androcentric author "thus suggests that men go to war to plunder for the sake of their women, and that this is something women want." The women in this scene basically then are "approving of their own imminent rape" ("Feminist Criticism," 74).

Exum takes one giant step further. The words of Sisera's mother and her ladies are placed by the androcentric author in the mouth of Deborah, so that now Deborah "is appropriated to advocate the male ideology of war in which rape is taken for granted as a weapon of terror and revenge" ("Feminist Criticism," 74). Thus as readers we "need to hold the narrator accountable, who, in the interests of his ideology, exploits women's voices to accept rapists who exploit women's bodies" (75).

Other authors seek to create an understanding of the sociological foundations of Israelite society from the text. So Block draws from the poem the conclusion that "Israel's sense of a national community consisting of at least nine (or ten) tribes antedated the monarchy, but internal tensions were created by varying levels of tribal loyalty to the confederate ideal" (216). Lindars concludes, on the other hand, that "the tribes (really clans) show no sign of political organization or central authority" (167). (See the extended treatment of the tribes in early Israel in the *Comment* on 5:14–18.)

Other authors want to demonstrate Israel's deep involvement in Canaanite religion from the text. Ackerman goes far beyond the literary evidence when she suggests "it is the influence of Canaanite myths concerning the warrior goddess Anat that has led Israelite tradition to promulgate and sustain a corpus of narratives in which women are portrayed as heroes in the battlefield" (*Warrior, Dancer,* 28–29). She goes even further, claiming, "The Israelite authors responsible for Judges 5 . . . derived their portrayal of Deborah as a female military hero in the battle against Sisera from older Canaanite paradigms of Anat, the warrior goddess." Even Ackerman must concede "the biblical text certainly does not assign to Deborah the same sorts of explicit associations with weaponry, and with the waging of war that are ascribed to Anat in Canaanite tradition" (58). Ackerman also sees Jael painted in the image of Anat, combining "militaristic imagery with imagery of sexuality and seduction" (59). These general traits of military images combined with seductive sexual ones would fit almost any female military hero in literary history. These are natural ways to portray heroines, not uses of language specific to Anat alone. Ackerman's larger agenda is seen as she goes on to insist that "myth and myth-like texts make possible depictions that historical reality does not. Because of its myth-like qualities, therefore, Judges 5 can transcend the cultural stereotypes of Israelite society regarding women and portray its female characters in ways that are not bound by the usual Israelite definitions of gender-appropriate behavior" (*Warrior, Dancer,* 68).

Is it necessary to turn to myth to find explanations for Israelite depiction of female heroes? Can it not be that Israel in exceptional cases welcomed females into the heroic annals and followed their leadership under God? Does a nation's normal prejudice and stereotypical behavior demand that it be so consistent in this that no heroic exceptions are allowed?

Block asserts that "the poet also wages a polemical war against the gods of the Canaanites" (218). Lindars reviews much of the literature on the relationship of the story to the Aqhat text in Ugarit, with scholars claiming that the Judges story "is a transference and transformation of the myth from its polytheistic cultural origin to Israelite religion," but Lindars concludes that "one or more of these myths may have been operative at the beginning of the oral tradition in which the story was evolved, but it is hard to think of this as a conscious process at the written stage, whether verse or prose" (170–71). Lindars appears to be even more on target when he writes, "Alternatively one can think of a parallel but independent use of conventional narrative themes in the traditions of Ugarit and Israel" (171).

The feminist concern is the most strongly represented and the most emotionally relevant of these issues. Obviously, the prose account centers on the issue of a woman replacing a masculine military general as the recipient of glory and fame. Thus Watts decides, "Gender is clearly at issue in ch. 4, where the initiative and power of the female characters, Deborah and Jael, are explicitly contrasted in Deborah's oracle with the humiliation of the main male characters, Sisera and Barak" (*Psalm and Story,* 88).

Despite Watts' understanding that in the poem, "gender is not made into an issue but rather affects the poetic imagery employed," the poem does feature three sensitive portrayals of feminine characters. Watts would call this "a woman's point of view which gives the psalm its distinctive feel" (88). Even Block agrees that in the poem "the feminine motif is obvious and intentional" (217). Olson decides properly that "both the prose and the poetic accounts defy any simple attempts to separate them into discrete masculine and feminine perspectives" (775). The unexpected reversal of gender roles is obviously at issue on the surface, not just below the surface in these texts. Block concludes, however, that "the biblical author was obviously interested in women's affairs and achievements, but in the final analysis Deborah and Jael are not heroic figures because of their revisionist challenges to prevailing social structures; they are heroines because of what they accomplish as agents of the divine agenda" (186). (For feminist literature on Judges 4–5, see Block 185, n. 149.)

I would question whether Block's summary does not dismiss too quickly and facilely the feminine component of the text in favor of a broad theological stroke. All biblical heroes are heroes because of what they accomplish in the divine agenda. Under this overarching umbrella of divine agenda, we must ask, what is the unique contribution of the text in question? Here in Judg 4–5 the role of females is at least an important part of the text's agenda. The question is, why are the females lifted up for notice here? Are these women lifted up as examples others are expected and encouraged to follow? Or are they used to depict the sorry state of Israelite society where priests disappear from the scene along with masculine prophets, where the only available masculine general must depend on a woman's leadership, and where the only hero able to encounter and kill the enemy general is a woman with only faint traces of kinship to Israel. Are women really praised in their own right? Or are they part of a battle parody showing how far men have sunk? Is this a call to liberate women or a call to revitalize the masculine element of the society?

Ackerman (*JBL* 121 [2002] 47–80) finds women pictured as anomalies, not examples, in Israelite society. Note her thesis, calling "into question the degree to which the women named as 'prophet' in the Bible can be considered examples of a positive role for women within Israelite religion" (50). She finds they "ultimately appear to be not so much exemplars as anomalies, their role as prophets exceptional rather than acceptable within Israelite religion" (50–51). From a similar perspective Yee writes:

> In creating the character of Jael for his story in chapter 4, our author uses the covert activity of women in war as a strategic entitlement to reinforce negative stereotypes of women in general. Instead of a warrior defending her people and her household, Jael becomes at the hands of the male author a temptress, deceiver, and ultimately a castrator. Likewise, Deborah's military leadership is subsumed under a larger story about male dishonor. As women warriors Deborah and Jael become for the male author metaphorical strategies of entitlement, functioning primarily as the agents of male shame. (*Semeia* 61 [1993] 116–17)

This is feminine reading with a vengeance, attacking one's best friend from a defensive stance.

The particular story does have as its main point the weak leadership in Israel, indeed, the weak male leadership in Israel. Women are the natural foils used to display this weakness in all its lack of glory. But because they are the agents used to portray national weakness, or masculine weakness and shame, does not mean the women are demeaned while the men are unmanned. As Watts phrases it, "Whether or not this issue as such is primarily a male or female concern is an interpretative value judgment; it is not indicated by the text" (*Psalm and Story*, 88).

Rather, the story presents the women as the only real heroes Israel has at this stage of its history. The story line itself may not highlight these female heroes as much as some readers would like, but the author of the narrative, the author of the poetic composition, and the framework narrator would all join in praise of "blessed Jael" and Deborah, the "mother in Israel." Each writer stands before them as amazed by the women's accomplishments as they are thrown into despair over the men's weakness. These women are not necessarily set up as examples for other women to follow, but they certainly are portrayed as heroes to whom all generations of Israelites owe a great debt. We can surely concur with Lindars that "the characterization of both Deborah and Jael shows an absence of stereotypes and presupposes a freedom of action which suggests a greater degree of social equality of women and men in old Israel than obtained after the rise of the monarchy" (172).

What can we conclude about the nature of Israelite history writing from this investigation? Soggin would warn us, "the whole narrative, like the song in ch. 5, has a culminating point: the killing of Sisera by a Kenite woman, in violation of all laws of hospitality; and this climax, with its individualistic, anecdotal, apolitical character, also suggests the perspective in which the two texts should be read: they are not history, but epic" (68).

Here is the central issue: can epic preserve history? Or more pointedly put, can biblical epic preserve history? Must one write in a style that fits a modern definition of scientific historical reporting to preserve historical memory of historical events? Can materials written for other than political reasons reflect actual historical events? To put the question specifically to chap. 4, can a battle parody or satire reflect historical reality? Several points come immediately to mind. Several of these seem too obvious to mention, but perhaps should be listed for clarity.

1. Prose narrative is the default form of Old Testament historical writing. Such narrative is not to be compared to the annals of other ancient Near Eastern kingdoms. This is not the type of literature preserved in Israel. Rather, we have narratives that display true literary art, even genius. The question is, can an author concentrate on literary genius and still write history? Murray typifies many writers in deciding that

> the narrator has an essentially literary rather than historical or quasi-historical interest. . . . The narrator is not concerned to give a report of any kind; nor is he primarily concerned with history as such: his concern is to narrate a story which appeared to him to comment with telling irony on the roles of two men and two women, and thus on the relationship of men and women in general. ("Narrative Structure and Technique," 185–86)

Thus Murray elects a moralizing purpose for the story rather than an artistic manner of preserving Israel's historic tradition. To this Murray would reply that we have "difficulty finding clear evidence that the present text was essentially an oral, as against an *ab initio written*, text" ("Narrative Structure and Technique," 186). I would ask if Israel's tradition—oral and written—simply created literary texts to give Israel identity, or if they preserved historical memory from which Israel had always gained their identity. One certainly must ask why Israel chose such negative examples to produce any kind of positive identity if all the examples are simply artistic creations.

2. Editors can use prose frameworks to incorporate poetic compositions into the sequential flow of historical writing.

3. Old Testament historical writing is done from a perspective of knowing the will, purpose, and action of the one God, but only at critical points in the narrative does God become the subject of narrative action; normally human beings carry the narrative action. This may be a characteristic that differentiates Hebrew historical narrative from mythological genres. Lindars is on target as he writes, "It is probably wisest to regard the story of the battle of the Kishon as one which was remembered precisely as a classic example of Yahweh's assistance to his people in war (cf. Ps. 83.10), which has a real basis

in history, but has tended to be conformed to the conventional pattern to some extent in the course of transmission" (171).

4. Hebrew historical narrative normally focuses narrative tension and resolution on an interpersonal level rather than on the national level even when the apparent genre and narrative report call for items crucial to national history. Thus the narrative of Judg 4 is concerned with personal honor much more than with victory over the enemy, and Judg 5 centers its attention much more on the problem of volunteering for Yahweh's service than it does on the defeat of the Canaanite army. It is the editor's framework that gives the narrative some focus on the national level, even though at this level the interests of the original narrative traditions used by the editor are far from being totally sublimated to national interests. Israelite historical narrative can combine reports of the same event told from two different perspectives and in combining them offer yet a third perspective on the narrative.

5. Prose narrative may lift up individuals as persons to emulate or persons whose examples should be avoided, while poetic narrative creates an emotional mood by directly pronouncing blessing and curse on individuals and/or groups. This encourages and empowers the singers and the audience to direct their praise to Yahweh, vent their emotions in relationship to other people, and learn the lessons of the national and individual past history.

6. We should not use some working hypothesis or almost unconscious code to limit Israelite history to national and international politics in the narrow sense, thus assuming it cannot include individual confrontations and stories. (See Bal, *Murder and Difference*, 25.) Note Soggin's complex historical reconstruction of a confrontation with a Canaanite/Philistine coalition even as he warns that "heroic poetry is a literary genre which it is difficult to use for history" (98–99). Still he sees the cities mentioned in these accounts not being destroyed but being "incorporated into the Israelite empire by means of a treaty or through some other peaceful means." Soggin then concludes that it is "difficult to say which version is closer to the events" (101).

7. Israelite history provides a complex picture of the early origins of Israel, yet presents a quite logical account of Israel's struggles against varied opponents in its attempts to gain control of, settle into, inhabit, and eventually rule the land. Judg 4–5 is key to this logic, showing Israel successfully gaining a victory over forces in central Canaan, thus helping Israel to unify its tribes and its military forces for future battles with the powerful Philistines.

8. Israelite historiography frequently "draws the reader into moral reflection without providing an explicit evaluation" (Olson, 783).

9. We have reason to assume that ancient oral tradition lies behind much of Israel's literature, but contemporary studies make it obvious that scholarly evaluation of the authenticity and historicity behind such tradition will continue to lead down various paths for the foreseeable future. I prefer to stand with Provan, Long, and Longman:

> The tentativeness with which these concluding observations are made is reflective of the fact that historical reconstruction is in a very real sense "underdetermined" by the evidence. Proving a particular reconstruction is simply not possible—at least not to everyone's satisfaction—any more than in a legal trial one can put a particular reconstruction of events beyond a *shadow* of a doubt. All that one should aspire to is presenting a reasonable reconstruction that does fullest justice to the greatest body of available evidence. As important as material evidence is—in history as in court—without *testimony* the past remains largely mysterious. . . . Unless someone tells a story, we are left to our own imaginative devices, which may as easily conjure up fantasies as facts. . . . In sum, then, we see little reason that an attempt to write a history of Israel's emergence in Canaan should take a path radically different

from the one that the biblical texts clearly suggest. (*Biblical History of Israel,* 191–92, emphasis original)

2. Gideon and Abimelech: Struggling to Be King (6:1–9:57)

a. Gideon Overcomes the Midianites (6:1–8:35)

Bibliography

Amit, Y. "The 'Men of Israel' and Gideon's Refusal to Reign" (Heb.). *Shnaton* 11 (1997) 25–31. **Ap-Thomas, D. R.** "The Ephah of Meal in Judges VI.19." *JTS* 41 (1940) 175–77. **Assis, E.** *Self-Interest or Communal Interest: An Ideology of Leadership in the Gideon, Abimelech, and Jephthah Narratives (Judges 6–12).* VTSup 106. Leiden: Brill, 2006. **Auld, A. G.** "Gideon: Hacking at the Heart of the Old Testament." *VT* 39 (1989) 257–67. **Barredo, M. A.** "Perfiles literarios y teológicos de Jue 7." *Anton* 75 (2000) 3–40. **Bellofiglio, N. F.** "The Gideon and Abimelech Narratives: The Contribution of Form Critical Analysis to the Current Debate on the Late Dating of Biblical Historiography as Illustrated in a Study of Judges VI–IX." PhD diss., University of Manchester, 1994. **Beyerlin, W.** "Geschichte und heilsgeschichtliche Traditionsbildung im Alten Testament: Ein Beitrag zur Traditionsgeschichte von Richter VI–VIII." *VT* 13 (1963) 1–25. **Birch, B. C.** "Choosing of Saul at Mizpah." *CBQ* 37 (1975) 447–57. **Block, D. I.** "Will the Real Gideon Please Stand Up? Narrative Style and Intention in Judges 6–9." *JETS* 40 (1997) 353–66. **Bluedorn, W.** "There Is Only One God." Paper presented at annual meeting, Evangelical Theological Society, 2002. ———. *Yahweh versus Baalism: A Theological Reading of the Gideon Abimelech Narrative.* JSOTSup 329. Sheffield: Sheffield Academic, 2001. **Böhme, W.** "Die älteste Darstellung in Richt. 6, 11–24 and 13, 2–24 und ihre Verwandtschaft mit der Jahweurkunde des Pentateuch." *ZAW* 5 (1995) 251–74. **Buber, M.** "The Gideon Passage." In *Kingship of God.* 59–65. **Castelbajac, I. de.** "Le cycle de Gédéon ou la condemnation du refus de la royauté." *VT* 57 (2007) 145–61. **Claassens, L. J. M.** "The Character of God in Judges 6–8: The Gideon Narrative as Theological and Moral Resource." *HBT* 23 (2001) 51–71. **Clark, G. R.** *The Word Hesed in the Hebrew Bible.* JSOTSup 157. Sheffield: JSOT Press, 1993. 221–22. **Culley, R. C.** *Themes and Variations: A Study of Action in Biblical Narrative.* SBLSymS. Atlanta: Scholars Press, 1992. **Daube, D.** "Gideon's Few." *JJS* 7 (1956) 155–61. **Davies, G. H.** "Judges viii 22–23." *VT* 13 (1963) 151–57. **Derby, J.** "Gideon or Jerubaal *[sic]*." *JBQ* 31 (2003) 181–85. **Dishon, J.** "Gideon and the Beginnings of the Monarchy in Israel" (Heb.). *Tarbiz* 41 (1972) 255–68. **Donner, H.** "Ophra in Manasse: Der Heimatort des Richters Gideon und des Königs Abimelech." In *Die Hebräische Bibel und ihre zweifache Nachgeschichte.* FS R. Rendtorff, ed. E. Blum, C. Macholz, and E. W. Stegemann. Neukirchen-Vluyn: Neukirchener Verlag, 1990. 193–206. **Dumbrell, W. J.** "Midian—A Land or a League?" *VT* 25 (1975) 323–37. **Edris, V.** "Yahweh versus Baal: A Narrative-Critical Reading of the Gideon-Abimelech Narrative." *JSOT* 33 (2008) 173–95. **Emerton, J. A.** "Gideon and Jerubbaal." *JTS* 27 (1976) 289–312. ———. "The 'Second Bull' in Judges 6,25–28." *ErIsr* 14 (1978) 52–55. **Feldman, L. H.** "Josephus' Portrait of Gideon." *REJ* 152 (1993) 5–28. **Fensham, F.** "Shamgar Ben Anath." *JNES* 20 (1961) 197–98. **Fontaine,**

C. R. *Traditional Sayings in the Old Testament*. Bible and Literature 5. Sheffield: Almond, 1982. 76–95. **Fritz, V.** "Abimelech and Sichem in Jdc IX." *VT* 32 (1982) 129–44. **Garsiel, M.** "Homiletic Name-Derivations as a Literary Device in the Gideon Narrative: Judges VI–VIII." *VT* 43 (1993) 302–17. **Glock, A. E.** "Early Israel as the Kingdom of Yahweh: The Influence of Archaeological Evidence on the Reconstruction of Religion in Early Israel." *CTM* 41 (1970) 558–605. **Guillaume, A.** "A Note on הפר השׁני, Judges VI.25.26.28." *JTS* 50 (1949) 52–53. **Haag, H.** "Gideon—Jerubbaal—Abimelek." *ZAW* 79 (1967) 305–14. **Habel, N.** "The Form and Significance of the Call Narratives." *ZAW* 77 (1965) 297–323. **Hentschel, G.** "Gideons Kämpfe mit den Midianitern (Ri 6,33–8,21)." In *Schätze der Schrift*. FS H. F. Fuhs, ed. A. Moenikes. Paderborner theologische Studien 47. Paderborn: Schöningh, 2007. **Hess, R. S.** "Asherah or Asherata?" *Or* 65 (1996) 209–19. ———. "Yahweh and His Asherah? Religious Pluralism in the Old Testament World." In *One God, One Lord: Christianity in a World of Religious Pluralism*. Ed. A. D. Clarke and B. W. Winter. Grand Rapids: Eerdmans, 1993. 13–42. **Himbaza, I.** "Retour sur Judges 7.5–6." *RB* 108 (2001) 26–36. **Jobling, D.** "Structuralist Criticism: The Text's World of Meaning." In *Judges and Method*. Ed. G. A. Yee. 91–118. **Kaufmann, Y.** "חסיפורים על גדעון—The Gideon Stories." *Tarbiz* 30 (1960–61) iv–v, 139–47. **Knauf, E. A.** "Eglon and Ophrah: Two Toponymic Notes on the Book of Judges." *JSOT* 51 (1991) 25–44. ———. *Midian: Untersuchungen zur Geschichte Palästinas und Nordarabians am Ende des 2. Jahrtausends v. Chr. ADPV.* Wiesbaden: Harrassowitz, 1988. **Kübel, P.** "Epiphanie und Alterbau." *ZAW* 83 (1971) 225–31. **Kutsch, E.** "Gideon's Berufung und Altarbau Jdc 6,11–24." *JTS* 81 (1956) 75–84. **Lee, B.** "Fragmentation of Reader Focus in the Preamble to Battle in Judges 6.1–7.14." *JSOT* 97 (2002) 65–86. **Légasse, S.** "Le cycle de Gédéon (Juges 6–8) d'après l'ancienne littérature juive." *BLE* 92 (1991) 163–80, 243–58. ———. "Exégèse juive ancienne et exégèse patristique: Le cycle biblique de Gédéon." *LASBF* 50 (2000) 181–262. **Lewis, T. J.** "The Identity and Function of El/Baal Berith." *JBL* 115 (1996) 401–23. **Lindars, B.** "Gideon and Kingship." *JTS* 16 (1965) 324–26. **Loewenstamm, S. E.** "The Lord Shall Rule over You (Judges VIII:23)" (Heb.). *Tarbiz* 41 (1972) 444–45. **Malamat, A.** "The Punishment of Succoth and Penuel by Gideon in the Light of Ancient Near Eastern Treaties." In *Sefer Moshe: The Moshe Weinfeld Jubilee Volume—Studies in the Bible and the Ancient Near East, Qumran, and Post-Biblical Judaism*. Winona Lake, IN: Eisenbrauns, 2004. 69–72. ———. "The War of Gideon and Midian: A Military Approach." *PEQ* 85 (1953) 61–65. **Margalith, B.** "The Episode of the Fleece (Judges 6:36–40) in the Light of Ugaritic." *Shnaton* 5–6 (1978–79) 40–42. **Martin, L. R.** "The Intrusive Prophet: The Narrative Function of the Nameless Prophet in Judges 6." *JSem* 16 (2007) 113–40. **Massot, R. M.** "Gideon and the Deliverance of Israel: A Literary and Theological Analysis of the Gideon Narrative in Judges 6–8." PhD diss., University of Cambridge, 1994. **McCartney, C.** *The Greatest Questions of the Bible and of Life*. Nashville: Abingdon-Cokesbury, 1948. 68–77. **McMillion, P. E.** "Judges 6–8 and the Study of Premonarchical Israel." PhD diss., Vanderbilt University, 1985. **Midden, P. J. van.** *Broederschap en koningschap: Een onderzoek naar de betekenis van Gideon en Abimelek in het boek Richteren*. Maastricht: Shaker, 1998. ———. "Gideon." In *The Rediscovery of the Hebrew Bible*. Ed. J. W. Dyk et al. ACEBTSup 1. Maastricht: Shaker, 1999. 51–67. **Mittmann, S.** "Die Steige des Sonnen-gottes (Ri 8,13)." *ZDPV* 81 (1965) 80–87. **Mobley, G.** *The Empty Men: The Heroic Tradition of Ancient Israel*. ABRL. New York: Doubleday, 2005. **Moenikes, A.** *Die grundsätzliche Ablehnung des Königstums in der hebräischen Bibel*. BBB 99. Weinheim: Belz Athenäum, 1995. **Müller, H. P.** "Die kultische Darstellung der Theophanie." *VT* 14 (1964) 183–91. **Müller, R.** *Königtum und Gottesherrschaft: Untersuchungen zur alttestamentlichen Monarchiekritik*. FAT 2/3. Tübingen: Mohr (Siebeck), 2004. **Na'aman, N.** "Pirathon and Ophrah." *BN* 50 (1989) 11–16. **Niesiolowski-Spano, L.** "Where Should One Look for Gideon's Ophra?" *Bib* 86 (2005) 478–93. **Olson, D.** "Buber, Kingship, and the Book of Judges: A Study of Judges 6–9 and 17–21." In *David and Zion*. FS J. J. M. Roberts, ed. B. F. Butto and K. L. Roberts. Winona Lake, IN: Eisenbrauns, 2004. 199–218. **Pury, A.** "Le raid de Gédéon (Jug 6, 25–32) et l'histoire de l'exclusivisme yahwiste." In *Lectio Diffi-*

cilior Probabilior? FS F. Smyth-Florentin, ed. T. Römer. DBAT 12. Heidelberg: Esprint, 1991. 173–205. **Rabin, C.** "The Origin of the Hebrew Word *Pīlegeš*." *JJS* 25 (1974) 353–64. **Richter, W.** *Die sogenannten vorprophetischen Berufungsberichte.* FRLANT 101. Göttingen: Vandenhoeck & Ruprecht, 1970. **Rösel, H. N.** "Studien zur Topographie der Kriege in den Büchern Josua und Richter: IV. Der Feldzug Gideons gegen die Midianiter, Ri 6–8." *ZDPV* 92 (1976) 10–46. **Rudman, D.** "The Second Bull in Judges 6:25–28." *JNSL* 26 (2000) 97–103. **Sakenfeld, K.** *The Meaning of Hesed in the Hebrew Bible.* HSM 17. Missoula, MT: Scholars Press, 1978. 54–58. **Sasaki, T.** "'To Clothe' or 'To Wear'? The Meaning of לבש in Judges 6:34." *Exeg* 8 (1997) 25–34. **Scherer, A.** "Gideon—ein Anti-Held? Ein Beitrag zur Auseinandersetzung mit dem sog. 'flawed-hero approach' am Beispiel von Jdc. vi 36–40." *VT* 55 (2005) 269–73. **Schmidt, L.** *Menschlicher Erfolg und Jahwes Initiative: Studien zu Traditions, Interpretation und Historie in Überlieferungen von Gideon, Saul und David.* WMANT 38. Neukirchen-Vluyn: Neukirchener Verlag, 1970. **Schmitt, H.-C.** "Das sogenannte vorprophetische Berufungsschema: Zur 'geistigen Heimat' des Berufungsformulars von Ex 3, 9–12; Jdg 6, 11–24; und I Sam 9, 1–10,16." *ZAW* 104 (1992) 202–16. **Schunck, K.-D.** "Wo lag Har Heres?" In *Altes Testament und Heiliges Land 1.* BEATAJ 17. Frankfurt am Main: Lang, 1989. 177–81. **Smelik, K. A. D.** "Gideon, held or antiheld? Karakterisering van een personage in het boek Richteren." *ACEBT* 19 (2001) 97–109. **Standaert, B.** "Adonai Shalom (Judges 6–9): The Persuasive Means of a Narrative and the Strategies of Inculturation of Yahwism in a New Context." In *Rhetoric, Scripture & Theology: Essays from the 1994 Pretoria Conference.* Ed. S. E. Porter and T. H. Olbricht. JSNTSup 133. Sheffield: Sheffield Academic, 1996. 195–202. **Tanner, J. P.** "The Gideon Narrative as the Focal Point of Judges." *BibSac* 149 (1992) 517–29. ———. "Textual Patterning in Biblical Hebrew Narrative: A Case Study of Judges 6–8." PhD diss., University of Texas, 1990. **Tolkowski, S.** "'Gideon's 300' (Judges vii and viii)." *JPOS* 5 (1925) 69–74. **Walton, J., V. H. Matthews,** and **M. W. Chavalas.** *The IVP Bible Background Commentary: Old Testament.* Downers Grove, IL: InterVarsity Press, 2000. **Whitley, K. W.** "The Sources of the Gideon Stories." *VT* 7 (1957) 157–64. **Winckler, H.** "Die quellenzusammensetzung der Gideonerzählungen." *Altorientalische Forschungen* (Leipzig) 1 (1893) 42–62. **Wong, G. T. K.** "Gideon: A New Moses?" In *Reflection and Refraction: Studies in Biblical Historiography.* FS A. G. Auld, ed. R. Rezetko, T. Lim, and B. Aucker. VTSup 113. Leiden: Brill, 2006. 529–45. **Zakovitch, Y.** "Assimilation in Biblical Narratives." In *Empirical Models of Biblical Criticism.* Ed. J. H. Tigay. Philadelphia: University of Pennsylvania Press, 1985. 192–95. ———. "The Sacrifice of Gideon (Jud 6,11–24) and the Sacrifice of Manoah (Jud 13)" (Heb., Eng. summary). *Shnaton* 1 (1975) 151–54. **Zimmermann, F.** "Reconstructions in Judg 7:25–8:25." *JBL* 71 (1952) 111–14.

Translation

⁶:¹ *The Israelites did evil in the eyes of Yahweh, and Yahweh gave them into the hand of Midian for seven years.* ² *The hand of Midian was harsh on Israel. Because of Midian, the Israelites fashioned for themselves hideouts in the mountains, caves, and refuges.* ³ *Whenever Israel sowed their fields,*[a] *Midian came up, along with Amalek and the Easterners,*[b] *and attacked them.*[c] ⁴ *They camped against them and destroyed the crops of the land*[a] *all the way until you come to Gaza. Nothing remained alive in Israel, neither sheep, nor ox, nor donkey.*[b] ⁵ *For they were coming up,*[a] *along with their cattle, and their tents*[b] *were appearing*[c] *like the enormous swarms of locusts. The number of them and their camels*[d] *was beyond counting. They entered the land*[e] *to ruin it.* ⁶ *Israel was totally humiliated before Midian. The Israelites cried out to Yahweh.*[a]

⁷ [a] *When the Israelites cried to Yahweh because of Midian,*[b] ⁸ *Yahweh sent a prophet to the Israelites. He told them, "Thus says Yahweh, the God of Israel, 'I brought you up from Egypt, and I brought you out of the house of servitude.*[a] ⁹ *I rescued you from the hand*

of Egypt and from the hand of all your oppressors. I drove them out before you, and I gave you their land. [10] *I said to you, "I am Yahweh your God. Do not fear the gods of the Amorites in whose land you are living. But you did not obey my voice."*"[a]

[11] *The messenger of Yahweh came and sat down under the oak tree in Ophrah. It belonged to Joash, the Abiezrite.*[a] *Gideon, his son, at that moment was threshing wheat in the winepress to hide from Midian.* [12] *The messenger of Yahweh appeared to him and told him, "Yahweh is with you, O mighty hero of war."*

[13] *Gideon replied to him, "With your permission, my*[a] *Lord, if Yahweh*[b] *is with us, then why has all this*[c] *happened to us? Where are all the wonders that*[d] *our fathers recounted for us? They said, 'Didn't Yahweh bring us up from Egypt?' But now Yahweh*[e] *has forsaken us and given us*[f] *into the palm of Midian."*

[14] *Yahweh*[a] *turned*[b] *to him and said,*[c] *"Go in this, your strength, and save Israel from the palm of Midian.*[d] *Have I not sent*[e] *you?"*

[15] *He*[a] *said to him, "With your permission, Lord.*[b] *With what can I save Israel? See! My clan is the smallest in Manasseh,*[c] *and I am the baby*[d] *in my father's house."*

[16] *Yahweh*[a] *said to him, "But I will be with you, and you will strike Midian dead as if they were one man."*

[17] *He*[a] *replied to him, "If now I have found favor in your eyes, then create this sign that you are speaking with me.*[b] [18] *Please do not leave here until I come to you bringing my offering out and placing it before you."*

He said, "I will stay until your return."

[19] *Now Gideon went in and readied a kid from the goats along with unleavened bread from an ephah of flour. He set the meat in a basket, while putting the broth in a pot. He brought it out to him under the oak tree. And he drew near.*[a]

[20] *The messenger of God*[a] *said to him, "Take the meat and the unleavened bread. Rest it on this rock, and pour out the broth." He did precisely that.* [21] *The messenger of Yahweh sent the end of the staff in his hand out and touched the meat and the bread. The fire came up from the rock and consumed the meat and the bread. Meanwhile, the messenger of Yahweh disappeared before his eyes.* [22] *Gideon realized he was the messenger of Yahweh.*

Gideon said, "Ah! It's true![a] *I have seen the messenger of Yahweh face to face."*

[23] *Yahweh said to him, "Peace. Don't worry. You will not die."*

[24] *Gideon built there an altar to Yahweh and called it, Yahweh is peace. It remains there until today in Ophrah of the Abiezrites.*

[25] *That night Yahweh said to him, "Take a bull from your father's oxen, the prize*[a] *bull which is seven years old. Destroy the altar to Baal that belongs to your father and cut down the Asherah*[b] *that is on it.* [26] *You shall build an altar to Yahweh, your God, on the top of this mountain refuge*[a] *with the proper arrangement.*[b] *You shall take the prize bull and offer it as a burnt offering on the wood of the Asherah that you cut down.*

[27] *Gideon took ten*[a] *men from his servants and did just what Yahweh had told him. His fear of his father's house and of the men of the city kept him from doing it in the daytime, so he did it at night.* [28] *The men of the city rose early in the morning. Look! The altar to Baal was broken down, and the Asherah that was on it was cut down. Also the prize bull*[a] *had been sacrificed*[b] *on the altar that had been built.*

[29] *Each man asked his neighbor, "Who has done this thing?" They investigated and inquired. Some of them said,*[a] *"Gideon, son of Joash, did*[b] *this thing."*

[30] *The men of the city said to Joash, "Bring out your son that he may die, for he has broken down the altar of Baal and because he has cut down the Asherah which was beside it."*

[31] *Joash told all*[a] *those standing around*[b] *him, "Do you have to defend Baal? Or must*

you save him? Whoever defends him will die before morning. If he is a god, let him defend himself when someone breaks down his altar." [32] *That day they gave Gideon[a] the name Jerubbaal.[b] They said, "Let Baal conduct his own defense against him because he broke down his altar."* [33] *All Midian, Amalek, and the sons of the East gathered together, crossed over, and camped in the Jezreel Valley.* [34] *The Spirit of Yahweh[a] clothed[b] Gideon, and he sounded the trumpet and called out Abiezer to follow him.[c]* [35] *He sent messengers through all[a] Manasseh and also called them together to follow him.[b] He sent messengers through Asher, Zebulun, and Naphtali. They went up to summon them out.*

[36] *Gideon said to God, "If you are really there saving Israel by my hand as you have promised,* [37] *Look! I am placing the wool fleece on the threshing floor. If dew is on the fleece by itself, but all the ground is dry, then I will know that you will save Israel by my hand just as you have said."* [38] *And it was so. He[a] rose early the next day. He squeezed the fleece, and dew dripped, filling a bowl full of water.* [39] *Gideon said to God, "Do not let your nostrils burn hot against me so I may speak yet once more. I will set up a test just one more time with the fleece. Please let dryness come to[a] the fleece by itself, but on all the ground, let there be dew."* [40] *That night God did just that. Only the fleece was dry, but on the ground was dew.*

[7:1] *Jerubbaal—that is, Gideon—rose early,[a] along with all the people with him. They camped by the spring[b] of Harod, the camp of Midian[c] being north of them in the valley of the Hill[d] of Moreh.* [2] *Yahweh said to Gideon, "The people with you are too many for me to give Midian into their hand.[a] Israel would glorify themselves over against me, saying, 'My hand delivered me.'* [3] *Therefore,[a] announce in the hearing[b] of the people, 'Whoever is afraid and trembling may turn around so that he may leave[c] from Mount Gilead.'"* Of the people twenty-two thousand turned back; ten thousand stayed.

[4] *Yahweh said to Gideon, "Still the people are too many. Take them down to the water, so I may test them for you there. When I tell you, 'This one will go with you,' then he will go with you. But everyone of whom I say to you, 'This one will not go with you,' he will not go."[a]* [5] *He took the people down to the water.*

Yahweh told Gideon, *"Everyone who laps with his tongue from the water like a dog laps, you will set to one side alone. Do the same for everyone who bends over on his knees to drink."[a]* [6] *The number of those who lapped with their hands to their mouth[a] was three hundred men. But all the rest of the people bent over on their knees to drink water.*

[7] *Yahweh told Gideon, "With the three hundred men who lapped I will deliver you. I will give Midian into your hand, and all the people will walk away, each to his place."* [8] *The people took the supplies from their hand[a] along with their trumpets. Every man of Israel he sent away, each to his tent. He retained three hundred men. Now the camp of Midian was below them in the valley.* [9] *That night Yahweh said to him, "Get up. Go down into the camp[a] for I have given it into your hands.*

[10] *"If you are afraid to go down, go down along with Purah,[a] your young assistant, to the camp.* [11] *You are to listen to what they are saying. Afterward your hands will be strengthened, and you will go down into the camp."* He went down, he and Purah,[a] his young assistant, to the edge[b] of the battle formation[c] which was in the camp. [12] Now Midian and Amalek and all the sons of the east were settling[a] down in the valley like a huge swarm of locusts. They had camels beyond counting; they were as many as the grains of sand on the seashore.

[13] *Gideon entered. Look! A man was relating a dream to his companion. He said, "See. I dreamed a dream. A loaf of barley[a] bread was tumbling into the camp of Midian. It came*

to the tent and struck it. It fell and turned upside down. Yes, the tent collapsed."[b]

[14]*His companion replied, "This can't be anything but the sword of Gideon, son of Joash, the man of Israel. The God*[a] *has given Midian into his hand along with all the camp."*

[15]*As soon as Gideon heard the account of the dream and its interpretation, he worshiped.*[a] *He returned to Israel's camp and said, "Get up, for God has given the camp of Midian into your*[b] *hand."* [16]*He divided the three hundred men into three companies.*[a] *He put a trumpet in the hand of each one along with an empty jar. Torches were in the center of*[b] *the jars.* [17]*He said, "You must look to me, and do just what I do. Look! I am going into the fringe*[a] *of the camp. Just as I do, so you must do.* [18]*I will blow the trumpet, yes, I and all who are with me. Then you also will blow the trumpets all*[a] *around the camp. You shall say, 'For*[b] *Yahweh and for Gideon!'"*

[19]*Gideon entered the fringe of the camp with the hundred men*[a] *who were with him at the start of the middle watch. (They had just changed the guards.) They blew the trumpets while smashing the jars in their hands.*[b] [20]*The three companies blew the trumpets and shattered the jars.*[a] *They held the torches in their left hand, and the trumpets they were blowing in their right. They called out, "The sword*[b] *of Yahweh and of Gideon."* [21]*Each man stood in his place surrounding the camp.*

All the camp of Midian[a] *ran,*[b] *shouted, and fled.*[c] [22]*The three hundred*[a] *trumpets sounded, and Yahweh set the sword of each man against his companion. Throughout*[b] *the camp the camp*[c] *fled clear to Beth-shittah in the direction of Zeredah*[d] *as far as the border of Abel-meholah near*[e] *Tabbath.*

[23]*Each man of Israel from Naphtali, from Asher, and from all of Manasseh was summoned.*[a] *They chased after Midian.* [24]*Meanwhile, Gideon sent messengers throughout the hill country of Ephraim, "Come down to confront Midian. Occupy ahead of them the waters as far as Beth-barah and the Jordan."*[a] *All the men of Ephraim were summoned, and they occupied the waters as far as Beth-barah and the Jordan.* [25]*They captured the two commanders of Midian—Oreb and Zeeb. They killed Oreb at the rock of Oreb, and Zeeb they killed at the winepress of Zeeb. They chased Midian,*[a] *while the head of Oreb and of Zeeb they brought back to Gideon across the Jordan.*

[8:1]*The men of Ephraim asked him,*[a] *"What is this thing you have done to us, not summoning*[b] *us when you went out to fight Midian?"*

[2]*He said to them, "What have I done now compared to*[a] *you? Are not the gleanings of Ephraim better than the grape harvest*[b] *of Abiezer?* [3]*God*[a] *gave the commanders of Midian—Oreb and Zeeb—into your hand. What have I been able to do compared to you?" Then by*[b] *his speaking this word, their spirit was soothed*[c] *in relationship to him.*

[4]*Gideon came to the Jordan. He, along with his three hundred men, was crossing over,*[a] *exhausted but still pursuing.*[b] [5]*He said to the men of Succoth, "Please give loaves of bread for the people following me,*[a] *for they are exhausted, and I am chasing Zebah and Zalmunnah, the kings of Midian."*

[6]*The leaders of Succoth said,*[a] *"Do you already have the palm*[b] *of the hand of Zebah and Zalmunnah in your hand*[c] *so that we should give bread to your hosts?"*

[7]*Gideon said, "Therefore when Yahweh gives Zebah and Zalmunnah into my hand, then I will thresh your flesh with thorns of the wilderness and with brambles."*[a]

[8]*He went up from there to Penuel and spoke to them in the same way. The men of Penuel answered him just as the men of Succoth had answered.* [9]*He*[a] *also told the men of Penuel, "When I return in peace, I will break down this tower."*

[10]*Now Zebah and Zalmunnah were in Karkor with an army of fifteen thousand. This was all that was left of the army of the sons of the east. One hundred twenty thou-*

sand men who draw the sword had fallen. [11] Gideon went up by way of those who were living[a] in tents east of Nobah and Jogbehah.[b] He struck the army dead, the army feeling secure.[c] [12] Zebah and Zalmunnah fled. He chased them, captured the two kings of Midian—namely, Zebah and Zalmunnah—and scattered[a] the whole army. [13] Gideon, the son of Joash, returned from the war by the Ascent of Heres.[a] [14] He captured a youth from among the men of Succoth. When they asked him, he wrote down for them the leaders[a] of Succoth and the elders—seventy-seven men. [15] He[a] came to the men[b] of Succoth and said, "Look. Zebah and Zalmunnah about whom you insulted me by saying, 'Do you already have the palm[c] of the hand of Zebah and Zalmunnah in your hand so that we should give bread to your weary men?'" [16] He selected the city elders.[a] With thorns of the wilderness and brambles he let them teach[b] the men of Succoth.[c] [17] The tower of Penuel he broke down, and he killed the men of the city. [18] He said to Zebah and Zalmunnah, "Where[a] are the men whom you killed at Tabor?"

They said, "No difference between you and them; each[b] has the appearance of a king's sons."

[19] He[a] said, "My brothers, the sons of my mother, were they. [b] As Yahweh lives, if you had let them live, I would not kill you."

[20] He told Jether, his firstborn son, "Get up! Kill them!" But the youth did not draw his sword, for he was afraid because he was still[a] a youth. [21] Zebah and Zalmunnah said, "Get up, you, and attack us yourself, for as a man so is his strength."[a]

Gideon got up and killed Zebah and Zalmunnah. He took the little moon ornaments on their camels' necks. [22] The men of Israel said[a] to Gideon, "Rule over us,[b] yes, you! Also your son and grandson,[c] for you have saved us from the hand of Midian." [23] Gideon said to them, "I will not rule over you, nor will my son rule over you. Yahweh rules over you." [24] Gideon continued, "Let me make one request of you: let each man give me an earring from the spoil." (They had gold earrings[a] because they were Ishmaelites.)

[25] They said, "We'll gladly give," and they spread out a piece of clothing,[a] and they each threw down an earring[b] from the spoil. [26] The weight of the gold earrings he asked for was seventeen hundred[a] shekels[b] of gold. This was aside from the little moon ornaments, the pendants,[c] and the purple clothing the Midianite kings wore and aside from the necklaces[d] which were on their camels' necks. [27] Gideon made himself an ephod[a] and placed it in his city—in Ophrah. All Israel prostituted themselves there with it. It became a snare to Gideon and to his house.

[28] Midian was subdued before the Israelites, unable again to lift their heads. The land had quiet forty years in the days[a] of Gideon. [29] Jerubbaal, son of Joash, went and lived in his house. [30] Gideon had seventy sons of his own[a] because he had many wives. [31] His concubine who lived in Shechem also bore him a son.[a] He named his name Abimelech.[b] [32] Gideon, son of Joash, died in a good old age.[a] He was buried in the tomb of Joash, his father, in Ophrah[b] of the Abiezrites.[c] [33] At the death of Gideon, the Israelites turned back and prostituted themselves with the Baals. They set up Baal Berith[a] as their god. [34] The Israelites did not remember Yahweh, their God, who saved them from the hand of all their enemies who surrounded them. [35] They did not show faithful love to the house of Jerubbaal, that is, Gideon, in relationship to all the good that he did for Israel.[a]

Notes

6:3.a. "Their fields" added for clarity. LXX[A] reads "the man of Israel," while LXX[B] reads "the sons of Israel," each adding a common phrase.

3.b. "Easterners" is lit. "the sons of the east." See *Comment.*

3.c. 4QJudgᵃ does not have "and attacked them," which *BHS* marks as an addition. MT actually represents the more difficult reading since one expects the camping of the next verse to precede attack. Webb points to the "sequence of iterative verb-forms in vv. 3–5" and sees them as capturing "the wave after wave of pillage and destruction" ([1987] 145).

4.a. LXXᴮ reads "their fruit" for "crops of the land" and then reads "in the land of Israel" for "in Israel," the first representing a free translation and the second a literary expansion inserting a common phrase. OL renders "boundaries" from גבול instead of "crops" from יבול.

4.b. 4QJudgᵃ does not have the *wāw*s before שׂה and שׁוֹר, creating a positive series—in Israel: sheep or ox or donkey.

5.a. Syr. and Vg. point to the deletion that *BHS* recommends, but both Gk. versions have two verbs here. These versions simplify the sentence while MT uses a verb of movement for men and animals and then gives the Israelite perspective of the onrushing enemy suddenly pitching camp like a horde of locusts lighting on a field.

5.b. 4QJudgᵃ, as reconstructed in J. Trebolle Barrera, "4QJudgᵃ 4QJudgᵇ," DJD 14, 162–63, adds "and their camels," a phrase not appearing later in the verse and perhaps transposed by a copyist here.

5.c. Lit. "were coming," reading the imperfect with many MSS and K along with *BHS*. Q reads perfect consecutive וּבָאוּ. LXXᴬ reads παρέφερον καὶ παρεγίνοντο ὡς, "they carried away their tents and appeared as," interpreting יבאו as a *hipʿil* form and adding a verb for clarity.

5.d. 4QJudgᵃ and some Latin evidence do not have "and of their camels," perhaps using it earlier in the verse where it appeared to fit better.

5.e. LXX reads "land of Israel"; LXXᴮ reads καὶ διέφθειρον αὐτήν, "and they were destroying it." The addition "of Israel" represents clarifying through addition of a common phrase. The LXXᴮ reading changes the text from an intention to an actual description.

7.a–10.a. 4QJudgᵃ does not contain vv 7–10. This leads J. Trebolle Barrera to conclude: "4QJudgᵃ can confidently be seen as an earlier literary form of the book than our traditional texts" ("4QJudgᵃ 4QJudgᵇ," DJD 14, 162). In a different writing Trebolle Barrera affirms that 4QJudgᵃ "ignores a literary development that entered into the Masoretic textual tradition and is reflected also in the Greek version" (*RevQ* 54 [1989] 238). Similarly, G. Mobley (*Empty Men,* 124–26) sees the omission as possibly an "idiosyncratic feature of one ancient version" but prefers the theory that it represents an earlier form of the text showing the Gideon narrative still under construction. E. Tov is a bit more uncertain: "If this minus did not stem from a textual accident, such as the omission of a complete paragraph ending with open sections, it could reflect an earlier edition of the book, in which part of the deuteronomistic framework, contained in these verses, was lacking" ("The Nature of the Large-Scale Differences between the LXX and MT S T V, Compared with Similar Evidence in Other Sources," in *Earliest Texts of the Hebrew Bible,* ed. A. Schenker, 135–36). N. Fernández Marcos agrees with Tov's possibility of a "slip from blank to blank space" but rules out "accidental haplography due to *homoio-teleuton.*" He thinks, however, that "four verses seem too much space to be omitted by this mechanical accident" ("The Hebrew and Greek Texts of Judges," in *Earliest Texts of the Hebrew Bible,* ed. A. Schenker, 4–5). R. S. Hess ("The Dead Sea Scrolls and Higher Criticism of the Hebrew Bible: The Case of 4QJudgᵃ," in *The Scrolls and the Scriptures: Qumran Fifty Years After,* ed. S. E. Porter and C. A. Evans, JSPSup 26 [Sheffield: Sheffield Academic, 1997] 122–28) takes a more conservative approach, seeing that all cases in Joshua and Judges which reverse the order or insert nonbiblical texts occur at the open points MT marks with *pārāšîôt.* This may witness to scribal liberty in moving passages or inserting sections for their own liturgical and other purposes. With no other textual evidence of this omission, Hess prefers to see the fragment belonging to a collection of biblical texts serving a particular purpose for the community.

In his DJD edition, Trebolle Barrera dates 4QJudgᵃ to 50–25 B.C.E., making it much later than the LXX versions. For the DSS text to represent an earlier literary form would mean it preserved a pristine text two hundred years after our first conclusive evidence for the longer text. Literary theory is not strong evidence for such textual conclusions (compare Fernández Marcos, "Hebrew and Greek Texts of Judges," 6). It remains possible that the DSS preserved this independent unit elsewhere, in parts of the DSS text that are no longer preserved, to avoid splitting the crisis description of vv 1–6 from the divine response in v 11. But splitting the two sections is precisely the artistic purpose of the writer as shown. O'Connell (*Rhetoric of the Book of Judges,* 141–48) finds it more likely that the Qumran text has omitted the text than that MT has added such a long block. (Compare Block, 254.) Amit states the conclusion emphatically and clearly: "These verses should not be seen as a later insertion, nor as an arbitrary combination of sources, but as part of the systematic and tendentious shaping of the editing of the cycle and its incorporation within the book" (*Book of Judges,* 251).

7.b. LXX[B] reads only "from before Midian," leading *BHS* and many commentators to see וַיְהִי כִּי־זָעֲקוּ
בְנֵי־יִשְׂרָאֵל אֶל־יְהוָה as duplication from v 6. The Heb. writer used the repetition to show the unexpected
change from focus on Israel and its need to focus on a scolding, rebuking prophet.

8.a. LXX[B] reads "land of Egypt" and "house of your servitude," supplying common phrases from
the tradition.

11.a. MT reads לְיוֹאָשׁ אֲבִי הָעֶזְרִי, "to Joash the father of the Ezraites." LXX[A] reads ὑπὸ τὴν δρῦν τὴν οὖσαν
ἐν Εφραθα τὴν τοῦ Ιωας πατρὸς Αβιεζρι, "under the oak tree which was in Ophrah, the one which
belonged to Joash, the father of the Abiezrite," while LXX[B] reads ὑπὸ τὴν τερέμινθον τὴν ἐν Εφραθα
τὴν Ιωας πατρὸς τοῦ Εσδρι, "under the terebinth tree which was in Ophrah which belonged to Joash,
the father of Esdri." 4QJudg[a] reads האביעזרי, "the Abiezrite." MT is definitely the harder reading and is
supported by both LXX traditions in reading the first half of the term as a separate word, אבי, father.
Perhaps we have haplography here in not copying one of two consecutive אבי original readings, though
all translations reflect the DSS reading of "Abiezrite" alone. Block (258, n. 508; compare *HALOT*) sees
MT as a "gentilic modification" of the combined term. The MT spelling also apears in Judg 6:24 and
8:32. The personal name remains one word in Josh 17:2; Judg 6:34; 8:2; and 1 Chr 7:18.

13.a. LXX[A] does not have "my."

13.b. 4QJudg[a] reads אלהים, "God," for "Yahweh," for literary diversity or to maintain the picture of
Gideon as following his father's religion at this point or to avoid using the sacred name in an oath
expressing unbelief.

13.c. LXX reads "all these bad things," making explicit the inference in the text.

13.d. 4QJudg[a] uses the abbreviated ש for MT's more common אשר, showing a use "characteristic of
Qumran texts between Late Biblical and Mishnaic Hebrew" (J. Trebolle Barrera, "4QJudg[a] 4QJudg[b],"
DJD 14, 164). See v 17 in MT.

13.e. LXX does not have second "the Lord," abbreviating to avoid unnecessary repetition.

13.f. A Cairo Genizah fragment omits "given us" as unnecessary in light of the preceding verb נְטָשָׁנוּ,
which can be understood as "handed or gave over."

14.a. LXX and OL read "angel of the Lord" with a secondary Heb. MS, bringing continuity to the
narrative from 6:11.

14.b. LXX[A] reads ἐπέβλεψεν, "he paid close attention to," rather than ἐπέστρεψεν, "he turned
to," of LXX[B].

14.c. LXX[A] reads "said to him," making the obvious explicit.

14.d. LXX[A] does not have "from the hand of Midian," providing a more generalized theological
statement.

14.e. LXX reads ἰδοῦ ἐξαπέστειλά σε, "See! I have sent you," an idiomatic translation of the Heb.,
avoiding the rhetorical question.

15.a. LXX reads "Gideon," clarifying the already obvious subject.

15.b. A few Heb. MSS and part of the Gk. tradition read "my Lord" as in v 13.

15.c. Niditch observes that "OL reads, 'thousands are diminished in Manasseh,' literalizing the
word for 'family group' or 'clan,' a grouping of a thousand people, and taking the 'poor, lowly' term
as a verbal root" (88).

15.d. Lit. "the smallest" or "the youngest."

16.a. LXX reads "the messenger (or angel) of the Lord" as in v 14 and so has to change "I will be
with you" to "the Lord will be with you."

17.a. LXX reads "Gideon," again making the subject clear.

17.b. LXX[B] (compare OL) reads ὀφθαλμοῖς σου καὶ ποιήσεις μοι σήμερον πᾶν ὅ τι ἐλάλησας μετ'
ἐμοῦ, "your eyes, and you will do for me today all that you have spoken with me," representing an inner
Gk. confusion between σημεῖον, "sign," and σήμερον, "today," leading to insertion of "all."

19.a. Bluedorn (*Yahweh versus Baalism*, 95) calls the Heb. וַיִּגַּשׁ "ambiguously vocalized," something
done intentionally to maintain Gideon's ambiguity and heighten narrative tension. LXX[A] maintains
the worship mood by translating Heb. וַיִּגַּשׁ, "and he approached," by προσεκύνησεν, "he bowed down
in worship," a possible translation for וַיִּגַּשׁ, "and he offered (an offering)." OL indicates that Gideon
took the offering to the messenger (see Niditch, 88). MT offers the more difficult reading. REB joins
the MT verb to the next verse. Text seems to emphasize Gideon's courage to approach, while later
copyists interpreted it in light of sacrificial language. *Preliminary and Interim Report* (2:88) wants to
change the text.

20.a. LXX[A] reads "the messenger of the Lord," substituting the more familiar phrase for the less
familiar "messenger of God."

25.a. Bluedorn (*Yahweh versus Baalism*, 91–96) surveys the long debate on the translation of פַר הַשֹּׁר

and other problems in this section. LXX[A] reads τὸν μόσχον τὸν σιτευτὸν τοῦ πατρός σου μόσχον τὸν ἑπταετῆ, "the fatted calf of your father, a seven-year-old calf," apparently not translating שׁנִי, while LXX[B] reads τὸν μόσχον τὸν ταῦρον ὅς ἐστιν τῷ πατρί σου καὶ μόσχον δεύτερον ἑπταετῆ, "the bull calf which is to your father and a second calf seven years old." OL has the "fatted calf." The Heb. expression פַּר הַשֵּׁנִי has traditionally troubled exegetes, for a "second calf" plays no role in the story. D. Rudman (*JNSL* 26 [2002] 97–103) argues that reference to the second bull is a glossator's addition based on the required sacrifice of two bulls in Lev 4:21 and Num 8:8. J. A. Emerton (*ErIsr* 14 [1978] 52), followed by Block (266), relates שׁנִי to cognate languages, creating a Heb. root meaning "be exalted, of high rank" and thus "premier or prize." Thus *Preliminary and Interim Report* correlates the textual questions in 6:25, 26, and 28: "MT seems to presuppose *one* sacrifice only with *one* bull only. Consequently, the description 'שׁנִי פַּר, a second bull' indicates the *quality* of the *only* bull sacrificed: it is the best bull which remains after the first, as firstborn, had been immolated immediately after birth" (2:89, emphasis original). This explanation results in a suggested translation of: "take your father's young bull, <that is> the second bull, seven years old." See *BHS*. One could tie the term to the similar Heb. word שׁנִי, meaning "red, crimson." See *Comment*.

25.b. אֲשֵׁרָה refers both to the Canaanite goddess, wife of El, and to the cultic pole used to symbolize her presence. LXX (compare OL) translates it with ἄλσος, "sacred groves." See *Comment*.

26.a. LXX[A] (compare OL) reads τῷ θεῷ σου τῷ ὀφθέντι σοι ἐπὶ τῆς κορυφῆς τοῦ ὄρους Μαωζ τούτου, "to your God to be seen by you on the top of this mountain Maos [a transliteration of Heb. term מָעוֹז, 'mountain stronghold']." LXX[B] simply transliterates מָעוֹז as Μαουεκ and consistently mentions the "second" calf, which LXX[A] never mentions; some Heb. MSS have הַמָּעוֹן, "lair" or "dwelling."

26.b. מַעֲרָכָה most often refers to an army in proper battle formation and is especially prominent in the Dead Sea Scrolls as seen in the citations in *DCH*. Here the term apparently refers to the proper formation of the altar with regular layers of stones.

27.a. LXX[A] reads "thirteen."

28.a. LXX[A] reads καὶ ὁ μόσχος ὁ σιτευτός, "the fatted calf," while LXX[B] reads καὶ εἶδαν τὸν μόσχον τὸν δεύτερον, "and they saw the second calf."

28.b. LXX[A] reads ἀνηνεγμένος εἰς ὁλοκαύτωμα ἐπὶ τὸ θυσιαστήριον, "had been sacrificed in a whole burnt offering on the altar," providing an extended meaning probably implied in the Heb. verb, an unusual *hoph'al* form.

29.a. Heb. reads lit. "and they said." LXX[B] reads ἠρεύνησαν καὶ ἔγνωσαν ὅτι Γεδεων, "they inquired and came to know that Gideon."

29.b. Many Heb. MSS add the sign of the direct object.

31.a. LXX[A] reads πρὸς τοὺς ἄνδρας τοὺς ἑσταμένους ἐπ' αὐτόν, "to the men who were standing by him," omitting the Heb. כל as implied by the context, while LXX[B] reads τοῖς ἀνδράσιν πᾶσιν οἳ ἐπανέστησαν αὐτῷ, "to all the men who were rising up against him," apparently turning the men into enemies.

31.b. Cairo Genizah fragment reads אֵלָיו, attesting a frequent Heb. confusion between the two similarly sounding prepositions.

32.a. Heb. reads "he called him."

32.b. LXX[A] reads ἐκάλεσεν αὐτὸ ἐν τῇ ἡμέρᾳ ἐκείνῃ Δικαστήριον τοῦ Βααλ ὅτι κατέσκαψεν τὸ θυσιαστήριον αὐτοῦ, "He called him in that day Justice Court of Baal because he destroyed his altar."

34.a. LXX[A] reads "Spirit of God," using an alternative divine title.

34.b. LXX[B] reads ἐνεδυνάμωσεν τὸν Γεδεων, "strengthened Gideon," while LXX[A] reads ἐνέδυσεν, "clothed," also represented in the OL. Niditch concludes: "Inner-Greek look-alike/sound-similar verbs have thus led to variants in the tradition, both of which make sense." (88).

34.c. LXX[B] reads ἐφοβήθη Αβιεζερ ὀπίσω αὐτοῦ, "Abiezer was afraid after him"; Heb. text reads lit. וַיִּזָּעֵק אֲבִיעֶזֶר אַחֲרָיו, "Abiezer was called together after him," referring to the mustering of the clan. *BHS* points to early Gk. evidence and suggests reading וַיִּזְעַק, the more usual *qal* form instead of MT's *niph'al* or passive/middle form. Niditch points out "the sound-alike Greek verbs for 'fear,' *ephobēthē* (Vat), and 'call,' *eboēsen* (A). . . . OL reads *'aḥărāyw* ('after him') as sound-similar, *'eḥāyw* ('his brother'): 'he called Abiezer his brother'" (88). MT represents the more difficult reading and leaves the command with God and Barak rather than with Abiezer.

35.a. Cairo Genizah fragment completes a familiar phrase: הר אפרים ו, "Mount Ephraim and."

35.b. LXX[B] reads simply εἰς πάντα Μανασση καὶ ἐν Ασηρ καὶ ἐν Ζαβουλων καὶ Νεφθαλι καὶ ἀνέβη εἰς συνάντησιν αὐτῶν, "into all Manasseh and in Asher and in Zebulun and Naphtali, and he went up to their meeting." This omits a part of the Heb. text that is a bit difficult syntactically and is missing in Cairo Genizah. LXX[A] reads ἀνέβησαν εἰς συνάντησιν αὐτοῦ, "his meeting," a reading adopted by *BHS* but one which highlights Gideon rather than the gathering of the various armies.

38.a. LXX^A reads "Gideon."

39.a. *BHS* suggests reading with many Heb. MSS על instead of MT אל based on the use in vv 37, 40. Texts frequently confuse the two prepositions. The reading here could be simply an editorial choice for variety.

7:1.a. OL reads "in the dawn I was vigilant."

1.b. LXX^A reads τὴν γῆν Αρωεδ, "land (earth) of Aroed (Harod)," while LXX^B reads ἐπὶ πηγὴν Αραδ, "at the spring of Arad," substituting better-known names for lesser-known ones.

1.c. LXX^A (compare OL) reads "Midian and Amalek," a reading *BHS* sees as original to the Gk. tradition, but which is drawn from 6:33 and 7:12 and levels the text.

1.d. LXX^B reads ἀπὸ Γαβααθ Αμωρα, "from Gibeah of Amorah (Moreh)," leading *BHS* to call MT a corruption and to propose מתחת מצפון לגבעת המורה, "from below north of the hill of Moreh," for מצפון מגבעת המורה בעמק, "Midian being north of them in the valley of the Hill of Moreh." Gk. transliterates the Heb. גבעת, "hill," as the place name Gibeah. The *BHS* proposal smooths the text a bit but has no textual basis.

2.a. OL reads, "the people are great, and I will hand Midian into their hands." Niditch notes that this omits "any sense of the deity's insecurity" (95).

3.a. LXX^A introduces the section with καὶ εἶπεν κύριος πρὸς αὐτόν, "and the Lord said to him," repeating the phrase from v 2.

3.b. Lit. "in the ears of."

3.c. *BHS* finds corruption here and restores the text in line with the Tg. and the following verse to read, "and Gideon sifted them." Compare Burney, Soggin, NRSV. OL reads, "go down." Niditch translates "fly away from," suggesting that "perhaps MT reflects confusion with the similar word for 'refine' or 'smelt' in v. 4" (92). *Preliminary and Interim Report* is cautiously correct as it concludes: "the meaning of the verb צפר is not certain; it may be either corrupt or a technical term for holy war. The translations of the versions depend more or less on the context and on the parallel of Deut 20:5–8. It may be translated 'and let him depart early in the morning from Mount Gilead'" (2:91–92). For a fuller discussion, see Barthélemy, *Critique textuelle*, 1:94–95.

4.a. LXX reads αὐτὸς οὐ πορεύσεται μετὰ σοῦ, "this one will not go with you."

5.a. LXX^A (compare OL) reads τοῦ πιεῖν μεταστήσεις αὐτὸν καθ' αὐτόν, "to drink, you shall remove him off by himself." *BHS* uses this with Syr. and Vg. evidence to restore תציג אותו לבד, "you shall leave him alone." Note the discussion by Niditch (95–96).

6.a. LXX^A reads πᾶς ὁ ἀριθμὸς τῶν λαψάντων ἐν τῇ γλώσσῃ αὐτῶν, "the total number of those lapping with their tongue." OL omits "with their hands to their mouth" and reads "who lapped with their tongue like a dog" from v 5. Amit (*Book of Judges*, 257, n. 47) follows many scholars in seeing "with their hands to their mouth" as an "exegetical gloss" that should be at the end of the verse but was inserted at the wrong place (see Moore, 202; Boling, 145; Soggin, 137). As Bluedorn notes (*Yahweh versus Baalism*, 118, n. 193), the Gk. reading enables a clear assignment of those drinking to Yahweh's prediction, but this is exactly what the Heb. does not want to do. *BHS* uses this to transpose "with their hands to their mouth" to the end of the sentence and to insert בלשונם, "with their tongues," here, giving a final reading of "lapping with their tongue three hundred men. But all the rest of the people bent over on their knees to drink water with their hands to their mouth." This again is a smoothing of the text without sufficient textual warrant. See *Preliminary and Interim Report*, 2:92–93.

8.a. *BHS* wants to write the story in its own fashion, seeing "perhaps" corruption from an original העם מידם (or צדה את־כדי) ויקח את־כדי, "and he took the necessities (or supplies) of the people from their hands." But see *Preliminary and Interim Report*, 2:93–94, and the complex grammatical discussion of Barthélemy, *Critique textuelle*, 1:95.

9.a. LXX^A (compare OL) reads κατάβηθι τὸ τάχος ἐντεῦθεν, "go down quickly from here."

10.a. Here and in the next verse LXX reads the name as "Para."

11.a. See *Note* 7:10.a.

11.b. For קצה, "end" or "edge," *BHS* suggests an unsupported change to לצפות.

11.c. LXX^A reads εἰς μέρος τῶν πεντήκοντα τῶν ἐν τῇ παρεμβολῇ, "into the part of the fifty of those in the camp," reading החמשים, "an army formation of fifty men," as חמשים, "fifty." LXX^B reads πρὸς ἀρχὴν τῶν πεντήκοντα, "to the beginning of the fifty." *BHS* accepts evidence of Gk. and two Heb. MSS to read חמשים, "fifty." The Heb. represents the more difficult reading without being nonsense and so should be retained.

12.a. Lit. "falling."

13.a. Cairo Genizah, many Heb. MSS, and Q reflect צליל for the written text צלול. Either reading represents a *hapax* that the versions translate as "barley loaf."

13.b. LXXᴬ reads ἐπάταξεν αὐτὴν καὶ κατέστρεψεν αὐτήν καὶ ἔπεσεν ἡ σκηνή, "it struck it and overthrew it, and the tent fell." *BHS* uses Gk. evidence to see both "it fell" and "the tent collapsed" as late additions that should be deleted. Again, such deletion is done to accommodate a certain literary theory and does not have sufficient supporting textual evidence.

14.a. LXXᴬ and OL read "the Lord," a frequent literary/textual substitution.

15.a. LXX reads "he worshiped the Lord"; compare *Note* 7:14.a above.

15.b. LXXᴮ reads, "our hand," picking up the self-centered picture of Gideon, but not providing sufficient evidence to alter the text.

16.a. Lit. "three heads."

16.b. LXXᴮ does not have "in the center of."

17.a. LXXᴬ reads "middle of the camp." OL adds "as the watch begins."

18.a. LXXᴬ does not have "all."

18.b. *BHS* lists strong Gk., Syr., and Tg. evidence to read "the sword of Yahweh and of Gideon," but quickly points to v 20 as the source for this reading. OL reads, "say to the Lord, 'Behold, Gideon.'" Niditch notes that this reading reduces "the impression that God and Gideon are military partners."

19.a. *BHS* proposes making איש articular on the basis of 8:14, where the noun is not articular. Judg 7:8 does give an articular example.

19.b. OL deletes "in their hands" as redundant. *BHS* uses Gk. evidence and v 20 to read sg. rather than pl.: ויתקע בשופר ונפוץ הכד אשר בידו. This uses weak evidence and a need for literary consistency to change a text that reads without problems.

20.a. OL reads "threw the jars of their hands and two battle lines were turned to them."

20.b. *BHS* proposes deleting השׁוֹפָרוֹת לתקוֹע and inserting הֶחָרֶב, "sword," to read "and in their right hand the sword, and they called, 'for Yahweh and for Gideon.'" This deletes a Heb. idiom, misses the point of the story with its emphasis on Gideon's search for self-sufficiency and praise, and has no basis in textual evidence. See *Preliminary and Interim Report,* 2:94.

21.a. "Of Midian" added for translation clarity. Based on a Genizah ms, *BHS* proposes העם, "the people," again without sufficient evidence and seeing the same textual ambiguity that leads us to add "of Midian" for clarity.

21.b. *BHS* proposes וַיִּקֶץ, apparently "he woke up, aroused from sleep," again a proposal without evidence or literary reason behind it. See *Preliminary and Interim Report,* 2:94.

21.c. Heb. has Kethib/Qere readings. Written text has וַיָּנִיסוּ, the *hip̄ʿil* form, while the marginal reading form is וַיָּנֻסוּ. Certainly, the latter is preferable in context. OL adds "and the camp of Midian and Amalek and all the enemy men feared."

22.a. Based on a bit of Gk. evidence, *BHS* suggests that perhaps the article should be added to the Heb. "hundred."

22.b. LXX evidence beyond LXXᴬ, LXXᴮ, Syr., and Vg. points to omission of the copula here.

22.c. Fewer than ten Heb. mss and the Syr. evidence point to the addition of כל here, perhaps showing scribal error in placing כל in this ms.

22.d. LXXᴬ translates צְרֵרָתָה, "in the direction of Zererah," as συνηγμένη, "gathered together." Fewer than twenty Heb. mss and 1 Kgs 11:26 read צרדתה, "Zeradathah," instead of MT's צררתה, apparently representing the correct name for the town here, a Heb. *dālet* being mistaken for a *rêš* in the MT copying tradition and thus removing mention of Jeroboam's home town. See *Preliminary and Interim Report,* 2:94–95; Barthélemy, *Critique textuelle,* 1:96.

22.e. *BHS* uses a few Heb. mss and the marginal Sebir ("supposed" or "expected") as evidence to suggest substituting Heb. על for MT עד, certainly choosing a simpler text than MT, which can be read sensibly.

23.a. LXX reads an active verb for MT's passive here and in the next verse.

24.a. *BHS* wants to read the preposition על, "on" or "beside," instead of MT's sign of the accusative. OL reads Beth-barah as "Bethel."

25.a. *BHS* proposes reading the sign of the accusative for MT's preposition אל on the basis of LXX, Syr., and Vg. evidence. This may be needed in light of the Heb. preposition meaning "towards," which does not fit the context here.

8:1.a. LXXᴮ reads "Gideon" with pl. verb (as does OL), making indirect object and collective interpretation of "man of Ephraim" clear.

1.b. Heb. mss differ on spelling of infinitive construct; many have קראה, and two have קרא.

2.a. Many Heb. mss read ב, "at, with, or against," here and in v 3 rather than MT כ, "comparing to, as," interpreting Gideon's statement as adversarial rather than diplomatic.

2.b. Heb. edition of Bombergiana reads the more usual *dāgēš* in the ב.

3.a. LXX, OL read "the Lord" instead of "God," not following the author's distinctive uses of the divine names.

3.b. Eastern MSS have ב rather than כ, an easy confusion as seen in vv 2 and 3, of similar letters, here having little semantic significance.

3.c. LXX^A reads κατέπαυσαν τότε ἀνῆκε τὸ πνεῦμα αὐτῶν, "they ceased; then he relieved their spirit," apparently incorporating two translations for the Heb. רָפְתָה or reading a *hip̄'il* form of נוח or שבת.

4.a. LXX, supported by Syr. and Vg., reads διέβη, leading to a frequent reading of the Heb. as וַיַּעַבְרוּ, an unnecessary fine tuning of grammar.

4.b. LXX^A reads ὀλιγοψυχοῦντες καὶ πεινῶντες, "discouraged and hungry," the latter possibly representing Heb. רעב. LXX^B reads πεινῶντες καὶ διώκοντες, "hungry and pursuing," possibly giving another witness to Heb. רעב. OL has "weak and hungry," again reflecting רעב. MT represents a more difficult reading in the context and maintains the story's theme of pursuit. Niditch (102) maintains, "The simplest sensible combination is probably 'tired and hungry,' and one might suggest that *rdp*, 'to pursue,' is a corruption of *r'b*, 'to be hungry.' On the other hand, the various images have been understood by receiving communities and operate as variants. There may have been versions that had only the term for 'tired.' *Rdp* enters under influence of the following verse, and some of the ancient translators/writers 'correct' it to 'hungry'" (102).

5.a. Lit. "people who are at my feet." LXX^A omits "loaves" and reads λαῷ τῷ μετ' ἐμοῦ ὅτι πεινῶσιν, "people with me because they are hungry." See *Note* 8:4.b above. LXX^B reads ἄρτους εἰς τροφὴν τῷ λαῷ τούτῳ τῷ ἐν ποσίν μου ὅτι ἐκλείπουσιν, "bread for food to the people at my feet because they are dying (or deserting)."

6.a. The Heb. subject is pl., but the verb sg.; thus *BHS* suggests reading the pl. verb with a few Heb. MSS, the marginal Sebir ("supposed" or "expected") notation, and the versions. MT apparently has the leaders speaking with one voice.

6.b. OL reads "head of Zebah and Zalmunna," giving a final touch to the wish for proof.

6.c. A few Heb. MSS, Syr., Arabic read the pl. "hands," which might be expected but is not necessary in the context.

7.a. LXX apparently did not know the meaning of Heb. הַבַּרְקָנִים, "brambles," and so transliterated it. *BHS* suggests, on the basis of the LXX, reading ב for the final two occurrences of את, another unneeded nicety of grammar.

9.a. LXX^B reads "Gideon," making the subject explicit.

11.a. *BHS* shows the proposal to read שֹׁכְנֵי, the simple participle, "dwellers," for MT's articular passive participle, thus supposing a much simpler reading.

11.b. LXX^A reads τῆς Ναβεθ ἐξ ἐναντίας Ζεβεε, "of Nobah from before Zebah," possibly representing Heb. מלפני זבח. Here and in Num 32:35 the Leningrad text places a *dāgēš* in the ב of "Jogbehah," a mark that does not appear in all other Heb. MSS and editions.

11.c. *BHS* points to a few Heb. MSS and LXX as evidence for reading sg. participle בֹּשֵׁם rather than noun בֶּטַח, again creating grammatical finery out of translations that do not always follow such fine distinctions. OL reads "the camp was in a place that they trusted."

12.a. *HALOT* interprets the meaning of the *hip̄'il* of חרד as "startle" or "cause to tremble, fear." *DCH* may be closer to the context here in reading "scatter." *BHS* suggests, on the basis of LXX^A (compare OL) ἐξέτριψεν and Josephus διέφθειρε, הכחיד, "destroy." The MT represents the more difficult and probably the original text.

13.a. LXX^B reads ἀπὸ τῆς παρατάξεως ἀπὸ ἐπάνωθεν τῆς παρατάξεως Αρες, "from the battle line from above the battle line of Heres," apparently an internal LXX dittography repeating τῆς παρατάξεως. OL reads "from the rise of the sea." *BHS* sees textual corruption here, suggesting on the basis of LXX, ממעלה, "from the ascent."

14.a. LXX^B reads τὰ ὀνόματα τῶν ἀρξόντων, "the names of the leaders."

15.a. LXX reads "Gideon."

15.b. LXX reads "leaders of Succoth."

15.c. See *Note* 8:6.b.

16.a. LXX^A (compare OL) reads ἔλαβεν τοὺς ἄρξοντά καὶ τοὺς πρεσβυτέρους τῆς πόλεως, "he took the leaders and the elders of the city."

16.b. MT וַיֹּדַע, "he caused to know"; *BHS* reads וַיָּדֹשׁ, "he threshed," with v 7 and with cross reference to LXX, Syr., Vg.

16.c. LXX^A reads κατέξανεν αὐτοὺς ἐν ταῖς ἀκάνθαις τῆς ἐρήμου καὶ ταῖς Βαρακηνιμ καὶ κατέξανεν ἐν αὐτοῖς ἄνδρας Σοκχωθ, "he tore them in pieces with the thorns of the wilderness and the Bapakenim [i.e., transliteration of Heb. 'brambles'], and he tore the men of Succoth to pieces with them." LXX^B (compare OL) reads καὶ ἔλαβεν τοὺς πρεσβυτέρους τῆς πόλεως ἐν ταῖς ἀκάνθαις τῆς ἐρήμου καὶ ταῖς βαρακηνιμ καὶ ἠλόησεν ἐν αὐτοῖς τοὺς ἄνδρας τῆς πόλεως, "and he took the elders of the city with the thorns of the wilderness and the Bapakenim [i.e., transliteration of Heb. 'brambles'], and with them he threshed the men of the city." This appears to reflect internal LXX dittography combined with a reading of יִדּשׁ, "to thresh," for יָדַע, "to know, to teach" *(hipʿil)*. (Compare v 7.) The latter reading also appears in LXX^B, which reads "men of the city" for "men of Succoth," perhaps taken from the ending of the next verse. With her oral literature approach, Niditch concludes, "Each version works well enough and reflects the oral-style variation that characterizes the manuscript traditions" (102).

18.a. OL reads, "Who and what kind were . . . ," questions Niditch (102) sees as more precisely suited to the response.

18.b. Based on Tg., supported by Vg., *BHS* suggests a possible reading of אָחַד אֶחָד. The word does not appear in a Heb. MS, LXX^R, Theodotian, and Syr.

19.a. LXX reads "Gideon."

19.b. OL adds, "and he swore to them," what Niditch calls "framing the form of the adjuration" (103).

20.a. LXX^A does not have "still."

21.a. LXX^B and LXX^C have second sg. suffix, not realizing this is a proverbial statement, not a direct reference to Gideon as in the previous part of the sentence.

22.a. A few Heb. MSS, the marginal Sebir ("supposed" or "expected") notation, and LXX^A, Origen, and LXX^L read verb as sg., not recognizing collective nature of the pl. subject אִישׁ־יִשְׂרָאֵל.

22.b. LXX^B reads κύριε ἄρχον ἡμῶν, "my Lord, rule us."

22.c. LXX does not have "grandson."

24.a. LXX^B reads "many golden earrings," probably a product of the tradition amplifying the grandeur of the story.

25.a. LXX reads ἀνέπτυξεν τὸ ἱμάτιον αὐτοῦ, "he [OL Gideon] spread out his garment."

25.b. LXX^A (compare OL) reads "golden earring," again magnifying the story's grandeur.

26.a. LXX^B reads "one thousand five hundred," one of many examples of the shift of numbers in the copying tradition.

26.b. Supplying "shekels" for clarity as did LXX.

26.c. LXX^A reads τῶν σιρώνων καὶ τῶν ὁρμίσκων ενφωθ, "the crescent ornaments [a transliteration from Heb.] and the necklaces of pendants [transliterating the Heb. for pendants]."

26.d. LXX^A reads τῶν κλοιῶν τῶν χρυσῶν, "gold chains," further enhancing the story, while LXX^B reads a much more blasé περιθεμάτων, "coverings."

27.a. LXX transliterates the technical Heb. term "ephod," just as we do in English.

28.a. כ has been proposed for ב to give a comparative meaning rather than a temporal one. Another proposal is to add כָּל, "all the days." The proposals simply make explicit the text's implication.

30.a. Lit. "sons, ones coming out of his loin."

31.a. OL expands the text with "he had concubines in Shechem."

31.b. Abimelech means, "my father is king."

32.a. Lit. "with good gray hair"; LXX^B reads ἐν πόλει αὐτοῦ, "in his city," a miscopying of the similar sounding and appearing ἐν πολιᾷ ἀγαθῇ, "with good gray hair."

32.b. A construct state עֶפְרָה is proposed in line with 6:24.

32.c. LXX^A reads Ιωας τοῦ πατρὸς αὐτοῦ ἐν Εφραθα πατρὸς Αβιεζρι, "Joash, his father, in Ophrah of the father of Abiezer," a case of translating אֲבִי as "my father" and then transliterating it in the name Abiezer.

33.a. LXX translated בַּעַל בְּרִית as "Baal of the covenant"; again LXX^A both translated and transliterated the term, coming out with ἔθεντο αὐτοῖς τὸν Βααλβεριθ εἰς διαθήκην τοῦ εἶναι αὐτοῖς αὐτῶν εἰς θεόν, "they appointed for themselves the Baal Berith in the covenant so that he was god for them."

35.a. A number of Heb. MSS read לְיִשְׂרָאֵל for MT עַם, "of Israel" for "people."

Form/Structure/Setting

The Gideon narrative brings Judges to its most ambiguous narrative point. Deborah and Barak have shown how the northern tribes lack unity and leadership, especially male leadership. Deborah's strengths are obvious. Her only problem is her gender. In Israelite society of her day, men were supposed to occupy the leading roles in the judiciary, the military, the political, and the religious segments. Deborah openly held judiciary and religious leadership as judge and prophet. Her military role, whatever it may have entailed, came as a result of Barak's refusal to take charge. Her political role can only be inferred from her military intervention. Nothing is said about Israel having peace during Deborah or Barak's lifetime. No credit comes to them for achieving and maintaining peace. Political leadership is absent from the narrative and apparently absent from Israel's life. Israel is simply a loosely formed coalition to which only a few tribes really feel loyalty.

These same few tribes will play central roles in the remainder of Judges, especially under Gideon. For these few tribes the stories of the central judges—Deborah/Barak, Gideon, Abimelech, and Jephthah—represent hero tales from the tribal standpoint, but gathered into a literary unity, they display the chaos that threatened and then overcame Israel. Gideon shows the best and worst of the leadership that brought final chaos. After him, one searches long and hard for things to praise in the lives of Abimelech, Jephthah, and especially Samson. At one time their tribes may have seen reason to tell their "heroic" tales, but seen from the perspective of tribal cooperation or confederation, they provide little to praise. This may well be another clue that the stories originally come from the north, but they are gathered under Rehoboam to show the real "strength" and "unity" of the seceding tribes. The northern tribes who want to separate themselves from Rehoboam can only point to "heroes" such as these self-centered, egotistical, self-seeking "leaders."

The religious scene becomes even more confused under Gideon. The introductory frame for Othniel says Israel did evil, forgot Yahweh their God, and worshiped the Baals and the Asherahs (3:7). The Ehud narrative starts with the quick reference to Israel doing evil (3:12). The Deborah/Barak cycle opens with Israel doing evil again (4:1), and the song mentions the choice of new gods (5:8) in passing. Only with Gideon do we find heretical worship practices and apparatus. Thus Matthews can say, "What differs here is the degree to which the storyteller develops the theme of apostasy among the people and by the judge" (81).

Form. The Gideon narrative cycle actually extends through chap. 9, brought to a conclusion only through the exploits of his son Abimelech. From one perspective these four chapters can be classified as a novella that "develops a point of tension to a final resolution. The perspective is this world. The structural character is complex: it may employ subplots. It is not set within the process of oral tradition" (G. W. Coats, *Genesis,* FOTL 1 [Grand Rapids: Eerdmans, 1983] 319). If this is the correct designation, then the novella is composed of separate units whose original home was in oral tradition. Most of the individual units fall under the category of "reports": "a brief, self-contained prose narrative about a single event or situation in the past" (S. J. De Vries, *1 and 2 Chronicles,* FOTL 11 [Grand Rapids: Eerdmans, 1989] 434).

See table 6.1 in the appendix to compare one possible example of narrative analysis with form-critical analysis for the entire Gideon/Abimelech complex in chaps. 6–9. The narrative elements follow the typical pattern of Hebrew narrative while the genre elements show the genre of each section with its component parts. Note how the narrator can use different genre elements and markers within or even across various narrative elements.

Structure. The Gideon novella is a complicated story with briefer narratives embedded in the larger complex. Mobley concludes that "the Gideon material contains confusing repetitions, a meandering plot, and multiple endings" (*Empty Men*, 114). Block goes so far as to call this the most complete and complex account in the book of Judges. He sees "a series of episodes that differ in foci and style" (247). Mobley sees at least "a blending of two versions" (*Empty Men*, 121) and then states that "the cathedral of Judges 6–9 remained under construction for centuries" (126). He concludes that we have "a narrative whose many chambers and details defy reduction to a simple organizing scheme for the entire complex" (127). Pressler explains the confusion on the basis of the interests of the compilers: "The stories were collected by compilers who were not primarily interested in consistency or accuracy, or in reporting historical or military data. Rather, they were interested in proclaiming the reliability and rule of Israel's God. The details of the Gideon story are often somewhat cloudy; its theological message, that God is sovereign and to be relied upon, is clear" (168).

Scholars such as U. Becker (*Richterzeit und Königtum*, 140–207) account for this complexity by identifying disparate preliterary traditions combined through several layers of Deuteronomistic editorial work. Earlier critics such as Moore sought to explain the complexity as a continuation of literary sources they had isolated in the Pentateuch. The newer historical minimalist approach, represented by A. G. Auld (*VT* 39 [1989] 257–67), regards the story of Gideon as an addition made to the book of Judges in the Persian period.

Various modern scholars provide distinctly different literary analyses of the Gideon block of material. Most add chap. 9 as an appendix giving final conclusion to the Gideon narrative. Mobley sees "three verbal structures that mark resolutions: military resolution through the defeat of the Midianites (Judg 7:22–23), rhetorical resolution through the initial and terminal images of the parts of a winepress (Judg 6:11; 7:25), and editorial resolution through the note that the land had rest (Judg 8:28)" (*Empty Men*, 116). But the long episode between Judg 8:3 and 8:28 presents a major structural problem for his analysis. Another frustration comes with the seven possible endings (8:3; 8:21; 8:24–27a; 8:27b; 8:28; 8:32; and chap. 9). Mobley introduces further complication when he isolates differing pictures of Gideon in the narrative: Moses, the reluctant leader (6:11–18); Lamech, the blood feuder (8:4–19); Aaron, the idolater (8:24–27); Othniel, the model judge (8:28); and the great man, like Eli, Solomon, and Josiah, whose son fails to measure up to the father's standards (ch. 9). However, for Mobley, "in the final version of the story, Gideon is a fearful hero (Judg 6:23, 27; 7:10) who habitually requires oracular reassurance (Judg 6:17, 36, 39; 7:10–11)" (155). Despite all the complexities he has raised, Mobley eventually isolates "a single heroic theme" that "appears again and again." This single theme is "the triumph of a small group over a vast army" (129–30).

O'Connell looks at plot structure and identifies three separate subplots. The following is a simplified version of his analysis:

1. Yahweh's rescue of Israel from the Midianites by means of Gideon (6:1–24; 33–40; 7:1–25; 8:1–4, 10–12, 28, 32)
2. Yahweh's judgment on Gideon and his tribe for holding on to foreign cult practices (6:25–32; 8:24–27, 33–34; 9:1–44, 46–49, 56–57)
3. Yahweh's judgment on Gideon, his sons, and his tribe for covenant injustices (8:5–9, 13–23, 29–31, 35; 9:1–49a, 50–57)

J. P. Turner ("The Gideon Narrative as the Focal Point of Judges," *BibSac* 149 [1992] 146–61) sees a chiastic pattern:

> A   6:1–10
>   B   6:11–32
>   C   6:33–7:18
>   B´   7:19–8:21
> A´   8:22–32

Block (250) finds three major parts: 6:1–8:3, 8:4–28, and 8:29–9:57.

Younger (167–68) also develops a symmetrical pattern with a "series of mini-climaxes" that lead to the ultimate climax in 8:22–32:

A   Prologue to Gideon (6:1–10)
B   God's plan of deliverance through the call of Gideon—the story of two altars (6:11–32)
     B1   The first altar—call and commissioning of Gideon (6:11–24)
     B2   The second altar—the charge to clean house (6:25–32)
C   Gideon's personal faith struggle (6:33–7:18)
    a   The Spirit-endowed Gideon mobilizes four tribes against the Midianites, though lacking confidence in God's promise (6:33–35)
      b   Gideon seeks a sign from God with the two fleecings to confirm the promise that Yahweh will give Midian into his hand (6:36–40)
        c   With the fearful Israelites having departed, God directs Gideon to go down to the water for the further reduction of his force (7:1–8)
        c´   With fear still in Gideon himself, God directs Gideon to go down to the enemy camp to overhear the enemy (7:9–11)
      b´   God provides a sign to Gideon with the dream of the Midianite and its interpretation to confirm the promise that Yahweh will give Midian into his hand (7:12–14)
    a´   The worshiping Gideon mobilizes his force of three hundred for a surprise attack against the Midianites, fully confident in God's promise (7:15–18)
B´   God's deliverance from the Midianites—the story of two battles (7:19–8:21)
     B1´   The first battle (Cisjordan) (7:19–8:3)
     B2´   The second battle (Transjordan) (8:4–21)
A´   Epilogue to Gideon (8:22–32)

Dorsey (110–11) offers a similar chiastic interpretation with 6:1–10, 6:11–40, and 7:1–14 being complemented by 7:23–8:21, 8:22–27, and 8:28–32 and with 7:15–22 serving as the fulcrum or turning point.

In his extensive description of the Gideon materials, Bluedorn (*Yahweh versus Baalism*) analyzes the text as expressing its theme in 6:7–10, namely, "Israel's apostasy and YHWH's claim to be worshipped instead of the Canaanite gods" (69). For Bluedorn, the narrator's focus lies in "the demonstration of YHWH's power and Gideon's selfish continuation of the battle against the Midianites to get credited [*sic*] himself" (*Yahweh versus Baalism*, 55). The Abimelech narrative then focuses on Baalism. Together the two narratives "show that YHWH has divine power and is God instead of Baal and indeed any other god" (56).

Amit (*Book of Judges*, 232–56) asserts that the editor has combined the individual units into two blocks of material, the first showing "the giving of signs and allusions to the active power of God" (6:11–7:23) and the second showing "problems of human leadership" (7:24–8:27a).

Robert Polzin also points to human egotism: "The Gideon story depicts the excessive concern men exhibit who seek by signs and tests to insure the success of their ventures" (*Moses and the Deuteronomist*, 168). He then quickly notes: "Yet, throughout all the venturesome incidents of the story, whether they involve successful enterprises or not, there is an aura of ultimate mystery surrounding the destiny of both man and nation, a destiny that is not finally predictable by any ideology."

The Gideon material is thus structured around human weakness in leadership mysteriously immersed in divine purpose. The extensive number of formal units are collected into a single structure. The major part of the structure is clearly marked as 6:1–8:28 by the conclusion in 8:28 pointing back to the introduction in 6:1–10. Just as clearly, 8:29–9:57 is marked off as a narrative appendix by the incorporation of Abimelech's birth report (8:31) within Gideon's "obituary."

The first major section (6:1–8:28) is introduced as a battle with Midian but explained as disobedience to God (6:1–10). The call narrative appears to alleviate this situation but instead shows the extensive control Baal worship exercised and the fear and lack of faith of the chosen leader so that the battle becomes Baal versus Yahweh. The actual extended battle narrative (6:33–8:21) results in victory for Israel but reveals the human reliance on superior numbers of troops, the leader's lack of faith in God, the leader's fear of the enemy, the divine plan leading to victory, and a human pursuit marked by tribal jealousy and human revenge. The theological conclusion (8:22–35) is that God is truly king even when the human leader leads a royal lifestyle.

The second major section opens with Jerubbaal's final years with his royal harem and seventy sons, plus the Shechemite concubine's son whose name is Abimelech, "my father is king." The theological exposition shows that Gideon's heritage was that of Baal worship, not obedience to Yahweh, and of disloyalty to Gideon and his family. Abimelech is then represented as relying on Baal worshipers for his election and achieving it through the murder of all but one of Gideon's seventy sons.

Jotham's fable gives narrative context to the following narratives, showing complex revenge motifs. This leads to the destruction of Shechem, where Joshua renewed God's covenant with his people (Josh 24), and of Abimelech, who tries to carry on Gideon's royal tradition through intrigue and royal murder. The Gideon narrative thus demonstrates the loss of true Yahweh worship, the control gained by Baal worship, the failure of Israel's first attempt at royal dynasty, and the shadow of things to come in the northern kingdom as capital cities vie for power, Baal worship emblems mark Israel's worship, and royal rebellions constantly do away with royal dynasties. Thus Schneider correctly concludes: "Many scholars seem almost annoyed at what the author or redactor of Judges has done by taking authority and power away from Gideon. These scholars miss the focus of the text which is structured to highlight just that point. According to the text the people strayed to such an extent that they no longer readily listened when the deity contacted someone directly" (100).

Setting. The narrative setting of the Gideon narrative is quite simple. The first major section deals with Midianite wars, while the second deals with Abimelech's attempt to rule from Shechem.

Niditch observes, "The Israelite tradition evidences genuine ambivalence and self-contradiction in attitudes expressed toward Israel's southeastern neighbor in northwestern Arabia. Moses is described as having close, positive, in-marrying relations with Midianites, while other passages describe them as enemies (Num 22:1–7) and seducers (Num 25:1–7, 16–18; 31:1–12)" (89). Midian was the Arabian tribe (Gen 25:2, 4) in whose territory Moses lived when he fled from Pharaoh (Exod 2:15). Midian joined Moab in opposing Israel in the wilderness (Num 22). Midianite women tempted Israelite men (Num 25). One of Moses' last acts was defeating the Midianites, but again Midianite women tempted Israel's men (Num 31). Thus again Israel faces opposition from people who do not claim Canaan as a homeland, just as Ehud faced the Moabites, Othniel opposed the Arameans, and Shamgar the Philistines. To this point, only Deborah and Barak have faced internal enemies. Bluedorn is right in seeing that the "Israelites appear to be more distressed by the Midianites than by any of the previous oppressors" (*Yahweh versus Baalism*, 60).

Abimelech made enemies of the people of Shechem in whose territory Israel had strong ties and traditions. Abraham (Gen 12:6) and Jacob (Gen 33:18) worshiped there. Trouble first arose when Shechem raped Leah's daughter Dinah and Israel's sons killed Shechem (Gen 34). Still Shechem was a sacred place for Jacob (Gen 35:4; compare 37:12). Moses expected Israel to be able to worship near Shechem (Deut 11:29; 27:4). Even with no narrative of conquest there, Joshua took Israel to Shechem for covenant ceremonies (Josh 8:30–34; 24) and made Shechem a Levitical city (Josh 20:7) and a city of refuge (Josh 21:21). There Joshua buried Joseph's bones (Josh 24:32), and there Gideon could find a concubine, have a son, and leave the woman to raise the son in Shechem (Judg 8:31). Thus the city in Canaan with the closest ties to Israel in patriarchal and covenant tradition becomes the center of controversy in Israel's first attempt at dynastic leadership. Quite readily, Shechem could be the Israelite center that preserved the Gideon/Abimelech traditions. Shechem also later became the launching point for the northern tribes to repudiate Rehoboam and enthrone Jeroboam (1 Kgs 12). The southern tribes then assimilated the Shechem traditions and used them to show the dark side of Shechem and Israel's dynastic tradition.

Comment

6:1–6 The story begins, as we expect all the stories in Judges to begin, with the framework report of Israel's evil and the formulaic announcement that Yahweh handed them over to an enemy, in this case, Midian. Bluedorn (*Yahweh versus Baalism*, 57), following L. G. Stone's dissertation ("From Tribal Confederation to Monarchic State," 302, 308), emphasizes the absence of וַיֹּסִפוּ, "they did again" (3:12; 4:1; 10:6; 13:1), to see here the beginning of a new sequence of judges leading up to Samson and an increase in Israel's evil actions. This is a small clue for such a large theological jump.

Suddenly the framework dies, replaced by an extensive description of Israel's plight under Midian. Midian exerts strong pressure on Israel, showing that what was happening to Israel was absolutely opposed to God's original plan. In God's plan the Midianites shelter and assist Moses (Exod 3), but here Midian is the enemy from whom Israel seeks shelter. So Israel flees to the hills, looking for caves and other places of refuge where they might hide from the enemy. Whenever Israel tries to resume normal agricultural life or carry out a shepherd's normal duties, the Midianites and their allies interfere. (For the Amalekites, see *Comment* on 3:13.)

The "Easterners" introduce a mysterious element here. They also appear in Gen 29:1; Judg 6:33; 8:10; and Ezek 25:4, 10. They seem to be "nomadic groups that migrated about the Arabic desert" (Block, 252), though they would not refer to themselves as Easterners, that being applied to them by peoples living west of them. Apparently, the Midianites recruited a coalition of nomadic tribesmen to harass Israel and to provide themselves with food and other goods. Mobley (*Empty Men,* 163, n. 31) thinks the reference to these two groups "is probably a secondary expansion of the story," a possible but unnecessary conclusion. Quite frequently, Near Eastern battles included major powers and their weaker allies.

As Judg 6:5 says, "They entered the land to ruin it." Israel suffers a plague of Midianites just as the Egyptians had suffered a plague of locusts (Exod 10:4–19). Israel becomes very small—in significance, in self-esteem, and in possessions. Mobley (*Empty Men,* 130) translates the Hebrew וַיִּדַּל מְאֹד (6:6) as "impoverished, thin, emaciated." This is probably too concrete for the meaning here. Israel is "humiliated" physically, socially, and spiritually. Finally, Israel cries out to Yahweh (v 6). This formula from the framework appears frequently in the Judges narratives, but as Block reminds us, "there is no hint of repentance, only a cry of pain" (253; compare Bluedorn, *Yahweh versus Baalism,* 62 with n. 15). The sudden appearance of this framework element, so deeply and securely embedded in the narrative, makes us ask if the framework formulas were not first part of the narratives and taken from them to form the formulaic introduction of chap. 2.

7–10 At this point the framework leads us to expect God to raise up a judge. This he does, but not with a formulaic expression. Rather, an entire call narrative replaces the simple formula. The narrative does not begin, however, with the appearance of the one called before God or his messenger. Instead, an unnamed prophet appears, marked unusually as a man, אִישׁ in the Hebrew text, placing him in contrast to Deborah, the woman, the prophetess, in 4:4. Younger notes that this is the only appearance of a prophet in the book of Judges: "God decided to try a different path: to send a prophet before raising up a deliverer" (169).

The prophet uses the traditional prophetic-messenger formula—"thus says Yahweh"—to open a prophetic-judgment speech and to repeat the traditional themes of salvation history:

"I brought you up from Egypt" (6:8; compare Judg 2:1)

"I brought you out of the house of servitude" (6:8; compare Exod 13:3, 14; 20:2; Deut 5:6; 6:12; 7:8; 8:14; 13:5, 10 [Heb. 6, 11]; Josh 24:17; Jer 34:13; Mic 6:4)

"I rescued you from the hand of Egypt" (6:9; compare Exod 3:8; 18:9–10; 1 Sam 10:18; see also Exod 14:30)

"and from the hand of all your oppressors" (6:9; compare Exod 3:9; Deut 26:7; Judg 1:34; 2:18; 4:3; 10:12; 1 Sam 10:18; 2 Kgs 13:4, 22; Pss 42:9 [Heb. 10]; 43:2; 44:24; 56:1 [Heb. 2]; 106:42; Isa 19:20; Jer 30:20)

"I drove them out before you" (6:9; compare Exod 23:28–31; 33:2; 34:11; Deut 33:27; Josh 24:12, 18; Judg 2:3; 1 Chr 17:21; Pss 78:55; 80:8 [Heb. 9]; see also Exod 6:1; 10:11; 11:1; 12:39; Num 22:6, 11; 2 Chr 20:11) "and I gave you their land" (6:9; compare Deut 4:38; 19:1; see also Gen 12:7; 15:7, 18; 24:7; 26:3; 28:4; 35:12; 48:4; Exod 6:4; 12:25; 13:5; 32:13; Lev 14:34; 23:10; 25:1, 38; Num 13:2; 14:8; 15:2; 20:12, 24; 27:12; 32:7, 9; 33:53; Deut 1:25; 2:12, 29; 3:18, 20; 4:38; 5:31; 6:23; 8:10; 9:6, 23; 11:17; 11:31; 12:1; 15:4; 16:20; 17:14; 18:9; 19:1, 8, 14; 24:4; 25:19; 26:1, 9; 27:2–3; 28:8, 52; 32:49, 52; Josh 1:2, 11, 13–15; 5:6; 18:3; 21:43; 23:16; 24:13; 1 Kgs 8:36, 48; 1 Chr 16:18; 2 Chr 6:27, 38; Neh 9:8, 36; Pss 105:11, 44; 135:12; 136:21; Jer 3:19; 7:7; 11:5; 30:3; 32:22; Ezek 11:15; 20:15; 33:24; 36:28; 37:25)

Block (255) correctly labels this "an expanded version of the earlier messenger's review (2:1) of Yahweh's gracious past actions for Israel's benefit," while Younger (169) points to the language of the covenant ceremony in Josh 24. Salvation history is recalled to remind Israel of God's expectations. Bluedorn sees chaps. 2 and 6 as having "different emphasis," but then resolves these differences by flattening their theological points: "both speeches contain the same message, that the Israelites should not fear the gods of the Canaanites" (*Yahweh versus Baalism*, 68).

Chap. 2 says little about Egypt but concentrates on covenants: the one Israel has with Yahweh and the ones they make with the native residents. Its conclusion is that God will not keep covenant because Israel has not kept covenant. Chap. 6, on the other hand, centers on God's treatment of Egypt and the Canaanite oppressors as a reason not to fear, specifically not to fear "the gods of the Amorites." Chap. 2 thus places the entire book of Judges under the theme of broken covenants leading to tempting gods. Chap. 6 places the Gideon/Abimelech narrative under the theme of fear, specifically the fear of local gods.

The prophet introduces "the most complete series of martial rituals, a full catalogue of Holy War, of any single biblical narrative" (Mobley, *Empty Men*, 152). He thus teaches Israel what it means to call upon Yahweh in time of trouble. In so doing he does not mean to cry to Yahweh and continue worshiping Baal, as the Israelites apparently did (see Amit, *Book of Judges*, 251). Willing to affirm God's covenant formulaic language under Joshua (24:15–17) and at the beginning of Judges (2:4–5), Israel has now refused to listen to Yahweh and apparently joined in covenants with Canaanite gods as well as with Yahweh (compare Bluedorn, *Yahweh versus Baalism*, 64–65). As Webb ([1987] 145) phrases it, "To call upon Yahweh is to invoke a relationship, but this relationship (acknowledged in the speech) is one which lays certain obligations upon Israel, obligations which she has not fulfilled." Yahweh has the right to expect something from Israel because "I am Yahweh your God" (Judg 6:10). Again the words from the exodus (Exod 6:7) authorize God's demands on his people (compare Exod 16:12; 29:46; Lev 11:44; 18:2, 4, 30; 19:2–4, 10, 25, 31, 34, 36; 20:7, 24; 23:22, 43; 24:22; 25:17, 38, 55; 26:1, 13, 44; Num 10:10; 15:41; Deut 29:6; Isa 41:13; 43:3; 48:17; Ezek 20:5, 7, 19–20; 28:26; 34:30; 39:22, 28; Joel 2:27; 3:17 [Heb. 4:17]; Zech 10:6). The anonymous, unexpected prophet "highlights the undeserved nature of Yahweh's intervention on her behalf" (Block, 254).

God's demand had been quite simple: "Do not fear [or reverence] the gods of the Amorites" (Judg 6:10), that is, the gods of the original inhabitants of the land prior to God's giving the land to Israel (Deut 6:14; 7:4, 16). But Israel would not listen to God's voice (Exod 4:1; Num 14:22; Deut 9:23; Judg 2:2; Jer 9:13; 22:21; 32:23; 40:3; Dan 9:14). Here is a summary of the wilderness wanderings, a summary of the period of the Judges, a summary of the monarchy, indeed a summary of the history of Israel and of the Old Testament. The biblical word is directed toward a people who have not and will not listen to God's voice (Judg 6:10). Abraham listened (Gen 22:18; 26:5). Pharaoh did not (Exod 5:2). God promised to heal if they listened (Exod 15:26). God's covenant called on them to listen to God (Exod 19:5; compare Deut 13:18; 15:5; 26:17; 27:10) and to his angel (Exod 23:20–22). Listening should bring blessing (Deut 26:12–15; 28:1–2). But Israel did not listen (Num 14:22; Deut 8:20; 9:23) and suffered in the wilderness (Josh 5:6) and in the promised land (Judg 2:2, 20). Only after punishment would they listen (Deut 4:30; 30:2, 8, 10, 20). Not listening brought covenant curse (Deut 28:15, 45, 62).

Bluedorn (*Yahweh versus Baalism*, 69) claims significance in the narrator's definition of the theme of the narrative "without any reference to Gideon." But that is the narrative style in Judges. The problem is stated in theological terms, then made more explicit with the introduction of the leading character, the judge. The narrative then takes one part of the major theme and applies it to Israel's leadership styles.

Amit remarks that the prophet's "rebuke concludes with accusation, leaving no opening for hope." As Gideon's response shows, "the prophet's rebuke thus accomplished the opposite of its intended goal: it led Gideon to doubt God's presence among his people" (*Book of Judges*, 250). The opening exposition to the Gideon narrative thus shows that if the Old Testament has any word of hope at all it is simply a miracle of God's love and grace. And yet the narrative does not mention divine love and grace. We must read that between the lines. Israel never did one thing to earn words of hope and directions toward a future with God. Consequently, the battle report with Midian gains strong theological overtones, leading us to expect stories of Yahweh's power as Bluedorn insists do follow. But the stories do not show God's power over the enemies as much as they show God's battle with his own chosen leader.

11–12 After this prophetic interlude sets out the theological exposition and backdrop for the story, the prophetic call narrative itself appears, one built along the same lines as those of Moses in Exod 3, Saul in 1 Sam 9–10, and Jeremiah in Jer 1. The call narrative has been thoroughly studied from differing perspectives. See N. Habel (*ZAW* 77 [1965] 297–323), W. Richter (*Die sogenannten vorprophetischen Berufungsberichte*), H.-C. Schmitt (*ZAW* 104 [1992] 202–16), and George W. Coats (*Exodus 1–18*, FOTL 2A [Grand Rapids: Eerdmans, 1999] 39–42). But the interpretation is too extreme when Block decides that "the narrator intentionally presents Gideon as sort of a second Moses" (257) or Bluedorn sees enough similarity in the call narratives "to let Gideon and his commission be on a par with Moses' call and his commission" (*Yahweh versus Baalism*, 77). Even though 6:1–10 sets the oppression stage for Gideon in much the same language as is used to describe the Egyptian oppression, certainly the task Moses faced was much more difficult than that which Gideon faces.

The similarities come not so much from an intentional literary reference as from the common elements of the call narratives themselves. The differences in the two call narratives are significant. Pressler misses the difference and defends Gideon: "The protest is a matter of humility and serves to make it clear that Gideon does not assume a leadership role out of his own initiative. God called him. . . . Gideon's dependence on signs reflects his readiness to rely on God. While timid and testing, Gideon still trusts Yahweh to show him what to do" (171–72). Niditch writes in similar fashion: "Even his attempt to refuse the call marks him as the quintessential biblical hero (cf. Exod 3:11; 4:10)" (89). This is what a call-narrative structure is intended to show, but the Gideon narratives add elements that show that fear, not humility, rule Gideon's conversations with God.

Matthews acknowledges one difference in the Gideon call narrative: "his 'fearfulness and reluctance' at each stage of his career" (83). Bluedorn (*Yahweh versus Baalism*, 77) points to the strongest difference: Moses recognizes the God who is calling him; Gideon demands a sign to discover which God is calling. I would rather see Gideon as becoming an antitype to Moses. Whereas Moses began weak in faith and insight and grew to become the model of all Israel's prophets and leaders, Gideon begins in obedience and courage but falls to the level of a typical Canaanite leader, seeking revenge, wealth, control of a cult, and a royal harem. Most of all, Gideon seeks the credit that belongs to Yahweh, thus never truly understanding or bowing to the transcendent character of Yahweh. Bluedorn offers this summary of the call-narrative message: "The call episode emphasizes Gideon's reluctance and weakness, so that it is not Gideon who will deliver Israel, but rather YHWH who calls him and promises to equip him with his divine power" (*Yahweh versus Baalism*, 90).

Pressler notes the subtlety here: "God raises up yet another deliverer for Israel. The shift is as unexpected as it is gracious" (170). The call is told in a simple form. God or his messenger appears to the person to be called. The messenger indicates God's presence and God's call. The one called hesitatingly objects with a reason he cannot serve. God provides words of assurance and a sign to validate the call. These motifs do not come in rigid form forced on the narrator. Rather, as Amit shows, "even when the author utilizes well-known motifs, he has a degree of autonomy in their adjustment to the editorial guideline and their incorporation within the context" (*Book of Judges*, 247).

Here God's messenger is called the יְהוָה מַלְאַךְ, "messenger of Yahweh" (Judg 6:11), a designation found fifty-eight times in the Old Testament (Gen 16:7, 9–11; 22:11, 15; Exod 3:2; Num 22:22–27, 31–32, 34–35; Judg 2:1, 4; 5:23; 6:11–12, 21–22; 13:3, 13, 15–18, 20–21; 2 Sam 24:16; 1 Kgs 19:7; 2 Kgs 1:3, 15; 19:35; 1 Chr 21:12, 15–16, 18, 30; Pss 34:8; 35:5–6; Isa 37:36; Hag 1:13; Zech 1:11–12; 3:1, 5–6; 12:8; Mal 2:7). "These human messengers are fully equated with their senders (Judg 11:13; 2 Sam 3:12, 13; 1 Kgs 20:2–40). . . . It was sometimes difficult to distinguish between human and angelic messengers (Judg 13:20; Mal 3:1) [for he] speaks in God's name and occasionally appears as Yahweh himself (e.g., Gen 16:7–14)" (S. F. Noll, "מַלְאָךְ," *NIDOTTE*, 2:941–43). Block calls the messenger "God's alter ego" (259).

The Judg 6 narrative leads us to believe the prophet of the previous message is now the messenger of Yahweh, but the ensuing story makes us step back and question this equation. This messenger of God fills the gap never filled in the Deborah and Barak narrative by explicitly calling the new judge to service. Deborah herself did the calling, but Barak refused to fulfill the role without Deborah's accompaniment. The book of Judges frequently lets us make assumptions that we must later question. We have seen the classic case in Judg 4, where Deborah insinuates that God will give her, not Barak, the glory of victory, when all along, Jael is the surprise glory-getter. This messenger paired with the prophet of 6:8 also serves as the first of several people and things paired together in the Gideon narrative. These include Gideon's two names (with Jerubbaal), two names for God (Yahweh and Elohim), Gideon's two fleece tests, two buildings of the altar in 6:24–32, two pairs of Midianite officers executed (7:25; 8:21), two tests of assurance of Yahweh's support (6:36–38, 39–40), and two tests God uses to reduce Gideon's army (7:2–3, 4–8). (See Mobley, *Empty Men*, 120–21.)

This messenger of God visits the family property allotted to the clan of Abiezer from the tribe of Manasseh (Josh 17:2; 1 Chr 7:18). The property was located in Ophrah, apparently somewhere in the center of the Jezreel Valley. The name appears here as a literary foreshadowing, for it will reappear at a couple of important moments in the stories that follow. As of yet, we are not supposed to know what those are.

The messenger comes to "the oak tree in Ophrah" (Judg 6:11). Sometimes translated as "terebinths," such massive trees often served as the home of religious high places and altars for the Baalistic fertility cult (Gen 35:4; Ezek 6:13; Hos 4:13; compare 1 Kgs 13:14; 1 Chr 10:12). But Israel seemed to use these Baal structures in what they would claim was Yahweh worship. The important element here is the name "Joash," Gideon's father and the head of the clan of Abiezer. His name contains the element "Jo," an abbreviated form of "Yahweh," and may mean, "Yah gives." His name clashes with his worship of Baal and shows the Israelites' worship confusion in which Baal worship and Yahweh worship are not easily distinguished. Bluedorn wants to make Joash the owner of Ophrah, not of the tree, and to see the reference to Joash with the title אבי העזרי, "Father of help" or Abiezrite, as unusual, since, in his reading, the title normally belongs to Ophrah. This leads to the somewhat stretched conclusion that "with the cultic character of the place and Joash's ownership assumed, this resemblance might characterize Joash as the priest of this idolatrous place, so that help is above all sought from the pagan god" (*Yahweh versus Baalism*, 72–73). This reading removes the narrator's intentional ambiguity as to the god Joash worships.

Now we see the importance of the earlier notice that the Midianites would not let Israel grow or reap their crops. Wheat was harvested in late spring (April to June). Apparently Joash and Gideon were clever enough to get a crop raised despite the Midianites and to be in the process of threshing it. Rather than thresh it on an open threshing floor using oxen and threshing sledges, Gideon apparently has only a small stick he holds in his hand with the grain hidden in an inconspicuous vat used for pressing out grape juice to make wine. He may well have chosen a place of worship (under the oak tree) as a place such activity would not be expected. He shows himself already to be a "trickster" (Matthews, 84). Note that the threshing floor also plays an important part in the story of Boaz and Ruth (Ruth 3) and in that of David (2 Sam 24:18–25).

The Lord's messenger has two great but strange and unexpected words of greeting for Gideon, enough to make anyone sit back and take notice. First, he informs Gideon "Yahweh is with you" (Judg 6:12). Such a greeting indicated material wealth and personal good fortune (Gen 26:28; Judg 1:22; Ruth 2:4; 1 Sam 16:18; 18:12, 14; 20:13; 2 Sam 7:3; 2 Kgs 18:7; 1 Chr 9:20; 22:11, 16; 15:2; 2 Chr 20:17; Zech 10:5; compare Num 14:43). It could be interpreted much more weakly as a personal greeting (see Bluedorn, *Yahweh versus Baalism*, 78) or as a promise of divine help in battle, thus showing that the name of Gideon's father, Joash, "Father of help," has come true in Yahweh's presence with Gideon. In the irony of Judges, this may be modified. R. G. Bowman concludes: "Divine presence only seems to confer the potential for human success; it does not confirm success as an inevitable result. Instead divine power is limited by the exercise of human freedom to obey or disobey God, to use or misuse human skills" ("Narrative Criticism: Human Purpose in Conflict with Divine Presence," in *Judges and Method,* ed. G. A. Yee [Minneapolis: Fortresss, 1995] 36). The remainder of the Gideon narrative revolves around Gideon's response when Yahweh is with Gideon.

Second, the messenger calls Gideon a גִּבּוֹר הֶחָיִל, "mighty hero of war." The title belonged to brave soldiers who fought for their country (Josh 1:14; 6:2 [men of Jericho]; 8:3; 10:7; 2 Kgs 24:14; 1 Chr 11:26; 12:8) and could indicate those belonging to the upper economic level of society (2 Kgs 15:20). The title confuses Amit, who concludes: "It is not at all clear to what might the angel is [referring].... The text fails to provide the reader with any guideposts for filling in this gap" (253). Apparently this was what God was calling Gideon to become and what God's presence would make of him. Gideon's immediate reaction shows that at the moment of address he was not aware of God's presence and did not see himself as a heroic warrior.

13 Gideon begs to differ. Block may be a bit strong in describing Gideon's answer as "a cheeky and sarcastic focus on the theological incongruity" (260). Younger (175–76) enumerates several of Gideon's more negative characteristics that anticipate later plot complications: an ignorance of Israel's sin problem, little awareness of God's recent mighty acts for Israel, an understanding that makes Yahweh less than god, an attempt to evade personal responsibility, and a preoccupation with tangible manifestations of the divine. Gideon takes the address as meaning the entire nation, not just himself personally, though the messenger has addressed him with the singular "you" in Hebrew. This does not justify the conclusion that Gideon "deliberately quotes him incorrectly to avoid the apparent implication that the angel addresses and calls him personally to action" (Bluedorn, *Yahweh versus Baalism,* 79). Rather, Gideon assumes that personal presence with God and personal power as a mighty hero of war could come only when the nation itself experienced God's presence and God's victories.

Nothing about present circumstances indicates Yahweh's presence. Here is one who had not experienced God's mighty acts for his people (2:10), but at least he remembers hearing his forefathers tell how God had performed miracles to lead Israel up from Egypt. But "for Gideon's generation, the stories of the Exodus were already just that, stories" (Schneider, 104). The forefathers painted an entirely different picture from that which Gideon has experienced. He knows only of a period when Yahweh has forsaken his people (1 Sam 12:22; 1 Kgs 8:57; 2 Kgs 21:14; Pss 27:9; 94:14; Isa 2:6; Jer 7:29; 23:33, 39). The evidence is clear, for Yahweh had handed them over to Midian. In such a circumstance Gideon has no desire to be a mighty hero in Israel's army. Staying in hiding seems the circumspect thing to do. In fact, as Younger points out, "although Gideon is aware of some of the traditions of Yahweh, for all practical purposes he and his family are worshipers of Baal and Asherah" (179), though Gideon and his family would probably see themselves as faithful worshipers of Yahweh at the same time. They simply are not at this time in Israel's nascent history monotheistic Yahwists.

14 Now Yahweh speaks clearly for himself, no longer hidden behind the "messenger." He has a clear commission for Gideon. Younger points out that "Gideon is the only judge in the book of Judges who is called by God personally through a theophany" (173; compare Bluedorn, *Yahweh versus Baalism,* 74 and n. 43). He is to "go in your ... strength" and deliver Israel from the hand of Midian. Before

Gideon can complain, Yahweh interjects the pregnant question: "Have I not sent you?" Here is the point of narrative tension, where the narrative changes from describing the call to describing the reaction to the call. The dominating question is not so much, will Gideon accept the call? Rather, the reader asks, will Gideon accept the call on God's terms, or will he accept it dependent on his own strength and looking for his own glory? Those familiar with the call-narrative genre expect plot complications before the call is accepted.

15 Complications arise immediately. Continuing to use exceptionally polite language, Gideon objects, an element that usually appears in divine-call narratives. Note Amit's observation (253 and n. 43) that this element aptly fits the context in each narrative and stresses "the unexpected choice." In what way could I possibly deliver Israel? See here, my family is the poorest in Manasseh, while I am the runt in my father's house (compare 1 Sam 9:21). The latter description may indicate that Gideon as the youngest brother is not even qualified to go to war (Amit, *Book of Judges*, 254). Gideon has not yet heard God's promise with these words through Isaiah: "The least will become a thousand, the smallest a mighty nation. I am the LORD; I will accomplish it quickly in its time" (Isa 60:22, HCSB). Gideon is not really a good talent scout for God. He calls his family the poorest one in the tribe, yet his father owns property and supports a worship place for Baal as we will soon learn. Far from being the poorest or weakest in the tribe, Gideon's father is a clan leader and one of the strongest economically and politically in the tribe. Despite this, Gideon makes it appear that he sees himself as a powerless runt without the ability to fulfill God's calling. God comes from another perspective.

16 In reassuring Gideon, God finds it necessary to repeat the messenger's words: "But I will be with you, and you will strike Midian dead as if they were one man." Yes, God will make Gideon a mighty warrior. But will Gideon agree to God's terms and back off from his desire to gain glory and power for himself rather than for God?

17–18 Gideon's response shows Gideon as "a fearful hero who habitually requires oracular reassurance" (Mobley, *Empty Men*, 155). Block finds a cynical tone here showing that Gideon "obviously does not yet recognize the person who has addressed him" (261). Gideon says, literally, "If now I have found favor in your eyes, then create (or make) for me the sign you yourself are discussing with me." Bluedorn, on the other hand, thinks Gideon simply seeks a needed "sign of assurance . . . that will demonstrate that it is YHWH who is speaking to him" (*Yahweh versus Baalism*, 84). Similarly, Amit sees that "the food was not an act of hospitality, but a means of ascertaining the guest's identity" (*Book of Judges*, 85; compare Matthews, 85). This conclusion may be questioned as an unnecessary exclusion of a double motif. Gideon does not necessarily expect the food he brings to result in a sign, though it does. Rather, he wants to carry out Near Eastern hospitality rituals to create an atmosphere favorable for a sign.

Gideon knows that proper etiquette of his day has not been completed. He needs to give his guest a gift or offering (Heb. מנחה). "The fact that the kid is prepared as meat and brought to the place rather than brought live and slaughtered there suggests more a meal than a sacrifice" (J. Walton et al., *IVP Bible Background Commentary*, 254). Amit (*Book of Judges*, 255) sees this as another test. If the messenger eats the food, he will show his humanity in that angels are prohibited from eating. Refusal to eat will reveal the messenger's heavenly nature. That we have sufficient evidence to show such a prohibition may be questioned. (Amit points to Judg 13; Tob 12.) The text makes no mention of the angel's refusal to eat. Rather, the angel turns it all to a burnt offering and disappears. The creation of fire and the mysterious disappearance, not refusal to eat, reveal the angel's identity and fulfill Gideon's request for a sign.

19–21   Gideon will not receive the sign of divine presence and victory until he enters battle (v 16), but he wants more assurance than that. He needs yet another sign. He thus continually finds ways to converse with God and delay battle. Before battle, as well as after an encounter with God, comes sacrifice. Thus the denouement of the story leads to Gideon's sacrifice, cementing his commitment to the task assigned. Now we see for sure that the oak actually represents a holy place, for there Gideon offers his sacrifice to God. Note Bluedorn's attempt (*Yahweh versus Baalism,* 86–87) to differentiate between the tree as an unacceptable place of sacrifice and the rock as the representation of God the Rock and thus acceptable for sacrifice. This makes too much distinction in a literary motif that simply prepares for the miracle of fire production. The sacrifice fits the huge appetite of deity—a whole goat, a half-bushel of flour, a whole pot of broth. (See Block, 263; J. Walton et al., *IVP Bible Background Commentary,* 254.) But Gideon's family also worships Baal and follows Baal's regulations in giving sacrifices, so God's messenger dictates precisely how a sacrifice to Yahweh is to be given. Gideon, unlike Israel (compare v 10), obediently follows instructions from the voice of God. Gideon does not have to find fire for the sacrifice. God's messenger provides that in a miraculous way. Is this letting Gideon begin to see the wonders of God that his generation has not experienced? Here Bluedorn correctly notes: "This implies that this god, who appears to be unable to accept an offering or to prevent an offering presented to him from being snatched away, is not god, and that YHWH, who takes the offering for himself, is rather god" (*Yahweh versus Baalism,* 87). God is calling Gideon away from the ambiguous worship of his Yahwistic-named, Baal-worshiping family to a total dedication to the God who is with him.

22–24   The wonderful fire and mysterious disappearance finally make the light dawn for Gideon. This is God's messenger he has seen. Gideon knows the danger he faces, for seeing God face to face brings death (compare Gen 32:30; Exod 33:20; contrast Exod 24:11; Num 20:6). God quiets Gideon's fears with a word even after the messenger has disappeared. God pronounces shalom, peace and wholeness and well-being, on Gideon. He instantly eases Gideon's fears, promising he will not suffer death. In response, Gideon builds an altar to Yahweh and names it "Yahweh is peace." The narrator of the story suddenly interrupts his narrative and interjects a word for his own day, explaining that the altar remains at the same place, Gideon's hometown, until that day. Form-critical analysis cannot define this narrative as an etiological story based on this one verse. The thrust of the narrative does not point to the present-day name but signifies Gideon's obedience thus far.

Apparently, Gideon assumes the messenger of Yahweh, that is, Yahweh, has spoken truthfully and that he has indeed found grace in God's eyes. With that assumption, Gideon is ready to get on with the second part of the greeting and of the commission. He is ready to become a great warrior. He is ready to defeat the Midianite army as if it comprised only one person. Bluedorn concludes, "He cannot ignore his call anymore and does not need to be concerned about his own incapability anymore" (*Yahweh versus Baalism,* 88).

25–27 The call narrative is complete with the hero answering the call, indicating his willingness to take on the task to which he is called, and offering a sacrifice to complete his commitment. As Block notes, "under normal circumstances the narrative should have proceeded directly from v 24 to vv 33–35 and then on to 7:1" (265). Still God's confirming sign is missing, as is the hero's actual fulfillment of his commitment. Thus narrative complication sets in. This is presented in the form of a testing narrative. Gideon must prove his commitment to Yahweh within his family before proving it in battle. He must prove it in adventurous religious practice before he proves it in dangerous battle. As Schneider points out, "The saviors of Israel no longer acted out of any sense of commitment to Israel or to their deity but had to be recruited. Baraq was recruited by a contemporary woman. The situation in this chapter has deteriorated to the point that now the deity had to oversee recruitment" (108).

Thus the second narrative is closely connected with the first, without introductory exposition. Rather, the moment of narrative tension appears immediately in a divine command: "Take a bull from your father's oxen, the prize bull which is seven years old." Here we see more evidence that Gideon's claim to belong to the poorest of families does not hold. Gideon would see this assignment as difficult enough. Dare he ask his father for the best of his animals? Or dare he take it without asking? The seven-year-old bull must have been "a prime breeding bull" (J. Walton et al., *IVP Bible Background Commentary*, 254). But this is not the center of Yahweh's commission here. For Gideon must destroy the altar to Baal that belongs to his father and cut down the Asherah that is on it. "You shall build an altar to Yahweh, your God, on the top of this mountain refuge with the proper arrangement. You shall take the prize bull and offer it as a burnt offering on the wood of the Asherah you cut down" (Judg 6:26). For Asherah, see *Comment* on 3:7. "The goddess was popular in the polytheistic deviations in Israel and was sometimes considered a mediator of Yahweh's blessings" (J. Walton et al., *IVP Bible Background Commentary*, 254). In a sense Bluedorn rightly interprets: "The fire is fed by the wood of the Asherah, so that the Asherah is sacrificed to YHWH" (*Yahweh versus Baalism*, 96).

The complications truly build for Gideon. He must destroy his family's worship place. The family has taught Gideon the traditions of the people of Yahweh (v 13), but they practice the rituals of Baal. Here is a clear indication of the syncretistic practices in Israel's religion at this period. People worshiped Baal and Yahweh together indiscriminately, either merging the two deities into one or allotting each deity controls and thus reason to be worshiped over various segments of daily personal and national life. The narrative, Polzin rightly says, "depicts in a graphic manner not only the indecision of Gideon and the Israelites whether to worship Yahweh or one of the gods of the Canaanites, but also and more fundamentally their inability to distinguish at times who the god was who now was delivering them from the Midianites, Yahweh or another" (*Moses and the Deuteronomist*, 170). As Schneider writes, "the Israelites did not see how the worship of the gods surrounding them angered the Israelite deity" (107). Matthews states this positively: "Like their Canaanite neighbors, these members of the tribe of Manasseh, living in a culturally diverse area, would have depended upon the good will of a number of gods, including Baal and Asherah and Yahweh, to provide for their needs. In that sense they seem to be totally unaware of their exclusive covenant with Yahweh and thus cannot be readily distinguished from the Canaanites" (86–87).

Gideon must cut down the images that represent the gods. He must replace Baal's altar with an altar to Yahweh, built in clear view of all his relatives and friends who worship Baal and apparently in view of the Midianite armies. Can Gideon pass such a test?

The narrator does nothing to build tension or complicate the plot. The divine challenge has set up the clear narrative tension. Gideon immediately does just what the Lord has told him. Oh, but a plot complication does arise. The narrative subtly slips it in after summarizing Gideon's obedience. "His fear of his father's house and of the men of the city kept him from doing it in the daytime, so he did it at night" (Judg 6:27). The one ready for Yahweh to be with him and make him a mighty hero is not ready to test God all the way or to pass God's test completely. Rather, he acts surreptitiously. Fear of Yahweh does not control his motivation and actions. Fear of his family and friends does. Block calls v 27 "a rare literary moment when the narrator offers us access to the internal motivation of a character by explicit reference to an emotion" (267).

28–30   Yet another narrative complicates the picture. This is a legal investigation. The men of the city, not Gideon's family, discover the incriminating evidence. The evidence has three components: altar broken down, Asherah cut down, and prize bull sacrificed on a new altar. Thus the question creating narrative tension: "Who has done this thing?" (Judg 6:29). Quick investigation solves the crime: Gideon is guilty. All that remains is the narrative denouement, executing sentence on the guilty party. In the meantime, the Israelites of Ophrah have proven themselves to be perfect Canaanites, protecting Baal in the face of Yahweh's self-evident victory. (See Block, 268.) But the narrator has a surprise twist for us. The one who owned the destroyed worship place and the prize bull that was sacrificed is not yet ready to execute the sentence. Joash, Gideon's father, turns the trial narrative around. He sets up a new defendant in the case. Not Gideon, but Baal is guilty. And those who would execute judgment on his son Gideon share Baal's guilt. Much more, in light of Israelite law, they deserve the death penalty, for they have encouraged people to worship a god other than Yahweh who brought them out of Egypt (Deut 13). Here is the theological climax of the entire chapter, the point the narrator wants to make with all his story complications.

"Do you have to defend [ריב] Baal? Or must you save [ישׁע, *hip̄ʿil*] him?" (Judg 6:31). Block (269) calls attention to the use of the same Hebrew verb הושׁיע (save) to define the role of the judges God raises up for his people. See Judg 2:16 and the *Comment* on Judg 8:12. The use of ריב sets up a play on Jerubbaal's name. As Block (269) says, "the irony is obvious. Instead of people needing deliverance from a hostile god, the god requires deliverance from the people." Joash's threat is just as obvious. The defenders of Baal want to kill Gideon. Anyone who continues to defend Baal and execute the sentence on Gideon will find the sentence being turned on him or her. Joash is apparently prepared to go all the way in defending and protecting his son. Such protection and defense create a new town hero in the person of Gideon. As Webb phrases it, "Nothing happens, the townsmen are impressed, and Gideon emerges as a hero. He is, as it were, reborn, and his father gives him a new name which marks him as living proof of Baal's impotence" ([1987] 149).

31–32   Again as in v 24 an etiological note ends the story, explaining the interesting fact of Israel's narrative history that Gideon had not one but two names.

Mobley thinks Gideon belonged to the original narrative throughout the materials but that other Israelite "oral traditions" told of a "warrior named Jerubbaal who fought against the Midianites in the premonarchical era," pointing to 1 Sam 12:11. "Parenthetical clauses in Judges 7:1 and 8:35 that emphasize the equivalence, are most likely mechanisms engineered to bridge two originally independent bodies of tradition about warriors from the era of Judges" (*Empty Men*, 122–23; compare Pressler, 174). Matthews opposes such a literary conclusion: "The elements of the narrative are sufficiently cohesive and the later tradition about this character is consistent enough to allow it to stand as is" (87).

Block's thorough study of the two names concludes that "his real name is Jerubbaal, and the god after whom he was named has taken up the challenge proposed by Josah (6:31–32) and, sad to say, has apparently successfully contended for himself and won" (*JETS* 40 [1997] (365).

Bluedorn (*Yahweh versus Baalism*, 96–97, with n. 126) concludes that Gideon and Jerubbaal are both nicknames coined by the narrator and perfectly fitting the narrative so that neither is the true name of the narrative's central figure. Gideon means "Hacker" or "Hewer." Jerubbaal, the name introduced here, raises great questions as to its meaning, as outlined by Bluedorn (101–5). The traditional interpretation is that of NIV and other modern translations: "Let Baal contend with him." Block (270) has shown convincingly that such a view results from pious interpretation rather than from linguistic analysis. Mobley (*Empty Men*, 160–61, n. 17) thinks the original name could be a Yahwistic one meaning "may the Lord (or 'Master') contend on my behalf," a meaning he knows is "contrary to that given in Judg 6:32 but historically more likely." Bluedorn (104) concludes that linguistic evidence points to a derivation from רבב, "increase, become great," but that the text makes a word play on ריב. (Compare Pressler, 173.)

The narrator thus mocks Baal who is "great" but cannot defend his own altar so that now Baal must defend himself. The Hebrew verb ריב is not used in the jussive, "let him," sense elsewhere. Names containing the name of a deity traditionally place the deity as subject of an active verb and praise the deity. The interpretation of the name thus becomes "Baal will take him to court" or "Baal will contend with him." Block sees this as a name defending Baal and showing that Joash is still a worshiper of Baal. I see it differently. The narrator ends the story by saying that Gideon who has answered God's call to be a mighty hero fights not just against Midian. He also fights against Baal, for Baal fights against him. Jerubbaal in obeying God's voice has created his first enemy—Baal. This contest between Baal and Jerubbaal sets the scene for the remainder of the Gideon/Jerubbaal narrative. Or as Webb expresses this viewpoint, "In this first major movement then, Gideon is a reluctant conscript, who distrusts his own competence and relies wholly upon Yahweh. In short, he is a model of Mosaic piety" (*Book of Judges*, 151). Note that Webb would apparently apply this description to Gideon's actions all the way through to 8:4. I would see the following attempts to test Yahweh with the fleece marking the beginning of Gideon's loss of faith.

33–35 Suddenly, again without exposition or introduction, the narrator switches to a new scene (6:33), a new story. The Midianites and their allies gather forces and camp in the Jezreel Valley, ready for war. Gideon does not have to initiate action to be God's mighty warrior. He has to respond to the enemy's initiative. Yahweh uses a unique way to demonstrate that he is with Gideon: "the Spirit of Yahweh clothed Gideon" (Judg 6:33; compare 1 Chr 12:19; 2 Chr 24:20). Such language thrills the modern reader and raises expectations of glorious divine actions, but Younger's caution is well taken:

> It is especially clear from the usages in the Jephthah narrative and the Samson episodes that the phrase does not necessarily carry a positive comment on the individual's spirituality. . . . To be filled with the Spirit in the New Testament speaks to spirituality; that is, the one who is filled is controlled by the Spirit with the consequent actions being spiritual activities (Eph 5:18b–20). In the Old Testament the notion is that of empowerment for a particular task, though it is apparent that the recipient might misuse this empowerment (e.g., 14:19). . . . Therefore in the case of Gideon, the Spirit's work reflects God's sovereign will to set things in motion for the deliverance he has planned, not Gideon's condition of faith or spirituality. (186–87)

The *IVP Bible Background Commentary* connects the coming of the Spirit in Judges with the mustering of an army:

> The measure of a leader in such situations was his ability to compel others to follow even though he had no office of command over them. In Israel this was a mark of the power of Yahweh, for it was he alone who had the authority to call out the armies of the tribes. . . . It was therefore a clear indication of the Lord's authority at work in someone when they exercised authority that was only Yahweh's by calling out the armies. (255)

Bluedorn sees the structural problem here: the repeated delay of the battle report with four episodes that "seem to contain the theme of fear and reassurance of divine support" (*Yahweh versus Baalism*, 107–8). When Bluedorn backs off this to change the theme to the "demonstration of Yahweh's divine power" (110), he misses the entire theme of Judges with its demonstration of the lack of human leadership. Thus Bluedorn is more on target when he speaks of a parallel theme of "Gideon's attempt to win the victory by himself and get glorified for YHWH's victory" (110) and when he sees an emphasis on "Gideon's fear of not achieving the victory on his own account" (111). Gideon is a man of fear, not faith, even after God passes the tests Gideon imposes.

Mobley (*Empty Men*, 137) sees "a crucial juncture" in vv 34–35. It allows Mobley to see three stages of the narrative: Abiezer troops and Manasseh troops represent "competing" versions, while 35b "represents a pan-Israelite editorial expansion." The latter appears only on the margins and "ends up having little effect on the story." Such analysis represents another version of source criticism gone wild and failure to see the complex literary skill of the author/editor.

Gideon raises the battle signal on the shofar or ram's horn trumpet. His own clan of Abiezer rallies to him, though in the previous narrative they were ready to kill him for apostasy. Then he sends messengers to his tribe and the surrounding tribes. Four Israelite tribes gather with him for battle: Asher, Zebulun, Naphtali, and Manasseh. This marks a change from Barak and Deborah. The prose account there centered on Naphtali and Zebulun (4:6, 10), while the song had a special word for Zebulun and Naphtali (5:18), at the same time also including Ephraim, Benjamin, Machir (part of Manasseh), and Issachar among those who answered the summons to battle. Asher, however, stood among those condemned (5:17). Here again we find a period with basic central tribes dedicated to Yahweh's call to battle along with a few peripheral ones. We continue to wonder what tribes composed the group called Israel in this period.

36–40   As we await the battle report, the narrator stops the battle action and shifts to another testing scene. This time Gideon is testing God with the famous fleece test. Here the narrator makes a subtle shift. The deity's personal name, *Yahweh*, which has dominated the story almost entirely to this point slips from view. The more generic, less personal, more transcendent term *Elohim*, "God," is used. By replacing *Yahweh* with *Elohim*, the narrator places some distance between Gideon and God, distance that had not been there when Gideon was making his commitments and following God's leadership. Block believes that "Gideon has difficulty distinguishing between Yahweh, the God of the Israelites, and God in a general sense" (273). Or as Polzin explains the selection of *Elohim* over *Yahweh*, "'God' refers to a deity whose identity, from the point of view of the speaker uttering his name or in view of the speaker's audience, is not Yahweh himself, or else a deity unable to be recognized as Yahweh in a particular instance of communication" (*Moses and the Deuteronomist*, 172).

Now facing the moment of truth and action, Gideon backs away from his commitment to God and seeks reassurance. With language tying back to v 14, Gideon says, "If you are really there saving Israel by my hand just as you promised" (Judg 6:36). We look in vain for the "then" clause to finish the conditional sentence. Instead we get the versatile Hebrew particle הִנֵּה, saying look right here at something I want to show you. Gideon does not say, If you keep your promise, then I will. Instead he backs off from his previous understanding and commitment and says he will know God's word is true if God will do the sign Gideon demands, not the sign God chooses to demonstrate. God does the sign just as Gideon asks, but Gideon is still not satisfied. After all, one would expect fleece to hold dampness longer than earth or grass. Gideon is cautious and tries to guard against any impatient anger God might display. He speaks to God, saying, "Do not let your nostrils burn hot against me so I may speak yet once more. I will set up a test just one more time with the fleece. Please let dryness come on the fleece by itself, but on all the ground, let there be dew" (Judg 6:39).

Sure enough, that night God does just as Gideon commanded. That ends the scene. Younger concludes, "This fleecing process is nothing short of a pagan divinatory test of the deity. . . . The narrator includes this pericope to construct a sharper picture of Gideon's unbelief and questionable religious practices" (188). The least we can say is that Gideon does everything in his power to delay the battle test and to find ways to garner as many signs as possible from this divine figure that confronts him.

Amit observes,

> The present order of units seems to imply that the appearance of the angel, the giving of the signs, the hearing of the divine speech, the fact that Gideon was not harmed by the destruction of the altar of the Baal and, finally, the divine spirit that possessed him and his ability to muster an army—all these did not give him enough confidence, and he places God to two additional tests. (*Book of Judges*, 227)

Younger (185) notes that the promise to save Israel by the hand of Gideon is repeated five times (6:36; 7:2, 7, 9, 14–15). Block finds that the words "just as he promised," appearing both in v 36 and in v 37, provide "the key to this text" (272). I must add to this the repetition of "by my hand" in vv 36–37. Gideon wants to be empowered so he can get credit for the victory. As Bluedorn notes, "YHWH is simply degraded to the one who silently has to provide Gideon's deliverance without intervening visibly" (*Yahweh versus Baalism*, 120).

"Gideon's problem is that with his limited experience with God he cannot believe that God always fulfills his word. The request for signs is not a sign of faith but of unbelief" (Block, 272–73). Polzin gives the theological interpretation in these terms: "By portraying the inability of his Israelite heroes often to understand Yahweh's words or even to recognize his salvific intervention, and by emphasizing their over reliance on tests and signs, the Deuteronomist suggests to his audience the danger of putting too much confidence in the ultimate test of an approved ideology, even that espoused by the author himself" (*Moses and the Deuteronomist*, 173).

Block asserts that "despite being clear about the will of God, being empowered by the Spirit of God, and being confirmed as a divinely chosen leader by the overwhelming response of his countrymen to his own summons to battle, [Gideon] uses every means available to try to get out of the mission to which he has been called" (273). We see only what God did. We do not hear how Gideon reacted. We never hear a word from God. Thus in this test narrative, we find a bit of distance developing between Gideon and God. We see God proving faithful even when Gideon fears divine anger. We hear Gideon asking for proof of God's saving presence, but we do not hear Gideon renewing his commitment. That response comes in the next narrative scene. This one leaves us knowing more about God, not more about Gideon. The narrative tension, or what narrative tension there is here, revolves around God's reaction and the possibility of God's anger. As Block has seen, we do discover that "unlike Yahweh, Gideon is not true to his word. Gideon's refusal to believe and/or accept the divine word and the divine sign leaves the reader suspicious that Gideon is trying to get out of his assignment" (273). Younger underlines the fact that "contrary to popular interpretation, these fleecings have nothing to do with discovering or determining God's will. The divine will is perfectly and absolutely clear in Gideon's own mind (note the wording in v. 36)" (187). But, as Amit describes the state of affairs, "he needed numerous signs like a person addicted to tranquilizers" (*Book of Judges*, 238).

7:1 The narrator gently slips us into a new narrative scene. God administers the tests this time. Bluedorn (*Yahweh versus Baalism*, 113–19; compare M. Sternberg, *Poetics of Biblical Narrative*, 365–66; R. M. Massot, "Gideon and the Deliverance of Israel," 77–78; S. Bar-Efrat, "Some Observations on the Analysis of Structure in Biblical Narrative," *VT* 30 [1980] 154–73) attempts to demonstrate minutely parallel construction between Gideon's tests in chap. 6 and Yahweh's tests here, creating what he calls a "negotiation based on a double interrogation" (*Yahweh versus Baalism*, 114). Certainly, the two sections form a narrative contrast, but that they are intentionally made parallel in every detail is not proven.

Gideon's "problem of faith" (Younger, 185) remains a central focus, or as Bluedorn describes it: "the issue of who will deliver Israel and be honoured for the deliverance" (116). Such an understanding sets the Gideon narrative in parallel to the Barak narrative in describing the problem of leadership and credit for achievements or honor. Barak forfeited honor that rightly belonged to him.

Gideon fights for honor that rightly belonged to Yahweh.

The narrator in chap. 7 first introduces Jerubbaal (i.e., Gideon) as the central character. Besides joining the narrative to the immediately previous one, the narrator is reminding the readers that the narrative remains a contest between Yahweh and Baal and is bringing to mind Gideon's original victory over Baal and his worshipers. Then he returns to the more familiar name Gideon. Gideon gathers the army he so carefully summoned at the spring of Harod or the "spring of trembling," ideally named for what follows. Traditionally, this is identified with the spring of 1 Sam 29:1 and located at modern Ain Jalud. The Midianites camped across the valley to the north at the Hill of Moreh, possibly modern Nebi Dahi. Wolf (3:424) locates Gideon at the foot of Mount Gilboa with the Midianites four miles (6.4 km) north in the Jezreel Valley, ten miles (16.1 km) west of the Jordan. Whatever the exact location, the Midianites have expanded their occupation to the north (Bluedorn, *Yahweh versus Baalism*, 124). Mobley keenly notes the importance of the place names: the Spring of Trembling (Harod) and the Hill of Seeing (Oracular) "symbolically underscore two motifs that run through the entire narrative, fear and divination" (*Empty Men*, 138). Bluedorn says, "the name of the well accurately reflects Gideon's and the Israelites' state of mind" (124).

2 God sees that Gideon has too many soldiers, while Gideon thinks the Midianites so outman him that victory is impossible. As J. C. Exum describes the situation, "no character in the book receives more divine assurance than Gideon, and none displays more doubt" ("The Centre Cannot Hold: Thematic and Textual Instabilities in Judges," *CBQ* 52 [1990] 416). This is again a testing scene, but now Gideon and his soldiers must pass the test. This time the divine name Yahweh returns to the narrative. Jerubbaal, or Gideon, leads his troops to the battlefield opposite the enemy camp. Matthews observes, "It is quite clear that this story follows the pattern set in Exod 17:8–16 (vs. Amalekites) and in Josh 6:1–21 (vs. Jericho) in which the divine warrior instructs Israelite leaders to employ a very unorthodox military strategy. This makes it clear that God gives them a victory that would otherwise be impossible given the military odds" (92).

God immediately injects narrative tension into the story. Yahweh has a word of surprise to test Gideon: "The people with you are too many for me to give Midian into their hand. Israel would glorify themselves over against me, saying, 'My hand delivered me'" (Judg 7:2). Schneider sees the meaning here: "Clearly the deity did not trust the people to acknowledge the deity for the victory" (110). The jealous God demands absolute worship from his people.

3 Now God announces the terms of his test for Gideon and his army. All fear-stricken people may return home and not fight. (Compare Deut 20:8.) Younger notes: "It is ironic in this context that one of the tests for eliminating unnecessary Israelite warriors (viz., 'fear') is the very problem that affects the leader, Gideon, himself" (189, n. 39). Twenty-two thousand accept God's offer and withdraw from battle. This is more than two-thirds of the army, as only ten thousand remain. Though scholars often question the large numbers here, Schneider (110) correctly insists: "The structure of the book, particularly the episodes involving Gideon/Jerubbaal, makes this theme primary and provides the framework for the episode."

Mount Gilead appears in Gen 31:21, 25; Deut 3:12; and Song 4:1 in reference to the mountainous country east of the Jordan. Nothing here indicates such an eastern location, prompting Walton, Matthews, and Chavalas to call this "a very obscure reference" (*IVP Bible Background Commentary*, 255). See *Note* 7:3.c above. Block calls it the "mount of trembling" (276) and observes that reading Mount Gilead "creates impossible problems" (n. 589). He suggests that the more likely reading is Mount Gilboa, but concludes that the best understanding results from associating the MT reading with the modern name of the spring Ain Galud. This is as close to a solution as modern information allows. Gaß sees Mount Gilead as evidently another name for a part of the Gilboa mountains (*Ortsnamen*, 336).

4   God is still not satisfied. Still too many people! "Take them down to the water so I may refine them." So God says he will determine who can go and who cannot. God is in charge. Gideon is not.

5   At the water's edge, Yahweh explains the test conditions. He wants to separate the people into two groups depending on how they drink: lapping with their tongue in the water like a dog, or kneeling down and scooping up the water with their hands. Note the discussion by Mobley, who argues that the canine imagery says nothing about posture but only refers to the action of tongues flapping like dogs' tongues as they lap up water (*Empty Men*, 139–41).

6   V 6 is somewhat confusing, for it apparently uses the verbs in opposite senses from their meaning in v 5. Now those who lap do not do so like dogs but rather bring water in their hands up to their mouths, while those who kneel are on their knees to stick their tongues in the water like dogs. See vv 5–6 in *Translation*.

7   Whatever the precise meaning of the approaches to drinking, the result is clear. God leaves Gideon with three hundred soldiers in his army, sending ninety-seven hundred "to his place" (NIV, an ambiguous note—see HCSB—that leaves room for their possible participation later if the phrase does not refer to "home" as in traditional interpretations [REB, NLT, NASB, NRSV, JPS, NAB]). Younger notes, "The reductions certainly are a way in which Yahweh is able to undermine any self-confidence that Gideon may have as a result of the fleece incidents" (189). The reductions may, indeed, bring Gideon's troop strength back to what he had with the original call of his own clan alone (Bluedorn, *Yahweh versus Baalism*, 127, n. 208).

Yahweh promises to deliver the nation (you, pl.) by the hand of Gideon (you, sg.). As with Barak, Yahweh opens the way for Gideon to receive sufficient honor for his obedient leadership while preventing both the leader and the nation from taking inordinate honor without giving due honor to Yahweh. Bluedorn concludes, "YHWH avoids accusing Gideon directly and opens a back door for Gideon that allows him without losing his face to let YHWH be honoured for the victory" (*Yahweh versus Baalism*, 125).

Schneider surmises that "the lappers were the less militarily able group" (111). Matthews sees the soldiers selected as "the most inattentive, least vigilant of his assembled forces" (92). Wolf sees the three hundred as displaying "a greater alertness in staying on their feet, but in actuality they may have been no more courageous than the 9,700 others" (3:425). He goes further to see the verb הֶחֱזִיק, "retained," as meaning, "hold against one's will." Amit decides "those who were chosen did not belong to either of the two designated groups" (*Book of Judges*, 257). Mobley follows the anthropological anecdotes of T. H. Gaster (*Myth, Legend, and Custom in the Old Testament* [New York: Harper & Row, 1969] 420) in suggesting that "the three hundred men selected for the battle maintained an alert, upright posture, bending enough 'to scoop up [the water] in their hands'" (*Empty Men,* 141). Younger concludes, "It seems best to understand the process as based on purely arbitrary criteria" (189). Or, as Bluedorn sees, "this criterion works in a rationally inexplicable way, which the narrator underlines by making it impossible to assign either group that actually drinks precisely to any of the predicted groups." Thus "any attempt to rationally explain the means by which the three hundred were selected among the soldiers is destined to fail" (*Yahweh versus Baalism,* 118, n. 193). Whatever the criteria for selection, the point is God has selected Gideon's army, a task one expects the general to carry out; and so God has won the victory by his hand, not by Gideon's (see Amit, *Book of Judges,* 259, following Ehrlich, 2:64).

8 Here is the narrative climax. What decision will Gideon make to resolve the tension? Gideon stands bravely on Yahweh's side, obeying his voice and sending the great majority of his army "to his tent," that is, to the military camp, not home. (See Schneider, 112; with NASB, NRSV, HCSB, NAB, NIV, but against JPS, NLT, REB.) These sent back "were still under some type of military command but not taking part in the battle itself" (Schneider, 112). All the while, Gideon is eyeing the Midianites and their allies in the valley below. Still, the reader must not miss the theological import here. In the previous narrative a woman had to call out the general to face the enemy. Now no human mediator appears. Schneider remarks, "The level of leadership in Israel had declined to such an extent that the deity no longer trusts even the deity-designated leaders with military strategy" (111). Or as Matthews phrases it, in strong contrast to Moses and Joshua, "Gideon is reluctant from the very beginning, and no matter how many proofs he is given there seems to be an assumption that he must be convinced each time he is called to lead the people" (92).

9–10 The narrative shifts to a new scene, in what Block calls a "second detour" arising from "Gideon's lack of personal faith," observing that "verses 10–15a seem quite superfluous" (278). The section is necessary because the deity was ready to use Gideon "but was testing his courage" (Schneider, 113). God calls on Gideon to enter the enemy camp by night. He is given a second choice. He may admit his fear and take his aide de camp with him. Of course, this is the option he takes. Schneider suggests that this young *na'ar* "was not even a soldier," whom Gideon took "possibly because he did not want his soldiers to see his fear evidenced in the next sentence, to follow the deity's command and investigate the enemy" (113). The promise stands, stated in the terms of the framework's divine-committal formula: "I will give Midian into your hand" (Judg 7:7; compare v 9).

11 This time the mission is not to fight but to listen. Having been told to "go in this, your strength" (6:14), Gideon now finds he will gain strength by obeying God on this fearful mission in the enemy camp.

12 First glance does not bring new strength. It provides reason for new fear. The enemy looks like a swarm of locusts spread out over the valley. (Compare Judg 6:5.) With Deborah and Barak, the problem was technological disadvantage (Judg 4:3); with Gideon, it is numerical disadvantage, a disadvantage made desperate by God's strategic test.

13–14 In God's timing, Gideon arrives just in time to hear a conversation between two enemy soldiers, one telling his dream to the other. Bluedorn observes, "It appears that the entire conversation is staged purely for their ears" (*Yahweh versus Baalism,* 132). The account follows the typical dream report, which "recounts the principal elements of a dream experience. Such reports use the verb 'dream' (ḥālam) extensively, especially in the introduction, and demarcate major shifts in subject matter with the particle 'and behold' (wĕhin-nēh). . . . Examples of dream reports are Gen 37:5–11; 40:9–11, 16–17; Judg 7:13–14" (B. O. Long, 2 Kings, FOTL 10 [Grand Rapids: Eerdmans, 1991] 299). For further discussion and bibliography, see Bluedorn, Yahweh versus Baalism, 132–36, and n. 220; A. L. Oppenheim, The Interpretation of Dreams in the Ancient Near East, Transactions of the American Philosophical Society 46 (Philadelphia: American Philosophical Society, 1956).

Younger rightly characterizes the dream as "absurd: a round loaf of barley bread tumbles into the Midianite camp, smashing into the tent with such force that it overturns and collapses" (190, n. 44). Bluedorn submits, "The symbols in the dream do not have any apparent equivalent in the interpretation" (Yahweh versus Baalism, 135), though he catalogues a number of past interpretations for the loaf of barley bread (Heb. צְלִיל) (134, n. 231).

The listening friend immediately interprets the dream as predicting Gideon's victory over the Midianite army. Bluedorn may be correct in thinking that "Gideon understands the interpretation and hence also the dream as if he himself represented the bread and destroyed the Midianite camp" (Yahweh versus Baalism, 136). Schneider points out that again the Gideon narrative moves away from the Deborah reports: "Deborah attributed the success to the deity whereas in the Gideon/Jerubbaal episode the deity had to orchestrate a scenario so that it would be difficult for Gideon to claim the victory for himself" (115).

15a Gideon and his aide immediately fall on their faces in worship to God, something Gideon will not do again (Younger, 191). Bluedorn (Yahweh versus Baalism, 136–37) goes too far in denying this as true worship. "The irony is rich," as Younger sees. "Hearing the promise directly from Yahweh did not convince Gideon (his fleece signs really didn't either), but hearing it from the lips of a Midianite soldier does convince him" (190). As Matthews sees, the Midianites portray "a faith in God's power that seems to be sorely lacking among the Israelites (compare Rahab's statement in Josh 2:8–11)" (92–93). The narrator adds further irony. The Midianite's words represent the last communication Gideon has with God, and the worship resulting from the Midianite's interpretation brings Gideon to his knees in worship for the final time in the narrative.

15b Returning to camp, Gideon calls his three hundred troops to immediate action, announcing to them what he has learned in his scouting mission. Block thinks, "The problem of Gideon's faithfulness had been resolved. Now he is ready to proceed with Yahweh's agenda" (280). And Younger concludes, "God must bring his servants to a moment when all human confidence is stripped away, when they sit silently in humble adoration of God as the One who is totally sufficient against all odds to accomplish his divine will. Then and only then are they ready to move forward to taste God's victory" (193). But Gideon still has a problem, as the next episode shows. Worship proves momentary, without further influence on his actions or attitudes. Still God maintains his committal-formula promise: "I will be with you" (Judg 6:16).

16–22 "The subsequent battle is almost an afterthought in the narrative," says Matthews (93). But it begins to dissolve the ambiguity of Gideon's character as he "takes the position of a commander" (Bluedorn, Yahweh versus Baalism,

138) and more and more ignores Yahweh. Instructing his men about the battle tactics, Gideon "emphasizes his own role" with the repetition of the first-person pronoun (Bluedorn, 138) and takes Yahweh's position in the battle (139). Under cover of darkness, Gideon issues lamps and trumpets to his soldiers, divides them into three companies, and sends them into battle to imitate what he does. This represents traditional strategy (1 Sam 11:11; 2 Sam 18:2), helping to "create the impression of being a much larger army" (Wolf, 3:427). Younger says, "The blowing of the trumpets, the breaking of the jars, the flashing of the torches, and the shouting of the men all proliferate utter chaos and horror in the Midianite camp" (196). Seeing the lighted lamps surrounding them in the middle of the night as the guard is changing, hearing the sound of the three hundred signaling horns and of the men shouting, "the sword of Yahweh and of Gideon" (Judg 7:20), the entire Midianite army panics and flees. The army is in such disarray that the men start killing their own troops.

Recent archaeological discovery of a dedicatory inscription from Ekron may shed some light on Gideon's battle cry. (See S. Gitin and M. Cogan, "A New Type of Dedicatory Inscription from Ekron," *IEJ* 49 [1999] 193–202.) Younger reads the inscription as "*lb'l wlpdy*" (for Ba'al and for Padi) and decides, "In light of this new inscription one must wonder if the narrator is using a stock phrase to make a subtle royal illusion *[sic]* in the text" (190–91, n. 46).

Here is what Block (282) calls the "magnificent irony: no one on the offense carried a sword." Yes, Gideon's three hundred unarmed men destroy the entire Midianite force. Schneider has isolated the theological problem here. Already before the battle, "the deity's fears were actualized; Gideon took partial responsibility for the victory even before it was accomplished" (115). Or, as Olson sees, "Gideon had earlier felt that he was nothing (6:15) and the Lord was everything (7:15). But now in this shout Gideon claims a piece of the spotlight along with God" (803). Olson also notes the subtle distinction from the similar tactics Joshua used in Josh 2, where Joshua gives full credit to God (Josh 2:16).

The further irony comes in God winning the battle for his fearful leader through Midian's groundless fears. Bluedorn rightly concludes, "YHWH fights the battle, and he does so with the weapons of his own enemies" (*Yahweh versus Baalism*, 142).

23–25 Here Amit (*Book of Judges*, 232) begins her second block of the Gideon narrative, a block devoted to "problems of human leadership." Amit sees that from here on in the Gideon narrative "time is not continuous," v 24 referring "to an earlier (past perfect) or simultaneous event." The text "is thus the result of the inherent inability of language to describe several events simultaneously, and of the narrator's wish to present complete stories" (240).

Gideon recalls his troops to join in the pursuit, complicating the plot, restoring the army that Yahweh had reduced to three hundred men, and bringing the focus directly on Gideon, not Yahweh (Bluedorn, *Yahweh versus Baalism*, 144–45). "Hence," as Bluedorn says, "his new recruitment appears unjustified" (148). Block scolds Gideon: "But having achieved the divinely intended goal with the three hundred core troops, Gideon appeared to forget the point of Yahweh's reduction of the troops. Instead of operating by faith and seeking guidance from God, he relied on human strength and mobilized the troops of Naphtali, Asher, and all Manasseh" (283; compare L. R. Klein, *Triumph of Irony*, 57–58).

Niditch admits the demise of Noth's amphictyonic hypothesis, but says, "it does seem likely that Israelite groups from various areas, some of whom had their own particular histories in relation to the land, would unify for military action and consider themselves related by bonds of kinship as well as by shared military and political interests" (98). I must agree with Schneider, though, that "the idea of 'summons' here refers to the lack of unity in Israel, which emphasizes the ongoing downward spiral" (118). As Amit sees,

> The author of Judges . . . expressed the typical reality of tribal division during the period he describes by both systematically refraining from using the term 'all Israel' or 'the children of Israel.' . . . Throughout Judges the leaders are represented, not as national, but as local leaders whose sphere of influence is determined in accordance with the conditions of time and place, one of the determining factors of the scope of their influence being the dimensions of foreign subjugation. (*Book of Judges*, 71)

That Judges "does not contain any tendencies towards nationalism" (Amit, *Book of Judges*, 71) overstates the case. The repeated mention of the various tribes shows that the author presumes Israel as a tribal alliance but describes a situation where the alliance has broken down.

The new situation of pursuit strategically requires more troops, and the repeated emphasis in Judges on only specific tribes being mustered appears here. The Ehud narrative and the furtherance of the Gideon narrative in chap. 8 show the pertinence of pursuit narratives to battle reports. (See Younger, 196, n. 49.) Mobley may be right in seeing that the involvement of more tribes "ends up having little effect on the story" (*Empty Men*, 137). That is, the narrative plot is changed little by the addition of these tribes. The theological definition of Israel, so important to Judges, is strongly affected, however, by the actions involving the larger number of tribes.

A special call goes to the hill country of Ephraim and the tribe of Ephraim to take control of the waterways so the enemy cannot cross the rivers and streams, especially the Jordan River. The men of Ephraim capture the enemy commanders or princes and kill them, killing Oreb at the rock of Oreb and Zeeb at the winepress of Zeeb. Younger observes, "Ironically, a winepress and rock in Ophrah were the setting for Gideon's call to deliver the Israelites from the Midianites (6:11–20)" (196). And Schneider notes that "throughout the Gideon story actions not related to the making of wine were carried out at a wine press" (118). Here then is the climax of the larger Gideon narrative begun in Judg 6:1. God's commissioned agent has carried out his commission and won the battle, showing that God is with him and that he is indeed a heroic warrior. (See Block, 274.) But another side of Gideon will soon appear.

8:1 Finally, the story of Gideon's call appears to be complete. God has given the sign he promised, that of his presence with Gideon and that of Gideon becoming a mighty hero. But more complication follows. Block reminds us that Hebrew narrative segments like this that seem unexpected and even unnecessary "are often the key to discovering the author's rhetorical goal" (287). As Block points out, "the plot is complicated by two persistent problems: the fractious nature of the Ephraimites (8:1–3) and character flaws in Gideon (8:4–27)" (284). The men of Ephraim are not pleased with the role they have played in the battle. They demand to know why Gideon did not call them out earlier. Here again the רִיב or "contend" part of Jerubbaal's name comes to the fore. Baal contended against him. So do the Ephraimites. Niditch tries to define the Ephraimites' case with more precision:

> The opening of ch. 8 portrays the sort of tensions that arise concerning the distribution of war spoils within decentralized political and military structures. Such disputes are frequent motifs in the bardic-style literary traditions about war. One might draw comparisons, for example, with tales of Achilles and Menelaus. Participants in battle fight with hopes of obtaining a piece of the victory spoils, and the Ephraimites complain that they were not called up sufficiently early in order to partake fully in the conquered goods and the glory. Gideon, able leader that he is, diffuses their anger by use of a proverbial saying. (103)

This may well represent another attack on Jeroboam, the Ephraimite (1 Kgs 11:26) who led in splitting Israel into two kingdoms. Ephraim in Judges stands in stark contrast to Ephraim in Joshua. There the tribe simply inherited land (Josh 16:4–9) with cities in Manasseh (17:8–10) and showed its need for even more land, Joshua showing them how to claim it (17:15–18). It could not take Gezer (16:10; compare Jdg 1:29). Naturally, cities of refuge (20:7) and priestly cities (21:5, 20–24) came from Ephraim as from all the tribes. Joshua, himself, received land in Ephraim (19:50), his own tribe (Num 13:8), and was buried there (24:30) as was Eleazar the priest (24:33). Thus Joshua pictures Ephraim as the large tribe to which Joshua himself belongs.

Judges paints a different picture. It takes over from Joshua the inability to control Gezer (Judg 1:29) and Joshua's burial (2:9). One assumes Ephraim joined Ehud (3:27), but this is not explicitly stated. Deborah apparently began her career in Ephraim (4:5), so Ephraim joined the battle (5:14). Gideon then assigns Ephraim an important task (7:24), but this does not satisfy Ephraim (8:1). Gideon has to exercise his best diplomatic skills to ease the tension and reassure the Ephraimites of their importance (8:2–3). An unusual coalition appears in Judg 10:9, where the Ammonites cross the Jordan to attack Judah, Benjamin, and Ephraim. Judah is the heart of David's territory. Benjamin represents Saul's territory. And Ephraim is the center of the northern kingdom and Jeroboam's home. Here the three apparently join forces, whereas in the later days of the writer of Judges, these represented opposing forces. In Judg 12:1 Ephraim reacts to Jephthah in a fashion similar to its reaction to Gideon, wanting to be the lead force in the battle. Jephthah uses brute force instead of Gideon's diplomacy, resulting in forty-two thousand Ephraimites dying (12:2–6). The Ephraimite judge Abdon is pictured in royal style (12:13–15). Micah apparently represents Ephraim as he steals from his mother, builds an idol, and installs a wandering Levite as his personal priest, expecting thus to find blessing from God (chap. 17). Micah proves a bit cowardly (18:26) and leaves the idol to become the center of worship at Dan, the idolatrous worship center Jeroboam established (1 Kgs 12:29). We find Israel, however, at its sociological worst, for it is clear that "the tribal cohesion is crumbling" and that Ephraim especially is a "self-centered and fractious lot, easily offended, and with an inflated estimation of their significance within the nation" (Block, 286)·

Here we see, at least, the great tension that permeates the book of Judges.

Who is Israel? Is there really a cohesive group called Israel that acts together in common interest? Or is Israel only an ideal about which you tell stories but which never really functions in real-life situations? Different judges work with different tribes or groups of tribes, rather than all working together. This is best illustrated in the Song of Deborah, in which some tribes are blessed for cooperating, others are cursed for not participating, and some are not even mentioned.

2–3 Gideon tries to dismiss the charges as insignificant by building up the importance of Ephraim at the expense of his own accomplishments and those of his own clan of Abiezer (8:2). The men of Ephraim accept his contention and let their anger subside. Gideon's leadership proves successful not only in battle but also in peaceful negotiations. Here we find Gideon "at his diplomatic best" (Block, 285). Block (286) goes too far in scolding Gideon for using "God" instead of "Yahweh," for saying nothing about his own call to divine service or his being clothed with the Holy Spirit, and for not mentioning God's desire to defeat the Midianites with a minimal human force. The psychological rather than theological nature of his arguments here comes precisely from the need for diplomacy, not for theological teaching in this situation. Younger observes, "If the narrative ended roughly with 8:3, Gideon would be considered one of the heroic judges of ancient Israel, notwithstanding his problems with fear and lack of faith" (197). He adds, "However, the narration continues, and the portrayal of Gideon becomes bleaker and bleaker." Block decides that "even in victory, Israel remains her own worst enemy" (286).

4 But this has been only an interlude in the battle report. Gideon's exhausted army remains in the chase after the Midianite kings. The chase propels them across the Jordan River into the territory of the tribe of Gad and the other Israelite peoples occupying the former kingdoms of Sihon and Og. Crossing the river marks a radical change in Gideon's military strategy and in his personality. Younger sees that "the moment that he and his men cross the Jordan, a whole new Gideon emerges" (197). "Clearly what he now achieves is by his own strength of character and tactical skill" (Younger, 198). No longer is Gideon fighting for a nation or a coalition of tribes. He is now on a personal crusade of vengeance. The narrator now proceeds without mentioning God.

5 Those Israelites occupying cities east of the Jordan show no hospitality to troops marching in from the other side of the river (compare Josh 22). Gideon's family picture dictates actions rather than his commission from Yahweh. Gideon's fear and reticence take a seat as aggressiveness and personal vendetta take charge. Younger asserts that he "is simply taking the law into his own hands as soon as events have permitted him a reasonable pretense and situation to do so" (198). Gideon now operates in Gideon's strength, not in the Lord's wisdom. Block, referring to the Transjordan wars as "Gideon's personal crusades" as opposed to his earlier "wars of liberation," goes so far as to say, "If 8:1–32 had been handed down without the literary context in which it is embedded, modern readers would reject Gideon as a tyrant, arbitrary in his treatment of the enemy and ruthless in his handling of his own countrymen" (287). Block asks if the narrator is "deliberately painting a picture of a human deliverer who is the antithesis of the divine Savior" (288).

Problems arise as Gideon and his forces enter Succoth, the ancient patriarchal city north of the Jabbok River east of the Jordan (Gen 33:17). Joshua had given the tribe of Gad this part of the former kingdom of Sihon of Heshbon (Josh 13:27; see also Pss 60:6 [8]; 108:7 [8]). Succoth is located at Tell Deir Alla and was known for its metal working. (See J. A. H. Seely, *ABD*, 6:417–18; Gaß, *Ortsnamen*, 439–44.) Gideon, the diplomat, seeks to make a deal with his Israelite relatives to get food for his troops as they relentlessly pursue Zebah and Zalmunna, two kings of Midian about whom nothing else is known except that their defeat along with that of Sisera and Jabin (Judg 4–5) and of Oreb and Zeeb became celebrated in Israel's lamentation (Ps 83:9–12).

6–7 Niditch (104) compares the scene to that of David and the foolish Nabal. The officials of Succoth are not willing to commit themselves until they determine who wins the final victory. This elicits a violent threat from Gideon. The Succoth experience is repeated at nearby Penuel with an equally violent reaction from Gideon. Thus the narrative tension is set up in a dual mode: Who will win the battle? Can Gideon carry out his threats? Niditch (104) sees the issue here as one of "just deserts" and supports Gideon's actions.

But a deeper crisis lies below the surface, the continuing crisis of Israelite identity. Why will Gideon's own relatives not help a leader from another tribe in his pursuit of enemies who have stifled and terrorized western Israelites for several years? Is Israel so divided and so unconscious of its divine calling as a nation that no leader can bring them together? Or is Gideon just not the right kind of leader to provide the unity Israel needs?

8–9 Gideon has similar results in dealing with the citizens of Penuel. Penuel, meaning "face of God," gained its name when Jacob wrestled with God (Gen 32:30–31 [31–32]). Significantly, it served as Jeroboam's capital city east of the Jordan (1 Kgs 12:25). Read in Jeroboam's day, the story shows how a pretender to rule and kingship could not gain the respect of the people east of the Jordan and so destroyed them.

10 The battle narrative, marked linguistically with a Hebrew disjunctive circumstantial clause opening a new episode (8:10), is told in a straightforward manner without introducing narrative tension or complication. It is also told without Yahweh, for, as Block notes, up to this point in the Gideon narrative "the deliverance of Israel from the Midianites is carefully credited to Yahweh," but in 8:4–28 (Block's B narrative), "his name appears only in flippant and falsely pious comments from the lips of Gideon" (250). The tattered 15,000 troops remaining from an original army of 120,000 rest at an apparently insignificant place named Karkor. Rainey gives the technical location: "in the Wadi Sirchan in the northern Chejaz, 93 miles (150 km) from Jubeihat and 50 miles (31 km) southeast of Azraq" (*Sacred Bridge*, 139). Block simplifies this to "100 miles east of the Dead Sea approaching the Midianite homeland" (291).

11–12 Gideon uses no subtle tactics, simply following the main trade route to the unsuspecting army. The two Midianite kings flee, but to no avail. Gideon captures them and destroys what remains of their army.

13–17 The narrator returns to what is for him the major story, the revengeful punishment of Succoth and Penuel. Capturing a young prisoner from Succoth, Gideon gets a list of the enemies from whom he seeks revenge. Then he carries out his threats against the two apparently Israelite cities who had refused him and his men hospitality. In fact, he goes beyond his threat against Penuel and kills all the men of the city. Block only slightly overstates when he writes, "he acted like a general out of control, no longer bound by rules of civility, let alone national loyalty" (293). Malamat ("Punishment of Succoth and Penuel," 69–72) uses Hittite treaties to attempt to indict the cities for not carrying out treaty promises to supply the treaty partner's troops.

18   The narrator then returns to the Midianite kings, using narrative stacking techniques to picture Gideon's victories and his reliability in carrying out his threats. The treatment of the Midianite kings brings a surprise element to the narrative forefront, for we learn that the Midianite kings did more than just challenge Gideon's army. They had also killed Gideon's brothers, eliciting the harshest of treatment from Gideon. Their description of those they had murdered allows the narrator to introduce an important theme into the book of Judges, that of kingship. The Midianite kings describe their now-dead enemies bluntly: "No difference between you and them; each has the appearance of a king's sons" (Judg 8:18). For the first time, the thought is slipped into the reader's mind that Gideon may have come from royal stock, or that he may be on the road to royal rule. But the Midianite kings, who should know, cannot describe Gideon as a king, only as one like his brothers with the appearance of princes who have not ascended the throne and who do not have royal authority. Thus, in reality, "this response is both evasive and ambiguous" (Block, 294).

19   Gideon responds to the conquered kings with a common Hebrew oath formula—"as Yahweh lives"—that occurs forty-four times in the Hebrew text of the Old Testament (Ruth 3:13; 1 Sam 14:39, 45; 19:6; 20:3, 21; 25:26, 34; 26:10, 16; 28:10; 29:6; 2 Sam 4:9; 12:5; 14:11; 15:21; 22:47; 1 Kgs 1:29; 2:24; 17:1, 12; 18:10, 15; 22:14; 2 Kgs 2:2, 4, 6; 3:14; 4:30; 5:16, 20; 2 Chr 18:13; Ps 18:47; Jer 4:2; 5:2; 12:16; 16:14–15; 23:7–8, 36; 38:16; Hos 4:15). Block's repeated reference to this phrase (295) as evidence of a flippant or glib attitude toward Yahweh on Gideon's part is a bit overdone in light of the frequency of this formula. Certainly, one would not say that Gideon had chosen his words carefully, but who does choose words carefully in a moment of intense emotion?

20   Gideon then commands Jether, his oldest son, to execute the Midianite kings. This "places his son in an awkward position" (Block, 295), but like his father, Jether fearfully refuses his first opportunity (see 6:27; 7:10). Thus Block sees the narrator portraying Jether as "an alter ego of Gideon's former (preferred) self," saying "the lad had not yet grown up and developed a stomach for violence" as had his father (295). Younger expresses a similar thought: "Jether . . . serves as an antithesis to his father and points up the contrast between Gideon as he was and Gideon as he is now" (199). Here again we must ask what motives lie behind Gideon's command. Is he seeking to provide leadership and war experience for his son? Or is he passing off an unwanted part of his job to the candidate least likely to rebel and most likely to be seen as next in line to do the job?

21   The Midianite kings taunt Gideon, challenging him to accomplish the task himself to prove his strength (גְּבוּרָתוֹ), a play on the earlier title given Gideon (6:12) as a heroic warrior (גִּבּוֹר הֶחָיִל). Niditch sees the kings as "noble enemies" who "are portrayed as negotiating their own execution" (105). Gideon has a chance to prove he has earned the title that Yahweh's messenger had conferred on him. So Gideon rises to act, in so doing taking the special ornaments hanging around the necks of the camels that the Midianite rulers rode. Does this simply portray a leader following precedent in showing his superiority by taking the conquered foes' special emblems (Block, 296), or is this a clue to an acquisitive, greedy part of Gideon's character? Niditch recognizes that "all great biblical heroes have their flaws and make errors. . . . The way in which the author concludes the chapter, however, strongly argues against the view that Gideon is a failed leader whose short-comings point to the need for a monarchy" (105). Block speaks for the perceptive reader when he says, "The greatest surprise of all is that in the end the reader's sympathies may have shifted completely from Gideon to the other participants in the scene, first the two kings, then his hapless son" (293).

22 Finally, we approach the narrator's climactic moment. In a totally unex-pected narrative twist, the men of Israel (literally, "the man of Israel," a collective term), "extremely impressed with his achievement" (Block, 296), speak up. No narrative exposition or scenic change has prepared us for the Israelites' imperative demand that frames the central issue of the book: "Rule over us, yes, you! Also your son and grandson" (Judg 8:22). Webb sees the offer of dynastic rule mark-ing "the peak of his power and influence," and "this, rather than his victory over the kings becomes the true climax of the second movement [for Webb, 8:4–28] and, retrospectively, of the story as a whole" ([1987] 146). Not just a few tribes, but Israel as a whole, are ready for a king like the nations. They see the weakness of their political system and want to change it drastically. They want not only a momentary king, but also a dynasty. Interestingly, they do not use the word "king." They refer only to the function of ruling, for they are interested in someone restor-ing strength, peace, prosperity, and possibly even tribal unity to Israel. As Block surmises, "the narrator may have avoided the term *melek* [that is, Hebrew for king] because the issue in Gideon's statement is not a title or an office but performance, which from beginning to end belongs to God" (297). The tribes' main concern is military deliverance, Hebrew ישע, a concept that appears in important places in the book and prompts God to raise up judges (Judg 2:16, 18; 3:9, 15, 31; 6:14–15, 31, 36–37; 7:2, 7; 8:22; 10:1, 12–14; 12:2–3; 13:5). But God knows that Israel will claim that deliverance comes from human power and will boast about their own strength (see Judg 7:2). For once it appears that Gideon has accomplished what before him only Joshua had done, uniting the tribes of Israel in a common cause; but as we will soon see, the unity is built around the wrong worship and the wrong theology, and is short-lived. Gideon in no way resembles the king described in Deut 17:14–20, a point that Block makes decisively (297–98).

23 Gideon's reply represents orthodox Israelite theology: "I will not rule over you, nor will my son rule over you. Yahweh rules over you" (v 23). Compare 1 Sam 8:7. As so often, however, practice does not always follow theology. The offer to Gideon may represent a request to certify officially what was already in place in practice. (See Block, 299.) Webb recognizes that

> the irony of the situation is that the impiety from which Gideon recoils is of his own mak-ing. From the moment he crossed the Jordan he has acted more and more like a king, especially in his dispensing of summary punishments on those who resist his authority. In crossing the Jordan he had already exceeded his commission and begun to move towards the kind of rule which is now formally offered to him. ([1987] 152)

24–27 Gideon proceeds to gather gold earrings from the plunder, each of the soldiers contributing one. This adds up to about forty-three pounds (20 kg) of gold, an amount which "takes on the character of a royal treasure" (Block, 299). Gideon also adds a few other garments and trinkets to his collection. And from this Gideon creates an ephod, apparently an elaborate priestly apron much like that worn by the high priest in Israel's true worship, but sometimes interpreted as a cultic image or idol. Younger is on target with his description:

> Perhaps Gideon's ephod refers to a high-priestly type garment with an unusual degree of gold ornamentation or to a replica of the high-priestly garment made of pure gold. However, the amount of gold and the verbs used to describe Gideon's action ("made," "set up") mitigate against this understanding. Here "ephod" is perhaps used figuratively to represent not only the garment that clothed a sacred image but also the image over which the garment was draped. (205–6)

The latter interpretation gains credibility because "all Israel prostituted themselves there with it. It became a snare to Gideon and to his house" (Judg 8:27b). Gideon began by transforming a Baal shrine in his own father's property to an altar for Yahweh. He concludes by turning the Ophrah shrine into a pagan one marked by an image or priestly garment that he himself has created. Block concludes, "In the beginning Ophrah is the scene of clan idolatry (6:25–32); in the end Ophrah is the focus of national idolatry (8:27)" (250). Younger suggests that Gideon reconstructed the Baal shrine he had earlier torn down (6:25–32): "However there is no indication that either altar to Yahweh is destroyed, and it seems better to understand the ephod as a syncretism of Yahwism and idolatrous practices. . . . If anything the ephod should have been made by a priest and then used in the tabernacle in the worship of Yahweh. But Gideon . . . fully intends for the ephod to bring himself and his family glory" (206–7). Ironically, Gideon, as one made in the image of God and clothed with the Spirit of Yahweh (6:34), creates his own image and clothes it with pagan materials (see Block, 300). Thus Gideon foreshadows the full-blown cultic apostasy that Jeroboam will inaugurate at Dan and Bethel.

28–32 The result of all this? Midian is defeated and cannot threaten Israel. The land has quiet and rest for forty years. Jerubbaal, the uncrowned king, goes back home to live out his remaining years, or perhaps to live enthroned his remaining years. There he is quite busy, collecting a harem of wives, concubines, and royal sons fit for a king, in open violation of Exod 34:15–16 and Deut 7:3–4; 17:14–20. Hauser argues that Gideon ruled after defeating Midian and making a treaty with Shechem sealed by marrying a Shechemite woman: "Abimelech's rise to kingship can only be explained on the presupposition that his father Gideon had been a ruler (9:1–6). . . . Gideon ruled over a substantial portion of the central hill country to the north and south of the valley of Jezreel" ("Unity and Diversity in Early Israel before Samuel," *JETS* 22 [1979] 299–300).

One son comes from a concubine in Shechem, a tantalizing piece of information, for Shechem was the site of Joshua's covenant ceremonies (Josh 8:30–35; 24:1–28). Shechem appears in the Ebla texts before 2000 B.C.E. and often in Egyptian texts from the nineteenth century onward. Gaß (*Ortsnamen,* 299) calls Shechem, even in its early appearances in foreign texts, an important strategic and political center which countries like Egypt considered dangerous. In the Amarna period Lab'ayu, king of Shechem, extended his control from the Valley of Jezreel to the environs of Jerusalem (L. E. Toombs, *ABD*, 5:1174) and gained a reputation as the secretive leader of rebellions against Egyptian overlords and Canaanite neighbors. Shechem, located between Mount Ebal and Mount Gerizim on Tell Balatah, slightly over forty miles (64.4 km) north of Jerusalem, has strategic highway and water resources.

What religion did this mother teach her son? And what did the son's name Abimelech, "my father is king," really signify? As Jordan notes,

> If the boy's mother had been the one to give him this name, it would be understandable. That Gideon gave it shows that his heart had been ensnared to some degree by the desire to rule over men as a potentate. The ephod had snared him, and now humanistic kingship had snared him. No father can harbor such desires without his son picking it up, and Abimelech acts out in life what his father had only dreamt of in his weaker moments. (156)

(For the various possibilities lying behind Abimelech's new name, see Bluedorn, *Yahweh versus Baalism*, 191–92.) Ultimately, Gideon dies and joins his father in burial. Niditch sees this as evidence that the editor portrays Gideon as "a hero fully deserving of God's favor and blessed with the interment of a good man" (106). It is interesting that this judge gains such a normal burial, but so does Samson. Respectful burial by the family does not prove a life well lived and pleasing to God. His true achievements are summarized by the previous and following verses.

33–35 Gideon's death returns Israel to Baal worship so that in the end Baal contends with Jerubbaal and wins the long-term victory, for "the Israelites did not remember Yahweh, their God, who saved them from the hand of all their enemies who surrounded them. They did not show faithful love to the house of Jerubbaal, that is, Gideon, in relationship to all the good that he did for Israel" (Judg 8:34). Younger aptly says,

> The final irony of the story is that Gideon, champion of Yahweh against Baal, presides over the national apostasy that after his death will become full-scale Baal worship again. . . . Therefore, Gideon's challenge to Baal has been answered in full, and Gideon himself has contributed significantly to the answer. The name Jerubbaal has acquired an ironic twist: Baal has indeed taken up his own cause (6:31–32) with the unknowing participation of his adversary. . . . The people come to Ophrah to worship Gideon's ephod, not to seek and honor God. Thus, Gideon's faith is turned into a superstition. (208)

Here then is the narrative of Gideon, actually a complex of several narratives tied together around his name. What are we supposed to learn from them, especially in the realm of leadership that is so central to the narratives and to the book of Judges? Certainly various scholars see different perspectives here. U. Becker sees the Deuteronomistic Historian (whom he calls DtrH) presenting through Gideon an office that offers an alternative to kingship. Most modern interpreters are much closer to Block as he concludes that "in the person of Gideon the narrator recognizes the schizophrenic nature of Israel's spiritual personality. On the one hand she treasures her call to be God's covenant people; on the other she cannot resist the allurements of the prevailing Canaanite culture" (250). Or as Younger describes him, "Gideon was apparently a man of great potential and natural ability but lacking in faith. . . . While not necessarily a professional soldier, Gideon is not a man devoid of resources or the natural potential for leadership" (193, 200; compare Webb, [1987] 149–50). Indeed, "Gideon's lifestyle contradicts his words" (Younger, 209).

So far as Gideon represents the end stage, the trap is sprung. God's people are caught. Their leader has moved down the spiral from one who made Baal contend with him to one who presumptuously assumes a leadership role God had not called him to and leaves a legacy of Baalism stronger than that he had learned at his father's feet and in his father's Baalistic shrine. Jordan remarks, "They were worshipping a half-breed god, so the Lord gave them into the hands of a half-breed man. . . . As always, God punished His people by giving them what they wanted" (157). Younger pictures Gideon in these words:

> Gideon is one of these faithless persons. He refuses at first to follow the call of God. Only after he has presumptuously subjected Yahweh to a series of tests and after he has witnessed Yahweh's gracious answers—ironically, ultimately in the mouth of a Midianite—does he finally accept the call to deliver his people. . . . Motivated by revenge, Gideon's excesses are spelled out in the extreme reprisals on his own countrymen. While the cities did not give support, the punishment is unduly severe. . . . Now he is a mighty warrior who does not need God to help him. (201)

Block succinctly describes Gideon's trek along the "typical pattern of oriental kings: (1) he treated his subjects/countrymen ruthlessly (8:5–9, 13–17); (2) his actions were driven by a personal agenda rather than theological or national ideals; (3) he reacted to the death of his brothers as if they were royal assassinations requiring blood vengeance; (4) he made ridiculous demands on his people (v. 20); (5) he claimed for himself the symbols of royalty taken from the enemy" (299). He also demanded a "symbolic gesture of submission" in asking for the golden earrings (v 24), collected what amounted to a royal treasury (v 26), took control of the worship place as kings usually did (v 27), made his own home town the de facto capital of the country (v 27), and assembled a family that can be compared only to royal harems (v 30). He even named a son Abimelech, meaning "my father is king." In addition to all this evidence that Gideon tacitly assumed the role of king of Israel, the wording in Judg 8:29 that he lived in his house may well mean he was enthroned (Block, 299–301). For Block, then, "the conclusion seems inescapable that despite his protestation, Gideon actually assumed the role of king 'over Israel.' But his was an aberrant and illicit kingship from the beginning," not initiated nor certified by Yahweh, the true King of Israel, and not devoted to Yahweh's law or to Yahweh's plan for his people. Rather, "for the first time idolatry is officially sponsored by a leader of the nation" (301).

Explanation

Gideon, then, the man called to live as a heroic warrior in God's presence, proves an enigma to himself, his nation, and to us. As Polzin so aptly describes the situation,

> The story of Gideon portrays how Israel even in the very process of being delivered by Yahweh vacillates between allegiance to him and allegiance to another god. More than this, it develops the irony that the result of Yahweh's deliverance through Gideon is Israel's transition from partial to total worship of Baal-Berith after Gideon's death (8:33). . . . It depicts Israel's confused efforts to decide which god, Yahweh or one of

the gods of the Amorites, would deliver them from their oppressors and ensure them peace. (*Moses and the Deuteronomist,* 171)

Niditch (compare Ryan) goes against the scholarly grain in pleading Gideon's case. She writes, "A close examination, however, reveals that those behind the Gideon cycle are far from enthusiastic monarchists, that Gideon is portrayed as a great hero, and that minor ambivalences about the nature of the hero and major ambivalences about the best form of polity are typical of Judges and the tradition as a whole" (103).

Certainly this narrative shows us the great potential of the leader God called to deliver his people. It depicts a fearful young man seeking reassurance at every step transformed into a vengeful leader punishing cities and people at the slightest whim. He brings death not only to the enemy but to villages of his own people. He illustrates the difficulty Israel's leaders had in developing any kind of unity and loyalty among the various entities that eventually were molded together under David and Solomon ever so briefly. It shows that leader following God's path and finding success as a leader, but it also shows a monumental failure as Gideon takes matters into his own hands, seeks family vengeance, and assumes all the outer appearances and trappings of a royal family even if he does give lip service to the theology that only Yahweh is king and so does not assume the title of king for himself. He prepares the way for his son Abimelech, "my father is king," to start the northern kingdom on the road to a series of revolutions, palace revolts, assassinations, and coups. He demonstrates that leadership that can seem so promising can end up leading a nation to ruin and apostasy.

b. Abimelech: Illegitimate, Self-seeking Rogue Warrior (9:1–57)

Bibliography

Abramsky, S. "Abimelech's Leadership—King, Chief, and Ruler" (Heb.). In *The Book of Sivan.* FS S. Sivan, ed. A. Even-Shoshan, B. Z. Luria, Ch. Rabin, and E. Talmi. Jerusalem: Kiryat Sefer, 1979. 163–76. **Adinolfi, M.** "Originalità dell'apologo di Jotham." *RivB* 7 (1959) 322–42. **Anderson, B. W.** "The Place of Shechem in the Bible." *BA* 20 (1957) 10–11. **Barredo, M. A.** "Abimelec: Paradigma de una actitud autónoma ante Dios, Estudio literario de Jue 9." *Car* 17 (2001) 1–66. **Bartelmus, R.** "Die sogenannte Jothamfabel—eine politisch—religiöse Parabeldichtung: Anmerkungen zu einem Teilaspekt der vordeuteronomischen israelitischen Literaturgeschichte." *TZ* 41 (1985) 97–120. **Bluedorn, W.** *Yahweh versus Baalism: A Theological Reading of the Gideon Abimelech Narrative.* JSOTSup 329. Sheffield: Sheffield Academic, 2001. **Boogart, T. A.** "Stone for Stone: Retribution in the Story of Abimelek and Shechem." *JSOT* 32 (1985) 45–56. **Bohmbach, K. G.** "Conventions/Contraventions: The Meanings of Public and Private for the Judges 19 Concubine." *JSOT* 83 (1999) 83–98. **Boling, R. G.** "'And Who Is Š-K-M?' (Judges IX 28)." *VT* 13 (1963) 479–82. **Braver, A. Y.** "And Abimelech Ruled over Israel" (Heb.). *Beit-Miqra* 7 (1963) 120–21. **Campbell, E. F., Jr.** "Judges 9 and Biblical Archaeology." In *Essays in Honor of David Noel Freedman in Celebration* *of His Sixtieth Birthday.* Ed. C. Meyers and M. O'Connor. Winona Lake, IN: Eisenbrauns, 1983. 263–67. ———. *Shechem III: The Stratigraphy and Architecture of Shechem/Tell Balatah.* ASORAR 6. Boston: ASOR, 2002. **Castelbajac, I. de.** "Histoire de la rédaction des Juges ix: Une solution." *VT* 51 (2001) 166–85. **Cathcart, K. J.** "The Trees, the Beasts and the Birds: Fables, Parables and Allegories in the Old Testament." In *Wisdom in Ancient Israel.* FS J. A. Emerton, ed. J. Day, R. P. Gordon, and H. G. M. Williamson. Cambridge: Cambridge UP, 1995. 212–21. **Clements, R. E.** "Baal-Berith of Shechem." *JSS* 13 (1968) 21–32. **Crown, A. D.** "A Reinterpretation of Judges IX in the Light of Its Humour." *AbrN* 3 (1963) 90–98. **Ebach, J.,** and **U. Rüterswörden.** "Pointen in der Jothamfabel." *BN* 31 (1986) 11–18. **Eshel, H.,** and **Z. Erlich.** "Abimelech's First Battle with the Lords of Shechem and the Question of the Navel of the Land." *Tarbiz* 58 (1988–1989) 111–16. **Fensham, F. C.** "The Numeral Seventy in the Old Testament and the Family of Jerubbaal, Ahab, Panammuwa, and Athirat." *PEQ* 109 (1977) 113–15. **Fokkelman, J. P.** "Structural Remarks on Judges 9 and 19." In *'Sha'arei Talmon': Studies in the Bible, Qumran, and the Ancient Near East.* FS S. Talmon, ed. M. Fishbane and E. Tov with W. W. Fields. Winona Lake, IN: Eisenbrauns, 1992. 33–45. **Fowler, M.** "A Closer Look at the Temple of El-Berith at Shechem." *PEQ* 115 (1983) 49–53. **Fritz, V.** "Abimelech und Sichem in Jdc. IX." *VT* 32 (1982) 129–44. ———. "Sichem." *TRE,* 31:245–47. **Gevirtz, S.** "Jericho and Shechem: A Religio-Literary Aspect of City Destruction." *VT* 13 (1963) 52–62. **Haag, H.** "Gideon-Jerubbaal-Abimelek." *ZAW* 79 (1967) 305–14. **Halpern, B.** "The Rise of Abimelech Ben-Jerubbaal." *HAR* 2 (1978) 79–100. **Hepner, G.** "Scatology in the Bible." *SJOT* 18 (2004) 278–95. **Herr, D. D.,** and **M. P. Boyd.** "A Watermelon Named Abimelech." *BAR* 28 (2002) 37–38, 62. **Honeyman, A. M.** "The Salting of Shechem." *VT* 3 (1953) 192. **Ilan, Z.** "The Location of the Navel of the Land." *Beit-Miqra* 27 (1981–1982) 122–26. **Jans, E.** *Abimelech und sein Königtum: Diachrone und synchrone Untersuchungen zu Ri 9.* Arbeiten zu Text und Sprache im Alten Testament 66. St. Ottilien: EOS, 2001. **Janzen, J. G.** "A Certain Woman in the Rhetoric of Judges 9." *JSOT* 38 (1987) 33–37. **Jarosh, K.** *Sichem: Eine archäologische und religionsgeschichtliche Studie mit besonderer Berücksichtigung von Jos 24.* OBO 11a. Freiburg: Universitätsverlag, 1976. ———. "Sichem." In *Neues Bibel-Lexikon.* Ed. M. Görg and B. Lang. Zurich: Benziger, 1988. 3.13:583–85. **Kautzsch, E.** "Richter 9,28." *ZAW* 102 (1990) 299–300. **Lewis, T. J.** "The Identity and Function of El/Baal Berith." *JBL* 115 (1996) 401–23. **Lindars, B.** "Jotham's Fable—A New Form-critical Analysis." *JTS* 24 NS (1973) 355–66. **Liss, H.** Die Fabel des Yotam in Ri 9,8–15—Versuch einer strukturellen Deutung." *BN* 89 (1997) 12–18. **Maly, E.** "The Jotham Fable—Anti-monarchical?" *CBQ* 22 (1960) 299–305. **Meersch, J. van der.** "Problema de Expugnatione Sichem ab Abimelech (Jud. IX,22–49)." *VD* 31 (1953) 335–43. **Na'aman, N.** "Migdal-Shechem and the 'House of El-Berith'" (Heb). *Zion* 51 (1986) 259–80. **Ogden, G. S.** "Jotham's Fable: Its Structure and Function in Judges 9." *BT* 45 (1995) 301–8. **Reviv, M.** "The Government of Sichem in the Amarna Period and in the Days of Abimelek." *IEJ* 16 (1966) 255. **Rösel, H. N.** "Studien zur Topographie der Kriege in den Büchern Josua und Richter." *ZDPV* 92 (1976) 10–46. ———. "Überlegungen zu 'Abimelech und Sichem in Jdc. ix.'" *VT* 33 (1983) 500. **Scham, S.** "The Days of the Judges: When Men and Women Were Animals and Trees Were Kings." *JSOT* 97 (2002) 48–53. **Schmid, H.** "Die Herrschaft Abimelechs (Jdc 9)." *Jud* 26 (1970) 1–11. **Schöpflin, K.** "Jotham's Speech and Fable as Prophetic Comment on Abimelech's Story: The Genesis of Judges 9." *SJOT* 18 (2004) 3–22. ———. "Jotham's Fable (Judges 9:8–15): A Prophetic Text within the Book of Judges." In *Basel und Bibel: Collected Communications to the XVIIth Congress of the International Organization for the Study of the Old Testament, Basel, 2001.* Ed. M. Augustin and H. M. Niemann. BEATAJ 51. Frankfurt: Lang, 2004. 97–102. **Schwegler, H.** "Aufstieg und Fall eines Gewaltmenschen: Abimelech (Richter 9)." In *Männer weinen heimlich.* Ed. D. Bauer and A. Meissner. Stuttgart: Katholisches Bibelwerk, 1993. 46–59. **Segal, M. Z.** "The Composition of the Chapter of Abimelech, Judges 9" (Heb.). In *Tradition and Criticism.* Jerusalem, 1957. 136–39. **Sellin, E.** *Wie wurde Sichem eine israelitische Stadt?* Leipzig: Deichert, 1922. **Simon, U.** "The Parable of Jotham: The Parable, Its Application and Their Narrative Framework" (Heb.). *Tarbiz* 34 (1965) i–ii, 1–34. **Soggin, J. A.** "The Migdal Temple: Migdal Sekem Judg 9 and the Artifact of Mount Ebal." In *Wünschet Jerusalem Frieden.* Ed. M. Augustin et al. Frankfurt am Main: Lang, 1988. 115–20. **Steger, L. E.** "The Shechem Temple: Where Abimelech Massacred a Thousand." *BAR* 29 (2003) 26–35, 66–69. **Steinberg, N.** "Social Scientific Criticism: Judges 9 and Issues of Kingship. In *Judges and Method: New Approaches in Biblical Studies.* Ed. G. Yee. Minneapolis: Fortress, 1996. 45–64. **Tatu, S.** "Jotham's Fable and the *Crux Interpretum* in Judges IX." *VT* 56 (2006) 105–24. **Terrien, S.** "The Omphalos Myth and Hebrew Religion." *VT* 20 (1970) 315–38. **Vater Solomon, A. M.** "Fable." In *Saga, Legend, Tale, Novella, Fable.* Ed. G. W. Coats. JSOTSup 35. Sheffield: JSOT Press, 1985. 114–25. **Waard, J. de.** "Jotham's Fable: An Exercise in Clearing Away the Unclear." In *Wissenschaft und Kirche.* FS E. Lohse, ed. K. Aland and S. Meurer. Texten und Arbeiten zur Bibel 4. Bielefeld: Luther, 1989. 362–70. **Wilkie, J. M.** "The Peshitta Translation of *tabbur ha'arets* in Judges ix 37." *VT* 1 (1951) 144. **Wright, G. R. H.** "The Mythology of Pre-Israelite Shechem." *VT* 20 (1970) 75–82. **Würthwein, E.** "Abimelech und der Untergang Sichems: Studien zu Jdc 9." In *Studien zum deuteronomistischen Geschichtswerk.* BZAW 227. Berlin: de Gruyter, 1994. 12–28. **Zenger, E.** "Ein Beispiel exegetischer Methoden aus dem Alten Testament." In *Einführung in die Methoden der biblischen Exegese.* Ed. J. Schreiner. Würzburg: Echter, 1971. 97–148.

Translation

[1] *Abimelech, the son of Jerubbaal, went to Shechem to his mother's brothers. He spoke to them and to all the clan of his maternal grandfather:* [a] [2] *"Please inquire of all the lords* [a] *of Shechem, 'Which is better for you?'* [b] *Should seventy men rule over you, that is, all the sons of Jerubbaal?* [c] *Or should one man rule over you?' Remind them that I am of the same bones* [d] *and flesh as you are."* [3] *His maternal uncles spoke for* [a] *him with all these words in the ears of all the lords of Shechem. Their hearts turned to support* [b] *Abimelech because they said, "He is our brother."* [4] *They gave him seventy shekels of silver from the house of Baal Berith. With the money* [a] *Abimelech hired men without discipline or principles,* [b] *and they followed him.* [5] *He went to his father's house in Ophrah and murdered his brothers, the sons of Jerubbaal—seventy men—on one stone.* [a] *Jotham, Jerubbaal's youngest son, was the only one left because he hid.*

[6] *All the lords* [a] *of Shechem met together with all Beth-millo.* [b] *They came and crowned Abimelech king* [c] *at the Oak of the Pillar* [d] *in Shechem.*

[7] *They told* [a] *Jotham, and he went and stood on the summit of Mount Gerizim. Raising his voice, he summoned* [b] *them, "Listen to me, lords of Shechem, so God may listen* [c] *to you.* [8] *Once upon a time the trees set out to anoint a king over them. They invited the olive tree, 'Rule* [a] *over us.'* [9] *The olive* [a] *told them, 'Should I stop producing my rich oil? Because of me,* [b] *both God and people are honored. Then I could hold sway over the trees.'* [10] *The trees said to the fig tree, 'You come, rule over us.'* [11] *The fig tree told them, 'Should I stop producing my sweet things, such good figs, so that I can go hold sway over the trees?'* [12] *The trees said to the vine, 'Come, rule* [a] *over us.'* [13] *The vine told them, 'Should I cease producing my new wine that causes both God and men* [a] *to rejoice so that I can go hold sway over the trees?'* [14] *All* [a] *the trees said to the bramble bush, 'You come, rule over us.'* [15] *The bramble bush told the trees, 'If in lasting faithfulness you are going to anoint me to rule over you, then come, find protection* [a] *in my shade. If that is not the case, then let fire come out from the bramble* [b] *bush so that it can consume the cedars of Lebanon.'*

[16] *"Therefore, if you have acted faithfully and with integrity when you crowned Abimelech king and if you have done the good thing in relation to Jerubbaal and to his house and*

if you have paid back to him what his work deserved[a]—[17]*when my father fought for you and put his soul on the line for you*[a] *to rescue you from the hand of Midian*—[18]*but you opposed my father's house today, you murdered his seventy sons, each on the same stone, and you crowned Abimelech, the son of his slave girl, king over the lords of Shechem just because he was your brother*—[19]*if in faithfulness and in integrity you have acted today in relation to Jerubbaal and to his house, then rejoice*[a] *in Abimelech so that he may, yes, even he, may rejoice in you.* [20]*But if that is not the case, may fire go out from Abimelech so that it consumes the lords of Shechem and Beth-millo*[a] *and so that fire may go out from the lords of Shechem and from Beth-millo so that it consumes Abimelech."*

[21]*Jotham fled and escaped.*[a] *He came to a well and lived there away from Abimelech, his brother.*

[22]*Abimelech reigned over Israel three years.* [23]*God sent an evil spirit between Abimelech and the lords of Shechem. The lords of Shechem dealt treacherously with Abimelech.*[a] [24]*This came about*[a] *so that the violent act against the seventy sons of Jerubbaal and their blood could be placed on Abimelech, their brother, who murdered them and on the lords of Shechem who gave him the power to murder his brothers.* [25]*The lords of Shechem set up an ambush on the tops of the hills. They robbed*[a] *all who passed by them on the way. This was reported*[b] *to Abimelech.*[c]

[26]*Gaal,*[a] *son of a slave,*[b] *came along with his brothers. They passed*[c] *through Shechem. The lords of Shechem trusted*[d] *him.* [27]*They went out to the field, gathered their harvest of grapes, and trampled on them to get the juice.*[a] *Then they celebrated a festival.*[b] *They entered*[c] *the house of their god*[d] *and ate and drank. They pronounced a curse on Abimelech.*

[28]*Gaal, the son of a slave,*[a] *said, "Who is Abimelech? On the other hand, who is Shechem?*[b] *Should we be his servants? Is he not the son of Jerubbaal? Is not Zebul his administrator? Serve the men of Hamor, Shechem's father.*[c] *Why should we, yes, even we, be servants?* [29]*If only this people were in my hands so that*[a] *I might depose Abimelech."*

He[b] *said to Abimelech,*[c] *"Get your army up to full strength,*[d] *and march out!"*

[30]*Zebul, the city's mayor, heard the speech by Gaal, son of a slave,*[a] *and anger*[b] *burned within him.* [31]*He sent messengers to Abimelech covertly,*[a] *saying, "Look here! Gaal, the son of a slave,*[b] *and his brothers have come to Shechem. Right this minute*[c] *they are besieging*[d] *the city in opposition to you.*[32]*Therefore, take your stand tonight, you and the people who are with you. Set up an ambush in the field.* [33]*As the sun rises in the morning, you must rise early and attack the city. At the moment Gaal*[a] *and the people with him are marching against you, you can do to him whatever your hand finds to do."*

[34]*Abimelech along with the people with him took their stand that night. They set an ambush beside Shechem in four companies.*[a] [35]*Gaal,*[a] *the son of a slave, marched out; and the city gate stood open. Then Abimelech along with the people with him made their move from the ambush.* [36]*Gaal*[a] *saw the people and told Zebul, "Look here! A people is going down from the summits of the mountains."*

Zebul replied to him, "You are seeing the shadow of the mountains appearing as men."[b]

[37]*Again Gaal*[a] *began talking, "Look here! A people is going down from the center of the earth,*[b] *and one company comes from the direction of the oak of the soothsayers."*[c]

[38]*Zebul said to him, "Where then is your oration? You're the one who said, 'Who is Abimelech that we should be his servants?' Is this not the people you rejected? March out now, and fight them."*

[39]*Gaal*[a] *marched out at the head of the lords of Shechem and fought Abimelech.* [40]*Abi-*

melech pursued him,[a] *and he fled from his presence. The mass of slain men fell clear to the entrance of the gate.*[b] [41]*Abimelech remained*[a] *in Arumah, and Zebul drove Gaal*[b] *and his brothers out so they could no longer live in Shechem.* [42]*The next day when the people went out to the field, they*[a] *told Abimelech.* [43]*He took the people and divided them into three companies. He set up an ambush in the field.*[a] *He looked up. Right then the people were marching out from the city, and he rose against them and defeated them.* [44]*Meanwhile, Abimelech and the companies with him*[a] *dashed ahead. They took their stand at the entrance of*[b] *the gate of the city. The other two companies dashed out against everyone in the field and defeated them.*[c] [45]*So Abimelech fought against the city all that day and captured*[a] *the city. He killed its people, tore down the city, and sowed salt on it.*

[46]*All the lords living in the tower of Shechem heard. They entered a secret tunnel of the house of El Berith.*[a] [47]*The report came to Abimelech that all the lords of the tower*[a] *of Shechem had joined together.* [48]*Abimelech went up Mount Zalmon,*[a] *he and all the people with him. Abimelech took hold of the battle axes*[b] *with his hand and cut down tree branches.*[c] *He lifted them up on his shoulder*[d] *and said to the people with him, "Whatever you see me doing, hurry up and do the same thing yourselves."* [49]*All the people also cut a branch*[a] *for himself and followed Abimelech. They set them against the secret tunnel and set the tunnel on fire. Every last one of the men of the tower of Shechem died, about a thousand men along with the women.*

[50]*Abimelech went to Thebez, set up a siege against Thebez,*[a] *and captured it.* [51]*But a strong tower was in the city center. All the men and women and the lords of the city fled there. They shut themselves in*[a] *and went up on the roof of the tower.* [52]*Abimelech came to the tower and fought against it. He*[a] *approached the entrance to the tower to burn it with fire.* [53]*A certain woman*[a] *threw an upper millstone down on Abimelech's head. She crushed*[b] *his skull.* [54]*He quickly called to his young aide who carried his weapons and said to him, "Draw your*[a] *sword and kill me lest they tell of me that a woman killed him." His young aide stabbed him, and he*[b] *died.* [55]*The men of Israel saw that Abimelech was dead and went each to his own home place.*

[56]*God repaid Abimelech's evil that he did to his father, killing his seventy brothers.* [57]*At the same time God repaid the men of Shechem, bringing to*[a] *them the curse of Jotham, the son of Jerubbaal.*

Notes

1.a. כָּל־מִשְׁפַּחַת בֵּית־אֲבִי אִמּוֹ, lit. "all the clan of the father's house of his mother." בֵּית־אָב represents a technical expression for all blood relatives on the father's side and denotes the extended family as a subdivision of the מִשְׁפָּחָה, "clan." LXX[A] does not have "of the father," apparently not seeing a way to make that meaningful in this syntactical situation. See *Comment.*

2.a. כָל־בַּעֲלֵי, lit. "all the baals," using the term in its common meaning of "lord" or "master" rather than as a proper name. LXX reads "the men of Shechem" without the "all" and reducing בעל to "men." Niditch (112) notes that LXX[B] (and apparently OL as well) employs this reading throughout the chapter, "perhaps avoiding the name of the Canaanite deity."

2.b. LXX[A] does not have "to you," possibly smoothing out the Gk. syntax. For Heb. syntax, see *IBHS,* 264, §14.4b.

2.c. OL reads "Gideon" for "Jerubbaal."

2.d. Apparently the Leningrad Codex represents a copyist's error in punctuation. More than twenty Heb. MSS read עִצְּמְכֶם for Leningrad עַצְמְכֶם.

3.a. DSS reads אליו for MT's עליו. This may represent a listening error by a copyist, but the MT is the more difficult reading here and fits significantly into the textual meaning.

3.b. וַיֵּט לִבָּם אַחֲרֵי, lit. "their heart stretched out after."

4.a. שִׁבְעִים כֶּסֶף, lit. "seventy of silver."

4.b. "Without discipline or principles" interprets רֵיקִים וּפֹחֲזִים, lit. "empty and insolent." LXX^A reads θαμβουμένους, "amazing, astounding," apparently reading פֹחֲדִים, "fearful," for MT פֹחֲזִים, "insolent, undisciplined." LXX^B reads δειλούς, "cowardly, fearful, reckless," possibly reading חֲפֹזִים. OL translates "fearless."

5.a. See *IBHS*, 251, §13.8.

6.a. LXX reads "men of" for Heb. בַּעֲלֵי, "baals" or "lords." OL reads "princes."

6.b. LXX^A reads "house of Millo," while LXX^B reads "house of Beth-millo," both translating and transliterating the Heb. בֵּית.

6.c. LXX^B does not have "king." OL refers to "anointing" rather than "making" king.

6.d. LXX reads στάσεως, apparently "military garrison." This would represent הַמַּצָּב instead of MT's מֻצָּב, "standing." LXX^B reads τῇ εὑρετῇ τῆς στάσεως, "found at the garrison," apparently translating מֻצָּב twice. OL reads "under the dense oak that was in Shechem." *BHS* suggests reading הַמַּצֵּבָה, "standing stone," or "pillar," a much simpler correction than the others but probably justified in this situation where "pagan" cultic practices are introduced into the text, a practice not expected from later copyists or interpreters. However, Bluedorn (*Yahweh versus Baalism*, 209, n. 90) argues for MT as original.

7.a. LXX^B reads ἀνηγγέλη, "it was told."

7.b. LXX^B reads ἔκλαυσεν, "he wept."

7.c. See syntax of purpose or "consequential force" in *IBHS*, 563, §33.4b.

8.a. Many Heb. MSS follow Q in reading the imperative form of the verb; the K reading in MT is a long form of the infinitive absolute and probably results from a copyist's error.

9.a. A few Heb. MSS read חַיָּה as a fem. noun and so make the verb fem.

9.b. *BHS* suggests following LXX^B in reading the third-person suffix. This is the simpler reading, while the MT represents the more difficult and appropriate reading of the text in which ב serves as a causal particle. OL reads "which the Lord and men glorified in me." For a different defense of the MT see *Preliminary and Interim Report*, 2:97. Barthélemy, *Critique textuelle*, 1:99, sees LXX^B as pietistic theological interpretation and so retains MT.

12.a. See *Note* 8.a above.

13.a. Heb. may be read "gods and men," but LXX and OL read the sg. OL apparently reads "which the Lord and men glorified in me."

14.a. LXX^A does not have "all."

15.a. LXX^A reads πεποίθατε ἐν τῇ σκέπῃ μου, "trust in my protection," while LXX^B reads ὑπόστητε ἐν τῇ σκιᾷ μου, "stand still in my shade."

15.b. LXX^B reads "from me" rather than "from the bramble bush," a simplifying of the original text.

16.a. כִּגְמוּל יָדָיו עֲשִׂיתֶם לוֹ is lit. "the accomplishments or benefits of his hands you have done to him." OL expands: "just as he did to you."

17.a. וַיַּשְׁלֵךְ אֶת־נַפְשׁוֹ מִנֶּגֶד is lit. "and he sent his soul straight ahead," though *BHS* and *HALOT* may be correct in seeing haplography here and reading נגדו with the pronominal suffix, *HALOT* translating "risked his life in it."

19.a. LXX^A reads εὐλογηθείητε, "may you be blessed." OL reads "may you be blessed and may you feast from Abimelech and may he feast from you."

20.a. LXX^A reads "house of Millo," while LXX^B reads "house of Beth-millo." See *Note* 6.b above.

21.a. LXX^A reads ἀπέδρα Ιωαθαμ καὶ ἐπορεύθη ἐν ὁδῷ καὶ ἔφυγεν εἰς Ραρα, "Jotham fled and came in the way and escaped to Beer."

23.a. LXX reads ἐν τῷ οἴκῳ Αβιμελεξ, "with the house of Abimelech," a copyist's addition of a common phrase.

24.a. LXX reads τοῦ ἐπαγαγεῖν, "of the bringing on," apparently a reading of an abbreviated form of the *hip̄'il* infinitive construct. The intrusion of infinitives in this verse suggests the author's special intent to show God's participation and purpose.

25.a. OL reads, "and they called upon all those who were passing through them on the way."

25.b. One Genizah MS reads *hip̄'il* here instead of *hop̄'al*, using the more common verb form but placing the lords of Shechem as the cause of the report to Abimelech.

25.c. LXX^B reads "to King Abimelech," attributing a title otherwise not used for Abimelech.

26.a. Josephus reads the name as Γυάλης, apparently representing Heb. גֻּעַל, "Goal."

26.b. A few Heb. MSS read עֶבֶד, "servant," while Gk. evidence combined with the Vg. leads many to propose the name Obed. Normal usage leads one to expect a proper name—Ebed or Obed—but the ironical style of the passage prompts suspicion that "son of a servant" is the correct reading here.

26.c. LXX^A does not have "they passed through." Some have proposed reading וַיֵּשְׁבוּ, "they resided," or וַיַּעַבְדוּ, "they served" (compare v 28), but עבר + בְ is a frequently used idiom for "to pass through" or "to pass by."

26.d. LXX[B] reads ἤλπισαν ἐν αὐτῷ, "hoped in him."

27.a. Lit. "they gathered the vineyard and they trod and they made festival."

27.b. הִלּוּלִים refers to a sacrifice of praise (Lev 19:24) and to celebratory activities during harvest festivals (Judg 21:21). LXX[B] with ελλουλιμ simply transliterated the Heb. term, while LXX[A] reads χορούς, "dance."

27.c. LXX[B] reads εἰσήνεγκαν, "to bring in," which continues the thought of the previous clause rather than turn attention to the worship place as the text does.

27.d. OL reads the pl. "gods," a possible translation of Heb. since אלהים can refer to the one God or many gods.

28.a. See *Notes* 26.a and 26.b above.

28.b. LXX reads "the son of Shechem," which would be a parallel title for Abimelech, fitting the following clause "that we should serve *him*," or more likely would be a contrast between Abimelech's shady family tree and the proud heritage of the citizens (sons) of Shechem. See Block, 326, n. 823.

28.c. LXX reads ἐπίσκοπος αὐτοῦ δοῦλος αὐτοῦ σὺν τοῖς ἀνδράσιν Εμμωρ πατρὸς Συχεμ, "his administrator, his servant with the men of Hamor, father of Shechem." OL reads "Was not the son of Gideon and Zebul his deputy among the men of Hamor . . . ?" MT reads עִבְדוּ, the imperative form. One expects the *qal* perfect pl. as often proposed and as reflected in the *Translation*. The conjecture is based on literary theories, not on textual evidence, as shown by *Preliminary and Interim Report*, 2:97–98. See Barthélemy's extensive study of the history of explanations (*Critique textuelle*, 1:99–100).

29.a. The simple *wāw* plus the imperfect plus the cohortative הָ- shows purpose or result. See T. O. Lambdin, *Introduction to Biblical Hebrew* (New York: Charles Scribner's Sons, 1971) 119, §107c.

29.b. 1QJudg reads "*they* said"; LXX reads ἐρῶ, "I would say." Both represent attempts to understand the indefinite subject of MT. Apparently, the narrator reenters the picture, concluding Gaal's speech to the leaders of Shechem, and introducing a speech directly challenging Abimelech. *Preliminary and Interim Report* (2:98) hesitates between two opinions here, offering a weak vote for MT and giving in finally to a literary decision, unlike their basic stance: "vv 28–29 are not a continuous discourse of Gaal, but the most offensive extracts of this discourse. This explains the repetition of 'and he said <moreover>' in v. 29b. The meaning of v. 29b is: 'and he said for Abimelech: multiply . . .' or, less likely, 'and he had it said to Abimelech.'" Barthélemy (*Critique textuelle*, 1:100–101) shows the relation to v 28 with a first direct address to Abimelech followed here by a second address to Abimelech. Bluedorn (*Yahweh versus Baalism*, 244, n. 217) argues for MT as *lectio difficilior*.

29.c. LXX[B] reads "him."

29.d. Lit. "make great (or multiply) your host." A few Heb. MSS read רַבָּה, a spelling variant of the *piʿel* imperative. Some propose reading the fem. adjective רַבָּה.

30.a. See *Notes* 26.a and 26.b above.

30.b. 1QJudg, Vg., OL read "very much anger," seeking to add emphasis.

31.a. Heb. term occurs only here; its meaning is disputed: "sly, cunning, in secret, faithless, betraying." LXX[A] (compare OL) reads μετὰ δώρω, "with gifts," a reading one might expect from the context. LXX[B] reads ἐν κρυφῇ, "secretly." *HALOT* concludes, "The different renderings of בְּתָרְמָה in the Vrss. shows that from very early on the meaning of the expression was no longer clear." Many scholars and *BHS* suggest reading בָּאֲרוּמָה, "in Arumah," as in v 41 below, or בֵּת אֲרֻמָה, "house of Arumah." Acknowledging the uncertainty of our knowledge, *Preliminary and Interim Report* (2:99) retains MT, translating "aside." Compare Barthélemy, *Critique textuelle*, 1:101–2. Block (327, n. 830; compare Bluedorn, *Yahweh versus Baalism*, 245–46, n. 221) sees the MT as supported by all the versions and as comprehensible here.

31.b. See *Notes* 26.a and 26.b above.

31.c. חִנָּה denotes immediate action (T. Lambdin, *Introduction*, 150, 168–69). DSS and LXX read והמה, "and they."

31.d. 1QJudg reads "they indeed are besieging against," possibly a case of dittography. See *Note* 30.b. *Preliminary and Interim Report* (2:99) points to RSV and JB conjecture of מְעִירִים, "stirring up" or "exciting," but dismisses it as without textual support. Compare Barthélemy, *Critique textuelle*, 1:102.

33.a. Heb. reads "he."

34.a. Lit. "four heads"; OL reads "and they sat in the field against Shechem in four groups."

35.a. LXX[A] (compare OL) reads καὶ ἐγένετο πρωὶ καὶ ἐξῆλθεν Γααλ, "and morning came and Gaal went out."

36.a. See *Note* 26.a. LXX reads "Gaal, son of Abed."

36.b. Leningrad Codex reading כְ is corrected by some other MSS to בְ.

37.a. See *Note* 26.a.

37.b. LXX (compare OL) has a double reading of מִעִם טַבּוּר הָאָרֶץ—κατὰ θάλασσαν ἀπὸ τοῦ ἐχόμενα τοῦ ὀμφαλοῦ τῆς γῆς, "down to the sea (or westward) from the area next to the navel of the earth." A Cairo Genizah fragment reads טיבור.

37.c. LXX^B reads ἀρχὴ ἑτέρα ἔρχεται διὰ ὁδοῦ Ηλωνμαωνενιμ, "another company comes through the way of Elonmawnenim" (transliteration of Heb.) where LXX^A reads ἀπὸ ὁδοῦ δρυὸς ἀποβλεπόντων, translating אֵלוֹן מְעוֹנְנִים, "oak of those watching."

39.a. See *Note* 26.a.

40.a. DSS reads "pursued them." MT follows scheme of Barak pursuing Sisera and of Gideon pursuing Zeba and Zalmunna, the pursuit being after leaders, not armies. See Bluedorn (*Yahweh versus Baalism*, 247, n. 227) for defense of MT's singular reading.

40.b. 1QJudg reads "to the entrance of the gate of the city"; LXX^A (compare OL) reads "to the entrance of the city." 1QJudg may represent a composite reading combining two text traditions. LXX may represent an attempt to clarify the meaning of city gate.

41.a. LXX^B reads εἰσῆλθεν, "he entered," apparently from בוא or perhaps שוב instead of MT ישׁב. BHS proposes וַיָּשָׁב אֲבִימֶלֶךְ אֲרוּמָה, "and Abimelech returned to Arumah," based on Lucianic readings in Gk. tradition. MT represents the more difficult reading. Again, *Preliminary and Interim Report* (2:99) resists this based on a lack of textual evidence.

41.b. See *Note* 26.a.

42.a. DSS, LXX^B read "he," while LXX^A reads "it was reported to," both efforts at clarifying the generalized "they" of MT.

43.a. LXX^A reads ἐν αὐτῷ, "in it," rather than ἐν ἀγρῷ, "in the field," of LXX^B.

44.a. Heb. הָרָאשִׁים, followed by *BHS*, is pl. in form and appears to refer to more than one "company" of soldiers, but the rest of the verse speaks of the action of the "the two companies," giving the impression that Abimelech had only one company with him. The pl. could be understood as a collective standing for all the troops or more literally "heads" in the company, or Abimelech had three companies with him and then one stayed with him at the gate while the others fought. LXX^B solves the problem with ἀρχηγοί, "princes."

44.b. LXX^A does not have "the entrance of."

44.c. LXX^A reads sg., "he defeated them" (more lit., "he struck them dead").

45.a. LXX^A reads pl., "they captured."

46.a. צְרִיחַ, "tunnel," is called a "vault" by *HALOT* (based on H. N. Rösel, *ZDPV* 92 [1976] 29), an area in the inner temple by K. Jarosh (*Sichem*, 113–14; compare K. Jarosh, "Zur Bedeutung von צריח in Ri 9:46.49," *AUSS* 15 [1977] 57–58) or particularly a subterranean room, crypt (Terrien, *VT* 20 [1970] 331). Carpenter and Grisanti in *NIDOTTE* call it "the stronghold in the house of El-Berith in Shechem . . . where persons sought additional security for either defensive or offensive purposes" (3:845). Block (332) follows Jarosh in calling it "a hold in the tower portion of the temple." Niditch sees it as a hideout (111, 114). Compare 1 Sam 13:6 for its use in hiding places in nature. Here it may refer to underground vaults that only the initiated would know existed. LXX^A (compare OL) reads τὸ ὀχύρωμα οἴκου τοῦ Βααλ διαθήκης, "fortress of the house of Baal of the covenant," while LXX^B reads συνέλευσιν Βαιθηλβεριθ, "stronghold (or gathering place) of Bethelberith" (transliteration of Heb.). LXX^A does not render אֵל, "God," i.e., the divine name *El*.

47.a. LXX^B reads pl., "towers."

48.a. LXX^B reads "Mount Hermon."

48.b. LXX^A reads sg. "ax," leading *BHS* to compare Syr. and propose אַחַת, "one of," for the direct object marker. This is a logical simplification of the more difficult Heb. reading. *Preliminary and Interim Report* (2:100) ignores suggestion to read a third sg. suffix here on lack of textual evidence. The *Report* also rejects הַקַּרְדֻּם, "the axe," saying we must consider elements in the Gk. syntax and grammar that forced translations to alter literal meaning of original language.

48.c. Here and in v 49, LXX^A reads φορτίον, "burden," normally Heb. מַשָּׂא, for MT שׂוֹכָה, "branch." LXX^B reads sg., "branch of the tree."

48.d. Heb. שִׁכְמוֹ, "shoulder," creates a wordplay with שְׁכֶם, "Shechem." LXX reads pl., "shoulders."

49.a. LXX^A reads καὶ ἔκοψαν καὶ αὐτοὶ ἕκαστος φορτίον καὶ ἦραν καὶ ἐπορεύθησαν, "and they cut even they each a burden and they lifted and went," while LXX^B reads καὶ ἔκοψαν καὶ γε ἀνὴρ κλάδον πᾶς ἀνὴρ καὶ ἐπορεύθησαν, "and they cut even each one a branch and went." A few Heb. mss read שׂוֹכוֹ, without the ה, leading *BHS* to propose שׂוֹכְתוֹ or perhaps שׂוֹכֹה from the previous verse.

50.a. LXX^B reads ἐκ Βαιθηλβεριθ καὶ παρενέβαλεν ἐν Θηβης, "out of Bethelberith [Heb. transliteration], and he set up camp in Thebez."

51.a. LXX[B] reads αἱ γυναῖκες τῆς πόλεως καὶ ἔκλεισαν ἔξωθεν αὐτῶν, "the women of the city, and they closed them from the outside," omitting reference to the lords of Shechem, apparently not recognizing the social organization within the text.

52.a. LXX reads "Abimelech."

53.a. GKC, §125b, sees this as one of the few passages where אֶחָד makes a noun "expressly indeterminate"; compare *IBHS*, 251, §13.8a.

53.b. Some MSS seek to restore the "normative" forms of *qal* for this unusual geminate verb that appears in MT to be a *hip̄ʿil*. GKC, §67p, refers to this as a "very peculiar form" and seeks to explain it as an imperfect *qal*.

54.a. LXX[B] reads "my."

54.b. LXX[A] reads "Abimelech."

57.a. A few Heb. MSS read the preposition עַל, "on," for MT.

Form/Structure/Setting

See chap. 6 for further comments on *Form/Structure/Setting* along with table 6.1 in the appendix, narrative and genre comparisons for chaps. 6–9.

The Abimelech narrative in chap. 9 forms an appendix to the Gideon narrative. It employs a complex set of literary forms to create a story of the rise and fall of Israel's first king, a story that completes the Gideon narrative as much as it functions independently, as seen by the repeated use of the name Jerubbaal through to the last word of chap. 9.

Gaß (*Ortsnamen*, 342) succinctly describes the common critical opinion: the Gideon composition was tied to the Abimelech composition only through redactional operations. The Abimelech narrative was originally independent of the Gideon narrative. Gaß then finds six independent small units that were tied together redactionally or simply created: 9:1–6, 7–21, 26–40, 41–45, 46–49, and 50–54. Such a view relegates the final verses (55–57) to the final redactor. See Gaß (342–44) for a history, particularly of German scholarship, on the critical analysis of each unit. Castelbajac (*VT* 51 [2001] 166–85) sees two northern traditions, one with Abimelech as a ruler of a Canaanite city-state (9:1–5a, 6, 26–41) and one with him as a judge of Israel (9:25, 42–54), then joined through a southern redaction using the Jotham material (8–21).

One cannot deny that separate traditions lie behind the various elements in their earliest history, but one need not see such a complex history of redaction. Block rightly concludes that the chapter is structurally complex "but not so complex as to be fragmented into a series of independent and secondary elements" (309, n. 736). One wonders how absolutely consistent a narrator would have to be in using traditions before the source critics would back off and proclaim a narrative as unified in its present telling rather than as the result of centuries of addition and subtraction.

Wong (*Compositional Strategy*, 205–6) argues for compositional techniques that integrate Abimelech into the editorial strategy of the entire book. For him, one key is the parallel between the retribution on Abimelech and that on Adoni-bezek in chap. 1, which he sees as intentionally foreshadowing the Abimelech narrative. This points to the "Canaanisation of this Israelite ruler." Likewise, Wong sees Judg 19 composed in light of Judg 9.

The major redaction brings all the Abimelech elements together as illustrative of the fall of Israelite leadership, using the major themes of the redaction of Judges as a whole—fight for honor and glory, importance of women, destruction of all that Joshua created, revenge and retaliation, choice of gods over God, and divine victory and punishment. Bluedorn reads the narrative from a different perspective, seeing a "double function": "It will show what effect idolatry, which is exemplified in Baal worship, has for Israel. Yet second, the Abimelech narrative will go further and provide the other side of the theological theme started with the Gideon narrative. It will demonstrate that Baal, who serves as an example for any other god, does not have divine power" (*Yahweh versus Baalism,* 183). Such a reading is achieved through constantly seeing analogies and symbolism. Mobley (*Empty Men,* 149) describes the story as a "morality tale about one, perhaps the central moral quality or virtue of ancient Israelite society: fidelity to covenant."

If one lets the Jotham fable set the tone for the entire narrative, then the responsibility for choosing and exercising leadership is much more at the center of the narrative, though fidelity to covenant should lead to proper choice and proper leadership. Thus Amit finds that "Jotham's parable brings out the problematic of the absence of monarchy. There is no place in the kingdom of God for ongoing human leadership; nevertheless, its existence does not negate the uncompromising need of society for authoritative human leadership" (*Book of Judges,* 111). In the end I must agree with Amit that "the issue of leadership is a central thematic axis integrating and unifying the various strands of the book of Judges into one continuous epic" (114). Israel seeks to find a way to follow God and to follow a human leader, a path that proves treacherous to take.

The Abimelech narrative pits unworthy foes against one another in a story anchored by dialogue. Abimelech speaks to his uncles (vv 1–2). They speak to the leaders of Shechem (v 3a), who respond (v 3b). Jotham speaks to the leaders of Shechem (vv 7–20) using a fable in which plants converse with one another (vv 8–15). Gaal, the slave's son, stirs up the leaders of Shechem (vv 28–29) but brings forth a warning to Abimelech from Mayor Zebul (vv 31–33). Even the battle introduction appears in the form of a dialogue between Gaal and Zebul (vv 36–38). Finally, Abimelech's death is preceded by his conversation with his young aide (v 54).

The interpretation of the story comes from the narrator's third-person report using the Hebrew narrative style with *wāw* consecutives (vv 5–6, 21–27, 34–35, 39–57). The major departures from this style appear in (1) the infinitives of v 24, the narrator's central explanatory statement indicting Abimelech and the leaders of Shechem and preparing the reader for the subsequent downfall of both; (2) the complex story of Gideon's ambush on Shechem (vv 43–45), told with disjunctive sentences representing immediate and simultaneous actions; and (3) the notation of God's simultaneous repayment of Abimelech and Shechem in fulfillment of Jotham's fable and curse. Thus syntax ties the entire chapter into one extended narrative.

The narrative belongs to Israel's traditions about Shechem. One set of these traditions portrays Shechem as the central location of Israel's conquest-period worship on Ebal and Gerizim (Deut 11:29; 27:4, 13; Josh 8:30, 33), climaxing in the covenant ceremony of Josh 24. The other set of Shechem narratives shows the wickedness of Shechem as here and as in the intriguing story of Gen 34 with the rape of Dinah, the negotiations to join forces and intermarry, the demand for circumcision, and the murder of Shechem's males, making Israel "odious" to the Canaanite inhabitants of the land. Shechem was also the center of Jeroboam's rebellion against Rehoboam (1 Kgs 12:1) and the site of Jeroboam's royal residence (1 Kgs 12:25). So Schneider sees "another reference in Judges with barely veiled allusions to the north/south conflict" (136).

Judg 9 features temples and worship centers, but it does not have Israel going to the top of Ebal and Gerizim. Rather, we have one temple or tower after another occupied by the lords of Shechem, not by Israelites. And one temple is called the house of El Berith, a strange name for Yahweh, but an interesting name for a blended worship of the Canaanite high god and Israel's covenant God. The story of Abimelech thus royally illustrates the danger and evil that come from kingship out of Shechem, kingship that is murderous and selfish and features false religious loyalties, kingship like that of Jeroboam I.

Comment

1–6 The narrator's introduction to Abimelech's coronation, in which he claims Baalistic heritage as justification for his kingship, stops the reader in his or her tracks. The location is correct, the place of Joshua's covenant renewal with Israel. But the actions are horrendous, seventy murders authorized by all the lords of Shechem, lords being expressed by the Hebrew term בעלי, which can also mean the "baals." Based on the analogy of Gen 14:13, Block sees these "aristocrats" as "the human signatories to the covenant with El/Baal-Berith" (311). Schneider is right in setting the tone for the entire narrative by noting, "It is not clear who the people of Shechem were presumed to be in this account and what their relationship was to Israel" (135). She continues by correcting Boling's view that "the objective of Gideon and Abimelech had been to weld together a nation-state centered in Shechem" (170). This would place Gideon's approval and perhaps even planning behind what Abimelech does and would expand the geographical setting of Abimelech's narrative far beyond its narrow confines. The narrator thus pictures Abimelech's coronation as "the result of human interests and not of divine choice" (Amit, *Book of Judges,* 103). Amit (112) sees a complex narrative theme here, citing both positive and negative characteristics of Abimelech so that despite the negative traits the men of Israel remain loyal to him. The men of Israel include the army supporting Abimelech and the group that offered the kingship to Gideon. If this is the case, the narrator does very little to make the connection and brings "Israel" into the picture only in quite subtle ways. Israel somehow lets Abimelech be a secondary ruler (v 22), but does not appear in the narrative except to slip away home after his demise.

1–2 We enter a section that in a strong narrative statement "underscores the tension between two forms of polity, one decentralized and the other centralized" (Niditch, 115). Abimelech was introduced in the final transition piece in chap. 8. He comes to the forefront at a time when Israel is devoted to the baals, especially Baal Berith, or the lord of the covenant, but is not devoted to the memory of Gideon or Jerubbaal. From a traditional viewpoint, Abimelech is the least likely to succeed, being the son of a secondary wife living away from the clan's center in Ophrah. Younger says, "Abimelech is not happy with his position as an outsider, and he is dominated by a ruthless craving to change his marginal existence. . . . He is inspired by his father in the desire to be king, but at the same time he rejects, hates, and despises his father" (220). Knowing he has no support among his father's family, Abimelech turns to his uncles on his mother's side and other members of their clan for support. See Matthews, 102–4, for marriage customs and regulations: "Where the legal difference [between a 'wife' and a 'concubine'] arose was in the sense of unquestioned membership in a specific household and in the inheritance rights of the children of a concubine" (103). Abimelech's mother is at home in Shechem, Tell Balatah. (For bibliography, see Younger, 228, n. 35; Gaß, *Ortsnamen*, 300–301, n. 2203.)

Schneider points out that "because of his mixed origin, [Abimelech] did not have authority in either community" (136). Lacking standing in Shechem, he appeals to clan members who do have standing to represent him to the leaders of Shechem. In so doing, he places himself under condemnation by Deuteronomic legal tradition (Deut 17) as shown by D. Daube ("One from among Your Brethren Shall You Set King over You," *JBL* 90 [1971] 480). Abimelech tries a logical argument. Should they let seventy brothers from another community rule them, or should they let a kinsman rule them? In so stating his case, he may well be purposely misrepresenting the intentions of his half brothers who remained at Ophrah, possibly still in mourning for their father (Jordan, 159). Nothing in the text would support Schneider's claim that "the nature of the question implies that Shechem was already under some kind of control by the seventy sons of Jerubbaal" (136). Rather, Abimelech uses the presence of the seventy sons as a threat against Shechem. "Abimelech makes up this threat to become leader himself" (Bluedorn, *Yahweh versus Baalism*, 205).

Apparently, Shechem is experiencing a leadership crisis and needs outside help. Abimelech has only one advantage and so uses that. He has kinship ties to Shechem that Gideon's other sons do not have. These kinship ties are not necessarily Israelite ones. As Matthews (104) sees it, "It is quite possible that the people of Shechem at that time were predominately Canaanite, which lowers Abimelech's status as an ethnically mixed member of Jerubbaal's household." If not Canaanite, the people of Shechem represent an Israel that has "become spiritually Canaanites" (Younger, 233).

3–4 Shechem's leaders make an emotional response. Kinship rules over logic or context. For their ruler they want a "brother," a term that possibly extends beyond blood relationships to include religious unity. If so, this implies that Abimelech is perceived to worship Baal. This religious brotherhood would be Abimelech's "most effective" argument (Jordan, 158). The Shechemite leaders pay Abimelech seventy pieces of silver for his support, funds taken from the temple of Baal Berith. So an Israelite leader becomes openly supported by a religious institution that is pagan at worst and a center of blended worship at best. And the institution "eventually financed its own destruction at the hands of its own people" (Jordan, 159).

Schneider identifies the sad trend that begins with this conflict: "This is the first example in Judges where lineage and clan loyalties influenced the community to such an extent that they chose their own leader. . . . The role of clan and tribal loyalties will grow to such an extent that it becomes a contributing factor to the civil war at the end of the book" (136).

Abimelech shows his financial abilities by using the money to hire "men without discipline or principles." Such men readily follow Abimelech. More literally one might translate the description of these men as "empty and reckless." This may refer to "rebellious have-nots" (see B. Kedar-Kopstein, רִיק *ryq, TDOT,* 13:482). They are impoverished people, empty of material resources (compare Judg 11:3; Prov 12:11; 28:19) and so are willing to accept Abimelech's money (see B. Kedar-Kopstein, רֵיק *ryq, TDOT,* 13:479–84). Mobley (*Empty Men,* 154) describes Abimelech's "empty men" as "mercenaries, misfits, the penniless and landless: empty men fell between the cracks of kinship structures and operated beyond the bonds of filial honor codes." The adjective, except when used in Jer 51:34, "always signifies that which is useless, to no purpose, in vain" (J. Shepherd, *NIDOTTE,* 3:1107). Interestingly 2 Chr 13:7 describes Jeroboam I's followers with the same term. Saul's daughter Michal uses the term to describe her despised husband, David (2 Sam 6:20).

The second term, פֹּחֵז, "characterizes reckless or arrogant people not restrained by the usual conventions of proper social behavior or the normal expectations for a a person in a sacred position. . . . They arrogantly follow their own desires and do not care about others" (G. V. Smith, *NIDOTTE,* 3:609), certainly an apt description of Abimelech and his band of rogues.

5 Abimelech marches from his unlocated home to his half brothers' home with their father in Ophrah. The terse narrative concentrates on only one action there—the murder of seventy men, the sons of Jerubbaal. The use of this form of the father's name may well be intended to underscore the Baal connection and emphasize how Gideon's actions have led to the worship of Baal (8:33). No matter how one rates Gideon's life, what he left at his death can in no way be acclaimed. Joshua left at least one generation of people who knew and followed God (Judg 2:7). Gideon has left only a people turned to Baal.

The killing "on one stone" leaves room for several interpretations. The meaning may be as simple as showing the intentionality of the killings by portraying them as a series carried out at one place. Thus Block describes the slaughter as "a calculated, brutal act of murder, not a quick slaughter of unsuspecting victims" (312). This may well be slaughterhouse language, as in 1 Sam 14:33–34 primarily (Block, 312), but sacrificial undertones may sound here, showing how far Abimelech has strayed from Yahwistic faith and practice (Boling, 171; Jordan, 159; Bluedorn, *Yahweh versus Baalism,* 207, with further bibliography). The killing effectively removes from Israel any legitimate leadership derived through family or dynastic ties and leaves the central figure in Israelite leadership as a half-breed with closer ties to the Canaanite Baal worshipers than to Israel. "YHWH is, so to speak, eradicated from the narrative" (Bluedorn, *Yahweh versus Baalism,* 206).

One son out of the seventy escapes, "because he hid." This prepares for the next narrative segment.

6 The Shechemite leaders officially crown Abimelech king. The people of Beth-millo join them. *Beth-millo* means "house of filling," probably referring to a construction technique of filling up or pouring material into a site to create an artificial terrace and may be identical to the tower of Judg 9:46 (Younger, 221; Boling, 171). The beth-millo would be the structure erected on the artificial terrace. Gaß (*Ortsnamen,* 311–12) identifies it most probably with the acropolis of Shechem with its temple and the buildings related to the temple organization. Block sees "all Beth-millo" as "another designation for the nobility, those who had authority to participate in Abimelech's installation as king, perhaps the official administrators of the city" (313). (Compare M. Görg, "Beth-Millo," *ABD,* 1:690, who concludes: "Beth-millo may thus be a term for the residential area of the king at Shechem [and Jerusalem, respectively] and may designate the administrative center of the city.")

The mention of "all Beth-millo" may consciously differentiate two groups, those from Shechem and those from Beth-millo, or it may point to a group who lived on the acropolis in Shechem and had special political, religious, or military power and privileges. The effect here is to point to the inclusion of everyone connected in any way with Shechem, especially those seeking to assert any kind of control or power. As such, this may separate Shechem in this time period from Israel. The generation(s) after Joshua apparently lost control of one of Israel's most sacred shrines. In so doing they ceded it in some fashion to Canaanites who worshiped Baal Berith or El Berith there, carrying on the Joshua covenant tradition perhaps, but in a paganized fashion. The two divine names here probably represent variations of the same type of worship, one using the name of the Canaanite high god El, the other representing a localized form of the worship, now dedicated to the fertility god Baal. See Judg 8:33; 9:34. (Compare T. J. Lewis, "The Identity and Function of El/Baal Berith," *JBL* 115 [1996] 401–23, who points to a Ugaritic mention of El Berith and sees El Berith as a pre-Israelite treaty partner in Shechem who also assumed the title baal or lord of the covenant.) I see no reason for H. Schmid's argument that Beth-millo represents an Israelite group within Shechem ("Der Tempelbau Salomos in religionsgeschichtlicher Sicht," in *Archäologie und Altes Testament*, FS K. Galling, ed. A. Kuschke and E. Kutsch [Tübingen: Mohr (Siebeck), 1970] 241–50).

The final phrases in the verse show the religious situation in Shechem and possibly the corruption of the text. If "at the Oak of the Pillar" is the correct reading (see *Note* 9:6.d above), then Shechemite worship had incorporated symbols foreign to Israelite religion. An אלון is a large tree, often translated "terebinth." Pagan gods were often worshiped under these trees (Ezek 6:13; Hos 4:13). Patriarchs also worshiped in connection with these trees (Gen 12:6; 13:18; 14:13; 18:1; 35:4). Josh 19:33 uses אלון in a compound to mark a boundary, the same compound reappearing in Judg 4:11 as the home of Heber the Kenite, Jael's husband. As frequently, Judges takes up a term used positively in Joshua (24:26) and turns it into negative religion and politics, having the king crowned not by priests in the tabernacle or temple but by the political leaders under the terebinth. Such a tree is distantly connected to the Jeroboam narrative in 1 Kgs 13:14. Thus Richter finds the parable directed against the reign of Jeroboam (*Traditionsgeschichtliche Untersuchungen*, 282–86).

Here אלון is closely connected with מֻצָּב, possibly meaning the "set up" or "propped up" terebinth (*DCH*, 5:736–37), though *BHS* is probably correct in emending the text to הַמַּצֵּבָה, "the terebinth of the pillar." This would represent a piling up of terms used for pagan practices (Exod 23:24; 34:13; Deut 7:5; 12:3) connected originally with patriarchal worship (Gen 28:18, 22; 31:13; 35:14; Exod 24:4) but forbidden for Israel (Lev 26:1; Deut 16:22). Joshua raised up a stone that is not directly called a *maṣṣēbâ* but may be regarded as one (Josh 24:26). Interestingly, the people of Judah under Rehoboam angered God with their pillars (1 Kgs 14:23).

Zevit (*Religions of Ancient Israel*, 256) finds in the archaeological evidence at least eight "Israelite cult places" featuring standing stones or *maṣṣēbôt*. These standing stones "were objects of veneration and worship, conventionalized aniconic representations of a deity—aniconic only in the sense that they did not attempt to represent a deity" (257). They apparently were "conceived as embodying a real presence" (258). But how Israel used them remains mysterious (260).

R. Albertz explains:

> The problem was that Yahweh simply entered this traditional cultic symbolism of Palestine with no prior reflection by the people on whether they could thus give appropriate expression to the special historical experiences of liberation that they had had with Yahweh. Massebas and asheras were from the start fertility symbols, and they represented the divine in the male-female duality which was so typical of the religions of the Near East (Jer. 2.27). (*History of Israelite Religion*, 1:85)

Zevit (*Religions of Ancient Israel*, 259) differentiates the cultic stones from memorial stones set up to celebrate events or mark funeral sites. He uses Gen 28 and 31 to describe "the ritual establishing of a bond between the person and the deity whose power indwelt the *masseba* that was declared a *byt 'lhym*, 'house of god(s)'" (261). The stones "represented, expressed, and guaranteed a continuous, immanent presence" (261). These stories, of course, are connected with patriarchal Bethel but may represent a charge against Jeroboam's founding of Bethel as a northern kingdom sanctuary, though Zevit argues that "apparently, Israelites established their own *massebot*, and Isa. 19:19 speaks positively about a *masseba* for YHWH. . . . It is likely that the *massebot* from Arad, the Bull Site, various loci at Dan, and Lachish loci 81 were Yahwistic, aniconic channels for the presence of YHWH" (261–62). These, at best questionable, cultic symbols are located explicitly in Shechem and not on Ebal or Gerizim, adding another negative note to religious practices in Shechem since the time of Joshua's covenant renewal. Thus Abimelech assumes a Canaanite kingship over a Canaanite people in a Canaanite temple. Schneider identifies this as "the theological low point in Israel's relationship to the deity. The Israelites no longer recognized their deity's preeminence" (138).

7 Here begins a narrative of revenge on Shechem, introduced by Jotham's bitter fable of the folly of monarchy. The news of Abimelech's coronation spreads fast. An anonymous group informs young Jotham in his hideout, prompting him to go to the site of the coronation, to Shechem. However, he goes to Mount Gerizim, the mount of blessing near Shechem (Deut 11:29; 27:12; compare Josh 8:33), not to the sacred tree and stone inside Shechem. He invites the "lords of Shechem" to come out and listen to him, promising them an audience with God. The lords believed their god(s) listened to them in the worship sites inside Shechem, but Jotham claims that God will listen only as he speaks from the top of Gerizim.

8 Jotham appears in parallel to the prophet of Judg 6:7–10. Just as that prophet's warning came true, so will Jotham's. His prophetic role does not mean that all he says or does is directed by God, for he never mentions the personal name of God—*Yahweh*—and only uses *Elohim*, the generic word for God, twice in ambiguous fashion. When he delivers his climactic curse, he does so in defense of his father, not in the name of God. (See Webb, [1987] 155.) Bluedorn argues that the narrator "accepts the viewpoint of Jotham's speech" which "articulates the theme for the Abimelech narrative" (*Yahweh versus Baalism*, 211). Jotham seeks to show "that benefits conferred entail an obligation to show loyalty to the one who conferred them" (Webb, [1987] 156).

Jotham employs the literary fable to catch their attention and deliver his message. This could even be an originally "Canaanite" fable from Shechem (Bluedorn, *Yahweh versus Baalism*, 218). The fable points to "the stupidity of the coronators"

(V. P. Hamilton, *Handbook on the Historical Books*, 136), while the interpretation focuses on the curse of both Abimelech and Shechem. Thus the interpretation of the fable does not reflect a one-to-one relationship with the elements of the fable, leading many critics to find separate literary sources and redaction here. (See Bluedorn, *Yahweh versus Baalism*, 212–17, for details.) Block lists seven marks of literary tension, but then answers the critics effectively:

> The points of disjunction are unmistakable. Nevertheless, to argue on these grounds that the fable has been artificially inserted into the narrative is to impose modern Western standards of literary consistency upon an ancient historiographic treatise with a distinct theological and rhetorical agenda. When rhetoricians employ illustrative stories, they do not generally insist that every element of the story be consistent with every element of the rest of the speech. . . . For all its distinctive features, it suits the original rhetorical context and fits in perfectly with its present literary environment. (316–17)

The use of fable is rare in the Old Testament, the other occurrence coming in 2 Kgs 14:9. A fable is "a short tale, usually involving animals or plants as characters, which implicitly makes a particular ideological statement or expresses a moral principle" (B. O. Long, *2 Kings*, FOTL 10 [Grand Rapids: Eerdmans, 1991] 300). In accordance with the genre, trees make a decision to anoint a king. This is the only time in Judges where מָשַׁח, "anoint," appears. This indicates the ritual act of pouring oil on a person inducted into an office. (See J. N. Oswalt, *NIDOTTE*, 2:1123–27.) Only the trees go through the proper procedure of installing a king. Later (1 Kgs 12:20) Israel would crown Jeroboam king without any mention of anointing him.

The olive stands as the trees' first choice. (See R. Frankel, *Wine and Oil Production in Antiquity in Israel and Other Mediterranean Countries*, JSOTMS 10 [Sheffield: Sheffield Academic, 1999].) Nearly every village had facilities to grind grain, crush olives to make oil, and press out grapes for wine. Olives were most important, being one of the three staples, along with grain and grapes, in Israelite life (M. D. Futato, *NIDOTTE*, 1:1097–98; compare Hos 2:8; Joel 2:19). They were beautiful (Hos 14:7), provided staple food, produced oil for cooking and lights (Exod 27:27), and served many other purposes. They represented God's gifts that Israel did not earn (Josh 24:13). Block describes olive oil as probably "the most valuable agricultural product in the ancient world" (318). Olives, grain, and wine also represented the resources cruel kings took away from the common people and gave to the servants employed in the royal court (1 Sam 8:14).

9   The chosen king olive refuses the offer. His product glorifies both humans and God; he has more important things to do. People use the olive's oil cosmetically, medicinally, and nutritionally. God receives sacrifices and anoints rulers with olive oil. Bringing honor and strength to others ranks higher than holding power over others.

10–11   The trees turn to the fig tree with the offer of rule. Fig trees often symbolized peace, safety, and prosperity (1 Kgs 4:25 [Heb. 5:5]; Mic 4:4; Zech 3:10). "When first ripe a fig was considered an unmatched delicacy, but when allowed to rot, it became a stomach-turning, nauseating product, good for nothing but the refuse pile" (see E. C. Hostetter, *NIDOTTE*, 4:268–69). In a land without sugar, figs and honey served as sweeteners. Fig leaves could even serve as clothing (Gen

3:7). "The fruit, fresh or dried, could be made into cakes and wine. . . . The leaves were woven into baskets, dishes, and umbrellas. Medicinally, the fruit proved an effective laxative and tonic, as well as a poultice. The fruit, pounded into a pulp, was used by King Hezekiah to cure a malignant swelling" (I. Jacob and W. Jacob, *ABD*, 2:806). Israel needs the fig's sweetness much more than it needs a king's bitter rule, and so the fig refuses the offer of kingship as well.

12–13 The grape vine becomes the next royal candidate. The source of wine, the vine symbolized life, fertility, and joy (Pss 4:7; 128:3; Eccl 9:7). "In the ancient Near East, with its scarcity of water, wine was a necessity rather than a luxury" (*DBI*, 953). "The fruit, grapes, may be consumed fresh or dried into raisins and currants. Its juice may be produced into wine or vinegar. The leaves are edible, and the remainder of the plant has been used for fodder and tannin. Wine was used as an anaesthetic and to reduce the anguish of capital punishment" (*ABD*, 2:810).

Grapes could defy expectations and become wild and sour (Isa 5:2; Jer 2:21). The presence of wine, olive oil, and grain symbolized God's covenant blessings, while their absence showed Israel's disobedience bringing divine covenant curses (Deut 28:39, 51; Hos 2:21–22; 9:2). The vine remains content to supply joy and merriment for God's people rather than rule over them, perhaps with the implication of making them drunk with their own sense of power.

14–15 Finally, in desperation, the trees turn to the bramble bush with the offer of rule. "The bramble grows where no other vegetation can, and thus it becomes an apt symbol of wilderness" (Matthews, 106–7). The precise identification of the plant indicated by Hebrew אָטָד is not known. Ps 58:9 (Heb. 10) identifies its use as fuel burned up under cooking pots. Otherwise, it is useless except to stick and prick. Irony oozes from the bramble's answer. Only the bramble speaks of anointing, echoing the trees' original purpose. The bramble wants to be sure he has all the official trappings, including religious certification, effectively asking the leaders to take an oath. Using the language Joshua used to bring the people back into covenant with God (Josh 24:14) and the language Jotham will soon use with Israel (Judg 9:16, 19), the bramble demands that Israel act "in lasting faithfulness," that is, with a true heart and a lifelong commitment.

Finally, the bramble offers an invitation that Younger (223) properly qualifies as a "physical absurdity." The Israelites can now find refuge or protection in the great amount of shade a bramble can offer, a shade marked by pricks and sticks. A further irony appears here, in that in Israel's environment, the shade of the king referred to special protection a king offered (Younger, 223, n. 20).

The bramble is ready for a negative reaction from the people. If they are not acting in truth and faithfulness, the bramble is not willing to return to life as normal, the alternative chosen by the olive and fig and vine. Rather the bramble threatens drastic action. The shrub capable of heating cooking pots before it disappears into ashes will send out a massive fire to consume the fabled "cedars of Lebanon," far to the northeast and far too extensive to fear what little heat the bramble can generate. Thus the parable indicates, according to Jordan, that "the only kind of men who desire political authority for its own sake are bramble men—unproductive men who seek to attain fame and fortune by taking it from others who are productive" (165). Or as Niditch perceives the meaning, the Israelite author may be suggesting that "monarchy is a necessary evil and that many kings are useless, but the political arrangement, flawed as it is, has a chance to work only when both parties enter into the agreement in good faith. Jotham's interpretation and application of the *mashal* continues this line of thought and directs a stinging critique at Abimelech's coup and his kingship" (116). The fable also seems to paint a picture by which to judge Jeroboam's coup and kingship.

16 The syntactical insertion of וְעַתָּה, "therefore," indicates the change of speaker here from the bramble to Jotham. The same syntactical tool appears in Josh 24:14 and 23 when Joshua calls the people, on the basis of his historical evidence, to serve God. Jotham uses the expression to call his people to attention to hear the prophetic judgment standing before them. They have heard in Jotham's prophetic fable the type of people willing to serve as king. Now they must examine their own motivation in crowning Abimelech king. To the bramble's call for faithful action, Jotham adds a request for תָּמִים, "integrity" (defined in *HALOT* as "complete, unscathed, intact" and as "in integrity, exclusively and honestly"). Jotham defines this as paying back to Jerubbaal "what his work deserved." The narrator has already informed us that Israel did not act in loyalty to Jerubbaal (Judg 8:35). This one who forced Baal to contend (Judg 6:32) and led armies to victory, even if vengefully and with selfish motives, left seventy sons as possible leaders for Israel. How could they possibly choose the one son who shares motivation with the bramble? Schneider perceives "the implication . . . that the people who designate the ruler have as much responsibility as the ruler" (140).

17 Jotham interrupts his conditional sentence to defend his father with typical youngest son enthusiasm and loyalty. In his view Gideon/Jerubbaal risked his own life to deliver Israel from Midian. Here he shares his father's opinion that God must at least share honor and glory for the victory, when God had done everything possible to show that God alone brought delivery. As Schneider points out, "Jotham claimed that in his eyes his family was wronged, whereas according to the rules established by the deity, the deity was wronged by the hero, his family, and the Israelites" (140).

18 A contrast sentence interrupts the narrative structure to lay blame on Jotham's audience. The narrative audience is simply "lords of Shechem" (Judg 9:7). They may have some kind of political/military alliance with Israel (Gen 34; Josh 24), but they worship and act like worshipers of Baal or El, not like loyal devotees of Yahweh. They have chosen Abimelech, not on the basis of what his family did for Israel but on the basis of kinship. And this kinship comes through his mother, an אָמָה, "slave girl," quite a derogatory categorization, "a taunt to diminish Abimelech's legitimacy" (Schneider, 141). Still, even they should choose a king on the basis of his gifts for the people, not on the basis of his threats to destroy the people. The narrative says Abimelech killed his brothers (Judg 9:5), but Jotham makes the Shechemite leaders share the blame. They have shown no respect for the family of Jerubbaal and have chosen a bramble-like king who claims more power than he has.

19 Having leveled his charge against the leaders of Shechem, Jotham returns to his conditional sentence from v 16. Jotham wants joy for all people. But joy can come only to a people who act "in faithfulness and in integrity."

20–21 Jotham finishes the condition with a curse, a curse on the basis of his father's honor, not Yahweh's honor or word. In so doing he shows he stands with his father in seeking family honor, not with God in seeking divine honor. If the people's actions are motivated by something beside faithfulness and integrity, then the bramble's curse will come on Shechem. But that is not all. Reciprocally, the curse will also come on Abimelech. Both parties to the agreement will face destruction.

Then Jotham follows the example of Hagar (Gen 21:14–21), living in the wilderness near a well. The reader's anticipation is built up, expecting Jotham to gain rightful political control over his father's territory, or at least over Shechem. But is Jotham to be placed alongside his father as the "noblest characters" and "real heroes" of the narrative (Bluedorn, *Yahweh versus Baalism*, 264)? Jotham never again appears. The narrator leaves him in the wilderness, having served his purpose. The narrator shows interest in Jotham's curse (Judg 9:57), not in Jotham's future. The theme is "the self-destructiveness of evil" (Jordan, 153), not the choice of a particular future leader (compare Schneider, 142). The narrator looks to God's swift retribution, "the swiftest in the book" (Younger, 224), not to Jotham's career. Thus Webb claims that "retribution remains the primary theme in the Abimelech narrative, for by interpreting the evil done by Abimelech and his followers as faithlessness, the narrator has established a firm thematic link with the Gideon narrative proper" ([1987] 156; compare Block, 336). The narrator's notes in vv 23–24 and 55–57 support such a claim.

Yet divine retribution is only a part of the story. Divine retribution is a means of demonstrating the ongoing power of Yahweh and the utter failure of kingship instigated by an individual's thirst for power rather than by divine calling. Retribution shows how God reacts to one experiment in leadership, but it does not replace leadership as the central theme of the book.

22–24 Only here does Judges use the Hebrew verb שָׂרַר, "to rule." This term places Abimelech in second place—like Sisera in Judg 4:2 and 7 or like Oreb and Zeeb in Judg 8:6 and 14—not as the authoritative king. (See Bluedorn, *Yahweh versus Baalism*, 230–31, for possible wordplays and puns here, and Wong, *Compositional Strategy*, 203, n. 46, for argument that Abimelech served as king over all Israel.) The minor judges שָׁפַט, "judge," Israel. Jotham's fable plays with the verb מָלַךְ, "to be king over."

In one way or another Abimelech led Israel for three years, the shortest period of leadership by an individual judge in the book and a notation that elsewhere comes at the end of a leader's rule, not at the beginning, where notation of enemy oppression usually occurs. Bluedorn (*Yahweh versus Baalism*, 212) may be correct in seeing the narrator suggest "Abimelech's reign as an oppression and Abimelech as Israel's enemy." Again, the mysterious designation appears to refer to the entire twelve tribes. But Block clarifies: "as elsewhere in the book, 'Israel' does not necessarily mean the entire nation but may be restricted to a local area the narrator recognizes as representative of the country as a whole" (322) or to Shechemite tribes only, who have recognized Abimelech's leadership (Younger, 224). How expansively the territory reaches beyond Shechem, the narrator does not say. The present context shows no sign of united Israelite effort nor any action of Abimelech for all Israel.

Controlling Israel's covenant center (Josh 24) provides the only claim to power over Israel as a whole, and even then Abimelech never appears to have resided in Shechem. Bluedorn (*Yahweh versus Baalism*, 198) puts us on the right track: "The idolatrous Shechemites represent idolatrous Israel." The people of Israel no longer take part in the narrative except as outside observers. What they see is what they have become in their worship of Baal Berith, forgetting all Yahweh has done for them. Bluedorn (*Yahweh versus Baalism*, 203) can go so far as stating, "The narrator thus remains the only distinctively Yahwistic character in the Abimelech narrative."

Abimelech stands out among the characters featured in Judges. The spirit of God does not come upon him as with Othniel (Judg 3:10), Gideon (6:34), Jephthah (11:29), and Samson (13:25; 14:6, 9; 15:14). Rather, "God sent an evil spirit between Abimelech and the lords of Shechem" (Judg 9:23). Here is "a chilling change in the operation of the 'Spirit of the Lord'" (Block, 335). The least that can be said here is Matthews' suggestion that this "may be a literary vehicle that allows the editor to make clear that there is a divine touch involved in these events" (109). This resembles the description of God's action with Saul (1 Sam 16:14–23; 18:10; 19:9; compare 1 Kgs 22:19–23; Job 2:10).

Here is a blatant and disturbing picture of God's sovereignty. Olson notes, "The divine spirit actually causes division and conflict between people rather than uniting them" (817). D. F. Watson describes the biblical stance: "While the nation of Israel was independent and flourishing, while the corporate body was doing well, evil was viewed as the retribution from God upon individuals for sin and breaking of covenant (Judg 2:11–15; 2 Sam 12:9–10; 1 Kgs 2:44). This evil served as a deterrent to pursuing further evil (Deut 19:20; Jer 36:3)" ("Evil," *ABD*, 2:678–79). "Thus God's spirit stirred up divisions among them so that their power would be diffused and their treachery finally ended," says Olson (818). John Goldingay offers a more philosophical description:

> a dynamic semipersonal force, semi-independent of Yhwh, the negative equivalent to Yhwh's commitment and steadfastness as forces that are semi-independent of Yhwh, forces Yhwh sends off to do things (Pss 23:6; 43:3). Anger is not a divine attribute in the same sense as love is; the instinct to love emerges from God without any outside stimulus, but God gets angry only as a reaction to outside stimulus. Yet God does get angry. (*Israel's Faith*, Old Testament Theology 2 [Downers Grove, IL: IVP Academic, 2006] 141)

The evil spirit represents God's angry response to both sides of a rebellious, treacherous situation. The term allows the narrator to make a play on good (טוב) and evil (רע). As Younger (224–25) phrases it: "Jerub-Baal had done 'good' to the Israelites (8:35), who repaid it with evil; what Abimelech argued was 'good/better' (9:2) became evil for the Israelies (9:23)." This evil spirit hangs over the rest of the Judges narrative and on into that of Saul. Webb sees it as "a reminder that God has a different principle of operation he can invoke at his discretion, and if it can be invoked against Abimelech and the men of Shechem, why not against Israel in general" ([1987] 159). Such treachery, disloyalty, and violent revenge belong in the evil camp in human vocabulary and assessment. Biblical theology attributes even such elements of history "to the work of God, whose hand may be hidden to the personalities involved but is obvious to the eyes of faith" (Block, 322) but whose moral nature as just and good is not affected by the sending of the evil spirit.

Both the lords of Shechem and Abimelech had flaunted their evil decisions in God's face. Now he pits them against one another to abolish both evil parties. Action begins as "the lords of Shechem dealt treacherously with Abimelech" (Judg

9:23). "Dealt treacherously" (בגד) describes action contrary to expectations based on past relationships and agreements. Isa 33:1 summarizes the context as one of treacherous action and then more closely defines this in Isa 33:8: "its oaths are despised, its obligation is disregarded" (NRSV). In Judges, God's purpose is clear. Abimelech has acted contrary to all family relationship expectations, putting political ambition above family loyalty. Shechem has acted contrary to all political laws by empowering Abimelech to kill his half brothers. "The implication," says R. Wakely, "is that the spirit of discord came in fulfillment of Jotham's curse and as inevitable retribution on the fratricidal Abimelech for his mass murder and on the Shechemites for their support of him (cf. 9:56–57)" (*NIDOTTE*, 1:582).

25 Shechem's treacherous act unrolls as an ambush story much like Josh 8, Judg 16, and Judg 20. The leaders were "feeling that they were not receiving adequate value for their support of the warlord" (Matthews, 109). Here the ambush is not a military strategy so much as an act of highway brigands attacking travelers (compare Judg 6:2–6).

26–29 The entrance of Gaal interrupts this narrative. Gaal is simply "the son of a slave" (v 26). Such a derogatory characterization leads the reader to expect the worst from this narrative newcomer. But Shechem does not share these negative expectations. Shechem's leaders "trusted him" (v 26). Trust (בטח) is certainly "a concept of central theological importance in the OT" (R. W. L. Moberly, *NIDOTTE*, 1:644). God is the ultimate object of trust as seen in texts like Pss 62:8 (Heb. 9); 115:9–11; Isa 26:3–4; 30:15. Moberly observes, "Some of the things in which people put their trust are substitutes for God, however naturally worthy of trust they may appear to be in themselves. . . . The logic of biblical monotheism requires that all these things be used in the service of God and not set up as alternatives to him" (*NIDOTTE*, 1:645).

The Shechemite leaders had heard Jotham's fable and knew the dangers of trusting in human allies rather than following God's directions. Thus they turn their trust from Abimelech to Gaal, the first potential leader to enter the scene. They show their trust by celebrating a religious festival, but a drunken one in keeping with baalistic fertility overtones. Block sees that "the scene of Shechem taken over by a mob of drunken men contrasts sharply with the picture of well-being Abimelech had promised the city" (326).

Based on the covenant nuances associated with Shechem, the leaders of Shechem may well have used the occasion to enter into covenant relationships with Gaal as their new leader. Part of such covenant making in the house of the lord of the covenant would be cursing their enemy, Abimelech. As the NET textual note says, "Here the verb probably describes more than a mental attitude. It is likely that the Shechemites made an alliance with Gaal and were now trusting him for protection in return for their loyalty (and probably tribute)." In so doing they show "not only their foolhardy bravado but also their nonworship of Yahweh" (Matthews, 109–10).

Gaal apparently sets up a contrast between Abimelech and Shechem, with Abimelech having no history or social standing and Shechem possessing ancient history and social importance. Such a contrast makes clear that Shechem has no reason to serve Abimelech, the son of one who forces Baal to contend for his place among the gods. Rather, Shechem should shift loyalty to Gaal, who claims to belong to the ancient Hamor tradition connected to Shechem (see Gen 33:19).

As is wont in this chapter, the character Zebul appears unexpectedly out of thin air. The original audience understood the meaning. The modern reader has to wait a bit. Likewise, Zebul's title פָּקִיד, "official," remains nebulous in its meaning here. Block (326, n. 824) sees it as "recruiter" or "party whip."

Has Abimelech appointed Zebul to office? Does Zebul represent Abimelech in political consultations? Or has Zebul exercised leadership over Abimelech? A social chasm separates Abimelech and Zebul from Shechem. And Gaal, the son of a servant, recognizes it. So Gaal calls Shechem back to its roots, serving the family line of Hamor and its tradition, not that of Abimelech, which has no tradition, especially in Shechem. The syntax adds an extraneous "we" in Hebrew at the end to show solidarity between Gaal and Shechem, not between Abimelech and Shechem. But who has better claim to the Shechemite tradition, a son of an Ophrahite's concubine or the son of a slave named Gaal, or "Loathsome" or perhaps "Defiled," who wandered in from nowhere ready to take over? Gaal boldly pleads for the people to put power in his hands to depose Abimelech. Just as the lords of Shechem had officially empowered Abimelech to kill his brothers, so now they are called on to empower Gaal to kill Abimelech. Having received the power, Gaal then challenges Abimelech to gather military reinforcements and march out to face him in battle.

30–33 Vv 30–49 provide a battle report describing Abimelech's defeat of Shechem. Gaal's challenge is accepted.

Zebul does not take mention of his name lightly. Here the reader learns the official title. Zebul is mayor (שַׂר) of Shechem. He apparently stands over against Gaal and the lords of Shechem in a house divided. Thus Gaal can refer to Zebul as Abimelech's official (פָּקִיד, Judg 9:28). Such reference angers Zebul, so he "covertly" sends messengers to Abimelech (see *Note* 9:31.a). Gaal describes the attacker as "the son of a slave" (Judg 9:31) and his cohorts as "brothers," which may signify family ties or allies.

The absent general and king, Abimelech, has to be told that his central stronghold is under attack by an unexpected enemy. He also has to learn proper battle strategy from his official. This stands in stark contrast to Joshua's battle of Jericho, where Joshua besieged the city, having learned strategy from God, not from a human subordinate. Joshua treated enemy spoils and captives in accordance with God's instructions. Abimelech follows a human plan to "do to him whatever your hand finds to do" (Judg 9:33). This points forward to the final chapters (17–21) marked by an Israel doing right in its own eyes. Schneider asserts, "Revenge has become a legitimate motivating factor and continues as a major cause for Israel's leaders throughout the rest of the book" (143).

34–45 A Hebrew disjunctive clause shows the beginning of a new narrative section. Schneider observes that Abimelech has gathered an army, "though from where and peopled by whom is not clear" (146). The battle report at Shechem describes Abimelech employing ambush strategy just as Joshua had at Ai. However, Joshua had been prompted by God's command, not human artifice. This ambush shows direct retaliation against the Shechemite ambush set for travelers in Judg 9:25. As they had first shown their treachery against Abimelech, so he would defeat them with the same treacherous tactics. Later, the Philistines would use similar strategy against Samson (Judg 16:2–12). Israel would eventually use such strategy to self-destruct in battle against the Benjaminites (Judg 20:29–38), the story climaxing with the Benjaminites lying in ambush seeking wives (Judg 21:20). Finally, the Saul stories would feature ambush tactics (1 Sam 15:5; 22:8, 13).

As the story progresses, the ambush army will gradually comprise fewer "companies" or heads (ראשים), starting in v 34 with four companies, which are reduced to three in v 43. Gaal falls for the trap, especially when Zebul tells him that he is seeing shadows in the mountains, that there are no people on "the summits of the mountains" (ראשי ההרים, v 36). Gaß (*Ortsnamen*, 328) follows E. Jans (*Abimelech und sein Königtum*, 235) in associating *rāšê hehārîm* with cultic activities, particularly reception of oracles.

A second look convinces Gaal that people are coming down from "the center of the earth" (טבּור הָאָרֶץ, v 37). Gaß (*Ortsnamen*, 328–29) notes the uncertainty about the meaning and location of this term, Tabbur perhaps referring to a high plane. Gaß points topographically to modern Ras Tabur, a small hill on the southwest slope of Gebel el-Kabir.

The Hebrew term is often identified as the center or navel (following LXX ὀμφαλός) of the earth. Some then identify it with Mount Gerizim (Younger, 226, n. 29; B. W. Anderson, *BA* 20 [1957] 10–11; S. Terrien, *VT* 20 [1970] 315–38), with Ras et-Tagur on Jebel el-Kabir northeast of Shechem (H. Eshel and Z. Erlich, *Tarbiz* 58 [1988–1989] 111–16; Z. Ilan, *Beit-Miqra* 27 [1981–1982] 122–26), or with Shechem or a specific stone object in Shechem (G. R. H. Wright, *VT* 20 [1970] 79). Gaß (*Ortsnamen*, 328) interprets the identification with Gerizim as placing the troops' starting point at Khirbet en-Nebi, approaching Gerizim from the southwest. Khirbet en-Nebi would be on the lower southeast slope of Gebel et-Tor, two and a half miles (4 km) south of Tell Balata.

Gaß finds, ultimately, that the term means Navel of the Land, referring to the center of Shechem, making it the middle point of the city-state. This points to the region around Nagmet Salim, which would have been a Shechemite quarry rather than a populated settlement. Block (329) sees the Hebrew טבּור as simply referring to "an elevated plateau without external fortifications." Another possibility is to see Navel of the Earth as mythical language pointing to the depths of the earth, giving an eerie, awesome tone to the narrative.

Gaal points to a further company marching down from "the directon of the oak of the soothsayers" (דֶּרֶךְ אֵלוֹן מְעוֹנְנִים), obviously a cultic location and perhaps one that is unpopulated. It is often compared to or identified with Elon-More from Gen 12:6. Here Gaß (*Ortsnamen*, 327) may be correct in surmising that perhaps an exact topographical location of the approaching companies was intended because the information given about the three directions can also possess mythical/cultic significance. In Gaal's eyes, this sets up Abimelech and his troops as a mystified, unconquerable force. If the information does lead to geographical locations, then Gaß (329) would place Elon-Meonenim on the road from Shechem leading to the south at Jacob's well, modern Bir Ya'qub, less than half a mile (680 m) southwest of Shechem. A second possible location would be Khirbet Ibn Nasir southeast of Shechem, which may never have been a permanent settlement. Whatever the precise location, this tree "marked a sacred spot, perhaps to which the Canaanites of the region resorted for a decision from the gods" (Block, 329).

Finally, Zebul jabs sarcastically at Gaal, asking him where all his "oration" (Judg 9:38), his big talk or boast, is now. You invited Abimelech to fight. Here he is. Go to it. As with the Gideon and Barak stories, the battle report says less about fighting and more about pursuit after the enemy leader. Meanwhile, the battlefield is littered with corpses all the way back to the city gate. The gate plays an important role in this narrative as in several Judges battle narratives (Judg 5:8, 11; 9:35, 40, 44; 16:2–3; 18:16–17).

Gaal's resistance is so feeble that Zebul completes the mopping up operations, while Abimelech remains in his headquarters at Arumah. Both Tiglath Pileser III and Ada-Nirari III mention such a place, but apparently refer to a different town (Gaß, *Ortsnamen*, 330). Similarity in names leads to placing Arumah at Khirbet el-'Orme (Jebel el-Urmeh), five miles (8 km) southeast of Shechem. Gaß (331, n. 2412) provides a lengthy list of proponents of this view.

Now the people of Shechem find themselves in an ironic position. They had chosen a ruler on kinship terms but then dealt treacherously with him so that he ruled through a mayor and lived outside the city. They tried to replace him with the son of a servant, but the appointed mayor took care of him. Lack of loyalty to chosen leaders seems to be the pattern for Shechem, one that proves deadly.

Having destroyed most of the soldiers, Abimelech turns his attention to the rebel city itself. Olson concludes, "Abimelech's frenzied attacks of unwarranted and extreme revenge show a portrait of of a madman out of control. . . . One senses that Abimelech is randomly slaughtering people for no apparent reason" (817). Four companies (v 34) are reduced to three (v 43), again setting up an ambush. For some untold reason, the people of Shechem march out against him rather than hiding behind city walls or defenses. Abimelech rises with his army and defeats the Shechemites. Then he hurriedly dashes toward the city gate from which the enemy had begun the attack. The mathematics get a bit difficult here. Abimelech has plural companies with him, dashing to attack the city gate, while two other companies dash into the field of battle to mop up the remaining enemy soldiers there. Perhaps the reference to three companies meant three besides the one Abimelech led directly. The narrative purpose is to show that the ambush strategy worked for Abimelech even when it was not directly commanded by God, whose absence in this report is awesomely present.

The summary (v 45) is simple. An all-day battle restores Abimelech as head of Shechem, but the newly restored head of the city kills its population and destroys the city's defenses. He blatantly shows his enmity toward the city by sowing salt on it. (See F. C. Fensham, "Salt as Curse in the Old Testament and the Ancient Near East," *BA* 25 [1962] 48–50.) This is certainly a ritual act "invoking an irrevocable curse on the site" (Block, 330). Deut 29:23 (Heb. 22) shows the effect of salting the land—vegetation will not grow, so the people will have no harvest (compare Ps 107:33–34; Jer 17:6; Zeph 2:9). This effectively makes it impossible for anyone to live in the region. Thus in contempt for Shechem's treachery, Abimelech makes the center of his own empire incapable of supporting a population, apparently destroying even his own mother's residence. As Younger phrases it, "Just as Abimelech has made Jerub-Baal's family barren, so now he makes Shechem barren" (228).

46–49 As the narrator prolonged the Gideon narrative with pursuit stories, so the Shechem story is prolonged even after victory seems complete. The lords of Shechem still remain in the "tower of Shechem" (מִגְדַּל־שְׁכֶם, v 46), having sent the common soldiers to their death. *Migdal* refers to an observation point, which could mean a fortress or a temple or a tower. This may refer to a specific part of Shechem or to a city within the city-state governed by Shechem (V. P. Hamilton,

Handbook on the Historical Books, 137). Block (331, n. 850) and Schneider (147) follow Boling (180) in equating it with Beth-millo. (For arguments and literature see Gaß, *Ortsnamen*, 305, n. 2237.) A separate village would fit the narrative of the salting of Shechem better (Gaß, 305). This would also place the temple of El Berith outside the city and make the people here distinct from the leaders of Shechem. Assuming separate cities, Gaß (306–11) lists six possible locations, Tell Sofar, Khirbet Kume, Tell er-Ras (south or north), et-Tananir, el-Burnat, and Khirbet esh-Sheh Nasralla, while reserving the possibility that it lies on Mount Zalmon itself. Gaß (332–33) finds Zalmon usually located either at Gebel el-Kabur or at Gebel Sheh Silman but sees no evidence supporting either one. Gaß opts for a symbolic name that describes the light-colored fire coming from the dark mountain: *ṣalmôn,* meaning "dark."

The leaders slip into the sanctuary of their god, El Berith. In Judg 8:33 and 9:4 the god was Baal Berith, the lord of the covenant. Here it is El Berith, the god of the covenant. The city leaders give their god one last chance to protect them. Using his information sources, Abimelech climbs Mount Zalmon with his army, takes his battle axes, and cuts down branches from the forest of trees. Finally speaking for the first time since v 2, Abimelech calls his followers to do what he is doing in collecting branches. They use these to set the not-so-secret tunnel to the temple on fire. The men of the tower do not represent a small group of select leaders. Rather, a thousand die. Block concludes, "Ironically, the building Gaal's men had crashed in their revelry in v. 27 had become their death trap" (332). And Bluedorn observes, "The idolaters are burned by the chief idolater in the temple of their own covenant-god" (*Yahweh versus Baalism,* 256). Abimelech has his revenge against all factions connected with Shechem. But that is not enough.

50–55 In a further battle report we learn that, inexplicably, Abimelech carries his revenge campaign to the unsuspecting village of Thebez. Block (333) conjectures that Abimelech wanted to expand his realm. This town is often identified with Tubas, thirteen miles (20.9 km) northeast of Shechem (Younger, 229, n. 28), but archaeological and linguistic evidence points against this. Other possibilities would be Khirbet ed-Der or Khirbet ed-Duq/Khirbet el-Fuhar. (See E. F. Campbell, Jr., *Shechem II: Portrait of a Hill Country Vale,* ASOR Archaeology Reports 2 [Atlanta: Scholars Press, 1991] 107; Gaß, *Ortsnamen,* 333–34.) Again a tower (מִגְדּוֹל) provides the last defense for the people. Again Abimelech plans to burn down the tower. As Gaal appeared from nowhere earlier, so now "a certain woman" appears without introduction. From the tower she throws down on Abimelech's head a common millstone the women use daily to grind grain. (Compare Shamgar's weapon in Judg 3:31 and Jael's in Judg 4:21.)

The narrator reports the result simply: "she crushed his skull" (Judg 9:53). Block aptly remarks, "To the end Abimelech remained belligerent, defiant, arrogant" (333). Knowing death is near, he asks his aide to kill him so he will not share with Sisera the ignominy of dying at the hand of a woman. Later, Saul's servant would fear to kill one God had anointed as king. Abimelech possesses no such anointing, and so his servant has no inhibitions. Even in death Abimelech does not attain his goal, for later reports still refer to him as the one a woman slaughtered (2 Sam 11:21). Abimelech uses his mother and her relatives to gain power, apparently kills them in the slaughter of Shechem, and then succumbs to the "certain woman" of Thebez in an unnecessary battle.

55 Without a leader, the "men of Israel" return home, in resignation, not in rest. Never again will Israel experience rest. The danger is no longer from outside opponents raised by God in punishment. Now the enemy lies within and may destroy Israel with Israel unawares. Certainly, Webb is offtrack in finding that the "Israelites as a whole benefit from the retribution worked upon their bramble king" ([1987] 158). No one benefits. All lose. Israel returns not to reap benefits but because no other alternative offers itself.

But who are these "men of Israel"? Schneider correctly paints the problematic situation here: "This comment appears out of context since no one of clearly defined Israelite origin or tribal affinity is mentioned throughout the story, nor are they ever rounded up to take part in any battle. It is a necessary statement to tie this episode into the larger context" (149). Webb thinks the phrase "men of Israel" in v 55 refers to Abimelech's followers ([1987] 156; compare Amit, *Book of Judges*, 197), while Block concludes that the "chapter reads like a page out of a Canaanite history notebook" (308–9), Abimelech's followers being "those relatives to whom he had appealed in the first instance (v. 1), as well as the retainers who had come with him from Ophrah" (328).

Later, Block speaks of Abimelech winning "the allegiance of many Israelites" (334), but this verse would be the only evidence for such a conclusion. These men of Israel have not appeared previously in the Abimelech narrative. The narrator reported in 8:33–34 that the Israelites had begun serving Baal Berith, forgetting God, their deliverer. Then 9:22 says Abimelech judged Israel for three years. Otherwise, the chapter has spoken only of the various elements in the population of Shechem, whether city or city-state. They are descendants of Hamor, not of Jacob/Israel. Their center is Shechem and the temple of Baal Berith, not Ebal and Gerizim, where Jotham appeared. Shechem has become Abimelech's enemy, and its population has disappeared. Meanwhile, Abimelech's personal army represents men without discipline or principles. This is not an army of men of Israel. Gaal challenged Abimelech to bring his army to full strength. Did Abimelech add Israelites to his army at that time? Where would they have come from? Why would they support him when he had killed Gideon's sons?

Has Israel actually been on the sidelines viewing Abimelech's test in kingship and seeing it fail? Is the narrator signaling us that the Israelites have given up on human leadership, so that each is returning home to do what is right in each individual's eyes? Has Israel come full circle to the place where Joshua left them—no one remembers what God has done for Israel? Block believes "Israel has been totally Canaanized; Baal has contended for himself and prevailed" (308).

56–57 Meanwhile, God declares the battle between Abimelech and treacherous Shechem a no contest. Both are losers, and God exacts his revenge on Abimelech and Shechem, fulfilling Jotham's fable. God is the only winner, proving, despite his virtual absence in the narrative, a strong presence as the king who did not abdicate (Younger, 232). God has to save Israel from one of its own and hope Israel never follows Shechem in making such a poor choice, a choice that will be quite nearly duplicated when Israel looks to Saul for leadership because he is so appealing physically (1 Sam 8–9, especially 9:2; see V. P. Hamilton, *Handbook on the Historical Books*, 136–37, and Wong, *Compositional Strategies*, 210–11, for similarities in the Abimelech and Saul narratives; Wong concludes that Saul is depicted as a "latter-day Abimelech").

God gave each precisely what was deserved. Abimelech proved to be untrue to his name in both its possible meanings: he did not prove true to the father who was king, whether that was Gideon or God. God brought him a shameful death. Shechem refused to listen to God's messenger Jotham, elected a briar as king, and suffered the fiery results. Thus ends not only the Abimelech narrative but also the Gideon cycle. Younger correctly points out that "all of the slaughters and destructions that are described in chapter 9 are the result of Gideon's sins in 8:27–32" (233). The royal lifestyle and vengeful warfare of the father found even more devastating results in the son of the concubine. Younger rightly observes that, through it all, "the moral degeneration within this major judge cycle underscores how great the unmerited favor of the Lord is toward Israel" (232).

Explanation

Niditch stretches the text as far as possible to provide "a more complex, ambivalent, and self-critical portrait of the monarchy and of preceding experiments in statehood. The judges belong to the 'old days,' before there were kings in Israel, but these early leaders are portrayed as clever, brave, inspired, charismatic, and flawed. They are heroic, engaging figures, and none of them is a king" (114).

I would hope to present a bit more nuanced statement with a more critical stance toward the "judges" as presented in the biblical text. God is king. Israel has trouble understanding its sociology. How does Israel function in a world where God has left enemies to oppose them? What kind of leader should emerge? God tries to show them—a leader with humility, patience, and obedience acting on God's election and God's direction. Gideon begins with the humility part, but a humility that almost stifles any leadership potential, a humility that brings him to test God, not trust God. Gradually, Gideon becomes the leader who contests with God for honor in victory. Ultimately, Gideon becomes the vengeful leader who neglects the needs of his troops, angrily punishes enemy kings, unreasonably carries out personal vendetta, and finally hides behind humble theological statements as he enjoys a royal lifestyle.

Meanwhile, none of Gideon's seventy sons proves strong enough or has the desire to follow the father's leadership, prolonging an Israelite tradition that does not honor family ties in selecting new leadership. The son with the least genealogical claims to power asserts himself through his "concubine" mother's family to gain leadership and becomes the first "king" in Israel's history. Backed by unprincipled soldiers with no apparent ties to Israel, he claims to rule the city-state of Shechem without ever moving his own residence there. He maintains a mysterious army without racial or national identity. He has no interaction with the divine until a divinely commissioned evil spirit pits treacherous Shechem against vengeful king. Ultimately, the subjects prove disloyal, while the king proves to have a bramble's ability and concern for the people. Israel learns that "the politics of Abimelech—ruthless violence, hunger for power, back-stabbing vengeance, irrational assault, the worship of other gods—are roundly condemned in the strongest terms" (Olson, 819). The result of such a dynastic approach to leadership is disaster, destruction, and death for all. The Israel the story represents—whatever sociological and national group that is—retreats home to search anew for a sociology of Israel, a leadership system that will prevent such disasters and unite all the potential members.

Later Israel tries a new dynasty, that of Jeroboam, only to see it end in total disaster and violence, having provoked God to intense anger (1 Kgs 15:29–30). One cannot point to the Gideon, the Abimelech, the Saul, or the Jeroboam narrative to pronounce a total end to the value of kingship for Israel. One simply sees various attempts at kingship that do not work because the king is not a man after God's own heart and because the people are no more loyal to the king than are the kings to the people. Webb rightly concludes, "Israel's future could not be secured by creating a new institution. Only a wholehearted return to Yahweh could do that. . . . Kingship is seen in an unfavourable light but it is not rejected in principle" ([1987] 159). But, as Block says, "Israel's Canaanite character has set. From here on it will all be downhill" (335).

3. Jephthah with Minor Judges (10:1–12:15)

a. Interim Report (10:1–18)

Bibliography

Assis, E. *Self-Interest or Communal Interest: An Ideology of Leadership in the Gideon, Abimelech, and Jephthah Narratives (Judges 6–12).* VTSup 106. Leiden: Brill, 2006. **Barredo, M. A.** "Aspectos sintácticos de Jueces 10,1–12:15." *Anton* 77 (2002) 211–33. **Beem, B.** "The Minor Judges: A Literary Reading of Some Very Short Stories." In *The Biblical Canon in Comparative Perspective.* Ed. K. L. Younger, Jr., W. W. Hallo, and B. F. Batto. Scripture in Context 4; ANETS 11. Lewiston, NY: Mellen, 1991. 147–72. **Berman, J. A.** *Narrative Analogy in the Hebrew Bible: Battle Stories and Their Equivalent Non-battle Narratives.* VTSup 103. Leiden: Brill, 2004. **Claassens, J.** "Notes on Characterisation in the Jephthah Narrative." *JNSL* 22 (1996) 107–15. ———. "Theme and Function in the Jephthah Narrative." *JNSL* 23 (1997) 203–19. **Day, P. L.** "From the Child Is Born the Woman: The Story of Jephthah's Daughter." In *Gender and Difference in Ancient Israel.* Ed. P. L. Day. Minneapolis: Fortress, 1989. 58–74. **DeMaris, R. E.,** and **C. S. Leeb,** "Judges——(Dis)Honor and Ritual Enactment: The Jephthah Story: Judges 10:16–12:1." In *Ancient Israel: The Old Testament in Its Social Context.* Ed. P. F. Esler. Minneapolis: Fortress, 2005. 177–90. **DeWitt, D. S.** "The Jephthah Traditions: A Rhetorical and Literary Study in the Deuteronomistic History." PhD diss., Andrews University, 1987. **Dus, J.** "Bethel und Mizpa in Jdc. 19–21 und Jdc. 10–12." *OrAnt* 3 (1964) 227–43. **Exum, J. C.** "The Tragic Vision and Biblical Narrative: The Case of Jephthah." In *Signs and Wonders.* Ed. J. C. Exum. 59–83. **Gunn, D. M.,** and **D. N. Fewell.** "Plots and Points of View: Judges 10–12." In *Narrative in the Hebrew Bible.* Oxford: Oxford UP, 1993. 112–19. **Hauser, A. J.** "The 'Minor Judges'—A Re-evaluation." *JBL* 94 (1975) 190–200. ———. "Unity and Diversity in Early Israel before Samuel." *JETS* 22.4 (1979) 289–303. **Hertzberg, H. W.** "Die kleinen Richter." *TLZ* 79 (1954) 285–90. **Martin, L. R.** "God at Risk: Divine Vulnerability in Judges 10:6–16." *OTE* 18 (2005) 722–40. **Mullen, E. T., Jr.** "The 'Minor Judges': Some Literary and Historical Considerations." *CBQ* 44 (1982) 185–201. **Nelson, R. D.** "Ideology, Geography, and the List of Minor Judges." *JSOT* 31 (2007) 347–64. **Noth, M.** "Das Amt des 'Richters Israels.'" In *Festschrift Alfred Bertholet.* Ed. W. Baumgartner et al. Tübingen: Mohr, 1950.

404–17. Olson, D. T. "Dialogues of Life and Monologues of Death: Jephthah and Jephthah's Daughter in Judges 10:6–12:7." In *Postmodern Interpretations of the Bible: A Reader.* Ed. A. K. M. Adam. Saint Louis: Chalice, 2001. 43–54. **Richter, W.** "Die Überlieferungen um Jephtah: Ri 10,17–12:6." *Bib* 47 (1966) 485–556. ———. "Zu den 'Richtern Israel.'" *ZAW* 77 (1965) 40–71. **Rösel, H. N.** "Jephtah and das Problem der Richter." *Bib* 61 (1980) 251–55. **Sasaki, T.** "What Triggers the Deliverance of Israel in the Book of Judg 10:6–16?" (Japanese). *Exeg* 14 (2003) 43–50. **Scherer, A.** "Die 'kleinen' Richter und ihre Funktion." *ZAW* 119 (2007) 190–200. **Schunck, K. D.** "Die Richter Israels und ihr Amt." In *Volume du Congrès Genève, 1965.* VTSup 15. Leiden: Brill, 1966. 252–62. **Selms, A. van.** "The Title 'Judge.'" *Di Ou Testamentiese Werkgemeenskap in Sud-Afrika* 1 (1959) 41–50. **Shveka, A.** "'וַתִּקְצַר נַפְשׁוֹ בַּעֲמַל יִשְׂרָאֵל,' (Jud 10:16): A New Understanding" (Heb.). *Beit-Miqra* 48 (2002) 77–86. **Sjöberg, M.** *Wrestling with Textual Violence: The Jephthah Narrative in Antiquity and Modernity.* Bible in the Modern World 4. Sheffield: Sheffield Phoenix, 2006. **Skolski, S.** "The Minor Judges" (Heb.). *Beit-Miqra* 13 (1968) 75–99. **Soggin, J. A.** "Das Amt der 'kleinen Richter' in Israel." *VT* 30 (1980) 245–48. **Stone, L. G.** "From Tribal Confederation." 383–85. **Tadmor, H.** "Jephthah and Jephthah's Daughter (Discussion at Helman Lecture)" (Heb). In *Studies in the Book of Judges.* Publications of the Israel Bible Society 10. Jerusalem, 1966. 345–47. **Webb, B. G.** "The Theme of the Jephthah Story (Judges 10:6–12:7)." *RTR* 45 (1986) 34–43. **Weinfeld, M.** "Judge and Officer in Ancient Israel and in the Ancient Near East." *IOS* 1 (1977) 65–88. **Weisman, Z.** "Charismatic Leaders in the Era of the Judges." *ZAW* 89 (1977) 399–411.

Translation

[1] *After Abimelech, Tola, the son of Puah, the son of Dodo,*[a] *rose to deliver Israel. He was a man from Issachar*[b] *and lived in Shamir*[c] *in the hill country of Ephraim.* [2] *He judged Israel twenty-three years, and he died. He was buried in Shamir.*[a]

[3] *After him, Jair the Gileadite rose. He judged Israel twenty-two years.* [4] *He had thirty*[a] *sons who rode on thirty donkeys.*[b] *They had thirty*[c] *towns*[d] *in*[e] *the land of Gilead. They are named*[f] *Havvoth*[g] *Jair to this day.* [5] *Jair died and was buried in Kamon.*

[6] *Again the sons of Israel did evil in the eyes of Yahweh. They served the Baals and the Ashtaroth—the gods of Aram,*[a] *the gods of Sidon, the gods of Moab, the gods of the Ammonites, and the gods of the Philistines. They abandoned Yahweh and did not serve him.* [7] *Yahweh's anger blazed against Israel, and he sold them into the hand of the Philistines and into the hand of the Ammonites.* [8] *They extinguished and exterminated the sons of Israel in that year. This lasted eighteen years for the sons of Israel who were beyond the Jordan in the land of the Amorites in Gilead.*[a] [9] *The Ammonites crossed over the Jordan to fight, even against Judah, against Benjamin, and against the house of*[a] *Ephraim. Israel*[b] *was in extreme trouble.* [10] *The sons of Israel cried out to Yahweh, "We have sinned against you; indeed,*[a] *we have abandoned our*[b] *God and served the Baals."*

[11] *Yahweh told the sons of Israel, "Is*[a] *it not true that some of the Egyptians, and some of the Amorites, and some of the sons of Ammon,*[b] *and some of the Philistines* [12] *and the Sidonians, and Amalek and Maon,*[a] *oppressed you. You cried out to me, and I delivered you from their hand.* [13] *But now you have abandoned me and served other gods. Therefore, I will not deliver you again.* [14] *Go, cry out to the gods*[a] *you have chosen. Let them deliver you in your time of need."* [15] *The sons of Israel said to Yahweh, "We have sinned. Treat us as it seems good in your eyes. Only, please*[a] *rescue us today."* [16] *They turned away from the foreign gods in their midst and served Yahweh. He could no longer stand to see Israel's trouble.*[a]

[17] *The sons of Ammon mustered*[a] *their army and camped in Gilead. The sons of Israel*

gathered their forces[b] *and camped in Mizpah.*[c 18] *The army*[a]—*the officials of Gilead—said each to his neighbor, "Who is the man who will lead the attack against the sons of Ammon? He will become the head of all the residents of Gilead."*

Notes

1.a. LXX reads υἱὸς πατραδέλφου αὐτοῦ, "son of his uncle," a translation rather than transliteration of the personal name. Niditch (120) shows that OL "offers an alternate expanded epithet, 'son of Ful, son of Charreon, his uncle.'"

1.b. Q has שָׂכָר; Ben Naftali reads שִׂשָּׂכָר; K has שִׂשָּׂכָר, which apparently indicates a reading of אִישׁ שָׂכָר, "man of Sacar," which may be be supported by the original Gk. reading Ισσαξαρ.

1.c. LXX[A] reads Σαμαρείᾳ, "Samaria," substituting a more familiar for a less familiar name.

2.a. LXX[A] reads Σαμαρείᾳ, "Samaria," substituting a more familiar for a less familiar name.

4.a. LXX reads "thirty-two sons," apparently dittography of καὶ δύο from the previous verse.

4.b. LXX reads "thirty-two colts," made necessary by the previous listing of "thirty-two sons."

4.c. LXX reads "thirty-two," made necessary by the previous listing of "thirty-two sons."

4.d. Following LXX πόλεις, "towns" (Heb. עָרִים), as indicated by *BHS,* eastern texts, and many versions rather than MT's dittography of עֲיָרִים, "donkeys."

4.e. MT has relative pronoun אֲשֶׁר, left untranslated here and not present in Cairo Genizah MSS.

4.f. Lit. "to them they called Havvoth Jair"; LXX[B] reads "he called to them."

4.g. LXX reads Ἐπαύλεις, "villages of Jair," translating the Heb. proper name חַוֹּת.

6.a. LXX[A] does not have וְאֶת־אֱלֹהֵי אֲרָם, "and the gods of Aram (or Syria)," while LXX[B] reads καὶ τοῖς θεοῖς Αραδ, "and the gods of Arad," a more difficult reading but one representing a copyist's error.

8.a. "This lasted" is added to translation for clarity. *BHS* notes that "in that year" may perhaps be a later addition since two dating systems appear to be juxtaposed here. No textual evidence supports the excision. LXX[B] reads more vaguely, "at that time." *Preliminary and Interim Report* (2:100) notes the possibility of reading שָׁעָה for שָׁנָה without providing textual support. Barthélemy (*Critique textuelle,* 1:103) sees nothing in original Gk. corresponding to "in that year" but places the decision on the literary-critical level rather than on the text-critical level.

9.a. LXX[B] does not have "house of," omitting a familiar but unnecessary phrase.

9.b. LXX[A] reads οἱ υἱοὶ Ισραηλ, "the sons of Israel," adding a familiar phrase.

10.a. *BHS* suggests deleting the ו before כִּי with many MSS, LXX, Syr., and Vg., though MT is the more difficult reading and can be seen as introducing a כי clause that explains and expands the previous "confession." The versions may not have understood the Heb. syntax at this point.

10.b. LXX[B] does not have "our." A few MSS and Vg. add יהוה, the divine name, to clarify the confession or simply to include the common phrase.

11.a. *BHS* sees the remainder of the verse as corrupt, proposing a reading of הֲלֹא מִמִּצְרַיִם וּמִן־הָאֱמֹרִי וּמִן־הָעַמּוֹן הוֹשַׁעְתִּי אֶתְכֶם וַאֲרָם וּבְנֵי עַמּוֹן וּפְלִשְׁתִּים, "Did I not deliver you from the Egyptians and from the Amorites and from the Canaanites, and Aram and the sons of Ammon and the Philistines." Speaking of anacoluthon, GKC, §67b, decides: "after a series of intermediate sentences, the predicate *I saved you* is suppressed; but the text can hardly be correct." (Compare Block, 346, n. 15; and O'Connell, *Rhetoric of the Book of Judges,* 467–68.)

11.b. LXX[A] has "and Moab," adding a familiar name to the list.

12.a. LXX reads Μαδιαμ, "Midian," for Maonites with LXX[A] reversing the order with Amalekites. *Preliminary and Interim Report* (2:101) attributes too little textual evidence and a possible lack of historical memory or scribal error for the substitution of the more familiar and much easier "Midian" for the original "Maon." Barthélemy (*Critique textuelle,* 1:103–4) shows the complex interchanges of names of nations in the text tradition here and in 2 Chr 20:1 and 26:8. Matthews (115, n. 215) sees the LXX source in the pairing of Midianites and Amalekites in 6:3.

14.a. OL omits "gods."

15.a. LXX[A] reads κατὰ πάντα ὅσα ἂν ἀρέσκῃ ἐνώπιόν σου πλήν κύριε ἐξελοῦ ἡμᾶς, "according to all which may be pleasing before you; nevertheless, O Lord, deliver us."

16.a. Lit. "and his soul became short (that is, impatient) with the trouble of Israel." LXX[A] reads καὶ οὐκ εὐηρέστησεν ἐν τῷ λαῷ καὶ ὠλιγοψύχησεν ἐν τῷ κόπῳ Ισραηλ, "and he was not pleased among the people and he was discouraged with Israel's troubles," while LXX[B] reads τῷ κυρίῳ μόνῳ καὶ ὠλιγώθη ἡ ψυχὴ αὐτοῦ ἐν κόπῳ Ισραηλ, "the Lord alone and his soul (lit. translation of Heb.) was diminished with the troubles of Israel." OL, according to Niditch (120), has "and they served the Lord God alone and they were disheartened in the labor of Israel." Niditch interprets this to mean "OL thus does not reflect the more emotional, empathetic, and perhaps guilty deity represented in MT."

17.a. Heb. וַיִּצְעֲקוּ, lit. "and they cried out for"; LXX reads ἀνέβησαν, "they went up."

17.b. Heb. וַיֵּאָסְפוּ, lit ."and they gathered together"; LXX^A reads ἐξῆλθον, "they went out."

17.c. LXX^B reads ἐν τῇ σκοπιᾷ, "in the watchtower," translating the proper noun *Mizpah*.

18.a. Or "the people"; LXX^A reads οἱ ἄρχοντες τοῦ λαοῦ Γαλααδ, "the rulers of the people of Gilead," giving a more natural order to the expression but missing the nuance that the "people" or perhaps "the army" is placed in apposition with the leaders or officials. *BHS* sees שָׂרֵי גִלְעָד as perhaps a gloss, referring to Judg 11:5.

Form/Structure/Setting

See table 10.1 in the appendix to compare one possible example of narrative analysis with form-critical analysis for chaps. 10–12. The narrative elements follow the typical pattern of Hebrew narrative while the genre elements show the genre of each section with its component parts. Note how the narrator can use different genre elements and markers within or even across various narrative elements.

Judg 10–12 offers as much difficulty for commentators as any section of the book. A new, totally unexpected type of material appears, usually referred to as the minor judges narratives. Amit (*Book of Judges*, 81) refers to these as "consecutive judges" as opposed to the other "disappointing judges." Amit sees that they, along with the other judges, have the same function—local heroes engaged in rule and sitting in judgment. Under them "we do not hear of any intermediate period of abandoning God or of periods of punishment and wars of deliverance" (84).

Hauser decides the difference is not so great: "We have one category—leadership—which could be developed in several different forms, forms that cross and interweave with one another" (*JETS* 22.4 [1979] 296–97). Hauser (301) finds Tola, Jair, and Jephthah to be military figures who gained prominence in their region through "military exploits." Ibzan and Abdon seem to be local clan leaders. Ehud and Barak appear to abandon leadership after danger has passed. Gideon and Abimelech almost establish a dynasty. Despite all his efforts, Jephthah controls only a limited number of people. For Hauser, then, "the pattern clearly is one of local separateness and autonomy which is occasionally interrupted by regional alliances that arise in order to counter the threat of foes but which returns once the threat has been removed and/or the delivering leader passes from the scene" (302).

Despite the sudden appearance of the minor judges narratives, Webb thinks "the material which precedes the introduction of Jephthah himself in 11:1 is closely integrated into the main body of the narrative" ([1987] 42). These narratives pick up language that has not been in the editorial framework sections since chap. 3. "Rose" (קום) appeared in framework materials in 2:10, 16, 18; 3:9 (Othniel), 15 (Ehud) but not in materials introducing Barak, Gideon, or Abimelech. The term did appear inside the narrative materials themselves in 3:20; 4:4, 14; 5:7, 12; 7:9, 15, 19; 8:20–21; 9:18, 32, 34–35, 43. Similarly, "deliver" (ישׁע) appears in 2:16, 18; 3:9 (Othniel), 15 (Ehud), 31 (Shamgar) but not in the frameworks to Barak, Gideon, or Abimelech. Again, within the narratives the term is seen in 6:14–15, 31, 36–37; 7:2, 7; 8:22. Now "rose" appears in 10:1, 3, while "deliver" is in 10:1, 12–14. The terms introduce the minor judges framework but do not appear within them in chap. 12. There, rather, the simple term "judged" (שׁפט) appears, defining the work of each of these minor judges as well as the work of

Samson. This use began in 3:10 (Othniel) and appears with each of the minor judges—10:2 (Tola), 10:3 (Jair), 12:7 (Jephthah), 12:8–9 (Ibzan), 12:11 repeated (Elon), 12:13–14 (Abdon), and 15:10 (Samson). Deborah (4:4) is said to have judged Israel, but that comes in a different formula in beginning the narrative rather than in the framework, and God is named the Judge in 11:27. Eli (1 Sam 4:18) and Samuel (1 Sam 7:15–17) also "judge Israel." Here we see a transitional structure that ties chaps. 10–12 (13–16) back to the framework of chap. 3 and its role-model judges and framework and that introduces the structure that will run through the Samson narrative. These structural markers almost make the reader think the narrator has started over on a second path.

The warrior leaders could not back up their claims to deliver Israel, so the attention turns to a different type of leader. The narrative content here then focuses on two of these potential deliverer/judges—Jephthah and Samson. Each of these goes his individual way and becomes more of a danger than a deliverer for Israel. Again, the term *Israel* remains a bit mysterious. Amit is on target: "The text gives no support for the tendency of some scholars to see the 'minor judges' as a national leadership. . . . The use of the name 'Israel' does not refer to all of Israel but is intended for purely rhetorical effect" (*Book of Judges*, 83–84). (For the complexity of the term *Israel* in Hebrew scriptures, see now S. Apóstolo, "On the Elusiveness and Malleability of 'Israel,'" *Journal of Hebrew Scriptures* 6 [2006] 1–15.)

The narratives combine several different formal genres into the larger minor judges cycle:

Annalistic citations of minor judges (10:1–5; 12:7–15)
The Jephthah cycle (10:6–12:6)
Extended narrator's framework (10:6–10)
Divine judgment speech or lawsuit (10:11–16)
Ammonite war report (10:17–11:33)
Vow narrative ([11:30], 11:34–30)
Intertribal battle report (12:1–6)
The Samson cycle (chaps. 13–16)

Niditch describes the annal form of the minor judges presentations:

The pattern of content in this little literary form is: allusion to the previous leader followed by the name of the new deliverer, his genealogical background or tribal/geographic origins, number of years that he judged, his death and place of burial (cf. vv. 1–2 concerning Tola and 12:11–12, 15 concerning Elon and Abdon). Additional information is offered in some of the annals concerning his offspring and their patrimonies, marriages, or mounts (v. 4 concerning Jair, and 12:8–9, 13–14 concerning Ibzan and Abdon, respectively). The mention of numerous sons, marriages contracted (Ibzan), donkeys on which the judges' sons rode (Jair, Abdon), and the villages named after the patriarch (Jair) are details that point to status and wealth in a traditional culture. These are the sort of stock details that characterize tales of heroes, their cultures' "big men." The conventionalized language in which these details are expressed further underscores the traditional nature of the material. (121)

The two sets of minor judges annals separate neatly the two individual narratives, that of Jephthah and Samson. But why? Matthews sees "the continuous spiral

downward, away from the divine direction of the judges and toward personal ca-
price" (113). In like manner, Schneider sees Tola's reign as showing that "Israel's
standards have slipped" (155). Amit may be right in claiming that "this editor
needed the consecutive judges in order to present the advantages of consecutive
rule" (*Book of Judges,* 85). Jordan is a bit off track in seeing the governing themes
here to be "aggrandizement" and "the tendency toward tyranny" (179). Brettler
honestly steps back: "This issue is intractable due to the paucity of evidence, and
for this reason, the 'minor judges' will not play a significant role in this study" (22).
I follow Block in thinking that "the differences in presentation probably derive
either from the sources used by the narrator (family/tribal chronicles for these
judges; folk narratives for the deliverer judges) or the individuals' significance for
the narrator's literary and theological agenda" (336–37). He also notes that these
leaders emerge "without the apparent involvement of God" (337).

These minor judges appear to establish times of peace and prosperity, while the
two militant individuals demonstrate military and physical strength but lead Israel
to civil war and loss of national freedom and security. The structure appears to
show the power of leaders from the smaller tribes and the danger of power coming from the more significant tribes of Benjamin, Ephraim, and Dan. The key to
understanding much of the material may be in understanding the role of Judah,
which suddenly appears both in the Ammonite war introduction and in the Samson
cycle. Certainly Benjamin, the tribe of Saul; Ephraim, the tribe of Jeroboam; and
Dan, the eventual home of Jeroboam's second sanctuary, come in for critique.
The role of Judah is much more complex and will have to be demonstrated in
the *Comment* below. Suffice it to note here that the major culprits or villains in the
narrative represent Ephraim and Dan. Again, the literary setting appears to be
amidst the north/south split brought on by Rehoboam and Jeroboam, while the
origin of the individual formal elements reaches back into the premonarchical
period. The individual cycles may well be the creation of the narrator in the time
of Jeroboam, though this remains open for much further study if enough evidence
can ever be brought forward to make a clear case.

Comment

The framework introduction referring to the evil that Israel has done (Judg
2:11; 3:7, 12; 4:1; 6:1; 10:6; 13:1) surprises by its absence. The only tie to what
precedes comes with the mention of Abimelech. This provides continuity for the
narrative while setting the following annals off as a new section, possibly showing
an alternative to Abimelech.

Many commentators want the reference to Abimelech to introduce Tola as
the one who delivers Israel from all that Abimelech caused. Thus Bluedorn says,
"The reference to Abimelech defines the Tola narrative as the continuation of
the whole Gideon-Abimelech narrative. . . . It may be implied, therefore, that he
delivers Israel from the effect of Abimelech's reign, and perhaps also from idolatry"
(*Yahweh versus Baalism,* 275). Brensinger decides that "Tola's responsibility likely
involves saving the Israelites, not from an external adversary, but from the dreadful
effects of Abimelech's butchery. Israel now requires deliverance and rebuilding
following *internal* oppression" (116, emphasis original). Block, pointing to Beem
("Minor Judges," 149), even concludes that "this probably reflects the seriousness

of the chaos produced in the wake of Abimilech's rampages" (338–39). Amit (*Book of Judges*, 43) insists on finding a cycle of sin, punishment, deliverance, and quiet in each of the narrative cycles, and so here finds Tola as the deliverance stage in the Gideon/Abimelech cycle with Jair providing the quiet cycle. This stretches the evidence, includes too many "judges," and makes the theoretical structure dominate the interpretation rather than following the text itself.

Amit is on the right trail in seeing Jair as establishing a time of peace and prosperity. Similarly, Block perceives the narrator to be giving the reader "brief if nostalgic glimpses of what normal life and rule in Israel could look like," providing "short periods of peace that offered Israel hope for the future" (337). In the eyes of Block, kingship is not the issue, these local rulers perhaps offering an alternative to kingship. Schneider (155) points out that Tola broke the dynastic chain that Abimelech sought to establish.

The use of אחר, "after," characterizes all the minor judges narratives and functions chronologically, not thematically. The minor judges form a contrast to Abimelech, Jephthah, and Samson, but they do not deliver Israel from the enemy Abimelech. In fact, little if any religious language enters these minor judges narratives, so deliverance from idolatry cannot be implied.

The purpose is again to deliver Israel, the same purpose as that of Ehud, Othniel, and Shamgar. The Gideon narrative framework does not mention deliverance, but the narrative from one perspective centers on who gets credit or honor for deliverance (Judg 6:14–15, 31, 36–37; 7:2, 7; 8:22). Gideon's narrative ends in Baal getting the credit and Israel forgetting Yahweh (8:33–35). Now the minor judges are called on to deliver Israel, but no record of fighting occurs. Rather, annals name them, demonstrate their wealth, detail the length of time the judge "judged" Israel, and cite his burial. The first minor judge is the only one mentioned as called to deliver Israel. The first set of minor judges leads to yet another period of doing evil in God's eyes (10:6), a time when God refuses to deliver Israel and challenges their new gods to deliver them (10:12–14). Then, Jephthah, as the new leader, claims Ephraim had the responsibility of deliverance but did not fulfill it (12:2–3). Eventually, God calls forth Samson, but his task is only to "begin to deliver" (13:5), something he accomplishes only in his own death. The opening framework (2:17–19) has said that God was with the judge he raised up and that he delivered Israel all the days of the judge. Thus one may read the minor judges as leaders who deliver Israel from foreign wars and provide a period of peace, only to see Jephthah and Samson win battles of deliverance but eventually lose the war of deliverance.

What is certain is that the minor judges represent tribes that are otherwise mainly insignificant in the biblical narrative, but they are blatantly presented as judging all Israel. The ambivalence of the Abimelech narrative disappears in the annalistic reports of the minor judges and their all-Israel context.

1–2 The first minor judge is Tola, about whom we know nothing except that his namesake was one of the sons of the tribal father Issachar (Gen 46:13; Num 26:23; 1 Chr 7:1–2). *Dôdô* means "his uncle," as the versions translate, but appears as a proper name here. The location of Shamir, his hometown, remains a mystery. (See Gaß, *Ortsnamen*, 345–46.) The narrator locates the town "in the hill country of Ephraim." This can either show the strength of Ephraim as the center of Israelite life, or it can show that to have a leader with strength, Ephraim had to look to the tribe of Issachar, a tribe that had supported Barak (5:15).

"He judged Israel." Previously, only Othniel, the role model judge from Judah (Judg 3:10), and Deborah, the woman called to enlist a general (Judg 4:4), had judged Israel. From this point forward, all the leaders explicitly judge Israel. But what do they do? Richard Schultz notes that

> the vb. *špṭ* (Heb. 202x; *šᵉpṭ*, Aram. 1x) describes a range of actions that restore or preserve order in society, so that justice, especially social justice, is guaranteed. Whether achieved by God (ca. 40 percent of the occurrences) or by a human agent (ca. the other 60 percent), as a continuous activity it can be translated as rule, govern; as a specific activity it can be translated as deliver, rescue, or judge. (*NIDOTTE*, 4:214)

Schulz is adamant that no one translation can be used in every instance. He finally decides that in Judges, aside from the special usage with Deborah, the term means "x *led*, i.e., served as the divinely designated *šōpēṭ* of Israel" (*NIDOTTE*, 4:215). Thus most modern translations choose one of the two ambiguous translations: "judge" (CJB, HCSB, REB, NRSV, NKJV, NLT, NJB, NASB, NAB) or "lead" (TNIV, NET, JPS, CEV). G. Liedke begins with the obvious: "The 'basic meaning' of the root has long been disputed" and cannot be restricted to "judicial decision making." The common description then is "an action [by a third party] that restores the disturbed order of a (legal) community" (compare Judg 11:27). The Judges formula "has overtones of governing over Israel," but still Liedke finds "no keys for the solution of the problem of the 'judges' in Israel's prenational period" (*TLOT*, 3:1394). *HALOT* decides, "Where שׁפט designates a prolonged action its meaning tends to be to rule, control" and sees where the term "means to pass judgement as well as including (or at least suggesting) to rule, or alternatively to govern—a) שׁפט אֶת־יִשְׂרָאֵל; Judg 3:10; 4:4; 10:2, 3; 12:7–9, 11, 13–14; 15:20; 16:31; 1 Sam 4:18; 7:6, 15–17; 8:2; 2 Kg 23:22" (4:1623). W. Richter surmises that "the judges of Israel originate in a town or a tribe during the transition from a tribal to a civil constitution; they are the appointed representatives from the elders of the tribe for ordering the administration of justice and civil affairs concerning a town and the corresponding territory" (*ZAW* 77 [1965] 71).

A more sociological model comes from P. McNutt. Her tentative conclusion is that

> it is possible that on the tribal level there were chiefs, or chieftains, who mediated in situations that could not be dealt with on the local level. . . . There may also have been a tendency for individual leaders within some of the lineages to act as spokesperson for a whole kinship group, to coordinate battles with the assistance of other lineages, and probably also to help resolve conflicts between individual families within the lineage. If this was the case, their status within their own group, as is typical of tribal societies, would have been based on the willingness of lineage members to take their advice and acknowledge their decisions, as long as they conformed to the members' expectations of them. . . . In all likelihood the head of the household of the most prominent family in the lineage would have served in such a capacity, although other individuals could have been considered as well. (*Reconstructing the Society of Ancient Israel*, 99–101)

The book of Judges shows in the minor judges the people who conform to McNutt's criteria—prominent, economically well-off leaders of large families. The individual narratives emphasize God's special choosing or Israel's false choosing of ill-equipped "weaklings." You have the left-handed Ehud; the woman Deborah; the unwilling Barak; the least of the least of the clans, Gideon; the self-proclaimed Abimelech with questions hanging over his family ties; the excluded prostitute's son, Jephthah; and the humble Danite family of Samson. They need to be seen in tribal light, not in modern monarchy light. They had no central palace and no central administrative staff. They relied on friendship or military ties for their followers. When battle finished, everyone went home to normal daily life, the "judge" more than likely joining the farmers in sowing and reaping the crops, simply available should decisions need to be made, advice given, or battles fought. Thus some left long tales of battles behind them. Others left nothing but annalistic notes reporting their family ties and their time of reign.

Tola, the first of the minor judges, leaves us the least amount of information—name, hometown, length of reign, tribe of origin, and death notice.

3–5 Tola's successor, Jair, provides a bit more information. His tribal affiliation raises questions, Gilead being territory east of the Jordan, not a tribal name. Yet Gileadites formed a unit within the clan of Machir in east Manasseh (Num 26:29) and could be listed parallel to other tribes in the ancient tribal list of Deborah's song (Judg 5:17; compare Hos 6:8). At some point, Gilead was strong enough among the East Jordan clans to claim tribal status. Jair uniquely conquers territory rather than defending against invaders. (See Hauser, *JETS* 22.4 [1979] 300.)

McNutt notes that "tribal structure and membership change constantly" (*Reconstructing the Society of Ancient Israel,* 82). Israel shows the complexity of this sociological conclusion. Apparently, quite early on Israel developed a concept of twelve tribes with a common ancestor and gave names to those tribes. But sociological changes altered the status of Levi, of the priests, and of the Joseph tribes. Military and social changes among the clans led to differing groups included in one of the most ancient listings of tribal names (Judg 5). Jair the Gileadite simply offers one more piece of evidence of the flexibility of the tribal system even with an ancient narrative defining the group.

Jair represents the strength of East Jordan tribes in a narrative dominated by the West Jordan tribes. Such strength would later play out in the Saul/David and Saul/Absalom struggles as well as in Jeroboam's necessity to establish a headquarters in East Jordan at Penuel. Jair's family includes thirty sons, each apparently with his own donkey, and each presumably controlling a separate town or village located within a district named after another ancient Jair (Num 32:41). Schneider notes how few people are "depicted as riding beasts of burden in Judges (1:14; 4:3, 7, 15; 6:5), only people who were powerful and part of the ruling elite" (157).

The region is referred to as Havvoth Jair. The strength of each of the villages was most likely small, the name Havvoth Jair (חוות יאיר) meaning an encampment of tents or tent villages (*HALOT*). Still, many commentators discern negative traits in Jair. Schneider (157) sees the villages being tied to Jair and separated from their original context with Moses (Num 32:39–40). Jordan contrasts him with Tola, perceiving Jair "moving in the direction of royal and dynastic privileges." In similar vein, Jordan sees the polygamous relationships of Jair, Ibzan, and Abdon as indicating that Israel's leaders "were drifting into a position of seeking special honors and privileges and of viewing themselves above certain provisions of the Law" (180).

This text shows the minor judges following in the footprints or familyprints of Gideon in amassing a harem, a formidable family, and great political and economic power. Still, Block correctly notes, "It is difficult to know the narrator's intent in this highly schematic picture." He decides that "the most likely interpretation is that the image of thirty sons riding on thirty donkeys conveys a picture of peace and prosperity in contrast to the insecurity and danger that characterized the days of Shamgar and Jael (5:6–10)" (340). Hauser concludes, "The picture of the many sons riding on their asses to the various cities suggests that Jair delegated authority to his sons in order that they could help govern the territory over which he had control" (*JETS* 22.4 [1979] 301).

What is lacking in all the minor judges' notices is any reference to their religious allegiances. So Jair's death notice bids him adieu.

6–18 Having introduced the first two minor judges without any framework, the narrator suddenly injects an extended framework setting up the Ammonite war and revealing the depraved status of Israel, with "the most elaborate description of Israelite apostasy in the book" (Block, 344). Structurally, these verses parallel the messenger's speech of 2:1–4, the prophetic speech of 6:7–10, and the narrative summary of 8:29–35. Each shows where Israel stands spiritually before God at a critical stage of history. The messenger shows that God is no longer bound to the covenant promises to give all the land to Israel, setting up the spiritual side of the ensuing warfare in the book. The prophet shows why unheeding, disobedient Israel is in such dreadful straits economically and militarily before the Ammonites, so that their cry for help does not bring automatic, immediate relief. The summary presents Israel's complete split with God, serving a Baal of the covenant and forgetting altogether the covenant of Yahweh and his deliverances. Chap. 10 then takes God's rejection one step further. God will not listen to a people who do not listen to him.

6 For Webb, Judg 10:6–16 contains "an exposition of the crisis out of which the plot is generated. It is a crisis with a double focus, one religious . . . and one political" ([1987] 42). "Sons of Israel" (בְּנֵי יִשְׂרָאֵל) is the favorite title for Israel in the book of Judges (1:1; 2:4, 6, 11; 3:2, 5, 7–9, 12, 14–15, 27; 4:1, 3, 5, 23–24; 6:1–2, 6–8; 8:28, 33–34; 10:6, 8, 10–11, 15, 17; 11:27, 33; 13:1; 19:12, 30–20:1; 20:3, 7, 13–14, 18–19, 23–27, 30, 32, 35; 21:5–6, 18, 24), but the spread in usage is interesting. The overwhelming majority of the occurrences in chaps. 1–11 and 13:1 appear in the framework materials (3:27; 4:5; 10:17; 11:27 being the only possible exceptions). Thereafter the Samson materials do not use the expression, but it becomes central to the narrative materials in the final three chapters. This provides one more piece of evidence that the "hero" narratives of the first half of the book focus more on individual tribes than on Israel as a whole, whereas the "appendix" chapters, especially Judg 19–21, zero in precisely on the sons of Israel.

"Again the sons of Israel did evil in the eyes of Yahweh" (Judg 10:6). With the minor judges as with the heroes, Judg 2:19 still remained in play: the judge changed only his generation as long as he lived. See Judg 2:11; 3:7, 12; 4:1; 6:1; 10:6; 13:1. The insertion of the יסף, "to do again," shows that evildoing has become a habit in Israel. This insertion, Sjöberg says, "signals that both the summary (10:6–8) and the scene of the dialogue (10:10–15) should be regarded as detailed accounts of what the Israelites had done many times before" (*Wrestling with Textual Violence*, 40). The evil is explicitly defined in v 6: "served the Baals and Ashtaroth" (עַשְׁתָּרוֹת; see 2:13). In Judg 2:11 and 8:33 the evil was serving the Baals, while in 3:7 they served the Baals and Asheroth (הָאֲשֵׁרוֹת). The narrative of 6:28, 30 tells of breaking down the altar of Baal and the "sacred pole" (הָאֲשֵׁרָה), and the narrative of 9:4 centers on the temple of Baal Berith (compare 9:46, El Berith). Israel's immediate confession mentions only the Baals (10:10). The purpose here is revealed in the following list of countries with their gods. This summary seeks to show Israel's evil at its worst. Rather than follow Joshua's example and annihilate the enemies of God and of his people, Israel lives with the nations and adopts their ways in culture and in worship.

Niditch believes that "the writer seeks to identify his people Israel and its God over against cultural enemies with whom much is shared in terms of language, worldview, and geography" (123). The gods of Aram let Israel maintain the close ties of the patriarchs with the Arameans or Syrians (Gen 24:2–4; 27:43–28:5; 29:1–30; Deut 26:5). Apparently the storm god Hadad led the Aramean gods. The gods of Sidon point to the Phoenicians to the northwest of Israel. Eshmun was the chief god of Sidon, while the partner city Tyre worshiped Melqart. We know little about either of these deities. Moab lay across the Jordan to the southeast, where Chemosh, the chief deity, led Moabite armies in battle. (See Num 21:29; Judg 11:24; 1 Kgs 11:7, 33; 2 Kgs 23:13; Jer 48:7, 13, 46.) The Ammonites claimed territory just north of Moab across the Jordan and were kin to Israel through Lot (Gen 19:36–38; compare Deut 2:19); among the Ammonites, Milcom was the main god (1 Kgs 11:5, 33; 2 Kgs 23:13; compare 2 Sam 12:30 = 1 Chr 20:2; Jer 49:1, 3; Amos 1:15; Zeph 1:5). Dagon was the chief god of the Philistines on the southwest coast (Judg 16:23; 1 Sam 5:1–7; 1 Chr 10:10; 1 Macc 10:83–84; 11:4). This "god list" then encompasses most of the people who had threatened Israel in the previous Judges stories, though Sidon does not appear there, and the Midianite gods are not included here. Ironically, Israel chose the gods of their enemies, the gods from whom Yahweh continually delivered them, and forsook their own God. Niditch would caution, "The links between these groups and the historical setting of late-second-millennium B.C.E., premonarchic Israel, a period assumed by the author, are difficult to make" (122).

Eventually this evil will be explained in a different way—doing right in one's own eyes. Refusal to seek and obey God's directions results in making oneself God and obeying only the self's desires. Josh 24:15 challenged Israel to "choose this day whom you would serve" (NRSV). Joshua's generation chose the impossible path of following Yahweh. The minor judges' generation tried to avoid choosing. They served every god they could find, every one except the true God, Yahweh. Preoccupied with pleasing foreign gods, Israel "abandoned Yahweh and did not serve him" (Judg 10:6). This refrain comes from the opening framework (Judg 2:12, 21; 10:6, 10, 13), again emphasizing that the minor judges did not fare any better than their better-known counterparts in changing the behavior of the Israelite people.

7 God's "anger blazed against Israel" (see Judg 2:14, 20; 3:8; 6:39). The Bible consistently pictures God as an emotional person who reacts to the choices his people make. Anger is a faithful response to Israel's rejection. All efforts to erase divine anger from Scripture fail, because God's anger continues to reappear in Torah, History, Poetry, Prophets, Apocalyptic, Gospels, Letters, and the Apocalypse. Anger leads God to sell Israel into the hands of the Philistines (Judg 3:3, 31; 10:6–7, 11; 13:1, 5; 14:3–4; 15:3, 5–6, 9, 11–12, 14, 20; 16:5, 8–9, 12, 14, 18, 20–21, 23, 27–28, 30) and the Ammonites (Judg 3:13; 10:6–7, 9, 11, 17–18; 11:4–6, 8–9, 12–15, 27–33, 36; 12:1–3), each of whom made a cameo appearance in chap. 3

and will take center stage in what follows. Jephthah will deal with the Ammonites, and Samson with the Philistines. The God-as-salesman image comes again from the early framework (Judg 2:14; 3:8; 4:2), having been used only once since (4:9). Thus 10:6–7 reinforces the opening framework and shows that its warnings remain in effect for a disobedient Israel.

8 Here we see what Sjöberg calls "temporal summary," showing the narrator "has made a selection with regard to which parts of the story are worthy of narration" (*Wrestling with Violence*, 44). The syntax of this sentence is a bit strained (see *Note* 10:8.a), but the major element is a shift of the center of emphasis back across the Jordan to Gilead. Gilead as a territory has been mentioned in Judges only in reference to Jair (10:4) unless one includes the "tribe" of Gilead in 5:17 or the geographically difficult mention of Mount Gilead in 7:3. Gideon's pursuits (chap. 8) centered in East Jordan with no explicit mention of Gilead. The mention here is opening the way for Gilead to take center stage in the narrative (10:17–11:2; 11:5, 7–11, 29; 12:4–5, 7; 20:1; 21:8–10, 12, 14). This is called the "land of the Amorites." Again, the Amorites have played little role up to this point, appearing in the opening chapter in reference to the tribes of Joseph and Dan (Judg 1:34–36) in the framework (3:5), and in the narrative of 6:10, which identified them as the original owner of the promised land. Mention of the Amorites here is a set-up for God's defense statement in Judg 10:11 and for the report in 11:19, 21–23.

The Ammonites both "extinguish" (רעע, a rare word appearing elsewhere only in Exod 15:6) and "exterminate" (רצץ, *po'lel*, a form used only here) the sons of Israel. The Hebrew syntax apparently indicates that Ammon (possibly in conjunction with the Philistines, since the Hebrew indicates the subject with only a plural verb form) made a determinative attack immediately upon God's selling the Israelites. The result of this is an eighteen-year bondage for Israel. The NET textual note explains a slightly different point of view:

> The phrase שְׁמֹנֶה עֶשְׂרֵה שָׁנָה (*shemoneh 'esreh shanah*) could be translated "eighteen years," but this would be difficult after the reference to "that year." It is possible that v. 8b is parenthetical, referring to an eighteen year long period of oppression east of the Jordan which culminated in hostilities against all Israel (including Judah, see v. 9) in the eighteenth year. It is simpler to translate the phrase as an ordinal number, though the context does not provide the point of reference. (See Gen 14:4–5.) In this case, the following statement specifies which "Israelites" are in view.

9 The Ammonites cross the Jordan from the east. The opponents, as in the hero narratives, are tribes, not the whole nation. The precise tribes named are of extreme interest for the book of Judges. Judah leads the list, having played the major role in chap. 1 (vv 2–4, 8–10, 16–19) and being primed to play a role in the Samson narrative and beyond (Judg 15:9–11; 17:7–9; 18:12; 19:1–2, 18; 20:18). Benjamin was marked briefly with failure in the first chapter (1:21) but praised for participating with Deborah and Barak (5:14). This mention prepares for the tragedy in the final chapters (19:14; 20:3–4, 10, 12–15, 17–18, 20–21, 23–25, 28, 30–32, 35–36, 39–41, 43–44, 46, 48–21:1; 21:6, 13–18, 20–21, 23). Ephraim is the most consistently represented tribe in the book. Most of the references, however, deal with the people's location, not their tribal action (2:9; 3:27; 4:5; 10:1; 12:15; 17:1, 8; 18:2, 13; 19:1, 16, 18). They failed their task in chap. 1 (v 29), gained praise for fighting for Deborah and Barak (5:14), and complained to Gideon for a greater share of battle honor (7:24; 8:1–2). This passage prepares for their decimating battle against Jephthah (12:1, 4–6). The editorial note here mentions each of the three tribes more for what is to come than for what has already occurred. But it appears to be no accident that precisely these three tribes are represented in this book dealing so strongly with leadership, for they represent the three sources of monarchs for Israel—the Davidic dynasty in Judah, the short-lived rule of Saul from Benjamin, and the disastrous role of Jeroboam from Ephraim.

Ammon's invasion against these three southerly tribes brings "extreme trouble," even terror, to Israel. This phrase "Israel was in extreme trouble" (וַתֵּצֶר לְיִשְׂרָאֵל מְאֹד) is picked up from the framework 2:15, another indication that this is written in terms of the narrator's purpose rather than in terms presented by the individual narratives themselves. The verb צרר, "to be in distress," does occur again in 11:7. The narrator thus signals that what is ahead is centered on the entire people Israel, not just on individual tribes.

10   Again, vocabulary from the framework appears as the Israelites surprisingly "cry out" (זעק, Judg 3:9, 15; 6:6–7; 10:10, 14) to Yahweh, not to the Baals and other national gods, for help. Note that the same term can be used for calling out or summoning the troops (4:10, 13; 6:34–35; 12:2; 18:22–23). Yahweh thus becomes the last resort when all other worship has failed. For the only time in the book, the people of Israel confess their "sin" (חטא, Judg 10:10, 15), defining sin precisely as the narrator described it in v 6—abandoning God, not worshiping or serving him, and worshiping or serving the Baals. Note here again the plural Baals denoting varied worship of Baal at different sanctuaries and possibly under different titles, such as that of Baal Berith in Shechem. Later Jephthah will use the term (חטא) to talk about missing the mark in international relationships (11:27), and the term will be used in its technical meaning of missing the mark in archery (20:16). The reader thus sees Israel reduced to its direst condition and finally doing as God and the narrator seem to have intended all the while.

The expectation is for God to forgive the people of Israel and restore them as his obedient people ruling the land. But is Brensinger right in seeing Israel here as "self-centered," the confession of sin being a "mere bargaining chip" (125)? Along a similar path, Polzin thinks that the Israelites attempt "once more to use Yahweh to insure their peace and tranquility" (178). Block notes that "Yahweh does not take the confession seriously" (346).

11–12   See *Note* 11.a for a discussion of the syntax that has caused problems for commentators and translators, many of whom add an "I delivered you" to the verse. So NRSV:

And the LORD said to the Israelites, "Did I not deliver you from the Egyptians and from the Amorites, from the Ammonites and from the Philistines? The Sidonians also, and the Amalekites, and the Maonites, oppressed you; and you cried to me, and I delivered you out of their hand."

The Complete Jewish Bible reads:

ADONAI said to the people of Isra'el, "I saved you from the Egyptians, the Emorim, the people of 'Amon, and the P'lishtim, didn't I? Likewise, when the people of Tzidon, 'Amalek and Ma'on oppressed you, you cried out to me; and I rescued you from their power."

NKJV renders:

So the LORD said to the children of Israel, "*Did I* not *deliver you* from the Egyptians and from the Amorites and from the people of Ammon and from the Philistines? Also the Sidonians and Amalekites and Maonites oppressed you; and you cried out to Me, and I delivered you from their hand." (emphasis original)

The second edition of the New Living Translation reads:

The LORD replied, "Did I not rescue you from the Egyptians, the Amorites, the Ammonites, the Philistines, the Sidonians, the Amalekites, and the Maonites? When they oppressed you, you cried out to me for help, and I rescued you."

MT sees the entire list of nations as oppressors from whom God delivered Israel after they had cried for help. The emendation proposed in *BHS* (see *Note* 11.a) speaks of God delivering Israel from the nations in v 11 and then listing other nations that oppressed Israel, leading Israel to cry out and God to deliver. NLT joins the two ideas by seeing God rescuing Israel from all the nations, and then referring back to times of oppression by each of them, leading to Israel's crying out and God's rescuing. The precise nuance of meaning may escape us due to textual uncertainty, but the theological presupposition is clear. Historically, the people of Israel must confess that God has faithfully defeated Israel's enemies when they have called for him to do so. Mention of Egypt refers to the exodus tradition.

The Amorites may well represent the conquest tradition under Joshua and all the nations that lived in Canaan: "The Amalekites live in the land of the Negeb; the Hittites, the Jebusites, and the Amorites live in the hill country; and the Canaanites live by the sea, and along the Jordan" (Num 13:29 NRSV; compare Deut 1:7; Jos 3:10; 9:1). Or it may refer to a group living east of the Jordan: "From there they set out, and camped on the other side of the Arnon, in the wilderness that extends from the boundary of the Amorites; for the Arnon is the boundary of Moab, between Moab and the Amorites" (Num 21:13 NRSV; compare 21:31).

Traditions about the Ammonites insist that God told Moses not to fight the Ammonites (Deut 2:19, 37). Yet the tribe of Gad received part of the territory of the Ammonites (Josh 13:24–25). The only specific "oppression" from the Ammonites would be in connection with Ehud's battles with the Moabites (Judg 3:13). The major battles with the Ammonites lay in the future under Jephthah (Judg 11–12), Saul (1 Sam 10:27; 11:11; 14:47), and David (2 Sam 8:12; 10:1–12:31).

The Philistines would also be a major foe in the immediate future with Samson, Saul, and David, the only time of oppression being that which Shamgar quelled (3:31; compare Josh 13:2; Judg 3:3). The Sidonians were oppressors only inasmuch as the tribe of Asher could not drive them out of their territory (1:31; compare Josh 13:6). The Sidonians really take center stage only under Queen Jezebel, the Sidonian (1 Kgs 16:31). The Amalekites inhabited the southern Negev (Num 13:29) and joined the Canaanites in defeating a disobedient Israel under Moses (Num 14:45). They also joined Eglon's Moabite coalition against Ehud (Judg 3:13) and the Midianite coalition against Gideon (Judg 6:3, 33; 7:12). Saul defeated them (1 Sam 14:48; 15:5–8), as did David (1 Sam 27:8; 30:1, 18).

The Maonites appear so infrequently (Josh 15:55; 1 Sam 23:24–25; 25:2; 1 Chr 2:45)—mainly in the story of David—that many want to change the text to Midian.

See *Note* 12.a and NAB, NJB, REB. Here, if we follow MT, we have a clear case of the narrator apparently knowing historical information that is no longer preserved for us. Block, referring to E. A. Knauf (*ABD,* 4:802), associates the name "with the Meunites, who were at home in the same region as the Midianites and may even have been a confederate or dependent group" (347).

God agrees with the Israelites' reading of their history with him. They have suffered persecution and oppression over and over. Each time they have had to call out in desperation for God's help. Each time they cried, God delivered. Matthews observes that "in God's set of place names each period from the exodus through the prior history of the settlement is chronicled" (115).

13 A strong disjunctive contrast sentence springs the divine surprise. The course of history changes. God agrees with the confessing Israel that they have sinned by abandoning him and serving other gods. This goes against God's basic covenant agreement with his people: "you shall have no other gods before me" (Exod 20:3 NRSV), a statement that occurs often in Deuteronomy and elsewhere (Exod 23:13; Deut 5:7; 6:14; 7:4; 8:19; 11:16, 28; 13:3, 7, 14; 17:3; 18:20; 28:14, 36, 64; 29:25; 30:17; 31:18, 20; compare Josh 23:16; 24:2, 16; Judg 2:12, 17, 19; 10:13; 1 Sam 8:8; 26:19; 1 Kgs 9:6, 9; 11:4, 10; 14:9; 2 Kgs 5:17; 17:7, 35, 37–38; 22:17; 2 Chr 7:19, 22; 28:25; 34:25; Jer 1:16; 7:6, 9, 18; 11:10; 13:10; 16:11, 13; 19:4, 13; 22:9; 25:6; 32:29; 35:15; 44:3, 5, 8, 15; Hos 3:1), frequently with the verb "worship" or "serve" (עבד). The speech ends echoing prophetic announcements of punishment—a punishment that involves negative action from Yahweh—"I will not deliver you again." Israel has played on God's covenant faithfulness and loving mercy too long and too often. God's patience is gone. His blazing anger does not disappear. He places limits on the repeated disobedience and "confessions" of his people. Ultimately, something real and constant must appear in the lives of God's people, something that eliminates "other gods" from the life of the people.

14 Block observes that "God sees past their pious words to their treacherous and parasitic hearts" (347). God goes so far as to suggest an alternative for his people. Go to the gods they have chosen to serve in the fertile, unhindered, unoppressed days. Let those "gods" deliver them in the time of need and oppression.

15–16a The people of Israel have no defense. They simply repeat their confession of sin and ask God to do what is good in his eyes for a people who have been doing evil in his eyes (v 6). The Israelites are ready for any action from God as long as it includes rescue from the enemies. "Rescue" (נצל) is used here rather than "deliver" (ישע). (Compare Judg 6:9; 8:34; 9:17; 10:15; 11:26; 18:28.) The two terms serve as synonyms for divine action in taking Israel out of the grasp of enemy oppressors. The people go one step further. They turn away from their gods and begin to serve Yahweh even before he rescues them. (See Josh 24:14, 23.) Now a new people faces God.

16b The divine response has elicited a tumult of scholarly responses. The text reads, literally, "And his soul *[nĕpēš]* was short with the trouble of Israel," "trouble" ambiguously referring to the trouble Israel caused Yahweh or the harm Israel suffered from enemies or the hard work oppressors were causing Israel to perform. The traditional interpretation is that God responded with his basic characteristic, gracious mercy. Thus NRSV reads: "he could no longer bear to see Israel suffer." (Compare NLT, JPS, CEV, NAB, NASB, NJB, NKJV, REB, TNIV.) Matthews continues to say that "Yahweh relents, but no specific divine action is taken or promised" (115).

The Complete Jewish Bible reads, however, "he became troubled by Isra'el's misery," while the HCSB has "He became weary of Israel's misery." The NET translation remains traditional: "Finally the LORD grew tired of seeing Israel suffer so much," but the textual note opens up the problem: "*Heb* 'And his spirit grew short [i.e., impatient] with the suffering of Israel.' The Hebrew noun נֶפֶשׁ (*nefesh*) also appears as the subject of the verb קָצַר (*qatsar*) in Num 21:4 (the Israelites grow impatient wandering in the wilderness), Judg 16:16 (Samson grows impatient with Delilah's constant nagging), and Zech 11:8 (Zechariah grows impatient with the three negligent 'shepherds')." Thus Bluedorn gives an ambiguous rendering: "In turn, YHWH acknowledges the Israelites' repentance and return to him, becomes impatient with their misery (10:16) and soon delivers them" (*Yahweh versus Baalism*, 276). Block, referring to Webb ([1987] 46–47), interprets the text to express "frustration, exasperation, and anger in the face of an intolerable situation" (349). For Block, Israel's is a "conversion of convenience." Webb (47) thus translates, "Yahweh could no longer tolerate their misery."

However one translates this final statement, Sjöberg rightly sees that "since there is no explicit description of either the original or the final state of the relationship between the people and Yhwh, it is not possible to say whether or not an original state of peace between the actors has been restored in the end" (*Wrestling with Textual Violence*, 32).

17–18 Having introduced the Ammonites as one of the two foes God used to punish his unfaithful people (vv 6–9) and having left ambiguous God's response to Israel's confession (v 16), the narrator sets the stage for his introduction of the next judge. Most often commentators set these verses up as the introduction to the Ammonite war, but the Hebrew disjunctive sentence changing focus comes at 18:1, not here. These verses conclude the transition from chaps. 4–9 to chaps. 10–16. They intimate that God's response to Israel's confession was to let the Ammonite army attack Israel in Gilead, the last judge's stronghold (v 4).

The Israelites "camped in Mizpah," which must be east of the Jordan but is difficult to locate. Its name simply means "watchtower" and is used for several locations. Becker (*Richterzeit und Königtum*, 220–21) has even tried to identify this with the Mizpah in Benjamin connected with Samuel and Saul. Gaß (*Ortsnamen*, 481) defends a location north of the Jabbok where Jephthah was at home, but then also sees the possibility of identifying it with Ramoth-mizpeh (Jos 13:26), apparently south of the Jabbok. He then surveys only southern locations (482–84), finding reasons not to support Khirbet es-Sar (too far south), Khirbet er-Rumman (too close to Ammonite territory), el-Mishrefe (lack of Iron Age archaeological evidence), and Khirbet Qurea (too far northwest of the village of Gilead). Thus Gaß sees er-Rashuni as the only site that comes into question. If one insists on a location north of the Jabbok, Gaß would place this at Suf.

The Gileadite officials (שָׂרֵי גִלְעָד) realize they have a major problem—no military commander. Thus the transition is complete. Israel's peacetime judges have disappeared for a season. Now a warrior is needed, but no likely candidate appears. And the Divine Warrior has made no promises. What can Israel do? The divine silence echoes loudly again. Block concludes, "Jephthah's emergence is treated as a purely human development" (350). Again, with Block, we find a leader "treating leadership as a matter of power rather than a call to service on behalf of those led. . . . There was no consciousness of being the people of Yahweh, no appeal to God to solve the crisis in leadership, and subsequently no reference to Yahweh raising a man. This was a purely secular moment" (351).

Explanation

Chap. 10 performs a most important function for the narrator of Judges. It marks the transition from the first set of Judges to the final set. The first have proved unacceptable as model leaders for Israel. Deborah, the prophet, served to call Barak to service, not to be the judge. Jael performed the decisive act that brought victory, and in so doing brought honor to herself and dishonor to Barak. Gideon proved unable to let God have the glory for victory, to forget his need for vengeance, and to reject the trappings of leadership. Abimelech selfishly and murderously claimed the kingship for himself, then ignored the people who crowned him, and finally murdered them before suffering an ignominious death of his own.

Thus chap. 10 introduces the new kind of judge, the "minor" judge of peaceful times. Even these create ambiguity for the reader, for Tola lived outside his own tribal territory and Jair rivaled Gideon in his materialistic lifestyle. Still, the narrator seems to accept these as having accomplished the purpose they were called to fulfill. Their counterparts in chap. 12 will let us see more of the function of the minor judges as they encase the judgeship of Jephthah. One thing the transition shows is a new weapon in the Israelites' arsenal. Now the Israelites are ready to confess their unfaithfulness in denying Yahweh and serving other gods. God reminds them of all that their only God has done for them. He has no further reason to hear their cry, accept it as genuine, and deliver them as previously. Israel replies that they trust what seems good in God's eyes while still pleading for deliverance. They apparently repent as they turn away from the foreign gods. God's ambiguous response is triggered by Israel's trouble or troubling.

Thus the people of Israel have to go to battle without a divine or human leader. They have to learn that God cannot be manipulated or predicted. They have to learn that serving God is a full-time job, not just an escape mechanism when trouble appears. They must learn to find God's peacetime leaders, not leaders like those they have followed previously. Cries to God in times of trouble should come from a faithful people, not a desperate people. Other nations do not provide the model for Israel. God's directions alone show them the path to follow. That goes for the community and especially for its leaders.

b. Jephthah: Sacrificing Family and a Tribe for Victory (11:1–12:15)

Bibliography

Bal, M. "Between Altar and Wandering Rock: Toward a Feminist Theology." In *Anti-Covenant.* Ed. M. Bal. 211–32. ———. "Dealing with Women: Daughters in the Book of Judges." In

The Book and the Text: The Bible and Literary Theory. Ed. R. Schwartz. Oxford: Blackwell, 1990. 16–39. ———. Death & Dissymmetry: The Politics of Coherence and the Hebrew Bible. Chicago: University of Chicago Press, 1988. **Bartelmus, R.** "Jephtha—Anmerkung eines Exegeten zu G. F. Händels musikalisch-theologischer Deutung einer 'entlegenen' alttestamentlichen Tradition." TZ 51 (1995) 106–27. **Bauks, M.** "La fille sans nom, la fille de Jephté." ETR 81 (2006) 81–94. **Beavis, M. A.** "A Daughter in Israel: Celebrating Bat Jephthah (Judg 11.39–40.)." Feminist Theology 13 (2004) 11–25. **Berlinerblau, J.** The Vow and the 'Popular' Religious Groups of Ancient Israel. JSOTSup 210. Sheffield: Sheffield Academic, 1996. **Berman, J.** "Medieval Monasticism and the Evolution of Jewish Interpretation of the Story of Jephthah's Daughter." JQR 95 (2005) 228–56. **Claassens, L. J. M.** "Herwaardering van die Ou Testament—verhaal in die prediking: met spesifieke verwysing na die Jefta-verhaal." NGTT 38 (1997) 397–407. ———. "Notes on Characterisation in the Jephtah Narrative." JNSL 22 (1996) 107–15. ———. "Theme and Function in the Jephthah Narrative." JNSL 23 (1997) 203–19. **Courtledge, T. W.** Vows in the Hebrew Bible and in the Ancient Near East. JSOTSup 147. Sheffield: JSOT Press, 1992. 175–85. **Craig, J. M., Jr.** "Bargaining in Tov: The Many Directions of So-called Direct Speech (Judges 11,4–11)." Bib 79 (1998) 76–85. **Culley, R. C.** Themes and Variations. 106–8. **Day, J.** "Bedan, Abdon, or Barak in 1 Samuel XII 11?" VT 43 (1993) 261–64. **Day, P. L.** "From the Child Is Born the Woman: The Story of Jephthah's Daughter." In Gender and Difference in Ancient Israel. Ed. P. L. Day. Minneapolis: Fortress, 1989. 58–74. **Dus, J.** "Bethel und Mizpa in Jdc 19–21 und Jdc. 10–12." OrAnt 3 (1964) 227–43. **Ellington, J.** "More on Shibboleth (Judges 12.6)." BT 43 (1992) 244–45. ———. "Translating Shibboleth and Sibboleth (Judges 12.6)." BT 41 (1990) 446. **Emerton, J. A.** "Some Comments on the Shibboleth Incident (Judges XII 6)." In Mélanges bibliques et orientaux. FS M. Delcor, ed. A. Caquot, S. Légasse, and M. Tardieu. AOAT 215. Neukirchen-Vluyn: Neukirchener Verlag, 1985. 149–57. **Exum, J. C.** "Feminist Criticism: Whose Interests Are Being Served?" In Judges and Method: New Approaches in Biblical Studies. Ed. G. A. Yee. Minneapolis: Fortress, 1995. 64–93. ———. "On Judges 11." In Feminist Companion to Judges (1993). Ed. A. Brenner. 131–44. ———. Tragedy and Biblical Narrative. ———. "The Tragic Vision and Biblical Narrative: The Case of Jephthah." In Signs and Wonders. Ed. J. C. Exum. 59–83. **Faber, A.** "Second Harvest: šibbōlεθ Revisited (Yet Again)." JSS 37 (1992) 1–10. **Fleishman, J.** "An Undone Evil in the Book of Judges" (Heb.). Beit-Miqra 153 (1998) 129–41. **Frymer-Kensky, T.** "Virginity in the Bible." In Gender and Law in the Hebrew Bible and the Ancient Near East. Ed. V. H. Matthews et al. JSOTSup 262. Sheffield: Sheffield Academic, 1998. 79–96. **Fuchs, E.** "Marginalization, Ambiguity, Silencing: The Story of Jephthah's Daughter." JFSR 5 (1989) 35–45. Reprinted in Feminist Companion to Judges (1993), ed. A. Brenner, 116–30. **Gandrup, R.** Jefta datter, fortaelling. Copenhagen: Gyldendalske Boghandel & Nordisk, 1922. **Gerstein, B.** "A Ritual Processed, a Look at Judges 11.40." In Anti-Covenant. Ed. M. Bal. 175–93. **Gilleo, M.** "Jephtah's Daughter: A Symbol of Omnicide." Proceedings of the Central States, Society of Biblical Literature and American Schools of Oriental Research 2 (1999) 44–52. **Good, R.** "The Just War in Ancient Israel." JBL 104 (1985) 385–400. **Greenstein, E., and D. Marcus.** "The Akkadian Inscription of Idrimi." JANESCU 8 (1976) 76–77. **Groß, W.** "Jiftachs Tochter." In Das Manna fällt auch heute noch: Beiträge zur Geschichte und Theologie des Alten, Ersten Testaments. FS E. Zenger, ed. F.-L. Hossfeld and L. Schwienhorst-Schönberger. HBS 44. Freiburg: Herder, 2004. 273–93. **Guest, P.** "Dangerous Liaisons in the Book of Judges." SJOT 11 (1997) 241–69. **Hendel, R.** "Sibilants and Shibbolet (Judges 12:6)." BASOR 301 (1996) 69–75. **Houtman, C.** "Die Bewertung eines Menschenopfers: Die Geschichte von Jefta und seiner Tochter in früher Auslegung." BN 117 (2003) 59–70. ———. "Rewriting a Dramatic Old Testament Story: The Story of Jephthah and His Daughter in Some Examples of Christian Devotional Literature." BibInt 13 (2005) 167–90. **Houtman, C., and K. Spronk.** Jefta's dochter: Tragiek van een vrouwenleven in theologie en kunst. Zoetermeer: Meinema, 1999. ———. Jefta und seine Tochter: Rezeptionsgeschichtliche Studien zu Richter, 11, 29–40. Altes Testament und Moderne 21. Zürich: LIT, 2007. **Hübner, U.** "Hermeneutische Möglichkeiten: Zur frühen

Rezeptionsgeschichte der Jefta-Tradition." In *Die Hebräischen Bibel und ihre zweifache Nachgeschichte*. Ed. E. Blum, C. Mackholz, and E. W. Stegemann. Neukirchen-Vluyn: Neukirchener Verlag, 1990. 489–501. **Hugo, P.** "'J'ai ouvert la bouche pour YHWH' (Jg 11:36): Parole et identité dans le voeu de Jephté." In *L'Ecrit et l'Esprit*. FS A. Schenker, ed. D. Böhler, I. Himbaza, and P. Hugo. OBO 214. Fribourg: Academic Press Fribourg, 2004. 112–27. **Humphreys, W. L.** "The Story of Jephthah and the Tragic Vision: A Response to J. Cheryl Exum." In *Signs and Wonders*. Ed. J. C. Exum. 85–96. **Janzen, D.** "Why the Deuteronomist Told about the Sacrifice of Jephthah's Daughter." *JSOT* 29 (2005) 339–57. **Jobling, D.** "Structuralist Criticism: The Text's World of Meaning." In *Judges and Method*. Ed. G. A. Yee. 91–118. **Kaiser, W.** *Hard Sayings in the Old Testament*. Downers Grove, IL: InterVarsity Press, 1988. 101–5. **Kallai, Z.** *Historical Geography of the Bible: The Tribal Territories of Israel*. Jerusalem: Magnes, 1986. **Karrer-Grube, C.** "Grenz-Überschreitung: Zum Körperkonzept in der Erzählung über Jepthas Tochter." In U. Bail et al., *Körperkonzepte im Ersten Testament: Aspekte einer Feministischen Anthropologie*. Hedwin-Jahnow Forschungsprojekt. Stuttgart: Kohlhammer, 2003. 94–121. **Kaswalder, P. A.** *La disputa diplomatica di Iefte (Gdc 11:12–28): La ricerca archeologica in Giordania e il problema della conquista*. Studium Biblicum Franciscanum, Analecta 29. Jerusalem: Franciscan Printing, 1990. **Keddell, J. S.** "A Dissertation on the Vow of Jephthah." London, 1840. **Keukens, K. H.** "Ri 11,37f: Rite de passage und Übersetzsprobleme." *BN* 19 (1982) 41–42. **Knauf, E. A.** "Hesbon, Sihons Stadt." *ZDPV* 106 (1990) 135–44. **Kramer, P. S.** "Jephthah's Daughter: A Thematic Approach to the Narrative as Seen in Selected Rabbinic Exegesis and in Artwork." In *Judges* (1999). Ed. A. Brenner. 67–89. **Kunz-Lübke, A.** "Interkulturell lesen? Die Geschichte von Jiftach und seiner Tochter in Jdc 11,30–40 in textsemantischer Perspektive." In *Was ist ein Text? Alttestamentliche, Ägyptologische, und altorientalische Perspektiven*. Ed. L. Morenz and S. Schorch. BZAW 362. New York: de Gruyter, 2007. 258–83. **Landers, S.** "Did Jephthah Kill His Daughter?" *BRev* 7 (1991) 27–31, 42. **Landy, F.** "Shibboleth: The Password." In *Proceedings of the Tenth World Congress of Jewish Studies*. Jerusalem: World Union of Jewish Studies, 1990. 91–98. **Lemaire, A.** "L'incident du sibbolet (Jg 12,6): perspective historique." In *Melanges bibliques et orientaux*. Ed. A. Caquot et al. Neukirchen-Vluyn: Neukirchener Verlag, 1985. 275–81. **Lenchak, T. A.** "Puzzling Passages: Judges 11:30–31." *TBT* 38 (2000) 248. **Levenson, J.** *The Death and Resurrection of the Beloved Son: The Transformation of Child Sacrifice in Judaism and Christianity*. New Haven: Yale UP, 1993. **Liptzin, S.** *Biblical Themes in World Literature*. Hoboken, NJ: Ktav, 1985. 102–12. **Marcus, D.** "The Bargaining between Jephthah and the Elders (Judges 11:4–11)." *JANES* 19 (1989) 95–110. ———. *Jephthah and His Vow*. Lubbock: Texas Tech UP, 1986. ———. "The Legal Dispute between Jephthah and the Elders." *HAR* 12 (1990) 107–11. ———. "Ridiculing the Ephraimites: The Shibboleth Incident (Judge 12:6)." *Maarav* 8 (1992) 95–105. **Marcus, R.** "The Word *sibboleth* Again." *BASOR* 87 (1942) 39. **Matthews, V.** "Female Voices: Upholding the Honor of the Household." *BTB* 24 (1994) 8–11. **Mehlman, I.** "Jephthah." *JBQ* 23 (1995) 73–78. ———. "Jephthah's Daughter." *JQR* 25 (1997) 73–78. **Mendelsohn, I.** "The Disinheritance of Jephthah in the Light of Paragraph 27 of the Lipit-Ishtar Code." *IEJ* 4 (1954) 116–19. **Milgrom, J.** *Numbers*. JPS Torah Commentary. Philadelphia: Jewish Publication Society, 1990. 488–90. **Miller, B.** *Tell It on the Mountain: The Daughter of Jephthah in Judges 11*. Collegeville, MN: Liturgical Press, 2005. **Mittmann, S.** "Aroer, Minnith und Abel Keramim (Jdc 11,33)." *ZDPV* 85 (1969) 63–75. **Mosca, P.** "Child Sacrifice in Canaanite and Israelite Religion: A Study of *mulk* and *mlk*." PhD diss., Harvard University, 1975. **Na'aman, N.** "Pirathon and Ophrah." *BN* 50 (1989) 11–16. **Neef, H.-D.** "Jephta und seine Tochter (Jdc. xi 29–40)." *VT* 49 (1999) 206–17. **Olson, D.** "Dialogues of Lie and Monologues of Death: Jephthah and Jephthah's Daughter in Judges 10:6–12:7." In *Postmodern Interpretations of the Bible—A Reader*. Ed. A. K. M. Adam. Saint Louis: Chalice, 2001. 43–54. **Orlinsky, H.** "On Gen 39:14,17; Jud 11:37." *JBL* 61 (1942) 87–97. **Ostriker, A.** "Jephthah's Daughter." *Cross Currents* 51 (2001) 201–18. ———. "Jephthah's Daughter: A Lament." In *On the Cutting Edge: The Study of Women in Biblical Worlds*. Ed. J. Schaberg, A. Bach, and E. Fuchs. New York: Continuum, 2003. 230–49. **Parker, S. B.** "The Vow in Ugaritic and Israelite Narrative Literature." *UF* 11 (1980) 693–700. **Penna, A.** "The Vow of Jephthah in the Interpretation of St. Jerome." *StPatr* 4 (1961) 162–70. **Pitt-Rivers, J.** *The Fate of Shechem or the Politics of Sex.* Cambridge: Cambridge UP, 1977. **Ramras-Rauch, G.** "Fathers and Daughters: Two Biblical Narratives." In *Mappings of the Biblical Terrain.* Ed. V. Tollers and J. Maier. Lewisburg, PA: Bucknell UP, 1990. 158–69. **Reinke, L.** "Über das Gelübde Jephthas." In *Beiträge zur Erklärung des Alten Testaments.* Münster: Copenrath, 1851. 1.3:419–526. **Reis, P. T.** "Spoiled Child: A Fresh Look at Jephthah's Daughter." *Proof* 71 (1997) 279–98. **Reviv, H.** "Elders and Saviors." *OrAnt* 16 (1977) 201–4. ———. *The Elders in Ancient Israel.* Jerusalem: Magnes, 1989. **Richter, W.** "Die Überlieferungen um Jephtah: Ri 10,17–12:6." *Bib* 47 (1966) 485–556. **Robinson, B. P.** "The Story of Jephthah and His Daughter: Then and Now." *Bib* 85 (2004) 331–48. **Römer, T. C.** "La fille de Jephté entre Jérusalem et Athènes: Réflexions à partir d'une triple intertextualité en Juges 11." In *Intertextualités: La Bible en echoes.* MdB 40. Geneva: Labor et Fides, 2000. 30–42. ———. "Why Would the Deuteronomists Tell about the Sacrifice of Jephthah's Daughter?" *JSOT* 77 (1998) 22–38. **Rooke, D. W.** "Sex and Death, or, the Death of Sex: Three Versions of Jephthah's Daughter (Judges 11:29–40)." In *Biblical Traditions in Transmission.* FS M. A. Knibb, ed. C. Hempel and J. M. Lieu. JSJSup 111. Leiden: Brill, 2006. 249–71. **Rösel, H. N.** "Jephtah und das Problem der Richter." *Bib* 61 (1980) 251–55. **Rottzoll, D. U.,** and **A. Rottzoll.** "Die Erzählung von Jiftach und seine Tochter (Jdg 11,30–40) in der mittelalterlichjüdischen und historisch-kritischen Bibelexegese." *ZAW* 115 (2003) 210–30. **Sasaki, T.** "The Ironic Use of צל in Judges 11:26" (Japanese). *Exeg* 13 (2003) 47–53. **Schenker, A.** "Gelübde im Alten Testament: Unbeachtete Aspekte." *VT* 39 (1989) 87–91. **Schmitt, H.-C.** "Das Hesbonlied Num 21,27ab–30 und die Geschichte der Stadt Hesbon." *ZDPV* 104 (1988) 26–43. **Schulte, H.** "Beobachtungen zum Begriff der Zona im Alten Testament." *ZAW* 104 (1992) 255–62. **Seters, J. van.** "The Conquest of Sihon's Kingdom: A Literary Examination." *JBL* 91 (1972) 182–97. **Sjöberg, M.** *Wrestling with Textual Violence: The Jephthah Narrative in Antiquity and Modernity.* Sheffield: Sheffield Phoenix, 2005. **Ska, J. L.** "De quelques elipses dans les récits bibliques." *Bib* 76 (1995) 63–71. **Smelik, K. A. D.** "The Use and Misuse of the Hebrew Bible as a Historical Source." In *The Rediscovery of the Hebrew Bible.* Ed. J. W. Dyk et al. ACEBTSup 1. Maastricht: Shaker, 1999. 121–39. **Speiser, E. A.** "The Shibboleth Incident (Jud. 12:6)." *BASOR* 85 (1942) 10–13. **Stanton, E. C.** *The Woman's Bible: The Original Feminist Attack on the Bible.* 2 vols. 1895–1898. Reprint, Seattle: Coalition Task Force on Women and Religion, 1974. **Steinberg, N.** "The Problem of Human Sacrifice in War: An Analysis of Judges 11." In *On the Way to Nineveh.* FS G. M. Landes, ed. S. L. Cook and S. C. Winter. ASOR Books 4. Atlanta: Scholars Press, 1999. 114–35. **Swiggers, P.** "The Word *Shibbolet* in Jud. xii.6." *JSS* 26 (1981) 205–7. **Sypherd, W. O.** *Jephthah and His Daughter: A Study in Comparative Literature.* Newark: University of Delaware Press, 1948. **Tapp, A. M.** "An Ideology of Expendability: Virgin Daughter Sacrifice in Genesis 19:1–11, Judges 11:30–39, and 19:22–26." In *Anti-Covenant.* Ed. M. Bal. 157–74. **Thompson, J. L.** "Preaching Texts of Terror in the Book of Judges: How Does the History of Interpretation Help?" *CTJ* 37 (2002) 49–61. **Trible, P.** "The Daughter of Jephthah: An Inhuman Sacrifice." In *Texts of Terror.* 93–116. ———. "A Daughter's Death: Feminism, Literary Criticism, and the Bible." In *Backgrounds for the Bible.* Ed. M. P. O'Connor and D. N. Freedman. Winona Lake, IN: Eisenbrauns, 1987. 1–14. ———. "A Meditation in Mourning: The Sacrifice of the Daughter of Jephthah." *USQR* 31 (1981) 59–73. **Tropper, J.** "Die *Shibbolet* Fälle (Richter 12,6)." *ZAH* 10 (1997) 198–200. **Valler, S.** "The Story of Jephthah's Daughter in the Midrash." In *Judges* (1999). Ed. A. Brenner. 48–66. **Walton, J., V. H. Matthews,** and **M. W. Chavalas.** *The IVP Bible Background Commentary: Old Testament.* Downers Grove, IL: InterVarsity Press, 2000. **Webb, B. G.** "The Theme of the Jephthah Story." *RTR* 45 (1986) 34–43. **Willis, T. M.** "The Nature of Jephthah's Authority." *CBQ* 59 (1997) 33–44. **Wuckelt, A.** "Sterben Frauen anders als Männer? Todeserzählungen geschlechterspezifisch betrachtet." *BK* 61 (2006) 22–26. **Wüst, M.** "Die Einschaltung in die

Jiftachgeschichte: Ri 11:13–26." *Bib* 56 (1975) 464–79. **Zapletal, V.** *Jephtas Tochter: Kulturbilder aus der Frühzeit des jüdischen Volkes.* Paderborn: Schöningh, 1920.

Translation

^{11:1}*Jephthah, the Gileadite, was a heroic warrior, but he was the son of a prostitute. Gilead had fathered Jephthah.* ²*Gilead's wife also bore him sons, and the wife's sons*[a] *matured. They drove Jephthah out, saying to him, "You will not inherit anything in our father's house, for you are the son of another woman."*[b] ³*Jephthah fled from his brothers and lived in the land of Tob. A group of unprincipled*[a] *men gathered around Jephthah and went out with him to fight.*[b]

⁴*Some*[a] *days later, the sons of Ammon fought with Israel.* ⁵*Just as the sons of Ammon began to fight with Israel, the elders of Gilead went to get Jephthah from*[a] *the land of Tob.* ⁶*They said to Jephthah, "Come! Become our commander so we can fight the sons of Ammon."*

⁷*Jephthah said to*[a] *the elders of Gilead, "Aren't you the ones who hated me and threw me out of my father's house?*[b] *Why have you come to me now when you're in trouble?"*

⁸*The elders of Gilead told Jephthah, "Granted that's the case. Now we are turning to you. You must go with us so we can fight*[a] *against the sons of Ammon. You will become our head over all the residents of Gilead."*

⁹*Jephthah told the elders of Gilead, "If you bring me back to fight against the sons of Ammon and if Yahweh gives them to me,*[a] *I, indeed I, will be your head."*[b]

¹⁰*The elders of Gilead told Jephthah, "Yahweh is listening between us. We take an oath that we will keep our word."*[a] ¹¹*Jephthah went with the elders of Gilead, and the army*[a] *put him over them as head and as commander. Jephthah spoke all his words before Yahweh in Mizpah.*

¹²*Jephthah sent messengers to the king of the sons of Ammon,*[a] *"What's at issue between me*[b] *and you that you have come against me to fight*[c] *against my country?"*

¹³*The king of the sons of Ammon told Jephthah's messengers, "Because Israel took my land—from the Arnon to*[a] *the Jabbok and to the Jordan—when they came up from Egypt. Now, therefore, give it*[b] *back in peace."*[c]

¹⁴*Once again Jephthah sent messengers*[a] *to the king of the sons of Ammon.* ¹⁵*He*[a] *said to him, "Thus says Jephthah, 'Israel did not take the land of Moab or the land of the sons of Ammon.*[b] ¹⁶*Indeed, when Israel went up from Egypt, they came into the wilderness clear to the Sea of Reeds*[a] *and came on to Kadesh.* ¹⁷*Israel sent messengers to the king of Edom, "Please, let me*[a] *pass through your land." But the king of Edom did not listen. In the same way they sent to the king of Moab, but he was not willing. Israel continued to live in Kadesh.* ¹⁸*They came through the wilderness, turned around the land of Edom and the land of Moab, and came to the eastern side of the land of Moab. They camped beyond the Arnon,*[a] *not coming into the territory of Moab, since the Arnon was the Moabite boundary.* ¹⁹*Israel sent messengers to Sihon, king of the Amorites, being king in Heshbon. Israel said to him, "Please, let us*[a] *pass though your land unto my place."* ²⁰*But Sihon did not trust*[a] *Israel to pass through his territory, so Sihon gathered all his army and camped at Jahaz. He fought with*[b] *Israel.* ²¹*Yahweh, the God of Israel, gave Sihon and all his army into Israel's hand. Israel struck them dead. They took possession of all the land of the Amorites who lived in that*[a] *land.* ²²*They*[a] *possessed all the Amorite territory*[b] *from the Arnon to the Jabbok*[c] *and from the wilderness to the Jordan.* ²³*Now therefore, Yahweh, the God of Israel, has taken possession away from the Amorites because*

of his people Israel. But you, will you now take possession from him?[a] [24] *Will you not take as possession whatever Chemosh, your god, takes as a possession for you?*[a] *At the same time everything that Yahweh, our God, takes as a possession*[b] *before us, we will take as a possession.* [25] *Now, therefore, are you better than Balak, son of Zippor, the king of Moab? Did he ever take Israel to court or*[a] *go into battle against them?* [26] *While Israel was living in Heshbon and its villages and in Aroer*[a] *and its villages and in all the towns on the banks of the Arnon*[b] *for three hundred years, why did you not rescue them*[c] *in that time?* [27] *As for me, I have not sinned against you, but you are treating me in an evil way in coming out to battle against me. May Yahweh, the Judge, judge today*[a] *between the sons of Israel and the sons of Ammon?'"*

[28] *The king of the sons of Ammon did not listen*[a] *to Jephthah's words that he sent to him.*

[29] *The Spirit of Yahweh came over Jephthah, and he crossed through Gilead*[a] *and Manasseh, and he crossed through Mizpah*[b] *of Gilead, and from Mizpah of Gilead,*[c] *he passed over*[d] *to the sons of Ammon.* [30] *Jephthah vowed a vow to Yahweh, "If you will truly give the sons of Ammon into my hand,* [31] *as I return in peace from the sons of Ammon, whatever comes out*[a] *when they come out of the door of my house to meet me will belong to Yahweh, and I will sacrifice it as a burnt offering."*[b]

[32] *Jephthah passed through to the sons of Ammon to engage in battle with them, and Yahweh gave them into his hand.* [33] *He struck them dead in twenty towns from Aroer to the entrance to Minnith*[a] *and*[b] *clear to Abel-keramim.*[c] *It was an exceedingly massive strike. The sons of Ammon were subdued before the sons of Israel.* [34] *Jephthah came to Mizpah to his house. Look! His daughter is coming out to meet him with tambourines and dancing. However, she was an only child.*[a] *Besides her, he had no son or daughter.* [35] [a] *As he saw her, he tore his clothes and said, "Oh, NO! My daughter, you make me bend over in pain.*[b] *At the same time you are*[c] *ruining me. Yes, I opened my mouth to Yahweh, and I cannot bring it back."*

[36] *She told him, "My father,*[a] *you opened your mouth to Yahweh. Do to me just what came out of your mouth after what Yahweh has done for you, avenging your enemies, the sons of Ammon."*[b] [37] *She told her father, "Do*[a] *this one thing for me. Leave me alone for two months. I will walk up and go down on the mountains and weep over my virginity, I and my friends."*[b]

[38] *He said, "Go!" and sent her away for two*[a] *months. She went with her friends and wept over her virginity on the mountains.* [39] *At the end of two months, she returned to her father, and he*[a] *did to her according to the vow that he had vowed. At that time she had not known a man. It has become*[b] *a statute in Israel:* [40] *"each year*[a] *Israel's daughters go out for four days in the year to recite*[b] *the story of the daughter of Jephthah the Gileadite."*

[12:1] *The men*[a] *of Ephraim were mustered for battle. They crossed over to Zaphon*[b] *and said to Jephthah, "Why did you cross over to fight with the sons of Ammon, but you did not summon us to go with you? We're going to burn your house with fire over you."*[c]

[2] *Jephthah told them, "A person of arbitration*[a] *have I been—I with my people and with the sons of Ammon. Exceedingly!*[b] *I issued the mustering cry for*[c] *you, but you did not rescue me from their hand.* [3] *I saw that you were*[a] *not a savior; then I took my life in my own hands, and I crossed over to the sons of Ammon. Yahweh gave them into my hand. Why do you (pl.) come up against me today to fight with me?"*

[4] *Jephthah gathered all the men of Gilead and fought Ephraim. The men of Gilead struck Ephraim dead because,*[a] *they said, "Fugitives from Ephraim are you. Gilead is in the midst of Ephraim in the midst*[b] *of Manasseh."* [5] *Gilead captured*[a] *the Jordan crossings belonging to Ephraim.*

Whenever an Ephraimite fugitive[b] said, "Let me cross over," the men of Gilead replied to him, "You are an Ephraimite." He would say, "No." [6]*They would say to him, "Please pronounce Shibboleth."[a] He would say, "Sibboleth." He was not in a habit[b] of so speaking. They would grab him and kill him at the Jordan crossings. From Ephraim at that time forty-two thousand fell.*

[7]*Jephthah judged Israel six[a] years, and Jephthah the Gileadite died. He was buried in the towns[b] of Gilead.*

[8]*Ibzan[a] from Bethlehem judged Israel after him.* [9]*He had thirty sons and thirty daughters. He sent his daughters outside, and brought in thirty daughters[a] for his sons from outside. He judged Israel seven years.* [10]*Ibzan[a] died and was buried in Bethlehem.*

[11]*After him Elon from Zebulun judged Israel. He judged Israel[a] ten years.* [12]*Elon[a] from Zebulun died and was buried in Aijalon[b] in the land of Zebulun.*

[13]*After him Abdon son of Hillel[a] from Pirathon judged Israel.* [14]*He had forty sons and thirty grandsons. They rode on seventy donkeys. He judged Israel eight years.* [15]*Abdon the son of Hillel from Pirathon died and was buried in Pirathon in the land of Ephraim in the hill country of the Amalekites.[a]*

Notes

11:2.a. OL does not have "wife also bore him sons" but expands the text in reading: "And the wife said to her husband, 'Throw these from my face, and the husband's sons.'" Niditch asks, "Could Gilead have had several illegitimate children in other versions?" (129).

2.b. LXX reads ὅτι γυναικὸς υἱὸς ἑταίρας εἶ σύ, "because you are the son of a courtesan woman (or concubine)," rather than the like-sounding ἕτερος, "other." OL has "fornicating woman."

3.a. OL reads, "Thieves gathered to him and they dwelt with him," a situation Niditch calls "an alternate image of the social bandit" (129).

3.b. "To fight" is implied in the verb but not actually stated.

4.a. LXX[B] does not contain v 4.

5.a. LXX[A] reads ἐν γῇ Τωβ, "in the land of Tob."

7.a. Many Heb. mss here and in v 9 read אל for MT ל, representing a confusion of prepositions with similar meanings and uses.

7.b. LXX reads ἐξεβάλετέ με ἐκ τοῦ οἴκου τοῦ πατρός μου καὶ ἐξαπεστείλατέ με ἀφ' ὑμῶν, "you threw me out of the house of my father, and you sent me out away from you," apparently taking both themes from v 2 or from Gen 26:27 and including them here.

8.a. LXX[A] reads οὐχ οὕτως νῦν ἤλθομεν πρὸς σέ καὶ συμπορεύσῃ ἡμῖν καὶ πολεμήσομεν, "is it not thus now: we have come to you even so that you should come to us and we will fight," while LXX[B] reads διὰ τοῦτο νῦν ἐπεστρέψαμεν πρὸς σέ καὶ πορεύσῃ μεθ' ἡμῶν καὶ παρατάξῃ, "therefore now we have turned to you even so that you would go with us and you would join the battle." This simply represents two styles of rendering the same Heb. source text, BHS's reference to Gen 4:15 notwithstanding. Sjöberg perceives LXX[A] as "more logical in context" yet sees MT as fitting "the pattern of the dispute as a whole" (*Wrestling with Textual Violence*, 59–60), the elders conceding to Jephthah.

9.a. Lit. "will give them to my face" or "before me." A few Heb. mss read the more frequent בְּיָדִי, "into my hand."

9.b. The last clause may be read as a question, "Will I indeed be your head?"

10.a. OL reads "the Lord is he who will hear among us that we do according to your word."

11.a. LXX[A] does not have "the army" (or "the people"), interpreting the text in the more natural way that elders would represent the people in setting up a king.

12.a. BHS suggests reading "Moab" here and throughout the chapter for "Ammon." This rests on literary or historical evidence, not textual evidence.

12.b. Lit. "what to me and to you?"

12.c. LXX reads "to fight me in my country," with the two LXX traditions each using its own vocabulary: ἥκεις πρός με σὺ πολεμῆσαί με ἐν τῇ γῇ μου and ἦλθες πρός με τοῦ παρατάξασθαι ἐν τῇ γῇ μου.

13.a. Many Heb. mss, LXX, and Vg. omit the Heb. ו as unnecessary here.

13.b. Heb. has a third fem. pl. suffix, while LXX[L], OL, and Vg. read the much easier sg. The pl.

suffix refers either to the cities of the land (NET notes) or to the three rivers and the land drained by them.

13.c. LXX^B, with Lucianic and other Gk. traditions, reads "in peace and I will go" (καὶ πορεύσομαι).

14.a. LXX^A reads καὶ ἀπέστρεψαν οἱ ἄγγελοι πρὸς Ιεφθαε καὶ ἀπέστειλεν, "and the messengers turned back to Jephthah, and he sent" = הַמַּלְאָכִים אֶל־יִפְתָּח. OL continues, "and the messengers returned to Jephthah."

15.a. A few MSS and the marginal Sebir ("supposed" or "expected") notation correct the syntax by making the verb pl., but this misses the point that messengers represented the voice of the king.

15.b. Consistent with its preference for "Moab" only, *BHS* suggests that the final phrase, "and the land of the sons of Ammon," is probably an addition to the original text.

16.a. Or "Red Sea"; LXX^B reads θαλάσσης Σιφ, "Sea of Ziph," transliterating Heb. סוּף.

17.a. A few Heb. MSS and Syr. read the pl. pronoun here as in v 19.

18.a. OL has "in Transjordan."

19.a. Many Heb. MSS, original LXX, and Vg. read sg. pronoun with v 17, agreeing with pronoun on "my place" at end of verse.

20.a. LXX^A reads οὐκ ἠθέλησεν Σηων διελθεῖν, "Sihon did not want Israel to pass through." *BHS* suggests a probable reading of תֵּת סִיחוֹן וַיְמָאֵן אָבָה, "and he was not willing and Sihon refused to give." Block sees MT as awkward and so says the emendation makes "better sense in the context and accords better with v 17 and Num 20:21" (361, n. 67). But parallel verses do not determine the present text, and the difficulty of the MT speaks for its authenticity, particularly in a context where trust was not being shown between Jephthah and the king of the Ammonites.

20.b. Many Heb. MSS join Gk. evidence for ב instead of the somewhat synonymous MT reading of עִם, though the MT does not imply "fight against" as strongly as the suggested reading would.

21.a. LXX^A does not have "that."

22.a. LXX^A reads "he," possibly a simple internal Gk. copying error: ἐκληρονόμησεν for ἐκληρονόμησαν.

22.b. LXX^B (compare OL) does not have "they possessed all the Amorite territory," eliminating the repetition from the preceding verse.

22.c. OL continues with "up to the boundary of the sons of Ammon."

23.a. Or "will you dispossess him" or "will you dispossess it"; LXX^A reads καὶ σὺ κληρονομήσεις αὐτὸν ἐπὶ σοῦ, "and you will dispossess him by yourself?"

24.a. *BHS* uses Gk. evidence and v 24b to propose deleting the second-person suffix.

24.b. LXX^B reads ἐξῆρεν κύριος, "the Lord carried away," instead of κατεκληρονόμησεν κύριος, "the Lord dispossessed."

25.a. Many MSS add the conjunction ו, but in a double question אם often introduces the second question. See *IBHS*, 684–85, §40.3.

26.a. LXX^A reads ἐν Ιαζηρ, "in Jazer." Other Gk. evidence joins Vg. in pointing to an original וּבְעַרְעֵר, MT representing an alternate spelling of the same term.

26.b. LXX (compare OL) reads παρὰ τὸν Ιορδάνην, "beside the Jordan," perhaps seeing the Jordan as more apt to have three hundred cities than would the smaller Arnon.

26.c. LXX^B C, followed in translation above in line with previous context, reads the verb as second sg. with a third pl. suffix instead of MT's second pl. without a suffix. MT represents the more difficult reading but creates an almost impossible syntax.

27.a. Niditch notes that "OL turns the preceding section into an oracle with the formula, 'The Lord says who judges today. . .'" (130).

28.a. LXX^A reads Αμμων καὶ οὐκ εἰσήκουσεν, "Ammon and did not listen," repeating the verb perhaps for stylistic reasons.

29.a. LXX^A reads "the land of Gilead," inserting a familiar phrase.

29.b. LXX translates "Mizpah" as σκοπιάν, "watchtower."

29.c. LXX^B does not have "and from Mizpah of Gilead," apparently through haplography. *BHS* uses a Heb. MS that reads עֵבֶר, "side, bank, edge," and the Gk. reading εἰς τὸ πέραν to propose a reading of מִמִּצְפֵּה נִלְעָד (לְ)עֵבֶר, "and he crossed over from Mizpah of Gilead to the border." This simplifies too greatly a complex text.

29.d. LXX apparently read עָבַר as עֵבֶר, "beyond, edge," translating εἰς τὸ πέραν, "into the side (or area beyond) the sons of Ammon." Many Heb. MSS, Syr., Tg., Vg. support the addition of אֶל, "to," which has to be understood here if not in the original MSS unless one reads "sons of Ammon" as a collective sg. and subject of the verb, resulting in "the sons of Ammon crossed over," but this is unlikely.

31.a. LXX^A reads καὶ ἔσται ὃς ἂν ἐξέλθῃ ἐκ τῶν θυρῶν, "and it will be whoever comes out of the doors" (compare OL and Vg.), not reproducing the Heb. repetition: וְהָיָה הַיּוֹצֵא אֲשֶׁר יֵצֵא מִדַּלְתֵי. Vg. adds *primus*.

31.b. A few MSS and Syr. read לְעֹלָה, adding a preposition for precise clarity: "for an offering."

33.a. LXX^B reads Αροηρ ἕως ἐλθεῖν ἄχρις Αρνων ἐν ἀριθμῷ εἴκοσι πόλεις, "Aroer as far as the entering even to Arnon, in number twenty cities."

33.b. Many MSS omit the conjunction.

33.c. LXX^A translates אָבֵל כְּרָמִים as Αβελ ἀμπελώνων, "Abel of the vineyards."

34.a. LXX^A (compare OL) reads καὶ αὕτη μονογενὴς αὐτῷ ἀγαπητή, "and she was the only one belonging to him, the beloved."

35.a. OL reads "immediately."

35.b. LXX^B C read ταραξῇ ἐτάραχάς με, "you have troubled me exceedingly." This leads to the proposal to transpose Heb. כרע, "bow down," to עכר, "to bring disaster, ruin."

35.c. Heb. וְאַתְּ הָיִית בְּעֹכְרָי reads, lit., "and you yourself are in my pains." OL interprets, "you have tripped me up and have become deprived (of life) before my eyes."

36.a. LXX^A reads Πάτερ μου εἰ ἐν ἐμοὶ ἤνοιξας, "my father, if about me you opened."

36.b. *BHS* sees "the sons of Ammon" as a gloss.

37.a. LXX^B reads ποιησάτω δὴ ὁ πατήρ μου, "do now, O my father."

37.b. K and Q offer different spellings of the same term.

38.a. A few MSS read שְׁנַיִם, reflecting the variant ways Heb. numerals are used.

39.a. LXX^A reads ἐπετέλεσεν Ιεφθαε τὴν εὐχὴν αὐτοῦ ἥν ηὔξατο, "and Jephthah completed the prayer which he prayed," inserting an explicit subject and omitting "to her" on stylistic grounds.

39.b. *BHS* suggests the reading וַיְהִי since the noun חֹק is normally masc. but appears to be read as fem. in MT: "Jephthah defends his honour by keeping his word." Sjöberg sees the emendation as "completely uncalled for . . . since no readings divergent from the MT motivate it" (*Wrestling with Textual Violence*, 65–66).

40.a. Lit. "from the days of her days."

40.b. LXX, supported by Vg., Syr., OL, and Tg., reads θρηνεῖν, "to lament"; Heb. meaning is not certain. See *Comment* on 11:40.

12:1.a. LXX^A reads καὶ συνήχθησαν οἱ υἱοὶ Εφραιμ καὶ ἦλθον, "and the sons of Ephraim were gathered together and went," substituting the more common reference for the less common one and not catching the military nuance of the verb.

1.b. LXX^B reads εἰς βορρᾶν, "to the north (or north wind)," translating rather than transliterating the proper name. Compare OL. Sefir and many Heb. MSS omit the *wāw*, reading simply צפנה.

1.c. LXX^A does not have "over you."

2.a. Or "a man of contention"; note LXX^A reads ἀνὴρ ἀντιδικῶν, "a man who goes to law," while LXX^B reads ἀνὴρ μαχητής, "a man who is a warrior."

2.b. LXX^A reads υἱοὶ Αμμων ἐταπείνουν με σφόδρα, "the sons of Ammon humiliated or oppressed me exceedingly," adding עִנּוּי. Niditch translates the OL as "I was an opponent, and my people (also), and the sons of Ammon humiliated me exceedingly" (137). Many commentators and translators follow this addition in an attempt to make sense of a tersely phrased text that reads, lit., "and he said, Jephthah, to them: a *rib* (ריב) man I have been (or become) I and my people and the sons of Ammon exceedingly." See *Comment* on 12:2.

> Jephthah said to them, "My people and I were engaged in conflict with the Ammonites who oppressed us severely." (NRSV)

Other translations take ריב as a verb:

> Jephthah answered them, "I and my people were in a bitter conflict with the Ammonites." (JPS)

> "My soldiers and I were engaged in a critical contest with the Ammonites." (NAB)

> "I and my people were engaged in a great struggle with the Ammonites." (NIV)

> "My people and I were entangled in controversy with the Ammonites. (REB)

Perhaps the *wāw*s may be understood to mean "with" (see R. J. Williams, *Hebrew Syntax*, 436), resulting in the translation above.

2.c. LXX reads πρὸς ὑμᾶς = אֲלֵיכֶם, either an easing of the Heb. syntax or a change to fit the Gk. lexicon.

3.a. LXX^A reads "he was not," leading *BHS* to read אִין, without the second-person suffix. OL does not witness: "I saw that you were not a savior."

4.a. *BHS* sees that the Gk. original (compare OL) does not translate the last half of this verse. *Preliminary and Interim Report* sees this as simplification of the text. NET follows Moore (307–8) and

Burney (327) in deciding כִּי אָמְרוּ פְּלִיטֵי אֶפְרַיִם ('because they said, "Refugees of Ephraim"') may have been accidentally copied from the next verse (cf. כִּי יֹאמְרוּ פְּלִיטֵי אֶפְרַיִם) and the following words ('you, O Gilead . . . Manasseh') then added in an attempt to make sense of the verse." REB is the major translation that omits the verses from the translation. Block says "it is difficult to imagine why a later hand would have added this (the text makes good sense without it)" (383, n. 153). Rather, he finds haplography in the Gk. text. Barthélemy (*Critique textuelle*, 1:104–5) concludes that the text may be literarily secondary but is not the result of textual accidents.

4.b. Many Heb. MSS, LXX, Syr., Vg. add the conjunction, thus making Ephraim and Manasseh parallel rather than possibly placing Ephraim in the midst of Manasseh. NRSV notes say, "Meaning of Heb is uncertain." Brown calls the Heb. "unintelligible" (236). Block sees the meaning as uncertain and adds the *wāw*. He translates in a "semignomic sense: 'being in Ephraim is like being in Manasseh'" (383). MT is definitely the harder reading, but the versions probably give the original meaning.

5.a. LXX^A reads προκατελάβοντο ἄνδρες Γαλααδ, "the men of Gilead captured."

5.b. Lit. "fugitives of Ephraim said (pl.), 'Let me . . .'"; LXX reads διαβῶμεν, "let us cross over," and maintains the pl. throughout the conversation.

6.a. LXX^A reads εἴπατε δὴ σύνθημα καὶ οὐ κατηύθυναν τοῦ λαλῆσαι οὕτως, "say (pl.) now the password, and they could not do it right to pronounce it so," while LXX^B reads εἰπὸν δὴ στάχυς καὶ οὐ κατεύθυνεν τοῦ λαλῆσαι οὕτως, "say (sg.) now 'ear of corn' (translation of *šibbōlet*), and he could not do it right to pronounce it so."

6.b. A number of Heb. MSS read יָבִין, "he could not understand," for MT יָכִין, representing a simplification of the MT, as Barthélemy (*Critique textuelle*, 1:105–6) decides. Compare *Preliminary and Interim Report* (2:103), which also points to adjustments needed in the target language. OL reads "give us a sign, and their ways of speaking did not agree."

7.a. LXX^B reads "sixty years."

7.b. LXX (compare OL) reads ἐν (τῇ) πόλει αὐτοῦ (ἐν) Γαλααδ, "in his city, in Gilead," so BHS suggests a probable reading of בְּעִירוֹ בַּגִּלְעָד, "in his town of Gilead." LXX^L reads Σεφ(ε), supported by Josephus reading in *Jewish Antiquities* of Σεβέη, which may represent a Heb. reading of בְּעִירוֹ בְּמִצְפֵּה גִלְעָד, "in his city, in Mizpah of Gilead." *Preliminary and Interim Report* (2:103–4) gives four possible readings: בְּעָרֵי גִלְעָד, "in the cities of Gilead"; בְּעִירוֹ גִלְעָד, "in his city, in Gilead"; בְּעִירוֹ מִצְפֵּה גִלְעָד, "in his city, Mizpah of Gilead"; בְּעִירוֹ בְּצָפָה גִלְעָד, "in his city, in Zepheh of Gilead." The latter presupposes that Mizpah and Zepheh are two names for the same place. *Preliminary and Interim Report* chooses the last alternative as a scribal error based on misunderstanding of historical data. Barthélemy (*Critique textuelle*, 1:106) opts for the simpler בְּעִירוֹ בְצָפָה. MT is certainly the most difficult of the readings. The addition of "Mizpah" represents interpretation added from previous texts. The singular "town" eases the text but corresponds to reality and may be original.

8.a. LXX^A reads "Heshbon," while other Gk. traditions witness various spellings.

9.a. LXX reads γυναῖκες (-ας), "women" or "wives" = Heb. נָשִׁים. Gk. represents simplification of Heb. parallel statements.

10.a. LXX^A reads "Heshbon."

11.a. LXX^B does not have "he judged Israel."

12.a. Leningrad Codex deleted the י from the name, corrected by many Heb. MSS.

12.b. LXX^A reads ὁ Ζαβουλωνίτης ἐν Αιλιμ καὶ ἔθαψαν αὐτόν, "the Zebulunite in Ailim, and they buried him." Rainey (*Sacred Bridge*, 141) uses this to identify the city as Elon. OL has "and Elon the Zebulunite died in Elim, and they buried him in Zebulun."

13.a. LXX^A reads Σελλημ here and in v 15, while OL reads *Ellen*.

15.a. Some scholars have proposed reading בְּהַר אֶפְרַיִם בְּאֶרֶץ שַׁעֲלִים, "in the hill country of Ephraim in the land of Sha'alim"; compare LXX^L Σελλημ, OL *Aellen*. *Preliminary and Interim Report* (2:104) sees the proposal as grounded on too small a textual basis, possibly representing an assimilation to other passages or editorial interpretation.

Form/Structure/Setting

For further notes on the *Form/Structure/Setting* of the larger unit, see chap. 10 with table 10.1 in the appendix, narrative and genre comparisons for chaps. 10–12.

The Jephthah story presents a heroic tragedy. Cast as a battle report, the narrative features political, theological, historical, and personal bargaining, devoting only two verses to battle results (Judg 11:32–33). The battle report, as Webb sees, does move "from complication, through increasing tension, to climax (32a) and, again via Yahweh's intervention, to resolution (11:33)" ([1987] 42). But, as Webb further notes, "This resolution gives rise to two further complications and crises, the first domestic (Jephthah and his daughter, 11:34–39) and the second political (Jephthah and the Ephraimites, 12:1–6)" (42). In these secondary complications, not the battle with Ammon, the narrator shows his greatest interest. Thus I would conclude with Webb that "as the inclusio between v. 30a and v. 39b suggests, the vow and its fulfilment is the axis along which the tension, and hence the dramatic interest, of the episode is built and resolved" ([1987] 63; compare Olson, 830).

This is done in the face of German devotion to new redaction criticism such as that of Römer, who insists, "It is quite obvious that the story of Jephthah's vow and sacrifice belongs to another literary level than the surrounding verses" (*JSOT* 77 [1998] 28). Janzen responds that the story is not to be seen as a "Hellenistic insertion," as per Römer, but as "an integral and interconnected part of the story of Jephthah as a whole" (*JSOT* 29 [2005] 339).

This loose connection of the narrative units has led many scholars, especially on the German scene, to do literary-critical surgery on the text. A recent example comes from Gaß (*Ortsnamen*, 502–4), following Richter and others. He sees a local Gileadite tradition secondarily expanded into an all-Israelite one. The original kernel of the narrative describes a battle over the town of Gilead in no man's land between Ammon and Gilead. Richter (*Bib* 47 [1966] 485–87) reduces the kernel to 11:29, 32–33. Kratz (*Composition of the Narrative Books*, 204–5) finds a kernel in 11:1a, 3, 5b, 6–8, 11a, given a Deuteronomistic framework in 10:6–10, 17–18; 11:29, 33b; 12:7, and then gradually expanded with the other narratives.

As so often in Hebrew narrative, conversation carries the narrative, as Webb observes: "The Israel/Ammon conflict is the link connecting all the episodes, but within each episode it provides the occasion, the background, for a dialogue, and it is in the dialogue that the real dramatic interest of each episode is centred" ([1987] 73).

Thus we have dialogue between

Jephthah and his brothers (11:1–3)
Jephthah and the elders (11:4–11)
Jephthah (his messengers) and the king of the Ammonites (11:12–28)
Jephthah and God (11:29–31)
Jephthah and his daughter (11:34–38; vv 39–40 form an etiology)
Jephthah and the men of Ephraim (12:1–4)
Men of Gilead and men of Ephraim (12:5–6)

Brensinger points out that each of the dialogue sessions "results in some form of death or destruction. The outcome grows increasingly more severe as the narrative proceeds" (122).

The Jephthah story takes up the information in the transition of chap. 10, where, Sjöberg says, the ambiguity of 10:16 and the threat of 10:17–18 indicate "that this story-line is not completely resolved, but rather begs for a continuation" (*Wrestling with Textual Violence*, 27). Still "nothing in the speech of the introduction ties it specifically to the situation of the Jephthah cycle" (69). Indeed, we have "two story-lines (10:6–18 and 11:1–12:7)" (70). For ease of commentary, I have divided chaps. 11–12 into four parts:

Ammonite war report (11:1–33)
Vow narrative (11:[30], 34–40)
Intertribal battle report (12:1–6)
Annalistic reports of minor judges (12:7–15)

For the narrator, however, only two sections are important: the Jephthah narrative (11:1–12:6) and the minor judges annals (12:7–15). The Jephthah narrative features an introduction (11:1–3) and an epilogue (12:1–6). The central narrative appears to be a battle report, but Sjöberg is surely correct in seeing that the "theologically central event, that is, the victory, is not its climax. At the same time, the consequence of fulfilling the goal of the story is its main complication" (*Wrestling with Textual Violence*, 28). On the other hand, he points out that "there is no evidence that the fulfilment of the vow changes the outcome of the story. In fact, it changes neither the relationship between Jephthah and God, nor that between Jephthah and the people of Gilead" (31). Indeed, the plot "ends neither in complete success or in complete failure" (33). The structure thus leaves the reader facing at least four questions resulting from the narrative's structural ambiguity. Sjöberg phrases them:

- Where does the centre of the story lie?
- Who is the driving force in the story?
- What is the narrator's explicit ideological stance towards the narrated events?
- What does the characterization of the main actors indicate about the narrator's implicit assessment of the narrated events?

The following commentary will seek to shed some light on these ambiguous issues.

Comment

The Jephthah narrative elicits squeals of anguish from all biblical students interested in the Bible's ethical teachings. The narrative cycle begins by underlining how starkly evil Israel has become, a fact then illustrated by the leader's lack of qualifications and by the leader's actions confirming his lack of qualifications to be a deliverer for God's people. And yet God still works with him to retard the progress of his people's enemies.

1:11 As so often in Judges, a new central character appears without narrative preparation. Webb ([1987] 50) and Younger (248) call this a flashback in an attempt to claim the major part of chap. 10 as the introduction or exposition of the Jephthah story. But a flashback goes back to a previous sequence. Here the intention is not to go back to a previous sequence but to introduce the major character. This is an alternative to the previous introductions of major judges in that it intentionally omits mention of Yahweh's participation in the appearance of the new central character. Chap. 10 served as transition preparing for both Jephthah and Samson, a transition parallel to 6:1–10, which prepared for Gideon and Abimelech.

The introduction offers nothing promising about Jephthah. He is from Gilead, far removed from the center of Israelite life, and apparently far removed from Jair, the previous Gileadite hero. Niditch observes that "as the outcast son of a harlot, banished by his paternal kin, Jephthah becomes a 'primitive rebel'" (131). Like David, Abimelech, and Jeroboam, he gathers around himself a band of military ruffians, men outside the institutional power base. The image of the hero surrounded by the outcasts of society is typical of the careers of successful bandit heroes (cf. Abimelech, 9:4; the displaced Danites, 18:25; and Jeroboam, 2 Chr 13:6–7).

In Josh 22, Israel's leadership brought understanding and peace between the tribes east of the Jordan and those west when a theological battle broke out. Gideon went across the Jordan to gain revenge against those who killed his brothers. Jephthah will set up a situation where Israelites east of the Jordan wreak havoc on a tribe west of the Jordan. His long speech to the king of the Ammonites shows that he knows Israel's theology, but his vow to sacrifice, resulting in the death of his daughter, shows that he does not have full faith in that theology.

Jephthah's mother is a "prostitute." Here we have the Hebrew term *zônâ* (זוֹנָה), one who is unfaithful or prostitutes herself, not *pîlegeš* (פִּילֶגֶשׁ), the secondary wife of Judg 8:31. The identity of a *zônâ* is more complex than simply a female prostitute doing business by the road or in the pagan temple. Sjöberg explains, "The precise meaning of the term remains obscure, largely due to the lack of proper sociological knowledge of the institutions of marriage and prostitution" (*Wrestling with Textual Violence*, 53). Schneider's comment is probably as close as we can get in defining the term: "The term *zonah* is understood to mean a professional prostitute who accepts payment for her services, but it could also apply to a woman who had sex before or outside the confines of marriage" (162; compare E. A. Goodfriend, "Prostitution [OT]," *ABD*, 5:505). Deuteronomic law described such an occupation as "abhorrent to the LORD" (Deut 23:18 [Heb. 19], NRSV; compare Prov 23:27; 29:3). Block explains: "As the rejected son of a prostitute Jephthah was a man without a physical or social home and without a future" (352–53). Still, in Joshua a *zônâ* became a savior and heroine for Israel (Josh 2:1; 6:17, 22, 25). The book of Judges recounts no heroics from a prostitute or her offspring. Nor does it condone the father who patronized prostitutes, as Block has shown (353).

Jephthah is a "heroic warrior," *gibbôr ḥayil* (גִּבּוֹר חַיִל), a term also applied to Saul (1 Sam 9:1), David (1 Sam 16:18), and Jeroboam (1 Kgs 11:28). R. Wakely offers this definition: "The phrase is frequently found in military contexts to refer to mighty warriors" (*NIDOTTE*, 2:119). Sjöberg prefers to define the term more broadly as "used for men whose life's purpose demands extraordinary strength or skills" (*Wrestling with Textual Violence*, 52). Jephthah, Saul, and Jeroboam show that such ability does not guarantee a person success or indicate God's blessing on one's endeavors.

Gilead fathered Jephthah. The original Gilead, the progenitor of the Gilead clan (tribe?), was the son of Machir and grandson of Manasseh (Num 26:29; 36:1), but Jephthah's father is simply named within the tribal heritage and appears nowhere else. The reader might well wonder if Gilead legally recognized his son as an heir. Matthews argues that he did: "Judg 11:1 makes it quite clear that Gilead is Jephthah's father, suggesting that a formal declaration has been made in his favor." But Matthews then says that Jephthah facing his brothers "had no legal recourse and is forced to flee" (117).

2–3 Gilead's half brothers do not accept him and fear he will take part of their inheritance. They call him "the son of another woman," another somewhat ambiguous term. How does this woman differ from the woman of comparison, the brothers' mother? Does she belong to a different tribe? Is she a secondary wife? Is she a foreigner? Does she worship foreign gods? Is she immoral? The text does not tell us. Sjöberg decides "unlawful female sexuality" is involved, pushing Jephthah into "an ethnically and socially inferior position" (*Wrestling with Textual Violence*, 54). At any rate, this other woman gives the brothers reason to drive Jephthah out of the family dwelling and inherited land. Younger (248–49) sees this as a complex legal case in which Gilead has officially adopted Jephthah, making him a legal heir; but then his brothers, at the father's death, go to court before the elders, who deny Jephthah's claim as an heir. In so doing they violate Israelite inheritance law. (See D. Marcus, *HAR* 12 [1990] 107–8; for a contradictory opinion see H. Schulte, *ZAW* 104 [1992] 255–62.)

Thus Jephthah is introduced as a counterpart to Abimelech, the previous judge featured in a long narrative. Sjöberg describes the comparison: they both are "empty men," are sons of "socially inferior women," have "conflict with their brothers, have tragic encounters with women," and are "outsiders who manoeuvre their way to become the leader of their people" (*Wrestling with Textual Violence*, 57; compare Block, 343). The comparison does not bode well for Jephthah, preparing the reader to expect the worst. One major difference will separate them: "Abimelech is nothing more than a destroyer; Jephthah is a deliverer" (Block, 343).

So Jephthah flees to "the land of Tob," literally "the good land." This may be either a village or a region but is apparently a small city-state mentioned by Thutmose III of Egypt and in the Amarna letters. In David's day and possibly in Jephthah's, Tob was allied with the Ammonites. Gaß (*Ortsnamen*, 494–96) shows three possible locations and points to et-Tayyibeh southeast of Edrei (modern Derʻa in Syria about sixty miles [97 km] south of Damascus) as the most likely. Rainey (*Sacred Bridge*, 140) agrees with this location. There Jephthah proves his military prowess and gathers a group of "unprincipled men," as had Abimelech (Judg 9:4). Thus he becomes a "guerrilla fighter or terrorist" (McCann, 80). Jephthah "went to a good land but gathered bad followers" (Schneider, 165).

4–11 Judg 11:4 appears to introduce a battle report just as had 10:17. The dialogue mirrors to an extent that of Israel and Yahweh in 10:7–16—having reference to the Ammonite oppression, an appeal to the dialogue partner, a sarcastic reply, a repetition of the appeal, and a final response, Yahweh refusing to let Israel use him while Jephthah seizes the opportunity. (See Block's table, 354.) The Ammonites begin to launch the attack, causing Israel to realize how unprepared they are, having no commander. "The Israelites appear desperate and disoriented" (Brensinger, 128). Hurriedly, the Gileadite elders send for Jephthah, apparently having no qualified or experienced leader among them. The elders served as decision makers for each city or tribe (Judg 2:7; 8:14,16; 11:5, 7–11; 21:16), yet, as Younger perceives, these "are pictured as irreligious opportunists, who seize the role of commissioning Jephthah, a role that belongs to Yahweh alone" (248). Schneider concludes, "The wrong people asked the wrong questions and offered wrong rewards" (166).

Shrinking from their decision in 10:18 to crown a "head" or *roʾš* (רֹאשׁ), the elders invite Jephthah to be their "commander" or *qāṣîn* (קָצִין), a general term for military commanders (Josh 10:24; Judg 11:6) or leaders in general (cf. Prov 6:7; 25:15; compare Judg 11:11; Isa 1:10; 3:6–7; 22:3; Dan 11:18; Mic 3:1, 9). Jephthah replies emphatically, "Aren't you, yes you, the ones who hated me and threw me out of my father's house?" (Judg 11:7). In so doing he identifies the elders with his brothers as participants in exiling him. This may be a charge of not interfering with the brothers' illegal action, or it may indicate that the elders in charge of legal dealings at the city gate had held court and approved the brothers' charges against Jephthah.

Jephthah continues his attack on the elders: "Why have you come to me now when you're in trouble?" I. Swart and R. Wakely explain the wide-ranging negative meanings of the word for "trouble," *ṣar* (צַר):

> The forms derived from צרר are applied to any kind of restricting, claustrophobic experience. Thus, the q[al] is used of the distress caused by military defeat (e.g., Judg 2:15; 10:9) and near revolt (1 Sam 30:6); the frustration of an individual tortured by unsatisfied lust (2 Sam 13:2); the foreboding and uncertainty experienced in response to an approaching danger (Gen 32:7 [8]); the anxiety suffered by the unscrupulous, avaricious person who undergoes a radical reversal of fortune at the very summit of success (Job 20:22); the fear, frustration, and cramped progress of one who rejects the unimpeded path of wisdom and righteousness in favor of folly and wickedness, which lead only to restriction, darkness, and death (Prov 4:12; cf. Job 18:7). (*NIDOTTE*, 3:854)

This reply apparently represents a bargaining maneuver. The elders cannot deny the charge and so make a counteroffer, using, as Webb ([1987] 53) points out, "the language of repentance" in saying they are turning to him with the request, Come, fight, and be our head or *ro'š* (רֹאשׁ). H. F. Van Rooy shows its various uses, explaining that the term

> is frequently used to denote different kinds of leaders. It can denote leaders in general (cf. Num 25:4; Deut 29:10 [9]; 33:5; Josh 23:2; 24:1; Job 29:25), important people in society (Isa 9:14, 15 [13, 14]), or leaders of specific groups. It is used frequently for heads of families (Exod 6:14, 25; Num 7:2) and the heads of the tribes of Israel (Num 1:16; 32:28; Deut 1:15; 1 Kgs 8:1; 2 Chr 5:2). There are also references to the leaders of Jacob (Mic 3:1), the leaders of the house of Judah (3:9), the leaders of the people (Neh 10:14 [15]), and provincial leaders (11:3).
> Jephthah is called a head in Judg 11:4–11. It must denote more than just a military leader in this instance, perhaps something like a governor. Saul is also called the leader of the tribes of Israel (1 Sam 15:17). The word is also used for leaders of non-Israelite tribes (Num 25:15) or of the world in general (Job 12:24). Moses elected leaders, on the recommendation of Jethro, to assist him in judging cases (Exod 18:25, 26). The king of Israel is denoted by this word as the one who is a leader amongst the nations (2 Sam 22:44; Ps 18:43 [44]; Jer 31:7). The word is often used in military contexts, e.g., for the head of the army (1 Chr 11:6), the leader of the Three (2 Sam 23:8, 18), and the thirty leaders of David's army (2 Sam 23:13). It is used for the high priest (2 Kgs 25:18; Jer 52:54) as well as for other important leading priests (Neh 12:7), and also for leaders of the Levites (Neh 12:24). In the cult a leader in thanksgiving and prayer is mentioned (Neh 11:17), and also leaders (directors) for the singers (Neh 12:46). (*NIDOTTE*, 3:1017–18)

For Jephthah, then, bargaining has brought him a higher position, apparently with political as well as military overtones. Brensinger observes, "Jephthah shrewdly capitalizes on the elders' obvious desperation, even extracting an oath so as to guarantee the validity of their proposal" (130). This action brings Jephthah "something more permanent, wide-ranging, and prestigious" (Webb, [1987] 52). But he also humbly provides a winning position for the elders in the face of their constituents, saying God must give him the victory before he takes the position. Despite claims by Schneider (168), following Exum (*Tragedy and Biblical Narrative*, 48), it is not clear at all that the differences between vv 6 and 8 show that the elders have also withdrawn from participating in the battle.

The dialogue does not reduce Jephthah's leadership "to that of a puppet" (Sjöberg, *Wrestling with Textual Violence*, 60). Jephthah gains a stronger position by accepting the responsibility for victory. The elders accept the agreement and commit themselves to it under oath. In fact, the elders go beyond the agreement and give Jephthah both titles, "as head and as commander" (11:11), prior to the battle. Still, Olson points out, "Jephthah is unable to unite even one entire tribe but only the district or clan of Gilead. . . . The judges seem less and less able to muster substantial coalitions of tribes as we move through the individual judge stories" (822, 831).

The agreement is more than a human bargain struck. It is spoken before God in the sanctuary at Mizpah, Jephthah's words forming what Block (356) calls an "oath of office." But Block (356) has probably gone too far in describing this as "a glib and calculated effort to manipulate Yahweh." Matthews is closer to reality: "He adds, as in ancient Near Eastern treaty language, the inclusion of the deity as witness to these terms. Any victory he gains will then be seen as divine affirmation of his position of leadership" (119).

Mizpah is not so much a false or unrecognized sacred site (see Younger, 251) as it is another example of the many sacred sites utilized by Israel in practice—as opposed to the pure theory of one chosen central sanctuary—in this time frame. If Schneider (169) should be correct in identifying this with the city in Benjamin, then the site is quite strongly connected with Saul (1 Sam 10:17) and prepares for Judg 20:1. But such identification of action here west of the Jordan is probably off base. Gaß (*Ortsnamen*, 481–84) lists five possible locations for Mizpah east of the Jordan and chooses er-Rasuni, about one mile (2 km) from Khirbet Gelʿad and one of the most significant Iron Age sites south of the Jabbok. This may be a different place from Jephthah's home further north (v 34), which Gaß (484) cautiously locates at Suf. Rainey (*Sacred Bridge*, 140) equates Mizpah with Ramoth-Mizpah of Josh 13:26, a site south of the Jabbok in the vicinity of Jebel Jelʾad and Khirbet Jelʾad.

Here, Jephthah and the Gileadite leaders go through the religious motions, fulfilling the ritual their tradition has taught them. The narrator does not reveal their motives in doing so unless one reads the divine silence in the previous narrative as rejection of Jephthah and his leadership.

12–28 Jephthah follows normal diplomatic procedure, sending messengers to the king of the Ammonites, seeking to avert military action. In so doing, Brown notes, "Jephthah speaks and acts more like a king than does any other judge" (224). The Ammonite leader adamantly refuses any kind of diplomatic compromise, but his case for war rests on action carried out by their ancestors many generations previous.

Niditch finds, "The interaction between Sihon and Moses, appearing several times in the biblical corpus, points to critical concerns: questions about divine right to the land and the desire to demarcate ancient boundaries; reflections upon Israel's relationships with neighboring peoples; and the desire to portray the people Israel as good international citizens" (131). Thus the narrator provides two perspectives on history, that of the Ammonites and that of the Israelites. The Ammonites believe that Israel stole their land from them and they have a right to take it back. The only way to solve the problem without bloodshed is for Israel to peacefully hand over the Ammonite territory. Rivers clearly mark the land, which stretches "from the Arnon to the Jabbok" (11:13), going south to north, with the Jordan as the western boundary. But the Ammonites face a problem because, as Block points out, their "heartland consisted of an amorphous region without distinct geographic boundaries between the desert to the east and the hills of Gilead in the west" (359).

Jephthah continues the diplomatic conversation through the messenger system, sending his representatives with power to speak in his name. The speech follows the "lawsuit" or *rîb* form evidenced in Israelite and Near Eastern literature as shown by O'Connell (*Rhetoric of the Book of Judges*, 195; compare T. Butler, "Announcements of Judgment," *Cracking Old Testament Codes*, ed. D. Sandy and R. Giese, Jr. [Nashville: Broadman & Holman, 1995] 163–64).

Jephthah states the Israelite version of the story of the crossing of the Sea of Reeds (Exod 13:18–15:22) to the camp in the wilderness of Paran at Kadesh (Num 12:16; 13:26). The king of Edom refused Israel's request for passage through Edomite territory (Num 20:14–21). The king of Moab also refused passage (compare Num 22; Deut 2:9). The Israelites carefully camped north of the Arnon, outside Moabite territory (Num 21:13).

Then Jephthah turns to dealings of early Israel with the Amorites and their King Sihon, who chose to fight Israel. Israel took his land from the Arnon to the Jabbok and settled there (Num 21:21–31), thus taking the land that the Ammonites now claim, though it did not belong to them then. Jephthah identifies this as more than a historical event. It was a theological act by Yahweh, the God of Israel. The Ammonites do not face merely Israel in their efforts to take the land between the Arnon and Jabbok rivers. They face Israel's God. They should be satisfied with what they can claim that the Moabite god Chemosh gave them. This has been the situation for "three hundred years" (11:26). Why try to turn back history now? Balak of Moab (Num 22) could not bring a curse on the people of Israel or defeat them (Num 22). Why should the Ammonites try now?

The three hundred years represent a round and perhaps "inflated" (Matthews, 122) number and so may not be open to precise calculation, though Brensinger says it "closely agrees with the 301 total years of oppression and liberation stated up to this point in the book (11:26)" (132). Block (363) questions the figure because it is a round number. Jephthah, in Block's view, has given other false information, and this is a political, not historical, speech. He does agree with Soggin (211) that the Moabite stone or Mesha Inscription says the men of Gad had dwelt in that region since time immemorial.

Niditch offers the viewpoint that "the passage seems to conflate Moabite and Ammonite in this detail, as in the larger historical overview. The comment on Chemosh suggests the belief that such gods do exist. They may succeed in battle on behalf of their nation." (132). Block overstates the case a bit in saying "he mixes up the facts and conflates Israel's encounters with Moabites, Ammonites, and Amorites" (360), as does Younger in speaking of "his great factual ignorance" (256). Block does see the omission of a reference to Ammon as "an intentional counter to the Ammonite charge. Far from robbing the territory of Gilead from the Ammonites, the latter were completely out of the picture when the Israelites had first arrived on the scene" (360). In similar fashion Younger concludes: "Jephthah's argument is in the main correct and therefore unanswerable" (258). Hamilton sees that "this may be more a part of the give-and-take for the courtesy of political diplomacy than an expression of Jephthah's theology" (*Handbook on the Historical Books*, 144). Or with Webb one can say that Jephthah "recognizes his opponent as legitimate ruler of *both* Ammon *and* Moab" ([1987] 56, emphasis original), having expanded his territory there before reaching into Gilead's land. As present ruler of Moab, the king of the Ammonites should follow earlier Moabite kings' examples and leave land north of the Arnon to Israel, not waging war for it.

Other biblical evidence points to the disputed territory as belonging to Moab at some times in history (Num 35:1; Deut 1:5; 1 Kgs 16:21–28), backed up by the Moabite stone. Jephthah does not note that Amorites had captured his territory up to the Arnon (Num 21:26). The Ehud story in chap. 3 also shows Moabite weakness, quite possibly having been taken advantage of by their Ammonite allies. So as Brensinger sees the situation, "the Ammonites take upon themselves Moab's former claims, including those to the region in question" (131). This explains the mention of Ammon and Moab in the Jephthah narrative and shows how Jephthah could refer to Chemosh, the god of the Moabites, as giving over land to the Ammonites. Schneider can go so far as to claim that Jephthah's historical review "does not deviate from those other references regarding Israel's relations with Moab and her neighbors. . . . This makes Jephthah the only leader in Judges who exhibited any knowledge of Israelite history or their conflicts" (172). Jephthah's story does fit the narrator's picture of Israelite history in 10:11–12. Jephthah is telling the story in such a way as to emphasize Ammonite fault and Israelite innocence.

The reference to Chemosh, though, has engendered great dispute among commentators. Block thinks Jephthah "displayed contempt for his own theological traditions . . . [since] Yahweh alone determines the boundaries of the nations" (362), with reference to Deut 2:5, 9, 19; 32:8–9; Amos 9:7. Brensinger asserts that Jephthah "applies a theological principle that the opposing king himself embraces. In so doing, Jephthah does not necessarily place Chemosh and the God of Israel on equal grounds. . . . Instead, he cleverly used mutually accepted categories that he no doubt considers irrefutable" (132). As Block (361) expresses the case, "these arguments would have been understood by all ancient Near Easterners who accepted that each nation had a patron deity whose duty and passion was to care for his people, which included providing them with a homeland." But Block does not accept a historical argument or a literary one claiming a tradition or text originally referring to Moab but now placed in the Ammonite war context. Rather Block points to Jephthah's political purposes so that he "is either engaging in propaganda for purposes of his own or is simply incorrect. . . . The error is intentional. The substitution of Chemosh for Milkom is of a piece with his earlier omission of Ammon in his historical survey of Israel's association with this territory" (362). Hamilton softens this a bit: "This may be more a part of the give-and-take for the courtesy of political diplomacy than an expression of Jephthah's theology" (*Handbook on the Historical Books*, 144). Or one can answer with Olson that "the questions imply that each nation has its legitimate god with a certain territory alloted to it, no more and no less. This view is in line with that of Deut 32:8–9" (830). Brown goes straight to the point:

> He placed their conflict within a larger context—a cosmic contest between their respective gods. This was the common way of understanding such conflicts, as evidenced in numerous other biblical and extrabiblical texts (cf. 1 Sam 4:1–6:6; 17:26, 36, 43–47) and will again be emphasized as the keynote of Jephthah's message to the Ammonite king (v. 27). Through these references, the Deuteronomic author (or the narrator) continues to press home his polemic against idolatry and to ridicule those who worship any god but the "one LORD" (Deut 6:4) as well as to reaffirm God's promise of the land for Israel. (224–25)

Brown adds later, "There is no compelling reason to think that a character like Jephthah was a strict monotheist. But in reality he affirms just the opposite, as did Gideon's father (6:31–32); if Chemosh were really a god, he would protect his interests" (226).

Having made the historical and political claim, Jephthah turns to personal diplomacy. He has not "sinned," the Hebrew term חטא (*ḥaṭa'*), against the king of the Ammonites; that is, Jephthah has not broken any treaty agreements or initiated aggression against the king. Rather, the king of the Ammonites is "treating me in an evil way" (Judg 11:27) or doing evil against me. The Ammonites have broken the peace, not Israel. So Jephthah places everything in the hands of Yahweh, the Judge, to decide. Gideon had called Yahweh the only king (8:23). Now Jephthah names him the "judge," or שפט (*šōpēṭ*). Compare Gen 18:25. This appears to set Yahweh up as the absolute ruler of Israel no matter what title one wants to use. God may set up and work through human judges (Judg 2:18), but the absolute Judge remains the God of Israel (compare 1 Sam 3:13; Pss 7:11 [Heb. 12]; 50:6; 75:7 [Heb. 8]; 94:2; Jer 11:20).

Jephthah proves a student of divine history. Unlike the generation following Joshua (Judg 2:10), he knows the works God had done for Israel and is willing to call on God to do similar works in his own generation. But his diplomacy does not work. The king of Ammon "did not listen" (Judg 11:28). That means one thing: war. Still, Jephthah has succeeded in "making Gilead's/Israel's right to the land ideologically legitimate" (Sjöberg, *Wrestling with Textual Violence*, 39). And he has laid out evidence before the divine Judge, whom he wants to intervene, as well as before the Ammonite king, whose acceptance of terms he never really expects (Webb, [1987] 59). Schneider observes, "Jephthah was originally depicted as an outsider, gathering the wrong crowd, the son of a prostitute or woman of low status. Suddenly he was a devoted Yahwist (i.e., he worshiped Israel's deity), knew his people's history, was prepared to negotiate before fighting, and pled his people's innocence while glorifying his deity, a completely different character" (173). But in the end, Brown is correct: "Jephthah was a smooth talker who knew how to use words to his advantage, but he also did not know when to keep his mouth shut" (223).

29–33 God responds to Jephthah's faithfulness by sending "the Spirit of Yahweh" (11:29) on him as he had on Othniel (3:10) and Gideon (6:34) and as he would on Samson (Judg 13:25; 14:6, 19; 15:4; compare 1 Sam 10:6; 16:13). Schneider, working from J. D. Levinson (*The Death and Resurrection of the Beloved*

Son: The Transformation of Child Sacrifice in Judaism and Christianity [New Haven: Yale UP, 1993] 14), sees from this that "the vow was what lured the deity to Jephthah's side. In that case the deity would condone and accept child sacrifice as the final element legitimating Jephthah as leader" (175). Surely the narrator would have made this connection clear had it been intended. God's coming is to give the enemy into Jephthah's hand, not to justify Jephthah's pagan vow.

Matthews comes closer to the mark in seeing that the Spirit is "a mark of divine presence and purpose and provides him with true legitimacy for his role as Gileadite leader and as charismatic marshal of a larger body of the Israelite tribes" (123). Brensinger acknowledges that God "sets aside his utter aggravation and graciously works through an instrument that he himself has not explicitly selected" (133). McCann reminds us that "the spirit may be an effectve power, but it seems that it is not automatically effective, at least not in terms of effecting deliverance. . . . The progression from Othniel to Samson suggests diminishing faithfulness on the part of the judges upon whom the spirit comes. . . . This diminishing faithfulness is paralleled by diminishing returns, in terms of deliverance" (82). God comes to battle on God's own terms, not on Jephthah's, and certainly not as a result of Jephthah's wheedling vow.

Jephthah thus passes through the Israelite territories east of the Jordan, apparently recruiting troops from at least east Manasseh and Gilead until he returns to his home base and then faces the Ammonite army.

Vv 30–31 present two of the most controversial verses in all the Old Testament. Barak had refused to answer the prophet Deborah's call to lead the battle without her involvement (4:6–9). Gideon had tested God before agreeing to lead in battle God's way and then gave way to personal vengeance (6:36–40; chap. 8). Abimelech seemingly ignored God and grabbed power on his own authority (chap. 9). Jephthah bargains with God, making a foolish promise to persuade God to be with him. The vow has two presuppositions: God will give Ammon into Jephthah's (not Israel's) hands, and Jephthah will return from the battle in "peace," or *šālôm* (שָׁלוֹם), that is, whole, not wounded or killed in battle (JPS, CEV, NASB95, NKJV, REB, HCSB, CJB, NET), though many translations read "in triumph" or something similar (NRSV, NLT, NIV, NAB, NJB). To the two presuppositions are attached two promises: whatever comes from Jephthah's house to meet him will be given "to Yahweh," and such gift will be given by means of a burnt offering.

This is the only time Jephthah speaks directly to God instead of about him. Matthews (124) sees this as a "signal that Jephthah should not be ad-libbing and instead should rely on the instruction provided by the investment of God's spirit." His vow can be read in many ways. It may be (1) "a challenge to the divine sovereign, an attempt to dictate Yhwh's future actions. As such, it also indicates a peak of self-assertiveness" (Sjöberg, *Wrestling with Textual Violence*, 61). Or it may be (2) "another demonstration of his shrewd and calculating nature, another attempt to manipulate circumstances to his own advantage. . . . He was outrightly pagan" (Block, 367). This stands in stark opposition to the statement of faith he had just made in v 27b.

In the face of battle, Jephthah decides he needs more than faith. He needs to make a deal with God. Apparently he has no idea what the real result of his vow will be. The content behind "whatever" (אֲשֶׁר) remains unexplained. It may be human or animal. Brensinger explains, "It is entirely possible for an animal to come out of the house. . . . Jephthah's entire household hangs precariously in the balance" (133; compare Younger, 263). But Webb represents many scholars in arguing that the phrase "to meet me" and the gravity of the situation "suggests that human rather than animal sacrifice is being contemplated" ([1987] 64; compare Amit, *Book of Judges*, 88; Walton et al., *IVP Bible Background*, 262). Brown (228, 230) sees the openness of the language but insists that the magnitude of the crisis demands a special kind of sacrifice, something above and beyond animal sacrifice. Jephthah expects a household servant, not his beloved daughter. (Compare Matthews, 125; D. Marcus, *Jephthah and His Vow*, 13–32.) Schneider points to Sisera's mother in the Song of Deborah to show that beloved women waited anxiously for loved ones to return from war so that "it is likely that a person who loved the military man would be as apt as an animal to come out of the house upon his return" (175). Olson rightly sees that "Jephthah's language is left intentionally ambivalent by the narrator so that the reader cannot know for sure what Jephthah's real intention was" (832; compare Howard, *Introduction to the Old Testament Historical Books*, 117). But McCann (83) reminds us of truth on the other side of the ledger: "The attempt to give Jephthah the benefit of the doubt only makes him look worse—stupid and thoughtless, as well as unfaithful."

Making vows was part of Israel's worship and practice (Gen 28:20; 31:13; Lev 7:16; 22:18, 21, 23; 23:38; 27:2, 8; Num 6:2, 5, 21; 15:3, 8; 21:2; 29:39; 30:3–15; Deut 12:6, 11, 17, 26; 23:19, 22–24; 1 Sam 1:11, 21; 2 Sam 15:7–8; Job 22:27; Pss 22:25 [Heb. 26]; 50:14; 56:12 [Heb. 13]; 61:5, 8 [Heb. 6, 9]; 65:1 [Heb. 2]; 66:13; 76:11 [Heb. 12]; 116:14, 18; 132:2; Prov 7:14; 31:2; Eccl 5:4–5 [Heb. 3–4]; Isa 19:21; Jonah 2:9 [Heb. 10]; Nah 1:15 [Heb. 2:1]; Mal 1:14). Jephthah had not learned the lesson of Prov 20:25: "It is a snare for one to say rashly, 'It is holy,' and begin to reflect only after making a vow" (NRSV). But Block (367) follows Webb ([1987] 64), who thinks "the vow is not impulsive; it is shrewd and calculating." Younger is to the point: "Jephthah's vow is both rash and manipulative" (262). Olson asserts, "Jephthah's vow in itself violates a deeply held Israelite norm in regard to the prohibition of gifts or bribes to judges" (832). The vow says nothing about God. It says multitudes about Jephthah.

Four other personal vows can be compared to this one: Jacob's (Gen 38:20–22), Israel's (Num 21:2), Hannah's (1 Sam 11), and Absalom's (2 Sam 15:7–8). All follow a basic form, as Block shows (366, n. 85). Block also notes the uniqueness of Jephthah's vow in that it has no connection with the object of the vow. "On the analogy of Num 21:2 he should have offered the inhabitants of the cities he would conquer" (368).

Brensinger gives three points related to the vow: (1) Jephthah has no previous conversation or direct relationship with Yahweh, only statements about him. (2) His earlier negotiation made his role as tribal head dependent on victory. (3) Negotiating is Jephthah's way of life. The vow "reflects Jephthah at his authentic and unmitigated best" (133).

God delivers on his side of Jephthah's bargain, though how the divine action relates to the human vow, the text does not say. The victory is only temporary, however, since later David would have to deal with the Ammonites (2 Sam 10; 12:26–31; 1 Chr 19:1–20:3). Surely Trible goes too far in saying that because the divine Spirit came on Jephthah, this "clearly establishes divine sanction for the events that follow" (*Texts of Terror*, 96). Webb ([1987] 63) is more on target in deciding that it is not clear where divine determinism operates in the vow sequence. Surely, the narrator has not pictured God accepting the sacrifice in any way, especially not in some causal fashion. The vow narrative joins with the following Ephraimite narrative to show the horrible end results of Jephthah's ambivalent lifestyle. The narrator shows Jephthah's unfaithfulness to God, not God's demand for faithfulness to a terror-filled vow.

Sjöberg identifies yet another ambiguity in the text: "whether Yhwh uses Jephthah or whether Jephthah uses Yhwh to win the victory" (*Wrestling with Textual Violence*, 51). The text underlines Yahweh's giving of the Spirit, an action the readers share with the narrator, perhaps without explicit awareness by Jephthah. The text also uses the traditional formula to indicate that the victory came from Yahweh, who gave the enemy into Jephthah's hands. Thus Yahweh proves to be the Judge who decides for Israel despite the claim of chap. 10 that he would not do so and the explicit anger of 10:7 and the divine impatience of 10:16. Jephthah may use pious language and ritual to influence deity, but God remains in control free from all human manipulation. The narrator would not say "Jephthah and Yhwh are identified as the joint architects of this tragedy, the former by opening his mouth and the latter by exacting his revenge," as Sjöberg suggests (*Wrestling with Textual Violence*, 67). Jephthah may well be, as Block describes, "a practical Yahwist . . . whom we wonder if God will use but who has no reservations about manipulating God for his own use" (364). God is not portrayed as a manipulative deity who forces a leader via the divine spirit to engage in an activity that is an abomination to God before giving victory. God retains his freedom to act as he chooses, no matter how faithful or unfaithful the earthly leader, as will be seen in even starker clarity in the Samson narratives.

The vow reflects an important element in the literary structure of the book since Caleb's vow in 1:12 and the Israelites' vow in 21:1 also deal with the fate of Israelite daughters. Caleb fulfills the vow and finds he has an assertive daughter. Jephthah shows "primary loyalty" to deity not daughter, making "no effort to circumvent his vow" (Sjöberg, *Wrestling with Textual Violence*, 62). The Israelites see the destructive nature of their vow and in compassion find ways to get around its results. Later, King Saul will inadvertently make a vow that threatens the life of his son Jonathan, but the people find a way to prevent its fulfillment (1 Sam 14:24, 45). Saul is thus pictured as a fruit of Israel's rescue of the Benjaminites and one who repeats Jephthah's rash vow.

Jephthah knew the history of God's deliverance of his people but did not fully trust God. Rather, he opened himself to the Moabite practice of child sacrifice (2 Kgs 3:27) and practices connected with the god Molech (Lev 18:21; 20:2–5; 2 Kgs 23:10; Jer 32:35) that 1 Kgs 11:7 links to the Ammonites. Jeremiah seems to connect the practice to Baal or Canaanite worship, perhaps performed by Israelites in the temple (Jer 7:31–32; 19:5–6, 11; compare Ezek 16:20–21; 20:26, 31; 23:37; see G. C. Heider, "Molech," *DDD*, cols. 1090–97). Younger sums up the irony: "Jephthah delivers the Israelites from the Ammonites, who along with their neighbors sacrifice their children to their gods; then he sacrifices his daughter to Yahweh, who does not accept human sacrifice!" (262).

Jephthah's path is not easy to follow. The Aroer in 11:33 is probably not the same place as that in 11:26, where it is described as being near the Arnon (Num 32:34; Deut 2:36; 3:12; 4:48; Josh 12:2; 13:9, 16; 2 Sam 24:5; 2 Kgs 10:33; 1 Chr 5:8; Jer 48:19). The Aroer mentioned in v 33 is evidently in the tribal territory of

Gad near Rabbah Ammon, modern Amman (Josh 13:25). Aroer on the Arnon is generally identified with Khirbet ʿAraʿir three miles (4.8 km) southeast of Dhiban, while Aroer near Rabbah is probably Khirbet Udena, three and a half miles (6 km) west of Rabbah (Gaß, *Ortsnamen*, 474–75). Many modern interpreters see a literary problem here and dismiss mention of Aroer as a later addition to the text (Gaß, 476, with n. 248). Rainey (*Sacred Bridge*, 140–41) understands this Aroer to be on the border between Gad and the Ammonites.

Minnith appears here and in Ezek 37:17. Rainey (*Sacred Bridge*, 141) places it at modern Umm el-Basatin, or Umm el-Hanafish as Gaß (*Ortsnamen*, 477–79) calls this same place. This is four and a half miles (7 km) from Heshbon. Abel-keramim is attested only here in the Bible but also appears in a list attributed to Tutmoses III and in the work of the Islamic geographer Tabari. Gaß (*Ortsnamen*, 465–73) uses this to isolate Tell el-ʿUmeri almost seven miles (11 km) southwest of Amman. Rainey offers several possible sites but makes no final decision. Knauf (*ABD*, 1:10–11) disputes the archaeological evidence at el-ʿUmeri and points to Sahab, which Rainey appears to favor. It lies seven and a half miles (12 km) southeast of Amman, but Gaß claims it cannot qualify because it was not settled in the time of Eusebius, who mentions it.

Whatever the exact location of the cities, Jephthah does not follow the pattern of Barak and Gideon in pursuing the enemy rulers. Block notes that "Jephthah appears not to have pursued the Ammonites into their own heartland. By destroying their border fortifications, he eliminated the pressure they were applying to his people" (370). Thus we see again that, as Schneider observes, "the book of Judges is not interested in the details of battle but in the story about the leader, how they were hired, their actions while in charge, and what they did with their power" (176).

Niditch (132–33) strongly supports Jephthah at this point:

> The eloquent, traditional style of Jephthah's speech with its formulaic renditions of history, rhetorical questions, recurring language, and emphatic flourishes ("And I . . . ," 11:27) contributes to Jephthah's characterization as a capable leader who knows his rights and defends his people. The language and literary form, moreover, are informed by juridical language and motifs such as the opening question in v. 12, the disclaimer at v. 27, and the reference to Yhwh as adjudicator in v. 27.

34–40 Victory turns to horror. The reader's mind returns to v 30 with alarm as the first one to greet Jephthah upon his victorious return is a celebrating daughter, dancing and playing, practicing "stereotypical female behaviour" (Sjöberg, *Wrestling with Textual Violence*, 65; compare Exod 15:20; 1 Sam 18:6–7; C. L. Meyers, "Of Drums and Damsels: Women's Performance in Ancient Israel," *BA* 54 [1991] 16–27). Unbeknown to her, hers is the dance of death. Still she appears to be "a paragon of faithfulness" (Ackerman, *Warrior, Dancer,* 110). Knowing he has to fulfill the vow by sacrificing her causes Jephthah great sorrow and anxiety. Her status as an only child only deepens the sorrow, guilt, and anxiety. He immediately acts out his grief symbolically by tearing his clothes. (Compare Gen 37:29, 34; 44:13; Num 14:6; Josh 7:6; Judg 11:35; 2 Sam 1:2, 11; 3:31; 4:12; 13:19, 31; 15:32; 1 Kgs 21:27; 2 Kgs 2:12; 5:7–8; 6:30; 11:14; 18:37; 19:1; 22:11, 19; 2 Chr 23:13; 34:19, 27; Ezra 9:3, 5; Esth 4:1; Job 1:20; 2:12; Isa 36:22; 37:1; Jer 36:24; 41:5; Joel 2:13.)

Even Webb with all his criticism of Jephthah must admit, "Face to face with her, he finds that he values her more, much more, after the battle than he had before" ([1987] 67). Pain and disaster now mark his life, not victory and military and political titles. Yet his words betray a patriarchal, self-centered perspective as he accuses the daughter of making him "bend over in pain" and "ruining" him (Judg 11:35). Brensinger remarks, "He offers no comfort or reassurance. The child, without siblings, therefore finds herself with no noticeable parental compassion either. How different is David's response a short time later . . . (2 Sam 18:33)" (135). Still he accepts responsibility because he "opened [his] mouth to Yahweh" (v 35). Again, ambiguity rules the narrative. Sjöberg claims, inappropriately, that "his responsibility for the course of events appears to be non-existent" (*Wrestling with Textual Violence*, 43).

The daughter knows that vows made are vows paid, for as Hamilton (*Handbook on the Historical Books*, 145) states, "Scripture makes no provision for withdrawing or annulling a vow made to God. That would be done later by postbiblical rabbinic tradition." Still, McCann is correct to declare that "to commend Jephthah for being a man of his word because he fulfills his vow amounts to saying that it does not matter what one believes as long as one is sincere. . . . Jephthah's story in its present canonical context thus has the effect of portraying Jephthah as a faithful Ammonite rather than a faithful Israelite!" (84).

She encourages her father to carry out the vow, knowing that this means her death. In so doing she "theologically legitimizes the sacrifice" (Sjöberg, *Wrestling with Textual Violence*, 67). She does add one condition to her agreement to suffer the consequences of her father's foolish vow. She wants two months of quiet time, a length of time that probably represents one of Israel's agricultural seasons as represented on the Gezer calendar (see Walton et al., *IVP Bible Background*, 263). She will spend the quiet time with her friends to mourn the fact that she must remain a virgin and never know the joy of the marriage relationship.

The Hebrew term *bĕtûlay* (בְּתוּלַי) is more complex than simply "virginity" (Judg 11:37). It designates a "girl under the guardianship of her father" (Walton, *NIDOTTE*, 1:783). Or, according to Sjöberg (*Wrestling with Textual Violence*, 65), it describes "a sexually available woman, about to be transferred from the realm of her father." Block notes that the term recognizes the desire to "realize the joy of motherhood, the natural longing of women, particularly in this ancient cultural context" (374, n. 123). Schneider disagrees:

> The assumption that Jephthah's daughter's distress is rooted in her lack of children is unfounded and goes against the pattern of women in the book thus far. . . . The emphasis on what she was missing lies not with what she could have created but those aspects of life that she would never have a chance to experience. The stress repeatedly on what she was missing emphasizes sexual experience. (181)

Niditch believes that "the women in the ritual are mourning the end of their old status as daughters while preparing for their new status with the full range of female adult responsibilities. Life passages such as these are marked in the myths and rituals of many cultures" (134).

The two months pass, and her father carries out the vow. Sjöberg concludes that "Jephthah defends his honour by keeping his word" (*Wrestling with Textual*

Violence, 55). In so doing he may be seen to be exercising "his rights as a father, sanctioned by Deuteronomistic law [Deut 21:10–17; 22:13–30], to determine his daughter's fate" (*Wrestling with Textual Violence*, 52). Jephthah receives no divine alternative, as did Abraham when he was willing to sacrifice his only son, Isaac (Gen 22). Brensinger elaborates on that contrast: "For Abraham, the entire event was a divinely ordained test. By way of contrast, Jephthah's dilemma has resulted from a self-motivated attempt to counteract his own faithlessness; God has nothing to do with it. He is left, therefore, to face the consequences of his own deeds, the OT's consistent abhorrence of human sacrifices notwithstanding (Lev 18:21; 20:1–5; Deut 12:31; 18:10; 2 Kgs 165:3; Jer 7:31)" (135). "His foolish, faithless act shows the horrible, terror-filled results of not enacting and embodying what God wills" (McCann, 85). It also shows that God in his love will not coerce obedience (McCann, 86–87).

Nor can exegetical ingenuity find an escape that condemns the daughter to perpetual virginity rather than death, as Keil and Delitzsch argued long ago (K&D, 388–95) and S. Landers (*BRev* 7 [1991] 27–31, 42) has more recently. Landers claims that a female would not be acceptable as a sacrifice. D. Marcus (*Jephthah and His Vow*, 52) uses the numerous ambiguities in the Jephthah narrative to argue for ambiguity at this point also. However, though the narrator's language here may involve circumlocution, it does not involve ambiguity. Reis (*Proof* 71 [1997] 279–98) argues that knowing Israel's history, Jephthah would also have known its legal tradition now reflected in Lev 27:1–8. Thus his intention was to dedicate a slave to God and then redeem the slave by paying the required amount to the priests. This assumes a great deal of knowledge and piety for a prostitute's son and builds on nothing at all in the text.

Jephthah does what he told God he would do. Brown remarks that "the text speaks volumes by its very silence. It refrains from saying what the father did in order to communicate more dramatically, more forcefully what he did" (231).

The daughter's fate institutes a statute among the Israelites wherein the Israelite virgins are required to spend four days a year reciting the story of Jephthah's daughter. The Hebrew *pi'el* form of the root *tnh* (תנה), often translated "lament" (NRSV, NLT, JPS, NJB; CJB; compare CEV), is more accurately rendered "recite" (Judg 11:40) or "commemorate" (see Judg 5:11; NASB95, REB, HCSB, TNIV, NET; compare Exum, "Feminist Criticism," 77). Notice that the word *ḥōq* (חק) carries the normal meaning "statute," "regulation," or "law" (CJB; Sjöberg, *Wrestling with Textual Violence*, 66), not the extended meaning of "custom" as it is often translated (NRSV, NLT, JPS, NAB, NASB95, NJB, NKJV, HCSB, NET). The daughter dies young and unfulfilled as a woman, but "she is commemorated by an official decree" (Sjöberg, *Wrestling with Textual Violence*, 66).

How does one picture the daughter of Jephthah? Does one agree with Sjöberg that "Jephthah determines every one of his daughter's acts. Her freedom lies solely in the attitude with which she carries out what her father allows her" (*Wrestling with Textual Violence*, 68)? Or does she show, as Brensinger suggests, "a more admirable and godly spirit than any seen elsewhere in the narrative. She, the unmistakable victim, becomes a devout encourager" (135)? Does she exhibit, as Block says, "sensitivity and submissiveness" (373)? Or is she, as McCann would have us believe, the "most likely candidate" in the book of Judges to be a "type of Jesus" (88)? The latter probably goes too far, but certainly her portrayal as loyal, obedient, brave, courageous, a bit independent, and loved by her friends makes her by far the most sympathetic character in the Jephthah narratives and possibly in the last half of the book of Judges.

Interestingly, the final verse of chap. 11 identifies Jephthah as "the Gileadite." What his brothers refused to accept and what caused the elders originally to hate him becomes in the end the identity of Jephthah. The son of a "prostitute" (v 1), of "another woman" (v 2), now becomes "the Gileadite." This leads Sjöberg (*Wrestling with Textual Violence*, 46) to see an expression of "anti-Gileadite ideology." Such a reading comes from the rest of the story in the next chapter, not obviously from chap. 11. Thus Block (372) sees Jephthah as "the tragic figure, presenting a pathetic picture of stupidity, brutality, ambition, and self-centeredness."

This appears to end Jephthah's saga, but it does not. Another story follows, a story that adds greater depth to the foolishness and inability of Jephthah to become the leader God seeks for his people. A man with the knowledge of Israel's history, the willingness to let God be Judge of Israel, and the patience to try to make diplomacy work before entering battle is also the man who makes foolish vows, leads an army of unprincipled men, and brings destruction to a major tribe in Israel.

12:1 Niditch says of the ensuing conflict between Jephthah and the Ephraimites in chap. 12, "This example of inner-Israelite strife highlights the weaknesses of epic models of leadership and polity and points to the ethnographic differences between two groups of Israelites. It continues the portrayal of Jephthah as a local chieftain who defends his power against other Israelite groups who would challenge him" (137).

The "men of Ephraim" appear even more suddenly than they did with Gideon in 7:24–8:3. Evidently not all the tribes accepted the leader the elders of Gilead had selected. Younger says, "Just as his half-brothers rejected him, so now his tribal 'brothers' seem to have rejected him" (273). The east-west divide of Josh 22 is not completely settled. The Ephraimites, having "no pride in greater Israel, let alone any respect for the Transjordanians" (Block, 381), gather for battle at Zaphon, a town seventeen miles (27.4 km) south-southeast of Beth-shan, just east of the Jordan in Gilead north of the Jabbok River and of Succoth as shown by Josh 13:27. Zaphon is one possible reading of a term in the Amarna correspondence, in a list from the time of Rameses II, and in the list of Shoshenq I. Gaß (*Ortsnamen*, 496–500) lists five possible sites: Tell el-Qosh, Khirbet Buweb, Khirbet Faqaris, Tell es-Saʿidiyeh, and Tell el-Mazar. He eliminates Buweb and Faqaris on archaeological grounds and expresses a preference for Tell el-Qosh. Rainey (*Sacred Bridge*, 141) lists Saʿidiyeh and Mazar as the two primary candidates.

Here again Ephraim in the west becomes involved in a campaign in the east, thus having to pass over the Jordan. The Ephraimites have one complaint with Jephthah—he did not call them to go with him. The emphasis in Judg 12:1 is on the "us" in the disjunctive clause: literally "but to us you did not call to go with you." As Niditch perceives, "Some of the deepest animus is reserved for fellow Israelites in the book of Judges" (138). Apparently the Ephraimite problem lies in thinking they were denied a share of the victors' booty (Niditch, 137). In chap. 8 Gideon was able to calm the protest and get on with the battle. Despite his skill shown in previous negotiations, here Jephthah does not display such diplomatic skills. Ephraim threatens to burn his house down. This could represent either his residence or his family, though the preceding unit did not leave him with much family. Matthews correctly notes: "The Ephraimites, this preeminent northern tribal group (and we would note the tribe of Jeroboam) is portrayed negatively, based on both their military stance and their incompetence in following simple instructions. In fact, the degree to which the Ephraimites are presented as positive or negative in Judges serves as a sort of literary-social barometer of the fortunes of the Israelites in this period" (129).

2–3 Jephthah identifies himself as a "person of arbitration," using the Hebrew *rîb* (ריב), a term central to Jerubbaal's name (6:31–32) and to Ephraim's contention with Gideon (8:1). Block sees this as a negative description of Jephthah, translating this difficult Hebrew verse as "I was a man of contention." He thinks the original tradition read, "I was an extremely contentious man" with the other words added by the narrator "to clarify the comment" (381). If the latter is so, the clarifying comment is surely unclear. Boling's "I was using diplomacy" (taken up by Younger, 272 n. 72) is not much too positive, as Block (381) would contend. The narrator is not having Jephthah belittle himself. Jephthah adequately summarizes his political life up to this point and could have added a note to include his religious relationship also.

Rîb, "contend with," also appears in Jephthah's historical review of Balak of Moab taking the Israelites to court or contending with them (11:25). It will also appear in the last chapter as the men of Shiloh contend with the Benjaminites who are seeking wives for themselves (21:22). The word has not previously been applied to Jephthah, but he has shown an ability to arbitrate in his dealings with the elders, with the Ammonites, and with God; however, his ability has never won the day without battle. (Compare Block, 381, who in n. 151 is surely correct that "nothing about the Hb. warrants the common pairing of 'I' and 'my people' against 'Bene Ammon.'") Thus the final narrative concerning Jephthah lets him identify himself as an arbitrator, one who takes people to court and tries to win the battle of wits and words. He has not been prejudiced in his arbitration, as he bargained with both "my people" and even more so with the "sons of Ammon" (Judg 12:2). Again he demonstrates his arbitration as he explains to the Ephraimites that he tried to muster their troops but they "did not rescue me." Receiving no help from Ephraim, Jephthah claims that he took his life in his hands to cross the Jordan away from the Ephraimites to face the Ammonites. Then Yahweh proved to be the savior or deliverer. Thus Ephraim has no reason to fight Jephthah. What are they up to?

Amit exaggerates only a bit as she concludes, "Jephthah did not exploit his diplomatic talents. . . . Instead, he preferred to irritate the Ephraimites and to set out against them in a cruel war" (*Book of Judges*, 89). Thus Block can conclude that "whereas Gideon's self-deprecating comments are known to contradict his heroic actions, Jephthah's heroic self-laudation flies in the face of the narrator's silence regarding any specific acts of heroism" (382). Olson goes too far in claiming, "the reader is led to conclude that this is a bald-faced lie" (837; compare Block 382; Younger, 272). The narrator is not so silent in 11:32–33 about Jephthah's exploits and gives no indication that the people of Gilead or those of Ephraim did not give Jephthah credit for the victory. Indeed, the narrator underlines God's part in giving the enemy into Jephthah's hands, but that does not make the pronoun of v 32 refer to God rather than to Jephthah. In the same vein, one cannot so blatantly accuse Jephthah, as Block does, of "feigned piety intended to impress his challengers" (382; compare Younger 272) when he confesses God's part in the victory as he addresses the Ephraimites. The narrator skillfully characterizes Jephthah as a person with ambivalent qualities, not someone who is totally bad.

4 The narrator provides no information about Ephraim's reaction, simply reporting that Jephthah gathered his troops for battle. This is what Olson calls "ruthless power politics" (838). Again, this condemns Jephthah a bit much. Neither he nor Ephraim carries all the blame. Thus ensues an intertribal war between Gilead and Ephraim, another piece of evidence of the lack of unity and support among the tribes of Israel. Finally, the narrator shows the basic source of the quarrel: Ephraim has been taunting the people of Gilead, claiming they do not have independent identity. They live totally dependent on Ephraim and Manasseh, the two Joseph tribes. They are "fugitives," precisely the Hebrew term *pilîṭî* (פְּלִיטֵי) that is applied to Ephraim in the next verse. Schneider argues, "What is important for the downward spiral of Judges is that the taunt was along tribal lines, which emphasizes Israel's increasing lack of unity and fragmentation into tribes" (185).

But what did the taunt mean, and how did it relate to reality? Block thinks the taunt "is a conscious and derogatory fabrication" (383), though it appears to have had enough truth behind it to upset the Gileadites in a masterful way. For Block, it alludes to Gilead living east of the Jordan "outside Israel's heartland" and to Jephthah being an outcast from his own family and warns that "they would find no refuge in Manasseh, their homeland" (383). It may well have been an Ephraimite way of saying that Gilead was not really a tribe of Israel and would not find acceptance or land among the Joseph tribes even though "historically Gilead was one of the clans from the tribe of Manasseh" (Walton et al., *IVP Bible Background,* 264).

5–6 Jephthah uses the same strategy as had Ehud and the Ephraimites (Judg 3:28). He gains military control of the Jordan crossings to trap the enemy. Gideon had also controlled the crossings thanks to the Ephraimites (7:24), to the extent that he could pursue the enemy across them (8:4). Jephthah does not ally with the Ephraimites to capture the crossings. Rather he uses the crossings to capture the Ephraimites. This shows how far the relationship with Ephraim had deteriorated—from allies to enemies—just as relationships would in the days of King Solomon and Jeroboam.

After the Gileadites' successful capture of the crossings, Ephraimites attempt to escape by crossing the river. The Gileadites put them to the test, first identifying them as Ephraimites, an identity the refugees deny, and then asking them to pronounce *Šibbōlet* (שִׁבֹּלֶת). Invariably, the Ephraimites replied with *Sibbōlet* (סִבֹּלֶת). This is surely a phonetic variant in pronunciation rather than a historical development as Block proposes (384; see the various theories in nn. 157–58). D. Marcus gives three translations (interpretations) of the phrase "he was not in the habit of so speaking" (Judg 12:6): "1) Not prepared to pronounce it correctly; 2) inattentive to pronounce it correctly; 3) did not have the ability to pronounce it correctly" (*Maarav* 8 [1992] 100–101). Most modern translations follow NRSV in reading "could not pronounce it right." The issue centers on the meaning of *yākîn* (יָכִין) and *kēn* (כֵּן). *Yākîn* has a variety of meanings, including "prepare, make ready, set up, determine, appoint, make firm or steady, be intent on, resolved." *Kēn* can mean either "correctly, accurately, honestly" or "thus, in the same way." I read the meaning to be prepared for the same thing they had just been told, that is, to be in a habit of doing it that way. This may well indicate not so much a physical inability as it does a lack of practice and usage. "As is always the case, consonant sounds that are not native to one's own speech dialect are difficult to reproduce without practice" (Walton et al., *IVP Bible Background*, 264).

The test reveals that the various tribes had enough distinct identity that they did not speak the same dialect. It also provides the Gileadites a way to kill forty-two thousand members of the tribe of Ephraim, almost as many as the Israelites would destroy in Benjamin just a bit later (20:35, 46). Othniel captured Arameans. Ehud killed the king of Moab. Shamgar slew Philistines. Barak defeated Canaanites, while Jael killed the Canaanite general. Gideon defeated the Midianites, leading to the murder of their generals, and killed their kings. He also destroyed two Israelite cities east of the Jordan, killing Israelite citizens. Abimelech killed his own half brothers and destroyed Shechem, murdering the inhabitants. Jephthah's rash vow led to his daughter's death, while the Ephraimites' inability to speak gives Jephthah a sign to kill forty-two thousand fellow Israelites. As Matthews concludes (130), "The ruthlessness of Jephthah's forces in executing thousands of Ephraimites is perhaps simply an extension of their leader's determination to win at all costs, a fatal flaw for both him and his people."

Still, this does not make the people of Ephraim the heroes or show a narrator's empathy for them. Indeed, as Younger says, "it is possible that Ephraim controlled some territories east of the Jordan (cf. 2 Sam 18:6, which mentions 'the forest of Ephraim'" (272). Younger (271) sees the Ephraimites using the language of "covenant disputation." Jobling's structuralist clues indicate "the Ephraimites seem to have the 'right' view (that is, the narrator's view)" ("Structuralist Criticism," 113), allowing that there may be some tension between the perspectives presented in the book of Judges. The progressively deteriorating picture of Ephraim from Ehud to here indicates otherwise. The tribe who could not drive out the residents of Gezer (1:29) followed Ehud's leadership (3:27) and Deborah's (5:14). They then obeyed Gideon (7:24) but then complained at not being the first ones called (8:1). Having to face the Ammonites proved a major obstacle for Ephraim and other tribes (10:9), but then Ephraim became distressed when not called to face the Ammonites (12:1), leading to a civil war and the almost complete destruction of the tribe (12:4). Finally comes the religious heresy of an Ephraimite and a Levite (chaps. 17–18) and the Ephraimite Levite of chap. 19. One finds it difficult to see the Ephraimites holding any right view in the perspective of storyteller, author, or reader/listener.

The "negative disposition toward the Ephraimites" (Block, 384) remains. Brettler judges them "bratty upstarts who want to be included where they do not belong" (*JBL* 108 [1989] 408), who are basically parodied or satirized as "an insufferable lot of bunglers, cowards, and dullards . . . and cannot even speak proper Hebrew," according to Block (387, following D. Marcus, *Maarav* 8 [1992] 95–105).

The Israel that God punished using other nations and then delivered from other nations has become the Israel intent on punishing and even destroying one another. Block declares, "Israel had become as fragmented as the Canaanite population they were commanded to expunge" (386). The narrator gives no interpretation of such action. Nor does the narrator show God's part in all this. Indeed, Block says, "God appears content to let the nation destroy itself" (384). The narrator lets the reader make the call. Is this the type of leadership Israel needs? Can Israel not find a leader who will bring the nation together rather than destroy its parts? Must Israel's leaders come from the unqualified and outcasts, the unwilling and untrusting? Are women the only heroes and martyrs in Israel? Has God finally given up on this people?

7 The narrator summarizes Jephthah's reign as judge in a form similar to that used in reporting on the minor judges, attributing to him only six years as Israel's judge. His burial has provided fodder for scholarly discussion. The Hebrew text has a plural in reference to the "towns" of his burial. Does that mean his body was severed into parts and scattered in various burial places? Or must the text be changed on the basis of Greek and Josephus? Or is the burial reference intended to report on various memorial services commemorating Jephthah's contributions to Gilead? We cannot be sure of the details at this point. As with the other minor judges and with Abimelech, no reference appears to a time of rest or peace. No mention is made of ending the Ammonite menace or securing the land (Block, 385). Now Israel and the judges, Brown says, "had set their course to chaos by their resolute waywardness" (235).

8–10 Ibzan follows Jephthah on the list of judges but stands on the opposite end of the fertility chain. His only notable achievement is siring children, "thirty sons and thirty daughters." Brown (236) sees this as a sign of divine covenant blessing, but the text does not mention this. One cannot argue on the basis of silence here nor in its absence of censure for Ibzan. The text is interested only in the children's marriages.

Ibzan apparently did what Solomon later would do, marry off his children to make political alliances (see 1 Kgs 11:1–13), paving the way for Jeroboam to become king of Israel and split the nation. Matthews interprets this, however, in a positive fashion, indicating, "how successful Ibzan was in acquiring a network of support through marriage alliances and how he added to his own territorial holdings through these extrafamilial links" (130–31). As Hauser expresses it, "Ibzan would have entered into such marital exhanges as a means of enhancing his role as leader in the region surrounding Bethlehem. Thus Ibzan is best understood as a local clan leader with ambitions stretching into the surrounding territory" (*JETS* 22 [1979] 301). However one sees the sociological and organizational structure at this time, the marriages represented good politics but bad religion just as in the later case of Solomon.

Ibzan's hometown of Bethlehem may be the famous southern city in Judah (Block, 388–89) or the northern town in Zebulun mentioned only in Josh 19:15. The context appears to point to the northern location, but a location in Zebulun that has Iron Age remains has not yet been discovered. The southern location would point forward to Judg 17:7–9; 19:1–2, 18. The attempt by Boling, Brown, and others to make Ibzan a representative of the tribe of Asher is inspired by a theory that all twelve tribes must be represented among the judges, not by anything the text says. Wong (*Compositional Strategy of the Book of Judges*, 239–41) makes the strongest case for seeing Asher represented here.

11–12 "Elon from Zebulun" led Israel for ten years, but has no special accomplishments listed. He was buried in Aijalon in Zebulun. Gaß (*Ortsnamen*, 175) locates this in Tell el-Butmeh.

13–15 Family matters highlight the judgeship of Abdon. Pirathon, Abdon's burial place, also appears in the list of David's heroes (2 Sam 23:30; 1 Chr 11:31;

27:14). Gaß (*Ortsnamen*, 352–55) considers four possible locations for Pirathon, but settles on Farʿata, six miles (9.7 km) southwest of Shechem, even though it is not in the territory of Ephraim. Block surmises that "Ephraim is being used loosely for the hill country south of the Wadi Fariʿa" (390). Rainey, who also opts for Farʿata, honestly admits, "Why a hill region in the land of Ephraim was called Amalekite is unknown" (*Sacred Bridge*, 41). Block has perhaps the best surmise: "Perhaps they had left their mark on this region during the earlier period of oppression prior to Gideon's acts of deliverance" (390). Abdon may be the judge listed as Bedan in 1 Sam 12:11. (See H. Jacobson, "The Judge Bedan [1 Samuel xii 11]," *VT* 42 [1992] 123–24.)

Abdon resembles Jair (10:4) in giving donkeys to his children and grandchildren, providing "evidence of their royal-type power over the region." He provides only "parodies of kingship," according to Younger (278). The question has to be raised whether mention of such possessions refers to a positive position in the community or a selfish accumulation of goods at the expense of those he "judged." Bluedorn sees the "focus on the rulership rather than on the rest or peace achieved, thus implying an unsuccessful rulership." He also finds that the geographical development implies "Israel's increasing dominance by foreign nations. . . . It appears, therefore, that the land becomes increasingly useless for the Israelites, and that the Israelites even lose portions of the promised land" (*Yahweh versus Baalism*, 278). Block thinks "periods of oppression were interspersed with periods of prosperity and political independence for Israel. (391). Brown sees the mention of children and grandchildren as indicating that "Abdon was blessed by the Lord and had a wide area of influence and jurisdiction" (237).

Brown adds that these three minor judges vignettes demonstrate "that the life of faith, or "unfaith," does not always move exactly in a straight line from point *a* to point *b*. Israel was on a collision course toward chaos, but there were some turns in the road. Despite the fact that the Lord was angry with Israel, he did not withdraw his blessing from them all at once" (237).

The clue here may come from the opening reference to Jephthah and Ibzan, both of whom obviously cannot be praised. Whereas the opening set of minor judges represented a time of peace, this set of minor judges shows that leadership cannot be fully trusted in the hands of this type of judge. Here for the first time, Schneider concludes, "Israel had a leader when there was no immediate threat necessitating one. . . . With the people's request to Gideon/Jerubbaal to rule over them, a new idea is introduced, that Israel needed constant leadership, someone to be in charge at all times. The minor judges introduce that theme in a non-dynastic way" (187, 190). Younger points to their material affluence and family numbers to claim that "from Gideon on judgeship is always on the verge of turning into kingship with sons succeeding fathers to office" (277; compare Webb, [1987] 161).

The minor judges follow the paths of Gideon, Abimelech, and Jephthah. They are interested in political alliances and family riches, not in the peace of Israel. Again, Matthews gives the other viewpoint, seeing this as pointing to "a long period of prosperity and apparent stability" (131). Matthews is more to the point in writing, "These figures, including Tola and Jair in 10:1–5, function as literary bookends demarking Jephthah's account and speeding the reader toward the growing apostasy and failure of the Israelites throughout the remainder of the book" (131).

Olson rightly characterizes these final minor judges. They

> do not compare favorably with the previous minor judges. No minor judge in this third group is said to "deliver" Israel. Their rule brings benefit only to themselves and not to the nation of Israel as a whole. The details about these judges involve only their own families and their deaths and burials. The lengths of their reigns (seven years, ten years, eight years) are relatively short in comparison to the previous minor judges. (839)

In the context of the final phrase of 12:15, Younger asks, "Have the Israelites dropped to such a level of living that they are being absorbed into the peoples of the land? This is not the note we would have hoped the noncyclical/minor judges' presentation to end on" (278). As Schneider concludes, "These minor judges needed no qualifications, did not do anything, nor did they hold the office in response to any crisis" (189).

Explanation

Summing up the meaning and intention of the Jephthah narrative proves as difficult as doing that for any other passage in the book. Webb concludes, "We are left to infer motivation from behavior. . . . The text is highly resistant to any simplistic, reductionist form of interpretation" ([1987] 77). The narrative thrives on ambiguity. Only as one interprets the ambiguities in one way or another can one ascribe meaning and purpose to the narrative. Such ambiguities refuse to let us simplify the characters into stock figures with simplistic motives and actions. The ambiguities, rather, add complexity and puzzlement to the characters, thus making them human in the deepest sense of the term.

On the surface, Jephthah is the outcast made good, the socially unaccepted become successful. He is a natural leader to whom men gravitate in time of need, whether it is the material needs of his unprincipled followers in Tob or the political, military needs of the elders of Gildead. Thus Niditch can conclude from a feminist reading:

> Some scholars consider this very positive portrayal to be at odds with the subsequent tale of a man who makes a rash oath; in fact, the two parts of ch. 11 are consistent. The tale of Jephthah's daughter, poignant and troubling, has to do with keeping one's word in a culture of vow making and covenants. The important social and political relationship is between the men, that is, Jephthah and the male deity, and it models such relationships between human men in which women serve as valuable exchange items and mediators. (133)

Jephthah, the leader, has thus simply made "a not untypical war vow, one that he fully comprehends on a mundane and tragic level only in the wake of war," according to Niditch (134).

Olson, in an attempt to understand the implications of Jephthah's actions, says, "We are left wondering . . . whether Jephthah, at his core, is a genuinely good and faithful person who has simply made the best of the unfortunate circumstances of his life, which were beyond his control. Or is Jephthah a cynical politician who is looking out only for his own interests, using religion to mask his quest for political power and position?" (827).

On the surface he is a man of faith, steeped in the religious and political traditions of his people. He knows that God is the ultimate Judge who determines affairs and distributes lands in international conflicts. He confesses that Yahweh must give him victory if victory is to be realized.

Yet he is a shrewd bargainer who can gain the title he wants and set forth the ideological foundation for his and his people's claim to their land. Olson observes that he is "both pious adherent to the Lord and shrewd negotiator for his own interests" (825). The problem comes in the time of crisis when he leaves behind the shrewd, clever bargaining skill and lays out a rash bargain before God. Here is a man who loses his cool and neglects to use his skills. This leads to the crisis of meeting his daughter, now doomed by his vow. Again the complexity of character appears as he bewails the inevitable loss of his only daughter and with it the only hope for his family to be carried into future generations. But at the same time, his bargaining skills come again to the fore as he tries to shift blame and pain to her rather than totally admit responsibility for foolishly opening his mouth before God. A man of powerful words, he finds the word can kill as well as exalt. As Olson says, "A key theme in the Jephthah narrative is the entrapment of human language that leads to death" (821).

Thus Jephthah shows us the skilled person God can use and also the misuse of skills in the name of God. Much like Saul who will follow him, he throws aside his skillful potential in the name of immediate expediency. Amit regrets that "Jephthah is a judge who arouses disappointment" (*Book of Judges,* 89), with which Webb concurs: "He has debased religion (a vow, an offering) into politics" ([1987] 74). Block thinks he is "an extremely tragic figure, . . . the consummate manipulator, . . . the ethical and spiritual low point" (385–86; compare Exum "Tragic Vision and Biblical Narrative"). Thus he is remembered, Brown says, "not as Israel's most heroic and brilliant judge but as the most heartless and barbaric of all Israel's judges" (227). He has killed more Ephraimites than all the other judges together kill of Israel's foreign enemies (Hamilton, *Handbook on the Historical Books,* 147). Amit declares, "His appearance, specifically after a period of consecutive judges, during which the people did not do what was evil in the eyes of God, strengthens the conclusion that the people need a strong, continuous central rule" (*Book of Judges,* 90), for, according to Hamilton, "Jephthah . . . is a far greater threat to Israel than are the Ammonites" (*Handbook on the Historical Books,* 148).

He has also debased the patriarchal system of the Bible and its care for children. If one reads Jephthah as a pure hero of faith, then his fulfillment of a rash vow becomes a heroic act. The biblical norm can be seen as one that puts the masculine honor above the safety and lives of women and children. Olson is more on target in arguing just the opposite: "The book of Judges suggests that the well-being and treatment of women and children (especially daughters) in a community or nation can serve as a measuring stick for the overall health and faithfulness of the community's religious and political life" (835).

At this point, we must ask how the canon of Scripture can place a positive affirmation on such a man as Jephthah and others of the judges as seen in 1 Sam 12:11 and Heb 11:32. The clearest theological reply comes from D. M. Howard, Jr.: "He was rash, foolish, and he sinned in doing this. If the Scriptures were to withhold commendation of people because of some sinful aspects to their lives, no commendations would ever have been issued, except in the case of Jesus. Jephthah's vow reflects a misguided application of the principle of offering to God the best of one's treasure. It also demonstrated a certain lack of faith" (*Introduction to the Old Testament Historical Books*, 117).

4. Samson's Self-centered Fight with Philistines and Women (13:1–16:31)

Bibliography

Ackerman, S. "What If Judges Had Been Written by a Philistine?" *BibInt* 8 (2000) 33–41. **Alter, R.** "How Convention Helps Us Read: The Case of the Bible's Annunciation Type-Scene." *Proof* 3 (1983) 115–30. ———. "Samson without Folklore." In *Text and Tradition.* Ed. S. Niditch. 47–56. **Amit, Y.** "Delilah: A Victim of Interpretation." In *First Person: Essays in Biblical Autobiography.* Ed. P. R. Davies. London; New York: Sheffield Academic, 2002. 59–76. ———. "Lifelong Nazirism—The Evolution of a Motif" (Heb.). In *Téuda.* Ed. M. A. Friedman and M. Gal. Tel Aviv, 1986. 4:23–36. ———. "The Life of Samson" (Heb.). *Tarbiz* 54 (1985) 299–305. ———. "'Manoah Promptly Followed His Wife' (Judges 13.11): On the Place of the Woman in Birth Narratives." In *Feminist Companion to Judges* (1993). Ed. A. Brenner. 146–56. ———. "There was a man . . . and his name was . . .": Editorial Variation and Its Purposes." *Beit-Miqra* 30 (1984–1985) 388–99. **Andersson, G.** *The Book and Its Narratives: A Critical Examination of Some Synchronic Studies of the Book of Judges.* Örebro Studies in Literary History and Criticism 1. Örebro: Universitetsbiblioteket, 2001. **Babcock-Abrahams, B.** "'A Tolerated Margin of Mess': The Trickster and His Tales Reconsidered." *Journal of the Folklore Institute* 11 (1975) 147. **Bader, W.** *Simson bei Delila: Computerlinguistische Interpretation des Textes Ri 13–16.* Tübingen: Francke, 1991. ———. "Traut Leserinnen etws zu! Eine unnötige textkritische Ergänzung in Ri 16,13.14." *BN* 75 (1994) 5–12. **Bal, M.** *Lethal Love: Feminist Literary Readings of Biblical Love Stories.* Bloomington: Indiana UP, 1987. 37–67. **Barredo, M. A.** "¿Acción de Dios en las Hazañas de Sansón? Enfoque Teológica de Jueces 13–16." *VyV* 60 (2002) 471–98. **Bauer, H.** "Zu Simsons Rätsel in Richter Kapitel 14." *ZDMG* 66 (1912) 473–74. **Blenkinsopp, J.** "Some Notes on the Saga of Samson and the Heroic Milieu." *Scr* 11 (1959) 81–89. ———. "Structure and Style in Judges 13–16." *JBL* 82 (1963) 65–76. **Blumenthal, F.** "Samson and Samuel: Two Styles of Leadership." *JBQ* 33 (2005) 108–12. **Böhme, W.** "Die älteste Darstellung in Richt. 6,11–24 und 13,2–24 und ihre Verwandtschaft mit der Jahveurkunde des Pentateuch." *ZAW* 5 (1885) 251–74. **Bömer, F.** "Die Römischen Ernteopfer und die Füchse im Philisterlande." *Wiener Studien* 69 (1956) 372–84. **Bowman, R. G.** "Narrative Criticism of Judges." In *Judges and Method.* Ed. G. A. Yee. 17–44. **Bowman, R. G.,** and **R. W. Swanson.** "Samson and the Son of God, or Dead Heroes and Dead Goats: Ethical Reading of Narrative Violence in Judges and Matthew." *Semeia* 77 (1997) 59–73. **Brenner, A.** "Female Social Behavior: Two Descriptive Patterns within the 'Birth of the Hero' Paradigm." *VT* 36 (1986) 257–73. **Brooks, S. S.** "Saul and the Samson Narrative." *JSOT* 71 (1996) 19–25. **Browne, E.** "Samson: Riddle and Paradox." *TBT* 22 (1984) 161–67. **Bynum, D. D.** *The Daemon in the Wood.* Cambridge, MA: Harvard UP, 1978. ———. "Samson as a Biblical φὴρ ὀρεσκῷος." In *Text and Tradition.* Ed. S. Niditch. 57–73. **Camp, C. V. van,** and **C. R. Fontaine.** "The Words of the Wise and Their Riddles." In *Text and Tradition.* Ed. S. Niditch. 127–52. **Carmy, S.** "The Sphinx as Leader: A Reading of Judges 13–16." *Tradition* 14 (1974) 66–79. **Cartledge, T. W.** "Were Nazirite Vows Unconditional?" *CBQ* 51 (1989) 409–22. **Carus, P.** *The Story of Samson and Its Place in the Religious Development of Mankind.*

Chicago: Open Court, 1907. **Chepey, S. D.** "Samson the 'Holy One': A Suggestion regarding the Reviser's Use of ἅγιος in Judg 13,7; 16,17 LXX Vaticanus." *Bib* 83 (2002) 97–99. **Chisholm, R. B., Jr.** "Identity Crisis: Assessing Samson's Birth and Career." Paper presented to Evangelical Theological Society National Conference, Valley Forge, PA, November, 2005. **Clanton, D. W., Jr.** "Samson et Dalila: What French Opera Reveals about the Biblical Duo." *BRev* 20 (2004) 12–18, 44–46. **Cohen, G. G.** "Samson and Hercules: A Comparison between the Feats of Samson and the Labours of Hercules." *EvQ* 42 (1970) 131–41. **Cook, S.** "The Theophanies of Gideon and Manoah." *JTS* 28 (1927) 368–83. **Crenshaw, J. L.** *Samson: A Secret Betrayed, a Vow Ignored.* Macon, GA: Mercer UP, 1978. ———. "The Samson Saga: Filial Devotion or Erotic Attachment?" *ZAW* 86 (1974) 470–504. **Culley, R. C.** *Themes and Variations.* 108–9. **Daalen, A. G. van.** *Simson: Een onderzoek naar de plaats, de opbouw en de funktie van het Simsonverhaal in het kader van de oudtestamentische geschiedschrijving.* Assen: Van Gorcum, 1966. **Dangl, O.** "Computerlinguistische Interpretation: Kritische Würdigung zu Winfried Bader." (Review of *Simson bei Delila: Computerlinguistische Interpretation of des Textes Ri 13–16,* by W. Bader.) *BN* 69 (1993) 56–86. **Diederichs, J. C. W.** *Zur Geschichte Simsons: Richter XIV–XVI.* Göttingen: Dieterich, 1778. **Doorninck, A. van.** "De Simsonsagen: Kritische Studiën over Richteren 14–16." *ThT* 28 (1894) 14–32. **Dundes, A.,** with **R. A. Georges.** "Toward a Structural Definition of the Riddle." In *Analytic Essays in Folklore.* Studies in Folklore 2. The Hague: Mouton, 1975. 95–102. Originally published in *Journal of American Folklore* 76 (1963) 111–18. **Eissfeldt, O.** "Die Rätsel in Jdc 14." *ZAW* 30 (1910) 132–35. **Emerton, J. A.** "Notes on Two Proposed Emendations in the Book of Judges (11,24 and 16,28)." *ZAW* 85 (1973) 220–23. **Emmrich, M.** "The Symbolism of the Lion and the Bees: Another Ironic Twist in the Samson Cycle." *JETS* 44 (2001) 67–74. **Exum, J. C.** "Aspects of Symmetry and Balance in the Samson Saga." *JSOT* 19 (1981) 3–29. ———. "Harvesting the Biblical Narrator's Scanty Plot of Ground: A Holistic Approach to Judges 16:4–22." In *Tehillah le-Moshe.* FS M. Greenberg, ed. M. Cogan, B. Eichler, and J. Tigay. Winona Lake, IN: Eisenbrauns, 1997. 39–46. ———. "Lethal Woman 2: Reflections on Delilah and Her Incarnation as Liz Hurley." In *Borders, Boundaries and the Bible.* Ed. M. O'Kane. London: Sheffield Academic, 2002. 254–73. ———. "Literary Patterns in the Samson Saga: An Investigation of Rhetorical Style in Biblical Prose." PhD diss., Columbia University, 1976. ———. "Lovis Corinth's *Blinded Samson.*" *BibInt* 6 (1988) 410–25. ———. "Promise and Fulfillment: Narrative Art in Judges 13." *JBL* 99 (1980) 43–59. ———. "Samson's Women." In *Fragmented Women: Feminist (Sub)versions of Biblical Narratives.* Valley Forge, PA: Trinity Press International, 1993. 61–93. ———. "The Theological Dimension of the Samson Saga." *VT* 33 (1983) 30–45. ———. "Why, Why, Why, Delilah?" In *Plotted, Shot, and Painted: Cultural Representations of Biblical Women.* JSOTSup 215. Sheffield: Sheffield Academic, 1996. 175–231. **Exum, J. C.,** and **J. W. Whedbee.** "Isaac, Samson, and Saul: Reflections on the Comic and Tragic Visions." In *Beyond Form Criticism, Essays in Old Testament Literary Criticism.* Ed. P. R. House. Sources for Biblical and Theological Study 2. Winona Lake, IN: Eisenbrauns, 1992. 272–309. Reprinted from *Semeia* 32 (1984) 5–40. **Feldman, L. H.** "Josephus' Version of Samson." *JSJ* 19 (1993) 171–214. **Fensham, F. C.** "The Shaving of Samson: A Note on Judges 16:19." *EvQ* 31 (1959) 97–98. **Fox, E.** "The Samson Cycle in an Oral Setting." *Ethnopoetics* 4 (1978) 51–68. **Freedman, D. N.** "A Note on Judges 15,5." *Bib* 52 (1971) 535. **Freeman, J. A.** "Samson's Dry Bones: A Structural Reading of Judges 13–16." In *Literary Interpretations of Biblical Narratives.* Ed. K. R. R. Gros Louis. Nashville: Abingdon, 1982. 2:145–60. **Frost, P.** "Sight, Sin, and Blindness in the Samson Narrative and in Milton's 'Samson Agonistes.'" *Dor le Dor* 15 (1987) 150–59. **Fuchs, E.** "The Literary Characterization of Mothers and Sexual Politics in the Hebrew Bible." In *Feminist Perspectives on Biblical Scholarship.* Ed. A. Y. Collins. Chico, CA: Scholars Press, 1985. 117–36. **Galpaz-Feller, P.** "'Let My Soul Die with the Philistines' (Judges 16.30)." *JSOT* 30 (2006) 315–25. ———. *Samson: The Hero and the Man. The Story of Samson (Judges 13–16).* Bible in History. Bern: Lang, 2006. **Gaß, E.** "Simson und die Philister, Historische und Archäologische Rückfragen." *RB* 114

(2007) 372–402. **Gaster, T. H.** *Myth, Legend, and Custom in the Old Testament.* New York: Harper, 1969. 433. **Gerstenberger, E.** "Boten, Engel, Hypostasen: Die Kommunikation Gottes mit den Menschen." In *Gott und Mensch im Dialog.* FS O. Kaiser, ed. M. Witte. 2 vols. BZAW 345. Berlin: de Gruyter, 2005. 139–54. **Gese, H.** "Die ältere Simsonüberlieferung (Richter c. 14–15)." *ZTK* 82 (1985) 261–80. Originally published in *Alttestamentliche Studien* (Tübingen: Mohr, 1991) 52–71. **Görg, M.** "Zu den Kleiderbezeichnungen in Ri 14,12f." *BN* 68 (1993) 5–9. **Gottlieb, F.** "Three Mothers." *Jud* 30 (1981) 194–203. **Greenberg, M.** *Biblical Prose Prayer as a Window to the Popular Religion of Ancient Israel.* Berkeley: University of California Press, 1983. **Greene, M.** "Enigma Variations: Aspects of the Samson Story (Judges 13–16)." *VE* 21 (1991) 53–79. **Greenstein, E. L.** "The Riddle of Samson." *Proof* 1 (1981) 237–60. **Grimm, D.** "Der Name der Gottesboten in Richter 13." *Bib* 62 (1981) 92–98. **Gunkel, H.** "Simson." In *Reden und Aufsätze.* Göttingen: Vandenhoeck & Ruprecht, 1913. 286–317. **Gunn, D. M.** "Narrative Patterns and Oral Tradition in Judges and Samuel." *VT* 24 (1974) 286–317. ———. "Samson of Sorrows: An Isaianic Gloss on Judges 13–16." In *Reading between Texts: Intertextuality and the Hebrew Bible.* Ed. D. N. Fewell. Louisville: Westminster John Knox, 1992. 225–53. **Hackett, J. A.** "Violence and Women's Lives in the Book of Judges." *Int* 58 (2004) 356–64. **Hart, R. van der.** "The Camp of Dan and the Camp of Yahweh." *VT* 25 (1975) 720. **Hartman, R.** "Simson's Füchse." *ZAW* 31 (1911) 69–72. **Haupt, P.** "Samson and the Ass's Jaw." *JBL* 33 (1914) 296–98. **Hoogewoud, F. J.** "Simson Revisited: In Memoriam Dr. Aleida G. van Daalen, leesmoeder in Amsterdam." *ACEBT* 19 (2001) 111–24. **Houtman, C.** "Simson en de leeuw: Richteren 14:6 verwoord en verbeeld." In *Om voor te lezen—Miqra.* FS F. J. Hoogewoud, ed. H. Blok, K. A. Deurloo, et al. ACEBTSup 4. Maastricht: Shaker, 2005. 73–80. **Houtman, C., and K. Spronk.** *Ein Held des Glaubens? Rezeptionsgeschichtliche Studien zu den Simson-Erzählungen.* Contributions to Biblical Exegesis and Theology 39. Leuven: Peeters, 2004. **Humbert, P.** "Les métamorphoses de Samson." *RHR* 80 (1919) 154–70. **Humphreys, W. L.** *The Tragic Vision and the Hebrew Tradition.* OBT. Philadelphia: Fortress, 1985. 68–73. **Jarrell, R. H.** "The Birth Narrative as Female Counterpart to Covenant." *JSOT* 97 (2002) 3–18. **Jonker, L. C.** "Samson in Double Vision: Judges 13–16 from Historical-Critical and Narrative Perspectives." *JNSL* 18 (1992) 49–66. **Jost, R.** "God of Love/God of Vengeance, or Samson's 'Prayer for Vengeance.'" In *Judges* (1999). Ed. A. Brenner. 117–25. ———. "Der Gott der Liebe—der Gott der Rache oder: Simson's Rachegebet." In *Von der Wurzel getragen: Christlich-feministische Exegese in Auseinandersetzung mit Antijudaismus.* Ed. L. Schottroff and M.-T. Wacker. Biblical Interpretation 17. Leiden: Brill, 1996. 103–13. **Kegler, J.** "Simson—Widerstandskämpfer und Volksheld." *CV* 18 (1985) 97–117. **Kelm, G. L.** *Timnah: A Biblical City in the Soreq Valley.* Winona Lake, IN: Eisenbrauns, 1995. **Kelm, G. L., and A. Mazar.** "Excavating in Samson Country." *BAR* (1989) 36–49. **Kim, J.** *The Structure of the Samson Cycle.* Kampen: Kok Pharos, 1993. **King, P. J.** "Circumcision—Who Did It, Who Didn't, and Why?" *BAR* 32 (2006) 48–55. **Kübel, P.** "Epiphanie und Altarbau." *ZAW* 83 (1971) 225–31. **Landy, F.** "Are We in the Place of Averroes?" *Sem* 32 (1984) 140–42. **Lehmann, G., H. M. Niemann, and W. Zwickel.** "Zora und Eschtaol: Ein archäologischer Oberflächensurvey im Gebiet nördlich von Bet Schemesch." *UF* 28 (1996) 343–442. **Leneman, H.** "Portrayals of Power in the Stories of Delilah and Bathsheba: Seduction in Song." In *Culture, Entertainment and the Bible.* Ed. G. Aichelle. JSOTSup 309. Sheffield: Sheffield Academic, 2000. 139–55. **Leuchter, M.** "'Now There Was a [Certain] Man': Compositional Chronology in Judges–1 Samuel." *CBQ* 69 (2007) 429–39. **Levy, L.** "Sexualsymbolik in der Simsonsage." *ZS* 3 (1916) 256–71. **Lods, A.** "Quelques remarques sur le Mythe de Samson." *RHPR* 4 (1924) 493–503. **Marcos, N. F.** "Héros et victime: Samson dans la LXX." In *L'apport de la Septante aux études sur l'Antiquité: Actes du colloque de Strasbourg 8–9 novembre 2002.* Ed. J. Joosten and P. le Moigne. LD 203. Paris: Cerf, 2005. 119–33. **Margalith, O.** "The Legend of Samson/Heracles." *VT* 37 (1987) 63–70. ———. "More Samson Legends." *VT* 36 (1986) 397–405. ———. "Samson's Foxes." *VT* 35 (1985) 224–29. ———. "Samson's Riddle and Samson's Magic Locks." *VT* 36 (1986) 225–34. **Margulies, H.** "Das Rätsel der Biene im Alten

Testament." *VT* 24 (1974) 56–76. **Matthews, V. H.** "Freedom and Entrapment in the Samson Narrative: A Literary Analysis." *PRSt* 16 (1989) 245–57. **Mayer, D.** "Samson ou l'anamorphose du récit." *Sémiotique et Bible* 93 (1999) 3–22. **Mayer-Opificius, R.** "Simson, der sechslockige Held?" *UF* 14 (1982) 149–51. **Mazar, A.** "The Emergence of the Philistine Material Culture." *IEJ* 35 (1985) 95–107. **McDaniel, C.** "Samson's Riddle." *Did* 12 (2001) 47–57. **Meissner, A.** "Alles oder Nichts: Die Tragik des Helden Simson (Richter 13–16)." In *Männer weinem heimlich: Geschichten aus dem Alten Testament.* Ed. D. Bauer and A. Meissner. Stuttgart: Katholisches Bibelwerk, 1993. 59–75. **Meredith, B.** "Desire and Danger: The Drama of Betrayal in Judges and Judith." In *Anti-Covenant.* Ed. M. Bal. 63–78. **Milgrom, J.** *Numbers.* JPS Torah Commentary. Philadelphia: The Jewish Publication Society, 1990. 43–50, 355–58. **Millard, M.** "Simson und das Ende des Richterbuches: Ein Beispiel einer Kanonexegese zwischen kompositions- und wirkungsgeschichtlicher Auslegung." In *The Biblical Canons.* Ed. J. M. Auwers and H. J. de Jonge. BETL 163. Leuven: Leuven UP; Peeters, 2003. 227–34. **Mobley, G.** *Samson and the Liminal Hero in the Ancient Near East.* LHBOTS 453. London: T&T Clark, 2006. ———. "The Wild Man in the Bible and the Ancient Near East." *JBL* 116 (1997) 217–33. **Müller, H. P.** "Der begriff 'Rätsel' im Alten Testament." *VT* 20 (1970) 465–89. **Nauerth, C.** "Simson's Taten: Motivgeschichtliche Überlegungen." *DBAT* 21 (1985) 94–120. **Neff, R. W.** "The Announcement in Old Testament Birth Stories." PhD diss., Yale University, 1969. **Nel, P.** "The Riddle of Samson (Judg 14,14,18)." *Bib* 66 (1985) 534–45. **Niditch, S.** *Folklore and the Hebrew Bible.* GBS. Minneapolis: Fortress, 1993. ———. "Samson as Culture Hero, Trickster, and Bandit: The Empowerment of the Weak." *CBQ* 52 (1990) 608–24. ———. *Underdogs and Tricksters: A Prelude to Biblical Folklore.* New Voices in Biblical Studies. San Francisco: Harper & Row, 1987. **Niemann, H. M.** "Zorah, Eshtaol, Beth Shemesh and Dan's Migration to the South: A Region and Its Traditions in the Late Bronze Age and Iron Ages." *JSOT* 86 (1999) 25–48. **Noy, D.** "Riddles at the Wedding Feast" (Heb.). *Mahanayim* 83 (1963) 64–71. **O'Connor, M.** "The Women of the Book of Judges." *HAR* 10 (1986) 277–93. **Olyan, S. M.** "What Do Shaving Rites Accomplish and What Do They Signal in Biblical Ritual Texts?" *JBL* 117 (1998) 611–22. **Palmer, A. S.** *The Samson Saga and Its Place in Comparative Religion.* London: Pitman, 1913; repr. New York: Arno, 1977. **Paris, C.** "Judges 14:4 and the Interlopers of the Biblical Narrative." Paper read to Southeastern Regional Meeting of Society of Biblical Literature, Nashville, 2007. **Parker, S. B.** "The Birth Announcement." In *Ascribe to the Lord.* FS P. C. Craigie, ed. L. Eslinger and G. Taylor. JSOT Sup 67. Sheffield: JSOT Press, 1988. 133–49. **Penchansky, D.** "Staying the Night: Intertextuality in Genesis and Judges." In *Reading between Texts.* Ed. D. N. Fewell. Louisville: Westminster John Knox, 1992. 77–88. **Pepicello, W. J.,** and **T. A. Green.** *The Language of Riddles.* Columbus: Ohio State UP, 1984. **Porter, J. R.** "Samson's Riddle: Judges xiv.18." *JTS* 13 (1962) 106–9. **Rad, G. von.** "Die Geschichte von Simson." In *Gottes Wirken in Israel.* Neukirchen-Vluyn: Neukirchener Verlag, 1974. 49–52. **Reinhartz, A.** "Samson's Mother: An Unnamed Protagonist." *JSOT* 55 (1992) 25–37. Reprinted in *Feminist Companion to Judges* (1993), ed. A. Brenner, 157–70. **Römheld, K. F. D.** "Von den Quellen der Kraft (Jdc 13)." *ZAW* 104 (1992) 28–52. **Roncace, M.** "Another Portrait of Josephus' Portrait of Samson." *JSJ* 35 (2004) 185–207. **Rosenblatt, N. H.** "Esther and Samson: Portraits in Heroism." *BRev* 15 (1999) 20–25, 47. **Roskoff, G.** *Die Simsonsage nach ihrer Entstehung, Form und Bedeutung und der Heraclesmythus.* Leipzig: Bredt, 1860. **Sasaki, T.** "Self-centered Vengeance or Legitimate Retaliation? The Meaning of נקם in the Prayer of Samson (Judg 16:28)" (Japanese). *Exeg* 15 (2004) 43–52. **Sasson, J. M.** "Who Cut Samson's Hair? (And Other Trifling Issues Raised by Judges 16)." *Proof* 8 (1988) 333–46. **Savron, G.** *Telling and Retelling: Quotation in Biblical Narrative.* Bloomington: Indiana UP, 1988. **Schniedewind, W.** "The Geo-Political History of Philistine Gath." *BASOR* 308 (1998) 69–78. **Segret, S.** "Paronomasia in the Samson Narrative in Judges 13–16." *VT* 34 (1984) 454–61. **Scheiber, A.** "Further Parallels to the Figure of Samson the Tree-Uprooter." *JQR* 52 (1961) 35–40. ———. "Samson Uprooting a Tree." *JQR* 50 (1959) 176–80. **Schipper, J.** "Narrative Obscurity of Samson's חידה in Judges 14.14

and 18." *JSOT* 27 (2003) 339–53. **Segert, S.** "Paranomasia in the Samson Narrative in Judges xiii–xvi." *VT* 34 (1984) 454–61. **Selms, A. van.** "The Best Man and Bride—from Sumer to St. John with a New Interpretation of Judges, Chapters 14 and 15." *JNES* 9 (1950) 65–75. **Seters, J. van.** "The Problem of Childlessness in Near Eastern Law and the Patriarchs of Israel." *JBL* 87 (1968) 401–8. **Shanks, H.** "Bible and Archaeology." *BAR* 34 (2008) 6, 84. **Siegert, F.** "L'Héraclès des Juifs." In *Discours religieux dans l'Antiquité: Actes du colloque—Besançon 27–28 janvier 1996.* Ed. M.-M. Mactoux and E. Geny. Paris: Belles Lettres, 1995. 151–76. **Simon, U.** "Samson and the Heroic." In *Ways of Reading the Bible.* Ed. M. Wadsworth. London: Sussex, 1981. 154–67. **Slotkin, E.** "Response to Professors Fontaine and Camp." In *Text and Tradition.* Ed. S. Niditch. 153–59. **Smith, C.** "Delilah: A Suitable Case for (Feminist) Treatment?" In *Judges* (1999). Ed. A. Brenner. 93–116. ———. "Samson and Delilah: A Parable of Power?" *JSOT* 76 (1997) 45–57. **Spronk, K.** "Samson as the Suffering Servant: Some Remarks on a Painting by Lovis Corinth." In *The New Things: Eschatology in Old Testament Prophecy.* FS H. Lenne, ed. F. Postma, K. Spronk, and E. Talstra. ACEBTSup 3. Maastricht: Shaker, 2002. 219–24. **Stahn, H.** *Die Simson-Saga: Eine religionsgeschichtliche Untersuchung.* Göttingen: Vandenhoeck & Ruprecht, 1908. **Stark, C.** *'Kultprostitution' im Alten Testament? Die Qedeschen der Hebräischen Bibel und das Motiv der Hurerei.* OBO 221. Göttingen: Vandenhoeck & Ruprecht, 2007. **Starke, R. A.** "Samson—The Last Judge." *Kerux* 17 (2002) 11–28. **Steinthal, H.** "The Legend of Samson." In *Mythology among the Hebrews.* Ed. I. Goldziher. Trans. R. Martineau. 1877. Reprint, New York: Cooper Square, 1967. **Stipp, H.-J.** "Samson, der Nasiräer." *VT* 45 (1995) 337–69. **Strawn, B.** *What Is Stronger Than a Lion? Leonine Image and Metaphor in the Hebrew Bible and the Ancient Near East.* OBO 212. Göttingen: Vandenhoeck & Ruprecht, 2005. **Täubler, E.** *Biblische Studien.* Tübingen: Mohr, 1958. 63–66, 85–89. **Thompson, Y.** "Samson in Timnah: Judges 14–15 Form and Function." *Dor le Dor* 15 (1987) 249–55. **Thompson-Smith, S.** *Motif-Index of Folk-Literature: A Classification of Narrative Elements in Folktales, Ballads, Myths, Fables, Mediaeval Romances, Exempla, Fabliaux, Jest-Books and Local Legends.* Rev. and enlarged ed. 6 vols. Bloomington: Indiana UP, 1989. **Toorn, K. van der.** "Female Prostitution in Payment for Vows in Ancient Israel." *JBL* 108 (1989) 193–205. ———. "Judges XVI 21 in the Light of Akkadian Sources." *VT* 36 (1986) 248–53. **Torcszyner, H. (Tor-Sinai).** "The Riddle in the Bible." *HUCA* 1 (1924) 125–49. ———. "Samson and His Riddle" (Heb.). In *Studies in the Book of Judges.* Publications of the Israel Bible Society 10. Jerusalem, 1966. 378–402. **Trau, H., N. Rubin,** and **S. Vargon.** "Symbolic Significance of Hair in the Biblical Narrative and in the Law." *Koroth* 9 (1988) 173–79. **Ulrich, S.** "Samson and the Heroic." In *Ways of Reading the Bible.* Ed. M. Wadsworth. Sussex: Harvester, 1981. 154–67. **Vanstiphout, H.** "The Importance of 'The Tale of the Fox.'" *Acta Sumerologica* 10 (1988) 191–228. **Vickery, J. B.** "In Strange Ways: The Story of Samson." In *Images of Man and God: Old Testament Short Stories in Literary Focus.* Ed. B. O. Long. Sheffield: Almond, 1981. 58–73. **Waldman, N. M.** "Concealment and Irony in the Samson Story." *Dor le Dor* 13 (1984–1985) 71–80. **Watson, W. G. E.** "Antecedents of a New Testament Proverb." *VT* 20 (1970) 368. **Webb, B. G.** "A Serious Reading of the Samson Story (Judges 13–16)." *RTR* 54 (1995) 110–20. **Weitzman, S.** "The Samson Story as Border Fiction." *BibInt* 10 (2002) 158–74. **Weldon, F.** "Samson and His Women." In *Out of the Garden: Women Writers on the Bible.* Ed. C. Buchmann et al. New York: Fawcett Columbine, 1994. 72–81. **Wenning, R.,** and **E. Zenger.** "Der siebenlockige Held Simson: Literarische und ikonographische Beobachtungen zu Ri 13–16." *BN* 17 (1982) 43–55. **Wharton, J. A.** "The Secret of Yahweh: Story and Affirmation in Judges 13–16." *Int* 27 (1973) 48–65. **Wieringen, W. C. G. van.** "'Wer . . . Ah, Dein name, Bitte?' Ein erster Versuch mit der Frau ohne Namen aus Richter 13 Bekanntschaft zu machen." In *Unless Someone Guide Me.* FS K. A. Deurloo, ed. J. W. Dyk et al. Maastricht: Shaker, 2001. 95–105. **Witte, M.** "Wie Simson in den Kanon kam: Redaktionsgeschichtliche Beobachtungen zu Jdc 13–16." *ZAW* 112 (2000) 526–49. **Yadin, A.** "Samson's *hîdâ*." *VT* 52 (2002) 407–26. **Yaron, R.** "Duobus Sororibus Coniunctio." *RIDA* 10 (1963) 115–36. **Zakovitch, Y.** *The Life of Samson* (Heb.). Jerusalem: Magnes, 1982. ———. "The Sacrifice of

Gideon (Jud 6,11–24) and the Sacrifice of Manoah (Jud 13)" (Heb., Eng. summary). *Shnaton* 1 (1975) 151–54. **Zapletal, V.** *Der biblische Samson.* Freiburg: Universitätsbuchhandlung, 1906.

Translation

¹³:¹ *Again the sons of Israel did evil in the eyes of Yahweh, and Yahweh gave them into the hand of the Philistines forty years.* ² *A certain man from Zorah from the clan* ᵃ *of the Danites was named Manoah; however, his wife was barren and bore no children.* ³ *A messenger of Yahweh appeared to the woman and told her, "Right now, you are barren and have borne no children. You will become pregnant and bear a son.* ᵃ ⁴ *Now therefore, be careful not* ᵃ *to drink wine or any intoxicating beverage. Do not eat anything ritually unclean.* ⁵ *Look out for yourself. You are pregnant* ᵃ *and will bear* ᵇ *a son. A razor* ᶜ *must never come upon his head, for the lad is to be a Nazirite* ᵈ *for God from the womb. He is the one who will begin to deliver Israel from the hand of the Philistines."*

⁶ *The woman went in and said* ᵃ *to her husband, "A man of God* ᵇ *came to me, and his appearance was like the appearance of an angel of God,* ᶜ *totally awesome.* ᵈ *I did not* ᵉ *ask him where he was from, while he did not tell me his name.* ⁷ *He said to me, 'Look out for yourself. You are pregnant and will bear* ᵃ *a son. Now, therefore, you must not drink wine or any intoxicating beverage. Do not eat anything unclean,* ᵇ *for the lad is to be a Nazirite* ᶜ *for God from the womb until* ᵈ *the day of his death.'"*

⁸ *Manoah begged Yahweh, "With your permission, my Lord,* ᵃ *let the man of God whom you sent* ᵇ *come, please, again* ᶜ *to us so he may teach* ᵈ *us what we should do for the lad who is to be born."* ᵉ ⁹ *God* ᵃ *listened to the voice of Manoah, and the messenger of God* ᵇ *came* ᶜ *again to the woman while she was sitting in the field, but Manoah, her husband, was not with her.*

¹⁰ *The woman hurried at a run and told her husband, "Look here! He has appeared to me, the man who came to me the other day."* ᵃ

¹¹ *Manoah rose and followed his wife and came* ᵃ *to the man. He said to him, "Are you the man who spoke with my wife?"*

He ᵇ *said, "I am."*

¹² *Manoah said, "Now may your words* ᵃ *come true. What will be the lad's destiny and his occupation?"*

¹³ *The messenger of Yahweh told Manoah, "Everything I told your wife, she must be careful* ᵃ *to do.* ¹⁴ *Everything that comes from the wine-producing* ᵃ *vine she must not eat. At the same time she must not drink wine,* ᵇ *and anything ritually unclean she must not eat. Everything I have commanded her, she must be careful to do."*

¹⁵ *Manoah told the messenger of Yahweh, "Let us detain you so we may prepare a kid from the goats for you."* ᵃ

¹⁶ *The messenger of Yahweh told Manoah, "If you detain me, I will not eat any of your food, but if you prepare* ᵃ *a burnt offering, offer it to Yahweh." For Manoah did not know that he was the messenger of Yahweh.* ᵇ

¹⁷ *Manoah told the messenger of Yahweh, "Who* ᵃ *is your name, because when your words* ᵇ *come true, we will be able to honor you."*

¹⁸ *The messenger of Yahweh said to him, "Why do you ask my name? It is Miraculous!"* ᵃ

¹⁹ *Manoah took a kid from the goats along with the grain offering and sacrificed it*

on a rock to Yahweh. He caused a miracle to happen,[a] and Manoah and his wife were watching. [20]When[a] the flame went up from the altar toward the heavens, the messenger of Yahweh went up in the flame of the altar.[b] Manoah and his wife were watching and fell down with their faces on the ground. [21]The messenger of Yahweh never again appeared[a] to Manoah or to his wife. Then Manoah knew that he was the messenger of Yahweh. [22]Manoah told his wife, "We will surely die because we have seen God."

[23]She said to him, "If Yahweh had desired to kill us, he would not have accepted from our hand[a] the burnt offering and the grain offering. He would not have shown us all these things, and at this time[b] he would not have informed us like this."

[24]The woman bore a son and called his name Samson. The lad grew, and Yahweh blessed him.[a] [25]The Spirit of Yahweh began to stir him[a] in Mahaneh-dan[b] between Zorah and Eshtaol.

[14:1]Samson went down to Timnah and saw a woman in[a] Timnah from the daughters of the Philistines.[b] [2]He went up and told his father and his mother,[a] "I saw a woman in[b] Timnah from the daughters of the Philistines. Now, therefore, take[c] her for me[d] as a wife." [3]His father and mother[a] said to him, "Is there not a woman among the daughters of your kinsfolk[b] or among all my people[c] that you must go and take a woman from the uncircumcised[d] Philistines?"

Samson told his father, "Take her for me because she is the right one in my eyes."

[4]His father and his mother did not know that this was from Yahweh, for he was seeking an occasion against the Philistines.[a] At that time the Philistines were ruling Israel.[b]

[5]Samson went down along with his father and his mother[a] to Timnah. They came[b] into the vineyards of Timnah.[c] Look! A young one from the lions is roaring to meet him. [6]The Spirit of Yahweh broke in[a] upon him, and he split it (the young lion) to pieces as he would split a young goat[b] with nothing at all in his hand. He did not tell his father or his[c] mother what he had done.

[7]He went down and spoke[a] to the woman, and she was right in his eyes. [8]He returned some days later to take her as his wife. He turned to see the lion's carcass. But look! A swarm of bees was in the body[a] of the lion along with some honey. [9]He scooped it into his hands[a] and continued on his way, eating as he went. He came to his father and mother and gave them some, and they ate. He did not tell them that he had scooped the honey from the body of the lion.[b]

[10]His father[a] went down to see the woman. Samson[b] prepared a banquet[c] there, for that was proper for bridegrooms to do. [11]When they saw[a] him, they took thirty companions[b] to be with him.

[12]Samson said to them, "Let me pose a riddle[a] for you. If you can report back to me during the seven days of the banquet, having found the answer,[b] I will give you thirty sets of underwear and thirty outfits. [13]But if you cannot report back to me, then you must give me thirty sets of underwear and thirty outfits."

They replied to him, "Pose your riddle, so we may hear it."

[14]He said to them, "From the eater comes out something to eat, and from the strong comes out something sweet."[a]

They were unable to report an answer to the riddle in three[b] days. [15]On the seventh[a] day, they said to Samson's wife, "Persuade your husband to tell us[b] the answer to the riddle so that we will not burn you and your father's house with fire. Was it for our possessions[c] you invited us here, or not?"[d]

[16]Samson's wife cried on him and claimed,[a] "You just hate me! You do not love me! You posed the riddle to the sons of my people, but you did not explain it to me."[b] He[c]

said to her, "Look here! I have not explained it to my father or my mother, but to you I should explain it?"[d]

[17]She cried on him the seven days[a] they had for the banquet. On the seventh day, he explained it to her because she pressured him. She told the riddle[b] to the sons of her people.

[18]The men of the town said to him on the seventh day just before the sun went down,[a] "What is sweeter than honey, and what is stronger than a lion."

He[b] said to them, "If you had not plowed[c] with my young cow, you would not have found out the riddle."

[19]The Spirit of Yahweh broke in[a] upon him, and he went down to Ashkelon. He struck dead[b] thirty men from them.[c] He took their clothes and gave outfits[d] to those who had answered the riddle. His[e] anger blazed, and he went up to his father's house. [20]Samson's wife now belonged to his companion who was his wedding companion.[a]

[15:1]Some time later during the wheat harvest, Samson took a young goat and visited his wife. He said, "I am going to my wife's room," but her father would not let him enter.[a]

[2]Her father said, "I told myself that you so totally hated her, and so I gave her to your companion. Isn't[a] her younger sister better looking? You may have her instead."

[3]Samson said to them,[a] "This time I cannot be blamed by the Philistines while I am creating havoc[b] with them."[c] [4]Samson went out and captured three hundred foxes. He took a torch, tied the foxes tail to tail, and set a torch between each pair of tails in the middle.[a] [5]He set fire with the torches and sent them (the foxes) into the Philistines' standing grain[a] crop. He burned up everything from sheaves to grain standing in the field, even the vineyards and[b] olive groves.

[6]The Philistines asked, "Who did this?"

The reply came, "Samson, the son-in-law of the man from Timnah,[a] because he took Samson's wife and gave her to his companion." The Philistines went up and burned her and her father[b] in the fire.

[7]Samson said to them, "If you are going to act like this, then I will get my revenge on you, and only then will I stop."[a] [8]He struck them on thigh and groin[a]—a horrendous attack.

He went down[b] and lived in a cave in the rock[c] of Etam. [9]The Philistines went up and camped in Judah. They spread out their forces in Lehi. [10]The men of Judah asked,[a] "Why have you come up against us?"

They[b] replied, "We have come up[c] to take Samson prisoner so we can do to him just what he did to us."

[11]Three thousand men went down from Judah to the cave in the rock of Etam. They said to Samson, "Don't you know that the Philistines rule over us? What is this you have done to us?"

He[a] said to them, "Just what they did to me,[b] so I have done to them."

[12]They said to him, "We have come down to take you prisoner so we can give you into the hand of the Philistines."

Samson said to them, "Take an oath for me that you, yes you, will not attempt to kill me."[a]

[13]They said to him, "Certainly not! For we will take you prisoner and give you into their hand. But murder! We will never murder you." They tied him up as a prisoner with two new ropes, and they led him up from the rock. [14]As soon as he[a] came near Lehi,[b] the Philistines came out to meet him shouting the victory cry.[c] The Spirit of Yahweh broke in upon him,[d] and the ropes on his arms became like linen burned in the fire.[e] His bindings

melted away from his hands.[f] [15]*He found the jawbone of a recently deceased donkey.*[a] *He reached out with his hand and took it and struck a thousand men dead with it.*

[16]*Samson said, "With the jawbone of a donkey, a heap, two heaps;*[a] *with the jawbone of a donkey I struck dead a thousand men."* [17]*As he finished speaking, he tossed the jawbone out of his hand. He named that place Ramath-Lehi.*[a]

[18]*Being parched with thirst,*[a] *he called out to Yahweh, "You yourself have given this great deliverance by the hand of your servant.*[b] *But now I am dying with thirst, and I will fall into the hand of the uncircumcised."* [19]*God*[a] *split open the hollow place*[b] *in Lehi, and water came out from it. He drank, his spirit returned,*[c] *and life was renewed. Therefore, it is named En-hakkore,*[d] *which remains in Lehi until this day.* [20]*He judged Israel in the days of the Philistines*[a] *twenty years.*

[16:1]*Samson went*[a] *to Gaza, saw a prostitute there, and visited her.* [2]*The citizens of Gaza were told,*[a] *"Samson has come here." They surrounded him and lay in ambush for him all night*[b] *at the city gate. They didn't make a sound all night, saying, "At the light*[c] *of day, we'll kill him."*[d] [3]*Samson lay in bed for half the night. He arose in the middle of the night, grasped hold of the door of the city gate as well as its two doorposts, tore them out along with the gate's bar, and set them on his shoulders. He carried them to the top of the hill in front of Hebron.*[a]

[4]*After this, he loved a woman in the Wadi Sorek. Her name was Delilah.* [5]*The Philistine rulers went up to her and said to her, "Entice him and see the source of his mighty strength and how we can defeat him. We will bind him up to humiliate him. At the same time we, each one of us, will give you eleven hundred shekels of silver."*

[6]*Delilah asked Samson, "Please tell me the source of your mighty strength and how you could be tied up to be humbled."*

[7]*Samson told her, "If you tie me with seven moist animal tendons that have never been dried, then I will become weak and be like any other man."*

[8]*The Philistine rulers brought up to her seven moist animal tendons that had never been dried, and she tied him with them.* [9]*The men in ambush were settled near her*[a] *in the room, and she called to him, "Samson, the Philistines have come upon you!" He snapped the tendons in two just as he would snap a fiber strand*[b] *singed by the fire. Still, the source of his strength was unknown.*

[10]*Delilah told Samson, "See now. You have deceived me. You told me a lie. Now, please, tell me how you can be tied up."*

[11]*He said to her, "If you tie me tight with new ropes*[a] *that have never been used in any kind of work, then I will become weak and be like any other man."*

[12]*Delilah took*[a] *new ropes and tied him with them.*[b] *She told him, "Samson, the Philistines have come upon you!" The men in ambush were still settled in the room. And he snapped them from his arms as if they were thread.* [13]*Delilah told Samson, "Up to now*[a] *you have deceived me. You have told me lies. Tell me how you may be tied up."*

He said to her, "If you weave seven strands of my hair with the web of the loom,[b] *[and push a pin through to secure them, then I will become weak and be like any other man."*

[14]*Delilah put him to sleep, began to weave the seven strands of his hair with the web of the loom,]*[a] *and pushed in the pin. She told him, "Samson, the Philistines have come upon you!" Waking from his sleep, he tore away the pin of the loom*[b] *and the web.*[c]

[15]*She*[a] *said to him,*[b] *"How can you say, 'I love you,' but your heart is not with me. This is the third time you have deceived me by not telling me the source of your mighty strength."*

[16]*When she harassed him daily*[a] *with her words*[b] *and had pestered him,*[c] *then he became sick to death.* [17]*He informed her of his whole heart and said to her, "A razor*[a] *has never*

come upon my head because from my mother's womb I have been a Nazirite dedicated to God.[b] *If I am shaved, then my strength would turn away from me; and I will become weak and be like any other*[c] *man."*

[18]*Delilah realized that he had informed her of all his heart, and she sent and summoned the*[a] *Philistine rulers, "Come up one more time*[b] *for he has informed me*[c] *of all his heart," with the result that the*[d] *Philistine rulers came up*[e] *to her. They brought the silver*[f] *in their hand.* [19]*She had put him*[a] *to sleep on her knees,*[b] *and so she summoned a man;*[c] *and she*[d] *shaved the seven strands of his head and began to humiliate him.*[e] *His strength turned away from him.*

[20]*She*[a] *called,*[b] *"Samson, the Philistines have come upon you!"*

He awoke from his sleep and thought, "I will go out as other times[c] *and shake loose."*[d] *But he did not know that Yahweh had turned away from him.* [21] *The Philistines seized him and gouged out his eyes. They brought him down to Gaza, tied him up with bronze*[a] *chains, and he was grinding in the house of the prisoners.*[b]

[22] *The hair on his head began to grow after it had been shaved.* [23] *The Philistine rulers gathered to sacrifice massive sacrifices to Dagon, their god, and to celebrate. They said, "Our god gave Samson, our enemy, into our hands."*

[24] [a]*The people saw him and praised their god because, they said,*[b] *"Our god has given our enemy*[c] *into our hands, the one who ruined our land and who multiplied our deaths."* [25]*When their heart felt good,*[a] *they said, "Summon Samson*[b] *so he can amuse us."*[c] *They summoned Samson from the prison house, and he entertained them.*[d]

They made him stand between the pillars.[e] [26]*Samson said to the young boy who held his hand, "Place me where I can feel*[a] *the pillars on which this building is built so I can lean on them."*[b] [27] *The house was at that time filled with men and women. All the Philistine rulers were there. On the roof about three thousand*[a] *men and women*[b] *were watching Samson's act.*

[28]*Samson called to Yahweh, "O Lord Yahweh, remember me and give me strength, just this*[a] *one time, please, O God.*[b] *Let me get revenge from the Philistines for one of my two eyes."*[c] [29]*Samson felt to get hold of the two pillars in the middle on which the building was built. He leaned*[a] *on them with his right hand on one and his left on the other.* [30]*Samson said, "Let me die with the Philistines!" He stretched out his arms with strength, and the house fell on the rulers and on all the people in it. The deaths he*[a] *caused in his own death outnumbered those he caused while alive.*

[31]*His brothers and all his father's house went down, picked him up, and took him away. They buried him between Zorah and Eshtaol in the tomb of Manoah, his father. He had judged Israel twenty years.*

Notes

13:2.a. LXX[A] reads ἐγένετο ἀνὴρ ἐκ Σαραα ἐκ τῆς φυλῆς, "a man came out of Zorah out of the tribe of," omitting "one" as unnecessary and changing "clan" to the more usual "tribe" of Dan. LXX[B] reads ἦν ἀνὴρ εἷς ἀπὸ Σαραα ἀπὸ δήμου συγγενείας, "one man was from Zorah from the people of the family of," adding "people of," perhaps giving a double translation of the ambiguous מִמִּשְׁפַּחַת.

3.a. LXX[A] reads καὶ ἐν γαστρὶ ἕξεις καὶ τέξῃ υἱόν, "and in the womb you will have and you will bear a son," paraphrasing וְהָרִית, "you will become pregnant," while LXX[B] reads καὶ συλλήμψῃ υἱόν, "and you will conceive a son," not witnessing to וְיָלַדְתְּ, "you will bear."

4.a. Many Heb. MSS, Syr., Vg. do not have the initial *wāw*. MT is the harder reading and to be preferred.

5.a. The NET translates "Look, you will conceive and have a son," but then in its note explains the translation problem here and in v 7:

Another option is to translate, "you are already pregnant and will have a son." The earlier reference to her being infertile (v. 3) suggests that her conception is still future, but it is possible that the earlier statement only reflects her perspective (as far as she is concerned, she is infertile). According to this interpretation, in v. 5 the angel reveals the truth to her—actually she has recently conceived and is now pregnant (see the translation in R. G. Boling, *Judges* [AB], 217). Usage favors this interpretation. The predicate adjective הָרָה (*harah*, "[be/become] pregnant") elsewhere has a past (1 Sam 4:19) or present (Gen 16:11; 38:25; 2 Sam 11:5) translation value. (The usage in Isa 7:14 is debated, but a present translation is definitely possible there.) A final, but less likely, possibility is that she miraculously conceived during the angel's speech, sometime between his statements recorded in vv. 3 and 5. See *Comment* on 13:5.

5.b. MT offers a mixed form וְיָלַדְתְּ, "you will bear," here and in v 7 with elements of the *qal* participle and the *qal* perfect along with Gen 16:11. The perfect fits the context here and parallels v 3, making the participle, evidenced by several Heb. MSS, the more difficult reading.

5.c. LXX reads σίδηρος, "iron implement," for מוֹרָה, "shearing knife, razor."

5.d. LXX^A reads ἡγιασμένον ναζιραῖον ἔσται τῷ θεῷ, "he will be sanctified as a Nazirite to God."

6.a. A number of MSS read וַיַּגֵּד, "to tell," a form used frequently in the Samson narrative, but that makes it the simpler reading here and thus not preferred.

6.b. Without MS evidence *BHS* says "God" is probably to be deleted on the basis of its absence in v 10. This misses the narrator's irony in what the wife tells and does not tell her husband.

6.c. Without MS evidence *BHS* thinks the probable reading would be "God" rather than "messenger of God," the latter being added from v 9. Again this rests on literary theory and subjectivity, not evidence.

6.d. LXX^A reads ἐπιφανής σφόδρα, "quite openly manifest," for נוֹרָא מְאֹד, "totally awesome," apparently reading a derivative of ראה, "to see," instead of ירא, "to fear."

6.e. LXX^A (compare OL) does not have the negative.

7.a. See *Note* 13:5.a.

7.b. Cairo Genizah Heb. MS reads טָמֵא rather than MT טְמֵאָה, both terms referring to ceremonial uncleanness.

7.c. LXX^B reads ὅτι ἅγιον θεοῦ ἔσται τὸ παιδάριον, "because holy to God will be the boy"; compare *Notes* 11:5.d; 16:17.b. Chepey (*Bib* 83 [2002] 97) suggests that the term "holy" comes from Num 6:5, 8.

7.d. Several Heb. MSS add a *waw* before עַד, apparently a minor grammatical "correction."

8.a. LXX^B reads κύριε Αδωναιε, "Lord Adonai," both translating and transliterating אֲדוֹנָי or יְהוָה אֲדֹנָי, the divine personal name. Crenshaw (*Samson*, 35) notes the "strong textual evidence for the personal name" (יהוה). Compare Vg, OL, Syr.

8.b. LXX^A reads "sent to us," a clarifying editorial addition.

8.c. LXX^A does not have "again."

8.d. *BHS* sees the original LXX reading καὶ φωτισάτω ἡμᾶς, which would retrovert to וִירֵנוּ. To emend the text requires strong faith that the translators were absolutely consistent in their translation of each Heb. term into a Gk. one.

8.e. Many MSS read הַיֶּלֶד, "the child," for MT הַיֻּלָּד, "the one to be born." This represents a simplification of the text.

9.a. Some Gk. MSS, OL, Vg., Syr. read κύριος, "Lord," for הָאֱלֹהִים, "God," a common textual change.

9.b. A Gk. MS and Syr. read κυρίου, "of the Lord."

9.c. One Heb. MS reads וַיֵּרָא, "and he appeared," either an errant reading by the copyist or an attempt to avoid the possible sexual connotations of בוא . . . אֶל.

10.a. LXX^A, representing the original LXX according to *BHS*, reads ἡμέρα ἐκείνη, "that day," the insertion of a common idiom.

11.a. LXX^A does not have "and came."

11.b. LXX reads "the angel (or messenger) said."

12.a. *BHS* reads the sg., "word," with many Heb. MSS, some LXX MSS, Syr., Vg. This represents strong MS evidence and probably the more difficult reading.

13.a. Jerusalem Bible in French read the verbs here and in v 14 as masc. rather than as MT's fem., but the third edition changed this in accord with MT. No evidence gives reason to emend the text. *Preliminary and Interim Report* (2:105) dismisses the emendation as too conjectural. See Stipp (*VT* 45 [1995] 350).

14.a. LXX^A does not have הַיָּיִן, "wine producing."

14.b. LXX^B reads σικερα μέθυσμα, "strong drink, intoxicating drink," translating the Heb. שֵׁכָר with two alternative readings.

15.a. *BHS* transposes to this place the second half of v 16: "For Manoah did not know that he was the messenger of Yahweh."

16.a. Several Heb. MSS and Syr. read תַּעֲלֶה for MT תַּעֲשֶׂה, an attempt to make the two verbs in the clause the same, missing the differentiation between "making" or "preparing" and "offering up."

16.b. See *Note* 13:15.a.

17.a. Several Heb. MSS read מה, "what," for MT מִי, "who," a natural change from a somewhat unusual reading.

17.b. Many eastern Heb. MSS, Gk., Syr., and Q read sg. while K reads pl. Compare *Note* 13:12.a.

18.a. Q has (א)פֶּלִי; a few MSS read פֶּלִיא; *BHS* says to read פֶּלְאִי with K.

19.a. LXX shows early difficulty in understanding this phrase. LXX^A reads τῷ κυρίῳ τῷ θαυμαστὰ ποιοῦντι κυρίῳ, "to the Lord, to the one doing wonders to the Lord," while LXX^B reads τῷ κυρίῳ καὶ διεχώρισεν ποιῆσαι, "to the Lord and he separated to act" (or possibly "he did a separate thing"). *BHS* suggests that the subject has probably dropped out due to haplography and suggests reading וְהוּא, "and that," as subject.

20.a. Many Heb. MSS read כ, "as," for MT ב, "when."

20.b. LXX^A does not have "of the altar."

21.a. *BHS* points out that the expected Heb. form would be לְהֵרָאֹת.

23.a. Many Heb. MSS, LXX^A read "our hands" for MT "our hand," which also appears in LXX^B.

23.b. LXX^A, OL, Vg. do not have "at this time," so *BHS* says to perhaps delete כעת, "as the time."

24.a. LXX^A (compare OL) reads καὶ ηὐλόγησεν αὐτὸν κύριος καὶ ηὐξήθη τὸ παιδάριον, "and the Lord blessed him and caused the lad to grow," reversing the clauses and apparently making it clearer that God was the growth agent.

25.a. LXX reads συμπορεύεσθαι or συνεκπορεύεσθαι, "to accompany him."

25.b. LXX reads "encampment of Dan," translating the Heb. proper noun.

14:1.a. LXX^B reads εἰς, "into," for "in."

1.b. LXX^A (compare OL) reads ἀλλοφύλων καὶ ἤρεσεν ἐνώπιον αὐτοῦ, "Philistines, and she pleased him."

2.a. Without evidence except literary theory, *BHS* calls for the deletion of "and his mother."

2.b. See *Note* 14:1.a.

2.c. One Heb. MS reads קא, leading to the proposal to read the sg. imperative קַח for MT pl. קְחוּ, based on the same literary theory as in *Note* 14:2.a.

2.d. The Leningrad MS of MT appears to stand alone in the Heb. tradition in inserting a *dāgēš* in the *lāmed* of לִּי, "to me."

3.a. See *Notes* 14:2.a and 14:2.c.

3.b. Syr. reads "in the house of your father," retroverted to Heb. as בְּבֵית אָבִיךְ, the tradition substituting a more familiar phrase for the less familiar of the MT.

3.c. LXX^L and Syr. read the second sg. suffix, leading *BHS* to give a probable Heb. reading of עַמְּךָ, "your people." OL reads "our people." Both these readings miss the father's self-centered and tradition-based reply emphasizing "my" family, from which the son's bride was expected to come.

3.d. OL does not have "uncircumcised."

4.a. LXX^A reads ὅτι ἀνταπόδομα αὐτοῦ ἐκζητεῖ ἐκ τῶν ἀλλοφύλων, "that he was seeking repayment from the Philistines"; LXX^B reads ὅτι ἐκδίκησιν αὐτὸς ζητεῖ ἐκ τῶν ἀλλοφύλων, "that he was seeking vengeance from the Philistines." Both give concrete meaning to the more neutral Heb.

4.b. LXX^A reads "the sons of Israel," adding a common phrase.

5.a. *BHS* suggests deleting reference to both parents, again based on literary theory, not textual evidence. See *Note* 14:2.a. *Preliminary and Interim Report* (2:105–6) sees this as too conjectural, but NEB and JB accept it.

5.b. LXX^A reads ἐξέκλινεν, "he turned away." LXX^B (compare OL) has ἦλθεν, "he went," leading *BHS* to say to read the sg., וַיָּבֹא. This again is built more on literary theory than on textual evidence. Compare Barthélemy (*Critique textuelle*, 1:106–7). *Preliminary and Interim Report* (2:106) sees MT as the more difficult reading with the emendation having too narrow a textual base to be accepted as NRSV, JPS, REB, NET, and NJB do. See NET note.

5.c. See *Note* 14:1.a.

6.a. LXX^A reads κατηυθύνεν, "came straight to him," while LXX^B reads ἥλατο, "jumped on him," consistently in the Samson narrative.

6.b. LXX^B does not have the second term for "goat" present in Heb. and in LXX^A.

6.c. LXX^A does not have "his."

7.a. LXX (compare OL) reads "they went down and spoke."

8.a. LXX reads στόματι, "mouth of," a Gk. copyist's hearing error for σώματι, "body of." OL reads "a honeycomb of bees was in the mouth of the lion," without adding "and honey." LXX^B reads ἰδοὺ συναγωγὴ μελισσῶν ἐν τῷ στόματι τοῦ λέοντος, "a gathering of bees was in the mouth of the lion."

9.a. LXX^A reads εἰς τὸ στόμα αὐτοῦ, "into his mouth," a translation from the sense of the content rather than word for word.

9.b. LXX^A reads ὅτι ἐκ τῆς ἕξεως τοῦ λέοντος ἐξεῖλεν τὸ μέλι, "that out of the habit (or use) of the lion he removed the honey." LXX^B reads ὅτι ἀπὸ τοῦ στόματος τοῦ λέοντος ἐξεῖλεν τὸ μέλι, "that from the mouth of the lion he removed the honey."

10.a. *BHS* suggests, without textual evidence, reading "Samson" here, as noted by Bartusch (*Understanding Dan*, 145), who points also to an inclusio with 14:10a and 19. *Preliminary and Interim Report* (2:106) sees this as too conjectural.

10.b. *BHS* suggests, without textual evidence, deleting "Samson."

10.c. LXX reads πότον ἡμέρας ἑπτά, "a seven-day drinking party," adopted by original JB but later corrected. *Preliminary and Interim Report* (2:106) sees this as an assimilation to a parallel passage.

11.a. LXX^A (compare OL) reads φοβεῖσθαι, "fearing," a simple misreading of Heb. בְּיִרְאָם for MT כְּרֹאותָם. Crenshaw calls this "a fortunate error in translation" (*Samson*, 85). *BHS* bases a new emendation on this: בְּיִרְאָם, "in their fearing." Bartusch sees LXX^A "as an interpretation of the original Hebrew רֹאה in an effort to explain the young men's action (the appointment of 30 companions)" (*Understanding Dan*, 145). See the discussion of Schneider (207). *Preliminary and Interim Report* (2:107) retains MT as the more difficult, the emendation not having a sufficient textual basis.

11.b. LXX^B reads κλητούς, "called ones" or "chosen ones" or "invited ones." OL completes the thought with "they brought to him thirty companions."

12.a. Yadin seeks to redefine the Heb. word for "riddle" as "'saying, proverb' with an accompanying sense of 'a singing that requires explication or interpretation'" (*VT* 52 [2002] 414).

12.b. Lit. "and you will have found," which LXX^A and OL do not have. Bartusch (*Understanding Dan*, 145) translates "and you guess," noting that, despite *BHS* deletion, the term does not appear in vv 13 and 14 in the similar construction, where one would expect the same editor to add it if this were an editorial addition. Again Bartusch sees an inclusio here with v 18.

14.a. OL retains only part of the riddle: "from the eater came forth sweetness."

14.b. One Heb. MS reads שִׁבְעַת, "seven," not enough evidence to change the text.

15.a. One Heb. MS does not have the opening temporal clause, while LXX and Syr. read "fourth," which *BHS* and Ackerman (*Warrior, Dancer*, 248, n. 56) accept as original, as do NRSV, NLT, NAB, NASB95, NJB, NET, NIV, HCSB, REB. Bartusch sees similar morphology between הַשְּׁבִיעִי and הָרְבִיעִ, "seventh" and "fourth," respectfully, as having caused Heb. corruption. Bartusch thus concludes: "the chronological markers throughout this text are not necessarily perfect. It is better to recognize the LXX as either a misreading of the Hebrew *Vorlage* [source text], or as a later attempt to smooth out the chronology" (*Understanding Dan*, 145). Schneider sees the text as

> confused concerning the timing of the next few events. It originally states that the marriage feast was to last seven days and that they had until the seventh day to solve the riddle. The previous verse stated that on the third day they still had not solved the riddle, which leads the reader to believe that the following event would happen either on the evening of the third day or on the fourth day. Instead the text states that the next event occurred on the seventh day, which would be the last possible day, which cannot be. (208)

Barthélemy (*Critique textuelle*, 1:107) retains the MT but with considerable doubt. *Preliminary and Interim Report* (2:106) retains MT, seeing the emendation as based on parallel texts. See NET note.

15.b. Lit. "so that he will report to us"; LXX (compare OL) reads ἀπαγγειλάτω σοι, "so that he will report to you," followed by REB, CEV. Barthélemy (*Critique textuelle*, 1:108) retains MT. *Preliminary and Interim Report* (2:107–8) sees the emendation as simplifying the text.

15.c. Lit. "was to dispossess (or disinherit) us you called to us? Was it not?" One Heb. MS reads הַלְיוֹרְשֵׁנוּ, apparently a *pi'el* reading for MT *qal*. LXX^A reads ἢ πτωχεῦσαι ἐκαλέσατε ἡμᾶς, "or did you call us to be poor?" LXX^B reads ἢ ἐκβιάσαι ἡμᾶς κεκλήκατε, "did you call to expel us?" *BHS* suggests a probable reading of הַלְהוֹרִישֵׁנוּ, the *hip'il* form.

15.d. Bartusch (*Understanding Dan*, 146) sees the MT הֲלֹא, "or not?" as an unusual construction and agrees with *BHS* and GKC, §150g, n. 1, that it should be emended, with a few Heb. MSS and Tg., to הֲלֹם, "to here," as appears in NRSV, JPS, CEV, NAB, NJB, NIV, REB, HCSB, NET. NET note sees the Heb. form here as "inexplicable." But with our small corpus of Heb. texts, an "unusual construction" may be unusual only because we do not have more text. Barthélemy (*Critique textuelle*, 1:109) points to two passages (Num 13:18; Jer 7:19) where the ה interrogative is repeated in the second part of a double question, as cited by E. König (*Historisch-comparative Syntax der hebräischen Sprache: Schlusstheil des historisch-kritischen Lehrgebäudes des Hebräischen* [Leipzig: Hinrich, 1897] §353). Thus Barthélemy retains MT. *Preliminary and Interim Report* (2:108) retains MT, saying that the interrogative *hê* means the same as אם לא after a clause introduced by the interrogative *hê* forming a double question.

16.a. LXX^A reads "to him."

16.b. The OL reading includes: "You hated me. You proposed a riddle to my countrymen. Why did you not tell it to me?"

16.c. LXX reads "Samson."

16.d. Or "but I will explain to you." LXX^B apparently clarifies the interrogative structure with the conditional clause: εἰ τῷ πατρί μου καὶ τῇ μητρί μου οὐκ ἀπήγγελκα σοὶ ἀπαγγείλω, "If to my father and to my mother I have not explained, to you I should explain?"

17.a. In solving the temporal problems, Block (434, n. 338) insists that "contextually Hb. שבעת הימים (lit. 'the seven days') must mean the remainder of the seven days of the feast." This, along with the emendation Block accepts for v 15, helps solve the chronological problem but strains the meaning of the text a bit too far. Possibly, she began nagging him the first day that he gave the riddle and accelerated the nagging on the seventh day when the men gave her motivation to do so.

17.b. LXX does not have "the riddle."

18.a. *BHS* proposes יבא החדרה, "he entered the room," based on Judg 15:1 and accepted by NJB, REB. LXX^B reads πρὸ τοῦ ἀνατεῖλαι τὸν ἥλιον, "before the rising of the sun," apparently providing time for the events of the next verse to occur on the same day or making sure the events occurred on the seventh day, the Sabbath. Bartusch (*Understanding Dan*, 146) prefers MT since it builds suspense toward the end of the story. Barthélemy (*Critique textuelle*, 1:109–10) shows the Syr. evidence is not sufficient to change the MT. *Preliminary and Interim Report* (2:108) retains MT, seeing the emendation as too conjectural.

18.b. LXX reads "Samson."

18.c. LXX^A reads κατεδαμάσατέ, "subdued."

19.a. LXX^A reads κατεύθυνεν, "came straight to him," while LXX^B reads ἥλατο, "jumped on him." See *Note* 14:6.a above.

19.b. LXX^A reads ἔπαισεν, "he played with" or "he mocked," a Gk. error for ἐπάταξεν of LXX^B.

19.c. LXX^A reads ἐκεῖθεν, "from there," a result of the previous change.

19.d. LXX^A does not have "their outfits."

19.e. LXX reads "Samson's."

20.a. The two LXX traditions interpret the enigmatic Heb. in slightly different ways: LXX^A reads καὶ συνῴκησεν ἡ γυνὴ Σαμψων τῷ νυμφαγωγῷ αὐτοῦ ὃς ἦν ἑταῖρος ἀτοῦ, "and Samson's wife lived together with his best man who was his companion," while LXX^B reads καὶ ἐγένετο ἡ γυνὴ Σαμψων ἑνὶ τῶν φίλων αὐτοῦ ὧν ἐφιλίασεν, "and Samson's wife became to one of his friends with whom he was friendly."

15:1.a. LXX^A reads "enter to her."

2.a. LXX^A reads οὐκ ἰδού, "is not, see here," perhaps an indication of an original Heb. הנה.

3.a. LXX^A reads "to him."

3.b. Lit. "when I am doing evil with them."

3.c. LXX, which *BHS* takes to represent the original LXX, and Vg. read "with you" (pl.).

4.a. LXX^B reads ἀνὰ μέσον τῶν δύο κέρκων καὶ ἔδησεν, "between the two tails and he tied."

5.a. *BHS* proposes reading the single construct form קמת for the MT pl. but has no supporting evidence for such a reading.

5.b. *BHS* inserts ועד on the basis of Tg., with comparative evidence from LXX and Vg.

6.a. LXX^B reads Σαμψων ὁ νυμφίος τοῦ Θαμνι, "Samson, the bridegroom of the Timnite."

6.b. LXX^A reads καὶ ἐνεπύρισαν τὴν οἰκίαν τοῦ πατρὸς αὐτῆς καὶ αὐτὴν καὶ τὸν πατέρα αὐτῆς, "and they burned the house of her father and her and her father." OL has "and her father's household." *BHS* uses this evidence, with many Heb. MSS and Syr., along with the threat in Judg 14:15 to insert בית, "house." Barthélemy (*Critique textuelle*, 1:110) defends MT because the suggested emendation is the easier reading. *Preliminary and Interim Report* (2:109) sees the emendation as assimilation to other passages. Exum summarizes the argument for MT succinctly: "LXX^A has a redundant reading which corresponds more exactly to 14:15, but may for that reason be an attempt to harmonize" (*JSOT* 19 [1981] 29).

7.a. LXX^A reads οὐκ εὐδοκήσω ἀλλὰ τὴν ἐκδίκησίν μου ἐξ ἑνὸς καὶ ἑκάστου ὑμῶν ποιησομαι, "I will not enjoy it, but I will take my vengeance out on each and every one of you," apparently a complex series of partial dittography and false copying in the Gk. tradition. OL reads, "if you do it this way, I will not forgive you; but I will take vengeance from each of you, and then I will stop."

8.a. LXX^A does not have "and groin."

8.b. Many Heb. MSS and Syr. read וַיֵּלֶךְ, "and he went," but this reading misses the literary use of ירד throughout the Samson narrative.

8.c. LXX^A reads καὶ κατῴκει παρὰ τῷ χειμάρρῳ ἐν τῷ σπηλαίῳ, "and settled by the river in the cave," while LXX^B reads ἐκάθισεν ἐν τρυμαλιᾷ τῆς πέτρας, "he sat down in a hole of the rock."

10.a. LXX^A reads εἶπαν αὐτοῖς πᾶς ἀνὴρ Ιουδα, "they said to them every man of Judah."

10.b. LXX reads "the Philistines."

10.c. LXX^A does not have "we came up."

11.a. LXX reads "Samson."

11.b. LXX reads "to us."

12.a. LXX^A reads ὀμόσατέ μοι μὴ ἀποκτεῖναί με ὑμεῖς καὶ παράδοτέ με αὐτοῖς μήποτε ἀπαντήσητε ὑμεῖς ἐν ἐμοί, "swear to me that you will not kill me nor give me over to them lest perhaps you might, yes you, come out to meet me with murderous intent."

14.a. LXX^B reads "they came," making the subject consistent with v 13.

14.b. LXX (compare OL) reads σιαγόνος, "jawbone," translating the proper name.

14.c. LXX^A reads καὶ οἱ ἀλλόφυλοι ἠλάλαξαν εἰς ἀπάντησιν αὐτοῦ καὶ ἔδραμον εἰς συνάντησιν αὐτοῦ, "and the Philistines shouted out into his meeting, and they ran to meet him," while LXX^B reads καὶ οἱ ἀλλόφυλοι ἠλάλαξαν καὶ ἔδραμον εἰς συνάντησιν αὐτοῦ, "and the Philistines shouted out and ran to meet him." This represents a double reading of Heb. הֵרִיעוּ, first as from רוע, "to raise the war cry or victory cry," and then from רוץ, "to run."

14.d. A Cairo Genizah fragment does not contain "the Spirit of Yahweh broke in upon him."

14.e. LXX^A reads ὡσεὶ στιππύον ἡνίκα ἂν ὀσφρανθῇ πυρός, "as flax whenever it smells the fire," introducing a figure of speech.

14.f. LXX^A reads "arms," consistent with the statement earlier in the verse.

15.a. LXX^A reads ὄνου ἐρριμμένην ἐν τῇ ὁδῷ, "a donkey cast off in the way," while LXX^B reads ὄνου ἐκρεριμμένην, "a donkey cast off."

16.a. That is, piles of bodies; lit. "with the jawbone of a donkey, a heap of two heaps"; "a heap of yoked donkeys"; "a donkey pile"; or, with slight change in the text, "I skinned them alive." Heb. "heaps" is spelled the same as Heb. "donkey." LXX^B (compare OL; see Niditch, 153) reads ἐν σιαγόνι ὄνου ἐξαλείφων ἐξήλειψα αὐτούς, "with a donkey's jawbone I completely wiped them out," utilizing the Hebraic syntactical construction of a participle followed by a conjugated verb of the same root. *BHS* sees this as the probable reading and retroverts it to חָמוֹר חֲמַרְתִּים, which Barthélemy (*Critique textuelle*, 1:110–11) accepts with considerable doubt, seeing MT as being made to correspond to Judg 5:30. Compare Vg. *Preliminary and Interim Report* (2:109) points to misunderstanding of linguistic data by the copyists and needed adjustments to the text to make translation possible. All this leads the *Report* scholars to accept the change in the text, with a resulting translation of "I have drubbed them well." NJB also appears to accept the emendation. NIV reads, "I have made donkeys of them." Compare REB, and see NET note. The "improvements" do not make the narrative any clearer than the MT, so it is retained.

17.a. That is, "the Hill of the Jawbone." LXX reads ἀναίρεσις σιαγόνος, "the raising up to bury from the Jawbone." OL reads, "The killing of the jawbone."

18.a. OL expands the text to read "even up to death."

18.b. LXX^B reads εὐδόκησας, "you were pleased," an inner-Greek miscopying of ἔδωκας (see LXX^A).

19.a. Vg. reads the personal name יהוה instead of אֱלֹהִים, the more generic word for deity.

19.b. LXX^A reads τὸ τραῦμα τῆς σιαγόνος, "the wound of the jawbone," while LXX^B reads τὸν λάκκον τὸν ἐν τῇ σιαγόνι, "the pit which is in the jawbone."

19.c. LXX^A reads ἐπέστρεψεν τὸ πνεῦμα αὐτοῦ ἐν αὐτῷ, "his spirit returned in him," making explicit the location implicit in MT and LXX^B.

19.d. As Niditch reports, LXX^B and OL "do not include Samson's foundational role as the one who names the place. Instead they read the passive. LXX^B reads, 'Because of this, its name is called, "The Well of One Who Calls Out"'; and OL reads, 'Because of this, its name is called, "The Invocation of the Jawbone"'" (153).

20.a. OL does not witness "in the days of the Philistines."

16:1.a. LXX^A reads ἐκεῖθεν εἰς Γάζαν, "from there to Gaza," dittography either of opening letters of שָׁמְשׁוֹן or of Gk. ἐκεῖ. *BHS* suggests that perhaps מִשָּׁם, "from there," should be inserted.

2.a. LXX reads (compare OL) καὶ ἀπηγγέλη τοῖς Γαζαίοις, "and it was reported to the Gazites." MT has no equivalent for the first two words, which may be retroverted as וַיֻּגַּד, "it was reported," or וַיֻּדַע, "it was told," with the former being central to the Samson narrative vocabulary. Barthélemy (*Critique textuelle*, 1:111) retains MT with considerable doubt, pointing to Jer 3:1 as instance of the infinitive לֵאמֹר, "saying" (often expressing simple quotation marks), being used without a finite verb. *Preliminary and Interim Report* (2:110) sees MT as elliptical and thus to be read, seeing the textual evidence as making translation changes to fit the syntax of the receiver language and as a simplification. Exum (*JSOT* 19 [1981] 4, 26; compare Niditch, 164) accepts LXX reading retroverted to וַיֻּגַּד.

2.b. *BHS* reads "all day" without textual evidence and with reference to v 2b.

2.c. LXX^A reads ἕως φωτὸς πρωὶ μείνωμεν, "let us wait until the light of morning."

2.d. Many Heb. MSS read וַהֲרַגְנֹהוּ, the normal pointing of the perfect first-person pl. with first-person sg. suffix.

3.a. LXX reads Χεβρων καὶ ἔθηκεν αὐτὰ ἐκεῖ, "Hebron, and he put them there," an editorial addition to state the implied action. *Preliminary and Interim Report* (2:110) sees "a gloss within the Septuagint tradition." The change is accepted by CEV. OL reads "he took the doors of the gate of the city and the two posts with the bar, and he put them on his shoulders."

9.a. LXX^A reads τὸ ἔνεδρον αὐτοῦ ἐκάθητο ἐν, "his ambush was sitting in," while LXX^B reads τὸ ἔνεδρον αὐτῇ ἐκάθητο ἐν, "the ambush for her was sitting in."

9.b. LXX^A reads ὃν τρόπον διασπᾶται κλῶσμα τοῦ ἀποτινάγματος, "in the manner he would tear apart a thread of sweepings (or tow)," while LXX^B reads ὡς εἴ τις ἀποσπάσοι στρέμμα στιππύου, "as if someone tore off thread of flax," a good example of variant Gk. renderings of the same Heb. text. OL reads "as a rope is split when it gets wind of fire."

11.a. LXX^A reads "seven new ropes."

12.a. LXX^A reads "took for him." OL includes "in that night."

12.b. LXX^B reverses the sentences and reads καὶ τὰ ἔνεδρα ἐξῆλθεν ἐκ τοῦ ταμιείου καὶ εἶπεν, "and the ambush came out of the store room and she said."

13.a. LXX^B reads ἰδού, "Look!" substituting the more frequent הִנֵּה for MT עַד־הֵנָּה, "up to here." Several Heb. MSS add the particle of entreaty נָא, as in vv 6 and 10. Bartusch thinks the particle "may have been intentionally omitted in v. 13 as a way to demonstrate Delilah's rising frustration at Samson's deception" (*Understanding Dan*, 153), the particle softening the imperative and so not needed here.

13.b–14.a. Words in brackets reconstructed from the LXX καὶ ἐγκρούσῃς ἐν τῷ πασσάλῳ εἰς τὸν τοῖχον καὶ ἔσομαι ἀσθενὴς ὡς εἷς τῶν ἀνθρώπων, "if you should knock with a pin (or peg) into the wall, I will be weak as one of the men." OL reads "if you take apart the seven locks of my head and you lay the warp of a web and you lay bare my hairs in it as if the web is covered over, I will become weak." Bartusch (*Understanding Dan*, 153) sees the verses as textually difficult and follows *BHS* in retroverting the Gk. into Heb. as וְתִקְעִם בַּיָּתֵד אֶל־הַקִּיר וְחָלִיתִי וְהָיִיתִי כְּאַחַד הָאָדָם. See the oral tradition–based explanation of Niditch (165).

LXX^A reads καὶ ἐκοίμισεν αὐτὸν Δαλιλα καὶ ἐδιάσατο τοὺς ἑπτὰ βοστρύχους τῆς κεφαλῆς αὐτοῦ μετὰ τῆς ἐκτάσεως καὶ κατέκρουσεν ἐν τοῖς πασσάλοις εἰς τὸν τοῖχον, "and Delilah put him to sleep and began to weave the locks of hair of his head with the extension and nailed the pen into the wall." The reference to nailing into the wall seems to be a Gk. interpretation from normal usage of the Gk. verbs. These clauses are apparently missing from the MT through homoioteleuton with הַמַּסֶּכֶת. LXX^B reads v 14a as καὶ ἐγένετο ἐν τῷ κοιμᾶσθαι αὐτὸν καὶ ἔλαβεν Δαλιδα τὰς ἑπτὰ σειρὰς τῆς κεφαλῆς αὐτοῦ καὶ ὕφανεν ἐν τῷ διάσματι καὶ ἔπηξεν τῷ πασσάλῳ εἰς τὸν τοῖχον, "and in his sleeping Delilah took the seven chains of his head and wove in the warp and fastened the pin into the wall." OL translates, "and Delilah made him sleep and she took apart the seven hairs of his head with fear, and she went out in the length of the room, and she fixed it in pins and she said to him, 'Foreigners are upon you, Samson.' And he rose up from his sleep, and he plucked out the pins with the loom and the 'division' [of his hair?] and his strength was not known."

The Heb. retroversion would be with *BHS* וַתִּישֵׁנֵהוּ וַתֶּאֱרֹג אֶת־שֶׁבַע מַחְלְפוֹת רֹאשׁוֹ עִם־הַמַּסֶּכֶת. Barthélemy (*Critique textuelle*, 1:112) takes the Greek addition to MT as most probable. *Preliminary and Interim Report* (2:111–13) accepts the Gk. additions. The Gk. addition of "into the wall" is retroverted as אֶל־הַקִּיר. Bartusch (*Understanding Dan*, 153–54) sees this as a part of the accidental omission in the Heb. text. At this point the evidence for this latter addition is not clear.

14.b. *BHS* sees the text as corrupt and proposes reading הַיָּתֵד, "the peg or pin," and omitting הָאֶרֶג, "of the loom." GKC, §127g, sees a conflation of two readings, the single noun being one reading and the combination forming the second reading. Barthélemy (*Critique textuelle*, 1:112) accepts MT despite its having the definite article on the construct noun. *Preliminary and Interim Report* apparently adds a sign of the direct object to read "and he awoke from his sleep and pulled away the pin, the loom, and the warp/the web" (2:113–14).

14.c. LXX^A reads καὶ ἐξέσπασεν τοὺς πασσάλους σὺν τῷ ὑφάσματι ἐκ τοῦ τοίχου καὶ τὸ δίασμα καὶ οὐκ ἐγνώσθη ἡ ἰσχὺς αὐτοῦ, "and he pulled the pen with the woven cloth out of the wall and the web, and the source of his strength was not known." LXX^B reads καὶ ἐξῆρεν τὸν πάσσαλον τοῦ ὑφάσματος ἐκ τοῦ τοίχου, "and he removed the pen of the woven cloth out of the wall." The LXX^A addition is probably made "in an effort to harmonize this verse with a previous one; compare the last part of v. 9" (Bartusch, *Understanding Dan*, 154).

15.a. LXX reads "Delilah" since the Gk. verb does not differentiate male and female.

15.b. LXX^B reads "Samson."

16.a. Lit. "all the days"; LXX^A reads ὅλην τὴν νύκτα, "the whole night." OL expands to "tricked him with words the whole night."

16.b. Or "with her concerns."

16.c. OL has "and she was vexing to him."

17.a. LXX^B reads σίδηρος, "an iron implement."

17.b. LXX^B reads ἅγιος θεοῦ, "holy to God"; compare Judg 13:7.

17.c. A few Heb. MSS miss the literary distinction and assimilate MT's כל, as "all" or "every," to כאחד, as "one member of mankind." Compare Bartusch, *Understanding Dan*, 154.

18.a. LXX^A reads "all the Philistine rulers."

18.b. LXX^B reads ἔτι τὸ ἅπαξ τοῦτο, "yet this once." OL does not have this term.

18.c. Following Q and LXX rather than K, which has לה, "to her," for לי, "to me." Bartusch (*Understanding Dan*, 154) sees this as assimilation to the same construction in v 17.

18.d. LXX^A reads ἀνέβησαν πρὸς αὐτὴν πᾶσαι αἱ σατραπίαι τῶν ἀλλοφύλων, "all the Philistine rulers went up to her."

18.e. Many Heb. MSS read the imperative consecutive rather than the perfect with simple *wāw* as in MT. This may represent a modal use of the perfect with *wāw* akin to the modal use of the imperfect with simple *wāw*. Bartusch (*Understanding Dan*, 154) thinks it possible that a *yôd* has dropped out in the sequence *wāw, wāw, yôd*, a copyist reading the *yôd* as a *wāw* and thinking it unnecessary. GKC, §112tt, also sees the text as corrupt here.

18.f. *BHS* proposes placing a *wāw*, "and," before "the silver" and omitting ויעל to read "and the silver was in their hand." Bartusch (*Understanding Dan*, 154) correctly observes that no MS evidence supports this and that it may well be unnecessary, "the silver" serving as an unmarked direct object.

19.a. LXX^B reads καὶ ἐκοίμισεν Δαλιδα τὸν Σαμψων, "and Delilah put Samson to sleep."

19.b. LXX^A reads ἀνὰ μέσον τῶν γονάτων αὐτῆς, "in the middle of (or between) her knees," leading to *BHS* suggesting that perhaps Heb. should read בין. Bartusch (*Understanding Dan*, 154) points, however, to Gen 30:3 for the MT reading and without further evidence retains MT.

19.c. LXX^A (compare OL) reads ἐκάλεσεν τὸν κουρέα, "called the barber."

19.d. One Heb. MS reads "and he shaved him" and is followed by *BHS*. LXX does not make gender distinctions here. Bartusch (*Understanding Dan*, 154) correctly sees MT as the more difficult text and, without more evidence, to be preferred.

19.e. LXX^A (compare OL) reads καὶ ἤρχατο ταπεινοῦσθαι, "and he began to be humbled." This appears to be a Gk. circumlocution or way to protect Samson a bit. It does not present strong enough evidence to change the text. Retroversion to ויחל לענות is not necessary. See Bartusch (*Understanding Dan*, 154) and *Preliminary and Interim Report* (2:114).

20.a. LXX reads "Delilah."

20.b. LXX^A reads "called to him."

20.c. OL reads "I will go and do what is necessary." Compare Judg 15:3; 16:8.

20.d. OL expands to include "and I will shake myself."

21.a. OL does not witness to "bronze."

21.b. For MT האסירים, "prisoners," many MSS and Q read אסורים, a passive participle denoting "the ones who are bound." With Bartusch (*Understanding Dan*, 154), I maintain the K.

24.a. *BHS* suggests transposing this verse after the next one, attributing the invitations to the Philistine leaders rather than to the people. Without evidence, this is much too subjective to follow. See Bartusch, *Understanding Dan*, 154.

24.b. LXX^B does not have "they said." Bartusch (*Understanding Dan*, 154) sees reason, with *BHS*, to delete these words but apparently prefers MT. Stronger evidence is needed for such a deletion.

24.c. One Heb. MS reads "Samson" for "our enemy"; another inserts "Samson" with "our enemy," and many others read the pl., "our enemies." *BHS* suggests inserting "Samson," which is unnecessary and does not have sufficient MS support. See Bartusch, *Understanding Dan*, 154–55.

25.a. The Heb. MS tradition reads and divides the consonantal text several ways. MT represents normal temporal clause and can be kept. See Bartusch, *Understanding Dan*, 155.

25.b. LXX reads καλέσατε τὸν Σαμψων ἐξ οἴκου φυλακῆς, "summon Samson out of the prison house," giving a complete parallel to the fulfillment of the summons later in the verse.

25.c. OL reads "dance."

25.d. LXX^A reads καὶ ἐνέπαιζον αὐτῷ, "and they mocked him," while LXX^B reads καὶ ἔπαιζεν ἐνώπιον αὐτῶν καὶ ἐρράπιζον αὐτὸν, "and he played before them, and they struck him." OL has "from the prison house, and they derided him." As Niditch notes, in OL "Samson does not sport nor do they beat" (167). I agree with Bartusch (*Understanding Dan*, 155) in reading MT.

25.e. LXX^A (compare OL) reads "between the two pillars," supplying the obvious information.

26.a. Many MSS and Q read וַהֲמִישֵׁנִי from מוש, "to handle, touch, feel." The K and a few Heb. MSS read וְהֵימֵ(י)שֵׁ(א)נִי from ימש, a root meaning "to touch" but not included in *HALOT*, but see *DCH*, 4:230. A few Heb. MSS read וַהֲשֵׁמֵנִי. BHS proposes וַהֲמִשֵׁנִי, the *hip̄'il* imperative from מוש, "to grasp, handle, allow to touch." Certainly Bartusch (*Understanding Dan*, 155) correctly describes the text as "confused," though its meaning "is clear."

26.b. LXX^A (compare OL) reads ὁ δὲ παῖς ἐποίησεν οὕτως, "now the child did this," easily retroverted as וַיַּעַשׂ הַנַּעַר כֵּן, a natural addition by an editor wanting to make sure the reader understood the implied action. See Bartusch, *Understanding Dan*, 155.

27.a. LXX^B reads ἑπτακόσιοι, "seven hundred."

27.b. BHS suggests that "all the Philistine rulers were there. On the roof about three thousand men and women" represents an editorial addition to the text, but gives no proof for this. See Bartusch, *Understanding Dan*, 155.

28.a. זֶה, "this," is questioned because פעם is usually fem. The BHS suggestion to replace it with the divine name goes too far in making emendations. Letting the biblical tradition make a slight grammatical error is better than such audacious handling of the text. See Bartusch, *Understanding Dan*, 155.

28.b. LXX^A and OL do not have "O God," leading BHS to delete it, but this is not sufficient evidence. See Bartusch, *Understanding Dan*, 155.

28.c. LXX, supported by Vg., reads ἀντὶ (περὶ) τῶν δύο ὀφθαλμῶν μου, "for my two eyes." Jost offers an interpretive explanation: "Does the Masoretic version put more emphasis on the fact that the 'revenge' to be exacted is more limited than it could be, while the Septuagint and Vulgate stress the full exercise of vengeance? Or, on the contrary, did the version in the ancient translations weaken a Hebrew text that expressed Samson's hope of being able to exact revenge for his second eye at a later time?" ("God of Love/God of Vengeance," 121).

29.a. LXX^B reads καὶ ἐπεστηρίχθη ἐπ' αὐτοὺς καὶ ἐκράτησεν, "and he supported himself on them and he grasped."

30.a. LXX reads "Samson."

Form/Structure/Setting

See table 13.1 in the appendix to compare one possible example of narrative analysis with form-critical analysis for chaps. 13–16. The narrative elements follow the typical pattern of Hebrew narrative while the genre elements show the genre of each section with its component parts. Note how the narrator can use different genre elements and markers within or even across various narrative elements.

Every scholar studying the Samson narratives today tries to outclass all his colleagues in describing the narrative artistry of these materials. James Crenshaw says this story "demonstrates Israelite narrative art at its zenith" (*Samson*, 149). Elsewhere Crenshaw writes, "The story weaves an intricate tapestry from separate strands of Hebrew rhetoric. Familiar themes, motifs, and rhetoric unite in a suspense-filled tale about squandered potential. The mighty Samson fell victim to his own fascination for foreign women" (*ABD*, 5:950). This narrative artistry is at least as apparent in what is not concretely specified as it is in what is explicitly noted. Each of the narrative units is a masterpiece in itself and often seems unrelated to what follows or precedes. However, careful reading reveals how seemingly unrelated units tie together to illustrate God's purpose with Samson and the traits of Samson's character that prevent him from accomplishing God's call. Exum in several articles (chiefly "Aspects of Symmetry and Balance in the Samson Saga," *JSOT* 19 [1981] 3–29) has demonstrated in detail the artistic relationship among the various segments of the Samson narrative, the linguistic details tying the materials together with leitmotifs, and the theological results of such linguistic artistry.

Wong has shown how the Samson narrative ties into the themes of the other sections of Judges. He claims (*Compositional Strategy*, 164–65), with only partial success, that the final part of chap. 15 shows that Samson's lack of faith is a deterioration from that of Gideon and Jephthah. He is more successful in demonstrating that self-interest is a greater motivating factor for Samson than it was even for Gideon and Jephthah, to which we might add for Barak and Abimelech. Wong concludes, "But it is not until one gets to Samson that the deterioration hits bottom" (174). Deterioration also occurs with regard to the decreasing participation of the tribes from Ehud to Samson whose "exploits against the Philistines was [sic] basically only a one-man affair" (178).

Wong does not mention Samson as he discusses "increasing harshness in dealing with internal dissent" (*Compositional Strategy*, 178–80), but one might note that for Samson internal dissent appears not among Israelites so much as among the Philistines, whom Samson repeatedly punishes, though Samson and the Judahites do have interaction leading to Samson's conflict with the Philistines. Finally, the cyclical pattern breaks down most thoroughly in the Samson narratives with only Samson crying out to God, and that in the midst of the narratives, not in the introduction; with the land not receiving rest; and with the enemy only beginning to be subdued.

Similarly, Wong shows that Samson represents the conclusion to a north-south orientation of the narratives as well as the deterioration theme, both reflecting the same orientation in chap. 1. Thus Wong argues that it is "extremely unlikely that the prologue could be a literary composition independently conceived and totally unrelated to the central section. Rather it is far more likely that the conquest report that makes up the core of the prologue was composed expressly as an introduction to the central section, offering important structural clues that would guide the interpretation of the latter" (*Compositional Strategy*, 189).

Wong stretches things only a bit as he ties the Samson narrative to the epilogue of chaps. 17–21. He sees the Levite's violation of every Levitical regulation echoing Samson's violation of practically every Nazirite regulation and the Levite's wooing and abandoning of his concubine echoing Samson's wooing and abandoning of his wife. He is on target in noting Samson doing what was right in his eyes (14:3, 7) in conjunction with the refrain of the epilogue (17:6; 21:25).

Olson (840–42) builds on the work of Webb ([1987] 162–74) and Greenstein (*Proof* 1 [1981] 237–60) to find in the Samson narrative sixteen thematic allusions to other parts of Judges:

- the role of Judah
- marrying with the nations
- the contrast to Othniel
- replacing the nation in crying out to Yahweh
- the theme of secrets as seen with Ehud
- unlikely weapons as with Shamgar

- the Hebrew term *taqaʿ*, "driving" (תקע), in 4:21 and 16:14
- destroying a pagan worship center as did Gideon
- personal vendetta as motivation, as with Gideon and Jephthah
- the divine-call genre shared with Gideon
- use of three hundred foxes compared to Gideon's three hundred men
- introduction of the Philistine threat from Judg 10:6–7
- refusal to keep a vow contrasted with Jephthah
- the burning of his wife compared to the burning of Jephthah's daughter
- the use of the phrase "to do what is right in one's own eyes" as in the epilogue
- the emergence of hope through his renewed hair growth and through the finding of wives for the nearly extinct Benjaminites

All this shows a literary unity to the book.

Niditch shows the internal themes that tie the Samson materials together:

> The tales of Samson are characterized by recurring language, motifs, and patterns of content. Repeatedly, Samson makes overtures to foreign women (Timnite, harlot, Delilah), performs superhuman feats (killing the lion with his bare hands, killing the Ashkelonites, jawbone killing, lifting the city gates, destroying the house of Dagon), and is associated with symbols of fertility (honey, water). He participates in and is countered by trickery (Samson's riddle, the Philistines' stealing the answer to the riddle, his feigning capture, his deceiving Delilah, and Delilah's treachery). He is involved in vengeance and countervengeance (Samson torches Philistine crops, they burn the Timnites; Samson kills Philistines, they capture and blind him; he takes vengeance by killing thousands of them). He frequently withdraws (to his parents, to the "cleft," finally to death itself). (153–54)

Such decisions concerning unifying qualities in the book fly in the face of opinions like those of Marc Zvi Brettler, who is so concerned to find the building blocks behind the narrative that narrative unity is ruled out: "The types of changes that are called for to create a truly coherent cycle went beyond what a biblical redactor would typically do. . . . The Samson cycle represents a model of redaction that is weak from a thematic and stylistic perspective. . . . We cannot always impose our desire to find order and coherence on ancient texts" (60). Brettler goes so far as to decide that "the Samson material came together from at least three different blocks of material (13:2–24; 14:1–15:19; 16:1–31a)," each unit having "a slightly different take on Samson" (44). Such remnants of the old documentary source theory provide little help in understanding Judges but do remind us that oral traditions of various shape and character lie behind the final written document.

Kratz limits the core of the tradition to Judg 14:1–15:8, with other parts added in stages and Deuteronomistic elements integrated in 13:1, 5, 25; 14:6, 19; 15:14, 20; 16:31, in which "the shadow of Saul may be recognized in Samson" (*Composition of the Narrative Books*, 205). (Compare Römer, *So-Called Deuteronomistic History*, 90–91, 136–39, 182; Stipp, *VT* 45 [1995] 344–55, who calls for a sixth- or fifth-century date due to the use of motifs from Gideon and the distanced, reflective style without narrative elements.) Even Olson reads the evidence to indicate that the Samson narrative was edited at a "late stage of the book's composition" (842).

As a whole, the larger Samson narrative falls into three parts that Younger labels "the birth account (13:1–25), the paralleled life accounts (14:1–15:20), and the death account (16:1–31)" (281). Mobley (*Empty Men*, 182) sees the three stories of women giving basic structure to a narrative introduced by a birth story, or what

Niditch calls "an annunciaton scene" (142). The annunciation scene is a "a form of theophany" that "often includes: the news for the woman, delivered by the deity or his emissary; particular instructions and information about the boy; an offering of sacrifice; the allusion to a divine name or identity; a miraculous passage revealing or sealing the importance of the event; and an expression of awe or fear on the part of those who experience the visitation. Judges 6:11–24 provides a close parallel to the theophany in ch. 13" (Niditch, 142).

Exum and Whedbee class the narrative as a comedy because of "its emphasis on restoration and resolution" that "exemplifies the comic vision" so that "only when viewed in its proper comic context can its tragic moments be rightly appreciated" ("Isaac, Samson, and Saul," 288–89). Samson's "wit and prowess provide the occasion to ridicule the Philistines and have a good laugh at their expense. He constantly gets the better of them, and the narrative shows a hearty, lusty approval of it all. . . . The frequently cruel laughter at the Philistines gives vent to Israelite hostility" (301). Niditch (*CBQ* 52 [1990] 608–24) shows how Samson is an Israelite version of the widespread hero, trickster, and bandit patterns. The Samson version is about authority and empowerment for Niditch, so that "the Samson tale deals with the desire to obtain and hold autonomy, both personal and political" (610).

Dorsey (113) finds a chiastic structure here as he does with virtually every segment of the Old Testament, but when everything is a chiasm, one asks what constitutes evidence for a chiasm. This structure puts 15:9–20 at the center of the narrative with "movement from negative to negative. The story is all bad" (112). Dorsey (114–15) does show parallels between Samson and Othniel as examples of the model judge and the worst judge.

Greene correctly finds that "a feature of the structure of the story [is] that its major peaks are followed by dramatic, unexpected reversals—intended intermarriage after theophany and blessing (13:20–14:2); return to Timnah after the apparent end of the affair (14:20–15:1); and sex with a prostitute after the great triumph of faith (15:18–16:3)" (*VE* 21 [1991] 70). Such an analysis sees the book of Judges as a carefully crafted narrative, not as a collection of materials undergoing a long series of editorial changes through many centuries. This does not mean that the component parts do not have individual histories. The stories may well have circulated independently in oral circles, but isolating the form and function of such stories is quite difficult, if not impossible, and does not lead to the understanding of the present text.

Margalith, in a series of articles in *Vetus Testamentum*, has argued that "the legends of Heracles are parallels of those of Samson and probably their source. . . . The Israelites became familiar through their contacts with their Philistine neighbours with these and other pictures and legends of Heracles, which were echoes of their original *Sitz im Leben* in the Aegean world" (*VT* 37 [1987] 63, 70). Such argumentation extends credulity a bit and ignores Israel's Near Eastern background.

Crenshaw (*Samson*, 41–50; compare Bartusch, *Understanding Dan*, 138, with n. 183; and Niditch, *CBQ* 52 [1990] 608–24) has made a case for folklore motifs being incorporated into the narrative. He examines six of these: barren wife, helpless hero facing a woman's wiles, quest for the deity's name, death wish, loss of charisma, and terror over a theophany. Interestingly, such motifs account for only a small portion of the Samson text. From this and other evidence, Crenshaw joins a long line of scholars who classify these chapters as a saga and see the saga as "legendary and of uncertain date," intended "to provide entertainment and to offer negative example" (*Samson*, 64). Bartusch goes so far as to find that "originally the stories told of a Danite hero who sucessfully and honorably wreaked havoc on the oppressive, neighboring Philistines" (*Understanding Dan*, 136). If such were true, it would explain the preservation and repetition of the narratives prior to their incorporation into the book of Judges, where the stories have been edited "so as to command a negative evaluation of the main character and, by extension, perhaps even of the Danites" (136).

In a similar vein Mobley thinks the Samson story "incorporates nearly every motif from the Israelite heroic tradition and, many assert, freely imports motifs from outside Israelite culture. . . . The uncommon feats of an extraordinaary—and criminally dangerous—misfit have been inflated to near-mythic proportions by the workings of popular storytelling over generations" (*Empty Men*, 174–75). Mobley classifies the narrative as an "outlaw ballad" of Samson and three women (187).

But we must pay attention to Greene: "The basic genre is taken as history, whatever roots it may or may not have in saga. . . . This authorial restraint suggests that this kind of historical narrative is intended to be read not just as historical record, not just as 'fictionalized history,' but as a kind of *mashal*, in which the hearer/reader is expected to mull over the implications of contrasts and comparisons himself" (*VE* 21 [1991] 54, 56).

Comment

1   As with most of the stories about the judges, Samson's begins with the editorial framework blaming the Israelites' evil deeds for their horrible situation. God is directly responsible for the situation, having handed his people Israel over to the Philistines. (Compare Judg 10:7.) This time the punishment lasts "forty years," a full generation and the time of the judgeship of Samson and Samuel (Crenshaw, *Samson*, 40). But no cry for help appears. Rather, we have a birth announcement. Chisholm ("What's Wrong with This Picture?") concludes that the people did not cry out because they had come to accept the Philistines as their overlords and no longer desired relief. This is certainly the case with the tribe of Judah as will be seen later in the narrative (see Judg 15:11).

2   As in the Gideon narrative, so here, the expected framework notice that God has raised up a judge is highly noticeable by its absence. Instead, a simple birth story ensues. Klein argues that "the annunciation type-scene arouses expectations which are diametrically opposed to the ensuing reality. The reader is set up for incongruity, for irony" (*Triumph of Irony*, 117).

The story takes the original readers and us into what later became Israel's northern border—the tribal territory of Dan—and what would become the home of Israel's most obvious violation of God's law, the sanctuary set up by King Jeroboam I. In Samson's day, however, Dan had not yet moved north, living instead on the southwestern coast where the Philistines had settled. The text refers to a *mišpaḥat*, or "clan" (מִשְׁפַּחַת), not to a *šebet*, or "tribe" (שֵׁבֶט). Bartusch says, "Judg. 13.2 portrays a precarious existence for Dan either as an independent group within Israel, or as a Danite enclave within the territory of Judah . . . depicted as a marginal, relatively weak, even oppressed group" (*Understanding Dan*, 168, referring to Josh 15:33).

As so often in ancient and biblical birth stories, the focus is on a woman who is barren, unable to bear children—Sarai, Gen 11:30; Rebekah, Gen 25:21; 29:31; Leah, Gen 29:31; Hannah, 1 Sam 1:5; Michal, 2 Sam 6:23; Elizabeth, Luke 1:36. Because of Israel's cultural norms, she carried a stigma and needed "to take extreme measures to secure a child" (Crenshaw, *Samson*, 42).

Crenshaw isolates (*Samson*, 42) five elements of barren-wife stories: the preferred wife, a mocking secondary wife, the wife begging for progeny, the promise of a son, and the birth. (Compare Alter, *Proof* 3 [1983] 115–30.) The Samson narrative replaces the nagging, mocking second wife with an ignorant, unbelieving, fearful husband. Samson's mother is not pictured as in any way desperate, for she does not ask for a child. God alone takes the initiative to fulfill divine purposes, not to relieve cultural shame. Ackerman contends that "the motif by which a child of promise is threatened with death before reaching full adulthood appears more common than not in the Bible's barren women stories" (*Warrior, Dancer*, 190–91). Manoah's wife hints at this in v 7. This leads Ackerman to decide that "the barren women stories reflect one theme, the God who fills a woman's womb has the right to demand, in some fashion, the life that comes forth from it" (193).

The law promised an obedient people that no woman among them would be barren or miscarry (Exod 23:26; Deut 7:14), so to be barren was often but not always seen as a curse from God (Gen 20:18; 1 Sam 1:5). God was praised for providing children for the barren (Ps 113:9). Yet here the barren-woman motif turns in a different direction.

The woman who will be the centerpiece of the story is not the first person introduced. McCann (95–96) identifies Samson's mother as the truly faithful hero and model in the Samson story. Since she virtually disappears after the first chapter of the story, this identification must be ruled out, as should the insistence that the story has a "faithful hero." Her husband enters the scene first in the narrator's quite individualistic, even "odd" (Block, 399), manner of introducing him. As Block remarks, "The male character is introduced by genus, geographic origin, tribal affiliation, and finally by name. The order is intentional, reflecting the fact that within the context of Samson's life as a whole his geographic setting and tribal identity were more important than the identity of his parents" (399).

The inclusion of a name would seem to afford more importance to Manoah than to his nameless wife, but this is an element of the narrator's art in leading you to expect one thing only to discover another. We shall see that, as Niditch states, "within the admittedly limiting contours of this culture, Manoah's wife is shown to be worthy of divine information, more worthy than her dolt of a husband. As in many traditional cultures, the empowerment of women takes place within the system and is imagined within stereotypical roles" (143).

3–5 Again, as in the Gideon story, the messenger or angel of Yahweh "appeared" (or "was seen") unexpectedly. This introduces a major theme for the Samson narrative: right and wrong seeing (Judg 13:3, 10, 19–23; 14:1–2, 8, 11; 16:1, 5, 18, 24, 27; compare Judg 1:24–25; 2:7; 3:24; 4:22; 5:8; 6:12, 22; 7:17; 9:36, 43, 48, 55; 11:35; 12:3; 18:7, 9, 26; 19:3, 17, 30; 20:36, 41; 21:21). Samson's wrong seeing precipitates the Timnah, Gaza, and Delilah incidents. Greene identifies the various examples of wrong seeing in this narrative: "[Samson] fails to see beneath the surface of others to the powers and allegiances that motivate them. . . . The Philistines fail to see what lies behind Samson, initially seeing him as a mere man, albeit a very strong one, and even after his fall, seeing only a humiliated hero and not the God behind him." But seeing must be seen as "rooted in the central theme of obedience" (*VE* 21 [1991] 76).

Rather than bringing a commission in a call narrative, the messenger brings God's birth announcement (13:3). Kim contends that "the woman's barrenness not only provides a fitting background for a miraculous birth but also reflects analogically the pathetic plight of the Israelites who by their apostasy have foreclosed the future" (*Structure of the Samson Cycle*, 181). With the announcement comes a demand. Block points to the use in 13:4 of the expression נָא הִשָּׁמְרִי עַתָּה, "now therefore be careful," in Deuteronomy calling for "diligence in the observance of the divine will. Cf. Deut 2:4; 4:9, 15; 6:12; 8:11; 12:13, 19, 30; 15:9; 24:8" (402).

The expectant mother must take a Nazirite vow (see Num 6:1–8) to abstain from strong drink, not to eat grapes or anything produced by the grapevine, not to touch anything dead, and to keep the food laws (13:4). The vow means she agrees not to drink alcoholic beverages, not to cut her hair, and not to touch anything associated with death. Then, as Hebrew narrative is wont to do, the messenger repeats the birth announcement, adding this time instructions for the new child's Nazirite vow. Only Samuel of all the Old Testament babies joins Samson in being given a life-long Nazirite vow from God (1 Sam 1:11, 21).

Scholars strongly and vociferously debate the nature of Samson's Nazirite status. No further mention of it is made until the final Delilah narrative in chap. 16, and there only the hair regulation is described unless the lad's destiny (מִשְׁפַּט־הַנַּעַר, v 12) means, as Chisholm suggests, "'the rule(s) of/for the boy' . . . the regulation(s) that the boy was to follow to fulfill his Nazirite status" ("Identity Crisis," 4, n. 14). On one side of the debate Wong (*Compositional Strategy*, 91) can claim, "Samson had violated almost every stipulation that defined his special status." He argues:

> The immediate context makes it clear that the reason she needed to observe these regulations was because of her pregnancy (13:5). For the child she would carry was to be a Nazirite to YHWH from the womb (מִן־בֶּטֶן) and not just from birth. . . . Thus, if the mother needed to observe these regulations for the sake of the child inside her, the implication is that these regulations would be of paramount importance for the child as well. (92, n. 36)

Wong notes the three repetitions of the prohibitions against strong drink and unclean food. If these were not functional for the rest of the narrative, the narrator has rendered "a significant part of the birth narrative irrelevant to the story as a whole" (*Compositional Strategy*, 93, n. 42). Gunn goes so far as to say, "the Nazirite vow permeates the narrative" ("Joshua and Judges," 118).

Olson (845), Bal (*Death and Dissymmetry*, 25), and Marais (*Representation in Old Testament Narrative Texts*, 127) agree that the Nazirite vow with all its components is central to the narrative. Exum (*VT* 33 [1983] 31) and Andersson (*Book and Its Narratives*, 179) join many who do not see Samson's Nazirite vow as a major factor in most of the narrative. Ackerman states the negative case simply: "Judges 13 does not prescribe these latter two restrictions [meaning strong drink and touching corpses] for Samson" (*Warrior, Dancer*, 113). Mobley believes "the emphatic effect of this [threefold] repetition [of the vow] loses much of its force because the conditions of the *nazir* state are formulated differently in each instance" (*Empty Men*, 176–77). Niditch insists "the 'hair growing' aspect of the Nazirite vow is central to the narrative, its plot, its hero's characterization, and its central themes" (*CBQ* 52 [1990] 612). Yet she also decides, "Staying away from alcohol, unclean food, and corpses (other aspects of the Nazirite vow as described in Priestly material at Numbers 6) are not the interest of the Samson writer" (613). Stipp (*VT* 45 [1995] 343) seeks to prove that Judg 13 was in no way intended to brand Samson as an undisciplined, duty-forgetting squanderer of his charisma.

Chisholm gives the best case for denying Samson full Nazirite status:

> It is possible that none of the actions prior to the Delilah incident violated the Nazirite code, at least technically speaking. The law about corpses may not have applied to animals, the text never says that he actually drank the prohibited beverages, and the situation described in Numbers 6:9 may not have applied to one whom God had commissioned to fight battles. So it is possible that Samson had not violated any of the Nazirite rules prior to the incident with Delilah. In this case the incident involving the animal corpse and Samson's appearance at the wedding may contribute to the story by creating an ominous mood where threats to Samson's Nazirite status lurk in his environment. ("Identity Crisis," 10–11)

Chisholm then concludes with discussion of the irony of the situation and says,

> The incidents that echo the Nazirite regulations fit well. Samson is a Nazirite, but not the usual type. He parades through the story seemingly or nearly violating Nazirite regulations right and left. However, he has not really done so, because only one rule applies in his case. This is incongruous, but for that reason it is exactly what one expects in this story, which might be subtitled, "What's Wrong with This Picture?" ("Identity Crisis," 12)

Thus Bartusch (*Understanding Dan*, 161–63; compare B. Levine, *Numbers 1–20: A New Translation with Introduction and Commentary*, AB 4 [New York: Doubleday, 1993] 230) sees the Nazirite note as a later addition to the narrative, always an easy way out to seal an argument.

Mobley (*Empty Men*, 179–81) also argues against Blenkinsopp's reading of the story as a story of three vows since that makes chap. 15 superfluous. Certainly, the Samson narrative is more complex than simply a story of three vows. Thus Mobley concludes finally that the three-vows element represents "the residue of another Samson story . . . left unfinished in the book of Judges but circulated in Israelite oral tradition and . . . preserved in fragmentary literary form here" (182). Exum and Whedbee chime in: "Commentators who condemn Samson for betraying his Nazirite vow engage in a moral evaluation which the narrative itself does not make" ("Isaac, Samson, and Saul," 297).

These and others who deny the Nazirite vow to Samson present a rather literalistic reading that leaves no explanation of why the mother should observe the regulations and the son not when the son is the center of interest. They expect explicit condemnation from a narrator who seldom utters an interpretive word. Even Exum and Whedbee note that "this lack of specific moral judgment finds its home in comedy" ("Isaac, Samson, and Saul," 297).

I would follow Greene: "At this point the reader is presumably to assume that the other elements apply, but that there is some particular reason for mentioning the razor" (*VE* 21 [1991] 59). The Nazirite theme prepares for Samson's final trial with Delilah but also appears along the way to help characterize Samson's complex relationship with deity.

Why must the child act this way? Because the child has a special mission! The child is to begin the process of delivering Israel from the Philistines. He will not end the process, but he will begin it. As Crenshaw shows (*Samson*, 56), "begin" (חלל) is a pregnant word in the Samson materials (13:5, 25; 16:19, 22) and, I would add, in the book of Judges as a whole (10:18; 20:31, 39–40). In 13:5 the beginning points to a conclusion under David. In 13:25 the beginning of the Spirit's work in Samson leaves open whether that work comes to its intended end. Delilah's shaving expedition accomplishes its goal (16:19), and Samson's renewed hair growth accomplishes its purpose even if it does not reach previous proportions.

To accomplish his mission, Samson must show his total devotion to Yahweh, the God of Israel, and to no one else. Thus the birth narrative begins to function as a call narrative. Here one needs to differentiate closely between the literary structure of a narrative and the literary function of a narrative. One of the points of the narrator's art is that he can hide an unexpected function within the expected format of a quite common literary form or genre. The Samson narrator has done just that. So Block can conclude:

> If we interpret this primarily as a birth narrative, as many do, then we fall into the same trap as Samson, thinking that he is both the occasion for and the goal of the story. But this is to take the account out of context. This is a call narrative, unconventional to be sure, but its purpose is to describe how God provides Israel with a deliverer to deal with the Philistines. (399).

6–7 The woman hurries home to her husband to share the news and her own confusion: "A man of God came to me." Matthews suggests that "Manoah may be concerned about unauthorized fraternization between his wife and an unknown man" (141). Brettler (45) deduces from this use of בָּא אֶל, "come to," that it can be used to indicate sexual relationships, that the man of God is the father of the child. (Compare Margalith, *VT* 36 [1986] 401.) Chisholm ("Identity Crisis," 2–3) provides a close linguistic argument, pointing especially to the use of בוא אֶל in vv 8 and 9 to dispute Brettler so that the language refers to appearance to and not to copulation with. Chisholm is ready to accept "the miraculous nature of Samson's conception and birth" (3), it being possible "that Manoah's wife became pregnant as the angel spoke with her. This could have occurred by a supernatural act apart from intimate contact with Manoah, although this need not be the case since conception does not occur immediately after copulation (she could have had relations with Manoah shortly before this)" (2).

Certainly the text gives no support to such sensationalist exegesis. Such a superhuman birth is not needed to explain the hero's "superhuman abilities" (Brettler, 46), nor is the story to be compared to the inimical passage in Gen 6:1–4. The Nazirite status of Samson does not come from his needing to be in the "human non-hereditary state closest to being divine" (47). Finally, this is not part of the evidence, as Brettler argues, which would lead to the conclusion that a group of female tradents willing to picture Manoah as foolish are responsible for the composition of chap. 13 (49).

Younger would join others in claiming that "Manoah's wife only perceives this to be a divine being but does not comprehend that this is the angel of Yahweh, Yahweh himself" (288). She played the game "ask me no questions, and I will tell you no lies" with the messenger. So she does not know his name. The text leads in a different direction. Samson's mother knows what the "totally awesome" (13:6) angel of God was supposed to look like and supposed that that is the identity of her visitor, though she is not certain. Younger notes that "the divine name [Yahweh] is used in narrative description, and the generic noun 'God' is used to signal a subjective conviction" (288).

Samson's mother repeats the messenger's birth announcement, the narrator thus pounding the same words home to the reader for the third time (see vv 5, 7). The demand for the woman's Nazirite vow is also repeated, this time tied to a reason for obedience—the new son will be a Nazirite from the womb. The woman must begin the vow for the son even before the son leaves the womb. The woman omits an important detail as Chisholm ("What's Wrong with This Picture?") indicates: Samson's mother fails to communicate what is most important—her son's divinely appointed destiny. Chisholm decides that apparently the angel expects Manoah's wife to inform her husband about these things, but there is no evidence that she does. In the story to follow, Samson never gives any indication that he understands himself to be God's deliverer. Thus for Chisholm, God began to deliver a people who did not seek deliverance through a deliverer who failed to see himself as such. (Compare G. W. Savran, *Telling and Retelling: Quotation in Biblical Narrative* [Bloomington: Indiana UP, 1988] 83–84; H. G. Peels *The Vengeance of God* [Leiden: Brill, 1995] 100–102.)

The woman adds a significant phrase and ignores one: "until the day of his death" (13:7) was not in the messenger's speech. Reference to Samson's mission of delivering Israel was in the message but not in the woman's report. Crenshaw remarks, "So Manoah's wife tempers jubilance with a hint of things to come." This is the beginning of a theme in the Samson narrative: what is told and what is not told (*Samson*, 74). But the woman's telling, as Chisholm observes, "foreshadows Israel's failure to recognize Samson as their God-given deliverer and Samson's own confusion about his role in life. . . . In the story to follow Samson never gives any indication he understood himself to be Israel's deliverer" ("Identity Crisis," 4–5).

Thus the narrator has set up an expectation for all that is to follow in the Samson narrative. The birth announcement has been transformed into a call narrative for a deliverer parallel to the call of Gideon. This call comes before the child leaves the mother's womb (see Jer 1). This opening exposition has given us the measuring stick for Samson's life. Will he maintain his Nazirite vow? Will he begin to deliver Israel from the Philistines? The narrative will proceed to address these issues in very subtle and unexpected ways, with popular folk stories and anecdotes originally told around Israelite and even Philistine campfires to the amusement of the crowd. We should find the same amusement in the stories, but then we must look deeper to see how these stories relate implicitly if not explicitly to this opening exposition of vow and mission.

8 Having heard the news, Manoah wants to hear it again, for himself, straight from the messenger's mouth. He prays to God to let this happen, stating as his main reason the desire to know precisely how to train the young son. Here the reader must look between the lines to discern Manoah's motivation. Do we read the narrative as straightforward reporting and remain content with Manoah's explanation, or do we find a sense of doubt or a sense of manipulation in Manoah's unwillingness to accept his wife's testimony? Why does he have to know for himself? Is he resentful, jealous, and hungry for power and domination in his own home? (See Block, 407; Younger, 289–90.)

9–11 The narrative appears to indicate that God accepts the request at face value and thus grants his request. Ironically, however, the second visit repeats the problem of the first; Manoah is nowhere to be seen or found. The woman leaves the messenger standing and hurries off to find her inquisitive husband and tell him of the messenger's return.

The Samson narrative repeatedly plays on what is told and what is not told. In 13:10 the wife again tells Manoah her experience. In 14:2 Samson tells his parents to get a Philistine girl for him as wife. In 14:6 he does *not* tell his parents of his experience with the lion. Nor does he tell them the source of the honey he gives them (14:9). Samson gives the Philistines seven days to "report back" (literally, "tell") with the answer to his riddle (14:12) and tells the consequences if they can-*not* tell (14:13), which they cannot (14:14). In desperation they force his wife to get Samson to tell (14:15). So in 14:16 she pleads with and cajoles Samson because he has *not* told her, and he explains that he has *not* even told his parents and so has no reason to tell her. So on the seventh day, because "she constantly insisted" or "nagged" (NRSV) him, he gives in and tells her, and she immediately tells her "people" (14:17). Samson disrobes the men of Ashkelon to pay the debt and gives the clothes to those who had told him the riddle (14:19). Similarly in the Delilah story, she demands that Samson tell her the secret of his strength (16:6, 10, 13). In frustrated anger Delilah chides Samson for *not* telling her (16:15). Finally, Samson tells her his whole heart (16:17), and she realizes that he has told her his whole heart and so tells the "Philistine rulers" (16:18). Thus "to tell" decides Samson's fate, as he refuses to tell his parents he has broken the Nazirite vow but tells his women the deep secrets that hold his fate. We learn through this key word that, as Crenshaw says, "Samson alone holds the key that unlocks the door to his riddle" (*Samson*, 67).

Responding to his wife's urgent summons, Manoah finally encounters the mysterious man and bluntly inquires if the man is his wife's previous visitor. In Hebrew the man's response is simply one word—I, meaning "I'm your man."

12–14 Manoah expresses his faith in the man's promise of a son who will begin to deliver Israel and wants to know his son's destiny, literally, "his justice and his deeds." (See the discussion of the translation difficulty at this point in Block, 408–9.) The messenger appears to ignore the question, reiterating instead his expectations of the wife. She must remember and do all that the messenger commanded. Again the messenger repeats the demands. Husband and wife cannot claim ignorance. They know what God expects of them as parents of Samson. Block concludes, "From this conversation with the heavenly visitor Manoah has learned nothing new, but he has been assured that his wife's report in vv. 6–7 was not the delusion of a woman frustrated over her barren condition. He may indeed look forward to the birth of a special child and share with his wife the burden of preparing him for divine service" (410).

15–18 As Gideon wanted to feed Yahweh's messenger (6:19), so does Manoah. (For a full comparison of the Gideon call narrative with the Samson birth/call narrative, see the chart by Block, 411, and his conclusion that "the narrator intends for vv.

17–23 to be interpreted in light of and in comparison/contrast to 6:17–24.") Again, Manoah's motivation comes under question. Is this simply a reference to Abraham's action in Gen 18? Is his intention, as Younger surmises, "to detain and obligate his divine visitor through feeding, a concept well-attested in ancient Near Eastern religions, where feeding a deity or his envoy provided the basis for the supplicant's expectation of divine action on his behalf" (290)? The messenger indicates that proper procedure is to offer sacrifice, not feed him. The narrator makes Manoah's ignorance explicit: "For Manoah did not know that he was the messenger of Yahweh" (Judg 13:16). Still, Block's repeated efforts (406–16) to paint Manoah as ignorant, bumbling, and impious appear to be a bit overdrawn.

Recognizing his ignorance, Manoah asks the messenger to reveal his name. Crenshaw (*Samson*, 44–46) notes the folklore motif of the quest for a deity's name here and points to the same motif in Gen 32:22–32 and in Exod 3:1–4:17. Elements of the motif include divine manifestation, human request for the divine name, divine refusal that includes a clue, and the successful use of the clue. Interestingly here in asking his question, "Manoah's syntax faltered" (46). He literally asks, "Who your name [מִי שְׁמֶךָ]?"

Why does Manoah ask? Younger (291) lists three possible suspect motives for Manoah's question: knowing the name provides power over the name; the desire to honor is pointed to the future after the words are fulfilled, reflecting Manoah's lingering doubts about Yahweh's words; and the desire to honor is directed at the person to whom he speaks rather than toward Yahweh, the only one worthy of honor. Ackerman (*Warrior, Dancer*, 112) says Manoah's asking points to his hubris or pride. The mysterious answer shows that God will not reveal himself completely. Manoah cannot have access to the inner reality of God represented by his name. That name is "Miraculous." This harks back to Jacob's fight with the messenger in Gen 32:29.

19–20 These verses again parallel the Gideon narrative, where at this point the messenger of Yahweh performs the miracle of setting the offering on fire and disappearing in the flames. A similar miracle occurs here, the text saying specifically that he causes a miracle to happen while Manoah and his wife are watching. Brettler attributes the parallels between the two stories to an editor trying to "create more unity and coherence in the book" (44). Such a perspective fails to see the literary purposes and artistry in connecting the materials of the entire book together and comparing the actions of one character to that of a previous one for narrative and theological reasons. For a strong, but a bit overdrawn, argument showing connections among the various sections of Judges, see Wong (*Compositional Strategy*; for Samson, see especially 89–110, 174–76, 184–85, 231–36).

The messenger does not necessarily light the fire this time, but he does disappear in its flames (13:20). This throws Manoah and his wife on their faces in worship. The miracle had not had this effect on Gideon. Only the interpretation of the Midianite soldier's dream could make Gideon worship (7:15).

21–23 The messenger's disappearance, rather than his appearance, brings revelation to Manoah. Now he "knew that he was the messenger of Yahweh" (Judg 13:21). Block observes, "When he stopped asking questions and offered the young goat to Yahweh, his questions concerning the divine visitor's identity were answered. Ironically, the presence of the envoy was a hindrance to Manoah's knowing. Only when he disappeared did he recognize him" (415).

As had Gideon (6:22; compare Exod 33:20), so Manoah expects to die when he realizes he has seen Yahweh's messenger. Crenshaw (*Samson*, 49–50) identifies the folklore motif of terror over theophany. This involves divine manifestation, overwhelming dread for the human witness, divine tempering of the fear, and the person's change of character. We see this in Jacob's wrestling with the divine messenger, Moses' taking off his shoes on the holy mountain, and Isaiah's call.

The wife reflects more calmly on the situation. God has done too much for them to kill them now. God would not accept an offering from someone he intends to kill. Nor would he reveal himself and his plans for his people to someone he plans to kill. As Block confirms, "God has spoken cultically, visually, and orally, declaring to them the future, which obviously depends upon their continued living" (416). They are safe, even with Manoah's many expressions of doubt and fear (compare Olson, 847). The narrative ends with one element conspicuously missing: the wife's lifestyle changes, but Manoah's character does not. Thus Ackerman thinks the wife "displays a theological acumen and sensitivity to Israel's covenant tradition that is reminiscent of the piety of Jephthah's daughter" (*Warrior, Dancer*, 112–13).

24–25 The revelation and commissioning element of the story out of the way, the narrator can turn to the birth itself. Unlike the announcement section, the birth is quickly covered in one sentence (v 24), a sentence that gives the child's name, "Samson," for the first time. Strangely, the name appears to be related to the Canaanite sun god Shemesh rather than to the God Yahweh, who has just spoken with her. Normally in birth announcements, the deity provides the name for the parents with some explanation of it, but here no explanation is given. Even as his mother names him, no explanation of the name is forthcoming. His name neither indicates his character nor describes his mission. (See Block, 416–17, for a discussion of the meaning of this name somehow connected to the sun.) Younger (292) calls the lack of a Yahwistic name "incredulous indeed!"

More important than the name or its meaning are the boy's growth and Yahweh's blessing. Interestly, however, physical growth does not lead to character development. As Exum and Whedbee see, "a typical comic hero, Samson displays a remarkable absence of character development" (302). The latter is shown in the coming of "the Spirit of Yahweh" (Judg 13:25) on him, but McCann regretfully notes, "The Spirit will come upon Samson more than upon any of the other judges, but with the least effect (see 14:6, 19; 15:14)" (101). The Spirit of Yahweh comes upon him to give him power to achieve God's mission. Yet, as R. G. Bowman says,

> Possession of the spirit of the Lord seems to result only in the personal protection of Samson from a variety of threats, some of which are caused by his own antics. . . . It again appears that divine power is constrained by the exercise of human freedom. . . . Divine success appears contingent upon an appropriate human response. . . . God will act to punish transgressions, but not to prevent them. ("Narrative Criticism of Judges," 38–39)

The Spirit does not show approval of Samson's spiritual condition, nor does it fill him with an inner spirituality. Again, as with Gideon and with Jephthah, the coming of the Spirit does not indicate a moral or devotional purity but a power to accomplish acts for God. In earlier instances, Matthews observes, "the theme of God's spirit "coming upon" or investing judges is intended to provide them with an aura of authority as they are called upon to lead the Israelites in battle. The phrase used in the Samson narrative, however, suggests physical possession by the spirit of God, infusing the hero with superhuman strength" (145). Matthews also suggests that in these Samson narratives the coming of the spirit occurs at "strategic moments" as a "narrative device dividing the tale into three parts. . . . Each of these events also functions as a signal that the 'romance' is doomed" (145–46).

Samson is active "in Mahaneh-dan between Zorah and Eshtaol" (Judg 13:25). Zorah is shown by the Amarna letters to be part of the kingdom of Gezer, which became one of the five major Philistine cities. Zorah is located in the Sorek Valley at modern Sar‘a, about two miles (3.2 km) north of Beth-shemesh and thirteen miles (20.9 km) southwest of Jerusalem. (See Gaß, *Ortsnamen*, 361–63.) It was Samson's home town (13:2). Eshtaol was in the eastern part of Dan's territory (Josh 19:41). Mahaneh-dan appears here and in 18:12, where it is located west of Kiriath-jearim. This causes Gaß (*Ortsnamen*, 364) to posit a possibility of two towns with the same name, but he then decides the name is literarily and theologically motivated so that no populated place is actually intended. B. Irwin (*ABD*, 4:473–74) leans toward the same conclusion, seeing any location of Mahaneh-dan as being "speculative." Rainey refers to the "camp of Dan" as a "folk epithet for places associated with the tribe of Dan within the territory of Judah" (*Sacred Bridge*, 141).

Gaß locates Eshtaol (see Josh 15:33; 19:41; Judg 16:31; 18:2, 8, 11) in modern Khirbet Deit Shubeib. He (*Ortsnamen*, 365–69) lists four other possible locations but eliminates them on archaeological grounds. (G. Greenberg, *ABD*, 2:617, agrees.) Thus Samson is active in the original territory of the tribe of Dan on the western coast of the Mediterranean amid Philistine neighbors and in the territory of Judah.

The opening birth story of Samson is full of expectations. It shows us God's demand that Samson fulfill his vow as a Nazirite. This means he is not to touch the dead, not to drink strong beverages, and not to cut his hair. The birth story also shows God's mission for Samson in Judg 13:5. He is to begin to deliver Israel from the Philistines. Here is a child experiencing God's Spirit, called to God's mission against the Philistines, and expected to show devotion and obedience through his keeping of a Nazirite vow his mother evidently had made while she waited for his birth. The reader is thus prepared for heroic battle stories showing the mighty Samson delivering Israel from the Philistines and constantly emphasizing his obedience to his vow and to his God. What we get is anything but that. Greene emphasizes the contrast with God's faithfulness: "These great expectations, however, are subordinated to the portrait of a God who is depicted as unmanipulatable but gracious to individual and nation, responsive to prayer, and taking the initiative to bless and reveal himself" (*VE* 21 [1991] 64–65).

The birth narrative has served its purpose, which Exum describes: "The story of Samson's birth in Judges 13 is an integral part of the saga and serves as the introduction to it. It introduces a number of motifs which we meet in chs. 14–16; e.g., the motif of life and death, the motif of answered prayer, the motif of knowing and not knowing, the motif of telling and not telling" (*JSOT* 19 [1981] 25).

14:1–4 Rather than the expected battle report, we are greeted with a romance novella. Instead of going up to battle, as we expect the Hebrew to say, we find Samson going down to Timnah, another Danite border city (Josh 19:43). This going up and down gives what Mobley (*Empty Men*, 184–85) calls "the rhythm" of the narrative, "going up" (עלה) or "going down" (ירד) occurring sixteen times (Judg 14:1, 2, 5, 7, 10, 19a, 19b; 15:6, 8, 9, 11, 13; 16:5, 21, 31a, 31b). Mobley lists the important boundaries he crosses in going up and down: Dan and Philistia, circumcised and foreskinned, highlanders and lowlanders, decentralized kinship society and centralized society, tribal leaders and city leaders, campsites of Dan and cities of the Philistines, rural and urban, nature and culture.

Timnah is the name of two cities, one in the Shephelah (Josh 15:10; 19:43; Judg 14:1–2, 5; 2 Chr 28:18) and the other in southern Judah (Gen 38:12–14; Josh 15:57). Founded about 1700 B.C.E., Samson's Timnah is located at Tell el-Batashi five and a half miles (8.9 km) west northwest of Beth-shemesh (compare Gaß, *Ortsnamen*, 369–72), but was originally assigned to Dan (Josh 19:43). It was alternately controlled by the Philistines and Israel. W. R. Kotter (*ABD*, 6:556–57) tentatively differentiates three towns called Timnah, isolating the town of Gen 38. Though Timnah was claimed as a city of Dan, all appearances indicate that the Philistines controlled and occupied it at this time.

Samson does not approach a Philistine city on military business, however. He has his eyes set on the Philistine girls, and he finds one. Crenshaw remarks, "The story illustrates the danger inherent in a relationship with a foreign woman whose chief asset is ravishing beauty" (*Samson*, 77). And Schneider chides, "The very thing which Samson pursued was what the deity had explicitly forbidden the Israelites throughout the text, intermarriage" (205).

We begin to sense something of Samson's character here, as he marches back home and insists that his father go through the normal Near Eastern procedures and obtain this woman as his wife. Samson's dispute with his parents represents two views of marriage in that culture. The parents' view, endogamy, forces a person to marry within his own clan or tribe or other group related by blood. Abraham has already modeled this view in sending a servant to his people to find a wife for Isaac. The dispute at Baal-Peor fights for this view (Num 25) as do Ezra and Nehemiah. But Moses, Ruth, and David point in the opposite direction, to exogamy, marriage outside blood ties. Crenshaw notes, "Opposition to intermarriage with foreigners arose from a valid intuition, the desire to assure integrity of worship" (*Samson*, 80). But "foreign women had the distinct advantage of the 'unknown' and the lure of the 'uninhibited'" (81). In the Samson narrative, Niditch observes, "exogamy leads not to peace with one's enemies but to a heightening of confrontation and destruction. No reconciliation is to be established between these enemies" (*CBQ* 52 [1990] 619).

Block summarizes Samson's misbehavior: "Samson is insensitive and disrespectful toward his parents and their grief over the matter and totally calloused toward the theological implications of his demand, let alone the implications for his mission" (426). Moreover, Younger says, "Samson is a man dominated by his senses, not logic. . . . These carnal proclivities overwhelm his perception of matters that any thinking man would know better" (300). Niditch would tone this down a bit to say, he "serves a larger divine purpose, to make war against the Philistines, Israel's political oppressors and cultural competitors. As in the tale of Samson's conception in ch. 13, a certain mystery surrounds the hero, an aura of the divinely sent and humanly uncontrollable" (155).

Normally, we would expect the parents to take a much more active role in the selection of a bride. Apparently, Samson's parents expected to have a larger role, too. Certainly, Samson's choice did not meet their major criterion. Where was a good Israelite girl for Samson? Biblical law forbade marriages to members of another nation (Exod 34:16; Deut 7:1–3), but this does not seem to be the major concern of Samson's parents. They are concerned that he has located his bride among those cultural barbarians, the Philistines, who are not even sophisticated enough to circumcise their sons. (See Block's discussion, 425, and nn. 308–9, concluding: "Because the Philistines did not adhere to this practice, culturally they were considered at the bottom rung.")

Samson allows no excuses. "She is the right one in my eyes," he insists, introducing the refrain that will highlight the last section of the book of Judges (17:6; 21:25). This give-me-what-I-want attitude seems to indicate that, in Block's words,

> left to himself, Samson would never have become involved in God's or even Israel's agenda; and left to themselves, the Israelites would have been satisfied to continue to coexist with the Philistines, but Yahweh has other plans. He must preserve his people as a separate entity. Therefore, through his Spirit, God intervenes in Samson's life so that the agenda set for him in 13:5–7 may begin to be fulfilled. (424)

Thus in Judg 14:4 the narrator tosses in an editorial aside to let the audience in on a secret the characters do not know: "His father and his mother did not know that this was from Yahweh, for he was seeking an occasion against the Philistines." Here Wong points out that "the parents' perspective would have constituted the normal and expected viewpoint" (*Compositional Strategy*, 100). But, instead, we find the unexpected intrusion of deity. Brettler (50–51) seeks to tie this to the wisdom tradition and place wisdom tradents behind chaps. 14–15, but this along with the appearance of riddles in a folklore narrative is weak evidence on which to build such a broad theory.

Understanding God in the Samson narrative requires theological freedom. We are challenged to confidently agree with Olson: "Remarkably, God steers Samson to disobey God's own covenant prohibitions against intermarriage in order to help Israel act against the Philistine oppressors. Yet we remain shy in exercising such freedom and want to absolve God by suggesting the language does not require divine causation but only divine permission or allowance" (849). (See Wong, *Compositional Strategy*, 101–2.) But the disjunctive sentence in v 4 emphasizes that what the parents opposed was "from God." Yet, marriage to a foreigner is strongly condemned in Judg 3:6. God is not a legalist in his dealings with human beings nor in his own decisions. God retains freedom to accomplish his purposes through the people and means he chooses. Olson concurs: "God works in mysterious and seemingly contradictory ways" (850).

Block points out the ominous foreshadowing that v 4 introduces: "Judges 14:4 is not only shocking, but it is also the key to chapters 14–15. Although Yahweh is largely absent from the narrative, in one way or another his agenda is being achieved in Samson's life. At the same time, while Yahweh's agenda is being achieved, the course of Samson's life is all downhill" (422). So the editor reminds us, God was at work in all this, and in case you do not remember from 13:1, the Philistines are ruling Israel. Gideon and Abimelech have already shown that Yahweh is supposed to rule Israel and that a human ruler does not fit the bill. Surely a foreign nation is not supposed to rule Israel. So the narrator pricks our attention, making us ask, how can God be at work when Samson is so bad, and the Philistines continue to rule? Block summarizes God's action in this matter: "Yahweh is determined to shatter the status quo. Samson is his tool chosen to rile up the Philistines, and this woman offers the opportunity to make it happen. . . . If the Israelites do not have the heart to take action against the Philistines, God will cause the Philistines to take action against them" (426).

We can conclude with Greene: "The issue of the relationship between divine sovereignty, human responsibility and punishment, was either not a significant issue for the contemporary reader, or one that the narrator chose to let him ponder" (VE 21 [1991] 64). Exum and Whedbee point out that "Yhwh controls Samson's folly and ludicrous escapades. . . . This fact allows perhaps for perplexity on the part of the reader, but not ambiguity. . . . Not simply sexual desire but also the spirit of Yhwh drives Samson to his confrontations with the Philistines" ("Isaac, Samson, and Saul," 299–300). This stands opposed to Saul's fate in not fulfilling God's mission for him (1 Sam 9:16–17).

Samson had been called before birth to begin to deliver Israel from the Philistines, but, as Block observes, "through it all he seems totally oblivious to what God is trying to accomplish through him" (423). His delivery style differs radically from that of the other judges or deliverers, so God sets him up in a different situation. Rather than gathering armies to fight the Philistines, Samson gathers girlfriends who create anger and violence between Samson, the individual, and certain Philistine families and cities. "Samson kills and steals," says Olson, "out of personal revenge and hot-headed anger, violations of the commandments against killing and stealing without community sanction (Deut 5:17, 19)" (851). Wharton contends, "Yahweh is underway in the world to free his people from Philistine tyranny, though not a soul in the story knows it and his chosen instrument looks very like an oversexed buffoon" (Int 27 [1973] 58).

How much of Samson's style is God-ordained is not always easily determined. Certainly, as he begins to break his Nazirite vow, he is not following God's leadership. Rather "he is an insolent and independent young man, unafraid to venture into the pagan world of the Philistines and undaunted by potentially compromising situations" (Block, 424). Still under and through it all, God continues to provide Samson opportunities to strike blows at the Philistines. Olson avers,

> God is free to contravene the very laws God has given to Israel for the sake of God's mercy and love for the people and for the sake of the punishment of the oppressive Philistines. Although laws and ordered structures are important and helpful, the priority remains on God's will and God's compassion, which may at times override institutional policy, governmental regulation, and even divine law. (851)

Chisholm puts it gently: "This does not mean that Yahweh overrode Samson's personality or natural inclinations, but it does suggest Samson would not have pursued the Philistine girl apart from a divine nudge" ("Identity Crisis," 5, n. 17).

5–7 Samson, along with his parents, journeys down to Timnah, the home of his bride-to-be, to make wedding plans. In the grape orchard near Timnah, suddenly "a young one from the lions is roaring to meet him" (Judg 14:5). Thus the Spirit-empowered Samson first encounters among the Philistines a wild lion rather than a Philistine army. Why is such a story told? Does it simply prepare the audience for future acts of strength, climaxing in the destruction of the Philistine temple? Is it a sly reference to his Nazirite vow? Or is M. P. O'Connor (142) correct in calling it a "shaggy dog story" created to introduce the riddle narrative that follows? Certainly, the major purpose here is to prepare for the riddle that follows, but the other two themes cannot be ignored in the complex structure of the narrative.

Quickly, Samson dispatches the lion. In so doing, he touches a dead animal and breaks his Nazirite vow. (See Stipp, *VT* 45 [1995] 337–69, for an argument that dead animals were not included in the Nazirite vow.) This unclean act required a lengthy period of cleansing and renewal (Num 6:9–12), which Samson ignores, refusing to let his parents know he was defiled. The narrator pushes mother and dad aside to concentrate on Samson and his woman. As Wharton points out, "Virtually the only role played by the parents in 14:5ff is to stress the fact that Samson alone knows the secret of the riddles" (*Int* 27 [1973] 55).

Samson communicates with his woman, and she continues to be right in his eyes, if not in anyone else's. Thus the lion episode has no sense of narrative tension. It is not cast in narrative form so much as in anecdotal form to characterize Samson's physical ability, to hint at his decision to ignore the responsibilities that accompany his Nazirite vow, and to confirm his decision about the woman despite others' opinions.

8 Days later, Samson again goes to Timnah to complete the wedding plans and claim his bride. He decides to turn from the road to see the lion's dead carcass. Now he is intentionally coming in contact with death, a clear volitional violation of his Nazirite vow (compare Num 6:6). Emmrich believes that Samson's status as a life-long Nazirite rather than one consecrated for a definite, limited period means that "ceremonial defilement, therefore, did not effect the termination of his unique status. . . . There is no indication that the meticulous rituals prescribed for the violation of the Nazirite vow . . . are of any concern to either God or Samson" (*JETS* 44 [2001] 71–72).

The corpse is no longer moist and attractive to flies and worms. Rather, the lion's body has dried out to the extent that a community of bees has set up a hive there and produced honey. Niditch sees the honey as "a symbol of fertility in many cultures and an appropriate food eaten on the way to form marriage relations" (156).

The Hebrew word עֵדָה, translated here as "swarm," normally refers to Israel as the community of God. Here the author pictures the bees as forming community when Israel has been unable to do so. Israel is represented by a vow-breaking lone ranger whose only sense of community lies in his fraternizing with the enemy's daughters and prostitutes. The bees have formed the community, but neither Samson nor Israel can. (Compare Block, 429.) Emmrich recognizes that "the lion's cadaver was an unlikely host for a 'community' of bees. But so was Canaan for Israel" because, as a cadaver, the land of Canaan was an unclean zone that could become habitable only through the death of God's enemies (*JETS* 44 [2001] 69–70).

9 Returning home, Samson becomes even more disruptive in his own family. Not only will he not accede to his parents' wedding wishes. Not only does he hide from them the breaking of his Nazirite vow. Now he deliberately leads them to break their own commitments to Israel's covenant laws by eating something that has come in contact with a dead animal (compare Lev 11:24–25, 39). Samson has leadership ability, but it is directed for the wrong purposes and blinded by pure self-interest.

10 Oblivious of his defilement, the father goes back to Timnah to complete wedding plans. The wedding may have been what is called a ṣādîqâ marriage in which the wife remains in her father's home while the husband lives there with his wife or simply makes occasional visits (Crenshaw, *Samson,* 82), but Matthews argues vehemently against this: it is "totally out of character for this lusty hero" (151). But what in the Samson narrative is not ironically out of character? Samson apparently accompanies his father to host a special feast traditionally associated with weddings (compare Gen 22:22; John 2:1–11). Wine and possibly other strong drink would be an essential element of the feast, so apparently Samson breaks this part of his Nazirite vow also.

11 The Philistines also maintain time-honored customs. A groom could not be alone during wedding preparations. He needed male companions, lots of them. So the Philistines kindly bestow thirty Philistine companions on Samson. Admittedly, the role of these companions remains unexplained. Are they more than companions to share the pre-wedding festivities? Niditch (156) sees the goal of the companions as forming a new sense of community and union. Block (432) may well have touched the right note in defining the action of providing such companions for Samson as "a potentially hostile act," their role being to serve as bodyguards who protect the Philistines from Samson rather than Samson from the Philistines. Their mention here is a foreshadowing of things to come.

12–15 Samson entertains the wedding crowd with a riddle and challenges them to solve it within the seven days of the wedding festivities. Niditch concludes:

> The riddle, cloaked in mystery and requiring interpretation, appropriately accompanies the wedding situation in which groups come together who are suspicious of one another, in which husband and wife are barely acquainted, and in which a major rite of passage is about to take place. The exogamous match between Samson and the Timnite is fraught with distrust, while the theme of secrecy runs throughout the tales of Samson. (157)

Earlier Niditch had written, "The battle of wits of the riddling context is a safe acting-out of animosities. . . . Here, however, . . . its outcome instead serves to pull the two groups apart, tensions becoming overt with destruction, departure, and dissolution" (*CBQ* 52 [1990] 618).

Yadin argues that no riddle competition is involved here, for the contest would be "patently unfair," the Philistines having no way to know the answer. He argues that the Hebrew term does not mean "riddle" here or in its other occurrences (Num 12:8; 1 Kgs 10:1–2; 2 Chr 3:1–3; Pss 44:4; 78:2; Prov 1:6; Ezek 17:2; Dan 8:23; Hab 2:6). Similarly, the common verb *nāgad* in the *hip̄ʿil* (הִגִּיד) means "to tell," not "to solve a riddle" (*VT* 52 [2002] 407–27).

The Philistine response does not mention Samson's miracles but is only a general statement about lions and honey. Thus the Philistines' saying has no reference to vv 5–9. The contest, then, is to see who can tell an enigmatic saying corresponding to the one first given. One understands this, according to Yadin, only by finding the context in Philistine weddings and ultimately in their Greek background. The bridegrooms' custom in v 10 has to be noted because it comes from Philistine, not Israelite, culture. The journey to the bride's house, the banquet there, and the bridal chamber consummation before one is truly married all come from

Greek practice, according to Yadin. Samson storms away without consummating the marriage so that she technically never becomes his wife, even though v 16 can in colloquial fashion refer to her as such. The companion who ultimately takes Samson's bride would have been a counterpart to the Greek doorkeeper at the bridal chamber. Greek contests to add a line to someone else's poem or "erotic saying" often in a wedding context give the parallel to Samson's "riddle." Greek parallels also refer to bees living in a carcass, as Maralith in his several articles has shown. The Philistines' answer thus takes up a familiar fable of bees and lions and transforms it into an erotic saying about sexual desire (Yadin, 416–22).

Yadin's explanation requires a long history of Philistines maintaining Greek customs, certainly an unproven assumption. It also removes the obvious connection between 14:5–9 and the wedding narrative. And it sees a redactor understanding Samson's saying as a riddle, thus interpreting Hebrew חִידָה as "riddle." All this then justifies removing the parents from the story. The much simpler explanation of the unity of chap. 14 and the contest as the solving of a riddle rather than the capping of an enigmatic saying is to be preferred to the complex history of custom, linguistic development, and text that Yadin proposes.

The riddle may not have been original with Samson, but its answers were. Originally, Samson's riddle could point to vomit as the result of eating. Another solution would be love or even the sexual act. The Philistine companions accept the challenge of the riddle. Crenshaw (*Samson*, 98–120) provides an extensive discussion of the nature and function of riddles. (Compare E. Slotkin, "Response to Professors Fontaine and Camp," 153–59.) Riddles depend on the innate ambiguity of language, employ double entendre, set a trap for those expected to solve them, and most frequently deal with sex or religion. Bartusch notes,

> If Samson's intention is purposely to deceive, contrary to what we may suppose, he is not automatically diminished in honor. While lying and deception strike the modern interpreter as always morally objectionable, they are dishonorable actions in the (ancient) Mediterranean culture only among one's kin group. It is acceptable, however, to lie for the purpose of deceiving an outsider who, it is held, has no right to the truth. (*Understanding Dan*, 147)

As Niditch summarizes (*CBQ* 52 [1990] 621), "The message is clear—the only way to relate to 'them' is through deception; truth and honesty bring defeat."

Samson's riddle involves a wager: thirty sets of men's clothing. The high stakes can be seen in that, according to Greene, "an individual would probably have only had one such set of clothing" (*VE* 21 [1991] 65). Samson may have quoted a familiar riddle and applied it to his own special circumstances, or he may have invented the riddle from those circumstances. (See Block, 432–33, for discussion of the possible original meaning of the riddle.) Whatever its source, the riddle proves impossible for the wedding companions to solve. Not wanting to be embarrassed or to pay the loser's debt, the companions seek help elsewhere. One person obviously stands closest to Samson and is most able to obtain the answer to the riddle. That is his wife. The men do not just suggest that the unnamed woman help them. They threaten her and her family's life and accuse her of being an accomplice to Samson's robbery of their possessions.

The temporal progression of the text in vv 14–18 has provided interpreters difficulty since the earliest days. See *Notes* 14:15.a, 14:17.a, and 14:18.a above. Bartusch decides that "it may not be required that the temporal/chronological notices fit perfectly (a preoccupation of a later age of interpreters?). Rather, what seems to be more important is the repetition of seven/seventh in the story (vv. 12, 15, 17 [twice], 18)" (*Understanding Dan*, 145). Crenshaw (*Samson*, 161, n. 3) says no satisfactory solution has been found. The main intention is to create suspense and hold the answer until the very last second so that the Philistine men appear to have failed to meet Samson's challenge and to have experienced dishonor. (See Bartusch, *Understanding Dan*, 148.)

16–18   So the girl turns to Samson with her feminine charms and cajolery. You can hear her now: "You just hate me! You don't love me! You posed the riddle to the sons of my people, but you didn't explain it to me!" (Judg 14:16). Schneider reminds us that "it is not clear at what point in the arrangements the woman officially became a wife" (209), though she is called his wife in v 16.

Samson has a ready answer: "I have not explained it to my father or my mother, but to you I should explain it?" (Judg 14:16). Still, constant nagging for "the seven days they had for the banquet" wins the day. At the last possible moment he explains the riddle to her. Why? Because she "pressured him," or more literally, she "oppressed him" or "squeezed him" or "harassed him." (Compare the same verb in 16:16.) As Mobley explains, "Samson's essential nature is to roam, and he cannot stand to be constricted. When bound (אסר) by ropes of men . . . or squeezed (צוק) by women's words, Samson explodes: he bursts bonds; he blurts secrets" (*Empty Men*, 189).

Of course, she immediately relays the solution to the wedding companions, her fellow countrymen. So just before the day ends at sunset, they answer the riddle for Samson, using interrogatives rather than the normal declarative answer. Crenshaw points out that "by stating their answer in interrogative form, the Philistines imply that any fool would have been able to solve Samson's riddle" (*Samson*, 113).

In fact, the riddle is open to several interpretations besides the reference to Samson's personal experiences. The companions ask Samson, "What is sweeter than honey, and what is stronger than a lion?" (Judg 14:18). This interrogative answer based on Samson's experience with the bees and lion leaves itself open to another answer: Love is sweeter than honey, and Samson is stronger than the lion. Thus, according to Block, "from the narrator's perspective, despite Samson's great physical strength and the force of his Nazirite vow, he is completely helpless when confronted with the love of women. From Yahweh's perspective the amorous desires of this man provide the occasions for the beginning of conflicts between Samson and the Philistines" (435). Mobley (*Empty Men*, 190) gives this a slightly different twist: "What proves stronger than the lion slayer Samson? What proves more irresistible to Samson than his wild honey, his natural foods regimen?"

Samson retorts with a traditional proverb with many applications. In it he "blamed the companions rather than the woman" (Schneider, 211): "If you had not plowed with my young cow, you would not have found out the riddle" (Judg 14:18). Marvin Sweeney ("Metaphor and Rhetorical Strategy in Zephaniah," in *Relating to the Text: Interdisciplinary and Form-Critical Insights on the Bible*, JSOTSup 384 [London: Clark International, 2003] 120–30) shows that the verb *hāraš* (הרש) has sexual connotations here. As Bartusch sees it, "the young men's violation of the sexual purity of Samson's wife is implied in Samson's saying." The young woman "brings shame to herself and dishonor to her husband. She acts inappropriately, and so violates her loyalty to her new family" (*Understanding Dan*, 149–50).

The riddle and the response it evokes thus communicate at different levels. At the strictly physical, experiential level, the riddle describes Samson's experience of eating sweet honey from the lion's carcass. On the emotional level, it shows Samson's attraction to women to be stronger than his physical strength, by which he performs seemingly impossible feats. On the more spiritual level, it shows the lack of commitment and faithfulness between Samson and his "lover."

Marriage festival becomes marriage failure. Bonds of trust and allegiance are obviously broken. The "right one in my eyes" becomes "my young cow" with whom Samson's companions have been plowing. Whatever love was there has vanished, ruined by greed, self-interest, and an amusing but catastrophic word game played prior to the wedding. Crenshaw concludes, "Samson's defeat comes because his wife performed the task of an animal. Later, Samson will himself carry out the work of oxen" (*Samson*, 119).

19 Finally, we find a battle report in the Samson narratives. God's Spirit takes control of an enraged man and sends him off to Ashkelon, another Philistine city. Samson is widening his territory among his Philistine opponents. For once he is not consorting with the enemy, especially enemy girls. Rather, he finds thirty Philistine men and kills them. Why? Because he is trying to deliver Israel from the hand of the Philistines? Afraid not! No, Samson, the sore loser, betrayed by his wife-to-be, kills thirty Philistines to pay off a bet. He does not want their lives so much as their clothes. Samson kills innocents to pay off the guilty. However, Chisholm points out, "Samson's very human, selfish response to Philistine trickery becomes a weapon of war in Yahweh's hand" ("Identity Crisis," 6).

In a burning rage Samson returns to his father's house, still not having a home of his own or a family of his own or an army to lead to battle. As Younger concludes, "This is murder and larceny. The motive is not to deliver Israel from the Philistines or even to bring judgment on them. It only serves his purposes. But even this does not placate his rage" (304). Yet, as Bartusch notes, in this social context the act is perceived as a necessary recovery of honor for a dishonored family (*Understanding Dan*, 150); it "shows Samson to be, to the end, an (ironically) honorable man, who honors his word and abides by his promises" (151).

20 The narrator's editorial note rounds off this narrative denouement with a surprise conclusion to Samson's marriage: his wife has been given to one of Samson's "wedding companions," which sets up the following narrative. Apparently, the narrator has just let the reader in on a piece of information hidden from Samson, namely, that his wife now belongs to his wedding companion.

In this narrative we have seen Samson's braggadocio character, his determination to do what is right in his own eyes, his self-centered actions that ignore his vows to God and bring guilt on his parents, and most of all his gullibility in dealing with women. The man God groomed before he was born to be a moral example and a military deliverer has fallen into an immoral, self-centered life with no thought for his own family's wishes, much less for the nation's need for deliverance.

15:1–3 At this point the narrative is unclear with regard to Samson's marriage, his chosen woman's relationship with the "best man," and the actions of the woman's father and the companions. See Schneider (212), who asserts that "in the eyes of the Israelites they were either never married or the woman was now an adulteress"

(213). With all his faults, Samson is tenacious, pugnacious, and persistent. He joins the Judges goat parade (compare Gideon in 6:19 and Manoah in 13:15, 19) and sets off to see his wife in Timnah, where by this time he has certainly become persona non grata. The goat kid he takes may have represented either "a mollifying gift or . . . the kind of gift expected in a marriage where the bride continued to live with her father" (Greene, VE 21 [1991] 66).

Samson barges in headlong, but the girl's father stands firmly in his way. What a self-defense testimony and proposition the father offers: "I told myself that you so totally hated her, and so I gave her to your companion. Isn't her younger sister better looking? You may have her instead" (Judg 15:2). Temperamental Samson will have none of that. Younger and prettier are not necessarily better. He has seen what was right in his eyes, and he wants it with no substitutes allowed. He leaves the father with one parting shot: "This time I cannot be blamed by the Philistines while I am creating havoc with them" (Judg 15:3).

4–5 And what havoc Samson creates. He catches "three hundred foxes," to use the traditional translation, though recent study shows that the animals were probably jackals rather than foxes. (See HALOT, שׁוּעָל; Neh 4:3 [Heb. 3:35]; Ps 63:10 [Heb. 11]; Cant 2:15; Lam 5:18; Ezek 13:4.) He sends the foxes through the ready-to-harvest crops, having tied the bushy tails of each pair of foxes together and implanted a flaming torch in each knot. Unharvested grain, harvested grain, even vineyards and olive groves fall victim to torch-bearing foxes in clear violation of Israelite law (Exod 22:6). The damage to grain, grapes, and olives rivals that which the Midianites wreaked on Israel in Gideon's time. As Matthews points out, "These three products are the economic and dietary staples of ancient Palestine" (151).

Obviously, in the oral telling of such a foxy story, the narrator expects the audience to laugh. This is only one indication of the humor drilled into the Samson stories. (See Crenshaw, *Samson,* 57.) The number three hundred may likewise represent one of several examples of hyperbole or exaggeration for the sake of humor (Crenshaw, *Samson,* 57).

But is this the way to deliver Israel from the hand of the Philistines, by outfoxing them and destroying their crops rather than their armies? It is Samson's way, the way of revenge. He does not honor Moses' words and leave revenge to Yahweh (Deut 32:35). Block evaluates Samson's character and behavior in light of this episode: "Samson's actions are all guerrilla tactics. All his achievements are personal, and all are provoked by his own [mis]behavior. Unlike the other deliverers, he never seeks to rid Israel of foreign oppressors, and he never calls out the Israelite troops. Samson is a man with a higher calling than any other deliverer in the book, but he spends his whole life 'doing his own thing'" (441).

6 As the men of Ophrah did in Judg 6:29, so the Philistines, not just the men of Timnah, set up court and conduct an investigation. They conclude that Samson is guilty but admit that his actions were justified. Thus, as Samson had announced earlier, he "cannot be blamed" (see Judg 15:3). The father-in-law is the one indicted for having given Samson's wife to another man. "So the Philistines went up and burned her and her father in the fire" (Judg 15:6). Ironically, as Block points out, "the woman draws the solution to the riddle out of Samson to prevent her and her family being burned, but in the end she succumbs to the very catastrophe she tried to avoid precisely because she got the answer from him" (433). (Compare Judg 14:15.) Again Samson's self-centered efforts do away with another Philistine family, this time by the hands of the Philistines themselves. What a way to begin to deliver Israel from the hand of the Philistines!

7–8 Block tell us, "The Philistines underestimated Samson's commitment to his wife, his preparedness to retaliate, and his physical strength" (442). Samson destroys the Philistine crops and fields and then sees the death sentence executed on the woman who betrayed him and her father who took his wife from him. Everything seems to be playing right into Samson's hands, giving him precisely what he wants. And how does he react? He swears an oath of revenge: "If you are going to act like this, then I will get my revenge on you, and only then will I stop" (Judg 15:7). Crenshaw includes this among the monologues in the Samson narrative. These occur "only in those places where someone expresses an intention that is later frustrated" (*Samson*, 58). (Compare Judg 15:1; 16:20.)

G. Mendenhall ("The 'Vengeance' of Yahweh," in *The Tenth Generation: The Origins of the Biblical Tradition* [Baltimore: Johns Hopkins UP, 1973] 69–104) sought to show that *nāqam* (נָקָם) refers to one's legal exercise of force to restore society's normal legal institutions. H. G. L. Peels echoes this understanding: "In the OT, however, the concept of 'vengeance' has a positive connotation, both from a semantic as well as from a theological point of view: 'vengeance' has to do with lawfulness, justice, and salvation. . . . Even Samson's 'revenge,' better 'vindication' (Judg 15:7; 16:28), is in accordance with the redemptive struggle against the enemy (Judg 14:4)" (*NIDOTTE*, 3:154, 156).

"He struck them on thigh and groin—a horrendous attack" (Judg 15:8). Block presumes this to be "a wrestling idiom for total victory" (442). Again we see Samson's singleness of purpose. He knows what is right in his own eyes (Judg 14:3) and wants that and nothing else. Escaping sentencing for his crimes is not enough. Samson sees his betrayer/wife suffer for his crimes and hers. Samson sees the man who gave his wife to another man suffer for his own crimes as well as Samson's. What he sees is not enough. Only one thing is right in Samson's eyes, and he has lost all possibility of attaining that. Samson remains focused on the harm that loss has done to him.

This time, however, Samson is wise enough not to return to his father's house. He hides in the caves of Etam, much as the Israelites had done in Gideon's time. Rainey (*Sacred Bridge*, 141) calls the location of Etam "something of a mystery." Gaß (*Ortsnamen*, 373) seeks Etam in the northern Shephelah and locates it at ʿIraq Ismaʿin. Ehrlich (*ABD*, 2:644) also places this rock or cave of Etam at ʿAraq Ismaʿin on the northern slope of the Sorek Valley near Zorah.

This sets the stage for the following narrative.

9–10 V 9 serves as the normal introduction for a battle report. The Philistine enemy stages forces for battle and conducts an opening raid to start the war. This time the scene is not in the territory of the Philistines nor in that of Samson's tribe of Dan. The army is ready for battle in the south with the tribe of Judah in Lehi. Gaß (*Ortsnamen*, 377–80) provides five possible locations for Lehi but is indecisive about making a final judgment. Rainey (*Sacred Bridge*, 141) decides that none of the suggestions carries conviction. M. Lubetski (*ABD*, 4:274–75) uses Akkadian evidence to see a deployment of forces along the borderline rather than a concentration at one locality, a theory Gaß also sees as a possibility.

After having taken a leading role in chap. 1, the people of Judah have disappeared from the Judges scene except for a cameo appearance in 10:9 as the Ammonites attack them. There the story shifted to Jephthah, a leader from Gilead, not to a hero from Judah. Block argues that "Samson's flight to Judah has escalated his personal feud with the Philistines into an international crisis—which is precisely what God wants" (443).

The men of Judah are not prepared to fight. They are not seeking an opportunity to begin to gain deliverance from the Philistines. The experience reveals much about the Israelite tribes, supposedly led by Judah (chap. 1). Block concludes,

> The Judahites would rather deliver their countrymen into the hands of the enemy and live under that enemy's domination than fulfill the mandate Yahweh had given them to occupy the land and drive out the enemy. . . . The Judahites are willing not only to substitute the rule of the Philistines for the rule of Yahweh, but also to sacrifice the divinely appointed leader to preserve the status quo. (444)

Yet Block gives a one-sided perspective on Judah and the tribes. Samson, not Judah, has the calling to deliver. The men of Judah would rather negotiate than fight, again taking up the negotiation theme from Gideon and Jephthah. Negotiations prove that the problem lies not with Judah but with Samson. Samson may be God's instrument to begin to deliver Israel from the Philistines, but, for Judah, Samson is just a hot-headed strong boy who has no leadership claims on them. Just as when Rehoboam started to attack the Israelites under Jeroboam and determined God did not want them to fight (1 Kgs 12:21–24), so here Judah determines not to fight against another Israelite or against the Philistines with whom Samson consorts. Judah has not heard a call that Judah shall go first, as at the opening (Judg 1:1–3) and in the ending (Judg 20:18) of the book. Unlike Samson and Gideon and Jephthah and Abimelech, the men of Judah know when to fight and when to withdraw.

11–13 So an astounding action ensues. An army of three thousand men of Judah march out to capture the one man, Samson. Again battle is not the aim. Judah wants to negotiate Samson's surrender to keep the peace with the Philistines. Status quo, not the beginning of the deliverance, is the desired result.

Samson remains consistent. He sees no reason for the Philistines to blame him for his actions. He has just practiced eye-for-an-eye retaliation. In fact, retaliation is the motive of all parties involved. As Younger (307) says, "For the Philistines, the Judahites, and Samson, the only thing that matters is reprisal and counter reprisal." The three thousand Judeans play no games. They bluntly inform Samson their one object is to arrest him and turn him over to the Philistines. So, grossly outnumbered, Samson puts forth only one deal-breaking point. The men of Judah must agree not to kill Samson, only to tie him up with new ropes and hand him over to the enemy. So Samson's first experience in pitched battle results in his own people taking him as a prisoner of war and handing him over to the enemy. Is this the way you begin to deliver Israel from the Philistines?

14–17 The scene shifts to the Philistine camp at Lehi (15:9, 14). Philistine forces pour forth to meet him, raising the cry of victory at the sight of a hand-cuffed Samson. Again, God's Spirit takes control of Samson, giving him that special gift of superhuman strength to meet the enemy. The ropes and bindings fall from his arms and wrists. Finally, Samson stands on a battlefield ready to fight the Philistine enemy. The battlefield is not auspicious for him, being in the center of the enemy camp. And he stands unarmed against the entire Philistine army with its technologically advanced weapons.

Carefully but quickly the narrator describes the scene of action: "He found the jawbone of a recently deceased donkey. He reached out with his hand and took it and struck a thousand men dead with it" (Judg 15:15). Mobley evaluates this description of Samson's actions: "Fierce as a lion, as socially marginal as a jackal, this animalistic portrait of Samson in Judges 14–15 is capped off when he happens upon and wields the most improbable of weapons, the jawbone of an ass" (*Empty Men*, 172).

Then Samson stands over the heaps of a thousand dead bodies and celebrates the victory with his own version of a victory hymn. In contrast to the Song of Deborah (chap. 5) or Miriam's Song (Exod 15:21), this one does not mention God. Maintaining his consistent attitude, he measures everything by himself and what he has achieved, as Crenshaw observes: "Samson's [song] breathes the spirit of braggadocio" (*Samson*, 36). In contrast, the Philistines' victory celebration in 16:23–24 ostensibly praises their god Dagon. Still, its eight references to first-person plural also point to self-interest. Having finished the task, Samson provides an etiological ending for the story by throwing away the jawbone, *leḥi* (לְחִי), and naming the place Ramath-Lehi, or Jawbone Heights.

At least he is taking the first steps toward beginning to deliver Israel from the hands of the Philistines. A thousand enemy soldiers is not a bad beginning. But again the deed is done through contact with a dead animal, emphatically described as recently deceased, and thus a renewed violation of the Nazirite oath. Here is individualistic leadership in Israel ignoring promises to God and giving all the credit for victory to self, a temptation Gideon, Abimelech, and Jephthah all faced unsuccessfully. Such leadership should not be surprised when every citizen of the nation does what is right in his or her own eyes.

18–19 Samson does not take the opportunity of the victory song of v 16 to pray to or even mention God. But then having exerted the effort to kill one thousand men, he realizes he is thirsty, thirsty enough to face death. And for the first time in the entire narrative complex of chaps. 13–15 Samson is prompted to mention God or speak to him. True to character, he does not address God in a time of national crisis, seeking help in delivering Israel from the hand of the Philistines. Rather, he seeks God in a moment of personal anguish when he wants something to drink. Seeing himself at death's door, Samson now gives God credit for the victory and asks if the only thanks he gets for his part is being killed by thirst and left in the hands of the uncircumcised Philistines. As much consorting as he has done with the Philistine enemies and their women, it seems strange for him suddenly to label them as uncultured and despised. It appears equally strange for him to identify himself as God's servant. As Crenshaw points out, "Nothing in the saga prepares the way for or justifies in the slightest this self-designation" (*Samson*, 31). Chisholm ("Identity Crisis," 6) sees this simply as a reflection of Samson's awareness of his Nazirite status.

It appears to Block that "his prayer is as narcissistic as his manner of life. Far from displaying any concern about the fate of his people or the work that is yet to be done, let alone concern for the glory of God, his intention in this prayer is purely personal: to avert his own death and to avoid capture by the Philistines" (447).

But is this prayer really a sign of lack of faith as Wong (*Compositional Strategy*, 163–65) argues? Or is Olson correct to say that it is a sign that "Samson stays connected to God" (853)? May Samson here be presented, as Greene suggests, "as a new Israel, faithful precisely where they [the wilderness generation] were not" (*VE* 21 [1991] 69)? Or is this an example of the desperation of lamentation? Laments do not attempt to exemplify great theology. They seek to find God's deliverance from a situation viewed as life-threatening. Connected to God or not, in dark crises people turn to God in lament and petition. However one answers these questions, Chisholm correctly notes that "great deliverance" (Judg 15:18) here "need not carry the connotation 'national deliverance'" ("Identity Crisis," 6). Still, the commentator dare not rush to paint Samson with totally evil colors. Samson has enough problems without Bible students giving him those he may not deserve. In the moment of tragedy, he knows to whom to turn for help. At least a bit of faith in and respect for God lies buried in his troubled breast.

No matter Samson's motivation or spiritual life, God takes care of this one through whom he plans to begin to deliver Israel from the hand of the Philistines. God miraculously provides water, so Samson "drank, his spirit returned, and life was renewed" (Judg 15:19). Younger points to the parallels with Israel in the wilderness, where God also provided water to a mumbling, grumbling people (Exod 17:1–7; Num 20:2–13): "Just as Israel's attitude was wrong in those contexts . . . so Samson's is wrong here. In spite of this, God provides in each instance" (309).

The narrator rounds the story off with another etiological note. Samson names the place En-hakkore, that is, "the spring, or fountain, of the one who calls," thus naming it obliquely for himself, he being the one who called on God at that place. The name, says Block, "memorializes the power of this man to manipulate and move the hand of God rather than the gracious action of God on his behalf" (447). Gaß (*Ortsnamen*, 380–82) mentions four possible locations for En-hakkore, but then points to the etiological form of the narrative and sees only a wordplay without an actual location. Lubetski (*ABD*, 2:503) agrees, citing evidence from the early translations. Crenshaw (*Samson*, 36) may be correct in seeing here an older name meaning "partridge spring." He is not so easily followed as he argues (41) for the etiology to be a late addition to the Samson narrative because the judging summary "legitimates an aetiolgy."

Greene gives a threefold impact of this incident, which "reestablishes Samson's typological identification with Israel, . . . shifts the focus off Samson's deeds and onto God's, [and] . . . shifts the focus away from Samson's conflict with the Philistines and onto his one-to-one relationship with God" (*VE* 21 [1991] 69).

20 Finally, the narrator supplies the reader with the information that Samson judged Israel for twenty years. As Schneider points out, "None of the other judges judged at a time when a foreign enemy was in control" (217). Commentators have debated the structural role of this editorial notation in relationship to a similar notation at the end of the next chapter. The notation appears to end a larger narrative segment, not prepare for a final chapter. Thus R. G. Boling finds, "The concluding formula in 16:31 ('He had judged . . .'), repeated from 15:20 but in perfect tense and disjunctive syntax, strongly suggests a second compiler. Chaps. 14 and 15 answer the question: Whatever became of 'Little Sun,' prodigal son of Manoah? He judged Israel. Chap. 16 answers the question: What became of Judge Samson?" (*ABD*, 3:1112). The first section marks Samson's rise, and the second, his fall.

Mobley follows Greenstein (*Proof* 1 [1981] 238) in seeing Judg 15:20 as representing narrative noise that "cannot be incorporated into any interpretative pattern." For Mobley it is "evidence of the friction between strata in a text" (*Empty Men*, 184). Chisholm ("What's Wrong with This Picture?") shows that the two notations (15:20 and 16:31b) end up as bookends for the story of Samson's descent into death. If then, Chisholm remarks, the placement of the truncated concluding formula in 15:20 is a rhetorical device, this means that it should not be utilized to construct theories of the text's composition and literary evolution as many have done.

This editorial summary in 15:20 is interesting, for it talks about judging a nation that still appears to be ruled by the Philistines. The narrator does not claim that Israel had rest. Samson has really only begun the process of deliverance. He may judge, but he has not fully delivered. Samson's ability to judge a people he never incorporates into his own plans and actions reveals something special about the God who called Samson to action. Block concludes: "God continues his work. The tools available to him may be crude and imperfect, but he will deliver his people. . . . Samson deserves no consideration from God. Yet Yahweh hears and delivers time and time again. His agenda for his people cannot fail, despite the people's seeming determination to commit national suicide" (448).

Or as Greene phrases it a bit optimistically, "The recording of Samson's elevation to judgeship at this point suggests that it had at least as much to do with the faith and dependence on God which he had demonstrated as with his great feats of strength" (*VE* 21 [1991] 69). At least, the narrator wants to see Samson as more complex an individual than commentators often paint him. His weaknesses are all too obvious, but he also had a sense of need for God's help, knew the source of his strength lay in his Nazirite vow, and called on God for help in his most threatening moments.

16:1–3 Chap. 16 begins with a brief story that serves as a prelude for the extended narrative that follows, ending in Samson's death, already implied in Judg 15:20. As Schneider observes, it "sets up Samson's personality in such a way that the following events are not out of character for Samson" (218). Mobley calls this a comic interlude which "emphasizes Samson's larger-than-life strength and potency" and compares it to Ehud's entering an enemy city, wreaking havoc, and escaping unharmed, with the difference that Ehud's escapade is by design and Samson's by impulse (*Empty Men,* 190).

Chisholm ("What's Wrong with This Picture?) notes that Samson's visit to the prostitute casts him in the role of a fool destined for destruction. Wisdom literature teaches that prostitutes reside in the gateway to death (Prov 6:26; 7:10; 23:27). So Chisholm concludes that despite Samson's flair for words and feeble efforts to display wisdom (see Judg 14:14, 18; 15:16), the narrator depicts him as one who violates a cardinal wisdom doctrine. This does not bode well for his future.

Wharton (*Int* 27 [1973] 53–54) sums up the nature of this brief narrative:

Judges 16:1–3 appears as a kind of prototypical Samson story in the Israelite tradition. At that level there is no weight of theological affirmation that we can discern. The story affords insight into two related realities of Israelite tribal existence in the twelfth or eleventh centuries, B.C.: the problem of conflict with a superior culture in areas of contact and friction; and the way in which folk narrative reduced that problem to manageable "memory" fraught with ribald adventure and the inchoate promise contained in "remembered" triumphs. . . . The bizarre character of Samson's exploits removes the

Philistine problem from the realm of direct action to the realm of the imagination. The ribald humor provides a low-risk outlet for anger, fear, and hope among people who had little means to press their cause against the Philistines.

Samson expands his geographical range in Philistine territory, going down to Gaza, the most southern of the major Philistine cities (Josh 13:2–4; compare Josh 10:41; Judg 1:18–19 and *Notes* and *Comment* there) and of Canaanite territory (Gen 10:19). It was forty-five miles (72.4 km) from his home base. The mention of Gaza here foreshadows the location of his last stand (Judg 16:21).

Samson expands not only his territorial range, but also his range of women. Here he finds a prostitute and "enters to her," apparently an intentional use of ambivalent language that can refer to sexual relationships. Surely, this was not permitted under his Nazirite vow. As usual, Samson pays the vow no mind.

Samson's reputation has also expanded its range, for the men of Gaza know he is on the Philistines' most-wanted list. To capture public enemy number one, they set up an ambush around the harlot's abode, a rather interesting reason for an army of men to be surrounding a house of prostitution. They expect Samson to depart at daylight, and so they determine to maintain their ambush until he does. They have one aim in mind: to kill Samson.

Samson remains bedded down until half the night is gone, then rises up and leaves the city, city gate and gateposts safe in hand. He takes them to the top of a hill overlooking Hebron, a journey of forty miles (64.4 km) with a climb of over three thousand feet (914 m) (Matthews, 156), and plants them there. In the canonical context, this prepares the way for the one who will not only begin but also complete the deliverance from the Philistines, for David's first headquarters are in Hebron (2 Sam 2:1–4). Once again Samson confronts the enemy and does nothing except preserve his own life. He does nothing to help his nation gain freedom from the oppressing Philistines. Rather he shows off his own strength for purposes of his own ego. Ironically, Matthews says, "Samson returned these pilfered gates to the men of Judah, who had helped the Philistines capture him" (156).

At first read, this section seems like an interlude, unconnected with what precedes or follows. But it expands the theme of Samson's sexual habit, foreshadows Samson's final desperation (16:21), and enforces the theme of Samson as an image of the nation. As Wong notes, "A key parallel between Samson and Israel is the repeated and almost compulsive involvement of each with things foreign and forbidden" (*Compositional Strategy*, 232). Wong may go too far in claiming that "the Gaza episode actually deconstructs Samson's 'love' for Delilah" (233). Olson is closer to reality as he contrasts this section with Josh 2 and Rahab: "Samson's liaison with the prostitute signifies Israel's lusting after other gods for the sake of personal gratification and self-centered desires. The Jericho spies were doing the opposite. They risked their lives and well-being for the sake of the larger community" (855). The episode illustrates yet again Samson's ability to get the best of male opponents and his inability to deal with women.

4 We turn now from an anecdote of the miraculous to the story of an extended test of love. E. Wurtzel sees the story as "the archetypal story of cross-cultural love between members of warring nations: this is Romeo and Juliet. . . . Essentially, the story of Samson and Delilah is one of fatal love, where someone is bound to die" (*Bitch: In Praise of Difficult Women* [New York: Doubleday, 1998] 329). Mobley

(*Empty Men*, 195) sees four clues that show love is the central theme of the entire Samson narrative: the plot's central search for female companionship, the answer to the Philistines' riddle being love, the wife and Delilah both accusing him of not loving them, and the use of love to introduce the Delilah narrative. This is true if one ends the narrative with Samson's being handed over to the Philistines. But the biblical structure makes this into more than a human battle of wits and love. The biblical structure turns this into a battle of deities and a test of human love for them.

Crenshaw (*Samson*, 43–44) categorizes this narrative as a folklore motif concerning the helpless hero before a woman's wiles. This motif has four parts: a woman's feigned friendship or love, the hero's submission, flirtatious teasing and tearful imploring, and the woman's eventual victory. He points to the stories of Jael, Esther, and Judith as examples. Samson extends the motif with his teasing of Delilah.

Ackerman (*Warrior, Dancer*, 232) compares the Delilah story to that of Samson's Timnite wife, finding that the plots of the two stories are the same. (Compare Exum, *JSOT* 19 [1981] 3–29.) Mobley compares the story of Samson to the traditional stories of folklore wild men, especially to the humanization of Enkidu in the Akkadian Gilgamesh Epic and more exactly to the Mesopotamian hairy man *lahmu* and the biblical Leviathan as chaos monsters. Samson thus becomes "YHWH's chaos monster sent to destroy Philistia" (*Empty Men*, 193, 200). But Mobley (196) perceives the wild-man theme to be reversed in that the humanizing of the wild man Samson is negative, not positive.

Niditch gives a mediating voice, noting that Samson is part of culture and concluding that he

> is, indeed, a mediator between the "raw and the cooked" like the transformer heroes of so many cultures. He is a bridge between what humans have transformed, neatened, shaped, institutionalized, and socialized and what is found in nature, wild and nonsocial. He moves between both worlds, but his source of strength, his unusual and emphasized qualities are in the realm of the raw, the wild, the natural, and the nonsocial. (*CBQ* 52 [1990] 613)

The Samson story does incorporate folklore elements in its telling. Still, this does not remove it from Yahweh's history with the people of God. As Mobley admits: "There is a grave danger in this mythological comparison if it obscures the humanity of our folk hero" (204). Samson is neither part of the divine world nor a symbol of the chaotic underworld. He is pictured as a human being endowed with almost divine strength and functioning to destroy the deity's enemies. Descriptions of his actions show him as all too human as he turns civilized cities into chaotic ruins.

People of all ages have loved to tell the story, but too seldom have we really concentrated on what it tells us about Samson and his mission to maintain his Nazirite vow and his mission to begin to free Israel from the hands of the Philistines. This "episode dramatizes the tragic effects of loving a woman who does not respond in kind" (Crenshaw, *Samson*, 92) even as it shows God's continued use of his chosen warrior in the hero's darkest hour.

But how does one evaluate Delilah? The first argument considers her nationality: Israelite, Philistine, or what? The text does not say, nor does it provide a genealogy for her, thereby stressing that Delilah does not gain her identity from family, ethnicity, or relationship to a man. Instead, Delilah has her own name and, consequently, an independent identity.

Based on her good Semitic name and the location of Valley of Sorek between Israelite and Philistine territory, J. Hackett decides Delilah is not necessarily Philistine though paid by Philistine lords. Thus hers would "perhaps be a more noble story if she had been Philistine, since at least she would have been in employ of her own people. . . . The narrative paints her simply as a woman interested in making money, and whose tolerance for the violent consequences of her act was high" (*Int* 58 [2004] 359).

More on target is Bartusch, as he adds, "While popularly [Delilah] may be assumed to be Samson's wife, Delilah is, in fact, portrayed throughout the story as an outsider to Samson, and thus as someone not to be trusted with the truth and only one more stranger to be deceived. Thus, Samson's downfall is not due to her unfaithfulness or shameless behavior, but only to his telling the truth to someone who is not entitled to it" (*Understanding Dan*, 157).

Smith looks at her from the Philistine perspective and sees "an example of a woman who is patriotic and shows initiative . . . a positive model of female independence, imagination and self-sufficiency" ("Delilah: A Suitable Case," 109). In similar vein, Fewell writes: "Delilah's identity is not bound to any man. Introduced simply by name, she is a woman who takes care of herself. She conducts her love affair with Samson and her business affairs with the lords of the Philistines without any father, brother, or husband acting as mediator. . . . Delilah, a woman without father, brother, or husband to support her, secures for herself financial stability" (73–74).

Smith hurries to modify this viewpoint:

> Nevertheless, the biblical text portrays various negative aspects of Delilah's character, and one cannot, with honesty, attribute all of the negative associations Delilah has had to patriarchal and misogynistic misrepresentations of the text, arising out of world-views of the commentators. She does whine, wheedle, and pester Samson. She does take money for betraying him to the Philistines. She does use the fact that he finds her sexually alluring to her own advantage. ("Delilah: A Suitable Case," 111)

Thus Smith adroitly concludes that "the narrative portrays Delilah *and* Samson as having both negative and positive qualities" (113, emphasis original).

Looking at one of the negative sides, Ackerman finds that Delilah "is depicted in the text as very prostitute-like in her behavior. . . . This is because, like a prostitute, she uses her sexuality and a man's desire for her in order to ensure her own well-being" (*Warrior, Dancer,* 231). Schneider rightly sees that Delilah's "liminal status between wife and prostitute is similar to the raped *pilegesh* whose story follows shortly" (221).

Matthews must be heard as he affirms "it is not possible to identify her unquestionably as a Philistine. . . . It is unlikely that the biblical writer was trying to portray Delilah as a heroine. . . . There is no sense of coercion, or, for that matter, of any reluctance by Delilah to betray her lover. Nor is there any real malice on her part either. It is simply a matter of business for this very business-like woman" (159–60). Or as Niditch expresses it, "She is no would-be wife, nor necessarily a harlot, but the sort of dangerous, traitorous woman about whom proverbial wisdom warns, one who underscores the impossibility of alliances with godless foreigners" (*CBQ* 52 [1990] 620).

The Hebrew syntax uses a temporal clause to clearly show that a new narrative segment begins here (v 4). "After this" also connects two of Samson's love affairs together, one with the Gaza prostitute, the other with Delilah. This is the first time that the narrator has credited Samson with love. It is the first time the text has given one of Samson's women a name, but in so doing it does not give her a country. "The text remains," points out Olson, "intentionally ambivalent about her ethnicity so that the reader may wonder whether Samson has at last 'come home' to Israel in obedience to his parents' wishes to find a woman to love from among 'our people' (14:3)" (858).

The meaning of her name puzzles scholars. Mobley (*Empty Men*, 191) notes several possibilities for the meaning of Delilah's name. These include "Dangling Hair," Devotee of Ishtar," and "Flirtatious." "One of the night" is a popular interpretation, set in contrast to the interpretation of Samson's name as "Sun," but Mobley sees this as the linguistically least likely interpretation.

What starts out like a love story quickly takes a new twist and turn. Philistine leaders continue to seek a way to capture Samson, but they realize he is too strong for them. Their only hope lies in robbing Samson of his strength.

Mobley notes, "The Bible says nothing about Samson's size, nothing about his physical appearance with the sole exception of a single detail: Samson wore his hair, uncut since birth, in seven braids" (*Empty Men*, 171). Thus Younger (316–17) interjects a useful warning about our traditional picture of Samson.

Samson is most commonly pictured as a hulk, a mammoth of incredible size and strength. While there is obviously in the biblical text a satirical characterization of the Philistines as ignorant, culturally challenged morons, they cannot be so stupid as to not recognize the obvious. If Samson were a Goliath-type behemoth, then obviously the "secret" to his strength would be in the size of his muscles. So the Philistines would be foolish to keep trying to overcome him. The Philistine rulers would be even dumber to pay such a price for the obvious, and Delilah would be the mother of all dummies if Samson were a man with fifty-inch biceps.

But Samson must have been a relatively ordinary-looking man in size and weight. His strength is not even in his long, seven-braided hair. Therefore, his strength is not in the obvious; it is in Yahweh, who is working through his special Yahweh-called, Nazirite status.

5 "The Philistine rulers" promise Samson's lover an enormous sum of money to betray him into their hands through her enticements. The Philistine leaders are referred to in Hebrew as the סַרְנֵי פְלִשְׁתִּים, that is, "governors of the Philistines." This is the title given each of the mayors or heads of the five major Philistine city-states (Josh 13:3; Judg 3:3; 1 Sam 6:4). Each of the five offered "eleven hundred shekels of silver." Herbert Wolf (3:475) estimates the weight of eleven hundred pieces of silver (compare Judg 17:2) to be 140 pounds (63.5 kg), meaning Delilah would receive 700 pounds (317.5 kg) of silver. Block (455) points to comparisons with Gen 24:15, 19; Exod 32:32; Judg 8:26; 2 Sam 24:24; and Jer 32:9. Younger describes the offer as "an absurdly fantastic amount for this time period" and notes that it represented 550 times the average annual wage (316, with n. 75). Projecting that to the modern scene and taking $25 thousand as the average annual wage, the governors' total offer to Delilah would approach $15 million. This lets us see how valuable the capture of public enemy number one was for the Philistine governors and what an incentive Delilah had to betray her lover.

6–15 The ensuing story of testing and enticing runs through three quite parallel rounds in which Samson passes the test. Block says, "Indeed, in this section every speech is a test" (452). The Philistines test Delilah; Delilah tests Samson and his love; Yahweh tests Samson's observation of his Nazirite vow; Yahweh tests Dagon, the Philistine god; and finally Samson tests Yahweh. These must be compared with the earlier enticing tests Samson endured with his wife from Timnah. Love blinds Samson's eyes and clogs his brain long before the Philistines capture him. Lovesick Samson cannot see through the simplest schemes of betrayal. Rather, he turns them into tests of mind and will to show that he can fool his women. Block concludes, "Infatuated with her and his own extraordinary talents, he is blinded to the reality she represents. In this man we witness a classic example of 'all brawn and no brain'" (452).

Each story gets shorter, and each ends with the betraying woman accusing her man of deception and lies. The very first story exposes Samson to fresh parts of a dead animal and thus again shows he has no fear in ignoring at least part of his Nazirite vow. The third time, she extends the accusing feminine wile of "you don't love me anymore."

16–22 Finally, testing gives way to nagging. Here the Hebrew term הֵצִיקָה means, "to press hard, to oppress, harass, to drive into a corner." One may translate v 16 to say: "When she harassed him daily with her words, she had pestered him so much that he became sick to death (or so impatient he was ready to die)." The narrator gives Samson a "figurative image that will soon become a literal fact" (Olson, 858). In such an agitated state, Samson breaks down and informs her of "his whole heart," revealing what would make him "be like any other man" (Judg 16:17). The precise interpretation of these words provokes scholarly debate. Crenshaw (*ZAW* 86 [1974] 498; compare Margalith, *VT* 36 [1986] 229) appears to argue that Samson claimed the credit for the strength rather than attributing it to God's Spirit. But Samson's express mention of the Nazirite status would argue against such an interpretation. Rather, the narrator of Judges has left the Nazirite theme in the background so that the attentive reader will be aware of its function through the other narratives but will still find a bit of a surprise when Samson reveals his awareness of the vow for the first time here in the climax of the narrative. Num 6:9–12 shows that shaving a Nazirite's head marks the conclusion of the period of the vow. No longer a Nazirite, Samson cannot expect to retain his strength. Samson's thought that he can again free himself occurs naturally as he awakes from sleep yet unaware of all that has occurred and of God's leaving him.

Webb ([1987] 169–70; compare Greene, *VE* 21 [1991] 72) argues that this is what Samson really wants, to be free of his obligations and calling, be free of his strength and abilities, and be like everyone else, left alone to enjoy love with the woman on whose knees his head rests. Thus for Webb, Yahweh ignores other violations of the Nazirite vow but does not ignore this one because he will not allow Samson to be like any other man. This reading is probably a bit cleverer than even the biblical narrator would dream up. Crenshaw (*ZAW* 86 [1974] 498) thinks Samson perceives Delilah as trying to keep Samson to herself, a fate not bad for one who loved so deeply. Vickery ("In Strange Ways," 71) thinks Samson has been so often betrayed that he desperately needs someone to trust. Alter ("Samson without Folklore," 53) sees Samson as drawn to the threat of danger. Wong correctly notes: "Intriguing as these suggestions may be, the text gives no support whatsoever to any of these conjectures" (*Compositional Strategy*, 93, n. 39).

Samson's confession draws the entire story beginning in chap. 13 back together. For the first time he acknowledges that he was bound to a Nazirite oath from birth. This means he has been dedicated to God from birth. Still, one must question Samson's thinking here. Long since, the Nazirite vow has been broken time and again. Does he think this is just one more escape mechanism and that breaking the vow in this way will not harm him either? Yet, he admits that this is how things should work out. Block correctly decides: "Samson's problem with his vow is not so much that he willfully violates it; he simply does not take it seriously. Like his strength, and the people around him, it is a toy to be played with, not a calling to be fulfilled" (459).

Surely Samson knows that Delilah will do what he describes this time, since both his wife from Timnah and Delilah have shown persistence in trying to find out his secret and in testing to see if his words are true. Schneider notes, "Yet he never questioned her motives. Samson was either so naïve as not to see what was happening, or so arrogant and confident in his strength that he had no fear" (222). Sure enough, Delilah senses that finally she has his "whole heart" and so goes for the jugular. Quite appropriately, she "put him to sleep on her knees" (Judg 16:19) for his first and final haircut. Ackerman points out that reference to the knees "ties together the mother, who first cradled the newborn Samson, bald, between her legs, and the lover, who ultimately betrays Samson as he lies, balded, between hers" (*Warrior, Dancer*, 234). (Compare Bal, *Death and Dissymmetry*, 202–3, 224–27.) Mobley can thus conclude: "When Delilah assumes this maternal posture and shears Samson, she severs the vow that had tied the Nazir to his biological mother and Samson, through the agency of this second mother, becomes something he had never been before, an ordinary man" (*Empty Men*, 194).

Who did the shaving? See *Notes* 16:19.c and 16:19.d. The Hebrew text says Delilah called a man and then she shaved Samson's head. Who is the mysterious man that is called? Exum (*JSOT* 19 [1981] 27) is probably correct in seeing this as one of the Philistines apparently hidden nearby (see Judg 16:9).

Then "his strength turned away from him" (Judg 16:19). Crenshaw (*Samson*, 48–49) calls this the loss-of-charisma folklore motif involving betrayal of vocation, withdrawal of divine blessing, adversity for the hero, and death at the hands of enemies. This also dominates the last days of Saul.

Once more Samson hears what by now should be a familiar cry, "Samson, the Philistines have come upon you" (Judg 16:20; see Judg 16:9, 12, 14). Appropriately, Samson's final battle with the Philistines occurs in a woman's bedroom, where he lies sleeping. Expecting nothing to be different, Samson rises for the battle; but the battle is lost. Once too often, he has neglected his vow and manipulated his God. So we hear these discouraging words: "The Philistines seized him and gouged out his eyes. They brought him down to Gaza, tied him up with bronze chains, and he was grinding in the house of the prisoners" (Judg 16:21). Schneider observes, "The Philistines were doing what seemed good in their hearts and, as it did for Samson and later will for the Israelites, it will cause their destruction" (225).

Niditch remarks that "the language and imagery here partake of the epic language of the defeated warrior as a sexually subdued woman in order to emphasize Samson's subdued and oppressed status" (*CBQ* 52 [1990] 617). Referring to Delilah's nagging, Crenshaw concludes that "Samson fared no better under a barrage of words than he did when flooded with tears" (*Samson*, 69). The narrative's nadir, according to Greene, thus pictures Samson "turned into a woman by being defeated by a woman; Samson, who made donkeys of the Philistines, becoming a donkey himself; Samson who demeaned his first wife as a heifer becoming a bovine himself" (*VE* 21 [1991] 73).

Olson rightly observes, "Samson's figurative blindness to his real condition of weakness and divine abandonment is made literal and physical" (858). Now, Block says,

> the ironies in his life have come to full fruition. Overnight this man is transformed from one whose life is governed by sight and whose actions are determined by what is right in his own eyes into a blind man with eyes gouged out. Overnight a life of coming and going as he pleases turns into a life of bondage and imprisonment. Overnight the person who had spent his life insulting and humiliating others becomes the object of their humiliation. Overnight a man with the highest conceivable calling, the divinely commissioned agent of deliverance for Israel, is cast down to the lowest position imaginable: grinding flour for others in prison. (462)

Being blinded, bound with chains and fetters, and forced to work like an animal milling grain was apparently a common fate for prisoners of war (Jer 52:11; compare van der Toorn, "Judges xvi 21 in the Light of the Akkadian Sources," *VT* 36 [1986] 248–53). "By these actions," says Bartusch, "the Philistines would strip Samson of his honor" (*Understanding Dan,* 160).

Apparently, we have come to the end of a sad story of leadership potential gone sour. The man called to begin to deliver Israel from the hand of the Philistines finds himself under their hand, acting like a slave or a woman (Exod 11:5; Judg 9:53), supplying power for the gristmill. The man able to kill a thousand soldiers with a donkey's jawbone has strength enough only to push the bars and make the grinding wheel go round. But the narrator throws in one final sentence to this narrative segment, one pregnant with meaning and anticipation: "The hair on his head began to grow after it had been shaved" (Judg 16:22).

23–24 Capture of public enemy number one is reason enough for the Philistines to celebrate. Whereas Samson had finally celebrated when he destroyed a thousand enemy soldiers and finally gave credit to God when he became deadly thirsty, the Philistine governors call for celebration when one man is captured. They immediately give credit to their god, Dagon, whose place in the story has been anticipated in Judg 10:6.

The non-Semitic Philistines with roots in the Aegean Sea region worshiped Dagon, a grain and agricultural god with Semitic roots reaching back before 2000 B.C.E. in Ebla. At Ugarit he was seen as the father of Baal. The Hebrew Bible mentions Dagon only in connection with the Philistines (1 Sam 5:2–5, 7; 1 Chr 10:10). (See J. F. Healey, "Dagon," *DDD,* cols. 407–13; L. K. Handy, "Dagon," *ABD,* 2:1–3.)

As Younger points out, mention of Dagon "raised the issue to another level. It is now Yahweh versus Dagon! [The Philistines] are, of course, wrong. The Philistines do not understand that it is precisely Yahweh who gave Samson into their hands"

(322). They accuse Samson of two crimes against the state (16:24): he "ruined our land and . . . multiplied our deaths" (Judg 16:24). This summarizes the story of the foxes war and the donkey war. Is this the epitaph of the one called to begin to deliver Israel from the hands of the Philistines?

25–26 The celebration leads to inebriation, described in Hebrew as "when their heart felt good." The drunken celebrants, in their national place of worship, feel the need to be entertained. Samson becomes the likely candidate to take center stage, which just happens to be located between the two supporting pillars of the temple. Blind Samson depends on a "young boy" to guide him, and he asks the lad to let him lean on the pillars that support the temple.

27–30 Now the narrator slows down the action to set the scene for the readers. They have a full house, both men and women. The five Philistine governors are in attendance. Another three thousand people line the roof, looking down into the temple below to watch the festivities and catch a glimpse of Samson the entertainer. The narrator's focus is not on the party people. Neither is it on the political powers. He centers our attention on blind Samson uttering his second prayer. As Olson perceives, "it is only when Samson reaches the end of his rope and slams up against his dependence on God that he comes to some realization of his need for God" (861). This prayer is not for water to deliver him *from* death, but for power to deliver him *to* death. This represents a variation on the folklore death-wish motif. Crenshaw (*Samson*, 46) isolates four elements of the motif: awareness of desperate straits, request for death, divine sustaining or reasoning with the person, choice to continue living. But Samson experiences no reasoning from God, nor does he express any will to live.

Again, Samson's motive is not religious. He does not ask God to help him fulfill a forgotten mission of deliverance. His motive is still selfish revenge. He wants payback "for one of my two eyes" (Judg 16:28; see *Note* 16:28.c). And he is willing to die himself to get it (16:30). Olson (860) notes others who requested death—Moses (Num 11:10–15), Elijah (1 Kgs 19:4), Jeremiah (20:17), and Jonah (4:3). Crenshaw (*Samson*, 47) adds two examples from Tobit. Olson concludes,

> God always refused the request to put the person to death and instead sent the person on to continue his mission. Samson's request for God to let him die is the only time such a request is granted in the Old Testament. . . . He embodies the office of the judge, which comes to an end with him. . . . He embodies Israel as a nation. . . . The exile will be a kind of death for Israel. (860)

Görg (86) reminds us that Samson is not trying to design a model prayer. Instead, he prays in reaction to a desperate situation in an all-too-human manner.

So "he stretched out his arms with strength, and the house fell on the rulers and on all the people in it" (Judg 16:30). Block appears to go a step too far in concluding that "with this utterance Samson declares his total and final identification with the enemy. . . . The Nazirite, set apart for the service of God, wants to die with the uncircumcised Philistines" (469). Crenshaw takes the same path: "Having made his bed with their daughters, he now chose to die in concert with the uncircumcised" (*Samson*, 29). However, he goes too far in the other direction when he claims, "Armed with faith alone, Samson grasped the columns and fell beneath the rubble" (*Samson*, 97). Similarly, Niditch sees Samson "dying a heroic death" (167).

Samson does not identify himself or join himself to the Philistines or commit himself to the unavoidable fact that to gain revenge on the Philistines he must die. Certainly, he does not identify himself with those on whom he seeks vengeance. On the other hand, he does not necessarily work on the basis of faith alone, his hunger for revenge impelling him to trust in God as the last resort. Perhaps ultimately Crenshaw does have the best way to phrase this situation: "Samson breathed his last gasp with a prayer on his oft-kissed lips" (*Samson*, 29). He identified himself with God even as he asked for one final opportunity for revenge.

Here we must see the complexity of Samson's last words and last act. Olson can picture Samson remaining "a tragic figure, forever blind to the larger purposes for which God had used him" (859). Crenshaw decides, "The appeal for remembrance functions to underscore Samson's great sense of abandonment" (*Samson*, 33). His prayer's selfish motivation coupled with its revenge factor may blind us so that we do not comprehend the import of his prayer: Yahweh is still his God, and his appeal is ultimately what God desires—the death of the Philistines—even if their reasons for desiring this common goal are not the same. Crenshaw believes "Samson's death breaks out of the domain of the tragic, inasmuch as he departs in communion with his God" (*Samson*, 130). So in the end, Webb says, "Samson is allowed to die with dignity and in so doing to fulfill the purpose for which he was born" ([1987] 172.) That such a death is "heroic" followed by a "noble" burial may take the praise of Samson too far (see Niditch, 171).

Webb, quoting an unpublished paper by David Gunn on Samson, artistically describes the scene:

> The ensuing scene of death and destruction is for Dagon a debacle of the greatest magnitude. The words of praise for their god must have died coldly on the lips of his devotees. Subtly, and without any crude fanfare of the explicit, the narrator underlines the power of Yahweh, the irrelevance of Dagon. The victory is unquestionably Yahweh's, even if it is only achieved through the suffering of his servant. ([1987] 165)

Samson has his revenge. But the narrator is interested in more than revenge. He wants to tally up Samson's lifetime contribution: "The deaths he caused in his own death outnumbered those he caused while alive" (Judg 16:30). Again Block is a bit too negative in his evaluation when he writes "the narrator's comment should not be interpreted as a compliment" (469). Finally, Samson has begun to deliver Israel from the hand of the Philistines, but only because the beginning of deliverance comes at the end of a misspent life when finally the Nazirite vow is fulfilled. Thus we can finally conclude, with Block, "With brilliant irony the narrator describes a free spirit, a rebel driven by selfish interests, doing whatever he pleases without any respect for his parents and with no respect for the claims of God on his life, but in the process he ends up doing the will of God" (426–27).

31 The narrator gives us one last glimpse of Samson as his brothers and all the families of his uncles gather for last rites at the same place where the Samson story began. He is placed in the family burial ground beside his father. Exum and Whedbee state, "His burial by his brothers in the tomb of Manoah his father serves as the final symbol of his integration into the society which he represents, but in which he has functioned so obstinately and independently" ("Isaac, Samson, and

Saul," 290).

To this the narrator simply adds the historical note, repeated from the end of the previous chapter: "He had judged Israel twenty years" (Judg 16:31). But he had not brought peace. He had not brought rest. He had only just begun to deliver Israel from the hand of the Philistine, and that perhaps more in the theological sphere than in the political sphere (Younger, 323). The rest of that mission would be left to Saul and Samuel and David.

"Ironically," as Younger concludes, "Samson, the strong man of the book, reveals himself as essentially the weakest, weaker than any of his predecessor judges, for Samson is subject, a slave to physical passion—the lowest kind of subjugation. Because his passions demand women, he is at the mercy of womankind—a deplorable situation from the point of view of a patriarchal society" (324). As Block summarizes Samson's story, "The deliverer never rallies the Israelite troops in battle against the oppressor, and there is no announcement of victory over the oppressor. . . . Divinely chosen leaders were part of Israel's problem rather than a lasting solution" (391).

The Samson narrative concludes the collection of stories about Israel's deliverers whom we call judges. A careful reading, leaving aside our natural romanticism when we approach Scripture, leads to Block's interesting conclusion:

> The Samson story represents the last of a series of cycles of apostasy-oppression-appeal-deliverance, in each of which, according to the narrator's own scheme, the depravity of the nation sank to a new low. Not only was this true of the nation in general, but it also applied to the men God raised up to provide deliverance from the enemy. . . . This and the following chapters must be interpreted as depicting the darkest period in the history of the Judges. (419)

But this dark picture is simply the backdrop against which the narrator paints a picture not of human judges but of a transcendent God. As Block phrases it,

> Israel may be moribund in its apostasy, but God is at work, graciously intervening, breaking in and preparing his agent of deliverance. The conception and birth of Samson declare emphatically God's refusal to let this nation die! Israel may be doing all in its power to destroy itself from within, but God must preserve this nation. The honor of his name and the cosmic mission of his grace are at stake. (420)

Olson expounds on how the Samson narrative exemplifies

> the kind of divine love that simply cannot let go. Samson loves even when the loved one repeatedly betrays that love and loyalty. . . . If we shake our heads in puzzlement over Samson's relentless love for those who betrayed him, then we must do the same for God's amazingly patient and relentless love for Israel throughout the book of Judges. Ironically, the most diobedient and ineffective of all Israel's judges becomes the best window into the heart and character of Israel's God. (843)

Is such naïve and self-defeating love really a picture of God's love? How can we see anything about Samson's womanizing that truly pictures divine love with its grace and its judgment? (See chap. 10.) Can Samson so easily image God's gracious love and, according to Olson, "symbolize the fickle love and loyalty of Israel" (854)?

From birth to death, the story of Samson provides as full a biography as we have in Judges. Yet it leaves us with a picture of a complex man, not a simple "hero." Here is a man chosen from birth for God's work, aware of that calling each time he touches his own hair, and yet drawn to the forbidden world of foreign women and exploits demonstrating his personal strength. In desperate situations, he remembers his God and seeks help from the one who is stronger than he. How does one judge this type of faith? It is faith that ultimately leads to a place in the roll call of faith in Heb 11. Yet it remains faith on the fringes of God's work, not faith dedicated to God's central purpose. It may be likened to mustard-seed faith that never grew. In the end, it is a faith willing to die to gain revenge on his and God's enemies. Thus Samson leaves us without easy answers and without easy sermons, but he forces us to contemplate deeply the meaning of being God's chosen and participating in God's mission even in the depths of human weakness and even human addiction.

Explanation

Olson declares, "All our expectations about what a judge should be fall apart in Samson" (840). And McCann explains, "The story of Samson is about what the entire book of Judges is about—God's will to oppose cruel oppression and the difficulties involved in the actual embodiment of God's will by God's people, especially in a Canaanite context" (83).

The human "star" of the narrative is given various roles: hero, underdog, dupe (Matthews, 137; Niditch, *Underdogs and Tricksters*, xi; and idem, *VT* 52 [1980] 608–24). Niditch recognizes Samson's positive characteristics in calling him

> a complex character, beloved by a deity, capable of grand and clever acts of deception, artful in his use of language, and able to perform superhuman feats. He is susceptible to women's attractions and to the delusion that his great power is self-generated. By succumbing to Delilah, he takes his place with Odysseus and other epic heroes who should keep key aspects of their identities to themselves. Instead, they boast by word or by action (168)

Block concludes:

> Samson's story is filled with irony. No other deliverer in the Book of Judges matches his potential. Yet Samson accomplishes less on behalf of his people than any of his predecessors. . . . Though Samson is impressive as an individual, he turns out to be anything but a military hero. He never leads Israel out in battle; he never engages the Philistines in martial combat; he never experiences a military victory. All his accomplishments are personal; all his victories, private. . . . On the one hand he is born and buried as a hero, but on the other he is a bandit, a trickster, and one who frivolously fritters away his extraordinary calling and gifts. (420–21)

In other words, McCann says, "as the final judge, Samson represents not the glorious culmination of the series of judges, but rather its abysmal conclusion" (93). Still, we must remember with Exum and Whedbee: "Each account leads to the same point: the strong man cannot save himself; Samson depends on Yahweh for life and death" ("Isaac, Samson, and Saul," 295). Thus we learn from Wharton that "the double implication is that Yahweh accomplishes what he sets out to do through human instrumentality; yet for the human instrument the choice of fidelity or infidelity is a fateful one" (*Int* 27 [1973] 61–62).

What was Samson's problem? Exum suggests, "He needs to prove his love by surrendering something uniquely his, a part of himself—the answer to his riddle (Judg 14), the source of his strength (16)—something that gives the woman power over him. Surrender is both attractive and dangerous" ("Feminist Criticism," 81). Exum finds in this patriarchal attitude that "women, as the account of the Timnite shows, are easily intimidated and manipulated, and as Delilah shows, morally deficient. . . . The story encourages women to become lawful and loyal mothers. This is the only role in which they can achieve status" (82–83). Still, she decides that "the fact that Samson loses his life in the process of establishing his superior position over the threat posed by woman's sexuality shows how costly the struggle to maintain supremacy is" (82). The story also calls readers to identify more with Samson's weaknesses than with his strengths (Mobley, *Empty Men*, 204).

But what does the narrative do from a positive perspective? I must concede to Greene that "the timelessness of some of the Samson story's themes and its broad appeal have, however, not led to any consensus or even majority view about its meaning" (*VE* 21 [1991] 53). Still, Greene has a solution: "Samson is implicitly a type for the whole people. This identification of Samson with Israel's history, which is intrinsic to the narrator's presentation makes the story a solemn warning against Israelite idolatry, a solemn summons to covenant holiness, and a solemn reminder that Israel is God's people" (77).

Jost reminds us that "in Jewish congregations, the Samson narrative can still be heard as an empowering story for a persecuted minority" ("God of Love/God of Vengeance," 124). She then modifies this in seeing that this narrative and others, especially New Testament ones, recognize that "the exercise of vengeance, the violent restoration of violated rights, is a matter for God and not for human beings."

Crenshaw perceives the story to be examining "competing loyalties . . . the tension between filial devotion and erotic attachment" (*Samson*, 65). In it Samson "experiences love's power and cruelty" (66). Crenshaw (*Samson*, 70) lists these loyalties: to an ideal Israelite woman or to physical attraction, to physical lust, and to unreciprocated love. Smith finds it to be "a story about power—who has it, who uses it, and how it is used" ("Delilah: A Suitable Case," 114).

Niditch centers on the role of women in the Samson narratives and finds that

> like Achsah (ch. 1), Jephthah's daughter (ch. 11), and the women in the troubling tale of civil war (chs. 19–21), women in Samson's adventures serve as commodities of exchange, the mediating doorways linking or separating groups of men. In Samson's case, exchange goes awry and women are sources of deception, betrayal, and destabilization rather than sources of stability and union. The clear message is not to create social connections with the hated enemy. (154)

In regard to Samson, Niditch knows of the criticisms levied against Samson and the psychoanalytic diagnoses made of his personality. However, she concludes:

> Samson is a complex, epic-style hero who would be incomplete without flaws. His

dangerous womanizing and his hubris, like his clever use of sayings and riddles and his Herculean acts of strength, all mark him as an Israelite version of an international character type who appears in a range of heroic or "epic" traditions. He is a worthy judge; the judge is to be understood, however, not as a seated and robed adjudicator of justice, but rather as an action hero. . . . Samson's power comes from God, his success is elicited by prayer, and the deity never completely deserts him, in spite of his weaknesses and failings. (154)

Certainly, later tradition has idolized the strong man of Israel, but the biblical narrative stops far short of identifying him as a worthy judge.

The rather simple narrative has complex things to say about God and divine freedom. God chooses unexpected people and families to produce chosen leaders. His spirit impels the hero into areas of activity that seem forbidden by divine law. As Emmrich sees it, "Yahweh seems to operate outside of the scope of 'orthodox' expectations" (*JETS* 44 [2001] 72).

God leads Samson to do what Samson's pious parents consider to be against all religious tradition. God works through one who operates in a totally different sphere from all his predecessors. God consistently overlooks the hero's ignorance of or lack of seriousness about the vow his parents made for him. God accomplishes the purpose for which the hero was called only through the hero's death. Crenshaw can thus conclude (*Samson*, 131–35) that God cannot ignore sin, that Israel remains God's chosen people, that God does not turn his back on his people forever, that victory comes as a divine gift, that Yahweh itches for a fight and delights in ritual purity while ethical behavior is irrelevant to this God, that God allows his hero to suffer so as to teach the need to rely wholly on God for strength, and that contrition of heart secures divine compassion. Thus, despite the many negative traits in the story, eventually it teaches those in trying circumstances a reason for renewed hope.

Samson and his experiences with a variety of women provide happy hunting grounds for biblical scholars searching for either patriarchal bias or gender equity in Scripture. Samson's nameless mother certainly presents a stronger picture of faith than does her vacillating, unseeing husband. Samson's wife offers much more than feminine beauty that catches Samson's eye and feminine wiles that learn his riddle. She provides a small portrait of a woman trying to do what she has to do to honor her country and protect her family, a tragic portrait of one who ultimately succeeded in the short-term goal but surrendered her life in the long term. The Gaza prostitute serves only as a narrative foil against which Samson's character and actions are painted. In total contrast, Delilah offers a strong, complex character with many ambivalent characteristics. She is independent, persuading, and determined. She is also deceptive, alluring, persistent, and dangerous.

Ackerman admits that Manoah's wife and other women receive preference over the character, faith, and life of their men. Still, she complains that the text imposes "limitations based on [the Deuteronomists'] notions of gender-appropriate behavior and gender-appropriate spheres of activity" (*Warrior, Dancer,* 116). In regard to Judg 13, Ackerman finds that the "narrator essentially portrays the woman as acting on *behalf* of her husband's patriarchal agenda" (116, emphasis original).

Olson sees the mother as "a positive model of faithfulness and trust," but then in one sweep of the brush paints all the other women as "objects of desire, nagging and tempting Samson into economic ruin, sexual immorality, and ultimately death." He does see that each woman "is in some way caught in the web of the pressures, economics, and powers of a male-dominated society" (860).

Exum sees "two kinds of women according to this story: the good (safe) woman and the bad (threatening) woman." Samson's mother is good: "If she is more favorably portrayed than her husband, it is because she poses no threat. She does nothing on her own, which is a trait that patriarchy finds desirable in a woman" ("Feminist Criticism," 78). Again, the patriarchal attitude "severs the relationship between eroticism and procreation" (80). Further, "none of the three women with whom Samson becomes amorously involved ever becomes a mother. (Motherhood redeems women, and these women are irredeemable.)" From another perspective, we are led to assume that "Israelite women behave respectably, while foreign women are disreputable and treacherous" (81). In all this we need to heed Matthews' reminder: "Realizing that the portrayal of women in ancient Israel is more complex may help to eliminate stereotypes or naïve conclusions" (132).

The Samson narrative shows the utter despair of spiritual growth and political maturity in Israel. That makes it simple to describe the naïve behavior and immature self-centeredness of this "hero of faith." As with Gideon and Jerubbaal in particular, we must not so quickly miss the complexity of their character and of their relationships to the God of Israel. They each know better than they do. Times of desperation sometimes lead them to lament and prayer, but at other times lead them to trust in self and to demand personal revenge. One of the signs of narrative artistry in the book is the ability to show the downward journey of Israel and its leaders while not caricaturing the characters or simplifying their portraits into totally negative pictures.

What does this wild fling of a life teach us about leadership? We can conclude with McCann, "Samson seems to have been an effective leader. Unfortunately, however, he will have led all the people in the wrong direction" (101). Or as Crenshaw phrases it, "Samson symbolizes a negative hero. . . . Samson's willingness to risk his neck seems to derive from inner compulsion" (*Samson*, 126–27).

We must finally ask, What leadership requirements were required for one who would be a judge in Israel? Or to phrase the question in simple terms: How does a person achieve God's will? Here we see the complexity of the book of Judges, especially in the story of Samson. For McCann is correct as he observes,

> If the story of Samson is a story about God's will, . . . it is primarily about the difficulties involved in the achievement of God's will. God's will for the deliverance of the people is clear enough; but Samson's unfaithfulness is clear, too. . . . In a story full of riddles, perhaps the greatest riddle of all is that God can accomplish anything at all through a character like Samson. (83)

Webb ([1987] 170) points us up the right trail as he describes the various judges: "Ehud is a devious assassin rather than a warrior; Shamgar is probably not an Israelite; Deborah is a woman." He could have added Barak is afraid to go alone even if it costs him the glory; Gideon overcomes his fear and weakness to become a tyrant ruler functioning in an office he claims not to hold; Abimelech is a blood-thirsty usurper, and on and on. To be a judge in Israel, then, is not to have perfect leadership skills or maybe any true leadership skills at all, but, as Webb explains, "to be a judge is to be the person in whom Yahweh's administration of Israel is realized at a particular time" ([1987] 171). This is not a call for current leaders to excuse their weaknesses in the light of the overwhelming weaknesses of Israel's judges. It is not a call to ignore God, knowing he will use you anyway. It is a call to realize that God can and will use you just as you are. He does not demand perfection, nor does he wait until you are perfectly committed to his call and his commission. He calls you to leadership, opens opportunities for leadership, and works through you to achieve his purposes even when your leadership is not all that he desires.

III. Epilogue: "Who is king when all is right in my eyes?" (17:1–21:25)

A. Saving Dan, the Cult Thief (17:1–18:31)

Bibliography

Abba, R. "Priests and Levites in Deuteronomy." *VT* 27 (1977) 256–67. **Ackroyd, P.** "The Teraphim." *ExpTim* 62 (1950–1951) 378–80. **Albright, W. F.** "Are the Ephod and the Teraphim Mentioned in Ugaritic Literature?" *BASOR* 83 (1941) 38–42. **Amit, Y.** "The End of the Book of Judges" (Heb.). In *Proceedings of the Ninth World Congress of Jewish Studies.* Jerusalem: World Union of Jewish Studies, 1986. 73–80. ———. "Endings—Especially Reversal Endings." *Scriptura* 87 (2004) 213–26. ———. "Hidden Polemic in the Conquest of Dan: Judges xvii–xviii." *VT* 40 (1990) 4–20. ———. "Literature in the Service of Political Studies in Judges 19–21." In *Politics and Theopolitics in the Bible and Postbiblical Literature.* Ed. H. G. Reventlow et al. Sheffield: JSOT Press, 1994. 28–40. **Arnold, W. R.** *Ephod and Ark.* HTS 3. Cambridge: Harvard UP, 1917. **Auberlen, C.** "Die drei Anhange des Buches der Richter in ihrer Bedeutung und Zusammengehörigkeit." *TSK* 33 (1860) 536–68. **Bartusch, M. W.** *Understanding Dan: An Exegetical Study of a Biblical City, Tribe and Ancestor.* JSOTSup 379. Sheffield: Sheffield Academic, 2003. **Bauer, U. F. W.** "Judges 18 as an Anti-Spy Story in the Context of an Anti-Conquest Story: The Creative Usage of Literary Genres." *JSOT* 88 (2000) 37–47. ———. "Eine Metaphorische Ätiologie in Richter 18:12." In *Unless Some One Guide Me.* Maastrict: Shaker, 2001. 107–13. Also published as "A Metaphorical Etiology in Judges 18.12," *Journal of Hebrew Scriptures* 3 (2001) 37–47. ———. "Richteren 17–18 als 'anti-verhaal' van teksten uit Genesis–2 Koningen." *ACEBT* 19 (2001) 139–57. ———. "Eine synchrone Lesart von Ri 18,13–18." In *Narrative and Comment.* Ed. E. Talstra. Kampen: Kok Pharos, 1995. 53–63. ———. *"Warum nun übertretet ihr SEIN Geheiss!"* למה זה אתם עברים את פי יהוה: *Eine synchrone Exegese der Anti-Erzählung von Richter 17–18.* BEATAJ 45. Frankfurt am Main: Lang, 1998. ———. "Zum Problem des Handelns Gottes nach Ri 17–18." In *YHWH—Kurios—Antitheism or the Power of the Word.* FS R. Zuurmond, ed. K. A. Deurloo and B. J. Diebner. DBAT 14. Heidelberg: DBAT, 1996. 77–84. **Begg, C. T.** "The Danites and Their Land according to Josephus." *ETL* 81 (2005) 177–85. **Bewer, J.** "The Composition of Judges, Chaps. 17, 18." *AJSL* 29 (1912–1913) 261–83. **Biran, A.** *Biblical Dan.* Jerusalem: Israel Exploration Society, 1994. ———. "The Collared-rim Jars and the Settlement of the Tribe of Dan." *AASOR* 49 (1989) 71–96. ———. *Dan: 25 Years of Excavations at Tel Dan* (Heb.). Tel Aviv: Hakibbutz Hameuchad, Israel Exploration Society, 1992. ———. "Tel Dan: Biblical Texts and Archaeological Data." In *Scripture and Other Artifacts: Essays on the Bible and Archaeology.* FS P. J. King, ed. M. D. Coogan, J. C. Exum, and L. E. Stager. Louisville: Westminster John Knox Press, 1994. 1–17. ———. "To the God Who Is in Dan." In *Temples and High Places in Biblical Times.* Ed. A. Biran. Jerusalem: Hebrew Union College, 1981. **Boling, R. G.** "In Those Days There Was No King in Israel." In *A Light unto My Path.* FS J. M. Myers, ed. H. N. Bream et al. Philadelphia: Temple UP, 1974. 33–48. **Bray, J. S.** *Sacred Dan: Religious Tradition and Cultic Practice in Judges 17–18.* Library of Hebrew Bible/Old Testament Studies 449. New York: T&T Clark, 2006. **Carroll, R. P.** "The Aniconic God and the Cult of Images." *ST* 31 (1977) 51–64. **Cody, A.** *A History of Old Testament Priesthood.* AnBib 35. Rome: Pontifical Biblical Institute, 1969. **Cryer, F. H.** *Divination in Ancient Israel and Its Near Eastern Environment.* JSOTSup 142. Sheffield: Sheffield UP, 1994. **Curtis, A. H. W.** "Some Observations on the 'Bull' Terminology in the Ugaritic Texts and the Old Testament." In *In Quest of the Past.* Ed. A. S. van der Woude. OtSt 26. Leiden: Brill, 1990. 17–31. **Curtis, E. M.** "The Theological Basis for the Prohibition of Images in the Old Testament." *JETS* 28 (1985) 277–87. **Davis, D. R.** "Comic Literature—Tragic Theology: A Study of Judges 17–18." *WTJ* 46 (1984) 156–63. **Day, J.** "The Destruction of the Shiloh Sanctuary and Jeremiah vii 12,14." In *Studies in the Historical Books of the Old Testament.* Ed. J. A. Emerton. VTSup 30. Leiden: Brill, 1979. **Dohmen, C.** "Das Heiligtum von Dan: Aspekte religionsgeschichtlicher Darstellung im Deuteronomistischen Geschichtswerk." *BN* 17 (1982) 17–22. **Dumbrell, W. J.** "'In Those Days There Was No King in Israel; Every Man Did What Was Right in His Own Eyes': The Purpose of the Book of Judges Reconsidered." *JSOT* 25 (1983) 23–33. **Edenburg, C.** *The Story of 'the Outrage of Gibeah' (Jdg 19–21): Its Composition, Sources, and Historical Background* (Heb.). Tel Aviv: Tel Aviv University, 2003. **Exum, J. C.** *Fragmented Women: Feminist Subversions of Biblical Narratives.* JSOTSup 163. Sheffield: Sheffield Academic, 1993. 176–98. **Faracone, C. A., B. Garnand,** and **C. López-Ruiz.** "Micah's Mother (Judg. 17:1–4) and a Curse from Carthage *KAI* 89: Canaanite Precedents for Greek and Latin Curses against Thieves?" *JNES* 64 (2005) 161–86. **Fernández, A.** "El santuario de Dan: Estudio critico-exegetico sobre Jud. 17–18." *Bib* 15 (1934) 237–64. **Gevaryahu, H. M. Y.** "Micah's Shrine in the Hill Country of Ephraim and the Journey of the Danites (Judges 17–18)" (Heb.). In *Studies in the Book of Judges.* Publications of the Israel Bible Society 10. Jerusalem, 1966. 547–84. **Grabbe, L. L.** "Prophets, Priests, Diviners, and Sages in Ancient Israel." In *Of Prophets' Visions and the Wisdom of Sages.* FS R. N. Whybray, ed. H. A. McKay and D. J. A. Clines. JSOTSup 16. Sheffield: Sheffield Academic, 1993. 43–62. **Greenspahn, F. E.** "An Egyptian Parallel to Judges 17:6 and 21:25." *JBL* 101 (1982) 129–35. **Güdemann, M.** "Tendenz und Abfassungszeit der letzten Kapitel des Buches der Richter." *MGWJ* 18 (1869) 357–68. **Gunneweg, A. H. J.** *Leviten und Priester.* FRLANT 89. Göttingen: Vandenhoeck & Ruprecht, 1965. **Hackett, J.** "'There Was No King in Israel.'" In *Oxford History of the Biblical World.* Ed. M. D. Coogan. New York: Oxford, 1998. 187–92. **Halévy, J.** "Recherches bibliques: XXI: L'histoire de Michée." *REJ* 21 (1890) 207–17. **Hallo, W. W.** "Cult Statue and Divine Image." In *Scripture in Context II.* Ed. W. W. Hallo, J. C. Moyer, and L. G. Perdue. Winona Lake, IN: Eisenbrauns, 1983. 1–17. **Halpern, B.** "Levitic Participation in the Reform Cult of Jeroboam I." *JBL* 95 (1976) 31–42. **Haran, M.** *Temples and Temple Service in Ancient Israel.* Oxford: Clarendon, 1978. **Hart, R. van der.** "The Camp of Dan and the Camp of Yahweh." *VT* 25 (1975) 720–28. **Hauret, C.** "Aux origines du sacerdoce danite." In *Mélanges bibliques rédigés en l'honneur de André Robert.* Travaux de l'Institute Catholique de Paris 4. Paris: Bloud & Gay, 1957. 103–13. **Hoffner, H. A.** "Hittite Tarpish and Hebrew Teraphim." *JNES* 27 (1968) 61–68. ———. "The Linguistic Origins of Teraphim." *BSac* 124 (1967) 230–38. **Jacobsen, T.** "The Graven Image." In *Ancient Israelite Religion.* FS F. M. Cross, ed. P. D. Miller, P. D. Hanson, and S. D. McBride. Philadelphia: Fortress, 1987. 15–33. **Jost, R.** "Die Fluch der Mutter: Feministischsozialgeschichtliche Überlegungen zu Ri 17,1–6." In *Gott an den Rändern: Sozialgeschichtliche Perspektiven auf die Bibel.* Ed. U. Bail and R. Jost. Gütersloh: Kaiser, 1996. 17–23. **Jüngling, H.-W.** *Richter 19—Ein Plädoyer für das Königtum: Stilistische Analyse der Tendenzerzählung Ri 19, 1–30a; 21,25.* AnBib 84. Rome: Pontifical Biblical Institute, 1981. **Keil, Y.** "'In Those Days There Was No King in Israel' (Comments on the Teaching of Judges 17–21)" (Heb.). In *Sofer Zeidel.* Publications of the Israel Bible Society 11. Jerusalem, 1962. 74–92. **Kennedy, J. M.** "The Social Background of Early Israel's Rejection of Cultic Images: A Proposal." *BTB* 17 (1987) 138–44. **Labuschag-ne, C. J.** "Teraphim: A Proposal for Its Etymology." *VT* 16 (1966) 115–17. **Landy, F.** "Between Centre and Periphery Her Story." Paper delivered at Annual Meeting of Society of Biblical Literature, 1989. **Lapsley, J.** *Whispering the Word: Hearing Women's Stories in the Old Testament.* Louisville: Westminster John Knox, 2005. **Leuchter, M.** "'Now There Was a [Certain] Man': Compositional Chronology in Judges–1 Samuel." *CBQ* 69 (2007) 429–39. **Loretz, O.** "Die Teraphim als 'Ahnen-Götter-Figur(in)en' im Licht der Texte aus Nuzi, Emar, und Ugarit." *UF* 24 (1992) 133–78.

Macdonald, J. "The Status and Role of the Na'ar in Israelite Society." *JNES* 36 (1976) 147–70. **Macintosh, A. A.** "The Meaning of *mklym* in Judges XVIII 7." *VT* 35 (1985) 68–77. **Malamat, A.** "... 'After the Manner of the Sidonians ... and How They Were Far from the Sidonians' (Judges 18.7)" (Heb. with Eng. summary). In *Avraham Biran Volume*. Ed. E. Stern and T. Levi. Jerusalem: Israel Exploration Society, 1992. 153, 194–95. ———. "The Danite Migration and the Pan-Israelite Exodus-Conquest: A Biblical Narrative Pattern." *Bib* 51 (1970) 1–16. ———. "Die Wanderung der Daniten und die panisraelitische Exodus-Landnahme: Ein biblisches Erzählmuster." In *Meqor Hajjim*. FS G. Molin, ed. I. Seybold. Graz: Akademische Druck- & Verlagsanstalt, 1983. 249–65. **Marcus, D.** "In Defence of Micah: Judges 17:2: He Was Not a Thief." *Shofar* 6 (1988) 72–80. **Mayes, A. D. H.** "Deuteronomistic Royal Ideology in Judges 17–21." *BibInt* 9 (2001) 241–58. **Mazar, A.** "On the Cult Places and Early Israelites: A Response to Michael Coogan." *BAR* 14 (1988) 45. **Mazar, B.** "The Cities of the Territory of Dan." In *Early Biblical Period: Historical Studies*. Ed. S. Ahituv and B. A. Levine. Jerusalem: Israel Exploration Society, 1986. **McConville, J. G.** "Priesthood in Joshua to Kings." *VT* 49 (1999) 73–87. **McMillion, P. E.** "Worship in Judges 17–18." In *Worship and the Hebrew Bible*. FS J. T. Willis, ed. M. P. Graham, R. P. Marrs, and S. L. McKenzie. JSOTSup 284. Sheffield: Sheffield Academic, 1999. 225–43. **Mettinger, T. N. D.** *No Graven Image? Israelite Aniconism in Its Ancient Near Eastern Context*. ConBOT 42. Lund: Almqvist & Wiksell, 1995. **Mueller, E. A.** *The Micah Story: A Morality Tale in the Book of Judges*. Studies in Biblical Literature 34. Frankfurt am Main: Lang, 2001. **Murtonen, A.** "Some Thoughts on Judges XVII sq." *VT* 1 (1951) 223–45. **Na'aman, N.** "The Danite Campaign Northward (Judges xvii–xviii) and the Migration of the Phocaeans to Massalia (strabo iv 1,4)." *VT* 55 (2005) 47–60. **Neef, H.-D.** "Michas Kult und Jahwes Gebot: Judc 17:1–18:31: Von kultischen Pluralismus zur Alleinverehrung YHWHs." *ZAW* 116 (2004) 206–22. **Nielsen, E.** "The Levites in Ancient Israel." In *Law, History and Tradition*. Copenhagen: Gads, 1983. 71–81. Originally published in *ASTI* 3 (1964) 16–27. **Niemann, H. M.** *Die Daniten: Studien zur Geschichte eines altisraelitischen Stämmes*. FRLANT 135. Göttingen: Vandenhoeck & Ruprecht, 1985. ———. "Zorah, Eshtaol, Beth-shemesh and Dan's Migration to the South." *JSOT* 86 (1999) 25–48. **Noth, M.** "The Background of Judges 17–18." In *Israel's Prophetic Heritage*. FS J. Muilenburg, ed. B. W. Anderson and W. Harrelson. New York: Harper & Brothers, 1962. 68–85. **Novick, P.** "There Was No King in Israel." In *That Noble Dream: The 'Objectivity Question' and the American Historical Profession*. Ideas in Context 13. Cambridge: Cambridge UP, 1988. 573–629. **Olson, D.** "Buber, Kingship, and the Book of Judges: A Study of Judges 6–9 and 17–21." In *David and Zion*. FS J. J. M. Roberts, ed. B. F. Butto and K. L. Roberts. Winona Lake, IN: Eisenbrauns, 2004. **Organ, B.** "Judges 17–21 and the Composition of the Book of Judges." PhD diss., University of Saint Michael's College, Toronto, 1987. **Parker, S. B.** "The Hebrew Bible and Homosexuality." *QR* 11 (1991) 4–19. **Peter, C. B.** "The Anti-Monarchic Tradition in the Old Testament and the Question of Diakonia." *IJT (Serampore)* 32 (1983) 9–18. **Pitkänen, P.** *Central Sanctuary and Centralization of Worship in Ancient Israel: From the Settlement to the Building of Solomon's Temple*. Gorgias Dissertations, Near Eastern Studies 5. Piscataway, NJ: Gorgias, 2003. **Porter, J. R.** "Ancient Israel." In *Divination and Oracles*. Ed. M. Loewe and C. Blacker. London: Allen & Unwin, 1981. 191–214. **Rudin-O'Brasky, T.** "The Appendices to the Book of Judges (Judges 17–21)" (Heb.). In *Beer-Sheva II*. Ed. M. Cogan. Jerusalem: Magnes, 1985. 141–65. **Sabourin, L.** *Priesthood: A Comparative Study*. Leiden: Brill, 1973. **Satterthwaite, P. E.** "Narrative Artistry and the Composition of Judges 17–21." PhD diss., Manchester University, 1989. ———. "'No King in Israel': Narrative Criticism and Judges 17–21." *TynBul* 44 (1993) 75–88. **Schley, D. G.** *Shiloh: A Biblical City in Tradition and History*. JSOTSup 63. Sheffield: Sheffield Academic, 1989. **Schmidt, B. B.** "The Aniconic Tradition." In *The Triumph of Elohim*. Ed. D. V. Edelman. Kampen: Kok, 1995. 75–105. **Schmoldt, H.** "Der Überfall auf Michas Haus (Jdc 18,13–18)." *ZAW* 105 (1993) 92–98. **Singer, S. F.** "Is the Cultic Installation at Dan Really an Olive Press?" *BAR* 10 (1984) 52–58. **Smith, S.** "What Were the Teraphim?" *JTS* 33 (1932)

33–36. **Spina, F.** "The Danite Story Historically Reconsidered." *JSOT* 1 (1977) 60–71. **Strange, J.** "The Inheritance of Dan." *ST* 20 (1966) 120–39. **Talmon, S.** "'In jenen Tag gab es keinen *mlk* in Israel' (Ri 17–21)." In *Gesellschaft und Literatur in der Hebräischen Bibel 1*. Ed. S. Talmon. Neukirchen-Vluyn: Neukirchen Verlag, 1988. 44–55. ———. "In Those Days There Was No מלך in Israel." In *King, Cult and Calendar in Ancient Israel*. Jerusalem: Magnes, 1986. ———. "Micah's Shrine in the Hill Country of Ephraim and the Journey of the Danites (Discussion at Gevaryahu Lecture)" (Heb.). In *Studies in the Book of Judges*. Publications of the Israel Bible Society 10. Jerusalem, 1966. 572–76. **Taylor, J. G.** "The Bible and Homosexuality." *Them* 21 (1995) 4–9. **Tidwell, N. L.** "The Linen Ephod." *VT* 24 (1974) 505–7. **Trible, P.** *Texts of Terror: Literary-Feminist Readings of Biblical Narratives*. OBT. Philadelphia: Fortress, 1984. **Uehlinger, C.** "Eine anthropomorphe Kultstatue des Gottes von Dan?" *BN* 72 (1994) 85–100. **Vaux, R. de.** "'Lévites' minéens et lévites israélites." In *Lex tua veritas*. FS H. Junker, ed. H. Gross and F. Mussner. Trier: Paulinus, 1961. 265–73. **Weitzman, S.** "Reopening the Case of the Suspiciously Suspended Nun in Judges 18:30." *CBQ* 61 (1999) 448–60. **Wilson, M. K.** "As You Like It: The Idolatry of Micah and the Danites (Judges 17–18)." *RTR* 54 (1995) 73–85. **Wood, B. G.** "From Ramesses to Shiloh: Archaeological Discoveries Bearing on the Exodus-Judges Period." In *Giving the Sense*. Ed. D. M. Howard, Jr., and M. A. Grisanti. Grand Rapids: Kregel, 2003. 256–82. **Wright, G. R. H.** "The Mother-Maid at Bethlehem: Cultic Fertility Themes in Judg 17–19 and Ruth." *ZAW* 98 (1986) 56–72. **Yadin, Y.** "'And Dan, Why Did He Remain with His Ships?'" *AJBA* 1 (1968) 9–23. **Yee, G.** "Ideological Criticism: Judges 17–21 and the Dismembered Body." In *Judges and Method*. Ed. G. Yee. 146–70. **Yeivin, S.** "The Benjaminite Settlement in the Western Part of Their Territory." *IEJ* 21 (1971) 141–54. **Zakovitch, Y.** "The Woman's Rights in the Biblical Law of Divorce." *JLA* 4 (1981) 28–46.

Translation

17:1 [a] A man from the hill country of Ephraim was named Micah. [2] He said to his mother, "The eleven hundred shekels of silver which were taken from you and which you[a] placed under a curse in my hearing,[b] Look here! I have the silver. I myself took it."[c]

His mother said to him, "May Yahweh bless you, my son."

[3] He returned the eleven hundred shekels of silver to his mother, and his mother said, "I totally dedicate my silver to Yahweh. It shall go from my hand to my son[a] to make a carved, overlaid image. Therefore, I give it back to you."[b]

[4] He returned the silver to his mother, and she took two hundred shekels of it and gave it to the smith. He made of it an idol and a metal image. It was in Micah's house. [5] Meanwhile, the man Micah had his own house of God.[a] He made an ephod and teraphim. He consecrated one of his sons, and he became the priest for him.

[6] In those days Israel had no king. Every person did what was right in his own eyes.

[7] A young man from Bethlehem of Judah,[a] part of the clan of Judah,[b] was a Levite.[c] He was an alien there.[d] [8] The man went from the town, that is, from Bethlehem of Judah,[a] to live as an alien wherever he might find a place. He came to the hill country of Ephraim, to the house of Micah, to make his own way.

[9] Micah said to him, "Where do you come from?"

He told him, "I am a Levite from Bethlehem of Judah, but I am going to live as an alien wherever I might find."

[10] Micah said to him, "Live with me. Be a father and a priest to me. In that case I will give you ten shekels of silver for a year,[a] necessary clothes, and food.[b]

The Levite went.[c] [11] The Levite eagerly accepted[a] the offer to live with the man. The youth became to him as one of his sons. [12] Micah consecrated the Levite, and the youth[a] became his priest. He was in Micah's house.

[13]*Micah said, "Now I know that Yahweh will be good*[a] *to me for I have a Levite as a priest."*

[18:1]*In those days Israel had no king.*

In those days the tribe of Dan was seeking an inheritance for themselves because nothing had fallen to them as an inheritance[a] *among the tribes of Israel until that day.*[b]

[2]*From their number,*[a] *the Danites sent from their clan*[b] *five men, heroic warriors, from Zorah and from Eshtaol to spy out the land and to search it. They told them,*[c] *"Go, search out the land."*

They entered the hill country of Ephraim and the house of Micah and spent the night[d] *there.* [3]*At Micah's house they recognized the voice of the young*[a] *Levite. They turned back there and said to him, "Who brought you here? What are you doing in this place? What is there for you here?"*

[4]*He said to them, "All this*[a] *Micah has done for me. He has hired me, and I have become his priest."*

[5]*They said to him, "Please ask God so we may know if you will bring success to our way that we are traveling."* [a]

[6]*The priest said to them, "Go in peace. Your way where you are traveling is under Yahweh's watch."*

[7]*The five men traveled on and came to Laish.*[a] *They saw the people in the middle of the town living in security*[b] *according to the Sidonians' system. They were quiet and secure.*[c] *Nothing brought shame*[d] *to the land, nor did anyone dispossess them oppressively.*[e] *But they lived far from the Sidonians and had no relationships with anyone else.*[f]

[8]*They*[a] *came to their kinfolk in Zorah and Eshtaol; and their kinfolk*[b] *asked them, "How are things with you?"*[c]

[9]*They said, "Get up*[a] *so we can go up against them,*[b] *for we have seen the land. Look! It is so very good. But you are lingering! Do not hesitate to get going to possess the land.* [10]*As you enter,*[a] *you will come upon a trusting people*[b] *with a wide expanse of land. Indeed, God*[c] *has given it into your hand. It is a place where nothing is lacking of anything on the earth."*[d]

[11]*From there,*[a] *that is, from Zorah and Eshtaol, six hundred men of the Danite clan set out dressed for battle.* [12]*They went up and camped in Kiriath-jearim in Judah. Therefore, they call the place Mahaneh-dan*[a] *until today. See, it lies behind Kiriath-jearim.* [13]*From there they crossed*[a] *into the hill country of Ephraim and came to Micah's home.*

[14]*The five men who had traveled to spy out the land of Laish*[a] *responded to their kinfolk, "You know that there is in these houses*[b] *an ephod, an image, an idol, and a metal image. Therefore, know what you are going to do."*

[15]*They turned in there and came to the house of the young Levite, that is, the house of Micah.*[a] *They greeted him, "Peace."*[b] [16]*Six hundred men*[a] *dressed for battle*[b] *stationed themselves at the entrance to the gate. They were Danites.* [17]*The five men who had traveled to spy out the land went up*[a] *and entered there. They took*[b] *the idol, the ephod, the image, and the metal image.*[c] *Meanwhile, the priest stationed himself at the entrance to the gate along with*[d] *the six hundred men dressed for battle.* [18]*At the time these*[a] *came to Micah's home*[b] *and took the idol, the ephod,*[c] *the image, and the metal image, the priest asked them, "What are you doing?"*

[19]*They said to him, "Keep quiet! Put your hand on your mouth, and come with us. You will be a father and a priest for us. Is it better for you to be a priest for the house of one man or for you to be a priest for a tribe and for a clan*[a] *in Israel?"* [20]*This made*

the priest glad of heart, and he took the ephod, the image, and the idol[a] *and entered in among the people.* [21] *They turned and traveled on, setting the little ones, the livestock, and their cherished possessions*[a] *in front of them.* [22] *They went a long way from Micah's home, but still the men*[a] *whose houses were near Micah's called for military help and caught up*[b] *with the Danites.* [23] *They called to the Danites,*[a] *who turned their faces around and said to Micah, "How are things with you that you called for military help?"* [24] *He*[a] *said, "The gods*[b] *that I made,*[c] *you have taken along with the priest, and have traveled on. What more do I own? So what is this you are saying to me, 'How are things with you?'"*[d] [25] *The Danites told him, "Don't make your voice heard with us? If you do, men embittered of soul will attack all of you; you will collect your soul*[a] *and those of your family."* [26] *The Danites traveled on their way, and Micah realized they were too strong for him, so he turned around*[a] *and returned to his house.* [27] *They*[a] *took*[b] *what Micah had made along with the priest who belonged to him and came to*[c] *Laish, to a people quiet and trusting.*[d] *They struck them*[e] *dead with the edge of the sword, while burning the city with fire.* [28] *No deliverer was there since it was so far from Sidon and they had no relationships with any men.*[a] *It lay in the valley at Beth-rahob.*[b] *They built the town and settled down there.* [29] *They named the town Dan after*[a] *the name of Dan,*[b] *their patriarchal father who was born to Israel, though in earlier times the name of the town was Laish.* [30] *The Danites erected for themselves the carved image.*[a] *Jonathan—the son of Gershom, son of Moses*[b]*—and his sons were priests for the Danite tribe until the day when the land*[c] *was captured.* [31] *They set up for themselves Micah's*[a] *idol that he*[b] *had made all the days the house of God was in Shiloh.*[c]

Notes

17:1.a. OL introduces another minor judge annal unknown elsewhere: "And there arose after him Asemada the son of Annan, and he slaughtered of the foreigners six hundred men, besides the animals, and the Lord made Israel safe."

2.a. Many Heb. MSS read with Q the regular form of the second fem. sg. pronoun, אַתְּ, in place of the older form אתי indicated by K. See GKC, §32h.

2.b. LXX[A] reads τοὺς λημφθέντας σοι καὶ ἐξώρκισας καὶ εἶπας ἐν τοῖς ὠσίν μου, "which was taken by (or from) you, and you put under a curse and spoke in my ears," while LXX[B] (compare OL) reads οὓς ἔλαβες ἀργυρίου σεαυτῇ καὶ με ἡράσω καὶ προσεῖπας ἐν ὠσί μου, "which you took of the silver yourself, and you put me under a curse and spoke in my ears." *BHS* suggests that a few words have dropped out here. Bartusch (*Understanding Dan*, 172) correctly retains MT, there being no textual evidence for a change. Note the extreme freedom Soggin (264–65) takes with the text along with "the majority of commentators," rearranging the verses in the order 2aα, 3bα, 2aβ, 3bβ, 2b, and 3a. This forces Soggin then to delete v 4a. Such extreme emendation should not be done without strong textual support, and this suggestion has none. *Preliminary and Interim Report* (2:114) does not comment on changes made on purely literary grounds but notes here that "though difficult MT makes good sense." Amit points in the right direction: "The proposed emendations obscure the ironic illusion, while preference of the Masoretic reading stresses the process of transfer from hand to hand" (*Book of Judges*, 324, n. 18).

2.c. *BHS* transposes 3bβ after "took it," again without evidence. See *Comment* on 17:2 and Bartusch (*Understanding Dan*, 172).

3.a. LXX[A] reads χειρός μου κατὰ μόνας τοῦ ποιῆσαι, "my hand solely for the purpose of making," omitting "to my son."

3.b. LXX[A] reads νῦν ἐπιστρέψω αὐτά σοι καὶ ἀποδώσω σοι αὐτό, "now I will return it to you and I will give it back to you."

5.a. LXX[B] reads καὶ ὁ οἶκος Μιχαια αὐτῷ οἶκος θεοῦ, "and the house of Micah was for him a house of God." The first two editions of Jerusalem Bible read והאיש בנה לו בית-אלהים, "and the man built for himself a house of God." Such evidence gives no reason to change MT.

7.a. LXX reads Βηθλεεμ δήμου Ιουδα, "Bethlehem of the people of Judah," explaining clearly the relationship to Judah.

7.b. LXXᴮ, a Heb. MS, and Syr. do not witness מִמִּשְׁפַּחַת יְהוּדָה, "part of the clan of Judah," possibly seen by the scribes as a doublet to the previous statement but missing the irony of the statement. *BHS* suggests the phrase is a gloss, but without sufficient evidence to be convincing. The variant reading may result from haplography. See the *Comment*, Bartusch (*Understanding Dan*, 172), and the description of the various positions by Amit (*Book of Judges*, 323, n. 17).

7.c. OL does not witness "and was a Levite."

7.d. *Preliminary and Interim Report* (2:116) notes the proposal to read וְהוּא גֵר־שָׁם as וְהוּא גֵרְשֹׁם, "and he was Gershom." This misses the literary strategy to hide the revelation of the Levite's identity to the end of the story in 18:30.

8.a. LXXᴬ reads ἐκ τῆς πόλεως Ιουδα ἐκ Βηθλεεμ, "out of the town of Judah, out of Bethlehem." LXXᴮ reads ἀπὸ Βηθλεεμ τῆς πόλεως Ιουδα, "from Bethlehem of the city of Judah." Both Gk. readings are attempts to add clarity to the statement.

10.a. Lit. "for days," an idiom meaning "years."

10.b. LXXᴸ adds καὶ εὐδόκησεν ὁ Λευίτη, apparently meaning, "he was glad to," a good translation of v 11a. OL adds *et coegit eum*, apparently "he pressed him," but Barthélemy (113) sees this as an internal Latin error and explains Gk. and Syr. evidence in a way to defend MT. *BHS* backtranslates to וַיִּאֶץ בְּלֵוִי, "he pressed (urged) on Levi." Bartusch says the *BHS* backtranslation into Heb. "does not appear to correspond to the variant texts cited" (*Understanding Dan*, 172). There appears no reason to introduce either of these variants into the MT. *Preliminary and Interim Report* sees this suggestion as lacking sufficient evidence and as simplifying the text.

10.c. OL ends with "and he compelled him." *BHS* suggests deleting "the Levite went" as dittography to the opening words of the next verse, but the text progresses from movement toward the house to eager acceptance of the offer. Bartusch (*Understanding Dan*, 172) sees correctly that no such change is needed without MSS evidence, the MT making sense. Block (489, n. 62) follows O'Connell (*Rhetoric of the Book of Judges*, 477) in using the Syriac Peshitta in attaching the words to v 11 and deleting one reference to the Levite: "And the Levite went and agreed to stay." Soggin follows G. R. Driver (*ALUOS* 4 [1962–1963] 18) in creating a new lexical item in Heb., לכך, "to hesitate" (266).

11.a. LXX reads καὶ ἤξατο παροικεῖν, "and he began to live as an alien," giving an alternate meaning of Heb. יָאֶל and making explicit here the alien relationship underlined previously.

12.a. LXXᴮ does not have "the youth," omitting an unnecessary reference, but missing the emphasis on the youth of the priest. See *Comment* on 17:12.

13.a. Heb. may be read as continuous present reality or future promise; LXXᴬ (compare OL) reads aorist or past, while LXXᴮ reads present.

18:1.a. A few Heb. MSS, LXX, and Syr. do not have the somewhat unexpected preposition ב attached to נחלה. Bartusch (*Understanding Dan*, 174) correctly retains MT as the more difficult reading.

1.b. LXXᴬ reads "until those days," repeating the expression earlier in the verse.

2.a. LXXᴬ reads ἀπὸ μέρους αὐτῶν, "from their part," a possible translation of מִקְצוֹתָם, but sg. rather than pl.; LXXᴮ, which for *BHS* represents the original Gk., and Syr. do not translate מִקְצוֹתָם אֲנָשִׁים, lit. "from the edges or ends of mankind," which may represent a conflate reading in the copying tradition with מִמִּשְׁפַּחְתָּם, "their clan."

2.b. LXX and Tg. read "clans" in the pl., even when the two Gk. traditions use different words to translate "clan." This represents a natural assumption that a tribe has more than one clan, but misses the ironical use of "tribe" and "clan" to refer to Dan in this passage. See *Comment*.

2.c. Cairo Genizah MS reads sg., "he told them." This is insufficient evidence to change MT.

2.d. LXXᴬᴿᴼ, supported by OL and Vg., read καὶ κατέπαυσαν, "and they stopped" or "rested," another interpretation of MT.

3.a. LXXᴬ reads παιδαρίου τοῦ νεωτέρου τοῦ Λευίτου, "of the boy of the youth the Levite," clearly a conflate reading, LXXᴮ having only τοῦ νεανίσκου τοῦ Λευίτου, "of the youth the Levite."

4.a. Heb. כָּזֹה וְכָזֶה, "according to this and to this." *BHS* proposes reading וכזה on the basis of 2 Sam 11:25, but Bartusch (*Understanding Dan*, 174) notes that *BHS* has misrepresented the Samuel passage here and that both it and 1 Kgs 14:5 are identical to MT here.

5.a. *BHS* suggests that we read הֲתִצְלַח with many Heb. MSS and Cairo Genizah evidence compared with LXX, Syr., Vg. This changes the subject to "our way," a fem. noun and makes the verb third-person fem. sg. in the basic *qal* rather than the MT's second-person fem. sg. causative *hif'il*, reading "so that we may know our way that we are traveling on it will be successful." The subject of the MT sentence is ambiguous, referring either to the priest or to God. Bartusch (*Understanding Dan*, 174–75) accepts the change as a smoother read, but that explanation goes against his decision, for the widespread change reflects the tradition trying to smooth out a textual ambiguity.

7.a. *BHS* suggests, without MS support, inserting צדנים כמשפט יֹשֶׁבֶת־לָבֶטַח, "living in security according to the Sidonians' system," from later in the verse. Bartusch (*Understanding Dan*, 175) rightfully calls this "unnecessary."

7.b. LXX^A reads εἶδον τὸν λαὸν τὸν κατοικοῦντα ἐν αὐτῇ καθήμενον ἐν ἐλπίδι, "saw the people who were residing in it living in hope." LXX^B also reads ἐν ἐλπίδι, "in hope."

7.c. Here also LXX^A reads ἐν ἐλπίδι, "in hope."

7.d. LXX^A (compare OL) reads καὶ μὴ δυναμένους λαλῆσαι ῥῆμα, "no one was able to speak a word." LXX^B reads ἡσυχάζουσα καὶ οὐκ ἔστιν διατρέπων ἤ καταισχύνων λόγον ἐν τῇ γῇ, "remaining at rest [a fem. participle] and there was no perverting or shaming a word (or a thing) in the land." For MT וְאֵין־מַכְלִים דָּבָר בָּאָרֶץ, "nothing brought shame to the land," *BHS* notes the proposal to read וְאֵין־מֶלֶךְ מַדְבִּר בָּאָרֶץ, "there was no king driving away" or "subduing" (see REB). *Preliminary and Interim Report* (2:116–18) lists three other separate changes to the Heb. text: וְאֵין־מַכְלִים דָּבָר בָּאָרֶץ יוֹרֵשׁ עֶצֶר. RSV and Luther read the text as וְאֵין־מַהְסוֹר כָּל־דְּבַר בָּאָרֶץ יוֹרֵשׁ עֶצֶר, "lacking nothing that is in the earth, and possessing wealth." The third edition of the Jerusalem Bible reads וְאֵין־מַהְסוֹר כָּל־דְּבַר בָּאָרֶץ יוֹרֵשׁ וָעֶצֶר, "and there was no lack of anything in the land, neither povety nor restriction." The first and second editions of the Jerusalem Bible read וְאֵין־מַהְסוֹר כָּל־דְּבַר בָּאָרֶץ, "and there was no lack of anything in the land." Again, such a conjecture cannot be accepted without MSS support. *Preliminary and Interim Report* (2:117–18) notes two possible translations of MT: "and there was no one who put to shame in anything, in the land, the power-holder" or "there was no power-holder who put <anyone> to shame in anything in the land." The problem is the Heb. term דָּבָר—"word, thing, matter." Block (500, n. 102) sees its appearance here as "awkward" but probably functioning adverbially, "in any matter." I have tied it to the negative to mean "nothing." See Macintosh (*VT* 35 [1985] 68–77). O'Connell (*Rhetoric of the Book of Judges*, 477–80) upholds the MT, and Barthélemy (*Critique textuelle*, 1:113) finds no evidence to lead him to restore a text preferable to the MT.

7.e. LXX^A does not have this sentence. LXX^B reads κληρονόμος ἐκπιέζων θησαυροῦ, "or an heir oppressing (or extorting) the treasury." *BHS* notes the proposal to read נֹגֵשׂ וְעֹצֵר, referring to LXX^B and Syr. Bartusch (*Understanding Dan*, 175) reads this as "drawing near and restraining." This requires the change noted in *Note* 7.d, neither of which is necessary or an improvement on MT.

7.f. Lit. "and a word (or thing) was not to them with a man" (Heb. אדם = Aram). LXX^A reads μετὰ Συρίας, "with Syria" (translating Heb. ארם), reflecting a common Heb. copyist's confusion of *reš* and *dālet*. *BHS* notes that Symmachus's Gk. tradition also supports this change and perhaps should be read. Several commentators follow this reading (Brensinger, 184; Amit, *Book of Judges*, 330, n. 23; Block, 501, n. 106; Boling, 263; Soggin, 273). Still Bartusch (*Understanding Dan*, 175) is to be followed: "The MT, nevertheless, makes sense and is to be preferred." *Preliminary and Interim Report* (2:118) points to simplification of the text, lack of historical information, and other scribal errors while voting for the MT here and in 18:28. Barthélemy (*Critique textuelle*, 1:114) shows reasons for pointing to the antiquity of the Gk. reading—Aram or Syria—but still retains MT reading as superior here and in 18:28.

8.a. LXX and OL read "the five men," making the pronominal subject explicit.

8.b. Lit. "their brothers." LXX^B (compare OL) reads "they said to their brothers," which makes sense the way LXX words the following question. OL continues: "because we entered and we went around the land of Geshem, and we saw a people dwelling in it in trust just like the Sidonians and far way from Sidon, and there was no correspondence between them and Syria."

8.c. Lit. "What you?" LXX reads τί ὑμεῖς κάθησθε, "Why are you sitting around?" Soggin (273) follows the *BHS* suggestion to read מִי אַתֶּם, "Who you?" with Ruth 3:16. Block (501, n. 109) calls this "no clearer." Bartusch (*Understanding Dan*, 175) compares the sentence here with Ruth 3:16 while noting that "the MT of Judg 18:8 expresses interrupted speech, and is clear." *Preliminary and Interim Report* (2:118) points to the need to adjust translation for the target language and retains the MT.

9.a. *BHS* wants to read the pl. imperative for the MT sg. with volative *hê* in accord with the eastern Q; several Heb. MSS; and the versions, including the LXX. Bartusch (*Understanding Dan*, 175) accepts the emendation as "a better Hebrew text . . . although the MT's singular may be interpreted distributively." The collective interpretation suffices without choosing the easier, simpler reading of the emendation.

9.b. *BHS* suggests that עֲלֵיהֶם, "against them," is a corruption from an original לְיִשָׁה, "to Laish." Bartusch (*Understanding Dan*, 175) correctly notes the lack of MS support for this and that the MT is both clear and understandable. LXX^A (compare note on OL in *Note* 18:8.b above) represents a complex case of dittography skipping back and repeating v 7 before continuing v 9: ἐπ' αὐτούς ὅτι εἰσήλθαμεν καὶ ἐνεπεριεπατήσαμεν ἐν τῇ γῇ ἕως Λαισα καὶ εἴδομεν τὸν λαὸν τὸν κατοικοῦντα ἐν αὐτῇ ἐν ἐλπίδι κατὰ τὸ σύγκριμα τῶν Σιδωνίων καὶ μακρὰν ἀπέχοντες ἐκ Σιδῶνος καὶ λόγος οὐκ ἦν αὐτοῖς μετὰ Συρίας ἀλλὰ ἀνάστητε καὶ ἀναβῶμεν ἐπ' αὐτούς ὅτι εὑρήκαμεν τὴν γῆν καὶ ἰδοὺ ἀγαθὴ σφόδρα, "against them because we have entered and walked around in the land unto Laish. We saw the people who are living in it in hope according to the pattern of the Sidonians, and they are far distant from Sidon. The matter (or word or relationship) is not to them with Syria but rise up and attack against them because we found the land. Look! It is very good . . ." OL reads "and you, you will be silent, lest you enter to possess the land. In your entrance . . ."

10.a. Several Heb. MSS supported by Syr. read the preposition ב, "in" or "when," for MT כ, "when" or "as." Bartusch notes the easy confusion between the two Heb. letters but still sees the emendation as "an expected improvement" (*Understanding Dan*, 175).

10.b. OL does not witness "you will come upon a trusting people."

10.c. A Heb. MS and the Vg. read the personal name YHWH for the generic 'elōhîm in the MT. Bartusch sees this as "a minority effort to bring this verse into conformity with the rest of the biblical tradition about the 'giving of the land,'" but still is not compelled by the support for the variant (*Understanding Dan*, 175).

10.d. OL reads "you will enter a land, having an outstretched hand because the Lord has given to us a place where there is not from nothing of all the deeds which are upon the land."

11.a. LXX^A does not have "from there."

12.a. That is, "Camp of Dan." LXX translates the name to Παρεμβολὴ Δαν, "Encampment of Dan."

13.a. LXX^A reads ἐκεῖνθεν καὶ ἦλθαν ἕως τοῦ ὄρους Εφραιμ καὶ ἦλθον, "from there and came to the hill country of Ephraim and came," duplicating the verb.

14.a. LXX^A does not have "of Laish," leading *BHS* to suggest it is a gloss. Bartusch (*Understanding Dan*, 175) is correct as he notes the absence of the phrase in the similar construction in v 2 but still prefers the clear MT.

14.b. LXX^B reads "in this house" (sg.).

15.a. Without citing evidence, *BHS* sees "the house of Micah" as a gloss, apparently because of the difficulty of the syntax. Bartusch (*Understanding Dan*, 175) suggests that the preposition אל, "to," does double duty for "house of young Levite" and for "house of Micah." Bartusch also suggests the possibility that "Levite" may be a construct form, meaning, "to the house of the young man, the Levite of the house of Micah." REB omits reference to the young Levite and his house.

15.b. Lit. "they asked of him peace"; LXX^A reads καὶ ἠσπάσαντο αὐτόν, "they greeted him."

16.a. Lit. "clothed with utensils of their war"; LXX^A does not have "their." *BHS* wants to read the definite article on the collective noun איש, "men," in line with the same expression in 18:17 and LXX^BL. Bartusch (*Understanding Dan*, 176) sees the possibility of haplography in v 16 but leaves open the possibility that "at their first mention the 600 men are 'indefinite,' while in later references to them they are 'definite.'"

16.b. *BHS* wants to transpose "they are Danites" here after "dressed for battle" based on Syrohexapla, but this may simply represent a way to adjust the translation to the needs of the target language. Amit finds "there was in fact an exchange of phrases and the conjunctive phrase ought to be moved" (*Book of Judges*, 331, n. 24). Bartusch decides correctly that MT "is likely to preserve a more original reading" (*Understanding Dan*, 175).

17.a. *BHS* notes the proposal to read ויאלו, "they eagerly accepted," as in 17:11 for MT ויעלו, "they went up." Lack of MS evidence votes against the proposal. LXX^B does not have the rest of the verse, apparently avoiding the repetition of content.

17.b. *BHS* notes the proposal to substitute the *qal* infinitive construct for the MT *qal* third-person pl., another attempt to force grammatical niceties on the biblical text.

17.c. Building on the insights of Boling and others, Soggin decides,

"The statue . . . the image" appear here and in v. 18 as two distinct objects, probably because the hendiadys (17:2) has been completely misunderstood here and unusual terms have therefore been repeated. *BHS* seems to want to remedy things by reading ". . . the statue of the ephod," an expression which seems absurd. LXX has a shorter text with few repetitions, another attempt to remedy the confused and repetitive character of the text. (275)

Exum goes a different direction: "There can be little doubt that the piling up of these terms is meant as ironic disapproval" (259). Mueller takes Exum's understanding a step further: "It may be assumed that he [the author] was well aware of the meaning of all three expressions . . . and that his readers were able to understand them" (*Micah Story*, 70).

17.d. *BHS* proposes that the rest of the verse beginning with "along with" is a later addition, but without supporting evidence this proposal should be ignored. See *Notes* 18:17.a and 18:18.a.

18.a. LXX[B] does not have "these" since it does not have the final part of the previous verse, but takes up "there" from previous verse, reading καὶ εἰσῆλθον ἐκεῖ, "they entered there." See *Notes* 18:17.a, c. *BHS* sees v 18a through "metal image" as probably a later addition.

18.b. LXX[B] reads Μιχαια καὶ ὁ ἱερεὺς ἑστώς, "of Micah and the priest was taking his stand," apparently incorporated here instead of in the previous verse.

18.c. MT might be read, "they took the image of the ephod." LXX reads το γλυπτὸν καὶ τὸ εφουδ (LXX[B] reads εφωδ) = אֶת־הַפֶּסֶל וְאֶת־הָאֵפוֹד. Bartusch is on the right track as he writes: "This appears to be an improvement of an original text thought to be defective by the LXX scribes" (*Understanding Dan*, 176). Amit (*Book of Judges*, 331, n. 24) sees dittography here in light of 18:16.

19.a. LXX[B] reads ἱερέα φυλῆς καὶ οἴκου εἰς δῆμον Ισραηλ, "priest of a tribe and a house in the people of Israel," interpreting מִשְׁפָּחָה as an extended family belonging to one "house" rather than the larger "clan" unit.

20.a. LXX reads καὶ τὸ χωνευτὸν, "and overlaid," which may have fallen out of the standard formula of the Heb. text.

21.a. LXX[A] reads καὶ ἔταξαν τὴν πανοικίαν καὶ τὴν κτῆσιν αὐτὸ τὴν ἔνδοξον, "and he stationed the entire household and his possessions, the glorious things," while LXX[B] reads ἔθηκαν τὰ τέκνα καὶ τὴν κτῆσιν καὶ τὸ βάρος, "he placed the children and the possessions and the baggage." OL has "they set the course of action and the glorious possessions." *Preliminary and Interim Report* (2:118–19) interprets טַף, "little ones" or "children," as referring to those "incapable of marching a long distance" and so translates "those who were not able to walk."

22.a. *BHS* notes the proposal to add וּמִיכָה, "with Micah," to make explicit that Micah was involved in the chase. Bartusch (*Understanding Dan*, 176) agrees, seeing possible haplography here. See *Note* 22.b. But the unexpressed subject of the passive verb נִזְעֲקוּ may well be understood as Micah, making his explicit mention unnecessary.

22.b. LXX[A] reads οἴκου Μιχα καὶ ἰδοὺ Μιχα καὶ οἱ ἄνδρες οἱ σὺν τῷ οἴκῳ μετὰ Μιχα ἔκραζον κατοπίσω υἱῶν Δαν, "the house of Micah, and look! Micah and the men who were with the house with Micah cried out after the sons of Dan."

23.a. LXX does not have "and they called to," beginning rather with "the sons of Dan turned."

24.a. LXX reads "Micah."

24.b. LXX reads τὸ γλυπτόν μου, "my carved image," avoiding the heretical "my god(s)."

24.c. LXX[A], supported by Vg., reads ἐμαυτῷ, "I made for myself (or by myself)" leading *BHS* to insert לִי due to haplography. Bartusch (*Understanding Dan*, 176) accepts the emendation, but this simplifies text and clarifies what MT left as self-evident in the context.

24.d. LXX[A] reads τί τοῦτο κράζεις, "What is this you cry out?" LXX[B] reads τί κράζεις, "Why are you calling out?"

25.a. That is, "you and your family will die"; LXX[A] reads καὶ προσθήσεις τὴν ψυχήν σου καὶ τὴν ψυχήν τοῦ οἴκου σου, "and you (sg.) will add your soul and the soul of your house," while LXX[B] has καὶ προσθήσουσιν ψυχὴν καὶ τὴν ψυχὴν τοῦ οἴκου σου, "and they will add soul and the soul of your house."

26.a. LXX[B] does not have "and so he turned around," apparently omitting the repetition.

27.a. LXX[B] reads "the sons of Dan," making the subject explicit.

27.b. Two Heb. MSS insert הַפֶּסֶל, "the idol," leading *BHS* to insert הָאֱלֹהִים, "the god(s)," parallel to 18:24. Bartusch notes that "if any addition is to be made, 'the idol and the ephod' would be added" (*Understanding Dan*, 176). A relative clause can follow the sign of the direct object, so that Bartusch rightly follows MT here.

27.c. *BHS* suggests perhaps reading, with many Heb. MSS and LXX, עַד, "unto," for MT עַל, "on, over, above, in front of, against." Two Heb. MSS, Syr., and Vg. support אֶל, "to." Bartusch notes that "since elsewhere the preposition of the MT is used to denote the Danites' movement against Laish, the MT is the preferable reading" (*Understanding Dan*, 176).

27.d. LXX[B] reads καὶ πεποιθότα ἐπ' ἐλπίδι, "and trusting in hope," giving two different readings for the Heb. term. OL has "resting and silent."

27.e. One Heb. MS and the marginal Sebir ("supposed" or "expected") notation change the third pl. pronoun "them," designating the people of the city, to the third fem. sg. pronoun, designating the actual word in the text, "city." *BHS* and Bartusch are right in retaining MT.

28.a. See *Note* 18:7.f.

28.b. LXX[B] apparently reads "Rahab" from Josh 2.

29.a. *BHS,* with many Heb. mss and the original lxx, suggests reading כְּשֶׁם, positing the easy confusion of the two Heb. prepositions ב and כ. Bartusch (*Understanding Dan,* 176–77) finds the mt form with "the meaning required by the context . . . nowhere else in the Hebrew Bible," the variant form appearing in Gen 4:17; Josh 19:47; 2 Sam 7:9; 1 Chr 17:8; Dan 4:8. So he, with good evidence, emends the text.

29.b. lxx^A does not have the second "Dan," apparently eliminating it as repetitious.

30.a. lxx^A reads "Micah's carved image."

30.b. Following Masoretic reading tradition (marked by raised *nûn* in the text), a few Heb. mss, Vg., OL, and lxx^A, supported by Syrohexapla. mt and lxx^B read "of Manasseh." Niditch says, "This variation offers a fascinating indication of the way in which a scribe could revise a text" (180). *Preliminary and Interim Report* sees the addition of the *nûn* as representing "interpretive modifications" (2:120). The scribal tradition apparently sought to protect the Mosaic reputation from such a heretical site as Dan, especially in light of its later connection with Jeroboam's golden calves. How Bray (*Sacred Dan,* 22) can join a "late date in the transmission of the canon" and "a continued polemic against Dan" is beyond me. Dan's existence as a city into the late periods is certainly attested by archaeology, but a cultic influence that would be strong enough to continue to raise polemical shots cannot be shown and even made a serious consideration. Bartusch (*Understanding Dan,* 177) supports reading "Moses" rather than "Manasseh." See *Comment.*

30.c. Scholars such as O'Connell (*Rhetoric of the Book of Judges,* 350) often change הָאָרֶץ, "land," to הָאָרוֹן, "ark," without textual support. This simply escapes a content problem that has better solutions. As Block notes, the emendation "is too speculative, too dependent on arguments from silence, and too driven by the need to interpret Judges as a pro-Davidic and anti-Saulide tractate" (513). See *Comment.*

31.a. lxx^B does not have "Micah's."

31.b. lxx^B reads "Micah made."

31.c. *BHS* notes proposals to read בְּלִישָׁה or בְּשַׁלְוָה, "in Laishah" or "in Shalwah," "at ease, at rest." *BHS* is the more difficult reading and should be retained without further evidence (with Bartusch, *Understanding Dan,* 177).

Form/Structure/Setting

See table 17.1 in the appendix to compare one possible example of narrative analysis with form-critical analysis for chaps. 17–18. The narrative elements follow the typical pattern of Hebrew narrative while the genre elements show the genre of each section with its component parts. Note how the narrator can use different genre elements and markers within or even across various narrative elements.

Where and how does Judges end? The scholarly debate goes on. Bartusch echoes Noth's view that the Deuteronomistic History did not contain these chapters which "depicted an (uncensored) religious attitude at odds with that of the Deuteronomists in the sixth century" (*Understanding Dan,* 184–85). This justifies for him the deletion of 17:6 and 18:1a from the original text, fragments that he ascribes to the latest Priestly editor who integrated the narrative into Judges. Bray can simply state that "chs. 17–18 and 19–21 are patently not by the same author, even though they are framed by the same redactional comments . . . that . . . are alien to both texts" (*Sacred Dan,* 31). Taking away the unifying elements is a simple way to deny unity to the texts.

Amit backs off this a bit, arguing that only 17:1–18:30 forms the conclusion to the book. Chaps. 19–21 forms "an appendix, reflecting different and later editorial tendencies that do not correspond to the editorial line of the book *per se.* Its inclusion . . . prepares the reader to deal with issues that will only be discussed in Samuel; that is, it does not answer the needs of the immediate context, but of the broader one" (*Book of Judges,* 311–12). Amit (312–13, nn. 6–9) surveys opinions as to the date of these materials and their claim as integral parts of the book of Judges.

Mayes (*BibInt* 9 [2001] 241–58), basing his work on Yee, Amit, and O'Connell, uses literary theories to separate chaps. 17–18 and 19—joined by a Deuteronomistic hand with the editorial refrain, including 21:25—into an account that may have introduced the Saul-David story before Judges was separated from Samuel. The Deuteronomistic Historian has modified the pro-Saul, anti-David slant and made the monarch responsible for implementing the Deuteronomic law. Jüngling (*Richter 19*, 245–84) identifies chaps. 20 and 21 as separate later additions by editors dissatisfied with the ending of the book. Guillaume goes so far as to claim "Judg. 17–18 and Judg. 19–21 have nothing in common" (*Waiting for Josiah*, 129). Kratz (*Composition of the Narrative Books*, 196–97, 207–9) considers chaps. 17–21 among the latest elements in Judges, being products of Deuteronomistic supplements akin to Priestly materials in Chronicles.

But many recent studies continue to show the integrity of the entire book, including the epilogue, even when the scholars do not agree on the origin and purpose of the book. Weinfeld (*VT* 17 [1967] 93–113) was one of the first to see Judg 17–18 as an integral part of the Deuteronomic tradition. Veijola (*Das Königtum*, 24–29; compare Jobling, "Deuteronomic Political Theory," 47–51) fits the epilogue structurally and theologically into the work of the Deuteronomistic History. Gooding (*ErIsr* 16 [1982] 70–79; compare Gunn and Fewell, *Narrative in the Hebrew Bible*, 120) displays the rhetorical symmetry of the book, especially the introduction and the epilogue. Brettler (80–81) sees true appendices—"new material relevant to that book . . . found after the book had been formed"—in 2 Sam 21–24 and Jer 52. In contrast, Judg 16 has "no major conclusion formula." Chap. 17 is "well-integrated into the previous material," 17:1 mimicking 13:2.

Block (474–75) notes nine features that link the two major sections of the epilogue together. Younger (30–33) puts in tabular form the parallel structure of the two introductory chapters and the five concluding ones. McCann sees that "these chapters provide a nearly perfect conclusion to the book in terms of the progressive deterioration that was anticipated in 1:1–2:5 and that has occurred since Gideon. For here the deterioration is complete, and terror reigns on all sides. There is no external enemy because the people are their own enemy" (117).

Wong, having displayed elements of chaps. 17–21 tied structurally and rhetorically to the central section of the book, concludes: "The epilogue of Judges is not a later appendage to a book it does not originally belong. On the contrary, it must have been conceived as a continuation of the central section of Judges, even at its very inception, and may indeed hold the interpretive key to understanding the unspoken assessment of the judges and of the era" (*Compositional Strategy*, 141).

The final chapters of Judges form a double conclusion parallel to the double introduction in the opening chapters. The conclusion is structured around the editor's comments repeated in Judg 17:6, 18:1, 19:1, and 21:25, but these structural markers do not separate narratives on the same structural level. The first two provide closure to a preceding section of a narrative. The latter two introduce and conclude the second half of this entire concluding section.

Judges disappear in the final five chapters of the book of Judges. So does divine deliverance. Names of all types of leaders virtually disappear. The emphasis turns to the lack of a king and the loss of national morality. Violence escalates. A tribe cedes its land and finds a new domicile in northern territory Joshua did not allot to any of the tribes. Another tribe sees some of its members commit a vile act violating all rules of hospitality, leading to the first true gathering of all the tribes of Israel in the entire book. All Israel then fights together, but the enemy is a tribe of Israel. Wong remarks, "The narratives seem full of inconsistencies, such that nearly all the main characters act in inexplicable ways and make decisions that appear self-contradictory and 'bizarre.' . . . Tucked away inconspicuously within almost every single one of these bizarre episodes is an echo of a specific event that took place in the life of a major judge in the central section of the book" (*Compositional Strategy*, 82–83).

Paradoxically, only in these chapters do priests appear. Only here do major worship places like Bethel and Shiloh function as gathering places for Israel. Only here do we find mention of Levites. Only here are the people united as they were in chaps. 1–3, but as McCann points out, "the unity is ironic; for the people come together, in essence, to destroy Benjamin" (118). Wong argues, "The focus of the epilogue seems . . . to be on spiritual, social and political chaos . . . generated entirely from within" (*Compositional Strategy*, 79). Thus the most immoral chapters in the book are at the same time those employing the most religious language.

Leuchter summarizes recent study showing opposing Samuel and Saul traditions in "a discernible form by the late eleventh century B.C.E." (*CBQ* 69 [2007] 432–33). Shiloh was the center of Samuel traditions based on Mosaic authority. Saul traditions rested on the Judges material, centering on Gideon and Abimelech. "Saul's kingship has replaced the normative Levitical religious authority that had once rested with the Shilonites" (435). Solomon and Jeroboam are also indicted as alienating the northern Levites. Saulide motifs were interpolated by Josianic writers into Judg 17–21 so "the sins of Jeroboam and Saul could be hermeneutically fused" (438).

However theoretical such tradition history results may prove to be, they do help us see the unsettled religious and political conditions of the era of the judges. This era was marked by tribes and clans attempting to work together while still protecting their individual traditions, loyalties, and places of worship.

The structure of these chapters is quite clear. Olson observes that "chapters 17–18 focus on the religious dimensions of Israel's decline . . . , and chaps. 19–21 deal more with the social dimensions of Israel's disintegration" as compared to chap. 1 dealing with social and political dimensions while chap. 2 centered on religious issues (863). Olson observes, "The conclusion of each section involves the preservation of an Israelite tribe through abhorrent but seemingly necessary means" (863). A story of lone individuals introduces the two major sections in chaps. 17 and 19. A Levite plays a central role. These stories provide the context for a tribe (Dan) or the nation to carry out incomprehensibly immoral actions. Each of the two major sections ends with the unsettled, threatened tribe able to resume normal life. Throughout, two statements echo to provide structural and thematic unity to this final section of Judges: "In those days Israel had no king in Israel. Every person did what was right in his own eyes" (Judg 17:6).

"One of the most unusual pericopes in the Hebrew Bible." So Bray (*Sacred Dan*, 4) characterizes Judg 17–18 as an introduction to the history of research (compare Mueller, *Micah Story*, 7–49) on a passage where there is "no overall scholarly agreement as to what the story is 'about.'" That history of research has featured a long series of attempts to break the chapters up, crediting either separate sources or a string of redactors, each adding a bit to an old story. In opposition to Noth, T.

Veijola (*Das Königtum*, 137–38) joins the chapters to the Deuteronomistic History, and indeed to DtrG, since these chapters appear to favor the monarchy and the Levite as a *gēr*, or resident alien.

Niemann (*Die Daniten*, 131–47) sees at least three redactions. One occurs under Jeroboam I, making the cultic changes of Jeroboam more acceptable. A second redaction after 733 is "pre-deuteronomistic." It is a negative edition adding *massekâ* or metal image (מַסֵּכָה) and 18:30b–31a, among other changes. The Deuteronomistic edition added Zorah and Eshtaol, 18:12, and 18:27*. An unknown source added other bits and pieces. Becker (*Richterzeit und Königtum*, 253–55) identifies DtrH as the basic formulator of these chapters, with hostile additions from DtrN. Postexilic editors then added comments about the monarchy. Becker takes us back to the heyday of source criticism, singling out individual words and brief phrases as later additions or as signs of a different editor. O'Connell (*Rhetoric of the Book of Judges*, 347–51) sees a compiler adding a few verses and parts of verses.

Bartusch (*Understanding Dan*, 181–202) offers two theories, the first basically unified except for the editorial notes on monarchy. Bartusch's second theory, and seemingly his preferred view, identifies an original etiological narrative explaining the city's name, with a second layer of strong redaction under Jeroboam that added all the cultic information to defend Jeroboam's choice of Dan and a third layer that represents a Judean critique of Jeroboam and his cult and priesthood. Even this Judean level (proto-Deuteronomistic) came from a "scribe living in Judah sometime late in the tenth or early in the ninth century, soon after the ascendency of Jeroboam in the Northern Kingdom and the establishment of royal sanctuaries at Bethel and Dan" (200). The complex theory to get to this final date for the materials can easily be simplified to an author of the entire narrative coming from the south in the time of Jeroboam and using ancient Danite materials to ridicule Dan.

Bartusch (*Understanding Dan*, 193) interprets the sparsity or lack of cultic evidence from Biran's excavations to mean no sanctuary older than Jeroboam's existed and that Jeroboam tried to "out-archaize" (197) David and Solomon's Jerusalem, a relative newcomer to Israel's cultic tradition.

Bray (*Sacred Dan*, 26–28) argues for a postexilic redactor who added idealistic, pro-monarchy comments and attacked the postexilic shrine of Dan, a quite improbable target. Pleading for late addition to the book because the chapters are out of order chronologically misses the whole structure and argument of the book of Judges. Yet, for his history of religion interests, Bray must point to elements of the text as early, preserving an early cult, but in so doing he legitimates the cult of Dan rather than allowing the text to humorously deride it with irony and satire. For Bray, even this early edition was written down after the destruction of Dan in 732, completely missing the relevance of the material for the cult of Jeroboam and its opponents. For earlier struggles to come to grips with the obviously negative elements of the material, see Amit (*Book of Judges*, 321–22, n. 16).

Despite Bray's contention (*Sacred Dan*, 25) that "it is improbable that Judges was composed as a whole," many scholars find unity in the material and exegete it as such. Already in 1934, Fernández (*Bib* 15 [1934] 237–64) argued for the literary unity of the material and noted a presentation of cultic facts without criticism. Similarly, R. H. Pfeiffer sees here the "earliest information on the priesthood in ancient Israel" (*Introduction to the Old Testament*, rev. ed. [London: A. & C. Black, 1948] 321). Vincent

(116) and Hertzberg (239–43) recognize polemic against the Danite sanctuary and thus against the cultic apostasy of Jeroboam I. Noth ("Background of Judges 17–18," 75–76) also saw polemic but only against the ancient Danite sanctuary and posed by Jeroboam's royal sanctuary there. T. C. Vriezen (*The Religion of Ancient Israel* [London: Lutterworth, 1967] 174) sees a foundation legend of the sanctuary at Dan, a legend that was later corrupted by editors or glossators. Soggin (269) sees Dan tradition used polemically to explain Assyria's destruction of the Danite sanctuary. (Compare W. I. Toews, *Monarchy and Religious Institution in Israel under Jeroboam,* SBLMS 47 [Atlanta: Scholars Press, 1993].) Haran (*Temples and Temple Service,* 38) sees the ironic polemic as the contribution of its southern author, not a redactor. Amit (*VT* 40 [1990] 4–20) sets the polemic against Bethel, not Dan.

I would agree with Auld in exclaiming: "What a stupid northerner! What a muddle-headed Ephraimite! There are no prizes for guessing the original audience for this story" (224). But then Auld points to Nah 1:14 and Deut 27:15 to date the story "quite late within the writings of the Old Testament" (225).

I would see the evidence and tendency of the work pointing to southerners at work defending their Bethlehem-born originator of the royal line against the foolish actions of a northern king who erects heretical cultic sites in unchosen places and places heretical images and cult implements there to be administered by self-serving priests.

The tone of the narrative helps one decide which elements to emphasize in trying to determine a genre for these chapters. Several subgenres are evident. Thus Malamat (*Bib* 51 [1970] 1–16) points to the spies and the battle report to call this a conquest story. Block speaks of "a parody on the earlier spy mission traditions" (492). Mueller (*Micah Story,* 75) sees parallels to the superscription (1:3) and temple sermon (chap. 7) of Jeremiah and emphasizes the opening story of Micah and his mother to find a "morality tale" created by a "morality teacher within the deuteronomic tradition who was active in the wake of the fall of Jerusalem in 587 B.C.E." Bray (*Sacred Dan,* 42–43, 46), building on H. Gressmann (*Die Anfänge Israels* [Göttingen: Vandenhoeck & Ruprecht, 1964]) and on Greek cultic stories, focuses on the repeated reference to cultic objects to see a cultic foundation story or etiology here, that is, "an historical account describing the foundation of a shrine in realistic terms" (46) as opposed to the cultic etiologies of Genesis. But Bray gives no generic elements of such a foundation story. He provides more of a description of what the story is not than of what it actually is. Yee finds that the Deuteronomist "conducts a propaganda war [supporting Josiah] against their clergy [i.e., those of northern cult centers such as Dan and Bethel], the country Levites . . . in an attempt . . . to break up the tribal body in service to the monarchy" ("Ideological Criticism," 167).

Auld finds the narrative tone that leads to discovery of the nature of these chapters as he discusses Judg 17: "How can anyone set up his own shrine? And as for installing one of his own sons as priest (v 5), that was doubly absurd: (a) there was a God-given special priestly clan; and (b) how anyway could your son be a proper 'father' to you (v 10)" (224). This tone of humorous, satirical polemic carries the day throughout these chapters. Micah, his mother, his son, his priest, his shrine, his tribe of Ephraim, and the Danites all stand in the bull's eye. The narrative as a whole quickly becomes a satire depicting everything an Israelite worship place should not be.

Younger (335–36; compare O'Connell, *Rhetoric of the Book of Judges,* 238–41) shows how Judg 17 and 18 give an antithetical picture of what Deut 12 legislated: cult sites on hills, idols, central shrine versus local shrines, doing what is right in one's eyes, supporting Levites, inheritance still in the future, a people living safe and secure, and the promise to expand territory. He concludes, "In doing what was right in their own eyes, the characters of this account are acting in defiance of the cultic ideals set forth in Deuteronomy 12" (336). Mueller sees the characters, including the tribe of Dan, as "mired in fear, immorality, and idolatry" so that they "violate eight of the ten commandments—stealing, dishonoring a mother, taking YHWH's name in vain, lying, coveting, and killing. And there is idolatry" (*Micah Story*, 2–3).

Niditch (180) says chaps. 17–18 form "a classic foundation myth, dealing with the conquest of land and the establishment of a tribal holding for Dan. . . . The ideology of expediency operates as one is made to see the workings of realpolitik in the ancient world." At the end of her discussion, she then notes: "The tale in chs. 17–18 serves ultimately as founding myth for an ancient and valued cultic center." Here she sees that the center of the double narrative is on cultic foundations, not conquest foundations. But she does not see that her own description sets the tone as satirical, not mythical or foundational.

Hebrew narrative markers introduce each of the chapters and divide the section into two major parts. The first begins in moral ambiguity and cursing and ends in religious ambiguity with expectation of blessing. The second (chap. 18) begins in territorial oblivion and ends in territorial conquest and religious syncretism. The first section features the complete editorial refrain: "In those days Israel had no king. Every person did what was right in his own eyes" (Judg 17:6). A partial echo of the refrain opens the second section: "In those days Israel had no king" (Judg 18:1). These guide the reader from here through the final repetition of the full refrain in Judg 21:25. In a real sense the entire final section of the book is a narrative exposition of this haunting, yet ambiguous refrain, one we can explain only when we get to the end of the complete narrative.

Judg 17:7 echoes the syntax of 17:1 in introducing a new character and the second stage of the Micah story of 17:1–6. As so often, dialogue and monologue dominate the structure of the section. The first narrative (Judg 17:1–6) is a simple report of private, unintended religious rebellion, while the second is a negotiation narrative bringing employment to a Levite in a private shrine. But the narratives are not straightforward. They are ironic and satirical parodies. The narrator's refrain in v 6, Amit rightfully says, "emphasizes that the two units share the nature of being exemplary variations of the same principle" (*Book of Judges*, 319).

Chap. 18 is longer and a bit more complex in its narrative structure. Two temporal clauses introduce the chapter. A spy narrative ensues, but this one overtly concerns search for land, not for enemy armies. The narrative intertwines with the previous one as the spies stop and make oracular inquiry of Micah's Levite (18:2b–6). The spy mission finds suitable land ready for the taking (18:7) and concludes with a report back to headquarters (18:8–10), including much repetition from v 7. Syntax marks no narrative change, but content shows a new form, ostensibly a battle report with an embedded etiology (18:12). A religious robbery report intervenes (18:13–20) followed by a chase and negotiation report (18:21–26). The battle report resumes and quickly ends (18:27–28a). The denouement then pictures the people of Dan rebuilding the city and dwelling in it with their stolen shrine and

Levite (18:28b–31). As frequently in Judges, the form of battle report is copied to report something quite distinctive, here the establishment of an illegitimate worship place, a worship place Jeroboam I would also establish, indicating yet again the northern kingdom's sin and senselessness (1 Kgs 12:29–30).

Comment

17:1 "There is humour in Judges 17 from the very beginning. The storyteller mocks Micah at almost every opportunity" (Auld, 224).

The opening phrase, "a man from," according to Block, "hints at a new focus. In the following chapters the narrator will offer the reader a series of glimpses at how ordinary Israelites fared in the dark days of the 'judges'" (474). This simple expression cannot, however, determine the dating and setting for this narrative and the entire epilogue as Mark Leuchter (*CBQ* 69 [2007] 429–39) and Serge Frolov (*The Turn of the Cycle: I Samuel 1–8 in Synchronic and Diachronic Perspectives*, BZAW 342 [Berlin: de Gruyter, 2004] 37–52) attempt to argue here and in 13:2 and 19:1. (See Gen 39:2; Judg 13:2; 17:1; 19:1; 1 Sam 1:1; 9:1; 2 Sam 21:20; 1 Chr 20:6.)

"The hill country of Ephraim" represents the best of Israel in its leaders Joshua and Phineas (Josh 17:15; 19:50; 20:7; 21:21; 24:30, 33; Judg 2:9) and in the work of Ehud and Deborah (Judg 3:27; 4:5). It also represents the beginning of disputes with the tribe of Ephraim (Judg 7:24) as well as the home of the Issacharite judge Tola (Judg 10:1).

This hill country plays a significant role in the following narratives (Judg 17:1, 8; 18:2, 13; 19:1, 16, 18). Samuel's family came from that area (1 Sam 1:1). Saul sought his donkeys there (1 Sam. 9:4), and Israelites hid from the Philistines there (1 Sam 14:22–23). Sheba, who rebelled against David, came from Ephraim's hill country (2 Sam 20:21). Solomon located an administrative district there (1 Kgs 4:8). And Jeroboam I resided there in Shechem (1 Kgs 12:25). There King Ahijah of Judah defiantly addressed Jeroboam I (2 Chr 13:4). See also 2 Kgs 5:22; 1 Chr 6:67; 2 Chr 15:8; 19:4; Jer 31:6.

Micah, or in Hebrew *mîkāyhû* (מִיכָיְהוּ), otherwise unknown, has a name glorifying God and meaning, "Who is like Yahweh?" Micah's ensuing actions may give an unexpected answer to the question his name asks. Wong observes, "What is most curious . . . is that in these initial episodes, the characters who were primarily responsible for commissioning the idols are actually portrayed as YHWHists, albeit YHWHists who seem totally oblivious to the glaring incongruity between their professions of faith and their actions" (*Compositional Strategy*, 84). Yet, as McCann emphasizes, "it seems that absolutely *no one* in chapters 17–18 knows what God is like!" The behavior of Micah and his mother is "ludicrous" (McCann, 121).

2 Micah confesses to thievery, deserving to be under the curse his mother uttered against a thief in Micah's hearing. The Hebrew for "curse," *'ālāh* (אָלָה), occurs only a few times in the Hebrew Bible and frequently in a negative context (1 Sam 14:24; 1 Kgs 8:31; 2 Chr 6:22; Hos 4:2; 10:4). O'Connell (*Rhetoric of the Book of Judges*, 232–34) sees the consequences of this curse as providing the major narrative plot in the story. Mueller shows its presence in the covenant oath with Yahweh in Deut 29:14–15 (Heb. 13–14) and concludes, "In the Micah story, the verb אלה (to curse, to take an oath) does not appear in a context of covenant making. Instead, it marks the verbal beginning of covenant breaking (Judg 17:2)"

(*Micah Story*, 83).

Amit argues that "Micah's acts are not to be seen as a step of 'repentance' or of recognition of wrong-doing, but only as motivated by fear of the punishment in wake of the curse" (*Book of Judges*, 324). The "eleven hundred shekels of silver" equal what each Philistine was willing to give Delilah to betray Samson (16:6). Rather than now cursing her thieving son, the mother blesses him in the name of Yahweh. One explanation for this is that, according to Brensinger, "the antidote for such a curse, after all, is the pronouncement of a blessing by the same person who has offered the original spell" (176).

3 The unnamed mother declares the silver sanctified to Yahweh, but sanctified for a special purpose: the making of a carved image or *pesel* (פֶּסֶל)—"the classic word for 'idol'" (Bray, *Sacred Dan*, 66), strictly forbidden to Israel in its earliest legal traditions (Exod 20:4; compare Lev 26:1; Deut 4:16, 23, 25; 5:8; 27:15; Judg 17:3–4; 18:14, 17–18, 20, 30–31; 2 Kgs 21:7; 2 Chr 33:7; Ps 97:7; Isa 40:19–20; 42:17; 44:9–10, 15, 17; 45:20; 48:5; Jer 10:14; 51:17; Nah 1:14; Hab 2:18)—and an overlaid image or *massēkâ* (מַסֵּכָה—notoriously connected with the golden calf of Aaron and the calves Jeroboam erected in Bethel and Dan; Exod 32:4, 8; 34:17; Lev 19:4; Deut 9:12, 16; 27:15; Judg 17:3–4; 18:14, 17–18; 2 Kgs 17:16; Neh 9:18; Ps 106:19; Isa 30:1; 42:17; Hos 13:2; Nah 1:14; Hab 2:18). Israel's obviously syncretistic worship, blending Baal fertility practices involving carved and cast metal images with traditional worship of Yahweh and his provision of victory in battle, started quite early in its history. Dan provided a model that Jeroboam quickly followed. Bray would deny that Jeroboam depended upon Dan to provide a model, perceiving "that the prophets and holy men of the Northern Kingdom were quite happy to accept the existence of these images in the sanctuaries" (*Sacred Dan*, 65–66). Such an argument from silence can prove many things. Bray (66–68) strains hard to justify פֶּסֶל as a neutral, not a negative, term meaning "carving." Bray claims that פֶּסֶל acquired its negative connotation from its appearance in the Decalogue, which Bray would obviously see as a later compilation, dating the first negative use of the term to the divided monarchy in the north. This enables Bray to conclude that the פֶּסֶל of Dan "may have been regarded as legitimate when the Danite story was written (i.e., some time in the later Divided Monarchy period), and only gained negative connotations later" (68). It remains a stretch to find the Decalogue not exercising influence in the north until the time of Hosea, who apparently presupposed that his audience knew the material and considered it authoritative.

But does the narrator refer to one or two images here? In 17:3–4 and in 18:14, the two terms are joined by the Hebrew conjunctive *wāw* and may be considered a hendiadys, or two terms used to describe the same object. The singular verb at the end of v 4 seems to support this interpretation. However, 18:17–18 expands the list of items and separates פֶּסֶל and מַסֵּכָה, seemingly identifying them as two distinct objects. Bray (64) resolves the problem the simple way, removing מַסֵּכָה from 18:17–18, where "it must be a gloss," and then using that to justify seeing it as a gloss inserted as a deliberate polemic in the other verses. Bray can conclude: "The word מַסֵּכָה is very firmly associated with the calf images of both Aaron and Jeroboam, and in view of this, it seems possible that the redactor of Judg 17–18 wanted to connect the shrine of Dan from its origins with the calves, and thus added the word to make the link more explicit" (*Sacred Dan*, 65). That it is possible does not mean it is probable.

Younger claims, "These terms . . . are more than a hendiadys. They are two fixed pairs used to encompass all aspects of idolatrous worship. . . . The terms, as used in the Judges narrative, stress humanity's part in either *making* the idol or in *using* it" (337–38, emphasis original).

The term מַסֵּכָה is of the essence of Judg 17–18, tying this sin of Dan to the sin of Aaron and to that of Jeroboam. Bray *(Sacred Dan,* 70) would argue that the 1 Kgs 12 account of Jeroboam is either "total fabrication" or a "thorough reworking." At the same time, Bray (71; compare Bartusch, 183) assumes that Micah's image was a bull image of Yahweh. Bray insists that Gen 49:24 shows that Yahweh can be "pictured in taurine form" and that the bulls of Jeroboam were more than pedestals for the deity. Haran (*Temples and Temple Service,* 29–30) sees two images in the royal Danite sanctuary—Micah's image of Yahweh in the central sanctuary and Jeroboam's golden calf in the open courtyard. Bartusch (*Understanding Dan,* 183, 198, n. 317) and Bray follow several scholars in seeing Jeroboam using the old Danite tradition to justify his new sanctuary as continuing ancient Israelite tradition. Bartusch says Jeroboam even retained Levites as priests in Dan, though employing non-Levitical priests elsewhere. (Compare B. Halpern, *JBL* 95 [1976] 31–42.)

Having received the money from her son, the mother ever so quickly returns it to him to provide her desired object, an image dedicated to Yahweh. Younger points out, "Ironically, while thinking that they are doing right, both Micah and his mother perform actions contrary to Yahweh's cultic requirements as prescribed in Deuteronomy 12" (338). Mueller says, "The text is silent about [the images'] function. Nothing is said about benefits anyone derives from their presence" (*Micah Story,* 85). Thus Niditch can claim, "The hewn and cast objects are not idols but iconic representations that allow worshipers to focus upon the deity and upon his/her qualities. The icon symbolizes the indwelling presence of the deity" (181).

The founding fathers of the cults at Dan and Bethel may have made such claims, but the editor who so carefully formulated the book of Judges certainly did not share that opinion. Thus, Block concludes, "If this was not an explicitly Canaanite image, it was certainly syncretistic" (480).

Each one did what was right in his or her own eyes. No king regulated their actions or represented Yahweh before the people. Mueller accurately notes, "The author is critical not only of the mother's own covenantal misbehavior but of her irresponsibility in raising her son (cf. Deut 6:7)" (*Micah Story,* 78). Olson states, "One senses the total absence of accountability and responsibility in this family" (870).

4 According to the Hebrew text, the silver keeps changing hands. This has caused scholars to see two versions of the narrative or errors in transmission (Bray, *Sacred Dan,* 32), again missing the irony and humor of the narrative. See *Notes* 17:2.b, 2.c, 3.a, and 3.b. Micah now again returns it to his mother, who transfers a small portion—two hundred shekels—to a smith to make the desired image, which she then places in Micah's house, not in a house of God. Block notes (480) that two hundred shekels of silver "would actually not have yielded a very impressive cult statue." What happens to the nine hundred shekels is a mystery. Bray (*Sacred Dan,* 32) suggests they went to create the ephod and teraphim and (33) that now Yahweh controlled the silver and chose to give it to the Danites. Nothing in the narrative suggests that Yahweh supports or blesses either the Danites or Micah. Amit (*Book of Judges,* 325) sees Micah acting as a middleman and taking a cut but still accepts the presence of "a certain information gap," noting that however the reader fills in the gap, the ironic dimension is strengthened.

The placement of an image in a private dwelling gives a bit of insight into Isra-elite popular religion in that a local family could have its own shrine with its own religious symbols and idols. Thus Albertz notes: "The kind of religion practised in the families of this time largely proves to be uninfluenced by the recent rise of Yahweh religion. . . . [Yahweh] made little impact on the religious everyday life of the families" (*A History of Israelite Religion in the Old Testament Period*, vol. 1, *From the Beginnings to the End of the Monarchy*, trans. John Bowden, Old Testament Library [Louisville: Westminster John Knox, 1994] 95). Micah's story puts a bit different slant on this. Micah and his mother do everything explicitly in the name of Yahweh, unlike some of the previous Judges narratives; but they do these things in religious forms alien to the Yahwism taught in the Torah and the prophets. Previously in Judges, Gideon had a similar family worship site, apparently dedicated to Baal. Thus Becker (*Richterzeit und Königtum*, 228) sees the explicit designation "house of Micah" (17:4, 8, 12; 18:2–3, 13, 15, 18, 22, 26) as central to the narrative's plot.

Yee concludes:

> Tribal Israel certainly does not escape caricature . . . depicted as uncivilized; no king ruled and cultic disorder was rampant. Furthermore, because this was a time when kin-ship relations were highly prized, the breakdown of these relations in this text is quite remarkable. A son betrays his mother. A "son" (the Levite) abandons his "father" (Micah). A shameless tribe violates the laws of hospitality and the host/guest relationship. . . . The Deuteronomist shifts the history of tribal collapse back two generations to the prestate period itself. He completely suppresses the fact that the monarchy deliberately broke up the "tribal body" in order to establish and preserve a tributary mode of production. ("Ideological Criticism," 161)

Albertz (*History of Israelite Religion*, 99) points to a house chapel with horned altars, cult stands, and goblets found in situ in Megiddo. P. D. Miller (*Religion of Ancient Israel*, 63) shows large-scale evidence of private cults in Tell Beit Mirsim, Beer-sheba, and Hazor with several having "a pillar-based female figurine" (64). (Compare J. S. Holladay, "Religion in Israel and Judah under the Monarchy," in *Ancient Israelite Religion*, FS F. M. Cross, ed. P. D. Miller, Jr., P. D. Hanson, and S. D. McBride [Philadelphia: Fortress, 1987] 249–99.) Turning to Judg 17, Albertz sees Micah's act as "by no means a special case" and points to Exod 21:6–7 as a text that "presupposes that every Israelite household had images of gods or at least a cultic niche" (100). The household cult would have offered incense offerings and made lamentations and thanksgivings, at the least. Brensinger, with refer-ence to Exod 20:24, notes, however, that "such a sanctuary has no clear claim to legitimacy. Nothing, for example, associates it in any way with genuine Israelite worship and tradition" (177). Miller concludes that "the complexity of Yahwism in both orthodox and heterodox forms was not confined to a particular group or place" (*Religion of Ancient Israel*, 56).

5 A disjunctive clause stops the narrative action to describe a major charac-teristic about Micah, here named with an abbreviated form of his name, *mîkâ*, without the Yahwistic element (*mîkāyhû*). Mueller contends that "the name change signals a new relationship between Micayhu and God . . . marks a distancing of the protagonist from YHWH" (*Micah Story*, 515).

Micah owns a "house of God" (בֵּית אֱלֹהִים). He equips it with an ephod and a teraphim, two items of cultic equipment whose identity and function are not clear. Wong observes, "One can say that the use of אפד [ephod] in a pejorative sense as an idolatrous cultic object is actually quite uncommon" (*Compositional Strategy*, 86). Guillaume sees the possibility that these two cultic elements could be "later additions, as these elements play no role in the story, although nothing permits us to affirm it" (*Waiting for Josiah*, 142). Guillaume again misses the ironic piling up of questionable cult objects in satirical polemic against Dan and ultimately against Jeroboam. As Exum phrases it, "The building up of terms is surely ironically emphatic" (*CBQ* 52 [1990] 426).

In Exod 28:4, 27–31 and 35:9, 27 (compare 1 Sam 2:18, 28), the ephod was clearly a part of the priestly garments. In 1 Sam 14:3 the priest carried the ephod, perhaps but not certainly a synonym for wearing it. Gideon's ephod became an object of worship (Judg 8:27). The ephod apparently hung on the wall in the worship place in storage waiting to be used (1 Sam 21:9 [Heb. 10]). All priests, not just the high priest, wore ephods (1 Sam 22:18). In 1 Sam 23:6–12 the ephod remained the property of the priest but was now carried in his hand and seemed to function as a divining tool enabling David to know God's directions for the war. (Compare 30:7.) This may indicate that the ephod carried the urim and thummim used for seeking answers from God. David himself wore the ephod, perhaps in the role of priest/king (2 Sam 6:14; 1 Chr 15:27). Hos 3:4–5, the only other passage where ephod and teraphim are paired according to Auld (226), threatened Israel with the loss of ephod and teraphim, so that these may not have been exclusive to the Jerusalem temple. P. Jenson (*NIDOTTE*, 1:476–77; compare Bray, *Sacred Dan*, 112–18) points to distinctions among the elaborate high priestly ephod, the linen garments for other priests, and "an independent cultic object used for oracles." "The third type has sometimes been regarded as different in kind, perhaps an idol, the garment of an idol . . . , a box . . . , or some other object." Jenson concludes that

> the Urim and Thummim, used for divination, are in the breastpiece that is attached to the ephod (Exod 28:30). . . . It is likely that ephods were found in a variety of different forms, the more practical garments of a simple design and the more ceremonial types made of costly materials and heavily ornamented. . . . An ephod was a prized ornament in a well-endowed shrine, probably used by the priest only on special occasions. (1:476)

In regards to the high priestly ephod, Jenson decides, "The details are unclear, but it appears to be a sleeveless overgarment with shoulder pieces (Exod 28:25) and bound by rings to the breastplate (28:28)" (*NIDOTTE*, 1:477). Similarly, Carol Myers feels that "a clear picture of what it looked like is difficult to obtain. It apparently was an apronlike garment, suspended from waist level downward and kept in place by shoulder pieces or straps; it probably completely encircled the lower body." Myers sees the possibility that at some stage(s) of Israel's religion the ephod represented a garment covering cultic statues. She concludes: "The ephod was both a special garment and a ritual object, and in either or both of these aspects it functioned symbolically to bring a human representative of the Israelite community into contact with the unseen God" (*ABD*, 2:550). Z. Zevit laments that "unfortunately, it is not exactly clear what made a garment recognizable as an 'epod'" (*Religions of Ancient Israel*, 256, n. 213).

Bray forthrightly admits, "It seems difficult to draw any firm conclusions about the nature and function of teraphim from the evidence of the Hebrew Bible" (*Sacred Dan*, 123; compare Block, 481). Bartusch (*Understanding Dan*, 195) sees their appearance in only northern traditions as significant. Judith M. Hadley (*NIDOTTE*, 4:339) perceives the teraphim to have different meanings in different passages. In Gen 31:19, 33, 35 she sees them as clan emblems that may confer "legal rights of leadership to the possessor." In contrast to the small figures of Genesis, in 1 Sam 19:13, 16 teraphim are big enough to appear to represent human bodies. The term normally has a negative connotation and can be associated with divination (1 Sam 15:23; 2 Kgs 23:24; Ezek 21:21 [Heb. 26]; Hos 3:4; Zech 10:2), though Bartusch (*Understanding Dan*, 196) sees them as positive instruments of divination for Jeroboam and Dan. Block uses the Zechariah passage to conclude that the teraphim are "some form of divinatory objects, comparable to oracular alabaster and hematite stones known from Akkadian sources" (481; compare T. J. Lewis, "Teraphim," *DDD*, 1588–1601).

In his religious reformation Josiah destroyed the teraphim (2 Kgs 23:24). Albertz sees the teraphim as small "figurines of deities in the possession of the family." They "served to secure the continuity of the family and the solidarity between one generation and the next" (*History of Israelite Religion*, 37). Judg 17–18 distinguishes the teraphim from the image of the deity and yet makes the teraphim a "part of the basic equipment of a regular household cult." So Albertz concludes they were "incidental and subordinate figurines around the precious cultic image" (37). They could be used in divining the god's purpose and will. Albertz will not rule out the possibility that teraphim "are meant to be images of deified ancestors" (1 Sam 28:13; *History of Israelite Religion*, 38). P. D. Miller goes so far as to see the teraphim as "ancestor figurines used in necromancy" (*Religion of Ancient Israel*, 56). Miller refers to K. van der Toorn, "The Nature of the Biblical Teraphim in the Light of the Cuneiform Evidence," *CBQ* 52 [1990] 202–23.

Micah "consecrated one of his sons" (וַיְמַלֵּא אֶת־יַד אַחַד מִבָּנָיו, 17:5), literally "and he filled the hand of one of his sons." This is a technical term in Hebrew for ordaining or consecrating a person to serve as priest (Exod 28:41; 29:9, 29, 33, 35; 32:29; Lev 8:33; 16:32; 21:10; Num 3:3; 1 Kgs 13:33; 1 Chr 29:5; 2 Chr 13:9; 29:31). Bray (*Sacred Dan*, 34, 90–94) tries to see the ordination here as so nearly parallel to that of the Levite later that both indicate ordination of one who has not served previously as a priest. (Compare Brensinger, 177.) That misses the whole point of the narrative, which shows the value of a Levite as priest and the assumption that a Levite is a priest and is desirable for a local or tribal or national sanctuary. The son's installation as priest may have represented desperate measures some local sanctuaries took, but it served as preparation for and contrast to the installation of the Levite as priest. Levites were scarce, most seemingly serving in national or tribal sanctuaries—perhaps at Beersheba, Arad, Gilgal, Bethel, Shiloh, Gibeah, and other such shrines. The point is that even Dan has a history of Levitical priests, a history Jeroboam ignored (1 Kgs 12:31).

Laity are "consecrated" only in 1 Chr 29:5 and 2 Chr 29:31. Consecration outside the Mosaic/Aaronic narratives occurs only here in Judges and in 1 Kgs 13:33 and 2 Chr 13:9, these latter two in connection with Jeroboam consecrating "illegitimate" priests. So again the Judges story in a unique fashion mirrors the sins of Jeroboam. Yet it also mirrors a form of family/clan religion in which families apparently had "friendly competition" to gain the best implements for worship and the most qualified worship leaders. Here the apparent clan leader is also the clan religious leader who selects and "consecrates" the worship leader/priest. Illegitimacy/legitimacy of the priesthood depended in their eyes on the perspective from which you viewed the religious history of Israel and its family components. One perspective appears to have been that Yahweh could be honored in family settings with locally consecrated religious leaders. Another restricted true religious ceremonies to the high places where Yahweh was worshiped through Canaanite practices. A different perspective limited worship to the central sanctuary (sanctuaries) Yahweh had chosen under priestly leadership from the family Yahweh had chosen. The clan of Micah surely originated this narrative in celebration of Micah's wit and financial power in bringing a qualified priest and special worship utensils to their clan shrine. The narrator who joined the narratives of the individual local heroes into the book of Judges used the narrative to show that even in their religious practices the people of Israel ignored Yahweh's teachings and worshiped however it seemed right in their own eyes.

6 "In those days Israel had no king. Every person did what was right in his own eyes." Mueller observes that "Judges 17:6 and 18:1a have received more scholarly attention than any other verses in the Micah story. . . . Both statements sum up a preceding scene and set the tone for what follows" (*Micah Story*, 103–4). (For a brief survey of opinions, see Olson, 864.) Schneider says, "Israel now enters a period when even a bad deity-designated leader no longer existed" (234).

Noth ("Background of Judges 17–18," 79) saw that these key verses, Judges 17:6 and 18:1a, "have been placed in their present location by someone who comprehended the interior structure of the narrative, and most probably this was the author himself." Mueller says that the comments "are critical of the actions of the protagonists in the Micah story. . . . The author points to the lack of competent leadership as a crucial reason accounting for the protagonists' covenantal misbehavior" (*Micah Story*, 105).

Talmon ("In Those Days," 242) sought a new meaning for the Hebrew מלך, "king," giving it the more general definition of hero or political leader. Wellhausen (*Composition des Hexateuchs*, 386) says the refrain "in those days Israel had no king" (17:6; 18:1) came from a writer during the monarchy who wanted to show that the monarchy was a great step forward from the period of the judges. Moore (382) saw a preexilic editor seeking to explain how such anarchy as that in the period of the judges could go unpunished. Mueller thinks the author is saying, "some particular king did not act as a king" (*Micah Story*, 105). Exum ("Judges," *Harper's Bible Commentary*, 258) decides that these key verses anticipate the monarchy as providing relief from the conditions when Israel had no king. O'Connell summarizes the key verses as meaning "kingship is implicitly endorsed as the means of attaining the covenant ideals of land occupation, intertribal covenant loyalty, social justice, and adherence to the cult" (*Rhetoric of the Book of Judges*, 10).

Klein shifts the focus from the advantage of the monarchy to a negative evaluation of the period when Israel had no king. Thus "the resolution of the book does not reflect regret of the absence of what is yet to come but recognition of the failure of the original goals" (*Triumph of Irony*, 141). McCann finds that chaps. 17–21 "do not offer ideological support for the monarchy; rather they fit into the larger pattern of Israel's persistent unfaithfulness and disobedience" (118). Olson concludes that the refrain and the final chapters of Judges "should be understood as both a negative portrayal of Israel in this period at the end of the Judges era and as an affirmation of the hope of God's continuing presence with the community in spite of its unfaithfulness" (864).

Boling (258) points to Israel's failure to recognize Yahweh as king and God's ongoing grace to such a people. Block sees no positive statement about the king; rather "the author's use of the formula deliberately extends to the citizenry in general the high-handed attitudes of later kings against the will of God" (476). Having listed four strong reasons to connect the description of the king here to Jeroboam, Block then shifts to the time of Manasseh and says that from that perspective,

> Israel did not need kings to lead them into idolatry, since the people did it on their own. . . . Everyone behaved just like later kings. . . . The difference between the period of the governors and the monarchy/ies is not the presence or absence of idolatry or evil. Rather, it is the source from which the evil springs. During the monarchy kings led the way in abominable acts; in pre-monarchic times the people did it on their own. (483–84)

Block then notes the article by F. E. Greenspahn (*JBL* 101 [1982] 129–30) arguing that a king could and would ensure the people's doing right in God's eyes. Block follows with this cryptic remark: "But the later one dates the insertion of this editorial comment, the less sense it makes" (484, n. 44). This should point Block back to Jeroboam, for whom he has provided so much evidence. Instead, it points him to the last portion of the monarchy when such comments make little sense. It may well be the case that from southern Judah's perspective, Israel, the northern kingdom, had no king, having rejected the Davidic monarch and having followed one who turned the worship of Yahweh upside down.

Mueller (*Micah Story*, 106) sees 17:6 and 18:1a as pointing forward to a special type of king, one who would lead the nation to obey covenant stipulations (compare Davis, *WTJ* 46 [1984] 158). In disagreement with Amit (*Book of Judges*, 336), Mayes sees the final redaction pointing forward to an ideal king: "It was not possible to identify the historical Judean king of the Davidic line as the dependable guarantor of Israel's welfare independent of the law" (*BibInt* 9 [2001] 257, n. 48).

Niditch goes a slightly different direction:

> This line ["in those days there was no king"] is not, as some have suggested, an indictment of early times of chaos, but an accepting commentary on a romantic, battle-ridden, foundation period in the history of the nation. The phrase is a reflection on the nature of power itself. The rubric also frames, in a neutral way, various forms of religious activity that would be considered highly irregular by Deuteronomic-style writers: the ad hoc priesthood whose founder begins his career as a retainer for a wealthy chieftain; the peculiar way in which various iconic objects are funded and created; and the very use of paraphernalia such as an ephod, condemned in the tale of Gideon by the voice of the theologian but here associated, at least in some manuscript traditions, with the genealogy of Gershom, son of Moses. The tale in chs. 17–18 serves ultimately as founding myth for an ancient and valued cultic center. In these tales can be heard the voice of the humanist [that is, Niditch's postexilic voice]. (180)

Later she recaps: "The phrase at 17:6 is far from an overt, zealous condemnation of the kind found elsewhere in the Hebrew Bible. Rather, he notes that these were early times, before the monarchy, when religious expression had not yet become uniform or orthodox" (182). It is doubtful that an original reader or listener to these narratives would see such a sophisticated meaning in them. Rather than explaining the one-time legitimacy of now-forbidden practices, the statement gives the audience a reason to support a certain variety of kingship, but not the northern variety that leads to such discredited religious practices.

A disjunctive temporal clause, "in those days," introduces the editorial recital. Interestingly, the two-part theological summary of 17:6 appears here at the juncture of two parts of the Micah narrative, not at the beginning or end of the whole narrative. As such, it is presented as integral to this narrative while other partial and entire quotations will serve as introductions (18:1; 19:1) to individual narratives or as conclusion to the entire epilogue. Amit notes that Micah's generation understood all the practices described in the following narrative as "legitimate and desired cultic behavior that will bring reward upon its owners. Precisely the fact that all of the parties acted in innocence and with the intention of doing what is right in the eyes of God rather than out of wickedness or contempt, reveals the distorted values of the period" (*Book of Judges*, 328).

The use of the editorial recital clearly joins chaps. 17–21 into a literary unit centered on two themes: (1) leadership and (2) moral/religious obedience. In the present context the full recital appears to signify that such unorthodox religious happenings in the center of the northern kingdom could not occur if the north had proper leadership. The reality appears to have been that they had Jeroboam, who consecrated national priests with as little claim to legitimacy as that which Micah's son possessed. Making leadership decisions, religious decisions, or personal decisions on the basis of personal preference did not work for the people of Yahweh.

7 Structurally and syntactically, v 7 mirrors v 1, introducing a new character into the narrative. This is not an adult man or *'îš* (אִישׁ). This is a "young man" or *na'ar* (נַעַר), leading Block (485) to point to Mosaic prescription of the age of thirty for a priest. Compare Num 4:3, 30 and 8:24–26.

Micah the grown man lives in the shadow of his mother, seeking to please her but also willing to stir her ire by stealing from her. In direct contrast, the young man of v 7 separates himself from his family to find his own place in life.

Block uses the designation of the Levite as a southerner from "Bethlehem of Judah" to deny a pro-Judean/Davidic bias in the book of Judges. However, even Block sees that the Levite's "roots had not been firmly planted in Bethlehem" (486). Rather, David's origin at Bethlehem looms bright in contrast to this misplaced Levite who has no business being in Bethlehem. Attachment to Bethlehem does not promise success. Attachment to the right person with Bethlehem roots does promise God's blessings (2 Sam 7).

Bethlehem is not represented among the Levitical cities of Josh 21, so sojourn there raises questions about why his family would live there. What is more, he is identified both as a Levite and as belonging to "part of the clan of Judah," apparently recognizing Levites not as a clan or tribe in Judah but as a profession. (See R. Nelson, *Raising Up a Faithful Priest: Community and Priesthood in Biblical Theology* [Louisville: Westminster John Knox, 1993] 4.) Scholars explain this problem in many different ways.

Brensinger finds from 18:30 that "while acknowledging a certain ambiguity in the language of 17:7, it seems appropriate here to retain a more traditional understanding of Jonathan's status. Jonathan was from the tribe of Levi, but he resided within the territory of Judah" (178). Brensinger blames the Levite for not being connected to one of the nine Levitic cities in Judah and Simeon's territory. Similarly, Younger says, "Micah evinces an ignorance of the Law in its most basic teachings" (339).

Bray (*Sacred Dan*, 19–21) sees a problem in translation here because the text places the Levite in Judah and a resident alien amidst his own tribe. Bray (20–21) thus translates *mišpāḥâ* (מִשְׁפָּחָה) with the wider meaning of "clansland." In so doing Bray, as throughout his work, misses the irony of the chapters. The text shows Dan unable to decide if it is simply a clan or has the strength of a tribe. These chapters picture a Levite expected to serve at a sanctuary as a priest but unable to find a satisfactory place to live or serve and so choosing to be a resident alien even in territory he refers to as his homeland. The final word of v 7 makes the ironic meaning evident. The Levite is a resident alien "there," that is, right among his own people. Even where he should be most at home, he feels most alienated and in need. Gunneweg (*Leviten und Priester*, 14–23) shows that one can be a member of a tribe and a resident alien within the tribal territory.

P. D. Miller describes the early situation:

> Many families from all over Israel would have dedicated their sons to the Levitical order, and, as Deuteronomy indicates (10:8–9; 18:1–8), they would have been landless and dependent upon patrons among the tribes or individual or corporate support for their livelihood, as was the case with the young Levite attached to the house of Micah. So while some were indeed born to the priesthood, others were recruited across clan and tribal boundaries. (*Religion of Ancient Israel*, 172)

Albertz concludes:

> The Levites purchased their right to priestly service by a readiness to sever their ancestral kinship relationships, take upon themselves the legally uncertain status of a *ger* (cf. Judg. 17:7; 19:1ff.), and thus become mobile. . . . The Levites of the early pre-exilic period can thus be defined as a mobile, religious association with a quasi-tribal organization which lived dispersed through the land. Some of them were engaged in priestly service, predominantly at the small sanctuaries of the country ("the high places"); those who could not find a fixed position probably earned their living by casual religious services, for example as experts in omens; . . . perhaps they were also active as helpers and teachers in the law (Deut. 33.10a). (*History of Old Testament Religion*, 58–59)

Albertz allows for the possibility that the Levitical association goes back to Moses.

Z. Zevit calls the Levites a "guild-caste of specialists in such lore," defining lore as "a body of cultic know-how" that various clans of Levites shared in serving as a uniting factor for the various tribes and cult places (*Religions of Ancient Israel*, 656). They brought uniformity to cultic ritual even if "myths may have been different" (657).

S. Tuell (*The Law of the Temple in Ezekiel 40–48*, HSM 49 [Atlanta: Scholars Press, 1992] 124–32) finds a complex system of priestly duties and privileges ranging from the priest, elders of priests, guardians of the threshold, second-order priests, Levites who carried the ark in processionals, to Levitical priests outside Jerusalem who mediated disputes, pronounced blessings, diagnosed disease, and led rituals.

M. D. Rehm decides "a clan constituted a blood relationship, and several such clans who had the common function of the priesthood joined together to form the tribe 'Levi.' Accordingly, the Levites comprised a group of clans who, taken together, could have been designated as a tribe." Rehm continues, "Levites were scarce during the period of the tribal league. This is understandable if their major function was caring for the central sanctuary with the tent and ark. Only gradually, as their numbers grew, would some Levites be free to serve at local sanctuaries" (*ABD*, 4:297–310).

Rehm uses evidence in Deuteronomy to distinguish between poor country Levites and Levites who served at central sanctuaries, poverty caused by Jeroboam I going outside Levitical circles to anoint priests and thus leaving many northern Levites unemployed and unsupported by the government. Rehm thus concludes:

> In the desert the Levites had been given the right to serve the ark. By virtue of this they became the keepers of the central sanctuary in the tribal league. It became their prerogative to expound the Mosaic law as well as sacrifice at the central sanctuary. As the Levites grew in number, not all of them could stay at the central sanctuary. This made some available for serving at local sanctuaries. Anyone could be a priest at a local sanctuary, but even there Levites were preferred. On the other hand, at the central sanctuary only the Levites could serve. These are the "Levitical priests" of Deuteronomy. All these Levites seem to be descendants of Moses and/or Ithamar. They were probably the Mushites and Libnites mentioned in Num 26:58a. (*ABD*, 4:305)

Rehm sees the south as equally unfriendly to Levites, the Zadokite priesthood appointed under David and Solomon eliminating the Levites from Jerusalem.

This Levite did not stand in the "biblical" tradition of Levites. Block (486–86) lists five ways he broke expectations of Levites: not going to a central shrine, not serving in the name of Yahweh, not serving with other Levites but taking the place of an unorthorized priest, not serving at a place God chose, and not receiving the proper recompense as Deut 18:1–5 describes.

Micah probably found it unusual, unexpected, and exciting to see a Levite coming to him. In his day, Levites were probably scarce commodities and possibly revered people. His presence appears to Micah to be a work of God, but the narrator does not intend for readers to see this as "an example of Yahweh using circumstances to his own ends" (contra Bray, *Sacred Dan*, 34). Rather, Bray correctly concludes, "Micah is presuming upon the divine will and is seeking to secure a blessing without consulting the deity" (35). This Levite, like many of them, is classified as a *gēr* (גֵּר) or resident "alien." The Levite and the old man in 19:1, 16 are also aliens. Dan was seen as an alien beside the ships (Judg 5:17). The patriarchs were viewed as aliens in the land of Canaan (Gen 20:1; Exod 6:4).

Israelite law called for incorporation of aliens into the Israelite community (Exod 12:48–49; Lev 19:33–34). Israelite law and custom demanded fair treatment and care for the alien, along with other economically challenged Israelites like orphans and widows (Deut 24:17; 26:13; Jer 7:6; Mal 3:5). A. H. Konkel summarizes the alien life:

> The sojourner is distinguished from the foreigner in that he has settled in the land for

some time and is recognized as having a special status. As individuals or a group they have abandoned their homeland for political or economic reasons and sought refuge in another community, as Abraham in Hebron (Gen 23:4), Moses in Midian (Exod 2:22), Elimelech and his family in Moab (Ruth 1:1), or the Israelites in Egypt (Exod 22:20).

The sojourner in Israel does not possess land and is generally in the service of an Israelite who is his master and protector (Deut 24:14). He is usually poor, but as a resident enjoys the rights of assistance, protection, and religious participation. He has the right of gleaning (Lev 19:10; 23:22), participation in the tithe (Deut 14:29), the Sabbath year (Lev 25:6), and the cities of refuge (Num 35:15). His participation in religious feasts assumes the acceptance of circumcision (Exod 12:48; cf. Deut 16:11, 14). He may bring offerings and is obligated to the regulations of purity (Lev 17:8–16). There is legislation for religious offenses (Lev 24:22), such as blasphemy of the name of Yahweh (Lev 24:16) or idolatrous practice (Lev 20:2). The sojourner is under divine protection (10:18; Ps 146:9); Israelites must love the alien as themselves (Deut 10:19), for that is what they themselves were. In daily life there was to be no barrier between the alien and the Israelite. (*NIDOTTE*, 1:837–38)

8–11 The Levite has no destination, just the intent to put down roots as an alien "wherever he might find a place." He is simply endeavoring "to make his own way," an expression that is unusual (Block, 487, n. 54) and whose meaning can be debated. NRSV reads, "to carry on his work"; NLT, "as he was traveling through." Apparently, the Levite has chosen to live away from his home as a resident alien, though the verb *gûr* (גּוּר) can simply mean "to dwell, abide." His is an aimless search, leading wherever events take him and someone accepts him.

Micah sees the chance of a lifetime to have a genuine Levite as his own priest. He thus invites him to be both "priest" and "father" to him (17:10). The latter term, "father," *'āb* (אָב), is a title of honor addressed to people with a special relationship: an older person (1 Sam 24:12), teacher (2 Kgs 2:12), prophet (2 Kgs 6:21), priest (Judg 17:10; 18:19), husband (Jer 3:4, 19), or adviser (Gen 45:8). To cement the relationship, Micah offers the Levite ten shekels of silver plus room and board, a much smaller amount than the eleven hundred shekels he had taken from his mother and the two hundred required to make an idol. The "necessary clothes" may refer to priestly garments (Block, 488, n. 60). Amit points out that "Micah's investment was not in fact very great" (*Book of Judges*, 326). However, the Levite "eagerly accepted" (17:11). The Levite is, according to Amit, thus portrayed as one "who tends to compromise with reality" (*Book of Judges*, 327). Or as Mueller puts it, "The Levite in the Micah story reverses most of what deuteronomic legislation stipulates" (*Micah Story*, 83). Ironically, the Levite hired as a "father" becomes a "youth," *hana'ar* (הַנַּעַר), like one of Micah's "sons." Yee observes, "The father-son relation becomes empty because it is reversible" ("Ideological Criticism," 159).

12 This new son with stronger priestly credentials is now consecrated in place of Micah's true son as priest in Micah's shrine (compare v 5). Again the narrator underlines that this man was a "youth," quite possibly younger than the son consecrated earlier. Bartusch (200, n. 324) sees the central critique in these chapters to be directed at the Levite, not at the cult apparatus. But the constant reference to man-made objects and lists of cultic items shows that the author is ironically condemning them. As Block sees, Micah's religion is not God-made; it is "a man-made religion" (488).

13 Micah makes his own kind of confession of faith: "Now I know that Yahweh will be good to me for I have a Levite as a priest." Block says, "Micah assumes that now that he has engaged a member of this clan, he has automatic access to the resources of heaven" (489). Or as Niditch phrases it, "Levites are wandering holy men who bring good luck with them. They are quintessential mediators between God and humans, have divinatory abilities, and are quite a catch for the repentant son, con man, and cult founder" (182).

Polzin sees this proclamation as connecting to the central theme of the stories in chaps. 3–16 as well as providing an introduction to chaps. 18–21: "Success or failure comes mysteriously to whomever it will" (*Moses and the Deuteronomist,* 198). In his own way Micah is a religious man dedicated to Yahweh and depending on Yahweh for blessing and prosperity. But, as with Gideon's ephod, Jephthah's vow, and Samson's neglected Nazirite vow and prayer for revenge, so Micah's expectation of blessing comes connected with the right name of God but the wrong practice of worship and life under that God. As Olson rightly observes, "Micah believes that just as God can be captured in a humanly crafted idol, so also God's favor can be guaranteed by buying the right priest" (870).

The book of Judges shows repeatedly that divine blessing depends not on "acceptable" cultic practitioners but on devotion and loyalty to God or simply on God's grace. Pride in a priest is no predictor of prosperity. Brensinger declares, "This section of the narrative concludes with what would have been unthinkable earlier: a Levite overseeing an idolatrous shrine, and a proprietor expecting God's blessing because of it" (179).

18:1 "In those days Israel had no king. In those days the tribe of Dan . . ." The repeated portion of the editorial refrain joined to a parallel temporal clause introducing the tribe of Dan appears to mark a shift to an entirely new narrative. So does a shift from imperfect consecutives to a participle in 18:1. But quite soon the Micah-and-his-priest narrative will link into the Dan-seeking-territory narrative. Dan marches out, eventually reaching Laish, twenty-five miles (40.2 km) north of the Sea of Galilee. Guillaume (*Waiting for Josiah,* 131, n. 6) appears to agree with J. M. Sasson ("Yarim-Lim Takes the Grand Tour," *BA* 47 [1986] 246–51) that the Laish mentioned in Near Eastern documents is near Aleppo and unconnected with Dan. Niemann (*Die Daniten,* 143) seeks to push the Danite migration down to 735 B.C.E., the migration being from Dan to Mahaneh-dan to escape Tiglath-pileser. According to Guillaume (*Waiting for Josiah,* 135–37, 142), Josiah used the story to invent the ideal Israel from Dan to Beersheba. Guillaume ties the migration to the Assyrian reorganization of the area in 701 B.C.E. as part of his Josianic portion of Judges, the migration being fictitious: "the only historically attested Danites are the inhabitants of the city of Dan" (142). Guillaume's reconstruction is so far from the actual text and so dependent on presumptions and theories that it goes beyond belief. Even Guillaume (138) admits that the story lacks "typically Deuteronomistic expressions."

Here again we see that the editorial purpose in assembling the Joshua and Judges narrative was not bound to strict chronology. Rather, the editor inserts the story of Dan spying out new territory at this point because it shows another side to Israel's decline, a whole tribe's loss of territory, a theme that will then be trumped by the Benjaminites who almost lose their entire identity as a tribe. All this occurs with no king in Israel.

Amit explains that the events of chaps. 17–21 "belong to the beginning of the period of the Judges rather than to its end, as in both sections appear figures belonging to the third generation following the Exodus" (*Book of Judges*, 311). Amit concludes that "in the final part of the book events appear to break its chronological flow" (312). Such a statement assumes a chronological flow in the first part of the book, where we have seen a geographical flow and a thematic flow of deterioration, but not a chronological flow. Amit does qualify her stance to conclude that "chronological inappropriateness is not a necessary and sufficient condition for characterizing an extant section as appended, just as chronological suitability does not make it an integral part of the composition" (314).

2 The narrative appears to be chronologically subsequent to the Samson materials wherein Samson as a part of the tribe of Dan worked on the southeastern coast near the Philistine cities and close to Judah, though Bartusch (*Understanding Dan*, 177 with n. 258) sees Samson typically dated after the Danite migration among a small remnant of southwestern Danites. Here Dan constitutes a "tribe" or *šebeṭ* (שֵׁבֶט) in Israel, while in Judg 13:2 Dan was simply a clan or *mišpāḥâ* (מִשְׁפָּחָה). Does this indicate that in Samson's day only a remnant of Dan remained in its original territory?

Bartusch finds "credible evidence to conclude that the tribe of Dan possibly may not ever have migrated northward and that the underlying story contained within Judges 17–18 may be better interpreted as an etiology explaining only how the city of Dan (Laish) at the northern border of Israel got its name" (*Understanding Dan*, 178). Thus Bartusch (178–81) does not see a time when Dan was not in the southwest and finds no history behind Judg 17–18. For him, a number of factors show that the story is without a historical basis: associations of Judahites and Danites (Num 1–2, 26); the literary nature of the Judges narrative as conquest story; the interpretation of Deut 33 as relating to city, not tribe; Josh 19 as literarily late; Judg 5 as not showing evidence of Dan in the north; six hundred as a standard literary number; and lack of archaeological evidence (see n. 265) for the emigration of new people.

Admittedly, a polemic such as these chapters present may rest on a skewed picture of history, but the existence of a city of Dan in the north is still best explained by association with the biblical tribe of Dan. Dan's place in the south seems secure, so a migration is the best explanation remaining for Dan's ability to name a city in the north.

For a review of theories concerning the history of the tribe of Dan, see Bray (*Sacred Dan*, 16–19). Evidence is based on several Scriptures where Dan appears and on recent excavations at Tel Dan: Gen 14:14 anachronistically marks Dan as the limit of Abraham's pursuit of the enemy armies, assuming that Dan is the northern limit of Canaan. Dan's birth narratives and appearance in tribal and genealogical lists include Gen 30:6, 35:25, 46:23, Exod 1:4, 1 Chr 2:2, and Ezek 48:1–2.

Individual members of the tribe of Dan appear in Exod 31:6, 35:34, 38:23, Lev 24:11, Num 7:66, 13:12, 34:22, 1 Chr 27:22, and 2 Chr 2:14 (Heb. 13), many skilled in making cultic materials. The blessing of Jacob in Gen 49:16–17 describes Dan as a judge in a wordplay on the meaning of the name and as a snake by the roadside ready to strike unwary travelers and their horses. Num 1:12, 38–39; 2:25, 31; 10:25; 26:42; and Ezek 48:32 give census figures, encampment configurations, and the order of march for the wilderness tribes or the new temple. The covenant ritual placed Dan among those tribes reciting the curses (Deut 27:13). The blessing of

Moses in Deut 33:22 describes Dan as a "lion's whelp that leaps forth from Bashan" (NRSV), thus locating the tribe in the north and pointing to its aggressive behavior. In Deut 34:1 the soon-to-die Moses views the promised land from Gilead to Dan, which appears to be an east to west description, placing Dan in the southwest, but which 34:2 modifies into a northern location beyond Gilead.

Josh 19:40–46 lists the cities of Dan's tribal allotment, but several of these cities later appear in Judah's allotment (Josh 15:13–63; compare Judg 1:18), or are seen as part of the Philistine territory (1 Kgs 15:27), as part of the Amorite settlement (Judg 1:34–35), or in Chronicles as part of Benjamin, Judah, or Ephraim (1 Chr 6:69 [Heb. 54]; 2 Chr 11:10; 28:18), showing Dan's inability to conquer the cities assigned. Josh 19:47–48 (compare Judg 1:34) describes Dan's forced northern migration, while Josh 21:5, 23 lists the Levitical cities. Judg 5:17 accuses Dan of abiding with the ships rather than joining the other tribes in battle. Samson's father was part of the tribe of Dan (Judg 13:25), and Dan was the proverbial northern limit of Israel's territory (Judg 20:1; 1 Sam 3:20; 2 Sam 3:10; 17:11; 24:2, 6, 15; 1 Kgs 4:25 [Heb. 5:5]; 1 Chr 21:2; 2 Chr 30:5). Dan became the infamous site of one of Jeroboam's golden calves (1 Kgs 12:29–30; 2 Kgs 10:29). Ben-hadad of Damascus conquered Dan (1 Kgs 15:20; 2 Chr 16:4). Jer 4:15 and 8:16 mention Dan, and Amos 8:14 refers to the god of Dan in a condemnatory context.

What is one to conclude from this evidence about the nature of the people of Dan? Were they nomads able only at a late time to settle down? Were they defeated and driven out by Amorites (Judg 1:34–35), or was their major problem with the Philistines, as in the Samson narratives? Are Danites somehow related to the Danuna of the Sea Peoples as seen by Spina (*JSOT* 1 [1977] 62), and supported by N. K. Sandars (*The Sea Peoples* [London: Thames & Hudson, 1978] 163–64) and T. Dothan (*The Philistines and Their Material Culture* [New Haven: Yale UP, 1982] 57)? Bray (*Sacred Dan*, 18) sees the question as so speculative that it must be left open, agreeing with Bartusch (*Understanding Dan*, 36).

Dan's fate has been hinted at in 1:34 and 1:17 along with the summary statement of Josh 19:47. Dan sought an "inheritance" in Israel, a *naḥălâ* (נַחֲלָה), an important theological term. C. J. H. Wright explains this term:

> The most common literal meaning . . . refers to the division of the land within the kinship structure of Israel and thus signifies the permanent family property allotted to the tribes, clans, and households of Israel. . . . There is a flexible "triangular" usage of both נַחַל and נַחֲלָה to signify the land as Israel's inheritance, the land as Yahweh's inheritance, Israel as Yahweh's inheritance, and even Yahweh as Israel's (or at least the Levites') inheritance. . . . The נַחֲלָה was the place of the family's security (breached by greedy oppressors, Mic 2:2), the place to which one returned after assembly or battle (Josh 24:28; Judg 21:24), and the place of burial (Josh 24:30). The family patrimony was inalienable (Lev 25:23). It was not "owned" by the current generation, but was held from "the fathers" for the sake of posterity; hence Naboth's staunch rejection of Ahab's proposal (1 Kgs 21:3–4). . . . נַחֲלָה can also be used of the territory of clans (Num 33:54; Josh 15:20; 18:28) and of tribes (Gen 48:6; Num 32:32). . . . [On the national level נַחֲלָה] is associated with the divine promise to the ancestors of Israel (Exod 32:13; Josh 1:6; Ps 105:11); therefore to enter into and live on the land thus promised was to enjoy the inheritance (Deut 4:21; 26:1, and passim). (*NIDOTTE*, 3:77–78)

The second half of the book of Joshua repeatedly uses the term נַחֲלָה to show the tribes receiving their "inheritance" by lot (Josh 13:23, 28, 32; 14:1–3, 13–14; 15:20; 16:4–5, 8–9; 18:20, 28; 19:1–51), and it becomes a leitmotif in Deuteronomy (Deut 4:21, 38; 12:9–10; 15:4; 19:3, 10, 14; 21:23; 24:4; 25:19; 26:1). "It is Joshua's task to bring Israel into possession of its *nachelah* (Deut 1:38; 3:28; 31:7; Josh 1:6; 11:23; 13:6–7)," as E. Lipinski points out (*TDOT*, 9:329). See *Comment* on Judg 2:6 and T. C. Butler, *Understanding the Basic Themes of Joshua* (Dallas: Word, 1991) 42–43.

G. Wanke explains the significance of נַחֲלָה for Deuteronomy:

> With the formulaic expression "the land that Yahweh (your God) will give you" (Deut 4:21, 38; 12:9; 15:4; 19:10; [20:16, cities; 21:23]; 24:4; 25:19; 26:1), Dtn emphasizes that Israel possesses the land only on the basis of the grant of its God, and that its claim to the land rests solely on the promise of Yahweh. In addition, Dtn understands the possession of the land as a realization of the promises to the patriarchs (6:10, 18, 23, etc.). It departs from this language only in dependence on firmly fixed traditions (10:9; 12:12; 14:27, 29; 18:1f.; 29:7). (*TLOT*, 2:732)

In contrast to the frequent use of this central theological concept in Deuteronomy and Joshua, it appears quite infrequently in Judges (Judg 2:6, 9; 18:1; 20:6; 21:23–24). Most of these references play directly back on Joshua.

The Hebrew expression describing Dan's search is a bit ambiguous, reading literally: "because there had not fallen to him until that day in the midst of the tribes of Israel an inheritance." Does this indicate that no lot had been cast to give Dan an inheritance, or does it somehow mean that in the inheritance given Dan in Josh 19 no inherited land had fallen to Dan's military efforts? Amit (*Book of Judges*, 330) suggests that "the Danites had not thus far found an inheritance because they were too selective and sought an area that was sufficiently broad and wealthy." The original Israelite spies found such a land but refused to believe they could take it. Joshua's spies had to be convinced by a pious prostitute that they could take the land. Dan knew they could take Laish, but the question was, did the land meet their specifications? Block uses linguistic evidence to argue that "the narrator's point here is simply that the land allotted as the grant of the tribe of Dan in Josh 19:40–48 had not come into their possession" (494).

The Danite strategy in finding land was simple. Five men were to spy out the land in a similar fashion to Moses sending representatives from each of the tribes to spy out the entire land of Israel (Num 13:1–14:45) and Joshua sending spies to Jericho before the battle there (Josh 2). Malamat (*Bib* 51 [1970] 1–16) has shown the resemblance of this narrative to earlier conquest stories. Webb ([1987] 185–86) has shown the distinct differences in the accounts of Dan compared to earlier conquest accounts. The Dan narrative has an Israelite tribe retreating, seeking an ungiven inheritance, marching out after Yahweh has withdrawn, fighting an isolated opponent—not one of the fortified city-states of interior Canaan—and accepting the spies' report of an easy conquest rather than a difficult one. The Dan narrative has more in common with the defeat at Ai in chap. 7 than with any real conquest narrative. Thus Brensinger calls the Danite mission "the direct antithesis of the Israelites' march to the Promised Land" (182).

Here Dan returns to clan status instead of the tribe status it had in the previous verse. The spies come from two cities—Zorah and Eshtaol—the same cities that play a role in the Samson narrative (Judg 13:2, 25; 16:31) but here definitely belonging to the tribe or clan of Dan (compare Josh 19:41). Block may well be right is saying that "the references to only two sites suggests that the Danites as a tribe had not established firm and permanent residence in the region. . . . These two cities, near the western border of Benjamin, would have been the first ones encountered when the Danies separated from the rest of Israel and headed for their territory" (494).

Following orders, the spies move out to the east, apparently one day's journey, and just happen to come to the town in the hill country of Ephraim where Micah lives. This must have been on a major roadway, for the Levite just happened to reach the same place earlier traveling north from Bethlehem. They "spent the night there," using a verb, *līn* (לין), that will become prominent in the final chapters of the book (Judg 18:2; 19:4, 6–7, 9–11, 13, 15, 20; 20:4). O'Connell (*Rhetoric of the Book of Judges*, 236) identifies seven comparisons and five contrasts between the Danite spy ventures and those of Num 12–14, Deut 1, and the Danite story. A major distinction, however, is that Numbers and Deuteronomy form true spy stories, while Judges uses the spy story format to introduce more important cultic information.

3 The narration departs from the normal consecutive tenses to spotlight or foreground a scene between the spies and Micah's Levite. The spies "recognized" the Levite's voice. Bray thinks the questions they ask show "they had met him at some time in the past, and were surprised to meet him here" (*Sacred Dan*, 35–36). Boling (263) is most likely correct in seeing this as an identification of a southern accent as opposed to the Ephraimites' northern accent, so that NET translates "accent" here. Compare the Jordan-crossing incident in Judg 12:1–6. The spies, apparently on their way out the next morning, stop for a moment to ask the Levite why in the world he would be in such an isolated place serving so few people. The spies could see no future for the Levite there.

4–6 The priest, grateful for a place of service anywhere, recites what Micah had done for him. "All this" (כזה וכזה) is, literally, "according to this and according to this," which Block labels "casual and flippant" (497, n. 87).

The spies, seemingly content at the answer, ask the Levite to perform a priestly duty for them, namely, the determining of God's (*'elohim*, not *Yahweh*) will in their journey. The priest obliges, promising "peace," or *šālôm* (שלום), with an answer that is "extremely glib" and "extremely vague" (Block, 498). Schneider points out, "The priest offered no prayer, did nothing with the cult paraphernalia, nor did he investigate the project" (237).

"Under the Lord's watch" is a bit ambiguous, literally, "positioned opposite of, that is, in front of, Yahweh." The rare Hebrew word *nōkaḥ* (נכח) apparently can signify both "in front of" and "opposite," so that the Danite's mission can be either "favorable" or "unfavorable" to God. Mueller says, "The reader is left to wonder whether this is indeed YHWH's response to the inquiry of the spies, or whether it is merely one fabricated by the priest" (*Micah Story*, 68).

Again Bray (*Sacred Dan*, 36) sees Yahweh at work through "chance encounters," deciding that the story "hinges upon the giving of the oracle in Judg 18:6" (50). But the narrator never credits Yahweh with involvement here. Instead, the inquiry seems almost an ambiguous sleight of hand by the Levite. Younger remarks, "Micah's illicit ephod and the teraphim (household gods) with their inherent ties to divination determine that the inquiry will automatically be considered unauthorized and unlawful" (344). Block says, "The reader can see through this charade. Yahweh would never sanction such a faithless mission" (498).

7 The spies complete their mission. This time they travel a long way, clear to the northern town of Laish. Egyptian execration texts and Mari letters show that Laish was an important commercial city about 2000 B.C.E. Abraham's armies chased the enemy here (Gen 14:14). The spies find the still well-to-do Late Bronze city, perhaps still relying on the Middle Bronze ramparts and fortifications. Thus they feel themselves to be "in security"—*beṭaḥ* (בֶּטַח)—or "with great trust or confidence." "Lifestyle" is an admittedly weak rendering of the Hebrew term *mišpaṭ* (מִשְׁפָּט) with its extremely wide range of meanings from a case in court to the claim of a person in court to the decision of the court to the justice behind that system to the measure by which justice is determined, etc. It is typically translated "in the manner of" or "according to the customs of." Mueller sees it as an ethical term: "the author regards the Laishan way of life as ethical, quite unlike that of the Danites" (*Micah Story*, 73). Block interprets the word to mean that the Laishites "lived under the umbrella of the Sidonians . . . within the sphere of influence of the coastal city of Sidon" (499–500).

It may also mean that Sidonian laws and legal claims controlled the city. The irony then would be that Sidon may have controlled the city but was too far removed to prevent attacks on it. The narrator goes to great lengths to show why Laish could be so easily taken. They were "quiet," *šōqēṭ* (שֹׁקֵט), having achieved the rest God sought to give Israel in the land (Josh 11:23; 14:15; Judg 3:11, 30; 5:31; 8:28).

Dan's enemies enjoyed the quiet rest God desired for Israel until Dan took peacefulness away from these people of Laish. People of Laish were "secure" or "trusting," *bōṭēaḥ* (בֹּטֵחַ), in this context often seen to mean "carefree, complacent, or unsuspecting" (compare Prov 11:15; 14:16; Isa 32:9–11; Amos 6:1). Again Bray (*Sacred Dan*, 37) sees Yahweh sacrificing these people to his will that the Danites might have the land. Rather, the description of the people serves to condemn the Danites' action, not to reveal God's will. How Bray (37) can justify saying that "the writers' sympathies are almost always on the side of the Hebrew heroes" is beyond any sensitive reading of the text of Judges, in which the great majority of the heroes come under condemnation and are painted with anything but purity. "Nothing brought shame to the land" represents an interpretation of a Hebrew text that is frequently emended. See *Note* 18:7.d. Laish lived so separated from other cities that no one harmed or shamed them. Block interprets this as "the effects of military defeat at the hands of external enemies"; that is, "Laish had not suffered military defeat and loss of independence" (500).

Textual questions also surround the phrase "nor did anyone dispossess them oppressively," the final word *'eṣer* (עֶצֶר) occurring only here in the Bible. This appears to stand parallel to the previous statement and mean that no other kingdom had succeeded in taking away their land and ruling over them. They were a free and independent people. This may represent the unoppressive way Sidon exercised control over them. The one major problem lay in that Laish "lived far from the Sidonians." In peaceful times this was a blessing, for there was no interference. However, when someone like the Danites attacked, Sidon could not come to help. In addition, Laish "had no relationships with anyone else"; that is, they had no allies to help in time of trouble. The author's ambiguous descriptions of the people of Laish, says Block, "transfers the reader's sympathies from the Israelite Danites to the Canaanite residents of this town" (499).

8–10 Returning to home base, the spies report. They rush the troops to action to capture the good land, delivering a report just the opposite of that Moses received from his spies, who said the land was good but unconquerable (Num 13:25–29; 14:36–37). The Danites' report is, however, somewhat parallel to the spies' report to Joshua (Josh 2:24). The land is as good in their eyes as creation was in God's (Gen 1:31). "Nothing is lacking." Most importantly, "God has given it into your hands" (Judg 18:10), the frequent and important conveyance formula that can be used for or against Israel. (Compare Exod 23:21; Deut 2:30; 3:3; 7:24; Josh 2:24; 6:2; 8:1; 10:32; 11:8; 21:44; 24:8, 11; Judg 1:2; 2:14, 23; 3:10; 4:7, 14; 6:1; 7:2, 7, 9, 14, 15; 11:30, 32; 12:3; 13:1; 20:28; contrast Judg 16:23–24.)

11–13 The narrator prepares the readers for a battle report as the Danite soldiers, six hundred strong, prepare to fight. First, an etiological note explains the existence of a place named for Dan but lying in the territory of Judah. Kiriath-jearim lies about seven miles (11.3 km) northwest of Jerusalem, meaning the Danites set up this first camp on their march about nine miles (14.5 km) from their original home and point of departure (Brensinger, 184). Taking the same route as the original spies, they march into the hill country of Ephraim and find Micah's home. But the battle and the search for land occupy little space and carry little importance in the narrative, as the repeated interruptions and the concluding statements show. The problem is not Dan's land but Dan's cult.

14–21 Bray (*Sacred Dan*, 38–39) sees a confused text in vv 14–18 with either textual corruption or two versions of an original text preserved side by side. His quandary involves who went in and took the cultic items from Micah's shrine. It seems clear to me that the MT shows a two-stage action. First, the five men go in the house and take away the items. Then, the priest accepts the Danites' offer and leaves with them, carrying out his assignment to transport the "holy" objects while in transit. By transporting the objects, the Danites break God's demands that they destroy all such images (Deut 7:5, 25; 12:3).

The spies had succeeded in more than finding the condition of Laish. They had also found the shrine of Micah. With that information they called the troops to battle, not for new land to live in but for new gods to worship. Having used the services of the Levite and to an extent endeared themselves to him earlier, they now seek him out. They also coerce him with the "six hundred soldiers" stationed at the gate (Judg 18:17). From v 16 on, the terminology changes from "young Levite" to "priest," showing the narrator's interest in priesthood at the Danite sanctuary, not the qualifications of tribal status (contra Bray, *Sacred Dan*, 39).

The spies, buttressed by the fearsome soldiers, enter Micah's shrine and steal its contents. The priest meekly joins the line of soldiers and watches the proceedings. Why does he not protest his loyalty to Micah as in v 4? He does try to interfere with the simple question, "What are you doing?" (Judg 18:18). But they brush him aside with a call to silence. The Danites also use a bit of a bribe, employing him as a tribal priest rather than a clan priest, though how big the tribe (clan) of Dan really was may be questioned. Guillaume reads Judg 17–18 as a "Josianic manifesto for the annexation of Israel" and thus sees the Danites' question of the Levite announcing "the Josianic programme of cultic centralization" (*Waiting for Josiah*, 138, 142). Such a reading is based on a division of editorial layers and a historical reconstruction, each of which is more contrived from scholarly theory than arrived at from textual observation.

Chisholm ("What Is Wrong with This Picture?) sees the disjunctive, offline structures in 18:17b and 17c and interprets them as showing that the narrator is so appalled by the Danites' audacity that he departs from the usual reportorial style of connecting verbs with the conjunction and speaks as if he is on the scene. We are transported into the scene and witness the crime firsthand. From another perspective, we could see appositional clauses indicating synchronic action followed by two disjunctive temporal clauses.

Even the Danites identify themselves as both a "tribe" and a "clan" (Judg 18:19). So the priest becomes "glad of heart" (Judg 18:20), literally, "it made good the heart of the priest." Bundling up his shrine, he marches off with the Danite soldiers. Mueller reminds us that "the Levite's fear cannot be overestimated, given that he is confronted with six hundred armed and mean spirited Danites" (*Micah Story*, 71).

21–26 The soldiers make an about face from Micah's gate and continue their journey, not spending the night there this time. They emulate Jacob in placing families and possessions in front of the troops (Gen 32:13–21). An enemy army might see these as tribute to be paid them and not realize an attack is in the offing. Or the Danites might be expecting an attack from Micah from the rear and choose to place the families in a safer location. This is the first indication that families have joined the six hundred soldiers.

Micah's clan and any allies he may have march together to challenge the Danite army, chasing them from the rear. They do not try an ambush or any such tactics. Rather they seek to negotiate the release of the stolen shrine and its Levite. But six hundred Danite soldiers have a better negotiating position. Micah understands their threat and chooses not to be attacked by men "embittered of soul" (Judg 18:25; see 2 Sam 17:8). Based on this phrase, Amit (*Book of Judges*, 331) describes Dan as "a wild and violent tribe . . . who developed their own scale of values."

Micah returns home without his prized shrine and its Levite, for which Younger denounces Micah: "Micah is concerned about the loss of gods who could not even protect themselves or their maker" (342). The narrator is concerned with a loss of political and moral control that allows the Danites to plunder at will and offers no protection or recourse for Micah. (See Amit, *Book of Judges*, 332.) Block concludes, "With delightful irony the despised Danites serve as agents of judgment upon this representative of the high and mighty Ephraimites" (490). But is this as a divine agent as Block implies? It may be in the realm of divine providence, but nothing in the text says so.

The text places neither Micah nor the Danites in the role of hero or as part of God's people. Rather the idolater is condemned along with the Levite and with the robbers who take priest and idolatrous cultic paraphernalia.

27–31 Enumeration of the cultic items ceases. Now they are simply "what Micah had made." So dialogue also ceases, raising the following to an implicit theological summary of the two chapters. Block states, "His consistently negative portrayal of the Levite and the Danites reaches its literary climax (but its spiritual nadir)" (510).

The Danite military comes to face the quiet, unassuming, carefree citizens of Laish. Such a people Israel could actually defeat. Block points out that "like Micah in chap. 17, the Danites are characterized as opportunists. They are not driven by any divine mandate, but solely by their need for living space and their own notions of where and how that need should be satisfied" (511). Apparently they employed the holy war *cherem*—or destruction of everything—on these people, one of the few times Israel carried out divine expectations, though nothing is mentioned here about God's involvement. Now the Danites have an inheritance, not one given by God and the priestly lot as in Josh 13–19 but one gained through annihilation of a peaceful people. Block concludes, "In the end the Danites have a territory they may claim as their home, but they have sold their souls to Canaanite values" (492).

Bray (*Sacred Dan*, 39–40) credits Danite success to Yahweh's blessing. The Danites may have interpreted it that way. The narrator certainly does not, maintaining mysterious silence about Yahweh's participation in or attitude toward the events. Just as Micah expected blessing and did not get it, so the Danites may have attributed "blessing" to their having the cultic items and cultic priest, but the narrator's ironic spirit stands against such a reading of events. Younger says, "The Danite conquest is described as a human achievement without any insinuations of God's involvement in the enterprise whatsoever. . . . As Samson moves from physical strength to weakness because of ritual impurity, so Dan moves from a position of military weakness to one of strength, albeit at the expense of cultic and covenantal loyalty" (342–43).

Finally, the narrator reveals the basic purpose behind the narrative as he reveals the name of the Levite priest. Jonathan is the son of Gershom and grandson of Moses (Exod 2:22; 18:3; 1 Chr 23:15–16; 26:24; see *Note* 18:30.b). This is the only biblical narrative mentioning Dan as tribe, city, and ancestor (Bartusch, *Understanding Dan*, 177). Yee finds that the preexilic Deuteronomistic editor "encodes the priestly rivalry between the Mushite and Zadokite families. The Deuteronomist represents the Levitic competitors of the Jerusalem priesthood as unscrupulous opportunists" ("Ideological Criticism," 160). Block opposes those who would see editorial work here: "To remove the Yahwistic name Jonathan and the names of Moses and his son robs this text of its prophetic punch. . . . The narrator . . . shocks the reader by associating the abominations committed in this chapter with Moses, the most venerable character in Israelite history" (512). Niditch explains:

> Are the Danites said to claim a priesthood that descends from the northern tribe of Manasseh, or, more likely, are they said to claim a priestly heritage in the line of Moses himself, through his son Gershom? The latter, more illustrious ancestry would no doubt have appealed to those who worshiped at an ancient northern shrine. One can understand political and theological reasons for the insertion of the *nun* by Judean, southern, pro-Davidic writers who would not want any shrine in the north, which was regarded as renegade by certain voices in the Hebrew Bible, to have the status of Mosaic origins.
>
> Many scholars thus suggest that the Danite foundation tale, with its icons of suspicious origins, is a Judean critique of apostate northerners and their shrines, a critique that further contributes to the message concerning the need for a Davidic king who would centralize and purify worship. The supposedly tainted origin of the shrine provides moral justification for the destruction of Dan and the northern kingdom by the Assyrians, who act as God's tools of vengeance (see Soggin 277–78). (184)

The present translation reads "Moses." Some traditions present and understand this tale as an important foundation myth. The priest's descent from the venerable Moses undermines the interpretation that views the tale of the Danites as propaganda against the north, as does the uncritical neutrality of the narrator. He may feel sorry for the people of Laish and consider the Danites to be pirates, but he presents the tale of the great old shrine as he understands it, ending his account with the etiological comments about the length of time that the "Mushite" priesthood, i.e., a priesthood claiming descent from Moses, served at the northern shrine and when that shrine existed.

Certainly the Danites trumpeted the fame and family of their priest, but the Jerusalem tradition held on to Aaronic priesthood, not Mosaic. Hiring a Mosaic priest, particularly a stolen Mosaic priest with a shrine of idols, did not meet divine qualifications. As Mueller evaluates the situation, "having an image and Jonathan, a grandson of Moses, for a Levitic priest cannot ensure YHWH's favor to the tribe of Dan any more than to Micah. . . . The narrator skillfully ties together what is most important to him within a span of one verse: the Danites introduce idolatrous worship, the priestly line keeps it going, and the land is lost to captivity" (*Micah Story*, 73). As the generation after Joshua forgot the historical acts of God, so this generation of Danites forgets the religious commands of God.

Judg 18:30b and 31 raise red flags for many commentators. Thus Amit states clearly: "Verse 31 of Chapter 18 is an editorial digression. . . . The reference to Shiloh in our passage is a remnant of a stage in which Chapter 18 constituted the end of Judges" (*Book of Judges*, 317–18). Bray sees v 30 coming from a northern refugee during the Assyrian invasions and v 31 being "part of a later, hostile redaction made when the narrative was incorporated into Judges" (*Sacred Dan*, 23), that is, in the postexilic period when the assumption that Shiloh was a forerunner of Jerusalem became commonly accepted. Bartusch (*Understanding Dan*, 201, n. 325) sees here a Jerusalem polemic against Shiloh in the territory of Ephraim.

This marked Dan's temple "until the day when the land was captured" (Judg 18:30). The meaning and dating of this note is difficult to determine. A. Biran, the excavator of Dan, concludes from the archaeological evidence:

> How the Assyrian conquest of N Israel affected Dan is not clear. In any case, the stone pavement continued to serve as a road leading northward into the city and to the sacred precinct. The houses of the 7th century were well built and in one quarter they were built around a large stone-paved courtyard. A large quantity of vessels, including decanters, storage jars, cooking pots, oil lamps, and a shard with the name Baal-Pelet, indicate that the settlement at Dan continued to prosper until the Babylonian Conquest. (*ABD*, 2:10–12)

Wood ("From Ramesses to Shiloh," 275–76; compare Brensinger, 187–88) dates the fall of Shiloh to the Philistines about 1100 B.C.E. and a fiery destruction of Dan about 1050 to the same people, using these dates to set Dan's migration between the late 1200s and 1100. He identifies the Philistine incursion about 1177 as the cause of the Danite migration and interprets the archaeological evidence to show a destruction of the city of Dan shortly after 1200, attributing the burning to the tribe of Dan. He sees that ten pithoi were made of foreign clay and so decides that newcomers brought these with them. Brensinger concludes, based on Wood's information, "Shiloh forever lost much of its importance following both the removal of the ark of the covenant as well as this apparent attack on the site itself. It may well be to this momentous decline, then, that the writer of Judges refers" (188).

Bray insists that v 30 refers to the exile of the northern kingdom that occurred long after the destruction of Shiloh since "there is, however, no good reason to assume the phrase does not refer to the Assyrian Exile" (*Sacred Dan*, 21–23). The only good reason for this is the text of Judg 18:30–31, a text Bray wants to divide into at least two redactional units. Bray does come to the interesting conclusion that the priest and his descendants "served the shrine for as long as it was possible in Northern Israel" (40). If this be true, then they also served as Jeroboam's priests and got one more promotion from tribal priest to national priest. Or it may be that the capture of Dan refers to Jeroboam's action in doing away with Dan's tribal shrine and priesthood and replacing it with a national shrine without Levites as priests (1 Kgs 12:31).

Could this dating statement in v 30 simply be parallel to v 31, which limits the use of Micah's idol to the period until Shiloh fell shortly after Eli's service as priest there (Jer 7:12–14; 26:6–9; compare Ps 78:60) or perhaps after Ahijah the prophet from Shiloh anointed Jeroboam as king over the north (1 Kgs 11:29; 14:1–18)? Though seeing the verse as an editorial addition, Amit believes the mention of Dan to be "preparing the way for the placing of a golden calf in the same site in the days of Jeroboam (1 Kgs 12:28–33)" (*Book of Judges*, 318). If, as I understand the situation, the book of Judges was composed in its entirety in Judah during or shortly after the reign of Jeroboam, then the downfall of Shiloh, the central sanctuary in Jeroboam's Ephraim, would be an important point of reference. The dual loss of Dan and Shiloh along with the destruction of Shechem under Abimelech should indicate that the site of the central sanctuary had been moved to Jerusalem.

Bartusch interprets the evidence to mean that "when the house of God was removed from Shiloh at the ascendency of David, at the same time the sanctuary at Dan (according to tradition), practically speaking, also ceased to exist" (*Understanding Dan*, 200). Satterthwaite ("Narrative Artistry," 117; compare O'Connell, *Rhetoric of the Book of Judges*, 284–85) sees the parallel with the removal of Shiloh as pointing to a destruction of Dan after the the battle of Aphek described in 1 Sam 4. Soggin (276–77) thinks Shiloh may have survived until a date well after Aphek, and J. D. Day argues that v 31 does not have to imply that Dan's sanctuary existed only as long as the Shiloh sanctuary "*and no longer*" ("Destruction of the Shiloh Sanctuary," 93). Shiloh will become central to the final chapters of Judges. See Josh 18:1, 8–10; 19:51; 21:2; 22:9, 12; Judg 21:12, 19, 21; 1 Sam 1:3, 9, 24; 2:14; 3:21; 4:3–4, 12; 14:3; 1 Kgs 2:27; 14:2, 4; Ps 78:60; Jer 7:12, 14; 26:6, 9; 41:5.

Mueller sums up the author's work well:

> The Shema (Deut 6:4), Decalogue (Deut 5:6–8; Exod 20:2–4), and Moses' sermon (Deut 4:16, 23, 25) explicitly prohibit behavior which the protagonists in the Micah story exhibit. Hand-crafted items forbidden by covenanat law are made (17:4–5; cf. 18:24, 27, 31) and kept in a household shrine dedicated to YHWH (Judg 17:4–5) until they are coveted (18:14), stolen (118:18, 20, 27), and set up in a tribal sanctuary (18:30–31). (*Micah Story*, 80)

Explanation

"Here sin succeeds! . . . God does not stifle every corrupt thought and scheme of the human heart" (Block, 514–15). Here is one thing on which commentators can agree from these chapters.

The great disagreeement among scholars about the nature and origin of these chapters leaves wide open the explanation of their meaning and purpose. O'Connell (*Rhetoric of the Book of Judges*) seeks to show these chapters fitting into support of the idealized Davidic monarchy, an idea that Bray (*Sacred Dan*, 25) endorses, adding that "the cult is the central concern of the original writer" (33) and also for Bray for the later redactor. But Bray (41) also wants to talk about God's blessing and providential care of his Danites, a theme ruled out by the ironical tone of the narrative and its care in not mentioning any action or attitude of Yahweh. Bray sees the story as told from the point of view of the Danites. That may be true for some tradition behind the story, but the unified story as now told is anything but pro-Danite. The "redactional elements" Bray so easily picks out to create a "pristine account" are precisely the only elements wherein the narrator reveals the authorial slant of the narrative. Even Bray has to conclude that "as it stands today, Judg 17–18 is a polemic against the ancient shrine of Dan" (42).

Halpern (*JBL* 95 [1976] 38) places the Micah story in the northern kingdom, justifying the new cultic innovations of Jeroboam as representing practices and personnel as old as Shiloh and connected to Moses. Dohmen (*BN* 17 [1982] 17–22) sees Jeroboam's supporters in Bethel polemicizing against the sanctuary at Dan only to have southerners take the material and aim it against Jeroboam I and his cults. Soggin (269) finds a southern pre-Deuteronomic polemic against the syncretistic worship in Dan not based on early traditions.

Brettler (398–416) sees support for the Davidic monarchy and condemnation of the northern kingship after 922 B.C.E. Similarly, Sweeney ("Davidic Polemics in the Book of Judges," *VT* 47 [1997] 517–29) sees the pro-David theme played out in polemic against Ephraim and Bethel.

Bartusch also sees the final edited version of Judges as wholly undermining "the legitimacy of the northern sanctuary and its priesthood at Dan" (*Understanding Dan*, 199). Amit shows the upside-down values of the narratives: "Micah, who practices hospitality and provides lodging to the five able men from Dan, is punished; the Levite, who drives a hard bargain and abandons values of loyalty and gratitude, ends up benefiting; while the Danites, who plunder others, end up victorious and achieving their goal" (*Book of Judges*, 333).

Thus the strong comment of Toews can be upheld: "There can be no doubt about its [Judg 17–18 as it now stands] intent to ridicule or to criticize the religious ventures of which it tells. . . . One must conclude that the primary intention of the narrative is to point out the illegitimacy of the sanctuary in Dan" (*Monarchy and Religious Institutions*, 163).

Brensinger is on target: "In these and other cases, the people of Israel simply equate God's blessing and acceptance with either the possession of religious property or the performance of religious rituals" (181).

Amit hears here "the final chord in the subject of leadership. . . . The function of these chapters is to arouse discussion, whose purpose is to summarize the failure of the judges' leadership and to recommend monarchy" (*Book of Judges*, 314). Analysis of the narrative structure leads Amit (321) to see the narrator influencing the reader to view royal rule positively. Amit summarizes by seeing chaps. 17–18 as predisposing the reader "to conclusions regarding the shortcomings of the age of the judges and to expectations from the monarchy" (336).

Mueller sees the Micah story emphasizing the absence of "covenant-promoting leadership in Israel because the king himself fails to uphold covenantal behavior among the people" (*Micah Story*, 3). Mueller decides chaps. 17–18 represent "the polemic of a preacher, aimed at those in leadership positions who disregard the covenant law . . . because they act in fear rather than from knowledge of God" (34).

Olson describes an ongoing process of different meanings within the editorial history of the book. At an early stage it served as an apologetic for the Judean monarchy. Editors who worked on the books of the Deuteronomistic History under Hezekiah and Josiah may be responsible for this stage. The entire exilic Deuteronomistic History showed that at each stage of political life, Israel first enjoyed success and then failure, so that "Israel came to know that each of these human political contexts and institutions was initially moderately successful but in the end ultimately flawed." Finally Judges "functions as a sober and realistic example of what eventually happens to any form of human governance or polity among the people of God. . . . The institution of Israelite judges was a paradigm of the way in which God must work in an imperfect world through necessary but inevitably flawed human structures, ideologies, and institutions" (865–66).

The ironic and satirical tones of the narrative sound forth the meaning and purpose of this section of Judges. Both Micah, with his local clan house of God, and the tribe of Dan, with its tribal/national sanctuary, come under literary attack. So do hand-made gods and self-centered priests. Parallel to chap. 2 and its emphasis on Yahweh's refusal to drive out the enemies, chaps. 17–18 show a tribe whose enemies God did not drive out and whose land remained unconquered. This was God's test to see if the people would walk in the way of Yahweh. Obviously, the family or clan of Micah failed the test. So did the people of Dan, whose tribe appeared to be reduced to clan size. They walked in the way of their neighbors in utilizing all sorts of cultic paraphernalia and images and in indiscriminate consecration of priests who sold their services to the highest bidder.

The central question appears to be the date of writing. When would Dan have enough pride of position to call such caricature and satire down on itself? When would Levites be going their own way, looking for work in any place they might find? When would the future of kingship be a true issue? The one place where these three major issues appear to converge is in the home of Jeroboam with his illegitimate shrine at Dan, his neglect of Levitic priests, and his claim to kingship so strongly opposed in Judah.

Chaps. 17–18 then show the horror of worship devised and led by human enterprise by means of man-made images and cultic items and expressed by oracles delivered without divine consultation or consent. These chapters picture Israelite religion at its worst when the nation served false gods under false priests and without a national leader to call them back to God's way. Religion must be more than human ritual pleasing in human eyes. Religion must be practiced according to God's way with God-called Levitical priests serving under a true descendant of Aaron in the place God has chosen, that is, in Jerusalem, Shiloh having lost its place of preeminence.

B. Saving Benjaminites, the Guest Rapers (19:1–21:25)

1. Uniquely Evil Benjamin Violates
Law of Hospitality (19:1–30)

Bibliography

Amit, Y. "Literature in the Service of Politics: Studies in Judges 19–21." In *Politics and Theopolitics in the Bible and Postbiblical Literature*. Ed. H. G. Reventlow, Y. Hoffman, and B. Uffenheimer. JSOTSup 171. Sheffield: Sheffield Academic, 1994. 28–40. ———. "The Saul Polemic in the Persian Period." In *Judah and the Judeans in the Persian Period*. Ed. O. Lipschits and M. Oeming. Winona Lake, IN: Eisenbrauns, 2006. 647–61. **Arnold, P. M.** *Gibeah: The Search for a Biblical City*. JSOTSup 79. Sheffield: Sheffield Academic, 1990. **Bach, A.** "Rereading the Body Politic: Women and Violence in Judges 21." *BibInt* 6 (1998) 1–19. Reprinted in *Judges* (1999), ed. A. Brenner, 143–59. **Bal, M.** "A Body of Writing: Judges 19." In *A Feminist Companion to Judges* (1993). Ed. A. Brenner. 208–30. ———. "The Rape of Narrative and the Narrative of Rape." In *Literature and the Body: Essays on Populations and Persons*. Ed. E. Scarry. Baltimore: Johns Hopkins UP, 1988. 1–32. **Bar-Magen, M.** "The Shiloh Sanctuary" (Heb.). *Beit-Miqra* 29 (1983–1984) 149–53. **Barnes, R. H.** "Marriage by Capture." *Journal of the Royal Anthropological Institute* 46 (1999) 57–73. **Berman, J. A.** *Narrative Analogy in the Hebrew Bible: Battle Stories and Their Equivalent Non-battle Narratives*. VTSup 103. Leiden: Brill, 2004. **Bewer, J. A.** "The Composition of Judges, Chaps. 17, 18." *AJSL* 29 (1912–1913) 261–83. ———. "The Composition of Judges, Chap. 19." *AJSL* 30 (1913–1914) 81–93. ———. "The Composition of Judges, Chaps. 20–21." *AJSL* 30 (1913–14) 149–65. **Beydon, F.** "Violence sous silence: Juges 19." *FoiVie: Cahiers bibliques* 28 (1989) 81–87. **Bledstein, A. J.** "Is Judges a Woman's Satire of Men Who Play God?" In *A Feminist Companion to Judges* (1993). Ed. A. Brenner. 34–53. **Blenkinsopp, J.** "Benjamin Traditions Read in the Early Persian Period." In *Judah and the Judeans in the Persian Period*. Ed. O. Lipschits and M. Oeming. Winona Lake, IN: Eisenbrauns, 2006. 629–45. ———. "The Judean Priesthood during the Neo-Babylonian and Achaemenid Periods: A Hypothetical Reconstruction." *CBQ* 60 (1998) 25–43. **Block, D. I.** "Echo Narrative Technique in Hebrew Literature: A Study of Judges 19." *WTJ* 52 (1990) 325–41. **Bohmbach, K. G.** "Conventions/Contraventions: The Meaning of Public and Private for the Judges 19 Concubine." *JSOT* 83 (1999) 83–98. **Bowman, R. G.** "Narrative Criticism in Judges: Human Purpose in Conflict with Divine Presence." In *Judges and Method*. Ed. G. Yee. 17–44. **Briend, J.** "Israël et les Gabaonites." In *La Protohistoire d'Israël: De l'exode à la monarchie*. Ed. E.-M. Laperrousaz. Paris: Cerf, 1990. 121–82. **Brooks, S. S.** "Was There a Concubine at Gibeah?" *BAIAS* 15 (1996–1997) 31–40. **Buuren, L. M. A. van.** "Het raadsel van de 'bijvrouw' te Gibea in Richteren 19." *ACEBT* 19 (2001) 159–75. **Carden, M.** "Homophobia and Rape in Sodom and Gibeah: A Response to Ken Stone." *JSOT* 82 (1999) 83–96. **Cazelles, H.** "Shiloh, Laws and the Return of the Ancient Kings." In *Proclamation and Presence*. FS G. H. Davies, ed. J. I. Durham and J. R. Porter. London: SCM Press, 1970. 239–51. **Cody, A.** *A History of Old Testament Priesthood*. AnBib 35. Rome: Pontifical Biblical Institute, 1969. **Coetzee, J. H.** "The 'Outcry' of the Dissected Woman in Judges 19–21: Embodiment of a Society." *OTE* 15 (2002) 52–63. **Culley, R. C.** *Studies in the Structure of Hebrew Narrative*. Missoula, MT: Scholars Press, 1976. 54–59. **Currie, S. D.** "Biblical Studies for a Seminar on Sexuality and the Human Community: I. Judges 19–21." *Austin Seminary Bulletin* 87 (1971) 13–20. **Davies, P. R.** "The Trouble with Benjamin." In

Reflection and Refraction: Studies in Biblical Historiography. FS A. G. Auld, ed. R. Rezetko, T. Lim, and B. Aucker. VTSup 113. Leiden: Brill, 2006. 93–112. **Delany, S.** "'This Borrowed Language': Body Politic in Judges 19." *Shofar* 11 (1993) 97–109. **Demsky, A.** "Geba, Gibeah and Gibeon—An Historico-Geographic Riddle." *BASOR* 212 (1973) 26–31. **Dickson, C.** "Response: Does the Hebrew Bible Have Anything to Say about Homosexuality?" *OTE* 15 (2002) 350–67. **Dus, J.** "Bethel und Mizpa in Jdc. 19–21 und Jdc. 10–12." *OrAnt* 3 (1964) 227–43. **Edenburg, C.** "The Story of the Outrage at Gibeah (Judg 19–21) and Its Relation to the Deuteronomistic History." Paper read at Society of Biblical Literature, Atlanta, 2003. ———. *The Story of the Outrage of Gibeah (Jdg 17–21): Its Composition, Sources, and Historical Background.* Tel Aviv: Tel Aviv UP, 2006. **Eissfeldt, O.** "Der geschichtliche Hintergrund der Erzählung von Gibeas Schandtat (Richter 19–21)." In *Festschrift Georg Beer zum siebzigsten Geburtstag.* Stuttgart, 1935. 19–40. Reprinted in *Kleine Schriften II*, ed. R. Sellheim and F. Maass (Tübingen: Mohr [Siebeck], 1963) 64–80. **Exum, J. C.** "Feminist Criticism: Whose Interests Are Being Served?" In *Judges and Method.* Ed. G. A. Yee. 65–90. ———. "Raped by the Pen." In *Fragmented Women: Feminist (Sub)versions of Biblical Narratives.* JSOTSup 163. Sheffield: JSOT Press, 1993. 176–94. **Fields, W. W.** "The Motif 'Night as Danger'" Associated with Three Biblical Destruction Narratives." In *'Sha'arei Talmon': Studies in the Bible, Qumran, and the Ancient Near East.* FS S. Talmon, ed. M. Fishbane and E. Tov with W. W. Fields. Winona Lake, IN: Eisenbrauns, 1992. 17–32. **Finkelstein, I.,** ed. *Shiloh: The Archaeology of a Biblical Site.* Tel Aviv: Institute of Archaeology, 1993. **Fokkelman, J. P.** "Structural Remarks on Judges 9 and 19." In *'Sha'arei Talmon': Studies in the Bible, Qumran, and the Ancient Near East.* FS S. Talmon, ed. M. Fishbane and E. Tov with W. W. Fields. Winona Lake, IN: Eisenbrauns, 1992. 33–45. **Frymer-Kensky, T.** "Law and Philosophy: The Case of Sex in the Bible." *Semeia* 45 (1989) 89–102. **Gage, W. A.** "Ruth upon the Threshing Floor and the Sin of Gibeah: A Biblical Theological Study." *WTJ* 51 (1989) 369–75. **Gagnon, R. A. J.** "The Old Testament and Homosexuality: A Critical Review of the Case Made by Phyllis Bird." *ZAW* 117 (2005) 367–94. **Gevirtz, S.** "Adumbrations of Dan in Jacob's Blessing on Judah." *ZAW* 93 (1981) 21–37. **Gomes, J. F.** *The Sanctuary of Bethel and the Configuration of Israelite Identity.* BZAW 368. Berlin: de Gruyter, 2006. **Greenspahn, F. E.** "An Egyptian Parallel to Judges 17,6 and 21,25." *JBL* 101 (1982) 129–30. **Güdemann, M.** "Tendenz und Abfassungszeit der letzten Capitel des Buches der Richter." *MGWJ* 18 (1869) 357–68. **Hentschel, G.,** and **C. Nießen.** "Der Bruderkrieg zwischen Israel und Benjamin (Ri 20)." *Bib* 89 (2008) 17–38. **Hobbs, T. R.** "Hospitality in the First Testament and the 'Teleological Fallacy.'" *JSOT* 95 (2001) 3–30. **Hudson, D. M.** "Living in a Land of Epithets: Anonymity in Judges 19–21." *JSOT* 62 (1994) 49–66. **Human, D.** "Homoseksualiteit—Perspektiewe uit die antieke Nabye Ooste." *OTE* 18 (2005) 629–36. **Ignatius, P.** "Gang Rape, Murder, and Dismemberment." *Vidyajyoti* 70 (2006) 417–32. **Jobling, D.** "Structuralist Criticism: The Text's World of Meaning." In *Judges and Method.* Ed. G. A. Yee. 91–118. **Jones-Warsaw, K.** "Toward a Womanist Hermeneutic: A Reading of Judges 19–21." In *A Feminist Companion to Judges* (1993). Ed. A. Brenner. 172–86. **Joosten, J.** "Le Benjaminites au milieu de Jérusalem: Jérémie VI, 1ss et Juges XIX–XX." *VT* 49 (1999) 65–72. **Jost, R.** *Frauenmacht und Männerliebe: Egalitäre Utopien aus der Frühzeit Israels.* Stuttgart: Kohlhammer, 2006. **Jüngling, H. W.** *Richter 19—Ein Plädoyer für das Königtum: Stilistische Analyse der Tendenzerzählung Ri 19, 1–30a; 21,25.* AnBib 84. Rome: Pontifical Biblical Institute, 1981. **Kamuf, P.** "Author of a Crime [Judg 19–21]." In *A Feminist Companion to Judges* (1993). Ed. A. Brenner. 187–207. **Kaufman, A. S.** "Fixing the Site of the Tabernacle at Shiloh." *BAR* 24 (1988) 46–52. **Keefe, A.** "Rapes of Women/Wars of Men." *Semeia* 61 (1993) 79–97. **Kellenbach, K. von.** "Am I a Murderer? Judges 19–21 as a Parable of Meaningless Suffering." In *Strange Fire: Reading the Bible after the Holocaust.* Ed. T. Linafelt. Sheffield: Sheffield Academic, 2000. 176–91. **Kirk-Duggan, C. A.** "What's Uncivil about Civil War? A Womanist Perspective on Pedagogical Issues in Ancient Biblical Battle Texts." SBL Forum, August 17, 2005 <http://www.sbl-site.org/Article.aspx?ArticleId=428>. **Knauf, E. A.** "Bethel: The Israelite Impact on Judean Language and

Literature." In *Judah and the Judeans in the Persian Period.* Ed. O. Lipschits and M. Oeming. Winona Lake, IN: Eisenbrauns, 2006. 291–349. **Köhlmoos, M.** *Bet-El-Erinnerungen an eine Stadt: Perspektiven der alttestamentlichen Bet-El-Überlieferungen.* FAT 49. Tübingen: Mohr (Siebeck), 2006. **Lapsley, J. E.** "A Gentle Guide: Attending to the Narrator's Perspective in Judges 19–21." In *Whispering the Word: Hearing Women's Stories in the Old Testament.* Louisville: Westminster John Knox, 2005. 39–67. **Lasine, S.** "Guest and Host in Judges 19: Lot's Hospitality in an Inverted World." *JSOT* 29 (1984) 37–59. **Leach, E.** "Anthropological Approaches to the Study of the Bible during the Twentieth Century." In E. Leach and D. A. Aycock, *Structuralist Interpretations of Biblical Myth.* Cambridge: Cambridge UP, 1983. 7–32. **Lefebvre, P.** "L'exemple de la concubine de Guibéa (Juges 19)." *FZPhTh* 54 (2007) 5–15. **Leshem, Y.** "The Date of the Composition of the Narrative Material in Judges: The 'Concubine of Gibeah' Story (Judges 19–21)" (Heb.). *Beit-Miqra* 46 (2001) 128–45. **Leuchter, M.** "'Now There Was a [Certain] Man': Compositional Chronology in Judges–1 Samuel." *CBQ* 69 (2007) 429–39. **Lipka, H.** *Sexual Transgression in the Hebrew Bible.* Hebrew Bible Monographs 7. Sheffield: Sheffield Phoenix, 2006. **Liverani, M.** "Messaggi, donne, ospitalità: Comunicazione intertribale in Giud. 19–21." *Studi storico-religiosi* 3 (1979) 303–41. **Luria, B. Z.** "The Incident of the Concubine at Gibeah" (Heb.). In *Studies in the Book of Judges.* Publications of the Israel Bible Society 10. Jerusalem, 1966. 463–94. **Macintosh, A. A.** "The Meaning of *MKLYM* in Judges XVIII 7." *VT* 35 (1985) 68–77. **Matthews, V.** "Hospitality and Hostility in Genesis 19 and Judges 19." *BTB* 22 (1992) 3–11. **Mayes, A. D. H.** "Deuteronomistic Royal Ideology in Judges 17–21." *BibInt* 9 (2001) 241–58. **McKenzie, S. L.** "Mizpah of Benjamin and the Date of the Deuteronomistic History." In *'Lasset uns Brücken bauen . . .': Collected Communications to the XVth Congress of the Organization for the Study of the Old Testament, Cambridge, 1995.* BEATAJ 42. Frankfurt am Main: Lang, 1998. 149–55. **Miller, G. P.** "Verbal Feud in the Hebrew Bible: Judges 3:12–30 and 19–21." *JNES* 55 (1996) 105–17. **Miller, J. M.** "Gibeah of Benjamin." *VT* 25 (1975) 145–66. **Miller, P. D.** *The Religion of Ancient Israel.* Ed. D. A. Knight. Library of Ancient Israel. Louisville: Westminster John Knox, 2000. **Müllner, I.** "Lethal Differences: Sexual Violence as Violence against Others in Judges 19." In *Judges* (1999). Ed. A. Brenner. 126–42. ———. "Tödliche Differenzen: Sexuelle Gewalt als Gewalt gegen Andere in Ri 19." In *Von der Wurzel getragen: Christlich-feministische Exegese in Auseinandersetzung mit Antijudaismus.* Ed. L. Schottroff and M.-T. Wacker. BibInt 17. Leiden: Brill, 1996. 81–100. **Nel, M.** "Homoseksualiteit en die Ou Testament: 'n studie van tekste." *IDS* 39 (2002) 365–78. **Nickelsburg, G. W. E.** "4Q551: A Vorlage to Susanna or a Text Related to Judges 19?" *JJS* 48 (1997) 349–51. **Niditch, S.** "The 'Sodomite' Theme in Judges 19–20: Family, Community, and Social Disintegration." *CBQ* 44 (1982) 365–78. **Olson, D.** "Buber, Kingship, and the Book of Judges: A Study of Judges 6–9 and 17–21." In *David and Zion.* FS J. J. M. Roberts, ed. B. F. Butto and K. L. Roberts. Winona Lake, IN: Eisenbrauns, 2004. 199–218. **Penchansky, D.** "Staying the Night: Intertextuality in Genesis and Judges." In *Reading between Texts: Intertextuality and the Hebrew Bible.* Ed. D. N. Fewell. Louisville: Westminster John Knox, 1992. 77–88. **Pfeiffer, H.** *Das Heiligtum von Bethel im Spiegel des Hoseabuches.* FRLANT 183. Göttingen: Vandenhoeck & Ruprecht, 1999. **Pitt-Rivers, J.** "The Stranger, the Guest, and the Hostile Host." In *Contributions to Mediterranean Sociology.* Ed. J. G. Peristiany. Paris: Mouton, 1968. 13–30. **Reich, R.** "Anonymity as a Literary Device in Judges 19–21" (Heb.). *Beit-Miqra* 158 (1999) 256–60. **Reis, P. T.** "The Levite's Concubine: New Light on a Dark Story." *SJOT* 20 (2006) 125–46. **Revell, E. J.** "The Battle with Benjamin (Judges xx 29–48) and Hebrew Narrative Techniques." *VT* 35 (1985) 417–33. **Reviv, H.** *The Elders in Ancient Israel.* Jerusalem: Magnes, 1989. **Sasaki, T.** "The Crime of Gibeah and the Punishment of the Benjaminites" (Japanese). *Exeg* 11 (2000) 53–62. **Satterthwaite, P. E.** "Narrative Artistry in the Composition of Judges xx 29ff." *VT* 42 (1992) 80–89. ———. "'No King in Israel': Narrative Criticism and Judges 17–21." *TynBul* 44 (1993) 75–88. **Schley, D. G.** *Shiloh: A Biblical City in Tradition and History.* JSOTSup 63. Sheffield: JSOT Press, 1989. **Schunck, K.-D.** *Benjamin: Untersuchungen zur Entstehung und Geschichte* *eines israelitischen Stammes.* BZAW 86. Berlin: Töpelmann, 1963. **Simons, L.** "An Immortality Rather Than a Life: Milton and the Concubine of Judges 19–21." In *Old Testament Women.* Ed. R. Frontain and J. Wojcik. Conway, AR: UCA Press, 1991. 144–73. **Stiebert, J.,** and **J. T. Walsh.** "Chaos Cries for a King." *TBT* 39 (2001) 210–15. **Stone, K.** "Gender and Homosexuality in Judges 19: Subject-Honor, Object-Shame?" *JSOT* 67 (1995) 87–107. ———. *Sex, Honor, and Power in the Deuteronomistic History.* JSOTSup 234. Sheffield: Sheffield Academic, 1996. 69–84. ———. "Sexual Practice and the Structure of Prestige: The Case of the Disputed Concubines." In *SBLSP 1993.* Ed. E. H. Lovering, Jr. Atlanta: Scholars Press, 1993. 554–73. **Talmon, S.** "In Those Days There Was No מֶלֶךְ in Israel." In *King, Cult, and Calendar in Ancient Israel.* Leiden: Brill, 1986. 39–48. **Tapp, A. M.** "An Ideology of Expendability: Virgin Daughter Sacrifice in Genesis 19:1–11, Judges 11:30–39, and 19:22–26." In *Anti-Covenant.* Ed. M. Bal. 157–74. **Tawil, H.** "Two Biblical Architectural Images in Light of Cuneiform Sources (Lexicographical Notes X)." *BASOR* 341 (2006) 37–52. **Theron, J.,** and **P. F. Theron.** "Die vless het Woord geword: Rigters 19." *NGTT* 42 (2001) 406–15. **Trible, P.** "An Unnamed Woman: The Extravagance of Violence." In *Texts of Terror.* Philadelphia: Fortress, 1984. 65–91. **Unterman, J.** "The Literary Influence of 'The Binding of Isaac' (Genesis 22) on 'The Outrage at Gibeah' (Judges 19)." *HAR* 4 (1980) 161–66. **Van Houten, C.** "The Rape of the Concubine." *Per* 12 (1977) 12–14. **Vile, J. R.** "Domestic Politics in the Book of Judges: The Story of Gibeah." *Journal of Political Science* 16 (1988) 33–42. **Wallis, G.** "Eine Parallele zu Richter 19,29ff und 1 Sam. 11,5ff. aus dem Briefarchiv von Mari." *ZAW* 64 (1952) 57–61. **Wolde, E. van.** "Does *ʿimma* Denote Rape? A Semantic Analysis of a Controversial Word." *VT* 52 (2002) 538–39. **Wright, R. A.** "Establishing Hospitality in the Old Testament: Testing the Tool of Linguistic Pragmatics." PhD diss., Yale University, 1989. **Wuckelt, A.** "Sterben Frauen anders als Männer? Todeserzählungen geschlechterspezifisch betrachtet." *BK* 61 (2006) 22–26. **Yamada, F. M.** "Configurations of Rape in the Hebrew Bible: A Literary Analysis of Three Rape Narratives." PhD diss., Princeton Theological Seminary, 2004. **Yee, G.** "Ideological Criticism: Judges 19–21 and the Dismembered Body." In *Judges and Method.* Ed. G. A. Yee. 146–70. **Yoo, Y.** "*Han*-Laden Women: Korean 'Comfort Women' and Women in Judges 19–21." *Semeia* 78 (1997) 37–46. **Zakovitch, Y.** "The Women's Rights in the Biblical Law of Divorce." *JLA* 4 (1981) 28–46.

Translation

[1] *In those days when Israel had no king, a man who was a Levite lived as an alien[a] in the most isolated parts of the hill country of Ephraim. He[b] took for himself a concubine from Bethlehem in Judah.* [2] *His concubine found him repulsive[a] and went away from him to her father's house in Bethlehem of Judah. She was there for a season, that is, four months.[b]* [3] *Her man rose and came after her to speak to her heart so as to bring her back.[a] His young servant was with him along with a pair of donkeys. She[b] let him enter her father's house, and when the bride's father saw him, he was overjoyed[c] to meet him.*

[4] *His father-in-law, the bride's father, prevailed on[a] him; and he stayed with him for three days. They ate and drank and spent the night[b] there.* [5] *On the fourth day they rose early in the morning, and he stood up to go. The bride's father said to his son-in-law,[a] "Sustain your heart with a bite to eat, and afterwards you may go."* [6] *The pair sat down and ate and drank together. The bride's father said to the man, "Please decide[a] to spend the night so that it may do your heart good."* [7] *The man stood to go, and his father-in-law urged him to spend the night there again.[a]* [8] *He rose early in the morning on the fifth day to go. The bride's father said, "Please sustain your heart and stay around[a] until the day has stretched out a bit." The pair ate.[b]* [9] *The man rose to go along with his concubine and his young servant. His father-in-law, the bride's father, said to him, "Look now! The day*

has sunk into evening. Please spend the night. Look, the day is disappearing. Spend the night here[a] *so that it may be good for your heart. All of you may rise up early tomorrow to be on your way, and you may go to your tent.*"[b]

[10] *The man did not want to spend the night. He rose to go and came near Jebus—that is, Jerusalem. With him were a pair of saddled donkeys. His concubine was also with him.*[a]

[11] *They were in the vicinity of Jebus when the day had almost disappeared.*[a] *The young servant said to his master, "Come, please, let's turn in to this city of the Jebusites so we may spend the night in it."* [12] *His master told him, "We*[a] *cannot turn in to a foreign*[b] *city who*[c] *are not part of the Israelites. We must cross over toward Gibeah."*[d] [13] *He said to his young servant, "Let's go,*[a] *so we can reach one*[b] *of the places, and we will spend the night in Gibeah or in Ramah."* [14] *They crossed over and journeyed on, and the sun set on them*[a] *near Gibeah, which belongs to Benjamin.* [15] *They turned in there*[a] *to go in to spend the night in Gibeah. Entering, he sat down*[b] *in the city plaza, but no one received them as guests to spend the night at their home.*[c]

[16] *Look! An old man came from his work in the field in the evening. The man was from the hill country of Ephraim, but he was an alien in Gibeah, the men of that place being Benjaminites.* [17] *He raised his eyes and saw the man who had wandered into the city plaza. The old man said, "Where are you going, and where have you come from?"* [18] *He told him, "We are crossing over from Bethlehem in Judah into the most isolated parts of the hill country of Ephraim. I am from there, and I went to Bethlehem in Judah, but it is to the house of Yahweh that I am going.*[a] *However, no one has received me as their house guest.* [19] *We have both*[a] *our own straw and food for our donkeys*[b] *as well as our own food and wine for me and for your maidservant, and for the young servant who is with your servants.*[c] *Nothing at all is needed."* [20] *The old man said, "Peace to you! Only everything you need is on me. You certainly are not going to spend the night in the plaza!"* [21] *He brought him to his house and fed the donkeys. They washed their feet and ate and drank.*

[22] *They were being good to their heart at the very moment when*[a] *the men of the city, men*[b] *who were sons*[c] *of Belial, had surrounded the house.*[d] *Pounding on the door, they told the old man, the lord of the house, "Bring out the man who came to your house that we may be intimate with him."* [23] *The man, the lord of the house, came out to them and told them,*[a] *"No, my kinsfolk! Don't be so evil. After all, this man came to*[b] *my house. Don't do this stupid sin!*

[24] *"Look! My virgin daughter is right here along with his concubine.*[a] *Allow me to bring them*[b] *out so you can humiliate them*[c] *and do to them*[d] *what is good*[e] *in your own eyes. But this man, you are not*[f] *to treat in this stupid sinful way."*

[25] *The men decided not to listen to him. The man seized his concubine and sent her out to them outside. They were intimate with her*[a] *and were sexually involved with her all night until morning. With*[b] *the coming of dawn, they sent her away.*

[26] *As morning came, the woman came and fell at the entrance*[a] *of the house of the man where her master was.*[b] *She was there until daylight.*

[27] *Her master rose in the morning and opened the doors of the house. He went out to go on his way. Look! Here was the woman, his concubine having fallen at the entrance to the house,*[a] *while her hands were on the threshold.* [28] *He said to her, "Get up so we can go."* *No answer!*[a] *He took her on the donkey, and the man got up*[b] *and went toward his place.* [29] *He came to his house*[a] *and took a knife*[b] *and seized hold of his concubine and cut her down to the bones*[c] *into twelve pieces. He sent her*[d] *among all the territory*[e] *of Israel.*

[30] *Whenever someone sees it, they will say,*[a] *"Nothing has been done or seen like this in*

all the days since the Israelites came up from the land[b] *of Egypt until today.*[c] *Now put yourself in her place.*[d] *Think about it.*[e] *Say something.*

Notes

1.a. For the appositional string used as subject, see *IBHS*, §4.4.1.b.9.

1.b. LXX[A] reads "the man."

2.a. Following LXX[A] (compare OL) ὠργίσθη, "grew angry," and Vg. along with *Tg. Jonathan, wbsrt ʿlwby,* "she despised him," and deriving תִּזְנֶה from a second root that appears only here in MT; compare *HALOT; DCH;* Boling (273–74). Younger (352) notes that זנה על is unique here in the MT. The normal root meaning of זנה would yield the translation "was unfaithful to him" or "gave herself sexually to another man." Wong tries to show that the following clause is explicative of this one, pointing to a figurative rather than a literal meaning of "unfaithful" (*Compositional Strategy,* 103 n. 69), and that the alleged Akkadian root is connected to Heb. זנח, not זנה (109, n. 81). Barthélemy (*Critique textuelle,* 1:116) opts for MT after a long discussion of history of study. BHS notes the proposal to read וַתִּזְנֶה, "to fornicate, be faithless." Webb ([1987] 261, n. 21) says that ὠργίσθη in LXX[A] regularly represents the Heb. חרה, but LXX may have used the same expression for this rare Heb. term. LXX[B] reads καὶ ἐπορεύθη, "and she went." Compare Zakovitch (*JLA* 4 [1981] 28–46), who interprets this to mean that the woman wanted a divorce. Webb sees LXX[B] as "an interpretation of the MT" ([1987] 261, n. 21). See *Comment* on 19:2.

2.b. Soggin points to ancient MSS with Palestinian vocalization, יָמִים וְאַרְבָּעָה חֳדָשִׁים, "for a year and four months," and finds it "a much better phrase syntactically; perhaps it should replace MT" (284–85). This extends the already overly long waiting period to farcical extremes.

3.a. MT K has masc. suffix, which would have to be interpreted as meaning "to cause to return to him"; but Q, "to bring her back," is followed here even though it is not the more difficult reading. LXX[A] (compare OL) reads τους διαλλάξαι αὐτὴν ἑαυτῷ καὶ ἀπαγαγεῖν αὐτὴν πάλιν πρὸς αὐτόν, "to reconcile her to him and to lead her back again to him," which appears to be a double translation incorporating both K and Q. LXX[B] reads τοῦ ἐπιστρέψαι αὐτὴν αὐτῷ, "to turn her back to him," again incorporating both pronouns. The latter is the correct meaning, whatever the original text. Lapsley decides, "Vaticanus follows the MT more closely, but Alexandrinus's use of *diallaxai* makes the Levite's motives more explicit, thus further underscoring the ironic difference between what *should* have happened to the woman (reconciliation) and what actually does happen to her (dismemberment)" ("Gentle Guide," 119, n. 19, emphasis original). Block (524, n. 200) sees an interesting literary play here. (See G. Fischer, "Die Bewendung דבר על־לב im AT—Ein Beitrag zum Verständnis von Jes 40,2," *Bib* 65 [1984] 247–48; and B. Costacurta, "Implicazioni semantiche in alcuni case di *Qere-Kethib*," *Bib* 71 [1990] 236–39.) *Preliminary and Interim Report* (2:120) decides on "she became angry."

3.b. On the basis of LXX[A]'s (compare OL) καὶ ἐπορεύθη, BHS proposes וַיָּבֹא, "he came," for MT's וַתְּבִיאֵהוּ, "she brought him." The change produces a less difficult text and involves too strong an interference in the text. See *Preliminary and Interim Report,* 2:120; Barthélemy, *Critique textuelle,* 1:116–17.

3.c. LXX[A] reads καὶ παρῆν, "and he was present," perhaps a copyist's error in the Gk. for LXX[B]'s ηὐφράνθη, "he was overjoyed."

4.a. Following MT; many Heb. MSS and editions, including BHS, read the *hipʿil* וַיַּחֲזֶק, "seized, held on to." LXX[A] reads καὶ εἰσήγαγεν αὐτόν, "he led him in" or "he introduced him," while LXX[B] reads καὶ κατέσχεν αὐτόν, "he restrained him."

4.b. Referring to LXX[L] and OL readings, BHS proposes reading the sg., "he spent the night." MT represents the more difficult reading and should be retained without stronger evidence.

5.a. LXX[B] reads νυμφίον, "bridegroom."

6.a. LXX[A] reads ἀρξάμενος, "beginning," using another meaning of יאל, while LXX[B] reads ἄγε, "come on and spend the night" or "extend your time and spend the night" or "celebrate and spend the night." OL has "stay and be with me."

7.a. OL reads "and he compelled him and he remained there." LXX[B] with ἐκάθισεν, along with LXX[R], LXX[C], and some Lucianic evidence, points to וַיֵּשֶׁב, "he abided" or "sat down." LXX[A] with πάλιν recognizes the Heb. idiom with שוב meaning "to repeat something, do it again." Either reading fits the context, and in an unpointed Heb. text could not be distinguished.

8.a. Lit. "strengthen" or "sustain, please, your heart." LXX[A] reads τὴν καρδίαν σου ἄρτῳ καὶ στρατεύθητι, "your heart with bread and march into battle," while LXX[B] reads καρδίαν σου καὶ στράτευσον, "your heart and march into battle," apparently witnessing to a Heb. לחם, which can be pointed in Heb.

to read either "bread" or "fight a battle." OL, according to Niditch (189), reads, "heart with a morsel of bread, and he [literally] made him different [perhaps "diverted his attention" or "changed his mind"] until the day passed." *BHS* suggests reading the imperfect וַיִּתְמַהְמָהּ in place of the imperative without textual evidence. See *Preliminary and Interim Report*, 2:121; Barthélemy, *Critique textuelle*, 1:117, who sees MT making excellent sense. "Stay around" is often debated or emended, but Fokkelman insists on reading MT as an imperative part of the father-in-law's speech, not a note from the narrator. He notes similar use with Lot in Gen 19:16, where the Heb. הִתְמַהְמֵהַּ "reveals a similar mentality (hanging on from love of ease)" ("Structural Remarks," 41, n. 17).

8.b. LXX^A reads ἔφαγον καὶ ἔπιον, "they ate and drink," picking up the common phrase from vv 4 and 6. See *Preliminary and Interim Report*, 2:121; Barthélemy, *Critique textuelle*, 1:118.

9.a. LXX^A reads ἰδοὺ δὴ εἰς ἑσπέραν κέκλικεν ἡ ἡμέρα κατάλυσον ὧδε ἔτι σήμερον, "Look, please! Into evening the day has tipped over. Lodge here yet today," having a text that did not contain the repetition of the MT. LXX^B has an even shorter text: ἰδοὺ δὴ ἠσθένησεν ἡ ἡμέρα εἰς τὴν ἑσπέραν αὐλίσθητι ὧδε, "Look, please! The day has weakened into the evening. Lodge here." This may point to a gradual expansion of an originally terse text, or it could represent a translator missing the literary emphasis on the garrulous nature of the father-in-law and the mood created by repeating reference to evening and night. The Gk. evidence could simply point to haplography.

9.b. Many Heb. MSS pluralize the noun to "your (sg.) tents." This is not necessary.

10.a. OL reads "and they set up/equipped a pair of donkeys and his lad, and he struck the donkeys and he took his concubine with him." *BHS* proposes reading וְעַרְרוֹ, "and his servant," with Lucianic and Syriac Hexapla support, to include the servant mentioned in the previous verse. This misses the literary style of placing the woman last in the series, almost as an afterthought following the donkeys, and assimilates this verse to the rest of the text. See *Preliminary and Interim Report*, 2:121–22. Barthélemy (*Critique textuelle*, 1:118) shows the emendation would represent a change in the Gk. pattern of translating נַעַר.

11.a. *BHS* says the LXX^A reading of κεκλικυῖα, a perfect participle, represents the original LXX reading so that Heb. should be read as יָרַד, the normal Heb. perfect. LXX^B reads the pluperfect προβεβήκει. GKC, §19i, says so-called aphaeresis of a weak consonant with a full vowel resulting in the perfect רַד in reality represents old copying errors.

12.a. LXX^A reads "I."

12.b. Or "foreign." LXX^B, LXX^C, and Syr. read the fem. adjective נָכְרִיָּה. *BHS* proposes pluralizing the term. The Gk. change represents perfect grammar, while the pl. would turn the expression into a construct: "the city of foreigners."

12.c. Literal Heb. reads, "which not from the sons of Israel they" (fem. pl.), or "here." A few Heb. MSS and Tg. read הֵמָּה, and a few read הֵם, both masc. pl. pronouns. The prounoun represents a collective representation of an understood "citizens" or "inhabitants." The fem. touch comes from עִיר, "city." *Preliminary and Interim Report* (2:122) translates, "into a city of the foreigner, here where (<people> are not Israelites)." See Barthélemy, *Critique textuelle*, 1:118–19.

12.d. *BHS* says נַעֲבֹרָה עַד־גִּבְעָה, "we must cross over toward Gibeah," should perhaps be considered an addition in light of v 13, but gives no reason for making such an addition. Translation with "must" as a statement of necessity relieves the problem to a great extent.

13.a. Q and several Heb. MSS read the lengthened imperative לְכָה while K reads the normal form לֵךְ. See GKC, §69x; *IBHS*, §34.5.1.b.13.

13.b. Many Heb. MSS read the fem. בְּאַחַת for MT masc. בְּאַחַד, "one," apparently accommodating to the ôt ending of הַמְּקֹמוֹת, which is the normal fem. pl. ending but serves as a masc. ending for מְקֹמוֹת, "places."

14.a. LXX^A does not have "on them."

15.a. Cairo Genizah witnesses a locative ה.

15.b. LXX has pl. verbs here. The Heb. sg. focuses on the Levite.

15.c. OL reads "no one to refresh them."

18.a. MT is supported by OL, Tg., Syr., and Vg. LXX reads καὶ εἰς τὸν οἶκόν μου, "and into my house." In light of v 29, this is often taken as the original reading (Message, NRSV, NAB, NASB95, NJB, REB, NET; compare Younger, 355, n. 18; O'Connell, *Rhetoric of the Book of Judges*, 483). Block says the MT "makes no sense in the context" (531, n. 227), following E. Tov (*Textual Criticism of the Hebrew Bible*, 256–57) in seeing בֵּיתִי, "my house," being mistaken for an abbreviation of בֵּית יהוה; however, the somewhat preposterous claim to be headed to the worship place in Shiloh may be part of the ironic, defensive portrait of the lead character painted in this narrative. Lapsley says the Gk. change shows "dissonance" on the part of the Gk. translators "trying to reconcile the conflicting information about the Levite's character" ("Gentle Guide," 43). Schneider sees that "explaining this [MT] away ignores this character's similar actions later in the story in his effort to initiate a civil war, where he provided only part of the story and deleted his role in the situation (20:4–6)" (259). Webb ([1987] 182) points to the end of the second narrative in 21:19–23 with its reference to Shiloh as a connecting link. *Preliminary and Interim Report* retains MT, seeing the projected change as assimilation to another passage and remarking that "the house of the LORD is the sanctuary where the Levite dwells" (2:121–22). See Barthélemy, *Critique textuelle*, 1:119.

19.a. For inclusive phrases and clauses, see F. I. Andersen, *Sentence in Biblical Hebrew*, 154–56.

19.b. Several Heb. MSS read the sg. noun, "our donkey."

19.c. *BHS* suggests reading עַבְדְּךָ, "your servant," with many MSS, Syr., and Tg., with support from Vg. The pl. apparently includes the secondary wife, for once elevating her above the young servant.

22.a. See GKC, §116u, for the apodosis introduced by הִנֵּה, in which the first action still continues on during the occurrence of the second.

22.b. LXX and Vg. do not witness "men of," perhaps the addition of a common phrase.

22.c. A few Heb. MSS and Syr. do not have "sons of."

22.d. See GKC, §117w, for the reflexive verb with an apparent direct object.

23.a. LXX[B] does not have "them."

23.b. Following many Heb. MSS, Edd, LXX reading אַל. MT reads אֶל־בֵּיתִי, "not my house."

24.a. *BHS* refers to v 25 to suggest deleting וּפִילַגְשׁוֹ, a literary decision without textual evidence that ignores the literary irony in MT. GKC, §91d, changes suffix to read וּפִילַגְשׁוֹ. See Barthélemy, *Critique textuelle*, 1:120.

24.b. *BHS* suggests, in light of its note a in v 24, changing the pl. suffix to fem. sg. GKC, §135o, explains: "Through a weakening in the distinction of gender, which is noticeable elsewhere (cf. § 110k, 144a, 145p, l, u) and which probably passed from the colloquial language into that of literature, *masculine* suffixes (especially in the plural) are not infrequently used to refer to *feminine* substantives." *Preliminary and Interim Report* (2:123) sees the dual role of the suffix that "might be an ancient dual suffix" and retains MT, dismissing the suggested emendation as making the text easier.

24.c. *BHS* suggests, in light of its note a in v 24, changing the pl. suffix to fem. sg.

24.d. *BHS* uses the evidence of many Heb. MSS which have fem. pl. suffix to suggest fem. sg. suffix, as in *Notes* 19:24.a, b, c.

24.e. Many Heb. MSS read כ, "as, according to," for MT's definite article. This ignores the parallel readings in 17:6 and 21:25 that use the definite article.

24.f. Many Heb. MSS, LXX, Vg. attest אַל instead of MT's לֹא. GKC, §107o, explains: "The imperfect with לֹא represents a more emphatic form of prohibition than the jussive with אַל־ (cf. § 109 c), and corresponds to our *thou shalt not do it!* with the strongest expectation of obedience, while אַל־ with the jussive is rather a simple warning, *do not that!*"

25.a. OL has "threw her to them outside" and then adds "and they humiliated her," "employing a verb," as Niditch notes, "connoting 'rape,' the term used in v. 24" (190).

25.b. Many Heb. MSS read כ, "as," for MT ב, "with."

26.a. LXX[A] reads παρὰ τὴν θύραν τοῦ πυλῶνος τοῦ οἴκου τοῦ ἀνδρός, "at the door of the gate of the house of the man."

26.b. LXX[B] reads οἴκου οὗ ἦν αὐτῆς ἐκεῖ ὁ ἀνήρ, "of the house where her man was there."

27.a. LXX[A] does not have "to the house."

28.a. LXX[A] (compare OL) reads ἀλλὰ τεθνήκει, "but she had died," while LXX[B] reads ὅτι ἦν νεκρά, "because she was dead." This is a natural editorial addition to a text, stating what the original text only implied, or, as Schneider explains, the LXX "is correcting a passage that was too difficult for its readers to bear. The absence of the phrase creates a more ambiguous situation, as the book of Judges does repeatedly" (264). Ackerman (*Warrior, Dancer*, 252, n. 84) argues for originality of LXX, reading Heb. as כִּי מֵתָה.

28.b. LXX[B] does not have "and he got up."

29.a. LXX[B] does not have "he came to his house," eliminating repetition.

29.b. LXX[B] (compare OL) reads ρομφαίαν, "sword."

29.c. LXX[B] does not have "down to the bones," which could be translated more loosely as "limb from limb."

29.d. OL interprets, "her limbs."

29.e. Or "border"; LXX[A] reads "tribes."

30.a. For the use of the perfect consecutives here, see GKC, §112dd, ee, and oo with 116w.

30.b. LXX[A] does not have "of the land."

30.c. LXX^A (compare OL) reads καὶ ἐνετείλατο τοῖς ἀνδράσιν οἷς ἐξαπέστειλεν λέγων τάδε ἐρεῖτε πρὸς πάντα ἄνδρα Ισραηλ εἰ γέγονεν κατὰ τὸ ῥῆμα τοῦτο ἀπὸ τῆς ἡμέρας ἀναβάσεως υἱῶν Ισραηλ ἐξ Αἰγύπτου ἕως τῆς ἡμέρας ταύτης, "and he commanded the men whom he sent out, saying, 'Thus you will tell all the men of Israel, "Has anything happened like this thing since the days of the sons of Israel coming up out of Egypt until this day?"'"

BHS thus suggests inserting וַיְצַו הָאֲנָשִׁים אֲשֶׁר שָׁלַח לֵאמֹר כֹּה תֹאמְרוּ לְכָל־אִישׁ יִשְׂרָאֵל הֲנִהְיְתָה כַּדָּבָר הַזֶּה לְמִיּוֹם עֲלוֹת בְּנֵי יִשְׂרָאֵל מֵאֶרֶץ מִצְרַיִם עַד הַיּוֹם הַזֶּה׃ This is often taken as the original text, but the LXX reading has no subject to issue the command. The command is then transformed into a rhetorical question. *Preliminary and Interim Report* (2:123–26) sees a sentence dropping from the Heb., but then emends the Gk. text, creating a conjectural text translated as: "and all who saw <it> said, '<Nothing> has ever happened or been seen like that from the day the sons of Israel came up out of the land of Egypt until this day.' And he commanded the men he sent saying, 'Thus shall you say to every man of Israel, "Has such <a thing> ever happened from the day the sons of Israel came up from Egypt until this day? Consider it, take counsel, and speak."'" (Compare NEB, NJB, CEV; Soggin, 289.) Barthélemy (*Critique textuelle*, 1:120) accepts Gk. reading (compare O'Connell, *Rhetoric of the Book of Judges*, 483–84). Boling translates LXX and then notes, "Since LXX and MT cannot be harmonized, the original was probably longer than either variant" (277). LXX^A must be seen as a conflate text containing repetition and duplication, though Block sees LXX as "much more natural reading" (548). Block is to be followed when he describes the verse as having "the appearance of the narrator's own call to his immediate readers" (548). Amit (*Book of Judges*, 345, n. 34) favors MT, "which supports the serious effect and there is no reason not to interpret the present text as intended to emphasize a change in the place of the events and the spontaneous, repeated reaction of all those who saw the pieces of the concubine." See *Comment* on 19:30.

30.d. A few Heb. MSS and Tg. read לִבְּכֶם, "set your heart upon it," importing a familiar phrase into this context.

30.e. BHS reports the proposal, based on LXX, to read עֻצוּ עֵצָה, "plan a plan," or "advise with advice."

Form/Structure/Setting

See table 19.1 in the appendix to compare one possible example of narrative analysis with form-critical analysis for chaps. 19–21. The narrative elements follow the typical pattern of Hebrew narrative while the genre elements show the genre of each section with its component parts. Note how the narrator can use different genre elements and markers within or even across various narrative elements.

Great debate rages over the function of the final three chapters of Judges, as was discussed in *Form/Structure/Setting* for chaps. 17–18. Traditionally seen as an appendix or later addition to the book (see Wong, *Compositional Strategy*, 80, n. 3–5), chaps. 19–21, along with chaps. 17–18, have more recently been viewed as an essential element in the narrative composition. Thus Block decides "this episode represents the climactic and supreme demonstration of the Canaanization of Israel" (519). Webb demonstrates that chaps. 17–21 complete the book by giving it aesthetically "a balanced, symmetrical shape" and by rhetorically "repeating or complementing elements from the introduction" ([1987] 197–201). Wong argues that "the same hand must have been responsible for the creation of both the prologue and epilogue of Judges" (*Compositional Strategy*, 77), while showing (79, n. 1) various scholars (Amit, Becker, Mayes, Noth, Jüngling) who contend for redactional history combining various parts of the epilogue.

Wong presupposes and seeks to prove that "tucked away inconspicuously within almost every single one of these bizarre episodes (chs. 17–21) is an echo of a specific event that took place in the life of a major judge in the central section of the book" (*Compositional Strategy*, 83).

Amit (*Book of Judges*, 337) remains unconvinced, seeing the chapters not as a thematic sequel to chaps. 17–18 but as an independent polemic against Benjamin featuring the twelve tribes functioning together, a unique occurrence in the book: "The community of Israel appears in this chapter [chap. 20] as a unified and well-run organization, that oversees morals, punishes sinners, and inquires of the Lord in legitimate ways—and not by a graven or molten image. . . . This incident provides an opportunity for praising the functioning of the community, the direct connection with God, and the longing for moral purity" (*Book of Judges*, 338, 341). Amit can go so far as to conclude that the final three chapters were "added artificially" and "do not contribute to the negative description of the period" (342).

Mayes also argues that chaps. 20–21 have been secondarily added to chap. 19 since chap. 19 shows the need for monarchy and chaps. 20–21 show the "effective functioning of the tribal assembly" (*BibInt* 9 [2001] 254–55). For Mayes, Israel's ultimate hope in the eyes of the "implied author" is an ideal king (257, n. 48).

This totally misses the ironic picture of a united Israel self-destructing "as one man" (Judg 19:1, 8, 11). Objecting to Boling's similar positive opinion, Wong sees Boling as "overly optimistic in his understanding of the final stories in Judges. . . . This negative interpretation of Shiloh is curious. . . . The stories punctuated by the refrain in the epilogue all turn out to be much more negative than Boling thought" (*Compositional Strategy*, 194–95).

These chapters picture Israel working together only to destroy one of its own tribes rather than in unity against foreign enemies. This Israel perceives Jerusalem as foreign territory and Benjamin as an enemy. That is what occurs when an entire nation does what is right in its own eyes without proper leadership, a strong conclusion to a book that started with tribes gathering to find who should lead them.

To see this as stressing the "capability of the congregation's leadership and its ability to mobilize all Israel 'as one man' (20:1, 11)" and to make the section a "'song of praise' to the functioning of the pre-monarchic frameworks," as does Amit (339), is to miss the irony that unifies the entire book and to miss the parallel of the conclusions with chaps. 1–2. As Schneider notes, "Irony abounds because by the end of the chapter the Israelites, who were righting this outrage, inflicted the same outrage on more women" (273). Block calls this "one of the most effective examples of ironic narrative in the Old Testament" (568).

Guillaume sees the final three chapters as "an internal settling of scores between Judah and Benjamin: the other tribes are never mentioned by name" (*Waiting for Josiah*, 203).

Here we have, Block says, the "longest coherent account in the book" (517). Schneider sees the final chapters as a summary of the entire book:

> The dramatic portrayal of the woman's ordeal is chilling. This episode is what the preceding stories in Judges have led up to and is itself the catalyst for what is to come. . . . Literary motifs and references made throughout the book culminate in this episode. This story contains most of the main questions raised thus far in the book: what happens when there is no leadership, what is the role of Judah versus Benjamin, what is the relationship between Israelites and non-Israelites, and more frightening, the relationships between the different Israelite tribes. (245–46)

Still, Block observes, "the plot is so complex that by the time a reader reaches the end of the book, the roots of the problem may have been forgotten" (515).

Younger (347) predictably finds a chiastic structure in these last chapters of Judges:

a   The rape of the concubine (19:1–30)
     b   ḥerem of Benjamin (20:1–48)
          c   Problem: the oaths—Benjamin threatened with extinction (21:1–5)
     b´ ḥerem of Jabesh-gilead (21:6–14)
a´ The rape of the daughters of Shiloh (21:15–25)

Equally predictable, Dorsey (117) finds a chiastic structure, but only in chap. 19, with chaps. 20–21 forming their own chiasm. For him, the turning point is the beginning of the journey home, forming the bridge between the concubine leaving home and her returning home. (Compare Younger, 351.) Again, we find the pan-chiasm of so much modern scholarship being quite subjective and identifying various elements as parallel structures. Finding a narrative structure leads to much more creative ways of analyzing the materials than does the search for chiasms everywhere. When every narrative contains a chiasm, then chiastic structures have lost their meaning and purpose.

Fokkelman ("Structural Remarks," 41) analyzes the story in chap. 19 according to journeying and staying, finding nine elements: introduction (vv 1–2), journey (vv 3–4), stay (vv 5–7), stay (vv 8–10), journey (vv 11–14), stay (vv 15–21), stay (vv 22–26), journey (vv 27–28), and appeal (vv 29–30), most marked off by time indications.

Chap. 19 is a happy hunting ground for critical scholars seeking literary history and sources behind the text, particularly in its use of titles and relationship terms. In supposing such source theories as they enter the study of the chapter, these scholars too often miss the irony and literary finesse the narrator employs to maintain a purposeful sense of confusion about the relationships and ties among the various characters. See the critique by Fokkelman, who accuses historical-critical scholars like Jüngling of a "lack of narratological knowledge and training" and practice of "diachronical hypercriticism" ("Structural Remarks," 42–43).

Chap. 19 also provides a hunting ground for intertextual studies. Unterman (HAR 4 [1980] 161–66) points to Gen 22, but Brettler (88) shows the weakness of this argument. Wong (Compositional Strategy, 103–11) looks to Samson wooing back his wife in Judg 15 and to Ehud in Judg 3. Niditch (CBQ 44 [1982] 374) sees a companion piece in Josh 22:10–34. Certainly, the dispute between east and west in Joshua is parodied to a great extent by Judg 20. Both involve the congregation assembling for action concerning "blatant sinning within the community" (Wong, 72). Both revolve around somewhat parallel questions (Josh 22:16; Judg 20:12). Phinehas, the priest, is involved in both instances but avoids civil war only in Joshua.

Joosten (VT 49 [1999] 65–72) sees Jer 6:1 as utilizing some form of Judg 19–20. O'Connell (Rhetoric of the Book of Judges, 299–304; compare Lasine, JSOT 29 [1984] 41–43) argues for dependence on the action of Saul in 1 Sam 11:7, but Block (547, n. 282) argues that the dependence goes in the reverse direction. Lasine thinks the parallel with 1 Sam 11 "shows what happens when one cannot call upon a newly chosen king to rally Israel 'as one man' in order to prevent or properly avenge a heinous crime" (42). Keefe lays responsibility solely at the feet of Saul: "By narrative allusion, responsibility for the civil war between Benjamin and the rest of the tribes of Israel is laid at the feet of Saul" (*Semeia* 61 [1993] 93, n. 10).

Lasine (*JSOT* 29 [1984] 37–59), with many others, points to the story of Lot in Gen 19. For Lasine, a comparison of the two stories shows "how the old host inverts Lot's hospitality into inhospitality, and how the action of the Levite-guest is the inverse of the action taken by Lot's divine guests." This develops an "'inverted world' where actions are often ludicrous, absurd, and self-defeating" (37). It is difficult to accept Lasine's argument that Lot's offering his own daughters "to a mob to fulfill one's duties as a host" is somehow on higher moral ground than offering "one's virgin daughter and the concubine of one's guest" (39).

Matthews (184) shows that the parallels to the Lot narrative are not as strong as they may at first seem, though Block (520) is able to list common vocabulary and ten "obvious links": small group of travelers arrive in evening, an alien sees the group, travelers prepare to stay in the city square (רחוב, *raḥôb*), alien host's insistence leads them to spend the night with him, host washes guests' feet, host and guest eat, depraved men of city surround the house, men of city demand guest for homosexual pleasure (i.e., gang rape), host protests, substitute female offered.

This represents a story plot dealing with hospitality and human lust and violence. In what form the writers of each variety knew it may be debated—as a genre plot, in oral tradition, in a source behind biblical texts, or in the form of the present biblical text. If the editor behind Judg 19 knew the story as connected to Lot in some form, then we may suppose an intentional reflection of the Lot narrative.

Niditch (*CBQ* 44 [1982] 356–78) and Guillaume (*Waiting for Josiah*, 226), however, argue for the priority of the Judges version, Niditch on the basis of the tight relationship to the larger context that is not necessarily the case with the Lot narrative. Niditch does admit that a definite conclusion is impossible and adds that the similar themes and phrases "are not used identically but vary according to context in a way that leads one to question the possibility of direct borrowing from a fixed version" (375). In her recent commentary Niditch decides that "each version, however, is best regarded as a variation on a theme, used for specific purposes in each context" (192). Guillaume calls Gen 19 "a Midrash of Judg 19, anticipating it and deepening the contrast to darken the 'period of the Judges' which is gradually being conceptualized" (226).

These chapters, particularly chap. 19, cry out for Hebrew instructors to use in introducing Hebrew sentence and clause structures as well as narrative techniques to their students. A temporal clause introduces the chapter and marks a new narrative opening. It is followed immediately by a disjunctive clause headed by a noun and giving a new structure to the editorial refrain that marks chaps. 17–21 as a separate unit.

The first verse among others overflows with appositional statements and compound construct relationships. Judg 19:3aβ adds a disjunctive clause to introduce the servant and donkeys. V 5 uses another temporal clause leading to a series of imperatives and a mixture of singular and plural subjects. V 6 again offers a combination of imperatives ending in a purpose clause. V 8 has a singular and plural imperative, including a rare *hitpalpel* form. V 9 presents a pair of הִנֵּה clauses, first with a perfect verb and then with an infinitive. Andersen (*Sentence in Biblical*

Hebrew, 94–96) classifies such a construction as a surprise clause, apparently one that predicts an impending event. Singular and plural imperatives again alternate, leading to a purpose clause with an imperfect. Two perfect consecutives continue the speech, shifting the time frame to the future. V 10 features a disjunctive negative clause with a perfect verb that shifts subjects. Imperfect consecutives continue the narrative, leading to an appositive phrase introduced by הִיא. A disjunctive clause then introduces contemporaneous facts.

Judg 19:11 apparently starts with an appositional sentence, joined to the previous clause without a conjunction (Andersen, *Sentence in Biblical Hebrew,* 36). Next appears a disjunctive clause expressing contrast with a perfect verb expressing a past perfect sense. Again, the *wāw*-consecutive clauses take over, with dialogue using imperatives leading to a purpose clause. V 12 features a relative clause without a verb. V 13 again uses imperatives plus a purpose clause with simple *wāw* followed by a perfect tense with *wāw* representing future action. V 14 then reverts to the standard narrative imperfect consecutive, ending with another verbless clause, with the preposition *lāmed* indicating possession. V 15 features a negative and thus disjunctive sentence with a *piʿel* participle and a locative *hê* attached to a noun. A surprise clause with *hinnē* (הִנֵּה), "Look!" opens v 16, breaking the succession of tenses so that a perfect is used.

Three disjunctive clauses then stop the action to introduce the elderly man and distinguish him from the residents of the city, Judg 19:17 reverting to the imperfect consecutives. The elderly man's questions then use the simple imperfects. To emphasize the present ongoing activity, the traveler uses a participle with personal pronoun to show the activity he is currently engaged in and a nonverbal clause to indicate his home before reverting to an imperfect consecutive to show a past action prior to the previous ones mentioned in the verse. A disjunctive clause with a participle and personal pronoun contrasts the past destination with the present destination, while a final negative disjunctive clause describes the present situation of lack of hospitality. In v 19 the Hebrew particle *gam* (גַּם), "both . . . and," has a double function, first at the phrase level to join two nouns in a both/and construction and then in an inclusive clause construction ("as well as") with *yēš* (יֵשׁ), "we have," the substantive marking existence or presence, to indicate possession of provisions for animals and for people. A negative appositional clause without the connecting *wāw* then repeats the previous meaning from a negative perspective.

The imperfect consecutive then reappears in Judg 19:20 along with the elderly man's greeting and speech, including a pair of exclusive constructions that are a bit ambiguous syntactically (see Andersen, *Sentence in Biblical Hebrew,* 169–78). V 21 again uses the imperfect consecutive, while v 22 uses a participle with a personal pronoun in an appositional clause to indicate the emotional side of their feasting. V 22b uses the surprise clause with *hinnē* (הִנֵּה), "at the very moment when," to introduce the men of the city who are further identified by an appositional phrase. Again the imperfect consecutive appears with a participial phrase showing present continuous action. The citizens' speech includes an appositional phrase indicating the addressee and ends with an imperative with a purpose clause. V 23 again uses an appositional phrase to identify the speaker and a perfect verb to describe past action. V 24 opens with the surprise clause indicating the host's unexpected offer. It uses a cohortative followed by two imperatives with *wāw,* which may express purpose or result or a straight imperative. A disjunctive clause then expresses contrast and uses a negated imperfect for a negative imperative.

Judg 19:25 then has a negative disjunctive marking contrast with a perfect verb followed by imperfect consecutives. The second half of v 27 introduces another surprise clause, highlighting the discovery of the woman at the door. An appositional word appears, as does a participle indicating continuing action in the past. The last clause of v 27 is disjunctive, indicating a contemporaneous state. The man's speech in v 28 includes a feminine imperative with a purpose clause followed by a contrasting negative disjunctive clause with a participial verb. The final verse puts the narrative in historical perspective and summarizes its importance with two perfect verbs with *wāw*s. The ending clause uses two imperatives, the last having the *wāw* attached.

This complex clause structure allows the reader to isolate conversation partners, time relationships, and narrative scenes. Here the latter are important to the understanding of the nature of the narrative. As usual, dialogue drives the narrative, marking scenes in which normally only two conversationalists participate. A temporal clause marks separation from the previous narrative and the opening scene in this one. The editorial refrain (v 1a) sets the historical situation and prepares the reader for the chaos to follow. The exposition (vv 1b–3) introduces the main participants, including the donkeys, and sets up scene 2 (vv 4–9) featuring the man, no longer referred to as a Levite, and his father-in-law. This is a delaying scene painting the character of the Levite. But his Levitical status plays no open role in this chapter. It functions in the larger context of chaps. 17–21 to show the weakness and untrustworthiness of religious leadership. The disjunctive clause of v 10 introduces scene 3, the delayed departure of the Levite and his entourage. This quickly turns to scene 4 in v 11 as the narrator repeats the geographic location to introduce the debate between the servant and the Levite and appears to set up a crisis over where they might lodge. This extends to the surprise clause of v 16 that introduces scene 5 with a new character, another alien from Ephraim in Gibeah.

This appears to be the resolution of the crisis, providing a good place to spend the night. Again an appositional clause in v 22 introduces a new scene, number 6, marking a contrast between the apparent situation for the night and what awaits them. A new crisis erupts. The surprise clause of v 24 then opens scene 7 and offers a bizarre climax as the elderly man introduces a new character, his virgin daughter, offering her and the Levite's concubine/wife. V 25 constitutes scene 8, beginning with a negative contrast clause, retarding the action briefly before changing characters from the old man to the Levite, who forces his concubine/wife into the revolting action. The time reference at the end of the verse gives way to scene 9 (v 26), describing the woman's action, again marking scene's end with a time reference. V 27 (scene 10) switches focus to the Levite again, only to interject a surprise clause in v 27b switching back to the woman. The scene continues with the man's address to the woman. Grammatical markers do not point to a scene shift until v 30, though one might see the repetition of place markers in v 29 as a scene marker. The final verse is a narrative summary and call to action.

But what kind of narrative is this? Nothing really comes to a resolution. The "marriage crisis" is resolved by the father-in-law's appreciation for the Levite, though the concubine/wife plays no part in that scene. The crisis of escape from the father-in-law's repeated invitations to dally and stay finally comes at the Levite's late evening initiative. The crisis of house hunting or bed hunting is briefly resolved only to be intensified. The life of the Levite is saved at the expense of his concubine/wife. The crisis of the inhospitality of the men of Gibeah is not resolved, its resolution being delayed until the next narrative.

Thus chap. 19 is not an independent narrative in the present context. Nor is its point that described by Ackerman: "men's mastery over the women who are under their control" (*Warrior, Dancer*, 238). It is only the exposition for the ensuing chapters, introducing a one-sided picture of a Levite and the shameful action of one part of the tribe of Benjamin. No positive character evaluation or depiction occurs in the narrative. Or, as Fokkelman phrases it, a mere incident "becomes the spark in a powder keg: it serves as the exposition to, and an opportunity for, the emotional chaos and civil war of chaps. 20–21" ("Structural Remarks," 43). The narrator simply wants to place this event in sharp contrast to the exodus event as its polar opposite. As the exodus is the center of the confession or credo, so this becomes the center of conversation to show the need for a political change.

The date of writing for these chapters is greatly debated. See Guillaume, *Waiting for Josiah*, 204–6, for most of the following suggestions:

Pre-monarchic confederacy	Niditch, *CBQ* 44 (1982) 366
Time of Saul	Jüngling, *Richter 19*, 291
	Unterman, *HAR* 4 (1980) 161–66
Before Hosea	Joosten, *VT* 49 (1999) 71
Syro-Ephraimite War	Tollington, "Book of Judges," 193
Seventh-century Deuteronomist	Yee, "Ideological Criticism," 152
Exile	Amit, *Hidden Polemics*, 185–89
Postexilic	Becker, *Richterzeit und Königtum*, 262, 297
Early Persian period	Blenkinsopp, *CBQ* 60 (1998) 30–31
About 500 B.C.E.	Guillaume, *Waiting for Josiah*, 206
Priestly	Kratz, *Composition of the Narrative Books*, 196

The story actually forms a triangle of influences: (1) Bethlehem in Judah and Jerusalem, (2) a Levite and a host from the depths of Ephraim, and (3) the Benjaminites of Gibeah. Such a triangle represents precisely the political chaos after Solomon's death when Saulides of Benjamin, Jeroboam of Ephraim, and Rehoboam of Judah vied for control.

Judg 19–21 thus portrays social chaos and political chaos that have developed from the social situation in Judg 1, Judg 17–18 having shown the religious chaos. Both sections, chaps. 17–18 and 19–21, begin with an individual or family problem and develop to a citywide and eventually a nationwide problem. (See Younger, 347.) Throughout, God remains "strangely silent" (Block, 519).

Comment

1   The editorial refrain takes a slightly different form from that in 17:6 and 18:1, bringing the reference to a king forward to an emphasized position in the sentence. A literal rendering of 17:6 and 18:1 would be "in those days there was not a king in Israel." In 19:1 we have, literally, "and it happened in those days and a king was not in Israel." This royal emphasis introduces all that follows in chaps. 19–21, not just a part of a narrative as in the previous occurrences. Lapsley notes that "these six [Hebrew] words cue the reader to interpret the story to come as one that could occur only when a vacuum in leadership allows such things to happen" ("Gentle Guide," 37). "In those days" is an implication on the part of the narrator that the situation described here no longer obtains. Yee perceives that the text supporting Josiah's reform "must conceal the social hardships and contradictions of a society actually governed by a king and his ruling elite" ("Ideological Criticism," 158). But it would not be hard for readers of the text to see strong comparisons between their world and the Levite's world in the days of Jeroboam even more than in the days of Josiah.

V 1 then introduces the major character in the narrative that follows, another "Levite alien" as in the previous chapters. In chaps. 17–18 the Levite was a piece of merchandise, valuable for his religious profession, and bought and sold by the major actors of the chapter. He was pictured as a negative character letting himself be sold to the highest bidder with the most power.

Here the Levitic identity is almost secondary, included to provide some credence for the testimony in chap. 20 regarding his earlier mistreatment by the Benjaminites. The Levite is most often referred to as "the man" with an occasional modifier to differentiate him from another character. All the characters remain anonymous, showing that none is a central hero in the story. Amit observes that "the protagonists are anonymous, and only the places are mentioned by name" (*Hidden Polemics,* 179).

Younger decides anonymity allows characters to stand for a larger group, "adopted to reflect the universality of Israel's Canaanization," and "reflects a dehumanization of the individual. . . . It denies individuality and humanity to both the criminals and the victims in the story" (348; compare Hudson, *JSOT* 62 [1994] 59–65; Block, 517–19). Block remarks, "By means of anonymity the narrator has depicted a sinister world of alienation, denigration, and deconstruction" (518).

Where Judg 17–18 featured action in the "hill country of Ephraim," this section begins with movement away from the "most isolated parts" of that area, but still identifies the Levite, along with Micah, as a representative of the religion of this area. This Levite takes a concubine or secondary wife just as Gideon did in 8:31. The term פִּילֶגֶשׁ (*pîlegeš*), "concubine," does not imply sexual misconduct outside marriage but often distinguishes "secondary wives from the primary wife who is the mother of the household" (V. H. Matthews and D. C. Benjamin, *Social World of Ancient Israel 1260–587* [Peabody MA: Hendrickson, 1993] 14; compare Schneider, 247–49; and Exum, "Feminist Criticism," 83). The ironic tone in this narrative comes from the absence of a primary wife.

Yee views this information from a different perspective: "In contrast to Israel's patrilineal ideology, where men typically marry and have sons to carry on the family name, the Levite apparently eschews a primary wife and uses his secondary wife for sexual gratification" ("Ideological Criticism," 151). Such conclusions come from a methodological decision in ideological criticism to pay "special heed to particular *absences* in the text" ("Ideological Criticism," 151, emphasis original). But argument from silence is quite vulnerable, especially in this case.

Exum goes so far as to define the issue in Judg 19 as "male ownership of women's bodies, control over women's sexuality" ("Feminist Criticism," 84), a quite narrowly focused reading of the text. The secondary wife will become the silent, tragic central character in the following narratives. Olson notes, "She remains an object passed from father to husband with no apparent opportunity for her to approve or disapprove of their decision concerning her fate" (876). Still, nothing notes approval of the way she is treated. The story is told to condemn such action, not validate it.

Her home in "Bethlehem of Judah" is the home of Ibzan (12:8) and of Micah's Levite (17:7) who fled to Ephraim. It is also the home of David (1 Sam 17:12), representing the birthplace of the Judahite monarchy. Thus in a real sense the Levite and his secondary wife represent the struggle between the Davidic monarchy of Rehoboam and the Ephraimite monarchy of Jeroboam. The fate of the secondary wife represents the fate of anyone who fled Judah to seek hospitality and protection in Ephraim.

2 Wong sees vv 2–3 as providing information that "really seems altogether superfluous" and is included only to provide "a more complete plot parallel with the Samson episode of 15:1–7" (*Compositional Strategy*, 108). Such a reading misses the need to provide reason for husband and father-in-law to meet and the need to introduce initial doubt about the secondary wife's character.

The secondary wife reacts against the Levite, but the meaning of the Hebrew term *zānâ* (זָנָה) remains debated. Thus NRSV (compare NJB, NET, REB) reads "became angry," but NLT (compare NIV, CEV, NAB, NASB95, NKJV, HCSB) reads "unfaithful." The NET note puts the problem succinctly: "Many have understood the Hebrew verb וַתִּזְנֶה (*wattizneh*) as being from זָנָה (*zanah*, 'to be a prostitute'), but it may be derived from a root meaning 'to be angry; to hate' attested in Akkadian" (see *HALOT*, 275, II זנה).

Wong thinks scholars choose the Akkadian root only because "the MT reading presents certain difficulties regarding logic and plausibility" (*Compositional Strategy*, 109). Soggin insists, "In no way can this be *zanah*, 'practice prostitution,' in the sense of 'betrayed him.' . . . The responsibility for the matrimonial crisis, on which the text gives us no information, must have lain with the husband, at least in view of his later behavior; however, the cause of the quarrel cannot have been very serious, if the wife and the father-in-law are so glad to be reconciled" (284).

Schneider reminds that

> while most would translate the previous verse as, "he took to himself a concubine," meaning that she was never his wife, in this verse they assume she was a legitimate wife. . . . If she were officially a wife and committed adultery, according to Deut 22:21 the woman should have been stoned to death. There are no rules in the MT governing what is considered adultery or unlawful procedures for a *pilegesh* because it is not a state that the laws recognize or regulate. (250)

Pressler (241) believes the narrator disapproves of the woman's actions, seeing rejection of the husband's authority "as in and of itself promiscuous." Schneider insightfully remarks, "Whether the *pilegesh* physically fornicated against him or metaphorically fornicated against him is not clear but that, at this point in Judges, is almost irrelevant. . . . All Israelites metaphorically fornicated against the deity and the *pilegesh*'s doing what was right in her eyes was no different than what the deity-appointed leaders did" (251; compare Yee, "Ideological Criticism," 162).

But Block (522–23) notes that nowhere else is a *pilegesh* relationship used as a metaphor of Israel's relationship to Yahweh. Indeed, Block suggests her father, on her return, may have "sent her out to work as a prostitute to contribute to the family economy" (523). Ultimately, Block opts for relying on the Akkadian root and reading "to be angry."

Lapsley ("Gentle Guide," 118–19, n. 12) points out that the story nowhere else refers to the woman's sexual misconduct and that the Levite's eventual attempt to get her back also does not fit such an image. The JPS reading, "deserted him," comes close to uniting the two possible meanings (as Lapsley, "Gentle Guide," 38, also sees), which may represent an intentional wordplay between the two Hebrew roots, if "to be angry" actually represents a Hebrew root. See *Note* 19:2.a.

Webb finds "grim irony" here that "suggests from the narrator's point of view there was an element of justice in the concubine's fate" ([1987] 188). Nothing else in the narrative points to the narrator passing judgment on the secondary wife, especially not such a harsh, grim judgment.

Dissatisfied with life in Ephraim, the secondary wife runs home to Daddy. Her reasoning and purpose are not clear. Matthews (180; compare Block, 522–23; Boling, 275) suggests divorce. This gives us another hint of the Levite's character—a wandering alien and a man unable to please his secondary wife, he waits four months to take action. Many have guessed at the reason for the wait. Yee ("Ideological Criticism," 162) sees it as a lack of care for his wife, while noting (n. 36) that wounded pride or the wife's secondary status accounts for the pause. Schneider (252–53) explains the four months as the time required to see if the woman is pregnant.

The narrative also makes us call into question what the man or woman has done to cause the woman to leave in spite of the serious consequences she faces by leaving. Lapsley argues, "A woman who had abandoned her husband could not expect to meet a warm reception elsewhere, even in the house of her father" ("Gentle Guide," 38; compare Matthews, 181.) But Schneider (251) wants to know an alternative place for her to go. Daddy's house is her only alternative.

Lapsley explains the silence and ambiguity of the text regarding the cause of the abandonment: "to dissuade the reader from attempting moral evaluations so early in the story" (38). The secondary wife's departure may well add to the miserable portrait of the Levite rather than saying anything about the woman. Some kind of dissatisfaction with him sparked the departure, and his four months of hesitation call into question any real devotion he has for her. Olson says, "Although subtly construed, the most sinister character in the narrative may be the Levite himself" (877). Younger (353) follows Webb ([1987] 188) and sees that her leaving involves some provocation on the man's part.

Certainly, the narrative does not justify Pressler's conclusion: "The concubine is female, she is lower class, and so, in the narrator's eyes, she is of little value" (241). The narrative is about the lack of proper valuation by the Levite, not the inherent value of the woman. The narrative does not justify the rape and dismemberment of the woman. Rather it condemns such activity and uses it to show the sordid nature and value system rampant in Israel. Later, even Pressler must conclude that "the Gibeonites, the Ephraimite host, the Levites, and (later) the Israelites all stand under the judgment of the text" (245). Thus, if the narrator stands on anyone's side, it would be the side of the secondary wife. Müllner concludes that "all the characters are given positive and negative attributes, and all are both victims and offenders. Thus in this narrative, the usual assumption that victims are not guilty does not apply" ("Lethal Differences," 137).

3 Another clue to the "marital relationship" comes as the narrator identifies the deserted man not as a Levite but as her man or "her husband." His intention is to speak to her heart or to persuade her to return with him. (See Block, 524, n. 199, for defense of NIV's "to try to persuade her.")

The Levite is not poor, having a young servant and a pair of donkeys. Perhaps he is kind enough to bring a donkey for the woman to ride on her return home. The exact succession of events becomes a bit inexact and incomplete. The woman brings the man to her father's house, comparable to Samson's relationship with the Timnite woman in Judg 14–15. I agree with Lapsley that the young woman is "pleased that he appears to be making some effort at reconciliation" ("Gentle Guide," 38).

Lapsley's emphasis on the father-in-law being overjoyed at the opportunity for reconciliation, thus sending reconciliation to the forefront of the motifs in the story, may be stretching the narrative a bit. The focus remains on the weakness of the Levite and his failure to talk to the girl's heart, not the problem of reconciliation, a minor motif in the story. Lapsley may be on the right track in seeing the father seeking "restoration of his daughter to social and economic stability" (39). Younger (353) sees an attempt to avoid disgrace for the family.

Now the narrative identifies the woman as a *na'ărâ* (נַעֲרָה), the feminine counterpart to the word used for the Levite's servant, which can also mean young, unmarried woman, a title used by parents for a newly married girl, or an attendant to another woman (*HALOT*). Here it means a new bride seen from the eyes of her father. The bride's father now takes charge of the narrative, again reducing the narrative's central character to a minor, weak role and causing the young bride to disappear completely from the scene. Lapsley says that by referring to her to identify her father, the narrator "draws the reader's attention to the absence of the young woman. . . . The young woman has been reduced to a trace in the text, but it is a trace to which the narrative itself is drawing attention" ("Gentle Guide," 40–41).

Father is overjoyed to see his son-in-law. Exactly why is not clear. Is he lonely and wanting a drinking companion? Does he truly want the couple to get back together? Does he see economic advantage for himself? Matthews suggests he simply put on the host's proper face "to adhere to the regimen of hospitality," or alternatively that the father had received a bride-price and/or other gifts that he did not want to pay back (181). Thus Pressler suggests that "the exchange of goods not only increased the bride's status; it also made dissolving the marriage costly and difficult," but then decides a concubine or secondary wife did not bring property into the marriage so that "dissolving the marriage was probably simple, entailing no financial settlement" (240–41).

4–9 A comic series of rising and sitting, eating and drinking follows with the father-in-law strongly in control, the Levite silently giving in to each of the father-in-law's tricks to make him stay, while the secondary wife does nothing and says nothing until it is time to stand to go. Block decides that "in this androcentric world she passively accepts the role expected of her" (528). Such a judgment reads too much into silence. The narrator in no way does anything to characterize this woman. She is portrayed as having done nothing to deserve her ultimate fate. Any intrusion into this masculine relationship might be read against her. The narrator reserves his surprise punch for later, relegating her to remain off stage until the crucial moment.

The hospitality show continues well into eventide on day five. Yee suggests, "The flamboyant display of generosity by the father-in-law toward the Levite symbolizes the moral and conceptual subordination of the guest to the host" ("Ideological Criticism," 163). Younger says the hospitality is normal for a three-day period and then "borders on the excessive. . . . Its redundancy conveys the potentially endless hospitality that the Levite may have enjoyed had he chosen to remain in Bethlehem" (353; compare Lasine, *JSOT* 29 [1984] 56–57, n. 34).

Block pronounces the hospitality not excessive. Indeed, for Block "the man is portrayed as a model of hospitality" (527; compare Niditch, *CBQ* 44 [1982] 366). Matthews (182–90) identifies examples of improper behavior in the hospitality exchanges and a possible contest between the Levite and his father-in-law and between the Levite and the old man, who has no right as an alien to offer hospitality in Benjamin. Fields shows the progression from full light to full dark in vv 8–14 with the counterparts in vv 25–26 showing progression from full dark to full light, "the plethora of expressions for the latter part of the day" creating "a sense of ominous foreboding" ("Motif 'Night as Danger,'" 23, n. 16). Fields perceives that "the narrative exudes anxiety, disquietude, and danger. . . . The apprehension, the suspense, the worry and concern formed in the emotions of the audience are all enhanced by the narrator's masterful employment of the danger-at-night motif" (24; compare Block, 539–40).

Repeatedly, the father-in-law picks up on the Levite's intention to speak to the girl's heart, asking the Levite to sustain his heart or do good to his heart (Judg 19:3, 5, 6, 8; compare v 22). Lapsley ("Gentle Guide," 39) emphasizes this as an attempt to promote reconciliation with the couple, although the father-in-law never allows the two to have time alone as he dominates the Levite's day into the evening. Lapsley explains: "The apparent absence of any communication between the two, and the Levite's imminent departure, prompt the father to drop some broad hints by means of the heart language" ("Gentle Guide," 120, n. 26).

The use of חֹתֵן (*hōtēn*), "father-in-law," raises a few questions about its meaning (see Exod 3:1; 4:18; 18:1–27; Num 10:29; Judg 1:16; 4:11; 19:7, 9) and its purpose in the present narrative. Though confusable with חָתָן (*hātān*), "son-in-law," the term here obviously refers to a relationship between a man and the father of his wife. This means that the narrator leads the reader to consider the relationship as one of husband and wife, an interpretation backed by the narrator's description of the young woman in his references to הַנַּעֲרָה, "bride." Schneider correctly suggests that "the author was trying to establish that even though the woman character was a *pilegesh*, she was considered a wife in this case" (256).

10–12 Finally, the man, still not called a Levite, "had had enough hospitality" (Schneider, 257). He exercises his will and leaves on a "virtual race against the sun" (Fields, "Motif 'Night as Danger,'" 25) to reach Jerusalem, less than six miles (9.7 km) to the north. The visitor takes with him his "saddled donkeys" (Judg 19:10) and his secondary wife (intentionally mentioned in that order to show the man's perspective on their value) and travels to Jebus, another name for Jerusalem because it was settled by Jebusites (1 Chr 11:4–5; Josh 18:28). This provides another chronological clue for the narrative. The narrative was placed in its current form some time after Israel took control of Jerusalem, that is, in the days of David. Joshua defeated the king of Jerusalem but did not capture the city (Josh 10; 12:10; 15:63). The men of Judah could take Adoni-bezek to Jerusalem, then attack the city and capture it (Judg 1:7–8), but the Benjaminites still faced Jebusites there whom they could not conquer (Judg 1:21). Here the citizens are still foreigners or strangers, unrelated to Israel.

The tired servant is ready to turn in for the night, but the Levite fears for his life among the foreigners of Jerusalem. Younger points out that "the nonevent [staying in Jebus/Jerusalem] furnishes the grounds for the evaluation of the event and action in Gibeah" (354). The following story will show that a foreign-dominated Jerusalem looks better in hindsight than an Israelite city in Benjamin. Amit concludes, "Gibeah is portrayed here as a thoroughly negative place. It is a city that has committed a wanton crime in Israel and whose inhabitants are base fellows and abominable people (Judg 19:22; 20:6, 10, 12–13)" (*Hidden Polemics,* 179).

So they travel about five more miles (8 km) to Gibeah in the territory allotted to Benjamin (Josh 18:28), the tribe which will play a central role in the final chapters of Judges. This was Saul's home (1 Sam 10:26; 11:4; 15:34; 22:6; 23:19; 26:1). There Jonathan would lead a company of Saul's army (1 Sam 13:2; compare 13:15; 14:16; see also Isa 10:29; Hos 5:8; 9:9; 10:9). For discussion of the anti-Saul polemic, see Brettler (88–91), though his postexilic dating of some anti-Saul polemic may well be stretching reality a bit. Leach ("Anthropological Approaches," 26–28) provides a brief structural analysis of Judg 19–21, emphasizing the competition between David of Bethlehem and Saul of Gibeah. (See the summary by Jobling, "Structuralist Criticism," 100.)

13–15 The Levite sees two acceptable cities—Gibeah and Ramah. Ramah was only four miles (7 km) north of Jerusalem. Near there Deborah sat to judge the nation (Judg 4:5). Ramah was apparently Samuel's home, if one emends the text of 1 Sam 1:1 to read "from Ramah, a Zuphite from the hill country of Ephraim" (see 1 Sam 1:19; 2:11; 7:17; 8:4; 15:34; 16:13; 25:1; 28:3). It had strong associations with Saul (1 Sam 10:10), his anointing as king taking place there (1 Sam 9:1–10:16), and with David (1 Sam 19:18; 20:1). Amit asserts, "The city of Ramah . . . does not serve the purposes of the story, but only the polemic needs; hence its mention is forced" (*Hidden Polemics,* 180). Or is Ramah made guilty by association with Gibeah, thus increasing the dark portrait of Saul?

Finally, the long day ends as the sun sets with them close to Gibeah. Entrance to the city only brings disappointment. They sit down in the "city plaza," but no one "received them as guests" (Judg 19:14–15). Olson says, "If the Israelites in the town of Gibeah had known their religious traditions and values well, they would have fallen all over each other to offer hospitality to this man who is both a sojourner and a Levite" (876). The father-in-law had been a bit too hospitable for the Levite's liking. Now the Benjaminites in Gibeah prove totally inhospitable. This appears to set up the crisis point for the narrative. Block observes, "The people of one tribe sense no obligation to the members of another. There is no sense of community" (531).

16–17 Suddenly, out of nowhere, appears an old man out of the field where he had been working into the evening. This man, like the Levite himself, had come from the "hill country of Ephraim" and so was an alien here in Benjamin.

The old man introduces himself with questions about the beginning and ending points of the Levite's travels, using singular verbs and thus ignoring the Levite's companions.

18–19 The Levite sets out his situation—traveling from Bethlehem and headed home to the isolated parts of the hill country of Ephraim. The Levite claims to be headed for the "house of Yahweh" (Judg 19:18), a way to show he is pious and offers no threat to the locals even though none of them has shown the expected hospitality and taken him in for the evening. The house of Yahweh could well be the Levite's home sanctuary. See *Note* 19:18.a.

Schneider finds that "while the Levite did not lie, he deleted information that the reader knows and added information that had not been included previously" (259). Lapsley aptly labels this "a mere façade of piety, offered for the consumption of the old man to make the Levite appear more sympathetic" ("Gentle Guide," 43). Matthews finds sarcasm "mixed with the polite speech expected of the stranger to his potential host" (184). The narrator does not provide the location of the sanctuary or the Levite's relationship to it. Nor does the Levite identify himself as a Levite. He does limit his reference to "me" as the one not being given hospitality (compare v 15 with the plural "them"). "Maidservant" (Heb. אָמָה, *'āmāh*; Judg 19:19) is a "negative and demeaning term" (Matthews, 184–85; compare Schneider, 259) and may give the old host reason to offer her to the gang later. We continue to see, along with Lapsley, "that the Levite is one who cares more for himself than he does for those in his care" ("Gentle Guide," 43).

The Levite claims not to need special provisions from a potential host. He has everything he, his companions, and his animals will need. Matthews (184) sees both this and the old man's questioning as breaking hospitality protocol.

20–21 Now the old man gives the official greeting of שָׁלוֹם (*šālôm*), "peace to you." The old man sounds horrified at the way people have ignored these wandering guests and so declares he will provide all that the visitors need, and they may come to his house. So he takes them home and provides all the gestures of hospitality the culture expects, including washing their tired, dirty feet. Just as with the father-in-law, they "ate and drank" (Judg 19:21).

22 The crisis appears to be resolved. Hospitality has been offered, even if by an alien. So the two men are "good to their heart," an unusual expression in Hebrew that seems to indicate they are enjoying themselves. The joy proves short-lived. What follows is certainly "among the most grotesque and sickening in the book" (Block, 532). Suddenly the "men of the city" have "surrounded the house" and are "pounding on the door." Fields avers, "Surrounding conveys a message of strength of opponents, imminent attack, and danger, especially when used in conjunction with the night motif" ("Motif 'Night as Danger,'" 31). The reader expects nothing good from these intruders, for the narrator informs us immediately that they are "sons of Belial," meaning they are useless, wicked, and good for nothing (Deut 13:13 [Heb. 14]; Judg 19:22; 20:13; 1 Sam 2:12; 10:27; 1 Kgs 21:10, 13; see *HALOT*; Block, 535–36 with nn. 236, 237, 238). Pressler tells us, "The term literally means sons of wickedness or worthlessness, and is used especially of groups who threaten the social order" (243).

They want the man who came to spend the night to spend it in intimacy with them. Here Block sees (536) a pitting of "the new morality, the new Canaanite ethic, against the old normative Israelite ethic. . . . Their demand represents a violation of three fundamental social/moral laws: the law of hospitality, the proscription on intercourse outside of marriage, and proscription on heterosexual [*sic*, homosexual?] intercourse."

23 The lord of the house protests strongly against such inhospitable demands. Surely they would not do such an evil thing. Such action is a "stupid sin." The Hebrew term *nĕbālâ* (נְבָלָה) belongs to a family of terms connected to foolish behavior but appears also to include the sense of sin against God *(HALOT)*. Such actions do not take place in Israel, being against the national sense of morality (2 Sam 13:12). The term will mark the following narrative (Judg 19:23–24; 20:6, 10; compare Josh 7:15; 8:29; 1 Sam 25:25; 2 Sam 13:12; 1 Kgs 13:22, 24–25, 28–30; 2 Kgs 9:37). A. Phillips asserts that "נְבָלָה is a general expression for serious, disorderly and unruly action resulting in the breaking up of an existing relationship whether between tribes, within the family, in a business arrangement, in marriage or with God" ("*Nebalah*," *VT* 25 [1975] 241). The term is applied to sexual acts such as those of Shechem in raping Dinah (Gen 34:7) and of Ammon against his half sister Tamar (2 Sam 13:12, 13). Jeremiah (29:23) applies it to committing adultery with a neighbor's wife. Promiscuity and loss of virginity were a "sacrilege in Israel" (Deut 22:21). (See Pan, *NIDOTTE*, 3:11.) Block (536–37) sees two dimensions to the crime—violation of sexual norms in a "perverse homosexual act" (compare Lev 18:22; 20:13) and violation of "customary norms of hospitality." Keefe concludes strongly:

> The cry against rape as *nebalah* points to an understanding in which the gravity of the crime is measured not primarily in terms of the consequences for the individuals involved, either victim or rapist, but as an *[sic]* disruption of and a violation against the order of community life. . . . Rape as *nebalah* is somehow, on the symbolic level at least, inherently generative of disorder, chaos, and the disintegration of *shalom* within a community. (*Semeia* 61 [1993] 82)

24 The old man pulls a surprise negotiating move, offering two for one—a virgin daughter and a new secondary bride in place of a perhaps not so young man—with free reign to do as they please. Younger comments, "That he volunteer either is unimaginable. But then, he is only doing what is right in his own eyes. . . . Hospitality and honor become more important than doing what is right in Yahweh's eyes" (357). Block concludes, "His sense of duty to a male guest supersedes his obligation to his own daughter, not to mention the man's concubine" (537). Webb ([1987] 189) blithely calls this a "comedy of correctness." That the host's actions are in any way correct may be greatly doubted. To think of them as comedic in any manner creates a tragedy.

Mention of a virgin may in a way prefigure the later Benjaminite hunt for virgin wives, as Schneider points out: "Here the Benjaminites rejected what all Israel must find for them later" (261). The unfinished refrain of v 1 is completed here: they may do what is good in their eyes. Just do not commit a stupid sin against the man. The editorial refrain in the elderly man's mouth, says Lapsley, "condemns the mob's action as the kind of atrocity that motivates the narrator's censorial remarks" ("Gentle Guide," 45).

Here may be seen the cultural distinction between the value of a male and that of a female, but as Matthews says, "women are legal extensions of their husbands and thus would come under the same protections guaranteed to their husbands—as long as their husbands identified them as such" (186).

But the biblical use of the story with its satirical elements shows that this is not the biblical viewpoint. The old man illustrates negative characteristics here after being the example of positive hospitality earlier. The characters are not pure or sinful. They are complex, capable of demonstrating the best in human behavior and the worst. As Fokkelman writes, Gen 19:8 and Judg 19:24 are "exceptional" and "show something that happens all over the world: under the pressures of terror and crime, good manners and morals crumble like a house of cards" ("Structural Remarks," 44, n. 20).

25 The men are not after young ladies; they demand that the old man obey their first request. They seek homosexual activity, or "homosexual gang rape" (see Younger, 359–60 with nn. 30 and 31, referring to J. G. Taylor, "The Bible and Homosexuality," *Them* 21 [1995] 4–9). Niditch puts this in some perspective:

> This passage is perhaps less about views of homosexuality, which priestly writers do condemn (Lev 18:22), than about a larger theme in sexual ethics in which one partner subdues, owns, and holds unequal power over the other. A most troubling feature of the Israelite version of the tale type is the apparent willingness of the men to hand over their women to violent miscreants. Implicit is a worldview in which women are regarded as disposable and replaceable. On the other hand, the narration that follows implies that the author does not condone the men's behavior. They emerge as cowardly, and their complicity in the rape and murder of the woman is a clear and reprehensible violation of covenant. The tale as told also emphasizes the ways in which women, the mediating gender, provide doorways in and out of war. (193)

Yee observes, "Shamed and feminized by his secondary wife and her father, the Levite is in danger of becoming even more humiliated and emasculated by degenerate men" ("Ideological Criticism," 164). Refusing to suffer further shame, the Levite, still not so identified, grasps his new secondary bride and tosses her out to the ravenous men. Pressler points out that "such an act would be reprehensible even in patriarchal culture" (244). Lapsley points to this as "the first narrated interaction between the Levite and his wife since the story began," making it "impossible to put a positive spin on the Levite's actions" ("Gentle Guide," 46). Block feels that "in his mind she has significance only as a potential sacrifice in defense of his own reputation" (538). One might say not his reputation but his physical life.

Younger observes, "This selfish act in the extreme saves him from the horde but reveals the depths of depravity in his heart" (357). Schneider calls this verse "one of the most powerful and frightening in the book. The book no longer recounts quaint folk tales. . . . The *pilegesh*'s nightmare is more poignant because the Levite had just taken her from her home, her father, and apparent security to ultimate horror" (261–62). What a strange way to speak to a woman's heart!

The men of Gibeah submit her to sexual activity all night, their deeds darker than the darkest night. Only as the sun comes up do they let up, sending her away. Fields finds that "the introduction of abnormal sexuality into the narrative allows the authors to win the sympathies of their audiences unawares, and having so won it *[sic]*, to count on their approbation for their causes and their understanding of their recriminatory messages" ("Motif 'Night as Danger,'" 30).

This is obviously one of the most despicably violent scenes in the Bible and has drawn much negative discussion, particularly among feminist exegetes such as Trible (*Texts of Terror*, 65–91), Exum ("Feminist Criticism," 83–88), and Ackerman (*Warrior, Dancer,* 235–39). Fields still seems to justify the men by concluding that "women were considered expendable if the alternative was harm to a man" ("Motif 'Night as Danger,'" 29).

Several recent studies have countered this tendency. (See especially Younger, 360–62.) Fokkelman calls such work

> a curious combination of good stylistic analysis and wrong value judgments. Feminist zeal leads Trible into some fundamental errors: (a) she takes for granted that the narrator is a man (!), and she puts him among all the wicked males of the story because she confuses his reticent art of storytelling with his point of view (pp. 76, 80, 86), but this overlooks the fact that the narrator reveals his moral stance unequivocally by disqualifying the men from Gibeah at the very moment that he introduces them; (b) she does not understand that quasi-objective narration and the precise description of horrors is a much more effective critique of violence than snorting out moral indignation, nor that the narrator is morally in order by the very creation and handing down of this story; (c) she overlooks that the transition from the accidental or personal to the national level arises out of the event; and (d) she ignores that the two men in 19:22 are themselves driven into an appalling predicament, in the face of which the reader should refrain from passing a quick and premature judgment. ("Structural Remarks," 40–41, n. 16)

Fokkelman does comment that "the story signifies how much the Levite is attached to 'carousing' (יָטַב לֵב and synonyms) and that such hedonism and materialism lead to a situation in which throwing women out as a sexual prey for the rabble will be called right" (43).

The biblical author lets the old man and the Levite make this decision, but the narrator obviously stands opposed to such an attitude and such actions. Block calls this "a portrait of patriarchy gone mad. . . . This is cancerous patriarchy expressed according to Canaanite standards. . . . In no way does this episode reflect acceptable treatment of women by men in any context" (543).

Schneider notes that "because of the nature of these new studies feminists have not tied this story into the larger narrative of Judges" (245). Lapsley cautions,

> Mere *depictions* of violence against women should not elicit outrage until attention has been paid to the way those depictions are presented in the text. . . . The shocking stories of women who are abused, raped, and killed do not appear here because these texts unreflectively mimic cultural attitudes toward women. While the stories in Judges are indisputably products of a patriarchal culture, they do not merely parrot that culture. . . . Everyone in the story, except the women, I would argue, is in some way censured by the narrative. ("Gentle Guide," 35–36, emphasis original)

Fields sums up the situation aptly: "Such brazen, public, shameless behavior seizes the attention of the reader because the sociological, religious, and legal climate should have precluded this kind of behavior" ("Motif 'Night as Danger,'" 29). Younger summarizes the text's meaning in contrast to feminists' evaluation: "The text blames the men: the men of Gibeah, the Levite, and the host. The woman is the victim of evil men. Good, godly men treat women differently—even in a patriarchal world" (360).

26 No longer called a "young woman or bride" or even a "secondary bride" (נערה or פילגש), the female companion is now a "woman" or "wife" (אִשָּׁה). Her man or husband has now become her "master" or "lord" (אָדוֹן), the same term the servant lad used in vv 11–12. Lapsley finds that the "terminology reflects her isolation and vulnerability" ("Gentle Guide," 46). Trible does have a perhaps somewhat overstated point in characterizing the manner in which the concubine is depicted:

> Of all the characters in scripture, she is the least. Appearing at the beginning and close of a story that rapes her, she is alone in a world of men. Neither the other characters nor the narrator recognizes her humanity. She is property, object, tool, and literary device. Without name, speech, or power, she has no friends to aid her in life or mourn her in death. Passing her back and forth among themselves, the men of Israel have obliterated her totally. (*Texts of Terror,* 80–81)

One must note it is men of Belial in Gibeah, not men of Israel, who treat her so badly, and it is the narrator's purpose to underline the cruel treatment given her, not just to use her as a "literary device."

Somehow the woman manages to get back to the old man's house as morning dawns. No one inside the house apparently notices her. She lies at the door until full daylight when the house begins to stir. Somehow Exum finds that "as narrative punishment for her sexual 'misconduct,' she is sexually abused, after which her sexuality is symbolically mutilated" ("Feminist Criticism," 84). How can one read the text as anti-wife rather than as anti-Levite? The text shows how drastically Israel had begun to do what is right in their own eyes, not what is right in Yahweh's eyes. In no way does the narrator justify the Levite's actions. Surely the story says something other than, "if you do anything that even remotely suggests improper sexual behavior, you invite male aggression" (Exum, "Feminist Criticism," 85). Seen from a wider perspective, the story says male aggression against women is the ultimate sign of self-serving amorality and reveals the sickness of a nation that tolerates it.

27 Block says "verses 27–28 portray the Levite as incredibly calloused" (541). Apparently unconcerned about his secondary wife, the Levite gets up early in the morning to go on his way. Surprise! Here is the woman, his secondary wife. Her hands are "on the threshold," stretching as far as she can to get into the house, but to no avail. As Lapsley observes, "The image of safety and rest inside the door stands in marked contrast to the image of suffering and abandonment outside the door. . . . This detail describing the disposition of the woman's hands functions like a zoom lens, mercilessly drawing the reader toward an excruciating vision of the woman's agony and the horror of the suffering she endured" ("Gentle Guide," 47–48).

28 Without investigating her condition or trying to help her, the Levite commands her, "Get up so we can go." Ominously, he receives no answer. Still uncaring, he gets up, puts her up on the donkey, and goes on to his destination. In getting up, Schneider observes, "the Levite did the thing his *pilegesh* could no longer do" (264). Thus, says Lapsley, the narrator exposes "the cultural problems that can provide the occasion for a woman to undergo this kind of abuse and wantonly inflicted suffering" ("Gentle Guide," 48).

Lasine sees that "the version in the Old Testament is designed to unmask the absurd callousness and obliviousness of the Levite. . . . The Levite's insensitivity reaches absurd proportions" (*JSOT* 29 [1984] 44–45). Keefe decides that "the narrative's graphic focalization upon the violence suffered by the woman in

Judges 19 evokes a powerful emotional response of sympathy and horror" (*Semeia* 61 [1993] 90).

Olson concludes: "The scene is a reversal of the first woman we encounter in the book of Judges, Achsah, daughter of Caleb. . . . The love, generosity, and promotion of life and well-being that characterized the relationship between women and men at the beginning of Judges are tragically absent here at the end of Judges" (877).

The MT leaves open the questions of when the woman died and who killed her, thus tantalizing the reader (Block, 541). See *Note* 19:28.a. The reader must assign guilt for murder or be content to leave the haunting question open.

29   Apparently aware that the woman is dead, the Levite's first action at home is to take a knife and cut his secondary wife into twelve pieces. Amit argues that "the dismemberment of the concubine seems an artificial and forced motif, intended to serve as an allusion to Saul's act [in 1 Sam 11]" (*Hidden Polemics,* 182), while Block says, "He desacralizes her body, treating her as if it were an animal carcass" (541). The text simply says "he sent her among all the territory of Israel," described by Fokkelman as "in a manner that is just as abhorrent as it is effective" ("Structural Remarks," 43). Younger concludes, "It is highly ironic that the one who issues such a call for justice is himself so selfishly insensitive and self-involved in the crime itself. But the outrageous dismemberment achieves its intended outrageous response" (358).

The implication appears to be that he sends one piece of his dismembered concubine to each tribe, though that is not explicitly stated. Block uses a Mari document (ARM 2.48) to show the purpose of such actions: "to mobilize the troops by creating shock and evoking fear" (546). This may represent a symbol of violated covenant agreements (see 1 Sam 11:7). It is also one of the few times in Judges that all twelve tribes of Israel are included in the narrative, an inclusion that leads to internal disaster rather than national unity and cooperation. Though denying any historicity to the story itself, Niditch draws from the nature of the narrative that its roots rest in the premonarchic period and gives evidence that some type of confederacy joined at least some of the tribes together. The story is "a statement of world-view, a model for the league, an example of how it should work" (*CBQ* 44 [1982] 374). The narrative here also provides a parody of what a unified league actually accomplishes.

This section of the narrative should be the resolution. Instead, it serves as a lead-in for the next narrative, setting up a national crisis rather than resolving an individual one. Sending the body parts throughout the land makes a national issue out of personal loss. The Levite lifts the stakes to the higher plane where they belong. The tribes of Israel must assess this outrage in light of their own religious and ethical traditions.

30   The narrator provides the meaning of the narrative in an unexpected manner, one not accepted by the various versions and many modern translators (NIV, NASB, NRSV, JPSV, REB, NJB; O'Connell, *Rhetoric of the Book of Judges,* 483–84). See *Note* 19:30.c. Block says MT "has the appearance of the narrator's own call to his immediate readers," but then appears to favor LXX (548). Following the MT, we see that the narrator involves the readers directly in the outcome of the story. They must compare it with the greatest of Israel's stories, the exodus from Egypt. Like the exodus, the death of the secondary wife represents a unique event in

Israel's history. People must consider this event and discuss it. As God's great acts of salvation should be remembered in Israel, so also dastardly deeds must not go unremembered and unrequited in Israel. (See Judg 2.)

Explanation

This story serves as the exposition to what follows rather than as a complete narrative in itself. It illustrates how degenerate Israel has become as represented by its Levitical leadership, by a central city, and by an important tribe. The story uses violence and sexual crimes as dastardly as anything in modern media. It shows the darkest side of moral life in Israel. In so doing, the narrative nowhere approves any action within the narrative. The secondary wife's leaving her husband to go back to Daddy receives no moral judgment. Neither the father's temptation to his son-in-law to carouse with him and to procrastinate in carrying out his plans nor the Levite's treatment of his secondary wife gain any sign of approval within the narrative. The only wisdom in the narrative comes from an otherwise silent servant who recommends stopping in a Jerusalem dominated by foreigners rather than waiting for the open-armed hospitality of an Israelite city. These individual Israelites, the city of Gibeah, and the Benjaminites, says Block, "have sunk to the level of those nations whom they were commanded to destroy and on whom the judgment of God hung. And in the words of Moses in Deut 8:19–20, when Israelites act like Canaanites, they may expect the same fate" (544).

The story can be read at many levels with many understandings. R. Bowman argues, "Like that of Jephthah's daughter, this story suggests that a human act of self-preservation results in innocent suffering. . . . The narrator's portrayals stress human responsibility, not divine accountability, and emphasize responsible human interaction, not responsive divine intervention" ("Narrative Criticism of Judges," 41).

Yee sees a sociological struggle behind the text: "Judges 17–21 tries to resolve ideologically the conflicts between the two modes of production" (the dominant native tributory mode giving taxes to the king and the "subordinate but still stubbornly present" familial/tribal mode) ("Ideological Criticism," 154). Yee (155) finds that Josiah took away the piece of the action the country Levites had had in collecting taxes for the government and instituted a model in which all money went to Jerusalem. But Mayes insists, "Any royal centralization objectives to be discerned in Judges 17–21 can in no sense be exclusively limited to supposed economic policies held by Josiah. . . . Yee has moved too quickly from a set of inadequately formulated literary observations to an unreliable set of historical conclusions" (*BibInt* 9 [2001] 251).

Müllner, concluding a complex argument, decides, "The narrative of Judges 19–20 reveals the great similarity between the desperate behavior towards differences and the search for identity that consists of the attempt to construct the self by distinguishing it from Others. It is a male self in search of itself that needs to take cognizance of, and deny Otherness as a threat" ("Lethal Differences," 142).

Olson details the decline of the treatment of women in Judges from bold leadership by Achsah, Deborah, and Jael to women becoming objects of foolish vows with Jephthah, objects of men's desires with Samson, to "purchased instruments for schemes of male vengeance" with Delilah, to the atrocity of this chapter. He sees also the climax of an individual or tribe symbolizing Israel as a whole in that the raped, dismembered concubine is "a gruesome metaphor for the social body of the twelve-tribe union of Israel" (872–73).

Mayes sees Judg 17–21 held together by the "inverted pattern of the refrain" "as evident illustrations of the religious and social anarchy to which Israel was subject without the centralizing control of the monarchic institution. The argument for the monarchy could scarcely be put in a stronger, more persuasive form" (*BibInt* 9 [2001] 242). Mayes finds that the "rhetorical purpose of the book" is "to enjoin all Israel to endorse the Judahite king who exemplified loyalty to the ideals of land occupation, inter-tribal unity, cultic order and social justice prescribed by Yahweh's covenant" (244, a thought provoked by O'Connell, *Rhetoric of the Book of Judges*, 266–67).

Judg 19 can be read from many perspectives with differing methodologies, resulting in widely divergent conclusions. Read as exposition to what follows, Judg 19 incriminates one city and the tribe that occupies it. Incrimination of that city is brought on, however, by two Ephraimites, one a Levite, protecting themselves at the expense of their women. This narrative thus illustrates not an Israel united in carving out territory under the leadership of God and a divinely chosen leader but an Israel united by unethical behavior ready to answer the call to action against one of its own tribes, not one of the Canaanite enemies. The uniqueness of this unethical, gruesome behavior must be remembered and taught to future generations in the same manner as the uniqueness of God's deliverance from Egypt is taught. Never again must such a foolish, evil act occur in Israel.

2. All Israel Gains Revenge on Benjamin (20:1–48)

Bibliography

See *Bibliography* for 19:1–30.

Translation

[1] *All the sons of Israel came out, and the congregation*[a] *assembled together to Yahweh at Mizpah. They were as one man*[b]*—those from Dan to Beersheba, even from Gilead.* [2] *The leaders*[a] *of all the people of all the tribes of Israel took their place in the assembly of the people of God, four hundred thousand infantrymen with drawn swords.*

[3] *The sons of Benjamin*[a] *heard that the sons of Israel had gone up*[b] *to Mizpah. The sons of Israel*[c] *said, "Tell us how*[d] *this evil thing happened."*

[4] *The Levite, husband of the murdered woman, answered, "I came to Gibeah which is in Benjamin along with my concubine to spend the night.* [5] *The lords of Gibeah rose up against me and surrounded the house against me at night. They planned to kill me; they humiliated*[a] *my concubine; and she died.* [6] *I grabbed up my concubine, cut her into pieces, and sent her into every territory of Israel's*[a] *inheritance, for they had committed a shameful act,*[b] *a stupid sin in Israel.* [7] *Look here, all you sons of Israel! Come up with your word of counsel here!"*[a]

[8]*All the people rose as one man, "No one will go to his tent, and no one will turn back to his house. *[9]*Now therefore, this is what we will do to Gibeah: against her*[a]* by lot. *[10]*We will take ten men of every hundred from all the tribes of Israel,*[a]* a hundred from a thousand, and a thousand from ten thousand to secure food for the army*[b]* so on their arrival they can do to Gibeah*[c]* of Benjamin according to all the stupid sin they did*[d]* in Israel." *[11]*All the men of Israel were mustered together to*[a]* the city as one man, a close-knit army.*[b]*

[12]*The tribes of Israel sent*[a]* men into all the tribes*[b]* of Benjamin asking, "What is this evil that was committed among you? *[13]*Now therefore, give up the men, the sons of Belial,*[a]* who were in Gibeah that we may kill them and banish the evil*[b]* from Israel."

But the sons*[c]* of Benjamin were not willing to listen to the voice of their kinsmen, the sons of Israel. *[14]*The sons of Benjamin mustered together from the towns*[a]* to Gibeah to go out to battle with the sons of Israel. *[15]*The sons of Benjamin mobilized in that day from the towns twenty-six thousand*[a]* men with drawn swords, not counting the residents of Gibeah who mobilized seven hundred elite troops.*[b]* *[16]*From all these people seven hundred men*[a]* were left-handed elite troops, each of whom could sling a stone to hit a hair without ever missing.

[17]*Meanwhile, the men*[a]* of Israel mobilized—apart from Benjamin*[b]*—four hundred thousand men with drawn swords, each one a warrior. *[18]*They rose and came up to Bethel*[a]* and inquired of God. The sons of Israel said, "Who should go up for us first*[b]* in the battle with the sons of Benjamin."

Yahweh said, "Judah is to be*[c]* first."

[19]*The sons of Israel rose in the morning*[a]* and pitched their camp against Gibeah. *[20]*The men*[a]* of Israel went out to battle with Benjamin.*[b]* The men of Israel lined up with them for battle*[c]* near Gibeah. *[21]* [a]*The sons of Benjamin went out from Gibeah,*[b]* and in that day destroyed twenty-two thousand men into the earth. *[22]* [a]*The army*[b]* of the men of Israel strengthened each other and lined up again for battle in the same place*[c]* where they had lined up the first time. *[23]*The sons of Israel went up*[a]* and cried before Yahweh until evening. They inquired of Yahweh, "Should I*[b]* again advance to battle with the sons of*[c]* Benjamin, my*[d]* kinsfolk?"

Yahweh said, "Go up to them."

[24]*The sons of Israel approached the sons of*[a]* Benjamin the second day. *[25]*Benjamin*[a]* went out to meet them from Gibeah on the second day. They*[b]* destroyed the sons of Israel*[c]* again, eighteen thousand men into the ground, every one of these with drawn swords. *[26]*All the sons of Israel went up with all the army and came to Bethel. They cried and sat there*[a]* before Yahweh. They fasted that day until evening*[b]* and offered up burnt offerings and peace offerings*[c]* before Yahweh. *[27]*The sons of Israel inquired of Yahweh,*[a]* the ark of the covenant of God*[b]* being there in those days.*[c]* *[28]*Also, Phinehas, the son of Eleazer, the son of Aaron,*[a]* was standing before it in those days asking,*[b]* "Should I yet again go out to battle with the sons of*[c]* Benjamin, my kinsfolk, or should I quit?"

Yahweh said, "Go up, for tomorrow I will give them into your individual hand."*[d]*

[29]*Israel*[a]* set an ambush surrounding Gibeah. *[30]*The sons of*[a]* Israel went up against the sons of Benjamin*[b]* on the third day and lined up against Gibeah as the other times. *[31]*When the sons of Benjamin went out to meet the army, they were lured away*[a]* from the town. They began*[b]* to strike down some of the army, killing*[c]* as the other times both on the roads—the one leading up to Bethel and the other to Gibeah*[d]*—and through the field.*[e]* About thirty men from Israel died. *[32]*The sons of Benjamin said, "They are being defeated*[a]* by us as the first time."

But the sons of Israel said, "Let's flee and lure them away from the town to the *roadway.* "[b] [33] *At that time all the men of Israel rose from their position and lined up at Baal Tamar. Israel's ambush was charging forth[a] from the unprotected side[b] of Gibeah.* [34] *Ten thousand men, elite troops from all Israel, came in front of[a] Gibeah. The battle was heavy, but they did not know that evil was approaching them.*

[35] *Yahweh defeated[a] Benjamin in the face of Israel.[b] The sons of Israel destroyed Benjamin in that day, 25,100 men dying, every one of these with drawn swords.* [36] *The sons of[a] Benjamin saw that they were defeated. The men of Israel had given their position to Benjamin because they trusted the ambush that they had set against[b] Gibeah.* [37] *At that moment the ambush[a] hurried forward in an attack against Gibeah. The ambush spread out and struck dead the whole town before the sword.* [38] *Now the men of Israel[a] had agreed on a sign with the ambush—the ambush[b] would make a huge[c] cloud of[d] smoke ascend from the town,* [39] *and the men of[a] Israel would turn back to the battle.[b]*

At that time Benjamin had begun to strike dead the men of Israel, about thirty men, when they said, "Surely, they are being severely defeated[c] before us as in the first battle." [40] *But when the cloud began ascending from the town in a column of smoke,[a] Benjamin turned around behind themselves. Look! The entire town was going up to heaven.* [41] *At that moment the men of Israel turned around, and the men of Benjamin were terrified because they saw that evil had come against[a] them.* [42] *They turned[a] around before the men of[b] Israel toward the way of the wilderness,[c] but the battle caught up with them, because those from the towns[d] were destroying[e] them in between.[f]* [43] *They surrounded Benjamin, pursued them without resting, and trampled them down[a] as far as the area of Gibeah[b] to the east.* [44] *There fell from Benjamin eighteen thousand men, each of these a heroic warrior.* [45] *They had turned[a] and fled to the wilderness to the rock of Rimmon, and they[b] had harvested in the roads five thousand men. They followed tightly after them[c] as far as Gidom,[d] and they struck dead two thousand of them.* [46] *The total number that fell from Benjamin in that day was twenty-five thousand men, each of these a heroic warrior.* [47] *Six hundred men turned and fled toward the wilderness to the rock of Rimmon. They stayed in the rock of Rimmon four months.*

[48] *But the men of[a] Israel returned[b] to the sons of Benjamin and struck them dead with the sword, each town totally,[c] including animals and everything found.[d] Also, every town that was found they set on fire.*

Notes

1.a. LXX[A] reads πᾶσα ἡ συναγωγή, "all the community," adding a common expression.

1.b. OL expands the opening to read, "And all the house of Israel gave instruction, and all the congregation made an assembly like one man."

2.a. LXX[A] reads ἔστη τὸ κλίμα παντὸς τοῦ λαοῦ πᾶσαι αἱ φυλαὶ Ισραηλ, "the region of all of the people of all the tribes of Israel stood," taking פנות geographically rather than as "chief" or "leader." LXX[B] (compare OL) reads ἐστάθησαν κατὰ πρόσωπον κυρίου πᾶσαι αἱ φυλαὶ τοῦ Ισραηλ, "they took their stand opposite the Lord, all the tribes of Israel," taking פנות in the familiar expression "face of the Lord" and omitting "all of the people," seen as an unnecessary doublet of "all the tribes," not seeing the emphasis on the complete, unified Israel.

3.a. Cairo Genizah fragment has "all the sons of Benjamin," creating a parallel with the previous verse.

3.b. LXX[A] reads "gone up to the Lord at Mizpah," adding a customary phrase to the text and interpreting Mizpah as a sanctuary. *BHS* points to several Heb. MSS to suggest that perhaps a verb has dropped out, proposing the following reading: [3a] [וַיִּשְׁמְעוּ בְּנֵי בִנְיָמִן כִּי־עָלוּ בְנֵי־יִשְׂרָאֵל הַמִּצְפָּה וַיְמָאֲנוּ לָבוֹא בְתוֹכָם], [2a] [וַיִּתְיַצְּבוּ פְנוֹת כָּל־הָעָם בִּקְהַל עַם הָאֱלֹהִים] , [3b] [וַיֹּאמְרוּ וְלֹבְנֵי יִשְׂרָאֵל] . . . , resulting in the translation "And the sons of Benjamin heard that the sons of Israel went up to Mizpah. And they refused to come into their midst. And the leaders of all the people took their stand in the assembly of the people of God. And they said to the sons of Israel . . ." This is an unnecessary evening of the text to bring clearer narrative logic. MT seeks to contrast Israel and Benjamin.

3.c. LXX[B] reads καὶ ἐλθόντες εἶπαν οἱ υἱοὶ Ισραηλ, "and coming, the sons of Israel said."

3.d. OL reads "where."

5.a. LXX[A] (compare OL) reads ἐταπείνωσαν καὶ ἐνέπαιξαν αὐτῇ καὶ ἀπέθανεν, "they humiliated and mocked her and she died," related to the LXX reading of 19:25 and apparently translating Heb. ענה two different ways.

6.a. LXX[B] reads κληρονομίας υἱῶν Ισραηλ, "the inheritance of the sons of Israel," adding a common phrase.

6.b. LXX[A] does not have an equivalent for זמה, "a shameful act," omitting a redundant, but significant, term. LXX[B] simply transliterates the Heb.

7.a. LXX[A] does not have "here," omitting it as unnecessary.

9.a. LXX (compare OL) reads ἀναβησόμεθα, "we will go up." This expresses the meaning of the Heb. if it does not represent the original reading. BHS proposes inserting נעלה, "let us go up against her by lot." *Preliminary and Interim Report* (2:126) sees two options: an exclamation or an elliptical expression assuming "let us go up" without expressing it. This would explain LXX as the easier reading and/or as a change in the text necessitated by target language. Barthélemy (*Critique textuelle,* 1:121–22) keeps MT, showing LXX as the first to gloss the text in light of the context.

10.a. LXX[A] does not have "all the tribes of Israel," perhaps an MT addition of a customary phrase.

10.b. Or "people"; LXX[B] does not have "for the people," reading ἐπισιτισμὸν τοῦ ποιῆσαι ἐλθεῖν αὐτοὺς εἰς Γαβαα Βενιαμιν ποιῆσαι αὐτῇ κατὰ πᾶν, "provisions so to make them come to Gibeah of Benjamin according to all," omitting "for the army." LXX[A] reads τοῖς εἰσπορευομένοις ἐπιτελέσαι τῇ Γαβαα, "who are going to repay Gibeah." See NRSV. BHS (compare Block, 556, n. 314) suggests reading לָבָאים לַעֲשׂוֹת, transposing the two words. *Preliminary and Interim Report* (2:126–27) retains MT as the more difficult reading, translating, "to do, when they come." Barthélemy (*Critique textuelle,* 1:122) retains MT, seeing the transposition of the two infinitives as unnecessary.

10.c. A Heb. MS reads לְגִבְעָה, so that BHS proposes לְגִבְעַת, a construct form. *Preliminary and Interim Report* (2:127) sees the proposal as a conjecture and appears to accept it. Barthélemy (*Critique textuelle,* 1:122–23) decides that one cannot appeal to textual criticism to distinguish Geba from Tell-el-Ful in the book of Judges.

10.d. BHS suggests reading the pl. with LXX and Syr. instead of MT's collective sg. עשׂה.

11.a. LXX[A] reads ἐκ τῶν πόλεων, "out of the towns," apparently interpreting the move as from the Israelite towns rather than in the direction of Gibeah.

11.b. LXX[A] reads חברים as הבאם, "those coming," while LXX[B] does not translate the term at all, missing the MT emphasis on unity.

12.a. A Heb. MS reads *pi'el* rather than *qal.*

12.b. LXX, Vg. read the expected sg., "tribe of Benjamin." Block (556, n. 316) sees שבט, "tribe," is to be interpreted as equal to מִשְׁפָּחָה, "clan."

13.a. Or "abominably wicked men." LXX[A] reads ἄνδρας τοὺς ἀσεβεῖς τοὺς ἐν Γαβαα τοὺς υἱοὺς Βελιαλ, "wicked men who are in Gibeah, the sons of Belial," apparently translating the Heb. term and then later transliterating it. OL reads "give the guilty men from the sons of Benjamin." As Niditch notes, OL is "making clear that only those who committed the crime will be punished. MT is more ambiguous" (200).

13.b. BHS proposes reading the definite article on רעה, "evil."

13.c. "Sons" is not in the written text but inserted as a Q by the Masoretes—i.e., MT has only the vowel points of בְּנֵי, "sons," without any consonants—one of ten instances in the Masoretic text wherein a word is inserted as a Q when nothing appears in the MT. Compare LXX, Syr., Tg.

14.a. LXX, Syr. read, "their towns," inserting the obvious.

15.a. LXX[A] reads "25,000," while LXX[B] reads "23,000"; compare vv 35, 46." *Preliminary and Interim Report* (2:128) follows MT, seeing too narrow a text base for the emendation, which represents accommodation to a parallel passage.

15.b. LXX[A] reads νεανίσκοι ἐκλεκτοί, "young, chosen," apparently giving two possible translations of Heb. בָּחוּר. BHS proposes deleting the last clause: שֶׁבַע מֵאוֹת אִישׁ בָּחוּר, "who mobilized seven hundred elite troops," on the basis of LXX, OL, Syr., Vg., thinking they have been taken out of v 16. See NRSV. *Preliminary and Interim Report* (2:128) follows MT, seeing too narrow a text base for change.

16.a. LXX[A] reads ἀμφοτεροδέξιοι πάντες οὗτοι σφενδονῆται βάλλοντες λίθους πρὸς τὴν τρίχα καὶ οὐ διαμαρτάνοντες, "left-handed (or ambidextrous) were they all, slingers who threw stones at the hair and did not miss." LXX[B] (compare OL) reads ἐκ παντὸς λαοῦ ἀμφοτεροδέξιοι πάντες οὗτοι σφενδονῆται ἐν λίθοις πρὸς τρίχα καὶ οὐκ ἐξαμαρτάνοντες, "out of all the people all these were left-handed who could sling with a stone at a hair and not miss." Thus REB omits "from all these people seven hundred . . . were . . . elite troops." *Preliminary and Interim Report* (2:128–29) maintains MT, seeing accidental omission in LXX. Barthélemy (*Critique textuelle*, 1:123) thinks the original text had two distinct numbers with the troops of Gibeah having the greater number. The MT explains the entire tradition, so that Barthélemy retains MT knowing it is not original.

17.a. LXX^A reads καὶ πᾶς ἀνήρ, "all the men," probably an addition of a customary phrase.

17.b. LXX^A reads "sons of Benjamin," again adding a customary phrase.

18.a. Vg. reads "Shiloh." Boling (285) translates the term as "the sanctuary" (lit., "house of God") and locates it at Mizpah. The text in its repetitions and mention of the ark leaves no real evidence for a location other than the ancient shrine of Bethel.

18.b. OL translates "play a leadership role."

18.c. MT does not have or have to have a verb. LXX^A reads Ιουδας ἀναβήσεται ἀφηγούμενος, "Judah will go up leading," while LXX^B reads Ιουδας ἐν ἀρξῇ ἀναβήσεται ἀφηγούμενος, "Judah at the first will go up leading." OL translates "play a leadership role." Both see the need for a verb in Gk., while LXX^B apparently translates the same word twice. OL reads "Judah will go up as leader."

19.a. LXX^A does not have "in the morning," apparently deleting the obvious.

20.a. LXX reads πᾶς ἀνὴρ Ισραηλ, "all the men of Israel," adding a customary phrase; compare *Note* 20:17.a.

20.b. Many Heb. MSS and Syr. read "sons of Benjamin," adding a customary phrase; compare *Note* 20:17.b.

20.c. LXX^BC do not have אִישׁ יִשְׂרָאֵל מִלְחָמָה, "men (lit. 'man') of Israel for battle," possibly eliminating repetitious language.

21.a. OL provides an expansive variant text: "And the sons of Israel gave to them one thousand men to besiege the cities. And they placed themselves on the way to Gibeah, and all the congregation commanded them saying, 'Go to that place which is above the ambushes, and it will be when the sons of Benjamin begin to come out from the city, you will mingle secretly, and you will enter it, and you will take away peace, and we will turn back hard upon their heels, and we will strike them.' And Benjamin went out from Gibeah, and all the men of Israel went out to Benjamin, all of Israel meeting with them in war against Gibeah, and Benjamin went out and exterminated from Israel in that day twenty-two thousand men, and Israel was overcome, and again they arrayed to fight there in the valley as on the first day."

21.b. LXX^A reads ἐκ τῆς πόλεως, "out of the town," a possible original reading later made specific.

22.a. *BHS* transposes this verse after v 23 without MS evidence. See NRSV, NIV, NJB.

22.b. LXX, Syr. do not have "the army" or "the people." *BHS*, followed by many modern translations, considers the word a gloss to be deleted, apparently not recognizing the technical meaning "army" that is appropriate and stylistically correct here.

22.c. Lit. "the place where they lined up there"; LXX^B does not have "there."

23.a. *BHS* uses vv 18 and 26 as evidence to insert "Beth-el" here. Without textual evidence, such an insertion is not necessary. *Preliminary and Interim Report* (2:129) calls the proposed emendation a conjecture.

23.b. LXX^B reads "we." MT forms a parallel to v 28 where first-person sg. spoken by the priest is correct.

23.c. LXX^A does not have "sons of," perhaps the addition of a customary phrase, so *BHS* deletes.

23.d. LXX^B reads "our." See *Note* 20:23.b.

24.a. Heb. MS, LXX^A do not have "sons of," so *BHS* deletes. This could be an example of MT introducing a familiar phrase into the text, making the shorter reading the preferred.

25.a. LXX^B reads "sons of," another addition of a customary phrase.

25.b. LXX^A reads "he," being grammatically precise, whereas MT is collective.

25.c. LXX^A reads διέφθειρεν ἐκ τοῦ λαοῦ, "he destroyed out of the people," again perhaps an original unspecific phrase for a later specific one.

26.a. LXX^A does not have "and sat there," omitting a possibly superfluous phrase.

26.b. LXX^A does not have "until evening," again omitting a possibly superfluous phrase.

26.c. LXX^A reads ὁλοκαυτώματα σωτηρίου, "burnt offerings of salvation," while LXX^B reads τελείας, "whole offerings."

27.a. LXX^B places "and the sons of Israel inquired of the Lord" in the middle of the next verse, beginning here simply "because there was the ark," giving a more normal interpretation of oracular proceedings. MT emphasizes the role of the priest. OL has a complex rendition of 20:26–28: "And they inquired of the Lord and they said 'Why, O Lord, has indignation and wrath been committed against Israel, and we your children have gathered together to take away the sons of iniquity who did impiety in Israel, and behold, we have fled from their face twice and now shall we set up again to go . . . ?'" See Niditch (200).

27.b. LXX^A, two Heb. MSS, Syr. read "ark of the covenant of the Lord," while two Heb. MSS, LXX^BR read "ark of the covenant of the Lord God." These appear to be expansions based on commonly used phrases. The use of אלהים, "God," appears to be a literary choice of the narrator, who often avoids the personal divine name in this chaotic context.

27.c. LXX^B does not have "in those days," which may be the original reading, MT adding an updating phrase to the text.

28.a. A few Heb. MSS, Syr. read, "the priest," a later updating and specifying of the text.

28.b. LXX^B reads ἐπηρώτησαν οἱ υἱοὶ Ισραηλ ἐν κυρίῳ λέγοντες, "and the sons of Israel asked the Lord saying," from v 27 and then changes the following pronouns to pl., a reading often accepted as original even though it is the easier reading. See BHS.

28.c. A few Heb. MSS do not have "sons of," so BHS suggests deleting, consistent with the BHS reading in 20:23, 24.

28.d. Two Heb. MSS read בידיך, "in your (pl.) hands."

29.a. LXX reads "the sons of," inserting a familiar phrase.

30.a. LXX^A does not have "the sons of," possibly reflecting MT's addition of a common phrase.

30.b. LXX^A reads καὶ ἔταχεν Ισραηλ πρὸς τὸν Βενιαμιν, "Israel set up in the direction of Benjamin," changing the verb and omitting "sons of."

31.a. BHS proposes on the basis of Josh 8:16 reading the *nip'al* וַיִּנָּתְקוּ for MT's *hop'al*, a form that appears only here in the Hebrew Bible.

31.b. BHS proposes transposing וַיָּחֵלּוּ לְהַכּוֹת מֵהָעָם חֲלָלִים כְּפַעַם בְּפַעַם, "they began to strike down some of the army, killing as the other times," to a position after גִּבְעָתָה, "to(ward) Gibeah." No MS evidence supports this transposition.

31.c. LXX^A does not have "killing," apparently seeing it as unneeded. OL reads "and the sons of Benjamin went out to the people; and they were drawn out from the city, and they began to fall wounded."

31.d. BHS proposes changing Gibeah to Gibeon without MS evidence. *Preliminary and Interim Report* (2:129) rejects the change as conjectural. Barthélemy (*Critique textuelle*, 1:123–24) says the text points to the two directions of the same road and thus maintains MT.

31.e. The syntactical relationship of "through the field" is variously interpreted. Thus NRSV reads "as well as in the open country." NJB reads "on the roads, one of which runs up to Bethel, and the other to Gibeah through open country." REB reads "on the highways which led across open country." JPS reads "they started out by striking some of the men dead in the open field."

32.a. LXX^A reads προσκόπτουσιν, "they are stumbling," a unique translation choice for LXX^A. Elsewhere in the chapter, LXX^A uses τροπόω to translate נגף (vv 32, 35, 36, 39). LXX^B is inconsistent in using πίπτω, πατάσσω, πλήσσω, and πτῶσις πίπτω.

32.b. LXX^B reads ὁδούς καὶ ἐποίησαν οὕτως, "roadway, and they did so," adding a natural conclusion to the passage.

33.a. LXX^A reads ἐπάλαιεν ἐκ, "struggled (or wrestled) from"; LXX^B reads ἐπήρχετο, apparently from επαρχέω, "come to the aid of."

33.b. LXX^A reads ἀπὸ δυσμῶν, "west of." The Heb. is not clear here (compare Block, 565, n. 350); possibly "from the clearing of Gibeah (or Geba)" or "from Maareh of Gibea," the reading of LXX^B. *Preliminary and Interim Report* (2:129–30) retains MT and translates "from the exposed point of Geba," seeing the changes as simplification of the text, lack of scribal knowledge, or simple scribal error. Barthélemy (*Critique textuelle*, 1:124) looks at the full panoply of early translations. The second half of v 33 corresponds to the first half in Vg., with the last words recalling the ancient Gk. Syr. has read מְעָרָה, "grotto." Tg. reads עֲרָבָה, "wilderness." The LXX appears to fit the context best, but it presupposes a Heb. ממערב, meaning "west," when that word did not become part of Heb. prose until quite late in Chronicles and Daniel. Barthélemy follows Rashi in interpreting MT to mean the unprotected side of Geba, the one on the other side from the battle. Rashi sees the word as עֶרְוָה, used for "nakedness" of the land in Gen 42:9, 12. The translation above follows Rashi's interpretation.

34.a. Many Heb. MSS, Tg. read מִנֶּגֶב, "from the Negev." The ambush narrative demands the MT reading.

35.a. LXX^A reads ἐτρόπωσεν, "he caused Benjamin to turn away."

35.b. LXX^B reads "sons of Israel," adding a common phrase.

36.a. LXX^A does not have "the sons of," again showing the flexibility of the tradition in using or not using the phrase.

36.b. Many Heb. MSS read עַל, the normal term for "against," for MT's אֶל, which more frequently means "to" or "toward." MT represents the more difficult reading.

37.a. LXX^B reads καὶ ἐν τῷ αὐτοὺς ὑποχωρῆσαι καὶ τὸ ἔνεδρον, "at their withdrawing, the ambush," adding a natural conclusion to the scene.

38.a. LXX^B reads "sons of Israel" for MT's "man of Israel," substituting one common phrase for another.

38.b. Lit. "they."

38.c. LXX^B reads μετὰ τοῦ ἐνέδρου τῆς μάχης, "with the ambush for battle," reading חֹרֵב for MT הֶרֶב, the reading of a few Heb. MSS. The term does not appear in Syr. or Vg. *BHS* compares LXX^L and deletes the term as a duplicate of הָאֹרֵב, "ambush." Niditch decides that LXX^A "may reflect an alternate Hebrew *Vorlage* that made more sense or a text that had been corrected to make more sense. It is also possible that the translator in A engaged in a form of creative exegesis in order to make sense of the same difficult Hebrew text found in MT" (201).

38.d. LXX^B reads σύσσημον, "signal," for MT's "cloud."

39.a. LXX^B reads "sons of," again substituting one common phrase for another.

39.b. LXX^B reads καὶ εἶδον οἱ υἱοὶ Ισραηλ ὅτι προκατελάβετο τὸ ἔνεδρον τὴν Γαβαα καὶ ἔστησαν ἐν τῇ παρατάξει, "and the sons of Israel saw that the ambush had surprised Gibeah, and they took their positions in the battle line," apparently adding a literary flourish to make the text read more smoothly.

39.c. LXX^A reads τροπούμενος τροποῦται, "they are surely put to flight," while LXX^B reads πτώσει πίπτουσιν, "they are surely falling." See *Note* 20:32.a.

40.a. LXX^B reads καὶ τὸ σύσσημον ἀνέβη ἐπὶ πλεῖον ἐπὶ τῆς πόλεως ὡς στῦλος καπνοῦ, "and the signal went up over the many (that is, more and more) over the city as a pillar of smoke." See *Note* 20:38.d. This may attempt to tie the narrative in some way to the Sinai signal of a cloud of smoke or represent a simple narrative expansion for clarity.

41.a. Many Heb. MSS have אֵלָיו for MT עָלָיו, a common exchange in the Heb. text; compare *Note* 20:36.b above.

42.a. *BHS* sees the probable reading to be the sg. וַיִּפֶן to gain consistency with the previous verse.

42.b. LXX^B reads "sons of," one of many examples of the tradition's flexibility in using common expressions.

42.c. LXX^B reads ἐρήμου καὶ ἔφυγον, "wilderness, and they fled," adding the obvious for narrative completeness. A few Heb. MSS add a locative ה to "wilderness," making movement toward the wilderness specific.

42.d. *BHS* cites LXX^u and LXX^{lll}, both Lucianic witnesses. The first reads ἐν τῇ πόλει, "in the city," while the second reads ἀπὸ τῆς πόλεως, "from the city." Referencing the Vg. also, *BHS* suggests reading מֵהָעִיר, "from the city," the MT resulting from dittography of the מ in the following word. MT apparently refers to towns on the path of retreat, while the emendation would refer to the ambush coming from Gibeah. Block (566, n. 375) sees the final *mêm* as a dittograph or duplication of the next word with a transposition of *'ayin* and *yôd*, creating the sg., "the city." *Preliminary and Interim Report* (2:130) sees simplification of the text at work here and translates: "And they turned away from the men of Israel towards the desert route; but the battle overtook them there and those coming from the cities exterminated them there in between." Barthélemy (*Critique textuelle*, 1:125) compares cities here with those of v 15 referring to small towns in Benjamin other than Gibeah and shows how the Masoretes have protected this reading with reference to Josh 20:4 and Ezek 25:9.

42.e. *BHS* suggests reading שֹׁתִים (הֵם), possibly meaning "they were drinking or banqueting."

42.f. With reference to the Syr., *BHS* proposes בְּתֹךְ, eliminating the suffix.

43.a. LXX^A reads καὶ ἔκοψαν τὸν Βενιαμιν καταπαῦσαι αὐτὸν κατάπαυσιν καὶ κατεπάτησαν αὐτόν, "and they cut down Benjamin, bringing him to a final end and trampling on him," while LXX^B reads καὶ κατέκοπτον τὸν Βενιαμιν καὶ ἐδίωξαν αὐτὸν ἀπὸ Νουα κατὰ πόδα αὐτοῦ, "they cut Benjamin in pieces and pursued him from Noua (transliteration of Heb. 'without rest') at his feet." Block (567, n. 360) sees the prefixed *mêm* as a partitive *min* (that is, as a preposition denoting separation from): "without rest." *BHS* sees LXX as pointing to Heb. וַיִּכְתֻהוּ or וַיִּרְדְפוּ, and so proposes the first as the original reading. *BHS* also uses the reading of LXX^{BC} καὶ ἔδιωξαν αὐτόν with the Lucianic LXX^{lll} to change the MT from the *hip'il* of רדף, "to pursue," to the *qal*. *BHS* notes LXX^{BRC} and LXX^{lll}'s ἀπὸ Νουα equals מִנּוּחָה, "from Nochah," a name of a son of Benjamin in 1 Chr 8:2. With reference to Tg. and Vg., *BHS* proposes מִמְּנוּחָה, "from Menochah," instead of "resting place" or "without resting." For MT הִדְרִיכֻהוּ, "to trample down" or "to catch up with," *BHS* proposes וַיַּדְבִּיקֻה, "follow hard" or "catch up with," on the basis of 20:42, 45 or וַיְּדַחֲקֻה, "afflict," as in Judg 2:18. *Preliminary and Interim Report* (2:130–31) follows MT, reading "<from their> resting place they trod them (lit. him) down." Barthélemy (*Critique textuelle*, 1:125) accepts the MT reading of the *hiph'il* of דרך as meaning "to attain to, to reach," and thus sees the meaning as to reach a troop's staging or resting place.

43.b. *BHS* proposes גֶּבַע, "Geba."

45.a. LXX^B reads καὶ ἐπέβλεψαν οἱ λοιποί, "and the rest eyed carefully."

45.b. LXX^B reads ἐκαλαμήσαντο ἐξ αὐτῶν οἱ υἱοὶ Ισραηλ πεντακισξιλίους ἄνδρας, "the sons of Israel had harvested out of them five thousand men," not translating "in the roads (or highways)."

45.c. LXX^B reads κατέβησαν ὀπίσω αὐτῶν οἱ υἱοὶ Ισραηλ, "the sons of Israel went down after them," inserting an explicit subject.

45.d. Heb. text is unclear at this point. LXX^R reads Γαδααμ, "Gadaam." LXX^B reads Γεδαν, "Dedan." Syr. reads (*l)gb' wn*, "to Gibeon." *BHS* on this evidence and the reading of 21:6 proposes גְּדַעֻם, "cut them off." Barthélemy (*Critique textuelle*, 1:126) suggests reading the simple *pi'el* infinitive of גדע, "to cut off." He points to similar constructions in 2 Sam 22:38, 1 Kgs 22:11, 2 Chr 18:10, and Ps 18:38. *Preliminary and Interim Report* (2:132), on the basis of a simplification of the text and scribal misunderstanding of linguistic and historical data, emends the text to read "until they had hewed them down."

48.a. LXX^B reads "sons of Israel, " substituting one familiar phrase for another.

48.b. LXX^A reads ἀπέκλεισεν, "shut up (or confined)."

48.c. *Translation* takes MT reading as meaning "sound, unhurt" as in Ps 38:4, 8 and Isa 1:6. See Barthélemy (*Critique textuelle*, 1:126–27), "of men (that is, inhabited)," rather than MT מְתֹם, "totally (or soundly)"; LXX^B reads ἀπὸ πόλεως Μεθλα, "from the city of Methla," probably an attempt at transliterating Heb. מְתֹם. *BHS* wants to add וָעִיר, "and the city," as a result of haplography, thus reading "and the city from its men [reading מִמְּתִים on basis of Heb., Syr., and Vg. evidence] unto beast and unto [adding the ו twice with several Heb. MSS] all that was found." *Preliminary and Interim Report* remarks: "Since the Massoretes no longer understood the expression עִיר מְתֹם (Deut 2.34; 3.6; Judg 20.48), they created two different vocalizations. But the meaning of the expression remains the same in the three places where it occurs" and is translated "male population" (2:132–33).

48.d. LXX^A reads ἀπὸ πόλεως ἑξῆς ἕως κτήνους ἕως παντὸς τοῦ εὑρεθέντος εἰς πάσας τὰς πόλεις, "from city one after another unto beasts unto all that was found in all the cities," while LXX^B reads ἀπὸ πόλεως Μεθλα καὶ ἕως κτήνους καὶ ἕως παντὸς τοῦ εὑρισκομένου εἰς πάσας τὰς πόλεις, "from the city of Methla and unto the beasts and unto all which is found in all the cities."

Form/Structure/Setting

The opening imperfect consecutives tie chap. 20 closely to chap. 19, as might be expected from the conclusion that chap. 19 serves as the exposition for chaps. 20 and 21. Most of the narrative consists of dialogue or monologue. I designate various scenes by the change of speakers and participants. Scene 1 describes the Israelites gathering for a national assembly to plot strategy (vv 1–3), a move the Benjaminites hear of. Scene 2 (vv 4–7) features the Levite's testimony concerning the happenings from chap. 19, concluding with a surprise clause calling on the assembly for action. Scene 3 (vv 8–11) describes the Israelites' decision making to oppose Benjamin and their mustering for battle. Scene 4 (vv 12–13) shows the negotiations between the two parties, with the Benjaminites refusing to accept the terms Israel offers. So scene 5 (vv 14–17) depicts the Benjaminites preparing for war in Gibeah and the Israelites mobilizing their troops. In scene 6 (v 18) the men of Israel go to Bethel to see who their leader is. Again as in chap. 1, the leader is Judah. The battle dominates scene 7 (vv 19–21) with Israel losing. Israel prepares for a return engagement in scene 8 and gains God's approval (vv 22–23). The second battle comes in scene 9 (vv 24–25). Scene 10 features Israelite lamentation at Bethel with the priest delivering a divine oracle promising victory (vv 26–28).

An ambush battle results in scene 11 (vv 29–35). Scene 12 switches perspectives on this battle, showing Benjaminite action (vv 36–41). The final scene (vv 42–48) shows Israel's mop-up action, carrying out the demands of holy war legislation.

This is an extended holy war battle report featuring an ambush, but a report with an edge on it, for the holy war is not against Canaanites but against a tribe of Israelites. Niditch shows the pattern of these repeated battle reports:

> The civil war is characterized by the recurring pattern of war: muster of each side (vv. 14, 15, 17, 19, 22, 29, 32), request for an oracle by the Israelites (vv. 18, 23, 26–28), response of the deity (vv. 18, 23, 28), going forth to battle (vv. 20, 21, 24, 25, 30, 31), the battle (vv. 25, 31, 33, 34, 35, 36–37, 39), and the outcome (vv. 39–48). The majority eventually take control of the crack troops of the enemy, the left-handed men of Benjamin. (203)

The report stands under the heading of "no king in Israel" and will lead to reaffirmation of the Israelites' doing what was right in their own eyes. Irony and sarcasm fill the report, as will be seen in the commentary below. The ambush narrative in 20:19–48 has an almost exact parallel in Josh 7:2–8:23, to the point of both being replete in irony. See Butler, *Joshua*, 81. Other ambush accounts in the Hebrew element "share little resemblance with each other" (Wong, *Compositional Strategy*, 58), but Josh 8 and Judg 20 share plot, vocabulary, and rhetoric (Wong, 58–63). See the comparison in table 20.1 in the appendix.

One can readily dissect the narrative of Judg 20 into doublets and various redactional elements as many commentators have done. (See the brief discussion by Block, 563; Wong, *Compositional Strategy*, 60 with n. 83.) In so doing these redaction critics again lose sight of the artistry of the whole, turning from Israel's perspective to Benjamin's perspective and to a final mopping-up exercise. (See Revell, *VT* 35 [1985] 417–33; Satterthwaite, *VT* 42 [1992] 80–89.) Niditch points out that "the repetitions in the present version, however, are thematically important, pointing to the very nature of war as an often pointless round of battles; power rises and falls, and justice is difficult to determine. The repetition of language exemplifies a variety of traditional registers but also helps to emphasize the push-and-pull dynamic of war" (203).

Satterthwaite demonstrates that "the shifts between narrative strands have produced striking juxtapositions of word and event or word and word; details are delayed until they can have a particularly telling effect; even the simple fact that repetition was necessary to sustain three separate narrative strands has been turned to literary gain, whether in the creation of suspense or in the depiction of relentless pursuit" (88–89).

In a certain way, this narrative serves as the exposition to the final chapter of Judges, introducing the crisis that has to be resolved there. Pressler thinks the final three chapters "paint a picture of utter disintegration of Israelite social, religious, and political life" (247). Brown says, "Contrasted with ch 1 the two final chapters of Judges serve to underscore the tragic irony of the entire story, that Israel never figured out who the real enemy was and thus expended a great deal of energy and many resources fighting the wrong battles" (278). Niditch sees that the "narrative thus offers a test of Israel's unity, as the events described challenge the very notion of peoplehood under the covenant" (201).

On its own, however, Judg 20 represents a complete narrative. Vv 1–3 introduce the characters or two battle sides. Vv 4–7 review the crisis situation introduced in Judg 19. Complication emerges as the two sides prepare for battle but fail in negotiations (20:8–11, 12–17). Benjamin wins two battles, complicating the crisis and delaying the resolution (20:18–25). Finally, with proper cultic procedure, Israel wins the battle through use of the ambush (20:26–35). The denouement shows the mop-up action of the battle and affirms Israel's obedience to holy war expectations. Here then is a holy war battle report that is "a parody of sacred assembly and holy war" (Pressler, 246). But this resolution of the Israel-versus-Benjamin crisis only leads to a new crisis that will be taken up in the next chapter. Chap. 20 actually causes a greater crisis than it resolves.

Comment

1 "Sons of Israel" represents the narrator's favorite designation for the chosen nation (Judg 1:1; 2:4, 6, 11; 3:2, 5, 7–9, 12, 14–15, 27; 4:1, 3, 5, 23–24; 6:1–2, 6–8; 8:28, 33–34; 10:6, 8, 10–11, 15, 17; 11:27, 33; 13:1; 19:12, 30–20:1; 20:3, 7, 13–14, 18–19, 23–27, 30, 32, 35; 21:5–6, 18, 24) but does not appear in the Abimelech narrative, the Samson chapters after the introductory 13:1, or the Danite chapters. The significant uses appear at three points in the book: in framework verses, in chaps. 2–3, and in the final three chapters. With this designation for the central entity of the narrative, the narrator applies to the entire nation stories each of whose basic narrative content features only a few tribes. What a portion of the nation does represents the nature and accomplishments of the entire nation. Only in Judg 3:27, 4:5, 6:2, 10:17, and 11:27 do the "sons of Israel" become actively involved in the narrative up to this point. The final three chapters now have much to say about their actions. Text notes show that the copying tradition utilized this frequent phrase in different contexts. Compare in chap. 20 alone *Notes* 6.a, 23.c, 24.a, 25.a, 28.b, 29.a, 30.b, 35.b, 38.a, 39.a, 42.b, 45.b, 45.c, and 48.a.

Israel "assembled together" (קהל, *nip'al*), a term often connected to Priestly literature in a nontechnical usage. (See H.-P. Müller, *TLOT,* 3:18–26.) *HALOT* (3:1079) offers only two other occurrences of the *nip'al* verb with an accusative of place—Josh 18:1 and 22:12. Naming these as Priestly materials requires seeing all of Josh 13–22 as coming from that source, a popular but unnecessary theory. Traditional source criticism would give Exod 32:1 to J or E, while 1 Sam 20:14 and 1 Kgs 8:2, both evidencing קהל, *nip'al*, certainly are older than P. Ascription of this language to P is enhanced by the use of *'ēdâ* (עֵדָה), "community" or "congregation." *HALOT* (2:790) lists Judg 20:1; 21:10, 13, 16; 1 Kgs 8:5 as "not in P, but influenced by P?" Again Josh 22:12 and 20 appear to represent uses outside P. Thus Webb sees עֵדָה as the "primary term, and it is the assembly as a pre-monarchical institution which is principally in view" ([1987] 262, n. 27). Block sees *'ēdâ* as "a legal term that denotes Israel as a vassal community covenantally committed to Yahweh" (551). According to Wong, the unique combination of these two terms "may represent a deliberate attempt to allude to a similar gathering described in Josh 22" (*Compositional Strategy,* 72), where Phinehas restored peace between east and west, while here the community under southern leadership puts a tribe of Israel under the total ban.

The community includes representatives of all the tribes gathered for worship or judgment or war. Here the latter predominates, though all three uses are involved. For once in the book of Judges, all Israel joins together to plot strategy, but it is strategy to punish one of their own, not to occupy the land and displace the native inhabitants who tempt them with foreign gods.

"To Yahweh" shows the worship emphasis and presents the people of Israel as turning to God for direction rather than doing what is right in their own eyes. They come to Mizpah in Benjamin. (See Josh 18:26.) It would be part of Samuel's route in judging Israel (1 Sam 7:16–17). Brensinger argues that "Mizpah functions simply as the place of assembly; Bethel, as the following verses indicate, serves as the sanctuary where oracles are sought" (202). Mizpah eventually became the government center after Jerusalem was destroyed (2 Kgs 25:23–25).

Gaß (*Ortsnamen*, 417–22) lists four possible locations for Mizpah—el-Bire, Tell es-Safiye, en-Nebi Samwil, and Tell en-Nasbe. He eliminates el-Bire for lack of archaeological evidence and Tell es-Safiye as located too far south and not having archaeological confirmation. En-Nebi Samwil is located too far south, is not suitable on strategic grounds, is only lightly settled, and does not have archaeological confirmation. Archaeological evidence, location six miles (9.7 km) north of Jerusalem, and a seal from the sixth century bearing the name Ya'azanyahu (identified with Jaazaniah in 2 Kgs 25:23) point to almost certain identification of Tell en-Nasbe with Mizpah. It lay just south of the border with Israel and served with Geba as border protection for Judah.

P. M. Arnold again uses the central role of Mizpah here to credit P with writing this material: "Literary evidence suggests that this information belongs to a postexilic Priestly redaction of the Gibeah Outrage tradition, and should not be regarded as historical (Arnold *Gibeah*, 159–65). These passages reflect, instead, the cultic significance of Mizpah in the exilic and postexilic period when it possessed a 'house of the Lord' (Jer 41:5). Priestly editors evidently wished to project this importance back into Israel's past" (*ABD*, 4:879).

But surely priestly vocabulary of worship and community definition did not suddenly appear in the exilic/postexilic community. Of all areas of life, the cultic is the most conservative in its use of language and rites. Finding language of later priestly traditions in an earlier tradition or narrative should not surprise. Such language was most likely dear to and definitive for Israel long before the exile. Mizpah is featured with Samuel and Saul narratives, for which this use prepares.

To this point Judges has highlighted the lack of cooperation among Israelite tribes. The almost entirely framework language of the Othniel account has him delivering the sons of Israel. Ehud worked with Israelites in the hill country of Ephraim. Shamgar fought the Philistines individually to deliver Israel. Deborah and Barak worked primarily with Zebulun and Naphtali in the prose account, joined by Ephraim, Benjamin, Machir, and Issachar in the poetic form. Following Gideon came Manasseh, Asher, Zebulun, and Naphtali, with Ephraim called belatedly. East of the Jordan the towns of Succoth and Penuel refused Gideon's requests. Abimelech killed Gideon's sons and fought with the support of a ragtag group of worthless hirelings. All his dealings centered on the city-state of Shechem. The minor judges represented specific tribes and/or areas of the country. Jephthah again represented an outcast, with outlaws forming his army, finally recalled by Gilead. Again, Ephraim entered the picture late with self-serving complaints and saw Gilead kill forty-two thousand of their men. Samson's narratives feature him, a southern Danite, fighting alone before being captured by Judah. Micah and his Levite bring northern Dan into the picture. The final chapters return us to Benjamin, Ehud's tribe.

But no judge has obviously gathered all the Israelite tribes together to fight the enemy. Rather, several—Gideon, Abimelech, Jephthah, and Samson—feature in-fighting among various groups of Israelites. Against this background comes the unexpected and ironic: "They were as one man."

God had promised Gideon he would strike down the Midianites as one man (Judg 6:16). Now suddenly the repeated phrase pictures Israel (20:1, 8, 11). In fact the Hebrew term "one" (אֶחָד) constantly reappears at interesting intersections in the narrative (Judg 4:16; 6:16; 8:18; 9:2, 5, 18, 37, 53; 13:2; 15:4; 16:7, 11, 28–29; 17:5, 11; 18:19; 19:13; 20:1, 8, 11, 31; 21:3, 6, 8). This unity is represented geographically. Othniel was in the southwest; Ehud, the southeast; Deborah and Barak, the north central; Gideon, the central and east Jordan; Abimelech, near Shechem in the center; Jephthah, east of Jordan; Samson, back to the southwest; and Micah and the Levite, central and far north. The Levite and his concubine represent the south, the central, and the borderland of Benjamin between north and south. Finally, in the closing chapters we meet Israel "from Dan to Beersheba, even from Gilead," that is, north to south (1 Sam 3:20; 2 Sam 3:10; 17:11; 24:2, 15; 1 Kgs 5:5), and even east of the Jordan, all territory claimed by Israel.

Earlier, Caleb had operated in the area of Beersheba and the Negev, while chaps. 17–18 concentrated on Dan. Gideon and Jephthah fought many of their battles in Gilead. Then in chaps. 19–21 the tribes all come out. The entire geographical span finds representation. Unity is Israel's goal but is achieved only in destroying one of its own tribes.

2 "The leaders" is literally "the corners" (פִּנּוֹת, 1 Sam 14:38; Isa 19:13; Zeph 3:6; Zech 10:4). Again, the narrator underlines the unity theme with the repetition of "all" and mention of "the tribes of Israel," an expression appearing only in the last chapters of the book (Judg 18:1; 20:2, 10, 12; 21:5, 8, 15). "Assembly" brings together the representatives of all the tribes and of the people. The term קָהָל, "assembly," occurs only in this final narrative in Judges and is related to the verb "assembled" in v 1 (Judg 20:2; 21:5, 8). The assembly gathers here for military purposes, as the men arrive with "drawn swords." In fact, the assembly of the Lord "identifies the nation as a body 'called out' by Yahweh to engage in holy war" (Block, 550–51).

They make up the "people of God" (עַם הָאֱלֹהִים), an expression that occurs elsewhere only in 2 Sam 14:13, the more frequent expression being "people of Yahweh" (Num 11:29; 17:6; Judg 5:11; 1 Sam 2:24; 2 Sam 1:12; 6:21; 2 Kgs 9:6; Ezek 36:20; Zeph 2:10). The unusual expression may show reluctance on the narrator's part to imply that Israel is truly the people of Yahweh though they may claim to be. The figure of "four hundred thousand" seems impossibly high, prompting some to translate as four hundred military units or to speak of hyperbole (Younger, 370, n. 52). Guillaume claims "such a demographic density was never reached in Benjaminite territory before the twentieth century c.e. These numbers are therefore historically unreliable, but they clearly convey the rage and hatred of the editors against their Benjaminite neighbours" (*Waiting for Josiah*, 204). Block (550) calls attention to the decrease in the population by one-third since the exodus (Num 1; 26), an indication of divine punishment on a people who refused to occupy the land according to divine instructions. (Compare Deut 28:18.) Brensinger admits "the function of such large figures throughout the OT remains frustratingly elusive" (202).

3 "The sons of Benjamin" are introduced as quickly as possible. They apparently received one of the pieces of the secondary wife and knew what was going on in all Israel. On the other hand they are contrasted with "the sons of Israel," who use the imperative plural to determine "how this evil thing happened."

4 The narrator obviously assumes knowledge of chap. 19. The Levite answers the request for information by putting his own spin on events. Lapsley points out that "the 'me' language crops up even where it is grammatically intrusive" ("Gentle Guide," 51). Pressler contends that "the Levite's testimony gives the impression that he narrowly escaped with his life and was unable to save his wife" (250).

The Levite says nothing of the previous actions or places or relationships in the narrative, starting only with the events in Gibeah, emphasizing that it was in Benjamin and repeatedly using the first-person singular pronoun. Even Niditch agrees that "his misrepresentation of the events contributes further to a negative portrayal of the Levite; readers and hearers of this tale already know about his despicable treatment of his wife and her body" (202).

5 No mention is made of the sons of Belial from 19:22. They become "lords of Gibeah" or "baals of Gibeah" (בַּעֲלֵי הַגִּבְעָה). Their plan suddenly becomes "to kill me," and the secondary wife's death becomes explicit, unlike in the narrative of chap. 19.

6 No mention appears of the insensitive treatment the Levite gave the injured (dead?) woman as he rose and exited the house. We skip to his actions at his house. He does not limit himself to twelve pieces, but gives a much wider possibility of distribution. He uses an unusual expression—"every territory (literally, field or pasture) of Israel's inheritance" (בְּכָל־שְׂדֵה נַחֲלַת יִשְׂרָאֵל). Taken literally, this could indicate that every family or clan received a piece. Webb says, "The facts are not grossly distorted, but quite a different impression is created from that which the narrator has given in the previous episode" ([1987] 190).

HALOT (2:687) calls *naḥalâ* (נַחֲלָה) "inalienable, hereditary property." Christopher J. H. Wright explains, "The most common literal meaning of both [i.e., noun and verb] refers to the division of the land within the kinship structure of Israel and thus signifies the permanent family property allotted to the tribes, clans, and households of Israel" (*NIDOTTE*, 3:77).

God giving the land to Israel and her tribes, clans, and families means the different social entities of Israel must protect their land, cannot dispose of the land, and are responsible under the covenant with God to obey God in using the land and in their daily life or face the consequences (Deut 24:4; Isa 58:14). God retains the right to withdraw the inheritance if the people refuse to maintain their covenant obligations or if they attempt to make their inherited part of the land a matter for commerce or real estate actions.

As Wright summarizes,

> The נַחֲלָה was the place of the family's security (breached by greedy oppressors, Mic 2:2), the place to which one returned after assembly or battle (Josh 24:28; Judg 21:24), and the place of burial (Josh 24:30). The family patrimony was inalienable (Lev 25:23). It was not "owned" by the current generation, but was held from "the fathers" for the sake of posterity; hence Naboth's staunch rejection of Ahab's proposal (1 Kgs 21:3–4). . . .
> It [the נַחֲלָה] is associated with the divine promise to the ancestors of Israel (Exod

32:13; Josh 1:6; Ps 105:11); therefore to enter into and live on the land thus promised was to enjoy the inheritance (Deut 4:21; 26:1, and passim). (*NIDOTTE*, 3:77)

Picking up on the sexual nature of the sins at the old host's home, the Levite describes what occurred as a "shameful (or lewd) act" (זִמָּה; Lev 18:17; 19:29; 20:14; 1 Chr 6:5, 27; 2 Chr 29:12; Job 17:11; 31:11; Pss 26:10; 119:150; Prov 10:23; 21:27; 24:9; Isa 32:7; Jer 13:27; Ezek 16:27, 43, 58; 22:9, 11; 23:21, 27, 29, 35, 44, 48–49; 24:13; Hos 6:9). The Levite in his witness picks up the language of Judg 19:23 (compare Josh 7:15) to confirm the words of the old host. In so doing he identifies a strong moral standard for the nation, a standard which he has totally failed to meet. See *Comment* on 19:23.

7 The witness ends his testimony like a judge asking a jury of peers for a verdict. He does not really want "counsel" as to what he should do but counsel as to what the nation as a whole, the "sons of Israel," should do. Younger contends, "Ironically, the Levite has sacrificed his concubine to save himself and now is willing to sacrifice the 'sons of Israel' to get his personal revenge on these Gibeahite 'sons of Belial'" (371). According to Schneider, "The irony is that the Levite man demanded that the Israelites go to war on account of the woman whom he had done nothing to help and whose situation he had caused in the first place" (268).

The Levite had shown no concern for his secondary wife and carefully avoided any mention of events that might incriminate him or call his character into question in any way. He ignores Yahweh, giving him no part in the events. Block says, "He transforms an explanation of the events into a self-centered apologia" (554).

With all the questions we may raise about the sincerity and accuracy of the Levite's sole testimony, Wong reminds us, "the overall guilt of the Gibeathites in the rape and subsequent death of the concubine was not in dispute" (*Compositional Strategy*, 111). Still, we must ask with Webb, "What will become of Israel when its assembly can be convened and used by a person of such dubious morals as this Levite?" ([1987] 192).

8 Younger observes, "To those at the assembly who have received the ghastly pieces it [the sending of the pieces] is interpreted as a zealous act of covenant fidelity and a call to religious war" (370). The Israelites not only assembled as one man, but they act as one man. Total unity within the eleven-tribe assembly meets the decision for war on a brother tribe. This calls for immediate action, no one returning home for any reason. Block notes, "It is truly remarkable that this nameless Levite from an obscure place in Ephraim was able to accomplish what none of the divinely called and empowered deliverers had been able to do" (550). But, says Lapsley, "it is a bogus unity that renders real unity even more remote. . . . Unity of purpose does not necessarily generate genuine, healthy unity" ("Gentle Guide," 52).

Still, I must agree with Niditch when she concludes that Noth may not be completely correct in details of his "amphictyony" hypothesis, but still "the notion that some means existed for allied military action on the part of various segments of Israel seems likely. The scene at Mizpah, however, explores how difficult such alliances are to maintain" (203).

The "tent" to which they may not return may represent the temporary shelter of a warrior mustered for battle, while the "house" would represent the permanent dwelling. Block (555, n. 311) sees an opposition between those in permanent housing and those still living in tents.

9–10 Going back to Joshua's way of determining God's will (Josh 13–20), the people determine by lot which 10 percent of the people will supply food while the rest go directly into battle. The decision is to follow the eye-for-an-eye principle and give Benjamin the same stupid treatment Benjamin had given the Levite and his secondary wife. This ignores the glaring fact that only some sons of Belial from one city in Benjamin had created the trouble, the tribe's only wrongdoing consisting of hiding the guilty and refusing to hand them over for trial and punishment. The sons of Belial have harmed one Israelite secondary wife. The sons of Israel decide to declare all-out war on Benjamin.

11 Again the narrator raises the unity flag. "All the men of Israel" muster to the same spot "as one man," forming a "close-knit army." "Close-knit" is an attempt to translate חֲבֵרִים, a relationship term that means to be joined closely together in a partnership or alliance whose purpose may be for good or for evil. The term proved troublesome here for early translators. See *Note* 20:11.b.

12–13 Israel seeks a peaceful solution, asking Benjamin to confess the crime of a few of its citizens and to give the guilty over for trial and the death penalty. Again, the unity strain appears as Israel is called Benjamin's "kinsmen," or more literally, "brothers." Surely, the people of Benjamin do not want to war against their brothers! But oh yes, these stubborn people do, all to protect a few men who raped and killed one woman. The value of a woman is raised to a high degree when her mistreatment leads to intertribal warfare.

14–17 The sides muster their troops, the narrator underlining the military ability of Benjamin's elite warriors and the heroic experiences of Israel's forces who are each a "warrior," literally, "man of war" (אִישׁ מִלְחָמָה; Exod 15:3; Josh 17:1; 1 Sam 16:18; 17:33; 2 Sam 17:8; Isa 3:2; Ezek 39:20). Ehud was another "left-handed" Benjaminite, but the meaning of *'iṭṭēr yad yĕmmînô* (אִטֵּר יַד־יְמִינוֹ) remains in dispute. See *Note* 20:16.a. Still, the numbers favor Israel overwhelmingly.

18 In strong holy war fashion, the Israelites move to the sanctuary at Bethel. Jeroboam I would dedicate Bethel in the south as the counterpart to Dan in the north as national worship places for the "renegade" northern kingdom in opposition to the southern kingdom's temple in Jerusalem. For one of only five times in the book (1:1; 18:5; 20:18, 23, 27), the Israelites seek an oracle from God. Auld observes, "Perhaps the problem which led to the Israelite blood-letting over two anxious days was too much speech and counsel *before* there had been any consultation of God" (250, emphasis original). Lapsley also questions the Israelites' wisdom in looking for guidance:

> The Israelites' reliance on the oracles to affirm their plans, when juxtaposed to the subsequent bloodshed, suggests a narrative critique of their arrogance in believing that they can co-opt YHWH in service to their ill-conceived schemes. . . . The repetition of inappropriate summonings of God in Judges suggests that the events in the final chapters of Judges are not mere isolated incidents, but rather constitute an ironic theme in the book as a whole. ("Gentle Guide," 55, 57)

As Pressler concludes, "Entrenched behaviors, attitudes, and habits can distort perceptions of God's will, can make wrong look right, and right look ungodly. Perhaps the people's relationship to God had so deteriorated that it was no longer possible for them to hear the divine word" (253).

As in 1:2, Yahweh answers that Judah will lead. The answer contains a bit of irony considering the location in Bethel. Thus the men of Israel can claim divine sanction for their work, but divine sanction comes from the soon-to-be condemned sanctuary. Wong points out that the "selection of Judah to lead the campaign against Benjamin seems puzzling. For in the immediately ensuing account of the war against Benjamin, Judah actually plays no distinguishable role from any of the other tribes within the Israelite coalition" (*Compositional Strategy*, 33). However, Wong's further comment that this is present primarily as a link to chap. 1 is a bit stretched since the oracle of v 18 begins a string of three oracles here with only the third one proving true.

Certainly, the oracle here ties back to chap. 1 to bring literary unity, but it also raises the questions of why Judah and why the oracle proves disastrous for the Israelites. It shows that Judah and Benjamin have fought one another long before Saul and David (Schneider, 274). It also replays the narrator's reluctance to mention the personal divine name. One can argue, a bit weakly because it is an argument from silence, that the lack of explicit Judahite leadership was one explanation for the first defeat. One can also argue that the answer gave no permission to war against the Benjaminites, since that was not the question asked but the assumption already made by the Israelites. Wong is correct in concluding, "Thus, the possibility exists that not only is the question מִי יַעֲלֶה־לָּנוּ (who will go up for us) in 20:18 inappropriate because the Israelites had yet to receive instructions from YHWH to fight against Benjamin, the very act of making such an inquiry may also be deemed problematic because this kind of pre-battle oracular inquiry is typically reserved for war against external enemies rather than brothers" (*Compositional Strategy*, 34).

19–21 Auld sees "a noticeable change (for the worse) in the quality of the narrative. It has lost the crisp terseness typical of so much of the Book of Judges, and has become complicated and turgid" (245). Auld has missed the narrator's changing of perspectives in his narration and his change of style to slow the narrative and to bring emphasis to the following section. Auld's only solution is to follow Soggin and others in dividing the material into two sources.

The narrator slows the action as battle becomes imminent, carefully marking each stage of the Israelite army's progress: they pitch the army's camp, march to battle, and line up in attack formation. The conclusion comes quickly: Benjamin gains overwhelming victory. The expression "into the earth," says Schneider, "is unusual" (275). Boling compares it to Onan's having "spilled his semen on the ground" in Gen 38:9 (NRSV). Schneider sees it as looking back at Jael's driving the pin through Sisera's temple into the ground (Judg 4:21). A simpler understanding sees it simply as a battle term for killing people, who fall to the earth and are eventually buried under the earth.

22–23 "The men of Israel strengthened each other," that is, encouraged one another to gain new hope and confidence for fighting another day. The narrative loses a bit of chronological clarity (the author's interest being "rhetorical," Block, 564), as the army returns to the battle line, and the "sons of Israel," perhaps the rest of the nation, seek to see if they have made a mistake in doing battle with "Benjamin, my kinsfolk." The sons of Israel cry as they had in Judg 2:4 when the angel warned them God would no longer drive out the foreign nations before them. Now they cry because God has not driven out their own brothers before them. In 11:37–38 Jephthah's daughter had cried over her perpetual virginity. In 14:16–17 Samson's wife cried for a week because he would not reveal the secret to her. These are real tears of anguish, frustration, and anger, not the crying out for help in the main sections of Judges. Again, at an unknown location, but presumably Bethel, they seek an oracle from God and receive the go-ahead.

24–25 The sides again march to battle. Israel's valiant warriors lose again.

26 Now, the army and the sons of Israel—again a united Israel—join in lamentation at Bethel. This time they consciously sit in Yahweh's presence, fast in proper lamentation procedure, offer proper sacrifices, acknowledge Yahweh's presence in the ark of the covenant, and let the proper Aaronic priest seek the oracle from God. This answers the northern kingdom's claims for Bethel. The narrator grants that at one time Bethel was God's chosen place of worship, but only when it could claim the proper religious accoutrements, namely, the proper sacrifices, the proper symbols of divine presence, and the proper priesthood. Without these, now safely in the temple at Jerusalem, Bethel could lay no claims to being a center of proper Yahweh worship. Its non-Aaronic priesthood, its calf images, and its man-devised sacrificial system disqualify Bethel from being a place of proper worship.

Fasting appears only here in the book of Judges and infrequently in the Hebrew Bible (1 Sam 7:6; 31:13; 2 Sam 1:12; 12:16, 21–23; 1 Kgs 21:9, 12, 27; 1 Chr 10:12; 2 Chr 20:3; Ezra 8:21, 23; Neh 1:4; 9:1; Esth 4:3,16; 9:31; Pss 35:13; 69:11; 109:24; Isa 58:3–6; Jer 14:12; 36:6, 9; Dan 9:3; Joel 1:14; 2:12, 15; Jonah 3:5; Zech 7:5; 8:19). It generally accompanies mourning ceremonies and is part of ritual self-humiliation or castigation designated by עָנָה ('ānâ; Lev 16:29, 31; 23:27, 32; Num 29:7; 30:14; Ps 35:13; Isa 58:3, 5). Fasting is one part of the mourning rituals that involved wearing sackcloth, expressing laments, and crying out loud (Esth 4:3).

J. E. Hartley defines fasting as "depriving the body of nourishment as a sign that one is experiencing great sorrow. . . . He who fasts claims to afflict himself or his soul, i.e., his inner person. . . . A true fast had to indicate that the people were intent on seeking righteousness, which included taking care of the poor and needy (Isa 58; cf. Jer 14:12; Zech 7:5)" (*TWOT*, 2:758).

R. J. Way notes: "A fast is a period of complete abstinence from food and sometimes from drink undertaken as a religious observance or as a plea to God. . . . Fasting expresses self-abnegation in order to assert the reality of God and the imperative of his law" (*NIDOTTE*, 3:780).

Burnt offerings involved the burning of entire animals on the altar. Lev 1 gives regulations for making such offerings. The blood was poured on the altar, and the animal then burnt up. Its function and motivation seems to be complex and diverse, involving both atonement and invocation. (See P. D. Miller, *Religion of Ancient Israel*, 107–9.) Peace offerings also elude specific definition. (See M. Modéus, *Sacrifice and Symbol: Biblical Šĕlāmîm in a Ritual Perspective*, ConBOT 52 [Stockholm: Almqvist & Wiksell, 2005].) Such offerings are often connected with *zebah* (זֶבַח), "a slain offering" occurring in Judges only in relationship to the Philistines and Dagon (Judg 16:23). The word for "peace offering," שְׁלָמִים (*šĕlāmîm*), always appears in a plural form and is also translated as "communion offering," "shared offering," "fellowship offering," and "offering of well-being." P. Miller explains: "The two most conspicuous features of the *shelem* offering are its consumption by human beings and its use on celebratory occasions" (*Religion of Ancient Israel*, 113). The ritual for the peace offering appears in Lev 3:1–17. Only the fat was burned on the altar. The rest of the sacrifice was eaten by the one making the offering and the accompanying family or group.

The offering here in Judges is, however, anything but celebratory. E. Merrill notes that "the fellowship offering, sometimes called the peace offering, was a voluntary act designed not to achieve fellowship with the Lord but to celebrate its reality" (*Everlasting Dominion: A Theology of the Old Testament* [Nashville: Broadman & Holman, 2006] 378).

The three cultic observances, notes Wong, seem "to signal steps taken to restore damaged relationship with YHWH" (*Compositional Strategy*, 68, n. 97). Brensinger says, "With two military defeats and God's disfavor, the presentation of both types seemingly reflects the Israelites' desire for forgiveness as well as acceptance" (207).

27 The ark of the covenant appears only here in Judges. Thus Guillaume sees it as a secondary addition to the narrative presupposing the end of the Priestly narrative in Josh 18:1. Its presence here simply harmonizes "Judges with the other books, once the collection of 'historical books' was appended to the Torah" (*Waiting for Josiah*, 207). This is traditional literary criticism gone wild without regard to literary artistry and history-of-religion reality.

S. T. Hague shows that the ark fits its Near Eastern context during the wilderness period (*NIDOTTE*, 1:5010). The ark led Israel through the desert wilderness, across the Jordan River, and around the walls of Jericho. In Judges, however, the brief mention in 20:27 is the ark's only appearance. Otherwise, it is centered at Shiloh (Josh 18:1; 1 Sam 1:3; 3:3) and captured there. After a hiatus of twenty years in Kiriath-jearim (1 Sam 5:1–7:2), the ark, under David's leadership, paraded into Jerusalem (2 Sam 6). In Israel's earliest period, the ark served as the clearest symbol of God's presence with Israel. Thus the ark played a strong role in obtaining God's marching orders in time of war, as here.

28 Phinehas is the high priest, occupying the position inaugurated by his grandfather Aaron (Exod 6:25; Num 25:7, 11; 31:6; Josh 22:13, 30–32; 24:33; 1 Chr 6:4, 50 [Heb. 5:30; 6:35]; 9:20; Ezra 7:5; Ps 106:30). Here we see the lack of chronological order as the structural key to the book of Judges. Phinehas served with Joshua (Josh 22) and thus was one of the survivors from Joshua's generation but certainly not one who had experienced the centuries covered by the book of Judges. His exemplary actions representing Yahweh against possible heresy appear in Num 25 and 31 and Josh 22. The priestly request for an oracle from God includes a question easily answered yes or no and a reference to Benjamin as "my kinsfolk" (lit. "brothers"). Wong observes, "The Israelites were becoming increasingly aware that their opponent's identity might have been a major issue" (*Compositional Strategy*, 66). This time the oracle succeeds in getting an indisputably positive response with the normal conveyance formula (see Judg 1:2). Having followed the proper procedures before battle, the sons of Israel are now ready for the third stage of the war against Benjamin, their brothers.

29 Having followed proper ritual procedure, Israel comes with new military tactics. It sets up an ambush much as Joshua did in fighting Ai (Josh 7–8). See *Form/Structure/Setting* above.

30–31 As on other days, the Israelite army sets up in battle array to attack Benjamin. It lets Benjamin mount the attack. This brings Benjamin into the field, away from the town of Gibeah. The battle carries into the fields and the highways. The Benjaminites inflict thirty casualties on Israel.

32 Two different perspectives result. Benjamin decides this is a repeat of the previous overwhelming victories over Israel. The men of Israel sees it as Benjamin falling into their ambush trap.

33 Israel has a two-pronged attack. The main army lines up at Baal Tamar. Gaß (*Ortsnamen*, 422–24) sees this as a sanctuary of Baal for which we have no future details and whose location near Gibeah cannot be determined exactly. It may be only a worship place without a settled population. Gaß has arguments against Ras et-Tawil and Khirbet beth Ta'amir as the location but has no positive suggestion. The ambush troops lie west of Gibeah or Geba. See *Note* 20:33.b.

34 The ambush apparently numbers ten thousand troops. They suddenly appear to confront Gibeah. The final clause of the verse sounds a somber, if ambiguous note, there being no explicit subject. Evil comes, but upon whom? Satterthwaite notes that repetitions in the following verses "build suspense simply by delaying the climax of the battle" (*VT* 42 [1992] 84).

35 A typical holy war note from the narrator follows, announcing Yahweh's victory over Benjamin, supplemented with details of Israel's victory.

Here we see Yahweh in action for the only time in this narrative (Wong, *Compositional Strategy*, 65). In fact, as Webb shows, "the present narrative incorporates virtually all its [holy war's] formal features . . . : the summons, the assembly of the people of God, the vow of concerted action . . . , inquiry for divine guidance, offerings in the face of reverses, divine assurance of victory, panic among the enemy, the execution of the ban . . . , dispersal of the assembly" ([1987] 192; compare Block, 567–68).

This ominous note adds a stern element to Israel's theology of warfare and punishment. God can use his own people to punish the deeds of a part of his people. It remains difficult to see how God was justified in inflicting such a decisive and destructive punishment on a people for the sin they committed. Still, that is a human way of thinking, prioritizing one type of disobedience as deserving greater punishment than another. We must always step back and let God define justice rather than trying to hold him accountable to our definitions of justice.

36–41 A flashback following the summary shows the fight from Benjamin's perspective, describing details of the fight. Wong (*Compositional Strategy*, 62) sees the change of perspective beginning at v 39b, but Benjamin's viewpoint is introduced after the summary statement of v 35. Wong's calling on the disjunctive clause of 39b to mark the change of perspective but then denying such a shift for the disjunction in v 41 defeats his own argument.

The ambush advances. The main army retreats to lure Benjamin into place away from the town. The trap is sprung. Yet the main body of Benjaminite soldiers does not recognize the situation immediately. They think their killing of thirty Israelite troops gives reason for renewed confidence. Satterthwaite says, "The most emphatic expression of Benjaminite confidence is telling, placed just before the point at which they realize they will be destroyed" (*VT* 42 [1992] 86). Eventually, the men of Benjamin see that their cause is lost. The ambush enters the city and destroys it. They burn it, giving the agreed-upon sign to the main army. Seeing the signal, the main army turns from its apparent retreat and confronts the Benjaminite army that now has no place to go. Here the ambiguity of v 34 becomes clear. Evil is against Benjamin.

42–48 Now Benjamin tries to escape but runs into the ambush coming out of the town and finds itself in between, being killed by both groups of Israelite troops. Trying to escape, the Benjaminites flee to the Rock of Rimmon. The name means "pomegranate" and is a title of the god Hadad. Thus it may represent a worship place where people could flee for asylum (Gaß, *Ortsnamen,* 424). It has been located at either Rammun, five and a half miles (9 km) northeast of Gibeah or at Mgareat el-Gha'ye over the Wadi es-Swenät, about one mile (2 km) east of Gibeah. (See Arnold, *ABD,* 5:774; Guillaume, *Waiting for Josiah,* 203.) Guillaume says it may be a "demythizing note. A local toponym connected to Baal Rimmon (2 Kgs 5:18 'Lord of Thunder') may have been reinterpreted as the Rock of the pomegranate, symbol of fertility, an obvious place to find refuge in order to remarry and produce offspring."

The Israelite army chases Benjamin clear to Gidom. Gaß (*Ortsnamen,* 427) finds the name is related to "being cut down" and means "clearing." He associates it etiologically with Judg 21:6, the cutting down of Benjamin, thus concluding that the name is a literary creation without geographical significance. Herion (*ADB,* 2:1015) thinks the term is temporal, "until they had been cut down" (see Boling).

Six hundred Benjaminites escape to the Rock of Rimmon, while the Israelites practice holy war *ḥerem* (חֵרֶם), destroying the towns and inhabitants of Benjamin. Wong notes, "Not only had Israel not treated Benjamin with the compassion of brothers, they even dealt with them more harshly than they did to the non-Israelite enemies at Ai" (*Compositional Strategy,* 70). With Israel losing so many soldiers in the first two encounters and Benjamin being decimated in the third, Webb says, "Yahweh takes his place at the head of the assembly and distributes victory and defeat in such a way that the punishment of Benjamin by the other tribes is made the occasion for the whole of Israel to be chastised by Yahweh" ([1987] 194).

Block concludes, "For once Yahweh has not operated in mercy. Justice is brutally exercised, but the criminals and their defenders are not the only ones who experience loss. All Israel suffers for the sin of one city, for with the annihilation of Benjamin they lose a brother and one-tenth of their own male population" (568). The six hundred escapees leave open the problem of the next chapter, while the Israelite victory closes out the crisis of the previous narrative in chap. 19.

Explanation

Block says, "This chapter portrays the nation of Israel finally whole-heartedly involved in the holy war against evil" (567). All the army, all the tribes, all the geographical areas, all the sons of Israel are ready and willing to act as one—except for one tribe that has become the enemy. Called out by a scheming, vengeful Levite's atrocious deed, the entire nation plots strategy against their own flesh and blood. As Joseph's brothers had plotted his death, so now the people of Israel seek to annihilate the tribe of Benjamin, Joseph's little brother and Jacob's favorite son. They involve God only at the last minute when they realize they have no leadership or authority for the attack.

Somehow the oracle sends them forth to battle in answer to an improper question with no evidence of priestly involvement or ritual preparation. The result: disastrous defeat. Again they try an oracle, with lamentation the only ritual. A positive answer obtained in some manner drives them to a second battle. They again meet defeat. Finally, all the Israelites, including the army, gather in Bethel for true worship with sacrifice, the ark symbolizing God's presence; full lamentation; and a famous priest seeking the oracle for the people. Everything in its proper place with a proper phrasing of the oracle, the people receive a true oracle promising victory. And victory is achieved, the most full-fledged victory in the book, the kind of holy war victory Israel was supposed to achieve over the Canaanites and other inhabitants of the land.

Schneider concludes, "The final judgment of the book is clarified in this episode; while a system of government dependent on the judges did not work for Israel, the concept of group leadership was even worse" (272). A corrupt priesthood, worship at places without the symbol of God's presence, desperation searches for oracles affirming action already determined, lamentation without sacrifice—all lead to defeat and desperation.

Such a narrative, told with irony and sarcasm, shows a northern kingdom with major worship centered in Bethel. Bethel's past history may reflect a true home for the ark and a true place of worship chosen by Yahweh for his people's central sanctuary. Legitimate past history, however, does not anoint Bethel as the place for future service. The location is not the central point. Location changes from Gilgal to Bethel to Shiloh. Location is not permanent. Prescribed ritual and personnel are. Weeping eyes do not take the place of sincere cries for help. Northern worship at Bethel without Aaronic priests and with bull images cannot produce a wholesome nation or a wholesome relationship with Yahweh, the God of Israel. Human plans will not be automatically ratified because people gather at an ancient, storied sanctuary. God's people must listen obediently to God before they can expect God to listen to their desperate cries.

The narrative also intrudes into Israel's understanding of justice. Justice differs from personal revenge. Human desire for victory over an enemy does not necessarily mirror God's understanding of justice and righteousness for the helpless segment of society. Instead of showing mercy and seeking justice for his secondary wife, who stood totally dependent upon him, the Levite sought to get the rascals who threatened him ever so slightly since he never had to face them openly. God said the most you could do was an eye for an eye, a tooth for a tooth. The Levite sought to destroy a tribe for the crimes of a few town ruffians. This was not justice. This was not divine. This was human rage. This was human revenge conceived totally apart from divine law, divine word, divine oracle, or divine presence.

Finally, the narrative shows that national unity means all tribes agreeing on what is best for all the rest. Benjamin stood guilty for not apprehending the guilty members of its tribe and making them face the rules of justice. Israel claimed to stand as one man when a whole tribe was missing. The leadership of the chosen tribe Judah, the leadership of the priestly tribe Levi, the leadership of the chosen priest Phinehas—despite his previous track record—could not lead God's people to live according to God's plan and follow the divine king. A new system must prevail, but it was not a system led by Benjamin, i.e., Saul, nor was it a system stemming from Ephraim and worshiping in a discredited Bethel, i.e., the northern kingdom under Jeroboam.

Brensinger concludes, "The shock of this entire scandal at Gibeah did not pass quickly, becoming instead an ugly benchmark in Israel's history (Hos 9:9; 10:9)" (203).

3. Israelites Work around Vow (21:1–25)

Bibliography

See *Bibliography* for 19:1–30.

Translation

[1] *The men of* [a] *Israel had sworn under oath in Mizpah, "No man from among us will give his daughter to Benjamin as a wife."* [2] *The people came* [a] *to Bethel* [b] *and sat there before God until evening. They lifted their voices and sobbed great tears.* [3] *They asked, "Why, Yahweh, God of Israel, has this happened in Israel, for one tribe to be missing from Israel today?"* [4] *The people rose early the next day and built an altar there. They offered up burnt offerings and peace offerings.* [a] [5] *The sons of Israel asked, "Who is there who did not go up with the assembly from all the tribes of Israel to Yahweh,"* *for a binding oath stated that whoever did not go up to Yahweh to Mizpah would surely be put to death.* [6] *The sons of Israel completed their mourning and were consoled concerning Benjamin, their kinsfolk.*

They said, "Today one tribe is cut off [a] *from Israel.* [7] *What can we do to get wives for those who remain,* [a] *it being the case that we ourselves have sworn under oath in the name of* [b] *Yahweh that we will not give them our daughters as wives."* [8] *They inquired, "Which one of the tribes of Israel did not go up to Yahweh at Mizpah?" Look! No men from Jabesh-gilead had come to the camp for the assembly.* [9] *The people counted off, and look here!* [a] *No one was there from the residents of Jabesh-gilead.* [10] *The congregation sent twelve thousand heroic warriors. They commanded them, "Go strike dead the residents* [a] *of Jabesh-gilead with the sword, including the women and children.* [b] [11] *This is what* [a] *you are to do. Every male as well as every woman with intimate experience bedding a male, you must put to the ban."* [b] [12] *They found among the residents of Jabesh-gilead four hundred young women who were virgins. They had had no intimate experience with a man, bedding a male. They brought them to the camp at Shiloh, which was in the land of Canaan.*

[13] *The entire congregation sent and spoke with the sons of* [a] *Benjamin who were by the rock of Rimmon, offering them peace.* [b]

[14] *Benjamin returned* [a] *at that time. They* [b] *gave them the women who were still living from the women of Jabesh-gilead. They did not* [c] *find the right number for them.* [d]

[15] *Meanwhile, the people relented* [a] *concerning Benjamin because Yahweh made a hole in the tribes of Israel.* [16] *The elders of the assembly said, "What can we do for wives for the remaining ones, because the female was destroyed from Benjamin?"* [17] *They added, "Is there a possession* [a] *for the survivors of Benjamin so that a tribe from Israel will not be wiped out?* [18] *We cannot give them wives from our daughters, for we sons of Israel swore under oath, 'Cursed is anyone who gives a wife to Benjamin!'"*

[19] *They said, "Right now* [a] *the annual festival for* [b] *Yahweh is taking place in Shiloh, which is north of Bethel, east of the road that goes up from Bethel to Shechem and south of Lebonah."* [c]

[20] *They commanded* [a] *the sons of Benjamin, "Go! Set an ambush in the vineyards.* [21] *Be on the lookout. The very moment the daughters of* [a] *Shiloh come out to dance among the dancers, move out from the vineyards and catch for yourselves, each man, a wife from the*

daughters of Shiloh. Then get going for[b] *the land of Benjamin.* [22] *When their fathers or their*[a] *kinsfolk come to file a complaint*[b] *with us,*[c] *we will tell them, 'Do us*[d] *a favor*[e] *with regard to them since we*[f] *did not capture a wife for each man in the war. Indeed, you did not actually give them anything. Then at the time*[g] *you would be guilty.'"*
[23] *The sons of Benjamin did exactly that. They carried away*[a] *the women according to their number from the dancers, whom they seized. They went and returned to their inheritance. They built cities and settled in them.* [24] *The sons of Israel went away from there at that time, each to his tribe and to his clan. They went out from there each to his inheritance.* [25] *In those days Israel had no king. Every person did what was right in his own eyes.*

Notes

1.a. LXX[B] reads "sons of, " substituting a common phrase.

2.a. Several Heb. MSS, LXX, Syr., and Vg. read a pl. verb rather than the Heb. collective sg., making a grammatical adjustment.

2.b. LXX[A] reads καὶ παρεγένοντο πᾶς ὁ λαὸς εἰς Μασσηφα καὶ Βαιθηλ, "and all the people came into Mizpah and Bethel," the additions of "all" and "Mizpah" coming from the following narrative.

4.a. LXX[A] reads "burnt offerings of salvation."

6.a. Several Heb. MSS read נִגְרַע, *nip'al* of גרע, "to be taken away," for MT נִגְדַּע, "be cut off," an easy copyist error but without sufficient support to allow emendation here.

7.a. LXX[B] reads τοῖς περισσοῖς τοῖς ὑπολειφθεῖσιν, "to those who are left to those who are remaining," giving alternate translations for the Heb. לַנּוֹתָרִים but not translating לָהֶם, "to them."

7.b. "In the name of" is implied in the oath formula.

9.a. LXX[B] does not have "Look here!"

10.a. LXX[A] reads "all the residents," giving a parallel construction to v 5 regarding the tribes of Israel.

10.b. LXX[A] reads "people" instead of "children," while LXX[B] does not have "and the women and the children," perhaps a theological change to ease the horror of the narrative.

11.a. LXX[B] does not have "is what," perhaps a simple target language choice.

11.b. LXX[BR] read ἀναθεματιεῖτε τὰς δὲ παρθένους περιποιήσεσθε καὶ ἐποίησαν οὕτως, "you must put to the ban. But you must save alive the virgins. And so they did." On this basis plus readings of LXX[L] and Vg., BHS says we should probably insert וְאֶת־הַבְּתוּלוֹת תְּחַיּוּ וַיַּעֲשׂוּ כֵן, "the virgins you (pl.) shall let live, and they did so." Soggin insists the LXX reading "is indispensable for producing a comprehensible text" (298). This clarifies the orders for the troops and sets up the execution of those orders in the next verse, but it also represents a much easier text and a natural expansion by the copyists from 21:12, 14. MT implies without explicit statement what LXX states. See Barthélemy (*Critique textuelle,* 1:127) and *Preliminary and Interim Report* (2:133) for rejection of the LXX expansion.

13.a. LXX[A] does not have "sons of." See *Note* 21:1.a.

13.b. Many Heb. MSS and LXX add the preposition ל, completing the normal idiom for offering a people a peace treaty.

14.a. LXX reads καὶ ἀπέστρεψεν (ἐπέστρεψεν) Βενιαμιν πρὸς τοὺς υἱοὺς Ισραηλ, "and Benjamin turned back to the sons of Israel," making the implied obvious.

14.b. LXX[B] reads "the sons of Israel," making the subject explicit. See *Notes* 21:1.a and 21:13.a.

14.c. LXX[L] does not have the negative, reversing the meaning in the context, perhaps not understanding the Heb. idiom. Guillaume (*Waiting for Josiah,* 212) sees the Gk. as original, evidence that the original draft moved from v 14 to v 24, vv 15–23 representing a slightly later edition.

14.d. LXX reads καὶ ἤρεσεν αὐτοῖς οὕτως, "and thus they were pleased," apparently a misunderstanding or reinterpretation of the Heb. context.

15.a. The disjunctive sentence with the Heb. verb נחם, as in v 6, has a variety of possible meanings and may need to be translated here differently from its occurrence in v 6. See *Comment* on 21:15. The clause is a "circumstantial clause" (Andersen, *Sentence in Biblical Hebrew,* 77). Such a clause "interrupts the sequence of events" and "generally reports an event contemporaneous, concomitant, or 'circumstantial' to the main clause." This marks "a new development" in the story (Andersen, *Sentence in Biblical Hebrew,* 79).

17.a. *BHS* sees the text as corrupt and turns to LXX^L πῶς ἔσται to propose אֵיךְ תִּשָּׁאֵר, "how can there be left," or יְרֻשָּׁה (from רשה; cf. Sir 3:22), "be given permission or empowered." MT has no verb in the first clause of the quotation, reading "and they said, 'a possession of the remnant of Benjamin.'" *Preliminary and Interim Report* (2:134) favors MT when translated as "<let> an endowment for survivors <be allocated> to Benjamin." Soggin (299) translates the LXX and Syr. text, saying MT is impossible. Barthélemy (*Critique textuelle*, 1:128) sees the Gk. as a simple paraphrase required by the terse Heb. text. 4QJudg^b apparently has no room for the suggested emendation (Trebolle Barrera, "4QJudg^a 4QJudg^b," 169). See *Comment* on 21:17.

19.a. LXX^A does not have "Look here!" See *Note* 21:9.a.

19.b. A few Heb. MSS and what *BHS* takes to be the original LXX read חג ליהוה, "a festival for Yahweh," with the preposition rather than the construct state of the noun. This may represent a translation choice in Gk. and the addition of a common idiom in Heb. MT has the more difficult reading.

19.c. LXX^A reads νότου τοῦ Λιβάνου τῆς Λεβωνα, "south of Lebanon, that is, Lebonah," perhaps a case of modified dittography or of two Gk. spellings of an unfamiliar place name.

20.a. Many Heb. MSS, versions, and the Q read the pl. verb, whereas the K has sg. The consistent use of pl. verbs in this section probably evidences the pl. here, a simple case of haplography.

21.a. LXX reads "daughters of the residents of Shiloh" (LXX^A "in Shiloh"), importing a familiar designation onto a different idiom.

21.b. A few Heb. MSS, LXX, and versions make the natural addition of the preposition אֶל, "to," which must be understood if one retains MT, which has no preposition.

22.a. The first two occurrences of "their" represent third-person pl. masc. pronouns in Heb. but have a third-person fem. pl. antecedent—"daughters of Shiloh." Guillaume sees this as a mark of "late biblical Hebrew" (*Waiting for Josiah*, 213–14; compare GKC, §130o).

22.b. Several Heb. MSS and Q have a י as the middle radical of the infinitive construct, while K has a ו, two different traditions of the spelling of the middle vowel infinitive construct.

22.c. LXX, Vg. read "to you (pl.)," a reading *BHS* adopts, misreading the situation of the assembly receiving complaints. *Preliminary and Interim Report* (2:134) says the MT means, "before us," that is, "before the elders of Israel." Barthélemy (*Critique textuelle*, 1:128) sees the syntax of this verse as very difficult and tortured by early witnesses and exegetes but chooses to retain MT.

22.d. LXX^A, Vg., Syr. do not have "us," again shifting to Benjamin action that MT portrays involving the assembly, a misreading of the narrative. *Preliminary and Interim Report* (2:135) retains MT, interpreting it to mean "grant them to us," that is, "be gracious to them on our account."

22.e. חנן is variously translated. Block (582) suggests "Be gracious to them for our sake," following JPS. NRSV reads "Be generous and allow us to have them"; NLT, "Please be understanding"; NIV, "Do us a kindness by helping them"; CEV, "Be kind enough to let those men"; NAB, "Release them to us as a kindness"; NASB95, "Give them to us voluntarily"; NJB, "Let us have them"; NKJV, "Be kind to them for our sakes"; REB, "Let them keep them with your approval"; HCSB, "Show favor to them"; NET, "Do us a favor and let them be"; GWT, "Have pity on them"; Message, "We did them a favor."

22.f. LXX, Syr., Vg. support a reading of third-person pl. subject rather than first-person pl., again reading the text with Benjamin in action rather than Israel. NET notes read, "'You did not give to them, now you are guilty.' The MT as it stands makes little sense. It is preferable to emend לֹא (*lo'*, 'not') to לוּא (*lu'*, 'if'). This particle introduces a purely hypothetical condition, 'If you had given to them [but you didn't].'" *Preliminary and Interim Report* (2:135) says the suggestion to omit the negative לֹא is too great a simplification.

22.g. Without citing textual support, *BHS* says we should probably read כִּי עַתָּ, "for now," a reading Guillaume (*Waiting for Josiah*, 213–14) apparently accepts to avoid the need for a "rather twisted translation" of the MT.

23.a. A few Heb. MSS, LXX^{54,55}, Syr. add לָהֶם, "for themselves," making the implicit obvious. 4QJudg^b does not appear to have room for the addition (Trebolle Barrera, "4QJudg^a 4QJudg^b," 169).

Form/Structure/Setting

The final chapter of Judges forms a self-contained narrative, while also completing the complex narrative in Judg 19–21. The opening disjunctive sentence sets this chapter off as an independent unit and provides a brief exposition. The main character is now "the men (literally, the man) of Israel." The location is Mizpah as in Judg 20:1. Again, Mizpah is a place of tribal assembly and discussion, not the place of worship. (See Soggin, 302.) The narrative crisis appears immediately. It centers on an oath the Israelites made, that is, a promise made in God's name not to provide their daughters for the six hundred remaining Benjaminites to marry.

Critical scholarship continues to debate the tradition history of this story. Moore summarized nineteenth-century scholarship: "It is not history, it is not legend, but the theocratic ideal of a scribe who had never handled a more dangerous weapon than an imaginative pen" (404). Boling finds the account to be "a rich mine of data on Israel's premonarchical organization, and the most explicit in the book" (278).

Hertzberg (254) finds behind the Benjaminite war a local Benjaminite tradition that explained how families of Jabesh-gilead and of Benjamin had such close relationships. Guillaume tries to show the independence of chap. 21 from chap. 20, based on a radical change of attitude and the sudden appearance of the previously unmentioned oath: "The story of Jabesh-gilead's massacre appears then to be preoccupied more with staining Saul's heroic deed than with offering a realistic solution to the near extinction of Benjamin" (*Waiting for Josiah*, 209).

Thus Guillaume finds,

> Looking for wives in Gilead could then be a realistic option for Benjaminites during the Persian period. However the method used in Judg. 21, through the banning of the rest of the town, is much more dubious. Heavy doubts remain over the real intentions of the narrators. . . . The story of Benjamin's destruction and the desperate search for women could be a distorted reflection of the economical crisis that prolonged itself in Benjamin in the Persian period. (*Waiting for Josiah*, 210–11)

According to Guillaume, in such a period returnees from exile viewed Mizpah and Bethel as "traitors, lackeys of Nebuchadnezzar . . . servants of a power that was now defeated" (*Waiting for Josiah*, 212; compare 224–25). This represents the ultimate use of redaction-critical tools and a great stretch of reality to push the narrative into the Persian period and explain all its incidentals in that historical context.

Here again we find the irony of the moment. Having destroyed Benjamin, their kinsfolk, in holy war, the people of Israel now mourn the destruction. Monologue dominates as they seek a solution before God in Bethel (21:2–9). Ironically, the solution is to conduct another holy war against another part of Israel. Even more ironically, the solution is only partial, falling two hundred women short of their goal.

So they avoid guilt for breaking an oath by using a religious festival with its drinking, entertaining, and dancing and by encouraging Benjaminites to steal wives. T. H. Gaster (*Myth, Legend, and Custom in the Old Testament* [New York: Harper, 1969] 445) would explain this as an etiology of an ancient practice of mass mating during seasonal festivals. The denouement sends Benjamin and Israel back to settle at home.

Soggin sees the two narratives as "independent and parallel," both being devoted to the "reconstitution of the tribe of Benjamin by bringing women from other groups" (300). Soggin also sees the story of the Levite in Judg 19–20 as supporting monarchy, while Judg 21 opposes monarchy. Guillaume sees the two narratives as coming from different dates in the Persian period and forming "an internal settling of scores between Judah and Benjamin: the other tribes are never mentioned by name" (*Waiting for Josiah*, 203).

Here is a variation on a holy war battle report, linking it with an ironic wife-stealing episode, to solve the marriage crisis in Benjamin, a crisis caused by a holy war against Benjamin. Thus, says Webb, "the conclusion of the story (21:1–24) turns out to be a highly satirical narrative episode in which the assembly, headed by the elders, resorts to a mixture of force, casuistry and guile to circumvent the oath sworn at Mizpah without actually breaking it" ([1987] 196). Younger believes that the chapter "could be described as a comical tragedy of legalism" (384). "No positive thing has really occurred in all the outcomes of the narrative. Not only have many wrongs occurred, but no rights have ultimately been championed" (383).

Chap. 21 presents a story without a hero or central figure. All receive blame. None receive praise. Action ceases, but chaos continues.

Comment

1 The singular collective "man of Israel" continues the unity theme from the previous chapter. Here the assembly acknowledges that it had sworn an oath not to undo, by providing wives for the six hundred escapees, what had been accomplished in the war against Benjamin (see 20:47). The time frame of this narrative is not absolutely clear but appears to point back in a "flashback" (Block, 569) to the original assembly in Mizpah (20:1), the oath being part of the declaration of holy war against Benjamin.

From a literary standpoint, the story, centered on giving of wives, ties back to the Caleb/Achsah narrative of the prologue (1:11–14; see *Comment* there and Wong, *Compositional Strategy*, 42–43). The Caleb narrative plays on the giving of blessing, while the Benjamin narrative seeks ways to avoid a curse. Wong remarks that the oath proves to "represent a rash and foolish decision made out of muddled thinking and excessive vindictiveness" (*Compositional Strategy*, 45).

Ironically, as Block points out, whereas "the Israelites had displayed few scruples in intermarriage with Canaanites, evidently they had pledged not to intermarry with their own countrymen. . . . In the mind of the narrator this grotesque application of Yahweh's prohibition on intermarriage with Canaanites (Deut 7:1–5) to their own kinfolks serves as a final acknowledgement of the Canaanization of Israel" (569). "Jacob's fears concerning his youngest son expressed centuries ago have come true: in bizarre fashion Joseph's brothers have taken Benjamin (Gen 42:36)" (570).

2–4 Ironically, the Israelites return to the same location in Bethel and repeat the ritual they performed as they sought God's oracle before the last battle with Benjamin (20:26)—sitting before God, crying, lamenting, and offering "burnt offerings and peace offerings." The reference to crying at Bethel ties the epilogue back to the prologue, in which Israel wept at Bochim, that is, "weepings" or "place of weeping" (2:1, 5; see *Comment* on 2:1 and Wong, *Compositional Strategy*, 40–41). Wong notes the irony of success being "what eventually also resulted in their weeping before YHWH. . . . While one records Israel's failure to do what was right, the other records Israel's success in doing what was wrong" (41).

Again the author has them sitting before Elohim, not before Yahweh, leaving the reader to decide whether the Israelites are coming to the true God. The cry is the lament of mourning, not the scream for help as in the earlier chapters of the book. As Lapsley phrases it, "The profound irony is, of course, that the moment of victory for which the Israelites have been longing is also the precise moment of their deepest grief" ("Gentle Guide," 58).

The people identify God explicitly: "Yahweh, Elohim of Israel" (21:3). Webb observes, "The inquiry is less a request for information than an oblique form of protest and an attempt by the inquirers to absolve themselves of responsibility" ([1987] 195).

Their interrogative lament is again ironic. They made the decision to fight Benjamin. They carried out holy war on Benjamin without specific divine instructions. Then they dare ask God, "Why . . . has this happened in Israel?" (21:3). Suddenly, the import of what they have done dawns on them, and they transfer the responsibility to God, or, as Pressler puts it, they make "a collective buck-passing gesture" (255). Block says, "The tone is accusatory. The Israelites are blaming God, as if Yahweh has failed to fulfill his role as divine patron protecting his people. Their query seems to represent an attempt to evade the requirements of covenant justice and to find a scapegoat" (571).

This all represents the "human propensity for denial" (Brown, 286). And yet as Lapsley points out, this is the third time the question of the reason for evil is asked (20:3, 12). Thus the search for "the causes of the unfolding disaster" becomes "the most profound theological moment in the entire story" ("Gentle Guide," 59).

Acting like one man (20:8, 11), Israel had caused one tribe to be missing in action. God does not respond. Webb declares, "In the previous episode he chastised them by speaking; in this one he chastises them by remaining silent. He will not be used by them" ([1987] 195). Thus, Brown says, Israel "found a way around their vow. But their way around turned out to be much more destructive, in terms of scope, than Jephthah's vow" (283).

The Israelites do the unexpected: they build an altar in the ancient worship place of Bethel. Pressler says, "Why they build a new altar is unclear" (255). Bethel's altar presupposed in 20:26 does not suffice for these important, tribe-saving sacrifices. Or, as we read in the *IVP Bible Background* commentary,

> If Bethel was only an assembly point for this episode and not the permanent cultic site for the ark, it is to be expected that a new Yahweh altar would have to be constructed for the use of the Israelites (see the legislation on construction of altars in Ex 20:24–26). It is also possible that a new altar would have been built in an open area or on a high place to accommodate the large numbers of Israelites assembled. (276)

5 The Israelites see that saving Benjamin and giving them a future "depends on finding loopholes in the law" (Block, 585). They devise a plan without mention of divine involvement. They hope beyond hope that someone failed to answer the call to the assembly at Mizpah and thus did not participate in the oath they made not to give their daughters to the remnant of Benjaminite men. There "as one man" (Judg 20:1) the Israelites had sworn that any nonparticipant at Mizpah should be "put to death," a linguistic formulation patterned after the formal death sentences in casuistic laws such as those in Lev 20:9–27. (See Block, 573, n. 376.) Now they want to find a violator of their rule so they can kill him. Niditch points to Num 31 and notes that "the banlike action is really invoked in order to free up virgin girls for Benjamin" (209).

But notice the way these stories are told. Webb sees the story as "essentially a piece of social criticism, and the criticism is of a moral nature. It shows how Israel's hospitality, warfare, justice, and politics were all debased because of the moral blindness and/or perversity of its citizens (including Levites and elders) and the consequent malfunctioning of its institutions" ([1987] 197).

Schneider sees that "the end of the book highlights how horrendous the situation had become for all Israel, but especially for the women of Israel" (272). Lapsley concludes, "This story is included in Scripture not because the biblical writers were indifferent to the violence and suffering of a women, but on the contrary, because they saw the violence depicted here as a major *theological* problem" ("Gentle Guide," 64–65, emphasis original). Hertzberg (255) shows that three of the Ten Commandments are broken here—killing, adultery, and stealing.

These stories are not told to amuse an audience or to laud a hero. If any narratives in the Hebrew Bible intend to raise the level of social consciousness and decry the present military, ethical, and moral situation in Israel, then these are the stories, stories in many ways with more power to transform than the great prophetic sermons.

6 The change of attitude moves from putting Benjamin under the holy war ban to termination of mourning rituals and letting themselves be "consoled" as *HALOT* (2:688) defines this use of the Hebrew *nip'al* of *nḥm* (םחנ). But *DCH* defines it as "be moved to compassion, have compassion on" (5:663). As M. Butterworth notes, "the detailed classification of the meanings of this root is difficult," but he decides on "have compassion on" (*NIDOTTE,* 3:82). This scholarly uncertainty leads to quite varying translations of the opening clause:

But the Israelites had compassion for Benjamin. (NRSV; compare HCSB)

The Israelites felt deep sadness for Benjamin. (NLT)

Now the Israelites grieved for their brothers, the Benjamites. (NIV; compare NKJV)

The Israelites were sad about what had happened to the Benjamin tribe. (CEV)

The Israelites were disconsolate over their brother Benjamin. (NAB)

And the sons of Israel were sorry for their brother Benjamin. (NASB95)

The Israelites regretted what had happened to their brother Benjamin. (NET)

The Israelites now relented toward their kinsmen the Benjaminites. (JPS)

The Israelites felt remorse over their kinsmen the Benjaminites. (REB)

One's interpretation of the term here depends totally on one's interpretation of the context. It does appear that this is a time of mourning that gives way to action. The Israelites find consolation through their lamentation and turn to finding a solution for their problem, stated once again: "Today one tribe is cut off from Israel." With only six hundred Benjaminite men remaining, desperate action is required. The obvious action is to allocate daughters from the other Israelite tribes.

7–8a The logical option is ruled out. An oath made in the name of Yahweh prevents this solution. Again, one must ask about irony here, for suddenly the Israelites become quite concerned about what is right in God's eyes rather than in their own. Does religious awe or magical fear drive their decision to maintain their oath? Whatever the absolute motivation, Israel squarely faces one question: Did any tribe not go up to the assembly at Mizpah? Lapsley laments, "The moment of clarity to which the anguished cry, 'Why, O YHWH, has this happened?' might have led has now evaporated. As a remedy for their distress, the people revert to the violence that ripped Israel apart in the first place" ("Gentle Guide," 59).

8b–9 A pair of surprise clauses in Hebrew underscores the discovery of an answer. Jabesh-gilead did not appear in Mizpah. Even a quick census of the people showed that Jabesh-gilead was absent and unaccounted for. Matthews insists that "this cannot be a coincidence and must be a contrived element designed once again to demonize Saul's tribe and family" (199).

The assembly is now called a "camp" (הַמַּחֲנֶה), the term used throughout Judges for the place an army has stationed its troops for battle and then for the troops who go to battle (Judg 4:15–16; 7:1, 8–11, 13–15, 17–19, 21–22; 8:10–12; 21:12; compare Exod 29:14; Num 1:52). Judges here appears to differentiate the "camp," set up for eating and sleeping, and the "assembly" (קהל), where national decisions are made.

Gilead, of course, is the central part of the territory east of the Jordan. The Wadi el-Yabis empties into the Jordan River about one mile (2 km) south of Tell Ghamain and seems to point to a location in the vicinity. Jabesh-gilead was a Saul-friendly town (1 Sam 11; 31). The Judges narrative characteristically demeans the locations linked with Saul, seeing his followers as uncooperative in not joining the tribal assembly and thus deserving death. Gaß (*Ortsnamen,* 504–9) offers four possible locations for Jabesh-gilead. Tell Abu Kharaz with its twin city Tell el-Meqbereh has Iron Age and especially Late Bronze Age pottery. The road to it may be too easily visible for it to serve as the city Saul defended. Tell Maqlub has both Iron Age and Bronze Age pottery and fits approximately the evidence from Eusebius. Der el-Chalaweh does not appear to have Iron Age pottery, only early Roman and Byzantine, so it is the least likely candidate for Jabesh-gilead. Khirbet Isnah has a few Iron Age pottery remains, but appears to have been settled only in the Persian period. Gaß (509) concludes that Tell el-Maqlub is the most likely location of ancient Jabesh-gilead. D. V. Edelman (*ABD,* 3:594–95) notes other suggested locations: ed-Deir/Deir el-Halawe and Miryamim. But she decides that "Tell Maqlub is the only possible candidate for Jabesh being located where the Roman Road crosses the Yabis." Block (574) locates Tell Maqlub seven miles (11.3 km) east of the Jordan and thirteen miles (21 km) southeast of Beth-shan.

10 Having struggled so valiantly and disastrously to eliminate the tribe of Benjamin, the Israelites find the "twelve thousand valiant warriors" (a number Pressler [256] designates "greatly exaggerated") still able to fight and send them to destroy Jabesh-gilead, apparently one of the leading towns east of the Jordan and a journey of forty-five miles (72.4 km) (Brensinger, 212). This time the actors are referred to not as "camp" or "assembly" but as "congregation" (עדה), perhaps a collection of synonyms, but also quite probably a fine distinction in authority and composition, the עדה being the technical term for the official, politically empowered assembly. The marching orders are clear: strike down the entire city, including women and little children. Pressler points out that only this verse, Num 31:15–18, and Deut 2:34 mention "children" or "little ones" (הטף). Thus Israel extends holy war practice to its furthest and most gruesome extent.

Implicit is the intent to capture all virgins as wives for the Benjaminites. Such a selective use of the ban may be read out of Num 31:17–18. Such action against Jabesh-gilead, Webb observes, is "legally justifiable, but morally dubious to say the least" ([1987] 195). Block says, "From a human perspective this is a clever strategy, exploiting one oath to circumvent another by the selective application of the law of *ḥerem*" (575), that is, the law requiring placing all enemies occupying the promised land under the ban or proscription requiring their death. Matthews points to Deut 22:28–29 and Exod 22:16–17 as relating to this incident: "Based on this law there are no circumstances in which the father could deny giving his daughter to her 'captor,' and the stipulation against divorce provides her with legal protections that could balance the father's ire at the loss of his child" (200).

11 A bit of irony or sarcasm needed for the plot enters the marching orders. In the midst of battle and at the end of battle during mopping-up operations, the soldiers have to distinguish between women who have had carnal knowledge of a male and those who have remained virgins. Exactly how they are to make such a quick determination is left to the reader's imagination.

12 Whatever the test, the Israelite soldiers discover "four hundred virgin girls" in Jabesh-gilead and bring them back to the "camp" (מחנה), now pitched at Shiloh (Josh 18:1, 8–10; 19:51; 21:2; 22:9, 12; Judg 18:31; 21:19, 21; 1 Sam 1:3, 9, 24; 2:14; 3:21; 4:3–4, 12; 14:3; 1 Kgs 2:27; 14:2, 4; Ps 78:60; Jer 7:12, 14; 26:6, 9; 41:5). The mathematically inclined reader will immediately find a problem to solve here. How do you divide four hundred women among six hundred soldiers? One hopes that you do not follow the Levite's example!

The assumption appears to be that at this point the ark of the covenant has moved from Bethel to Shiloh (see 1 Sam 4:3), which has displaced Bethel as God's chosen assembly and worship place. Shiloh would also be the center of activity for Eli and Samuel, only to have its priesthood banished and disenfranchised because of the actions of Eli and his sons (1 Kgs 2:27).

Block (576), however, notes the military neutrality of Shiloh as compared to Mizpah and Bethel, which had apparently served as military mustering points. Block may be correct in his supposition that the Israelites "felt that they could sanctify their decisions by bringing the women here and presenting them to the Benjamites before the priest" (576). Leuchter uses an interesting interpretation of 1 Sam 1:1 to draw "a strong connection between the religious circles of Eph-ratah-Bethlehem in Judah and the Shilonites of the Ephraimite hinterland" (*JBL* 125 [2006] 61). The connection in Judg 17–21 among Bethlehem, Shiloh, Bethel, and the hinterlands of Ephraim may add a bit of support for this supposition. These chapters do not, however (contra Leuchter), add support for Jeroboam to claim Davidic legacy and for Jeroboam to seek to incorporate Shiloh tradition into his regime.

Shiloh is located "in the land of Canaan." Is this another indicator of the ancient age of this tradition, that is, of a time of origin when Israel still had not settled the entire land so that its worship place was an outpost in the land still controlled by Canaanites? Or is "land of Canaan" simply a standard phrase for Palestine, including parts Israel failed to conquer? Or is it the land promised Abraham? The answer appears to be the promised land in its entirety (Gen 13:12; 16:3; 17:8; 23:2, 19; 33:18; 35:6; 36:5–6; 37:1; 42:5, 7, 13, 32; 44:8; 45:25; 46:6, 12, 31; 47:1, 4, 13–15; 48:3, 7; 49:30; 50:5; Exod 6:4; 16:35; Lev 14:34; 18:3; 25:38; Num 13:2, 17; 26:19; 32:30, 32; 33:40, 51; 34:2, 29; 35:14; Deut 32:49; Josh 5:12; 14:1; 21:2; 22:9–11, 32; 24:3; 1 Chr 16:18; Ps 105:11; Ezek 16:29; 17:4). Block says this is the only Old Testament passage where "land of Canaan" applies to the postconquest period. So, for Block, the least the expression can show is that "the material in these last chapters derives from the nation's earliest history within the land" (576). Rhetorically, according to Block, "the narrator makes the shocking suggestion that Shiloh is fundamentally a Canaanite site" (576); but this reads a bit too much into the text here. The reference to "land of Canaan" more likely situates this central sanctuary in the land Israel was supposed to conquer, shows they did conquer something in the land, and points to Israelite selfish action that led to Shiloh's destruction, the ark's loss to the Philistines, and Shiloh's replacement by Jerusalem as the place where God wanted his people to worship.

Younger remarks, "The addition of the phrase 'in Canaan' at the end of v 12 heightens the irony that the *ḥerem* which was designed for application to the Canaanites (which Israel did not fully obey, Judg 1), here is being applied to an Israelite city because it did not participate in the civil war against Benjamin (one of Israel's own tribes); and it is applied to almost utter extinction" (381).

Also, the narrator suddenly has to locate Shiloh for his readers. Gaß (*Ortsnamen*, 401) suggests that perhaps a second, lesser-known Shiloh is indicated here, not the major central sanctuary. Gaß (401) sees this town located at Khirbet Seilun, where excavations seem to indicate only a cultic place without permanent settlement until Iron I. But the very existence of a cultic place in either the Bronze Age or the early Iron Age is often disputed. (For literature, see Gaß, *Ortsnamen*, 403–4, along with final n. 2905, which refers to a horned altar found near Khirbet Seilun.) Gaß cannot give a clue as to the site of the major sanctuary of Shiloh that he separates from the Shiloh of Judg 21.

B. Halpern (*ABD*, 5:1213) recognizes only one town of Shiloh and places it without argument at Khirbet Seilun. I. Finkelstein ("Seilun, Khirbet," *ABD*, 5:1069–72) also has no doubt of the identification of Shiloh at Khirbet Seilun. From his own excavations, Finkelstein concludes:

> The excavation results shed light on several aspects concerning the role of Shiloh in the Israelite Settlement process. First, it is now clear that in the beginning of the Iron Age Seilun/Shiloh was the outstanding candidate to become the sacred center of the hill-country population, since it was an ancient cult site that now stood deserted in an area with only a sparse Canaanite population and a high concentration of "Israelite" sites. The exact date Shiloh was first settled by the Israelites is not yet clear; however, it seems that major construction did not begin before the middle of the 12th century B.C.E. (*ABD*, 5:172)

The important role Shiloh played is reflected in the density of the Iron I sites around it, which is two and even three times greater than that of the other regions in the land of Ephraim. The size of the settlement was about two and a half to three acres (1–1.2 ha). Since a considerable part of it was probably occupied by the shrine complex and other public buildings, the possibility that Shiloh was primarily a sacred *temenos*, or cut-off piece of land dedicated to a sanctuary and/or its god, rather than an ordinary village should not be ruled out. According to the data from the excavations, the shrine was probably at the summit of the tell. Unfortunately, this area was badly eroded and destroyed by later occupation.

The Bible does not directly report Shiloh's destruction, but it most likely occurred as the Philistines gained mastery over much Israelite territory in the days of Samuel and Saul (compare Jer 7:12, 14; 26:6, 9; Ps 78:60). The depiction in 1 Kgs 14 indicates a Shiloh tradition that totally opposes the way Jeroboam ruled Israel. Despite all God did for him, Jeroboam set up a totally false cultic worship at Dan and Bethel, apparently in opposition to the cult at Shiloh. Gaß's suggestion of two Shilohs might explain several issues involved in this chapter, but the inference of this chapter is that it distinguishes a Shiloh in the land of Canaan north of Bethel here from a Shiloh either farther north or in the land of Gilead across the Jordan from the land of Canaan. If that were the case, the reader would expect the Shiloh not in the land of Canaan to figure in this chapter, which it explicitly does not. Thus we seem to be left with the common opinion, represented by Finkelstein, that there was only one Shiloh.

Shiloh is the central sanctuary for Israel at the end of the period of the judges, but quite possibly not at the beginning. This may help locate the narrative in time. For this narrative, Shiloh is in Canaan, is located in reference to Bethel (21:19), and has a festival that the Israelites have to learn about (21:19). Pressler says this makes the narrative "a late addition" coming from an era when "the site was no longer well-known" (256).

The pains the narrator takes to locate and describe the site seem rather to point to an early period when Israel did not yet recognize Shiloh as a centralized cult place, Bethel being the major sanctuary and meeting place. Shiloh may have been a neutral site where Israel and Benjamin could meet, Israel setting up camp, not cult, there to meet Benjamin.

13 Having begun the process of finding wives for the Benjaminites, Israel's congregation tries to make peace with Benjamin's remnant.

14 The men of Benjamin turn back, apparently returning to their own land. Israel gives the Jabesh-gilead women to the Benjaminites, realizing that they "did not have the right number," or more literally, "they had not found for them the right." Guillaume (*Waiting for Josiah*, 212) sees this marking the end of a first draft that skipped to its final verse in v 24, the negative element here and the four hundred in v 12 being added to connect the later edition. This again shows the length to which new-redaction critics are willing to go to push portions of an artistic narrative late into Israel's postexilic history.

15 Again the word *nḥm* appears and receives the same variety of translations as in v 6. Does it still point to Israel concluding their mourning and being "consoled," as I have translated in 21:6? Or does it indicate that the people of Israel have finally "relented" of their animosity toward Benjamin and are seeking reconciliation, as I have translated in 21:15?

The reason behind Israel's reaction is Yahweh's deed. In Israel's theology, God has made a break or "a hole" in the tribes of Israel. Again, this is Israel speaking, not Yahweh, though Block believes "the narrator places responsibility for the loss of Benjamin squarely on the shoulders of Yahweh," admitting, however, that the verse is intentionally ambiguous (573).

Lapsley sees "an instance of free indirect discourse in which a change of perspective occurs within a single sentence," switching from the narrator's perspective in the first part of the verse to the people's perspective in the latter half ("Gentle Guide," 60). This fluctuating perspective shows "the depth of the people's self-deception.... The line between divine sovereignty and human action is often indistinct" (61).

The sons of Israel had gone to war on their own and gotten thoroughly defeated until finally they let a priest seek an oracle and gained the permission to fight Benjamin. Israel did not treat Benjamin as a member tribe to be punished and brought back into the fold. Rather Israel treated Benjamin as a foreign occupant of the land and "put them to the ban" (Judg 21:11). Having destroyed Benjamin, the men of Israel apparently went far beyond Yahweh's commands. Now, seeing the extent of their actions and looking at the long-range results, they find themselves in a situation they do not like. So they turn all the blame on God.

16   This is the only appearance of elders in Judges since 2:7, where they were the last ones to keep the Joshua tradition of covenant renewal and obedience alive. Now they are dedicated to death for part of Israel.

The elders turn to the practical situation, ignoring theological language and divine involvement: "What can we do for wives?" The arithmetic finally catches up with them. Two hundred men still need marriage partners. The onus is on "we" to get the job done and square the mathematical equation. Niditch thinks that "in this section, 'elders' of the congregation play a leadership role as the storyteller projects an image of polity in the days before there were kings in Israel" (210). Or could it be that elders actually performed the leading roles in Israel's polity prior to the monarchy?

Wong sees "conscious literary design so that the episodes are reworked to echo the incident about Jephthah's daughter. ... If the elders' decision was indeed bizarre, it is at least not unprecedented because a similarly bizarre conclusion involving rash vows has happened before in the life of one of Israel's judges" (*Compositional Strategy*, 134–35).

17   Block is certainly correct when he understates reality: "The Hebrew of v 17 is difficult" (578). See *Note* 21:17.a. The unexpected appearance of the Hebrew noun יְרֻשַּׁת (*yĕruššat*), "possession," and the lack of a verb in the opening clause of the quote have led to many translations:

There must be heirs for the survivors of Benjamin. (NRSV, NLT; compare NIV)

If they don't have children . . . (CEV)

There must be an inheritance for the survivors of Benjamin. (NASB95, NKJV)

There must be a saving remnant for Benjamin. (JPS)

The remnant of Benjamin must be preserved. (NET)

There has to be a way to help the survivors preserve Binyamin's inheritance. (CJB)

Translators who use "heir" or "inheritance" stretch the meaning of יְרֻשָּׁה from its normal meaning of land conquered and possessed to that of a family receiving children as a special possession, ensuring that an inheritance can be passed down. Block (579, n. 395) says "heirs" is an unlikely rendering. He suggests: "It is a [territorial] possession of a survivor belonging to Benjamin" (n. 396).

Some mystery thus remains in translating and understanding the verse. Whatever the exact translation, the text pictures Israelites recognizing the loss they have inflicted on the nation by wiping out one tribe. What is to prevent "my" tribe from being next? How can we face our enemies when we are fighting among ourselves and destroying ourselves? A selfish look at reality shows Israel its mistake in doing what for the moment was right in their own eyes. Block says, "The awkward construction captures the vexed emotional state of the elders" (579).

Note that the Hebrew behind "be wiped out" is *māḥāh* (מחה), which normally "describes the disappearance of the name or the memory of a person or group" (Block, 579; reference Gen 6:7; 7:4, 23; Exod 17:14; 32:32–33; Num 5:23; 34:11; Deut 9:14; 25:6, 19; 29:19; 2 Kgs 14:27; 21:13; Neh 3:37; 13:14; Pss 9:6; 51:3, 11; 69:29; 109:13–14; Prov 6:33; 30:20; 31:3; Isa 25:6, 8; 43:25; 44:22; Jer 18:23; Ezek 6:6).

18 A contrast clause sets Israel's desperate desire to help Benjamin over against the gross facts of reality. They cannot take the logical step and let Benjamin marry daughters from the other tribes. They established that early in the narrative based on their oath made in the name of Yahweh (Judg 21:1, 7). Such a person would stand under a curse that cut the offender off from the people Israel and their God Yahweh (Gen 3:14; 4:11; 9:25; 27:29; 49:7; Num 24:9; Deut 27:15–26; 28:16–19; Josh 6:26; Judg 5:23; 1 Sam 14:24, 28; Jer 11:3; 17:5; 20:14–15; 48:10; Mal 1:14).

R. P. Gordon explains, "The effectiveness of a curse depends on the status of the speaker and the receptivity of the cursed; moreover, the tendency is for God to be invoked to bring the curse into effect" (*NIDOTTE*, 1:525). The Israelite curse against Benjamin may well imply that Yahweh would be the one to carry out the punishment of a curse breaker, but that is not made explicit. What becomes clear, as Wong states, is that the "oath itself had become a curse to the community" (*Compositional Strategy*, 45).

19 A surprise clause indicates that a new idea registers with the elders or with the ones to whom the elders speak. Ackerman notes, "Ironic juxtaposition is redolent here. In 19:1–20:48 Benjamin's taking of the Levite's wife for sexual purposes was deemed to be criminal, but in 21:15–25 these same Benjaminites are encouraged to go forth and take sexual partners—*cum* wives from the gathering of Shiloh's young women" (*Warrior, Dancer,* 254).

Leuchter sees that "the details regarding the Shiloh sanctuary, its geographic situation, and its festival and sacrificial schedule" (*CBQ* 69 [2007] 431, n. 11) "correspond to institutions to which later writers did not have acccess or with which they would not have been concerned or familiar" (431).

The "annual festival" is taking place at Shiloh. The following description seems to indicate a local festival rather than a national one, but it could refer to the Feast of Tabernacles (Wong, *Compositional Strategy*, 74, n. 107; compare Younger, 382). Soggin believes the "topographical description of the location of Shiloh can hardly be put on the lips of the 'elders of the assembly': it would be too artificial" (299). Thus Soggin sees the description as a later note added to the text. Block finds the expression so vague that it may indicate "they do not really know what they are talking of. . . . These festivals seem either to have been neglected for a long time or to have been transformed/debased beyond recognition" (580). Ackerman says that "this notion of unfamiliarity is patently absurd. . . . The elaborate description of Shiloh's backwoods location in Judg 21:19 is thus an out-of-kilter twist . . . totally at odds with what the rest of biblical literature would lead us to expect. It is present in the text only to accentuate the peculiar parallelism that ties Judge 19–20:48 and 21:15–25 together" (*Warrior, Dancer,* 255).

This text paints a complex portrait of Shiloh as a religious center since it appears to serve as the central shrine for Israel, yet its festival remains a local affair featuring the daughters of Shiloh. The description may well represent a very early text before Shiloh had yet become an important worship center for all Israel (compare Brensinger, 212). The narrative raises a number of mind-numbing questions, as Brensinger points out: "If the Shilohites are in fact Israelites, however, then why are they unaware of the ongoing proceedings? Did they not have representation at the intertribal assembly? Or if the people of Shiloh constitute a Canaanite settlement not yet under Israelite control, then how can they be held accountable for honoring the oath (21:18, 22)? Worse yet, if they are Canaanites, then why are they considered desirable for marriage?" (213).

Ackerman shows that "the notion that sees eroticism as the focus of women's music-making at the vineyard festival lies very close to the surface of at least the Judges 21 and 1 Samuel 1–2 tales" (*Warrior, Dancer,* 263–64). It becomes, Wong says, "the place where sexual purity was taken away from innocent young women against their will" (*Compositional Strategy,* 74). As Niditch describes the rituals based on anthropological parallels, "Like the tale of Jephthah's daughter, the tale of the women of Shiloh may well be an etiology for customs involving marriage, key passages in the lives of young women. In this case, the story describes a yearly 'wife-stealing' ritual in which matches are made between men of Benjamin and daughters of Shiloh. Such rituals are common in other cultures" (210).

Lebonah is mentioned to help locate Shiloh, but this place name appears only here in the Hebrew Bible. Gaß (*Ortsnamen,* 427–28) places it at Lubban (esh-Sharqi). Block (580, n. 401) sees the location as uncertain.

20–21 The mention of hiding in the vineyards in Judg 21:20 may indicate that the festival involves the grape harvest. The emphasis is on speed and watchfulness. The men of Benjamin must strike at exactly the right moment, just as an army in ambush, to catch their brides. First each must catch a wife and then head for home just as fast as he appeared. "Catch" is the strong but rare Hebrew word *ḥāṭap* (חטף) that *HALOT* renders "abduct." See its only other appearance in Ps 10:9.

Combined with the language of v 23, Lapsley says, "the word choice reflects the narrator's view that the women have been forcibly seized, plundered, robbed, stolen" ("Gentle Guide," 62). Younger concludes, "The rape of the daughters of Shiloh is an ironic counterpoint to the rape of the concubine, just as the campaign against Jabesh Gilead is an ironic counterpoint to the war against Benjamin" (383).

The story of the abduction of the Shiloh daughters draws comparisons with many ancient parallel laws and narratives as shown especially by Guillaume (*Waiting for Josiah,* 215–24; Ackerman, *Warrior, Dancer,* 267–76). Guillaume concludes that "some elements do indicate that rape was an option to acquire wives." Ancient Near Eastern laws seem to indicate that "the Shiloh festival cannot be considered as a particular time of sexual license providing special relaxation of rules in order to facilitate matrimonial endeavors" (*Waiting for Josiah*, 218). Thus the elders' plan to hijack Shiloh women is "at least more realistic than the ban on Jabesh." Still, for Guillaume (219), Shiloh may refer to mythological rapes more than historical ones. Nothing, however, in the present narrative represents mythology as opposed to history. Not every story whose ethical conduct we question must have its origin among the gods.

The narrator suddenly "telescopes the account" (Block, 580). Evidently, Shiloh had representatives at the assembly in Mizpah and so could not give their daughters willingly. Just as evidently, Shiloh did not participate in this later decision making since they would hardly have agreed to let men steal away their daughters. Again ambush strategy is involved, this time to be employed by the Benjaminites. Such strategy worked for Joshua against Ai (Josh 8) and ultimately for Israel against the Benjaminites (Judg 20:29–46). It led Israel to mourn their success. Thus we see with Wong that the epilogue highlights "the lack of discernment of a generation who knew only to superficially copy past strategies of success without understanding how to appropriately apply them in their own context" (*Compositional Strategy*, 70).

Block (581) may read too much into "daughters of Shiloh" when he sees a reference to "cultic dancers," a professional class taken from Canaanite religion.

22 Guillaume claims that Judg 21:22 presents a "rather complicated argument," but that "the understanding of the Shiloh episode hangs on the understanding of this verse" (*Waiting for Josiah*, 213). He translates the third clause as "because we did not take each his wife in the war," interpreting this to mean that, unlike the other tribes, the men of Shiloh had taken wives for themselves in the war with Benjamin, reference to the murder of Benjaminite women being implicit but not explicit in the narrative. He then translates כִּי לֹא אַתֶּם נְתַתֶּם לָהֶם as "because it is not you who gave to them," thinking that "the elders seem to reproach the fathers and brothers [for] the fact that they were prevented by these very fathers and brothers to take [*sic*] women captives for themselves because they did not give them" (214). But the Hebrew syntax, if an apposition statement, should place the redundant pronoun אַתֶּם before the negative לֹא. Thus for Guillaume "two ideas seem to be entangled: firstly, the families whose girls were abducted by the Benjaminite survivors happen to be the ones who kept some Benjaminite female prisoners alive, they are therefore guilty and should not claim compensation. Secondly, the oath was not broken because the Shiloh girls were taken and not given" (215).

This intricate attempt to reinterpret the entire story on the basis of one convoluted verse fails at one simple point. The "we did not capture" is not a personal testimony representing an unfulfilled wish to gain something for themselves. It is a collective statement saying that the troops who represented the elders in going to war did not fulfill their mission since they did not capture a sufficient number of women for Benjamin, not for themselves. Guillaume does come to an interesting conclusion: perhaps the text "was meant to be tortuous from the start, expressing mumbo jumbo bargaining between rogues, rather than a convincing argument to afford protection to the Benjaminite survivors" (*Waiting for Josiah*, 215).

A temporal clause sets up the future scene when Benjamin has left and the Shiloh men find that their young women have disappeared. At that time the elders of Israel expect the men of Shiloh to file a legal "complaint" or *rîb* (רִיב). The legal action will be "with us." That is, the complaint will be brought before the official assembly. The assembly will ask "a favor." Here another ironic touch appears. God had told Israel:

When the LORD your God brings you into the land that you are about to enter and
occupy, and he clears away many nations before you—the Hittites, the Girgashites, the
Amorites, the Canaanites, the Perizzites, the Hivites, and the Jebusites, seven nations
mightier and more numerous than you—and when the LORD your God gives them over
to you and you defeat them, then you must utterly destroy them. Make no covenant with
them and show them no mercy. (Deut 7:1–2, NRSV)

The last term—*ḥānan* (חָנַן), "mercy"—is the same as used in Judg 21:22 for "do
a favor." The men of Israel had made war on both Benjamin and Jabesh-gilead
as if they were conquering pagan inhabitants of the land. Now they have turned
around seeking a favor on behalf of the tribe they annihilated because they could
not gain sufficient women from the city they placed under the ban.

The elders thus justify violence, Pressler says, "framing the rape of the virgins
as an act of grace for the men of Shiloh, who did not have to break their oaths
and incur guilt. The justification is another example of blatant hypocrisy" (257).
Their interesting reasoning is that by letting their daughters go to the men who
had kidnapped them, the men of Shiloh would not come under the guilt of giving
their daughters to Benjamin and thus would not come under the terms of the curse
the tribal assembly had made at Mizpah. The reverse of this is that, according to
Younger, "if the fathers do not accept the abductions, the elders will hold them
guilty . . . , and they will come under the oath's curse" (382).

Block concedes that "although it transgresses every standard of morality and
decency, this rationalization satisfies the letter of the law. . . . The rationalization
puts the protesting fathers and brothers in a bad light for putting personal and
family interests ahead of the interests of the tribe and nation" (582). Doing a favor
by giving their daughters now was a way to get around the curse of giving their
daughters previously. Webb concludes, "In effect the men of Shiloh are asked
to accept the rape as a *fait accompli,* just as Micah had to accept the plundering
of his shrine by the Danites (18:22–26)" ([1987] 196). Matthews argues that the
men of Shiloh "have no real choice given the political decision of the elders of
the other tribes" (200).

Thus we appear to have a "happy ending" for all. Guillaume wants to modify this:
"The trouble-free accomplishment of the advice in v 23 remains baffling, and it is
hard to accept this conclusion of a happy ending without wondering if this is not
another instance of Judean derision of the Benjaminites." Lapsley denies a happy
ending: "The story refuses to sweep this problem under the rug by formulating a
happy ending. . . . After the civil war comes to its pathetic conclusion (abducting
the women of Shiloh), each tribe of Israel limps back home. The whole of Israel
has suffered a major wound to its integrity. Such is the cost of victory" ("Gentle
Guide," 67).

Kamuf sees that "the Levite's avengers, after punishing Benjamin, find themselves forced to identify with the criminals they have punished and to refuse any
demand for vengeance (by the fathers of Shiloh) of the very sort they have just
carried out" ("Author of a Crime," 193).

23 The people of Benjamin obey orders. They seize Shiloh's young women
and race back to their inheritance. In so doing they commit a crime worthy of the
death penalty (Exod 21:16; Deut 24:7). "Seized" is another strong Hebrew term,
gāzal (גּוּל). *HALOT* translates it as "tear off: the skin (Mic 3:2) . . . ; to tear away,

to seize (Lev 5:23; Deut 28:31; Judg 21:23; Jer 21:12; 22:3; Ezek 18:7, 12, 16, 18; 22:29) . . . ; wells (Gen 21:25); women (Gen 31:31); fields (Mic 2:2); houses (Job 20:19); . . . to rob a person of his right (Isa 10:2); . . . to snatch from (Job 24:9); to snatch away the snow waters (Job 24:19); to rob (Lev 19:13; Judg 9:25; Pss 35:10; 69:4 [Heb. 69:5]; Pr 22:22; 28:24); . . . to steal a flock (Job 24:2)."

Yes, despite being victims of holy war from their kinsfolk, Benjamin's small remnant retains an inherited share among the Israelite tribes. Six hundred men with their new wives "built cities and settled in them." Here the narrator points to the long-term success of the endeavor to get wives for Benjamin. But the success comes as Israel's tribal leaders decide strategy for themselves and carry out actions of holy war and kidnapping to make up for the damage they have inflicted on their own kinsfolk. Never do they ask God for directions. Rather they blame God for the predicament they have caused. And Younger points out that rebuilding cities means "the entire implementation of the *cherem* has been undercut" (383). Ackerman concludes,

> What we have, then, in Judg 19:1–20:48 and 21:15–25 is a paradox, where two episodes stand paralleled within the telling of the larger Judges 19–21 tale, yet stand paralleled in a manner curiously askew. The result is outcomes disconcertingly "out of sync," whereby a story that begins by condemning Benjamin's assault of an Ephraimite's woman concludes by condoning the Benjaminites' ravaging of the Ephraimites' women. (*Warrior, Dancer*, 254–55)

24 Having solved the Levites' problem by waging holy war on one of their own and having solved the Benjaminites' problem by putting the ban on an Israelite city and planning the kidnapping of the women of Shiloh while they are celebrating a religious festival, Israel disbands its assembly so that each representative returns home to his own "inheritance." Niditch sees a positive note bringing a happy ending to Judges:

> With wives obtained, the Benjaminites go off to build cities and dwell in them. Reunited with their kin and their problems resolved, the Israelites return as well to their various tribes and clans. The final imagery is not of chaos but of cosmogony. The world is set and ordered, cities inhabited, and people properly and peacefully divided into social kinship groups, even while recognizing the ties that unify all Israelites. For the time being, the group as a whole has asserted itself over against more circumscribed kin-based loyalties within one tribe. . . . It was all so long ago when each man did what was right in his own eyes (21:25). Yet Judges does not end with chaos; it ends with wholeness, reconciliation, rehabilitation, and peace, made possible in men's eyes through the taking of women. (210–11)

The return home does bring an end to the narrative of Judges, just as return to the inheritances brought an end to the Joshua narrative (Josh 24:28) and an end to the unfinished mission given in Judg 2:6.

One difference catches the reader's attention: Joshua sent the people back having led them to renew their covenant with God; the people in Judges go back on their own having narrowly averted destroying a tribe of their kinsfolk by putting one of their own cities to the ban. This ending to the Judges narrative then stands in parallel form but in opposing meaning in relationship to Joshua. The seemingly innocuous denouement to Judges actually shows that throughout the entire book no narrative progress is made. Israel stands in the same position at the end of Judges as it did at the end of Joshua, people returning to live on their inherited land. What is more, as Lapsley shows, the narrator emphasizes "the separateness and isolation of each of the tribes and even of each individual Israelite" ("Gentle Guide," 63). The verbal form, for Lapsley, carries a specific connotation of going in different directions and can convey a randomness of direction. "This return is characterized not by unity, but by fragmentation" (63).

This was a different people. Joshua's people chose the impossible assignment—to follow Yahweh. The Israelites under the judges ultimately choose to do what is right in their own eyes. The people of Joshua looked up to a servant of God and back to a series of conquests in which God was faithful in fulfilling all his promises. The people at the end of Judges look up to no leader and back to a series of inept, unfaithful attempts to escape the dangers of foreign rulers. They see a God who has kept a promise not to deliver them again (10:13). For Joshua, God had fulfilled all his promises and provided land and rest (Josh 21:43–45). For the Israelites of Judges, God lets them wander back to their inheritances still under threat from Philistines and Amorites (Judg 10:7–8). What land remained for Joshua to conquer (Josh 13:1–7) still remained for Israel to conquer, the judges having really gained no new land. The judges have let leadership deteriorate to a new low from its acme under Joshua.

25 "In those days Israel had no king. Every person did what was right in his own eyes." The last verse of chap. 21, the most important verse in the book, lends itself to a wide variety of contradictory interpretations. A few things seem evident:

Israel needed leadership. To do right in one's own eyes certainly cannot be construed as a positive action. It parallels doing evil in the eyes of Yahweh.

The remaining nations existed to "test Israel . . . to determine if they would obey Yahweh's commandments which he had commanded their fathers by the hand of Moses" (Judg 3:4). But nowhere else in Judges do the commandments of Moses appear (compare Judg 1:16, 20; 4:11; 18:30), while Moses is referred to fifty-seven times in Joshua. Younger says, "In a sense Judges is the antithesis to Joshua. In Joshua the Israelites attempt to Hebraize Canaan; in Judges they Canaanize themselves" (383).

Doing what was right in their own eyes was Israelites' posture before they entered their inheritance (Deut 12:8), certainly not the posture expected of them after they have entered their inheritance and established themselves in the land. This is a far cry from Josh 21:43–45.

The verse points beyond itself to hope for a future time, that of the writer or beyond.

Much remains far from evident. Scholars carry on strong debates about this verse in its dating, its view of kingship, its moral intention, and its relationship to other instances of the refrain in part and in whole. (See Wong, *Compositional Strategy,* 191, nn. 1–2.)

The relationship to other instances of the refrain appears to be the simplest to answer. The narrator has carefully created an inclusio with 17:6, placing part of the refrain in 18:1, complemented by 18:26, and in 19:1, complemented by 19:24. All references look back to Samson's experience in 14:3, 7 and serve the same function as reporting evil that Israel did in Yahweh's eyes (2:11; 3:7, 12; 4:1; 6:1; 10:6; 13:1). Briefly, Israel called for God to do to them as was good in God's eyes (10:15). As Samson had his eyes gouged out so that he could not determine what was good in his eyes (16:21, 28), so Israel walked in moral darkness as they did what was right in their eyes.

The refrain seems to connect the various elements of the book into a whole—introduction, main body with Samson, and epilogue. But, of course, scholars do not agree. They separate the refrain literarily, chronologically, and even theologically.

Boling sees the refrain as copied from earlier editions, including 17:6, and affirming Yahweh's kingship: "Added to the book in a period perhaps as late as the Babylonian exile, it meant that the time had arrived once again for every man to do what was right before Yahweh without any sacral political apparatus to get in the way" (293).

Soggin (300) follows Jüngling (335 ff.) in seeing the refrain's original position at the end of chap. 19. Mayes builds on Jüngling and Becker and finds that "Judges 19–21 is not all of one piece. In particular, ch. 19 stands apart as an originally independent story to which chs. 20–21 have been secondarily added" (*BibInt* 9 [2001] 254), and thus attaches 21:25 to chap. 19.

Guillaume (*Waiting for Josiah*, 227–42) sees Judg 21:25 as part of the last editorial stage of the book. Dumbrell extends the work of Crüsemann (*Der Widerstand gegen das Königtum* [Neukirchener-Vluyn: Neukirchener Verlag, 1978] 156–67) to show that the "concluding statement of the book (21:25) closes comment on the dubious social character of Shiloh and yet serves to introduce further material which follows in 1 Samuel 1–3. In 1 Samuel, however, the standpoint is pan-Israelite, not tribal as in Judges" (*JSOT* 25 [1983] 24). He does find (25) the pan-Israelite view in Judg 17–21. For Dumbrell, "the replacement of the office of Judge by kingship and the struggle which ensued for political control between Samuel and Saul displays the view that judgeship and kingship were incompatible, and that, at least in Samuel's view, kingship was a political degeneration from earlier ideals" (26).

Seeing the work as a unified redactional work of an exilic editor, Dumbrell concludes,

> But in spite of the tremendous social upheavals of the age, in spite of the fact that there was a lack of a strong authoritarian administration such as that which the later monarchy produced, something of value remained at the end of this period of total debacle. After the glaring apostasy which the accounts present, what remained, surprisingly (from a human point of view), was the ideal which was Israel. Despite the absence of the sort of human support which might have preserved a human religious or political ideal, in spite of the fact that every man did what was right in his own eyes, Yahweh has preserved the reality of a united Israel with which the book had commenced. . . . The author . . . is suggesting that the pattern of direct divine intervention, with theocratic leadership, upon which Israel's well-being had always hung, had been never so really demonstrated as it had been in the age of the Judges. It is the revival of this manner of leadership which alone would hold the key to Israel's future. (31)

Dumbrell's idealistic vision of the leadership of the Judges and of the enduring unity of Israel does not come close to the meaning and picture of the narratives as we have seen them. Neither is his recourse to an exilic date convincing. The oft-mentioned theme of the grace of God in relationship to Judges also is more popular than it is clear from the biblical text. Thus Wong judges that "the likelihood that the refrain is meant to function as a positive encouragement for the book's target audience is therefore very slim at best" (*Compositional Strategy*, 199).

Exum, having displayed to her satisfaction the negative role God plays in Judges and the total breakdown of the opening framework, concludes: "In Judges 17–21 Yhwh's rule is ineffectual, either because Yhwh does not intervene in events or because Yhwh intervenes in ways that result in destruction rather than benefit. Yhwh thus shares with Israel responsibility for the disorder with which Judges ends" (*CBQ* 52 [1990] 431).

Ackerman says, "The editor signals that the whole Judges 19–21 complex depicts a world gone grossly awry, where God's cult site is so hidden in the hinterlands that it almost has been forgotten, in which elders have come to perpetuate evil and oaths have lost any sense of obligation, and where rape—whatever the rhetoric of retaliation and revenge in Judges 20 may suggest—is an act whose perpetrators are ultimately recompensed and rewarded" (*Warrior, Dancer*, 257).

Schneider sees that the notion "that when there is a king people do not do as they please but rather as the king pleases is inherent in that statement, thereby promoting the idea that kingship is preferred" (284). Wong sees the refrain as a "lament against pervasive anarchy in Israel in the absence of a higher authority" (*Compositional Strategy*, 197).

For Brensinger the period of the judges ends in nothing short of chaos. No discernible standards exist. "Even the apparently effective operations of the inter-tribal assembly merely mask the godless choices and strategies employed. . . . The statement itself anticipates a brighter future. Such chaos, after all, will eventually give way to the type of stability and order that must have characterized the writer's own time" (215).

But such a brighter, more stable time did not really become established under Josiah, nor did the exiles know of such a time. Only the period of David and Solomon represented such a time, and it was destroyed by Jeroboam.

Block sees the meaning of 21:25 from a bit different perspective: "Nothing about the foregoing events is right in Yahweh's eyes. These are apostate Israelites acknowledging no king, neither divine nor human. But then there is no need for a king in the estimation of the narrator. Wickedness is democratized; everyone does what is right in his own eyes, and the results are disastrous" (583).

I would surely follow Block (583, n. 411) in rejecting an exilic or postexilic setting for a verse seen to favor kingship, kingship having already proved disastrous for the exiled nation. That there is no need for a king in the narrator's eyes certainly lies open to debate. The "proper response" of Gideon (8:23) is not the narrator's theological summary, being set as it is in a context of irony and sarcasm. Gideon's own lifestyle belies his allegiance to his confession. It does appear that the writer seeks a time when a proper king will illustrate a proper lifestyle and when the nation will find itself obligated to and wanting to follow. That proper time comes with David and Saul and will return when Israel refuses to follow the Abimelech-like usurper Jeroboam and comes back to the united Israelite fold under Judah.

Auld decides "the anti-Saul propaganda and hints like the mention of Bethlehem in Judah suggest to me that these chapters do not look for salvation from any king, but look forward beyond Saul to a proper king" (256). But he shoves this to postexilic times with a rather weak note: "The problem stated is a refusal of marriage relations. Benjamin may represent a community whether in Palestine or in the Diaspora whose ostracism had to be overcome, who had to be brought back into fellowship. It may be that the royal, 'messianic' ideal of the end of Judges is an ecumenical ideal as well" (257).

Auld's own exegesis has pointed to Saulides and Davidic kings, not messianic ones, and that "a refusal of marriage relations" is the central theme is far from obvious. That king of course would be David as well as his son Solomon. Israel did right in their eyes when they rejected Solomon and his son Rehoboam and chose to follow a different king without ties to the south.

Thus many questions remain unanswered and strongly debated:

Does this verse intend to summarize the entire book, or only the part from 17:6, the verse with which 21:25 forms an inclusio? The opening study of this verse's relationships to other parts of Judges shows a clear narrative structure anchored by the refrain and tied directly to its parallel statement concerning the evil that Israel does in Yahweh's eyes.

Obviously, the verse points directly back to 17:6 to show the social, religious, military, and political chaos in which Israel finds itself. Indirectly, it points on back to Samson, who chose a wife because it was right in his eyes (14:3). It points further back to Abimelech, whose name meant "my father is king" and whose actions illustrated the coups that would plague the northern kingdom throughout its existence. It points further back to Jotham and his sarcastic fable denying the power and purpose of monarchy. It points further back to Gideon, who refused the offer of becoming king but demanded royal harem, royal money, royal insignia, and a royal lifestyle. But does the concluding verse point further back? The kingship motif as such is absent in the first seven chapters of the book, where the "did evil in the eyes of Yahweh" motif is set up.

Does this verse support kingship as a government system or oppose it? At first read, the stories of Judges strongly oppose kingship. They oppose the type of rogue, violent, self-interest-dominated government exercised by Abimelech living apart from his people. They oppose the type of weak, ill-qualified kingship Jotham illustrated with the fable of the briar. They oppose the kingship of Gideon based on vengeance, wealth seeking, and false religion.

Schneider observes,

> The book examines many different forms of leadership, employing a large range of terminology to refer to those positions of control. Judges examines how leaders are chosen, attributes they need to be successful, personality and character flaws which cause trouble, and how all of these features impact the leaders and their ability to rule. . . . Despite the gradually building idea that kingship is the answer to Israel's predicament, monarchy is not condoned by Judges. Monarchy is the answer when the alternative is anarchy, but monarchy is not described in glowing terms. (287–88)

Still, the clearest reading points to a future hope for a king of some kind, a kind not illustrated in Judges but pointing back to the example of Joshua, the model leader after Moses. Thus Mayes blatantly states, "The argument for the monarchy could scarcely be put in a stronger, more persuasive, form" (*BibInt* 9 [2001] 242).

Does this verse conclude a polemic against Saul and support for David? The final chapters go out of their way to polemicize against places and actions connected with Saul. Ramah, Jabesh-gilead, Gibeah, Mizpah, the tribe of Benjamin, the sending of the pieces of the concubine as Saul would later send pieces of an oxen—all point to continuing feuds between Davidides and Saulides. Amit summarizes the situation quite tersely: "The members of the tribe of Benjamin and the descendants of the house of Saul continued to cultivate their hope for a return to the monarchy. Moreover, it enjoyed extensive public support, as may be seen from the description of the massive participation in the two rebellions that broke out in the days of David: Absalom's rebellion and that led by Sheba son of Bichri" (*Hidden Polemics*, 170). In the midst of this, Judges repeats the call for Judah to lead the armies of Israel and sets up the southern judge Othniel as the pattern all others should follow.

But the situation is not quite so simple. Judges also exercises a strong polemic against Ephraim as the troublesome tribe constantly demanding leadership roles and being the home of unheroic characters. Judges does not paint Ephraim as totally evil. The people of Ephraim helped Ehud (3:27). Deborah resided there (4:5). They assisted Deborah and Barak (5:14). They fought for Gideon (7:24). They suffered with Judah and Benjamin from the attack of the Ammonites, leading to a confession of sin and God's threat never to deliver them again. But the narrative abandons the western tribes and focuses on Jephthah's leadership and events in Gilead (10:9). A judge, Tola, comes from Ephraim (10:1) but accomplishes none of the explicitly great deeds of the other judges.

Judges features another side of the people of Ephraim: their inability to defeat Canaanites (1:29), their argument with Gideon (8:1–2), the devastating defeat at the hands of Jephthah (12:1–5), and their identity as the tribe of Micah who created the false cult and images and their position as the home of both the not-so-nice Levites (17:8; 19:1) and the aged host with his connivery (19:16). In a real sense Judges portrays Ephraim as the corrupter of Levites and the origin of the fatal religion at Dan.

The polemic of the book of Judges is thus not simply an anti-Saul, anti-Benjamin polemic. It is also an anti-Ephraim, anti-Bethel, anti-Dan polemic. Certainly some form of southern rule is preferred to that from Benjamin or Ephraim. The Saul connection seems to preface an attack on northern kingship personified more strongly by Jeroboam from Ephraim with his direct connections to Dan and Bethel. Brettler can conclude: "In those days there was no king in Israel (17:6; 18:1; 19:1; 21:25) and Saul wouldn't be much better, either" (91).

I would add that neither would Jeroboam, for the fight seems to be three ways as the kingdoms separate—Saul, Rehoboam, Jeroboam—or Judah, Benjamin, Ephraim. This three-way fight is not to be thrust forward to the weak state of Jehud under Persia as Jerusalem seeks to take back political leadership from Mizpah and Bethel. It must be placed in a three-way living argument among Jerusalem, Ephraim, and Benjamin. The rise of Jeroboam is the logical time to place this controversy and thus the logical time for Judges to have been formulated and issued by Judean supporters of Rehoboam and the Davidic line in opposition to Jeroboam's usurpation.

Does this verse complete a program of support for Judah against Israel? This is the most difficult of the questions raised. The polemic against the tribes fighting with Judah for supremacy is stronger than the support for Judah. Judah is twice designated as leader (1:1–2; 20:18). Judah's judge Othniel is the model. Judah defeats Jerusalem when Benjamin cannot (1:8, 21). Judah makes a deal with Samson and turns him over to the Philistine (15:9–20). Judah joins Benjamin and Ephraim as the central tribes the Ammonites attack, indicating their leadership so that a defeat of these tribes would provide the upper hand in all of Israel. The Levite of 17:7 is from Judah but lives in Ephraim, where he conducts his self-promoting cultic exchanges. The secondary wife is also from Judah, where hospitality is a bit overdone but is at least done in safety and joy. The retreat from Judah brings a decision against a non-Israelite Jerusalem as a city of foreigners.

Webb thus concludes that

> the way Judah is handled in the finished form of the book does not seem to indicate that either chapters 17–21 or the work as a whole is simply pro-monarchical or anti-monarchical, and discussions of theme have, in my judgment, been dominated too much by this issue. . . . The narrator speaks as one who has seen kingship come and go, as judgeship had come and gone, and recognizes that both, in their time, had a role to play in Yahweh's administration of Israel. The refrain of 17:6, 18:1, 19:1 and 21:25 intimates that kingship will be the subject-matter of a sequel to the present work and that the positive contribution of kingship will be to bring a measure of order and stability to Israel's internal affairs. But the clear message of the two narratives brought together in these chapters is that no institution can make Israel proof against divine chastisement, and paradoxically, that it is that very chastisement which preserves Israel, not its institutions. ([1987] 202–3)

Sweeney argues just the opposite. He thinks "the northerners are incompetent, vindictive, and increasingly compromised by the presence of Canaanites in the land" (*VT* 47 [1997] 517–29). Both of the concluding narratives present a Levite as "somehow compromised by northern tribes who act in a non-YHWHistic fashion" (525). He also sees that "a very clear polemic against Bethel (and Ephraim) appears to be hidden within Judg xvii–xxi, together with the more overt polemics against Dan and Benjamin" (526). Following this line, Brettler declares, "A clear pattern falls into place, which mirrors chapter 1: It is the Judean judges who are unambiguously good, and the northern leaders who are bad. Noting that the judges, like the tribes in chaper 1, are described geographically from south to north is not sufficient—it is critical to realize that this geographical patterning is connected to a set of value judgments as in chapter 1" (113). O'Connell (*Rhetoric of the Book of Judges*, 268) perceives the rhetorical purpose of the book of Judges to be "idealizing the monarchy of Judah."

The present reading of Judges follows the line of thinking that sees a pro-Judean bias in the story, knowing full well that this is not as clear as the negative biases against Benjamin, Ephraim, Dan, Bethel.

Does this verse summarize a support for Josiah and his reform movements? The argument that this verse supports Josiah has been promoted on sociological and ideological grounds by Gale Yee ("Ideological Criticism") with much of the evidence on what is not said and on a restoration of the history of the Levites. Guillaume *(Waiting for Josiah),* following contemporary redaction-critical methodology and presuppositions, sets a major editorial stage of the book in Josiah's time, but has to find many other periods to account for the entire book. Josiah and Hezekiah may represent the closest Israel came to restoring unity and morality to the nation as Judges calls for, but they certainly did not achieve enough for a significant period of time to claim they are the king(s) who led Israel to do what was right in the eyes of Yahweh and not what was right in their own eyes.

From a commentator's viewpoint, Boling sees the unified book defending the cult in Jerusalem against other "competitors" and thus as a legitimation of King Josiah, but with the opening chapter and chaps. 19–21 stemming from a final exilic redactor. Block (66–67) tends toward a date under Manasseh or possibly Josiah but at least not before 700 B.C.E. based on 18:30. Amit (*Book of Judges*, 363–75) reverses traditional scholarship and sees Judges as witnessing to pre-Deuteronomistic language coming from about 700 B.C.E.

I have tried to demonstrate, with a growing number of scholars, that insufficient Deuteronomic/Deuteronomistic language appears in the book to warrant attributing the book to one or more Deuteronomistic History writers. The book, instead, represents an early collection of premonarchical oral narratives collected together in the early monarchy and "published" to support the Davidic monarchy, especially in the time of Jeroboam I's establishment of a northern alternative to David. Without a presupposition of a Deuteronomistic History including Judges, most justification for positioning the book of Judges in the time of Josiah or of the exilic/postexilic period vanishes. The narratives ring of real historical polemic, not of idealistic fiction writing when kingship is no longer an alternative for Israel.

Does this verse point into the exilic/postexilic period to call Israel back to a form of government without a king? Critique of Dumbrell's view above sets this theory on its end. Such a theory rests too strongly on acceptance of Noth's Deuteronomistic History or more recently of Cross's modification of Noth that sees the central portion of that work edited under Josiah. If more recent work done in this commentary and many of the recent studies on which it rests is at all correct, then this book is an independent whole with its own date, setting, and purpose apart from any later connections with a larger historical work. As an independent work, Judges shows much more affinity as a literary weapon launched in the middle of the monarchy's division than as a subtle, divided part of a larger literary work with many stages in its development. The exilic/postexilic view also builds on a conception of the development of canon in which an originally unified Judges and Samuel were separated at a late date. This understanding comes from a view that Judges functions as an introduction to Samuel rather than, the view of this commentary, that Judges is produced as a strong contrast to Joshua, the true model of leadership in Israel.

As questions abound, so do suggested answers. Wong (*Compositional Strategy*, 201) argues against Judg 21:25 advocating a human king because "this interpretation jars with reality depicted elsewhere in the book." The central narratives of the book—Gideon and Abimelech—deal with Israelite kings. For Wong the main problem with seeing 21:25 as referring positively to an Israelite king is that "one is hard pressed to come up with a Sitz im Leben in which an unqualified endorsement of the institution would make sense" (211). Thus Wong (212–23) settles for Yahweh as the one referred to as king. He follows Block (59, 476; compare Gunn and Fewell, 121) in seeing the negative reference in 21:25 to mean that the nation no longer recognized anyone, not even Yahweh, as king. The other side of that reality is the silence and lack of divine action in the latter part of the book (Wong, 216).

But certainly no reader of Judges would see Abimelech as any kind of legitimate king over all Israel. He was simply a local king in Shechem backed by only a small portion of the population for a very limited period of time. To back away from the issue by centering attention on Yahweh as king is to ignore the entire book's wrestling with the problem of human leadership and its search for a human leader who will follow the divine leader. For Judges as a whole, if not for each of its original sources and parts, Israel is a twelve-tribe whole created by Yahweh and needing a leader like Joshua, the prime example of leadership after Moses. Such a leader must be tied to the Torah of Moses, to the covenant with God, and to the unity of the people Israel.

Explanation

Proper interpretation of chaps. 17–21 and especially of the refrain at the front and back of the narrative leads to proper interpretation of the entire book. Until one understands the royal perspective of the book of Judges, one cannot understand the nature and intent of the book. In ancient Near Eastern society a king was expected to drive out enemies, maintain peace, make treaties, and maintain religious temples and rituals to preserve his subjects' right and opportunity to live on a land and farm it. A portion of the crop and service in the king's army seemed a small price to pay for a people in a land threatened by enemies on all sides. Israel needed a leader because Israel had no one to defend the land from enemy advances.

The Gideon narrative (Judg 6–9) opens unexpectedly with the appearance of a prophet. Normally, such an appearance would occur in the court of the king or in the central sanctuary. This prophet had no court in which to ply his trade and deliver his message. Israel had no spokesman to reply to the prophet. (Contrast Isa 7.) The prophet's central charge was religious: Israel had worshiped other gods (Judg 6:10). Gideon's extended call narrative paints a picture that makes one think of David and issues a call to a task fit for a king, while illustrating the weakness of leadership in Israel. By confronting Zebah and Zalmunnah, the kings of Midian, Gideon and his brothers displayed the outward appearance if not the royal title or all the privileges of royalty. Refusing the title of king, Gideon took up the booty of war and the insignia of royalty (8:26). Creating an ephod, he subtly put control of the priestly and possibly the prophetic functions, too, in his own hands.

In function Gideon was the royal priest/king/judge even if he did not assume the title. He played out the royal function by establishing a harem and producing a large family fit only for a king. His "orthodox theology" claimed God was the only king, but Gideon continued to exercise strong powers without such titles. Thus an interesting phenomenon results: the narrative refrains from saying Gideon judged Israel. Rather, it says Israel did not show the expected kindness to the "house of Jerubbaal" (8:35). Gideon did not just judge. He established a house. At worst, Gideon could be judged as having perverted the leadership role in Israel, making Israel play the harlot, having left no religious memory in Israel and having opened the door for the son of his concubine to usurp the office as well as the power. At best, he could be regarded as having established a house of leadership that Israel needed and as having done so within the parameters of orthodox theology.

The hereditary monarchy that Gideon declined, Abimelech assumed as a given. Abimelech began his life at the religious center Joshua had established, the city of

Shechem (Josh 8:30–35; 24:1–32). To gain the kingship, he killed his half brothers, setting the stage for later royal revolts, such as Jeroboam's in the northern kingdom. Jotham, Abimelech's youngest brother, escaped to taunt Abimelech with his fable, claiming that only those who had no value to God or men except the offer of refuge should consider the call of kingship. But such a task belonged to God as did the royal title. Thus Jotham showed kingship's other possibility—becoming a destroying fire against insincerity. Jotham presupposed kingship but saw that kingship must be based on a qualified candidate and a people committed to the royal house, that is, the royal dynasty.

Abimelech ruled as *śar* for three years over Israel (9:22), the verb pointing to an office different from that of king, especially king over Shechem. As king of Shechem and prince over Israel, Abimelech failed to meet Jotham's standards. The people crowning him also failed to meet those standards. Thus they could expect neither refuge nor rejoicing, only judgment by fire (9:23). The Jotham/Abimelech narrative leaves the impression that kingship under God done in sincerity and truth with the right man could work, but kingship done in bloodshed and suspicion has no chance.

Jephthah assumed new titles for the leader—chief and head—who acted on a par with foreign kings (11:11–12). He introduced another component of leadership not seen in Judges, the ability to recite salvation history. His problem lay not in his devotion to God, as with many of the other judges, but in his foolish piety, his making of a pious vow without thinking through the consequences.

Samson faced another enemy ruling over Israel—the Philistines. Unlike Jephthah, he refused to keep the vows given him by God. Doing what was right in his own eyes (14:3, 7), he showed no concern for tribes or nation, being a one-man show for his own pride and enjoyment.

Ultimately, the narrator gives us a set of narratives bracketed by the inclusio: no king; all did what was right in their own eyes (17:6; 21:25). Idolatry, dependence on religious office and tradition rather than on God's action and true worship, robbery, self-centered ambition, immoral actions so that Israelites find more security among foreigners than among Israelites, unspeakable immorality, destruction of a tribe and a city in Israel, kidnapping of Israelite women—all mark the life of the people of Israel as they do right in their own eyes. Phinehas, the agent of peace in Josh 22, becomes the agent of war (Judg 20:28).

Thus the call for a king in 21:25 seeks to stop Israel's selfish individualism. That call does not ring into a vacuum. The case for a king has been carefully built. The conditions under which kingship could work have been laid. The case for kingship in Israel rests on the negative qualities of those seeking kingship. Israel has to find God's way to kingship. Setting up personal power structures and imitating the neighboring monarchs with all their emblems of power and wealth are not the way.

The king must show true humility, unlike Gideon. The king must show true piety, unlike Jephthah. The king must show loyalty to a people, unlike Abimelech. The king must know that kingship is a function in Israel but not an exclusive office to meet selfish desires for power, riches, and a large family. The office belongs by rights to God. The human occupant must enter the office only as the people under God's leadership place him there, not through usurpation as had Abimelech.

The book of Judges was self-consciously a continuation of the book of Joshua in its beginning and a contrast to Joshua through its content. In its ending Judges is self-consciously a middle point leading forward to kingship. The author of Judges has written a self-contained work, but he knows the rest of the story. To find the qualities of the perfect leader, one must look back to Joshua. To find the nature of kingship as it might work for Israel, one must look forward to Samuel. To find the nature of a people without a king, one can readily explore the negative examples of Judges, examples which show Israel's drastic need created not by lack of divine leadership but through lack of devoted human leadership.

The final verses do not bring a resolution to the book's own narrative tension. If anything, they simply deepen the tragedy by escalating the tension, leaving Israel isolated under Philistine rule in individual groups serving false gods in false ways at false sanctuaries with false priests through false rituals. All the while, they ignore the commandments of Moses, the very standard by which God judges them. Joshua marched to an overwhelming success. Judges flounders to social, moral, military, political, and spiritual failure. Judges thus provides a complete narrative in structure as shown in the introduction, but the narrative remains open ended. It is an intentional interlude, pointing from the front backward to the days of Joshua, the ideal leader meditating on Moses' law, and from the back forward to the day of a true king, one not like the usurper Jeroboam. The new king from Judah would save Israel from the situation of unresolved tension, self-centered leadership, moral impasse, and international weakness.

Olson concludes: "The book of Judges is a sober and mature portrait of the necessity of human structures of leadership and power" ("Buber, Kingship, and the Book of Judges," 218). This is undoubtedly true. When Olson continues, saying, "the inevitability of their corruption and eventual decline, and the gracious willingness of God to work in and through such flawed human structures and communities in order to accomplish God's purpose," one hears a bit of modern theologizing that does not necessarily arise directly from the text. Yahweh constantly opened doors of hope to Israel, consistently called new leaders, and showered grace on the people. But Judges speaks much more of threat and judgment and punishment than of hope. It tells stories of failed leaders but yet points forward to a new king. It shows Israel could place no demands or controls on God but almost goes out of its way to avoid making theological statements about the deity.

Appendix of Tables

Table I.1 479

Table I.1. Comparison of Joshua and Judges

Topic	Joshua		Judges	
Death of leader	1:1	Moses	1:1	Joshua
Commission	1:2–9 1:10–11	Prepare army and meditate on book. Alert nation.	1:1–2 1:3	Judah to go up. Judah calls Simeon.
Call to unity	1:12–18	East commits to west.	1:4–36	Individual tribes fight and fail from south to north.
Divine revelation	2:1–24	Prostitute prophet shows God has given the land.	2:1–5	Angel reveals God will not give the land.
Divinely blessed leadership provides for future training	3:1–4:24	Joshua and priests lead people across Jordan, setting up stones to train new generation.	2:6–15	Leaderless generation abandons Yahweh and suffers defeat.
Cultic cleansing of the people	5:1–12	Circumcision and Passover for the people.	2:16–22	People serve other gods and transgress the covenant.
Reaffirmation of leader	5:13–15	Joshua affirmed after fashion of Moses.	3:1–6	God affirms foreign nations' role to test and punish Israel.
God uses victory to elevate leader	6:1–27	Obedient people defeat Jericho, and God makes Joshua famous.	3:7–11	Disobedient people cry to God for help, and God raises up Othniel, who brings victory by God's spirit.
Disobedient people experience punishment	7:1–26	Disobedient Achan brings defeat at Ai, but people follow God's directions to turn away divine anger.	3:12–31	Disobedient people bring defeat by foreign alliance, but God raises Benjaminite to deliver them with help of Ephraimites.
Obedience to war rules brings victory for God's leader and leaves memorial for future generations	8:1–29	Forgiven people under Joshua follow God's regulations and defeat Ai, leaving memorial to this day.	4:1–24	Disobedient people cry for divine help, and God uses women to defeat northern Canaanites.
Victors celebrate and worship	8:30–35	All Israel renews covenant and obeys Mosaic law at Shechem.	5:1–31	Deborah and Barak celebrate victory by six tribes while cursing and making fun of enemies.
Deceived people incorporate foreigners into worship	9:1–27	Fearful Gibeonites deceive Israel, but Joshua incorporates them as temple servants into Israelite worship.	6:1–32	Disobedient Israel suffers from Midianites, hears prophetic judgment, and gains fearful leader, who turns Baal cult to Yahweh cult.

Table I.1. Comparison of Joshua and Judges (continued)

Topic	Joshua		Judges	
Joshua leads Israel to deliver treaty partners against foreign alliance	10:1–15	Joshua keeps Israel true to treaty with Gibeonites, and God provides miraculous deliverance.	6:33–8:3	Fearful Gideon calls out Israelite allies but tests God before defeating foreign alliance and alienating Ephraimites.
God gives victories over foreign kings	10:16–43	God gives hiding kings to Joshua, quiets enemies, and fights victoriously against southern opponents.	8:4–21	Pursuing kings, Gideon finds no support from "Israelite" cities east of Jordan or from his own son as he defeats the kings.
Leader's final response to victory and law	11:1–12:24	Following Moses' law, Joshua defeats northern kings, completes conquest of land, and gives land to the people.	8:22–35	Gideon outwardly refuses kingship, acclaims God as king, but sets up royal lifestyle and pagan cult site, leading people astray to the Baal of the covenant.
The land that remains, the land already divided, and the role of the Levitic priests	13:1–33	God commands aged Joshua to ignore land that remains, remember land Moses divided east of Jordan, and provide for priests as God's inheritance.		(no equivalent)
The southern inheritance	14:1–15:63	Caleb's reward, Judah's inheritance, Caleb's presents to his daughter, and failure in Jerusalem constitute inheritance.		(Judah, Caleb material incorporated in 1:1–20)
The Josephite inheritances	16:1–17:18	Joseph tribes' lot including Canaanites among Ephraim, women inheriting in Manasseh according to Moses' command, and blessing on Josephites' demand for more are inheritance.	9:1–10:2	Shechem, worship center in Joseph tribes, becomes center of violence, family slaughter, and ruin in Abimelech's demand for kingship; Tola from Ephraim rises to deliver Israel.
Benjaminite inheritance and Simeon within Judah	18:1–19:9	Joshua rebukes slackness of Israel, recalls eastern allotments, has land charted, and gives lots to Benjamin and Simeon in Judah.	10:3–16	Jair, eastern judge, lives like king; Ammonites fight Judah, Benjamin, and Ephraim; apostasy, cry for help, divine refusal, repentence, divine compassion.
Northern tribes' inheritances	19:10–39	Joshua allots land to Zebulun, Issachar, Asher, and Naphtali.	10:17–13:15	Jephthah disputes sacred history with and defeats Ammonites, sacrifices daughter, defeats northern Ephraimites, and is followed by northern judges Ibzan, Elon, and Abdon.

Table I.1 continued 481

Table I.1. Comparison of Joshua and Judges *(continued)*

Topic	Joshua		Judges	
Dan's inheritance	19:40–48	Joshua allots land to Dan, who lost territory and went to take Leshem.	14:1–16:27	Samson, the Danite, ignores his people, flirts with Philistines, finally dies, and thus sets stage for Dan to lose western territory.
Cities of refuge	20:1–9	Joshua assigns cities of refuge for accused murderers.	16:28–31	Philistine house of worship becomes Samson's refuge in death.
Cities of Levites and theological summary	21:1–45	Joshua allots cities to landless Levites, and summary shows God fulfills promises.	17:1–18:31	With no Israelite king, landless Danites rob Judahite Levite with Mosaic connections from idolatrous Micah while God was in Shiloh (compare Josh 18:1–21:9).
Resolving tribal feuds	22:1–34	Phinehas and chiefs mediate altar dispute between east and west, testifying that Yahweh is God.	19:1–20:48	United Israel destroys tribe of Benjamin over hospitality issue.
Covenant warning	23:1–16	Joshua warns Israel of disaster for breaking covenant.	21:1–23	Israelites religiously circumvent covenant among themselves to let remnant of Benjaminites steal wives during festival at Shiloh.
Covenant renewal and return home	24:1–28	Joshua renews covenant between Israel and God and sends people to their inheritances.	21:24–25	People return home to do what is right in their own eyes without a king.
Obedience to past and death of leaders	24:29–33	Israel buries Joseph's bones and then serves God until Joshua, Eleazar, and their generation dies.		Past forgotten, no leaders to bury, no obedience to report (compare chap. 2).

Table I.2. Thematic inconsistency in the book of Judges

Schema element	Occurrences in narrative	Occurrences in Dtr Hist (!)
"Sons of Israel did evil," וַיַּעֲשׂוּ בְנֵי־יִשְׂרָאֵל אֶת־הָרַע (2:11)	Othniel, 3:7 Ehud, 3:12 Deborah, 4:1 Gideon, 6:1 Jephthah, 10:6 Samson, 13:1	Num 32:13; Deut 4:25; 9:18; 17:2; 31:29; 1 Sam 15:19; 2 Sam 12:9; 1 Kgs 11:6; 14:22; 15:26; 34; 16:19, 25, 30; 21:20, 25; 22:52; 2 Kgs 3:2; 8:18, 27; 13:2, 11; 14:24; 15:9, 18, 24, 28; 17:2, 17; 21:2, 6, 15–16, 20; 23:32, 37; 24:9, 19; cf. Num 32:13; 2 Kgs 21:9; 2 Chr 12:14; 21:6; 22:4; 29:6; 33:2, 6, 9, 22; 36:5, 9, 12; Neh 9:28; Pss 34:16 (17); 51:4 (6); Prov 2:14; Eccl 5:1 (4:17); 8:11–12; Isa 56:2; 65:12; 66:4; Jer 7:30; 18:10; 32:30; 52:2; Mal 2:17
"Served Baal(s)," וַיַּעַבְדוּ אֶת־הַבְּעָלִים (2:11, 13; 3:6)	Othniel, 3:7 Jephthah, 10:6, 10, 13	1 Sam 12:10; 1 Kgs 16:31; 22:53 (54); 2 Kgs 10:18–19, 21–23; 17:16
"Abandoned Yahweh," וַיַּעַזְבוּ אֶת־יְהוָה (2:12, 13)	Othniel, 3:7 Jephthah, 10:6, (13)	Josh 24:20; 1 Sam (8:8); 12:10; 1 Kgs 9:9; (11:33); 2 Kgs 21:22; (22:17); cf. Deut 29:25; Josh 24:16; 1 Kgs 6:13; 8:57; 18:18; 19:10, 14; 2 Kgs 17:16; 2 Chr 7:22; (12:1); 21:10; (24:18); 24:20, 24; 28:6; Ps 38:21 (22); Isa 1:4, 28; 65:11; Jer 2:17, 19; (22:9)
"Followed after other gods," וַיֵּלְכוּ אַחֲרֵי אֱלֹהִים אֲחֵרִים (2:12, 19)		Deut (6:14); 8:19; 11:28; 13:2 (3); 28:14; 1 Kgs 11:10; cf. (Josh 23:16); (2 Chr 7:19); Jer 7:6, 9; 11:10; 13:10; 16:11; 25:6; 35:15
"They worshiped them," וַיִּשְׁתַּחֲווּ לָהֶם (2:12, 17, 19)		Deut 4:19; 5:9; 8:19; 11:16; 17:3; 29:26; 30:17; Josh 23:7, 16; 1 Kgs 9:6, 9; 11:33; 16:31; 22:53 (54); 2 Kgs 17:16, 35; 21:3, 21; cf. Exod 20:5; 23:24; 32:8; 34:14; Lev 26:1; Num 25:2; 2 Chr 7:19, 22; 25:14; 33:3; Pss 81:9 [10]; 106:19; Isa 2:8, 20; 44:15, 17; 46:6; Jer 1:16; 8:2; 13:10; 16:11; 22:9; 25:6; Ezek 8:16; Mic 5:12 (13); Zeph 1:5
"They angered Yahweh," וַיַּכְעִסוּ אֶת־יְהוָה (2:12)		1 Kgs 14:9, 15; 15:30; 16:2, 7, 13, 26, 33; 21:22; 22:53 (54); 17:11, 17; 21:6, 15; 22:17; 23:19, 26; 2 Chr 28:25; Jer 7:19
"They served the Ashtaroth," וַיַּעַבְדוּ לָעַשְׁתָּרוֹת (2:13)	Jephthah, 10:6	1 Sam 7:3 12:10; 1 Kgs 11:5, 33; 23:13
"Yahweh burned with anger against Israel," וַיִּחַר־אַף יְהוָה בְּיִשְׂרָאֵל (2:14, 20)	Othniel, 3:8 Jephthah, 10:7	2 Kgs 13:3; cf. Num 25:3; 32:13

Table I.2 continued 483

Table I.2. Thematic inconsistency in the book of Judges *(continued)*

Schema element	Occurrences in narrative	Occurrences in Dtr Hist (!)
"He gave them into the hand of plunderers," ביד־שסים (2:14)		2 Kgs 17:20
"He sold them into the hand of their enemies," ביד איביהם (2:14)	Othniel, 3:8 Deborah, 4:2 Samson, 10:7	Deut 32:30; 1 Sam 12:9; cf. Joel 3:8 (4:8)
"The hand of Yahweh was against them," יד־יהוה (2:15)		Deut 2:15
"The hand of Yahweh was against them for evil," יד יהוה היתה בם לרעה (2:15)		
"They were in extreme trouble," צר להם מאד (2:15)	Cf. Othniel, 3:9	Cf. 1 Sam 28:15; 2 Sam 24:14; 1 Chr 21:13
"Yahweh raised up judges," ויקם יהוה שפטים (2:16, 18)		
"They delivered them from the hand," ויושיעם (2:16, 18)	Othniel, 3:9 Gideon, 8:22 Cf. Jephthah, 10:12	1 Sam 7:8; 2 Kgs 14:27; cf. Neh 9:27; Ps 106:10; Isa 37:20
"They did not obey," לא שמעו (2:17, 20)	Gideon, 6:10 Jephthah, (11:17, 28)	Deut 1:43; 8:20; 9:23; 11:28; 18:19; 21:18; 28:15, 45, 62; 30:17; Josh 1:18; 5:6; Judg 2:2; 1 Sam 2:25; 12:15; 15:19; 28:18; 1 Kgs 12:15; 20:36; 2 Kgs 17:14; 18:12; 21:9; 22:13; cf. Gen 42:21–22; Exod 4:1, 8–9; 6:9, 12; 7:4, 13, 16, 22; 8:15, 19; 9:12; 11:9; 16:20; Lev 26:14, 18, 27; Num 14:22; et al.
"They became harlots with other gods," אלהים אחרים (2:17)	Gideon, 8:33	Deut 31:16; cf. Exod 34:15; Lev 17:7; 20:5–6; 1 Chr 5:25; Ezek 6:9

Table I.2. Thematic inconsistency in the book of Judges (*continued*)

Schema element	Occurrences in narrative	Occurrences in Dtr Hist (!)
"They turned quickly from the way," סרו מהר מן הדרך (2:17)		Deut 9:12; 16; 11:28; 31:29; cf. Exod 32:8; Isa 30:11; Mal 2:8
"Obey commandments," שמע מצות (2:17; 3:4)		Deut 11:13, 27–28; 28:13; cf. Neh 9:16, 29
"Yahweh was with," היה עם (2:18)	Gideon, 6:12–13	Judg 1:22; 1 Sam 16:18; 18:12, 14, 28; 20:13; 2 Sam 7:3; 2 Kgs 1:37; 18:7; cf. Gen 26:28; Exod 10:10; Num 14:43; Ruth 2:4; 1 Chr 9:20; 22:11, 16; 2 Chr 15:2; 17:3; 19:11; 20:17; 25:7; Zech 10:5
"Yahweh showed compassion," נחם יהוה (2:18)		2 Sam 24:16; cf. Gen 6:6; Exod 32:14; Jer 26:13; 26:19; Amos 7:3, 6
"They behaved more corruptly," השחית (2:19)		Deut 4:16, 25; 31:29; cf. 2 Chr 26:16; Isa 1:4; 11:9; 65:25; Jer 6:28
"They have disobeyed my covenant," עברו את בריתי (2:20)		Deut 17:2; Josh 7:11, 15; 23:16; 2 Kgs 18:12; Jer 34:18; Hos 6:7; 8:1
"I will not drive out," לא אוריש (2:21, 23)	Jephthah, 11:23–24	Deut 4:38; 7:17; 9:3–5; 11:23; 18:12; Josh 3:10; 13:6, 13; 14:12; 15:63; 16:10; 17:13, 18; 23:5, 9, 13; Judg 1:19–21, 27–33; 1 Sam 2:7; 1 Kgs 14:24; 21:26; 2 Kgs 16:3; 17:8; 21:2; cf. Exod 34:24; Num 32:21; 33:52, 55; 2 Chr 20:7; 28:3; 33:2; Ps 44:2 (3); Zech 9:4
"To test," נסה (2:22; 3:1, 4)		Deut 8:2,16; 13:3; cf. Gen 22:1; Exod 15:25; 16:4; 20:20; 2 Chr 32:31; Ps 26:2
"To guard or keep the way of Yahweh," שמר דרך יהוה (2:22)		2 Sam 22:22; 1 Kgs 2:4; 8:25; cf. Gen 3:24; 18:19; 2 Chr 6:16; Pss 18:21 (22); 37:34; 39:1 (2); Prov 16:17; Mal 2:9
"They take (foreign) daughters," לקח את בנותיהם (3:6)		1 Kgs 3:1; 16:31; cf. Gen 27:46; 28:1, 6; Exod 34:16

Table I.3 485

Table I.3. New elements from the "ideal narrative"

Schema element	Occurrences in narrative	Occurrences in Dtr Hist (!)
They served the enemy king a definite number of years, וַיַּעַבְדוּ בְנֵי־יִשְׂרָאֵל מִסְפַּר שָׁנִים (3:8)	Ehud, 3:14; Abimelech, 9:28	1 Sam 1:11; 17:9; 2 Kgs 18:7; 25:24
"Sons of Israel cried out to Yahweh," וַיִּזְעֲקוּ בְנֵי־יִשְׂרָאֵל אֶל־יְהוָה (4:3)	Othniel, 3:9; Ehud, 3:15; Gideon, 6:6–7; Jephthah, 10:10; cf. 10:14	1 Sam 7:9; 12:8, 10; cf. Exod 2:23; 1 Chr 5:20; 2 Chr 18:31; 20:9; 32:20; Neh 9:4, Pss 22:5 (6); 107:13, 19; 142:1, 5 (2, 6); Lam 3:8; Ezek 9:8; 11:13; Hos 7:14; Joel 1:14; Mic 3:4; Hab 1:2; 28
"Yahweh raised up a deliverer," וַיָּקֶם יְהוָה מוֹשִׁיעַ (cf. 2:16)	Othniel, 3:9; Ehud, 3:15; Gideon, cf. 6:36; Jephthah, cf. 12:3	Deut 22:27; 28:29, 31; 1 Sam 11:3; 2 Kgs 13:5; cf. Isa 19:20
"The Spirit of Yahweh (God) was upon him," וַתְּהִי עָלָיו רוּחַ יְהוָה	Othniel, 3:10; Gideon, 6:34; Jephthah, 11:29; Samson, 13:25; 14:6, 19; 15:14	1 Sam 10:6, 10; 11:6; 16:13–14, 23; 19:20, 23; 2 Sam 23:2; 1 Kgs 18:12; 22:24; 2 Kgs 2:16; cf. Gen 1:2; 6:3; 41:38; Exod 3:13; 35:31; Num 11:29; 24:2; 2 Chr 15:1; 18:23; 20:14; 24:20; Pss 104:30; 139:7; 143:10; Isa 11:2; 30:1; 34:16; 40:13; 42:1; 44:3; 48:16; 59:19, 21; 63:14; Ezek 11:5, 24; 36:27; 37:1, 14; 39:29; Joel 2:28 (3:1); Mic 2:7; 3:8; Zech 4:6; 7:12
"He judged Israel," וַיִּשְׁפֹּט אֶת־יִשְׂרָאֵל	Othniel, 3:10; Deborah, 4:4; Abimelech, 10:2 (Tola); 10:3 (Jair); Jephthah, 12:7; 12:8–9 (Ibzan); 12:11 (Elon); 12:13–14 (Abdon); Samson, 15:20; 16:31	1 Sam 4:18; 7:6, 15–17; 8:2; 2 Kgs 23:22; cf. Ruth 1:1; Hos 7:7; Amos 2:3; Mic 5:1 (4:14)
"The land was quiet," וַתִּשְׁקֹט הָאָרֶץ	Othniel, 3:11; Ehud, 3:30; Deborah, 5:31; Gideon, 8:28	Josh 11:23; 14:15; 2 Chr 14:1, 6 (13:23; 14:5)
Judge died	Othniel, 3:11; Ehud, 4:1; Gideon, 8:32–33; Abimelech, 9:54–55; 10:2 (Tola); 10:5 (Jair); Jephthah, 12:7; 12:10 (Ibzan); 12:12 (Elon); 12:15 (Abdon); Samson, 16:30	Josh 24:29, 33; Judg 2:8, 19; 1 Sam 4:11, 18

Table I.4. The Israelites' failures in the book of Judges

Judges	Leader	Cultic failure	Moral failure	Political failure
3:7–11	Othniel	Forgot God; served Baals		
3:12–30	Ehud	Did evil in God's sight		
4:1–24	Deborah			Weak masculine leadership bringing honor to feminine leader
	Barak		Refused to answer God's summons alone	
5:1–31	Deborah and Barak			Lack of tribal unity
6:1–8:35	Gideon	People did evil; leader created ephod for false worship and acted contrary to theological pronouncement (8:27)	Did not obey God (6:10)	Complaining leader (6:13) without faith (6:15), fearful (6:27; 7:10–11)
9:1–57	Abimelech		Wicked (9:56)	Usurped power and killed brothers
10:6–12:7	Jephthah	Foolish vow and disastrous sacrifice (11:30–31); people did evil and served foreign gods (10:6, 10, 13)	Leader was son of a harlot	Leader hated by people (11:7)
13:1–16:31	Samson	Did evil; violated Nazirite vow to God; failed to take God's calling seriously	Gave in to lust and women's requests and wiles	Acted solo without helping Israel

Table I.5 487

Table I.5. Chronology from the exodus through Solomon's reign

Passage	Leadership	Number of years
Num 14:33; Deut 2:7 (cf. 2:14; Josh 14:7)	Moses in wilderness wandering	40
Josh 14:10 (cf. Deut 2:14; Josh 14:7)	Caleb and Joshua conquering land	(45–7=) 38 (7+ yrs. of conquest)
Judg 3:8	Cushan-Rishathaim controls Israel	8
Judg 3:11	Rest for land under Othniel	40
Judg 3:14	Eglon of Moab controls Israel	18
Judg 3:30	Rest for land under Ehud	80
Judg 4:3	Jabin of Hazor controls Israel	20
Judg 5:31	Rest for land under Deborah/Barak	40
Judg 6:1	King of Midian controls Israel	7
Judg 8:28	Rest for land under Gideon	40
Judg 9:22	Abimelech rules Israel	3
Judg 10:2	Tola rules Israel	23
Judg 10:3	Jair rules Israel	22
Judg 10:8	Philistines and Ammonites control Israel	18
Judg 12:7	Jephthah rules Israel	6
Judg 12:9	Ibzan rules Israel	7
Judg 12:11	Elon rules Israel	10
Judg 12:14	Abdon rules Israel	8
Judg 13:1	Philistine king(s) control Israel	40
Judg 15:20 (16:31)	Samson rules Israel	20
Judg 17–21	Anarchy in Israel	?
1 Sam 4:18	Eli rules Israel	40
Josephus, *Ant.* 6.13.5 (cf. 1 Sam 7:2)	Samuel rules Israel	12
1 Sam 13:1 (broken text)	Saul rules Israel	?
Acts 13:21	Saul rules Israel	40
1 Kgs 2:11	David rules Israel	40 (7 in Hebron; 33 in Jerusalem)
1 Kgs 6:1	Solomon rules Israel	4
TOTAL		624
Total from 1 Kgs 6:1		480
Total from Josephus, *Ant.* 20.10.1		612
Total from Josephus, *Ant.* 8.3.1		592

Table I.6. Use of assumptions to reconcile chronology in Judges

Type of assumption	Example of problem	Scholars
Rounded numbers	Times of rest	Noth, *Überlieferungsgeschichtliche Studien;* de Vaux, *Early History of Israel;* Boling; Soggin; Gray; Block; Provan, Long, and Longman, *Biblical History*
Symbolic numbers	Twelve generations	Wellhausen, *Prolegomena;* Burney; Block; Provan, Long, and Longman, *Biblical History*
Forty-year generation	1. 1 Kgs 6:1 2. Active life span of warrior	1. Wellhausen, *Prolegomena;* Burney 2. Noth, *Überlieferungsgeschichtliche Studien*
Overlapping periods	1. Philistines and minor judges 2. Philistines and Samuel and Saul 3. Eli and Samuel 4. Imprecise 5. Ammonites and Philistines and Samuel and Eli all overlap 6. Shamgar and Ehud; Ammonites and Philistines, including Jephthah, Ibzan, Elon, and Samson 7. Any combination possible, even Deborah and Samson or all the minor judges 8. Philistines, Samson, Samuel, Eli	1. Wellhausen, *Prolegomena* 2. Noth, *Überlieferungsgeschichtliche Studien* 3. Burney 4. Howard, *Introduction;* Kaiser, *History* 5. Provan, Long, and Longman, *Biblical History* 6. Steinmann, *JETS* 48 (2005) 491–500 7. Soggin 8. Galil, *Bib* 85 (2004) 413–21
Limited authority	Local judges	Wellhausen, *Prolegomena;* Moore; Howard, *Introduction;* Kaiser, *History*
Lack of chronological intention	Developed by geographical adjacency rather than chronological adjacency	Wellhausen, *Prolegomena;* Moore; Boling; Warner, *VT* 28 (1978) 455–63; Block
Ignoring years of foreign oppression	Edomite, Midianite, Canaanite, Ammonite, Philistine	Moore; (Nöldeke, "Chronologie")
Omit section on literary grounds	1. Abimelech 2. Eli (1 Sam 4:18b) 3. Abimelech, Shamgar, minor judges 4. Minor judges	1. Moore; Gray 2. Noth, *Überlieferungsgeschichtliche Studien* 3. Burney 4. Budde; Gray; Galil, *Bib* 85 (2004) 413–21
Omit illegitimate rulers	1. Saul 2. Shamgar, Abimelech	1. Moore 2. Richter, *Bearbeitungen*
Artificial reckoning system	1 Kgs 6:1	Burney; de Vaux, *Early History*
Key on Judg 11:26	Demands early exodus (1446 B.C.E.)	Howard, *Introduction;* Kaiser, *History;* cf. Warner, *VT* 28 (1978) 455–63; Provan, Long, and Longman, *Biblical History*
Accept biblical numbers as fitting Near Eastern system	Precise dates for every part of list	Steinmann, *JETS* 48 (2005) 491–500
Interpretation hopeless	1. Hopeless 2. 420-year total too high in view of historical critical/literary results	1. Block; Burney 2. Boling; Soggin

Table I.7 / Table I.8 489

Table I.7.
Richter's calculation of the historical years of Israel's history

Wilderness years	40
Joshua and Elders	5
Oppression of Aram	8
Othniel	40
Moabites	18
Ehud	80
Jabin	20
Deborah and Barak	40
Midianites	7
Gideon	40
Tola	23
Jair	22
Jephthah	6
Ibzan	7
Elon	10
Abdon	8
Samson	20
Eli	40
Saul	2
David	40
Four years of Solomon	4
Total	**480**

Table I.8. Steinmann's calculation of the historical years of Israel

Date	Event	Date	Event
1406–1400	Joshua's conquest		
1399–1379	Joshua and the elders die		
1378–1371	Oppression by Cushan-Rishathaim		
1371–1332	Othniel cycle		
1332–1315	Eglon's oppression		
1315–1236	Ehud/Shamgar cycle		
1236–1217	Jabin's oppression		
1217–1178	Deborah		
1178–1172	Midianite oppression		
1172–1133	Gideon cycle		
1133–1131	Abimelech		
1131–1109	Tola		
1109–1088	Jair		
1099–1060	Eli as priest and judge		
1088–1071	Ammonite oppression	1088–1049	Philistine oppression
		1088–1083	Jephthah
		1083–1077	Ibzan
		1077–1068	Elon
		1068–1061	Abdon
		1049–1030(?)	Samson
1060–1049	Samuel as sole judge		
1048–1021	Saul as king with Samuel		
1021–1009	Saul reigns alone		
1009–970	David		
970–967	Solomon to building of temple		

Table I.9. A proposed relative chronology for the book of Judges

Passage and judge	Enemy	Central cult/tribe	Relative chronology
Judg 1 (Othniel)	Canaanites	(Jerusalem)/Judah, Joseph	Initial mop-up efforts after initial conquest; perhaps differing time periods beginning before Joshua's death; Joseph tribes not divided (?)
Judg 3:7–11 Othniel	Cushan-Rishathaim of Syria	None/(Judah)	Relation to Caleb; not fighting northern Canaanites
Judg 3:31 Shamgar	Philistines	None/Unknown	Early victory over Philistines, who have not established dominance
Judg 4–5 Deborah (and Barak)	North-central Canaanites	Mount Tabor (?)/Zebulun and Naphtali	After Shamgar; Kenite relationships; still fighting Canaanites; no established central shrine; break-up of tribal allegiances; Zebulun and Naphtali strong
Judg 13–16 Samson	Philistines (and Judah?)	None/Dan	Philistine domination; weak tribe of Dan in southwest; tribal cooperation disintegrated
Judg 17–18 (no judge)	Dan versus Levite Micah (both enemies; no heroes)	Dan/Dan	Dissolution of tribal cooperation; Dan lost territory in southwest and forced north (compare 5:17); Yahwistic religion totally compromised; Jonathan, grandson of Moses, as priest
Judg 3:12–31 Ehud	King Eglon of Moab	Gilgal (?)/Benjamin (Ephraim)	Benjamin in good graces, strong; Gilgal important
Judg 19–21 (no judge)	Benjamin, Jabesh Gilead, Shiloh	Bethel/Judah; elders of Israel	Benjamin weakened but has time to recover before Saul; Shiloh insignificant; assembly of tribes still functioning
Judg 10–12 Jephthah	Ammonites, (Ephraim)	Eastern Mizpah (?)/Gilead (and east Manasseh?)	Break-up of east/west ties solidified by Joshua (Josh 22); Gilead assumed leadership in east as in Judg 19–21
Judg 6–8 Gideon	Midianites (Penuel, Succoth, Ephraim)	Ophrah/West Manasseh, Asher, Naphtali, Zebulun	No central cult; east/west conflict; continued conflict with Ephraim; central tribes still strong
Judg 9 Abimelech	Sons of Gideon; Shechem; Thebez	Shechem (conflated worship with El or Baal and Yahweh traditions?)/West Manasseh	Internal fighting escalates; ancient central sanctuary for Joshua deteriorated to conflated or pure Baal worship; connection to Gideon

Table I.10 491

Table I.10. Dating the book of Judges and its sources

Modern author	Original narratives	J or original collection	E or secondary collection	JE or first major editor	Deuteronomist	Second Deuteronomist	Final additions
Keil, 1865	Under Saul or first years of David's reign						
Moore, 1895		Shortly after 900: J	Shortly after 800: E; about 700: E2	About 650: JE with all but Othniel	Shortly after 600: 2:6–16:31 with Othniel; without Abimelech, minor judges		About 400: joined JE and D, restoring 1:1–2:5, chaps. 9, 17–21, and minor judges
Burney, 1918		850	750	700	RE^2 about 650	Exile	Priestly in exile or later
Noth, *Überlieferungsgeschichtliche Studien*, 1943	Individual narratives, even "doublets"	Collection of stories in two complexes: hero stories and annotated list of minor judges			One Dtr compiled entire history		11:12–28 later addition
Richter, *Bearbeitungen*, 1963–64	Individual legends	Book of Saviors or Deliverers: Ehud, Barak, Gideon, Abimelech—in reign of Jehu (841–14) by prophetic circles	Holy war edition	Rdt^1 Adds framework	Rdt^2 adds Othniel and sharpens retribution	Postexilic Dtr^G additions to chaps. 2 and 10, minor judges, Samson	Chaps. 1, 17–21 later additions

Table I.10. Dating the book of Judges and its sources (*continued*)

Modern author	Original narratives	J or original collection	E or secondary collection	JE or first major editor	Deuteronomist	Second Deuteronomist	Final additions
Gray, 1967	Contemporary oral sagas collected in local tribal centers: Ehud, Gideon, Jephthah, Othniel; hero legends with mythical influence: Samson & Shamgar; local saga and cult hymn: Deborah	Collection from fast and penitence liturgy—Othniel, Ehud, Deborah and Barak, Gideon, Jephthah—with frame (3:7-11, 12-15a, 30; 4:1a, 2a, 3a, 23-24; 5:31c; 6:1-2a, 7-10; 8:28, 33-35; 10:6-16; 11:33b)			Ca. 600: 1:1-3:6, Abimelech, Samson cycle, minor judges, Shamgar	Chaps. 17-18 based on Dan traditions from 734 to 732	Chaps. 19-21: postexilic redactor based on two old sources from Mizpah and Bethel
Cundall, 1968	Contemporary oral traditions			980 written; possible later addition of chaps. 9 & 16-21; then 1:1-2:5	Exile: minor shaping		
Boling, 1975	Premonarchic folklore style of stories	Formation of early Israelite epic		Pragmatic, didactic edition, eighth century	Seventh century with 2:1-5; 6:7-10; 10:6-16; 16:1-18:31	Sixth century with 1:1-36; 19:1-21:25	
Van Seters, *In Search of History*, 1983	Ancient folk legends				Dtr History	Chaps. 17-21	Priestly additions: 1:1-2:5; 2:22-3:4; 10:1-5; 12:8-15
Webb, 1987				One of edited series of books, each an independent literary unit			

Table I.10 continued 493

Table I.10. Dating the book of Judges and its sources (*continued*)

Modern author	Original narratives	J or original collection	E or secondary collection	JE or first major editor	Deuteronomist	Second Deuteronomist	Final additions
Becker, *Richterzeit und Königtum*, 1990	Anecdotes and sagas about heroes	None			2:11–16:31 DtrH	DtrN adds 1:21, 27–36; 2:1–5; 8:24–27; 17–18 and moral notes to chaps. 2, 3, 9	R² supplies 1:1–18, 22–26; 19:1–21:25
Wolf, 1992				Written by associate of Samuel before David's capture of Jerusalem	Some later additions		
O'Connell, *Rhetoric*, 1996				Basic book collected and written early in David's reign			
Olson, 1998	Local tribal hero stories			Hezekiah shaping	Josiah editing		
Block, 1999	Secondary "judge" list or annal, local primary hero stories, conquest records, prophetic traditions, victory hymn	Anthology of hero stories, collection of prophetic traditions in prophetic circles, Priestly records behind chaps. 17–21 collected at Shiloh and temple		Materials collected and final book written about 650 under Manasseh by prophetic figure in Judah			
Schmid, *Erzväter und Exodus*, 1999							Judges integrated into Dtr in second century

Table I.10. Dating the book of Judges and its sources (*continued*)

Modern author	Original narratives	J or original collection	E or secondary collection	JE or first major editor	Deuteronomist	Second Deuteronomist	Final additions
Campbell/ O'Brien, *Unfolding*, 2000	Deliverance collection: Ehud, Deborah/ Barak, Gideon	Other pre-Dtr material			Josianic Dtr	Revisions with national focus	Later revisions
Brown, 2000	Original tribal stories; joined into cycles like Samson cycle, Jephthah cycle	Judges stories collected without minor judges			Dtr collection preexilic after Josiah with 2:6–3:6 framework	Dtr editing exilic; 1:1–2:5 added; chaps. 17–21 added here or later	
Kraz, *Komposition*, 2000 (Eng. 2005)	Loose collection without narrative thread or frame				Secondary Dtr[8] in 3:7–16:31 adding framework and binding Exodus-Joshua with Samuel-Kings	Further Dtr[s]	Priestly additions
Müller, *Micah Story*, 2001	Early narratives				Early exilic morality teacher takes up Deuteronomic concerns		
Younger, 2002	Blocks of material about each of the judges				Exilic or postexilic final book		
McCann, 2002	1200–1020 B.C.E. original stories	Propaganda supporting David over Saul			722 B.C.E. original Dtr; later editions 2:6–3:6	Exilic or postexilic final edition	

Table I.10 continued   495

Table I.10. Dating the book of Judges and its sources *(continued)*

Modern author	Original narratives	J or original collection	E or secondary collection	JE or first major editor	Deuteronomist	Second Deuteronomist	Final additions
Guillaume, *Waiting for Josiah*, 2004	Original stories	Book of Saviors: Ehud, Barak, Deborah, Gideon, Abimelech—720 in Bethel	Edited under Manasseh after 700: 1:4–18, 27–34; 3:8–10*	Josiah's Judges about 620: 1:35–36; 2:1–5, 11–19; 6:7–10; 10:1–3; 12:9–15; 17:1–18:30	Babylonian Bethel demythologization about 580: 10:6–11; 11:29–16:31	Jerusalem and Bethel insertions about 500: 1:22–26; 19–21	Dtr created about 200: 1:1–3, 10–21, 36; 2:6–10; 4:5; 21:25; then additions about 150: 2:20–3:6; 4:11, 17, 21; 5:24; 11:12–28
Stone, *DOTHB*, 2005	Deliverers stories	Stories remembered and celebrated	Stories of emerging order, the moralist	Voice of the monarchy			
Assis, *Self-Interest*, 2005	Premonarchy						
Wong, 2006	Sources of central section				Self-contained Deuteronomic story of unstated date but independent of other Deuteronomic materials		
Ryan, 2007						Sixth-century editor with long line of storytellers and editors	
Niditch, 2008	Epic-bardic voice of twelfth century				Theologian's voice of seventh century akin to northern Levites	Humanist voice from postexilic era	

Table I.11. The narratives of Judges

Judge's name	Judge's tribe	Battle location(s)	Enemy(ies)	Tribes involved
Othniel	Kenaz (Judah?)	(not given)	Cushan-Rishathaim of Aram-Naharaim/Syria (?)	Israelites
Ehud	Benjamin	City of Palms	Eglon of Moab with Ammonites and Amalekites	Israelites of hill country of Ephraim
Shamgar	Anath (Philistia?)	(not given)	Philistines	(not given)
Deborah/ Barak	Ephraim (?) and Naphtali	Mount Tabor, Wadi Kishon, Harosheth-ha-goim, Kedesh; in poem Taanach by Megiddo	Jabin of Canaan in Hazor with Sisera of Harosheth-ha-goim	Naphtali and Zebulun joined in poem by Ephraim, Benjamin, Machir, Issachar with Reuben, Gilead, Dan; Asher condemned for not participating; Meroz also cursed
Gideon	Abiezer in Manasseh	Ophrah, Valley of Jezreel, hill of Moreh, Beth-shittah to Abel-meholah near Tabbath, Beth-barrah, Succoth, Penuel, Karkor, Nobah, Jogbehah	Midian with Amalekites and people of the east; as far as Gaza	Abiezrites then Manasseh, Asher, Zebulun, and Naphtali; later Ephraim
Abimelech	Abiezer in Manasseh	Shechem, Ophrah, Beer, Arumah, Mount Zalmon, Thebez	Shechem, Thebez	Worthless men
Tola	Issachar	Shamir in hill country of Ephraim		
Jair	Gilead	(Havvoth-Jair, Kamon)		
Jephthah	Gilead	Gilead, Mizpah, Aroer, Minnith, Abel-keramim, Zaphon	Ammonites, Ephraim	Israelites, Gilead, Manasseh, Ephraim
Ibzan	Bethlehem (of Zebulun?)			
Elon	Zebulun			
Abdon	Pirathon of Ephraim			
Samson	Dan	Zorah, Eshtaol, Timnah, Ashkelon, Etam, Lehi, Gaza, Hebron, Valley of Sorek	Philistines, Judah	(works alone)

Table 1.1 497

Table 1.1. Syntactical breaks in Judg 1

Passage in Judges	Syntactical form	Central character	Function	Notes
1:1	Temporal clause + *wāw* consecutive	Sons of Israel/ Judah	Connect to/ contrast with book of Joshua	See Josh 1:1; 2 Sam 1:1
1:9	Temporal clause + *wāw* consecutive	Sons of Judah	Create sequential element	See 1:1
1:14	Temporal clause	Achsah	Episode transition fronting Achsah	New episode features Achsah, not Caleb
1:16	Contrast clause	Sons of the Kenite	Identify Kenites with Judah	Foreshadows appearance in chaps. 4–5
1:21	Contrast clause	Jebusites of Jerusalem/sons of Benjamin	Front Jebusites in contrast to Judah's results there (v 8)	Judah/Benjamin contrast
1:22b	Circumstantial clause	Yahweh	Highlight parallel of Yahweh's presence with Joseph and Judah (v 19)	Judah takes hill country; Joseph sends out spies (compare Josh 7)
1:25b	Contrast clause	Citizen of Bethel	Highlight obedience, doing *hesed*	See Josh 2:12, 14; Judg 8:35
1:27	Negative sentence	Manasseh	Emphasize failure	
1:28	Temporal clause + *wāw* consecutive + heightened negative contrast clause	Israel (compare 1:1)	Sequence to future and emphasize continued negative action	Israel continued not to obey, not taking over possession of the land
1:29	Disjunctive circumstantial clause	Ephraim	Place Ephraim as part of Israel's action or as acting simultaneously	Appears to equate Israel with north
1:30, 31, 33	Apposition clauses	Zebulon, Asher, Naphtali	Place these tribes on equal level in time and action with Ephraim	Appears to equate Israel with north
1:34–35a	*Wāw* consecutives resume narrative thread	Amorites	Places Amorites on syntactical par with other Israelite tribes and subordinates Dan to them	Surprises with attention to Amorites to complete narrative
1:35b	*Wāw* consecutive	House of Joseph	Awkwardly brings Amorites under corvée	
1:36	Concluding circumstantial clause	Amorites	Concludes narrative with Amorite territory	

Table 1.2. Tribal conquests and failures in Judg 1

Judges	Tribe	Dispossessed	Resided among	Corvée
1:1–20	Judah	V 19 possessed hill but did not dispossess residents of plain; v 20 Caleb dispossessed from Hebron "three sons of Anak"	Not mentioned	Not mentioned
1:3, 17	Simeon	Not mentioned	Not mentioned	Not mentioned
1:21	Benjamin	Did not dispossess Jebusites	Jebusites reside with sons of Benjamin in Jerusalem to this day	Not mentioned
1:22–26	Joseph	Not mentioned	Not mentioned	Not mentioned
1:27–28	Manasseh	Manasseh did not dispossess residents of Beth-shan, Taanach, Dor, Ibleam, Megiddo	Canaanites persisted in living in this land (territory, area)	"When Israel became strong, they put the Canaanites to corvée."
1:29	Ephraim	Ephraim did not dispossess Canaanites who resided in Gezer	"Canaanites resided among them in Gezer."	Not mentioned
1:30	Zebulun	Did not dispossess residents of Kitron, Nahalal	"Canaanites resided among them."	They became corvée
1:31–32	Asher	Did not dispossess residents of Acco or Sidon and Ahlab, Achzib, Helbah, Aphik, and Rehob	"Asherites resided among the Canaanites who resided in the land."	Not mentioned
1:33	Naphtali	Did not dispossess residents of Beth-shemesh or Beth-anath	"They resided among the Canaanites who resided in the land."	"Residents of Beth-shemesh and Beth-anath became corvée."
1:34	Dan	Not mentioned	"Amorites pushed the sons of Dan into the hill country. Indeed, they did not allow them to go down into the valley."	Not mentioned
1:35	House of Joseph	"Amorites were determined to reside in Har-heres, in Aijalon, and in Shaalbim."	Not mentioned	"Hand of the house of Joseph grew heavy, and they became corvée."

Table 1.3   499

Table 1.3. Instances of יָשַׁב, "to reside, live," in Judg 1

Judges	Peoples	Location of residence	Dispossessed
1:9	Canaanites	Hill country, Negev, and Shephelah	Not mentioned
1:10	Canaanites	Hebron	"Struck Sheshai, Ahiman, and Talmai dead"
1:11, 13	Debir	Debir	"Othniel . . . captured it"
1:16	Sons of the Kenite with sons of Judah	Negev of Arad	"Resided with the people"
1:17	Canaanites	Zephath (Hormah)	"Devoted it to the ban"
1:19	Residents of the valley		Judah could not dispossess
1:21	"Jebusites, the residents of Jerusalem"	"Reside with sons of Benjamin in Jerusalem to the present day"	Could not dispossess
1:27	Residents of Dor, of Ibleam, of Megiddo	Canaanites determined to reside in this land	Manasseh did not dispossess
1:29	Canaanites	Gezer; "resided among them in Gezer"	Ephraim did not dispossess the Canaanites
1:30	Residents of Kitron, of Nahalol	"Canaanites resided among them"	Zebulun did not dispossess
1:31–32	Residents of Acco, residents of Sidon,	"Asherites resided among the Canaanites who resided in the land"	Asher did not dispossess
1:33	Residents of Beth-shemesh, of Beth-anath	Naphtali "resided among the Canaanites who resided in the land"	Naphtali did not dispossess but made them to be corvée for them
1:35	Amorites	Har-heres, Aijalon, Shaalbim	Not mentioned; "hand of the house of Joseph grew heavy, and they became corvée"

Table 1.4. Comparison of Judges 1 with Joshua

Judges passage	Joshua passage	Apparent inconsistencies
אדני בזק 1:4–7:	אדני־צדק 10:1–5:	Jerusalem connection in both but similar names may point to related traditions
1:8, 21 Judah captured Jerusalem; Benjamin did not possess it; lived with Jebusites	15:63 Judah not able to possess; lived with Jebusites	Parallel wording in Judg 1:21 and Josh 15:63 with different tribe
1:10–15, 20 יהודה ויכו את־ששׁי ואת־אחימן ואת־תלמי:	15:13–19; compare 14:6–15 וירשׁ משׁם כלב את־שׁלושׁה בני הענק את־ששׁי ואת־אחימן ואת־תלמי ילידי הענק:	Judg 1:10//Josh 15:14 Who defeated/killed the sons of Anak?
1:11 וילך משׁם אל־יושׁבי דביר ושׁם־דביר לפנים קרית־ספר:	15:15 ויעל משׁם אל־ישׁבי דבר ושׁם־דבר לפנים קרית־ספר:	Only opening verb different Who captured Debir? When?
1:12	15:16	Identical text When did this occur?
1:13	15:17	Judges adds after "brother of Caleb": הקטן ממנו (the younger from him)
1:14	15:18	Judges has article before "field": השׂדה
1:15 ותאמר לו הבה־לי ברכה כי ארץ הנגב נתתני ונתחה לי גלת מים ויתן־לה כלב את גלת עלית ואת גלת תחתית:	15:19 ותאמר תנה־לי ברכה כי ארץ הנגב נתתני ונתחה לי גלת מים ויתן־לה את נלת עליות ואת גלת תחתיות:	Judges has "to him" explicit after "she said," uses הבה for "give," and makes Caleb explicit subject of "he gave"; Joshua uses תנה for "give."
1:18–19	13:2–3	Joshua has five Philistine cities as part of territory Joshua left; Judges has Judah capture three of the cities. Chronological sequence unclear
1:19; compare 4:3, 13	17:16–18	Joshua has Joseph facing Canaanite iron chariots, but Joshua promising to drive them out. Judges has Judah unable to occupy the plain because of iron chariots.

Table 1.4

501

Table 1.4. Comparison of Judges 1 with Joshua *(continued)*

Judges passage	Joshua passage	Apparent inconsistencies
1:27–28 ולא־הוריש מנשה את־בית־שאן ואת־בנותיה ואת־תענך ואת־בנתיה ואת־ישב ן־ישבי] דור ואת־בנותיה ואת־יושבי יבלעם ואת־בנותיה ואת־יושבי מגדו ואת־בנותיה ויואל הכנעני לשבת בארץ הזאת: ויהי כי־חזק ישראל וישם את־הכנעני למס והורש לא הוריש:	17:11–13 ויהי למנשה ביששכר ובאשר בית־שאן ובנותיה ויבלעם ובנותיה ואת־ישבי דאר ובנותיה וישבי עין־דר ובנתיה וישבי תענך ובנתיה מגדו ובנותיה שלשת הנפת: ולא יכלו בני מנשה להוריש את־הערים האלה ויואל הכנעני לשבת בארץ הזאת ויהי כי חזק בני ישראל ויתנו את־הכנעני למס והורש לא הורישו:	Same information given in different sequence. Judges begins segment with inability to conquer, Joshua with list of cities. Judges does not include En Dor, either through haplography or without understanding that En Dor was separate town. Joshua ends with the mysterious "three of the Napheth," perhaps an attempt to identify Dor as Naphoth Dor. Judg 1:27b and Josh 17:12b are identical. In v 13 Joshua has sons of Israel with plural verbs; Judges has Israel with singular and a different verb for "put to corvée."
1:29	16:10	Judges introduces Ephraim here, Joshua in preceding verses. Joshua uses plural verb. Judges reads "in its midst in Gezer"; Joshua, "in the midst of Ephraim this day, and they became slaves doing forced labor"
1:30	19:10–16	Judges lists only two towns in Zebulun; gives variant spelling on Kitron (Kattah).
1:31–32	19:24–31	Judges lists seven towns in Asher. Acco relates to a textually corrupt Ummah in Josh 19:30; similarly Ahlab and Helbah to Mechebel (or Mahallib or Mahalab) of 19:29. Sidon = Sidon the Great from 19:28; Achzib appears in 19:29; Aphek and Rehob both appear in 19:30.
1:33	19:32–39	The two cities Judges mentions for Naphtali are the final two of Josh 19:38. Joshua has nothing to say about failure or about corvée.
1:34–35	19:41–48; compare 15:10	Three cities in Judges represent the first two cities of Josh 19:42 and possibly a secondary name or translation of Ir-shemesh, "city of the sun," in 19:41. Judges tells Dan's failure from view of Amorite strength without mention of Joshua story of Danite migration. Joshua does not mention strength of Joseph.

Table 2.1. Narrative and genre comparisons for chap. 2

Narrative			Genre		
Element	*Passage*	*Marker*	*Element*	*Passage*	*Marker*
Exposition	2:1–2a	New speaker	Angelic theophany	2:1–5	Appearance and speech of מלאך־יהוה
Complication: disobedience	2:2b	Disjunctive contrast sentence			
Change: divine threat	2:3	כ clause			
Resolution: national weeping	2:4a	Temporal clause			
Ending: etiology and sacrifice	2:5				
Exposition: flashback to Joshua's generation	2:6–7	Change of subject	Interpretative flashback	2:6–10	Repetition from Josh 24
Complication: Joshua's death	2:8–9	Change of theme and place			
Change: new generation not knowing Yahweh	2:10	כ clause and new theme			
Resolution and ending: not given					
Exposition: Israel's disobedience	2:11–13	Change of subject and theme	Narrative preview	2:11–19	Closing formula in v 10; change of subject
Complication: Yahweh's anger	2:14–15	Change of subject			
Change: Yahweh raised up judges	2:16a	Change of theme and subject			
Resolution: deliverance by judges	2:16b	Change of subject			
Ending: contrast between divine compassion and human disobedience as ongoing condition	2:16b–23	Change of mood and theme: temporary obedience and ongoing testing	Divine judgment speech	2:20–22	Change of speakers to speech of Yahweh with announcement of judgment
			Narrative summary	2:23	Change of speaker to narrator with summary explanation

Table 3.1 503

Table 3.1. Narrative and genre comparisons for chap. 3

Narrative			Genre		
Element	Passage	Marker	Element	Passage	Marker
			Testing conditions	3:1-6	
Exposition: Yahweh's reason and method for testing	3:1-4	אלה opening	List of testing nations with purpose statements	3:1-3	אלה (these are the), with exclusive clauses
			Central test statement	3:4	ל יהוה (they were for the purpose of), purpose introduction
Complication: Israel's intermarriage and false worship	3:5-6		Test failure	3:5-6	Disjunctive contrast clause
Change: none Resolution: none Ending: none			Pattern narrative: all formal components without any unique items	3:7-11	
Exposition: disobedience	3:7	Change of theme	The charge: Israel did evil and served gods	3:7	Evil-in-eyes-of-God formula
Complication: divine anger and punishment	3:8	Change of subject	Punishment: sold to foreign king	3:8a	Sale formula
			Sentence: eight years	3:8b	Served formula
Change: "Israel cried out to Yahweh"	3:9a	Change of subject	Cry for help	3:9a	Cry-to-Yahweh formula
Resolution: Yahweh raises up deliverer	3:9b-10	Change of subject	Deliverer raised	3:9b	Divine-deliverer formula
			Battle report of victory	3:10	Spirit and conveyance formulas
Ending: land is quiet and Othniel dies	3:11	Change of subject	Rest restored	3:11a	Land-had-quiet formula
			Death of judge	3:11b	"He died" formula
			Individual duel report	3:12-15	
Exposition	3:12a	Change of subject	The charge: Israel did evil	3:12a	Evil-in-eyes-of-God formula

Table 3.1. Narrative and genre comparisons for chap. 3 *(continued)*

Narrative			Genre		
Element	*Passage*	*Marker*	*Element*	*Passage*	*Marker*
Complication: Yahweh raises enemy king	3:12b–14	Change of subject	Punishment: strengthened foreign king	3:12b	
			Battle summary: defeat	3:13	Defeated Israel
			Sentence: eighteen years	3:14	Served formula
Change: Israel's cry for help	3:15a	Change of theme	Cry for help	3:15a	Cry-to-Yahweh formula
Resolution: Yahweh raised deliverer	3:15b	Change of subject	Deliverer raised	3:15b	Divine-deliverer formula
Ending = test-of-wits narrative	3:15c–30	Change of subject and locale			
Exposition: Ehud's mission	3:15d–17a	Change of locale	Individual ironic duel report	3:16–22	
Complication: solo appearance before king after sending his escorts home	3:17b–19a	Change of locale			
Change: Ehud kills fat Eglon	3:19b–23	Change of subject	Hero escapes	3:23	Change of scene
Resolution: servants find king dead	3:24–26	Change of subject	Fearful royal servants discover stinking truth	3:24–25	Contrast clause
			Mop-up battle report	3:26–31	
			Hero escapes	3:26	Contrast clause
Ending: Israel's army summoned and Moab defeated, bringing rest	3:27–30		Summons to battle	3:27	Temporal clause: blew the horn
			Encouragement cry	3:28	"Follow after me" with conveyance formula
			Battle summary	3:29–30a	Smiting formula
			Rest restored	3:30b	Land-had-quiet formula
Notation: Shamgar's deliverance	3:31	Change of subject	Shamgar annal	3:31	"After [him] . . . saved Israel"

Table 4.1 505

Table 4.1. Narrative and genre comparisons for chap. 4

Narrative			Genre		
Element	*Passage*	*Marker*	*Element*	*Passage*	*Marker*
Exposition: introducing problem and combatants	4:1–5 Sale formula	Change of locale	Divine-battle report with ironic twist	4:1–22	
			The charge: "Israel again did evil"	4:1	Evil-in-eyes-of-God formula
			Punishment: sold to foreign king	4:2a	Sale formula
			Introduction of enemy	4:2b	Disjunctive conditional clause
			Cry for help	4:3a	Cry-to-Yahweh formula
			Sentence: twenty years	4:3b	Disjunctive contrast clause
			Heroine's introduction	4:4–5	Disjunctive conditional clause
Complication: Chosen general sets conditions	4:6–9	New subject introduced	Commissioning of general	4:6–7	Yahweh commanded
			General's conditional acceptance speech	4:8	Change of speakers; presence formula
			Punishment for making conditions	4:9a	Change of speakers; sale formula
Change: opposing armies set for battle	4:10–13		Preparations for battle report	4:9b–10	Summons formula
			Ironic introduction of secondary character	4:11	Disjunctive conditional clause
			Enemy preparations for battle report	4:12–13	Change of subject; summons formula

Table 4.1. Narrative and genre comparisons for chap. 4 (*continued*)

Narrative			Genre		
Element	*Passage*	*Marker*	*Element*	*Passage*	*Marker*
Resolution: God wins the battle	4:14–16		Ironic summons to battle for general from prophetess	4:14a	Change of subject; divine-presence formula; conveyance formula
			March-to-battle report	4:14b	Change of subject
			Divine-battle report	4:15	Panic formula
			Ironic pursuit report	4:16a	Disjunctive contrast clause; pursuit formula
			Battle-results report	4:16b	Holy war victory report
Ending = new narrative tension	4:17–22				
Exposition: enemy general escapes to ally with Israelite general pursuing wrong direction	4:17	Disjunctive contrast clause changing subjects	Enemy general seeks refuge	4:17	Disjunctive contrast clause with ironic tie to v 11
Complication	4:18–20	Romantic atmosphere created with new subject	Ironic love-trap murder report	4:18–21	Change of characters
Change: murder in the lady's tent	4:21	New theme			
Resolution: Israelite general loses honor	4:22	Change of subject	General ironically loses honor	4:22	Disjunctive surprise clause
Ending: editorial summary	4:23–24	Summary formula with change of subject	Editorial summary	4:23–24	Change of subjects with "on that day"

Table 4.2 507

Table 4.2. Structural formulas in Judg 4

Type of formula	Hebrew element	English element	Judg 4–5 wording	Other occurrences
Negative evaluation (2:11; cf. 2:12–13, 17, 19)	וַיַּעֲשׂוּ בְנֵי־יִשְׂרָאֵל אֶת־הָרַע בְּעֵינֵי יהוה וַיַּעַבְדוּ אֶת־הַבְּעָלִים	"The Israelites did evil in Yahweh's eyes: they served the Baals."	וַיֹּסִפוּ בְּנֵי יִשְׂרָאֵל לַעֲשׂוֹת הָרַע בְּעֵינֵי יהוה (4:1)	Judg 2:11; 3:7, 12; 6:1; 10:6; 13:1; cf. Deut 31:29; (2 Kgs 21:15)
Divine anger (2:14)	וַיִּחַר־אַף יהוה בְּיִשְׂרָאֵל	"Yahweh burned with anger against Israel."		Judg 2:14, 20; 3:8; 10:7; cf. Exod 4:14; Num 11:10; 12:9; 25:3; 32:10, 13; Deut 6:15; 7:4; 11:17; 29:26; Josh 7:1; 23:16; 2 Sam 6:7; 2 Kgs 13:3; 1 Chr 13:10; 2 Chr 25:15; 32:13; Ps 106:40; Isa 5:25
Divine committal (2:14)	וַיִּתְּנֵם בְּיַד	"He gave them into the hand of . . ."	וַיִּתְּנֵם בְּיַד (4:7, 14)	Judg 1:2; 2:14, 23; 3:10, 28; 6:1; 7:7, 9, 15; 8:3, 7; 9:29; 11:30, 32; 12:3; 13:1; 15:12–13; 18:10; 20:28; cf. Num 21:34; Deut 2:30; 3:2; Josh 2:24; 21:44; 24:8, 11; 1 Sam 14:37; 17:47; 23:4; 2 Sam 5:19; 21:9; 1 Kgs 15:18; 20:13; 2 Kgs 3:18; 13:3; 17:20; 21:14; 1 Chr 14:10; 2 Chr 16:8; 25:20; 28:9; Neh 9:24, 27, 30; Ps 106:41; Isa 47:6; Jer 22:25; 38:16; 46:26; Ezek 7:21; 16:39; 21:36; 23:9, 28; 31:11; 39:23
Divine sale (2:14)	וַיִּמְכְּרֵם בְּיַד אֹיְבֵיהֶם	"He sold them into the hand of their enemies."	וַיִּמְכְּרֵם יהוה (4:2)	Judg 2:14; 3:8; 10:7; cf. Exod 21:7; 22:2; Deut 32:30; Judg 4:7; 1 Sam 12:9; Ps 44:13; Isa 50:1; Joel 3:8
Weakness (2:14)	וְלֹא־יָכְלוּ עוֹד לַעֲמֹד לִפְנֵי אוֹיְבֵיהֶם	"They were no longer able to stand before their enemies."		
Divine opposition (2:15)	יַד־יהוה הָיְתָה בָּם לְרָעָה	"The hand of Yahweh was against them to bring evil."		cf. Exod 9:3; Deut 2:15

Table 4.2. Structural formulas in Judg 4 (*continued*)

Type of formula	Hebrew element	English element	Judg 4–5 wording	Other occurrences
Cry of distress (4:3; compare 2:14, 18)	ויזעקו בני־ישראל אל־יהוה	"The sons of Israel cried out to Yahweh."	ויצעקו בני־ישראל אל־יהוה (4:3)	Judg 3:9, 15; 6:6–7; 10:10; cf. Exod 8:8; 14:10; 15:25; 17:4; Num 20:16; Deut 26:7; Josh 24:7; Judg 10:14; 1 Sam 7:8; Neh 9:27; Ps 107:6, 28; Isa 19:20
Provision of leadership (2:16)	ויקם יהוה שפטים	"Yahweh raised up judges."		Judg 2:18; 3:9, 15; cf. Deut 18:15, 18; 1 Sam 2:35; 1 Kgs 14:14; Jer 30:9
Human deliverance (2:16, 18)	שפטם ויושיעם מיד	"Judges, and they delivered them from the hand."		Judg 8:22
Divine presence (2:18)	והיה יהוה עם־השפט	"Yahweh was with the judge."		cf. Gen 26:28; Num 14:43 (neg.); 1 Sam 18:12; 20:13; 1 Kgs 1:37; 2 Kgs 18:7; 1 Chr 22:11, 16; 2 Chr 17:3; 19:11
Divine deliverance (2:18)	והושיעם מיד כל איביהם כל ימי השפט	"So that he delivered them from the hand of their enemies all the days of the judge."	ויכנע אלהים ביום ההוא את יבן מלך־כנען לפני בני ישראל (4:23; compare 3:30; Deut 9:3)	cf. 1 Sam 7:8; Ps 106:10; Isa 37:20
Divine compassion (2:18)	וינחם יהוה מנאקתם מפני לחציהם ודחקיהם	"Yahweh showed compassion on account of their groaning before those who tormented and oppressed them."		cf. Gen 6:6 (regret); Exod 32:14 (relent); 2 Sam 24:16 (relent); Jer 26:13, 19; (relent); Amos 7:3, 6 (relent)
Subjugation (4:23)		"God subdued."	ויכנע אלהים (4:23)	Judg 3:30; 8:28; cf. Lev 26:41; Judg 11:33; 1 Sam 7:13; 1 Chr 20:4; 2 Chr 13:18; 28:19; Ps 106:42
Death report (2:19)	...במות השפט	"At the death of the judge . . ."		Judg 3:11; 4:1b; 8:32; 12:7
Land-rest report (3:30)	ותשקט הארץ שמנים שנה	"The land was quiet eighty years."	ותשקט הארץ ארבעים שנה (5:31b)	Judg 3:11; 8:28; cf. 2 Chr 14:1, 6

Table 5.1   509

Table 5.1. Narrative and genre comparisons for chap. 5

Narrative			Genre		
Element	*Passage*	*Marker*	*Element*	*Passage*	*Marker*
Exposition: scene of praise and theophany	5:2–5	Language of praise	Opening call to individual praise	5:2–3	"Bless Yahweh! I will sing . . . make music"
			Report of a theophany	5:4–5	God marching from Seir amid weather phenomena
Complication: economic and religious conditions changed	5:6–8	Change of time with temporal clause	Historical setting	5:6–9	"In the days of"— temporal phrase
Change: some people volunteer and lead as tribes decide to march to battle or stay home	5:9–18	First-person language and listing of participants and nonparticipants	Call to ponder peasant praise	5:10–11	Ponder this with praise
			Call to battle	5:12–13	Arousal formulas
			Response to the call	5:14–18	"From . . . they came"
Resolution: God wins the war with Jael's help	5:19–27	Language of war and murder	Holy war report	5:19–22	"Kings fought. . . . stars fought"
			Curse and blessing	5:23–27	"Curse. . . . Blessed above all . . . is"
Ending: mother of enemy general mourns; narrator calls for destruction of all enemies	5:28–31	Temporal phrase, language of mourning	A mother's mourning	5:28–30	"She cried"
			Concluding petition	5:31	"So may all your enemies"

Table 6.1. Narrative and genre comparisons for chaps. 6–9

Narrative			Genre		
Element	Passage	Marker	Element	Passage	Marker
Exposition: Midianite threat	6:1–10		Novella composed of individual reports	6:1–9:57	
			Framework and exposition: Midianite control	6:1–6	Evil-in-eyes-of-God formula; conveyance formula; sentence; cry-to-Yahweh formula
			Prophetic judgment speech	6:7–10	Historical prologue; "you did not obey"
Complication: God calls reluctant Gideon	6:11–40	Change of locale and subject	Call narrative	6:11–24	
			Theophanic appearance of deity	6:11–12	Messenger of Yahweh appears
			Complaint: Where is God's salvation?	6:13	Interrogatives
			Commission: Deliver Israel in might of your hand.	6:14	Command to save Israel
			Objection: too weak, no credentials	6:15	Interrogatives
			Divine reassurance: "I will be with you."	6:16a	Divine-presence formula
			Promise of a sign: I will defeat Midianites.	6:16b	
			Acceptance of commission: Wait for me to sacrifice.	6:17–18	Call for sign
			Commission sealed through sacrifice	6:19	
			Divine confirmation: creates fire, disappears	6:20–21	Messenger disappeared
			Response of fear and awe: Help! I saw God.	6:22	"I have seen the messenger of Yahweh"
			Divine reassurance: "Peace. . . . You will not die."	6:23	Shalom greeting; salvation-oracle formula
			Etiological editorial explanation: Ophrah altar	6:24	"Until today"
			Divine-testing narrative	6:25–32	
			Divine commission: destroy Baal altar	6:25–26	Divine imperatives
			Human obedience: obey	6:27a	He did just as Yahweh said
			Human reluctance: in secrecy of night	6:27b	"Did it at night"
			Discovery and investigation: Gideon discovered	6:28–29	Surprise clause: הנה

Table 6.1. Narrative and genre comparisons for chaps. 6–9 (continued)

Table 6.1 continued   511

Narrative			Genre		
Element	*Passage*	*Marker*	*Element*	*Passage*	*Marker*
Complication: God calls reluctant Gideon (cont'd)	6:11–40 (cont'd)	Change of locale and subject (cont'd)	Sentence demanded from father: death for son	6:30	"That he may die"
			Father's defense: let Baal defend self	6:31	"Let him defend himself"
			Etiological editorial expansion: Gideon = Jerubbaal	6:32	"That day"
			Battle report with embedded testing narratives	6:33–8:21	
			Battle exposition: Midian and Gideon amass troops	6:33–35	Disjunctive clause; "gathered together"
			Human-testing narrative: questions God's promise	6:36–40	"If . . . then I will know"
Change: God reduces Gideon's army but gives encouraging dream	7:1–18	Change of locale and subjects	Battle exposition resumed: sides encamped	7:1	"Jerubbaal—that is, Gideon—rose early, along with all the people with him."
			Divine testing narrative: God reduces troop size	7:2–8	"People are too many . . . so I may test them"
			Divine encouragement narrative: God allays fears	7:9–15	Disjunctive temporal clause; conveyance formula
Resolution: victory report	7:19–25		Battle narrative: battle orders carried out for victory	7:16–22	Just as I do, so you must do
			Pursuit narrative: expanded army captures captains	7:23–25	"Chased after"
Ending: Ephraim appeased	8:1–3	New setting and subjects	Complaint complication: Ephraim soothed	8:1–3	"What is this thing you have done?"
Exposition: tired army pursuing enemy	8:4	New setting and theme	Battle-pursuit narrative with revenge stories embedded (see 8:5–9)	8:4, 10–12	"Pursuing"
Complication: reasons for vengeance	8:5–21	Change of subjects and theme	Embedded revenge stories	8:5–9	"When" with conveyance formula, "then I will"
			Revenge narratives concluded: Succoth, Penuel punished	8:13–17	"He let them teach. . . . He killed the men."
			Battle narrative concluded: brothers revenged	8:18–21	Oath formula

Table 6.1. Narrative and genre comparisons for chaps. 6–9 *(continued)*

Narrative			Genre		
Element	*Passage*	*Marker*	*Element*	*Passage*	*Marker*
Change: invitation to rule	8:22	Change of theme	Theological conclusion	8:22–35	"with the Baals"
Resolution: invitation refused	8:23	Change of speaker	God is King	8:22–23	"Rule over us. . . . Yahweh rules over you."
Ending: Gideon's royal life and burial lead to idolatry	8:24–35	New theme	Gideon lives as a king	8:24–28	"Give me . . . from the spoil . . . made an ephod . . . all Israel prostituted themselves . . . land had quiet forty years."
			Failure to overcome Baalistic menace	8:29–9:57	
			Report of last days of Jerubbaal and royal harem	8:29–30	"Seventy sons . . . many wives . . . concubine"
			First days of "my father is king"	8:31	He named his name Abimelech
			Gideon's death and burial	8:32	Died, buried
			Theological exposition: Gideon's heritage is Baal worship	8:33–35	"All Israel prostituted themselves . . . with the Baals . . . set up Baal Berith . . . did not remember Yahweh . . . did not show faithful love"
Exposition: Abimelech kills brother and is crowned king of Shechem	9:1–6	New locale	Enthronement account	9:1–6	"Which is better for you? Murdered his brothers . . . crowned Abimelech king . . . in Shechem."

Table 6.1 continued   513

Table 6.1. Narrative and genre comparisons for chaps. 6–9 (*continued*)

Narrative			**Genre**		
Element	*Passage*	*Marker*	*Element*	*Passage*	*Marker*
			Revenge-on-Shechem account	9:7-57	
Complication: Jotham's parable and charge indict Shechem and Abimelech	9:7-21	New subject	Jotham's fable	9:7-15	"Listen to me so God may listen to you . . . the trees . . . rule over us."
			Jotham's charge	9:16-21	"Therefore [הִנֵּה] . . . if you have acted faithfully . . . if . . . if . . ."
Change: King Abimelech faces rebellion	9:22-29	New subjects and locale	Account of Abimelech's rule	9:22-25	"Abimelech reigned . . . God sent evil spirit . . . dealt treacherously . . . set up ambush."
			Account of Gaal's coup	9:26-29	"Trusted him . . . curse on Abimelech"
Resolution: Abimelech defeats Gaal and Shechem	9:30-55	New theme: battle reports	Battle report	9:30-49	"Set up ambush . . . marching against you . . . took their stand . . . marched out and fought"
			Battle report	9:50-55	"Set up an ambush and captured . . . fought against it . . . crushed his skull"
Ending: theological explanation	9:56-57	Narrator reports God's viewpoint	Theological exposition	9:56-57	"God repaid Abimelech's evil. . . . God repaid the men of Shechem."

Table 10.1. Narrative and genre comparisons for chaps. 10–12

Narrative			Genre		
Element	*Passage*	*Marker*	*Element*	*Passage*	*Marker*
Exposition: minor judges introduced; divine reluctance and Israelite obedience; divine compassion; armies mustered	10:1–17	Time change	Annals of minor judges	10:1–5	"After . . . judged Israel . . . years . . . died . . . was buried."
			Jephthah novella	10:6–12:6	
			Extended narrator's framework	10:6–10	Evil-in-eyes-of-Yahweh formula; served formula; abandoned-Yahweh formula; Yahweh's anger formula; sale formula; defeated Israel; time-of-service formula; Israel in trouble; cry-to-Yahweh formula; confession-of-sin formula
			Divine-judgment speech	10:11–16	Salvation history recital with oppression, cry-to-Yaweh, abandon, deliverance, and serve-othergods formulas; "therefore" transition; confession-of-sin formula; cry for rescue; pledge to serve God
			Ammonite war report	10:17–11:33	

Table 10.1 continued   515

Table 10.1. Narrative and genre comparisons for chaps. 10–12 (continued)

Narrative

Element	Passage	Marker
Complication: Israel lacks a leader	10:18–11:11	Change of subject
Change: king of Ammon refuses negotiated agreement	11:12–28	Change of subject, theme, and locale
Resolution: apparent holy war victory under vow	11:29–33	Change of locale and theme
Ending = new narrative	11:34–40	Change of locale, subject, and theme

Genre

Element	Passage	Marker
Preparation for battle	10:17–18	Mustered, gathered-forces formula; search for Israelite leader
Introduction-of-leader report	11:1–3	Disjunctive clause introducing new episode; biographical elements
Negotiations with new leader	11:4–11	Temporal disjunctive clauses; invitation-to-lead formula; original refusal; negotiated offers and final agreement
Negotiations with Ammonite king	11:12–28	Versions of history compared; rhetorical questions; confession of innocence; call for divine judgment; Ammonite refusal of negotiations
Vow	11:29–31	Spirit of Yahweh coming; mustering expedition; vow to God to sacrifice
Battle report	11:32–33	Conveyance formula; extent-of-victory report

Table 10.1. Narrative and genre comparisons for chaps. 10–12 (continued)

Narrative			Genre		
Element	Passage	Marker	Element	Passage	Marker
Exposition: return	11:34a	Change of locale	Fulfillment-of-vow report	11:34–40	Surprise clause; lament; call to obedience; plea for condition; condition fulfilled in lamentation; fulfillment report; etiological update
Complication: daughter greets him	11:34b	Change of subject			
Change: lament	11:35	Change of subject			
Resolution: daughter accepts conditions of vow with her own stipulations	11:36–37	Change of subject			
Ending: conditions of daughter's stipulations and of father's vow fulfilled, leading to updated etiology	11:38–40	Change of subject			
Exposition: complaint	12:1	Change of locale, subjects, time	Intertribal battle report	12:1–6	Muster formula; complaint with threat; explanatory response and defense; battle report with test narrative; results formula
Complication: arbitration attempt fails	12:2–3	Change of subject			
Change: battle begun	12:4a	Change of locale, theme			
Resolution: Israel wins over tribe of Ephraim	12:4b–6	Change of subject			
Ending: history continues with minor judges	12:7–15	Change of subjects and locales	Annals of minor judges	12:7–15	Judged . . . years formulas; death-and-burial formulas; after-him formulas; family information

Table 13.1   517

Table 13.1. Narrative and genre comparisons for chaps. 13–16

Narrative			Genre		
Element	Passage	Marker	Element	Passage	Marker
Exposition to chaps. 13–16	13:1–25	New subjects and locale			
Exposition: barren wife	13:1–2	New subjects and locale	Framework	13:1	Evil-in-eyes-of-Yahweh formula; conveyance formula; time formula
			Birth story	13:2–25	
			Exposition	13:2	There was "a certain man"; barren-wife motif
Complication: birth announcement and doubtful reactions to it	13:3–14	Change of subject	Theophanic birth announcement	13:3–5	
			Theophany	13:3a	Messenger-of-Yahweh formula
			Birth announcement	13:3b	"You are barren . . . you will become pregnant"
			Instructions for mother's Nazirite vow	13:4–5a	Nazirite vow commands
			Instructions for son's Nazirite vow and mission	13:5b	Nazirite vow commands; salvation oracle
			Family birth announcement	13:6–7	
			Description of theophany	13:6	"Man of Yahweh came"
			Repetition of birth announcement	13:7a	Birth announcement repeated
			Repetition of Nazirite vows	13:7b	Nazirite vow commands
			Repeated theophanic birth announcement for husband	13:8–14	
			Prayer for repeated theophany	13:8	"Begged Yahweh"
			Reappearance of divine messenger to woman	13:9	Messenger-of-Yahweh formula
			Bringing husband onto scene	13:10	
			Reiteration of wife's Nazirite instructions	13:11–14	Identification formula; Nazirite vow commands

Table 13.1. Narrative and genre comparisons for chaps. 13–16 (continued)

Narrative			Genre		
Element	Passage	Marker	Element	Passage	Marker
Change: sacrifice for messenger and "revelation" of name	13:15–21	Change of theme	Sacrifice and miraculous revelation	13:15–23	
			Man's offer of sacrifice (or meal?)	13:15	
			Instructions to offer sacrifice to Yahweh	13:16	"Offer it to Yahweh"
			Request for and denial of name revelation	13:17–18	"Who is your name?" "Why do you ask?"
			Sacrifice to Yahweh	13:19a	Sacrificed to Yahweh
			Miraculous ascent of messenger as revelation	13:19b–21	"Caused a miracle to happen"; "fell down . . . on the ground"; "Manoah knew"
Resolution: fear of death for seeing God resolved	13:22–23	Change of theme	Man's fear of death	13:22	"We will surely die . . . have seen God."
			Wife's reassurance	13:23	
Ending: birth and coming of the Spirit	13:24–25	Change of subject and theme	Birth of son and preparation for Spirit's work	13:24–25	
			Birth and naming	13:24a	"Bore a son . . . called his name"
			Physical and spiritual growth	13:24b	"Lad grew . . . Yahweh blessed"
			Spirit of Yahweh stirring Samson	13:25	"Spirit of Yahweh began to stir"
			Wedding tale gone sour	14:1–20	
			Choosing a bride	14:1–4	"Take her for me as a wife. . . . She is the right one in my eyes."

Table 13.1 continued   519

Table 13.1. Narrative and genre comparisons for chaps. 13–16 (*continued*)

Narrative			**Genre**		
Element	*Passage*	*Marker*	*Element*	*Passage*	*Marker*
Exposition: dispute over wife as "right one in my eyes"; "uncircumcised Philistines"; "did not know that this was from Yahweh"	14:1–4	Change of time and locale	Meeting the girl	14:1	
			Requesting parental action	14:2	
			Parental objection	14:3a	
			Samson's insistence	14:3b	
			Yahweh's secret plan against the Philistines	14:4a	"This was from Yahweh"
			Historical note	14:4b	"At that time"
			Wedding plans riddled with broken vows	14:5–7	
Complication: content of riddle experienced and expressed	14:5–14	Change of locale and theme	Visit to fiancée displays power of the Spirit in killing lion	14:5–6	"Spirit of Yahweh broke in"
			Family visit to bride	14:5a	
			Appearance of lion	14:5b	
			Appearance of Spirit of Yahweh	14:6a	
			Killing of lion without cleansing for vows	14:6b	
			Keeping the tale silent	14:6c	"Did not tell"
			Reassurance the girl is the right one	14:7	"She was right in his eyes"
			Riddling the riddler and the wedding	14:8–18	
			Wedding march discovery	14:8–9	"Take her as his wife"
			Return for wedding	14:8a	
			Discovery of bees and honey in the lion's carcass and breaking of vows	14:8b–9a	
			Keeping the tale silent and leading parents to break vows	14:9b	"Did not tell"
			Finalizing wedding preparations, breaking marital trust, and breaking off wedding	14:10–18	"Father went . . . to see the woman"
			Father and son finalize preparations	14:10–11	

Table 13.1. Narrative and genre comparisons for chaps. 13–16 (continued)

Narrative

Element	Passage	Marker
Change: wife becomes foil of enemies	14:15–17	Change of subject
Resolution: Philistines "solve" riddle and hear Samson's proverbial reply	14:18	Change of subject
Ending: Spirit broke in; kills in Ashkelon for riddle payment; returns home; wife given another = exposition for next chapter	14:19–20	Change of subject
Exposition: Samson loses wife, gets revenge, retreats to cave	15:1–8	Disjunctive clause; change of locale

Genre

Element	Passage	Marker
Riddle posed	14:12–15	"Let me pose a riddle.... If you ... but if you cannot ..." "Pose your riddle."
Wife involved and trust broken	14:16a	"Did not explain it to me"
Secret revealed and confidence betrayed	14:16b–17	"She cried ... seven days"
Riddle answered and accusations lodged	14:18	"Men said ..." "He said ..."
Spirit empowers Samson but marriage destroyed	14:19–20	
Spirit-empowered	14:19a	"Spirit of Yahweh broke in"
Riddle debt paid through deadly deed	14:19b	"Those who had answered the riddle"
Back home in anger	14:19c	"His anger blazed"
Wife lost to wedding companion	14:20	
Donkey-and-fox-style deliverance	15:1–20	Disjunctive clause
Seeking revenge for a marriage gone sour	15:1–8	
Visit to wife thwarted with better offer given	15:1–2	
Harvest havoc created with foxes	15:3–5	
Enemy's revenge on their own	15:6	
Samson's revenge on the Philistines	15:7–8a	"If you ... then"
Samson's retreat	15:8b	"He went down and lived"
Samson captured by his own people	15:9–13	

Table 13.1 continued   521

Table 13.1. Narrative and genre comparisons for chaps. 13–16 *(continued)*

Narrative			Genre		
Element	*Passage*	*Marker*	*Element*	*Passage*	*Marker*
Complication: fellow tribe of Judah makes deal with Philistines and with Samson to imprison him	15:9–13	Change of locale and subjects	Philistine threat	15:9–10	"Went up and camped"
			Judean expedition to capture Samson	15:11–12a	"Three thousand men went down"
			Negotiated capture	15:12b–13	"Take an oath"
			Donkey battle report	**15:14–17**	
Change: Samson defeats Philistines	15:14–17	Disjunctive clause; change of subject and locale	Engagement with celebrating enemies	15:14a	Disjunctive clause; "came out to meet him shouting the victory cry"
			Spirit empowerment	15:14b	"Spirit of Yahweh broke in"
			Victory with a donkey jawbone	15:15–16	Victory hymn
			Editorial etiology	15:17	Temporal clause; "named that place"
			Divine deliverance for thirsty warrior	**15:18–19**	
Resolution: further demands made on God and fulfilled	15:18–19	Change of subject, theme, and locale	Praise for deliverance and prayer for drink	15:18	"Called out to Yahweh"
			Divinely provided drink	15:19a	"God split open"
			Editorial etiology	15:19b	"Therefore, it is named"
Ending: he judged Israel twenty years	15:20	Change of theme	Framework: Samson as judge	15:20	"He judged Israel . . . twenty years"
			Prostituting Gaza	**16:1–3**	
Exposition: Samson in Gaza with prostitute	16:1	Change of location	Visit to a prostitute	16:1	
Complication: men of Gaza in ambush	16:2	Change of subject	Ambush set against Samson	16:2	"Lay in ambush"

Table 13.1. Narrative and genre comparisons for chaps. 13–16 (*continued*)

Narrative			Genre		
Element	*Passage*	*Marker*	*Element*	*Passage*	*Marker*
Change: Samson escapes	16:3a	Change of subject	Samson's escape with the city gates	16:3	
Resolution: carried them to Hebron	16:3b	Change of locale			
Ending: missing			Deceiver deceived by Delilah	16:4–22	
Exposition: Samson loves Delilah, who agrees to deal to betray him	16:4–5	Disjunctive clause; change of locale, theme, subjects	Love affair with Delilah	16:4	Temporal clause
			Delilah's contract to deceive	16:5	"Went up to her" "Will give you"
Complication: Samson resists Delilah's tests	16:6–15	Change of locale and subjects	Samson's first deception of Delilah	16:6–9	"Please tell me …" "Then I will become weak." "Samson, the Philistines have come." "Source of his strength was unknown"
			Samson's second deception of Delilah	16:10–12	"Deceived me, … told me a lie. … Tell me." "If … then …" "Philistines have come"
			Samson's third deception of Delilah	16:13–14	"Deceived me … told me lies … tell me." "If … then …" "Philistines have come"
			Pestered almost to death	16:15–21	
Change: Samson reveals truth and loses strength	16:16–19	Disjunctive clause and theme	Daily harassment brings true information about Nazirite vow	16:15–17	"You have deceived me"; temporal clause; "informed her of his whole heart." "If … then …"
			Philistines summoned, ready to pay	16:18	"Philistine rulers came up … brought the silver"
			A close shave destroys a vow	16:19	"His strength turned away"

Table 13.1 continued 523

Table 13.1. Narrative and genre comparisons for chaps. 13–16 *(continued)*

Narrative			Genre		
Element	*Passage*	*Marker*	*Element*	*Passage*	*Marker*
Resolution: Samson imprisoned and mocked as entertainment for Philistine festival	16:20–25	Change of subject, theme, and locale	Away from Yahweh and away to prison	16:20–21	"She called." "He did not know that Yahweh had turned away."
			The hair returns	16:22	"Hair began to grow"
			Samson sacrifices the Philistines	16:23–30	
			Philistine religious celebration and sacrifice	16:23–24	"Gathered to sacrifice"; conveyance formula; "praised their god"
			Intoxicated with joy and juice, but demanding amusement	16:25	"Summon Samson so he can amuse"
Ending: Samson gains revenge, dies, is buried	16:26–31	Change of subject, theme, and locale	Entertainer entertains execution plans	16:26	
			Editorial note enumerating potential victims	16:27	Disjunctive clause
			Entertainer implores God for one last revenge effort	16:28	"Called to Yahweh . . . 'Let me get revenge'"
			Suicidal success Samson's greatest	16:29–30	"Let me die with the Philistines"
			Epilogue: Samson's family burial and judgeship	16:31	"Went down, picked him up, and took him away . . . buried him. . . . He had judged . . . twenty years."

Table 17.1. Narrative and genre comparisons for chaps. 17–18

Narrative			Genre		
Element	Passage	Marker	Element	Passage	Marker
Ending to 1:1–16:31	17:1–21:25	Introduces theme of "no king" and "did what was right in his own eyes" (17:6)			
Exposition to 17:1–21:25	17:1–18:31	Introduces shrines of Micah and Danites	Cultic founding narrative	17:1–18:31	"Micah had his own house of God." "Yahweh will be good to me for I have a Levite as a priest."
Exposition: establishment of private house of God	17:1–13	Introduces Micah, his shrine, and Levite	Establishing house of God with no king in Israel and all doing what was right in his own eyes	17:1–6	"Micah had his own house of God."
			Establishing of priest for local shrine	17:7–13	"Be a father and priest to me." "Yahweh will be good to me for I have a Levite as a priest."
Complication: Danites find Micah's shrine and get oracle from his priest	18:1–10	Introduces Danites and new locale	Spy narrative converted to cultic founding narrative	18:1–31	"Sent men ... to spy out the land"
			Discovery of local shrine and test of local Levite	18:1–6	Paired disjunctive temporal clauses
			End of spy report	18:7–10	"Men traveled on ... get going to possess the land"; conveyance formula

Table 17.1 continued   525

Table 17.1. Narrative and genre comparisons for chaps. 17–18 (*continued*)

Narrative			Genre		
Element	*Marker*	*Passage*	*Passage*	*Element*	*Marker*
Change: Danites take Micah's shrine and priest	Change of locale and theme	18:11–26	18:11–13	Travel report as opening of battle report ending at Micah's shrine with etiology	"Set out dressed for battle"; "camped in … call the place until today"
			18:14–20	Thievery of shrine and priest	"Took idol, ephod, image, and metal image"
			18:21–26	Battle report without battle	"Traveled on … called for military help and caught up … will attack you … traveled on their way … turned around and returned to his house"
Resolution: Danites take new territory	Change of locale and theme	18:27–29	18:27–28	Battle report	"Struck them dead … burning the city with fire … built the town and settled down there"
			18:29	Etiology	"Named the town"
Ending: Dan sets up idolatrous shrine with Mosaic priest	Change of theme	18:30–31	18:30–31	Cult founding	"Erected carved image … were priests … until the day … set up Micah's idol"

Table 19.1. Narrative and genre comparisons for chaps. 19–21

Narrative			Genre		
Element	Passage	Marker	Element	Passage	Marker
Complication to 17:1–21:25: Benjaminite city allows rape of southern visitors Exposition to chaps. 19–21: lack of hospitality between tribes	19:1–30	Disjunctive temporal clause; new locale, characters, time, theme	Sexual violation of guest narrative	19:1–30	
Exposition: "Israel had no king"; southern hospitality to northern "husband"	19:1–9	Disjunctive temporal clause; new locale, characters, time, theme	Introduction of players	19:1–3	"In those days ... Israel had no king ... man who was an alien ... took for himself a concubine." She went away to her father's house.
			Hospitality shown	19:4–9	Ate, drank, and spent the night (repeated elements)
Complication: no hospitality in Gibeah	19:10–21	Negative disjunctive clause and disjunctive appositive; change of locale, subject	Hospitality rejected	19:10–13	"Did not want to spend the night ... came near Jebus"; "let's turn in to this city"; "cannot turn in to a foreign city"; "let's go, so we can reach"
			Travel note leads to lack of hospitality	19:14–15	"Crossed over and journeyed"; "turned in ... to spend the night"; "no one received them"
			Hospitality given by alien	19:16–21	Surprise clause; "old man came from his work ... but was an alien"; "no one has received me"; "peace to you ... not going to spend the night in the plaza"; "brought him to his house ... washed their feet and ate and drank"
Change: sons of Belial attack concubine all night	19:22–26	Disjunctive appositive clause; change of subjects	Negotiations with sons of Belial	19:22–25a	Men of the city ... surrounded the house"; "bring out the man"; "don't be so evil ... don't do this stupid sin"; "my virgin daughter ... with concubine"; "do to them what is good in your own eyes"; "men decided not to listen"
			Sexual violence report	19:25b–26	"Seized his concubine and sent her out"; "intimate with her"; "woman came and fell at the entrance of the house"

Table 19.1 continued 527

Table 19.1. Narrative and genre comparisons for chaps. 19–21 (continued)

Narrative			Genre		
Element	*Passage*	*Marker*	*Element*	*Passage*	*Marker*
Resolution: Levite cuts concubine to pieces and distributes	19:27–29	Change of locale, time, and subjects	Report of Levite's inhumane treatment	19:27–28	"Went out to go on his way"; "get up so we can go"; "no answer"; "took her on the donkey"
			Call to national assembly	19:29	"Came to his house and took a knife"; "cut her . . . into twelve pieces"
Ending; editorial call to remember	19:30	Change of voice and verbal tense; change of subject	Editorial instruction	19:30	"Nothing has been done or seen like this. . . . Put yourself in her place. Think about it. Say something."
Crisis to 17:1–21:25; Benjamin faces extinction without wives	20:1–48	Change of subject and locale	Holy war battle report against kinsmen	20:1–48	
Exposition: general assembly hears Levite's charge against Benjamin	20:1–7	Change of subject and locale	Confederacy gathering to consider war	20:1–2	"Congregation assembled . . . took their place in the assembly"
			Call for and giving of testimony	20:3–7	"Tell us how this evil thing happened"; "they had committed a shameful act, a stupid sin in Israel!"; "come up with your word of counsel"
Complication: Israel prepares for war; Benjamin refuses to return guilty for punishment	20:8–13	Change of subject and theme	Declaration of war	20:8–11	"Rose as one man"; "no one will go to his tent"; "they can do . . . according to all the stupid sin they did"
			Pre-battle negotiations fail	20:12–13	"What is this evil that was committed among you? . . . Give up the men . . . that we may kill them and banish the evil from Israel"; "were not willing to listen"

Table 19.1. Narrative and genre comparisons for chaps. 19–21 (continued)

Narrative			Genre		
Element	Passage	Marker	Element	Passage	Marker
Change: Israel loses battles with Benjamin	20:14–25	Change of locale and subject	Troops mobilize for battle	20:14–17	"Mustered together . . . mobilized in that day . . . mobilized"
			Oracle report	20:18	"Inquired of God . . . Yahweh said"
			Report of defeats	20:19–25	"Rose . . . pitched their camp . . . went out to battle . . . lined up with them for battle . . . went out . . . destroyed . . . strengthened each other . . . lined up again for battle . . . approached . . . went out to meet them . . . destroyed"
Resolution: Israel wins battle after correct cultic practice	20:26–46	Change of theme	Lamentation and oracle request	20:23, 26–27	"Went up and cried before Yahweh"; "inquired of Yahweh"; "Yahweh said"; "cried and sat there before the Yahweh . . . fasted . . . offered up burnt offerings and peace offerings . . . inquired of Yahweh. . . . Should I yet again go out to battle?"
			Salvation oracle	20:18, 23, 28	"Judah is to be first . . . go up to them . . . go up, for tomorrow I will give them into your individual hand"
			Preparation of ambush	20:29	"Set an ambush"
			Attack and flight before the enemy	20:30–36	"Went up against . . . lined up . . . went out to meet the army . . . were lured away . . . strike down some of the army . . . rose from their position and lined up . . . ambush was charging forth . . . battle was heavy . . . Yahweh defeated . . . destroyed . . . trusted the ambush"
			Attack from ambush	20:37	"Ambush hurried forward . . . ambush spread out and struck dead"
			Signal of smoke from city	20:38–41	"Agreed on a sign . . . cloud began ascending . . . Benjamin turned around . . . men of Israel turned around . . . were terrified because they saw that evil had come against them"

Table 19.1 continued 529

Table 19.1. Narrative and genre comparisons for chaps. 19–21 (*continued*)

Narrative			Genre		
Element	*Passage*	*Marker*	**Element**	*Passage*	*Marker*
Ending: Holy war instituted but six hundred left	20:47–48	Change of theme	Holy war victory accomplished	20:42–48	"Battle caught up with them . . . surrounded . . . pursued . . . trampled them down . . . there fell . . . struck them dead . . . each town totally"
			Ironic holy war battle report	21:1–15	
Exposition: Israel mourns loss of tribe in Israel	21:1–6	Flashback; change of locale and theme	Reason for battle: lamentation for enemy	21:1–6	"Sworn under oath . . . sat there before God . . . lifted their voices and sobbed . . . asked, 'Why, Yahweh?' . . . rose early . . . built an altar . . . offered up burnt offerings and peace offerings . . . surely be put to death . . . were consoled"
Complication: search for wives for remaining men	21:7–9	Change of locale and theme	Plan for battle; discovering the opponent	21:7–9	"Sworn under oath . . . inquired" (but not of God); surprise clauses
Change: successful war does not provide enough wives	21:10–14		Battle report: kill all but virgins	21:10–12	"Sent . . . heroic warriors", "strike dead the residents . . . put to the ban", "found . . . virgins"; "brought them to the camp"
			Battle treaty report: peace with former enemies	21:13–15	"Entire congregation sent and spoke . . . offering them peace . . . did not find the right number . . . relented concerning"
Resolution: steal wives from Shiloh	21:15–23a	Change of subject, theme, and locale	Cultic wife-stealing episode	21:16–25	
			Self-interrogation?	21:16–18	"What can we do? . . . cannot give them . . . swore under oath"
			Battle plan against cultic festival	21:19–21	"Set an ambush . . . be on the lookout . . . get going"
			Civil plan against lawsuit	21:22	"Do us a favor . . . you would be guilty"

Table 19.1. Narrative and genre comparisons for chaps. 19–21 (continued)

Narrative			Genre		
Element	Passage	Marker	Element	Passage	Marker
Ending: Benjamin returns home, as does Israel, without king and with all doing right in their own eyes	21:23b–25	Change of locale and theme	Battle plan carried out	21:23–24	"Did exactly that . . . returned to their inheritance . . . . built cities and settled . . . went away . . . to his tribe and to his clan . . . to his inheritance"
			Editorial summation	21:25	"No king. . . . Every person did what was right in his own eyes."

Table 20.1. Comparison of ambush narratives in Joshua and Judges

Formal element	Joshua	Judges	Notes
Initial defeat	7:2–5	20:19–25	Individual versus national sin
Lamentation	7:6–9	20:23, 26–27	Joshua and elders parallel people and then priest
Salvation oracle	8:1–2	20:18, 23, 28	First two in Judges do not bring salvation
Preparation of ambush	8:3–9	20:29	
Attack and flight before the enemy	8:10–17	20:30–36	
Signal to ambush	8:18		Implied in Judges
Attack from ambush	8:19	20:37	
Signal of smoke from city	8:20–21	20:38–41	
Victory accomplished	8:21b–23	20:42–48	Judges leaves six hundred survivors

Map: The Judges of Israel

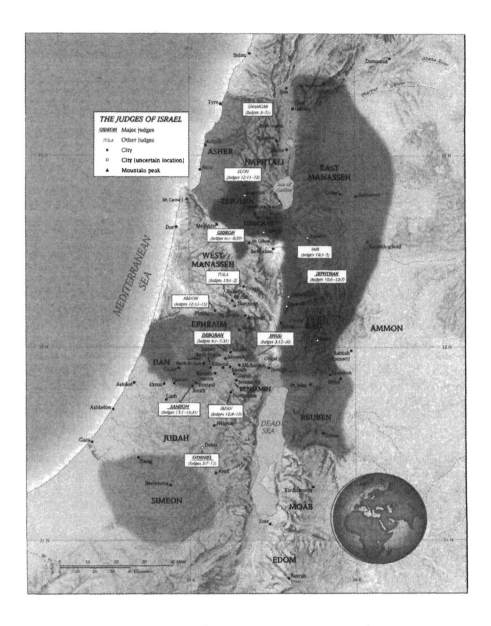

Index of Modern Authors Cited

Citations in *Notes* section are not included.

Index of Subjects and Names

Since God (Yahweh) appears on the scene or behind the scene in every page, reference to God does not appear in the index except for special divine names or characteristics.

Index of Selected Hebrew Terms